FSE University

Equipping Christians to Engage the Culture with the Gospel

Copyright © 2018 by Edward A. Croteau

Images used in this book with lawful excuse under Fair Use Law 17 U.S. Code §107 for nonprofit classroom educational purposes only.

This material is part of the teaching ministry of Missouri non-profit corporation N01345108, 'Faith, Substance and Evidence'.

The Foundation of FSE University = The Faith, Substance & Evidence (FSE) Pyramid

This book uses **Hebrews 11:1** as it's foundation for studying the basis for the Christian worldview and the reality of Jesus Christ. We start at the base of the Pyramid (the Gospel) and then work our way up to the top (God's will for my life), building a firm foundation for Christianity layer by layer as we investigate the evidence for Jesus Christ as the source of the answers to life's most pressing questions:

1) Is what I believe true?
2) Who am I?
3) Where did I come from?
4) Why am I here?

The substance of our faith is the Person of Jesus Christ. We will examine the evidence for why faith in Christ is the key to finding the answers to these questions.

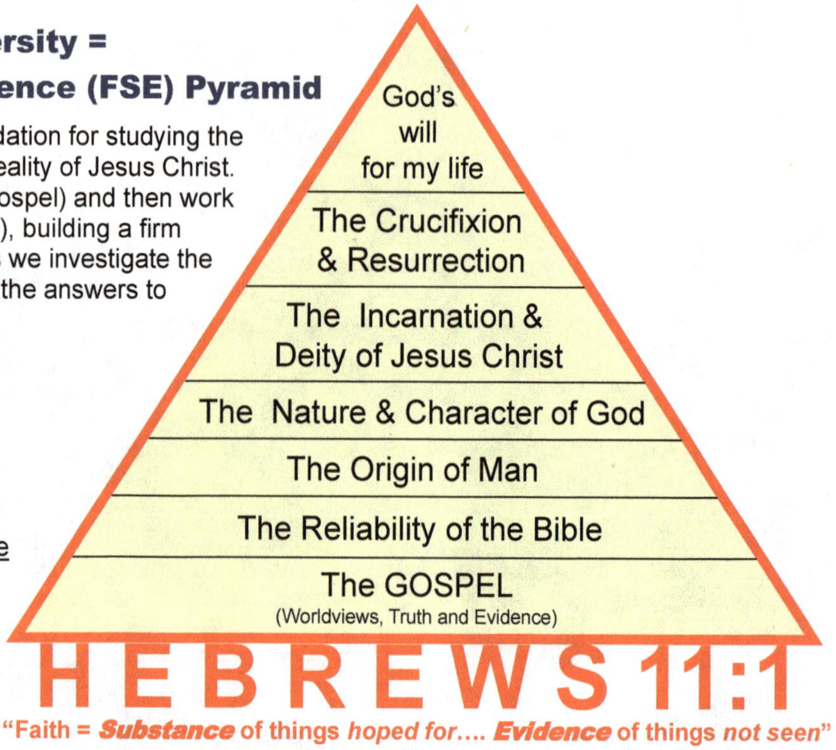
God's will for my life
The Crucifixion & Resurrection
The Incarnation & Deity of Jesus Christ
The Nature & Character of God
The Origin of Man
The Reliability of the Bible
The GOSPEL
(Worldviews, Truth and Evidence)
HEBREWS 11:1
"Faith = Substance of things hoped for.... Evidence of things not seen"

- **The Layers of the Pyramid:** This book combines *four books* that tie together to guide us in a systematic study of the Pyramid's layers from it's foundation (The Gospel) to the top (God's Will for my life).

Book 1 = Worldviews, Truth and Evidence (answers the two questions *'Is what I believe true?'* and '*Who Am I?*')
Book 2 = The Origin of Man (answers the question '*Where did I come from?*')
Book 3 = The Reliability of the Bible and the Person of Jesus Christ (further answers the question *'Who am I?'*)
Book 4 = God's Will for My Life, The Nature & Character of God (answers the question '*Why am I here?*')

- **How to use this book:** 1) With the WEBSITE LESSONS = Each book's lessons are accompanied by a short video lesson on the 'Faith, Substance & Evidence' website www.fse.life. You can watch the condensed version of the book's lesson on the website, then read that lesson in the book for more in-depth analysis.

2) In DISCUSSION GROUPS = each of us can examine today's culture against biblical truth, then challenge each others' views and learn from one another with the goal of 'renewing our minds' with a biblical worldview.

The FSE Ministry Focus: A Challenge to "Know What I Believe and Why"

The following are excerpts from Dinesh D'Souza's book 'What's So Great About Christianity'[13]

"Today's Christians know that they do not, as their ancestors did, live in a society where God's presence was unavoidable... Many of us now reside in secular communities, where arguments drawn from the Bible or Christian revelation carry no weight, and where we hear a different language than that spoken in church.

Instead of engaging this secular world, most Christians have taken the easy way out. They have retreated into a Christian subculture where they engage Christian concerns. Then they step back into secular society, where their Christianity is kept out of sight until the next church service. Without realizing it, Christians have become postmodernists of a sort: they live by a gospel of the two truths. There is *religious truth*, reserved for Sundays and days of worship, and there is *secular truth*, which applies to the rest of the time... they have sought a workable, comfortable 'modus vivendi' in which they agree to leave the secular world alone if the secular world agrees to leave them alone.

But a group of prominent atheists – many of them evolutionary biologists – has launched a powerful public attack on religion in general and Christianity in particular; they have no interest in being nice... The atheists no longer want to be tolerated. They want to monopolize the public square and to expel Christians from it. They want political questions like abortion to be divorced from religious and moral claims. They want to control school curricula so they can promote a secular ideology and undermine Christianity... In short, they want to make religion – and especially the Christian religion – disappear from the face of the earth... the atheists have had it too easy. Their arguments have gone largely unanswered.

The Bible in Matthew 5:13-14 calls Christians to be the 'salt of the earth' and the 'light of the world'... That includes confronting the challenge of modern atheism and secularism."

BOOK 1: WHO AM I? Worldviews, Truth & Evidence

			Page
Chapter 1	**Christianity: Substance with Evidence**	Hebrews 11:1	**15**
1.1	Does God Exist? The 5 Religious Worldviews		16
	Dr. Antony Flew: "There is a God" (How the World's Most Notorious Atheist Changed His Mind)		19
1.2	What the World Believes: Three Major Global Religions outside Christianity		20
1.3	My Personal Worldview = how I see Truth	Romans 12:2, John 1:10	22
1.4	Worldview #1 in America: Postmodernism		26
1.5	Worldview #2 in America: Secular Humanism		30
1.6	Why Christianity is on the rise: The Empty Message in Secular Humanism		32
1.7	Worldview #3 in America: Christianity		38
1.8	Christian Worldview: Faith requires Logical Thinking	Ephesians 3:14-19	40
Chapter 2	**The Essence of the Christian Worldview = The Gospel**	2Corinthians 5:21	**42**
2.1	The Christian mandate = Emphasizing the Essentials		43
	Greg Kohkl: "Tactics" (Game Plan for Discussing Your Christian Convictions)		46
2.2	The Gospel = Creating a Christ-centered worldview	John 12:19	47
2.3	The Gospel = Turning Greeks into Jews	1Corinthians 1:22-23	49
2.4	The Gospel = A Reasoned Presentation of Jesus Christ	Acts 17:2-4, 18:4	51
2.5	The Gospel = God uses people to reach people	Genesis 6:3,5	53
2.6	The Gospel = God works through the Base Things	1Corinthians 1:26-29	55
2.7	The Gospel = Scattering the Seed	Matthew 13:3-8	56
Chapter 3	**The Battle for the Beginning**	Genesis 1:1	**57**
3.1	What is Creationism? What is Darwinian Evolution?		57
3.2	How Strong is the Belief in Evolution in the Scientific Community?		59
	What difference does it make whether I believe in Darwinian Evolution or Creation?		60
	Secular Humanism's 10 Lies to promote Darwinian Evolution		60
3.3	Science, Truth and Faith	Romans 1:18-20	63
	Dr. Thomas Nagel: "Mind & Cosmos" (Why Materialist Neo-Darwinian Concept of Nature is False)		64
3.4	Are Science and Faith compatible in the search for Truth?		65
3.5	The History of Scientific Inquiry is rooted in Christianity		67
3.6	The History of Science & Religion: The Great Scientists		70
Chapter 4	**Science and Reason: The Evidence for Christianity**		**71**
4.1	'Operation Science' vs. 'Origin Science'		71
	Applying Origin Science to the Bible and the Person of Jesus Christ		73
4.2	Is the Bible Reliable? Corroborating Evidence: 53 Measurable Data Points		74
4.3	Is Jesus Christ the Messiah? Corroborating Evidence: 87 Measurable Data Points		75
	Applying Origin Science to Origins		78
4.4	Universe & Life: specially created? Corroborating Evidence: 60 Measurable Data Points		78
4.5	Applying Probability Science to Origins, The Bible & Deity of Christ		80
	Origin of Life: Probability and Precision point to an Intelligent Designer!		83
Chapter 5	**Who I am: made in the "image of God"**	Genesis 1:26	**84**
5.1	What does it mean to be a 'person'?		84
5.2	The "Table of Nations" (Genealogy & Origin of Mankind)	Genesis 10	86
5.3	My Christian Roots	Matthew 1	98
5.4	Book of Isaiah: Who I am, Where I came from, Why I'm here	Isaiah	100
5.5	Jesus Christ = The True Vine and Chief Cornerstone	John 15:1-5	102

Glossary of Terms   **105**

Frank Turek[6]: "Can't I just have Faith?"

"Contrary to popular opinion, Christians are not supposed to 'just have faith'. We are COMMANDED to know what we believe and why we believe it, as well as to:

1) <u>Give answers to those who ask</u> → 1Peter 3:15 *"...sanctify the Lord God in your hearts, and always be ready to give a DEFENSE to everyone who asks you a reason for the hope that is in you, with meekness and fear..."*

2) <u>Demolish arguments against Christianity</u> → 2Corinthians 10:4-5 *"...the weapons of our warfare are not carnal but mighty in God for pulling down strongholds, CASTING DOWN ARGUMENTS and every high thing that exalts itself against the knowledge of God..."*

"We give evidence for Christianity because we ought to live our lives based on TRUTH. Socrates once said that the unexamined life is not worth living. We believe that the unexamined faith is not worth believing. Since God is reasonable (Isaiah 1:18), and wants us to use our reason, Christians don't get brownie points for being stupid. In fact, using reason is part of the greatest commandment which, according to Jesus, is to *"Love the Lord your God with all your heart and with all your soul and with all your MIND"* (Matthew 22:37)."

So what's the ultimate goal in "knowing what and why I believe"?

After I evaluate the evidence behind the claims of Jesus Christ, I must decide if I am willing to allow Him unrestricted access to transform my life, from how I live my life today to surrendering my life to His control.

We'll use the *"Proverbs Ladder of Character"* (to the right) to look at each of the four major phases in growing in the Christian life:

1) Only when God takes the initiative to put wisdom in my heart can I know Him.

2) He gives me His wisdom to grow our relationship.

3) He grows our relationship by molding my character to be more like His Son.

4) The more I allow Him unrestricted access to mold my character, the more I radiate Christ in my life... and the more He is GLORIFIED in me.

for His glory	My Renewed character = glorifies God	Matt. 5:16
	My Giving = promises God's blessing	Prov. 21:26
	My Forgiveness = answer to bitterness	Prov. 14:10
	God's Forgiveness = His gift of love	Prov. 17:9
	God's Kindness/ Mercy = love in action	Prov. 19:22
	My Love = why I obey	Prov. 3:12
	God's Love = "agape"	Prov. 10:12
by molding my character	My Truthfulness = delights Him	Prov. 12:22
	God's Truthfulness = buy it, don't sell it	Prov. 23:23
	My Faithfulness = requires risk	Prov. 3:5-6
	My Self-Control = my understanding	Prov. 17:27
	My Submission = my servanthood	Prov. 16:3
	My Humility = draws God to me	Prov. 3:34
	My Reverence = where I begin	Prov. 1:7
to grow our relationship	My Character: must walk in the Spirit	Gal. 5:16
	My Character: can defeat my nature	Romans 6
	My Character: fights against my nature	Prov. 20:9
	My Character: requires renewal	Prov. 28:13
	My Character: is relational	Prov. 23:26
	My Character: a heart issue	Prov. 4:23
	My Character: God's definition	Prov. 21:3
God imparts His wisdom into my heart	God's Character = diligent towards me	Prov. 4:1-2
	God's Character: His concern	Prov. 22:1
	God's Wisdom: seen in His Character	Prov. 18:10
	God's Wisdom: vs. world's foolishness	Prov. 14:02
	God's Wisdom: foolish to the world	Prov. 21:30
	God's Wisdom: only through His Son	Prov. 8:1-36
	God's Wisdom: only by His instruction	Prov. 6:23
	God's Wisdom: I must seek diligently	Prov. 8:17
	God's Wisdom: the key to knowing Him	Prov. 2:1-5

Dr. Geisler and Dr. Turek[6]: *"No amount of evidence will convince you because evidence is not what's in your way - you are."*

Book 1 References

1. Charles Darwin — "The Origin of the Species" — Bantam Books — 1859
2. John Stott — "Your Mind Matters" — Inter-Varsity Press Books — 1972
3. Nancy Pearcey — "Total Truth" — Crossway Books — 2004
4. Greg Koukl — "Tactics" — Zondervan Publishers — 2009
5. Antony Flew — "There is A God" — Harper One Publishers — 2007
6. F. Turek, N. Geisler — "I Don't have…Faith to be an Atheist" — Crossway Books — 2004
7. Thomas Nagel — "Mind & Cosmos" — Oxford University Press — 2012
8. John Ankerberg — "Darwin's Leap of Faith" — Harvest House Publishers — 1998
9. Philip Johnson — "Darwin on Trial" — Inter-Varsity Press Books — 1991
10. M.R. DeHann, MD — "Portraits of Christ in Genesis" — Zondervan Publishers — 2002
11. Josh McDowell — "Evidence that Demands A Verdict" — Here's Life Publishing — 1986
12. Norman Geisler — "When Skeptics Ask" — Baker Book Publishers — 2008
13. Dinesh D'Souza — "What's So Great About Christianity" — Tyndale House Publishers — 2007
14. Hugh Ross, PhD — "The Creator and the Cosmos" — Navpress Publishers — 1993
15. Richard A. Swenson, M.D. — "More than meets the Eye" — Navpress Publishers — 2000
16. Michael J. Behe, PhD — "Darwin's Black Box" — Touchstone Books — 1996
17. Michael Patton — "Representing Christ to Postmodern" — www.Bible.org — 2004
18. Henry M. Morris, PhD — "Scientific Creationism" — Creation-Life Publishers — 1974
19. Michael Denton, PhD — "Evolution: A Theory in Crisis" — Adler and Adler Publishers — 1986
20. Steve Herzig/ Ken Ham — "On Darwin and Evolution" — Israel My Glory, July/ August — 2005
21. Jonathan Wells, PhD — "Icons of Evolution" — Regnery Publishing, Inc. — 2000
22. Lee Strobel — "The Case for a Creator" — Zondervan Publishers — 2004
23. G.S. McLean — "The Evidence for Creation" — Understand the Times Publisher — 1995
24. A.E. Wilder Smith, PhD — "Man's Origin, Man's Destiny" — Bethany House Publishers — 1968
25. John MacArthur — "The Gospel According to Jesus" — Zondervan Publishers — 1994
26. John MacArthur — "The Battle for the Beginning" — Word Publishing Group — 2001
27. Tim Osterholm — "The Table of Nations" — www.soundchristian.com — 2005
28. Mark Robinson — "Israel: God's Answer to Skeptics" — Israel My Glory, June/ July — 2006
29. Norman Geisler — "Christian Apologetics" — Baker Book Publishers — 1989
30. Duane Arthur Schmidt — "And God Created Darwin" — Allegiance Press — 2001
31. Bertrand Russell — "Why I am not a Christian" — Simon & Schuster — 1957
32. Ergun & Emir Caner — "Unveiling Islam" — Kregel Publications — 2002
33. Walter Martin — "The Kingdom of the Cults" — Bethany House Publishers — 1985
34. John Stott — "Basic Christianity" — Eerdsmann Publishing — 1971

Book 1 Additional Reading

35. F.F. Bruce — "The Canon of Scripture" — Intervarsity Press — 1988
36. Timothy Keller — "The Reason for God" — Riverhead Books — 2008
37. Henry M. Morris, PhD — "Many Infallible Proofs" — Master Books — 1974
38. Henry M. Morris, PhD — "The Genesis Record" — Baker Book Publishers — 1976
39. A.E. Wilder Smith, PhD — "He who Thinks has to Believe" — TWFT Publishing — 1981
40. Hugh Ross, PhD — "The Fingerprint of God" — Navpress Publishers — 1993
41. William Lane Craig, PhD — "On Guard" — David C Cook Distributors — 2010
42. Jay W. Richards, PhD — "The Privileged Planet" — Regnery Publishing, Inc. — 2004
43. J. Warner Wallace — "God's Crime Scene" — David C Cook Distributors — 2015
44. Josh McDowell — "Beyond Belief to Convictions" — Tyndale House Publishers — 2002
45. Chuck Colson, N. Pearcey — "How Now Shall We Live?" — Tyndale House Publishers — 1999
46. John C. Lennox — "God and Stephen Hawking" — Lion Books — 2011
47. Henry M. Morris, PhD — "Biblical Creationism" — Baker Book Publishers — 1993
48. Robert Jastrow — "God and the Astronomers" — W.W. Norton & Co, Inc. — 1978
49. Charles Darwin — "The Descent of Man" — Bantam Books — 1871
50. Nabeel Qureshi — "No God But One – Allah or Jesus?" — Zondervan Publishers — 2016

BOOK 2: WHERE DID I COME FROM? The Origin of Man

			Page
Chapter 1	**Argument #1 for God = The Origin of the Universe**	Genesis 1:1-3	**109**
1.1	Four Scientific Theories today to explain the Origin of the Universe		109
	Genesis → Revelation: 124X God claims He created the Universe		111
1.2	How does Science explain the Existence of the Universe?		119
1.3	What leading Scientists say: Universe began as a 1-Time Creative Act by an Intelligent Mind		121
1.4	Evidence ①: Einstein's General Theory of Relativity (1907-1915)		125
	Einstein's Greatest Failure: He denied the Intelligent Creator he discovered was Personal		126
1.5	Evidence ②: The Hubble Constant, Doppler Red Shift, Expansion Rate of the Universe		127
1.6	Evidence ⑤: The Cosmic Background Radiation		129
	How the "Big Bang" got its name → An Explosion of a 'Singularity'		130
1.7	Evidence ⑥: 1st Law of Thermodynamics ("Conservation of Energy")		131
	$E=mc^2$ Explained - Energy Transfer & the Atom Bomb		132
1.8	Evidence ⑦: 2nd Law of Thermodynamics ("Disintegration of Energy")		133
	==Dr. A.E. Wilder Smith: "Man's Origin, Man's Destiny" = Why 2nd Law of Thermodynamics points to Creation, falsifies Evolution==		==134==
1.9	Evidence ⑧: Newton's Laws of Causality		135
1.10	**Argument #2 for God = Existential Causality**		137
	==Dr. Robert Jastrow: "God and the Astronomers" (Strange Developments in Astronomy)==		==140==
Chapter 2	**Argument #3 for God = DESIGN in the Universe**		**141**
2.1	What leading Scientists say: Design in the Universe is a Creative Act by an Intelligent Mind		142
	==Dr. Douglas Axe: "Undeniable" (How Biology Confirms Our Intuition that Life is Designed)==		==144==
2.2	The Logos = Creative Mind of the Universe	John 1:1-2	145
	To do Science requires faith in a *Mathematically Ordered, Intelligible Universe*		146
2.3	God's Orderly Design: The Mathematical Laws of Motion		147
	The Mind behind the Universe: Speaking in the Language of Math Equations		148
	God's Orderly Design: The 4 Forces in the Universe		149
	Nuclear Fission: God's Strong Nuclear Force = the source of Unimaginable Power		151
	What is the universe made of? How is it held together? How is it kept together?		152
	Genesis 1:1-2 2Peter 3:10 Hebrews 1:1-5 Colossians 1:15-17		
Chapter 3	**Argument #4 for God = FINE-TUNING in the Universe**	Psalm 19:1-4a	**155**
3.1	Origin of Life: Probability & Precision point to an Intelligent Designer!		156
	What leading Scientists say: Precision in the Universe is a Creative Act by an Intelligent Mind		157
	What Designers Do: Precisely Control Multiple Independent Variables		159
3.2	Fine-Tuned Precision in the Universe: 25 Measurable Variables		160
	==Dr. Hugh Ross: "The Creator and the Cosmos" (Why the Anthropic Principle points to a personal Creator: Life requires the precise controls)==		==162==
	of multiple, independent variables		
3.3	God personally cares for me: Earth's precise location	Psalm 8:3-4	164
3.4	God personally cares for me: Earth's precise design	Job 12:8-9, Isaiah 45:18	166
	Earth's Hydrologic Cycle: God's Fine-Tuning for life on earth	Ecclesiastes 1:7	167
3.5	The "Sun of Righteousness"	Psalm 19: 4b-6	168
3.6	==Dr. Jay Richards, Dr. Guillermo Gonzales: "The Priviledged Planet" (How Our Place in Cosmos is Designed for Discovery)==		==170==
3.7	God's Word, not His creation, points me to Him	Psalm 19:7-11	173
3.8	What Reward is there for "keeping" God's Word?	Psalm 19:11	174
3.9	Christian "Wisdom" = walking daily in His Light	Psalm 19:12-14	175
Chapter 4	**Argument #5 for God = DESIGN in Animal Kingdom**	Job 12:7,9	**177**
4.1	Bat Echolocation		177
	Godwit Migration		178
	Giraffe Blood Circulation		179
	Camel Blood Design		181
	Bombadier Beetle Defense System	Genesis 1:24-25	182

Chapter 5	**Argument #6 for God = *IRREDUCIBLE COMPLEXITY***	Psalm 139	**183**
5.1	God's Omniscience = He knows me perfectly	Psalm 139:1-4	183
	Irreducible Complexity (IC): Reveals Design, Falsifies "Natural Selection"		184
	Dr. Michael Behe: "Darwin's Black Box" (The Biochemical Challenge to Evolution)		185
	The Human Eye, The Human Ear	Psalm 94:9	186
5.2	"An Eye for Creation"		188
	"Microbiology kills Darwin's theory that the Human Eye evolved"		190
5.3	Blood = God's Irreducibly Complex Design for Life	Genesis 9:3-4	191
	"Blood Clotting 101": What happens when I cut myself?		193
	How do evolutionists explain the process of Blood Clotting?		194
	Blood = "God's Design for Eternal Life: the Forgiveness of my sin"	Leviticus 17:11	195
5.4	God's Omnipresence = He surrounds me completely	Psalm 139:5-12	196
	God's gift of my Brain – how I receive and understand information		196
Chapter 6	**Argument #7 for God = The *LANGUAGE* of Life**	Psalm 139	**198**
6.1	God's Omnipotence = He designed me fearfully	Psalm 139:13-18	198
	DNA: Put in Perspective when compared to LEGOS, The "Book of Life"		199
6.2	The Double Helix DNA: God's detailed Language that "fashions" me		200
	Using Probability Science (again): Could DNA's messaging have formed by Chance?		201
6.3	The Cell: God's micro-machinery that designs and sustains me		202
6.4	A.E. Wilder-Smith: The Cell, DNA & ATP: Information Theory, Von-Neumann Machines		204
	ATP → The Cell's Energy Information Source to accomplish Life's work		205
Chapter 7	**Argument #8 for God = The Human *SOUL***	Psalm 139	**207**
7.1	My Heart = where my God becomes my Lord	Psalm 139:23	207
	My Physical Heart – God's amazing Design		207
	My Spiritual Heart – how does God show me who I really am on the *inside*?		207
	God's Power: He leads me in "the way everlasting"	Psalm 139:24	208
7.2	My Conscience and Intelligence (heart, soul and spirit)	Matthew 22:37	209
	Men and Women are 3-Part Beings: Spirit, Soul and Body	1Thessalonians 5:23	211
Chapter 8	**How Darwinian Evolution is taught in Schools**		**212**
	Dr. Jonathan Wells: "Icons of Evolution" = 10 Questions to ask about Darwinian Evolution		212
	Answers from Evolution: Who am I? Why am I here? Where did I come from?		212
8.1	What our kids learn in High School: 11 Evidences for Darwinian Evolution		213
8.2	Scrutinizing Darwinian Evolution → Life from Non-Life: Miller-Urey Experiment		217
8.3	Scrutinizing Darwinian Evolution → Common Ancestor: Darwin's Tree of Life		219
8.4	Scrutinizing Darwinian Evolution → Common Ancestor: Embryology		220
8.5	Scrutinizing Darwinian Evolution → Common Ancestor: Homology		223
8.6	Vestigial Organs infer Common Ancestry? Imperfections infer anti-Design?		225
8.7	Scrutinizing Darwinian Evolution → Natural Selection via DNA Mutations		226
	The Scientific Definition of Natural Selection		227
	DNA Mutations: Agents of Natural Selection that drive Evolution?		227
8.8	The Peppered Moth & Industrial Mellanism: Creation's Natural Selection		229
8.9	Galapagos Finches & Adaptive Radiation: Creation's Natural Selection		231
8.10	Can we reconcile the Bible with Natural Selection?		233
8.11	Scrutinizing Darwinian Evolution → Transitional Forms: Fossil Record		234
	The Cambrian Explosion: Discovery that reinforces a Designer; Evidence for Genesis ch. 1		235
	Dr. Stephen Meyer: "Darwin's Doubt" (Explosive Origin of Animal Life & Case for Intelligent Design)		236
8.12	Scrutinizing Darwinian Evolution → The Human Fossil Record		238
	The History of the *Evidence* for "Missing Links"		240
	Prof. Marvin Lubenow: "Bones of Contention" (Creationist Assessment of Human Fossils)		241
8.13	The Scientific Evidence: I am not descended from animals		242
	The Biblical Evidence: I am uniquely created by God		243
Glossary of Terms			**245**

Book 2 References

1. Charles Darwin	"The Origin of the Species"	Bantam Books	1859
2. Charles Darwin	"The Descent of Man"	Bantam Books	1871
3. Henry M. Morris, PhD	"The Genesis Record"	Baker Book Publishers	1976
4. Henry M. Morris, PhD	"Scientific Creationism"	Creation-Life Publishers	1974
5. Henry M. Morris, PhD	"Biblical Creationism"	Baker Book Publishers	1993
6. Henry M. Morris, PhD	"Many Infallible Proofs"	Master Books	1974
7. John MacArthur	"The Battle for the Beginning"	Word Publishing Group	2001
8. Lee Strobel	"The Case for a Creator"	Zondervan Publishers	2004
9. F. Turek, N. Geisler	"I Don't have...Faith to be an Atheist"	Crossway Books	2004
10. Dinesh D'Souza	"What's So Great about Christianity"	Tyndale Books	2007
11. A.E. Wilder Smith, PhD	"Man's Origin, Man's Destiny"	Bethany House Publishers	1968
12. A.E. Wilder Smith, PhD	"He who Thinks has to Believe"	TWFT Publishing	1981
13. G.S. McLean	"The Evidence for Creation"	Understand the Times Publisher	1995
14. John Ankerberg	"Darwin's Leap of Faith"	Harvest House Publishers	1998
15. Richard A. Swenson, M.D.	"More than meets the Eye"	Navpress Publishers	2000
16. Michael J. Behe, PhD	"Darwin's Black Box"	Touchstone Books	1996
17. Jonathan Wells, PhD	"Icons of Evolution"	Regnery Publishing, Inc.	2000
18. Hugh Ross, PhD	"The Creator and the Cosmos"	Navpress Publishers	1993
19. Hugh Ross, PhD	"The Fingerprint of God"	Navpress Publishers	1993
20. Michael Denton, PhD	"Evolution: A Theory in Crisis"	Adler and Adler Publishers	1986
21. Ken Ham	"The Genesis Solution"	Baker Book Publishers	1988
22. Jerry Bergman, PhD	"ATP: Cell's Energy Currency"	Creation Research Society	1999
23. Robert Jastrow, PhD	"God and the Astronomers"	W.W. Norton & Co., Inc.	1978
24. Donald B. DeYoung	"Astronomy and the Bible"	Baker Book Publishers	1988
25. Charles H. Spurgeon	"The Treasury of David"	MacDonald Publishing Co.	1950
26. Jay W. Richards, PhD	"The Privileged Planet"	Regnery Publishing, Inc.	2004
27. John MacArthur	"The Gospel According to Jesus"	Zondervan Publishers	1994
28. Nancy Pearcey	"Total Truth"	Crossway Books	2004
29. Doug Axe, PhD	"Undeniable"	Harper One Publishing	2016
30. Duane Arthur Schmidt	"And God Created Darwin"	Allegiance Press	2001
31. Dr. Norman Geisler	"When Skeptics Ask"	Baker Books	2008
32. Dr. Norman Geisler	"Christian Apologetics"	Baker Books	1976
33. Dr. Dave Miller	www.Apologetics Press.org	Website Article	
34. Melinda Christian	"Answers in Genesis"	Oct-Dec. 2006 Publication	2006
35. Chuck Colson, N. Pearcey	"How Now Shall We Live?"	Tyndale House Publishers	1999

Book 2   Additional Reading

36. Susanna Van Rose	"Eyewitness Earth"	DK Publishing, Inc..	2005
37. Dr. Jonathan Henry	"The Astronomy Book"	Master Books	2002
38. Philip Johnson	"Darwin on Trial"	Inter-Varsity Press Books	1991
39. Dr. Stephen Meyer	"Darwin's Doubt"	HarperCollins Publishers	2013
40. Dr. Stephen Meyer	"Signature of the Cell"	HarperOne Publishers	2009
41. Dr. Marvin Lubenow	"Bones of Contention"	Baker Books	2004
42. Stuart Clark	"The Big Questions: The Universe"	Metro Books	2011
43. Michael Brook	"The Big Questions: Physics"	Metro Books	2011
44. Francis Collins, PhD	"The Language of God"	Free Press Publishers	2006
45. Curt Sewell	"Creation Overviews"	Website Article	1999
46. Curt Sewell	"Scopes Trial and Inherit the Wind"	Website Article	1999
47. Tom Bethell	"Darwin's House of Cards"	Discovery Institute Press	2017
48. J.P. Moreland	"Three Views on Creation & Evolution"	Zondervan Publishers	1999

BOOK 3: The Reliability of the Bible, The Person of Jesus Christ — Page

Chapter 1 — The Uniqueness of the Bible — 256
- 1.1 Top 5 Reasons Skeptics Give for Rejecting the Authority of the Bible — 257
- The Bible: Reasonable, Intellectual, True — 258
- 1.2 The Bible: Unique in its Continuity, Circulation, Translation, Influence — 259
- 1.3 The Bible: Unique in its Survival — 261
- The Diocletian Persecution — 262
- William Tyndale: Translating the Bible for the "Common Man" — 263
- 1.4 God has deeply invested in His Bible — 2Timothy 3:16 — 264
- 1.5 What the Bible can do in My Life: 8 Pictures of God's Word — Jeremiah 20:8-9 — 266

Chapter 2 — Manuscripts (Bibliographic Evidence Test) — 268
- 2.1 The New Testament — 268
- Examining the Evidence: Time Gap from the Originals, Transmission Errors in the Bible — 270
- Dr. Daniel Wallace: Expert Testimony on Transmission Errors in the New Testament — 270
- 2.2 Sir William Ramsay: "Bearing of Recent Discovery on Trustworthiness of New Testament" — 273
- 2.3 Dr. Bruce Metzger: Expert Testimony on the Text of the New Testament — 275
- 2.4 The Old Testament — 278
- Dr. Robert Wilson: "Scientific Investigation of the Old Testament" — 279
- Dr. William F. Albright: Expert Testimony on Archaeology and the Biblical Record — 280
- 2.5 The Dead Sea Scrolls: QIsaiah[a]: Proof of Isaiah's Prophecies of Jesus Christ in 730 BC — 281

Chapter 3 — Archaeology (External Evidence Test) — 286
- 3.1 Archaeology & the Bible: Ba'al Worship — 287
- Archaeology & the Bible: The Philistines — 288
- 3.2 Archaeology & the Bible: The Hittite Empire — 289
- 3.3 Archaeology & the Bible: The Assyrian Empire — 294
- The Biblical Record: Assyria, Israel & Judah (256 years) — 295
- 3.4 Archaeology and the Kings of Assyria — 296
- 3.5 The Assyrian Empire & Kingdom of Judah — 303

Chapter 4 — Fulfilled Prophecy & Archaeology (Internal Evidence Test) — 305
- 4.1 Why does God give Fulfilled Prophecies in the Bible? — 305
- 4.2 Prophecy #1: The Destruction of Tyre — 3,000BC-1,600AD — 306
- 4.3 Prophecy #2: The Destruction of Nineveh — 2,000 - 612BC — 309
- 4.4 Prophecy #3: Thebes & Memphis — 3,100BC - 641AD — 311
- 4.5 Prophecy #4: The Destruction of Babylon — 2,112 - 536BC — 313
- 4.6 Prophecy #5: Moab & Ammon — 1,200 - 580BC — 318
- 4.7 Prophecy #6: The Destruction of Samaria — 880BC - 66AD — 321
- 4.8 Prophecy #7: Gaza-Ashkelon — 2,000BC - 1,250AD — 323
- 4.9 Prophecy #8: The Destruction of Petra & Edom — 1,010 - 312BC — 325
- 4.10 Prophecy #9: Palestine — 1,200BC - Today — 328

Chapter 5 — Non-Biblical Sources (External Evidence Test) — 332
- 5.1 Early Church Writings: Irenaeus, "Against Heresies III" — 332
- Eusebius: "Ecclesiastical History III" — 332
- Plinius Secundus: "Letter to Emperor Trajan" — 332
- Cornelius Tacitus: "Christus, the leader of the Christians" — 332
- Flavius Josephus: "Antiquities" — 333
- Lucian: "The Crucified Sage of the Christians" — 334
- Babylonian Talmud: "Yeshu was hanged on the eve of the Passover" — 334
- 5.2 Dr. William Lane Craig: Answering the Skeptics' Question: Did Jesus Christ really exist? — 334

Chapter 6	**Eyewitness Accounts**	**(Internal Evidence Test)**		**336**
6.1	Peter:	Eyewitness to the Resurrection (from coward to courage)		337
	Dr. John Piper:	8 Reasons why I believe Jesus rose from the dead		338
6.2	Dr. William Lane Craig:	Expert Testimony on the Historical Resurrection of Jesus Christ		339
6.3	Theories:	Explaining Away the Resurrection of Jesus Christ		341
6.4	Forensic Science:	Expert Testimony on the Crucifixion of Jesus Christ		344
Chapter 7	**Argument #9 for God = The Person of Jesus Christ**			**354**
7.1	Peter Stoner: "Science Speaks: Scientific Proof of Accuracy of Bible Prophecy"			354
7.2	The Deity of Jesus Christ		John 8:56-59	356
7.3	Dr. John H. Gerstner: "A Primer on the Deity of Christ"			357
7.4	Evidence #1 for the Deity of Jesus Christ: Messiah's Lineage		Genesis	360
7.5	Evidence #2 for the Deity of Jesus Christ: The Incarnation		Isaiah 7:14, John 1:1-2,14	361
7.6	Evidence #3 for the Deity of Jesus Christ: 'Immanuel'		Joshua 1:9, Matthew 1:23	362
7.7	Evidence #4 for the Deity of Jesus Christ: God in the Flesh		Isaiah 9:6	364
7.8	Evidence #5 for the Deity of Jesus Christ: The Son of Man		Daniel 7:13	365
7.9	Evidence #6 for the Deity of Jesus Christ: Messiah's 1st Coming		Daniel 9:24-26	366
7.10	Evidence #7 for the Deity of Jesus Christ: The Suffering Messiah		Isaiah 53:1-12	368
7.11	Evidence #8 for the Deity of Jesus Christ: The Crucifixion		Psalm 22	370
7.12	Evidence #9 for the Deity of Jesus Christ: The Creator, Life & Light		John 1:3-5	371

Book 3 References

1.	Josh McDowell	"The New Evidence that Demands a Verdict"	Here's Life Publishing	1999
2.	Josh McDowell	"The Resurrection Factor"	Here's Life Publishing	1989
3.	Josh McDowell	"He Walked Among Us"	Here's Life Publishing	1988
4.	Lee Strobel	"The Case for Christ"	Zondervan Publishing House	1998
5.	Henry M. Morris	"Many Infallible Proofs"	Master Books	1990
6.	James MacDonald	"God Wrote A Book"	Crossway Books	2005
7.	C.S. Lewis	"Mere Christianity"	Barbour & Co. Publishers	1952
8.	John Foxe	"Foxe's Book of Martyrs"	Hendrickson Publishers	2004
9.	John H. Gerstner	"A Primer on the Deity of Christ"	Presbyt. & Reformed Publishers	1984
10.	Emir/ Ergun Caner	"More Than A Prophet"	Kregel Publications	2003
11.	Robert Anderson	"The Coming Prince"	Kregel Publications	1954
12.	Eric Blehm	"Fearless"	Waterbrook Press	2012
13.	Dan Brown	"The DaVinci Code"	Knopf Doubleday Publishing	2009
14.	Randall N. Baer	"Inside the New Age Movement"	Huntington House Inc.	1989
15.	Peter Stoner	"Science Speaks"	Moody Bible Institute	1968
16.	Victor Buksbazen	"Commentary on the Prophet Isaiah"	Friends of Israel, Inc.	2008
17.	Victor Buksbazen	"Isaiah's Messiah"	Friends of Israel, Inc.	2002
18.	Sir William Ramsey	"Bearing of Recent Discovery on the Trustworthiness of the New Testament"	Hodder & Stoughton Publishers	1915
19.	Dr. Robert Wilson	"Scientific Investigation of the Old Testament"	Harper Books	1929
20.	Dr. Paul L. Maier	"Josephus: The Essential Writings"	Kregel Publications	1988
21.	Dr. Craig Evans	"Dead Sea Scrolls"	B&H Publishing Group	2010
22.	Werner Keller	"The Bible as History"	Bantam Books	1998
23.	W. D. Edwards, MD	"On the Physical Death of Jesus Christ"	JAMA	1986
24.	Al Hoerth	"Bible Archaeology"	Baker Books	2005
25.	Gaalyah Cornfeld	"Archaeology of the Bible: Book by Book"	Hendrickson Publishers	1989
26.	Hershel Shanks	"The Dead Sea Scrolls After 40 Years"	Biblical Archaeology Society	1991
27.	J. Barton Payne	"Encyclopedia of Biblical Prophecy"	Baker Book House	1989
28.	Alfred Edersheim	"Bible History: The Old Testament"	Hendrickson Publishers	1995
29.	Alfred Edersheim	"Life & Times of Jesus the Messiah"	Hendrickson Publishers	1995

BOOK 4: WHY AM I HERE? God's Will for my Life

			Page
Chapter 1	**God's Will: 4 Rules for knowing it**	Colossians 1:9-10	**374**
1.1	What is a person's will?		375
	The Dignity God bestows on Man: Free Will	Psalm 8:3-9	376
1.2	Finding God's hidden will for my life	Psalm 37:3-6	377
1.3	God's will is fully revealed in Jesus Christ	Isaiah 61:1-3	379
	Jesus Christ = God's Work in Salvation	John 4:34, John 5:17	380
Chapter 2	**God's Will: my Justification**	Acts 13:39, Romans 5:16	**382**
	Sin: It's Definition / It's Operation		384
2.2	Jesus explains Justification	Luke 18:9-14	385
	The Reformation: The Battle over Justification	Romans 1:16-17	385
2.3	What is Saving Faith?	Ephesians 2:8-9	387
	Factual Faith, Temporary Faith: the kind that cannot save you	Book of Exodus	389
2.4	God's Way of Salvation	Matthew 7:13-14	391
	The Rich Young Ruler: The Cost of Eternal Life	Mark 10:17-27	394
2.5	The Gospel according to Jesus	Matthew 16:24-25	395
2.6	What is Repentance?	1Thessalonians 1:9	397
	The Prodigal Son: Repentance to Salvation	Luke 15:11-32	398
2.7	God's Gift of Salvation: His Covenant Vow	Genesis 15:5-12,17	399
	Jesus as the Bridegroom: He keeps His vows	Isaiah 62:5	400
2.8	God's Gift of Salvation: A Consecration	Hebrews 9:16-18	401
	The Cross: Consecration's Power is in Brokenness	Isaiah 53:5,10	402
2.9	Eternal Security: can it impact how I live?	John 10:28	403
Chapter 3	**God's Will: my Sanctification**	1Thessalonians 4:3,7	**405**
3.1	Christ freed me from the power of sin	Romans 6:6-7,14	406
	God's Character = His Will for my life	Book of Proverbs	408
3.2	God's Wisdom: is seen in His moral character	Proverbs 18:10	409
	11 Old Testament Names for God that reveal His Moral Character		411
	Dr. William Lane Craig: Answering the Objection from the Euthyphro Dilemma		413
	Argument #10 for God = The Objective Moral Law	Habakkuk 2:13	415
	Ravi Zacharias: Answering the Objection from Epicurus		416
	CS Lewis: "Mere Christianity" = Three Arguments for the Objective Moral Law		417
3.3	God's Character: is His concern	Proverbs 22:1	419
3.4	My Character: God's Definition	Proverbs 21:3	421
3.5	My Character: a Heart Issue	Proverbs 4:23	423
	Jesus: He Guards My Heart	Isaiah 59:9-17	426
3.6	My Character: is relational	Proverbs 23:26	427
3.7	My Character: requires renewal	Proverbs 28:13	429
3.8	My Moral Character: fights against my immoral nature	Proverbs 20:19	431
	The Moral Law and the 'War Within'	Romans 7:14-25	432
	Dr. Francis Collins: "The Language of God" = The Moral Law and the Battle Within		433
	Winning the Battle: I must die to myself if I want to live	Colossians 3:3-10	434
	Watchman Nee: "The Normal Christian Life"		435
3.9	My Moral Character: can defeat my immoral nature	Romans 6:6-7,11,19	436
3.10	My Reverence: where I begin	Proverbs 1:7	439
	God's Love requires Him to judge Evil	Psalm 145:17-20	440
	Hell = The Greatest Monument to Human Free Will	Romans 1:24-25	441
3.11	My Humility: draws God to me	Proverbs 3:34	442
3.12	My Submission: demonstrates my humility	Proverbs 16:3	444
3.13	My Meekness: reveals my understanding	Proverbs 17:27	446
3.14	My Faithfulness: requires risk	Proverbs 3:5-6	448
	Dangerous Faith	Mark 5:22-34	449
3.15	My Truthfulness: delights Him	Proverbs 15:22	450

Chapter 4 God's Will: His Glorification

		Isaiah 42:8	**452**
4.2	My Fruit: based on the character of the power producing it	Matthew 7:16-20	453
	Why some people reject Christ: they watch Christians	Ezekiel 36:21	455
4.3	God's Love for me: is called 'agape'	Proverbs 10:12	456
4.4	My Love for God: is why I obey	Proverbs 3:12	460
4.5	God's Kindness and Mercy: His love in action	Proverbs 19:22	462
	Propitiation = God's Mercy Seat	Rom. 3:23-26, Heb. 2:17	463
4.6	God's Forgiveness: His gift of love	Proverbs 17:9	464
	Jesus = God's Scapegoat to forgive my sins	Leviticus 16:10,21-22	467
4.7	My Forgiveness: the answer to bitterness	Proverbs 14:10	468
4.8	My Giving: promises God's blessings	Proverbs 11:25	470
4.9	My Diligence: prompts a promise from God	Proverbs 8:17	472
4.10	God's Suffering: fulfills His own righteousness	Hebrews 5:8	476
	Jeremiah = Jesus in the O.T.: the 'Weeping Prophet'	Jeremiah 20:8-11	476
	Argument #11 for God = Evil & Suffering Exists	1Peter 3:18	478
	Dr. William Lane Craig: Argument Against Naturalism: Objective Moral Values		479
	Dr. Fazale Rana: What about Natural Evil and the Suffering it causes?		480
4.11	My Suffering: grows my character	Romans 5:3-4	481
4.12	My Evangelism: fulfills the vision of Jesus	Matthew 5:16	483
	Effective Evangelism: First 'Come and See', then 'Go and Tell'	Mark 1:17	484
4.13	God's Rewards: different for Christians vs. non-Christians	Revelation 20:11-15	485
	The Rich Man and Lazarus – The Reality of Hell	Luke 16:24-31	486
4.14	My Rewards: based on my motives	1Corinthians 3:11-15	488

Book 4 References

1.	Rick Warren	"The Purpose Driven Life"	Zondervan Books	2002
2.	John MacArthur, Jr.	"The Gospel According to Jesus"	Zondervan Books	1994
3.	John MacArthur, Jr.	"Hard to Believe"	Nelson Publishing	2003
4.	John MacArthur, Jr.	"Found: God's Will"	Victor Books	1973
5.	John MacArthur, Jr.	"The God Who Loves"	Word Publishing	2001
6.	C.S. Lewis	"Mere Christianity"	Barbour & Co.	1943
7.	C.S. Lewis	"Virtue & Vice"	Hayser-Collins	2005
8.	Dinesh D'Souza	"What's So Great About Christianity?"	Tyndale House	2007
9.	Charles Stanley	"Eternal Security: Can You Be Sure?"	Nelson Books	1990
10.	Charles C. Ryrie	"So Great Salvation"	Victor Books	1989
11.	Andy Stanley	"Louder than Words"	Multnomah Publishers	2004
12.	Max Lucado	"He Still Moves Stones"	Word Publishing	1993
13.	Max Lucado	"A Heart Like Jesus"	Word Publishing	1998
14.	Timothy Keller	"The Reason for God"	Riverhead Books	2008
15.	Francis Collins	"The Language of God"	Free Press Publishing	2006
16.	Ergun & Emir Caner	"Unveiling Islam"	Kregel Publications	2002
17.	Walter Martin	"The Kingdom of the Cults"	Bethany House	1985
18.	Norman Geisler	"When Skeptics Ask"	Baker Books	2008
19.	John Stott	"Your Mind Matters"	Inter-Varsity Press	1972
20.	John Stott	"Basic Christianity"	Eerdsman Publishing	1971
21.	Bertrand Russell	"Why I am not a Christian"	Simon & Schuster	1957

Book 4 Additional Reading

22.	Watchman Nee	"The Normal Christian Life"	Tyndale House	1957
23.	Dietrich Bonhoeffer	"The Cost of Discipleship"	Collier Books	1937
24.	Alan Redpath	"The Making of A Man of God"	Baker Books	1962
25.	J.I. Packer	"A Quest for Godliness"	Crossway Books	1990
26.	Donald Whitney	"Spiritual Disciplines for the Christian Life"	Navpress Books	1991

FSE University

Book 1 of 4

Worldviews, Truth & Evidence

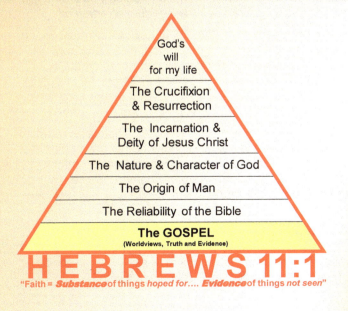

Is what I believe true?

HEBREWS 11:1
"Faith = *Substance* of things *hoped* for.... *Evidence* of things *not seen*"

YOUNG ADULTS = Teenagers and Millennials - Our Future Hope

Teenagers don't want a lecture. They want to talk.

The most recent Barna research shows that about 80% of all Americans who claim Jesus Christ as their savior do so before reaching the age of 21.

Teenagers are the biggest ministry opportunity for the church. What do they claim is most important to them spiritually?

Barna says 45% want "to worship and connect with God", and close behind is 42% who want "to better understand what I believe".

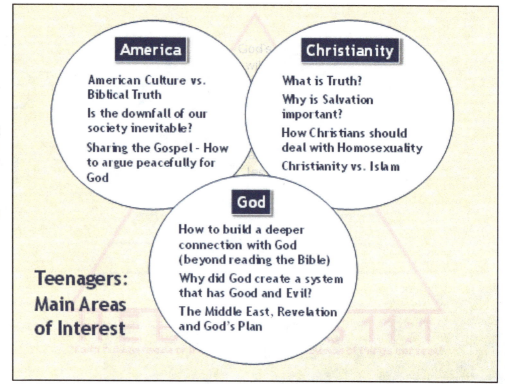

What is a "Millennial"?

The Pew Research Center defines them by age: from 18-35. In terms of size, they are a force to reckon with. The Pew Center also reports that *"As of April 2016, 69.2 million Millennials were voting-age U.S. citizens... almost equal to the 69.7 million Baby Boomers (ages 52-70) in the nation's electorate."* They now are a critical group in defining the future of our constitutional republic. There has only been one other time in American history where Millennials played such a crucial role in our Constitution. But it wasn't in protecting it – it was in creating it.

On August 2, 1776, our founding fathers – those who led the American Revolution to establish the greatest nation the world has ever seen - signed the Declaration of Independence. Just 11 years later (September 17, 1787), our Constitution was signed by many of the same people. Their average age? Only 44, with nearly half under 40.

Our "Founding Fathers" were actually "Founding Millennials". And what did these "Founding Millennials" make priority #1 in the Constitution? In his article 'The US Constitution and Religious Liberty', political writer and lawyer David Limbaugh gives us the answer: *"The freedom of religion and the freedom of religious worship were of such paramount importance to the Framers that they guaranteed them in the very first two clauses of the very first amendment to the Constitution, the establishment clause and the free exercise clause.... which was a dedication to the idea that the federal government should not establish a national church -- because to do so would diminish religious liberty. The free exercise clause, by its very terms, expressly guarantees the freedom of worship."*

So our founders thought religious liberty is the most important liberty any American could have. And where would such a young generation come up with such a scandalous idea? In crafting the Constitution, they purposely divided the government into three distinct branches (Judicial, Legislative and Executive) in order to create a system of checks and balances that would prevent any one of them becoming too powerful. Where did this idea come from? The Old Testament Book of Isaiah: *"The Lord is our Judge; the Lord is our Lawgiver; the Lord is our King; he will save us."* (Isaiah 33:22).

And who is this King whom our Millennial founders looked to for salvation? On April 18, 1775, about a year before signing the Declaration of Independence, Paul Revere arrived at Reverend Jonas Clarke's home to warn him that the Redcoats were approaching. The next morning British Major Pitcairn shouted to a regiment of Minutemen: *"Disperse, ye villains, lay down your arms in the name of George the Sovereign King of England."* Reverend Clarke, the new leader of the militia, responded with what is known as the Battle Cry of the American Revolution: *"We recognize no Sovereign but God and no King but Jesus."*

Now, 240 years later, with over 30% of the vote, our Millennials are again at a place in history where they can be a critical player in America's future. But this time what is at stake isn't whether or not America will be born. Rather, it's whether or not America's Christian foundation will remain. For those of us who claim Jesus Christ as their King, we have a responsibility to help guide our millennial population into a deeper relationship with Him.

CHAPTER 1   Hebrews 11:1   Christianity ⇨ *Substance* with *Evidence*   1.1

"①FAITH is the ②SUBSTANCE of things hoped for, the ③EVIDENCE of things not seen."

① FAITH = Gr. *"pistis"* = a firm conviction; to "cling" to; the object of faith is a Person (it is not faith in God's promises, which are the occasions to exercise my faith, but rather in God Himself)
② SUBSTANCE = Gr. *"hupostasis"* ⇨ "hupo" = under, "stasis" = stand upon; what I "stand upon, under me" (i.e., "understanding") that defines my future hope and assurance (can be objective by facts or subjective by opinion)
③ EVIDENCE = Gr. *"elegehos"* = convincing proofs that lead to *conviction* (i.e., faith) in or on a matter or subject

What is Evidence?
Webster's Dictionary = *"that which, when presented clearly, tends to prove or disprove something; an indication or sign; data presented to a court to decide an alleged matter or fact"*
Romans 1:20 *"For since the creation of the world His INVISIBLE ATTRIBUTES ARE CLEARLY SEEN, being understood by the things which are made, even His eternal power and Godhead, so that they are without excuse."*

What "Evidence" in Hebrews 11:1 is my faith based on?
God provides much empirical evidence for anyone to believe, but my faith does not rest only on the evidence. Its foundation is its *SUBSTANCE*: a *DIVINE ASSURANCE*, which is a *GIFT* from Him (Ephesians 2:8). It's the God-given *conviction* in my *heart* of a future *reality*, made real in history in the Person and work of Jesus Christ.
Acts 3:16 *"And His name, through faith in His name, has made this man strong, whom you see and know. Yes, the faith WHICH COMES THROUGH HIM has given him this perfect soundness in the presence of you all."*
Ephesians 2:8-9 *"...by grace you have been saved through faith, and that NOT OF YOURSELVES; it is the GIFT OF GOD, not of works, lest anyone should boast."*
Romans 8:24-25 *"For WE WERE SAVED IN THIS HOPE, but hope that is seen is not hope; for why does one still hope for what one sees? But if we hope for what we do not see, then we eagerly wait for it with perseverance."*

Josh McDowell[11]: "The Evidence provides any honest seeker a basis for faith in the Lord Jesus Christ"
"The evidence confirming the deity of the Lord Jesus Christ is overwhelmingly conclusive to any honest, objective seeker after truth… But watch your Attitude: The proper motivation behind the use of this material is to glorify and magnify Jesus Christ – not to win an argument. Evidence is not for proving the Word of God but simply for providing a basis for FAITH."

Stephen Meyer (PhD Physics, Geology)[12]: "The Scientific Evidence reminds me my faith is in the Lord"
"For a 2-year period in my life, I was attracted to Nietzsche's version of existentialism. He asked, 'Why should God rule and I serve?' That resonated within me. Why should a condition of my happiness be submission to the will of God? I sensed I couldn't be happy without Him; I knew my bad lifestyle only brought misery. The intellectual rebellion the apostle Paul talks about is very true in my own life. Even in my Christian thinking today, I find a tendency to slide back into what Paul refers to as the natural mind.
And here's what the scientific evidence for God does for me: it realigns me. It helps me recognize that despite my natural tendency toward self-focus and self-absorption, I can't ignore God's accomplishment in this world to let everyone know that He is real, that He is the Creator, and that we need to get right with Him."

What is the foundation of my Faith: God's Sovereignty or Man's Understanding?	
God's Sovereignty	**Man's Understanding**
Daniel 4:35 *"All the inhabitants of the earth are reputed as nothing; HE DOES ACCORDING TO HIS WILL in the army of heaven and among the inhabitants of the earth. No one can restrain His hand or say to Him, 'What have You done?'"*	Bertrand Russell[31](Nobel Prize philosopher, atheist): *"If one day I stand before God and He asks me, 'Why didn't you believe in Me?', I would say, 'Not enough evidence, God! Not enough evidence!'"*
Psalm 115:3 *"Our God is in heaven; HE DOES WHATEVER HE PLEASES."*	Francisco Ayala[8]: *"There is no evidence of any vital force directing the evolutionary process toward the production of specified kinds of organisms."*
Isaiah 43:13 *"… Indeed before the day was, I am He. And there is no one who can deliver out of My hand; I work, and WHO WILL REVERSE IT?"* 1Chronicles 16:31 *"Let the heavens rejoice, and let the earth be glad; and let them say among the nations, 'THE LORD REIGNS'"*	William Provine, Cornell Univ. evolutionist and Historian[8]: *"If Darwinism is true, then there are five inescapable conclusions: 1) there's no evidence for God, 2) there's no life after death, 3) there's no absolute foundation for right and wrong, 4) there's no ultimate meaning for life, 5) people don't really have free will."*

DOES GOD EXIST? The 5 Religious Worldviews — Dr. Geisler ('Christian Apologetics')[29]

Worldview	Where it contributes…	Where it fails as a Worldview…
DEISM • God created the natural world but is beyond the world, never operating in it in miraculous ways; • The world operates by natural and self-sustaining laws of the Creator. • Deny the Trinity, Deity of Christ, Virgin Birth. • Deny miracles *Forms of Naturalism*	1) God reveals something personal about Himself through His creation; 2) emphasizes using reason in religious matters, to separate truth from falsehood 3) use reason to evaluate miracles (don't use miracles as answer for anything you don't understand) 4) historical attacks on Christianity gave rise to scholarly defenses of orthodox Christianity	1) it is self-defeating to admit the miracle of creation but deny other lesser miracles (like the Virgin Birth, walking on water) are possible. 2) It is inconsistent to disallow personal communication from the supernatural to the natural realm once admitting God is personal. 3) A God concerned enough and strong enough to create man should be concerned and strong enough to help. So, God's nature is compatible with miraculous intervention in the natural world when He deems it. 4) Deist arguments to eliminate belief in supernatural revelation also apply to eliminate belief in creation. 5) Deism has failed to cast sufficient doubt on the supernatural either in principle or in fact (Deist criticism of trustworthiness of biblical documents and writers is definitely lacking): (a) archaeological confirmation of Scripture is overwhelming (> 25,000 finds confirm biblical world), (b) integrity of eyewitnesses has been sufficiently established, (c) Bible's alleged contradictions have been answered, (d) no scientific errors have been proven in the Bible
PANTHEISM • Polar opposite of Deism • God is the world, and the world is God. • God does not transcend reality but is imminent in reality (all reality is in God). Beyond God is only illusion. • Creation from nothing is meaningless since creation flows from God. • God is an It, not a He (impersonal, beyond rational knowledge). • God is beyond good or evil, and just is. Evil is an illusion. • God is understood not by sensible observation nor by rational inference but by mystical intuition that is beyond the law of noncontradiction (opposing statements on God can both be true). *Hinduism, Taoism, Native American Religion, Gnosticism*	1) It is both metaphysical and comprehensive (not a piecemeal philosophy) = this is essential in any worldview. 2) emphasizes unity (since there is a uni-verse, there must be a basis in reality for uni-ty). 3) emphasizes that God is really in the world, at least within the depths of the human soul. 4) emphasizes that only one God is absolute and necessary – none of creation is independent or ontologically detached – all is completely dependent on God who is All in all. 5) emphasizes the direct and unmediated intimacy with God, the object of knowledge. 6) often expresses God in terms of what he is not – 'via negativa' – God can't be expressed in positive terms with limited meaning, since he is infinite and transcendent (all limitations must be negated from terms applied to him).	1) It is unaffirmable by man, since no finite reality exists that is different from God (the pantheist must affirm, 'God is but I am not', which is self-defeating, since one must exist in order to affirm he doesn't). 2) to avoid the above self-defeating argument, pantheists allow some reality to finite man, as only a *self*-conscious mode or aspect of God. But if this is true, why aren't people conscious of this? If I am unconscious of my own existence, how does a pantheist know he is not being deceived when he claims to be conscious of reality as an aspect of God? 3) Fellowship and worship is impossible since finite man is not real but only a mode or aspect of God, who is ultimate reality. 4) If evil is not real, why is it so persistent and seem so real? Making evil a part of God does not explain evil – it puts God beyond the laws of logic, with no distinction between good and evil. 5) God is not personal, but an impersonal force driven by metaphysical necessity and not by volitional and loving choice. 6) Since God is 'All' with the universe (the Whole is a collection of all its finite parts or aspects), pantheism is metaphysically the same as atheism ('the universe is all there is, all there was, and all there will ever be'). The only difference is pantheism attributes religious significance to the All, and atheism doesn't. 7) To say 'God is All', including things that are opposite, violates the Law of Noncontradiction and says nothing meaningful about him. 8) Claiming only what God is not tells one nothing about Him and is meaningless. Pantheist writings contain no information, so why write? It is self-defeating to communicate a view on God only to inform the audience that he has not done so.

DOES GOD EXIST?	**The 5 Religious Worldviews**	Dr. Geisler ('Christian Apologetics')[29]
Worldview	**Where it contributes…**	**Where it fails as a Worldview…**
ATHEISM There is no God, either in or beyond the world. Secular Humanism, Buddhism	1) The principle of Sufficient Reason (that everything needs a cause or explanation) leads to an infinite regress and not to God. 2) God cannot have the cause of himself within himself (a self-caused Being is impossible). 3) If a moral law exists, it either results from God's will or it doesn't. If by his will, it's arbitrary since he can call anything good. If not from his will, he is subject to it and not God. 4) An all-powerful God could destroy evil; an all-good God would destroy evil. But evil exists, so God is either: (a) impotent and can't destroy evil, (b) malevolent and won't destroy evil, (c) both a and b, (d) doesn't exist. 5) An all-wise, all-powerful, all-good God would not allow any unjust suffering. One injustice in the world argues against God being all-just. 6) It is possible the world happened by blind chance. The universe may be just a 'happy accident'. 7) I am free to determine myself, and be accountable to my own actions, so there is no God.	1) The principle of Causality does not demand that everything needs a cause, but only finite, changing, dependent beings need a cause. 2) The principle of causality leads to an infinite, necessary and uncaused Being, which is not contradictory as self-caused. 3) Moral law doesn't flow from God's arbitrary will – it is rooted in His unchanging good and loving nature. He is bound by who He is, the very essence of His Person. 4) Just because evil is not yet defeated in time by an all-loving, all-powerful God, doesn't mean He never will. And God has done something to this point to defeat evil. Christians believe evil was defeated by Christ on the Cross, and evil will be destroyed when Christ returns. In fact, I can trust in His guarantee that He will one day do just that. A finite God cannot offer such hope. Rather than evil eliminating the logical possibility of God, only God can guarantee the elimination of evil. 5) If atheism claims there is unjust suffering in the world, there must be a standard of justice beyond this world, otherwise how can anyone judge what is unjust? But this brings us back to God, the ultimate standard for justice. So atheism's claim there exists a just standard is self-defeating since it points to God. 6) The odds against a chance explanation of such an immense universe are great, while the evidences for a designed universe exist. 7) Knowing what men will do with their freedom isn't the same as ordaining what men must do against their freedom. Love is persuasive, but never coercive, making God responsible for the fact of freedom but not responsible for the acts of freedom, thus allowing men to determine their own destiny.
PANEN-THEISM • God is *in* the world (Pantheism says God *is* the world). • The world is the 'body' of God. God is to the world as the mind is to the body. • God is finite and limited, in a continual process of change. • God isn't the Creator, but a Cosmic Director.	1) argue metaphysics that allow classical truth testing (ontology, teleology, morality). 2) God transcends the world, so they avoid the self-defeating identification of God and the real world (i.e., Pantheism). 3) stresses God's personal interaction with the real world. 4) God's being in the world is what saves it from chaos (without Him the world would not exist). 5) points to the need to explain the God of Scripture as a personal God of ceaseless creative activity (He actively sustains the creative world process, and is active in history and manifest in nature). Hinduism, Ba'Hai Faith, Sikhism,	1) the bipolar concept of God as eternal potential seeking temporal actualization is self-defeating (no potential can actualize itself - it must be activated by something outside itself, which would lead to a theistic God of pure act in order to account for a panentheistic god). 2) A finite, changing god must have an infinite and unchanging basis for its change. Change makes no sense unless there is an unchanging basis by which change is measured (the relative presupposes the absolute). 3) A finite god cannot guarantee the defeat of evil, and holds out little prospect for a better world: (a) how does a finite, limited god who cannot triumph over evil assure us there is any real growth in value in the universe? (b) does the supposed increase in value justify the countless numbers of evils suffered to gain it? What significance is there in suffering for the individual? 4) the concept of god is based on what he does, not what he is (the error of man creating god in his own image) – there is activity but no Actor, movement but no Mover, creation but no Creator. This god is impotent in being limited in power and always changing.

DOES GOD EXIST? The 5 Religious Worldviews — Dr. Geisler ('Christian Apologetics')[29]

Worldview	Where it contributes…	Where it fails as a Worldview…
THEISM • God is both beyond and within the world, a Creator and Sustainer who sovereignly controls the world and supernaturally intervenes in it. _3 Important Points_: 1) Reality must be viewed in terms of the possible, the impossible, or the necessary – there are no other logical possibilities (and logic can be applied to reality). 2) The world and God are either caused, self-caused or uncaused - there are no other logical possibilities. 3) Based on 1) and 2) above, forming a metaphysical world-view that includes all the possibilities about reality and to eliminate some as actually impossible, and to establish the remaining one as actually necessary, is not an arbitrary position but a logical one. Monotheism = Christianity, Judaism, Islam, Zoroastrianism Polytheism = Hinduism, Egyptian & Greek Religions	**1) Every finite effect has a cause; the world is a finite effect; therefore, the world has a cause** (whatever exists that has the potential to not exist, i.e., might not exist, is an 'effect' caused to exist by another, i.e., is contingent on another causing it to exist). **2) The world is a whole, not just its parts, needs a cause** (the very nature of the caused parts demands that the whole group of them taken together must be caused – for example, by the very nature of a wooden table, if each part is made of wood, then the whole table must be wooden). **3) An Infinite Regress of causes is impossible** (in an infinite series every cause is being caused by another – if there were one cause that was causing but not being caused it would be the uncaused cause which the infinite series seeks to avoid. So, this one (or more) cause that is doing the causing of every other cause must be causing itself, since it too is being caused by the causality in the series. But the only causality in the series is being given to the series by that cause itself. So, this one cause would be causing itself - it would be a self-caused being, which is impossible. **4) The terms 'Necessary Being' and 'Uncaused Cause' are meaningful** (God is not a logically necessary Being; i.e., we're not making an A Priori argument, but the statement 'God exists' is a logically necessary statement, based on #1 above). An actual effect demands an actual cause, and a contingent being demands a necessary Being to ground it. So, it follows that the actual contingent world demands an actually necessary Being as its cause.	1) _A Priori Arguments Alone_ for God are logically invalid – no reality, including God, can be established by logical necessity (you can't argue for God's existence based on the _concept_ of an absolutely perfect or necessary Being (even if it is logically necessary to _conceive_ of a necessary Being as necessarily existing, it does not follow that It necessarily exists). 2) _A Posteriori Arguments Alone_ for God are also logically invalid (experience is never logically necessary – the existence of God cannot be proven without appealing to some principle that is independent of experience). If it is logically possible that _something(s)_ can exist without a cause, then any theistic argument based on this principle fail. • Most criticisms of theism miss the significance of the argument based on existential causality and are directed toward invalid A Priori arguments, such as the ontological argument, or toward insufficient A Posteriori arguments that either assume an unjustified causal premise (as the teleological and moral arguments), or else are based on a rationally unjustified form of the principle of sufficient reason. In this sense neither A Priori nor A Posteriori proofs for God's existence are rationally inescapable. • There is however a valid argument that COMBINES both the A Priori self-evident principle of existential causality and the undeniable A Posteriori fact that something exists (e.g., I exist). The criticisms of this argument are insufficient. • **_Theism has found a firm ground in existence for the conclusion that God exists. This is a theistic universe._"** 

"There is A God" by Dr. Antony Flew[5]

Dr. Antony Flew was the author of over 30 professional philosophical works that helped set the agenda for atheism for over half a century. His 'Theology and Falsification', presented first to the Oxford University Socratic Club (chaired by C.S. Lewis) in 1950, became the most widely printed philosophical publication of the last century. As Ravi Zacharias once said, Flew was the standard for studying atheistic philosophy in his university education.

Dr. Flew wrote for over 50 years on anti-theology with an admired approach that was systematic, comprehensive, original and extremely influential. Why?

There is a God – How the World's Most Notorious Atheist Changed His Mind

"My discovery of the Divine has been a pilgrimage of reason and not faith."
Antony Flew
Page 93

"It speaks very well of Professor Flew's honesty. After all these years of opposing the idea of a Creator, he reverses his position on the basis of the evidence."
Alvin Plantinga

Because unlike so many others such as Dr. Bertrand Russell, Flew's writings didn't originate from a disdain for organized religion. Rather, his focus was on, as he claimed from the very beginning, developing arguments to support HIS position, grounded in the Socratic Method: "We must follow the argument wherever it leads."

Dr. Flew makes two straight-forward confessions in this book that not only prompted many Christian apologists and theologians to praise his openness and courage, but also raised the hostility of atheist leaders to denounce him as "old and senile". On page 12, he says this: *"I have said in some of my later atheist writings that I reached the conclusion about the nonexistence of God much too quickly, much too easily, and for what later seemed to me the wrong reasons"*. Ouch. Then, on pages 29 and 32: *"No one is as surprised as I am that my exploration of the Divine has after all these years turned from denial to discovery… it took years for my philosophical views to mature and solidify. By the time they did so, I had arrived at the guiding principles that would not only govern my lifetime of writing and reasoning, but also eventually dictate a dramatic turn FROM ATHEISM TO THEISM."*

So what exactly prompted Dr. Flew to become a theist? On page 88, Dr. Flew explains: *"It's time for me to lay my cards on the table, to set my own views and the reasons that support them. I now believe that the universe was brought into existence by an Infinite Intelligence. I believe that this universe's intricate laws manifest what scientists have called the Mind of God. I believe that life and reproduction originate in a divine Source. Why do I believe this, given that I expounded and defended atheism for more than half a century (about 60 years)? The short answer is this: this is the world picture, as I see it, that has emerged from modern science… and a renewed study of the classical philosophical arguments."*

Dr. Flew's book was published around the same time many of the New Atheists were gaining in popularity and the phenomenon on college campuses of the Veritas Forum was taking center stage, as a more collegial debate structure also gained popularity in pitting the best Christian apologists against the New Atheism spokesmen.

But Dr. Flew's arguments against atheism, and for theism, have gone largely unnoticed in this age of internet instant information and rhetorical arguments supplanting good old "butt in the seat" diligent study. On page 89, Dr. Flew himself explains what actually led him away from atheism and to theism: *"My departure from atheism was not occasioned by any new phenomenon or argument. Over the past two decades, my whole framework of thought has been in a state of migration. This was my consequence of MY CONTINUING ASSESSMENT OF THE EVIDENCE OF NATURE.*

When I finally came to recognize the existence of a God, it was not a paradigm shift, because my paradigm remains, as Plato in his 'Republic' scripted Socrates to insist: 'WE MUST FOLLOW THE ARGUMENT WHEREVER IT LEADS."

In his book, Dr. Flew asks 32 questions to his fellow atheists. These questions are not new – but they are coming from one of the greatest, if not the greatest, atheist philosophical minds in history – and they are meant to be a challenge to atheists to really examine the evidence, because it will lead any open-minded seeker away from atheism and to theism.

What the World Believes:
Understanding the Three Major Global Religions outside Christianity

ISLAM (Ergun and Emir Caner, "Unveiling Islam"[32]) – Middle East, Africa

Allah: the "Distant One"

The Allah we worshipped as Muslims was a remote judge.

When Christians speak of the intimacy and grace of God, it confuses a Muslim.

In all the terms and titles of Allah, one does not encounter terms of intimacy.

Even the most faithful and devout Muslim refers to Allah only as a servant to master; Allah is a distant sovereign.

Allah: the "Cold Judge"

Islam looks to a god of the scales, as opposed to the atoning Son of God.

Allah forgives only at the repentance of the Muslim, and all consequences for sin and the debt of guilt fall on the Muslim, who comes to Allah in terror, hoping for commutation of his sentence.

One sees a judge, as opposed to a God of Love.

Allah: the "Hater"

Allah's heart is set against the infidel.

He has no love for the unbeliever, nor is a Muslim to "evangelize" the unbelieving world.

Allah is to be worshipped, period.

The theme is conquest, not conversion, of the unbelieving world.

Middle East

Country	Population	Muslim		Christian	
Pakistan	156,483,155	150,349,015	96.1%	3,614,761	2.3%
Iran	67,702,199	67,038,717	99.0%	223,417	0.3%
Turkey	66,590,940	66,351,213	99.6%	213,091	0.3%
Uzbekistan	24,317,851	20,305,406	83.5%	316,132	1.3%
Iraq	23,114,884	22,386,765	96.9%	358,281	1.6%
Afghanistan	22,720,000	22,240,608	97.9%	4,544	0.0%
Saudi Arabia	21,606,691	20,057,491	92.8%	980,944	4.5%
Yemen	18,112,066	18,101,199	99.9%	9,056	0.1%
Syria	16,124,618	14,560,530	90.3%	822,356	5.1%
Turkmenistan	4,459,293	4,095,415	91.8%	120,401	2.7%
Oman	2,541,739	2,355,175	92.7%	64,560	2.5%
United Arab Emirates	2,441,436	1,623,555	66.5%	227,054	9.3%
Kuwait	1,971,634	1,723,800	87.4%	161,082	8.2%
	428,186,506	411,188,889	96.0%	7,115,678	1.7%

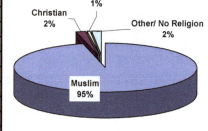

Africa

Country	Population	Muslim		Christian	
Nigeria	111,506,095	45,717,499	41.0%	58,652,206	52.6%
Egypt	68,469,695	59,239,980	86.5%	8,887,366	13.0%
Algeria	31,471,278	30,426,432	96.7%	91,267	0.3%
Sudan	29,489,719	19,168,317	65.0%	6,841,615	23.2%
Morocco	28,220,843	28,178,512	99.9%	14,110	0.1%
Somalia	10,097,177	10,092,128	100.0%	5,049	0.1%
Tunisia	9,585,611	9,553,020	99.7%	21,088	0.2%
Libya	5,604,722	5,408,557	96.5%	168,142	3.0%
Mauritania	2,669,547	2,665,276	99.8%	4,271	0.2%
	297,114,687	210,449,721	70.8%	74,685,114	25.1%

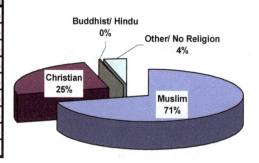

BUDDHISM (Lit-Sen-Chang, "Zen-Existentialism: The Spiritual Decline of the West") – Far East

Zen Buddhism is a subtle form of Atheism: it is the love of self first, last and always.
It denies the infinity and transcendence of a living, personal God.
It denies the need of a Savior, thus denying the true God and the gift of His grace, by exalting and deifying man.
Salvation can be secured by man's own power and wisdom.
In Zen Buddhism, there is no supernatural intervention. We bear the whole responsibility for our actions and no Sage whosoever he be has the right to encroach on our free will.

HINDUISM (Walter Martin, "The Kingdom of the Cults"[33]) – Far East

There is no single Hindu idea of God.
He can be pantheist (all existence), animist (all nonhuman objects such as rocks, trees, animals, etc.), polytheist (many gods to worship), henotheist (many gods, but only one worshipped), monotheist (only one god).
Hinduism believes that all souls are eternal and accountable for their actions throughout time.
There is no need for a personal relationship to a Savior, who by grace takes the punishment for their sins.
Rather, it is through "karma" (wheel of suffering) and "reincarnation" (soul inhabits successive human bodies) their bad actions are atoned for as they strive to achieve self-realization ("nirvana") through ritualistic sacrifice and discipline.

Far East

Country	Population	Other or No Religion		Buddhist/ Hindu		Muslim		Christian	
China	1,262,556,787	1039968025	82.4%	105,802,259	8.4%	25,251,136	2.0%	91,535,367	7.3%
India	1,013,661,777	45614780	4.5%	817,011,392	80.6%	126,707,722	12.5%	24,327,883	2.4%
Indonesia	212,991,926	3194879	1.5%	4,685,822	2.2%	171,032,517	80.3%	34,078,708	16.0%
Bangladesh	129,155,152	839508	0.7%	16,790,170	13.0%	110,595,557	85.6%	929,917	0.7%
Vietnam	79,831,650	29649475	37.1%	43,109,091	54.0%	558,822	0.7%	6,514,263	8.2%
Burma	45,611,177	1870058	4.1%	38,039,722	83.4%	1,733,225	3.8%	3,968,172	8.7%
North Korea	24,039,193	22551167	93.8%	1,081,764	4.5%	0	0.0%	406,262	1.7%
Nepal	23,930,490	552794	2.3%	21,728,885	90.8%	1,196,525	5.0%	452,286	1.9%
Malaysia	22,244,062	1379132	6.2%	5,916,920	26.6%	12,901,556	58.0%	2,046,454	9.2%
Sri Lanka	18,827,054	84722	0.4%	15,801,546	83.9%	1,506,164	8.0%	1,434,622	7.6%
Tajikistan	6,188,201	564364	9.1%	0	0.0%	5,538,440	89.5%	85,397	1.4%
Laos	5,433,036	1953176	36.0%	3,319,585	61.1%	59,763	1.1%	100,511	1.9%
Tibet	2,500,000	490000	19.6%	2,000,000	80.0%	5,000	0.2%	5,000	0.2%
	2,846,970,505	1,148,712,081	40.3%	1,075,287,156	37.8%	457,086,425	16.1%	165,884,842	5.8%

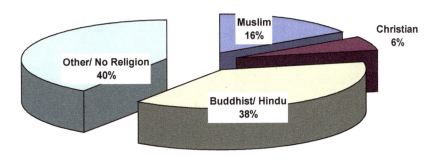

Romans 12:2, John 1:10 "My Personal Worldview = how I see TRUTH" 1.3

"...do not be conformed to this ①WORLD, but be transformed by the renewing of your mind..."
"He was in the ②WORLD, and all things in the world were made through Him, and the world didn't know Him."

① WORLD = Greek *"aión"* = age or period in time, marked by its spiritual or moral characteristics

Matthew 13:22 *"...the cares of this WORLD and the deceitfulness of riches choke the word, and he becomes unfruitful."*
Luke 16:8 *"... the sons of this WORLD are more shrewd in their generation than the sons of light."*
Galatians 1:3-4 *"Grace to you and peace from God the Father and our Lord Jesus Christ, who gave Himself for our sins, that He might deliver us from this present evil AGE, according to the will of our God and Father."*

② WORLD = Greek *"kosmos"* = mankind's world system which is alienated from and in opposition to God

John 7:7 *"The WORLD cannot hate you; but it hates Me because I testify of it that its works are evil."*
1John 4:5 *"They are of the WORLD. Therefore they speak as of the world, and the world hears them."*
1Corin. 1:20 *"... Has not God made foolish the wisdom of this WORLD?"*
Coloss. 2:8 *"Beware lest anyone take you captive through philosophy and empty deceit, according to the tradition of men, according to the basic principles of the WORLD, and not according to Christ."*

What is a "WORLDVIEW"?[3] "The term means literally 'a view of the world'. It is the window by which a person views the world and decides, often subconsciously, what is real and important, or unreal and unimportant. It may be that a worldview is commonly a collection of prejudices. If so, prejudices are necessary, because we can't start from a blank slate and investigate everything from scratch by ourselves. Understanding worldview is a bit like trying to see the lens of one's own eye. We do not ordinarily see our own worldview, but we see everything else by looking through it."

The Three Worldviews in Our Culture

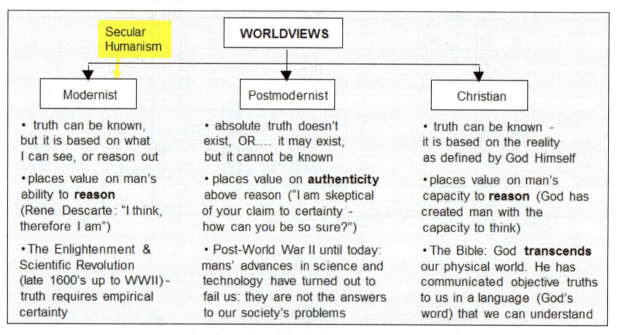

What is "TRUTH"? What corresponds to reality (i.e. "telling it like it is").

Dr. Geisler[12]: Both the Bible and Philosophy are based on the Correspondence view of Truth: *"The Scriptures use the correspondence view of truth quite a bit. The ninth commandment certainly presupposes it. 'You shall not bear false witness against your neighbor' (Exodus 20:16) implies that the truth or falsity of a statement can be tested by whether it checks out with the facts. When Satan said, 'You shall not surely die,' it is called a lie because it does not correspond to what God actually said... Anything that does not correspond to God's Law is considered false (Psalm 119:163). And in the New Testament, Jesus says that His claims can be verified by John the Baptist, saying, 'You have sent to John and he has borne witness to the truth.'*

Philosophically, lying is impossible without a correspondence to reality. If our words do not need to correspond to the facts, then they can never be factually incorrect. Without a correspondence view of truth, there can be no true or false. There would be no real difference in the accuracy of how a system describes a given fact because we could never appeal to the fact as evidence. There has got to be a real difference between our thoughts about things and the things themselves for us to say whether something is true or false."

Truth Test #1 = The Correspondence Test. Truth about reality is what corresponds to the way things really are. Truth is "telling it like it is." There is a reality, and truth accurately expresses it. Falsehood tells or claims things like they are not, misrepresenting the facts or the way things are. So if someone makes a truth claim that does not correspond to reality and the facts, their claim is false.

This way of testing whether someone's claim is true or false is how most people live their lives everyday and matches up with what the Bible has to say as well. According to the Bible, a claim is true only if it accords with factual reality. There are numerous passages that contrast truth claims with lies. For example, Deuteronomy 18:22 warns against false prophets whose words do not correspond to reality: *"If what a prophet proclaims in the name of the Lord does not take place or come true, that is a message the Lord has not spoken"*. The 9th Commandment specifically warns against bearing false testimony. For example, in John 14:6, when Jesus says "I am the way, the truth, and the life," there is a correspondence to reality. Since He is the full revelation of God, Jesus is showing us who God is in actual reality.

How People *Test* for Truth

Correspondence Test
Does the claim accurately describe (i.e., correspond to) the way things actually *are* (reality)- the FACTS?

Coherence Test
Truth is rational or logical within some set of propositions or beliefs. Allows for the *evidence* for different perspectives to be weighed against each other.

For my BELIEF to be TRUE... It must satisfy both tests:
Correspondency: the truth claim must conform to objective features of the world (i.e. reality, or facts).
Coherency: the truth claim must make sense when measured against competing claims on the same belief or topic.

Truth Test #2 = The Coherence Test. Truth is what is self-consistent. But by itself it is inadequate for testing truth. For example, to say "All bachelors are unmarried men" is by itself consistent, but it doesn't tell us anything about reality. The statement would be true, even if there were no bachelors. It really means, "If there is a bachelor, he must be single." But it does not inform us if bachelors exist in reality. At best, coherence is a negative test of truth. Statements are wrong if they are inconsistent, but not necessarily true if they are.

Truth Decision #1 = Objective versus Subjective. By "objective truth" we mean "independent of people's (including my own) opinion." The opposite of "objective" is "subjective", which means "it's just a matter of personal opinion." For example, if objective moral values and obligations do exist, then everyone would be obligated or forbidden from doing certain actions, regardless of what we think.

Truth Decision #2 = Absolute versus Relative. By "absolute truth" we mean "independent of people's circumstances or situation." The opposite of "absolute" is "relative", which means something can be true depending on my circumstances or the situation I'm in. For example, killing another person may be justifiably true depending on the circumstance, such as if an intruder breaks into my home and physically threatens my family.

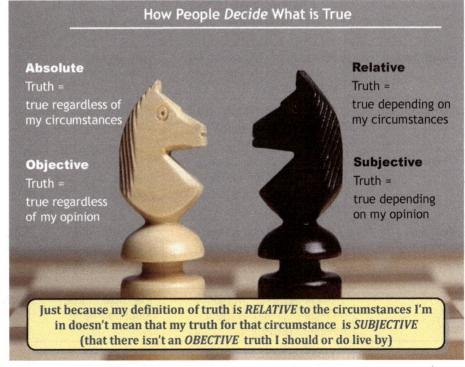

How People *Decide* What is True

Absolute
Truth = true regardless of my circumstances

Objective
Truth = true regardless of my opinion

Relative
Truth = true depending on my circumstances

Subjective
Truth = true depending on my opinion

Just because my definition of truth is *RELATIVE* to the circumstances I'm in doesn't mean that my truth for that circumstance is *SUBJECTIVE* (that there isn't an *OBECTIVE* truth I should or do live by)

Epistemology = The Study of "How We Know" (How People determine what is *TRUE* for them)

People often discover, when they really stop and think about WHY they believe a particular view is true, that it's more of an EMOTIONAL reason than an INTELLECTUAL one (it's something they grew up with, that their parents or a close friend taught them, rather than something they've investigated and convinced themselves it's true).

In order to build a solid foundation for what I believe is true, I first have to honestly answer these questions:
1) How did I come to believe what I believe? What is my belief based on (what is the *foundation* of my belief)?
2) How certain am I that the particular things I believe are *really* true?
 - Is it OK to be uncertain in areas of my Christian faith (what happens if I admit I'm not sure what I believe)?
 - Are there "essential" beliefs I hold in my Christian faith where I should be absolutely certain that it's really true?
3) Do I have a *standard* to determine my essential Christian beliefs? For example, am I as certain of the doctrine of creation, or the Trinity, as I am of the Deity of Christ?

What do I mean when I say I "believe" something is true?
1) Does this belief become something that I am *consciously aware of*?
2) Does this belief *satisfy* the thing that caused me to previously doubt (by whatever means I've chosen)?
3) Does this belief *motivate* me to start cultivating within me a 'rule of action' based on that belief?
4) Does this belief *convict* me to maintain the 'rule of action' in spite of times I fail or others' contrary views?

Ten Epistemologies people use to build their worldview

Epistemology	What it is	What it sounds like	Example	Worldview
Relativism	truth is defined by the group you associate with or the culture in which you grow up	"I believe that because that's the way I was raised"	growing up in India	Postmodernism
Subjectivism	truth is defined based on what you personally believe is true	"That's my opinion. Don't try to convince me otherwise"	personal preference	Postmodernism, Modernism
Perspectivism	truth is synthesized with others' views (take into account the other person's perspective)	"my spouse's view weighs in on any decision I make"	marriage	Postmodernism
Pragmaticism	truth is defined based on what works for that person	"I'm just not happy, so my situation needs to change"	divorce	Postmodernism
Skepticism	truth requires verification (the skeptic *doubts* that anything can be known)	"why should I believe that?"	TV commercials	Postmodernism
Agnosticism	means 'no knowledge'; we know reality is true, but we *can't know* what it is	"if God created man, who created God?"	belief in the supernatural is illogical	Postmodernism, Modernism
Rationalism	Truth is defined by what is knowable through human reasoning (evidence is not necessary)	"The cosmos is all there is, was, and ever will be"	mathematical equations	Modernism
Realism	Some truth can be known when supporting evidence resolves any reasonable doubts	"innocent until proven guilty beyond reasonable doubt"	America's Legal System	Modernism, Christian
Fideism	Truth is personal (subjective), so I just believe it without having to prove it	"the Bible is true because I have faith"	emotional commitment	Modernism, Christian
Objectivism	Truth is defined by reality; truth transcends culture, people, situations; it applies to all	"I'm bound by it, whether I like it or not"	Law of Gravity	Christian

Aristotle's 'On Rhetoric': How we can be persuaded to adopt a worldview

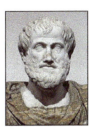

American has gone through a major cultural shift. We have moved from a world of absolutes and objectivity to one of relativism, subjectivism, and tolerance. The greatest commandment in our society today is *'thou shalt tolerate one another'*. But does the behavior of the apostle Paul in Acts 19:8 still hold true today – is Christianity persuasive as a worldview in today's supposed 'enlightened' America? That raises more questions: how do you choose between so many different beliefs? What criteria do you use to decide what is believable? They all can't be right.

While many of my skeptical friends like to claim they live according to the evidence and form their worldview based on reasoning alone, Aristotle, credited as the 'father of Western civilization' and 'the originator of today's scientific method', would disagree.

He believed that a person's worldview is shaped by much more than logical reasoning. In his famous treatise called 'On Rhetoric', he explains how people are persuaded toward belief. First of all, let's define 'rhetoric'. It's really an art form, where the goal of the speaker or writer is to inform, persuade, or motivate their audience in specific topics. Aristotle explains the three ways you or I are persuaded by rhetorical arguments towards believing something. He calls these three ways *'Logos'*, *'Ethos'* and *'Pathos.'*

'LOGOS'
Evidence-based
(Correspondence, Coherence)

'ETHOS'
Expert's knowledge or character

'PATHOS'
Emotion-based
(my feelings)

The first, **'LOGOS'**, is where we get today's word 'logic'. This form of persuasion is evidence-based, where the depth of the facts presented gives strong reasons for believing. This is Luke's appeal in Acts 1:3 when he writes *"to whom He (Jesus) presented Himself alive after His suffering by many unmistakable proofs…"*. Christianity, unlike other world religions, opens itself up to scrutiny by the skeptic and invites anyone to test its claims.

The second form of persuasion is **'ETHOS'**, where the speaker's personal character or their depth of knowledge on the subject persuades us that he or she is credible. 'Ethos' can be achieved in many ways. One could be a noted expert in the field, like a college professor or a company executive. Or the speaker may have a vested interest in the subject, like a couple who has been married fifty years and is a source of wisdom on marriage. Or the speaker could use impressive 'Logos' that shows he or she is knowledgeable on the topic. Jesus Christ often employed 'Ethos' persuasion, as Matthew 7:28-29 tells us: *"And so it was, when Jesus had ended these sayings, that the people were astonished at His teaching, for He taught as one having authority, and not as the scribes."*

And finally, Aristotle's third form of persuasion is **'PATHOS'**, which appeals to the audience's emotions. We get the words *'pathetic'* and *'empathy'* from it. Pathos can be very effective when it appeals to audience's hopes - where the speaker paints a scenario of positive future results of following the course of action proposed. This is the distinguishing element of the good news of Jesus Christ, and the essence of the most beloved verse in the Bible, spoken by Jesus Himself: *"For God so loved the world, that He gave His only begotten Son, that whosoever believes in Him should not perish but have everlasting life."* (John 3:16).

Now you can understand why Paul, in Acts 19:8, was so bold to proclaim publically the gospel of Jesus Christ. It meets Aristotle's criteria for the three elements of persuasion. Are Christians in America like Paul, boldly sharing the exclusive claims of Jesus Christ? Or is it that we as Christians have not put in the time and effort to examine our beliefs and discuss them in open with others. We cave into our culture, which tells us to keep our Christianity at home or on Sundays in church. Our faith resides in our private world, safe from the critique of those around us.

There is no good reason a Christian can give for why their faith in Jesus Christ should blend into American culture as just one of the many beliefs to be tolerated. Based on Aristotle's dictums, Christianity stands alone. And more importantly, based on the historical reality of the Person of Jesus Christ, it is true. Share it.

Worldview #1 in America: *POSTMODERNISM*

Michael Patton[17]: sections from article 'How to Represent Christ in a *POSTMODERN* World'

"Our world is going through a major cultural shift. We have moved from a world of absolutes and objectivity, to one of **relativism, subjectivism,** and **tolerance**. The greatest commandment in this postmodern society is this, *thou shalt tolerate one another.* As one writer has put it, "Tolerance has become so important that no exception is tolerated. A person may have his or her religion, and may believe it, but he or she has no right to try to persuade another of his or her belief. Why? Because what you are saying is that your belief is superior to their belief. This is the supreme act of intolerance, the primary postmodern taboo.

RELATIVISM = the heart of the Postmodern.

Because postmoderns are skeptical that there can be absolute truths, relativism is their creed. It is the idea that truth is contained in the eye of the beholder. It is not uncommon to hear, "Christ is *my* way to God, but I don't push *my* beliefs on others." Or, "It doesn't matter what you believe as long as you are sincere."

To the relative postmodern, all truth is contingent upon the situation, culture, or language of the person. With relativism, a moral truth can be true and binding for one person, while for another it is not. Having an abortion may be wrong for one person and right for another.

OBJECTIVISM = ABSOLUTE TRUTHS do exist in and of themselves (the opposite of relative truths).

They *do not* depend upon the situation, culture, language, or any other variable. They are true even if nobody believes them to be true. An example of an objective truth is that the sun shines. These are truths that exist independently. They do not need anything to affirm them in order for them to be true.

The existence of objective truths is one of the bedrocks of Christianity. It is because of the objective truth of the atonement that you and I can have access to God. It is because of the objective truth that God created us that we exist. There is no room for relativity in these matters. We defend many of these objective truths at all costs.

What is Christian Tolerance towards non-Christians?

The only truth that the postmodern believes is that there is no truth, or at least no objective access to that truth. Whatever our conclusions are, they are merely our opinions, and our opinions are no better than those of another. To the postmodern, all of us are imprisoned behind the unbreakable walls of this subjective reality, and therefore we must all *"tolerate"* each other. It is not uncommon to hear statements like this: "If you believe that the Bible is God's Word, that is fine and good, but you must also tolerate the person who believes in the Quran or any other religious literature they may choose."

What do the postmoderns mean by "tolerate"? Do they mean the same as the *American Heritage Dictionary's* definition of what it means to tolerate: "To allow without prohibiting or opposing; permit"? Do they simply mean that if I have a neighbor who adheres to a belief system other than mine, that I am supposed to live at peace with him, not prohibiting or oppressing him? If this is the case, I agree.

But this is not what typical postmoderns mean when they cry for "tolerance." They are not asking people to simply tolerate and get along with the opposing belief. The fact is that they are asking people to **compromise** their beliefs. They are asking me to concede that my neighbor's beliefs are just as true as mine, to forfeit my notion of objectivity, and to surrender my view of **exclusivism**.

The result would accomplish nothing less than to render a death blow to my belief in the Scriptures. What they are implying when they push their definition of "tolerance" is that people should never stand up for their beliefs, if standing up for them means stating that their beliefs are the only true beliefs—that they are exclusive. They are not asking people to tolerate the homosexual, but to *change their belief* that homosexuality is wrong *for everyone*.

By tolerance, the postmodern means that we compromise the **objectivity** of God's Word. By tolerance, the postmodern cries for us to stop reaching out to others with the Gospel. By tolerance, the postmodern demands that we approve of their lifestyles. By tolerance, the postmodern is essentially asking us to give up our faith. This we cannot do.

Dr. Norman Geisler ('When Skeptics Ask')[12]:
"Dealing with the Postmodern - Skeptics and Agnostics"

"One great philosopher had an effective way to deal with skepticism. When encountered by people who claimed to doubt everything, he would ask, 'Do you doubt your own existence?' If they answered yes, then he would point out that they must exist in order to doubt and that certainty should remove their doubts. If they answered no, then he could show them that there are at least some things which are beyond doubt.

To counter this assault on their doctrines, the skeptics decided to simply remain silent. Then they would not be caught in this trap. The philosopher was not shaken though. At that point, he said, 'I guess there is nobody here after all. I may as well go talk to somebody else who exists.' And he walked away."

Dr. Norman Geisler[12]: "The Impossibility of Denying Absolutes"

"… there is a fundamental inconsistency to a denial of absolutes: in order to deny absolutes, one must imply that there are absolutes in the process of the denial. To deny absolutes, you have to make an absolute denial. It's just like saying, 'Never say never.' You just did. Or, 'It's always wrong to say always.' You have to say it to say it. How can you be absolutely sure that there are no absolutes?

Besides, if relativity were true, then there must be something to which all things are relative, but which is not relative itself. In other words, something has to be absolute before we can see that everything else is relative to it. This is the nature of relations: they exist between two or more things. Nothing can be relative by itself, and if everything else is relative, then no other relations are real. There has to be something which does not change by which we can measure the change in everything else. Even Einstein recognized this and posited absolute Spirit as something to which all else is related (see Book 3 on 'Einstein and Theory of Relativity')."

<u>RELEVANCE</u> = how to evangelize in the world today

Can we tolerate the postmodern? What are the issues which we are to tolerate? We do not panic when someone says that truth is relative, we explain that they are right, but only *some* truth is relative. When they cry for tolerance, we cry with them, and explain to them the difference between tolerance and compromise.

How do we represent CHRIST to the postmodern? We approach them like we do any other unbeliever of any time, or culture, or language — we hand them the crucified and risen Savior. We bring them what is *RELEVANT.*

"American Christianity's Abandonment of Truth (*we've lost our minds*)"[3]

1) Churches *withdrew* from intellectually confronting the secular world, limiting their attention to the realm of practical Christian living.

2) Churches *gave up* the truth of Christianity as the framework to interpret all of life (Christianity became trapped in the 'upper story').

3) Christianity *gave in* to the demand that the academic disciplines must be separated from religion, not realizing that it was a cover to introduce new philosophies like secular humanism and naturalism."

OK…. so what now? The first step in reclaiming a Christian worldview is to overcome this divide between "heart" and "brain". We have to reject the division of life into a sacred realm, limited to things like worship and personal morality, against a secular realm that includes science, politics, economics, and the rest of the public arena. This dichotomy in our own minds is the greatest barrier to liberating the power of the gospel in our culture today.

What has never changed: while our culture is changing at an incredible speed, God's definition of TRUTH has remained steadfast. Jesus still asks me the same FOUR QUESTIONS. How I answer them they will determine where I spend eternity – regardless of what the world defines as their truth.

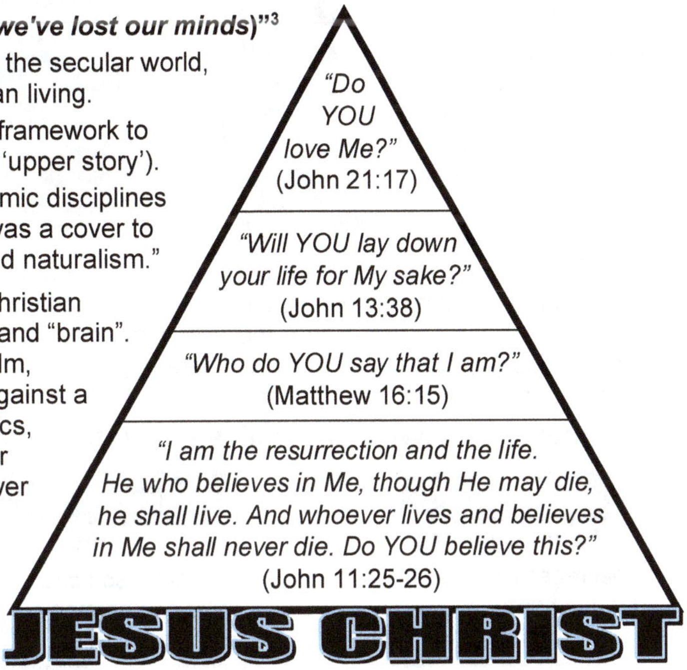
"Do YOU love Me?" (John 21:17)
"Will YOU lay down your life for My sake?" (John 13:38)
"Who do YOU say that I am?" (Matthew 16:15)
"I am the resurrection and the life. He who believes in Me, though He may die, he shall live. And whoever lives and believes in Me shall never die. Do YOU believe this?" (John 11:25-26)
JESUS CHRIST

1Corin. 3:11 *"No other foundation can anyone lay than that which is laid, which is Jesus Christ"*

Dr. Norman Geisler[12]: "You Christians Are So *Close-Minded*"

glad tidings assembly
www.gtalondon.org
WELCOME
DON'T BE SO
OPEN-MINDED
YOUR BRAINS
FALL OUT

"Open-mindedness has become a self-evident virtue in our society and a closed mind, a sign of ignorance and depravity. However, this thinking is based on HALF-TRUTHS. Surely, it is good to admit the possibility that one might be wrong and never good to maintain a position no matter what the evidence against it. Also, one should never make a firm decision without examining all the evidence without prejudice.

*That is the half-truth that ropes us into this view, but a half-truth is a whole lie. Are we still to remain open-minded when all reason says that there can be only one conclusion? That is the same as the error of the closed mind. In fact, **openness is the most closed-minded position of all** because it eliminates any absolute view from consideration.*

What if the absolute view is true? Isn't openness taken to be absolute? In the long run, openness cannot really be true unless it is open to some real absolutes that cannot be denied. Open-mindedness should not be confused with empty-mindedness. One should never remain open to a second alternative when only one can be true."

Nancy Pearcey[3]: 'History's Path to a Postmodern America'

"Francis Schaeffer depicted Greek philosophy's classical thought of truth and reality as a 2-Story Building because it drew a stark dichotomy between matter and spirit, treating the material realm as though it were less valuable than the spiritual realm (and sometimes outright evil). Salvation was defined in terms of ascetic exercises aimed at liberating the spirit from the material world so that it could ascend to God.

This concept of what is TRUE and REAL is divided by this "building": In the Lower Story are science and reason, which are considered Public Truth, binding on everyone. Over against it is an Upper Story of noncognitive experience, which is the center of personal meaning. This is the realm of Private Truth, where we hear people say, 'That may be true for you but it's not true for me.'

Upper Story
- Values & Meaning
- Personal Preferences
- Private Truth
- Sacred Realm
- Spiritual
- "Heart"

Lower Story
- Science & Reason
- Binding on Everyone
- Public Truth
- Secular Realm
- Material
- "Brain"

The first step in forming a Christian worldview is to overcome the sharp divide between 'heart' and 'brain'. We must reject the division of life into a sacred realm, limited to things like worship and personal morality, versus a secular realm that includes science, politics, economics, and the rest of the public arena. This dichotomy in our own minds is the greatest barrier to liberating the power of the gospel across our culture today."

How 'Upper and Lower Story' Philosophy infiltrated the Early Church

Plato (350 BC)

Form (spiritual)
- eternal reason and rationality
- order and harmony
- spirit = goodness, truth, beauty

Matter (material)
- eternally formless and irrational
- disorderly, irrational
- evil, chaotic

Earliest believers: surrounded by a culture steeped in Greek paganism.
Plato: material world is inferior to eternal spiritual ideals of truth and beauty.

The Problem: Plato identified the source of chaos and evil with matter (part of God's creation). Creation was divided into 2 parts: spiritual (good) vs. material (evil).
This opposes a biblical worldview, where God created matter and has absolute control over it, and humanity's problem is MORAL.

Augustine (430 AD)

Spiritual
- eternal reason and rationality
- order and harmony
- spirit = goodness, truth, beauty

Material
- ✓ creation is from God and good
- physical world and bodily functions inferior and causes sin

Reaching higher levels of spiritual life meant avoiding, suppressing and escaping material aspects of life.
- Manual labor - less valuable than prayer and meditation.
- Marriage and sexuality - rejected in favor of celibacy.
- Ordinary social life - on a lower plane than life in a monastery.

The Problem: Augustine kept part of Plato's philosophy (inferiority of the material) in the church, which fostered the concept of spiritual elitism over living a normal life.

Aquinas (1270 AD)

Grace
- supernatural "add-on" to nature
- gift from God, nature, allowing man to have a relationship with Him.

Nature
- ✓ creation (physical world) is good since it's by a good Creator
- "nature", or the "purpose" of things (its goal to which it strives), can be found within the world

He recovered a more biblical view of creation: God and His physical creation are both good; the goodness of the Creation are evidence of the goodness of God.

The Problem: Aquinas allowed the "nature" or purpose of things to be found within the world, so the world didn't need God but was capable of reaching their full potential by its own resources. The problem for people: Don't I have a higher purpose? Don't I need to be in relationship to God to be fulfilled?

N. Pearcey[3]: "From the Reformers (Luther) to Today: The 2-Story Framework is alive and well"

In her book "Total Truth"[3], Nancy Pearcey gives us a history lesson of how Schaeffer's "2-Story View of Truth & Reality" has so infiltrated our culture that, as she says, "the very concept of being 'professional' has come to have connotations of being secular. Faith is often reduced to a separate 'add-on' for personal and private life - on the order of a private indulgence, like a weakness for chocolates - and not an appropriate topic in the public arena."
Picking up from Aquinas, the Reformers flatly rejected this 2-Story framework of Truth but were unable to extinguish it. The "2 Stories" permeate our culture today, many times subconsciously, leading Christians to feel their spiritual life should be kept in isolation for Sunday mornings, separate from their careers and other areas of their life (Christianity is held captive in the "Upper Story" of "subjective, private truth"). Pearcey explains that "by understanding how these secular dualisms (Upper-vs-Lower Story') developed throughout history, we can strike them right at the root with an effective strategy that has the potential to: 1) bring Christian truth back into the public sphere, 2) evangelize our world in this post-modern age."

Luther & Calvin (1500-1600's)

Reformation
- rejected spiritual elitism (monks, priests) and emphasized priesthood of all believers (1Peter 2:9)
- medieval scholarship accommodated pagan philosophy (like Aristotle)
- reason and truth don't exist apart from God's word

They preached that the Christian life is not a summons to a life *separate* from family and work, but is *embedded within* it. Running a business or a household was as important as being a priest or a nun, because all were ways of participating in God's work in maintaining and caring for His creation.

The Problem: They didn't give their followers any tools to defend their new insights against philosophical attack. Their successors went right back to teaching Greek philosophy's dualistic approach to Christian living ("separate from the world").

Descartes (1700's)

Romanticism
- religion and humanities
- MIND (spirit, thought, emotion, will)
- proof of human spirit: "*I think, therefore I am*"

Enlightenment
- science and reason
- MATTER (mechanical, deterministic machine)
- natural laws with fixed patterns

The Secularization Process: Romanticism conceded the study of nature to the Enlightenment, wanting only their own parallel arena for the arts and humanities. Enlightenment: successes of the scientific revolution led to science enthroned as the path to knowledge and truth. Romanticism: rejected science for religion, philosophy, humanities & the arts (beauty and creativity).

The Problem: Descartes' intention to elevate the mind failed: it was cast into the Upper Story, irrelevant to scientific materialism.

Kant (1700-1800's)

Freedom
- autonomy = individual is subject only to laws imposed on oneself by oneself (personal morality)
- socially constructed *values* (what I can't help believing to be true)

Nature
- Newtonian Physics (not Aquinas' purpose/ goal')
- "*everything taking place is infallibly determined by the laws of nature*"
- publicly verifiable *facts* (what I know to be true)

Kant knew that a 'machine' image of the universe would be rejected by artists, writers and religious thinkers as an enemy to human values.

The Problems:
1) Kant arrogated God's role of creating moral law to each individual's rational will.
2) Kant's 2 Stories were *contradictory* (if nature is the deterministic machine of Newtonian physics, how can I ever have real freedom?)

Darwin (1800-1900's)

Value
- social values that give personal meaning
- Kant's *freedom*

Fact
- public truth verified by science (naturalistic mechanism for life's origin)
- naturalism became a comprehensive philosophy

R. Dawkins: "*Darwin made it possible to be an intellectually fulfilled atheist.*" The "Lower Story" became self-contained (God not needed for life itself, nevermind moral laws).

The Problems:
1) "Upper Story" cut off from history, science, reason (if evolutionary forces produced the mind, then religion and morality aren't truths but only ideas; I create my own morality and meaning through my choices).
2) This opposes a biblical worldview, where God as Creator is sovereign over everything, including me.

Today (1900's on)

Postmodernism
- morality = values
- personal preference
- subjective (private) truth in ethics and morality
- people have moral freedom and dignity

Scientific Naturalism
- evolutionary science = facts binding on everyone
- objective (public) truth in science & history
- people are data-processing machines

The Postmodern Contradiction = science says the human mind is just a complex data-processing machine, while the possibility of morality depends on the idea that we are more than machines, capable of making free choices (S. Pinker: "*a human being is a machine and a sentient free agent, depending on whether we're playing the science game or the ethics game*").

The Problem: real people don't act like machines; what matters most (purpose, free will, meaning) is reduced to nothing more than useful fiction.

Worldview #2 in America: *SECULAR HUMANISM*

Stephen Gould ("Ever Since Darwin"): *"Before Darwin, we thought that a benevolent God had created us. No intervening spirit watches lovingly over the affairs of nature. No vital forces propel evolutionary change. And whatever we think of God, his existence is not manifest in the products of nature."*

Richard Dawkins ("The Blind Watchmaker"): *"Darwin made it possible to be an intellectually fulfilled atheist."*

Isaac Asimov (Pres., American Humanist Assoc.): *"Humanism is a NON-THEISTIC RELIGION. Emotionally, I am an atheist. I don't have the evidence to prove that God doesn't exist, but I so strongly suspect that he doesn't that I don't want to waste my time."*

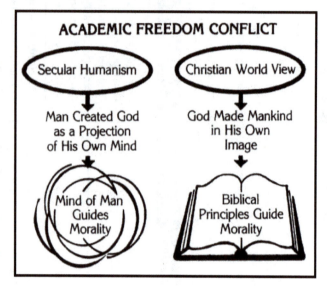

The Humanist Manifesto (1933):

1) "The universe is self-existing and not created;
2) "Man is a part of nature and has emerged as a result of a continuous process;
3) "The universe, by *modern science*, makes unacceptable any supernatural guarantees of human values;
4) "Realization of human personality is the end of man's life; the goal is its development and fulfillment in the here and now;
5) *"Man is the result of a blind and random process that does not necessitate any kind of meaning*;
6) "*Humanism is fostered by the teaching of EVOLUTION.*"

Isaiah 44:9-10, 13-20 "Idol Worship of 'self': Secular Humanism"

"Those who make a graven image, all of them are useless, and their precious things shall not profit; they are their own witnesses; they neither see nor know, that they may be ashamed. Who would form a god or cast a graven image that profits him nothing? The craftsman stretches out his rule, he marks one out with chalk; he fashions it with a plane, he marks it out with the compass, and MAKES IT LIKE THE FIGURE OF A MAN. According to the beauty of a man, that it may remain in the house. He hews down cedars for himself, and takes the cypress and the oak; he secures it FOR HIMSELF among the trees of the forest. He plants a pine, and the rain nourishes it.

Then it shall be for a man to burn, for he will take some of it and warm himself; yes, he kindles it and bakes bread; indeed he MAKES A GOD and WORSHIPS IT; he makes a carved image, and falls down to it. He burns half of it in the fire; with this half he eats meat; he roasts a roast, and is satisfied. He even warms himself and says, 'Ah! I am warm, I have seen the fire.' And the rest of it he makes into a god, his carved image. He falls down before it and worships it, prays to it and says, 'Deliver me, for you are my god.'

They do not know nor understand; for He has shut their eyes, so that they cannot see, and their hearts, so that they cannot understand. And no one considers in his heart, nor is there knowledge nor understanding to say, 'I have burned half of it in the fire, yes, I have also baked bread on its coals; I have roasted meat and eaten it; and shall I make the rest of it an abomination? Shall I fall down before a BLOCK OF WOOD?' He feeds on ashes; a DECEIVED HEART has turned him aside; and he cannot deliver his soul, nor say, 'IS THERE NOT A LIE IN MY RIGHT HAND?'"

> **John MacArthur** (commentary on Isaiah): *"Like eating ashes, which provide no nourishment, idolatry is a deception, from which the sinner gets nothing but judgment."*

What's an *IDOL*, anyway?

1) Greek *"eidōlon"* = an image or IDEA made to represent a false god, that is worshipped (1Corin. 8:4-6).
2) Hebrew *"ĕlyil"* = "vanity", or "thing of naught" (Leviticus 19:4) – this is what Paul meant in Acts 14:15-17 when he said what represented a deity to Gentiles was a "vain thing".
3) Romans 1:22-25 = God traces idolatry (sin of the mind against God) and immorality (sins of the flesh) to a lack of acknowledging Him and showing Him gratitude.
4) An idolater = slave to the depraved ideas his idols represent (Galatians 4:8-9).

N. Pearcey[3]: "Its not *if* I worship…. It's the *object* of my worship that determines my destiny"

"Humans are inherently religious beings, created to be in relationship with God - and if they reject God, they don't stop being religious; they simply find some other ultimate principle upon which to base their lives. Often that idol is something concrete, like financial security or professional success; in other cases, it may be an ideology or set of beliefs that substitutes for religion. They are far from religiously neutral."

John 18:37-38   Which Worldview is *TRUE?*

"'Everyone who is of the truth hears My voice.'   Pilate said to Him, 'What is Truth?'"

	Secular Humanism Worldview	Christian Worldview
Ultimate Reality	Ultimate reality is impersonal matter; no God exists. Carl Sagan[8]: *"The cosmos is all that is, or ever was, or ever will be".... "We live on a hunk of rock and metal that circles a humdrum star that is one of 400 billion other stars that make up the Milky Way Galaxy, which is one of billions of other galaxies, which make up a universe, which may be one of a very large number – perhaps an infinite number – of other universes. That is a perspective on human life and our culture that is well worth pondering."*	Ultimate reality is an infinite, personal, loving God. Isaiah 42:8 *"I am the Lord, that is My name; and My glory I will not give to another."* Psalm 100:3 *"Know that the Lord, He is God; it is He who made us, and not we ourselves; we are His people, and the sheep of His pasture."* Psalm 14:1 *"The fool says in his heart, 'There is no God.'"*
Universe	The universe was created by chance, accidental events without ultimate purpose. C.S. Lewis[8]: *"If the solar system was brought about by an accidental collision, then the appearance of life was also an accident, and the whole evolution of man was an accident too. If so, then all our present thoughts are accidents – the accidental by-product of the movement of atoms. And this holds for the thoughts of the materialists and astronomers as well as for anyone else's. But if their thoughts are merely accidental by-products, why should we believe them to be true? I see no reason for believing that one accident should be able to give me a correct account of all the other accidents."*	The universe was created by God for a purpose. Isaiah 45:12 *"I have made the earth, and created man on it. It was I – My hands stretched out the heavens, and all their host I commanded."* Isaiah 45:18 *"For thus says the Lord, who created the heavens, who is God, who formed the earth and made it, who has established it, who did not create it in vain, who formed it to be inhabited."* Psalm 19:1-3 *"The heavens declare the glory of God; the firmament shows His handwork. Day unto day utters speech and night unto night reveals knowledge. There is no speech nor language where their voice is not heard."*
Man	Man is the product of the evolutionary process (time plus chance plus matter). Man's value, dignity or meaning is subjectively derived. Donald Kalish (UCLA Prof.)[8]: *"There are no ethical truths. You are mistaken to think that anyone ever had the answers. There are none. Be brave and face up to it."* J.W. Burrow (evolutionist)[8]: *"Nature, according to Darwin, was the product of blind chance and a blind struggle, and man is a lonely, intelligent mutation, scrambling with the brutes for his sustenance."*	Man was created by God in His image and is loved by Him. All men have eternal value and dignity. Their value is not derived from them, but from God. Genesis 1:26 *"Let Us make man in Our image, according to Our likeness."* Jeremiah 29:11-13 *"I know the thoughts that I think toward you, says the Lord, thoughts of peace and not of evil, to give you a future and a hope... you will seek Me and find Me, when you search for Me with all your heart."*
Morality	Morality is defined by each person by his views and interests. Every person is the final authority. Nietzche[8]: *"Everything lacks meaning. The advantage of our times is that nothing is true, everything is permitted."* Jeremiah 18:12 *"And they said, 'That is hopeless! So we will walk according to our own plans, and we will every one do the imagination of his evil heart."*	Morality is defined by God and immutable because it is based on God's unchanging character. Proverbs 21:30 *"There is no wisdom or understanding or counsel against the Lord."* Micah 6:8 *"He has shown you, O man, what is good; and what does the Lord require of you but to do justly, to love mercy, and to walk humbly with your God?"*
Afterlife	The afterlife = eternal annihilation (personal extinction) for everyone. William Provine, Cornell Univ. Evolutionary Biologist and Historian[8]: *"If Darwinism is true, then there are five inescapable conclusions: 1) there's no evidence for God, 2) there's no life after death, 3) there's no absolute foundation for right and wrong, 4) there's no ultimate meaning for life, 5) people don't really have free will."*	The afterlife: either eternal life with God (personal immortality) or eternal separation from Him (personal judgment). Prov. 23:17-18 *"Do not let your heart envy sinners, but in the fear of the Lord continue all day long; for surely there is a hereafter, and your hope will not be cut off."* Matthew 25:46 *"...these will go away into everlasting punishment, but the righteous into eternal life."*

Why Christianity is on the rise: The Empty Message in Secular Humanism

The following are excerpts from Dinesh D'Souza's book 'What's So Great About Christianity'[13]

- "The traditional churches, not the liberal churches, are growing in America. In 1960, for example, the churches affiliated with the Southern Baptist Convention had 8.7 million members. Now (2007) they have 16.4 million… If secularization were proceeding inexorably, then religious people should be getting less religious, and so conservative churches should be shrinking and liberal churches growing. In fact, the opposite is the case.

- This is the way of secularization: the idea that as an inevitable result of science, reason, progress, and modernization, the West will continue to grow more secular, followed by the rest of the world. The secularization thesis was based on the presumption that science and modernity would satisfy the impulses and needs once met by religion. But a rebellion against secularization suggests that perhaps important needs are still unmet, and so people are seeking a revival of religion – perhaps in a new form – to address their specific concerns within a secular society.

- Biologists like Dawkins and Wilson say there simply must be some natural and evolutionary explanation for the universality and persistence of religious belief, and they are right. There is such an explanation, and I am pleased to provide one in this chapter. The Reverend Randy Alcorn, founder of Eternal Perspective Ministries in Oregon, sometimes presents his audiences with two creation stories (Secular 'Tribe', or worldview vs. Christian 'Tribe', or worldview, parenthesis added) and asks them whether it matters which one is true:

Christian 'Tribe'	Secular 'Tribe'
'You are a special creation of a good and all-powerful God. You are created in His image, with capacities to think, feel, and worship that set you above all other life forms. You differ from the animals not simply in degree but in kind. Not only is your kind unique, but you are unique among your kind. Your Creator loves you so much and so intensely desires your companionship and affection that He has a perfect plan for your life. In addition, God gave the life of His only Son that you might spend eternity with Him. If you are willing to accept the gift of salvation, you can become a child of God.'	'You are the descendant of a tiny cell of primordial protoplasm washed up on an empty beach three and a half billion years ago. You are the blind and arbitrary product of time, chance, and natural forces. You are a mere grab bag of atomic particles, a conglomeration of genetic substance. You exist on a tiny planet in a minute solar system in an empty corner of a meaningless universe. You are a purely biological entity, different only in degree but not in kind from a microbe, virus, or amoeba. You have no essence beyond your body, and at death you will cease to exist. In short, you came from nothing and are going nowhere.'
Which of the two tribes is more likely to survive, prosper, and multiply?	
The religious tribe is made up of people who have an animating sense of purpose.	The secular tribe is made up of people who are not sure why they exist at all.
The religious tribe is composed of individuals who view their every thought and action as consequential.	The secular tribe is made up of matter that cannot explain why it is able to think at all.
Should evolutionists like Dennett, Dawkins, Pinker, and Wilson be surprised, then, to see that religious tribes are flourishing? Throughout the world, religious groups attract astounding numbers of followers and religious people are showing their confidence in their way of life and in the future by having more children. By contrast, atheist conventions draw only a handful of embittered souls. The important point is not just that atheism is unable to compete with religion in attracting followers, but also that the lifestyle of practical atheism seems to produce listless tribes that cannot even reproduce themselves."	

- …Modernization helps people triumph over necessity but it also produces a profound crisis of purpose in modern life. The greater the effects of modernization, the stronger the social anxiety and the striving for 'something more'. As Wolfhart Pannenberg puts it, 'Secular culture itself produces a deep need for meaning in life and therefore also for religion.'… GK Chesterton calls this the '**REVOLT INTO ORTHODOXY.**' Like Chesterton, I find myself rebelling against extreme secularism and finding in Christianity some remarkable answers to both intellectual and practical concerns… Christianity is winning, and secularism is losing. The future is always unpredictable, but one thing seems clear. God is in the future, and atheism is on its way out.

- …it is not religion but atheism that requires a Darwinian explanation. Atheism is a bit like homosexuality: one is not sure where it fits into a doctrine of natural selection. Why would nature select people who mate with others of the same sex, a process with no reproductive advantage at all? It seems equally perplexing why nature would breed a group of people who see no brighter purpose to life or the universe. Here is where the biological expertise of Dawkins, Pinker or Wilson could prove illuminating. Maybe they can turn their Darwinian lens on themselves and help us understand how atheism, like the human tailbone and the panda's thumb, somehow survived as an evolutionary leftover of our primitive past."

In his book 'What's So Great About Christianity'[13], Dinesh D'Souza explains how the combination of science and education have become the atheist's greatest tools for de-Christianizing the American culture:

SCIENCE = The *Method* to spread Secular Humanism and minimize Christianity

- *"Alarmed by the rising power of religion around the world, atheists in the west today have grown more outspoken and militant. What we are witnessing in America is 'atheist backlash.' The atheists thought they were winning, but now they realize that, far from dying quietly, religion is on the global upswing. So the atheists are striking back, using all the resources they can command.*

- *Statistics suggest that in America the number of atheists is growing. The Pluralism Project at Harvard reports that people with no religious affiliation now number nearly forty million. That's almost 15 percent of the population, up from less than 10 percent in 1990, and so a virtual doubling of the atheist ranks in a single decade. In this book I use the term 'atheist' in its broad sense to refer to those who deny God and live as if He did not exist.*

- *The distinguishing element of modern atheism is its intellectual militancy and moral self-confidence. Yes, there is a bit of arrogance here, but in the view of the atheists it is justified. What gives the atheists such confidence? The answer, in a word, is* **SCIENCE**. *Many atheists believe that modern science – the best known way to accumulate knowledge, the proven technique for giving us airplanes and computers and drugs that kill bacteria – has vindicated the nonbeliever's position.*

- *While science relies on the principle that 'nothing is more sacred than the facts', Sam Harris charges that 'theology is now little more than a branch of human ignorance. Indeed it is ignorance with wings.'*

EDUCATION = The *Means* to spread Secular Humanism and minimize Christianity

- *"<u>How then should religion be eliminated</u>? Our atheist educators have a short answer: through the power of science. One way in which science can undermine the plausibility of religion, according to biologist E.O. Wilson, is by showing that the mind is the product of* **EVOLUTION** *and that free moral choice is an illusion. 'If religion… can be systematically analyzed and explained as a product of the brain's evolution, its power as an external source of morality will be gone forever.' The objective of science education, according to biologist Richard Lewontin, 'is not to provide the public with knowledge of how far it is to the nearest star and what genes are made of.' Rather, 'the problem is to get them to reject irrational and supernatural explanations of the world, the demons that exist only in their imaginations, and to accept a social and intellectual apparatus, science, as the only begetter of truth.'*

- *<u>How is all this to be achieved</u>?... through* **INDOCTRINATION IN THE SCHOOLS**. *Some educators argue that children should be taught to have reverence for science, which can replace religion as the object of human veneration. 'We should let the success of the religious formula guide us', urged Carolyn Porco, a research scientist at the Space Science Institute in Colorado, at a 2006 conference on science and religion. 'Let's teach our children from a very young age about the story of the universe and its incredible richness and beauty. It is already so much more glorious and awesome and even comforting than anything offered by any scripture or God concept I know.'*

- *Philosopher Richard Rorty argued that secular professors in universities ought to 'arrange things so that students who enter as bigoted, homophobic religious fundamentalists will leave college with views more like their own.'… Indeed, parents who send their children to colleges should recognize that as professors 'we are going to go right on trying to discredit you in the eyes of your children, trying to strip your fundamentalist religious community of dignity, trying to make your views seem silly rather than discussable.'*

- *Biologist Kenneth Miller, who has testified in favor of evolution in court trials, admits that 'a presumption of atheism or agnosticism is universal in academic life… the conventions of academic life, almost universally, revolve around the assumption that religious belief is something that people grow out of as they become educated.'*

- *Children spend the majority of their waking hours in school. Parents invest a good portion of their life savings in college education to entrust their offspring to people who are supposed to educate them. Isn't it wonderful that educators have figured out a way to make parents the instruments of their own undoing? Isn't it brilliant that they have persuaded Christian moms and dads to finance the destruction of their own beliefs and values? <u>Who said atheists weren't clever</u>?*

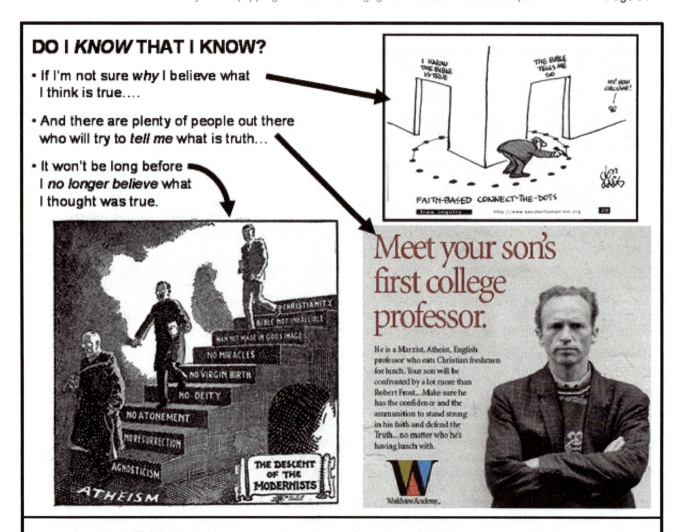

Are Our Kids ready for College? Do they know what they believe, and why they believe it?

"Every child in America entering school at the age of 5 is insane because he comes to school with certain allegiances toward our founding fathers, toward his parents, toward a belief in a supernatural being, toward the sovereignty of this nation as a separate entity... its up to you TEACHERS to make all of these sick children well by creating the international children of the future." - Chester M. Pierce, Professor of Education and Psychiatry, Harvard University, Address to the Association for Childhood Education International, April 1972.

"And in fact, if Jesus did come back, the most likely people to put him back on the cross would be the Christians, and the most likely people to nail him to the cross would be the fundamentalist Christians. They would be the ones who would be nailing that !$%@# back to the cross, because he'd be the one who'd be refuting what they believe, and they wouldn't want that. Fair enough? So the most likely guys to be hammering in the nails, they are the guys who elected George Bush, and believe in the literal truth of the Bible, and don't believe in evolution, because they don't want to use reason, and they don't want to think, they'd rather stick to their illusions that hopefully may convince them that they don't have to be afraid at night when they are all alone, and the devil may whisper in their ears." - Dr. Lee Carter, Arizona State University, Sept. 2007 during classroom lecture.

"The battle for humankind's future must be waged and won in the PUBLIC SCHOOL CLASSROOM by teachers who correctly perceive their role as the proselytizers of a new faith: a religion of humanity - utilizing a classroom instead of a pulpit to carry humanist values into whatever they teach. The classroom must and will become an arena of conflict between the old and the new - the rotting corpse of Christianity, together with its adjacent evils and misery, and the new faith of humanism." - John J. Dunphy, The Humanist, 1983

"I think the most important factor leading us to a secular society has been the EDUCATIONAL FACTOR. Our schools may not teach Johnny to read properly, but the fact that Johnny is in school until he is 16 tends to lead toward the elimination of religious superstition. The average child now acquires a high school education, and this militates against Adam and Eve and all other myths of alleged history." - Paul Blanchard. '3 Cheers for our Secular Sate' (The Humanist, April 1976).

"The Declaration in Defense of Science and Secularism"
published Nov., 2006 at the press conference for the opening of The Center for Inquiry, in Washington, D.C.

"We are deeply concerned about the ability of the United States to confront the many challenges it faces, both at home and abroad. Our concern has been compounded by the failure exhibited by far too many Americans, including influential decision-makers, to understand the nature of scientific inquiry and the integrity of empirical research. This disdain for science is aggravated by the excessive influence of religious doctrine on our public policies.

We are concerned with the resurgence of fundamentalist religions across the nation, and their alliance with political-ideological movements to block science. We are troubled by the persistence of paranormal and occult beliefs, and by the denial of the findings of scientific research. This retreat into mysticism is reinforced by the emergence in universities of "post-modernism," which undermines the objectivity of science.

These disturbing trends can be illustrated by the push for intelligent design (a new name for creationism) and the insistence that it be taught along with evolution. Some 37 states have considered legislation to mandate this. This is both troubling and puzzling since the hypotheses and theories of evolution are central to modern science. Moreover, the resilience of anti-evolution movements is supported not only by religious dogmatism but also by the abysmal public ignorance of basic scientific principles. Consider these facts:

- A recent poll by the Pew Research Center revealed that 64% of Americans are open to the idea of teaching intelligent design or creationism in public schools.
- Some 42% totally reject evolution or believe that present forms of life existed since the beginning of time. 38% would teach only creationism instead of evolutionary theory.
- Only 26% agree with the predominant scientific view that life evolved by processes of natural selection without the need for divine intervention.
- The percentage of individuals who accept the theory of evolution is lower in the United States than in any other developed country, with the exception of Turkey.

We think that these dismal facts portend a clear and present danger to the role of science in the U.S. In our view it is not enough to teach specific technical subjects—important as that is—but to convey to the public a general understanding of how science works. This requires both some comprehension of the methods of scientific inquiry and an understanding of the scientific outlook. The cultivation of critical thinking is essential not only for science but also for an educated citizenry—especially if democracy is to flourish. Unfortunately, not only do too many well-meaning people base their conceptions of the universe on ancient books—such as the Bible and the Koran—rather than scientific inquiry, but politicians of all parties encourage and abet this scientific ignorance.

It is vital that the public be exposed to the scientific perspective, and this presupposes the separation of church and state and public policies that are based on secular principles, not religious doctrine... Science transcends borders and provides the most reliable basis for finding solutions to our problems. We maintain that secular, not religious, principles must govern our public policy. This is not an anti-religious viewpoint; it is a scientific viewpoint.

To find common ground, we must reason together, and we can do so only if we are willing to put personal religious beliefs aside when we craft public policy. For these reasons, we call upon political leaders of all parties:
1) to protect and promote scientific inquiry,
2) to base public policy insofar as possible on empirical evidence instead of religious faith,
3) to provide an impartial and reliable source of scientific analysis to assist Congress, for example, by reviving the Congressional Office of Technology Assessment, and
4) to maintain a strict separation between church and state and, in particular, not to permit legislation or executive action to be influenced by religious beliefs.

Science and secularism are inextricably linked and both are indispensable if we are to have sound public policies that will promote the common good, not only of Americans but of the global community."

So what would the founder of Evolutionary Theory think of this *Declaration*?
Charles Darwin: Letter to Asa Gray (22 May 1860):

"I cannot anyhow be content to view this wonderful universe, and especially the nature of man, and to conclude that everything is the result of brute force. I am inclined to look at everything as resulting from designed laws, with the details, whether good or bad, left to the working out of what we call chance.

Not that this notion at all satisfies me. I feel most deeply that the whole subject is too profound for the human intellect. A dog might as well speculate on the mind of Newton. Let each man hope and believe what he can."

Just Thinking:
The Atheist Science Professor and the Christian Student debate FAITH

Professor: "You are a Christian, aren't you, son?"
Student: "Yes, sir."
Professor: "So, you believe in God?"
Student: "Absolutely, sir."
Professor: "Is God good?"
Student: "Sure."
Professor: "Is God all powerful?"
Student: "Yes."

Professor: "My brother died of cancer even though he prayed to God to heal him. Most of us would attempt to help others who are ill. But God didn't. How is this God good then, hmm?"
(Student was silent).
Professor: "You can't answer, can you? Let's start again, young fella. Is God good?"
Student: "Yes".
Professor: "Is Satan good?"
Student: "No."
Professor: "Where does Satan come from?"
Student: "From God."
Professor: "That's right. Tell me, son, is there evil in this world?"
Student: "Yes."
Professor: "Evil is everywhere, isn't it?" And God did make everything. Correct?"
Student: "Yes."
Professor: "So who created evil?"
(Student didn't answer).
Professor: "Is there sickness? Immorality? Hatred? Ugliness? All these terrible things exist in the world, don't they?"
Student: "Yes, sir."
Professor: "So, who created them?"
(Student didn't answer).
Professor: "Science says you have 5 senses you use to identify and observe the world around you. Tell me, son, have you ever seen God?"
Student: "No, sir."
Professor: "Tell us if you have ever heard your God?"
Student: "No, sir."
Professor: "Have you ever felt your God, tasted your God, smelt your God? Have you ever had any sensory perception of God for that matter?"
Student: "No sir, I'm afraid I haven't."
Professor: "Yet you still believe in Him?"
Student: "Yes."
Professor: "According to empirical, testable, demonstrable protocol, Science says your God doesn't exist. What do you say to that, son?"
Student: "Nothing. I only have my FAITH."
Professor: "Yes, *FAITH*. And that is the problem Science has."
Student: "Professor, is there such a thing as heat?"
Professor: "Yes."
Student: "And is there such a thing as cold?"
Professor: "Yes."

CHRISTIANITY:
The belief that some cosmic Jewish Zombie can make you live forever if you symbolically eat his flesh and telepathically tell him that you accept him as your master, so he can remove an evil force from your soul that is present in humanity because a rib-woman was convinced by a talking snake to eat from a magical tree.

Makes perfect sense.

Student: "No, sir. There isn't."

(The Lecture Hall became very quiet with this turn of events).

Student: "Sir, you can have lots of heat, even more heat, superheat, mega heat, white heat, a little heat or no heat. But we don't have anything called cold. We can hit 458 degrees below zero which is no heat, but we can't go any further after that. There is no such thing as cold. Cold is only a word we use to describe the absence of heat. We cannot measure cold. Heat is energy. Cold is not the opposite of heat, sir, just the absence of it."

(There was pin-drop silence in the Lecture Hall).

Student: "What about darkness, Professor? Is there such a thing as darkness?"

Professor: "Yes. What is night if there isn't darkness?"

Student: "You're wrong again, sir. Darkness is the absence of something. You can have low light, normal light, bright light, flashing light. But if you have no light constantly, you have nothing and it's called darkness, isn't it? In reality, darkness isn't. If it is, well you would be able to make darkness darker, wouldn't you?"

Professor: "So what is the point you are making, young man?"

Student: "Sir, my point is your philosophical premise is flawed."

Professor: "Flawed? Can you explain how?"

Student: "Sir, you are working on the *premise of duality*. You argue that there is life and then there is death, a good God and a bad God. You are viewing the concept of God as something finite, something we can measure. Sir, Science can't even explain a thought. It uses electricity and magnetism, but has never seen, much less fully understood, either one. To view death as the opposite of life is to be ignorant of the fact that death cannot exist as a substantive thing. *Death is not the opposite of life, just the absence of it*. Now tell me Professor, do you teach your students that they evolved from a monkey?"

Professor: "If you are referring to the natural evolutionary process, yes, of course I do."

Student: "Have you ever observed evolution with your own eyes, sir?"

(The Professor shook his head with a smile, beginning to realize where the argument was going).

Student: "Since no one has ever observed the process of evolution at work and cannot even prove that this process is an on-going endeavor, are you teaching your opinion, sir? Are you not a scientist but a preacher?"

(The class was in an uproar).

Student: "Is there anyone in the class who has ever seen the Professor's brain?"

(The class broke out in laughter).

Student: "Is there anyone here who has ever heard the Professor's brain, felt it, touched or smelt it? No one appears to have done so. So, according to the established rules of empirical, stable, demonstrable protocol, Science says that you have no brain, sir. With all due respect, sir, how do we then trust your lectures, sir?"

(The room was silent. The Professor stared at the student, his face unfathomable).

Professor: "I guess you'll have to take them on FAITH, son."

Student: "That is it sir... exactly! The link between man and God is *FAITH*. That is all that keeps things alive and moving."

Atheism

The belief that there was nothing and nothing happened to nothing and then nothing magically exploded for no reason, creating everything and then a bunch of everything magically rearranged itself for no reason what so ever into self-replicating bits which then turned into dinosaurs.

Makes perfect sense.

Hebrews 11:1 *"FAITH is the substance of things hoped for, the EVIDENCE of things not seen."*

Hebrews 11:3 *"By FAITH we UNDERSTAND that the worlds were framed by the word of God, so that the things which are seen were not made of things which are visible."*

2Corin. 5:7 *"We WALK by FAITH, not by SIGHT."*

Romans 1:17 *"...the JUST shall LIVE by FAITH."*

Romans 4:5 *"...to him who does not work but BELIEVES on Him who justifies the ungodly, his FAITH is accounted for righteousness."*

Romans 11:20 *"....because of unbelief they were broken off, and you STAND by FAITH."*

Everyone has faith... It's where you place your faith that counts

Worldview #3 in America: *CHRISTIANITY*

1.7

"To claim Christianity is the truth about reality means the Bible provides the direction to understand what is real. As Nancy Pearcey explains in 'Total Truth'[3], *"A worldview is like a mental map that tells us how to navigate the world effectively. It is the imprint of God's objective truth on our inner life...it's far more than a mental strategy or a new spring on current events. At the core, it is a deepening of the spiritual character of our lives. It begins with the submission of our MINDS to the Lord of the universe – a willingness to be taught by Him."*

The goal in developing a worldview that aligns with reality is the commitment to 'love the Lord your God with all your heart, soul, strength, and mind" (see Luke 10:27). We see God's desire for this love throughout the Bible:

Proverbs 23:26   *"My son, GIVE ME YOUR HEART, and let your eyes observe My ways."*
Proverbs 3:5   *"Trust in the Lord with ALL YOUR HEART, and lean not on your own understanding."*

If one desires to develop a worldview that aligns with reality, 2Corinthians 10:4-5 explains that to achieve the goal of intellectual growth, where one can 'pull down strongholds and casting down arguments', one must first grow spiritually. That means surrendering to God's Lordship so that God can be your Teacher, where the interpretation of all thoughts and actions is made according to God's Bible. This surrender is not easy. It takes work and discipline because a Christian must be willing to give himself or herself to God as Romans 12:1 describes as a 'living sacrifice'. That requires whole-hearted devotion to God in both the heart and the mind.

Nancy Pearcey[3]: "My Search for *TRUTH* led me to a Personal Relationship with Jesus Christ"

"To some people, 'worldview' may be a stuffy academic-sounding term that conjures up images of tweedy professors and dusty lecture halls.... but 'worldview' is not something abstract and academic, but intensely personal. Our worldview is the way we answer the core questions of life that everyone has to struggle with:
1) What are we here for?   2) What is ultimate truth?   3) Is there anything worth living for?

I began by asking these question in a serious way myself as a teenager. I had a good background in knowing WHAT Christianity teaches. But I came to realize I didn't know WHY it was true... I had no reason for believing Christianity was true over against the other belief systems I was encountering. When I asked my parents and pastors questions, the typical response was a patronizing pat on the head. One pastor told me, 'Don't worry, we all have doubts sometimes.' No one grasped that I was not merely troubled by 'doubts' but had stepped outside the circle of faith and was questioning the truth of the whole system.

Failing to find answers, I took a significant step: I decided the most intellectually honest course would be to reject my faith and then to analyze it objectively alongside all the other major religions and philosophies, in order to decide which one was really true. I'd had a genuine faith, even though it was only a child's faith: I knew God created me, that He loved me, that He had a wonderful purpose for my life. These principles seem very simple – until you reject them. Then suddenly I became acutely aware that I had no answers for the most basic questions – where did I come from? Was life just a chance accident of blind forces? Did it have any purpose? Were there any principles so true and so real that I could build my life on them?

Then I stumbled across the ministry of Francis Schaeffer (L'Abri in Switzerland). It was the first time I had ever encountered Christians who actually answered my questions – who gave reasonable arguments for the truth of Christianity instead of simply urging me to have faith. At that time, it was extremely rare to discover Christian ministries capable of crossing the countercultural divide to reach alienated young people, and my curiosity was sparked: Who were these Christians? I had to admit (rather ruefully) that I was already convinced that Christianity was true. Through my discussions at L'Abri and my readings in apologetics, I had come to realize there were good arguments against moral relativism, physical determinism, epistemological subjectivism, and a host of other 'isms' I had been carrying around in my head... The only step that remained was to acknowledge that I had been persuaded - and then give my life to the Lord of Truth.

What I hope you take from my experience is that 'worldview' is not an abstract, academic concept. Instead, the term describes our search for answers to those intensely personal questions everyone must wrestle with – the cry of the human heart for purpose, meaning, and a truth big enough to live by. No one can live without a sense of purpose and direction, a sense that his or her life has significance as part of a cosmic story. We may limp along for a while, extracting small installments of meaning from short-term goals like earning a degree, landing a job, getting married, establishing a family. But at some point, these temporal things fail to fulfill the deep hunger for eternity in the human spirit. For we were made by God, and every part of our personality is oriented toward a RELATIONSHIP WITH HIM. 'Our hearts are restless', Augustine said, 'until we find rest in Him.'

Once we discover that the Christian worldview is really true, then LIVING IT OUT means offering up to God all our powers – practical, intellectual, emotional, artistic – to live for Him in every area of life. Biblical truth takes hold of our inner being, and we see that it is not only a message of salvation but also the truth about all reality. GOD'S WORD becomes a light to all our paths, providing the foundational principles for bringing every part of our lives under the Lordship of Christ, to glorify Him and to cultivate His creation."

Christian Worldview: Engages the *MIND* to discern *TRUTH*

> Matthew 22:37 *"You shall love the Lord your God with all your ①HEART, with all your soul and all your ②MIND."*
>   ①HEART = Greek *"kardia"* = feelings, thoughts   ②MIND = Greek *"dianoia"* = intellect, understanding
>
> Romans 12:2 *"...do not be conformed to this world, but be transformed by the renewing of your ④MIND"*
> Romans 1:28 *"as they did not like to ③RETAIN God in their knowledge, God gave them over to a debased ④MIND..."*
>   ③RETAIN = Greek *"echō"* = possess, hold onto   ④MIND = Greek *"nous"* = intellect, understanding

In his book 'Basic Christianity'[2], John Stott explains in the two headings below, "Avoiding Mindless Christianity" and "Why Use My Mind – to discover what is TRUE", why it is so crucial to use your mind, your intellect, to develop a worldview that maps with reality:

Avoiding Mindless Christianity ⇨ "What Paul wrote about unbelieving Jews in his day could be said, I fear, of some believing Christians in ours: Romans 10:2 *'I bear them witness that they have a zeal for God, but not according to knowledge.'* Many have zeal without knowledge, enthusiasm without enlightenment. In more modern jargon, they are keen but clueless. Now I thank God for zeal. Heaven forbid that knowledge without zeal should replace zeal without knowledge! God's purpose is both: zeal directed by knowledge, knowledge fired with zeal.

Why Use My Mind – to discover what is *TRUE* ⇨ I was created to *think* = God made man in His own image, and one of the noblest features of the divine likeness in man is his capacity to think. Right from the beginning, God expects man to understand: He expects man to cooperate with Him, consciously and intelligently, in tilling and keeping the garden in which he has placed him, and to discriminate – rationally as well as morally – between what he is permitted to do and the one thing he is prohibited from doing. Scripture bases the regular argument that since man is different from the animals he should *behave* differently (Psalm 32:9 *"Do not be like the horse or like the mule, which have no understanding..."*). While there are many similarities between man and the animals, animals were created to behave by instinct, human beings by intelligent choice. And in spite of the fallenness of man's mind, commands to think, to use his mind, are still addressed to him as a human being.

Christianity is a *revealed* religion (in *words* to *minds*) = If there is a religion in the world which exalts the office of teaching, it is the religion of Jesus Christ. In pagan religions the doctrine is at a minimum. The chief thing is the performance of a *ritual*. But this is precisely where Christianity separates itself from other religions:
  1 - it does contain *DOCTRINE*   2 - it comes to men with definite, positive *teaching*
  3 - it claims to be the *TRUTH*   4 - it bases religion on *knowledge* attainable only under moral conditions

Some people reach the opposite conclusion: since man is finite and fallen, they argue, since he cannot discover God by his intellect and God must reveal Himself, therefore the mind is unimportant. But no. The Christian doctrine of revelation, far from making the human mind unnecessary, actually makes it indispensable and assigns to it its proper place. God has revealed Himself in *words* to *minds*. His revelation is a rational revelation to rational creatures. One of the highest and noblest functions of man's mind is to listen to God's Word, and so to read His mind and think His thoughts after Him.

God will one day judge me on my response to His revelation = Having achieved redemption of mankind through the death and resurrection of His Son, God now announces this redemption through His servants. The proclamation of the gospel – again addressed in *words* to *minds* – is the chief means which God has appointed to bring salvation to sinners. One thing is clear... He will judge me by my knowledge, by my response (or lack of response) to His revelation. This principle of judgment our Lord Himself endorsed in John 12:48 *'He who rejects Me, and does not receive My words, has that which judges him – the word which I have spoken will judge him in the last day.'* God has made us thinking beings; He has treated us as such by communicating with us in words. It is a solemn thought that by our own anti-intellectualism, in which we either refuse or cannot be bothered to listen to God's word, we may be storing up for ourselves the judgment of God."

The Bible's Emphasis: the goal of Knowledge, Understanding and Wisdom is to *KNOW THE TRUTH*

Proverbs 3:13-14 *"Happy is the man who finds WISDOM, and the man who gains UNDERSTANDING, for her proceeds are better than the profits of silver, and her gain than fine gold."*

Proverbs 4:7 *"WISDOM is the principal thing; therefore get wisdom. And in all your getting, get UNDERSTANDING."*

Ephesians 1:17-18 *"...the God of our Lord Jesus Christ, the Father of glory, may give to you the spirit of WISDOM and revelation in the KNOWLEDGE of Him, the eyes of your UNDERSTANDING being enlightened, that you may KNOW what is the hope of His calling, what are the riches of the glory of His inheritance in the saints..."*

Colossians 1:9-10 *"...(we) do not cease to pray for you, and to ask that you may be filled with the KNOWLEDGE of His will in all WISDOM and spiritual UNDERSTANDING; that you may have a walk worthy of the Lord, fully pleasing Him, being fruitful in every good work and increasing in the KNOWLEDGE of God.."*

Proverbs 23:23 *"BUY THE TRUTH, and don't sell it, also wisdom and instruction and understanding."*

Ephesians 3:14-19   Christian Worldview: Faith requires Logical Thinking   1.8

"...I bow my knees to the Father of our Lord Jesus Christ, from whom the whole family in heaven and earth is named, that He would grant you, according to the riches of His glory, to be strengthened with might through His Spirit in the inner man, that Christ may dwell in your hearts through ①FAITH; that you, being rooted and grounded in love, may be able to ②COMPREHEND with all the saints what is the width and length and depth and height – to ③KNOW the love of Christ which passes ④KNOWLEDGE; that you may be filled with all the fullness of God."

① FAITH = Gr. *"pistis"* = moral conviction; persuasive assurance; trust in God based on His character
② COMPREHEND = Gr. *"katalambanô"* = take eagerly or seize; attain; possess; perceive
③ KNOW = Gr. *"ginôskô"* = to be sure of; to be resolved; to fully understand
④ KNOWLEDGE = Gr. *"gnôsis"* = the act of knowing; science (form of *"ginôskô"*)

John Stott[2]: Faith ≠ credulity   "H.L. Mencken says 'Faith may be defined briefly as an illogical belief in the occurrence of the improbable'. But Mencken was wrong – faith is not credulity. To be credulous is to be gullible, to be entirely uncritical, undiscerning and even unreasonable in one's beliefs. It is a great mistake to suppose that faith and reason are incompatible. Faith and sight are set in opposition to each other in Scripture (see 2Corin. 5:7), but not faith and reason. On the contrary, true faith is essentially reasonable because it trusts in God's character and promises. A Christian is one whose mind reflects and rests on these certitudes.

John Stott[2]: Faith ≠ optimism (positive thinking)
This seems to be the confusion made by Norman Vincent Peale. His fundamental conviction concerns the power of the human mind... Dr. Peale develops

his thesis about positive thinking, which he goes on (mistakenly) to equate with faith. In his book 'The Power of Positive Thinking' he says 'According to your faith in yourself, according to your faith in your job, according to your faith in God this far will get you and no farther.' Dr. Peale apparently draws no distinction between faith in God and faith in oneself. Indeed, he does not seem to be at all concerned about faith's object. To Dr. Peale faith is really another word for self-confidence, for a largely ungrounded optimism.

Matthew 6:28-30   Faith and Evidence belong together (Believing requires Thinking)

"⑤CONSIDER the lilies of the field.... Now if God so clothes the grass of the field, which today is, and tomorrow is thrown into the oven, will He not much more clothe you, O you of ⑥LITTLE FAITH?"

⑤ CONSIDER = Gr. *"katalambanô"* = to learn thoroughly; to note carefully; to seize (same as "comprehend")
⑥ LITTLE FAITH = Gr. *"oligopistos"* = lacking confidence or assurance

We must study our Lord's lessons in *observation* and *deduction* from the evidence. The bible is full of logic, and we must never think of faith as something purely mystical. Look at the birds about you, and draw your deductions. Look at the grass, look at the lilies of the field, consider them. Faith, can be defined like this: *it is a man insisting upon thinking when everything seems determined to knock him down in an intellectual sense.*

John Stott[2]: Faith = Logically Thinking upon the Trustworthiness of God   "Christian faith reckons thoughtfully and confidently upon the trustworthiness of God. 1Samuel 30:6 says that *"David strengthened himself in the Lord his God"*. This is true faith. David did not shut his eyes to the facts. Nor did he try to build up his self-confidence or tell himself that he was really feeling fine. No. He remembered the Lord his God, the God of creation and the God of the covenant, the God who had promised to be his God and to set him on the throne of Israel. As David recalled the promises and faithfulness of God, he grew strong in faith. He 'strengthened himself in the Lord his God.' The trouble with the person of little faith is that, instead of controlling his own thought, his thought is being controlled by something else, and as we put it, he goes round and round in circles. That is the essence of WORRY... that is not thought; that is the absence of thought, a FAILURE TO THINK."

The foundation of my faith = clear and logical *knowledge* of Jesus Christ.

Logically Thinking through the Problems of Christianity

1) Problem #1 = there are many **intellectual** reasons to question Christianity
   - a) where did life come from? — The Bible says God created life
   - b) where does evil come from? — The Bible says from man's nature
   - c) how can the Bible have no errors? — The Bible says it is error-free

2) Problem #2 = there are **emotional** obstacles with Christianity
   - a) aren't there many ways to heaven? — The Bible says Jesus is the only way to eternal life
   - b) how can a loving God create hell? — The Bible says hell is a real place of torment
   - c) why is there so much hypocrisy in Christianity? — The Bible says Christianity is a heart issue

3) Problem #3 = there are **volitional** reasons to reject Christianity
   - a) why should I have to answer to anyone? — The Bible says to deny yourself and follow Jesus
   - b) why deny myself fun today for promises someday? — The Bible says true rewards are in heaven
   - c) why would I put others ahead of my own desires? — The Bible says esteem others better than yourself

In their book 'I Don't Have Enough Faith to be an Atheist'[6], Norman Geisler and Frank Turek explain below that the reasonableness of Christianity must withstand the test of evidence in order for faith to make sense:

Is Christianity reasonable? "We believe it is. But unless you make a thorough investigation of the *evidence* with an open mind, belief in Christianity may appear to be problematic. Once one looks at the *evidence*, we think it takes more faith to be a non-Christian than it does to be a Christian. The claim that religion is simply a matter of faith is a modern myth - it's just not true. While religion certainly requires faith, religion is not only about faith. Facts are also central to all religions because all religious worldviews - including atheism - make *TRUTH CLAIMS*, and many of those truth claims can be evaluated through *SCIENTIFIC* and *HISTORICAL* investigation."

Why does every religious worldview require faith? "As limited human beings, we do not possess the type of knowledge that will provide us with *ABSOLUTE PROOF* of God's existence. Outside of the knowledge of our own existence (I know I exist because I have to exist in order to ponder the question), we deal in *PROBABILITY*. Whatever we've concluded about the existence of God, it's always possible that the opposite conclusion is true. In fact, it is possible that our conclusions in this book ("*I Don't Have Enough Faith to be an Atheist*") are wrong. We don't think they are because we have good *evidence* to support them. Indeed, we think our conclusions are true beyond a REASONABLE DOUBT. This type of certainty, say, 95-plus percent certain, is the best that fallible and finite beings can attain for most questions, and it is more than sufficient for even the biggest decisions in life. Nevertheless, some faith is required to overcome the possibility that we are wrong."

The Faith of an Atheist[6]

"While some faith is required for our conclusions, it's often forgotten that faith is also required to believe any worldview, including atheism. We were reminded of this recently when we met an atheist named Barry at one of our seminars. Barry was incredulous that a mutual friend, Steve, had become a Christian.

He said, 'I can't figure Steve out. He claims to be an intellectual, but he can't answer all my objections I pose to him about Christianity. He says he doesn't have all the answers because he's new and still learning.'

I (Frank) said, 'Barry, it's virtually impossible to know everything about a particular topic, and it's certainly impossible when that topic is an infinite God. So there has to be a point where you realize you have enough information to come to a conclusion, even if unanswered questions remain.'

Barry had decided his view - atheism - was correct even though he did not have exhaustive information to support it. Did he know for sure there is no God? Had he investigated every argument and evidence for the existence of God? Could he answer every objection to atheism? Of course not. It would be impossible to do so. Since Barry, like Steve, is dealing in the realm of probability rather than absolute certainty, he has to have a certain amount of faith to believe that God does not exist.

"FAITH = what I use to cover any gap in my knowledge"[6]

When thinking through issues of faith, the question is: who has more *evidence* for their conclusion? Which conclusion is more reasonable? The less evidence you have for your position, the more faith you need to believe it (and vice versa).

As we'll see, the empirical, forensic, and philosophical *evidence* strongly supports conclusions consistent with Christianity and inconsistent with any other worldview."

The Essence of the Christian Worldview = The GOSPEL

What *essential beliefs* must a person hold, to become a Christian? 2.1

The "centermost circle" of the target contains the six core **ESSENTIALS** as defined in the Bible that any person must confess to belief in, in order to be saved and call themselves by the name "Christian".

1) Existence of God
2) Deity of Jesus Christ
3) The Atonement
4) Repentance from my sin
5) The Death, Burial & Resurrection of Jesus Christ
6) "Sola Fidei" = Salvation is by God's Grace alone, through my faith in the Lord Jesus Christ alone.

The Gospel by John MacArthur: *"He [the Father] made Him [the Son] to be sin who knew no sin, so that in Him we might become the righteousness of God"* (2 Cor. 5:21).

"Jesus was guilty of nothing. Yet on the cross, the Father treated Him as if He had committed personally every sin ever committed by every individual who would ever believe.

Though He was blameless, He faced the full fury of God's wrath, enduring the penalty of sin on behalf of those He came to save. In this way, the sinless Son of God became the perfect substitute for the sinful sons of men.

As a result of Christ's sacrifice, the elect become the righteousness of God in Him. In the same way that the Father treated the Son as a sinner, even though the Son was sinless, the Father now treats believers as righteous, even though they were unrighteous.

Jesus exchanged His life for sinners in order to fulfill the elective plan of God. And He did it so that, in the end, He might give back to the Father the love gift that the Father gave to Him."

1) **The Existence of God (Hebrews 11:6, Psalm 14:1) –** BOOKS 1 & 4
   I must believe that God exists (I cannot be an atheist and call myself a Christian).

2) **The Deity of Christ – The Incarnation (John 1:1,14, John 8:56-59) –** BOOK 3
   I must believe Jesus Christ is God who revealed Himself to mankind (as promised in Scripture).

3) **The Atonement (John 1:29, Mark 10:45, 1Corin. 15:3, 2Corinthians 5:21) –** BOOK 4
   I must believe Jesus atoned for my sins by dying *for* me, thus paying the ransom owed to God the Father (to satisfy His standard for holiness).

4) **Repentance (Luke 13:3,5; Acts 11:18, 2Corinthians 7:9-10) –** BOOK 4
   I must admit I am a sinner and be willing to repent (turn from my sin and turn to Jesus Christ as my only means to be forgiven by God).

5) **The Death, Burial and Resurrection of Jesus Christ (1Corinthians 15:1-22) –** BOOK 3
   I must believe Jesus Christ died for my sins and was buried, then rose physically from the dead, to not only affirm my faith in a risen Savior but to make Him my "first fruits" (vs. 20) of my new life ("born again": only by His resurrection can I now be resurrected to new life *in Him*).

6) **"Sola Fidei" = Salvation is by God's grace alone through my faith in the Lord Jesus Christ alone (John 3:16, Romans 1:17, Ephesians 2:8) –** BOOK 4
   I must actively trust *in* Him (who He is = God the Son) and *in* what He accomplished *for* me (dying for my sins and rising from the dead), by willingly surrendering the control of my life into His hands.

The Christian mandate = Emphasizing the Essentials

In his article 'Representing Christ to a Postmodern World'[17], Michael Patton explains how to distinguish between what are the essential tenets of the Christian faith versus those things that may be interesting but not essential:

"What beliefs are the **'sine qua non'** (without which, not) of the true Christian? What are the essentials of the Christian faith versus the non-essentials? Concerning salvation, we need to be able to state exactly what the Bible says is essential for salvation — *what exactly is the content of what a person needs to believe to be saved.* Does one simply have to "believe in the Lord Jesus" (Acts 16:31)? If so what does that entail? What does one have to know about Christ? Does he have to know that He is God? Does he have to believe that Christ vicariously took his place on the cross? Does he have to believe *and* turn from his sin? Or does he just have to believe, as the thief on the cross did, that Christ was the messianic King going to His Kingdom? Do you have to believe in the Trinity, the virgin birth, the inspiration of Scripture, the Second Coming of Christ, or the existence of Hell? Are these all doctrines (the "list") that the unbeliever must accept *before* he or she is considered a believer? It is extremely important that we categorize just exactly what the Bible says about salvation.

The "4-Block" Chart: Help me define what I consider Relative vs. Objective, Essential vs. Non-Essential

This chart (below) has two broad categories, each divided into two sections. Following are the category definitions. Observe the patterns on the chart as you read.

1. **True Relativity**: Everything that exists on the left side of the quadrant is truly relative. It is either completely independent of right or wrong, or the right or wrong is determined by the situation.
   a. *Situational Relativity*: The right and the wrong of those in this category are dependent upon the culture, time, situation, or some other variable. Its sinfulness was dependent upon the cultural expression. The same sin may be expressed in our culture but in a different way.
   b. *Autonomous Relativity*: This category contains those that are truly relative. There is no right or wrong. This category is filled with opinions and customs that are not right nor wrong. One's opinion on the best song is an example of something that is autonomously relative. There is no one correct answer — it's always relative.

2. **True Objectivity**: Everything on the right side has a definite right or wrong. There is always an objective truth that is true no matter whether one believes it. It is not dependent upon time, culture, or any situation. It exists as true or false in and of itself. All biblical principles and doctrines belong on this side.
   a. *Essential Objectivity*: This category contains only those that are essential for salvation. This should contain only those truths which you believe a person must accept to be considered a true Christian.
   b. *Non-Essential Objectivity*: This category contains doctrinal and non-doctrinal issues which are not necessary for one's salvation. An example is the gift of tongues. Tongues either did or didn't cease. The truth is objective. But it is non-essential because it is not necessary to believe one way or the other to be saved.

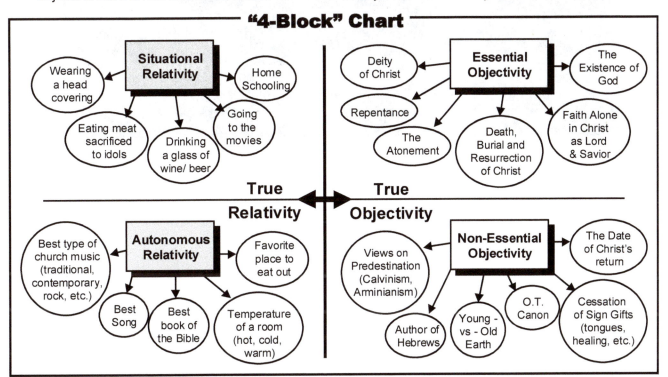

> **Construct my own chart:** When issues arise, decide the category in which they belong. BE CRITICAL OF MYSELF. This chart is extremely valuable in understanding that these categories exist. It is not an ironclad never-fail chart that I can use in all situations. My chart will probably look different from the one shown.
>
> **The value of my chart:** It shows the necessity of THINKING ABOUT THESE THINGS MORE DEEPLY.
> I live in a postmodern culture in which people live their lives on the left side of the quadrant (relativism). I have a Church that wants to counter by living on the right side (objectivism). Being familiar with the principles of this chart allows me to express truth in a more RELEVANT fashion.

A big problem within the Church = we major in the MINORS

Many Christians overly stress their views on certain issues to an unbelieving postmodern, giving them the wrong impression. We express our opinions about having a glass of wine, rock-and-roll, or some other area just as emphatically as we would the death, burial, and resurrection of Christ. We will argue all day long with the unbeliever about the theory of evolution and never tell them about Christ. We never even give them a chance to believe what is most important.

Let me make this clear: There is nothing wrong with discussing or even debating the non-essentials, but we must keep in mind that the non-essentials do not save. They can be used as primers or springboards for the Gospel, but they cannot replace it. We must get to the Gospel in every witnessing opportunity we have.

Eleven of the twelve sermons in Acts contain the death, burial, and resurrection of Christ. The only one that did not was Stephen's, and if it were not cut short, he surely would have presented the risen Christ to the Sanhedrin. It is imperative that we emphasize the Gospel; it is the only message that contains eternal life.

We do so as if we believe that convincing someone that rock-and-roll is wrong is the same as convincing them of the Gospel. We must understand that convincing someone of any area outside of the objective essential will not save them.

Another Value of the "4-Block" chart = place emphasis where emphasis is due

We have to continually ask ourselves what things we have placed as ESSENTIALS in our lives and if they should be there. If too much emphasis is placed on the non-essentials, it makes the essentials less important. We end up destroying the "object of our enthusiasm"— the Gospel of Christ.

Most people's lives are filled with opinions, pet peeves and disputes. When the unbelieving postmodern looks at you, what would he say that you have in italics in your life? We should have very few things that we greatly emphasize in order to save our stress for the things that really matter. We can give no greater honor to Christ than to emphasize the things that He emphasized."

**The list of the 6 Essentials of the Gospel is NOT intended to be dogmatic.
We all can come up with what we think is the right "list".**

The intention of the "List" = to make you THINK

**As John Stott said, can I clearly and accurately share the GOSPEL?
Do I focus on the "majors"… or do I focus on the "minors"?**

Essential #1 has become a Contradiction in Terms → "CHRISTIAN ATHEISM"

Are there people out there today who would describe themselves as "Christian Atheists"? Believe it or not, the answer is yes. For most of us, this sounds like a contradiction in terms. So what is a Christian Atheist? Thomas Ogletree (Assistant Professor of Constructive Theology, Chicago Theological Seminary), explains the four common beliefs of a "Christian Atheist":

1) the UNREALITY OF GOD for our age, including traditional Christian theology's understandings of God
2) the need to RESHAPE the Christian message to fit in contemporary culture
3) varying degrees and forms of SEPARATION from today's church
4) the importance of centralizing the person of JESUS in theological reflection

1) Unreality of God Christian atheists believe that there is no God because there is no evidence of Him. In essence, Christian atheists are MODERNISTS – they generally do not believe in things which cannot be proven empirically. To them, God has ceased to be "a 'need fulfiller' and 'problem solver'". Most Christian atheists believe that God never existed, but there are a few (such as Thomas J.J. Altizer) who believe in the death of God literally (not only is God absent, but that His death was an actual historical event). Most Christian atheists do not tend to see God's death literally, though. They see it in the non-literal, atheistic sense. When they say that God is dead, they mean that there is not and never has been such a Being.

2) Reshaping Christianity to fit the culture Christian atheism was created by theologians who attempted to reconcile Christianity and America's increasingly secular culture. Theologians looked at the scientific, empirical culture of today and tried to find religion's place in it. They reject the current state of the Christian message and want to make Christianity more meaningful to people in the modern world. Colin Lyas, a Philosophy lecturer at Lancaster University, stated that "*Christian atheists are united also in the belief that any satisfactory answer to these problems must be an answer that will make life tolerable in this world, here and now and which will direct attention to the social and other problems of this life*". They want something that will help them with life now rather than a religion whose focus is on things of the next life. According to them, people living in today's world are skeptical and can no longer believe in such a Being as God. Instead of looking to the past, they say that Christians must look to the future and reshape theology to fit current culture.

3) Separation from the church Christian atheists believe that the way to true Christianity is through the culture of the world and not the worship of God. They see religions which withdraw from the world as moving away from TRUTH. They say that a belief in God is an escape from the world around us. To a Christian atheist, God is a restrictive and illogical idea; it keeps people from connecting with the world around them. One of the major problems Christian atheists have with Christian beliefs is how ABSOLUTE they are. Christian atheists are RELATIVISTS; they believe that what's true depends on each person's own views and on the cultural circumstances. They criticize Christians for their hypocrisy, by separating themselves from the world. Christian atheists see separating from the world as separating from what a Christian is supposed to be, which is someone who suffers along with everyone else in the world.

4) The centrality of Jesus Most Christian atheists think of Jesus as a wise and good man, accepting His moral teachings but rejecting the idea of His divinity. They look to Jesus as an example of what a Christian should be, but they do not see him as a God. Instead of seeing Jesus as the way to heaven, Christian atheists see Him as the way to humanity. To them, following Jesus means being "alongside the neighbor, being for him". So, to follow Jesus means to be human, to help other humans, and to further mankind. In doing this, they see Jesus as an example of a really good human being, nothing more. They want to become the kind of human being Jesus was; they want to be thoroughly human.

Psalm 14:1 *"The fool has said in his heart, 'There is no God.'"*

The Gospel & 'TACTICS'[4]: How to get your friends to open up

Greg Kohkl: M.A. in Philosophy of Religion & Ethics, Talbot School of Theology; M.A. in Christian Apologetics, Simon Greenleaf School of Law; Founding director of 'Stand to Reason' and CPA (Center for Public Christianity).

The most effective way to respond to someone's claim is ...

to understand where they are coming from.

The most effective way to understand where they are coming from is...

to **ASK THEM**.

So often, we think our job is to defend our position...

we think we are the ones being backed in a corner, being put on the defensive – DON'T FALL FOR THE TRICK.

> Who bears the burden of proof in any conversation?
> The person who is making the claim!

Greg Kohkl: 'You do not have to be an expert in Apologetics' (4:34)

Sharing the Gospel in Today's Culture: The COLUMBO Tactic

Question #1 = "What do you mean by that?"
   The Goal: I want to gain information –
       understand what the person means

Question #2 = "How did you reach that conclusion?"
   The Goal: I want to gain information –
       on what evidence is their view based?

Question #3 = "May I ask you a question?"
   The Goal: Take command of the conversation –
       get THEM to now defend their claim.

> Most people associate Apologetics with conflict – it's not!
> The Goal is to guide someone from their faulty thinking toward TRUTH

Greg Kohkl: 'The Columbo Tactic in Apologetics' (4:06)

John 12:19 The Gospel = Creating a Christ-centered worldview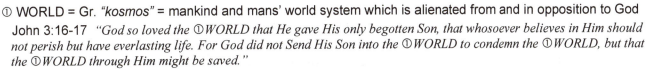

"The Pharisees.. said among themselves, 'You see that you are accomplishing nothing. Look, the ①WORLD HAS GONE AFTER HIM!'"

① WORLD = Gr. *"kosmos"* = mankind and mans' world system which is alienated from and in opposition to God

John 3:16-17 *"God so loved the ①WORLD that He gave His only begotten Son, that whosoever believes in Him should not perish but have everlasting life. For God did not Send His Son into the ①WORLD to condemn the ①WORLD, but that the ①WORLD through Him might be saved."*

John 7:7 *"The ①WORLD cannot hate you; but it hates Me because I testify of it that its works are evil."*

The context of John chapter 12: A Clash of Worldviews

"worldview" = the window by which a person views and decides what is real and valuable, unreal and worthless.

1) Jesus confronted the religious elite with who He is by His actions (healing the blind man, raising Lazarus) and His words (the Light of the world, the Door to heaven, the Bread of eternal life).

2) Jesus turned everyone's worldview upside down: people followed Him because His words and actions fit their worldview; the religious elite felt threatened because the "world" followed Him, not them.

3) Jesus' message = John 12:32 ➔ His sacrificial death on the cross will draw *all people* to Him (John 3:14-15) and fulfill God's requirement for the only way for anyone to be righteous in His eyes.

John ch. 12: "A Clash of Worldviews"	
The Religious Elite	**Jesus Christ**
They (and everyone else) believed they were righteous and destined for heaven	He openly rebuked them as unrighteousness and destined for hell (Matt. 5:20, Matt. 16:12)
They instituted a man-made legal system that everyone was required to follow to please God	He preached heartfelt repentance over personal sin for forgiveness and restoration back to God (Mark 1:15)
They claimed their laws came from God as His requirements for personal righteousness	He claimed to not only be the Law but that He came to fulfill the law for our sakes (John 8:51, Matt. 5:17)
They claimed God-given authority to judge rightly	He claimed to be God (John 8:56-58)
They claimed to know truth concerning God	He claimed to be Truth (John 14:6)
They claimed to know the way to eternal life	He claimed to be Eternal Life (John 11:25-26)
They claimed to be God's shepherds to the people	He claimed to be the Shepherd (John 10:11)

John chapter 12 shows a worldview system centered around Jewish culture... but it applies to any culture. Now.... jump forward in time 2,000 years to the culture in America today –

America Today: "A Clash of Worldviews"		
Secular Humanism	⇄	**Biblical Christianity**
Cosmology: the universe is self-existing and not created	⇄	Cosmology: the effect of the universe's existence must have a suitable CAUSE
Morality: modern science's universe is self-existing; supernatural guarantees of human values are unacceptable	⇄	Morality: man's built-in sense of right and wrong can be accounted for only by an innate awareness of a code of law IMPLANTED by God
Rational: man is a part of nature and has emerged as a result of a continuous process	⇄	Rational: the operation of the universe, by order and natural law, implies a MIND behind it
Ontology: realizing my personality is the end of life; the goal is its development and fulfillment now	⇄	Ontology: man's ideas of God imply a God who IMPRINTED such a consciousness
Teleology: man is the result of a blind and random process that does not require any kind of meaning	⇄	Teleology: the design of the universe implies a PURPOSE behind it
Humanism: foundation is in the teaching of Evolution	⇄	Christianity: foundation is in teaching the Bible

N. Pearcey[3]: A Worldview must fit with Reality *"If our worldview doesn't fit the larger reality we're trying to explain, then at some point we will find that WE CANNOT FOLLOW IT. C.S. Lewis once wrote, 'The Christian and the Materialist hold different beliefs about the universe. They can't both be right.'"*

N. Pearcey, 'Total Truth'[3]: "The Best Way to debunk a false worldview is to offer a Good One"

"When the only form of cultural commentary Christians offer is moral condemnation, no wonder we come across to nonbelievers as angry and scolding. The best way to drive out a bad worldview is by offering a good one, and Christians need to move beyond CRITICIZING culture to CREATING culture. Whether we work with our brains or with our hands, whether we are analytical or artistic, whether we work with people or with things, in every calling we are CULTURE-CREATORS, offering up our work as a service to God."

Christian Worldview: ① God's Creation ➔ ② mans' Fall ➔ ③ mans' Redemption

- Genesis 1:27-28 = God originally *created* me to subdue the earth in *His name*
- Romans 3:23 = My sin short-changed God of *His glory* He would have revealed through me
- Ephesians 4:22-24 = God is *sanctifying* me to restore *His name*

Effective Evangelism = giving solid answers to the same fundamental questions

Question #1 – CREATION: "How did it all begin? Where did we come from?"
Question #2 – FALL: "What went wrong? What is the source of evil and suffering?"
Question #3 – REDEMPTION: "What has been done about it? How will the world be set right again?"

America Today: 2 Reasons for Creation as the starting point for Evangelism

Today, as we address the biblically illiterate Americans of the 21st century, we need to follow Paul's model (in Acts 17), building a case from Creation before expecting people to understand the message of sin and salvation.

Reason #1: in our secular culture, starting with the Fall renders the rest of our message incoherent

"In an earlier age, when most Americans were brought up in the church, they were familiar with basic theological concepts. When people said, 'You're a sinner', they had the context to understand what it meant, and many were moved to repentance. But contemporary Americans often have no background in biblical teaching – which means that the concept of sin makes no sense to them. The response is likely to be, *'What right does God have to judge me? How do you even know He exists?'*"

Reason #2: in our secular culture, starting with the Fall doesn't allow us to explain Redemption

"The goal of Redemption is to restore us to our original created state. If it were true that we are worthless, and that being sinners is our core identity, then in order to have something of value God would have to destroy the human race and start over. But He doesn't do that; instead He restores us to the high dignity originally endowed at Creation – recovering our true identity and renewing the image of God in us."

Today's World: A Battleground for the Souls of People

"Picture the world as God's territory by right of CREATION. Because of the FALL, it has been invaded and occupied by Satan and his minions, who constantly wage war against God's people. At the central turning point in history, God Himself, the 2nd Person of the Trinity, enters the world in the person of Jesus Christ and deals Satan a deathblow through His resurrection. The enemy has been fatally wounded; the outcome of the war is certain; yet the occupied territory has not actually been liberated.

There is now a period of time where God's people are called to participate in the follow-up battle, pushing the enemy back and reclaiming territory for God. This is the period in which we now live – between Christ's resurrection and the final victory over sin and Satan. Our calling is to apply the finished work of Christ on the cross to OUR LIVES and the world around us, without expecting perfect results until Christ returns."

Today's Evangelism: Fulfilling Psalm 126:1-6   Compassion Towards Those Trapped in our Culture

"When the Lord brought back the captivity of Zion, we were like those who dream. Then our mouth was filled with laughter, and our tongues with singing. Then THEY SAID AMONG THE NATIONS, 'The Lord has done great things for them.' The Lord has done great things for us, whereof we are glad... Those who SOW IN TEARS shall reap in joy. He who continually goes forth WEEPING, bearing seed for sowing, shall doubtless come again with rejoicing, bringing his sheaves with him."

"Even when Schaeffer raised serious criticisms in our culture, he expressed a burning compassion for people caught in the trap of false and harmful worldviews. 'These works of art are the expression of men struggling with their lostness. Dare we laugh at such things? Dare we feel superior when we view their tortured expressions in their art? The men and women who produce such things are dying while they live; yet where is our compassion for them?' How many Christians reach out in compassion? How many do the hard work of crafting real answers to their questions? How many cry out to God on behalf of people struggling in the coils of false worldviews?'"

Ps 107:2 *"Let the redeemed of the Lord say so, whom He has redeemed from the hand of the enemy."*

1Corinthians 1:22-23   The Gospel = Turning Greeks into Jews   2.3

"...①JEWS request a ②SIGN, and ③GREEKS seek after ④WISDOM; but we ⑤PREACH Christ crucified, to the Jews a ⑥STUMBLING BLOCK and to the Greeks ⑦FOOLISHNESS."

① JEWS = Gr. "*Ioudaios*" = originates from JUDAH (Hebrew *"Yehudah"*) in Genesis 49:8-12; Judah was one of Jacob's (Israel's) children - his descendants were called Yehudim ("Judahites"). The word **"Jew"** is a shortened form of the word "Judahite"). A "Jew" in the OT would be a "Judahite;" and a "Jew" in the NT would be a "Judean."

② SIGN = Gr. "*sēmeion*" = a supernatural indication; a miracle

  Mark 8:11-12 "Jesus rebukes hard-hearted people (they demand a sign in order to believe in Him)"
  "..the Pharisees came out and began to dispute with Him, seeking from Him a SIGN from heaven, testing Him. But He sighed deeply in His spirit, and said, 'Why does this generation seek a sign?'"

  Matthew 11:2-6 "Jesus encourages sincere seekers to pay attention to the OT signs"
  "...when John had heard in prison about the works of Christ, he sent 2 of his disciples and said to Him, 'Are You the Coming One, or do we look for another?' Jesus answered and said to them, 'Go and tell John the things which you hear and see: the blind receive their sight and the lame walk; the lepers are cleansed and the deaf hear; the dead are raised up and the people have the gospel preached to them. And blessed is he who is not OFFENDED because of Me,'"

  Luke 10:13 "Jesus' miracles should have brought repentance and belief (not testing)"
  "Woe to you, Chorazin! Woe to you, Bethsaida! For if the MIGHTY WORKS (Gr. "dunamis" = power; miracles) which were done in you had been done in Tyre and Sidon, they would have repented long ago, sitting in sackcloth and ashes."

> John 5:39-40 "Use OT Messianic miracles and prophecies as the *evidence* that Jesus is Messiah"
> *"You search the Scriptures, for in them you think you have eternal life, and these are they which TESTIFY OF ME. But you are NOT WILLING to come to Me, that you may have life."*
>
> This is the essence of what Paul means in 1Corinthians 1:22 – the Jews have the OT Scriptures: they were given much detailed evidence by Jesus that He fulfilled the OT requirements for Messiah. But it boils down to a person's *will*, to choose to respond to His offer for eternal life and surrender their life to His control.

③ GREEKS = Gr. "*Hellēn*" = an inhabitant of Hellas; a Greek-speaking person; a non-Jew; a Gentile
④ WISDOM = Gr. "*sophia*" = human wisdom (earthly, natural)
⑤ PREACH = Gr. "*kērussó*" = herald (as in publicly crying out); proclaim; publish
⑥ STUMBLING BLOCK = Gr. "*skandalon*" = snare; cause for displeasure or sin; thing that offends
⑦ FOOLISHNESS = Gr. "*mōria*" = silliness; absurdity (where we get the English word "moron")

Why have western countries continually declined in Christian morality, despite numerous evangelistic campaigns? It comes down to understanding the difference between 'Jews' and 'Greeks'.

Acts 2:14-47   "Peter's message to Jews = God's Messianic fulfillment in Christ through His signs and wonders"

- Peter's audience = Jews who believed in the OT God of creation
   a) they knew what God expected of them and knew they fell short (they understood sin and mankind's' fall)
   b) they had the Law of Moses (God's Word was sacred in their eyes)
   c) they understood the need for a sacrifice for sin
   d) they weren't indoctrinated with evolutionary ideas
- Peter's main message = Jesus' death and resurrection and mankind's need for salvation
- Peter's results = 3,000 people responded

> The Jews understood creation and sin: both are necessary to understand the message of salvation (Peter didn't have to convince them that God was Creator or that man had sinned – he concentrated on the cross)

Acts 17:16-21   "Paul's message to Greeks = Jesus' death and resurrection are sufficient for salvation"

- Paul's audience = Greek philosophers who knew nothing of the OT God of creation
   a) they believed in many gods
   b) Jewish Scriptures had no value to them
   c) they had no understanding of sin and had no understanding of their need for a sacrifice for sin
   d) their culture was based on evolution (Epicureans, the atheists of their day, believed man evolved from dirt)
- Paul's main message = same as Peter's
- Paul's results = no one responded – they labeled him a 'babbler' (they brought him to Mars Hill)

> The Greeks had no foundational knowledge of God as Creator and mankind' sin; God's Word had no value to them (Paul's preaching was completely foreign to them – they saw it as foolishness)

Paul's message to Greeks (Acts 17:22-32) = God created man to seek Him and know Him

→ vs. 22-23 "Paul focuses them on the one 'unknown God' they worship"

"...Paul stood in the midst of the Areopagus and said, 'Men of Athens, I perceive that in all things you are very religious; for as I was passing through and considering the objects of your worship, I even found an altar with this inscription: 'To the Unknown God'. Therefore, the One whom YOU WORSHIP WITHOUT KNOWING, Him I proclaim to you: ....

→ vs. 24-25 "Paul identifies this 'Unknown God' as the true and only Creator of all"

"God, who MADE THE WORLD and everything in it, since He is Lord of heaven and earth, does not dwell in temples made with hands. Nor is He worshipped with men's hands, as though He needed anything, since He gives to all life, breath, and all things."

→ vs. 26-28 "Paul credits this 'God' with creating all men from one blood, challenging their evolutionary ideas"

"He has MADE FROM ONE BLOOD every nation of men to dwell on all the face of the earth, and has determined their preappointed times and the boundaries of their habitation, so that THEY SHOULD SEEK THE LORD, in the hope that they might grope for Him and find Him, though He is not far from each one of us; for in Him we live and move and have our being, as also some of your own poets have said, 'For we are also His offspring.'

→ vs. 29-32 "Paul calls them to repent (change their worldview), and returns to Christ and His resurrection"

"Therefore, since we are the offspring of God, we ought not to think that the Divine Nature is like gold or silver or stone, something shaped by art and MAN'S DEVISING. Truly, these times of ignorance God overlooked, but now commands all men everywhere to REPENT, because He has appointed a day on which He will judge the world in righteousness by THE MAN whom He has ordained. He has given us assurance of this to all by RAISING HIM FROM THE DEAD. And when they heard of the resurrection of the dead, some mocked, while others said, 'We will hear you again on this matter.'"

Paul's challenge is the same today - turning 'Greeks' into 'Jews'

In his article 'On Darwin and Evolution'[20], Ken Ham explains the challenge Christians have today is the same challenge Paul faced in the early days of Christianity: "Unlike Peter, Paul had to take pagan, evolutionist Greeks and change their entire way of thinking about life and the universe, and then get them to think like Jewish people concerning the true foundation of history. No wonder only a few came to Christ at first. Such a change is dramatic. Imagine trying to get an Australian Aborigine to think like an American. Such a change would be extremely difficult to say the least.

Generations ago: the culture was somewhat like that of the 'JEWS'. People were familiar with their Bible. Most knew the basic concepts of Christianity concerning creation, sin and the message of salvation. When an evangelist preached the message of the cross, it was somewhat like Peter preaching to the Jewish people in Acts 2. Most people had the foundational knowledge to understand the message and respond accordingly. But most church leaders didn't understand that people who were responding were already 'Greeks' in their thinking about reality. Students were being taught evolutionary ideas in a low-key way that was undermining the credibility of the Bible's history. Consequently, there was no real, lasting impact on western culture, which has become more anti-Christian. Underneath it all, people had questions about the validity of the Bible.... and evolution is taught as fact throughout the education system. Generations of people now have little or no knowledge of the Bible. They have been thoroughly indoctrinated in an atheistic, evolutionary philosophy.

Western culture today: no longer one of mainly 'JEWS' but is more like 'GREEKS' – genuine, pagan 'Greeks' – increasingly anti-Christian with a predominantly atheistic, evolutionary, secular philosophy.

Children don't automatically go to Sunday School or church programs as they used to. Ministers of religion find it more difficult to conduct programs in schools. And most church leaders tell their congregations its fine to believe in evolutionary ideas, as long as God is somehow involved. After years of subtle indoctrination and an emphasis on rejecting the book of Genesis as literal, generations today doubt the reliability of the entire Bible.

How can we reach today's 'GREEKS'?

STEP 1 = their faulty foundation of evolution needs to be rebuilt: they need to understand and believe that the Bible's account of creation and the fall of man (i.e., that man is a sinner) is true.

STEP 2 = once they have the foundation, they can better understand the message of the Messiah who came to provide forgiveness for them by being the final blood sacrifice for their sin.

Effectively Evangelizing our American Culture

#1. The cross will not be understood until people can be changed from 'Greeks' into 'Jews'.

#2. Today's culture needs answers from the Bible and science to counter evolutionary teaching.

#3. Teach Genesis 1-11 as literal history, to return the gospel's credibility in our 'Greek' culture.

Acts 17:2-4, 18:4   The Gospel = A *Reasoned* Presentation of Jesus Christ — 2.4

"Paul, as his custom was, went in to them, and for 3 Sabbaths ①REASONED with them from the Scriptures, ②EXPLAINING and ③DEMONSTRATING that the Christ had to suffer and rise again from the dead, and saying, 'This Jesus whom I ④PREACH to you is the Christ.' And some of them were ⑤PERSUADED... And he reasoned in the synagogue every Sabbath, and persuaded both Jews and Greeks."

① REASONED = Gr. "*dialegomai*" = to bring together different viewpoints and reckon them up in open discussion
② EXPLAINING = Gr. "*dianoigó*" = to open up completely or expound upon
③ DEMONSTRATING = Gr. "*paratithēmi*" = to place alongside or present; to set before (to bring forward the truth)
④ PREACH = Gr. "*kataggellô*" = declare; proclaim; challenge with facts (different than teach: 'present the facts')
⑤ PERSUADED = Gr. "*peithô*" = to convince by argument or debate; to consent to evidence or authority

> In his book 'Basic Christianity'[34], John Stott explains how Paul, In Romans 10:14-17, argues for "the necessity of preaching the gospel if people are to become Christians. Sinners are saved, he says, by calling on the name of the Lord Jesus. That much is clear. But...
>
> > Question #1 = How can men call on someone in whom they have no faith?
> > Question #2 = And how can they have faith in someone of whom they have never heard?
> > Question #3 = And how can they hear of Him unless a preacher tells them?
>
> He concludes his argument: 'So faith comes from what is heard, and hearing comes by preaching Christ.'
>
> His argument implies that there must be a SOLID CONTENT in our evangelistic proclamation of Christ. It is our responsibility to set Jesus Christ forth in the fullness of His divine-human person and saving work so that through this 'preaching of Christ' God may arouse faith in the hearer. Such evangelistic preaching is far removed... from what is all too common today, namely an emotional, anti-intellectual appeal for 'decisions' when the hearers have but the haziest notion what they are to decide about or why."

Two New Testament Reasons for a Rational Proclamation of the Gospel:

Reason #1 = to "persuade men" (Acts 17:2-4, 18:4)
• to "persuade" = to marshal arguments in order to prevail on people to change their mind about something.
• Paul was teaching DOCTRINE and arguing toward a conclusion (he sought to convince in order to convert).

Reason #2 = to "respond to the truth" (Ephesians 1:12-13)
• becoming a Christian is "believing the truth", "obeying the truth", "acknowledging the truth".
• early Christian evangelists, in preaching Christ, were actually teaching DOCTRINE ("truth") about Christ.

The Gospel is not Academic – its Rational:
• The gospel is for everybody, whatever their education or lack of it... the kind of evangelism for which I am pleading, which sets Jesus Christ forth in His fullness, is relevant to all kinds of people, children as well as adults, the uncultured as well as the cultured...
• This evangelism is not academic (couched in philosophical terms and complicated vocabulary) but RATIONAL. And the uneducated are just as rational as the educated. Their minds may not be trained to think a certain way... but they still think. All human beings think, because God made a human being a thinking creature.
• The teaching of Jesus Himself, although simple, made His listeners THINK. He presented GREAT TRUTHS about God and man, about Himself and the kingdom, about His life and the next. And He often ended His parables with a teasing question to force His hearers to MAKE UP THEIR MINDS on the issue under discussion.

Our Duty in Evangelism = Present a Gospel that is Understandable:
Again, as John Stott says in Basic Christianity'[34], "Our duty is to avoid distorting or diluting the gospel, and at the same time to MAKE IT PLAIN, to cut the word of truth STRAIGHT so that people can FOLLOW IT, lest *'when any one hears the word of the kingdom and does not ①UNDERSTAND it, the evil one comes and snatches away what is sown in his heart* (Matthew 13:19).'

① UNDERSTAND = Gr. "*suniémi*" = to put together mentally; to consider to level of mentally grasping
I fear that our clumsy explanations can give the devil this very opportunity which he ought never to be allowed."

Do Doctrine and Arguments negate the work of the Holy Spirit?

- Evangelism is impossible without the Holy Spirit's power, but reasoned evangelism doesn't replace His working.

- <u>Paul's evangelistic approach</u>: to rely on the Holy Spirit but used doctrine, evidence and arguments to appeal to his audience's minds (Acts 17:16-17), then to argue with their mind, plead with their heart, to move their will, trusting in the Holy Spirit (2Cor. 5:17-21).

- John Gresham Machen, former Professor of New Testament at Princeton Theological Seminary, explains the importance of arguments from the evidence and it's alignment with the working of the Holy Spirit: *"There must be the mysterious work of the Spirit of God in the new birth. Without that, all our arguments are quite useless. But because argument is insufficient, it does not follow that it is unnecessary. What the Holy Spirit does in the new birth is not to make a man a Christian regardless of the evidence, but on the contrary to clear away the mists from his eyes and* enable him to attend to the evidence*."*

---

813 Times: God says He wants people to *KNOW* Him and His great truths

To the atheist, agnostic, 'religious': you are ignorant because you won't respond to the *knowledge* He gives.
To the Christian: I recall the great truths about myself, and I meditate on them until they grip my mind and mold my character. God's way is to remind me who I truly am because He made me that way in Christ.

<u>The Old and New Testament's constant urging to us</u>: "Don't be *ignorant* (don't *'not know'*)"

- **"ignorant"** = Hebr. "*lô' lô' lôh yâdá*" = not knowing; not understanding nor recognizing

Isaiah 56:10 *"His watchmen are blind, they are all IGNORANT; they are all DUMB DOGS, they cannot bark..."*

- **"ignorant"** or "not know" = Gr. "*agnoeô*" = not understanding due to lack of information or intelligence

1Corinthians 12:1-2 *"...concerning spiritual gifts, brethren, I do not want you to be IGNORANT: you KNOW that you were Gentiles, carried away to these DUMB idols, however you were led."*

<u>The Old and New Testament's constant urging to us</u>: "*Know with full understanding*"

- **"know"** = Hebr. "*yâdá*" = to know by recognizing; to be sure; to have understanding
  "understand" = Hebr. "*bîyn*" = to separate out mentally; to regard and discern wisely

Exodus 7:5 *"...the Egyptians shall KNOW that I am the Lord, when I stretch out My hand on Egypt and bring out the children of Israel from among them."*

Isaiah 43:10 *"'You are My witnesses,' says the Lord, 'and My servant whom I have chosen, that you may KNOW and believe Me, and UNDERSTAND that I am He. Before Me there was no God formed, nor shall there be after Me.'"*

Hosea 14:9 *"Who is wise, Let him UNDERSTAND these things. Who is prudent? Let him KNOW them. For the ways of the Lord are right; the righteous walk in them, but transgressor stumble in them."*

- **"know"** = Gr. "*ginóskó*" = to know absolutely; to be mentally sure in understanding

John 8:32 *"...you shall KNOW the truth, and the truth shall make you free."*

John 7:17 *"If anyone wants to do His will, he shall KNOW concerning the doctrine, whether it is from God or whether I speak on My own authority."*

John 17:3 *"...this is eternal life, that they may KNOW You, the only true God, and Jesus Christ whom You have sent."*

- **"know"** = Gr. "*eidó*" = to know as in seeing; to be sure of

John 3:2 *"This man came to Jesus by night and said to Him, 'Rabbi, we KNOW that You are a teacher come from God, for no one can do these signs that You do unless God is with him."*

1John 5:13 *"These things I have written to you who believe in the name of the Son of God, that you may KNOW that you have eternal life, and that you may continue to believe in the name of the Son of God."*

- **"understand"** = Gr. "*noieô*" = to exercise the mind; to think upon; to consider to the point of understanding

Hebrews 11:3 *"By faith we UNDERSTAND that the worlds were framed by the word of God, so that the things which are seen were not made of things which are visible."*

John 12:39-40 *"they could not believe, because Isaiah said again, 'He has blinded their eyes and hardened their heart, lest they should see with their eyes and UNDERSTAND with their heart, lest they should turn, so I should heal them.'"*

- **"understand"** = Gr. "*suniémi*" = to put together mentally; to consider to level of mentally grasping

Matthew 15:10 *"...He called the multitude and said to them, "Hear and UNDERSTAND.."*

Luke 8:9-10 *"...His disciples asked Him, saying, 'What does this parable mean?' And He said, 'To you it has been given to KNOW the mysteries of the kingdom of God, but to the rest it is given in parables, that "Seeing they may not see, and hearing they may not UNDERSTAND."'"*

God regards knowledge, understanding and wisdom as *foundations* of my faith (Psalm 11:3)

Genesis 6:3,5   The Gospel = God *uses* people to *reach* people   2.5

"'My Spirit shall not strive with man forever, for he is indeed flesh, yet his days shall be 120 years.' Then the Lord saw that the ①WICKEDNESS of man was great in the earth, and that every intent of the thoughts of his heart was only ①EVIL continually."

① WICKEDNESS, EVIL = Hebrew "*ra' râ âh*" = can mean either physical calamity (like earthquakes, tsunamis, etc.) or moral corruption that originates from the heart; in this verse, it is clearly moral.

② WICKEDNESS = Hebrew "*resha*" = iniquity (doing what you know is wrong according to God's law)

Habakkuk 1:13   *"...You are of purer eyes than to behold ①EVIL, and cannot look on iniquity."*

Psalm 5:4   *"...You are not a God who takes pleasure in ②WICKEDNESS, nor shall ①EVIL dwell with You."*

- **The Holy Spirit is active in the O.T.:** Genesis 6:3,5 is the second reference to the Holy Spirit. In Genesis 1:2, He energizes and activates the created cosmos. Here, He is STRIVING and LONGSUFFERING with man, calling them to repentance during the 120-year period before the Flood, through the preaching of Noah and Enoch:

1Peter 3:20, 2:5   *"...the longsuffering of God waited patiently in the days of Noah, while the ark was being prepared, in which a few, that is, eight souls, were saved through water...He did not spare the ancient world, but saved Noah, one of eight people, A PREACHER OF RIGHTEOUSNESS,, bringing in the flood on the world of the ungodly."*

Jude 14-15   *"Now Enoch, the 7th from Adam, PROPHESIED about these men also, saying, 'Behold, the Lord comes with 10,000's of His saints, to execute judgment on all, to convict all who are ungodly among them of all their ungodly deeds which they have committed in an ungodly way, and of all the harsh things which ungodly sinners have spoken against Him."*

- **John 16: 7-11**   **Jesus confirms the Holy Spirit's continuing ministry of striving with sinful man to repent**

"...It is to your advantage that I go away; for if I do not go away, the Helper will not come to you; but if I depart, I will send Him to you. And when He has come, He will convict the world of sin, and of righteousness, and of judgment: of sin, because they do not believe Me; of righteousness, because I go to the Father and you see Me no more; of judgment because the ruler of this world is judged."

The Holy Spirit doesn't condemn man – He strives WITH man, to CONVICT us of our *need* to be saved.

- **Romans 1:9, 14-17**   **God always reserves a FAITHFUL REMNANT to serve Him**

Paul, following in the same footsteps as Enoch and Noah, was *used* by the Holy Spirit to witness to all mankind of God's gift of salvation through His grace. Paul says God has revealed Himself to man through His creation, but man not only refuses God's truth but *suppresses* the truth in their man-made lies, showing themselves to be fools.

"...God is my witness, whom I SERVE in my spirit in the gospel of His Son, that without ceasing I make mention of you always in my prayers...I AM A DEBTOR both to the Greeks and to barbarians, both to wise and unwise. So much as is in me, I AM READY to preach the gospel to you who are in Rome also. For I AM NOT ASHAMED of the gospel of Christ, for it is the power of God to salvation for everyone who believes, for the Jew first and also for the Greek. For in it the righteousness of God is revealed from faith to faith: as it is written: 'The just shall live by faith.'"

- **1Corinthians 2:1-5**   **God demonstrates His power as He works through Paul**

"...I, brethren, when I came to you, did not come with excellence of speech or of wisdom declaring to you the mystery of God. For I determined not to know anything among you except JESUS CHRIST and HIM CRUCIFIED. I was with you in weakness, in fear, and in much trembling. And my speech and my preaching were not with persuasive words of human wisdom, but in DEMONSTRATION OF THE SPIRIT and of power, that your faith should not be in the wisdom of men but in the power of God."

This is exactly what God means in **2Chronicles 16:9** – *"...the eyes of the Lord run to and fro throughout the whole earth, to SHOW HIMSELF STRONG on behalf of those whose HEART IS LOYAL TO HIM."*

Isaiah 66:1-2 "God is looking for Humble Hearts to dwell in"

"Heaven is My throne, and earth is My footstool. Where is the house that you will build Me? And where is the place of My rest? For all those things My hand has made, and all those things exist," says the Lord. "But on this one I will look: on him who is POOR and of a CONTRITE SPIRIT, and who TREMBLES AT MY WORD."

John MacArthur[25]: *"Isaiah reminds us that God is not looking for a temple of stone, since as Creator of all things, the whole universe is His dwelling place... God is looking for a HEART TO DWELL IN, a heart that is tender and broken, not one concerned with the externalities of religion (Matthew 5:3-9). God desires to dwell in the heart of a person who takes HIS WORD seriously by LIVING IT OUT (Isaiah 66:5, John 14:23)."*

- **Philippians 3:3-6** Paul's achievements, which he saw as required for salvation, before he knew Jesus

"We are the circumcision, who worship God in the Spirit, rejoice in Christ Jesus, and have no confidence in the flesh, though I also might have confidence in the flesh. If anyone else thinks he has confidence in the flesh, I more so:
1) *circumcised the 8th day* (Genesis 17:12, Leviticus 12:3 – the prescribed day per the law)
2) *of the stock of Israel* (Paul is a true Jew because he descended directly through Abraham, Isaac and Jacob)
3) *of the tribe of Benjamin* (Genesis 35:18, 1Kings 12:21 - Benjamin was one of the elite tribes of Israel who, with Judah, stayed loyal to David and formed the southern kingdom)
4) *a Hebrew of the Hebrews* (Acts 26:4-5, 21:40 - Paul was born a Hebrew and kept his Hebrew traditions)
5) *concerning the law, a Pharisee* (Acts 26:5 – Pharisees were the legalists of Judaism, whose zeal to apply the OT Scriptures directly to life led to their complex system of tradition and works righteousness)
6) *concerning zeal, persecuting the church* (Acts 8:1-3 – to a Jew, "zeal" combines love and hate, and is the highest single religious virtue. Paul loved Judaism - he hated the church because it threatened what he loved).
7) *concerning the righteousness which is in the law, blameless* (Paul outwardly kept the law, so that no one could accuse him of breaking it. He was sinful and self-righteous – not an OT believer, but a proud and lost legalist).

- **Philippians 3:7-11** Paul contrasts his achievements against personally knowing Jesus Christ

"But what things were ①GAIN to me, these things I have counted ②LOSS for Christ. But indeed I also count all things loss for the excellency of the ③KNOWLEDGE of Christ Jesus my Lord, for whom I have suffered the loss of all things, and count them as rubbish, that I may gain Christ, and be found in Him, not having my own righteousness, which is from the law, but that which is through ④FAITH in Christ, the righteousness which is from God by faith; that I may ③KNOW Him and the power of His resurrection, and the fellowship of His sufferings, being conformed to His death. If, by any means, I may arrive at the resurrection from the dead."

① GAIN = Gr. "*kerdos*" = an accounting term meaning "to make a profit"
② LOSS = Gr. "*zēmia*" = an accounting term meaning "to enter a business loss"
   John MacArthur: *"Paul used the language of business to describe the spiritual transaction that occurred when Christ redeemed him. All his Jewish religious credentials that he thought were in his profit column, were actually worthless and damning….he only put them in his loss column when he saw the glories of Christ."*
③ KNOW = Gr. "*ginōskō*" = moving toward total understanding (compared to Gr. "*oida*", which is having full knowledge) in a personal relation between the one knowing and the object known (what is known is highly important to the one who knows, which cements the relationship). Paul's emphasis is on gaining a deeper knowledge and intimacy with Christ.
John 17:3 *"…this is eternal life, that they may KNOW You, the one true God, and Jesus Christ whom You have sent."*
④ FAITH IN CHRIST = Gr. "*pistis*" or "*pisteuo*" =
   1) to "cling" to: a firm conviction based upon hearing, resulting in a pledge of fidelity (commitment to promise)
   2) a personal surrender to the invisible God, and the conduct inspired by that surrender (2Corin. 5:7)
   3) its object is a Person: not God's promises (the occasion to exercise faith), but in Him (the object of faith)
   John MacArthur: *"Faith is the confident, continuous confession of total dependence on and trust in Jesus for God's necessary requirement to enter His kingdom…and that requirement He demands is the righteousness of Christ Himself, which God imputes to every believer who places his/ her faith in Him."*

Romans 1:16-17 *"…I am not ashamed of the gospel of Christ, for it is the power of God to salvation for everyone who believes, for the Jew 1st and then the Greek. For in it the righteousness of God is revealed from faith to faith: as it is written, 'The just shall live by faith.'"*

> **People don't impress God – *Psalm 1:10-11, Acts 10:34***
> **He is only impressed with His Son – *Luke 3:21***
> **He gives me 1 way to please Him: make Him my #1 priority by…**
> 1) **obeying Him and…**
> 2) **using the gifts He has given me to glorify Him on earth as I…**
> 3) **strive to be more like His Son everyday – *John 8:29***

1 Corinthians 1:26-29 The Gospel = God works through the *Base Things* 2.6

"For you see your calling, brethren, that not many ①WISE according to the flesh, not many ②MIGHTY, not many ③NOBLE, are called. But God has chosen the ④FOOLISH THINGS of the world to put to shame the wise, and God has chosen the ⑤WEAK THINGS of the world to put to shame the things which are mighty, and the ⑥BASE THINGS of the world and the things which are despised God has chosen, and the things which are ⑦NOT, to bring to nothing the things that ⑦ARE, that no flesh should glory in His presence."

① WISE = Gr. "*sophos*" = naturally learned (often used in context with the world system: "according to the flesh")
② MIGHTY = Gr. "*dunatos*" = able or capable; strong
③ NOBLE = Gr. "*eugenēs*" = well born, as to a family of high society
④ FOOLISH = Gr. "*mōria*" = silly; absurd (our English word "moron")
⑤ WEAK = Gr. "*asthenēs*" = strengthless; impotent; feeble or sick (unable to do anything on their own power)
⑥ BASE = Gr. "*agenēs*" = despised; of no account or reputation by the world's standards
⑦ NOT = Gr. "*may*" = lack; seen as nothing   ⑦ ARE = Gr. "*ousa*" = have; seen as something

John MacArthur[25]: "If the world calls you a fool for publicly following Christ, thank God"

• God disdained human wisdom, not only by disallowing it as a means to knowing Him, but also choosing to save the lowly; He doesn't call to salvation many whom the world would call wise, mighty and noble.

• God's wisdom is revealed to the foolish, weak and common (those considered nothing): He gets the glory when the "lowly" come to know Him – saved sinners cannot boast that they have achieved salvation by their intellect

Zechariah 4:6 *"'... Not by might nor by power, but by My Spirit', says the Lord of hosts."*

Matthew 11:25 *"I thank You, Father, Lord of heaven and earth, because You have hidden these things from the wise and prudent and have revealed them to babes."*

Isaiah 40:29-31 *"He gives power to the WEAK, and to those who have NO MIGHT He increases strength. Even the youths shall faint and be weary, and the young men shall utterly fail. But those who WAIT ON THE LORD shall renew their strength; they shall mount up with wings like eagles, they shall run and not be weary, they shall walk and not faint."*

"Entrusted with the Gospel: The Story of Edward Kimball" (Harvest OnLine.com)

Question #1: If you were asked today what the main purpose of your life is, what would you say?
Answer: The Bible teaches that we were put on this earth to bring glory to God.
Question #1: How am I personally taking care of this responsibility to get the gospel out?
Answer: Not every Christian is called as an evangelist, every Christian is called to evangelize.

Edward Kimball was a faithful Christian who wanted to be used by God. He was not a pastor or a missionary, but he knew that he should go and share the gospel. Kimball felt especially burdened for a young man named Dwight, who worked in a Chicago shoe store. He mustered up the courage to go and tell Dwight about Jesus. Much to Kimball's delight, he responded and gave his life to Christ. Dwight later began a preaching ministry. He became known as **D.L. Moody**, one of the greatest evangelists in church history.

When Moody was out preaching one day, a man named Frederick Meyer was listening. Meyer was already a Christian, but Moody's preaching motivated him to enter full-time ministry. We know him as **F.B. Meyer**. Kimball reached Moody, and Moody reached Meyer, but the story doesn't end there.

When Meyer was preaching, a young man named **Wilbur Chapman** responded and gave his life to Christ. Chapman became an evangelist. One of the young men he mentored was a former professional baseball player who also wanted to preach the gospel and did so with great success. His name was **Billy Sunday**.

Sunday held a crusade in Charlotte, North Carolina, where many people came to faith. The people there were so thrilled that they wanted to have another crusade. Sunday wasn't available, so an evangelist named **Mordecai Hamm** was invited to speak. While the campaign wasn't considered as successful as the first one, a young, lanky farm boy walked down the aisle on one of the final nights. We know him as **Billy Graham**.

You may not be a Billy Graham, but you are an Edward Kimball - Kimball reached Moody, who touched Meyer, who reached Chapman, who helped Sunday, who reached the businessmen in Charlotte who invited Hamm, who then touched Billy Graham. We all have been entrusted with the gospel. We all have a part to play.

It comes down to this: One day, when you stand before God, He will want to know what you did with His sacred charge of the gospel. You are entrusted with the gospel. He said in Luke 19, "Do business until I come."

What are you going to do with what God has entrusted to you?

Matthew 13:3-8 The Gospel = Scattering the Seed 2.7

"Behold, a sower went out to sow. And as he sowed, some seed fell by the ①WAYSIDE; and the birds came and devoured them. Some fell on ②STONY PLACES, where they did not have much earth; and they immediately sprang up because they had no depth of earth. But when the sun was up they were scorched, and because they had no root they withered away. And some fell among ③THORNS, and the thorns sprang up and choked them. But others fell on ④GOOD GROUND and yielded a crop: some a hundredfold, some sixty, some thirty."

① **"Wayside Soil"** = hard-packed dirt of the travelers' paths, bordering the farmers' fields (no fences separated fields from dirt roads). Because of the continual foot traffic, the dry hot climate, and the fact this soil was never loosened and turned over as the field soil, the ground became as hard as pavement. As the sower broadcast the seed, some fell directly on the hard-packed earth of these paths. This seed never gets a chance to germinate – it gets eaten by the birds (Satan – Luke 8:12).

② **"Shallow Soil"** = the "stony places" doesn't mean soil with stones in it. Farmers removed stones from any soil. Because Israel has natural limestone beds in many places just beneath topsoil, any seed falling in this type of soil germinates quickly but its roots can't penetrate the limestone. At first, these plants look spectacular – until the hot sun comes up. These plants were the first to die, never bearing fruit. Their roots cannot reach the moisture.

③ **"Thorny Soil"** = this soil looks good –it is deep, tilled and fertile. At sowing time the seed would germinate, but hidden with the seed were weeds. The weeds have the advantage because they are native to the soil, while the seed was a foreigner. The weeds need no care, but the foreign seed requires care from the farmer to survive. If the weeds gain a foothold, they dominate and steal the moisture and sun. They choke out the good plants.

④ **"Good Soil"** = this soil is soft (unlike "wayside soil"), it is deep (unlike "shallow soil"), and it is clean (unlike "thorny soil"). This seed, under the farmer's care, bursts into life and yields a huge harvest – hundredfold, sixtyfold, thirtyfold.

A simple parable with a DEEPER MEANING that many miss:
Jesus exhorts people to heed its message (vs. 9), but only those who have Him to teach them can understand it, and only those who truly want to know even bother to ask (Mark 4:10).

• **"SEED"** = the Gospel (vs. 19); Luke 8:11 says it is the "word of God." Seed, like the message of the gospel, is not created but reproduced. God doesn't call us to create our own seed – the only seed to spread is His Gospel.

• **"SOWER"** = anyone who "spreads" the gospel in hearts by sharing God's word (Jesus = the ultimate Sower).

• **"SOIL"** = the human heart (vs. 19). The heart of the hearer = the soil receiving the sower's seed.

• **THE MORALE** = nothing is wrong with the sower, or the seed, or the way the sower spreads the seed, or the soil composition. The problem is the condition of the soil (the *HEART*): whether hard-packed, shallow, weedy or deep, it's the same soil. All soil can receive the seed if it is prepared. Soil not prepared will never bear a crop.

The Hardened, Unresponsive Heart = the poorly-conditioned soil = the UNSAVED (NO CROP)

• **"Wayside Heart"** (verse 19) = REJECTOR
Hearts so hardened by sin, they are indifferent to the gospel - never broken up by sorrow for offending God, and they hate anyone trying to share what the Bible says. They are unregenerate – they don't even pretend to believe.

• **"Shallow Heart"** (verse 20-21) = PRETENDER #1
Superficial response with no commitment. It receives the promises (joy, fellowship), but rejects the command to "deny yourself, take your cross, follow Me." Under the thin veneer of "good soil" is an unrepentant heart.

• **"Thorny Heart"** (verse) = PRETENDER #2
People who live for the things of this world (career, possessions, looks, hobbies), but not for Him. They say they are Christians, but they care nothing about the things of God. This "weedy soil", which at first looked so good, gets overwhelmed with thorns of worldliness (eventually, you can't tell if there ever was good soil).

Truth #1 = God doesn't hold the sower responsible for where the seed lands

Truth #2 = God doesn't hold the sower responsible for whether or not there is a harvest

Truth #3 = God only holds the sower responsible for *scattering* the seed

CHAPTER 3   Genesis 1:1   The Battle for the Beginning   3.1

"In the beginning God ①CREATED the heavens and the earth."

① CREATED = Hebr. *"bara"* = only God can call into existence what never existed ("something out of nothing")

What is "Creationism"?   G.S. McLean, "The Evidence for Creation"[23]

"A creationist is a person willing to accept that the biblical account of origins and the history of the earth are accurate and reliable. A creationist also believes that the statements made in God's Word should be able to be backed up and supported by *physical evidence* from the world that God has created. A creationist apologizes to no one that Scriptures are used as a key for understanding the principle of origins and the history of the earth."

What is "Darwinian Evolution"?   Henry M. Morris, PhD "Scientific Creationism"[18]

"Evolution attempts to explain the origin, development, and meaning of all things by natural laws and processes which operate today as they have in the past. No extraneous processes, requiring the special activity of an external agent, or Creator, are permitted. The universe, in all its aspects, evolves itself into higher levels of order ("particles to people") by means of its innate properties. Evolution is a process occurring in time, which in its course gives rise to an increase of variety and an increasingly high level of organization. Particles evolve into elements, elements into complex chemicals, complex chemicals into simple living systems, simple life forms into complex life, complex animal life into man."

Michael Denton, "Evolution: A Theory in Crisis"[19]

"Evolution has as its core idea that living things have originated gradually as a result of the interplay of chance and selection. According to Darwin, all the design, order and complexity of life and the eerie purposefulness of living systems were the result of a simple blind random process – natural selection. He believed that life was all related by common descent from an original ancestral species (i.e, that new species had arisen from pre-existing species in nature) and that, therefore, species were not the fixed immutable entities most biologists supposed."

Who was Charles Darwin?[20]

Charles Darwin was born February 12, **1809** in Shrewsbury, England. His grandfather, Erasmus Darwin, was a naturalist and philosopher. His father, Robert, was a successful and wealthy doctor. His mother died when he was eight.

As a youngster, Charles was very interested in science and nature. At his father's urging, he studied medicine at the University of Edinburgh. But after 2 years he found he didn't like it and transferred to Christ's College in Cambridge for a major in theology, where he seriously was considering entering the clergy of the Church of England. He later wrote, *"I did not then in the least doubt the strict and literal truth of every word in the Bible."*

After graduating in **1831**, he served on a 5-year British science expedition as a naturalist aboard the *HMS Beagle*. In South America, Darwin found fossils of extinct animals that were similar to modern species. On the Galapagos Islands he recorded many variations among plants and animals of the same general type as he observed in South America. It was at this time that he read Charles Lyell's work, *Principles of Geology*, and his religious beliefs came into direct conflict with his expanding knowledge of science.

By **1836**, at the close of the expedition, he confessed in his writings that he wrestled over 2 theological issues:
1. the presence of evil in a world created by God: *"There seems to me too much misery in the world. I cannot persuade myself that a beneficent and omnipotent God would have designedly created the Ichneumonidae with the express intention of feeding within the living bodies of caterpillars, or that a cat should play with mice."*
2. the inerrancy of Scripture: *"I had gradually come by this time (1836–1839) to see that the Old Testament as no more to be trusted than the sacred books of the Hindus or the beliefs of any barbarian."*

In 1838, he began writing up his notes from the *Beagle* expedition. A 230-page paper was published in 1844, and in **1859** he published *The Origin of Species by Means of Natural Selection*. He laid out his view that all life came not from the hand of a creator but from the process of 'survival of the fittest'. In a letter to a friend he said *"my deity is Natural Selection."* In **1871** Darwin published his 2nd book, *The Descent of Man*. In it he argued that humans are no different from other forms of life and that we, too, evolved through natural selection.

Darwin's son, Francis, quotes him as saying *"I never gave up Christianity until I was 40 years of age"*. The death of his eldest daughter Annie from fever at this same time in his life hammered the final nail in the coffin of his Christianity. In a letter written in **1880** Darwin stated, *"I am sorry to have to inform you that I do not believe in the Bible as a divine revelation and therefore not in Jesus Christ as the Son of God. Thus disbelief crept over me at a very slow rate, but was at last complete. The rate was so slow that I felt no distress."* He proclaimed himself an agnostic.

As an old man in failing health, Darwin wrote *"Science has nothing to do with Christ, except in so far as the habit of scientific research makes a man cautious in admitting evidence. For myself, I do not believe that there has ever been any revelation. As for a future life, every man must judge for himself between CONFLICTING VAGUE PROBABILITIES."*

More Definitions: What is "Darwinian Evolution"?

Michael J. Behe, PhD[16] "Evolution is a flexible word. It can be used by one person to mean something as simple as change over time, or by another person to mean the descent of all life forms from a common ancestor, leaving the mechanism of change unspecified. In its full-throated, biological sense, however, evolution means a process whereby life arose from nonliving matter and subsequently developed by entirely natural means. This is the sense that Darwin gave to the word, and the meaning that it holds in the scientific community."

John Ankerberg and John Weldon[8] "The general theory that all life on earth has evolved from non-living matter and progressed to more complex forms with time; hence, it refers to *macroevolution* and not *microevolution* (minor changes within species illustrated in crossbreeding, such as varieties of dogs or varieties of corn)."

Richard A. Swenson, MD[15] "The theory of first things goes something like this: first you start with nothing, which then becomes something. The something then becomes a prebiotic soup with hydrogen, carbon, nitrogen, and water vapor (free oxygen arrives later). The soup bubbles into compounds like methane and ammonia. Lightning strikes periodically, stirring the pot. This frightens various molecules into each other's arms. Eventually, after this happens enough, you get an AMINO ACID. Then several. These get frightened into each other's arms (they don't like lightning either), and you get a PROTEIN. Then larger and larger proteins. Then more and more of them. And pretty soon (well, actually, not so soon) you have an ORGANISM with 100,000 proteins made by DNA that has 3,000,000,000 base pairs – all because of random benefit mutations. When the pot stops bubbling and the smoke clears, out of the cave steps Arnold Schwarzenegger: tens of trillions of cells with 100,000,000,000 neurons, 60,000 miles of blood vessels, and a retina that in a fraction of a second solves nonlinear differential equations that would take a Cray-2 supercomputer 100 years to solve."

Jonathan Wells, PhD[21] "Biological evolution is the theory that all living things are modified descendants of a common ancestor that lived in the distant past. It claims that you and I are descendants of ape-like ancestors, and that they in turn came from still more primitive animals. This is the primary meaning of "evolution" among biologists. 'Biological evolution', according to the National Academy, explains that living things share common ancestors. Over time, evolutionary change gives rise to new species. Darwin called the process 'descent with modification,' and it remains a good definition of biological evolution today. For Charles Darwin, descent with modification was the origin of all living things after the first organisms. He wrote in *The Origin of Species*, 'I view all beings not as special creations, but as the lineal descendants of some few beings' that lived in the distant past'. The reason living things are now so different from each other, Darwin believed, is that they have been modified by natural selection, or survival of the fittest: 'I am convinced that Natural Selection has been the most important, but not exclusive, means of modification.'"

Lee Strobel[22] "...you don't need a Creator if life can emerge unassisted from the primordial slime of the primitive earth, and you don't need God to create human beings in his image if we are merely the product of the impersonal forces of natural selection. In short, you don't need the Bible if you've got The Origin of Species."

Hugh Ross, PhD[14] "Evolution is the belief that inorganic material evolves into simple cells and later into advanced life without any input from a divine being."

G.S. McLean[23] "The foundation of evolution is the belief that the origin of all ordered, complex systems including living creatures can be explained by the operation of natural laws without the initiation or the intervention of God. According to evolution, all living creatures including man are the product of billions of years of random chance events which have worked together to produce design and order out of randomness."

A.E. Wilder Smith, PhD[24] "The development of life from nonliving matter took place spontaneously by stages, the first stage being that simple organic compounds (such as hydrocarbons) arose spontaneously under the influence of various radiations on a lifeless earth (in other words, spontaneous chemical evolution up to simple organic compounds occurred). In the second stage of evolution, very complicated molecules (protein-like substances, nucleic acids, etc.) arose. The lithosphere, atmosphere and hydrosphere were the 'theatre of operation', with the general laws of chemistry and physics as known today, combined with chance events over long time spans. The third stage in the spontaneous evolutionary process up to life was reached when the complex molecules formed during the second stage were acted upon and changed under the influence of the external medium and which then underwent selection. Thus arose the most primitive primary organisms under the influence of nothing but chance, time, a suitable environment and simple chemicals."

How Strong is the *Belief* in Evolution in the Scientific Community?[8]   3.2

- Associated Press, "Biology Textbooks OK'd" (Nov. 8, 2003): *"The State of Texas Board of Education voted overwhelmingly to approve biology textbooks that drew criticism from the religious academia who say the books fail to present the anti-evolution point of view. Most of the scientists and educators argued that the theory of evolution is widely believed and is a cornerstone of modern scientific research. Texas, California and Florida account for more than 30% of the nation's $4 billion public school book market."*
- Carl Sagan (Cornell Univ. Astronomer, Pulitzer Prize winner): *"Evolution is a fact, not a theory."*
- Julian Huxley ("Evolution and Genetics"): *"Evolution can be defined as a directional and essentially irreversible process occurring in time, which in its course gives rise to an increase in variety and an increasingly high level of organization in its products. Our present knowledge indeed forces us to the view that the whole of reality is evolution – a single process of self-transformation."*
- Francisco Ayala ("Biology as an Autonomous Science") *"Biological evolution can be explained without recourse to a Creator or a planning agent external to the organisms themselves. There is no evidence of any vital force directing the evolutionary process toward the production of specified kinds of organisms."*
- George Gaylord Simpson (Prof. of vertebrate paleontology at Harvard's Museum of Comparative Zoology): *"Ample proof has been repeatedly presented and is available to anyone who really wants to know the truth. In the present study the factual truth of organic evolution is taken as established."*
- Ashley Montagu (Prof. Princeton University): *"The attack on evolution, the most thoroughly authenticated fact in the history of science, is an attack on science itself."*
- American Association for the Advancement of Science: *"The evidences in favor of evolution of man are sufficient to convince every scientist of note in the world."*
- Rene Dubos ("Humanistic Biology") *"Most enlightened persons now accept as a fact that everything in the cosmos – from heavenly bodies to human beings – has developed and continues to develop through evolutionary processes."*
- American Institute of Biological Sciences: *"The theory of evolution is the only scientifically defensible explanation for the origin of life and development of species. As a community, biologists agree that evolution occurred and that the forces driving the evolutionary process are still active today. This consensus is based on more than a century of scientific data gathering and analysis."*
- American Society of Parasitologists: *"Evolution is believed by nearly all professional life scientists. Virtually all scientists accept the evolution of current species from fewer, simpler ancestral ones as undisputed."*
- American Geological Institute: *"Scientific evidence indicates beyond any doubt that life has existed on Earth for billions of years. This life evolved through time producing vast numbers of species of plants and animals."*
- Geological Society of America: *"We geologists find incontrovertible evidence in the rocks that life has existed here on earth for several billions of years and that it has evolved through time."*
- Society of Vertebrate Paleontology: *"Scientists do not argue about whether evolution took place: that is a fact."*

The 7 Assumptions of Evolution (G.A. Kerkut, evolutionist and author, "Implications of Evolution"[8])

"The *evidence* we have at present is insufficient to allow us to decide the answer to these problems. Evolution has to be taken on pure faith. *The evidence is circumstantial and can be argued either way*."	
Assumption	Comment
#1. non-living things gave rise to living material ("abiogenesis")	There is little if any evidence for abiogenesis; we have no indication it can be performed. It's a matter of faith by the biologist that it occurred.
#2. non-living things gave rise to living material ("abiogenesis") only once	This is again purely a matter of belief rather than proof.
#3. viruses, bacteria, protozoa and higher animals were all interrelated	We have as yet no definite evidence about the way in which viruses, bacteria or protozoa are interrelated
#4. protozoa gave rise to the metazoa	Here again, nothing definite is known.
#5. various invertebrate phyla are interrelated	Evidence for the affinities of the invertebrates is circumstantial; not the type of evidence needed to form a verdict of definite relationships.
#6. invertebrates led to vertebrates	In a sense, this account is science fiction.
#7. fish, amphibia, reptiles, birds and mammals are interrelated	many of the key transitional forms are not well documented and we have as yet to obtain a satisfactory objective method of dating fossils.

What difference does it make whether I believe in Darwinian Evolution or Creation?

1. **Man is an advanced animal and has no unique relevance other than what he chooses to give himself**
   - George Gaylord Simpson (evolutionist)[8]: *"man has no special status other than his definition as a distinct species of animal. He is in the fullest sense a part of nature and not apart from it. He is literally kin to every living thing, be it an amoeba, a tapeworm, a seaweed, an oak tree, or a monkey…"*

2. **If man is just an animal and an accident of nature, where does he get ultimate meaning, dignity, or absolute values?**
   - William Provine (Prof., Cornell University)[8]: *"The implications of modern science are clearly inconsistent with most religious traditions. No inherent moral or ethical laws exist, nor are there absolute guiding principles for human society. The universe cares nothing for us and we have no ultimate meaning in life."*
   - Leslie Paul ("The Annihilation of Man")[8]: *"No one knows what time this lonely planet will cool, all life will die, all minds will cease, and it will all be as if it had never happened. That is the goal to which evolution is traveling… life is no more than a match struck in the dark and blown out again. The end is to deprive life of meaning."*

3. **If the universe is meaningless, why bother with morals? Isn't it "survival of the fittest"?**

HITLER and NAZISM[8] Nazi General Friedrich von Bernhardi: *"…from an evolutionary viewpoint, it is biologically right to crush the weaker peoples of the earth. War is not only a biological law, but a moral obligation."*

Sir Arthur Keith (evolutionist): *"It was often said in 1914 that Darwin's doctrine of evolution had bred war in Europe, particularly in Germany. There is no question that evolution was basic in all Nazi thought, from beginning to end. Yet, it is a remarkable phenomenon how few are aware of this fact today."*

Adolf Hitler: *"I regard Christianity as the most fatal, seductive lie that ever existed. He who would live must fight; he who does not wish to fight in this world where permanent struggle is the law of life, has no right to exist. I do not see why man should not be as cruel as nature; all that is not of pure race in this world is trash."*

John Koster (historical philosopher): *"Many names have been cited beside that of Hitler to explain the Holocaust. Oddly enough, Charles Darwin's is almost never among them. Yet, Darwin's picture of man's place in the universe prepared the way for the Holocaust…the term neo-Darwinism was openly used to describe Nazi racial theories. The expression 'natural selection', as applied to human beings, turns up at the Western Conference in the prime document of the Holocaust."*

STALIN and COMMUNISM[8] G. Gludjidze, "Landmarks in the Life of Stalin": *"At a very early age, the young Stalin was a seminary student, studying to become a priest in the Russian Orthodox Church. We were discussing religion: Joseph heard me out, and then said: 'You know, they are fooling us, there is no God.' I was astonished at these words. I had never heard anything like it before. 'I'll lend you a book to read; it will show you that the world and all living things are quite different from what you imagine, and all this talk about God is sheer nonsense,' Joseph said. 'What book is that?' I inquired. 'Darwin. You must read it.' Having become an atheist, Stalin murdered millions of his own people in his attempt to construct an official atheistic state."*

MAO TSE TUNG and COMMUNISM[8] *"Being a Marxist and an atheist and a firm believer in evolutionism himself, Mao mandated that the reading material used in this early day "Great Leap Forward" in literacy would be the writings of Charles Darwin and other materials supportive of the evolution paradigm."*

Secular Humanism's 10 Lies to promote Darwinian Evolution

From his book 'And God created Darwin'[30], we can learn from Duane Schmidt ten lies that evolutionists who hold to a worldview of secular humanism use, as Schmidt says, to "ease me on in" to the *theory* of evolution, in an effort to make evolution tolerable for me to accept as a *proven fact*…

#	Lie	Description	Example	The Truth
1	"I'm really on your side"	Evolutionists quote or mention a Scripture reference, in an attempt to pacify Creationists that they share some "common ground"	Stephen Gould (Harvard Prof. Geology) refers to Biblical stories in his essays, and Darwin himself quotes Bible passages without referencing the verses	1) Gallup polls: while only 9% of Americans believe in evolution, 87% believe God created the universe all at once or used evolution. But 84% of American scientists interviewed don't believe God created the universe, 96% don't believe in hell, and only 8% believe in heaven. 2) Creation claims there is a reason for being - humans have a specific God-based purpose; evolution claims there is no reason for being (you can't get more apart than that).

Secular Humanism's 10 Lies to promote Darwinian Evolution

Evolutionists who hold to a worldview of secular humanism use a variety of outright lies to "ease me on in" to the *theory* of evolution in an effort to make evolution tolerable for me to accept as a *proven fact*...

#	Lie	Description	Example	The Truth
2	"discredit the messenger"	Anti-evolutionists are derogatorily called creationists, religious freaks, the "Religious Right", "Bible Thumpers", "Genesis Freaks", who "believe in such nonsense as Noah and the Flood, etc.	Dawkins: *"anti-evolutionist propagandists try to buy credibility by concealing fact; an opponent of evolution is a person who is ignorant, stupid or insane (or wicked, but I'd rather not consider that); opposition to evolution is 'redneck creationism'; those who find no merit in the evolution argument are 'backwoodsmen', pretending scientific credentials."*	There is an enormous body of scientists with credentials equal to or greater than Dawkins, who strongly oppose evolution. There is also a rich history of Christian creationists, who *invented* many fields of science. Evolutionists use an old tactic: by charging his antagonist with religious bias, he puts the questioner on the defensive, removing his need to defend his position (an evolutionist offense is far easier than mounting a good defense of evolution).
3	"the flat-out statement"	School textbooks flatly state that evolution "has been proven", or "is a scientific fact", or "can be seen in nature", without a single fact to support their statement	American Association for the Advancement of Science: *"The evidences in favor of evolution of man are sufficient to convince every scientist of note in the world."*	Einstein published his theories for the scientific community to test. They tested them, found them credible, and used them as keystones of science. But there is no published proof on evolution that scientists have tested and found credible.
4	"drop names"	Prestigious university names and titles and positions can cause people, especially students, to take their statements as truth	National Geographic and Nature magazines, Smithsonian museum, Harvard/ Yale/ Cambridge universities: all install a sense of respect in people – when these institutions publish evolutionary information, most take it as unquestionable truth.	(a) Jan. 2000: Nature and National Geographic magazines published the hoaxes "archaeoraptor" and "bambiraptor" as true intermediary species between birds and dinosaurs, only to be embarrassed when found to be deceptions by Chinese peasant farmers. (b) Michael Behe researched past issues of the Journal of Molecular Evolution and didn't find even ONE article in over 10,000 published that offered a scenario for the evolution of complex biological systems!
5	"invent a vocabulary"	Evolutionists invent words that attach "evolution" to them, so people grow comfortable with developing an evolutionary mindset. It was Russian entomologist Iuri Philipchenko, a secular scientist, who, in 1927, first introduced the terms "micro" vs. "macro" evolution... Christians have bought it ever since.	The word *"microevolution"* never existed until evolutionists made it up. No one disputes dogs or roses come in many varieties. But evolutionists reclassify varieties as microevolution, suggesting that there is some sort of analogy to be made between variation within a species and creating a new species gradually over time (which is true evolution, disguised by the word, you guessed it, *"macroevolution"*). But "a rose is still a rose", as is a dog or a cat or anything else.	1) Variation is no proof for evolution, just as conformity is worlds apart from adaptation (another clever word game played by evolutionists). Just because a species fits its environment doesn't mean it adapted to get there. These words are meaningless and contribute nothing to science literature. 2) The word *"evolve"* is now being used to describe everything, from governments to language and art. Yet "evolve" as originally used in biology means accidental change that is gradual, over time....not by plan or design or intentional (as used so often today).

Secular Humanism's 10 Lies to promote Darwinian Evolution

Evolutionists who hold to a worldview of secular humanism use a variety of outright lies to "ease me on in" to the *theory* of evolution in an effort to make evolution tolerable for me to accept as a *proven fact*...

#	Lie	Description	Example	The Truth
6	"semantic browbeating"	The language of science originates mainly from Greek and Latin - many scientists arguing evolution slip back into this language (everyday folks get lost in their meaning)	Steven Gould: "...*contemporary science has massively substituted notions of indeterminacy, historical contingency, chaos and punctuation for previous convictions about graduated, progressive, predictable determinism.*" (what he really meant: "the reason you don't see fossils of in-between species is we now agree that's not how evolution works").	1) Science is not that complicated that it can't be explained. US District Judge James Graham (May 2000): *"Science is not an inscrutable priesthood. Any person of reasonable intelligence should, with some diligence, be able to understand and critically evaluate a scientific theory."* 2) remove the invalidated, unverified, irrelevant, unproven statements: you'll be amazed at how little is left of evolution literature.
7	"circular reasoning (tautology)"	Giving the answer that only restates the problem	Q: "What species survive?" A: "The fittest." Q: "Which are the fittest?" A: "Those that survive." "Survival of the Fittest" is one of those Darwinian phrases that means nothing. After hearing it defined, you know absolutely nothing about survivors.	Darwin saw right through circular reasoning in other scientists: *"Authors sometimes argue in a circle when they state that important organs never vary; for these same authors rank these parts as important because they do not vary."* Since he nailed circular reasoning in others, it's amazing he failed to see it in his own answers.
8	The "Just So" Explanation	Evolutionists give answers to explain something after it has happened - not to try to be right, but to avoid ever being wrong. Their answer need not be correct, since it can't be disproved; but it must sound like it could or should be a suitable answer.	Evolutionists point to marmots, which cling together in tight family communities, as an example of how evolution favors closeness and cooperation. They will then point to bears, which live solitary lives of hermits, as an example of evolution favoring animals that spread themselves far and wide to forage for nourishment.	There is no evidence for each individual case that can link directly back to the subject of evolutionary development in an organism. Rather than pursuing the truth through the use of the scientific method, evolutionists spend a lot of energy deflecting questions that lead to exposing the lie. *"A lie, repeated often enough and loud enough, remains a lie. What thinking people really want are proofs beyond nimble argument."*
9	"drown the argument with extraneous data"	Evolutionists lull people into belief by constant repetition of irrelevant technical details that make the theory appear scientific	High school science books publish detailed technical data on the Galapagos Islands "Darwin" finch population's migratory patterns, food types, and interbreeding patterns, without publishing exact data to support their claim for evolutionary origins.	Reviewing the scientific literature shows that almost no direct research is going on in evolution.
10	present "favorable mutations" as if a fact	Since the theory of evolution requires favorable mutations, they "must" be there. The fact that we can't point to any is just a stupid inconvenience.	How can an eye, just beginning to be an eye, and yet can't see, benefit the organism over no eye at all? If the eye developed such complexity, and evolution occurs in tiny steps of favorable mutations, each of the millions of mutations it would take to reach the present form of the eye had to be *favorable*.	The exact opposite is true: no favorable mutation has ever been observed – Michael Denton: *"Most mutations damage function." "What is very remarkable about this whole issue is that, as is typical of any 'unquestioned article of faith,' evidence for the doctrine of spontaneous mutation is hardly ever presented."*

Romans 1:18-20   "Science, Truth and Faith"   3.3

"The wrath of God is revealed from heaven against all ①UNGODLINESS and UNRIGHTEOUSNESS of men, who ②SUPPRESS the truth in unrighteousness, because what may be known of God is ③MANIFEST in them, for God has shown it to them. For since the creation of the world His invisible attributes are clearly seen, being understood by the ④THINGS THAT ARE MADE, even His eternal power and Godhead, so they are ⑤WITHOUT EXCUSE."

① UNGODLINESS = Gr. ""*asebeia*" = lack of reverence to, and worship of, God (no relationship with Him)
UNRIGHTEOUSNESS = Gr. ""*adikia*" = result of ungodliness = moral wrongfulness (of character)

② SUPPRESS = Gr. ""*katechō*" = although God has provided the *evidence* from conscience (1:19, 2:14) and creation (1:20), as well as His Word (2Tim. 3:16), men choose to "hold down" and oppose His truth.

③ MANIFEST = Gr. ""*phaneros*" = shine, make public; intelligence, conscience = *evidence* (1:20,21,28,32, 2:15).

④ THINGS MADE = Gr. ""*poiēma*" = products, workmanship (Ps 19:1-8, Ps 94:9, Acts 14:15-17, Acts 17:23-28).

⑤ WITHOUT EXCUSE = Gr. ""*anapologētos*" = indefensible; but when anyone who responds to God's revelation, even if only nature, God provides for that person to hear the gospel (Acts 17:24-31).

Are Scientists interested in finding Truth about Origins, whether Creation or Evolution?
Linus Pauling (2X Nobel Prize winner)[21]: *"Science is the search for TRUTH"*
Bruce Alberts (president, US National Academy of Sciences)[21]: *"Science and lies cannot coexist."*

How can distinguished scientists get such opposing views from the same information?
Philip Johnson (Berkeley Law Prof., "Reason in the Balance: The Case Against Naturalism in Science, Law and Education"):
- What is reasonable" is not based on searching for truth but on pre-conceived definition of what is reasonable.
- The accepted definition today of "science" = MATTER is the final absolute and only cause for all existence.
- Any supernatural or nonphysical explanation for reality is unacceptable and unreasonable in the field of science.
- Sir Julian Huxley[8]: *"the idea of God is entirely removed from the sphere of rational discussion."*

I'm not a scientist – how can I be expected to determine TRUTH from lies?
- Jonathan Wells[21]: *"In a surprising number of instances, the average person is as competent to make a judgment as the most highly trained scientist. If a theory of gravity predicts heavy objects will fall upwards, it doesn't take an astrophysicist to see the theory is wrong. And if a picture of an embryo doesn't look like the real thing, it doesn't take an embryologist to see that the picture is false. So an average person with access to the evidence should be able to understand and evaluate many scientific claims."*
- Dr. L.R. Wysong[8], "The Creation/ Evolution Controversy": *"Evolution is not a form of true scientific method… evolution means the initial formation of unknown organisms from unknown chemicals produced in an unknown atmosphere or ocean of unknown composition under unknown conditions, which organisms have then climbed an unknown evolutionary ladder by an unknown process leaving unknown evidence."*
- US District Judge James Graham[21]: *"Science is not an inscrutable priesthood. Any person of reasonable intelligence should, with some diligence, be able to understand and critically evaluate a scientific theory."*

Jonathan Wells (1979 -) - two Ph.D's: 1) Molecular and Cell Biology, Univ. of California at Berkeley, 2) Religious Studies, Yale University; former Research biologist at the Univ. of California at Berkeley; former Prof. Biology at California State University in Hayward; currently, Senior Fellow at Discovery Institute's Center for Science and Culture, where he is a proponent of the Intelligent Design movement and critic of evolution. The quote below is from his book "Icons of Evolution"[21]:

"Truth must tie to evidence: If science wasn't the search for TRUTH, our bridges wouldn't support the weight we put on them, our lives wouldn't be as long as they are, and modern technological civilization wouldn't exist. Storytelling is a valuable enterprise, too. Without stories, we would have no culture. But we do not call on storytellers to build bridges or perform surgery. For such tasks, we prefer people who have disciplined themselves to understand the realities of steel or flesh.

Any theory that purports to be scientific must somehow, at some point, be compared with observations or experiments. Theories that survive repeated testing may be tentatively regarded as true statements. But if there is persistent conflict between a theory and evidence, the former must yield to the latter. When science fails to obey nature, bridges collapse and patients die on the operating table."

Deuteronomy 4:32   *"... ask now concerning the days that are past, which were before you, since the day that God created man on the earth...."*

"Mind & Cosmos" by Dr. Thomas Nagel[7]

Dr. Thomas Nagel, Professor of Philosophy and the School of Law at New York University, is one of the most influential atheist philosophers in America.

Winner of the 2008 Rolf Schock Prize in Logic and Philosophy, he is known for his expertise in the philosophy of the mind, political philosophy and ethics. He is also well known for his critique of material reductionism and especially Darwinian evolution, focusing on the failure of evolution to account for consciousness, cognition, reasoning and moral value judgments.

Mind and Cosmos – Why the Materialist Neo-Darwinian Conception of Nature is almost certainly False

"My guiding conviction is that mind is not an afterthought or an accident or an add-on, but a basic aspect of nature. The intelligibility of the world is no accident."

Thomas Nagel
Page 16, 17

"A theistic account has the advantage over a reductive naturalistic one in that it admits the reality of more of what is so evidently the case." (page 25)

He further takes evolutionary biology to task on its inability to even stand up to the common sense of anyone, regardless of whether they are trained in the biological sciences: *"It is prima facie highly implausible that life as we know it is the result of a sequence of physical accidents together with the mechanism of natural selection. My skepticism is not based on religious belief, or on a belief in any definite alternative. It is just a belief that the available scientific evidence, in spite of the consensus of scientific opinion, does not in this matter rationally require us to subordinate the incredulity of common sense."*

He also explains why people find this position outrageous – because the scientific community continues to browbeat anyone who raised the same doubts as he is in this book: *"I realize that such doubts will strike many people as outrageous, but that is because almost everyone in our secular culture has been browbeaten into regarding the reductive research program as sacrosanct, on the ground that anything else would not be science."*

He further explains why current evolutionary theory is in serious need of repair – because of discoveries in science!: *"Doubts about the reductionist account of life go against the dominant scientific consensus, but that consensus faces problems of probability that I believe are not taken seriously enough, both with respect to the evolution of life forms through accidental mutation and natural selection and with respect to the formation from dead matter of physical systems capable of such evolution. The more we learn about the intricacy of the genetic code and its control of the chemical processes of life, the harder those problems seem."*

He goes deeper in his critique of evolution: *"With regard to evolution, the process of natural selection cannot account for the actual history without an adequate supply of viable mutations, and I believe it remains an open question whether this could have been provided in geological time merely as a result of chemical accident, without the operation of some other factors determining and restricting the forms of genetic variation. It is no longer legitimate simply to imagine a sequence of gradually evolving phenotypes, as if their appearance through mutations in the DNA were unproblematic – as Richard Dawkins does for the evolution of the eye."*.

Then he goes to the origin of life, explaining how our discovery of the DNA molecule eliminates materialistic naturalism as a sufficient explanation for life's origins: *"With regard to the origin of life, the problem is much harder, since the option of natural selection as an explanation is not available. And the coming into existence of the genetic code – an arbitrary mapping of nucleotide sequences into amino acids, together with mechanisms that can read the code and carry out its instructions – seems particularly resistant to being revealed as probable given physical law alone."*

In his book, Dr. Nagel asks 36 questions to proponents of evolution. These questions are not new – but they are coming from one of the most respected analytical atheist philosophical minds today – and they are meant to be a challenge to evolutionists to examine the evidence, because it will lead open-minded seekers away from evolution.

Are Science and Faith compatible in the search for *TRUTH*?
22 World-renown Scientists say *YES*

1 Michael Faraday (1791-1867) – British Physicist, founder of electromagnetism: *"…his religious belief in a single Creator encouraged his scientific belief in the "unity of forces", the idea that magnetism, electricity and the other forces have a common origin."* (B. Bowers, Michael Faraday and Electricity, 1974).

2 Sir George Gabriel Stokes (1819-1903) – Irish Mathematician and Physicist; Lucasian Prof. of Mathematics, Cambridge Univ.: *"A deeply religious man and a renowned physicist and mathematician, Stokes tries to combine his religiosity with his determined belief in the existence of natural laws."* (J. Petrunic, Abstract of Stoke's Gifford Lectures, 'Natural Theology', delivered before the Univ. of Edinburgh, 1891-1893).

3 Lord William Kelvin (1824-1907) – Scottish Mathematical Physicist: *"Do not be afraid of being free thinkers. If you think strongly enough you will be forced by science to the belief in God, which is the foundation of all Religion. You will find science not antagonistic, but helpful to Religion."* (The Times, May 2, 1903, Lord Kelvin speaking at Univ. College of London, on Religion and Science).

4 James Clerk Maxwell (1831-1879) – Scottish Mathematician and Theoretical Physicist: *"I think men of science as well as other men need to learn from Christ, and I think Christians whose minds are scientific are bound to study science that their view of the glory of God may be as extensive as their being is capable of."* (Campbell and Garnet, *'The Life of James Clerk Maxwell'*, London 1882).

5 Lord Rayleigh (1842-1919) – 1904 Nobel Prize in Physics: *"…I may say that in my opinion true Science and true Religion neither are nor could be opposed."* (Religion and Health, James John Walsh, 1920).

6 Max Planck (1858-1947) – 1918 Nobel Prize in Physics: *"Anybody who has been seriously engaged in scientific work of any kind realizes that over the entrance to the gates of the temple of science are written the words: Ye must have faith. It is a quality which the scientist cannot dispense with… There can never be any real opposition between religion and science; for one is the complement of the other. Every serious and reflective person realizes, I think, that the religious element in his nature must be recognized and cultivated if all the powers of the human soul are to act together in perfect balance and harmony. And indeed it was not by accident that the greatest thinkers of all ages were deeply religious souls."* ('Where Is Science Going?', 1932).

7 Robert Millikan (1868-1953) – PhD Physics; 1923 Nobel Prize in Physics *"…the combination of science and religion provides today the sole basis for rational intelligent living… religion and science are the two great sister forces which have pulled, and are still pulling, mankind onward and upward."* ('The Autobiography of Robert A. Millikan', Prentice-Hall, New York, 1950).

8 Albert Einstein (1879-1955) – PhD Theoretical Physics; 1921 Nobel Prize in Physics; Time Person of the Century, *"…everyone who is seriously involved in the pursuit of science becomes convinced that a spirit is manifest in the laws of the Universe - a spirit vastly superior to that of man, and one in the face of which we with our modest powers must feel humble."* (Letter, Jan. 24, 1936, quoted in Helen Dukas and Banesh Hoffman, 'Albert Einstein: The Human Side',1981).

9 Erwin Schrödinger (1887-1961) – PhD Physics; 1933 Nobel Prize in Physics: *"In the presentation of a scientific problem, the other player is the good Lord. He has not only set the problem but also has devised the rules of the game--but they are not completely known, half of them are left for you to discover or deduce…"* ('Schrödinger: Life and Thought', Walter Moore, Cambridge: Cambridge Univ. Press, 1990).

10 Arthur Compton (1892-1962) – PhD Theoretical Physics; 1927 Nobel Prize in Physics: *"Science has created a world in which Christianity is a necessity… I believe that its insistence on the inherent value of individual men and women Christianity has the key to survival and the good life in the modern world… In their essence there can be no conflict between science and religion. Science is a reliable method of finding truth. Religion is the search for a satisfying basis for life."* ('The Human Meaning of Science', 1940).

11 William Henry Bragg (1890–1971) – MA Theoretical Physics, Cambridge Univ.; 1915 Nobel Prize in Physics: "In 1940 Bragg identified 'two sad mistakes' current in science-religion debates: *'The one is to suppose that science, that is to say, the study of Nature, leads to materialism. The other that the worship of God can be carried on without the equipment which science provides."…"From religion comes a man's purpose; from science, his power to achieve it. Sometimes people ask if religion and science are not opposed to one another. They are: in the sense that the thumb and fingers of my hand are opposed to one another. It is an opposition by means of which anything can be grasped."* ('The Scientific God Journal', April 2010, ISSN 2153-831X).

12 Werner Heisenberg (1901-1976) – PhD Physics; 1932 Nobel Prize in Physics: *"In the history of science, ever since the famous trial of Galileo, it has repeatedly been claimed that scientific truth cannot be reconciled with the religious interpretation of the world. Although I am now convinced that scientific truth is unassailable in its own field, I have never found it possible to dismiss the content of religious thinking as simply part of an outmoded phase in the consciousness of mankind, a part we shall have to give up from now on, Thus in the course of my life I have repeatedly been compelled to ponder on the relationship of these two regions of thought, for I have never been able to doubt the reality of that to which they point."* ('Das Universum – Hinweis auf Gott?', 1988).

13 Wernher von Braun (1912-1977) – PhD Physics; NASA Director of Marshall Space Flight Center and chief architect of the Saturn V launch vehicle: *"I find it as difficult to understand a scientist who does not acknowledge the presence of a superior rationality behind the existence of the universe as it is to comprehend a theologian who would deny the advances of science."* ('The Skeptical Inquirer',10:258-276).

14 Charles Townes (1915 -) – PhD Physics, CalTech; 1964 Nobel Prize in Physics: "Townes' answer to interview question 'If science and religion share a common purpose, why have their proponents tended to be at loggerheads throughout history?' = *"Science and religion have had a long interaction: some of it has been good and some of it hasn't. As Western science grew, Newtonian mechanics had scientists thinking that everything is predictable, meaning there's no room for God - so-called determinism. Religious people didn't want to agree with that. Then Darwin came along, and they really didn't want to agree with what he was saying, because it seemed to negate the idea of a creator. So there was a real clash for a while between science and religions.* But science has been digging deeper and deeper, and as it has done so, particularly in the basic sciences like physics and astronomy, we have begun to understand more. We have found that the world is not deterministic: quantum mechanics has revolutionized physics by showing that things are not completely predictable. That doesn't mean that we've found just where God comes in, but we know now that things are not as predictable as we thought and that there are things we don't understand. *So as science encounters mysteries, it is starting to recognize its limitations and become somewhat more open. There are still scientists who differ strongly with religion and vice versa. But I think people are being more open-minded about recognizing the limitations in our frame of understanding."* (2005 interview for *Berkeley News* by Bonnie Powell).

15 Richard Feynman (1918-1988) – PhD Quantum Physics);1965 Nobel Prize in Physics: "*I also agree that a belief in science and religion is consistent*… science cannot produce 'the meaning of life' nor can it tell us 'the right moral values'. These must come from somewhere else." ('*The Meaning of It All*', 1998, p. 36).

16 Robert Jastrow (1925-2008) – PhD Theoretical Physics; 1961 Director of NASA's Goddard Institute for Space Studies; *"For the scientist who has lived by faith in the power of reason, the story ends like a bad dream. He has scaled the mountains of ignorance; he is about to conquer the highest peak; as he pulls himself over the final rock, he is greeted by a band of theologians who have been sitting there for centuries."* ('God and the Astronomers', 2nd edition, New York and London: W.W. Norton & Company, 199).

17 Arthur L. Schawlow (1921-1999) – PhD Physics; 1981 Nobel Prize in Physics: "*The context of religion is a great background for doing science.* In the words of Psalm 19, 'The heavens declare the glory of God and the firmament showeth his handiwork'. Thus *scientific research is a worshipful act, in that it reveals more of the wonders of God's creation.*" (quoted by Margenau & Varghese,1997).

18 Arno Penzias (1933 -) – PhD Physics; 1978 Nobel prize in Physics: "*The best data we have are exactly what I would have predicted, had I had nothing to go on but the five books of Moses, the Psalms, the Bible as a whole.*" (New York Times on March 12, 1978).

19 Henry "Fritz" Schaefer (1944 -) – PhD Chemical Physics; Director of the Center for Computational Quantum Chemistry, Univ. of Georgia: "*Why are there so few atheists among physicists? Many scientists are considering the facts before them.* They say things like: 'The present arrangement of matter indicates a very special choice of initial conditions.' (Paul Davies). 'In fact, if one considers the possible constants and laws that could have emerged, the odds against a universe that produced life like ours are immense.' (Stephen Hawking), 'A common sense interpretation of the facts suggests that a superintellect has monkeyed with physics, as well as with chemistry and biology, and that there are no blind forces worth speaking about in nature.' (Fred Hoyle). As the Apostle Paul said in his epistle to the Romans: 'Since the creation of the world, God's invisible qualities—His eternal power and divine nature—have been clearly seen, being understood from what has been made.'" ('Scientists and their Gods: Science and Christianity, Conflict or Coherence?',1999).

20 George Smoot (1945 -) – PhD Particle Physics; 2006 Nobel Prize in Physics: "George Smoot commenting on the discovery by the COBE Science Working Group of the expected "ripples" in the microwave background radiation. He called these fluctuations "*the fingerprints from the Maker.*" Smoot draws attention not only to the fact that his team had provided more *evidence* for the creation event, but for a 'finely orchestrated' creation event."

21 Frank Tipler (1947 -) – PhD Physics; Prof. of Mathematics and Physics, Tulane Univ.: "*From the perspective of the latest physical theories, Christianity is not a mere religion, but an experimentally testable science.*" ('The Physics Of Immortality', New York, Doubleday, 2007).

22 William Philips (1948 -) – PhD Physics; 1997 Nobel Prize in Physics: "*Many scientists are also people with quite conventional religious faith. I, a physicist, am one example. I believe in God as both creator and friend. That is, I believe that God is personal and interacts with us.*" (Lecture "Ordinary Faith, Ordinary Science", delivered at the conference "Science and the Spiritual Quest", April 2002); "*There are probably more Nobel Laureates who are people of faith than is generally believed.* Most people in most professions don't make a special point to make their religious views known, since these are very personal." ("Letter to the compiler T. Dimitrov", May 19, 2002).

3.5 Dinesh D'Souza[13]: The History of Scientific Inquiry is rooted in Christianity

"We often hear that science was founded in the 17th century in revolt against religious dogma. In reality, science was founded between the 13th and 14th centuries through a dispute between two kinds of religious dogma. The first kind held that scholastic debate, operating according to the strict principles of DEDUCTIVE REASON, was the best way to discover God's hand in the universe. The other held that INDUCTIVE EXPERIENCE, including the use of experiments to 'interrogate nature,' was the preferred approach. Science benefited from both methods, using experiments to test propositions and then rigorous criticism and arguments to establish their significance.

In the 16th century the Reformation introduced a new idea. This was the notion that knowledge is not simply the province of ecclesiastical institutions but that, especially when it comes to matters of conscience, each man should decide for himself. The 'priesthood of the individual believer' was an immensely powerful notion because it rejected the papal hierarchy, and by implication all institutional hierarchy as well... it was a charter of independent thought, carried out not by institutions but by individuals. The early Protestants didn't know it, but they were introducing new theological concepts that would give new vitality to the emerging scientific culture of Europe."

> *"It is widely accepted on all sides that, far from undermining it, science is deeply indebted to Christianity and has been so from at least the scientific revolution. Recent historical research has uncovered many unexpected links between scientific enterprise and Biblical theology."* (Russell, 1984, 777).

The following 20 Scientists were not only Christians, but are credited with discovery of their science discipline:

Johannes Kepler (1571-1630) - Celestial Mechanics He was a German mathematician and astronomer who postulated that the Earth and planets travel about the sun in elliptical orbits. He is chiefly remembered for discovering the 3 laws of planetary motion that bear his name. He did important work in optics (1604, 1611), gave the first proof of how logarithms worked (1624), and contributed to the development of calculus (1615, 1616). He calculated the most exact astronomical tables known today, whose continued accuracy established the truth of heliocentric astronomy.

Blaise Pascal (1623-1662) - Hydrostatics, Probability Science French mathematician, physicist and religious philosopher. He was a child prodigy, educated by his father. His earliest work was in the natural and applied sciences, where he made important contributions to the construction of mechanical calculators, the study of fluids, and clarified the concepts of pressure and the vacuum. Pascal wrote powerfully to defend the scientific method. Pascal helped create 2 major new areas of research. He wrote a significant treatise on the subject of projective geometry at the age of 16 and later on probability theory, strongly influencing the development of modern economics.

Robert Boyle (1627-1691) - Chemistry and Gas Dynamics He is regarded as the first modern chemist. Among his works, *The Sceptical Chymist* is seen as a cornerstone book in the field of chemistry. Boyle was also a major apologist for the new science, reflecting at length on the mutual relations between science and religion. He made important contributions to physics and chemistry and is best known for Boyle's law, describing an ideal gas. Boyle's great merit as a scientific investigator is that he carried out the principles of scientific investigation. On several occasions he mentions that in order to keep his judgment as unbiased as possible with any of the modern theories of philosophy, he "provided with experiments" to help him judge of them. Nothing was more alien to his mental temperament than the spinning of hypotheses.

Sir Isaac Newton (1643-1727) - Calculus and Dynamics He was the greatest English mathematician of his generation. He laid the foundation for differential and integral calculus. His work on optics and gravitation make him one of the greatest scientists the world has known. Newton is regarded as the founding exemplar of modern physical science, his achievements in experimental investigation being as innovative as those in mathematical research. With equal, if not greater, energy and originality he also plunged into chemistry, the early history of Western civilization, and theology; among his special studies was an investigation of the form and dimensions, as described in the Bible, of Solomon's Temple in Jerusalem.

Sir William Herschel (1738-1822) - Galactic Astronomy Probably the most famous astronomer of the 18th century, Sir William Herschel discovered, in addition to the planet Uranus, many new nebulae, clusters of stars and binary stars. He was the first person to correctly describe the form of our Galaxy, The Milky Way. During the course of his career, he constructed more than 400 telescopes. The largest and most famous of these was a reflecting telescope with a 40 ft focal length. Herschel discovered that unfilled telescope apertures can be used to obtain high angular resolution, something which became the essential basis for interferometric imaging in astronomy.

Sir David Brewster (1781-1868) - Optical Mineralogy Brewster was a Scottish scientist, inventor and writer. His most important scientific work falls under 5 headings: (1) The laws of polarization by reflection and refraction; (2) The discovery of the polarizing structure induced by heat and pressure; (3) The discovery of crystals with 2 axes of double refraction, and many of the laws of their phenomena, including the connection between optical structure and crystalline forms; (4) The laws of metallic reflection; (5) Experiments on the absorption of light.

Michael Faraday (1791-1867) - Electromagnetics and Field Theory He was one of the greatest experimenters ever. He formulated the second law of electrolysis: "the amounts of bodies which are equivalent to each other in their ordinary chemical action have equal quantities of electricity naturally associated with them." He published many of his results in the three-volume *Experimental Researches in Electricity* (1839-1855). One of his most important contributions to physics was his development of the concept of a field to describe magnetic and electric forces in 1845.

Charles Babbage (1791-1871) - Computer Science Known as the "Father of Computing" for his contributions to the basic design of the computer through his Analytical machine. He is widely regarded as the first computer pioneer and the great ancestral figure in the history of computing. Babbage's present-day reputation rests largely on the invention and design of his vast mechanical calculating engines. His Analytical Engine conceived in 1834 is one of the startling intellectual feats of the nineteenth century. The design of this machine has all the essential logical features of the modern general purpose computer.

Matthew Maury (1806-1873) - Oceanography, Hydrology He was nicknamed *Pathfinder of the Seas* and *Father of modern Oceanography* and later, *Scientist of the Seas*, due to the publication of his extensive works. He charted winds and ocean currents, including pathways for ships at sea. He published his *Wind and Current Chart of the North Atlantic* which showed sailors how to use the ocean's currents and winds to their advantage, drastically reducing the length of ocean voyages. Maury's uniform system of recording synoptic oceanographic data was adopted by navies and merchant marines around the world and was used to develop charts for all the major trade routes.

Louis Agassiz (1807-1873) - Glacial Geology, Ichthyology One of the "founding fathers" of modern American science. A renowned teacher and promoter of science in America, he was also a lifelong opponent of Darwin's theory of evolution. He worked in paleontology, systematics, and glaciology. In 1848 he accepted a professorship at Harvard, where he acquired funding for a great museum of natural history, and founded the Museum of Comparative Zoology in 1860. He was a founding member of the National Academy of Sciences in 1863, and was appointed a regent of the Smithsonian Institution.

Sir George Gabriel Stokes (1819-1903) - Fluid Mechanics, Mathematics Stokes was an Irish mathematician and physicist, who at Cambridge made important contributions to fluid dynamics, optics and mathematical physics (including Stokes' theorem). His work on fluid motion and viscosity led to his calculating the terminal velocity for a sphere falling in a viscous medium. This became known as Stokes' Law. His best-known research dealt with the wave theory of light. In 1852, in his famous paper on the change of wavelength of light, he described the phenomenon of fluorescence. The Stokes' shift, which describes this conversion, is named in Stokes' honor.

Louis Pasteur (1822-1895) - Bacteriology He solved the mysteries of rabies, anthrax, chicken cholera, and silkworm diseases, and helped develop the first vaccines. He debunked the widely accepted myth of spontaneous generation, setting the stage for modern biology and biochemistry. Pasteur's work gave birth to many branches of science. He is revered for possessing the most important qualities of a scientist: the ability to survey all the known data and link the data for all possible hypotheses, the patience and drive to conduct experiments under controlled conditions, and the brilliance to uncover the road to the solution from the results. On the discipline of rigid and strict experimental tests he said, "Imagination should give wings to our thoughts but we always need decisive experimental proof. When the moment comes to draw conclusions and to interpret the observations, imagination must be checked and documented by the factual results of the experiment."

Gregor Mendel (1822-1884) - Genetics His work became the foundation for modern genetics. His work in heredity was so brilliant and unprecedented that it took 34 years for the rest of the scientific community to catch up to it. In his *Experiments with Plant Hybrids*, Mendel described how traits were inherited. It has become one of the most influential publications in the history of science. He was the first person to trace the characteristics of successive generations of a living thing, He was an Augustinian monk who taught natural science to high school students. The practical result of Mendel's research is that it not only changed the way we perceive the world, but also the way we live in it.

Lord William Thomson Kelvin (1824-1907) - Energetics Scottish mathematician and physicist who contributed to many branches of physics. He calculated the age of the earth from its cooling rate and concluded that it was too short to fit with Lyell's theory of gradual geological change or Darwin's theory of the evolution of animals though natural selection. He used the field concept to explain electromagnetic interactions. He speculated that electromagnetic forces were propagated as linear and rotational strains in an elastic solid, producing "vortex atoms" which generated the field. He proposed that these atoms consisted of tiny knotted strings, and the type of knot determined the type of atom. With Tait, Kelvin published *Treatise on Natural Philosophy* (1867), which was important for establishing energy within the structure of the theory of mechanics.

Bernhard Riemann (1826-1866) - Non-Euclidean Geometry He was the most influential mathematician of the mid-19th century. He was a German mathematician who made important contributions to analysis and differential geometry, some paving the way for the later development of general relativity. These would subsequently be major parts of the theories of Riemannian geometry, algebraic geometry and complex manifold theory. The theory of Riemann surfaces became an area of mathematics that was foundational in topology, and in the 21st century is still being applied to mathematical physics.

Joseph Lister (1827-1912) - Antiseptic Surgery He is known as the 'Father of Antiseptic Surgery'. He discovered the link between lack of cleanliness in hospitals and deaths after operations. Lister believed that it was microbes carried in the air that caused diseases to be spread in wards. People who had been operated on were especially vulnerable: their bodies were weak and their skin had been cut open, so germs could enter the body easily. Lister covered the wound with a piece of lint covered in carbolic acid. His success rate for survival was very high. Lister then developed his idea further by devising a machine that pumped out a fine mist of carbolic acid into the air around an operation.

James Clerk Maxwell (1831-1879) - Electrodynamics, Magnetics Maxwell, a Scottish mathematical physicist, had one of the finest mathematical minds of any theoretical physicist of any time. Maxwell is widely regarded as the 19th century scientist who had the greatest influence on 20th century physics, making contributions to the fundamental models of nature. In 1931, on the centennial anniversary of Maxwell's birthday, Einstein described Maxwell's work as the "*most profound and the most fruitful that physics has experienced since the time of Newton.*" Maxwell demonstrated that electric and magnetic fields travel through space, in the form of waves, at a constant velocity of 3.0×10^8 m/s.

Lord Rayleigh (1842-1919) - Dimensional and Model Analysis His real name was John Strutt. He was an English physicist and winner of the Nobel Prize in Physics in 1904 "for his investigations of the densities of the most important gases and for his discovery of argon in connection with these studies". He also discovered the phenomenon now called "Rayleigh scattering" and predicted the existence of the surface waves now known as "Rayleigh waves". Lord Rayleigh's first researches were mainly mathematical, concerning optics and vibrating systems, but his later work ranged over almost the whole field of physics. His experiments led to the standards of resistance, current, and electromotive force. His later work was concentrated on electric and magnetic problems.

John Ambrose Fleming (1849-1945) - Electronics He was an English electrical engineer and physicist. He was the first professor of Electrical Engineering, where he lectured at the Univ. of Cambridge, Univ. of Nottingham and Univ. College of London. In 1904, he invented and patented the 2-electrode vacuum-tube rectifier, which he called the oscillation valve. It was also called the Fleming valve. This invention is often considered to have been the beginning of electronics, for this was the first vacuum tube. Fleming's contributions to electronic communications and radar were of vital importance in winning World War II. He was awarded the IRE Medal of Honor in 1933 for "the conspicuous part he played in introducing physical and engineering principles into the radio art."

Sir William Ramsay (1852-1916) - Inorganic Chemistry He was a Scottish chemist who discovered the noble gases and received the Nobel Prize in Physics along with Lord Rayleigh in1904 (without working together, he and Lord Rayleigh proved there must exist a previously unknown gas in the atmosphere- argon). In 1887 he held the prestigious chair of Chemistry at the University College of London, where his most celebrated discoveries were made. He published several notable papers on the oxides of nitrogen. His most notable discoveries included the elements of argon, helium, neon, krypton, and xenon.

The History of Science & Religion ⇔ The Great Scientists

| | 1600's | 1800's | 1900's | 2000's | Today |

Johannes Kepler (1571-1630) German Astronomer, Mathematician; Founder: Laws of Planetary Motion

Blaise Pascal (1623-1662) French Mathematician, Physicist, Philosopher; Founder: Statistics

Isaac Newton (1643-1727) British Mathematician, Physicist, Invented Differential Calculus; Founder: Law of Gravity, Laws of Motion

William Herschel (1738-1822) British Astronomer, Founder: Galactic Astronomy; Telescope Designer, Detailed description of Milky Way Galaxy

Bernard Riemann (1826-1866) German Mathematician; Founder: Riemannian Geometry; Paved way for Theory of Relativity by proposing how light bends in space

Michael Faraday (1791-1867) British Physicist, Mathematician; Greatest Experimenter in History; Founder: 2nd Law of Electrolysis, Science of Electromagnetism

James Maxwell (1831-1879) Scottish Physicist; 19th century's greatest scientist; Founder: equations for a unified model of electromagnetism

George Stokes (1819-1903) Irish Mathematician, Physicist; Founder: Stokes Law, Fluid Dynamics, Mathematical Physics

Lord William Kelvin (1824-1907) Scottish Mathematician, Physicist; Founder: Absolute Zero; helped derive 1st & 2nd Laws of Thermodynamics

Lord Rayleigh (1842-1919) British Physicist; 1904 Nobel Prize; Founder: Argon, "Rayleigh Waves"

Arthur Eddington (1882-1944) British Astrophysicist; Director, Cambridge Observatory; helped Einstein with Theory of Relativity

John Fleming (1849-1945) English Physicist; 1st Prof. of Electrical Engineering; Founder: "Fleming Valve" (started field of Electronics)

Max Planck (1858-1947) German Physicist; 1918 Nobel Prize; Founder: Quantum Theory

Robert Milliken (1868-1953) American Physicist; 1923 Nobel Prize; Founder: electron charge

Albert Einstein (1879-1955) German Physicist; 1921 Nobel Prize; Founder: Theory of Relativity

Erwin Schrödinger (1887-1961) Austrian Physicist; 1933 Nobel Prize; Founder: Wave Mechanics, Schrödinger Equation

Arthur Compton (1892-1962) American Physicist; 1927 Nobel Prize; Founder: Compton Effect

William Bragg (1890-1971) British Physicist; 1915 Nobel Prize; Founder: Crystal Structures via X-rays

Werner Heisenberg (1901-1976); German Physicist; 1932 Nobel Prize; Founder: Quantum Mechanics

Wernher von Braun (1912-1977) German Physicist; 1st Rocket Scientist; Director of Marshall Space Center

Richard Feynman (1918-1988) American Physicist; 1965 Nobel Prize; Founder: Quantum Electrodynamics

Arthur Schawlow (1921-1999) American Physicist; 1981 Nobel Prize; Founder: Laser Spectroscopy

Fred Hoyle (1915-2001) British Astrophysicist; Founder: Institute of Theoretical Astronomy

Robert Jastrow (1925-2008) American Physicist; Director NASA Institute for Space Studies

Alan Sandage (1926-2010) American Astronomer, Founder: Observational Cosmology; measured universe size and age

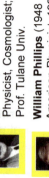

Charles Townes (1915-) American Physicist; 1964 Nobel Prize; Founder: Maser Technology

Steven Weinberg (1933-) American Physicist; 1975 Nobel Prize; Founder, Electroweak Unification Theory

Arno Penzias (1933-) American Physicist; 1978 Nobel Prize; Co-founder: Cosmic Background Radiation

Robert Wilson (1936-) American Physicist; 1978 Nobel Prize; Co-founder, Cosmic Background Radiation

George Ellis (1939-) South African Mathematician & Physicist; one of world's leading Theorists in Cosmology

Paul Davies (1942-) British Physicist; Chair, Post-Detection Science of International Academy of Aeronautics

Stephen Hawking (1942-) British Physicist & Cosmologist; Director, Cambridge Center for Theoretical Cosmology

Henry Schaefer (1944-) American Physicist & Chemist; Director, Center Computational Quantum Chemistry

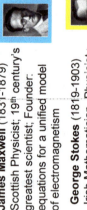

George Smootz (1945-) American Physicist; 2006 Nobel Prize; Senior Scientist, Berkeley National Lab

Frank Tipler (1947-) American Mathematician, Physicist, Cosmologist; Prof. Tulane Univ.

William Phillips (1948-) American Physicist; 1997 Nobel Prize; Founder: Laser Cooling

Christian — yellow
Pantheist — blue
Deist — grey
Agnostic — black
Atheist — red

"I strongly believe in the existence of God, based on intuition, observations, logic, and scientific knowledge."
(Charles Townes, 1964 Nobel Prize in Physics)

CHAPTER 4 *Science* and *Reason*: The Evidence for Christianity

In today's debates over the origin of the universe, the origin of life, the reliability of the Bible, and the Person of Jesus Christ, we may not appreciate the fundamental problem people have in trying to apply the discipline of science to uncover solid evidences for *events that occurred in the past and can't be repeated today.*

We would all agree that in its most basic definition, science is the disciplined approach to finding the *CAUSE* for the effects we *observe* in the world. But is there a difference in the *type* of science we use when trying to find the cause for non-repeatable events of the past that we cannot observe today (like creation, or the Resurrection)?

In his book 'When Skeptics Ask'[12], Dr. Norman Geisler explains there are really two kinds of 'science' we are dealing with when investigating any event, depending on whether the event we wish to study is observable in the present or occurred in the past and thus cannot be repeated (so it could be observed):
1) The first type of science he calls 'Operation Science' = it deals with how observable events work.
2) The second type he calls 'Origins Science" = it deals with how nonobservable events happened in the past.

Operation Science = It looks at how things presently WORK, and follows the classical scientific method (see below). It seeks answers that are TESTABLE by repeating the experiment over and over, and falsifiable if the cause does not always yield the same effect. Its conclusions should allow one to project what will happen in future experiments. Operation science likes things to be very regular and predictable. No changes; no surprises. So the idea of a supernatural being coming around to stir things up occasionally is strongly resisted.

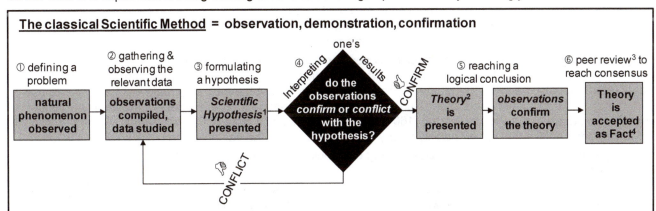

The classical Scientific Method = observation, demonstration, confirmation

1) **Hypothesis** = a well-supported speculation for the probable cause of an event, based on observed data.
2) **Theory** = an explanation based on observation, experimentation and testing, that helps explain and predict natural phenomenon. A theory must be verifiable, and is grounded upon observed facts. If *evidence* is found that contradicts the stated theory, the theory must be modified or discarded.
3) **Peer Review** = *public scrutiny* of theories, to test them objectively and so they don't become subjective myths. Peer Reviews work to eliminate individual bias and subjectivity, because others must also be able to determine whether a proposed explanation is consistent with the available *evidence*.
4) **Fact (law)** = a statement of something that is always observed to be true in certain conditions. Scientific theories don't become laws or facts - they explain them (example: the law of gravity states all airborne objects left to themselves fall to the ground - the theory of gravity explains why).

Origin Science = It looks at how things BEGAN, not how they work. It studies things that happened ONCE and don't happen again. Rather than being an empirical science like physics or biology, it is more like a FORENSIC SCIENCE. Origin Science works on different principles than Operation Science. Since the past events that it studies cannot be repeated today, ...it does not claim to give definitive answers but only plausible ones. We did not observe the events of origins, and we cannot repeat them. So the remaining EVIDENCE must be STUDIED and interpretations of it MEASURED by what seems MOST LIKELY (*i.e.,* PROBABILITY SCIENCE – my italics added, and explained on next page) to explain the evidence.

What is Forensic Science? *'Forensic'* is a synonym for "legal" or "related to courts". *Forensics* is related to the notion of AUTHENTICATION, where the goal is to determine, through accepted scholarly or scientific methods of investigation, if the FACTS regarding an event, an artifact, or some other physical item (such as a corpse) can be verified beyond a reasonable doubt as being the case.

The word *forensic* comes from the Latin adjective *forensis*, meaning *'of or before the forum.'* In Roman times, a criminal charge meant presenting the case before public individuals in the forum.

Both the person accused of the crime and the accuser would give speeches based on their side of the story. The individual with the best argument and delivery determines the outcome of the case. This origin is the source of the two modern usages of the word *forensic* – as a form of legal evidence and as a category of public presentation.

Columbia College, MO: Requirements for a Bachelor of Science in FORENSIC SCIENCE	
The major in *Forensic Science* draws from the biological sciences, physics and chemistry as well as from the fields of criminal justice and the law. The degree is generated from a cross-disciplinary perspective, blending expertise from both the criminal justice and science program areas. The program focus is on professions in the criminal justice and science areas, which require specific coursework as shown below:	
Criminalist I - Physical Evidence	Coursework: ≥ 2 natural science classes, algebra, and trigonometry (coursework in calculus can be substituted for the algebra and trigonometry).
Criminalist I - DNA	Coursework: 20 semester hours in genetics, biochemistry, molecular biology to provide a basic understanding of forensic DNA analysis
Criminalist I – Trace Evidence	Coursework: ≥ 20 hours of chemistry (organic and inorganic)
Criminalist I - Toxicology	Coursework: 20 hours of chemistry (2 semesters of general chemistry, 2 semesters of organic chemistry, and 1 semester of quantitative analysis)
Criminalist I - Latent Prints	Coursework should include ≥ 2 natural science classes
The Goal = Become skilled in uncovering *evidence* for an event that occurred in the past, to make conclusions that can be upheld in a court of law with a reasonably high degree (≥ 95%) of certainty	

What is Probability Science? It is the discipline used to calculate the CHANCE of a future event occurring, to a certain degree of accuracy. It first came into use when situations presented themselves that had potential for great GAINS, but also had RISKS that the desired outcomes might not happen, so people wanted a way to use facts (data) to PREDICT the gains and the chance of the risks happening. The "Fathers of Probability Science" were Pascal (1623-1662), Pier de Fermat (1601-1665). It was the initial work of Pascal, Fermat, Graunt, Bernoulli, DeMoivre, and Laplace that set probability theory on its way to being the valuable inferential science it is today.

• Accomplishment #1 (1600's) = the realization that one could actually predict to a certain degree of accuracy events which were yet to come.

• Accomplishment #2 (1800's) = probability and statistics could converge to form a well defined, firmly grounded science, with limitless applications and possibilities.

Question: "When I roll dice, what's the chance of getting a pair of 6's?"

Answer = 36 → since there are 6 sides to each dice, and each possible combination of numbers has an equal likelihood of occurring when the dice are randomly rolled, multiply the number of possible "events" to get the chance of the desired event.

So.... what are the odds of rolling a pair of 6's when you pick up a pair of dice?
 - 1 chance in 36 rolls = 1: 36, or 1 divided by 36 (1/ 36) = 2.8% chance of rolling 6's
 - or.... there's a 97.2% chance of not rolling 6's (high risk of failure)

• Back to the Dice Example: You've got a 2.8% chance of rolling a pair of 6's. You're offered $100,000 if, on your one and only chance, you roll a pair of 6's. But you have to wager $10 to have the chance of playing for the $100,000.... would you take the risk of losing $10 for the chance to gain $100,000? What if you had to wager $10,000 (not $10) to gain $100,000 – would you? WHY or WHY NOT?

Dice #1: if it rolls a "6"... it could just as likely roll 1-5
Dice #2: if it rolls a "1"... it could just as likely roll 2-6

6	1
6	2
6	3
6	4
6	5
6	6

• Examples: Odds of an Event: 1: 6,357 to die in auto accident   1: 600,000 to be struck by lightning
                                1: 19,000 to contract AIDS   1: 11,000,000 to be in a plane crash

Summarizing: 'Operation' Science vs. 'Origin' Science	
Operation Science	**Origin Science**
Studies how present events work	Studies how past events happened
Studies testable, repeatable, observable events	Studies untestable, unrepeatable, unobservable events
Can recreate and retest events, so any conclusion can be *proven* false	Cannot recreate events, so any conclusion cannot be *proven* false (only *inferences* can be made)
Data collected during event (direct evidence)	Data collected after event (circumstantial evidence)

The TYPES of Evidence available when evaluating a Hypothesis

1) **Direct evidence** = Supports the truth of a hypothesis *directly* (if repeatable, it's Operational Science; if not, it's Origin Science); an example would be if credible eyewitnesses *observed* the event from start to finish.

2) **Circumstantial Evidence** = Evidence after an unobserved, nonrepeatable, nontestable event occurred that can *infer* towards a hypothesis, but does not directly support it (example: fingerprints at a crime scene). A hypothesis based on circumstantial evidence becomes more valid when any alternative explanations can be ruled out.

3) **Corroborating Evidence** = Circumstantial evidence becomes stronger when there are *multiple pieces* that all point to the same hypothesis (together, the pieces give weight to one hypothesis over another).

4) **Forensic Evidence** = Type of circumstantial evidence that is supplied by an *expert witness*.
   - A forensic scientist who testifies that ballistics *proves* the defendant's gun was used to shoot the victim gives circumstantial evidence from which the defendant's guilt may be *inferred*, but this inference of guilt could be incorrect if it was someone else who actually pulled the trigger.
   - But if there was additional circumstantial evidence of the defendant's fingerprint on the trigger, it would strengthen the conclusion by the corroborating evidence.

Whenever no one is there to *see* the event, we have no direct evidence to support any hypothesis, so *circumstantial evidence* is the most important evidence available.

Applying Origin Science to the *Bible* and the *Person of Jesus Christ*

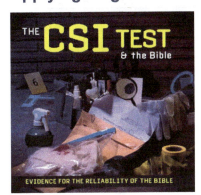

I start with the questions I am trying to solve.... How can I **trust** the content and events recorded in the Bible? → Can I have a high level of certainty that the Bible is God's revelation to me about Himself, and His instructions for how to live my life? → How do I gather *evidence* so I can test the certainty of my faith? → Using Dr. Geisler's method of 'Origin Science', can I collect facts to measure how reliable the Bible is as a truth source (especially when checked against all the other ancient writings that people have trusted)?

In his book *Evidence that Demands a Verdict*[11], Josh McDowell uses three tests taken from the book *Introduction to Research in English Literary History* by military historian **Dr. Chauncey Sanders** (a non-Christian). These three tests are used in this series as the method of Forensic Science to validate the historicity and reliability of the Bible.

TEST #1: Bibliographical Test   This test exams the textual transmission of the manuscripts through time. Since I don't have the hand-written originals, how reliable are the copies I do have in terms of their *number* and the *time interval* between the original writing and the earliest existing copy? I'll apply this test not only to the most famous secular literature taught today in our schools and universities, but also to both the New Testament and Old Testament.

TEST #2: Internal Evidence Test   This test asks the question "Does the internal evidence of the document itself contain any inaccuracies or contradictions that would bring to question its reliability and trustworthiness? It is based on <u>Aristotle's dictum</u>: *"The benefit of the doubt is given to the document itself; don't assume fraud or error unless I can prove contradictions by the author within the text or known factual inaccuracies."* I'll again apply this test to both the New and Old Testaments, examining the *Eyewitness Accounts* of Jesus Christ and Old Testament *Fulfilled Prophecies*.

TEST #3: External Evidence Test   This test evaluates sources outside the document: "do other historical documents confirm or deny the internal testimony provided by the documents themselves? What sources exist apart from the literature under examination that confirm its accuracy, reliability and authenticity?" I'll once again apply this test to both the New Testament and Old Testaments, using the evidence of *Non-biblical sources* (writings outside the Bible) and the findings of *Archaeology*.

#	**Is the Bible Reliable? (Book 3)** **Corroborating Evidence: 53 Measurable Data Points** (applying Dr. Chauncey Saunders Tests) 4.2	Manuscript Test	Internal Test	External Test
1	Bible's continuity	✓		
2	Bible's circulation and transmission	✓		
3	Bible's survival	✓		
4	Bible's influence	✓		
5	Bibliographic Test: New Testament manuscripts	✓		
6	Bibliographic Test: Old Testament manuscripts	✓		
7	Bibliographic Test: Dead Sea Scrolls	✓		
8	Eyewitness Testimony: The Incarnation of Jesus Christ		✓	
9	Eyewitness Testimony: The Death, Burial and Resurrection of Jesus Christ		✓	
10	Prophecy: Destruction of Tyre		✓	
11	Prophecy: Destruction of Nineveh		✓	
12	Prophecy: Destruction of Memphis and Thebes		✓	
13	Prophecy: Destruction of Babylon		✓	
14	Prophecy: Destruction of Moab and Ammon		✓	
15	Prophecy: Destruction of Petra and Edom		✓	
16	Prophecy: Destruction of Samaria		✓	
17	Prophecy: Gaza-Ashkelon		✓	
18	Prophecy: Palestine		✓	
19	Archaeology: The walls of Jericho			✓
20	Archaeology: The Ebla Tablets and Kings of Mesopotamia			✓
21	Archaeology: The Roman Census			✓
22	Archaeology: The Hittite Empire			✓
23	Archaeology: The Assyrian Empire and The Library of King Assurbanipal			✓
24	Archaeology: The Black Obelisk of King Shalmaneser III			✓
25	Archaeology: King Shalmaneser III attacking Hamath			✓
26	Archaeology: King Tiglath-pileser conquering cities			✓
27	Archaeology: King Sargon II capturing and deporting Israel			✓
28	Archaeology: King Sennacherib exiling Lachish of Judah			✓
29	Archaeology: Nabonidus Stele: King Sennacherib murdered by his sons			✓
30	Archaeology: Siloam Inscription: King Sennacherib attacks King Hezekiah			✓
31	Archaeology: King Esarhaddon restoring Babylon			✓
32	Archaeology: King Assurbanipal royal bodyguards			✓
33	Archaeology: King Assurbanipal conquering Hamanu in Elam			✓
34	Archaeology: Mesha Stele: King of Moab war on Omri (King of Israel)			✓
35	Archaeology: Canaanite gods Molech, Chemosh			✓
36	Archaeology: Canaanite god Ba'al			✓
37	Archaeology: Philistine god Dagon (sanctuary of Tell Qasileh)			✓
38	Archaeology: Philistine warrior carvings (Thebes)			✓

#	Is the Bible Reliable? (Book 3) *Corroborating Evidence: 53 Measurable Data Points* (applying Dr. Chauncey Saunders Tests)	Manuscript Test	Internal Test	External Test
39	Archaeology: Ruins of Petra			✓
40	Archaeology: Ruins of Tyre			✓
41	Archaeology: Ruins of Nineveh			✓
42	Archaeology: Ruins of Babylon			✓
43	Archaeology: Ruins of Samaria			✓
44	Archaeology: Amaran Letters (King Yidya of Ashkelon)			✓
45	Archaeology: Merneptah Stele (King Merneptah conquers Israel, others)			✓
46	Archaeology: The Practice of Crucifixion			✓
47	Early Church manuscripts: Irenaeus "Against Heresies III"			✓
48	Secular Historians: Eusebius "Ecclesiastical History III"			✓
49	Secular Historians: Plinius Secundus "Writings to Emperor Trajan"			✓
50	Secular Historians: Cornelius Tacitus "Nero blames Christians for 64AD Fire"			✓
51	Secular Historians: Flavius Josephus "Antiquities XVIII, 63"			✓
52	Secular Historians: Flavius Josephus "Antiquities XX, 197"			✓
53	Secular Historians: Flavius Josephus "Antiquities XVIII, 106"			✓

After weighing these 53 pieces of circumstantial evidence as a whole…
Does the *evidence* favor the Bible as historically accurate and reliably transmitted?

4.3

#	Require-ment	Is Jesus Christ the Messiah? (Book 3) *Corroborating Evidence: 87 Measurable Data Points* (confirm Old Testament Prophecies by New Testament facts)	New Testament Evidence Test
1	Messiah Lineage	Genesis 22:18 ➔ Jesus is a Hebrew	Matt. 1:1; Luke 3:34; Gal.3:16
2		Genesis 21:12 ➔ Jesus descended from Isaac	Matt. 1:2; Luke 3:34
3		Genesis 35:10-12 ➔ Jesus descended from Jacob	Matt. 1:2; Luke 1:33, 3:34
4		Genesis 49:10; Jeremiah33:14 ➔ Jesus descended from Judah	Matt. 1:2,2:6; Luke 3:33
5		Isaiah 11:1,10 ➔ Jesus descended from Jesse	Matt. 1:5; Luke 3:32
6		Isaiah 9:7; Jerem. 23:5,33:15-17 ➔ Jesus descended from David	Matt. 1:6; Luke 1:32, 3:30
7	Messiah Titles	Genesis 3:15 ➔ Jesus is our Victor over Satan	John 8:41-44; 1John 3:8; Rom. 16:20; Hebr. 2:14-15
8		Genesis 22:7-14 ➔ Jesus is our Sin Offering	John 1:29; Hebr. 7:27, 9:26
9		Genesis 49:10 ➔ Jesus is the 'One who brings Peace' (Shiloh)	Rom. 5:1; Eph. 1:2, 2:14-16
10		Exodus 3:13-15 ➔ Jesus is the 'I AM'	John 8:24, 56-59
11		Exodus 12:21-27 ➔ Jesus is the Passover Lamb	1Cor. 5:7; Rom. 3:21-26
12		Exodus 16:32 ➔ Jesus is the Bread of Life	John 6:31-35,48-51,63
13		Exodus 25:17-22 ➔ Jesus is the Way to meet with God	Matt. 27:51; Heb. 10:19-20
14		Exodus 33:18-23 ➔ Jesus is the Rock through which we see God	John 1:14, 14:7-9; 1Cor. 10:4
15		Leviticus 9:15-18 ➔ Jesus is our High Priest	Hebr. 2:17, 4:14-15, 10:11-12
16		Leviticus 14:1-7 ➔ Jesus is our Cleansing from Sin	1John 1:7-9; Matt. 8:2-4

#	Requirement	Is Jesus Christ the Messiah? (Book 3) *Corroborating Evidence: 87 Measurable Data Points* (confirm Old Testament Prophecies by New Testament facts)	New Testament Evidence Test
17		Leviticus 16:8-9,15-19 ➔ Jesus is our Sin Atonement	1John 3:5, 1Peter 1:18-19
18		Leviticus 16:10,20-22 ➔ Jesus is our Sin Scapegoat	Mark 15:33-34, Gal. 3:13
19		Leviticus 16:14-17 ➔ Jesus is our Propitiation for our sin	Romans 3:21-26
20		Leviticus 17:11 ➔ Jesus is the Blood of the Covenant	Luke 22:20, Hebr. 9:14-15
21		Numbers 20:7-13 ➔ Jesus is the Water of Life	John 4:10-14, 7:37-38
22		Numbers 21:7-9 ➔ Jesus is the Bronze Serpent	John 3:14-17
23		Numbers 24:8 ➔ Jesus is God's Son out of Egypt	Matthew 2:13-15
24		Deuteronomy 18:18-19 ➔ Jesus is the Prophet	John 6:14, 12:49-50, 17:8
25		Job 19:25-27 ➔ Jesus is the Redeemer who lives forever	Gal. 4:4-5, Col. 1:14, Rev. 5:9
26		Psalm 16:10 ➔ Jesus is the Resurrection	John 11:25-26, 14:19
27		Psalm 118:22-23, Isaiah 28:16 ➔ Jesus is the Cornerstone	Matthew 21:33-46
28		Proverbs 8:14-31 ➔ Jesus is the Creative 'Logos'	John 1:1-3,14, 1Corin. 1:24,30
29		Isaiah 5:1-7 (Psalm 80:8-16, Jeremiah 2:21) ➔ Jesus is the True Vine	Matt. 21:33-45, Luke 20:9-19, John 15:1-7
30		Isaiah 7:14 ➔ Jesus is 'God with us'	Matthew 1:22-23, Luke 7:16
31		Isaiah 9:6 ➔ Jesus is the God-Child	Luke 2:10-21,25-35,40
32	Messiah Titles	Isaiah 9:6 ➔ Jesus is God's Son given to man	John 3:16, Galatians 2:20
33		Isaiah 9:6 ➔ Jesus is El Gibbor ('Mighty God')	John 1:1, 8:58, Hebr. 1:8
34		Isaiah 9:6 ➔ Jesus is equal to the Father	John 10:30, 14:7-9
35		Isaiah 9:6 ➔ Jesus is the Prince of Peace	John 14:27, 16:33, Rom. 5:1
36		Isaiah 11:1-2 ➔ Jesus is anointed with the Holy Spirit	John 1:32-34, Matt. 3:13-17
37		Isaiah 12:2 ➔ Jesus is our Savior	Matt. 1:21, 18:11, Acts 4:12
38		Isaiah 28:16 ➔ Jesus is our Foundation Stone	Luke 20:17-18, Rom. 9:31-33
39		Isaiah 40:10-11 ➔ Jesus is the Great Shepherd	John 10:11-16
40		Isaiah 42:6-7, 49:6 ➔ Jesus is the Light of Salvation to Gentiles	Luke 2:28-32, Acts 13:46-48
41		Isaiah 52:10 ➔ Jesus is the Arm of Salvation	John 14:6, Rom. 1:16, Phil. 2:9
42		Isaiah 53:5-6,8 ➔ Jesus is our Sin-Bearer	John 1:29, 2Corin. 5:21
43		Isaiah 53:10-11 = Jesus is God's Pleasing Sacrifice for our sins	Matt. 3:17, Mark 10:45
44		Isaiah 59:16-17 ➔ Jesus is the Armor of Salvation	Rom. 13:14, Eph. 6:10
45		Jeremiah 23:5-6, 33:15-17 ➔ Jesus is our Righteousness	Rom. 1:17, 3:22, 2Corin. 5:21
46		Daniel 3:24-25 ➔ Jesus is the 4th Man in the Furnace Fire	John 11:43-44, Hebr. 13:5-6
47		Daniel 7:13 ➔ Jesus is the "Son of Man"	Mark 14:61-64
48		Daniel 9:24-26 ➔ Jesus is the Coming Messiah Prince	Luke 19:41-44, Hebr. 10:5-7
49		Zechariah 13:1 ➔ Jesus is our Fountain of Water	John 4:10, Rev. 21:6
50		Malachi 4:2, Psalm 19:4-6 ➔ Jesus is the Sun of Righteousness	Matt. 4:16, Luke 1:78-79
51	Messiah Beginnings	Isaiah 7:14 (Isaiah 53:9) ➔ Jesus is virgin-born (without sin)	John 8:45-46, 1Peter 1:19
52		Isaiah 40:3-5 ➔ Jesus' forerunner (prepares for His arrival)	Luke 1:76-77, John 1:22-29
53		Isaiah 53:1-2 ➔ Jesus' poor, humble upbringing	Luke 1:27, 2:22-24, John 6:42
54		Micah 5:2 ➔ Jesus is born in Bethlehem Ephrathah	Matt. 2:6, Luke 2:4, John 7:42

#	Requirement	Is Jesus Christ the Messiah? (Book 3) *Corroborating Evidence: 87 Measurable Data Points* (confirm Old Testament Prophecies by New Testament facts)	New Testament Evidence Test
55	Messiah Public Displays & Pronouncements	Psalm 69:9 → Jesus is zealous for God	John 2:14-17
56		Psalm 78:2 → Jesus teaches in Parables	Matt. 13:34-35, Mark 4:33-34
57		Isaiah 9:1-2 → Jesus starts His ministry in Galilee	Matt. 4:12-17, John 2:11
58		Isaiah 35:4-6 → Jesus performs miracles of physical healing	Mark 7:37, Luke 7:20-23
59		Isaiah 42:1-4 → Jesus is meek but resolute	Matt. 11:28-30, 12:15-21
60		Isaiah 50:4-9 → Jesus 'sets His face' to do His Father's will	Matt. 26:39, Luke 9:51, John 8:29
61		Isaiah 55:1-3 → Jesus invites everyone to come to Him	Matt. 11:28-30, John 7:37-38
62		Isaiah 61:1-2 → Jesus came to bring salvation from sin	Luke 4:17-21, John 8:32-36
63		Isaiah 61:2-3 → Jesus came to console, comfort and bring joy	Matt. 22:9-12, Luke 15:22-24
64		Zechariah 9:9 → Jesus enters Jerusalem on a donkey	Matt. 21:1-5, John 12:14-15
65		Malachi 3:1 → Jesus comes before Temple destroyed	Matt. 24:1-2, Mark 11:11
66	Events leading up to Messiah Death	Psalm 27:12, 35:11 → Jesus is falsely accused	Matt. 26:59-62, Mark 14:55-60
67		Psalm 41:9 → Jesus is betrayed by a close friend	John 13:11,18-30, Luke 22:48
68		Psalm 35:19, 69:4, 109:3-5 → Jesus is hated for no reason	John 15:18-25
69		Isaiah 50:6, 52:13-15 (Matt. 20:17-19, Mark 10:32-34) → Jesus is publicly mocked, spit on, beaten, scourged, physically mutilated	Matt 26:67, 27:26-30, Mark 14:65, 15:15-20, John 19:1-3
70		Isaiah 53:3-4 → Jesus is rejected by the people	Luke 4:28-29, John 19:14-16
71		Isaiah 53:7 (Psalm 38:13-14) → Jesus is silent during accusations	Matt 26:63, 27:12-14
72		Jeremiah 20:8-11, Psalm 38:12 (Nehemiah 6:10-13) → Jesus is persecuted throughout His ministry	Matt 9:23-24, 12:10-14, 22-24, 13:54-58, 21:23-46, 22:34-46, Mark 6:2-3, Luke 20:20-26
73		Zechariah 11:12 → Jesus is betrayed for 30 pieces of silver	Matt 26:14-16, Luke 22:3-6
74		Zechariah 11:13 → 30pcs silver thrown in God's house, buys Field	Matt 27:3-10, Acts 1:18-19
75		Zechariah 13:7 (Matt 26:31, Mark 14:27) → Disciples forsake Jesus	Matt 26:56, Mark 14:50
76	Events during and after Messiah Death	Psalm 22:1 → Jesus is forsaken by God on the cross	Matt 27:46, Mark 15:34
77		Psalm 22:7-8 → Jesus is publicly ridiculed on the cross	Matt. 27:39-44, Mark 15:32
78		Psalm 22:15, 69:21 → Jesus thirsts on the cross (gall/ vinegar mix)	Matt 27:48, John 19:28-30
79		Psalm 22:14-16 → Jesus is crucified	Matt 27:35, John 19:17-22
80		Psalm 22:18 → Jesus' clothing gambled for while He dies	Matt 27:35, John 19:23-24
81		Psalm 31:5 → Jesus commits His soul to God as He dies	Luke 23:46
82		Psalm 34:20 (Exo.12:46) → Jesus' bones not broken on the cross	John 19:33,36
83		Psalm 38:11 → Jesus' friends watch Him die on the cross	Matt 27:55, Mark 15:40, Luke 23:49 (2:35), John 19:25-27
84		Isaiah 53:9 → Jesus is buried in rich man's tomb	Matt 27:57-60, John 19:38-42
85		Isaiah 53:9,12 (Luke 22:37) → Jesus is crucified with criminals	Mark 15:27-28, Luke 23:33-43
86		Isaiah 53:12 → Jesus intercedes for sinners	Luke 23:34, Heb. 7:25, 9:15,24
87		Zechariah 12:10 → Jesus' side pierced on the cross	John 19:34-37, 20:24-27

After weighing these 87 pieces of circumstantial evidence as a whole...
Does the *evidence* point to Jesus Christ as the Messiah predicted in the Old Testament?

Applying Origin Science to *Origins*

I start with the questions I am trying to solve.... Does the
Bible provide greater PROBABILITY that I was created by God,
or is there more convincing evidence that Natural Laws and/ or Evolution
is more PROBABLE to be the basis for my origin? ➔ **Who am I?** ➔
Where did I come from? ➔ **Why am I here?**

Using Dr. Geisler's method of 'Origin Science', can I gather *circumstantial evidence* (data, facts) to help me answer these questions?

Albert Einstein November 28, 1919 "The Times" magazine article "Time, Space and Gravitation":
Analytics (measurable data) = circumstantial evidence to reach sound conclusions
"The theory of relativity belongs to the class of 'principle-theories'. As such it employs an Analytic method.
1. The elements which comprise this theory are not based on *hypothesis* but on empirical discovery.
2. The *empirical* discovery leads to understanding the general characteristics of natural processes.
3. *Mathematical models* are used to separate natural processes into theoretical-mathematical descriptions.
4. Therefore, by analytical means the necessary conditions that have to be satisfied are *deduced*.
5. Separate events must satisfy these *conditions*.
6. Experience should then match these *conclusions*."

#	Universe & Life: specially created? (Book 2) *Corroborating Evidence: 60 Measurable Data Points* (Bible explanations match Scientific Findings)	Biblical Reference(s)
1	Kepler's 3rd Law of Planetary Motion	Isaiah 40:26, Rom. 1:19-20
2	Newton's 2nd & 3rd Laws of the Universe	Gen. 1:1, Ps 90:2, Heb 1:8-11
3	1st Law of Thermodynamics (Conservation of Mass/Energy: $E = mc^2$)	John 1:3, Gen. 2:2, Heb 1:3
4	2nd Law of Thermodynamics (Disintegration of Energy)	1Ki. 2:1-2, Ps 102:26, Rom. 8:21
5	Einstein's General Theory of Relativity	Psalm 8:3, 89:11-12, 124:8
6	Hubble Constant	Ps 104:1-2, Isa. 42:5, Jer 10:12
7	Doppler Red Shifts, Cosmic Microwave Background Radiation	Gen. 1:1,3
8	Corotation Circle	Psalm 8:3-4, Isaiah 45:8, Hebrews 11:3
9	Circumstellar Habitable Zone	
10	Precision of the Expansion Rate of the Universe	Job 38:4-6, Isaiah 40:21-22
11	Precision of Gravitational Exponent	Genesis 1:1-26, Job 38:4-6, Psalm 8:3-4, Psalm 19:1-4a, Romans 1:19-20, Colossians 1:15-17, 2Peter 3:10, Hebrews 1:1-5, Hebrews 11:1-3
12	Precision of Electromagnetic Force	
13	Precision of Ratio of Electromagnetic Force – to – Gravitational Force	
14	Precision of Atomic Strong Nuclear Force	
15	Precision of Atomic Weak Nuclear Force	
16	Precision of # Protons – to – # Neutrons in the Universe	
17	Precision of Electron – to – Proton Mass in Atomic Nucleus	
18	Precision of Neutron – to – Proton Mass in Atomic Nucleus	
19	Precision of nuclear ground state energies of He, BE, C, O_2	
20	Precision of mass density of the Universe	
21	Precision of velocity of light	
22	Precision of Fine Structure Constant (splitting of spectral lines)	
23	Precision of decay rate of a proton	
24	Precision of Carbon – to – Oxygen Energy Level in the Universe	

4.4

#	**Universe & Life: specially created? (Book 2)** *Corroborating Evidence: 60 Measurable Data Points* (Bible explanations match Scientific Findings)	**Biblical Reference(s)**
25	Precision of decay rate of Beryllium	Gen 1:1-26, Ps 8:3-4, 19:1-4a, Rom 1:19-20, Coloss 1:15-17, 2Peter 3:10, Heb 1:1-5, 11:1-3
26	Ratio of exotic – to – ordinary matter in the Universe	
27	Earth's location and position in the *spiral* Milky Way Galaxy	Psalm 8:3-4, Psalm 115:14-16, Job 12:8-9, Isaiah 45:18
28	Earth's protection from asteroid hits	
29	Earth's distance from the Sun	
30	Earth's Water and Carbon	
31	Precision of Earth's Rotational Axial Tilt	
32	Precision of size of Earth's Moon	
33	Earth's suspension in space, as a sphere	Job 40:22, Isaiah 40:22
34	Earth's Hydrologic Cycle	Ecclesiastes 1:7
35	Sun's Uniqueness as Earth's Energy Source	Ps 19:4b-6, John 1:4-5, 8:12
36	Stability of Sun's energy output	Mal 3:6, Heb 1:12, 13:8
37	Fact that our Sun is only star in Solar System	Matt 17:2-3,6,8, John 14:6
38	Sun's mass (dwarfs the Earth) and metal composition	Exo 33:20, Isa 40:22, Heb 12:29
39	Bat's echolocation system	Genesis 1:24-25, Job 12:7,9, Job 39:26, Jeremiah 8:7
40	Godwit's migratory flight patterns	
41	Giraffe's rete mirable caroticum (blood control valves)	
42	Camel's oval-shaped red blood cells	
43	Bombadier Beetle's inhibitor chemical reservoir	
44	Precision/ complexity of Human Eye (light to electrical impulse)	Psalm 139:1-18, Psalm 66:3, 94:8-9, 103:11-14, 119:73 Genesis 9:3-4, 16:13, Deuteronomy 12:15-16, 23-25, Ezekiel 18:4, 48:35, Matt 28:20, Luke 15:31, Revelation 21:3, Daniel 5:23, Isaiah 43:7, Jeremiah 1:5
45	Precision/ complexity of Human Ear (sound to electrical impulse)	
46	Precision/ complexity of Human Brain (control center)	
47	Precision/ complexity of Human Heart (auto-rhythmic pumping of blood)	
48	Precision/ complexity of DNA (specific instructions for each organism)	
49	Precision/ complexity of ATP to create energy packets for life	
50	Precision/ complexity of Blood Clotting (auto-catalytic cascade)	
51	Precision/ complexity of Eukaryote Cell to regulate its own health	
52	Precision/ complexity of Human Body to regulate its own health	
53	Human intelligence (example: vocabulary of > 20,000 words)	Ps 139:23-24, 4:4-5, 23:2, 46:10, Matt 10:28, 22:37, Luke 2:19, John 8:7-9, Acts 24:16, Gen. 2:7, 1Ki 18:21, 1Thes 5:23, Heb 4:12
54	Human consciousness (example: capacity for self-awareness)	
55	Human Soul (example: people have a free will – we can make choices)	
56	Homologous Structures (unique creations at earliest stages)	Genesis 1:11-12, Genesis 1: 20-22, 24-27, Ecclesiastes 1:9-10, Psalm 102:26, John 1:1-3, Colossians 1:16-17, Romans 8:20-21
57	Embryology (unique creations at earliest stages)	
58	Natural Selection (operates within range of a species' DNA)	
59	The Cambrian Explosion (abrupt appearance in fossil record)	
60	Foramen Magnum (unique only to humans – allows for bipedalism)	

After weighing these 60 pieces of circumstantial evidence as a whole…
Does the *evidence* point to the Universe and Life as originating by an Intelligent Designer?

Applying Probability Science to *Origins, The Bible & Deity of Christ*   4.5

There are three methods commonly used in Probability Science to determine the chance that someone is right or wrong when they make a statement about an event that happened in the past, that cannot be repeated.

Method #1: use historical data to calculate the odds of an event occurring

We can use statistics to calculate the odds that any historical event happened by chance, as well as the odds of its reoccurrence in the future, if we have historical data for its occurrence or for the steps leading to its occurrence.

The table gives examples of how often an event will occur when its odds are reduced (from 1:100 to 1:100,000). In order to reduce these odds (since these are undesirable events), we must implement ORDERLY, SUSTAINABLE CONTROLS in the processes by which the events occur.

An Event's chance of occurrence when "as-is" process is '99% Good' (1:100 chance for a defect)	Same Event's chance of occurrence if we could improve it's process to '99.99999% Good' (1:100,000 chance for a defect)
Unsafe drinking water 15 minutes each day	Unsafe drinking water 1 minute every seven months
2 short or long landings at most major airports each day	One short or long landing at most major airports every five years
No electricity for 7 hours each month	No electricity for 1 hour every 34 years
20,000 lost articles of mail each hour	7 lost articles of mail each hour
300,000 incorrect invoices each year	102 incorrect invoices each year
2,500 improperly handled cargo claims each year	1 improperly handled cargo claim each year
1,500 inaccurate expense reports each year	1 inaccurate expense report every 2 years

Another example is the chance of building a defect-free Jet Engine. Say a company wants to hire me to build jet engines for them, and they ask me to prove I can build them defect-free. I can use historical data to answer that question. As shown below, there are six main assemblies that must be built separately, then come together, in a final assembly of a jet engine. The historical data shows each assembly's chance of being built without defects. Unfortunately for me, history shows I only have a 28% chance of building a defect-free engine (a 72% chance that my engines won't work). I doubt the company would hire me, based on my history of building engines.

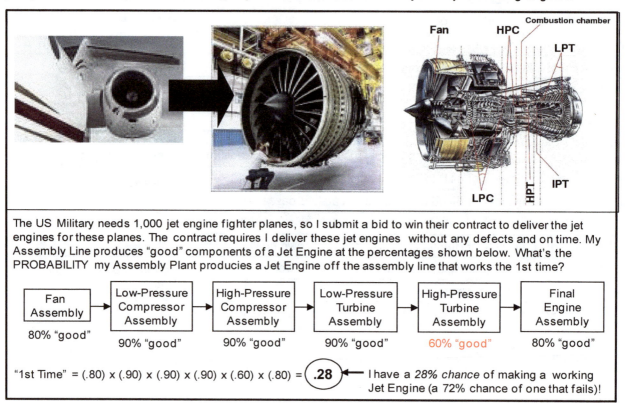

The US Military needs 1,000 jet engine fighter planes, so I submit a bid to win their contract to deliver the jet engines for these planes. The contract requires I deliver these jet engines without any defects and on time. My Assembly Line produces "good" components of a Jet Engine at the percentages shown below. What's the PROBABILITY my Assembly Plant producies a Jet Engine off the assembly line that works the 1st time?

Fan Assembly 80% "good" → Low-Pressure Compressor Assembly 90% "good" → High-Pressure Compressor Assembly 90% "good" → Low-Pressure Turbine Assembly 90% "good" → High-Pressure Turbine Assembly 60% "good" → Final Engine Assembly 80% "good"

"1st Time" = (.80) × (.90) × (.90) × (.90) × (.60) × (.80) = .28 ← I have a 28% chance of making a working Jet Engine (a 72% chance of one that fails)!

We'll use this method when pondering these questions: ① "What are the odds that the Old Testament prophecies against nations could have been fulfilled by chance?", ② "What are the odds that any one person could fulfill the Old Testament prophecies on the Messiah by chance?", ③ "What are the odds that life could have arisen by chance?" ④ "What are the odds that life processes (blood clotting, eyesight) occurred randomly?"

Method #2: use historical data to prove causal relationships This is commonly used in sports, where statistics measure the performance of an athlete or team to try and predict future results. For example, if we have data on how many points a basketball team scores per game, and we have data on how many practice hours they spent in preparing for the games, we can use statistics to see if there is a relationship between these two factors.

The graph to the right shows there is greater than *74% certainty* that the amount of practice time the team puts in each month directly affects how many points they score each week in their games.

We'll use this method when pondering the question:
① "Does the data support that the universe was CAUSED (and not a random occurrence)?"

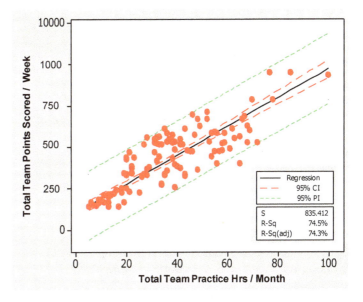

Method #3: use historical data to prove the precision and order in a system By analyzing the historical data from the operation of an event, process or system, we can determine whether that event operates by *random chance* or it is *designed*. How do we do this? We are looking for evidence of: Simplicity and Randomness versus Complexity, Order, and / or Precision.

1) **Simple** = plain; lacks intelligence
2) **Complex** = intricate assembly of parts, units
3) **Order** = correctness according to a set of rules or laws; the state of effectively controlled operation
4) **Precise** = being minutely accurate, rigidly strict (i.e., "tuned" to its standard)
5) **Tuned** = the act of adjusting for proper functioning; to be precise to a known standard (ex: the correct pitch of a musical instrument to achieve its intended function)
6) **Design** = an intended outline or plan; to plan or fashion skillfully, especially for a definite purpose
7) **Random or Unguided** = without plan or order

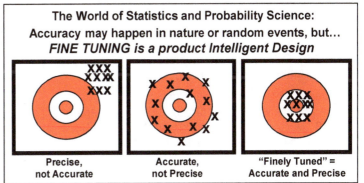

An example of how statistics is used to assess a system or process for whether it behaves *randomly* or is under *intentional control* is by evaluating the precision or stability in its output data with a tool called the "Precision" or "Stability" Factor.

- The "Stability" or "Precision" Factor is simply the ratio of Q_1 to Q_3: $SF = Q_1 / Q_3$
- It is often used in statistics to get an idea of how repeatable or "stable" a process is over time ("over time" means "the data being observed includes all sources of long-term variation that it should be exposed to")
- Q_3, or the 3rd Quartile, also contains within its population the Q_1, or 1st Quartile, data.
- When SF is close to "1": The closer the Q_1 value is to the Q_3 value, the closer the SF is to a value of "1". The closer SF is to "1", the *TIGHTER* (or more "spiked") the histogram is. And the tighter it is, the more *REPEATABLE* or *PRECISE* the process variation is over time. This type of process is what you see in intelligent, intentional design.
- When SF is far from "1": Q_1 is a smaller number than Q_3, so the histogram isn't tight but instead very "flat" or "spread out", which represents a process with a lot of variation. This type of process is what you see with unguided, naturally-occurring systems or processes, and are much harder to control).

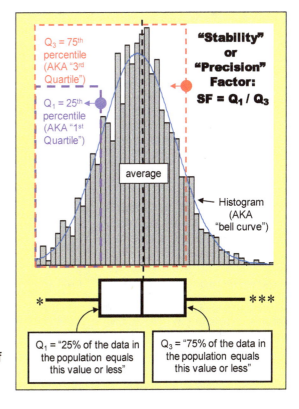

An example of using Stability Factors to assess a system's or process's precision is shown to the right, where two different Telecommunication Call Centers "A" and "B" are being compared over the same period of time for their capability to resolve the same customer issue.

There is nothing different about the "inputs" into the process or system of customer resolution at these two call centers:

1) Both centers have the same customer issues being communicated to their agents manning the phones and taking these customer calls.
2) The time period when this analysis was performed was the same for both call centers.
3) Both centers are located within the same geographic region of the country (same state).

But as the data shows, both visually (looking at each histogram) and analytically (looking at each center's resulting Stability Factor), the capability of these two Call Centers is very different:

Call Center "A": As a collective group, the agents at this center are not only accurate in resolving the customer issues (they average a 95.3% resolution rate, close to the 95% target), they are also precise (SF = .99). Call Center "A" resolves customer issues at a very stable rate and on target.

Call Center "B": As a collective group, the agents at this center are way off the target of 95%, averaging only 80.1% (they are not very accurate). Plus, these agents as a collective group are very imprecise and unstable in resolving the customers' issues, with a SF = .79 and a histogram that is very spread out.

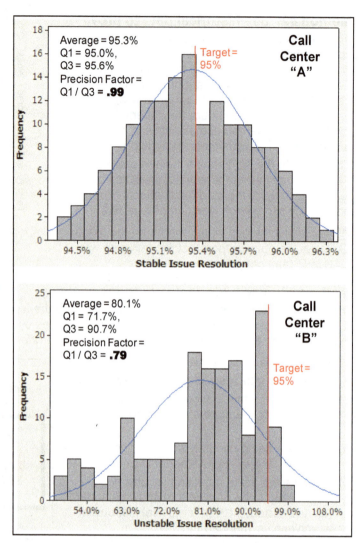

What did we find when we investigated the CAUSE for the huge difference between these centers (notice how we used the Law of Causality… more later)?

Center "A" implemented DESIGN CONTROLS, where each agent follows standard operating procedures for how to resolve customer issues, with weekly follow-up supports from their supervisors when they run into problems.

Center "B" allowed the agents to operate base on each agent's own experience and skill level, with no external controls in place. Solution: implement Center "A" external controls at Center "B".

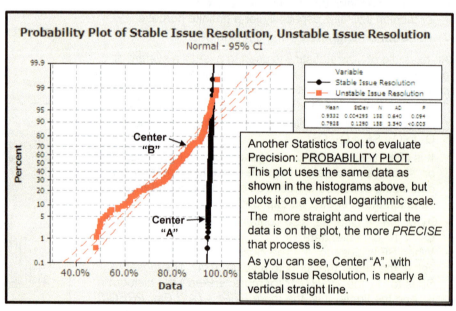

Another Statistics Tool to evaluate Precision: PROBABILITY PLOT. This plot uses the same data as shown in the histograms above, but plots it on a vertical logarithmic scale.

The more straight and vertical the data is on the plot, the more PRECISE that process is.

As you can see, Center "A", with stable Issue Resolution, is nearly a vertical straight line.

We'll use this method when pondering these questions: ① "What's the explanation for the incredible precision of the constants in the universe, which scientists have proven are responsible for sustaining life on earth today?", ② "What's the explanation for the incredible precision in the bat's echolocation system? The giraffe's rete mirabile caroticum?" ③ "What's the explanation for the incredible precision in the cell's functioning as a mini metropolitan 'city'?" ④ "What's the explanation for the incredible precision in the DNA protein (not to mention ATP, and others), which scientists have proven is responsible for the information that defines each living organism?"

ORIGIN OF LIFE:
Probability & Precision point to an Intelligent Designer!

UNIVERSE
Expansion Rate
Electromagnetic Force
Gravitational Force

- Electromagnetic-to-Gravitational force = *precise* to 1×10^{40} [18]
- Gravitational Constant = *precise* to 5 decimals (2.00000) [18]
- Universe Expansion rate = *precise* to 1×10^{55} [18]

MILKY WAY, SOLAR SYSTEM

- Stars: *odds* - only .001% have the right location and have host star properties that could support life [18]
- Milky Way is spiral galaxy = req'd for life to exist (*odds* are only 5% of all galaxies are spiral) [18]

SUN, EARTH

 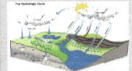 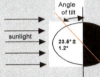

- Earth *precise* tilt = 23.5° ± 1.2° [18]
- Sun's *precise* energy output = constant to 0.1% [18]

BODY, MIND, BRAIN

 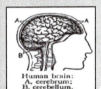

- my brain's *precision*: 1,000x storage capacity of a supercomputer; holds and sorts 10^{14} bits of information [15]
- *odds* that a human being formed by *chance* = $1 \times 10^{2,000,000,000}$ [15]

HEART, EYE, EAR

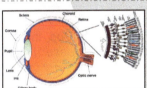

- 100 years of supercomputer processing to simulate the *precision* of what occurs in my eye millions of times every second [15,16]
- no one knows what causes my heart's *precise* "auto-rhythmic" beat 100,000X/day, so I can have life [15]

BLOOD CELL

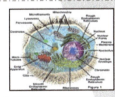 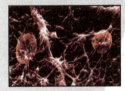

- Blood Clotting: *odds* of getting just the one factor TPA and its activator to work = 1×10^{31} (there are at least 32 others) [16]
- Each cell has an all-powerful city hall (nucleus) surrounded by communication centers, factories, power plants, with the complete DNA for my unique design [15]

DNA, ATP

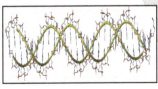 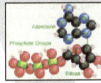

- DNA code formation = 1 in 10^{600} by *chance* [15]
- ATP = mini "motors" 200,000X smaller than a pinhead spinning at 6,000 rpm (faster than any made-made engines) [15]
- *odds* of all proteins needed for life might be formed in one place by random events = $1 \times 10^{40,000}$ [15]

Matter
Atoms, Molecules

Nuclear Forces
Strong nuclear force
Weak nuclear force

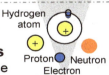

- Strong nuclear force = *precise* to 2% [18]
- neutron-to-proton mass = *precise* to 0.1% [18]
- #electrons-to-protons = *precise* to 1×10^{37} [18]

> "The probability of life originating at random is so utterly miniscule as to make it absurd...
> The favorable properties of physics on which life depends are in every respect deliberate...
> It is therefore almost inevitable that our own measure of intelligence must reflect higher intelligences...
> Even to the limit of God ... such a theory is so obvious that one wonders why it is not widely accepted as being self-evident. The reasons are psychological rather than scientific."
>
> (Fred Hoyle, Cambridge Professor of Astrophysics and Natural Philosophy, 1981)

CHAPTER 5   Genesis 1:26   Who I am: made in the "image of God"   5.1

"Let Us make man in Our ①IMAGE, according to Our ①LIKENESS; let them have dominion over the birds of the air, over the cattle, over all the earth and over every creeping thing that creeps on the earth."

① IMAGE, LIKENESS = Hebrew *"tselem"* = carving, pattern (same word used for graven images in Exodus 20:4); parallel Hebrew terms used for *emphasis*: God Himself is the pattern from which mankind's personhood was carved (directly opposes evolutionary theory of our origins).

- man's spiritual makeup: God is Spirit and not flesh (John 4:24), He is a person, and man is like God: a person.

What does it mean to be a "person"?

1) I have the power to reason (Isaiah 1:18)

Acts 17:2 *"Then Paul, as his custom was, went in to them, and for 3 Sabbaths REASONED with them from the Scriptures, explaining and demonstrating that the Christ had to suffer and rise again from the dead..."*

2) I have a conscience

Romans 7:18,22-23 *"...I know that in me nothing good dwells; for to will is present with me, but how to perform what is good I do not find. For I delight in the law of God according to the inward man, but I see another law in my members, warring against the law of my mind, and bringing me into captivity to the law of sin, which is in my members."*

> Paradox #1: In the Christian life, as I mature in Christ I become less conscious of self and more conscious of my responsibility to others (Phil. 2:3-4). This forgetfulness of self leads to the highest fulfillment of the self. The fact that I find life by losing my own is a fundamental law of life only discovered in Christ (Matt. 16:24-25).

3) I feel a sense of moral responsibility

Mark 12:29-31 *"'The first of all the commandments is: "Hear O Israel, the Lord our God, the Lord is one. And you shall love the Lord your God with all your heart, with all your soul, with all your mind, and with all your strength." ... And the second, like it, is "You shall love your neighbor as yourself.' There is no other commandment greater than these."*

> Paradox #2: My highest self-development is reached when my moral responsibility is first to God and His expectations on me. My highest level of living is reached when my devotion to God and service to people goes from a sense of obligation and duty to a natural result of my inward desire to please Him, not me (John 8:29).

4) I have a capacity for fellowship and communication

- anything that limits or destroys my fellowship with others will impoverish my personality.
    Genesis 2:18 *"...the Lord God said, 'It is not good for man to be alone; I will make him a helper comparable to him."*
- it is my capacity to commune with God that makes me a being created in God's image.
- God's image within me finds its fulfillment in my fellowship with Him as my Creator, since He is the source of the image and He is the perfect embodiment of that which is so imperfectly expressed by me.

> Paradox #3: God, who is all-powerful, all-knowing, all-present, limits Himself by my willingness to spend time with Him. I must *respond* to Him for there to be real communication (Isa. 50:2, Jer. 2:5, Matt. 11:28-30)

What has sin done to the image of God in me?

- I was created in the image of God, but became "recreated" in the image of sin in 2 ways:
1. Romans 5:12 = sin became an integral part of my heritage
2. Romans 3:10 = sin became a very *personal* experience in my life (Jew and Gentile alike: no one is excluded)
- Everyone, regardless of nationality, position or gender, has "de-glorified" God and fallen under condemnation
    Romans 3:23 *"...all have sinned and fallen short of the glory of God."*

Has sin destroyed God's image in me? marred it? or left it largely untouched?

- Galatians 3:28 = Respect for the human personality is based on the fact that *every single person* was created in God's image.
- If God's image was completely destroyed in man, there would be no reason for universally respecting men (the only people with any real worth and dignity would be those who had the image restored through God's grace).
- But God's image wasn't completely destroyed through sin. Mankind after sin was still sacred in God's eyes.
    Genesis 9:6 *"Whoever sheds man's blood, by man his blood shall be shed; for in the image of God He made man."*

- Why we proclaim the gospel: there is enough of God's image left in every person
  1. while an unsaved person can't communicate with God due to sin, each person has the *potential* because God created each person for that purpose.
  2. Each individual person is still held responsible to God for his or her sin

So if sin hasn't completely destroyed that image, what has it done?
- While all people have the capacity to reason, and feel a sense self-consciousness and responsibility, sin has definitely marred mankind's' capacity to communicate with each other and with God.
- At its core: SIN IS SEPARATION (first from God, then from each other)
  Genesis 3:24 *"So He DROVE OUT THE MAN; and He placed cherubim at the east end of the garden of Eden, and a flaming sword which turned every way, to GUARD the way to the tree of life."*
  Isaiah 59:1-2 *"... the Lord's hand is not shortened, that it can't save; nor His ear heavy, that it cannot hear. But your iniquities have SEPARATED you from your God, and your sins have hidden His face from you, so that He will not hear."*
  Genesis 4:6-9 *"...the Lord said to Cain, 'why are you angry? Any why has your countenance fallen? If you do well, will you not be accepted? And if you do not do well, sin lies at the door. And its desire is for you, but you should rule over it.'... it came to pass, when they were in the field, that Cain rose against Abel his brother and killed him. Then the Lord said to Cain, 'Where is Abel your brother?' ...he said, "I do not know. AM I MY BROTHER'S KEEPER?'"*

How does God's image in me become restored?
- Jesus Christ = the "visible image of the invisible God"
  Colossians 1:15,19 *"He is the (EXACT) IMAGE of the invisible God, the firstborn ("preeminent") over all creation. For it pleased the Father that in Him all the FULLNESS should dwell."*
  Hebrews 1:1-3 *"...who being the EXPRESS IMAGE of His person, and upholding all things by the word of His power..."*
- God Almighty, the invisible and unseen, is seen in His Son
  1. Jesus = not only reflects the glory of God, but He is the "exact image" of His person.
  2. Jesus = the "very stamp" of God's nature; the "perfect representation" of God's being
  3. Just as a seal on a document reflects the official seal, so Jesus is the exact reproduction of God the Father
     John 14:9 *"...He who has seen Me has seen the Father. How can you say, 'Show us the Father?'"*
- Jesus Christ = sent into the world in the LIKENESS OF OUR SINFUL FLESH
  1. Jesus came to do what the law couldn't: FREE me from law's penalty for sin (death = separation from God).
     Romans 8:3 *"...what the law could not do in that it was weak through the flesh, GOD DID by sending His own Son in the LIKENESS OF SINFUL FLESH, on account of sin: He condemned sin in the flesh."*
  2. Real Freedom = I am now united with Jesus, living under the guidance of the Spirit who lives within me
     John 14:26 *"...the Comforter, the Holy Spirit, whom the Father will send in My name, He will teach you all things..."*
     Galatians 5:16 *"...walk in the Spirit, and you shall not fulfill the lust of the flesh."*
- God's purpose in uniting me with Jesus = conform me to His image (who is the exact image of God Himself)
  1. I am freed: FROM sin and death (negative), IN the Spirit (positive) = God's marred image in me is restored
  2. To be conformed to the image of His Son = "bear the family likeness"
     Romans 8:29 *"...whom He foreknew He also predestined to be CONFORMED TO THE IMAGE OF HIS SON, that He might be the firstborn among many brethren."*
  3. Being conformed to the image of Jesus (God's exact image) = being conformed to the original image of God in man. CHRIST IN ME is the only hope for restoring God's image (and isn't completed until I *see* Him).
     Colossians 1:27 *"To them God willed to make known what are the riches of the glory of this mystery among the Gentiles: which is CHRIST IN YOU, THE HOPE OF GLORY."*
     Philippians 1:6 *"...He who has begun a good work in you will complete it until the day of Jesus Christ."*
     1John 3:2 *"Beloved, now we are children of God; and it has not yet been revealed what we shall be, but we know that when He is revealed, we shall be like Him, for we shall see Him as He is."*

Am I allowing Christ in me to *mold me* each day towards *His* image?
How much of my lifestyle shows Jesus to those around me?
HOW MUCH OTHERS *SEE* JESUS IN ME = HOW WELL I *KNOW* HIM PERSONALLY

Genesis 10 The "Table of Nations" (Genealogy & Origin of Mankind) 5.2

Darwin's theory on where we came from:	What Darwin's theory implies of our origins:
people are modified descendants of an ancestor we shared with other animals (probably apes)	people are nothing but animals (we are not the preordained goal of any directed purpose)
our distinctive features form different "races": they are due mostly to natural selection acting randomly on small variations over a long time	J.W. Burrow (evolutionist): *"Nature, according to Darwin, was the product of blind chance and a blind struggle, and man is a lonely, intelligent mutation, scrambling with the brutes for his sustenance."*

Darwin (Origin of Species[1]): *"Man bears in his bodily structure clear traces of his descent from some lower form."*

➔ **What is a "race" of people?** Definition: the dictionary defines race as "a class or kind of individuals with common characteristics, interests, appearances, or habits as if derived from a common ancestor."

1) Race is not based on skin color: biologically, a race is thought of as a subspecies, within a given species.
   (a) we have made the term race to apply to skin color, but race does not apply to skin color alone.
   (b) Skin color is the only biological difference in race. Science can't tell what causes the difference in skin cell pigmentation. This superficial distinction is the basis for how we divide mankind.
2) Genetics determines racial characteristics: Modern genetics shows that when a large, interbreeding group is broken into smaller groups which then breed only among themselves (as the Biblical description of the language dispersion at Babel implies), different racial characteristics will arise very rapidly.
   (a) One pair of middle-brown parents can produce all shades, from very white to very black, in *one* generation.
   (b) The racial characteristics which exist today have not evolved. They are simply different combinations of pre-existing (created) genetic (hereditary) information.
3) Genesis 10 details origin of NATIONS: Biblical viewpoint: there is not a black race, white race, yellow race, etc. Genesis 10 is a historical document of the three distinct families of mankind, indicating how the present population of the world originated and spread after the flood.

➔ **Genesis 9:1 (1:18), 9:19, 10:   I descended from Noah's family**

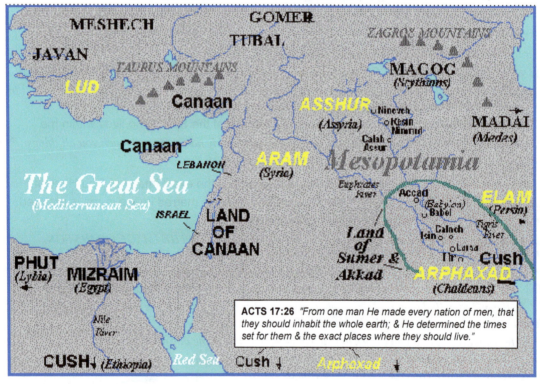

1) Genesis 9:19 we all descended from one of the sons of Noah (Shem, Ham, Japheth), including so-called fossil man, primitive peoples and modern man.

2) Genesis 10:32 Gen. 10 refers to people and nations by genealogies: *persons or families* (ethnology), then *nations or tribes* (ethnography).

3) Genesis 10 Nations settled (geography). They began as hunter-gatherers (live off land as migrated).

ACTS 17:26 "From one man He made every nation of men, that they should inhabit the whole earth; & He determined the times set for them & the exact places where they should live."

- The descendants of Japheth (oldest): the Greeks, Romans, Spanish, Celts, Scythians, and Medes ➔ They migrated into Europe and parts of Central Asia. Some people groups merged to form one nation, as did the Persians (Shem) and the Medes (Japheth), which later became the Medo-Persian empire.
- The descendants of Shem: the Hebrews, Persians and Assyrians ➔ They mostly remained in the Middle East.
- The descendants of Ham (youngest): the Egyptians, Ethiopians, Canaanites, Phoenicians and Hittites ➔ His descendants were the 1st to fill the earth (early settlers of Africa, Asia, Australia, South Pacific, and Americas).

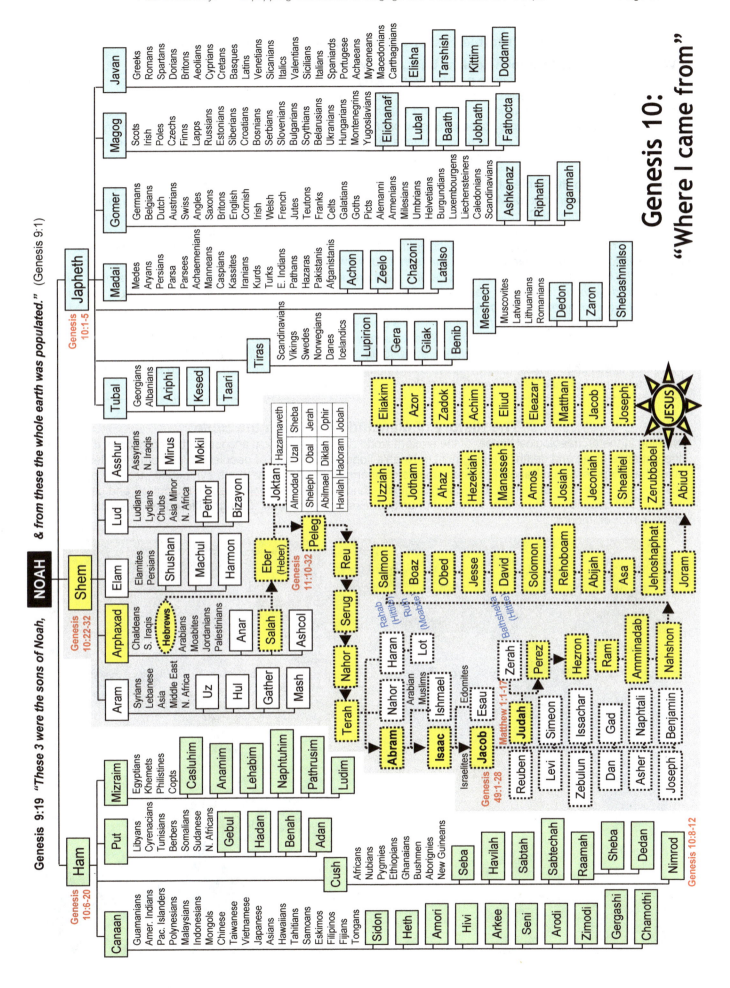

The Incredible Historicity of the Bible's Table of Nations

William F. Albright, PhD John Hopkins Univ., renowned Archaeologist: *"It stands absolutely alone in ancient literature, without a remote parallel even among the Greeks, where we find the closest approach to a distribution of peoples in genealogical framework. But among the Greeks the framework is mythological. In view of the inextricable confusion of racial and national strains in the ancient near East it would be quite impossible to draw up a simple scheme which would satisfy all scholars; no one system could satisfy all the claims made on the basis of ethnic predominance, ethnographic diffusion, language, physical type, culture, historical tradition. The Table of Nations remains an astonishingly accurate document."*

Martin Luther on the Table of Nations: *"Whenever I read these names, I think of the wretched state of the human race. If it were not for Moses, what would you know about the origin of man?...Hence one must consider this chapter of Genesis a mirror in which to discern what we human beings are, namely, creatures so marred by sin that we have no knowledge of our own origin, not even of God Himself, our Creator, unless the Word of God reveals these sparks of divine light to us from afar. Then what is more futile than boasting of one's wisdom, riches, power, and other things that pass away completely? Therefore we have reason to regard the Holy Bible highly and to consider it a most precious treasure. This very chapter, even though it is considered by many to be full of dead words, has in it the thread that is drawn from the first world to the middle and to the end of all things. From Adam the promise concerning Christ is passed on to Seth; from Seth to Noah; from Noah to Shem; and from Shem to this Eber, from whom the Hebrew nation received its name as the heir for whom the promise about the Christ was intended in preference to all other peoples of the whole world. This knowledge the Holy Scriptures reveal to us. Those who are without them live in error, uncertainty, and boundless ungodliness; for they have no knowledge about who they are and whence they came."*
(Martin Luther, Luther's Works, Vol. 2, pp. 2-2.)

The History of Mankind flows from the *Bible*

Nothing in the archaeological history of the ancient world denies the biblical account of the creation of the world, the entrance of sin and death, the judgment of Noah's flood, and the rise of people groups from their descendants after their dispersal from Babel. The descendants of Shem, Ham and Japheth are evidenced, not only by Biblical history, but archeological, anthropological, biological, ethnographical, ethnological, etymological, and geological history. The question is not one of worth but of uniqueness of contribution. Though differences exist, one group is not superior or inferior.

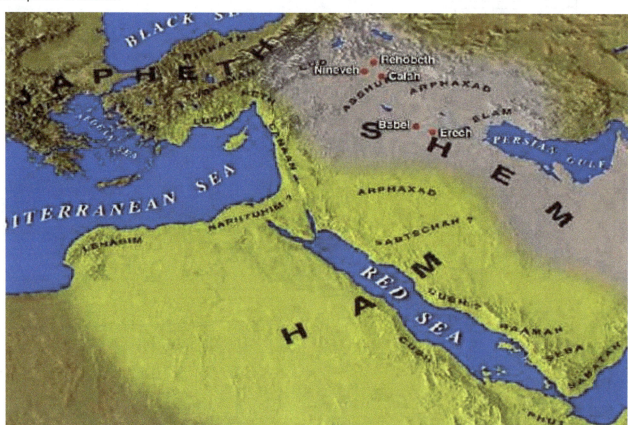

Genesis 10:22-32 SHEM[27] or *Sem* - means *named or renown* (father of Semitic races - *Shemites*)

The sons of Shem were:

(1) Elam *"eternity"* (sons = Shushan, Machul and Harmon) - Elamites, Persians

(2) Asshur *"a step"* or *"strong"* (sons = Mirus and Mokil) - Assyrians/Northern Iraqis

(3) Arphaxad *"I shall fail"* (sons = Shelach, Anar and Ashcol) - Chaldeans/Southern Iraqis, Hebrews/ Israelites/ Jews[1], Arabians/Bedouins, Moabites/ Jordanians/ Palestinians

(4) Lud *"strife"* (sons = Pethor and Bizayon) - Ludim, Lubim, Ludians, Ludu, Lydians, Chubs, related groups in Asia Minor and North Africa);

(5) Aram *"exalted"* (sons = Uz, Chul, Gather and Mash) - Aramaeans/Syrians, Lebanese

- Noah's sons kept together at first, then broke up into small groups and eventually arrived from the east in the southern Mesopotamian Plain (**Genesis 11:2**). The descendants of Elam, the first born son of Shem, were the first people to enter Mesopotamia.

- Susa, the capital city of the Elamites (Shemitic Elamites), gave rise to other early cities like Al-Ubaid (which later gave rise to Hamitic settlements—including the Sumerian civilization) and Jemdet Nasr. Recent excavations have provided very strong evidence of direct cultural links between some of the earliest cities in Babylonia and the lowest layers uncovered at Susa. These people established themselves first in the south and then spread toward the north, but without losing the cultural links. There are no known modern descendants of the Elamites.

- Other excavations have shown that one of the first Hamitic groups, the Sumerians, gave rise to considerable cultural advance and power in that region. Other people groups known very early included the Japhethites, noted especially for their fairness of skin, in the hill country east of the Tigris. Soon the great Babylonian empire arose.

- The descendants of Shem are often called **Semites**, a term first used in the late 18th century for peoples listed in the Bible as descended from Shem. Today the term Semite refers to peoples who speak any of the Semitic languages, including the ancient peoples who inhabited Babylonia. Modern peoples speaking Semitic languages include the Arabs and Jews. Shem's descendants are well documented. Modern day Arabs and Jews trace their lineage to Shem. Many Arabic nomad tribes still claim they descended from Shem.

- Centuries before the Christian Era, many ancient Semitic populations migrated from Arabia to Mesopotamia, the coasts of the Mediterranean Sea, and the Nile River delta. Jews and other Semites settled in Judea (southern Palestine). Today, the Semitic-speaking peoples are concentrated in the Middle East and northern Africa.

The Hebrews descended from Eber (Heber), a great-grandsons of Shem.

1) Both Sunnite Arabs and Jews are Semites *and* Hebrews.

2) **Genesis 11:26** = Abram (Abraham): born 6 generations after Heber– he was both a **Hebrew** and a **Semite**, born of the line of Heber and Shem (people interchange "Jew" and Israelite, though Abraham was not an Israelite or a Jew. The word "Jew" is not used in the Bible until nearly 1,000 years after Abraham).

3) **Genesis 12-15** = God forms His covenant promises with Abram through His grace as Abram exercises his faith in God's promises (Romans 4:1-4).

4) **Genesis 16, 21:9-21**= Sunnite Arabs (specifically Arabian Muslims): consider themselves to be descendants of Ishmael, calling themselves Ishmaelites, and thus are both Semitic and Hebrews (Ishmael born 1st of Abraham).

5) **Genesis 17:18-21, 21:1-8** = Isaac born of Abraham after Ishmael, but God forms His covenant with Isaac.

6) **Genesis 25:21-34** = Isaac had twin sons named Esau and Jacob. Esau was firstborn, and so had the right to inheritance (as was custom), but instead sold his birthright to Jacob during a time of hunger. Esau's name was changed to Edom, and Jacob's name was changed to Israel. The descendants of Esau (Edom) were called Edomites, and the descendants of Jacob (Israel) were called *Israelites*. Jacob fathered twelve sons which became the twelve tribes of Israel (Genesis 29:31-35, 30:1-24, 35:22-26)..

7) **Genesis 49:8-12** = JUDAH (Hebrew *"Yehudah"*): one of Jacob's (Israel's) children - His descendants were called Yehudim ("Judahites"). In Greek the name is *Ioudaioi* ("Judeans"). Most all Bible translations use the word **"Jew"** (it's a modern, shortened form of the word "Judahite"). A "Jew" in the Old Testament would be a "Judahite;" and a "Jew" in the New Testament would be a "Judean."

8) **Genesis 26:34, 27:1-45, 28:1-9** = A bitter rivalry between the descendants of Esau and Jacob continued throughout history, and as they lived in close proximity for hundreds of years, their hatred worsened.

- The Romans called the *Edomites Idumeans*, separate from Israelites, when they lived in Palestine together.
- The Romans later divided Palestine into districts, with Idumea (land of Edomites) being one of the districts. As the Roman Empire faded, Idumea fell to an Ishmaelite Moslem army led by Caliph Umar in 8 A.D.
- Historians suggest the remaining Edomites embraced Islam at that time and remained in the land, blending with the Arabs, and uniting against the Israelites.

9) Jerusalem soon became a focal point for the Moslems, being the third most holy city of Islam, after the cities of Mecca and Medina (though Jerusalem is never mentioned in the Koran, it is mentioned over 800X in the Bible).

10) By 691 A.D., the Mosque of Omar (also called the "Dome of the Rock") was completed on the Temple Mount, where Moslems/Muslims believe that Mohammed ascended to heaven from. The Arabic term for the holy place is "al-Haram as-Sharif" meaning "The Noble Sanctuary."

11) To Israelites and Jews, Jerusalem was the city of the great prophets and the capital of the Kingdom of Israel and Judah under King David and his son King Solomon. The first and second temples were the center of worship until the destruction of the city by the Romans in 70 A.D. Christians revere the city as the place where Jesus Christ taught in the temple, and was later crucified.

The Tower of Babel - Genesis 11:1-9

- The rulers of Babylon attempted to avert dispersal of the people by proposing the building of a monument as a visible rallying point on the flat plain of Mesopotamia.

- Scripture and historical texts note that the tower of Babel, the building of which Nimrod (a Sumerian) supervised, was to have two great significances:
1) The city of Babel would be the metropolis of the world and unite its inhabitants under the rule of Nimrod.
2) The tower was to be a monument to man to stand as a symbol of Babel.

- Given the present knowledge of Babylonian history, **Genesis 11** has a solid historical foundation in early Mesopotamia. Nimrod hoped to prevent the people from scattering abroad into colonies as God intended, thus bringing upon themselves a judgment which led to confusion of the languages and rapid scattering throughout the earth. Babel means *confusion*.

- Urbanization did not occur until after the dispersal of languages. The history of linguistic development and settlement patterns in Mesopotamia support this. There are many unclassified and isolated languages throughout the world, such as Basque, Ainu and Ticuna, testifying to the widespread language distribution at Babel.

- From here the three families of man populate the earth.

Genesis 10:6-20 HAM[27] Also *Cham or Kham.* Literal meanings are *passionate, hot, burnt or dark*

(father of the Mongoloid and Negroid races - *Hamites*). His four sons were:

(1) Canaan "down low" (sons were Zidon, Heth, Amori, Gergashi, Hivi, Arkee, Seni, Arodi, Zimodi and Chamothi) - also *Canaanites, Cana, Chna, Chanani, Chanana, Canaana, Kana, Kenaanah, Kena'ani, Kena'an, Kn'nw, Kyn'nw, Kinnahu, Kinahhi, Kinahni, Kinahna, Kinahne* (Mongols, Chinese, Taiwanese, Thais, Vietnamese, Japanese, Asians, Eskimos, American Indians, Malaysians, Indonesians, Filipinos, Hawaiians, Polynesians, Tahitians, Guamanians, Samoans, Fijians, Tongans, Pacific Islanders and related groups);

(2) Cush "black" (sons were Seba, Havilah, Sabta, Raama and Satecha) - also *Chus, Kush, Kosh* (Nubians, Ethiopians, Ghanaians, Africans, Bushmen, Pygmies, Australian Aborigines, New Guineans);

(3) Mizraim "double straits" (sons were Lud, Anom, Pathros, Chasloth and Chaphtor) - also *Misraim, Mitzraim, Mizraite, Mitsrayim* (Egyptians, Khemets, Copts, other related groups);

(4) Phut "a bow" (sons were Gebul, Hadan, Benah and Adan) - also *Punt, Puta, Put, Puni, Phoud, Pul, Fula, Putaya, Putiya, Libia, Libya* (Libyans, Cyrenacians, Tunisians, Berbers, Somalians, Sudanese, North Africans).

- Tribes in other parts of Africa, Arabia and Asia, aboriginal groups in Australia, native Pacific Islanders, American Indians and Eskimos were birthed from descendants of Canaan, Cush, Mizraim and Phut.

- Looking at history, whichever region is considered, Africa, Europe, Australia, or America, the major migrations have always been from Asia. In every area of the world where Japhethites have subsequently settled, they have always been preceded by Hamites. This pattern applies in every continent.

- In early historic times the circumstance seems always to be true, the earliest fossil remains of man being Mongoloid or Negroid in character and in head shape, whereas those that came last belong to the family of Japheth (Caucasoid). If you study ancient history and technological achievements, which were in many ways the equal of, or superior of, much that we have today, were founded and carried to a high technological proficiency by Hamitic people, showing an amazing adaptability to the world in which they live.

- Their achievements were exploited by Japhetic and Semitic peoples, who became great scientific discoverers. The Hamitic migrations indicate they sought a way of life, not an understanding or a control of nature beyond what was immediately useful.

- **Canaanites:**

a) Ham's first born son was Canaan. **Genesis 10:15-19** identifies a distinctive characteristic of the sons of Canaan: they liked to spread out. The Canaanites are specifically mentioned as migrating far and wide, and afterward the families of the Canaanites were spread abroad.

The territory of the Canaanites extended from Sidon as you go toward Gerar, as far as Gaza; as you go toward Sodom and Gomorrah and Admah and Zeboiim, as far as Lasha." History indicates they did have a propensity for sprawl. The descendants of Canaan would later make up the vast populations of Asia, Africa and the Western Hemisphere.

b) **Zidon (or Sidon)** = he and his descendants settled on the Mediterranean coast of present-day Lebanon, then known as the land of Canaan. The Sidonians called themselves Kena'ani, or **Canaanites**.

c) The Canaanites spoke a Semitic language, probably adopted from a large migration of Semites who came from land and sea, and introduced their language and a sophisticated maritime technology about 1800 B.C.

d) Historians suggest these Canaanites succumbed to racial and linguistic intermixture with the invading Semites, which led to the loss of their own ethnic predominance, as evidenced by modern excavations.

e) They eventually moved westward and occupied a very narrow coastal strip of the east Mediterranean, building new cities, and establishing significant trade with neighboring nations.

f) The Israelite name for **"Canaan"** came to mean "traders," though some suggest the name Canaan is from the Hebrew name *Hurrian*, meaning "land of red purple." The Canaanites were known for their red and purple cloth (a purple dye was extracted from murex snails found near the shores of Palestine, a method now lost).

g) The Greeks called the land of Canaan **"Phoenicia"** which meant "purple." The Phoenicians became a nation of great trade, language, and culture. Phoenician, Hebrew and Moabite were a group of west Semitic languages, all dialects from Canaan, as referred to in **Isaiah 19:18**.

h) The writing system of the Phoenicians is the source of the writing systems of nearly all of Europe, including Greek, Russian, Hebrew, Arabic and the Roman alphabet.

i) The Phoenician empire fell under Hellenistic rule after being conquered by Alexander the Great about 332BC. In 64BC the name of Phoenicia disappeared entirely, becoming a part of the Roman providence of Syria.

j) At the beginning of the Christian era, remaining Phoenicians were the first to accept the Christian faith after the Jews. Zidon's name is still perpetuated in the modern-day city of Sidon (Saidoon is the Phoenician name, Saida in Arabic) in southern Lebanon.

- **Native American Indians:**

a) Evidence for migrations into the Americas comes from research on living **American Indian** populations, which includes data from Mitochondrial DNA (DNA that is passed down from a mother to her children from one generation to the next intact). DNA haplogroups (haplogroups are used in DNA tests for markers that give a broad or regional picture; haplotypes are one person's results on various DNA tests). These studies have consistently shown similarities (deep ancestry) between American Indians and recent populations in Asia, Siberia and northern Scandinavia. These groups include the Lapps in northern Europe/Scandinavia, the Chukchi and Yukaghir in Siberia, plus Indians and Eskimos/Aleuts throughout Canada and America.

b) There is genetic relationship between early Taiwanese populations and southeast Asian, Oceanic (South Pacific) and Native American descendants. Ancient American Indian skeletal remains show a range of physical attributes (round-headed) suggesting separate migrations of different populations from Asia *and* the South Pacific, representing 95 percent of all modern American Indian populations. What of the other five percent?

c) There are exceptions. For example, the Siouan family of tribes (**Sioux Indians**), the popular red-skinned tribes having a long-head shape similar to that of early Italic peoples in Europe. They are thought to be descendants of Canaanites who intermarried with Indo-Europeans while migrating across Europe, and subsequently sailing to America. Settling along the eastern shores of America, and according to tradition, they populated the Carolinas, then migrated to the regions of Louisiana, Mississippi, Missouri, and eventually Minnesota and the Dakotas.

d) Many tribes had fortified villages similar to ancient Canaanites (who lived along the Mediterranean coast, including parts of Egypt and the Jordan Valley). Archeological evidence shows they constructed towns and cities with pyramids and vast road systems throughout the Mississippi Valley. With them came a tradition that is thought to be a reference to the wives of Noah and his three sons. Four women are identified as "mothers of origin" whose names (possibly Canaanite) have been preserved down through the generations.

e) Additionally, there are striking similarities between the languages of ancient Egypt and those of the Native Americans that inhabited the areas around Louisiana about the time of Christ. Epigraphy experts have stated that the languages of the Attakapa, Tunica and Chitimacha tribes have affinities with Nile Valley (Egyptian) languages involving certain words associated with Egyptian trading communities of 2,000 years ago.

- **Aztecs:**

a) Many American Indian people groups migrated southwest into Oklahoma, Texas, New Mexico and eventually Mexico, establishing the powerful **Aztec** tribes with their beautiful fortified cities, integrating with the **Mayas** (who had been there hundreds of years before, and thought of the Aztecs as barbarians).

b) Likely there was a mixing of cultures as they migrated, as there was no conquest of the Maya world by the Aztecs; that title would be given to the Spaniards in the late 17th century.

c) The Aztec's traditions and legends are largely ignored by modern scholars as myths and fables. The Aztecs, according to their own legends, departed from a region in the north called Chicomoztoc, a region that is today the areas of Texas, Oklahoma and New Mexico. Later establishing a city known as Aztlan, somewhere in north or northwest Mexico (now lost), their tribal name *Aztec* was born. Being nomadic, they eventually reached the valley of Mexico in the 12th century A.D.

d) They were known as fearless warriors and pragmatic builders who raised an enormous city called Tenochtitlan, their capital city (now Mexico City).

e) They later called themselves "Mexica" (where Mexico is derived). Their language, Nahuatl, was linguistically related to other native language groups throughout the U.S. southwest and northern Mexico. Linguists note, for instance, the Shoshoni language in the Utah-Nevada region was understood by all the tribes from Mexico, without difficulty. Other related tribes included the Paiute, Hopi, Pima, Yaqui/Apache, Tepehuan, Kiowas and Mayos.

f) Catholic missionaries in the 1850's established that all of those peoples were of one language family. While there are other examples of language similarities, studies of the native languages of the Americas show them to be extremely diverse, representing nearly 200 distinct families, some consisting of a single isolated language.

- **Pacific Islanders:**

a) They have a diverse and unique history. These oceanic peoples of the South Pacific, whom we know as Polynesians, Tahitians, Samoans, Fijians, Tongans and others, have their roots in southern China.

b) Prior to the Mongols establishing themselves in southern China, there were migrations of Negroid peoples from east Africa and the Sahara. Many African cultures kept documents and ancient texts, as well as strong oral history and legends, of migrations to ancient China from Africa.

c) Mongol groups later migrated into southern China, resulting in a mixing of cultures. Southern China is thought to have first come into being out of the mixture of Mongoloids and Negroids. These peoples were likely driven out by other aggressive Mongoloids. Being master seafarers, they sailed into Polynesia and the surrounding region, populating the islands of the South Pacific.

- **Hittites:**

a) Most of the peoples who are classified as **Mongoloid**, who settled the Far East, have been difficult to fit into the Table of Nations. Evidence shows they are Hamitic, although some have reasoned that the Chinese were of Japhetic stock, and the Japanese were either Japhetic or Semitic. There are two names which provide clues.

b) Two of Canaan's sons, *Heth* (Hittites) and *Sin* (Sinites), are presumed to be the progenitors of Chinese and Mongoloid stock. The **Hittites** were known as the *Hatti* or *Chatti*.

c) In Egyptian monuments the Hittite peoples were depicted with prominent noses, full lips, high check-bones, hairless faces, varying skin color from brown to yellowish and reddish, straight black hair and dark brown eyes.

d) The term *Hittite* in Cuneiform (the earliest form of writing invented by the Sumerians) appears as *Khittae* representing a once powerful nation from the Far East known as the *Khitai*, and has been preserved through the centuries in the more familiar term, *Cathay*. The Cathay were Mongoloids, a part of early Chinese stock.

e) There are links between the Hittites and Cathay, for example, their modes of dress, their shoes with turned-up toes, their manner of doing their hair in a pigtail, and so forth. Representations show them to have possessed high cheekbones, and craniologists have observed that they had common characteristics of Mongoloids.

- **Chinese = Sin (or Seni)**, a brother of Heth, has many occurrences in variant forms in the Far East.

a) There is one significant feature concerning the likely mode of origin of Chinese civilization. The place most closely associated by the Chinese themselves with the origin of their civilization is the capital of Shensi, namely, *Siang-fu* (Father Sin). Siang-fu appears in Assyrian records as *Sianu*. Today, Siang-fu can be loosely translated, "Peace to the Western Capital of China."

b) The Chinese have a tradition that their *first* king, Fu-hi or Fohi (Chinese Noah), made his appearance on the Mountains of Chin, was surrounded by a rainbow after the world had been covered with water, and sacrificed animals to God (corresponding to the Genesis record).

c) Sin himself was the third generation from Noah, a circumstance which would provide the right time interval for the formation of early Chinese culture. In addition, the Miao tribe of southwest China had a tradition similar to the Genesis account, even before they met Christian missionaries.

d) According to their tradition, God destroyed the whole world by a flood because of the wickedness of man, and Nuah (Noah) the righteous man and his wife, their three sons, Lo Han (Ham), Lo Shen (Shem), and Jah-hu (Japheth) survived by building a very broad ship and taking on it pairs of animals.

e) Those who came from the Far East to trade were called Sinæ (Sin) by the Scythians. Ptolemy, a Greek astronomer, called China the land of *Sinim or Sinæ*. Reference to the *Sinim* in **Isaiah 49:12** notes they came "from afar," specifically *not* from the north and *not* from the west. Arabs called China *Sin, Chin, Mahachin, Machin*. The Sinæ were spoken of as a people in the remotest parts of Asia.

f) For the Sinæ, the most important town was Thinæ, a great trading emporium in western China. The city Thinæ is now known as Thsin or Tin, and it lies in the province of Shensi. Much of China was ruled by the *Sino-Khitan* Empire (960-1126A.D.), which Beijing became the southern capital. The Sinæ became independent in western China, their princes reigning there for some 650 years before they finally gained dominion over the whole land.

g) In 3rd century B.C., the dynasty of Tsin became supreme. The word Tsin itself came to have the meaning of purebred. This word was assumed as a title by the Manchu Emperors and was changed into the form Tchina. From there the term was brought into Europe as *China,* from the Ch'in or Qin dynasty (255-206B.C.).

h) The Greek word for China is Kina (Latin is Sina). As well, Chinese and surrounding languages are part of the *Sino-Tibetan* language family. Years ago, American newspapers regularly carried headlines with reference to the conflict between the Chinese and Japanese in which the ancient name reappeared in its original form, the *Sino-Japanese* war. *Sinology* refers to the study of Chinese history.

i) With respect to the Cathay people, it would make sense to suppose that the remnants of the Hittites, after the destruction of their empire, traveled towards the east and settled among the Sinites who were relatives, contributing to their civilization, and thus becoming the ancestors of the Asian people groups. Still others migrated throughout the region and beyond, making up present-day Mongoloid races in Asia and the Americas.

j) The evidence strongly suggests that Ham's grandsons, Heth (Hittites/Cathay) and Sin (Sinites/China), are the ancestors of the Mongoloid peoples.

- **Africans =** There are many native African tribes which trace themselves back traditionally to Ham.

a) The Yoruba, who are black skinned, for example, claim to be descendants of Nimrod, son of Cush, whereas the Libyans, who are much lighter skinned, are traced back to Phut (Phut is the Hebrew name for Libya). Ethiopians still trace their ancestry back to Cush.

b) The Egyptians were descendants of Mizraim (the Hebrew name for Egypt). Ancient Egyptians are considered the greatest technicians in all human history. Other African groups trace their roots back to Ham or one of his descendants, so it is suggested that all of Africa was initially settled by members of this one Hamitic family.

c) In the course of time, some of these people groups had migrations to Australia, Melanesia, New Guinea and the surrounding region. For example, there is evidence of similarities in the form of horticulture found in the Sahara and in Papua New Guinea. Recent studies from archaeology have discovered there was once extensive trade between east Africa and New Guinea.

d) The evidence appears to point consistently in the same direction, supporting that not only Africa with its black races, but the Far East, the Americas, Australia and the Oceanic nations with their colored races were all descendants of Ham.

e) The Hamitic people were the first to reach the distant lands of the world, preparing the way for the future. Their inventions and discoveries made a significant impact on the world, and provided inspiration for those to follow.

Genesis 10:1-8 JAPHETH[27] or *Diphath*. Means *opened, enlarged, light* (father of the Caucasoid/Indo-Europoid, Indo-European, Indo-Germanic, or Indo-Aryan races - *Japhethites*). His seven sons were:

(1) Gomer "complete" (sons were Ashkenaz, Riphath and Togarmah) - Caledonians, Picts, Milesians, Umbrians, Helvetians, Celts, Galatians, Ostrogoths, Visigoths, Goths, Vandals, Scandinavians, Jutes, Teutons, Franks, Burgundians, Alemanni, Armenians, Germans, Belgians, Dutch, Luxembourgers, Liechensteiners, Austrians, Swiss, Angles, Saxons, Britons, English, Cornish, Irish, Welsh, French.

(2) Magog "land of God" (sons were Elichanaf, Lubal, Baath, Jobhath and Fathochta) - Scythians, Scots, Irish, Russians, Belarusians, Ukrainians, Hungarians, Finns, Lapps, Estonians, Siberians, Yugoslavians, Croatians, Bosnians, Montenegrins, Serbians, Slovenians, Slovakians, Bulgarians, Poles, Czechs.

(3) Madai "middle land" (sons were Achon, Zeelo, Chazoni and Lotalso) - Medes, Aryans, Persians, Parsa, Parsees, Achaemenians, Manneans, Caspians, Kassites, Iranians, Kurds, Turks, East Indians, Pathans, Hazaras, Afghanistan, Pakistan, Azerbaijan, Khazachstan, Turkmenistan, Uzbekistan, Tajikstan and Kyrgyzstan.

(4) Javan "miry" (sons were Elisha, Tarshish, Kittim and Dodanim) - Grecians, Greeks, Elysians, Spartans, Dorians, Britons, Aeolians, Achaeans, Myceneans, Macedonians, Carthaginians, Cyprians, Cretans, Basques, Latins, Venetians, Sicanians, Italics, Romans, Valentians, Sicilians, Italians, Spaniards, Portugese.

(5) Tubal "brought" (sons were Ariphi, Kesed and Taari) - Georgians, Albanians, others.

(6) Meshech "drawing out" (sons were Dedon, Zaron and Shebashnialso) - Muscovites, Latvians, Lithuanians, Romanians.

(7) Tiras "desire" (sons were Benib, Gera, Lupirion and Gilak) - Pelasgians, Scandinavians, Varangians, Vikings, Swedes, Norwegians, Danes, Icelandics.

- The Japhetic people are, in general, the peoples of India and Europe (Indo-European stock), with which any demographer is familiar.

- **Celts:**

a) Celtic race descended from Gomer, though history suggests modern Celts descended from Gomer and Magog. Archaeologists and ethnologists agree that the first Indo-European group to spread across Europe were Celts.

b) The Irish Celts claim to be to the descendants of Magog, while the Welsh Celts claim to be to the descendants of Gomer. Irish chronicles, genealogies, plus an extensive number of manuscripts which have survived from ancient times, reveal their roots.

c) The **Irish** were descendants of **Scythians**, also known as Magogians. Archaeological evidence shows that both the Celts (from Gomer) and Scythians (from Magog) mingled cultures at their earliest stages. Russian and eastern European excavations plainly reveal the blending of these two groups. Their geographical locations (what is now eastern Europe, southern Russia and Asia Minor) were referred to by the Greeks under the name of Celto-Scythae, which was populated by the Celts to the south and west, and the Scythians to the north.

d) The ancient Greeks first called the northern peoples by the general name of Scythae; but when they became acquainted with the nations in the west, they began to call them by the different names of Celts, including the Celto-Scythae. Celts and **Scythians** were considered essentially the same peoples, based on geography, though many independent tribes of Celts and Scythians existed.

e) The Latins called them "Galli," and the Romans referred to them as "**Gauls**." Later names used by Greeks were the Galatai or Galatae, Getae, Celtae and Keltoi. In the third century before Christ (about 280 B.C.), the Gauls invaded Rome and were ultimately repelled into Greece, where they migrated into the north-central part of Asia Minor (Anatolia). Known as fiercely independent peoples, they conquered the indigenous peoples of that region and established their own independent kingdom. The land became known as **Galatia**. The Apostle Paul wrote his famous epistle to their descendants, the Galatians. Jewish historian Flavius Josephus wrote that the Galatians or Gauls of his day (93A.D.) were previously called Gomerites.

f) Early Celtic tribes (from Gomer) settled in Europe, prior to contact with Scythians. France was called Gaul, after the Celtic descendants of Gomer, whom ceded the territory to Romans and Germanic/Teutonic Franks (whence *France*) in the 4th century A.D. Northwest Spain is called Galicia to this day.

g) Some of the Gomerites migrated further to what is now called **Wales**. The Welsh claim their ancestors "first landed on the Isle of Britain from France, about three hundred years after the flood." The Celtic language survives today mainly in the two variants of Welsh and Irish/Scottish Gaelic. The Welsh call their language Gomeraeg (after Gomer). The Celts of today are descendants of Gomer, and of the blended tribes of Magog and Gomer.

- **Germans:**

a) Present-day Germanic people groups are descendants of both Japheth and Shem, and there are several references from recent and ancient history. Recent history records the descendants of Gomer migrated and settled in the region that is now northern Europe (Germany and Scandinavia).

b) These tribes became the Goths, Ostrogoths, Visigoths, Teutons and Burgundians, descendants of some of the first peoples to migrate to northern Europe from ancient times—the Askaeni. The Askaeni were descendants of Ashkenaz, son of Gomer, son of Japheth. When the Askaeni arrived in northern Europe, they named the land Ascania after themselves, which later translated Scandia, then **Scandinavia**.

c) Later in history, we find the Askaeni being referred to as Sakasenoi, which became Sachsen, and finally Saxon. The **Saxons** played an large part in European and English history. Ashkenaz has been one of the most well preserved names throughout European history.

d) Semitic peoples also migrated to central Europe (southern Germany, Austria and Switzerland). These people were the descendants of Asshur, son of Shem, where Germans originated. Asshur is well known in history as the father of the **Assyrians**.

e) The land of the Assyrians was called "Athur," which became "Tyr" or "Teiw" by early Germanic peoples. Later, the name changes to "Ziu." Germans likely derived their identity and language from these ancestral names.

f) The earliest known name of the German language was called "*Diu*tisc," which later becomes Deutsch (which Germans call themselves today). Deutschland (land of the Deutsch) could be called Asshurland. The Romans referred to the *Deu*tschen as *Teu*tons.

g) The term "German" comes from Latin (Roman) sources. The Assyrians occupied a Mesopotamian city on the lower Tigris River called "Kir" and placed captive slaves there (also referenced in **2 Kings 16:9**). The city was populated by the Assyrians for years, and the inhabitants were known as "Kir-man." The Assyrians (Kerman) were driven from their land shortly after their fall about 610B.C. They migrated into central Europe where they were called "German" or "Germanni," a general name used by the Romans to represent all Assyrian tribes.

h) The known Assyrian tribes were the Khatti (also Hatti, Hessians)—Chatti is still the Hebrew term for German, and Khatti was also used by the Romans to represent Germanic tribes; the Akkadians (Latins called them Quadians); the Kassites (or Cossaei); and the Almani (or Halmani, Allemani was the Latin name).

- **Russians:**

a) Ancient peoples known as the Sarmatians (not to be confused with the Samaritans) and Alans lived in the area around the Caspian Sea from about 900B.C. Sarmatian and Alani tribes were later called **Scythians** (Slavs of today), who were also known as the Rukhs-As, Rashu, Rasapu, Rosh, Ros, and Rus.

b) There is no debate that they were the inhabitants of southern Russia, and the existence of the names of rivers, such as the "Ros," refer to Rus populations.

c) About 739 A.D., the word Rus appears again in eastern Europe, from a different source. Finnish peoples referred to Swedes as "Ruotsi," "Rotsi" or "Rus" in contrast with Slavic peoples, which was derived from the name of the Swedish maritime district in Uppland, "Roslagen," and its inhabitants, called "Rodskarlar."

d) Rodskarlar or Rothskarlar meant "rowers" or "seamen." Those Swedish conquerors (called *Varangians* [**Vikings**] by the Slavs), settled in eastern Europe, adopted the names of local tribes, integrated with the Slavs, and eventually the word "Rusi," "Rhos" or "Rus" came to refer to the inhabitants.

e) Russia means "land of the Rus." Scholars continue to debate the origin of the word Rus, which has derived from two sources: the *Ruotsi* or *Rhos*, the Finnish names for the Swedes, and earlier from the Scythians called the *Rashu* or *Rosh* in southern Russia.

- **Medes and Persians:**

a) The Aryans first come into historical view about a thousand years before Christ, invading India and threatening Babylonia. Historians of old reference an Aryan chief called Cyaxeres, king of the Medes and Persians.

b) The Medes and Persians seem to have been tribes of one nation, more or less united under the rule of Cyaxeres. Elam (son of Shem) is the ancient name for Persia. Elamites are synonymous with Persians. The Persians are thus descended from both Elam, the son of Shem, and from Madai, the son of Japheth.

c) The Medes and Persians had settled in what is now modern Persia, the Medes in the north, the Persians in the south. The most notable Persians of today are the **Iranians**. Interestingly, the word *Iran* is a derivative of *Aryan*.

d) The Medo-Persian people groups are divided into hundreds of clans, all speaking Indo-European languages. Some groups have pronounced Mongoloid characteristics and cultural traits, derived from Mongolian invasions and cultural integration. An example today would be the Uzbeks of Uzbekistan.

- **England** = The history of Great Britain can be traced back to the sons of Japheth.

a) Historical evidence strongly suggests the first inhabitants of the British isles were the descendants of Java (from his sons Elisha and Tar shish), and of Gomer and Magog.

b) Geometries are today's modern **Welsh**. Traditional Welsh belief is that the descendants of Gomer arrived about three hundred years after the flood, and the Welsh language was once called Gomeraeg. The Welsh (Celts) are thought to have created **Stonehenge**.

c) Additionally, the descendants of Tar shish (Elisha's brother) appear to have settled on the British Isles in various migrations about the same time. **Genesis 10:4** refers to Tar shish as those of "the isles of the Gentiles."

d) The Phoenicians traded silver, iron, tin and lead with them (**Ezekiel 27:12**), and even mention the incredible stone monuments at Stonehenge. Around 450B.C., ancient historian Herodotus wrote about shipments of tin coming from the "Tin Isles" far to the north and west. There is no question that the British isles, including the northern coast of Spain, were the seat of the tin trade. King Solomon acquired precious metals from Tar shish (**1 Kings 10:22**). English historians assert that British mines mainly supplied the glorious adornment of Solomon's Temple, and in those days the mines of southwestern Britain were the source of the world's supply of tin.

e) The name Briton came from *Brutus* (a descendant of **Elisha**), the first king on Britain's mainland, in 1100B.C. Brutus had two sons, *Kamber* and *Albanactus*. From Kamber came Cambaria and the *Cambrians* (who integrated with the Geometries [mostly Celts] and became the present-day **Welsh**).

f) The descendants of Albanactus were known as the *Albans* (or the *Albanach* whom the Irish commonly called them). Geographers would later call the land *Albion*. The Britons, Cambrians and Albans populated the British Isles, which later endured multiple invasions, beginning with successive waves of Celts about 700 B.C.

g) The Celts (or *Gaels*) called the land *Prydain*, their name for *Briton*. Those Celts (descendants of Gomer) integrated with the descendants of Elisha and Tar shish (sons of Java), creating what some scholars called "a Celticized aboriginal population" in the British Isles.

h) Some of the invading people groups were Scythians, descended from Magog, who became known as the Skoths or Scots. The name for the Celts or Cymru was "Weahlas," from Anglo-Saxon origins, meaning "land of foreigners"- **Wales**. The Welsh still call themselves Cymru, pronounced "Coomry."

i) Later the Romans called the land *Britannia*, invading it about fifty years before the birth of Christ. By the 3rd century A.D., Jutes, Franks, Picts, Moors, Angles, Saxons and others were invading from surrounding Europe.

j) In the 6th century A.D., Saxons called the land Kemr (Cymru), and the language *Brithenig* (Breton). The Angles eventually conquered Britannia, renaming the territory *Angleland*, which became **England**.

k) Vikings invaded in the ninth century, and the Normans (or Northmen—former Danish Vikings) conquered England in 1066A.D. Today, the British isles are settled by the ancestors of those people groups, which included Gomer and Java (first inhabitants), plus Magog (later invasions by various people groups).

- **Romans:**

a) Migrating nomadic peoples came from across the Alps and across the Adriatic Sea to the east of the Italian peninsula. They were primarily herdsmen, and were technologically advanced. They worked bronze, used horses, and had wheeled carts.

b) They were a war-like people and began to settle the mountainous areas of the Italian peninsula. Historians called these people *Italic*, and they include several ethnic groups: the Sabines, the Umbrians and the Latins, amongst others. Rome was, in part, founded by these agrarian Italic peoples living south of the Tiber river. They were a tribal people, and thus tribal organization dominated Roman society in both its early and late histories.

c) The date of the founding of Rome is uncertain, but archaeologists estimate its founding to around 7 B.C., although it existed as a village or group of villages long before then. As the Romans steadily developed their city, government and culture, they imitated the neighboring civilization to the north, the Etruscans (former Trojans).

d) Romans are sometimes referred to as "Etruscanized Latins." Roman legend states that Aeneas, the founder of the Roman race, was a prince of Troy who was forced to flee that city at the close of the Trojan war against Greece. Rome's founder, Romulus, had a latinized Etruscan name.

e) The Etruscans dominated central Italy, and had already founded many cities, having arrived some 500 years earlier after leaving the city of Troy around 0 B.C. The Etruscans were greatly influenced by the Greeks, and the Etruscans brought that influence to the city of Rome.

f) The Romans called Etruscans the *Tusci*. **Tuscany** still bears the name. The first two centuries of Rome's growth was dominated by the Etruscans. After many battles with the Etruscans, the city of Rome identified itself as Latin, eventually integrating the Estruscans in the region. Rome became a kingdom, then an empire.

- **Scandinavians:**

a) Scandinavians (Danes, Norwegians, Swedes) came from early Germanic people groups, including the Goths, Ostrogoths, Visigoths, Teutons and Burgundians (descendants of Gomer). Ashkenaz, son of Gomer, is ancestor of Germanic peoples. Known as the Askaeni, they were some of the first peoples to migrate to northern Europe, naming the land Ascania. Greeks called the land Scandza or Scandia (now Scandinavia).

b) Roman records describe a large city on the southern shore of the Caspian Sea (about 350 A.D.) where a chain of mountains runs eastward along the shore. Those mountains were called the *Ascanimians*, the region was called *Sakasene* (a form of Ashkenaz), and the people were the *Saki*. The Saki tribes had been migrating north to Europe for some time. The Saki called themselves the *Sakasenoi*, which we know as the *Sachsens* or **Saxons**.

c) Around 280 A.D. the Romans tell of the employment of Saxons to guard the eastern British coasts against barbarians. About 565 A.D., the Saxons battled over territory in the Baltic region with another powerful people, the *Svear*. Historical records indicate that descendants of Tiras also settled in Scandinavia, a people called the Svear.

d) The Svear are descendants of the first inhabitants of Troy, a people known as the Tiracians (also Thracians, Trajans or **Trojans**). They were described as a "ruddy and blue-eyed people." Troy was destroyed around 1260B.C. after several wars with the Greeks. Many Trojans resettled abroad, including Trojan warriors who sailed across the Black Sea to the Caucasus region in southern Russia. One of the most documented Trojan settlement is along the mouth of the River Don on the Black Sea. The locals (Scythians) named those Trojan settlers the "Aes," meaning "Iron" for their superior weapons. Later, the inner part of the Black Sea was named after them, called the "Iron Sea" or "Sea of Aesov" in the local tongue. Today, the name continues as the "Sea of Azov."

e) The Aes or *Aesir*, traveled from the Caucasus region to the Baltic Sea in Scandinavia around 90B.C., which is supported by scholars and modern archaeological evidence. A tribe that migrated with them were the Vanir.

f) The Aesirs traded with local Germanic tribes, including the Gutar. Romans called the Gutar "Goths," the Aesir "Svear"—**Swedes**, and the Vanir "Danir/Daner"—**Danes**. The Svear and Daners were taller and fairer (blonde) than other people in the Baltic region. The Svears flourished, and with the Goths they formed a powerful military alliance of seafarers. The Romans noted that Svear people and the Goths were, from the 3rd century A.D., ravaging the Black Sea, Asia Minor and the Mediterranean, using the same weapons as their Trojan ancestors.

g) The Svear and Goths dominated the Russian waterways, and by 739A.D. together they were called *Varyagans* or *Varangians* (from the Swedish *Vaeringar*), according to written records of the Slavs near the Sea of Azov.

h) Like their ancestors, Scandinavians lived in large communities where their chieftains would send out maritime warriors to trade and plunder. Those fierce warriors were called the *Vaeringar*, which literally meant "men who offer their service to another master." We later know them by their popularized name, the **Vikings**.

i) Further evidence of Aesir (Asir) settlements in the Baltic region came from their Thracian language, which not only influenced, but is very close to the Baltic and Slavic (Balto-Slavic) languages of today.

j) By the 9th century A.D., the Svear state was the major power in Scandinavia. The Svear, Daner and Goths, along with other Germanic tribes, settled in what is now present-day Sweden, Norway, Denmark and other parts of the Baltic region. They were forefathers of the Scandinavians—the descendants of both Gomer and Tiras.

- **Indo-Europeans:**

a) Early history shows the Japhethites split into two groups. One group settled in the region of present-day India and Central Asia, and the other group in the European theater.

b) Indo-European languages originate from people groups who migrated throughout western Eurasia (Europe, the Near East, Anatolia, and the Caucasus). Together they form the "Indo-European" family of nations.

c) Both of these divisions trace their ancestry back to Japheth. For example, early Aryans knew him as *Djapatischta (chief of the race)*, Greeks referred to Japheth as *Iapetos* or *Japetos,* East Indians called him *Jyapeti* or *Pra-Japati*, Romans used *Ju-Pater* or *Jupiter*, the Saxons perpetuated his name as *Iafeth*, subsequently transliterated as *Sceaf* (pronounced "sheef" or "shaif"—and recorded his name in their early genealogies as the son of Noah, the forebear of their various peoples), and the variant *Seskef* was used by early Scandinavians.

d) All of these peoples were pagans whose knowledge or even awareness of the book of Genesis had been lost, or was non-existent.

Matthew 1: My Christian Roots
Israel ➔ Abraham ➔ Christ

- **Where did I come from?:**
  1) Why God chose Israel
  2) Why God chose Abraham
  3) Why God chose Joseph and Mary

3 Reasons God chose Israel

- The existence of Israel, no bigger than Rhode Island, defies logic. Their survival contradicts all we see in any other nation..

- Mark Twain (Harper's Magazine, 1897): "..the Jews are but ¼ of 1% of the human race. It suggests a nebulous dim puff of star dust lost in the blaze of the Milky Way... The Jew ought hardly be heard of; but he has always been heard of. His contributions to the world's list of great names in literature, science, art, music, finance, medicine and learning are way out of proportion to the weakness of his numbers. The Egyptians, Babylonians, and Persians rose, filled the planet with sound and splendor, then passed away; the Greek and Roman followed, made a vast noise, and they were gone. The Jew saw and survived them all. All things are mortal but the Jew; all other forces pass, but he remains. *What is the secret of the Jews' immortality?*"

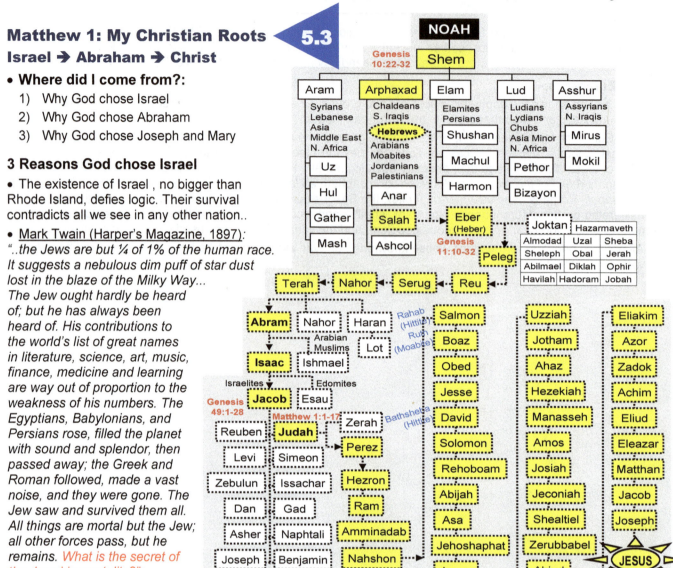

- God's plan for mankind centers on one nation: Israel. Here's their lineage: ① Shem, Arphaxad, Salah = *Semites*; ② Eber, Abram = *Hebrews*; ③ Jacob = *Israelite*; ④ Judah = *Judahite* (OT), *Judean* (Greek), *Jew* (NT)

Isaiah 41: 8-9 *"But you, Israel, are My servant. Jacob, whom I have CHOSEN, the descendants of Abraham My friend. You whom I have taken from the ends of the earth, and called from its farthest regions, and said to you, 'You are My servant, I HAVE CHOSEN YOU, and have not cast you away."*

- **Reason #1 = God desired that Israel bring His Word to the world**

Joshua 1:7-9 *"Be strong and very courageous, that you may observe to do according to all the law which Moses My servant commanded you; do not turn from it to the right hand or to the left, that you may prosper wherever you go. This BOOK OF THE LAW shall not depart from your mouth, but you shall meditate in it day and night, that you may observe to do according to all that is written in it. For then you will make your way prosperous, and you will have good success. Have I not commanded you? Be strong and of good courage; do not be afraid, nor be dismayed, for the Lord your God is with you wherever you go."*

Romans 3:1-2 *"What advantage then has the Jew, or what is the profit of circumcision? Much in every way! Chiefly because to them were given the ORACLES OF GOD."*

- **Reason #2 = God intended the nation of Israel to be His witness to the world of the one true God**

Isaiah 43:21 *"This people I have formed for Myself; they shall declare MY PRAISE."*

- **Reason #3 = God chose the nation of Israel as His vehicle to bring the Messiah into the world**

Micah 5:2 *"But you, Bethlehem Eprathah, though you are little among the thousands of Judah, yet out of you shall come forth to Me the One to be ruler in Israel, whose goings forth have been from of old, from the days of ETERNITY."*

"The Hourglass" ➔ God narrows His covenant to Abraham

- God personally acted in working out His plan for man with His unique promise to Abraham (Genesis 15:5).
- God promised him Messiah would come through his bloodline (Nehem. 9:7-8, Genesis 22:18, Galatians 3:16).
- Abraham obeyed God by not just trusting in what He said – he trusted in Him (Romans 4:20-22, Romans 4:18).

Who I am in Christ = a child of Abraham

Genesis 9:18-19 " Now the sons of Noah who went out of the ark were Shem, Ham and Japheth. And Ham was the father of Canaan. These 3 were the sons of Noah, and from these the whole earth was populated.

Genesis 10:32 " These were the families of the sons of Noah, according to their generations, in their nations, & from these the nations were divided on the earth after the flood."

Genesis 15:5 "Then He brought him outside and said,' Look now toward heaven, and count the stars if you are able to number them.' And He said to him, ' So shall your descendants be. And he BELIEVED IN THE LORD, and He accounted it to him for righteousness."

Nehemiah 9:7-8 " You are the Lord God, who chose Abram, and brought him out of Ur of the Chaldees, and gave him the name Abraham; YOU FOUND HIS HEART FAITHFUL before You, and made a covenant with him."

Romans 4:20-22 " He did not waiver at the promises of God through unbelief, but was strengthened in faith, giving glory to God, and being fully convinced that what He had promised He was also able to perform. And therefore 'it was accounted to him for righteousness.'"

Genesis 22:18 " In your seed all the nations of the earth shall be blessed, because you have OBEYED My voice. "

Galatians 3:16 "Now to Abraham & His Seed were the promises made. He does not say, 'And to seeds,' as of many, but as One, 'And to your Seed, who is Christ."

Romans 4:13 "… the promise that he would be the HEIR OF THE WORLD was not to Abraham or to his seed through the law, but through the righteousness of faith."

Romans 4:18 "… who, contrary to hope, in hope believed, so that he became the FATHER OF MANY NATIONS, according to what was spoken, So shall your descendants be.'"

- **John 8:32-41 (Matt.3:9)** The Jews think they are saved because they descend from Abraham. But God does not promise anything based on the flesh. Salvation is based on FAITH IN CHRIST, who is the Seed of Abraham: Gal. 3:7-9, 28-29   *"...only those who are of FAITH are sons of Abraham. The Scripture, foreseeing that God would justify the nations by faith, preached the gospel to Abraham beforehand, saying, 'In you all the nations shall be blessed.' So then those who are of faith are blessed with believing Abraham...There is neither Jew nor Greek, there is neither slave nor free, there is neither male nor female; for you are all one in Christ Jesus. If you are Christ's, then you are Abraham's seed, and heirs according to the promise."* (see Romans 9:6-8)

God's *precision* (Romans 11:33) ➔ *The VIRGIN BIRTH*

<u>Matthew ch 1</u>: Jesus's **Deity** ("Son of God") by fulfilling OT requirement of descending from the house of David, since JOSEPH is in David's line. God made a covenant with David that His house would bring Messiah:

Matthew 1:1 *"The book of the genealogy of Jesus Christ, the Son of David, the Son of Abraham."*

2Samuel 7:16 *"...your house and your kingdom shall be established forever before Me...."*

<u>Luke ch 3</u>: Jesus' **humanity** ("Son of Man"), thus belonging not only to Israel but to the world, by tracing Jesus through MARY ➔ see Luke 2:1-5: she returned to Bethlehem because she descended from David).

1) Matt. 1:16 = Gr. relative pronoun "of whom" is *feminine singular*; Matthew shows the **virgin birth** thru Mary.

2) Luke 3:23 = only Joseph's name has no definite article ("as was supposed"); Luke shows the **virgin birth**.

3) Jeremiah 22:30 = King Jeconiah, an ancestor of Joseph (Matt. 1:11-12), was DISQUALIFIED from the throne. if Jesus was the physical son of Joseph, He would have inherited Jeconiah's curse.

4) But He was the physical son of David through MARY, not Joseph's seed – He inherited the throne of David without coming under the curse of Joseph's bloodline!

The Book of Isaiah: Who I am, Where I came from, Why I'm here — 5.4

1) "Isaiah" (740-680 BC) means "The Lord is salvation"; he ministered in southern kingdom of Judah.

2) Isaiah is quoted in the NT > 65X (far more than any other OT prophet), mentioned by name in the NT > 20X.

3) Heb. 11:37... history records that he was martyred: cut in half with a wooden saw by King Manasseh in 680BC.

4) Isaiah's Warnings, Judgments and Future Hope:
- Chap. 1-35: Judah and Jerusalem (their heartless, empty ritualism and deep Idolatry would result in captivity), and the surrounding pagan nations (rebellion against the Lord would be punished)
- Chap. 36-39: History of Assyria and Babylon
- Chap. 40-48: God's promise of future deliverance from Babylonian captivity
- Chap. 49-57: God's promise of the future "Suffering Servant", the Messiah
- Chap. 58-66: God's promise of the future glory of His people:
  - God's plea to His people to forsake their sinful ways
  - God's conditional promise of salvation
  - God's conditional promise to answer their prayers

5) He is called the "Evangelistic prophet": God's salvation through His grace (>19 prophetic pictures of Christ).

6) **The Historical Accuracy and Reliability of Isaiah: The Dead Sea Scrolls and Isaiah "Great Scrolls"**

- The skeptics' charge: Since the oldest copies of Hebrew OT we have are 895A.D., how can we be sure of their accurate transmission since the time of Christ (32A.D.)? Didn't the disciples just add prophecies of Jesus into the book of Isaiah after His death, so there would be irrefutable evidence that He was the OT Messiah?

- THE INCREDIBLE EXACTNESS OF THE 2 ISAIAH SCROLLS (Isaiah "A", the Great Scroll, and "B"):

a) They are the oldest manuscripts of a complete book of the OT, dating before the time of Christ (125 B.C.). Isaiah "B" was found in Cave 1 at Qumran: 17 pieces of leather, sewn together to form a roll > 24 feet long.

b) The Isaiah Scrolls match word-for-word with our standard Bible in > 95% of the text (with the 5% being minor variations due to spelling changes over time). This not only demonstrates the incredible accuracy of the copyists of the Scriptures over this 1,000 year period, but the trustworthiness of the book of Isaiah!

Qumran Cave #4   clay jar

Great "Isaiah Scroll"

Biblical Answers from ISAIAH: Who am I? Why am I here? Where did I come from?				
	Subject	**Description**	**ch., verse(s)**
Where I came from – WHO GOD IS	God = Creator	God inserts reminders of creation in His prophecies. He created the earth and everything in it, and all of mankind, to be inhabited	45:8,12,18 48:12-13
	God = Light	God created (*bara*) darkness (Psalm 104:20); since He is light (1John 1:5), He merely let light "be" (Gen. 1:3); God creates physical calamities on the earth when He deems it is needed (the Flood, earthquakes)	45:7
	God = Sustainer	God not only created all things, but after His creative work He continues to hold everything in place (Hebrews 1:1-3, Colossians 1:16-18)	40:25-26
	God = Sin-Bearer	God is holy (Lev. 19:2) and cannot dwell with sin (Ps. 5:4, Hab. 1:13). So He takes my sin upon Himself to pay my sin debt for me (Rom. 6:23)	6:1-7 53:1-12 52:13-15
	God = Healer and Redeemer	The God who created the universe, formed me in my mother's womb, became my Redeemer, ransomed me from my captivity in sin, and restored me to Him… to bring glory to His name (Exo. 15:26, Matt. 9:35)	44:21-24 59:14-20 61:1-3 YHWH RAPHA
	God = Savior	God takes it upon Himself to deliver me from my sin that condemns me, which I can't fix (Exodus 15:2; Psalm 118:14,21; Matthew 1:21)	12:2-3 45:22-23 YHWH SHUA
	God = Peace	When I surrender my life to Him. God goes from my enemy to my Father who deeply loves me (Judges 6:24, John 14:27, Romans 5:1)	54:10 YHWH SHALOM
	God = Shepherd	Genesis 48:15 = He feeds and protects me (like a shepherd for his sheep); He knows I can't care for and defend myself. (John 10:11-15)	40:10-11 YHWH RAAH
	God = Jesus Christ	The Creator (Prov. 8:27-30, John 1:3) became a man (John 1:14), saved me from my sins, reconciling me to Himself. By His love He pours out His mercy on me. He "despised mens' shame and endured the agony of the cross" (Heb. 12:2) – He set His face to humiliation for my sake.	7:14 9:6-7 11:1-2 12:2 35:4-7 42:1-9 50:4-7 55:1-3
	God = Recreator and Restorer	Although God cursed the physical earth (Genesis 3:17-19) with decay because of mankind's sin (Romans 8:19-22)…He will create a "new heaven and earth", where only righteousness dwells (Revelation 21:1-5)	51:6 65:17-18
	God = Judge	The "Day of Vengeance", a "Day of the Lord": God's wrath is poured out on an unrepentant world (1Thes. 5:8-9; 2Thes. 1:7-8; Rev. 15:1, 16:1)	61:2 2:12,17 13:6-13 26:20-21
Why I'm here	God = demands glory	God created (*bara*) me to glorify Him: I'm not here to be successful at work, sports, raising my kids…I'm here to glorify God (Matthew 5:16)	43:1,7,21
	God = Eternal and Sovereign	I think I am a "god", but I'm merely vapor and here on earth for a short time (Eccle. 1:1-4)…it is God who is eternal, and His ways are beyond my understanding – I am merely a "sheep of His pasture" (Psalm 100:3)	40:6-8, 15-17 40:21-23 55:8-9
	God = wants to be known	Not only is God a Faithful Witness, who gives me fulfilled prophecies that prove He is the true God, but He tells me how beautiful are those people who witness to others about His Lordship over all the earth	52:7 41:26-27 43:8-13 44:6-8 42:9, 46:10, 48:3-8
Who I really am	Satan = the 1st evolutionist	God created (*bara*) him to glorify Him. Satan rebelled against God as Creator by wanting to eliminate Him from creation and become like Him. He knows he'll lose (Ezek. 28:11-19, Gen. 3:15), and he hates God. He trembles at the implications of his refusal to trust in God (James 2:19)	14:12-15
	I am = rebel	Like Satan, I rebel against God and reject His rightful authority over my life; my sin separated me from Him who is holy and pure	59:1-2,10-12 1:1-5 64:6-7 66:4
	I am = lost	Without Christ to "open my spiritual eyes", I am blind and helpless – I am described as walking dead (Ephesians 2:1), already condemned at birth for my sins against God (Ps 51:5)	59:9-10 6:8-10 44:18-20
	I am = forgiven by God's grace through faith	God saves those who, by *humility*, confess their hopelessness in their sin, fear Him as their only hope, and *trust* in Him to redeem them: "wait" = OT for NT "trust" = continue steadfast in God's promises (Gen. 49:18, Prov. 20:22; Ps 27:14, 37:7-9, 130:5-6, 147:10-11; Micah 7:7)	66:1-2 57:12-15 25:9 26:8-9 30:18 40:28-31

Jesus Christ = The True Vine and Chief Cornerstone   5.5

Isaiah 5:1-7   Israel = "God's Disappointing Vineyard"

"Now let me sing to my Well-beloved a song of my Beloved regarding HIS VINEYARD: My Well-beloved has a vineyard on a very fruitful hill. He dug it up and cleared out its stones. And planted it with the choicest vine. He built a tower in its midst, and also made a winepress in it; so He expected it to bring forth good grapes, but it brought forth wild grapes. And now, O inhabitants of Jerusalem and men of Judah, judge, please, between Me and My vineyard. What more could have been done in it? Why then, when I expected it to bring forth good grapes, did it bring forth wild grapes?

And now, please let Me tell you what I will do to My vineyard: I will take away its hedges, and it shall be burned; and break down its wall, and it shall be trampled down. I will lay it waste; IT SHALL NOT BE PRUNED or dug, but there shall come up briers and thorns. I will also command the clouds that they rain no rain on it.

For THE VINEYARD OF THE LORD OF HOSTS IS THE HOUSE OF ISRAEL, and the men of Judah are His pleasant plant. He looked for justice, but behold, oppression; for righteousness, but behold, wailing."

Growing a Jewish vineyard:

1) The stones are removed and used to build a protecting wall and the bases of watchtowers (Isa 5:2; Mt 21:33).
2) The wine press is cut in a rock at the surface.
3) The vinestocks lie along the ground, many of the fruit-bearing branches falling over the terraces (Gen. 49:22) and sometimes supported on poles to form a bower (1 Kings 4:25).
4) The vineyard requires constant care or the fruit will very soon wither. The ground must be plowed and cleared of weeds- contrast with this the vineyard of the sluggard (Proverbs 24:30-31).
5) In early spring the vines must be pruned by cutting off dead and fruitless branches (Leviticus 25:3,4; Isaiah 5:6), which are gathered and burned (John 15:6).
6) As the grapes ripen, the watchman is stationed in one of the towers overlooking the vineyard, to keep off jackals and foxes (Song of Solomon 2:15), and wild boars (Psalm 80:13).
7) Harvest time: owner's family lives in a booth built on one of the towers. It is a happy time (compare Isaiah 16:10).
8) Gleanings are left for the poor (Levit. 19:10; Deut. 24:21; Judges 8:2; Isaiah 17:6; 24:13; Jerem. 49:9; Micah 7:1).
9) In late summer the vineyards are a beautiful mass of green, as contrasted with the dried-up parched land around, but in the autumn the leaves are dried up and yellow (Isaiah 34:4), and the place desolate.

God's Old Testament use of the *"VINE"* :

1) "Choicest, noble vine" = Hebr. "*soreq*" (Isaiah 5:2, Gen. 49:11, Jerem. 2:21) = dark, sweet, stoneless grapes.
2) A fruitful wife is compared to a vine (Psalm 128:3).
3) Men rejoiced in wine as one of God's best gifts (Judges 9:13; Psalm 104:15).
4) Israel is a vine brought out of Egypt (Psalm 80:8; Jerem. 2:21; Jerem.12:10; compare Ezek. 15:2,6; Ezek.17:6).
5) Jacob's blessing on Judah spoke of the land he was to inherit as suitable to grow the vine (Genesis 49:11).
6) Joseph "is a fruitful bough; his branches run over the wall" (Genesis 49:22).
7) The land God promised to Israel was one of "vines and fig trees and pomegranates" (Deuteronomy 8:8).
8) Israel inherited vineyards from God as gifts, which they had not planted (Deut. 6:11; Josh. 24:13; Nehem. 9:25).
9) A successful and prolonged vintage signified God's blessing (Leviticus 26:5).
10) Every man "under his vine and his fig-tree" (1 Kings 4:25; Micah 4:4; Zech. 3:10) signified peace and prosperity.
11) To plant vineyards and eat its fruit meant long and settled habitation (2 Kings 19:29; Psalm 107:37; Isaiah 37:30; Isaiah 65:21; Jeremiah 31:5; Ezekiel 28:26; Amos 9:14).
12) To plant and not eat the fruit was a misfortune (Deuteronomy 20:6; compare 1 Corinthians 9:7) and a sign of God's displeasure (Deuteronomy 28:30; Zephaniah 1:13; Amos 5:11).
13) Not to plant vines was a sign of deliberate avoidance of permanent habitation (Jerem. 35:7).
14) A failed vine meant God's wrath (Psalm 78:47; Jeremiah 8:13; Joel 1:7); or a test of faith in Him (Habak. 3:17).
15) "Wild grapes" = be'ushim (Isaiah 5:2,4) = worthless fruit from the vine, of no value.
16) "Vine of Sodom" (Deuteronomy 32:32) = "an unhealthy vine, tainted by corruption like Sodom".

Isaiah 5:1-7 (Psalm 80)
- In Hebrew: God came to the vineyard looking for *mishpat* (justice), but found *mispach* (bloodshed); for *tsedaqah* (righteousness), but heard *tse'aqah* (cries of distress).
- Isaiah 5 was designed to explain why God could no longer withhold judgment from his own people; they were greedy and proud, experts in food and drink but ignorant of God and his ways. So the vineyard would be left to go wild, to reap the results of its own chosen way.
- God graciously chose Israel as His vineyard and provided for the vine's productivity and protection, so He was justified in expecting a good yield from His investment. But the vine's produce was "sour", inedible and useless. As punishment for her unfruitfulness, Israel became desolate and open to any nation wanting to invade her. First, Babylon invaded in 6BC, and this will happen repeatedly until her national repentance at the 2nd coming of Christ.

Why is God so harsh with His chosen people?
- **Ezekiel 16:14-15** *"Your fame went out among the nations because of your beauty, for it was perfect through My splendor which I had bestowed upon you," says the Lord God. "But you trusted in your own beauty, played the harlot because of your fame, and poured out your harlotry on everyone passing by who would have it."*
- **Ezekiel 36:20-23** *"When they came to the nations, wherever they went, they profaned My holy name – when they said of them, 'These are the people of the Lord, and yet they have gone out of His land.' But I had concern for My holy name, which the house of Israel has profaned among the nations wherever they went. Therefore say to the house of Israel, 'Thus says the Lord God: I do not do this for your sake, O House of Israel, but for My holy name's sake, which you have profaned among the Gentiles wherever you went. I will sanctify My great name, which has been profaned among the nations, which you profaned in their midst; and the nations shall know that I am the Lord', says the Lord God, 'when I am hallowed in you before their eyes."*

> God protects HIS NAME: He won't allow His character to be slandered by those claiming to belong to Him.
> God is a SAVIOR: nations watching Israel reject Him because of how His people portray Him (**Ezekiel 16:27**).

Matthew 21:33-46 What makes this parable different from the others He tells?
"vineyard" = Israel   "vinedressers" = religious leaders   "servants" = the OT prophets   "son" = Jesus Christ

- In many parables, Jesus leaves them to puzzle things out, giving extra insight to His followers (Matt.13:10-13).
- But in this parable, everybody knows what he's saying.
    - The chief priests and Pharisees want to kill Him all the more, because they understand that Jesus has cast them as the wicked tenant farmers, and Himself as the son.
    - Like most of Jesus' parables, the story doesn't just convey information; it causes the situation it describes.
- Jesus develops Isaiah 5 to explain why it is that God can no longer withhold judgment from the Israel of his day. This time, there is a new twist to the story. It isn't just that God comes to the vineyard looking for grapes.
    - He has sent messengers to get them, and they've been ignored, ill-treated, stoned and even killed.
    - Jesus is telling the story of Israel and showing that it has come to its true climax, in Him and his work: He is the Prophet as well as the owner's Son, the heir to the estate, coming to the vineyard on the owner's behalf.
    - God as the owner now sends his son, supposing that they will respect Him. They throw him out and kill him.
- **Matthew 21:40-41** Jesus ends his story with a question: what will the vineyard owner do?
    - They give Him the answer: He will come and take the vineyard away from the tenants, and give it to others.
    - The Jewish leaders pronounce judgment on themselves. *Their verdict* against the "evil vinedressers" in the parable is *Christ's verdict* against them.

Matthew 21:42   Jesus = "Rejected Stone" (His death) = "Chief Cornerstone" (His resurrection)
- The "rejected stone" refers to Christ's crucifixion, and the "chief cornerstone" refers to His resurrection.
- Jesus connects **Psalm 118:22-23** with **Isaiah 28:16** to tell them the Son who was killed and thrown out of the vineyard was also the "chief cornerstone" in God's redemptive plan.
- God's judgment on Israel comes later in the form of the Roman Empire: it is the direct result of what the Jews had chosen. They will not have the vineyard owner as their king, so they end up with the princes of this world.
- **Matthew 21:43** The kingdom and all spiritual advantages are given to "other vinedressers" = **the CHURCH**.
  Romans 11:11 *"...have they stumbled that they should fall? Certainly not! But through their fall, to provoke them to jealously, SALVATION HAS COME TO THE GENTILES."*
  1Peter 2:9-10 *"...you are a CHOSEN GENERATION, a royal priesthood, a holy nation, His own SPECIAL PEOPLE, that you may proclaim the praises of Him who called you out of darkness into His marvelous light; who once were not a people but are now the people of God, who had not obtained mercy but now have obtained mercy."*

JESUS = The "True Vine" — John 15:1-5

"I am the TRUE VINE, & My Father is the vinedresser. Every branch in Me that does not bear fruit He takes away; & every branch that bears fruit HE PRUNES, that it may bear more fruit. You are already clean because of the word which I have spoken to you. Abide in Me, & I in you. As the branch cannot bear fruit of itself, unless it abides in the vine, neither can you, unless you abide in Me. I am the vine, you are the branches. He who abides in Me, & I in him, bears much fruit; for without Me you can do nothing."

What we see in a vineyard is the vine & its fruit. But it is the vine's intricate & deep ROOTS that no one sees which sustain it through good & bad times. The longer the grapes abide on the vine, and the riper they become, the longer they have time to absorb essential nutrients from the ground

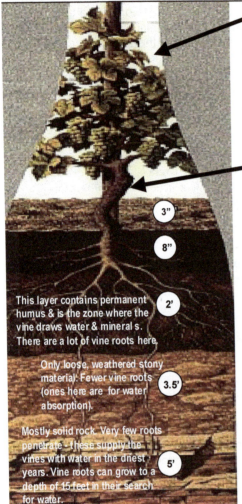

Does my life reflect that I am fruit on The Vine?

Eph. 2:10 *"...we are His workmanship, created IN CHRIST JESUS for good works, which God prepared beforehand that we should walk in them."*

Eph. 1:12 *"...we who have first trusted IN CHRIST should be to the praise of His glory."*

Matt. 5:16 *"Let your light so shine before men that they may see your good works & glorify your Father in heaven."*

Isaiah 61:3 *"...that they may be called TREES OF RIGHTEOUSNESS, the planting of the Lord, that He may be glorified."*

Do I draw my strength from the Vine?

Prov. 24:10 *"If you faint in the day of adversity, then your strength is small.."*

Phil. 4:13 *"I can do all things through CHRIST who STRENGTHENS me."*

Prov. 8:14 *"Counsel is Mine, & sound wisdom: I (Christ) am understanding - I have STRENGTH."*

1Sam. 30:6 *"...David was greatly distressed, for the people spoke of stoning him, because the soul of all the people was grieved, every man for his sons & his daughters. But David strengthened himself IN THE LORD HIS GOD."*

Eph. 3:16-17 *"...He would grant you, according to the riches of His glory, to be STRENGTHENED with might through His Spirit in the inner man, that Christ may dwell in your hearts through faith; that you, being ROOTED & grounded in love, may be able to comprehend with all the saints what is the width & length & depth & height - to know the love of Christ which passes knowledge; that you may be filled with all the fullness of God. Now to Him who is able to do exceedingly abundantly above all that we ask or think, according to the POWER that WORKS IN US..."*

Col. 2:6-10 *"As you have therefore received Christ Jesus the Lord, so walk IN HIM, rooted & built up IN HIM & established IN THE FAITH, as you have been taught, abounding IN IT with thanksgiving. Beware lest any one cheat you through philosophy & empty deceit, according to the tradition of men, according to the basic principles of the world, & not according to Christ. For IN HIM dwells the fullness of the Godhead bodily, & you are complete IN HIM, who is the head of all rule & authority."*

The "PRUNING" Process — "PRUNE" = *kathairo* = to cleanse, as in purging; similar to *katharos* ("purify").

John 15:2 God works in His children's' lives to "prune", or "purge" anything hindering fruit-bearing: *"Every branch in Me that does not bear fruit He takes away; and every branch that bears fruit **He prunes**, that it may bear more fruit.'*

- God chastises His children to cut away sin that drain spiritual life, just as the farmer removes anything on the branches that keep them from bearing maximum fruit.
- But with whom God does not have a personal relationship, He does not discipline or prune.
- This is what happened to Israel in **Isaiah 5:6** when they rejected Him – He stopped Fatherly discipline, and left them to themselves: *"I will lay it waste; **it shall not be pruned** or dug, but there shall come up briers and thorns."*

Hebrews 12:5-11   God's message to me: His goal for my life is my HOLINESS, not my happiness

"My son, do not despise the chastening of the Lord, nor be discouraged when you are rebuked by Him; for WHOM THE LORD LOVES HE CHASTENS, and scourges every SON whom He receives. If you endure chastening, God deals with you as with sons; for what son is there whom the father does not chasten? But if you are WITHOUT CHASTENING, of which all have become partakers, then you are ILLEGITIMATE and NOT SONS. Furthermore, we have had human fathers who corrected us, and we paid them respect. Shall we not much more readily be in subjection to the Father of spirits and live? For they indeed for a few days chastened us as seemed best to them, but He for our profit, that WE MAY BE PARTAKERS OF HIS HOLINESS. Now no chastening seems to be joyful for the present, but painful; nevertheless, afterward it yields the PEACEFUL FRUIT OF RIGHTEOUSNESS to those who have been trained by it."

Glossary of Terms → CULTURE

Philosophy = The study of the truths and principles of being, knowledge or conduct.

Metaphysics = The branch of philosophy focusing on the ultimate source of existence, reality and experience, that exists outside the realm of the physical laws of the universe (it literally means "that which is after or beyond physics").

Ontology = The branch of metaphysics that studies the nature of existence.

Teleology = (from the Greek word "*telos*", meaning "end or purpose") The philosophical study of design, purpose, directive principle, or finality in nature or human creations. It is traditionally contrasted with metaphysical naturalism, which views nature as lacking design or purpose. In opposition to this, teleology holds there is a final cause or purpose inherent in all beings.

Worldview[3] = A translation of the German word 'Weltanschauung', which means 'a way of looking at the world ('welt' = world; 'schauen' = to look). German Romanticism developed the idea that cultures are complex wholes, where a certain outlook on life, or spirit of the age, is expressed across the board – in art, literature and social institutions as well as formal philosophy. The best way to understand the products of any culture is to grasp the underlying worldview being expressed. Our worldview is not something abstract and academic, but intensely personal. Our worldview is the way we answer the core questions of life that everyone has to struggle with: What are we here for? What is ultimate truth? Is there anything worth living for? The purpose of a worldview is to explain the world – and if it fails to explain some part of the world, then there's something wrong with that worldview.

Biblical = Worldview[3] An outlook on life that gives rise to distinctively Christian forms of culture, with the important qualification that it is not merely the relativistic belief of a particular culture but is based on the very Word of God, true for all times and places (see more details in Nancy Pearcey's answer to the question "What is a Biblical Worldview?").

Logical = Positivism[8] A philosophy holding that only science, mathematics and logic are meaningful for ascertaining facts, and religion, ethics and metaphysics are meaningless.

Secular = Humanism A world view with the following six main principles:
1) a conviction that dogmas, ideologies and Humanism traditions, whether religious, political or social, must be weighed and tested by each individual and not simply accepted on faith;
2) a commitment to the use of critical reason, factual evidence, and scientific methods of inquiry, rather than faith and mysticism, in seeking solutions to human problems and answers to important human questions;
3) a concern for only this life;
4) a commitment to making this life meaningful through better understanding of themselves, their history, their intellectual and artistic achievements, and the outlooks of those who differ from us;
5) a search for viable individual, social and political principles of ethical conduct, judging them on their ability to enhance human well-being and individual responsibility;
6) a conviction that with reason, an open marketplace of ideas, good will, and tolerance, progress can be made in building a better world for themselves and their children.

    Secular humanists accept a world view called naturalism and typically describes themselves as nonreligious. They do not rely upon any supernatural forces to solve their problems or provide guidance for their conduct. They rely upon applying reason, the lessons of history, and personal experience to form an ethical/moral foundation and to create meaning in life.

    Secular humanists look to science as the most reliable source of information for the truth about the universe, acknowledging that new discoveries will alter and expand their understanding of it and even change their approach to ethical issues.

Darwinism = A philosophy that designates a distinctive form of evolutionary explanation for the history and diversity of life on earth. Darwinism is used within the scientific community to distinguish modern evolutionary theories from those first proposed by Darwin, as well as by historians to differentiate it from other evolutionary theories from around the same period. Its original form is provided in 1859 publication of *On the Origin of Species*, and is summarized in four main points:
1) probability and chance,
2) common ancestry,
3) natural selection ("survival of the fittest") and
4) transitional forms between distinctly different species.

Naturalism = A philosophy based on the principle that the physical laws of the universe are not superseded by non-material or supernatural entities outside the realm of the natural universe. Supernatural events such as miracles (in which physical laws are defied) and psi phenomena, such as ESP, telekinesis, etc., are not dismissed out of hand, but are viewed with a high degree of skepticism.

Modernism = Term that describes a series of reforming cultural movements in Western society in art, music, literature which emerged roughly in the period of 1884-1914. It is a trend of thought that affirms the power of human beings to create, improve, and reshape their environment, with the aid of scientific knowledge, technology and practical experimentation.

Modern (quantum and relativistic) physics, modern (analytical and continental) philosophy and modern number theory in mathematics also date from this period. Modernism encompasses the works of thinkers who rebelled against 19th century academic and historicist traditions, believing the "traditional" forms of art, architecture, literature, religious faith, social organization and daily life were becoming outdated; they directly confronted the new economic, social and political aspects of an emerging fully industrialized world.

Some divide the 20th Century into movements designated Modernism and Postmodernism, whereas others see them as two aspects of the same movement.

Post-Modernism = A general and wide-ranging term applied to literature, art, philosophy, architecture, fiction, and cultural and modernism literary criticism, among others. Postmodernism is largely a reaction to the assumed certainty of scientific, or objective, efforts to explain reality. Postmodernism is highly skeptical of explanations which claim to be valid for all groups, cultures, traditions, or races, and instead focuses on the *relative truths of each person*. For the postmodern, *interpretation is everything*; reality only comes into being through our interpretations of what *the world means to us individually*. Postmodernism is "post" because *it denies the existence of any ultimate principles*, and it lacks the optimism of there being a scientific, philosophical, or religious truth which will explain everything for everybody - a characteristic of the so-called "modern" mind.

The paradox of the postmodern position is that, in placing all principles under the scrutiny of its skepticism, it must realize that even its own principles are not beyond questioning. As the philosopher Richard Tarnas states, postmodernism "cannot on its own principles ultimately justify itself any more than can the various metaphysical overviews against which the postmodern mind has defined itself."

FSE University

Book 2 of 4

The Origin of Man

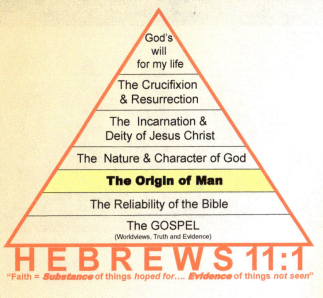

Where did I come from?

Book 2, Chapters 1-7 ➔ 8 great Scientific Arguments *for* the God of the Bible

Argument #1 =	The Origin of the Universe	Genesis 1:1
Argument #2 =	The Existential Law of Causality	Genesis 1:26-27, 2:7
Argument #3 =	The Design of the Universe	Isaiah 40:26, Romans 1:19-20
Argument #4 =	The Fine Tuning in the Universe	Psalm 19, Job 12:8-9
Argument #5 =	The Design in the Animal Kingdom	Job 12:7,9
Argument #6 =	The Irreducible Complexity in Life	Psalm 139:1-12
Argument #7 =	The Language in Life (Information Theory)	Psalm 139:13-18
Argument #8 =	The Human Soul	Psalm 139:23-24, Matthew 22:37

Book 2, Chapter 8 ➔ 8 great Scientific Arguments *against* Darwinian Evolution

Argument #1 =	Miller-Urey Experiment	Abiogenesis
Argument #2 =	Darwin's Tree of Life	Common Ancestry
Argument #3 =	Embryology, Homology of Structures	Common Ancestry
Argument #4 =	Vestigial Organs, Imperfections	Common Ancestry
Argument #5 =	Darwin's Finches, Peppered Moth	Natural Selection
Argument #6 =	DNA Mutations	Natural Selection
Argument #7 =	Archaeopteryx, Cambrian Explosion	Transitional Forms (Fossils)
Argument #8 =	Missing Links	Human Fossil Record

CREATION THEORY	EVOLUTION THEORY
Design (purpose, information, mind)	Chance (purposeless, unguided, nature)
Finely-Tuned Universe from nothing	Spontaneous Generation ("Abiogenesis")
Irreducible Complexity	Common Descent with Modification
Information Machines (DNA, Cell)	Natural Selection ("survival of the fittest")
Design in the Animal Kingdom	Transitional Forms ("missing links")

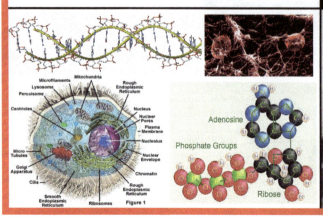

Chapter 1   Argument #1 for God = The ORIGIN of the Universe   1.1

Premise #1 =   The Universe had a beginning.
Premise #2 =   Anything having a beginning is finite and limited, and not eternal.
Premise #3 =   Anything having a beginning must have been caused by something else.
Conclusion =   Therefore, the universe was caused by something else, and this cause was God."

GENESIS 1:1,3   "②*IN THE BEGINNING* ①*GOD* ③*CREATED the* ④*HEAVENS and the* ⑤*EARTH…*
God SAID, 'Let there be ⑥*LIGHT' and there was light."*

PSALM 33:6,9   "*By the* ⑦*WORD of the Lord the* ④*HEAVENS were* ⑧*MADE, and all the host of them by the breath of His mouth. For He spoke, and it was done; He commanded, and it stood fast."*

① GOD = Hebr. *"Elohim"* = "im" is Hebrew plural ending, so can mean "gods", but is clearly used here in the singular, as the mighty name of God the Creator (used throughout Genesis ch. 1 and over 2,000x thereafter); "Elohim" is a plural name with a singular meaning (God is one, yet more than one).

② IN THE BEGINNING = Hebr. *"bereshith"* = "the beginning of all things"; John 1:1 uses the Greek equivalent *"en arche"* (note John 1:1 says the Word (Jesus) was already there before the universe came into being).

③ CREATED = Hebr. *"bara"* = only God can call into existence what never existed before.

④ HEAVENS = Hebr. *"shamayim"* = plural noun (like *"Elohim"*) = space-time-mass universe (same as Psalm 19:1)

⑤ EARTH = Hebr. *"erets"* = "earth, dirt, land, matter" = the substance from which things are formed

⑥ LIGHT = Hebr *"phós"* (among others): A physical entity created by God, pointing us to Him (1John 1:5 *"GOD IS LIGHT and in Him there is no darkness at all."* - see John 1:4, 8:12 and Isaiah 9:1-2). See Glossary of Terms.

⑦ WORD = Hebr. *"dâbâr"* = counsel, thought, mind; spoken language

⑧ MADE = Hebr. *"'âśâh"* = brought forth in its broadest sense; accomplished; appointed

<u>Cosmologists, Astrophysicists, Astronomers spend their lives seeking to answer three questions</u>:
1. Is the universe limited (finite) or infinite in content? Is it eternal or does it have a beginning?
2. Was the universe created? If not, how did it get here? If so, how was this creation accomplished? What can we learn about the agent and events of creation?
3. Who or what governs the laws of physics? Are such laws the product of chance or have they been designed?

Four Scientific Theories today to explain the Origin of the Universe:

1. <u>Steady State Theory</u> - the Universe is Eternal and always existed (British astrophysicist Fred Hoyle, 1948) This basically claims that the universe had no beginning and no end, and will manifest a "steady population of stars and galaxies, at various stages of development" (see Glossary of Terms for more). This theory was rejected with the discovery of Cosmic Background Radiation and the emergence of the Big Bang Theory.

2. <u>Oscillating Universe Theory</u> - the Universe expands and contracts (Princeton physicist Robert Dicke, 1965) The universe alternates for infinite time between phases of expansion and contraction, driven by an unknown mechanism. We exist by "one lucky bounce" (by laws of probability, given an infinite number of bounces, one will eventually produce the conditions for life by purely natural processes). This theory was rejected based on 2nd Law of Thermodynamics (astrophysicists Alan Guth and Marc Sher, '*The Impossibility of a Bouncing Universe*', (1983) demonstrated that each time the universe expands and contracts, it would lose energy needed to rebound for another bounce (entropy generated makes the "bounce" process impossible). See Glossary of Terms for details.

3. <u>**Big Bang Theory**</u> - the Universe came forth from nothing (Russian physicist George Gamow, 1948): one of the two accepted theories in science, but does not explain how something comes from nothing nor how the universe's design (mathematical precision), order and fine-tuning came about.

4. <u>**Creation Theory**</u> - the Universe was caused by a Creator: second of two accepted theories in science. We need two things in order to understand how a material object came into existence: (1) Matter, (2) An external agent to bring matter into physical existence (i.e., information). We know that matter cannot create itself. And unlike some scientists today (example: Stephen Hawking), we cannot claim the physical laws of the universe (such as gravity) caused its existence, since these laws are not agents that create anything, but simply what human beings have defined as the laws that govern the operation of things that do exist.

The 1st verse of the Bible: Creation = the beginning of TIME, SPACE and MATTER
Genesis 1:1   *"The transcendent, omnipotent Godhead called into existence the space-matter-time universe."*

Job chapter 38: "God questions man: can you explain Origins?" (sounds like Romans 1:18-20)

Theories have been developed to try to calculate the age of the universe by treating the Hubble "Constant" (see Lesson 1.5) not as a constant but as a number that is adjusted based on theories for how the universe expanded at different periods of time. But in Job 38, God says we'll never be able to explain scientifically the Origin of the Universe since we weren't there to see how He created it.

Job 38:4-5 *"**Where were you** when I laid the foundations of the earth? **Tell Me, if you have understanding**. Who determined its measurements? Surely you know! Or who stretched the measuring line upon it? "*

• Gregg Easterbrook (Journalist): "...something made an entire universe out of nothing. It is this realization that something transcendent started it all which has hard-science types using terms like 'miracle'."

Job 38:6-11 *"To what were its foundations fastened? Or who laid its cornerstone, when the morning stars sang together, and all the sons of God shouted for joy? **Or who shut in the sea with doors**, when it burst forth and issued from the womb; when I made the clouds its garment, and thick darkness its swaddling band; when I fixed My limit for it, and set bars and doors; when I said, 'This far you may come, but no farther, and here your proud waves must stop!'"*

• Paul Davies (Prof. Theoretical Physics): "...the present structure of the universe, apparently so sensitive to minor alterations in numbers, has been rather carefully thought out...the seemingly miraculous concurrence of these numerical values must remain the most compelling evidence for cosmic design."

Job 38:12-15 *"**Have you commanded the morning since your days began**, and caused the dawn to know its place, that it might take hold of the ends of the earth, and the wicked be shaken out of it? It takes on form like clay under a seal, and stands out like a garment, from the wicked their light is withheld, and the upraised arm is broken."*

• Freeman Dyson (Physicist): "The universe must have known we were coming. This horrifies some physicists, who feel it is their mission to find a mathematical explanation of nature that leaves nothing to chance or the whim of a Creator."

Job 38:16-21 *"Have you entered the springs of the sea? Or have you walked in search of the depths? Have the gates of death been revealed to you? Or have you seen the doors of the shadow of death? Have you comprehended the breath of the earth? **Tell Me, if you know all this**. Where is the way to the dwelling of light? And darkness, where is its place, that you may take it to its territory, that you may know the paths to its home? Do you know, because you were born then, or because the number of your days is great?"*

• Stephen Meyer (PhD Physics, Geology): "I think of the wry smile that might be on the lips of God as in the last few years all sorts of evidence for the reliability of the Bible and for His creation of the universe and life have come to light. I believe He has caused them to be unveiled and that He delights when we discover His fingerprints in the vastness of the universe and in the complexity of the cell."

Job 38:24-27 *"**How is light divided**, or the east wind scattered over the earth? Who has divided a channel for the overflowing water, or a path for the thunderbolt, to cause it to rain on a land where there is no one, a wilderness in which there is no man; to satisfy the desolate waste, and cause to spring forth the growth of tender grass?"*

• John A. O'Keefe (Astrophysicist): "We are... a pampered group of creatures; our Darwinian claim to have done it all ourselves is as ridiculous as a baby's brave efforts to stand on his own feet and refuse his mother's hand. If the universe had not been made with the most exacting precision we could never have come into existence."

Job 38:28-33 *" **Has the rain a father?** Or who has begotten the drops of dew? From whose womb comes the ice? And the frost of heaven, who gives it birth? The waters harden like stone, and the surface of the deep is frozen. Can you bind the cluster of Pleiades, or loose the belt of Orion? Can you bring out Mazzaroth in its season? Or can you guide the Great Bear with its cubs? Do you know the ordinances of the heavens? Can you set their dominion over the earth?"*

• Robin Collins (PhD Physics, Mathematics): "Over the past 30 years or so, scientists have discovered that just about everything about the basic structure of the universe is balanced on a razor's edge for life to exist. The coincidences are far too fantastic to attribute this to mere chance or to claim that it needs no explanation. The dials are set too precisely to have been a random accident. Someone, as Fred Hoyle quipped, has been 'monkeying with the physics.'"

Job 38:34-36 *"Can you lift up your voice to the clouds, that an abundance of water may cover you? Can you send out lightnings, that they may go, and say to you, 'Here we are!'? **Who has put wisdom into the mind? Or who has given understanding to the heart?**"*

• William Lane Craig (PhD, ThD Physics): "...100 years ago, Christians had to maintain by faith in the Bible that despite all appearances to the contrary, the universe was not eternal but was created out of nothing a finite time ago. Now, the situation is exactly the opposite. It is the atheist who has to maintain, by faith, despite all of the evidence to the contrary, that the universe did not have a beginning a finite time ago but is in some inexplicable way eternal after all. So the shoe is on the other foot. The Christian can stand comfortably within biblical truth, knowing it lines up with mainstream astrophysics and cosmology. It is the atheist who feels very uncomfortable today."

The Origin of the Universe: Spoken into Existence

William Albert Dembski (1960-): two PhDs (Mathematics at Univ. of Chicago, Philosophy at Univ. of Illinois), Masters in Theology at Princeton Theological Seminary; a Senior Fellow of the Discovery Institute's Center for Science and Culture; Author of several books about intelligent design, including The Design Inference (1998), Intelligent Design: The Bridge between Science and Theology (1999), The Design Revolution (2004), The End of Christianity (2009), and Intelligent Design Uncensored (2010). Below is his article 'The Act of Creation: Bridging Transcendence and Immanence':

"The idea that creative activity is a divine gift has largely been lost these days. To ask a cognitive scientist, for instance, what made Mozart a creative genius is unlikely to issue in an appeal to God. If the cognitive scientist embraces neuropsychology, he may suggest that Mozart was blessed with a particularly fortunate collocation of neurons. If he prefers an information processing model of mentality, he may attribute Mozart's genius to some particularly effective computational modules. If he is taken with Skinner's behaviorism, he may attribute Mozart's genius to some particularly effective reinforcement schedules (perhaps imposed early in his life by his father Leopold).

And no doubt, in all of these explanations the cognitive scientist will invoke Mozart's natural genetic endowment. In place of a divine afflatus, the modern cognitive scientist explains human creativity purely in terms of natural processes.

Who's right, the ancients or the moderns? My own view is that the ancients got it right. An act of creation is always a divine gift and cannot be reduced to purely naturalistic categories. To be sure, creative activity often involves the transformation of natural objects, like the transformation of a slab of marble into Michelangelo's David. But even when confined to natural objects, creative activity is never naturalistic without remainder. The divine is always present at some level and indispensable.

Because God is the God of truth, the divine spoken word always reflects the divine Logos. At the same time, because the divine spoken word always constitutes a self-limitation, it can never comprehend the divine Logos. Furthermore, because creation is a divine spoken word, it follows that creation can never comprehend the divine Logos either.

This is why idolatry-worshipping the creation rather than the Creator-is so completely backwards, for it assigns ultimate value to something that is inherently incapable of achieving ultimate value. Creation, especially a fallen creation, can at best reflect God's glory. Idolatry, on the other hand, contends that creation fully comprehends God's glory. Idolatry turns the creation into the ultimate reality. We've seen this before. It's called naturalism. No doubt, contemporary scientific naturalism is a lot more sophisticated than pagan fertility cults, but the difference is superficial. Naturalism is idolatry by another name.

Though intuitively appealing, Paley's argument had until recently fallen into disuse. This is now changing. In the last five years, design has witnessed an explosive resurgence. **Scientists are beginning to realize that design can be rigorously formulated as a scientific theory.**

The creation of the world by God is the most magnificent of all acts of creation. It, along with humanity's redemption through Jesus Christ, are the two key instances of God's self-revelation. The revelation of God in creation is typically called general revelation whereas the revelation of God in redemption is typically called special revelation. Consequently, theologians sometimes speak of two books, the Book of Nature, which is God's self-revelation in creation, and the Book of Scripture, which is God's self-revelation in redemption.

If you want to know who God is, you need to know God through both creation and redemption. According to Scripture, the angels praise God chiefly for two things: God's creation of the world and God's redemption of the world through Jesus Christ. Let us follow the angels' example."

Genesis → Revelation: 124X God claims He created the Universe
CREATION = a Biblical Doctrine (not just a Genesis account)

GENESIS (1425 BC)

1:1 *"In the beginning, God created the heavens and the earth."*

1:21 *"...God created great sea creatures and every living thing that moves, with which the waters abounded, according to their kind, and every winged bird according to its kind. And God saw that it was good."*

1:27 *"...God created man in His own image; in the image of God He created him; male and female He created them."*

1:31 *"God saw everything that He had made, and indeed it was very good. So the evening and the morning were the 6th day."*

2:4 *"This is the history of the heavens and the earth when they were created, in the day that the Lord God made the earth and the heavens..."*

2:7 *"...the Lord God formed man of the dust of the ground, and breathed into his nostrils the breath of life; and man became a living being."*

2:21-22 *"...the Lord God caused a deep sleep to fall on Adam, and he slept; and He took 1 of his ribs, and closed up the flesh in its place. Then the rib which the Lord God had taken from man He made into a woman, and He brought her to the man."*

5:1-2 *"This is the book of the genealogy of Adam. In the day that God created man. He made him in the likeness of God. He created them male and female, and blessed them and called them Mankind in the day they were created."*

9:6 *"Whoever sheds man's blood, by man his blood shall be shed; for in the image of God He made man."*

JOB (1500 BC)

5:8-10 *"...as for me, I would seek God, and to God I would commit my cause – who does great things, and unsearchable, marvelous things without number. He gives rain on the earth, and sends waters on the fields."*

9:8-9 *"He alone spreads out the heavens, and treads on the waves of the sea; He made the Bear, Orion, and the Pleiades, and the chambers of the south..."*

10:8-12 *"Your hands have made me and fashioned me, an intricate unity; yet You would destroy me. Remember, I pray, that You have made me like clay, and will You turn me into dust again? Did You not pour me out like milk, and curdle me like cheese, clothe me with skin and flesh, and knit me together with bones and sinews? You have granted me life and favor, and Your care has preserved my spirit."*

12:7-10 *"...ask the beasts, and they will teach you; and the birds of the air, and they will tell you; or speak to the earth, and it will teach you; and the fish of the sea will explain to you. Who among all these does not know that the hand of the Lord has done this, in whose hand is the life of every living thing, and the breath of all mankind?"*

26:13-14 *"By His Spirit He adorned the heavens; His hand pierced the fleeing serpent. Indeed these are the mere edges of His ways, and how small a whisper we hear of Him! But the thunder of His power who can understand?"*

33:4 *"The Spirit of God has made me, and the breath of the Almighty gives me life."*

38:1-38 *"...Who is this who darkens counsel, by words without knowledge? Now prepare yourself like a man; I will question you, and you shall answer Me. Where were you when I laid the foundations of the earth? Tell Me, if you have understanding. Who determined its measurements? Surely you know! Or who stretched the measuring line upon it? To what were its foundations fastened? Or who laid its cornerstone, when the morning stars sang together, and all the sons of God shouted for joy? Or who shut in the sea with doors, when it burst forth and issued from the womb; when I made the clouds its garment, and thick darkness its swaddling band; when I fixed My limit for it, and set bars and doors; when I said, 'This far you may come, but no farther, and here your proud waves must stop!*

"Have you commanded the morning since your days began, and caused the dawn to know its place, that it might take hold of the ends of the earth, and the wicked be shaken out of it? It takes on form like clay under a seal, and stands out like a garment, from the wicked their light is withheld, and the upraised arm is broken. Have you entered the springs of the sea? Or have you walked in search of the depths? Have the gates of death been revealed to you? Or have you seen the doors of the shadow of death? Have you comprehended the breath of the earth? Tell Me, if you know all this. Where is the way to the dwelling of light? And darkness, where is its place, that you may take it to its territory, that you may know the paths to its home? Do you know, because you were born then, or because the number of your days is great?

Have you entered the treasury of snow, or have you seen the treasury of hail, which I have reserved for the time of trouble, for the day of battle and war? By what way is light divided, or the east wind scattered over the earth? Who has divided a channel for the overflowing water, or a path for the thunderbolt, to cause it to rain on a land where there is no one, a wilderness in which there is no man; to satisfy the desolate waste, and cause to spring forth the growth of tender grass? Has the rain a father? Or who has begotten the drops of dew? From whose womb comes the ice? And the frost of heaven, who gives it birth? The waters harden like stone, and the surface of the deep is frozen.

Can you bind the cluster of Pleiades, or loose the belt of Orion? Can you bring out Mazzaroth in its season? Or can you guide the Great Bear with its cubs? Do you know the ordinances of the heavens? Can you set their dominion over the earth?

Can you lift up your voice to the clouds, that an abundance of water may cover you? Can you send out lightnings, that they may go, and say to you, 'Here we are!'? Who has put wisdom into the mind? Or who has given understanding to the heart? Who can number the clouds by wisdom? Or who can pour out the bottles of heaven, when the dust hardens in clumps, and the clods cling together?"

EXODUS (1445 BC)

20:11 *"...in 6 days the Lord made the heavens and the earth, the sea and all that is in them, and rested the 7th day. Therefore the Lord blessed the Sabbath day and hallowed it."*

DEUTERONOMY (1420 BC)

4:32 *"...ask now concerning the days that are past, which were before you, since the day that God created man on the earth..."*

PSALMS (1100 BC)

8:3-5 *"When I consider Your heavens, the work of Your fingers, the moon and the stars, which You have ordained. What is man that You are mindful of him, and the son of man that You care for him? For You have made him a little lower than the angels, and You have crowned him with glory and honor."*

19:1-3 *"The heavens declare the GLORY of God; and the expanse of heaven reveals the work of His hands. Day unto day utters speech and night unto night reveals knowledge. There is no speech nor language where their voice isn't heard."*

24:1-2 *"The earth is the Lord's, and all its fullness. The world and those who dwell therein. For He has founded it upon the seas, and established it upon the waters."*

33:6-9,13-15 *"By the word of the Lord the heavens were made, and all the host of them by the breath of His mouth. He gathers the waters of the sea together as a heap; He lays up the deep in storehouses. Let all the earth fear the Lord; let all the inhabitants of the world stand in awe of Him. For He spoke, and it was done; He commanded, and it stood fast. The Lord looks from heaven; He sees all the sons of men. From the place of His habitation He looks on all the inhabitants of the earth; He fashions their hearts individually; He considers all their works."*

50:10-12 *"...every beast of the forest is Mine, and the cattle on 1,000 hills. I know all the birds of the mountains, and the wild beasts of the field are Mine. If I were hungry, I would not tell you; for the world is Mine, and all its fullness."*

74:16-17 *"The day is Yours, the night also is Yours; You have prepared the light and the sun. You have set all the borders of the earth; You have made summer and winter."*

89:11-12 *"The heavens are Yours, the earth also is Yours; the world and all its fullness, You have founded them. The north and the south, You have created them..."*

90:1-2 *"Lord, You have been our dwelling place in all generations. Before the mountains were brought forth, or ever You had formed the earth and the world, even from everlasting to everlasting, You are God."*

94:8-9 *"Understand, you senseless among the people, and you fools, when will you be wise? He who planted the ear, shall He not hear? He who formed the eye, shall He not see?"*

95:3-7 *"...the Lord is the great God, and the great King above all gods. In His hand are the deep places of the earth; the heights of the hills are His also. The sea is His, for He made it; and His hands formed the dry land. Oh come, let us worship and bow down; let us kneel before the Lord our Maker. For He is our God. And we are the people of His pasture, and the sheep of His hand."*

96:4-6 *"...the Lord is great and greatly to be praised; He is to be feared above all gods. For all the gods of the peoples are idols, but the Lord made the heavens. Honor and majesty are before Him; strength and beauty are in His sanctuary."*

97:1-6 *"The Lord reigns, let the earth rejoice; let the multitude of isles be glad! Clouds and darkness surround Him; righteousness and justice are the foundation of His throne. A fire goes before Him, and burns up His enemies round about. His lightnings light up the world; the earth sees and trembles. The mountains melt like wax at the presence of the Lord, at the presence of the Lord of the whole earth. The heavens declare His righteousness, and all the peoples see His glory."*

98:4,7,8 *"Shout joyfully to the Lord, all the earth; break forth in song, rejoice, and sing praises. Let the sea roar, and all its fullness, the world and those who dwell in it; let the rivers clap their hands; let the hills be joyful together before the Lord."*

100:3 *"Know that the Lord, He is God: it is He who has made us, and not we ourselves; we are His people, and the sheep of His pasture."*

104:1-6 *"O Lord my God, You are very great; You are clothed with honor and majesty, who cover Yourself with light as with a garment, who stretch out the heavens like a curtain. He lays the beams of His upper chambers in the waters, who makes the clouds His chariot, who walks on the wings of the wind, who makes His angels spirits, His ministers a flame of fire. You who laid the foundations of the earth, so that it should not be moved forever, You covered it with the deep as with a garment; the waters stood above the mountains."*

104:24-26 *O Lord, how manifold are Your works! In wisdom You have made them all. The earth is full of Your possessions – this great and wide sea, in which are innumerable teeming things, living things both small and great. There the ships sail about; and there is that Leviathan which You have made to play there."*

115:14-16 *"May the Lord give you increase more and more, you and your children. May you be blessed by the Lord, who made heaven and earth. The heaven, even the heavens, are the Lord's, but the earth He has given to the children of men."*

119:73 *"Your hands have made me and fashioned me; give me understanding, that I may learn Your commandments."*

119:90-91 *"Your faithfulness endures to all generations; You established the earth, and it abides. They continue this day according to Your ordinances, for all are Your servants."*

121:1-2 *"I will lift up my eyes to the hills – from whence comes my help? My help comes from the Lord, who made heaven and earth."*

124:8 *"Our help is in the name of the Lord, who made heaven and earth."*

134:2-3 *"Lift up your hands in the sanctuary, and bless the Lord. The Lord who made heaven and earth..."*

135:5-7 *"...I know that the Lord is great, and our Lord is above all gods. Whatever the Lord pleases He does, in heaven and in earth. In the seas and in all deep places. He causes the vapors to ascend from the ends of the earth; He makes lightning for the rain; He brings the wind out of His treasuries."*

136:5-9 *"To Him who by wisdom made the heavens, for His mercy endures forever; to Him who laid out the earth above the waters, for His mercy endures forever; to Him who made great lights, for His mercy endures forever – the sun to rule by day, for His mercy endures forever; the moon and stars to rule by night, for His mercy endures forever."*

139:13-16 *"...You have formed my inward parts; You have covered me in my mother's womb. I will praise You, for I am fearfully and wonderfully made; marvelous are Your works, and that my soul knows very well. My frame was not hidden from You, when I was made in secret, and skillfully wrought in the lowest parts of the earth. Your eyes saw my substance, being yet unformed. And in Your book they all were written, the days fashioned for me, when as yet there were none of them."*

146:5-6 *"Happy is he who has the God of Jacob for his help, whose hope is in the Lord his God, who made heaven and earth, the sea, and all that is in them..."*

147:4-5,8-9,16-18 *"He counts the number of stars; He calls them all by name. Great is our Lord, and mighty in power; His understanding is infinite...who covers the heavens with clouds, who prepares rain for the earth, who makes grass to grow on the mountains. He gives the beast its food, and to the young ravens that cry. He gives snow like wool; He scatters the frost like ashes; He casts out His hail like morsels; who can stand before His cold? He sends out His word and melts them; He causes His wind to blow, and the waters flow."*

148:1-5 *"Praise the Lord! Praise the Lord from the heavens; praise Him in the heights! Praise Him, all His angels; praise Him, all His hosts! Praise Him, sun and moon. Praise Him, all you stars of light! Praise Him, you heavens of heavens, and you waters above the heavens! Let them praise the name of the Lord, for He commanded and they were created."*

PROVERBS (950 BC)

8:27-30 *"When He prepared the heavens, I was there. When He drew a circle on the face of the deep, when He established the clouds above, when He strengthened the fountains of the deep, when He assigned to the sea its limit, so that the waters would not transgress His command, when He marked out the foundations of the earth, then I was beside Him, as a master craftsman..."*

ECCLESIASTES (930 BC)

7:29 *"Truly, this only I have found: that God made man upright, but they have sought out many schemes."*

12:6-7 *"Remember your Creator before the silver cord is loosed, or the golden bowl is broken, or the pitcher shattered at the fountain, or the wheel broken at the well. Then the dust will return to the earth as it was, and the spirit will return to God who gave it."*

12:1 *"Remember now your Creator in the days of your youth, before the difficult days come, and the years draw near when you say, 'I have no pleasure in them.'"*

JONAH (760 BC)

1:9 *"...he said to them, 'I am a Hebrew; and I fear the Lord, the God of heaven, who made the sea and the dry land.'"*

4:6-11 *"...the Lord God prepared a plant and made it come up over Jonah, that it might be shade for his head to deliver him from his misery. So Jonah was very grateful for the plant. But as morning dawned the next day God prepared a worm, and it so damaged the plant that it withered. And it happened, when the sun arose, that God prepared a vehement east wind; and the sun beat on Jonah's head, so that he grew faint. Then he wished death for himself, and said, 'It is better for me to die than to live.' Then God said to Jonah, 'Is it right for you to be angry about the plant?' And he said, 'It is right for me to be angry, even to death!' But the Lord said, 'You have had pity on the plant, for which you have not labored, nor made it grow, which came up in a night and perished in a night. And should I not pity Nineveh, that great city, in which are more than 120,000 persons who cannot discern between their right hand and their left, and also much livestock?'"*

AMOS (750 BC)

4:13 *"...behold, He who forms mountains, and creates the wind, who declares to man what his thought is, and makes the morning darkness, who treads the high places of the earth – the Lord God of hosts is His name."*

8:8 *"He made the Pleiades and Orion; He turns the shadow of death into morning, and makes the day dark as night; He calls for the waters of the sea and pours them out on the face of the earth; the Lord is His name."*

9:6 *"He who builds His layers in the sky, and has founded His strata in the earth; who calls for the waters of the sea, and pours them out on the face of the earth – the Lord is His name."*

HOSEA (740 BC)

8:14 *"...Israel has forgotten his Maker, and has built palaces; Judah also has multiplied fortified cities, but I will send fire upon his cities, and it shall devour his palaces."*

ISAIAH (720 BC)

40:21-26 *"Have you not known? Have you not heard? Has it not been told to you from the beginning? Have you not understood from the foundations of the earth? It is He who sits above the circle of the earth, and its inhabitants are like grasshoppers, who stretches out the heavens like a curtain, and spreads them out like a tent to dwell in. He reduces the princes to nothing; He makes the judges of the earth useless. Scarcely shall they be planted, scarcely shall they be sown, scarcely shall their stock take root in the earth, when He will also blow on them, and they will wither, and the whirlwind will take them away like stubble. 'To whom then will you liken Me, or to whom shall I be equal?' says the HOLY ONE. Lift up your eyes on high, and see WHO HAS CREATED THESE THINGS, who brings out their host by number; He calls them all by name by the greatness of His might and the strength of His power..."*

40:28 *"Have you not known? Have you not heard? The everlasting God, the Lord, the Creator of the ends of the earth, neither faints nor is weary. There is no searching of His understanding."*

41:20 *"...they may see and know, and consider and understand together, that the hand of the Lord has done this, and the Holy One of Israel has created it."*

42:5 *"Thus says God the Lord, who created the heavens and stretched them out, who spread forth the earth and that which comes from it. Who gives breath to the people on it, and spirit to those who walk on it..."*

43:1 *"...thus says the Lord, who created you, O Jacob, and He who formed you, O Israel: 'Fear not, for I have redeemed you; I have called you by your name; you are Mine."*

43:7 *"Everyone who is called by My name, whom I have created for My glory; I have formed him, yes, I have made him."*

45:8 *"Rain down, you heavens, from above, and let the skies pour down righteousness; let the earth open, let them bring forth salvation, and let righteousness spring up together. I, the Lord, have created it."*

45:12 *"I have made the earth, and created man on it. It was I – My hands that stretched out the heavens, and all their host I have commanded."*

45:18 *"...thus says the Lord, who created the heavens, who is God, who formed the earth and made it, who has established it, who did not create it in vain, who formed it to be inhabited."*

HABAKKUK (610 BC)

3:3-6 *"God came from Teman, the Holy One from Mount Paran. His glory covered the heavens, and the earth was full of His praise. His brightness was like the light. He had rays flashing from His hand, and there His power was hidden. Before Him went pestilence, and fever followed at His feet. He stood and measured His earth, He looked and startled the nations. And the everlasting mountains were scattered, the perpetual hills bowed. His ways are everlasting."*

3:10-11 *"The mountains saw You and trembled; the overflowing of the water passed by. The deep uttered its voice, and lifted its hands on high. The sun and moon stood still in their habitation; at the light of Your arrows they went. At the shining of Your glittering spear."*

JEREMIAH (600 BC)

1:5 *"Before I formed you in the womb I knew you; before you were born I sanctified you; and I ordained you a prophet to the nations."*

5:22 *"'Do you not fear Me?' says the Lord. 'Will you not tremble at My presence, who have placed the sand as the bound of the sea, by a perpetual decree, that it cannot pass beyond it? And though its waves toss to and fro, yet they cannot prevail; though they roar, yet they cannot pass over it.'"*

23:24 *"'Can anyone hide himself in secret places, so I shall not see him?' says the Lord; 'Do I not fill heaven and earth?'"*

10:10-13 *"...the Lord is the true God; He is the living God and the everlasting King. At His wrath the earth will tremble, and the nations will not be able to abide His indignation. Thus you shall say to them: 'The gods that have not made the heavens and earth shall perish from the earth and from under these heavens.' He has made the earth by His power, He has established the world by His wisdom, and has stretched out the heavens at His discretion. When He utters His voice, there is a multitude waters in the heavens; and He causes the vapors to ascend from the ends of the earth. He makes lightning for the rain, He brings the wind out of His treasuries."*

31:35-37 *"Thus says the Lord, who gives the sun for a light by day, and the ordinances of the moon and the stars for a light by night, who disturbs the sea, and its waves roar (the Lord of hosts is His name): 'If those ordinances depart from before Me, says the Lord, Then the seed of Israel shall also cease from being a nation before Me forever.' Thus says the Lord, 'If heaven above can be measured, and the foundations of the earth searched out beneath, I will also cast off all the seed of Israel for all that they have done,' says the Lord."*

32:17,26-27 *"Ah, Lord God! Behold, You have made the heavens and the earth by Your great power and outstretched arm. There is nothing too hard for You. Then the word of the Lord came to Jeremiah, saying: 'Behold, I am the Lord, the God of all flesh. Is there anything too hard for Me?'"*

51:15-16 *"He has made the earth by His power; He has established the world by His wisdom, and stretched out the heaven by His understanding. When He utters His voice - there is a multitude of waters in the heavens; He causes the vapors to ascend from the ends of the earth; He makes lightnings for the rain; He brings the wind out of His treasuries."*

EZEKIEL (580 BC)

18:4 *"Behold, all souls are Mine; the soul of the father as well as the soul of the son is Mine; the soul that sins shall die."*

28:12-13,15 *"...thus says the Lord God: 'You were the seal of perfection, full of wisdom and perfect in beauty. You were in Eden, the garden of God; every precious stone was your covering: the sardius, topaz, and diamond, beryl, onyx, and jasper, sapphire, turquoise, and emerald with gold. The workmanship of your timbrels and pipes was prepared for you on the day you were created. You were perfect in your ways from the day you were created, till iniquity was found in you.'"*

DANIEL (535 BC)

5:23 *"...the God who holds your breath in His hand and owns all your ways, you have not glorified."*

7:9-10 *"I watched till thrones were put in place, and the Ancient of Days was seated; His garment was white as snow, and the hair of His head was like pure wool. His throne was a fiery flame, its wheels a burning fire; a fiery stream issued and came forth from before Him. A thousand thousands ministered to Him; ten thousand times ten thousand stood before Him. The court was seated, and the books were opened."*

7:13-14 *"I was watching in the night visions, and behold, One like the Son of Man, coming with the clouds of heaven! He came to the Ancient of Days, and they brought Him near before Him. Then to Him was given dominion and glory and a kingdom, that all peoples, nations, and languages should serve Him. His dominion is an everlasting dominion, which shall not pass away, and His kingdom the one which shall not be destroyed."*

HAGGAI (520 BC)

2:6-8 *"...thus says the Lord of hosts: 'Once more (it is a little while) I will shake heaven and earth, the sea and dry land; and I will shake all nations, and they shall come to the Desire of Nations, and I will fill this temple with glory', says the Lord of hosts. 'The silver is Mine, and the gold is Mine,' says the Lord of hosts."*

ZECHARIAH (500 BC)

12:1 *"...thus says the Lord, who stretches out the heavens, lays the foundation of the earth, and forms the spirit of man within him..."*

MALACHI (430 BC)

2:10 *"Have we not all one Father? Has not one God created us?"*

1CHRONICLES (430 BC)

16:25-26 *"...the Lord is great and greatly to be praised; He is also to be feared above all gods. For all the gods of the peoples are idols, but the Lord made the heavens."*

NEHEMIAH (420 BC)

9:5-6 *"Stand up and bless the Lord your God forever and ever! Blessed be Your glorious name, which is exalted above all blessing and praise! You alone are the Lord; You have made heaven; the heaven of heavens, with all their host, the earth and all things on it, the seas and all that is in them. And You preserve them all. The host of heaven worships You."*

JAMES (AD 45)

1:17-18 *"Every good gift and every perfect gift is from above, and comes down from the Father of lights, with whom there is no variation or shadow of turning. Of His own will He brought us forth by the word of truth, that we might be a kind of firstfruits of His creatures."*

ROMANS (AD 55)

1:19-20 *"...because what may be known of God is evident among them, for God has shown it to them. For since the creation of the world His invisible attributes are clearly seen, being understood by the things that are made, even His eternal power and divine nature, so that they are without excuse."*

1:24-25 *"...God also gave them up to uncleanness, in the lusts of their hearts, to dishonor their bodies among themselves, who exchanged the truth of God for the lie, and worshiped and served the creature rather than the Creator, who is blessed forever. Amen."*

8:20-22 *"...the creation was subjected to futility, not willingly, but because of Him who subjected it in hope; because the creation itself also will be delivered from the bondage of corruption into the glorious liberty of the children of God. For we know that the whole creation groans and labors with birth pangs together until now."*

9:20-21 *"...indeed, O man, who are you to reply against God? Will the thing formed say to Him who formed it, 'Why have you made me like this?' Does not the potter have power over the clay, from the same lump to make 1 vessel for honor and another for dishonor?"*

11:34-36 *"...who has known the mind of the Lord? Or who has become His counselor? Or who has 1st given to Him and is shall be repaid to him? For of Him and through Him and to Him are all things, to whom be the glory forever. Amen."*

1CORINTHIANS (AD 55)

11:8-9 *"...man is not from woman, but woman from man. Nor was man created for the woman, but woman for the man."*

15:38-39 *"...God gives it a body as He pleases, and to each seed its own body. All flesh is not the same flesh, but there is 1 kind of flesh of men, another flesh of beasts, another of fish, and another of birds."*

15:45-49 *"...so it is written, 'The 1st man Adam became a living being.' The last Adam became a life-giving spirit. However, the spiritual is not 1st, but the natural, and afterward the spiritual. The 1st man was of the earth, made of dust; the 2nd Man is the Lord from heaven. As was the man of dust, so also are those who are made of dust; and as is the heavenly Man, so also are those who are heavenly. And as we have borne the image of the man of dust, we shall also bear the image of the heavenly Man."*

2CORINTHIANS (AD 56)

4:6 *"...it is the God who commanded the light to shine out of darkness who has shone in our hearts to give the light of the knowledge of the glory of God in the face of Jesus Christ."*

11:3 *"...I fear, lest somehow, as the serpent deceived Eve by his craftiness, so your minds may be corrupted from the simplicity that is in Christ."*

MATTHEW (AD 60)

8:26-27 *"...He said to them, 'Why are you fearful, O you of little faith?' Then He arose and rebuked the winds and the sea. And there was a great calm. And the men marveled, saying, 'Who can this be, that even the winds and the sea obey Him?'"*

11:25 *"...Jesus answered and said, 'I thank You, Father, Lord of heaven and earth, because You have hidden these things from the wise and prudent, and have revealed them to babes.'"*

28:18 *"...Jesus came and spoke to them, saying, 'All authority has been given to Me in heaven and on earth.'"*

MARK (AD 60)

10:6-9 *"...from the beginning of the creation, 'God made them male and female.' For this reason a man shall leave his father and mother and be joined to his wife, and the two shall become one flesh'; so them they are no longer two, but one flesh. Therefore what God has joined together, let no man separate."*

13:19 *"For in those days there will be tribulation, such as has not been from the beginning of creation which God created until this time, nor ever shall be."*

LUKE (AD 60)

21:33 *"Heaven and earth will pass away, but My words will by no means pass away."*

ACTS (AD 60)

4:24,29 *"So when they heard that, they raised their voice to God with 1 accord and said, 'Lord, You are God, who made heaven and earth and the sea, and all that is in them...Now, Lord, look on their threats, and grant to Your servants that with all boldness they may speak Your word..."*

14:15-17 *"...we also are men with the same nature as you, and preach to you that you should turn from these vain things to the living God, who made the heaven, the earth, the sea, and all things that are in them, who in bygone generations allowed all nations to walk in their own ways. Nevertheless He did not leave Himself without witness, in that He did good, gave us rain from heaven and fruitful seasons, filling our hearts with food and gladness."*

17:22-30 *"Then Paul stood in the midst of Mars Hill and said, 'Men of Athens, I perceive that in all things you are very religious; for as I was passing through and considering the objects of your worship, I even found an altar with this inscription: TO THE UNKNOWN GOD. Therefore, the One whom you worship without knowing, Him I proclaim to you: God, who made the world and everything in it, since He is Lord of heaven and earth, does not dwell in temples made with hands. Nor is He worshipped with mans' hands, as though He needed anything, since He gives to all life, breath, and all things.*

And He has made from 1 blood every nation of men to dwell on all the face of the earth, and has determined their preappointed times and the boundaries of their habitation, so that they should seek the Lord, in the hope that they might grope for Him and find Him, though He is not far from each one of us; for in Him we live and move and have our being, as also some of your own poets have said, "For we are also His offspring." Therefore, since we are the offspring of God, we ought not to think that the Divine Nature is like gold or silver or stone, something shaped by art and man's devising. Truly, these times of ignorance God overlooked, but now commands all men everywhere to repent..."

EPHESIANS (AD 60)

2:10 *"...we are His workmanship, created in Christ Jesus for good works..."*

3:9 *"...God who created all things through Jesus Christ..."*

COLOSSIANS (AD 60)

1:15-17 *"He is the image of the invisible God, the firstborn over all creation. For by Him all things were created that are in heaven and that are on earth, visible and invisible, whether thrones or dominions or principalities or powers. All things were created through Him and for Him. And He is before all things, and in Him all things consist."*

3:9-10 *"Do not lie to one another, since you have put off the old man with his deeds, and have put on the new man who is renewed in knowledge according to the image of Him who created him..."*

1TIMOTHY (AD 63)

4:1-3 *"Now the Spirit expressly says that in latter times some will depart from the faith, giving heed to deceiving and doctrines of demons, speaking lies in hypocrisy, having their conscience seared with a hot iron, forbidding to marry, and commanding to abstain from foods which God created to be received with thanksgiving by those who believe and know the truth."*

1PETER (AD 64)

1:20 *"He (Jesus) indeed was foreordained before the foundation of the world, but was manifest in these last times for you..."*

4:19 *"...let those who suffer according to the will of God commit their souls to Him in doing good, as to a faithful Creator."*

2PETER (AD 65)

3:3-6 *"...scoffers will come in the last days, walking according to their own lusts, and saying, 'Where is the promise of His coming? For since the fathers fell asleep, all things continue as they were from the beginning of creation.' For this they willingly forget, that by the word of God the heavens were of old, and the earth standing out of water and in the water, by which the world that then existed perished, being flooded with water."*

HEBREWS (AD 68)

1:1-3 *"God, who at various times and in different ways spoke in times past to the fathers by the prophets, has in these last days spoken to us by His Son, whom He has appointed heir of all things, through whom also He made the worlds; who being the brightness of His glory and the express image of His person, and upholding all things by the word of His power, when He had by Himself purged our sins, sat down at the right hand of the Majesty on high..."*

1:10 *"You, Lord, in the beginning laid the foundation of the earth, and the heavens are the work of Your hands..."*

2:6-8 *"...one testified in a certain place, saying: 'What is man, that You are mindful of him, or the son of man that You take care of him? You made him a little lower than the angels. You crowned him with glory and honor, and set him over the works of Your hands. You have put all things in subjection under his feet."*

3:4 *"...every house is built by someone, but He who built all things is God."*

4:3-4 *"...we who have believed do enter that rest, as He has said: 'So I swore in My wrath, they shall not enter My rest,' although the works were finished from the foundation of the world. For He who has spoken in a certain place of the 7th day in this way: 'And God rested on the 7th day from all His works...'"*.

4:10 *"...he who has entered His rest has himself also ceased from his works as God did from His."*

11:1-3,6 *"Now faith is the realization of things hoped for, the evidence of things not seen. For by it the elders obtained a good testimony. By faith we understand that the worlds were framed by the word of God, so that the things which are seen were not made of things which are visible. But without faith it is impossible to please Him, for he who comes to God must believe that He is, and that He is a rewarder of those who diligently seek Him."*

JOHN (AD 85)

1:1-5,10 *"In the beginning was the Word, and the Word was with God, and the Word was God. He was in the beginning with God. All things were made through Him, and without Him nothing was made that was made. In Him was life, and the life was the light of men. And the light shines in the darkness, and the darkness did not comprehend it. He was in the world, and the world was made through Him, and the world did not know Him."*

17:24 *"Father, I desire that they also whom You gave Me may be with Me where I am, that they may behold My glory which You have given Me; for You loved Me before the foundation of the world."*

REVELATION (AD 95)

4:11 *"...You created all things, and by Your will they exist and were created."*

10:5-6 *"...the angel whom I saw standing on the sea and on the land lifted up his hand to heaven and swore by Him who lives forever and ever, who created heaven and the things that are in it, the earth and the things that are in it, and the sea and the things that are in it, that there should be delay no longer..."*

14:7 *"... worship Him who made heaven and earth, the sea and springs of water."*

How does *SCIENCE* explain the Existence of the Universe? 1.2

The "Big Bang" Theory ➔ It *BEGAN* with a Random "Explosion" of a "Singularity"

- The physical universe (the four dimensions of matter, energy, space and time) exploded from a *singularity* ("kernel" of mass energy of near-infinite density, temperature and pressure about the size of a pinhead), about 13-15 billion years ago. The universe expanded, and continues to expand today, from this explosion.

- As radiation expanded from this *random explosion*, the *precise* Laws of Thermodynamics require its simultaneous *cooling*. This rapid cooling down explains how hydrogen and helium atoms formed (today's universe: 73% H, 24% He, 3% heavy elements).

- The first stars formed from the cooling gas in the young universe. This star-forming process led to planets and galaxies.

Big Bang Theory: Outline of Events (initial explosion-to-origin of Solar System-to-me)

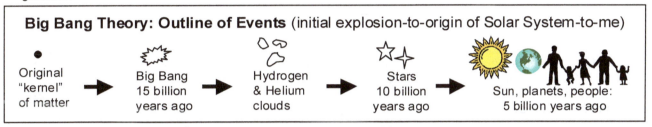

Original "kernel" of matter ➔ Big Bang 15 billion years ago ➔ Hydrogen & Helium clouds ➔ Stars 10 billion years ago ➔ Sun, planets, people: 5 billion years ago

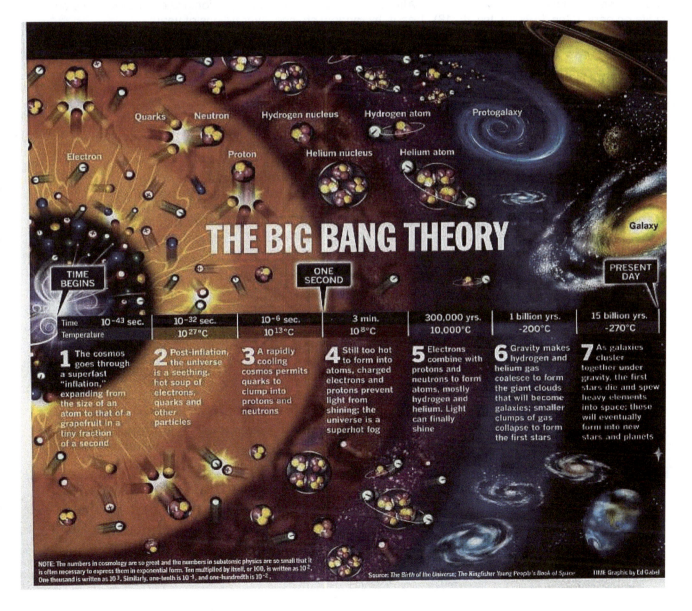

Source: The Birth of the Universe; The Kingfisher Young People's Book of Space. TIME Graphic by Ed Gabel

Is the "Big Bang" Theory biblical?

The Bible	The Big Bang
All elements made together - Gen. 1:1	Elements beyond H and He formed after millions of years
Origin of matter = God simply said so (predicts 1st Law of Thermodynamics) – Ps 33:9	Origin of matter = from *nothing* (violates 1st Law of Thermodynamics: matter can't be created without violating energy conservation; the 1st Law says total amount of energy in the universe is a constant).
Earth formed before the stars; sun was formed on the 4th day, after the earth Gen. 1:1-5 Day #1 = earth, light Gen. 1:14-19 Day #4 = stars, Sun, Moon	Earth formed long after the stars; Sun was formed before the earth
Sun, moon and stars formed together (Gen. 1:14-19)	Sun was formed from older stars
God fine-tuned His creation, without a "Big Bang" (Gen. 1:14, Job 9:8-9 = He formed the planets, stars and galaxies and set them into precise motions)	*An explosion is random, not precise: it throws matter apart and expands outward until its energy dissipates, but the Big Bang mysteriously produced the opposite effect: intricate planets, stars and entire galaxies evolved when the initial matter exploded).*
God precisely designed the universe for life on earth (Gen.1, Ps 19, Isa. 45:18).	After the Big Bang's random explosion, life eventually arose on earth by random chance, over billions of years.

If the "Big Bang Theory" isn't biblical, why is it important?

• Michael Behe (The Problem for Scientists = Big Bang implies Intelligent Design): *"Saying that the universe began in a Big Bang is one thing, but saying life was designed by an intelligence is another. The phrase 'Big Bang' itself evokes only images of an explosion, not necessarily a person. The phrase 'Intelligent Design' seems more urgent and quickly invites questions about who the designer might have been."*

Steady State, Big Bang, Creation: which of these 3 Theories for the Origin of the Universe fits the evidence?	
Secular Models of Origins (Big Bang, Steady State): neither can be observed; both *CONTRADICT* the two proven scientific Laws of Thermodynamics	**Creation Model of Origins:** can't be observed, but it *PREDICTS* the two proven scientific Laws of Thermodynamics
Steady State Theory = matter evolved into its present structure far out into non-observable space (to offset the tendency toward universal decay, new matter is continually evolving into existence out of nothing somewhere out in space). **Big Bang Theory** = a primeval explosion of some kind (perhaps due to a previous gravitational collapse into a super-dense state) is supposed to have converted energy into matter ("something comes from nothing").	what it states: all major systems and categories in nature – including stars and galaxies – were created in the beginning, each with a distinctive structure to serve a distinctive purpose. what it predicts: stars and galaxies won't change (especially not to enable them to advance to higher levels in the hierarchy of stars). what is observed: no stars or galaxies have ever changed (confirming the creation model)

What is God teaching us?   Psalm 90: The ETERNITY OF GOD and the FRALITY OF MAN
vs. 12 *"Teach us to number our days, that we may gain a heart of wisdom."* (Ps 95:6-7, Ps 100:3)

What leading Scientists say:
The Universe began as a 1-Time Creative Act by an *Intelligent Mind*

1.3

Some of the most influential physicists in history are quoted as saying the scientific evidence for the creation of the Universe best fits the idea of an Intelligent First Cause, as best explained in the Christian Bible:

1 Lord William Kelvin (1824-1907) - Scottish Mathematical Physicist: "*Science positively affirms Creative Power. It is not in dead matter that we live and move and have our being, but in the creating and directing Power which science compels us to accept as an article of belief.*"

2 John Ambrose Fleming (1849-1945) - PhD Physics Univ. College of London; first Professor of Physics and Mathematics at Univ. of Nottingham; first Professor of Electrical Engineering at Univ. of Cambridge: "'*it (the Bible) is, and always has been, revered as the communication to us from the Creator of the Universe, the Supreme and Everlasting God.*'"

3 Albert Einstein (1879-1955) - PhD Theoretical Physics; 1921 Nobel Prize in Physics; Time Person of the Century, 1999: "*That deeply emotional conviction of the presence of a superior Reasoning Power, which is revealed in the incomprehensible Universe, forms my idea of God.*" (Memorial speech for Christian Anfinsen at Memorial Garden Dedication, Weizmann Institute. Nov. 16, 1995).

4 Arthur Eddington (1882-1944) - British Astrophysicist; Cambridge Prof. of Astronomy and Philosophy; Director of Cambridge Observatory: "*Philosophically, the notion of an ubrupt beginning to the present order of Nature is repugnant to me … even those who would welcome a proof of the intervention of a Creator will probably consider that a single winding up at some remote epoch is not really the kind of relation between God and his world that brings satisfaction to the mind.*" ("*Cosmos and Creator*", S. Jaki, 1980).

5 Arthur Compton (1892-1962) - PhD Physics, 1927 Nobel Prize in Physics, Chairman Univ. of Chicago Physics Dept., Head of WWII Plutonium Project (first self-sustaining nuclear reaction): "*For myself, faith begins with the realization that a supreme intelligence brought the universe into being and created man. It is not difficult for me to have this faith, for it is incontrovertible that where there is a plan there is intelligence. An orderly, unfolding universe testifies to the truth of the most majestic statement ever uttered: 'In the beginning God ...'*" (quoted in Chicago Daily News when asked his view of the 1st verse of the Bible, 1936).

6 Sir Fred Hoyle (1915-2001) - Cambridge Prof. of Astrophysics and Natural Philosophy; Founder, Institute of Theoretical Astronomy in Cambridge: "*The big bang theory requires a recent origin of the Universe that openly invites the concept of creation.*" ('The Intelligent Universe', Holt, Rinehard, and Winston, 1983).

7 Wernher von Braun (1912-1977) - PhD Physics, 1975 winner, National Medal of Science; Leader of rocket technology in both Germany and US; NASA Director of Marshall Space Flight Center: "*To be forced to believe only one conclusion--that everything in the universe happened by chance--would violate the very objectivity of science itself. What random process could produce the brains of a man or the system of the human eye?*"

8 Robert Jastrow (1925-2008) - PhD Theoretical Physics, Director of NASA's Goddard Institute for Space Studies: "*Astronomers now find they have painted themselves into a corner because they have proven, by their own methods, that the world began abruptly in an act of creation to which you can trace the seeds of every star, every planet, every living thing in this cosmos and on the earth. And they have found that all this happened as a product of forces they cannot hope to discover. That there are what I or anyone would call supernatural forces at work is now, I think, a scientifically proven fact.*" (Christianity Today, Aug. 6, 1982); "*Now three lines of evidence – the motion of the galaxies, the laws of thermodynamics, and the life story of the stars – pointed to one conclusion: all indicated the Universe had a beginning.*" ('God and the Astronomers', Warner Books, 1978).

9 Charles Townes (1915 -) - PhD Physics, 1964 Nobel Prize in Physics, Prof. Astrophysics, Univ. of Berkeley: "*I strongly believe in the existence of God, based on intuition, observations, logic, and also scientific knowledge.*" (letter to T. Dimitrov, 2002, on the question, "What do you think about the existence of God?")

10 Robert W. Wilson (1936 -) - PhD Physics, 1978 Nobel Prize in Physics, Professor of Physics, State Univ. of New York: "*Certainly there was something that set it all off. Certainly, if you are religious, I can't think of a better theory of the origin of the universe to match with Genesis.*" ('Show Me God: What the Message from Space Is Telling Us About God', Day Star Publications, 2000).

11 George Smoot (1945 -) - PhD Particle Physics, 2006 Nobel Prize in Physics; Prof. of Physics at Univ. of California Berkeley: "*There is no doubt that a parallel exists between the big bang as an event and the Christian notion of creation from nothing…*" ('Wrinkles in Time', William Morrow and Company, 1993).

The History of Science & Religion ⇨ Mathematics, Physics, Astronomy, Cosmology

| 1600's | 1800's | 1900's | 2000's | Today |

Johannes Kepler (1571-1630) German Astronomer, Mathematician, Founder: Laws of Planetary Motion

Blaise Pascal (1623-1662) French Mathematician, Physicist, Philosopher; Founder: Statistics

Isaac Newton (1643-1727) British Mathematician, Physicist, Invented Differential Calculus; Founder: Law of Gravity, Laws of Motion

William Herschel (1738-1822) British Astronomer, Founder: Galactic Astronomy; Telescope Designer, Detailed description of Milky Way Galaxy

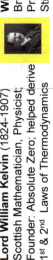

Bernard Riemann (1826-1866) German Mathematician; Founder: Riemannian Geometry; Paved way for Theory of Relativity by proposing how light bends in space

Michael Faraday (1791-1867) British Physicist, Mathematician; Greatest Experimenter in History; Founder: 2nd Law of Electrolysis, Science of Electromagnetism

James Maxwell (1831-1879) Scottish Physicist; 19th century's greatest scientist; Founder: equations for a unified model of electromagnetism

George Stokes (1819-1903) Irish Mathematician, Physicist ; Founder: Stokes Law, Fluid Dynamics, Mathematical Physics

Lord William Kelvin (1824-1907) Scottish Mathematician, Physicist; Founder: Absolute Zero; helped derive 1st & 2nd Laws of Thermodynamics

Lord Rayleigh (1842-1919) British Physicist; 1904 Nobel Prize; Founder: Argon, "Rayleigh Waves"

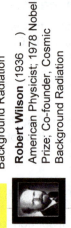

Arthur Eddington (1882-1944) British Astrophysicist; Director, Cambridge Observatory; helped Einstein with Theory of Relativity

John Fleming (1849-1945) English Physicist; 1st Prof. of Electrical Engineering; Founder: "Fleming Valve" (started field of Electronics)

Max Planck (1858-1947) German Physicist; 1918 Nobel Prize; Founder: Quantum Theory

Robert Milliken (1868-1953) American Physicist; 1923 Nobel Prize; Founder: electron charge

Albert Einstein (1879-1955) German Physicist; 1921 Nobel Prize; Founder: Theory of Relativity

Erwin Schrödinger (1887-1961) Austrian Physicist; 1933 Nobel Prize; Founder: Wave Mechanics, Schrödinger Equation

Arthur Compton (1892-1962) American Physicist; 1927 Nobel Prize; Founder: Compton Effect

William Bragg (1890-1971) British Physicist; 1915 Nobel Prize; Founder: Crystal Structures via X-rays

Werner Heisenberg (1901-1976) German Physicist; 1932 Nobel Prize; Founder: Quantum Mechanics

Wernher von Braun (1912-1977) German Physicist; 1st Rocket Scientist; Director of Marshall Space Center

Richard Feynman (1918-1988) American Physicist; 1965 Nobel Prize; Founder: Quantum Electrodynamics

Arthur Schawlow (1921-1999) American Physicist; 1981 Nobel Prize; Founder: Laser Spectroscopy

Fred Hoyle (1915-2001) British Astrophysicist; Founder: Institute of Theoretical Astronomy

Robert Jastrow (1925-2008) American Physicist; Director NASA Institute for Space Studies

Alan Sandage (1926-2010) American Astronomer; Founder: Observational Cosmology; measured universe size and age

Charles Townes (1915 -) American Physicist; 1964 Nobel Prize; Founder: Maser Technology

Steven Weinberg (1933 -) American Physicist; 1975 Nobel Prize; Founder, Electroweak Unification Theory

Arno Penzias (1933 -) American Physicist; 1978 Nobel Prize; Co-founder: Cosmic Background Radiation

Robert Wilson (1936 -) American Physicist; 1978 Nobel Prize; Co-founder, Cosmic Background Radiation

George Ellis (1939 -) South African Mathematician & Physicist, one of world's leading Theorists in Cosmology

Paul Davies (1942 -) British Physicist; Chair, Post-Detection Science of International Academy of Aeronautics

Stephen Hawking (1942 -) British Physicist & Cosmologist; Director, Cambridge Center for Theoretical Cosmology

Henry Schaefer (1944 -) American Physicist & Chemist; Director, Center Computational Quantum Chemistry

George Smootz (1945 -) American Physicist; 2006 Nobel Prize; Senior Scientist, Berkeley National Lab

Frank Tipler(1947 -) American Mathematician, Physicist, Cosmologist; Prof. Tulane Univ.

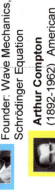

William Phillips (1948 -) American Physicist; 1997 Nobel Prize; Founder: Laser Cooling

Christian — yellow
Pantheist — blue
Deist — grey
Agnostic — black
Atheist — orange/red

"I strongly believe in the existence of God, based on intuition, observations, logic, and scientific knowledge."
(Charles Townes, 1964 Nobel Prize in Physics)

What the Bible says:
The Beginning of the Universe was a 1-Time Creative Act from 'No-Thing'[6]

→ <u>Jesus contradicts today's Big Bang Theory</u> "In Mark's account of Christ's response to the Pharisees concerning marriage and divorce, he repeats Christ's words as follows: *'But from the beginning of creation God made them male and female'* (Mark 10:6; see also Matthew 19:4-6). This is a reference to the creation of Adam and Eve – in fact, it includes an actual quote from Genesis 1:27 – on the sixth day of the primeval week of creation. The important point is that 'God made them male and female' from the beginning of the creation – not 4.6 billion years after creation began!

Modern evolutionists believe that the 'creation' started with the 'Big Bang' perhaps 15 billion years ago, and human life about one million years ago – long, long after the beginning of creation! Jesus Christ, however, who was there at the beginning of creation, said that man and woman were there, too!

'Christian evolution' is a contradiction in terms; there is no such thing. The Lord Jesus Christ was no evolutionist. As God, He was the Creator; as man, He was a creationist. Furthermore, He was a 'young-earth creationist'; the very idea of billions of years of meaningless history before man appeared on earth is directly contradicted by this straightforward statement of His."

→ <u>Luke's Gospel contradicts today's Big Bang Theory</u> *"At the birth of John the Baptist, his father Zacharias offered praise to God because of his imminent fulfillment of all God's ancient messianic promises given 'by the mouth of His holy prophets, which have been since the world began'* (Luke 1:70). Note his testimony that God's prophets had been prophesying 'since the world began' – not beginning over 4 billion years later! Luke (as does Matthew) mentions *'the blood of Abel'* as the first in a long line of martyred prophets, the blood of whom *'was shed from the foundation of the world'* (Luke 11:50, 51), not starting four billion years after the foundation of the world."

→ <u>Acts contradicts today's Big Bang Theory</u> "Peter reminded the people of God's primeval promises, which were now in the process of fulfillment. *'And He shall send Jesus Christ, which before was preached unto you: whom the heaven must receive until the times of restitution (that is, restoration) of all things, which God hath spoken by the mouth of His holy prophets since the world began'* (Acts 3:20,21). Contrary to the opinions of pagan philosophers, there had been a beginning! And from the beginning (not several billion years after the beginning), God had been promising the coming Savior. In fact, the word here for "world" is the Greek aion, meaning "time" or "age" or even "space/ time". Peter was saying that the promise had been given through the prophets since the very beginning of the space/ time universe. There was no room for any evolutionary gaps before man in this context!"

→ <u>Hebrews contradicts today's Big Bang Theory</u> "In Hebrews 4, there is an explicit confirmation that the creation was completed at the end of creation week, in a context comparing God's rest after completing His work of creation to the believer's rest in Christ after he ceases trusting in his works for salvation. *'The works were finished from the foundation of the world. For He spake in a certain place of the seventh day on this wise, And God did rest the seventh day from all His works.'* (Hebrews 4:3,4). This is further confirmed in Hebrews 4:10: *'He that is entered into His rest, he also hath ceased from his own works, as God did from His.'* God has not ceased from His work of sustaining and saving His creation, but He, long ago, finished His work of creating and making all things. This reminder once again stresses clearly that no 'creation' (that is, no evolution – not even theistic evolution) is going on today. Everything was finished and functioning from the beginning. The weekly rest every seventh day is a worldwide commemoration of that fact."

John MacArthur[7]: The Bible's *DAY 7* points to a 1-Time Creation from 'No-Thing'

"Genesis 2:1-2 says that the uniqueness of the seventh day stems first from the fact that God had ended the work of creation. *'Thus the heavens and the earth, and all the host of them, were FINISHED. And on the seventh day God ENDED His work which He had done, and He RESTED on the seventh day from ALL His work which He had done.'* The entire work of creation was complete in six days, just as God had planned. And with the dawn of the seventh day, God ceased from creating. Four times in the first three verses of Genesis 2, the text states that God had finished ALL the work of creation. This argues against evolution, which suggests that creation is a work still in process. The biblical emphasis is on the utter PERFECTION of everything God created and the wondrously brief time in which He accomplished it all. The clear statement of Scripture is that 'the heavens and the earth, and all the host of them, were FINISHED'.

Interestingly, science itself offers evidence that Genesis 2:1 is true. The 1st Law of Thermodynamics rules out the possibility of ongoing creation, and the 2nd Law of Thermodynamics eliminates the possibility that an ordered universe evolved naturally from chaos. The Bible consistently says that God created it all in six days, and Genesis 2:1 says that on the seventh day He ceased from His creative work. There is no ongoing creation of matter and energy; It is neither eternal nor self-sufficient. It is the product of God's creative genius."

9 Evidences for Argument #1 (Universe originated out of 'NO-THING')
Scientific Facts #1-8, Philosophical Fact #9

We will provide well known scientific facts for the universe being created by God, as well as one indisputable philosophical fact that the universe had to have a beginning. The eight scientific evidences are listed below, with a quote from Michael Behe serving as the introduction to our investigation. Our ninth evidence is taken from Norman Geisler, and is the argument that the universe had to have a starting point. We'll review that first.

Evidence #1 = General Theory of Relativity	Evidence #2 = The Hubble Constant
Evidence #3 = The Doppler Red Shift	Evidence #4 = The Expansion Rate of the Universe
Evidence #5 = The Cosmic Background Radiation	Evidence #6 = First Law of Thermodynamics
Evidence #7 = Second Law of Thermodynamics	Evidence #8 = The Law of Causality
Evidence #9 = Time had a beginning (it cannot go back into the past forever)	

Michael Behe, "Darwin's Black Box"[16] **– Evidences #1-5:** *"About 70 years ago most scientists thought the universe was infinite in age and size. In contrast Judaism and Christianity thought the universe was created in time and was not eternal. Einstein discovered that his ① GENERAL THEORY OF RELATIVITY predicted an unstable universe – one that would expand or contract, but would not remain stationary. Einstein, in what he later admitted was the greatest mistake of his career, inserted a 'correction factor' into his equations to make them predict a stationary, eternal universe.*

A short time later the astronomer ② EDWIN HUBBLE observed that wherever in the sky he pointed his telescope, the stars appeared to be moving away from the earth at a speed that was proportional to their distance from the earth (he couldn't actually see stars moving. He inferred their motion from a phenomenon called a ③ DOPPLER SHIFT, where stars that are moving away from an observer emit light of a longer wavelength – the faster they move, the greater the change in the wavelength). This was the first observable evidence that Einstein's unfudged equations were correct in predicting the ④ EXPANSION OF THE UNIVERSE. It didn't take a rocket scientist to mentally reverse the expanding universe and conclude that at some time in the past, all of the matter in the universe was concentrated into a very small place. This was the beginning of the Big Bang hypothesis... Despite its religious implications, the Big Bang was a scientific theory that flowed from <u>observable data</u>, not from holy writings or visions. Most physicists adopted the Big Bang theory and set research programs accordingly. A few didn't like the implications of the theory and tried to develop alternatives.

The astronomer Fred Hoyle championed another theory of the universe, called Steady-State theory. Hoyle proposed that the universe was infinite and eternal, but he also admitted that the universe was expanding. Since a universe that has been expanding for an infinite period of time would become infinitely thinned out, even if it started with an infinite amount of matter, Hoyle had to explain why our present universe is relatively dense. He proposed that matter was continually coming into existence in outer space at the rate of about one hydrogen atom per cubic mile of space per year. Now, it must be emphasized that Hoyle was proposing creation of hydrogen from nothing and with no cause. Since he had no <u>observable evidence</u> to support this notion, why did he propose it? Hoyle thought the Big Bang strongly implied the supernatural and found the prospect extremely distasteful.

In the 1960's the astronomers Penzias and Wilson finally put Hoyle's steady-state theory out of its misery with their observation of ⑤ BACKGROUND RADIATION. They saw that microwaves are bombarding the earth from every direction with uniform intensity. Such background radiation was predicted to be an indirect result of the Big Bang. But the theory justified itself by reference to <u>observable data</u> – the expansion of the universe - and not by invoking sacred texts or mystical experiences of holy men. The model came right from <u>observable evidence</u>." The observation of the background radiation was, and still is, taken to be the crowning glory of the Big Bang theory. The success of the Big Bang model had nothing to do with its religious implications. It seems to agree with the Judaeo-Christian dogma of a beginning to the universe...."

Norman Geisler, "When Skeptics Ask"[31] **– Evidence #9:** *"Beyond the scientific evidence that shows the universe began, there is a philosophical reason to believe that the world had a starting point. This argument shows that TIME CANNOT GO BACK INTO THE PAST FOREVER. You see it is impossible to pass through an infinite series of moments. You might be able to imagine passing through an infinite number of dimensionless points on a line by moving your finger from one end to the other, but time is not dimensionless or imaginary. It is real and each moment that passes uses up real time that we can't go back to....*

If the past is infinite (which is another way of saying, 'If the universe had always existed without a beginning'), then we could never have passed through time to get to today. If the past is an infinite series of moments, and right now is where that series stops, then we would have passed through an infinite series and that is impossible. If the world never had a beginning, then we could not have reached today.

But we have reached today; so time must have begun at a particular point in the past, and today has come at a definite time since then. Therefore, the world is a finite event after all and it needs a CAUSE for its beginning."

Evidence ①: Einstein's General Theory of Relativity (1907-1915)   1.4

"Without gravity (i.e., a vacuum), space and time are not constant nor have absolute value - they CHANGE based on the velocity of a moving object relative to the frame of reference of whoever is observing the object."

Some concepts introduced by General Relativity:
1) Measurements of various objects are *relative* to the velocities of observers.
2) Space and time are measured relative to each other.
3) The speed of light is constant for all observers (it doesn't matter how the observers are moving relative to each other, or how the source of the light is moving).
4) Gravity is not actually a force (as previously defined by Newtonian physics), but instead is a *curved field* in space created by mass (matter causes space to curve).

$G_{\mu v} = 8\pi G T_{\mu v}$
G = gravity
μ = mass
v = velocity

"Everything should be made as simple as possible, but not simpler".
Albert Einstein

Einstein's equation isn't used to calculate anything. He developed it to simplify a very complex phenomenon: there is a relationship between matter, time and space.

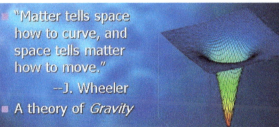

"Matter tells space how to curve, and space tells matter how to move."
   --J. Wheeler
■ A theory of *Gravity*

Some consequences of General Relativity:
1) Observers moving at constant speeds are subject to the same physical laws.
2) Light rays bend when in a gravitational field.
3) 'Frame-dragging' = Rotating masses "drag along" the space-time around them..
4) The Universe is expanding, and its farthest parts move away from us faster than the speed of light.

Your GPS = a perfect example of General Relativity's use today:

GPS devices store vast amounts of electronic maps to guide you from one destination point on Earth's surface to another. But how do they accurately locate the place you want to go, and guide you to that location, instead of sending you off on a wild goose chase? What makes the system so precise? GPS satellites orbit about 16,000 miles above Earth. In order to stay in orbit, these satellites must move at over 8,000 mph relative to Earth's surface. They travel faster than any reference point on the Earth, so a clock on one of them would run about .0000072 seconds/ day *slower* than a clock on Earth.

But besides this small difference in clock speeds (between a clock on the satellite and the same clock on Earth's surface), there is a second difference: the same GPS satellite orbiting 16,000 miles above Earth is in a lower gravitational field than if it were on Earth's surface. Since we know the force of gravity decreases as the distance between objects increases (see definition of Gravity, where the equation $G = m_1 \times m_2 / distance^2$). This means that the gravitational force of attraction between the satellite and Earth, due to a 16,000-mile distance between them, results in the satellite's clock running about .0000046 seconds/ day *faster in space* than on Earth's surface.

So, due to Einstein's General Relativity, these two differences in a satellite clock's time combine to cause the clock on the satellite to run about .0000038 seconds/day *faster* than if that clock were on Earth. That increased speed would cause your GPS receiver to build up errors in location that result in it being off by 5-6 miles per day,

Fortunately, your GPS is designed to correct for these errors by setting the satellite's atomic clocks to run *slower* than they would on Earth *before* the satellite is launched. Once set in orbit, where the effects of relativity act on it, the satellite's clocks speed up and very closely match its reference point on Earth (i.e., your GPS in your car)

Why General Relativity matters: *Scientific EVIDENCE pointing to a BEGINNER of the Universe*

- Hugh Ross[18] (Albert Einstein discovers God): *"Einstein's equations of General Relativity show the universe is simultaneously expanding and slowing down, which means there must have been a beginning to the expansion. By the simple Law of Cause and Effect, it must have had a Beginner. But Einstein hypothesized a new force of physics that canceled out the deceleration and expansion factors. In 1929, Edwin Hubble proved from his measurements on 40 different galaxies that they are expanding away from one another, and this expansion is actually predicted by Einstein's original equations. In the face of this proof, Einstein abandoned his hypothesized force and acknowledged 'the necessity for a beginning' and 'the presence of a superior reasoning power.'"*

- Henry Morris ("Scientific Creationism"[4]): *"Einstein emphasized that all frames of reference as to size, position, time and motion in the world are relative, not absolute. This argues that the universe cannot be absolute in itself, and therefore can have no independent or absolute existence. Since it could not produce itself, it must be in existence due to the omnipotence of an EXTERNAL CREATOR, who is Himself its absolute standard."*

PSALM 124:8 *"Our help is in the name of the Lord, who MADE heaven and earth."*

Einstein's Greatest Failure:
He denied the Intelligent Creator he discovered was Personal[18]

Albert Einstein, Edwin Hubble, and Walter Adams (l-r) in 1931 at the Mount Wilson Observatory 100" telescope, in the San Gabriel Mountains of southern California. It was here in 1929 that Hubble discovered the cosmic expansion of the universe. *Courtesy of the Archives, California Institute of Technology*

"Astronomer Edwin Hubble in 1929 proved from his measurements on 40 different galaxies that the galaxies are expanding away from one another. Moreover, he demonstrated that expansion was in the same manner predicted by Einstein's original formula of general relativity. In the face of this proof, Einstein abandoned his hypotheses and acknowledged 'the necessity for a beginning' and 'the presence of a superior reasoning power.' Einstein held unswervingly, against enormous peer pressure, to belief in a Creator, but like many other powerful intellects through the centuries, ruled out the existence of a personal God. Though he confessed to the rabbis and priests who came to congratulate him on his discovery of God that he was convinced God brought the universe into existence and was intelligent and creative, he denied that God was personal.

The clergy had a stock response to Einstein's denial: 'How can a Being who is intelligent and creative not also be personal? Einstein brushed past their valid objection by raising the paradox of God's omnipotence and man's responsibility for his choices: 'If this being is omnipotent, then every occurrence, including every human action, every human thought, and every human feeling and aspiration is also His work; how is it possible to think of holding men responsible for their deeds and thoughts before such an almighty Being? In giving out punishments and rewards He would to a certain extent be *passing judgment on Himself*. How can this be combined with the *goodness and righteousness ascribed to Him*?'

The clergy responded by saying that God has not yet revealed the answer. They encouraged him to endure patiently and blindly trust the 'All-Knowing One.' Einstein lacked the persistence to pursue an answer for himself. He took for granted the biblical knowledge of these religious professionals and assumed the Bible failed to address this crucially important issue. He also didn't live long enough to see the accumulation of scientific evidence for a personal, caring Creator."

How C.H. Spurgeon would have answered Einstein = The INCARNATION[25]

God personally *identifies* with me ➔ He personally *pays* for my sin ➔ He *makes me right* with Him

"The Word became flesh and dwelt among us in the world that He might thereby MAKE OUR PEACE, reconciling God to man and man to God... The Son of God is become the Son of Man, even flesh of our flesh and bone of our bones; and the sons of men are made the sons of God... *My sin is His sin*, and *His righteousness is my righteousness*. He who knew no sin, *for my sake was made sin*, and I having no good thing, am MADE the righteousness of God IN HIM (2Corinthians 5:21)".

Romans 3:21-26 "Jesus Christ = How God revealed to everyone He is both good and righteous
"...now the righteousness of God apart from the law is revealed, being witnessed by the Law and the Prophets, even the righteousness of God which is through faith in Jesus Christ TO ALL and ON ALL who believe, for there is no difference.
For ALL HAVE SINNED and fallen short of the glory of God, being justified FREELY by HIS GRACE through the redemption that is in Christ Jesus, whom God set forth to be a propitiation by His blood, through faith, to DEMONSTRATE HIS RIGHTEOUSNESS, because in His forbearance God had passed over the sins that were previously committed, to demonstrate at the present time His righteousness, that HE MIGHT BE JUST and the JUSTIFIER of the one who has faith in Jesus."

Galatians 3:11-13 "Jesus Christ = How God passed judgment on Himself for the sin we commit
"...that no one is justified by the law in the sight of God is evident, for 'The just shall live by faith.' Yet the law is not of faith, but 'The man who does them shall live by them.'
Christ has redeemed us from the CURSE OF THE LAW, having become a CURSE FOR US (for it is written, 'Cursed is everyone who hangs on a tree.')"

John 17:3 *"This is eternal life, that they may KNOW YOU, the only true God, and Jesus Christ whom You have sent."*

Evidence ②: The Hubble Constant

1.5

Robert Jastrow (1925-2008), Director of NASA's Goddard Institute for Space Studies: *"The Hubble Law is one of the great discoveries in science; it is one of the main supports of the scientific story of Genesis."*

Astronomer Edwin Hubble (1889-1953) fit data obtained into a MATHEMATICAL EQUATION that showed the relationship between the *radial velocities* of galaxies and their *distance* from each other. The slope of the fitted line is called the **Hubble constant, H_o**. In 1996, astronomers Riess, Press and Kirshnerfurther confirmed Hubble's initial equation by showing an even tighter correlation in their graph, with H_o = 67-72 km/sec/Mpc.

Hubble Constant: proving the Expansion Rate of the Universe by *the SCIENCE of STATISTICS*

GRAPH TO THE RIGHT: Hubble's constant was calculated by plotting the measurements of 1,355 galaxies' velocities against their distances from that point of measurement. Then, a statistics program fits a straight line to these points (see red line in graph) and the *slope 'm'* of the fitted line is calculated. This slope is the Hubble constant.
These 1,355 points seem to be in a straight line that slopes left-to-right. But can you prove it? How can we be certain? After all, the implications are enormous – it would mean the 1,355 measurements collected over time confirm the Universe has been expanding from some starting point, discrediting past theories of a static, eternal universe

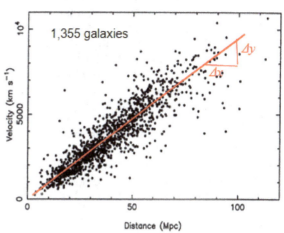

GRAPH TO THE RIGHT: The statistics program is called a Linear Regression Model, where the computer "fits" a straight line to the plotted points, calculates the slope "m" of the fitted line, and provides a value called $Rsq_{(adj)}$, which is derived through calculations measuring each point's distance off the fitted line, known as it's "residual error" (if a point isn't on the line, its distance off the line is the amount of error the computer model incurred in trying to fit that point to its fitted line). The higher $Rsq_{(adj)}$ (max. is 100%, which means all points fall exactly on the line), the higher the certainty the fitted line defines the relationship of the X-axis variable to the Y-axis variable (in this case, galaxy velocity to galaxy distance). The lower the $Rsq_{(adj)}$, the less certain you are in claiming any relationship.

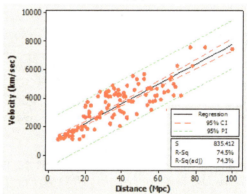

EQUATION TO THE RIGHT: We know by the Laws of Cause and Effect that if data can be expressed in the form of a line "$Y = mX + b$", the Effect "Y" (expansion of the universe) has a Cause "X" that set it in its motion at a certain rate (the slope "m") that can be tested for its explanatory power (R_{sq}).

$Y = mX + b$, where
Y = Effect = motion of the universe and its bodies
X = Cause = the Factor that causes the universe to move
$m = H_o$ = Hubble constant = slope of fitted line = $\Delta y / \Delta x$
$m = \Delta_{velocity\ between\ 2\ galaxies} / \Delta_{distance\ between\ 2\ galaxies}$

GRAPH TO THE RIGHT: Linear Regression Modeling is nothing new. We use it today to define the cause for effects we see in everyday life.
One such example is tracking the quarterly change in unemployment as the CAUSE ("X") for the quarterly change in the US Gross Domestic Product (GDP), the EFFECT ("Y"). Like the expanding universe, we use the *EVIDENCE* from the DATA to assess how the nations' unemployment is impacting our ability to produce goods. Having tracked this data for a long time, we *TRUST* that, if we implement practices that reduce our unemployment, we will produce more as a nation. Sound familiar?.....

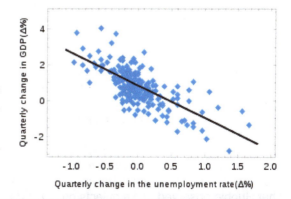

Isaiah 42:5 *"God the Lord, who created the heavens and STRETCHED THEM OUT (Hebr. "nâtâh" = to extend outward), who SPREAD FORTH (Hebr. "râqa" = to expand by spreading abroad) the earth and that which comes from it."*

Evidence ③: The Doppler Red Shift

As we observe the stars and galaxies, their light has distinct wavelengths that are characteristic of the atoms that make up the gases around the stars. These wavelengths are shifted toward the RED end of the spectrum, which by the "Doppler Shift" means all of the galaxies are moving AWAY from us.

The "Doppler Shift" is defined as "a shift in the frequency of acoustic or electromagnetic radiation emitted by an object as it moves relative to the position of the observer:" This Doppler Shift of the observed object will be to higher frequencies, and emit a BLUE spectrum, when the object is moving TOWARD the observer. When the object is moving away from the observer, the Doppler Shift will be to lower frequencies, and emit a RED spectrum.

Doppler

- **Blue Shift**
  - higher frequencies, shorter wavelength
  - the observer moves toward the source
  - the source moves toward the observer
- **Red Shift**
  - lower frequencies, longer wavelengths
  - the observer moves away from the source
  - the source moves away from the observer

$$r = \frac{v}{H_0} = \frac{\beta c}{H_0} = \left[\frac{(z+1)^2 - 1}{(z+1)^2 + 1}\right]\frac{c}{H_0}$$

Hubble's equation for defining the relationship between an observed galaxy's velocity away from an observed point and its distance from that same observed point is based on measurements of the Doppler Red Shift. The red shift of the spectral lines in the light emitted from the observed object is expressed as the z-parameter, (defined as the "shift in the spectral wavelength"). The more detailed equation in the above box defines the Hubble distance "r" in relationship to this z-parameter.

Evidence ④: The Expansion Rate of the Universe

Job 38:4-6 (see also Job 9:8-9) *"Where were you when I laid the foundations of the earth? Tell Me, if you have understanding. Who determined its measurements? Surely you know! Or who ①STRETCHED the measuring line upon it? To what were its foundations fastened?"*

Psalm 104:1-2 *"O Lord my God, You are very great; You are clothed with honor and majesty; who cover Yourself with light as with a garment, who ①STRETCH OUT the heavens like a curtain."*

Isaiah 40:21-22 (see also Isaiah 42:5, 45:12) *"Have you not known? Have you not heard? Has it not been told to you from the beginning? Have you not understood from the foundations of the earth? It is He who sits above the circle of the earth, and its inhabitants are like grasshoppers, who ①STRETCHES OUT the heavens like a curtain, and ①SPREADS them out like a tent to dwell in."*

Jeremiah 10:12 (see also Jeremiah 51:15-16) *"He has made the earth by His power, He has established the world by His wisdom, and has ①STRETCHED OUT the heavens at His discretion."*

Zechariah 1:1 *"...thus says the Lord, who ①STRETCHES OUT the heavens, lays the foundation of the earth, and forms the spirit of man within him..."*

① "SPREAD/STRETCH", "SPREAD OUT/ STRETCH OUT" = Hebrew *"nâtâh"* = to stretch, extend outward
② "SPREAD FORTH" = Hebrew *"râqa"* = to make broad or spread abroad, to stamp or stretch

In the verses above, we can see that the Bible declares the expansion of the universe before scientists quantified it by Hubble's equation.

God "spreading / stretching out the heavens" can be illustrated by the surface of an expanding balloon. If we glue objects on the balloon's surface and begin inflating it, they move farther apart without actually moving themselves. The *farther* the objects are from the point of inflation, the *faster* they move away from each other. Objects can be stationary yet move away from each other at the same time! This is what Hubble observed. Like objects on the balloon's surface, galaxies are moving away from each other at speeds in relation to their distances from the point of measurement.

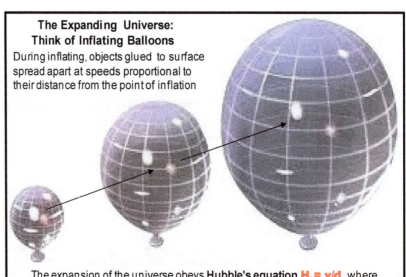

The Expanding Universe: Think of Inflating Balloons
During inflating, objects glued to surface spread apart at speeds proportional to their distance from the point of inflation

The expansion of the universe obeys **Hubble's equation $H_0 = v/d$**, where H_0 = Hubble's constant, v = galaxy's radial velocity, d = distance from Earth.

Evidence ⑤: The Cosmic Background Radiation
1.6
The following is directly quoted from sections in pages 21-24 of "The Creator and the Cosmos"[18]

- **The 'Cosmic Oven'**: Astronomers knew, based on the deductions by physicist Richard Tolman (1922) and George Gamow (1948) that the universe's beginning and subsequent development resembled a hot kitchen oven. When the door of the oven is opened, heat that was trapped inside escapes. Dissipation of the oven's heat takes place as the heat expands outward from the oven. Radiant energy that was confined to a few cubic feet now spreads throughout the kitchen's several hundred cubic feet. As it does, the oven cavity eventually cools down to a temperature of the room, which is now just a little warmer than it was before. If one knows the peak temperature of the oven cavity, the volume of that cavity, and the volume of the room throughout which the oven's heat is dissipated, then the amount by which the room will warm up can be determined. If one were using the opening of the oven door to dry out some wet towels, it would be important to control the temperature of the oven as well as the rate at which the oven disperses its heat to the room. If the oven were too hot, or the dissipation too rapid (say the room was too large or the towels too far away), the towels would stay wet. Similarly, if the universe were to expand too slowly, too many of the nucleons (protons and neutrons) would fuse together to form heavier elements. This would result in too few of the lighter elements essential for life chemistry. On the other hand, if the expansion were more rapid, too many of the nucleons would fuse into lighter elements. This would result in too few of the heavier elements essential for life chemistry.

Following this oven analogy, Gamow's research team in 1948 calculated what temperature conditions would be necessary to yield the currently observed abundances of elements. They concluded that a faint glow measuring only 5° Centigrade above absolute zero (-273° Centigrade or -460° Fahrenheit) should be found everywhere throughout the universe. At the time, such a low temperature was hopelessly beyond the capabilities of telescopes and detectors to measure. But by 1964 astronomers Arno Penzias and Robert Wilson put together an instrument that successfully measured at radio wavelengths the cosmic background radiation (i.e., heat) to be about 3° Centigrade above absolute zero. Since that initial discovery, the cosmic background radiation has been measured to much greater accuracy and at many more wavelengths (see below).

- **First COBE Discovery (January 1990)**: They showed the universe to match a perfect radiator, dissipating virtually all its available energy. The data showed the background radiation temperature to be very low and smooth. No irregularities in the temperature larger than one part in 10,000 were detected. This extraordinarily low and smooth temperature in the cosmic background radiation convinced astronomers that the universe must have had an **EXTREMELY HOT BEGINNING** about 15 to 20 billion years ago. The finding essentially ruled out many alternative models for the universe's beginning such as the Steady State Model.

- **Second COBE Discovery (April 1992)**: The smoothness of the cosmic background radiation helped confirm a **HOT BIG BANG** beginning of the universe. But astronomers knew that the background radiation could not be perfectly smooth. At least some level of non-uniformity in the cosmic background radiation would be necessary to explain the formation of galaxies and clusters of galaxies. The whole range of reasonable theories for how galaxies can come together required temperature fluctuations roughly ten times smaller than what COBE had the capability to detect in 1990. Fortunately, the newly refined COBE measurements, announced on April 24, 1992, showed irregularities in the background radiation as large as about one part in 100,000, just what astronomers thought they would find.

- **Third COBE Discovery (January 1993)**: The deviations between the 1990 COBE results and the spectrum for a perfect radiator measured less than 1% over the entire range of observed frequencies. Data released from the COBE research team at an American Astronomical Society meeting in January 1993 reduce the deviation to less than 0.03%. The new data also yield the most precise measure to date of the temperature of the cosmic background radiation, 2.726° Kelvin (that is 2.726° Centigrade above absolute zero), a measure that is accurate to within 0.01° Kelvin.

- **Proof for the Big Bang**: These new results do more than just prove that the universe began with a hot big bang. They tell us which kind of hot big bang. The universe must have erupted from a **SINGLE EXPLOSIVE EVENT** that by itself accounts for at least 99.97% of the radiant energy in the universe. With a single explosive creation event accounting for so much of the radiation in the universe, astronomers can conclude that the temperature fluctuations in the cosmic background radiation… must have transformed the smooth primordial cosmos into today's universe of clumped clusters of galaxies."

George Smoot (UC Berkeley astronomer, winner 2006 Nobel Prize in Physics for COBE):
"What we have found is evidence for the birth of the universe. It's like looking at God."

How the "Big Bang" got its name ➔ An Explosion of a 'Singularity'
The following is directly quoted from sections in pages 23-24 of "The Creator and the Cosmos"[18]

"Suppose our hypothetical 'kitchen oven' were surrounded by thousands of thermometers, each placed at exactly the same distance from the oven. Suppose also that some time after the oven had been heated, turned off, and its door opened, each thermometer indicated the same temperature. The only possible conclusion we could draw would be that the heat flow from the oven cavity to the room totally dominated the normal temperature-disturbing air flows in the room. Such dominance would imply that *the original temperature of the oven cavity must have been very much greater than the room's temperature*.

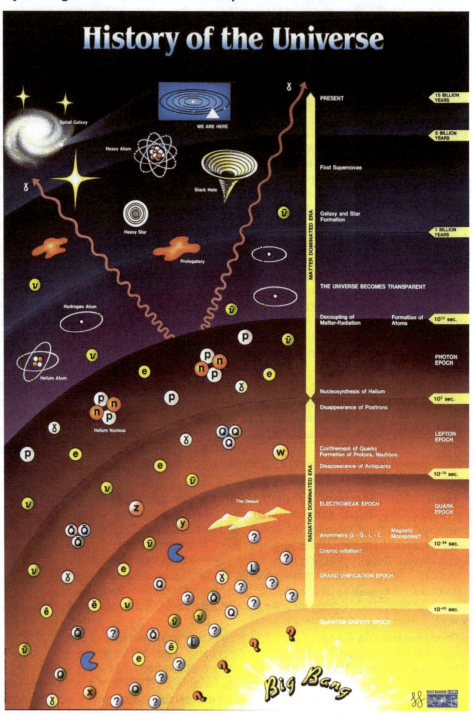

In addition, if all those thousands of thermometers indicated a very low temperature, we would conclude that considerable time had passed since the opening of the oven door.

The temperature measurements from COBE provide convincing evidence of a hot origin for the cosmos some billions of years in the past. Astronomers normally refer to this hot beginning as the BIG BANG for good reason.

The cool and uniform temperature of the cosmic background radiation and its close fit to the spectrum of a perfect radiator establishes that the universe has suffered an enormous degradation of energy, typical of a LARGE EXPLOSION. This energy degradation is called entropy. Entropy describes the degree to which energy in a closed system disperses, or radiates (as heat), and thus ceases to be available to perform work. Specific entropy is the measure for a particular system of the amount of entropy per proton.

A burning candle is a good example of a highly entropic system, one that efficiently radiates energy away. It has a specific entropy of about two. Only very hot explosions have much higher specific entropies. The specific entropy of the universe – about one billion – is enormous beyond all comparison.

Even supernova explosions, the most entropic (and radiant) of events now occurring in the universe, have specific entropies a hundred times less. Only a hot big bang could account for such a huge specific entropy for the universe… it can be demonstrated, further, that if the specific entropy were any greater or any less, stars and planets would never have existed at any time in the history of the universe."

Evidence ⑥: 1ˢᵗ Law of Thermodynamics ("Conservation of Energy") 1.7

- No new matter (mass/energy) is coming into existence anywhere in the universe, and every bit of that original matter is still here.
- Nothing is created nor destroyed; systems using energy don't use it up – they convert it to other energy forms.
- Heat and work are forms of energy transfer. A system's energy is conserved but it changes as heat and work transfer in or out of it.
- The universe didn't create itself (nothing in natural law can explain the universe's own origin).
- **Ecclesiastes 1:9-10** *"…there is NOTHING NEW under the sun. Is there anything of which it may be said, 'See, this is new'? It has already been in ancient times before us."*

1ˢᵗ Law of Thermodynamics of any closed system:

$$E_2 - E_1 = Q - W$$

E_1 = initial energy state,
E_2 = resulting energy state,
Q = heat transferred into the system,
W = work done by the system.

The Conservation of mass-energy (The 1ˢᵗ Law)

This law was developed in the nineteenth century, after Isaac Newton (1643-1727) discovered his Laws of Motion and Gravity (see previous section) and Albert Einstein (1879-1955), leveraging Newton's work, discovered his famous equations for energy-mass relationship and his General Theory of Relativity.

In physics, the law of conservation of **energy** states that energy cannot be created nor destroyed. Energy exists in many forms, such as heat, electricity, light or sound. We can change one type of energy into another (a car engine converts the chemical energy in gasoline into mechanical energy, solar cells change radiant energy into electrical energy), and we can move energy from one place to another, but the total quantity of energy in the universe is constant and cannot be changed.

There is also the law of conservation of **mass**. Mass is the property of an object to resist a change in its motion. Anything with a lot of mass is heavy; anything with little mass is light. Just as with energy, we can change one type of mass into another (for example, with a chemical reaction) and we can move mass from one place to another, but mass cannot be created nor destroyed. So both mass and energy are **conserved**.

Einstein quantified this law in his famous equation $E=mc^2$, which states that *matter and energy are really different forms of the same thing*. Matter can be turned into energy, and energy into matter. So the 1ˢᵗ Law of Thermodynamics says the amount of "stuff" in the universe is constant.

Conservation of mass-energy is what we find in the Bible.

1) The Bible says no new material comes into existence:

John 1:3 says all things were made by Jesus, and nothing has come into existence apart from Him: *"ALL THINGS were made through Him (Jesus Christ), and without Him nothing was made that was made."*

Genesis 2:2 states that God ended His work of creation by the seventh day of the creation week: *"And on the 7ᵗʰ day God ENDED HIS WORK which He had done, and He rested on the 7ᵗʰ day from all His work which He had done."*

Prof. Albert Einstein delivers the 11th Josiah Willard Gibbs lecture at the meeting of the American Association for the Advancement of Science in the auditorium of the Carnegie Institute of Technology Little Theater at Pittsburgh, Pa., on Dec. 28, 1934. Photo by AP

Since only God can bring new things into existence from nothing, and since God ended His work of bringing new things into existence (i.e., creation) by the 7ᵗʰ day, no new "stuff" will come into existence today

2) The Bible shows that no matter or energy originally created by God will cease to exist:

Hebrews 1:3 states that God is upholding all things by His sustaining power: *"…who being the brightness of His glory and the express image of His person, and upholding ALL THINGS by the word of His power…"*

Colossians 1:17 states that by Jesus Christ all things consist (i.e., are held together): *"…He is before all things, and in Him ALL THINGS consist."*

---

1) Since nothing new will be created, the amount of matter in the universe is constant.
2) Neither matter nor energy will cease to exist, because God is sustaining them.
3) CONCLUSION: The universe obeys the 1ˢᵗ Law (Law of conservation of mass-energy).

E=mc² Explained - Energy Transfer & the Atom Bomb (excerpts from Bill Willis, 1999)

EQUATION OF THE WEEK
Einstein's Equation

In honour of the International Year of Physics, Ideas asked 10 Canadian scientists and mathematicians to share their favourite equations. This is the fourth instalment.

$$E = mc^2$$

where: E = energy, m = mass, c = speed of light

Who loves it:
Diane deKerckhove, a physics professor at Marianopolis College (and soon to be at Guelph University) who has used scanning proton microscopy to analyze the hair of Napoleon Bonaparte. She is also a jazz singer, with several CDs released under the name Diane Nalini.

What it all means:
"What it says is that every massive object, whether it's moving or not, has a certain amount of energy stored into it, and if you can overcome the energy required to separate atoms apart or break quarks apart, then you can convert all of that mass into raw energy."

Why it's her fave:
"There's something deeply satisfying about it, because it tells you that mass and energy are the same thing, basically. I find that philosophically very interesting, very deep. It's not obvious to our everyday experience, and to me that's what makes it magical."

One of Einstein's great insights was to realize that matter and energy are really different forms of the same thing. Matter can be turned into energy, and energy into matter.

For example, consider a simple hydrogen atom, basically composed of a single proton. This subatomic particle has a mass of 0.000 000 000 000 000 000 000 000 001 672 kg. This is a tiny mass indeed. But in everyday quantities of matter there are *a lot* of atoms! For instance, in one kilogram of pure water, the mass of hydrogen atoms amounts to just slightly more than 111 grams, or 0.111 kg. Einstein's formula tells us the *amount* of energy this mass would be equivalent to, if it were all suddenly *turned* into energy. It says that to find the energy, multiply the mass by the square of the speed of light, this number being 300,000,000 meters/ second (a *very* large number): $E = mc^2$ = 0.111 x 300,000,000 x 300,000,000 = 10,000,000,000,000,000 Joules.

This is an incredible amount of energy! A Joule is not a large unit of energy ... one Joule is about the energy released when you drop a textbook to the floor. But the amount of energy in 30 grams of hydrogen atoms is equivalent to burning hundreds of thousands of gallons of gasoline! If you consider all the energy in the full kilogram of water, which also contains oxygen atoms, the total energy is close to 10 million gallons of gasoline!

Another phenomenon peculiar to small elementary particles like protons is that they combine. A single proton forms the nucleus of a hydrogen atom. Two protons are found in the nucleus of a helium atom. This is how the elements are formed ... all the way up to the heaviest naturally occurring substance, uranium, which has 92 protons in its nucleus. It is possible to make two free protons (Hydrogen nuclei) come together to make the beginnings of a helium nucleus. This requires that the protons be hurled at each other at a very high speed. This process occurs in the *sun*, but can also be replicated on earth with lasers, magnets, or in the center of an atomic bomb. The process is called *nuclear fusion*. When the protons are forced together, this extra mass is released ... as energy... predictable using the formula $E = mc^2$.

Elements heavier than iron are unstable. Some of them are *very* unstable! This means that their nuclei, composed of many positively charged protons, which *want* to repel from each other, are liable to fall apart at any moment! We call atoms like this *radioactive*. Uranium, for example, is radioactive. Every second, many of the atoms in a chunk of uranium are falling apart. When this happens, the pieces, which are now new elements (with fewer protons) are less massive in total than the original uranium atoms. The extra mass disappears as energy ... again according to the formula $E=mc^2$! This process is called *nuclear fission*.

Both these nuclear reactions release a small portion of the mass involved as energy. Large amounts of energy! You are probably more familiar with their uses. Nuclear fusion is what powers a modern nuclear warhead. Nuclear fission (less powerful) is what happens in an atomic bomb (like the ones used against Japan in WWII), or in a nuclear power plant.

Albert Einstein was able to see where an understanding of this formula would lead. Although peaceful by nature and politics, he helped write a letter to the President of the United States, urging him to fund research into the development of an atomic bomb ... before the Nazis or Japan developed their own first. The result was the *Manhattan Project*, which did in fact produce the first tangible evidence of E=mc²... the *ATOMIC BOMB*!

Evidence ⑦: 2nd Law of Thermodynamics ("Disintegration of Energy") — 1.8

Since the total energy in the cosmos is constant (1st Law), the amount of energy available for a closed or isolated system such as the cosmos (i.e., system left to its own devices) to do useful work is always decreasing.

<u>Entropy</u> = The amount of a system's unavailable energy, as it moves to *lower levels of usefulness* (from order to disorder), eventually reaching equilibrium (complete randomness) and unavailability for further work.

Romans 8:21 "The 2nd Law of Thermodynamics" *"...the creation itself also will be delivered from the bondage of CORRUPTION (decay) into the glorious liberty of the children of God."*

The 2nd Law: An *ENERGY SOURCE* is required to counteract *Entropy* in Biological Systems

If entropy and the 2nd Law state that systems naturally move from order to disorder, how do biological systems maintain such a high degree of order? Doesn't this violate the 2nd Law?

Order in a system is not a natural by-product of that system. Order can only be produced by the input of information, in the form of ENERGY, from a source outside of that system, allowing the system to create and then expend its own energy to maintain order. Energy is defined as the ability to do work. By expending energy, the order we see in life on the earth is produced by the input of information from sources external to that life.

In the plant world: The external information, or energy, source is the SUN, where plants use the process of photosynthesis to convert the sun's energy into storable potential energy (energy available but not yet used) as sugar, so now a plant can put that energy to use (i.e., kinetic energy) and perform work. So what was the source of information that produced the Sun? **Genesis 1:16-19** says God, as the External Source, made the Sun (and the moon) of our solar system on the 4th day of creation:

"God made two great lights, the GREATER LIGHT to rule the day, and the lesser light to rule the night. He made the stars also. God set them in the firmament of the heavens to give light on the earth, and to rule over the day and over the night, and to divide the light from the darkness. And God saw that it was good. So the evening and the morning were the 4th day."

In the animal world: Mitochondria are the "power plants" within each cell, which use the potential energy stored in sugar molecules (carbohydrates) from the food we eat to form more highly ordered proteins called ATP (Adenosine Tri-Phosphate) which release the energy in the carbs whenever we perform useful work. Next to DNA, ATP is one of the most complex molecules ever discovered (much more on mitochondria, DNA and ATP later). So what was the source of information that produced animal cells, and how could so complex a machine as ATP exist by itself? **Psalm 139:14-16** says God, as the External Source, made these things:

"I will praise You, for I am fearfully and wonderfully made; marvelous are Your works, and that my soul knows very well. My frame was not hidden from You, when I was made in secret, and skillfully wrought in the lowest parts of the earth. Your eyes saw my substance, being as yet unformed. And in Your book they were all written, the days fashioned for me, when as yet there were none of them."

When the potential energy (energy stored in carbohydrates) is converted into kinetic energy (energy in motion), animals get no more energy until they input it again from an outside source. As energy transfers back and forth between potential and kinetic, some energy is lost as heat, which is a form of kinetic energy (all systems are not 100% efficient in converting potential to kinetic energy). The flow of potential-to-kinetic energy is what sustains order and life. Some of the more popular examples of Potential-to-Kinetic Energy transfer are:

1) <u>Gasoline</u> has potential energy to be converted into kinetic energy by the engine. When the potential is used up, the engine stops performing useful work.

2) <u>Batteries</u> have potential energy. When placed into an electronic device and its turned on, that potential in the batteries is transformed into kinetic energy to run the device. When the batteries' potential energy is all used up, the device stops performing its useful work.

3) <u>Earth's Hydrologic Cycle</u> depends on the sun to continuously recharge it. When it rains or snows, water falls to earth and flows toward the oceans. Without the sun, the water would still reach sea-level, but never be evaporated to recharge the cycle (more details n the Hydrologic Cycle later).

On Earth – Entropy always wins: The only defense a living system has against decay = take in energy. But every living thing cannot maintain its order forever. All living systems will break down, moving from order to disorder, with the final outcome that all organisms cease to take in energy and die. This, again, is exactly how the Bible describes life. David states this truth in **1Kings 2:1-2**: *"Then the days of David drew near that he should die, and he commanded Solomon his son, saying: 'I go THE WAY OF ALL THE EARTH....'"*

---

3 Facts No One can argue (intelligently): the 2nd Law *requires* an External Agent

1. Any isolated, natural process, left to its own, runs down. This is a proven fact.
2. For organisms to evolve, there must be: gained *ENERGY*, increased *ORDER*, added *INFORMATION*.
3. Evolution never happens in an isolated, natural process unless *EXTERNAL FORCES* make it happen.

Why 2nd Law of Thermodynamics points to Creation, falsifies Evolution: Life cannot arise from Nonlife without an External Energy Source ('Motor')

Dr. A.E. Wilder-Smith (1915-1995): 3 PhD's (Organic Chemistry and Pharmacology); Visiting Prof. at Univ. of Illinois Medical Center, Professor of Pharmacology of the University of Bergen Medical School in Norway ➔ The following is quoted from his book "**Man's Origin, Man's Destiny**"[11] on the section entitled "Elaboration of Second Law":

1) Energy constantly Decreases, Randomness and Chaos constantly Increases: "Neither matter nor energy are today being created as far as we know. Nevertheless, the energy available for work is relentlessly getting less as time advances, which means that the amount of unavailable energy in the universe is ever increasing. A measure of the amount of this unavailable energy is known as entropy. These same facts can be expressed otherwise by saying that in nature everything is continually moving toward greater probability... everything in nature tends toward the area of highest entropy or greatest probability.

Either expression means that the area of least orderliness or greatest chaos or 'rundownness' will tend to be reached. Order is improbable and order tends to disintegrate into disorder..., just as a city with no cleaning, repair and disposal services descends to chaos with the passage of time. If one doubts this universal fact, it is only necessary to place one's shiny new car under a tree in a forest and leave it there for twenty years with no attention. Chaos will certainly have overtaken the once orderly car by then.

2) What was the External Energy Source that overcame the 2nd Law so life came into being? Quoting Dr. Harold Blum (in his book 'Time's Arrow and Evolution'): 'How, when no life existed, did substances come into being which, today, are absolutely essential to living systems, yet which can only be formed by those systems?... If living systems were to evolve (from nonliving systems) – free energy had to be supplied. The source of this free energy is a fundamental problem we must eventually face...' Dr. Blum's fundamental problem that of building a protein metabolic motor to support life before life was present to build it. This motor has to be built under the choking restriction imposed by Darwinism, by chance in a nonliving medium by chemical evolution.

In order to reduce chaos and randomness to order, a motor to supply the energy is necessary... Work must be done… What Dr. Blum is saying is: How was the motor to extract the energy from the environment built before life processes had arisen to build it?... Dr. Blum has shown that it is inconceivable to account even for the building of a simple protein by chance. But chemical evolution taking place before the advent of life could only rely upon chance. Dr. Blum says precisely this and hopes we shall find ways and processes which would explain how nature overcame this otherwise insuperable mathematical problem without invoking extramaterial interference."

3) Can't life happen if given enough time? "Dr. Blum: 'I think if I were rewriting this chapter (on the origin of life) completely, I should want to play down still more the importance of the great amount of time available for highly improbable events to occur. One may take the view that the greater the time elapsed the greater should be the approach to equilibrium, the most probable state, and it seems that this ought to take precedence in our thinking over the idea that time provides the possibility for the occurrence of the highly improbable.'

Dr. Blum is saying here, in effect, that increasing time will increase the chances of finding things at equilibrium, that is, randomness.... Dr. Blum is saying that huge spans of time will bring likely equilibrium randomness and not unlikely synthesis such as the Darwinians have supposed with impunity for a century. To put things crudely, as infinite time is approached, infinite randomness will be achieved, namely, complete lack of order."

4) Won't the availability of solar energy (heat) make life possible? "It is often maintained by evolutionists that the energy for these synthetic processes was obtained from the sun. Living matter uses this supply of solar energy to carry out its syntheses, so why should nonliving matter not do the same in using the same source?

The whole force of Blum's argument on just this problem lies in his emphasis of the fact that solar energy, even though it may bathe nonliving matter, is not available to it for syntheses of the type in which we are interested. A complex metabolic motor is a necessary intermediate in making solar energy available. Chlorophyll (chloroplasts) functions as just such a motor, but is far too complex to have arisen by chance processes from nonliving matter."

Proponents of this view of energy sources available for synthesis in nonliving matter may reflect that, such kinetic energy, though surrounding them on all sides, is not available to supply energy for synthesis. Solar energy may surround nonliving matter, but it is not available to it for synthetic purposes without the intermediary of a motor.

The energy of sunlight cannot be used directly for molecular synthesis without the medium of a 'motor'. Sunlight cannot work on nonliving molecules of matter to yield organic synthesis. Just as the energy in petroleum cannot be conveniently used and harnessed without the intermediary of a properly designed internal-combustion or steam engine, neither can sunlight quanta be used without a properly constructed photosynthetic motor, which is not present in nonliving matter, for reducing carbon dioxide to sugars and starch.

The problem of providing a complex motor to utilize solar energy has to be solved. And such complex motors do not arise by chance from nonliving matter. This is basically the problem which Darwinists avoid or beg."

Evidence ⑧: Newton's Laws of Causality 1.9

When we think of "causality" in terms of our everyday experiences, we usually think of the relationship we observe between the result of something we can actually see (the "effect") and what it was that originally made that result happen in time (the "cause").

For example, if we turn on our TV and catch the end of a boxing match, where we see the result is one of the boxers lying unconscious on the canvas, and the other boxer circling the ring with his hands in the air, we immediate assume the "cause" of the resulting knockout is that other boxer taking his victory lap.

Causality is also studied within the disciplines of philosophy and statistics, but it is fundamental to all of natural science, especially physics. Causality is the most universally accepted scientific principle in experimental science, and was brought to mathematical formulation by Isaac Newton's LAWS OF CAUSALITY, or the Laws of motion for all objects (whether microscopic particles or planets).

Isaac Newton's 3 Laws of Motion of *Any* Objects (particles, people, planets...)

Newton's (1642-1727) famous three laws of motion have been validated by experiment and observation for over 200 years. These three laws, combined with his Law of Gravity and the math behind calculus, allow man to explain, through quantitative equations, the vast majority of physical phenomena we see and feel.

1st Law (Law of Inertia): $\Sigma F = 0 \succ dv/dt = 0$
If the net force exerted on any object (i.e., the vector sum of all forces) is zero, then the velocity of the object is constant. Another way of saying the same thing: Objects at rest stay at rest, or objects in uniform motion in a straight line stay in motion, unless acted upon by an unbalanced external force.

2nd Law (Law of Cause-and-Effect): $F = (m)(dv/dt) = ma$
When a net force acts on an object, the object accelerates in the direction of the force. If the mass of an object is held constant, increasing force will increase acceleration. If the force on an object remains constant, increasing mass will decrease acceleration (force and acceleration are directly proportional, while mass and acceleration are inversely proportional). In honor of him, the official unit of force is called a "Newton", or N, and equals 1 kilogram-meter per second^2. In our English units, 1 pound = 4.448 N.

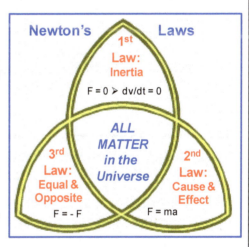

3rd Law (Law of Action-vs-Reaction): $\Sigma F_{a,b} = -\Sigma F_{b,a}$
When two objects exert forces on each other, there will be action and reaction forces equal in magnitude, but opposite in direction (to every action there is always an equal and opposite reaction). All forces are interactions between objects ($F_{a,b}$ = forces of object a on object b, and $F_{b,a}$ = forces of object b on object a).

Every Event is an Effect originating from a Cause I know by experience that nothing happens in isolation. Every event can be traced to one or more events which preceded it and *caused* it. I ask: "How did this happen?" "What caused this?" "Where did this come from?" "When did it start?" When I try to trace the event to its cause, or causes, I never seem to reach a stopping point. The cause of the event was itself caused by a prior cause, which was affected by a previous cause, and so on. Forensic Science uses the Law of Causality every day, by collecting the *evidence* from observable effects, to answer the above questions.

A scientific experiment tries to relate effects to causes, with quantitative equations. If the same experiment is repeated with the same factors, the same results are reproduced. The "scientific method" is based on this Law of Causality - that effects are in and like their causes, and like causes produce like effects. Science is impossible if cause and effect didn't occur.

The Effect: *Any effect has a greater cause.* Every cause will produce an effect that is less than its cause.

If we trace the 1st Law of Thermodynamics backwards, we are left with only two choices:

(1) There is an infinite chain of nonprimary causes, or

(2) There is an "Uncaused Source", by which observable effects occur.

Newton's 2nd & 3rd Laws:
"Cause & Effect / Action-Reaction"

$$Y = f(x_1, x_2, x_3 ...)$$

Y = Effect, and is a "function of"
x_1, x_2, x_3 = factors causing the Effect

"If one body exerts a force on a 2nd body (2nd Law), the 2nd body exerts an equal and opposite force on the 1st body (3rd Law)."

- Every force is exerted by something and on something else
- Forces exist in equal and opposite (action-reaction) pairs.

Henry Morris ("Scientific Creationism"⁴): *"If the evolutionist prefers not to believe in God, he must still believe in some kind of uncaused First Cause. He must either postulate matter coming into existence out of nothing or else matter having always existed in some primitive form.*

In either case, matter itself becomes its own Cause, and the creationist may well ask, 'But, then, who made Matter?' In either case, one must simply believe – either in eternal, omnipotent Matter or else in an eternal, omnipotent Creator God. The individual may decide which he considers more reasonable, but he should recognize this is not completely a scientific decision either way.

In justification of his own decision, however, the creationist utilizes the scientific law of Cause-and-Effect. This law, which is universally accepted and followed in every field of science, relates every phenomenon as an effect to a cause. No effect is ever quantitatively 'greater' nor qualitatively 'superior' to its cause. An effect can be lower than its cause but never higher. Using causal reasoning,… we conclude from the law of cause-and-effect that the First Cause of all things must be an infinite, eternal, omnipotent, omnipresent, omniscient, moral, spiritual, volitional, truthful, loving, living Being (see table below)! Do such adjectives describe Matter? Can random motion of primeval particles produce intelligent thought?"

the 1st Cause of	must be	the 1st Cause of	must be	the 1st Cause of	must be
Limitless Space	infinite	Endless Time	timeless	Boundless Energy	omnipotent
Universal Interrelationships	omnipresent	Infinite Complexity	omniscient	Human Responsibility	volitional
Moral Values	Moral	Spiritual Values	spiritual	Human Integrity	truthful
Human Love	loving	Life	living		
HEBREWS 11:1 (ISAIAH 41:20)		The most logical answer to the *EVIDENCE* in the universe is the existence of an uncaused Source, an omnipotent, omniscient, eternal, and Primary, *First Cause.*			

Psalm 90:2 *"Before the mountains were ①BROUGHT FORTH, or ever You had ②FORMED the ③EARTH and the ④WORLD, even from everlasting to everlasting, You are God."*

① BROUGHT FORTH = "*yâlad*" = given birth to, as in child bearing
② FORMED = "*chûl chîyl*" = to writhe, twist, wrestle through as in the process of childbirth
③ EARTH = "*erets*" = earth, dirt, land, matter (the substance from which material things are formed)
④ WORLD = "*têbêl*" = the inhabited part of the land

N. Geisler[31]: Answering Skeptics' Questions on "First Cause"

Question #1 = "If Everything Needs a Cause, then What Caused God?"

"This question comes up a lot. The problem is that people don't listen well to what we have to say. We didn't say that everything needs a cause; we said everything that has a beginning needs a cause. Only finite, contingent things need a cause.

God didn't have a beginning; He is infinite and He is necessary. God is the uncaused cause of all finite things. If God needed a cause, we would begin an infinite regress of causes that would never answer the question. As it is, we can't ask 'Who caused God?' because God is the FIRST CAUSE. You can't go back any farther than a first."

Question #2 = "If God created all things, how did He create Himself?"

"Again, only finite, contingent beings need causes. Necessary beings don't. We never said that God is a self-caused Being. That would be impossible. However, we can turn this objection into an argument for God. There are only three possible kinds of beings:
1) self-caused,
2) caused by another, and
3) uncaused.

Which are we? Self-caused is impossible with respect to existence. Uncaused would mean that we are necessary, eternal, infinite beings, which we are not; so we must be caused by another.

If we are caused by another, what kind of being is He? Again, self-caused is impossible; if He were caused by another, that leads to infinite regress; so He must be uncaused."

Argument #2 for God = *EXISTENTIAL CAUSALITY*

The following are excerpts from pages 239-250 of Dr. Geisler's book 'Christian Apologetics'[32]

Dr. Norman Geisler holds a Ph.D. in Philosophy from Loyola University. He is a Christian apologist and co-founder of the Southern Evangelical Seminary (Charlotte, North Carolina) and the Veritas Evangelical Seminary (Murrieta, California), where he has been the Chairman of Christian Apologetics.

"The theist need not claim that everything has a cause. Rather, he or she can return to the claim of **existential causality** *which claims that EVERY FINITE, CONTINGENT AND CHANGING THING HAS A CAUSE. If this principle is sound and leads to an infinite, necessary, and unchanging Being, then this Being need not have a cause. God will be the Uncaused Cause of everything else that exists. This is the direction taken in developing proof for the existence of God."*

Premise #1 It is undeniable that *I exist* → One must exist in order to deny that he or she exists, which is self-defeating (whatever is undeniable is true, and whatever is unaffirmable is false, so it is undeniably true that I exist). It is *logically possible* that I do not exist, but since I do exist, it is *actually undeniable* that I do exist.

Premise #2 My existence is undeniable but **contingent** → It is logically possible that I not exist, and therefore I am not **necessary** (a necessary existence is one that cannot not exist). Once I establish that I have the potential to not exist, whatever has the potential not to exist is currently caused to exist by another. My *potential existence* is either self-caused, caused by another, or uncaused; there are no other possibilities.

 (1) I cannot be self-caused, since a self-caused being would have to exist prior to itself, simultaneously in a state of actuality and potentiality in regard to being. But potentiality is not actuality; nothing is not something. In order to cause one's own existence one must simultaneously exist and not exist, which is impossible.

 (2) I cannot be uncaused, since I had the potential to not exist. Whatever can come to be (like me) must be caused to be. For something cannot come from nothing; the mere potential for being cannot actualize itself. No finite being can actualize its own existence. The actualization of a potentiality is what is meant by **causality**. Hence, to actualize one's own potential for being would mean to cause one's own being, which is impossible.

 (3) I must be caused. No potential can actualize itself. There must be a cause outside the known existence of potential things since potential things (like me) exist. But the potential for being does not account for the existence of something. Many things which could possibly exist do not exist (mermaids, Pegasus, etc.). Why then do other things which might not exist actually exist? *The only adequate explanation for why there is something rather than nothing at all is that the something that could be nothing is caused to exist by something that cannot be nothing...* All contingent beings are caused by a necessary Being. Whatever is but might not be is dependent on what is but cannot not be.

Premise #3 A necessary Being has pure actuality with **no potentiality** → If there was any potential for existence, then it would be possible not to exist. The nonexistence of a necessary Being is impossible (if there is a necessary Being, then it must exist necessarily).

Premise #4 A necessary Being is **changeless** → Whatever could change has potential for change, but a necessary Being has no potentiality; therefore a necessary Being cannot change.

Premise #5 A necessary Being is **nontemporal** and **nonspatial** → A necessary Being can't change, but time involves change in moment and space involves change in position. So a necessary Being cannot be temporal or spatial.

Premise #6 A necessary Being is **eternal** → There is no potential for nonexistence since a necessary Being has no potentiality. A necessary Being cannot *come to be* or *cease to be*, for whatever comes to be or ceases to be moves from a state of potentiality to a state of actuality with regard to existence.

Premise #7 A necessary Being can only have **one** existence → In a Being of pure actuality, with no potentiality, all must be one since there is no way for one thing to differ from another in it's being unless there is some real potentiality for differentiation.

Premise #8 A necessary Being is **simple** and **undivided** → It cannot be composed of different arts or elements. There is no principle of differentiation in it – all is simply one. And if it exists at all, than it must be and cannot not be, so it is impossible to destroy the existence of a necessary Being.

Premise #9 A necessary Being is **infinite** in whatever attributes it possesses → Only what has potentiality can be limited. 'Limitation' means that which differentiates one thing from another, while 'pure actuality' is being pure and simple, and is unlimited. The only limitations on pure actuality are those of possibility *outside* of it. Therefore, If it is knowing, it must be all-knowing. If powerful, it must be all-powerful. If good, it must be all-good.

Premise #10 A necessary Being is **uncaused** → Whatever is caused passes from potentiality to actuality, for that is what causality means. A necessary Being has no potentiality and it cannot change. Therefore, it is clear that a necessary Being cannot be caused. And since a self-caused being is impossible, it must be concluded that a necessary Being is an uncaused Being.

Premise #11 This Uncaused Being is *__all-powerful__* ➔ By power we mean what can cause something else to be or not to be in some way, which is what the uncaused cause is: it causes the very being of all that exists.

Premise #12 This Uncaused Being is *__all-knowing__* ➔ It must be knowing because knowing beings exist (I am a knowing being, and I know it). The ability to know (which I possess) is caused to be by the Cause of all finite beings. If my mind or ability to know is received, then there must be Mind or Knower who gave it to me. The intellectual does not arise from the non-intellectual; something cannot arise from nothing. The cause of knowing is infinite, so it knows infinitely. With us some knowledge is possible; with the Creator all knowledge is actual.

Premise #13 This Uncaused Being is *__all-good__* ➔ 'Good' is that which is desired for its own sake. Persons do want to be desired for their own sake... to be loved and not used... to have intrinsic value. The proof is the way they *expect* others to act toward them (the most effective way to find out if a man believes it is wrong to break promises is to break a promise made to him). There are values or goods desired for their own sake, and... the cause of good must be Good, since it cannot give what it does not have to give (all actualities actualized in the effect must preexist in the Cause). But since the Cause of all goodness is infinite, it follows that the Cause must be infinitely good. The Cause of personhood cannot be less than personhood himself. He may be much more than is meant by finite persons but he cannot be less.

Premise #14 'God' = This Uncaused infinitely Perfect Being ➔ By 'God' we mean what is worthy of worship... The Ultimate who is deserving of ultimate commitment. 'God' is that which has ultimate intrinsic value – what can be desired for his own sake as a person. Nothing has more intrinsic value than the ultimate ground and source of all value. Hence, nothing is more worthy of worship than the infinitely perfect uncaused Cause of all else that exists. Therefore, it is appropriate to call this infinitely perfect cause 'God'.

Premise #15 God exists ➔ What in religion is known as the ultimate object of worship or commitment is by REASON known to exist. Hence, what philosophy leads to by the above argument is not an abstract 'unmoved Mover' but a real concrete Ground for our being, and a personal Object whom we can love 'with all our soul, strength, heart, and mind.' *The God the heart needs, the heart has good reason to believe really exists.*

Premise #16 The God who exists matches the **God of the Bible** ➔ The God of the Bible is described as:
ETERNAL – John 8:58 *"Most assuredly, I say to you, before Abraham was, I AM."*; Colossians 1:17 *"All things were created through Him and for Him. And He is before all things, and in Him all things consist."* ; Hebrews 1:1-2 *"God, who at various times and in different ways spoke in times past to the fathers through the prophets, has in these last days spoken to us by His Son, whom He has appointed heir of all things, through whom also He made the worlds..."*

INFINITE – 1Kings 8:27 *"Will God indeed dwell on the earth? Behold, heaven and the heaven of the heavens cannot contain You. How much less this temple which I have built!"*; Isaiah 66:1-2 *"Heaven is My throne, and earth is My footstool. Where is the house that you will build Me? And where is the place of My rest? For all those things My hand has made, and all those things exist', says the Lord."*

CHANGELESS – Malachi 3:6 *"I am the Lord, I do not change..."*; Hebrews 6:17-18 *"God, determining to show more abundantly the unchangeableness of His purpose, guaranteed it by an oath, that by two unchangeable things, in which it is impossible for God to lie, we have strong consolation, who have fled for refuge to lay hold of the hope set before us."*

ALL-LOVING – John 3:16 *"God so loved the world that He gave His only begotten Son, that whoever believes in Him should not perish but have everlasting life."*; 1John 4:16 *"We have known and believed the love that God has for us. God is love, and he who abides in love abides in God, and God in him."*

ALL-POWERFUL – Hebrews 1:3 *"... being the brightness of His glory and the express image of His person, and upholding all things by the word of His power..."*; Matthew 19:26 *"Jesus looked at them and said to them, 'With men this is impossible, but with God all things are possible.'"*

ALL-KNOWING – John 2:24-25 *"Jesus did not commit Himself to them, because He knew all men, and had no need that anyone should testify of man, for He knew what was in man."*; Matthew 26:33-34 *"Peter answered and said to Him, 'Even if all are made to stumble because of You, I will never be made to stumble.' Jesus said to him, 'Assuredly, I say to you that this night, before the rooster crows, you will deny Me three times.'"*

First, there can be only one infinite and necessary Being, as shown in #7 above. Second, there is only one absolutely perfect Being (there could not be two beings who have all possible perfections attributed to them - to have two Beings, one would have to differ from the other). But if there cannot be two such beings, then the God described in the Bible is identical to the God concluded from the above argument.

CONCLUSION The God described in the Bible exists ➔ There cannot be two infinitely perfect beings; there cannot be two such ultimates or absolutes; and so forth. Hence, *the God portrayed in Scripture does indeed exist.*

ISAIAH 45:22 *"Look to Me, and be saved, all you ends of the earth! For I am God, and there is no other."*

"God and the Astronomers"[23] by Dr. Robert Jastrow

God and the Astronomers – The Strange Developments Going On In Astronomy

Dr. Robert Jastrow, a self-described agnostic when it comes to the existence of God, was the founder and director of NASA's Goddard Institute for Space Studies. He was also professor of Astronomy and Geology at Columbia University, and professor of Earth Sciences at Dartmouth College. He was internationally recognized as an authority on both astronomy (the branch of science that deals with the physical universe as a whole) and cosmology (the branch of science that deals with the origin and development of the universe). Modern astronomy is dominated by the Big Bang theory, which brings together observational astronomy, particle physics and cosmology. Dr. Jastrow will always be included in the most famous and learned experts in these fields.

> "For the scientist who has lived out his faith in the power of reason, the story end like a bad dream. He has scaled the mountains of ignorance; he is about to conquer the highest peak; as he pulls himself over the final rock, he is greeted by a band of theologians who have been sitting there for centuries."
>
> Robert Jastrow, Page 116

> "It turns out that the scientist behaves the way the rest of us do when our beliefs are in conflict with the evidence. We become irritated, we pretend the conflict doesn't exist, or we paper it over with meaningless phrases." (page 16)

In the book's introduction, the publishers summarize what readers will discover: *"'Strange developments are going on in astronomy' writes Dr. Jastrow. 'They are fascinating partly because of their theological implications, and partly because of the peculiar reactions of scientists… astronomers have proven the Universe was created in a fiery explosion 20 billion years ago. In the searing heat of the first moment, all the evidence was melted down and destroyed that science might have used to determine the cause of the great explosion… This is the crux of the story of Genesis.'*

The publishers go on: *"According to Jastrow, scientists did not expect to find evidence for an abrupt beginning. When the evidence began to accumulate, they were repelled by their own findings. Einstein wrote, 'Such possibilities seem senseless', and the great astronomer Eddington declared, 'The notion of a beginning is repugnant.' Dr. Jastrow comments, 'There is a strong ring of feeling and emotion in these reactions. They come from the heart, whereas you would expect the judgments to come from the brain. Why?'"*

Dr. Jastrow himself states on page 14: *"Now we see how the astronomical evidence leads to a biblical view of the origin of the world. The details differ, but the essential elements in the astronomical and biblical accounts of Genesis are the same: the chain of events leading to man commenced suddenly at a definite moment in time, in a flash of light and energy."*

Dr. Jastrow titles his book "God and the Astronomers" because he takes you on a journey through the major discoveries in the recent century which point to a universe beginning from nothing and the scientists who, during these discoveries, came to grips with the evidence. Of special note are Jastrow's accounts of Albert Einstein's journey in coming to grips with a universe that is not eternal but rather came to be from nothing.

Jastrow on Einstein (pages 27-28): *"Around this time (1923, when Friedmann's correction of Einstein's error in GTR calculations was published and acknowledged), signs of irritation began to appear among scientists. Einstein was the first to complain. He was disturbed by the idea of a Universe that blows up, because it implied that the world had a beginning. In a letter to de Sitter – discovered in a box of old records in Leiden a few years ago – Einstein wrote 'The circumstance (of an expanding universe) irritates me,' and in another letter about the expanding universe, 'To admit such possibilities seems senseless.'*

This is curiously emotional language for a discussion of some mathematical formulas. I suppose that the idea of a beginning in time annoyed Einstein because of its theological implications. We know he had well-defined feelings about God, but not as the Creator or Prime Mover.

The theory and observation (Hubble's measurements) pointed to an expanding universe and a beginning in time. Still Einstein resisted the new developments and held onto his idea of a static, unchanging Universe until 1930, when he traveled halfway around the world from Berlin to Pasadena to visit Hubble. He studied Hubble's plates, looked through his telescope, and announced himself convinced. He said, 'New observations by Hubble and Humason concerning the red shift of light in distant nebulae make it appear likely that the general structure of the Universe is not static.'"

Chapter 2   Argument #3 for God = *DESIGN* in the Universe
The Mathematics in the Universe infer an Intelligent Designer

This argument, that the presence of design in the Universe means there must be a Designer who caused it, is proposed and then explained by philosopher Dr. Norman Geisler in his book "*When Skeptics Ask*"[31]:

> "Premise #1 =   All designs infer a designer.
> Premise #2 =   There is great design in the universe.
> Conclusion =   Therefore, there must be a Great Designer of the universe."

"**Premise #1** we know from experience. Anytime we see a COMPLEX DESIGN, we know by previous experience that it came from the mind of a designer. Watches imply watchmakers; buildings imply architects; paintings imply artists; and coded messages imply an intelligent sender. It is always our expectation because we see it happening over and over. This is another way of stating the PRINCIPLE OF CAUSALITY.

Also, the greater the design, the greater the designer. Beavers make log dams, but they never constructed anything like Hoover Dam. Likewise, a thousand monkeys sitting at typewriters would never write Hamlet. But Shakespeare did it on the first try. The more complex the design, the greater the intelligence needed to produce it.

There is a difference between simple patterns and complex design. Snowflakes or quartz crystals have simple patterns repeated over and over, but have completely natural causes. The difference is that snowflakes and crystals have a simple repeated pattern. But language communicates COMPLEX INFORMATION, not just the same thing over and over. Complex information occurs when the natural elements are given boundary conditions.

So when a rockhound sees small round rocks in a stream, it doesn't surprise him because natural erosion rounds them that way. But when he finds an arrowhead he realizes that some intelligent being has deliberately altered the natural form of the rock. He sees complexity here that cannot be explained by natural forces. Now the design that we are talking about in this argument is COMPLEX DESIGN, not simple patterns; the more complex that design is, the greater the intelligence required to produce it.

That's where **Premise #2** comes in. The design we see in the universe is COMPLEX. The universe is a very intricate system of forces that work together for the mutual benefit of the whole. Life is a very complex development. A single DNA molecule, the building block of all life, carries the same amount of information as one volume of an encyclopedia. No one seeing an encyclopedia lying in the forest would hesitate to think that it had an intelligent cause; so when we find a living creature composed of millions of DNA-based cells, we ought to assume that it likewise has an intelligent cause.

Some have objected to this argument (**Premise #3**) on the basis of chance. They claim that when the dice are rolled any combination could happen. However, that is not very convincing for several reasons.

First…
1) The design argument is not really an argument from chance but from design, which we know from repeated observation to have an intelligent cause.

Second…
2) Science is based on repeated observation, not on chance. So this objection to the design argument is not scientific.

Finally….
3) Even if it were a chance (probability) argument, the chances are a lot higher that there is a designer. One scientist figured the odds for a one-cell animal to emerge by pure chance at 1 in $10^{40,000}$. The odds for an infinitely more complex human being to emerge by chance are too high to calculate!

The only REASONABLE conclusion is that there is a great Designer behind the design in the world."

What leading Scientists say:
The Design & Order in the Universe is a Creative Act by an *Intelligent Mind*

Many of the most influential physicists, mathematicians and astronomers in history also point to the order and design in the Universe through the physical laws and forces as evidence for an Intelligent First Cause:

1 Johannes Kepler (1571-1630) - German Mathematician and Astronomer: *"When things are in order, if the cause of the orderliness cannot be deduced from the motion of the elements or from the composition of matter, it is quite possibly a cause possessing a MIND."* (Somnium: Posthumous Work on Lunar Astronomy).

2 Isaac Newton (1643-1727) - British Mathematician and Physicist, founder of modern physical science: *"...whence is it that Nature doth nothing in vain; and whence arises all that Order and Beauty which we see in the World? ... does it not appear from phaenomena that there is a Being incorporeal, living, intelligent, omnipresent, who in infinite space, as it were in his Sensory, sees the things themselves intimately, and thoroughly perceives them, and comprehends them wholly by their immediate presence to Himself."*

3 Sir William Herschel (1738-1822) - British Astronomer: *"Herschel strongly believed that God's universe was characterized by order and planning. His discovery of that order led him to conclude that 'the undevout astronomer must be mad'".* (Ann Lamont, 'Sir William Herschel – Founder of Modern Stellar Astronomy' 2000).

4 Michael Faraday (1791-1867) - British Physicist, founder of electromagnetism: *"...his religious belief in a single Creator encouraged his scientific belief in the "unity of forces", the idea that magnetism, electricity and the other forces have a common origin."* (B. Bowers, Michael Faraday and Electricity, 1974).

5 Sir George Gabriel Stokes (1819-1903) - Irish Mathematician and Physicist; Lucasian Prof. of Mathematics, Cambridge Univ.: *"In thus referring the motions of the planets in their orbits to a general property of matter, that of gravitation, we introduce an idea of causation... this leads us to the conception of a designing MIND lying behind the furthest causes... that we could even conceivably attain to by purely scientific investigation."* (Gifford Lecture #1, 'Natural Theology',1891).

6 Lord William Kelvin (1824-1907) - Scottish Mathematical Physicist: *"Overwhelming strong proofs of intelligent and benevolent design lie around us....I believe that the more thoroughly science is studied, the further does it take us from anything comparable to atheism…The more thoroughly I conduct scientific research, the more I believe that science excludes atheism."*

7 James Clerk Maxwell (1831-1879) - Scottish Mathematician and Theoretical Physicist, widely regarded as the 19th century scientist who had the greatest influence on 20th century physics: *"No theory of evolution can be formed to account for the similarity of molecules, for evolution necessarily implies continuous change.. The exact equality of each molecule to all others of the same kind gives it.. the essential character of a manufactured article, and precludes the idea of its being eternal and self-existent."* ('Discourse on Molecules', a paper presented to the British Assoc. For the Advancement of Science, 1873).

8 Max Planck (1858-1947) - PhD Theoretical Physics (age 21), 1918 Nobel Prize in Physics: *"As a man who has devoted his whole life to the most clear headed science, to the study of matter, I can tell you as a result of my research about atoms this much: All matter originates and exists only by virtue of a force which brings the particle of an atom to vibration and holds this most minute solar system of the atom together. We must assume behind this force the existence of a conscious and intelligent MIND."* ('Nature of Matter', 1944).

9 Albert Einstein (1879-1955) - PhD Theoretical Physics; 1921 Nobel Prize in Physics; Time Person of the Century, 1999: *"The scientist is possessed by the sense of universal causation ... His religious feeling takes the form of a rapturous amazement at the harmony of natural law, which reveals an intelligence of such superiority that, compared with it, all the systematic thinking and acting of human beings is an utterly insignificant reflection... In the view of such harmony in the cosmos which I, with my limited human mind, am able to recognize, there are yet people who say there is no God. But what makes me really angry is that they quote me for support for such views..."* ('The Expanded Quotable Einstein', Princeton Univ. Press, 2000).

10 Robert Millikan (1868-1953) - PhD Physics; 1923 Nobel Prize in Physics: *"The laws of physics allowed humankind to know a God not of caprice and whim, such as were all the gods of the ancient world, but a God who works through law who revealed a nature of orderliness, and a nature capable of being known..."* ('Evolution in Science and Religion', Yale University Press,1927).

11 Arthur Compton (1892-1962) - PhD Physics; 1927 Nobel Prize in Physics: *"The scientist who recognizes God knows only the God of Newton. He feels that God is in nature, that the orderly ways in which nature works are themselves the manifestations of God's will and purpose. Its laws are his orderly way of working."* ('The Human Meaning of Science', 1940).

12 Sir Fred Hoyle (1915-2001) - Cambridge Prof. of Astrophysics and Natural Philosophy: *"A common sense interpretation of the facts suggests that a superintellect has monkeyed with the physics, as well as with chemistry and biology, and that there are no blind forces worth speaking about in nature. The numbers one calculates from the facts seem to me so overwhelming as to put this conclusion almost beyond question."*

13 Wernher von Braun (1912-1977) - PhD Physics, NASA's 'greatest rocket scientist in history': *"I find it as difficult to understand a scientist who does not acknowledge the presence of a superior rationality behind the existence of the universe as it is to comprehend a theologian who would deny the advances of science."* ('The Skeptical Inquirer',10:258-276).

14 Charles Townes (1915 -) - PhD Physics, 1964 Nobel Prize in Physics: "*Intelligent design, as one sees it from a scientific point of view, seems to be quite real. This is a very special universe: it's remarkable that it came out just this way. If the laws of physics weren't just the way they are, we couldn't be here at all.*" (2005 interview for Berkeley News by Bonnie Powell).

15 Arthur L. Schawlow (1921-1999) - PhD Physics, 1981 Nobel Prize in Physics: *"It seems to me that when confronted with the marvels of life and the universe, one must ask why and not just how. The only possible answers are religious. . . . I find a need for God in the universe and in my own life."* ('Cosmos, Bios, Theos: Scientists Reflect on Science, God, and the Origins of the Universe, Open Court Pub. Co., 1992).

16 Alan Sandage (1926-2010) - PhD Astronomy, the most influential astronomer of the last half-century: *"I find it quite improbable that such order came out of chaos. There has to be some organizing principle. God to me is a mystery but is the explanation for the miracle of existence, why there is something instead of nothing."* ('Sizing up the Cosmos: An Astronomer's Quest', NY Times, 1991).

17 Arno Penzias (1933 -) - PhD Physics, 1978 Nobel Prize in Physics: *"By looking at the order in the world, we can infer purpose and from purpose we begin to get some knowledge of the Creator, the Planner of all this. This is, then, how I look at God. I look at God through the works of God's hands and from those works imply intentions. From these intentions, I receive an impression of the Almighty."* ('The God I Believe In', 1994).

18 Stephen Hawking (1942 -) - PhD Cosmology & Theoretical Physics: *"The whole history of science has been the gradual realization that events do not happen in an arbitrary manner, but that they reflect a certain underlying order, which may or may not be divinely inspired."*

19 Henry "Fritz" Schaefer (1944 -) - PhD Chemical Physics, Professor of Chemistry and Director of the Center for Computational Quantum Chemistry, Univ. of Georgia: *"Why are there so few atheists among physicists? Many scientists are considering the facts before them. They say things like: 'The present arrangement of matter indicates a very special choice of initial conditions.' (Paul Davies). 'In fact, if one considers the possible constants and laws that could have emerged, the odds against a universe that produced life like ours are immense.' (Stephen Hawking)… As the Apostle Paul said in his epistle to the Romans: 'Since the creation of the world, God's invisible qualities—His eternal power and divine nature—have been clearly seen, being understood from what has been made.'"* ('Scientists and their Gods (Science and Christianity, Conflict or Coherence?',1999).

20 George Smoot (1945 -) - PhD Particle Physics, 2006 Nobel Prize in Physics: *"George Smoot commenting on the discovery by the COBE Science Working Group of the expected "ripples" in the microwave background radiation, called these fluctuations 'the fingerprints from the Maker.' Smoot draws attention not only to the fact that his team had provided more evidence for the creation event, but for a "finely orchestrated" creation event. Stephen Hawking was so impressed with this finding that he called it "the most important discovery of the century, if not of all time."*

21 Frank Tipler (1947 -) - PhD Physics, Prof. of Mathematics and Physics, Tulane Univ., *"When I began my career as a cosmologist some twenty years ago, I was a convinced atheist. I never in my wildest dreams imagined that one day I would be writing a book purporting to show that the central claims of Judeo-Christian theology are in fact true, that these claims are straightforward deductions of the laws of physics as we now understand them."* ('The Physics Of Immortality', Doubleday, 1994).

22 William Philips (1948 -) - PhD Physics, 1997 Nobel Prize in Physics, Prof. of Physics at Univ of Maryland: *"I believe in God. In fact, I believe in a personal God who acts in and interacts with the creation. I believe the observations about the orderliness of the physical universe, and the apparently exceptional fine-tuning of the conditions of the universe for the development of life suggest that an intelligent Creator is responsible. I believe in God because of a personal faith, a faith consistent with what I know about science."* (Letter to T. Dimitrov, 2002).

How Science (and you) test for Design: the *IMPROBABILITY* in Nature

Knowing the difference between a process or event that occurred naturally (*random chance*), or by *Design* (intentional purpose): look for highly improbable ORDER (Accuracy *with* Precision to a Standard).

1) **Simple** = plain, straightforward; lacking in intelligence
2) **Complex** = an intricate assembly of parts, units, etc.
3) **Order** = correctness according to a set of rules or laws; the state of effectively controlled operation
4) **Accurate** = degree of closeness to a prescribed target of a set of measurements from a process or system
5) **Precise** = degree to which a process or system's measurements repeat themselves in unchanged conditions
6) **Finely Tuned** = precision of a process or system's measurements to a *standard* that was designed to achieve it's purpose (example: the correct pitch of a musical instrument to achieve its intended sound)
7) **Design** = an intended outline or plan; to plan or fashion skillfully, especially for a definite purpose
8) **Random** = without plan or order, thereby lacking in purpose (we will also refer to this as *unguided*)

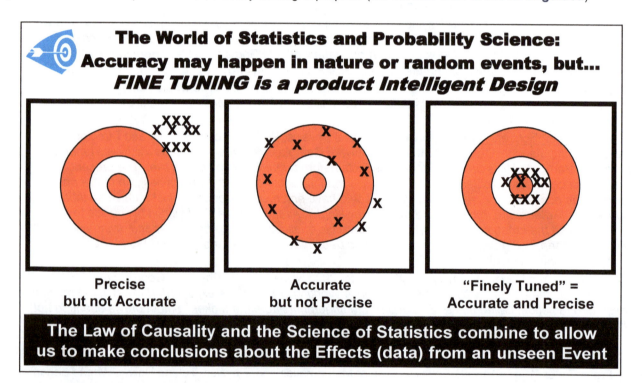

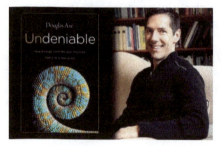

Professor Doug Axe, PhD in molecular biology (Caltech) is the Director of Biologic Institute. In his latest book 'Undeniable: How Biology Confirms Our Intuition that Life is Designed'[29], he claims there are two key facts that demonstrate that 'all humans are scientists': *"Fact #1: Everyone validates their design intuition through firsthand experience. Fact #2: Experience is scientific in nature."* Dr. Axe goes in to explain:

"Basic science is an integral part of how we live. We are all careful observers of our world. We all make mental notes of what we observe. We all use those notes to build conceptual models of how things work. And we all continually refine these models as needed. Without a doubt, this is science. I call it 'common science' to emphasize the connection to common sense." Dr. Axe then explains what any person needs in order to apply their 'common science': *"All you need is a healthy dose of curiosity and a healthy tolerance of the good kind of awkwardness – the kind that comes from challenging claims that ought to be challenged."*

> *"People who lack formal scientific credentials are nonetheless qualified to speak with authority on matters of common science."* — Professor Doug Axe, 'Undeniable'

JOHN 1:1-2   The Logos = Creative MIND of the Universe   2.2

"②*In the beginning was the* ①*Word, and the Word was with God, and the Word was God. He was in the beginning with God.*"

① Word = Greek 'Logos' = rationality, thought, reasoning
② In the beginning = Greek 'ejn ajrch' – a direct reference for Jews to Genesis 1:1.

John's Gospel was written to both a Jewish and Greek culture – he is reaching out to both Jews and Greeks in these first verses by pointing to the MIND in the Universe, who existed from eternity with God.

George Wald (1906-1997) – 1967 Noble Prize in Physiology, PhD Zoology, Columbia Univ., Professor of Biology at Harvard University: *"It has occurred to me lately—I must confess with some shock at first to my scientific sensibilities—that both questions [the origin of consciousness in humans and of life from non-living matter] might be brought into some degree of congruence. This is with the assumption that MIND, rather than emerging as a late outgrowth in the evolution of life, has existed always as the matrix, the source and condition of physical reality—that stuff of which physical reality is composed is mind-stuff. It is mind that has composed a physical universe that breeds life and so eventually evolves creatures that know and create: science-, art-, and technology-making animals. In them the universe begins to know itself."* (from his article entitled "Life and Mind in the Universe" which appeared in the peer-reviewed journal *The International Journal of Quantum Chemistry: Quantum Biology*, symposium 11, 1984).

The Greeks: 'Logos' of Stoicism

The Stoics were the prevailing Greek culture in John's day. They originated as a school of Hellenistic philosophy, founded in Athens by Zeno of Citium in the early third century BC. It became the most popular philosophy among the educated elite in the Greco-Roman Empire, to the point where the majority of the successors of Alexander the Great professed themselves Stoics

They thought of the Universe as pervaded by "logos", the 'World-Soul', the creative energy, the eternal Reason. They used the term "logos" to express their conviction of the ultimate rationality of the universe. It was the 'force' that originated and permeated and directed all things - the supreme governing principle of the universe. Stoicism holds that becoming a clear and unbiased thinker allows one to understand the universal reason (*logos*).

But the Stoics did not think of the "logos" as knowable in a personal sense. They believed that all things came from it, and men derived their wisdom from it. This impersonal "logos" is "always existent", and "all things happen through this "logos".

Stoicism focuses on an active relationship between cosmic determinism and human freedom: Stoics believe it is virtuous to maintain a will that is in accord with NATURE.

The Stoics presented their philosophy as a way of life: the best indication of an individual's philosophy was not what a person said but how they behaved. They emphasized ethics as the main focus of human knowledge.

The Jews: 'Logos' of Wisdom

John's use of the 'Word' also points to the "logos", the eternal WISDOM of God, in Psalm 33:6, *"By the word of Yahweh the heavens were made..."*. His Jewish audience knew the Old Testament pointed to the wisdom of God in creation (Psalm 33:6 and Prov. 8) and salvation (Psalm 107:19-20),

The Jewish Targums (translations of the Hebrew OT into Aramaic, ≈ 300 BC) substituted *Memra* ("Word") in many places as a designation for God (Exodus 19:17, *"And Moses brought the people out of the camp to meet God...".*).

- The Palestinian Targum reads "to meet the *Word* of God."
- Targum Jonathan uses this expression "the *Word* of God" some 320 times.

Where the Jew and Greek would have a common understanding of "Logos":

"Logos" represents the ruling fact of the universe, and represents the self-expression of God. The Jew remembers that 'by the Word of the Lord the heavens were made'; the Greek thinks of the rational principle of which all natural laws are expressed. Both will agree that this Logos is the starting-point of all things.

John used "Logos" because it was in common use everywhere. He knew all men caught his essential meaning. But for John, the Word was not a principle, but a living, divine PERSON, who is the source of life for all people.

Jesus: 'Logos' gets an Identity

Did you notice that John never uses the term "Logos" after verse 13 of his first chapter? It's because John's Prologue focuses on the PRE-EXISTENCE of this universal wisdom and reason. But then, JOHN 1:14 is his point of transition. 'Logos' is now Jesus of Nazareth. The "Logos" is the pre-existent Christ.

"To DO Science requires faith in a *Mathematically Ordered, Intelligible Universe*"[10]

"Lists of the great ideas of modern science typically contain a major omission. On such lists we are sure to find Copernicus's heliocentric theory, Kepler's laws, Newton's laws, and Einstein's theory of relativity, yet the greatest idea of modern science is almost never included. It is such a big idea that it makes possible all the other ideas. And it is invisible to us because it is an assumption taken for granted rather than a theory that has been formulated. Oddly enough, the greatest idea of modern science is based not on reason but on FAITH.

Scientists today take for granted the idea that the universe operates according to LAWS, and that these laws are comprehensible to the **HUMAN MIND**. Science is based on what author James Trefil calls the principle of universality: *'It says that the laws of nature we discover here and now in our laboratories are true everywhere in the universe and have been in force for all time.'*

The laws that govern the universe seem to be written in the language of **MATHEMATICS**. The greatest scientists have been struck by how strange this is. In his essay 'The Unreasonable Effectiveness of Mathematics in the Natural Sciences', physicist Eugene Wigner confesses that the mathematical underpinning of nature *'is something bordering on the mysterious and there is no rational explanation for it.'* Feynman confesses, *'Why nature is mathematical is a mystery… The fact that there are rules at all is a kind of miracle.'* This astonishment springs from the recognition that the universe doesn't have to be this way. There is no special reason why the laws of nature we find on earth should also govern a star billions of light years away. It is easy to imagine a universe in which conditions change unpredictably from instant to instant, or even a universe in which things pop in and out of existence. There is no logical necessity for a universe that OBEYS RULES, let alone one that abides by the rules of mathematics.

Yet the universe seems to be ordered. I say 'seems' because there is no way to prove this is so. Even so, **scientists cling to their long-held faith in the fundamental rationality of the cosmos**. Convinced in advance that rules exist, and that human reason is up to the task of uncovering these rules, scientists continue to try to find them. These ARTICLES OF FAITH are essential for science to function.

Without the 'irrational' belief that we live in an ordered universe, modern science is impossible. Science also relies on the equally unsupported belief that the rationality of the universe is mirrored in the rationality of our human minds.

So where did Western man get this faith in a unified, ordered, and accessible universe? How did we go from chaos to cosmos? My answer, in a word, is **CHRISTIANITY**. Christianity reinvigorated the idea of an ordered cosmos by envisioning the universe as following laws that embody the rationality of God the creator."

John 1:1 *"In the beginning was the ①WORD; the Word was with God; the Word was God."*
①**WORD** = Greek "Logos" = rationality, thought, reasoning ⇨ God created the universe, and it operates according to the laws He, by His divine reasoning, has put in place.

God's Orderly Design: The Mathematical Laws of Motion **2.3**
God's Universe can be accessed and understood by man

Romans 1:19-20 *"...what may be known of God is ①MANIFEST among them, for God has ①SHOWN IT TO THEM. For since the creation of the world His invisible attributes are ②CLEARLY SEEN, being ③UNDERSTOOD by the things that are made, even His eternal power and divine nature, so they are without excuse."*
① MANIFEST, SHOWN IT TO THEM = Gr. *"phaneros"* = rendered publicly apparent or obvious
② CLEARLY SEEN = Gr. *"kathoraō"* = fully beheld, distinctly apparent
③ UNDERSTOOD = Gr. *"noieō"* = intellectually perceived by observing, then exercising the mind

Isaiah 40:26 *"①LIFT UP YOUR EYES ON HIGH, and ②SEE who has ③CREATED these things, who brings out their ④HOST by ⑤NUMBER; He ⑥CALLS them all by ⑦NAME, by the greatness of His might and the strength of His power; not one is ⑧MISSING."*
① LIFT UP = Hebr. *"nâśâ nâsâh"* = bring forth, regard your gaze upward
② SEE = Hebr. *"râ'âh"* = joyfully behold, consider, discern for yourself, take heed
③ CREATED = Hebr. *"bârâ'"* = to dispatch into existence what never existed before (same as Genesis 1:1)
④ HOST = Hebr. *"tsâbâ' tseâb'âh"* = an organized army, under one's command for service
⑤ NUMBER = Hebr. *"mispâr"* = abundance (can be finite or infinite)
⑥ CALLS THEM = Hebr. *"qârâ'"* = to address someone; to bid or call forth by public proclamation
⑦ NAME = Hebr. *"shêm"* = an individually-applied mark or memorial, done to bestow honor and authority
⑧ MISSING = Hebr. *"âdar"* = found wanting, as in battle; failing to keep rank

Celestial Mechanics → Cosmology → Astronomy → Physics = *Scientific Evidence* of ORDER, not chaos
The following is directly quoted from sections in pages 104-105 of "The Privileged Planet"[26]

"The mere presence of the Moon and other planets in the Solar System fostered the development of *celestial mechanics and modern cosmology*. Danish astronomer **Tycho Brahe**'s (1546-1601) observations of the paths of the planets against the background stars allowed **Johannes Keplar** (1571-1630) to formulate his three famous laws of planetary motion. Keplar's discovery of the 3rd law (that the square of the orbital period of a planet is proportional to the cube of its mean distance from the Sun) required several visible planets. It also helped that the planets span a large range of distance from the Sun. As Keplar's discovery of his 1st Law – that the orbits are not circles but ellipses – required that at least one such planet have a discernible eccentric orbit. For Keplar, Mars served the purpose. If, like many of the extra Solar Systems discussed..., Earth had lacked "wandering neighbors" (the word "planet", by the way, derives from the Greek word meaning "wanderer"), we might never have discovered these laws.

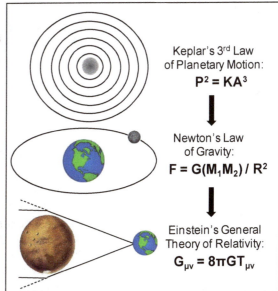

Keplar's 3rd Law of Planetary Motion:
$$P^2 = KA^3$$

Newton's Law of Gravity:
$$F = G(M_1 M_2) / R^2$$

Einstein's General Theory of Relativity:
$$G_{\mu\nu} = 8\pi G T_{\mu\nu}$$

Kepler's three empirical laws served as the foundation of **Isaac Newton's** (1643-1727) more general physical laws of motion and gravity, which became the foundation for **Einstein's** (1879-1955) General Theory of Relativity two centuries later. The planets may have inspired Keplar, but the Moon inspired Newton to apply his Earthly laws to the broader universe. Without the Earth-centered motion of the Moon, the conceptual leap from falling bodies on Earth's surface to the motions of the Sun-centered planets would have been much more difficult. By linking the motions of the Moon and planets to experiments on Earth's surface, Newton gave a physical basis to Keplar's 3rd Law would have remained a mathematical curiosity, more an indication of the cleverness of a mathematician with too much time on his hands than of a deep truth of the universe. As it is, *astronomy gave birth to physics*.

The most habitable locale happens to be near a star with several other planets whose orbital periods are substantially shorter than a human life span. Not only is a free-floating planet in interstellar space (or even in an open cluster) a poor home for complex life, it doesn't even provide the opportunity to DISCOVER these universal laws. Even geniuses like Keplar and Newton needed a planetary playpen to discover the laws of motion and gravity and to realize that they apply throughout the cosmos. And since General Relativity now forms the basis of cosmological models, once astronomers understood the motions of planets, they were well on their way to understanding the structure and history of the universe."

Mathematical Equations = Intelligent Design → Order, Control, Precision

The Mind behind the Universe: Speaking in the Language of Math Equations

"Mathematics" = Greek word 'knowledge, learning' → Abstract study of quantities, structures, space and other properties of the universe. Using logical reasoning, mathematics developed from counting, calculating and measuring phenomena, and then progressed to the systematic study of the shapes and motions of physical objects. Mathematical research establishes the TRUTH or falsity of claims through rigorous deduction from appropriately chosen axioms and definitions.

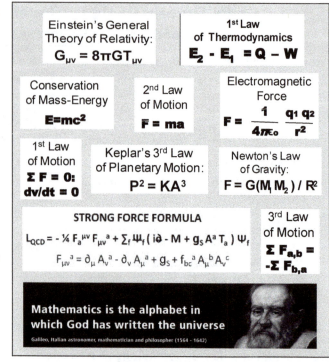

Einstein's General Theory of Relativity: $G_{\mu\nu} = 8\pi G T_{\mu\nu}$

1st Law of Thermodynamics: $E_2 - E_1 = Q - W$

Conservation of Mass-Energy: $E=mc^2$

2nd Law of Motion: $\bar{F} = ma$

Electromagnetic Force: $F = \dfrac{1}{4\pi\epsilon_0} \dfrac{q_1 q_2}{r^2}$

1st Law of Motion: $\Sigma F = 0;\ dv/dt = 0$

Keplar's 3rd Law of Planetary Motion: $P^2 = KA^3$

Newton's Law of Gravity: $F = G(M_1 M_2)/R^2$

STRONG FORCE FORMULA: $L_{QCD} = -\tfrac{1}{4} F_a^{\mu\nu} F_{\mu\nu}^a + \Sigma_f \Psi_f (i\partial - M + g_S A^a T_a) \Psi_f$

$F_{\mu\nu}^a = \partial_\mu A_\nu^a - \partial_\nu A_\mu^a + g_S + f_{bc}^a A_\mu^b A_\nu^c$

3rd Law of Motion: $\Sigma F_{a,b} = -\Sigma F_{b,a}$

"Mathematics is the alphabet in which God has written the universe"
Galileo, Italian astronomer, mathematician and philosopher (1564 - 1642)

 Alfred Russell Wallace (1823-1913): British naturalist best known for conceiving the theory of evolution through natural selection (led Darwin to publish 'Origin of Species'): *"Nothing in evolution can account for the soul of man. The difference between man and the other animals is unbridgeable. **MATHEMATICS** is alone sufficient to prove in man the possession of a faculty inexistent in other creatures. Then you have music and the artistic faculty. No, the soul was a separate creation."* ('New Thoughts on Evolution', 1910).

 Albert Einstein (1879-1955): Nobel Prize Physics 1921: *"The theory of relativity belongs to the class of 'principle-theories'. As such it employs an Analytic method. The elements which comprise this theory are not based on hypothesis but on empirical discovery. The empirical discovery leads to understanding the general characteristics of natural processes. **MATHEMATICAL MODELS** are used to separate natural processes into theoretical descriptions. Therefore, by analytical means the necessary conditions that have to be satisfied are deduced. Separate events must satisfy these conditions. Experience should then match these conclusions."* (1919 'The Times' article "Time, Space and Gravitation").

 Eugene Wigner (1902-1995): Nobel Prize Physics 1963, Prof. Mathematical Physics, Princeton Univ.: *"Certainly it is hard to believe that our reasoning power was brought, by Darwin's process of natural selection, to the perfection which it seems to possess... It is difficult to avoid the impression that a miracle confronts us here, quite comparable in its striking nature to the miracle that the human mind can string a thousand arguments together without getting itself into contradictions, or to the two miracles of the existence of laws of nature and of the human mind's capacity to divine them. The miracle of the appropriateness of the language of **MATHEMATICS** for the formulation of the laws of physics is a wonderful gift which we neither understand nor deserve."* ('The Unreasonable Effectiveness of Mathematics in the Natural Sciences', 1960).

 Richard Feynman (1918-1988): Nobel Prize Physics 1965, Prof. Theoretical Physics, Cornell Univ.: *"To those who do not know **MATHEMATICS** it is difficult to get across a real feeling as to the beauty, the deepest beauty, of nature.. If you want to learn about nature, to appreciate nature, it is necessary to understand the language that she speaks in. Mathematics is like a language plus logic. Mathematics is a tool for reasoning."* ('Lecture Series: The Character of Physical Law', Cornell Univ., 1964).

 David Berlinski (1942 -): PhD Philosophy (Princeton Univ.), Post doctorate fellow, mathematics and molecular biology, Columbia Univ.: *"Across the vast range of arguments offered, assessed, embraced, deferred, delayed or defeated, it is only within **MATHEMATICS** that arguments achieve the power to compel allegiance because they are seen to command assent. And it is only by means of mathematics that the powerful ideas of an alien discipline such as theoretical physics may step by step be returned to the ordinary human power to grasp things... the reason Darwinian biologists and evolutionary psychologists don't need math is that most of what they are doing isn't science..."* ('Why Math is really important', May 2013).

 Walter L. Bradley (1943 -): PhD Materials Science, Distinguished Prof. of Engineering, Baylor Univ.: *"Only in the 20th century have we come to fully understand that the incredibly diverse phenomena that we observe in nature are the outworking of a very small number of physical laws, each of which may be described by a simple **MATHEMATICAL** relationship. Indeed, so simple in mathematical form and small in number are these physical laws that they can all be written on one side of one sheet of paper... the universe assumes a remarkably simple and elegant mathematical form."* ('How the Recent Discoveries Support a Designed Universe').

God's Orderly Design: The 4 Forces in the Universe   2.4

There are four basic forces in the natural world: gravity, electromagnetic force, a "strong" and a "weak" nuclear force. Gravity acts between all mass in the universe and it has infinite range. The electromagnetic force acts between electrically charged particles. Electricity, magnetism, and light are all produced by this force and it also has infinite range. The strong nuclear force binds neutrons and protons together in the cores of atoms and is a short range force. The weak nuclear force causes Beta decay (the conversion of a neutron to a proton, an electron and an antineutrino). Like the strong force, the weak force is also short range.

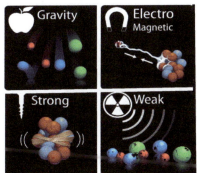

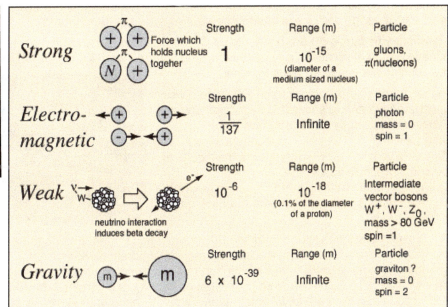

Gravity and electromagnetism decrease in strength inversely with the square of the distance between two objects. The electromagnetic force is weaker than the strong force but stronger than the weak force and gravity, which is weakest.

➔ **What is Gravity?**[24] Gravity is the force of attraction that exists between all objects. It acts through the vacuum of space and is the only force strong enough to extend (like invisible cords) through vast distances. Gravity cannot be turned off (no anti-gravity machine has yet been invented). For example:
  a) the Earth's gravity keeps the moon in orbit
  b) the moon pulls back on Earth and causes the tides
  c) the Earth also pulls downward and gives objects their "weight"
  d) on the Moon you would weigh 6X less than on Earth because lunar gravity is less than the Earth's
  e) on Earth, gravity causes the rain to "fall"
  f) on Earth, gravity makes us tired since we work against its force all day long, every day

God gives gravity the correct strength to make life possible on earth (its this gravitational attraction that causes all the objects in our solar system to move with clockwise perfection). The following incredible facts about our universe are never even noticed by us, since God's faithful gravity force ensures Earth's atmosphere and inhabitants remain firmly in place:
1. Earth's rotation on its axis, as it orbits the sun, results in a surface speed of 1,000 mph at its equator.
2. Earth's orbital speed around the sun is 66X greater than its rotation (that's 66,600 mph) – this equates to moving 30X faster than a rifle bullet.
3. Our solar system travels around the Milky Way Galaxy at 500,000 mph.
4. The Milky Way Galaxy moves at 1.1 million mph.

$F_{gravity} = G (m_1 \times m_2) / r^2$

G (the gravitational constant) = 6.67×10^{-11} Nm²/kg²
m_1, m_2 = masses of the two objects
r = distance between the two objects

If mass increases, the force of gravity increases.

If distance increases, the force of gravity decreases.

The Incredibly Designed Precision of Gravity:
Isaac Newton's famous equation: all masses attract each other with a force that varies inversely as the SQUARE of the separation distance between the masses. Scientists have long wondered about this factor of "2": it just looks too perfect. Why not 1.999? or 2.001? This gravity force has been repeatedly tested with sensitive torsion balances – the result is always the same: it's exactly "2" to five decimal places (2.00000). Any value other than 2.00000 would lead to an eventual catastrophic decay of orbits and thus the entire universe.

The strength of gravity determines how hot a star's nuclear furnace in its core burns. A planet that sustains life must be supported by a star that is stable and long-burning. If gravity was any stronger: stars would be so hot they'd burn up too quickly for life. If gravity was any weaker: stars would never get hot enough to ignite nuclear fusion. In such a universe, no elements heavier than H and He would be produced, making life *impossible*).

➔ What is Electromagnetic Force?
The force resulting from the interaction of charged particles (all charged particles attract oppositely charged particles and repel identically charged particles). It is responsible for the atomic structure of elements because it holds electrons in orbit around atomic nuclei, and atoms in molecules (it *holds together* all matter in the universe – hint: study Colossians 1:17). Like gravity, the electromagnetic force has an infinite range and obeys the inverse-square law.

Electromagnetic forces (F) are governed by **Coulomb's Law**. The motion of charged particles produces a magnetic field, which causes a force on a moving charged particle. That is why we call this an *electromagnetic* force: electric and magnetic exist together.

The magnitude of electrostatic force F between two point charges q_1 and q_2 separated by a distance r in air/vacuum is given by Coulomb's law, where:
- $1/(4\pi E_0) = 9 \times 10^9$ N m^2/C^2 is a constant, and
- $E_0 = 8\text{-}85 \times 10^{-12}$ C^2 N^{-1} m^{-2}, is absolute electrical permittivity of free space.

The smallest magnitude of charge found in nature is the charge of an electron or a proton represented by $e = 1\text{-}6 \times 10^{-19}$ C

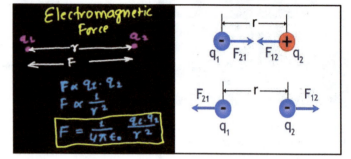

The Incredibly Designed Precision of the Electromagnetic Force: For life to exist, more than 40 different elements must be able to bond to form molecules. But molecular bonding depends on 2 factors: 1) strength of electromagnetic force, and 2) ratio of electron mass to proton mass. If electromagnetic force was any larger: atoms would hold onto electrons so tightly that no sharing of electrons between other atoms would occur. If this electromagnetic force were any weaker: atoms wouldn't hang onto electrons at all, so again no sharing. In either case, molecules could never form, making life *impossible*.

The Incredibly Designed Precision of the Ratio of the Electromagnetic Force-to-Gravitational Force: If the electromagnetic force relative to the gravitational force increased by only 1 part in 10^{40}, only small stars could form. If this ratio decreased by 1 part in 10^{40}, only large stars could form. But life is *impossible* without small and large stars. We need large stars: only within their thermonuclear furnaces can most life-essential elements be made. We need small stars (such as our sun): they burn long enough and stable enough to sustain planetary life.

➔ What is the Strong Nuclear Force?
The force governing the degree to which protons and neutrons stick together in atomic nuclei. It is very strong but short-range, extending only to the atomic nucleus. Its value is so delicately set that any change in it, whether stronger or weaker, would make life impossible on earth.

STRONG FORCE FORMULA

$$L_{QCD} = -\tfrac{1}{4} F_a^{\mu\nu} F_{\mu\nu}^a + \sum_f \Psi_f (i\partial - M + g_s A^a T_a) \Psi_f$$

$$F_{\mu\nu}^a = \partial_\mu A_\nu^a - \partial_\nu A_\mu^a + g_s + f_{bc}^a A_\mu^b A_\nu^c$$

The Incredibly Designed Precision of the Strong Nuclear Force: If it was too weak, protons and neutrons wouldn't stick together – only Hydrogen (H) would exist (H has just one proton and no neutrons in its nucleus). If it was too strong, protons and neutrons would be so attracted to each other that none would remain alone in the universe. In that case, there would be no hydrogen (only heavy elements). Life is impossible without hydrogen. How delicate is the balance for the strong nuclear force? If it was **2%** weaker, or **0.3%** stronger, than it actually is: life would be *impossible* at any time and any place within the universe.

➔ What is the Weak Nuclear Force?
The force governing the conversion of protons to neutrons and vice-versa, and the interaction of neutrinos with other particles. Without this force, there would not be enough essential elements available for life. The derivation of this force is so complex, no simple equation can describe it.

The Incredibly Designed Precision of the Weak Nuclear Force: If it was stronger, the matter in the universe would quickly convert into heavy elements. If it was weaker, the matter in the universe would stay as only the lightest elements. Thus, those elements essential for life (C, O_2, N_2, Ph) would either not exist at all or in too small quantities for all life-essential chemicals to be built, making life *impossible*.

Colossians 1:17 *"Jesus is before all things, and in Him all things HOLD TOGETHER."*

Hebrews 1:2-3 *"His Son.. UPHOLDS all things by the word of His power…"*

Nuclear Fission: God's **Strong Nuclear Force** = the source of Unimaginable Power

- **What's Nuclear Fission?** The process of *splitting atoms*, or fissioning them

Imagine about 200 marbles lying on a flat surface, all jumbled together, roughly forming a circle. What would happen if someone took another marble and threw it into them? They would fly all around in different directions and groups. That is exactly what happens in nuclear fission. The filled circle is like an atom's nucleus. The marble being thrown is like a "neutron bullet". The only differences are that the marbles are protons and neutrons, and the protons and neutrons aren't in a filled circle, but in the actual atom's nucleus.

- **Why use a neutron as the "bullet"?**

The neutron is electrically neutral and thus would not get repelled from a positive nucleus (remember: the nucleus has positively-charged protons and neutral neutrons, so anything else would be repelled by the nucleus).

- **Anything else special about the "neutron bullet"?**

The speed at which the bombarding neutron is moving. If the neutron is highly energetic (and thus moving very quickly), it can cause fission in some elements that a slower neutron would not. For example, Thorium 2 requires a very fast neutron to induce fission. However, Uranium 2 (2U) needs slower neutrons. If a neutron is too fast, it will pass right through a 2U atom without affecting it at all.

- **Why use Uranium 2 in nuclear reactors and atomic bombs?**

When a stray neutron strikes a 2U nucleus, it is at first absorbed into it. This creates 236U. 236U is unstable and this causes the atom to fission. The fissioning of 236U can produce over 20 different products and a tremendous release of ENERGY (the reaction = the bomb). However, the products' masses always add up to 236. The following two equations are examples of the different products that can be produced when 2U fissions:

2U + 1 "neutron bullet" = 2 neutrons + Kr + Ba + ENERGY
2U + 1 "neutron bullet" = 2 neutrons + Sr + Xe + ENERGY

- **But what really causes the "nuclear reaction"?**

In each of the above reactions, one neutron splits the atom. When the atom is split, one additional neutron is released. This is how a chain reaction works. If more 2U is present, those two neutrons can cause two more atoms to split. Each of those atoms releases one more neutron bringing the total neutrons to four. Those four neutrons can strike four more 2U atoms, releasing even more neutrons. The chain reaction will continue until all the 2U fuel is spent. This is roughly what happens in an atomic bomb. It is called a *runaway nuclear reaction*

- **So where does this "energy" come from?**

The mass of an atom is more than the sum of the individual masses of its protons and neutrons. Extra mass is a result of the *BINDING ENERGY* that holds the protons and neutrons of the nucleus together. This is the "strong nuclear force" we discussed previously (i.e., the force governing the degree to which protons and neutrons stick together in atomic nuclei. It is as short-range as it is strong, extending no farther than the atom's nucleus. Its value is so delicately set that any change in it, whether stronger or weaker, would make life impossible on earth).

So when the uranium atom is split, some of the energy that held it together is released as radiation in the form of HEAT. Because energy and mass are one and the same, the energy released is also mass released. In essence, man is taking the perfectly-tuned forces designed by God to hold atomic particles in place and releasing that incredible energy to harness it for his use.

- **WWII: Nuclear Fission's Incredible Power to destroy life**

The plane carrying the bomb, Enola Gay, dropped a nuclear fission bomb named "Little Boy" on the Japanese city of Hiroshima. After it hit the ground, the bomb sustained a nuclear fission reaction, releasing huge amounts of energy as the "strong nuclear force" that once held it together is now set free. The pilots described seeing blinding light fill their aircraft and the ground below obscured by the billowing mushroom-shaped column of smoke. The co-pilot said he could taste the fission as lead in the air.

About 70,000 Japanese were instantly vaporized by the explosion. The tremendous levels of radiation caused radiation sickness in nearly everyone that was close to the explosion but survived it. For the next generations, radiation-related genetic mutations caused deaths and diseases in children born by those exposed to the radiation. **200,000 deaths** were the estimated final number from dropping "Little Boy"..

The area of the destruction caused by the bomb was **4 square miles**. In this area an estimated 48,000 buildings were completely destroyed.

Genesis 1:1-2	The UNIVERSE: What is it made of?	2.5
Colossians 1:15-17	How is it held together?	
2Peter 3:10	How is it kept together?	
Hebrews 1:1-5		

Genesis 1:1-2 *"In the beginning God created the heavens and the earth. The earth was ①WITHOUT FORM, AND VOID."*

The first verse of the Bible speaks of the beginning of TIME and the creation of SPACE and MATTER.

G.S. McLean[13]: "In order to begin any kind of building project, the designer must first assemble the raw materials. It's interesting that the biblical account of creation begins by giving a detailed explanation of the raw materials, or "building blocks", that God assembled to construct the universe."

H. Morris[3]: "At the time of the initial creation, there were no other planets, stars, or other material bodies in the universe; nor did any of them come into being until the fourth day. The earth essentially had no form to it, so this verse must speak essentially of the creation of the basic elements of MATTER, which thereafter were to be organized into the structured earth and later into other material bodies."

> Genesis 1:1 can legitimately be paraphrased as:
> "The transcendent, omnipotent Godhead called into existence the space-matter-time universe."

① WITHOUT FORM, AND VOID = Hebrew *"tohu wavohu"* or *"tohu waw bohu"* = without form, random

- H. Morris[3]: "The word *'TOHU'* carries various meanings; it occurs 20x in the Old Testament and is translated in the KJ Version no less than 10 different ways ('vanity', 'confusion', 'empty space', 'nothing', etc.). The best translation in the context of Genesis 1:1 is exactly as the KJ scholars render it: 'without form'. Similarly, the context of **Isaiah 45:18** (having to do with God's purpose for the land of Israel) makes the best translation there of "tohu waw bohu" to be "in vain". Or to paraphrase, *"God created not the earth to be forever unformed and uninhabited; He formed it to be inhabited."* Likewise, the word *'BOHU'* does not connote a desolation, but simply 'emptiness'. When initially created, the earth had no inhabitants; it was 'void'. Genesis 1:1 essentially says: *'In the beginning God created the heaven and the earth (or space and matter), and the **MATTER** so created was at first unformed and uninhabited.'"*

- G.S. McLean[13]: "God hadn't put matter into any meaningful form or design at that time (randomness). It's the same as a child's building blocks being tossed on the floor – the blocks would be random, with no order."

What is MATTER? It all starts with the ATOM:

The basic structure making up all matter (the "building blocks" found in everything in the universe).

- they can't be seen with our eyes, but today's microscopes can "see" the magnified images of atoms.
- a small coin contains > 20,000,000,000,000,000,000,000 atoms.
- 1 breath of air contains 6,000,000,000,000,000,000,000,000 oxygen atoms.

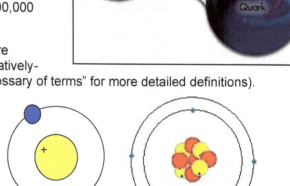

NUCLEUS = the atom's core; it contains particles that are positively charged (protons) and neutral (neutrons); negatively-charged particles (electrons) circle the nucleus (see "Glossary of terms" for more detailed definitions).

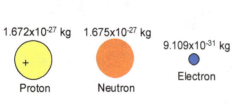

1.672×10^{-27} kg — Proton
1.675×10^{-27} kg — Neutron
9.109×10^{-31} kg — Electron

Hydrogen atom

Beryllium atom

Colossians 1:15-17 *"He is the image of the invisible God, the first-born of all creation; for in Him all things were created, in heaven and on earth, visible and invisible, whether thrones or dominions or principalities or authorities- all things were created through Him and for Him. He is before all things, and in Him all things ①HOLD TOGETHER."*

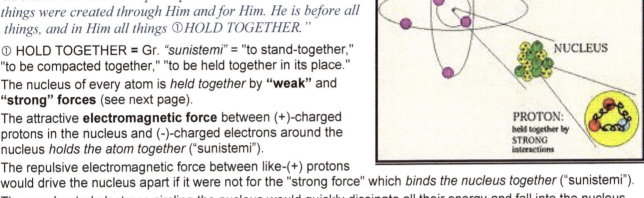

① HOLD TOGETHER = Gr. *"sunistemi"* = "to stand-together," "to be compacted together," "to be held together in its place."

The nucleus of every atom is *held together* by **"weak"** and **"strong" forces** (see next page).

The attractive **electromagnetic force** between (+)-charged protons in the nucleus and (−)-charged electrons around the nucleus *holds the atom together* ("sunistemi").

The repulsive electromagnetic force between like-(+) protons would drive the nucleus apart if it were not for the "strong force" which *binds the nucleus together* ("sunistemi").

The accelerated electrons circling the nucleus would quickly dissipate all their energy and fall into the nucleus unless there exists an invisible electromagnetic force to counteract this and *hold them in place* ("sunistemi").

> Verse 15 says all things (both visible and invisible) in the entire universe *were* created through Jesus and for Jesus. It doesn't say "are still being created". That's because God says in **Genesis 2:1-2** that after He finished His creation He ended His work and rested (Colossians confirms the Genesis account).
>
> Verse 15 also says Jesus was my Creator long before He took on human form and became my Redeemer and Savior: so I need Jesus to save me from my sins is because I first rebelled against Him as my Creator.

2 Peter 3:10 *"But the day of the Lord will come as a thief in the night, in which the heavens will pass away with a ③GREAT NOISE and the ②ELEMENTS will be ④DISSOLVED with fervent heat; both the earth and the works that are in it will be burned up."*

② ELEMENTS = Gr. *"stoicheion"* = ordered arrangement of things, building blocks of the universe, atomic elements; each element is made up of only one type of atom (it can't be broken into simpler components).

- 99% of our planet earth is made of only ten of these elements
- scientists organize them in a "Periodic Table" based on properties, so they can be understood (see below)

The 10 Most Abundant Elements

Element		% of Earth's Mass
Oxygen	O	46.6
Silicon	Si	27.7
Aluminum	Al	8.1
Iron	Fe	5.0
Calcium	Ca	3.6
Sodium	Na	2.8
Potassium	K	2.6
Magnesium	Mg	2.1
Titanium	Ti	0.4
Hydrogen	H	0.1

Periodic Table of the Elements

③ GREAT NOISE = Gr. *"rhoizedon"* = a rushing roar; ④ DISSOLVED = Gr. *"luo"* = unloosed

- there will come a time in the future when God *lets go* of the nuclear forces that hold the atom together.
- 2Peter, like Colossians, strongly suggests that the active power of God is behind the strong nuclear force and electromagnetic force that holds every atomic nucleus together. If this is so, all the other fundamental forces of nature are likewise forces that originate with Christ and His sustaining direction of the original creation.

Hebrews 1:1-5 *"God, who at various times and in different ways spoke in time past to the fathers by the prophets, has in these last days spoken to us by His Son, whom He has appointed ①HEIR of all things, through whom also He ②MADE the ③WORLDS ; who being the ④BRIGHTNESS of His glory and the ⑤EXPRESS IMAGE of His person, and ⑥UPHOLDING all things by the word of His power, when He had by Himself purged our sins, sat down at the right hand of the Majesty on high, having become so much better than the angels, as He has by inheritance obtained a more excellent name than they."*

① HEIR of *all* things" = Gr. "*klēronomos*" = He has been assigned by God the Father the possession of all things which He will one day enter into – it means that we are house guests in Someone Else's universe!

② MADE = Gr. "*poieō*" = to construct or produce (refers to His creative act, emphasizing action; see John 14:23)

③ WORLDS = Gr. "*kosmos*" and/ or "*aiōn*" = "ages" (all periods of time) – it refers to the reaches of time, space, energy and matter – the entire universe and everything that makes it function (John 1:3).
  - Jesus → made, produced, built, operated, and arranged the universe and everything in it in order.

④ BRIGHTNESS of His glory" = Gr. "*apaugasma*" = shining forth, as coming from a luminous body
  - John MacArthur: "the term is used only here in the New Testament; it expresses the concept of sending forth light or shining; the meaning of "reflection" isn't appropriate here – the Son is not just reflecting God's glory: He is God and radiates His own essential glory.

⑤ EXPRESS IMAGE of His Person" = Gr. "*eikon*" = God's nature and essence represented in space and time.

⑥ UPHOLDING ALL THINGS = Gr. "*pherō*" = to bear, carry or support
  - John MacArthur: "the universe and everything in it is sustained by the Son's powerful word (Colossians 1:17); this term also conveys the concept of movement or progress – the Son of God directs all things in accordance with God's sovereign purpose (He maintains, guides and propels the universe by His mighty word of power)."

> **CONCLUSION =** There is an active force imposed on the universe, which *actively holds* the very atoms of the material world together moment by moment, day by day, century by century.

So Jesus is Creator and Sustainer: what does this mean to *me*?   **PSALM 95:1-9**

"O come, let us sing to the Lord; let us make a joyful noise to the rock of our salvation! Let us come into His presence with THANKSGIVING; let us make a joyful noise to Him with songs of PRAISE! For the Lord is the great God, and the great King above all gods. In His hand are the depths of the earth; the heights of the mountains are His also. The sea is His, for He made it; and His hands formed the dry land.

O come, let us WORSHIP and BOW DOWN, let us KNEEL before the LORD, our Maker! For He is our God, and we are the people of His pasture, and the sheep under His care. O that today you would hearken to His voice! Do not harden your hearts, as in the rebellion, and as in the day of testing in the wilderness, when your fathers tested Me; they proved Me, though they saw My work.""

- David gives us five names for God: Lord, Rock of our salvation, great God, great King, and Maker/ Creator.
- When I meditate on God's character and His awesome majesty in this Psalm, and I study these four verses that detail out for me how He created and sustains the universe, I can't help but respond to Him in the five actions described in this Psalm: thanksgiving, praise, worship, bowing down, kneeling.

> **Jesus Christ is the present Sustainer of the universe**
> - He is not uninvolved, remote, detached nor impersonal. He doesn't leave things to run by themselves.
>   Our moment-by-moment existence depends on Him sustaining every electron, atom, molecule and every spiritual entity as well. We are safe when we place our trust in Him and put our whole lives into His hands!
> - Whatever we may think of God and physics, the Bible leaves us with no room to doubt that God does care about the sparrow that falls to the ground, the widow, the orphan, and the homeless. He does not lose track of His children and watches over them with infinite, patient, intimate Fatherly care.
>
> He is also Lord of all lords, Head of the church, Firstborn of the new creation, the Way to God, the eternal Word, the Life of the believer, the Hope of Israel, and the High Priest of every true worshiper. He holds the keys of death and hell, and stands as Advocate and Surety for everyone who believes on Him in truth.
>
> **Salvation comes not by "accepting His finished work", or "deciding for Christ"…**
> Salvation comes by believing on the Lord Jesus Christ, the whole, living, victorious Lord who, as God created me, as God and man, fought my fight and won it, accepted my debt as His own and paid it, took my sins and died under them, and rose again to set me free.
> This is the true Christ preached by Paul in **Galatians 2:20** in a very personal and real way; nothing less will do.

Chapter 3   Argument #4 for God = *FINE-TUNING* in the Universe   3.1
The Precision (Fine-Tuning) in Life's Variables infers an Intelligent Designer

> "Premise #1 = Precision in a system or process infers an intelligent designer.
> Premise #2 = There is great precision in the universe.
> Conclusion = Therefore, there must be an Intelligent Designer of the universe."

PSALM 19:1-4a *"The ①HEAVENS ②DECLARE the ③GLORY of God; and the ④FIRMAMENT shows His ⑤HANDIWORK. Day unto day utters speech, and night unto night reveals knowledge. There is no speech nor language where their voice is not heard. Their line goes out through all the earth, and their words to the end of the world."*

① HEAVENS = Hebrew *"shamayim"* = plural noun (like *"Elohim"*) = "space-time-mass universe" (same as Genesis 1:1); the sun, moon and stars give light (without their light, everything is dark and indiscernible).

② DECLARE = Hebrew *"sâphar"* = continuous form, meaning "are declaring" – every moment, day and night, God's existence, power, wisdom and goodness are *preached*: they are put on *open display* by the heavens:
1) Sovereignty (seen in the expanse of the stars); 2) Wisdom (seen in the precise balance of heavenly bodies)
3) Control (seen in the regularity of planetary motions); 4) Power (seen in the universal laws and forces)

③ GLORY (of God) = Hebrew *"kâbôd kâbôd"* = splendor, full weight = The heavens proclaim arguments for a conscious, intelligent, planning, controlling and presiding Creator. The heavens don't hint at the possibility of Intelligence – it is a plain, unmistakable, constant DECLARATION.

④ FIRMAMENT = Hebrew *"raqia"* (Gen. 1:6) = expanse, or "spread-out-thinness" (akin to today's term "space")

⑤ HANDIWORK = Hebrew *"ma'ăśeh"* = God's labor or activity during creation is continuously and openly displayed to all in the product His labor produced (i.e., the material universe and all it includes).

In his early days: David, as a keeper of his father Jesse's flocks (1Samuel 16:11), studied God's two great books: nature and Scripture. In Psalm 19, David magnifies God's excellency in both nature and the Bible.

Psalm 19's three sections: Creation reveals God's glory in vs. 1-6; Scripture reveals God's grace in vs. 7-11; I personally pray for God's grace to be applied to my life in vs. 12-14 (C. Spurgeon[25] : *"Praise and prayer are mingled, and he who sings the works of God in the world without, pleads for a work of grace in himself within"*).

Psalm 19:2-4a ➔ Three ways nature "preaches" God's wisdom, power and glory

vs. 2: *"day unto day"*, *"night unto night"* = ① **they preach with no intermissions** (all day and night, everyday)
- If all preachers on earth were silenced, and no one spoke of God's glory, the heavens above would never cease to proclaim His glory. They are ever preaching, their message delivered day after day and night after night.

vs. 2: *"reveals knowledge"* = God puts Himself on open display, to inspire man's reverence

Romans 1:20 *"...since the creation of the world His invisible attributes are clearly seen, being understood by the things that are made, even His eternal power and Godhead, so that they are without excuse."*

Proverbs 1:7 *"The fear of the Lord is the beginning of knowledge, but fools despise wisdom and instruction."*

- Fools = God's description of people who reject creation's witness and rely on their own wisdom

  Psalm 14:1 *"The fool has said in his heart, 'There is no God...'"*

  Rom. 1:21-22 *"...although they knew God, they did not glorify Him as God, nor were thankful, but became futile in their thoughts, and their foolish hearts were darkened. Professing to be wise, they became fools..."*

vs. 3: *"no speech nor language"* = Acts 14:15-17 - ② **they preach in every language** (everyone understands their message because it's not in audible sounds - it is PICTORIAL, directed to the eye and heart).

Acts 14:15-17 *"...We also are men with the same nature as you, and preach to you that you should turn from these vain things to the living God, who made the heaven, the earth, the sea, and all things that are in them, who in bygone generations allowed all nations to walk in their own ways. Nevertheless He did not leave Himself without witness, in that He did good, gave us rain from heaven and fruitful seasons, filling our hearts with food and gladness."*

vs. 4a: *"their line....their words"* = they preach a language of signs (not literal words): their "line" = the measure of their domain (how they act and operate = their brightness, orbiting patterns, properties, etc.)

vs. 4a: *"through all the earth, to end of the world"* = ③ **they preach in every corner of the world** (it may be easy to escape from the light of ministers, but all mankind is overshadowed by the heavenly preaching).

- John Boys[25]: *"The heavens are diligent pastors, as preaching at all times; and learned pastors, as preaching in all tongues; and catholic (universal, or broad-minded) pastors, as preaching in all towns."*

ORIGIN OF LIFE:
Probability & Precision point to an Intelligent Designer!

UNIVERSE
Expansion Rate
Electromagnetic Force
Gravitational Force

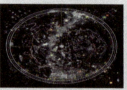 

- Electromagnetic-to-Gravitational force = *precise* to 1×10^{40} [18]
- Gravitational Constant = *precise* to 5 decimals (2.00000) [18]
- Universe Expansion rate = *precise* to 1×10^{55} [18]

MILKY WAY, SOLAR SYSTEM

- Stars: *odds* - only .001% have the right location and have host star properties that could support life [18]
- Milky Way is spiral galaxy = req'd for life to exist (*odds* are only 5% of all galaxies are spiral) [18]

SUN, EARTH

  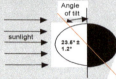

- Earth *precise* tilt = $23.5° \pm 1.2°$ [18]
- Sun's *precise* energy output = constant to 0.1% [18]

BODY, MIND, BRAIN

  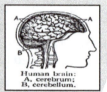

- my brain's *precision*: 1,000x storage capacity of a supercomputer; holds and sorts 10^{14} bits of information [15]
- *odds* that a human being formed by *chance* = $1 \times 10^{2,000,000,000}$ [15]

HEART, EYE, EAR

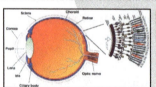

- 100 years of supercomputer processing to simulate the *precision* of what occurs in my eye millions of times every second [15,16]
- no one knows what causes my heart's *precise* "auto-rhythmic" beat 100,000X/day, so I can have life [15]

BLOOD CELL

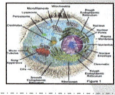 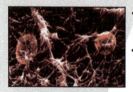

- Blood Clotting: *odds* of getting just the one factor TPA and its activator to work = 1×10^{31} (there are at least 32 others) [16]
- Each cell has an all-powerful city hall (nucleus) surrounded by communication centers, factories, power plants, with the complete DNA for my unique design [15]

DNA, ATP

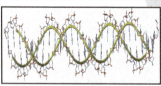 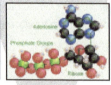

- DNA code formation = 1 in 10^{600} by *chance* [15]
- ATP = mini "motors" 200,000X smaller than a pinhead spinning at 6,000 rpm (faster than any made-made engines) [15]
- *odds* of all proteins needed for life might be formed in one place by random events = $1 \times 10^{40,000}$ [15]

Matter
Atoms, Molecules

Nuclear Forces
Strong nuclear force
Weak nuclear force

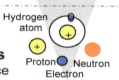

- Strong nuclear force = *precise* to 2% [18]
- neutron-to-proton mass = *precise* to 0.1% [18]
- #electrons-to-protons = *precise* to 1×10^{37} [18]

ORDER = correctness according to a set of rules or laws; the state of effectively controlled operation
PRECISION = degree to which a system's measurements repeat themselves in unchanged conditions
FINE TUNING = precision of a process or system's operation to a set standard designed to achieve it's purpose (example: the correct pitch of a musical instrument to achieve the designer's intended sound)
DESIGN = an intended outline or plan, fashioned skillfully, to meet the designer's purpose

What leading Scientists say:
Finely-Tuned Precision in the Universe is a Creative Act by an *Intelligent Mind*

Some of the most influential physicists, astronomers and mathematicians in history use the scientific evidence for the precision in the variables of the Universe that determine life as best explained by an Intelligent Creator:

1 Isaac Newton (1643-1727) – British Mathematician and Physicist: *"Did blind chance know that there was light and what was its refraction and fit the eyes of all creatures after the most curious manner to make use of it? These and such like considerations always have and ever will prevail with mankind to believe that there is a being who made all things and has all things in his power and who is therefore to be feared."*

2 James Clerk Maxwell (1831-1879) - Scottish Mathematician and Theoretical Physicist, widely regarded as the 19th century scientist who had the greatest influence on 20th century physics: *"No theory of evolution can be formed to account for the similarity of molecules, for evolution necessarily implies continuous change.. The exact equality of each molecule to all others of the same kind gives it.. the essential character of a manufactured article, and precludes the idea of its being eternal and self-existent."* ('Discourse on Molecules', a paper presented to the British Assoc. For the Advancement of Science, 1873).

3 Albert Einstein (1879-1955) - PhD Theoretical Physics; 1921 Nobel Prize in Physics; Time Person of the Century, 1999: *"I see a pattern, but my imagination cannot picture the maker of that pattern. I see a clock, but I cannot envision the clockmaker. The human mind is unable to conceive of the four dimensions, so how can it conceive of a God, before whom a thousand years and a thousand dimensions are as one?... What I see in Nature is a magnificent structure that we can comprehend only very imperfectly, and that must fill a thinking person with a feeling of 'humility'. This is a genuinely religious feeling that has nothing to do with mysticism."*

4 Sir Fred Hoyle (1915-2001) - Cambridge Prof. of Astrophysics and Natural Philosophy: *"Life cannot have had a random beginning... The trouble is that there are about two thousand enzymes, and the chance of obtaining them all in a random trial is only one part in $10^{40,000}$, an outrageously small probability that could not be faced even if the whole universe consisted of organic soup.... Once we see, however, that the probability of life originating at random is so utterly miniscule as to make it absurd, it becomes sensible to think that the favorable properties of physics on which life depends are in every respect deliberate ... . It is therefore almost inevitable that our own measure of intelligence must reflect ... higher intelligences ... even to the limit of God ... such a theory is so obvious that one wonders why it is not widely accepted as being self-evident. The reasons are psychological rather than scientific."* (Fred Hoyle, 'Evolution from Space' (London: J.M. Dent & Sons, 1981).

5 Wernher von Braun (1912-1977) - PhD Physics, NASA's 'greatest rocket scientist in history': *"To be forced to believe only one conclusion--that everything in the universe happened by chance--would violate the very objectivity of science itself. What random process could produce the brains of a man or the system of the human eye?"* ('Profiles in Christianity and Science: Wernher von Braun', Ray and Gale Lawson, Sept. 2005.

6 Charles Townes (1915 -) - PhD Physics, 1964 Nobel Prize in Physics: *"The sun couldn't be there, the laws of gravity and nuclear laws and magnetic theory, quantum mechanics, and so on have to be just the way they are for us to be here. Some scientists argue that 'well, there's an enormous number of universes and each one is a little different. This one just happened to turn out right.' Well, that's a postulate, and it's a pretty fantastic postulate - it assumes there really are an enormous number of universes and that the laws could be different for each of them. The other possibility is that ours was planned, and that's why it has come out so specially."* (2005 interview for Berkeley News by Bonnie Powell).

7 John A. O'Keefe (1916-2000) - PhD Astronomy, Univ. Chicago, NASA Astronomer: *"We are, by astronomical standards, a pampered, cosseted, cherished group of creatures.. ... If the Universe had not been made with the most exacting precision we could never have come into existence. It is my view that these circumstances indicate the universe was created for man to live in."* (Heeren, F. 1995. 'Show Me God'. Wheeling, IL, Searchlight Publications).

8 Edward R. "Ted" Harrison (1919-2007) - Prof. Physics and Astronomy, UMass: *"Here is the cosmological proof of the existence of God – the design argument of Paley – updated and refurbished. The fine tuning of the universe provides prima facie evidence of deistic design. Take your choice: blind chance that requires multitudes of universes or design that requires only one.... Many scientists, when they admit their views, incline toward the teleological or design argument."* ('Masks of the Universe', Collier Books, 1985).

9 Vera Kistiakowsky (1928 -) - PhD Chemistry, Berkeley, Prof. Particle Physics, MIT: *"The exquisite order displayed by our scientific understanding of the physical world calls for the divine."* ('Cosmos, Bios, and Theos', Margenau, H and R.A. Varghese,1992).

10 George F. Ellis (1933 -) - PhD. Applied Mathematics and Theoretical Physics: *"Amazing fine tuning occurs in the laws that make this [complexity] possible. Realization of the complexity of what is accomplished makes it very difficult not to use the word 'miraculous' without taking a stand as to the ontological status of the word."* ('The Anthropic Principle', F. Bertola and U.Curi, ed. New York, Cambridge University Press).

11 Arno Penzias (1933 -) - PhD Physics, 1978 Nobel prize in Physics: ""If God created the universe, he would have done it *elegantly*... You don't need somebody diddling around like Frank Morgan in The Wizard of Oz to keep the universe going. Instead, what you have is half a page of mathematics that describes everything. In some sense, the power of the creation lies in its underlying simplicity." ('Scientists Talk about Why They Believe in God', Gordy Slack 1997).

12 George S. Greenstein (1940 -) - PhD Astronomy, Yale, Prof. Astronomy Amherst College: "As we survey all the evidence, the thought insistently arises that some supernatural agency - or, rather, Agency - must be involved. Is it possible that suddenly, without intending to, we have stumbled upon *scientific proof of the existence of a Supreme Being*? Was it God who stepped in and so providentially *crafted the cosmos* for our benefit?" ('The Symbiotic Universe', William Morrow, 1988).

13 Paul Davies (1942 -) - PhD Theoretical Physics, Prof. of Physics. at Arizona State Univ. "There is for me powerful evidence that there is something going on behind it all....It seems as though somebody has *fine-tuned nature's numbers to make the Universe*....The impression of *design* is overwhelming." ("The Cosmic Blueprint: New Discoveries in Nature's Creative Ability To Order the Universe. New York: Simon and Schuster).... "The really amazing thing is not that life on Earth is balanced on a knife-edge, but that *the entire universe is balanced on a knife-edge*, and *would be total chaos if any of the natural 'constants' were off even slightly*. You see," Davies adds, "even if you dismiss man as a chance happening, the fact remains that the universe seems unreasonably suited to the existence of life—almost contrived—you might say a 'put-up job'.".

14 Stephen Hawking (1942 -) - PhD Cosmology and Theoretical Physics: "The laws of science, as we know them at present, contain many fundamental numbers, like the size of the electric charge of the electron and the ratio of the masses of the proton and the electron …. *The remarkable fact is that the values of these numbers seem to have been finely adjusted to make possible the development of life*." ('A Brief History of Time - From the Big Bang to Black Holes, New York: Bantam Books, 1988).

15 Henry "Fritz" Schaefer (1944 -) - PhD Chemical Physics, Professor of Chemistry and Director of the Center for Computational Quantum Chemistry, Univ. of Georgia: "Why Are There So Few Atheists Among Physicists? Many scientists are considering the facts before them. They say things like: 'The present arrangement of matter indicates a very *special choice* of initial conditions.' (Paul Davies). 'In fact, if one considers the possible *constants and laws* that could have emerged, the odds against a universe that produced life like ours are immense.' (Stephen Hawking)... As the Apostle Paul said in his epistle to the Romans: 'Since the creation of the world, *God*'s invisible qualities—His eternal power and divine nature—have been clearly seen, being understood from what has been *made*.'" ('Scientists and their Gods (Science and Christianity, Conflict or Coherence?',1999).

16 George Smoot (1945 -) - PhD Particle Physics, 2006 Nobel Prize in Physics: "The big bang, the most cataclysmic event we can imagine, on closer inspection appears *finely orchestrated*." ('Show Me God: What the Message from Space Is Telling Us About God', Day Star Publications, 2000).

17 Hugh Ross (1945 -) – PhD Astronomy from Univ. of Toronto: "If the strong nuclear force were slightly weaker, multi-proton nuclei would not *hold together*. Hydrogen would be the only element in the universe." ('The Fingerprint of God', Promise Publishing Co.,1991).

18 William Philips (1948 -) - PhD Physics, 1997 Nobel Prize in Physics, Prof. of Physics at Univ of Maryland: "I believe in *God*. In fact, I believe in a personal God who acts in and interacts with the creation. I believe the observations about the orderliness of the physical universe, and the apparently exceptional *fine-tuning of the conditions of the universe for the development of life* suggest that an *intelligent Creator* is responsible. I believe in God because of a personal faith, consistent with what I know about science." (Letter to T. Dimitrov, 2002).

19 Steven Weinberg (1948 -) - PhD Physics, Princeton Univ.,1979 Nobel Prize in Physics, Prof. of Physics at Harvard Univ.: "...how surprising it is that the laws of nature and the initial conditions of the universe should allow for the existence of beings who could observe it. *Life as we know it would be impossible if any one of several physical quantities had slightly different values*." (Scientific American Journal)

20 Idit Zehavi (PhD Physics, Prof. Astronomy and Physics, Case Western Reserve Univ.), Avishai Dekel (1951- , PhD Physics, Hebrew Univ., Researcher Astrophysics and Cosmology): "This type of universe, however, seems to require a degree of *fine tuning* of the initial conditions that is in apparent conflict with 'common wisdom'." ('Evidence for a positive cosmological constant from flows of galaxies and distant supernovae', Nature, 1999).

21 Tony Rothman (1953-) - PhD Theoretical Physics, Lecturer in Cosmology/ Physics, Princeton Univ.: "When confronted with the *order and beauty of the universe* and the strange coincidences of nature, it's very tempting to take the leap of faith from science into religion. I am sure many physicists want to. I only wish they would admit it." (Casti, J.L. 1989. Paradigms Lost. New York, Avon Books).

What Designers Do: Precisely Control Multiple Independent Variables

Let's say I like to make decorative wood assemblies of three oak cubes that fit into a pretty oak box as Christmas presents for my friends. After making a few of these hand-crafted gifts in my workshop, pretty soon word gets around and I'm getting orders from a lot of people!

I could make some good money off of this, as more and more people start contacting me. So I put a price out there just for kicks, and wow – people will actually pay money for these! Now I'm really excited when I realize if I spread the word and get the same kind of response on an internet site…. maybe I can retire and do nothing but this for a living!

But then I realize I have a problem. You see, I customize each of the three cubes that go into the box by hand, to make sure they look great and fit snugly in each box with just a little clearance. The problem is I just received my first order for 1,000 assemblies. That's 3,000 cubes and 1,000 boxes! I don't have time to do the necessary filing and sanding that I used to do on each cube, to make sure I get the look I want and they always fit in the box. It's time for mass production.

For each gift, if the three cubes don't fit, no sale – I generate junk! And the cubes have to fit snug in the box or they break during shipment – more junk! How can I make sure the three cubes will always correctly fit in the box?

Why not just make a ton of cubes, and a ton of boxes, and just "hope for the best"? Because common sense tells me that an *UNGUIDED PROCESS* of cube-making and box-making will not produce the assembly I need. I know that, left to its own, the natural result of these 1,000 assemblies all fitting together is highly *improbable* (i.e., the statistical probability of randomly making the 1,000 assemblies with all three cubes fitting snugly is almost zero).

In order to have these assemblies have a *HIGH PROBABILITY* of meeting my requirements, I must *DESIGN* a way to do this. The answer: use Mathematics and Probability theory. First, define the equation for the *nominal* assembly clearance, and then the equation for the amount of *variation* (the standard deviation) in the assembly clearance. Here they are:

- Equation 1 = Nominal Assembly Clearance = 'CLR_{NOM}'

$CLR_{NOM} = W_{box} - w_1 - w_2 - w_3$

W_{box} = overall box width
w_1 = cube #1 width, w_2 = cube #2 width, w_3 = cube #3 width

- Equation 2 = Standard Deviation in CLR_{NOM} = 'σ_{CLR}'
(based on technical paper 'Combining Error Sigmas', GE Schenectady Research Center, 1987).

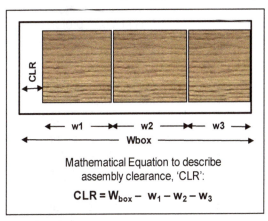

Mathematical Equation to describe assembly clearance, 'CLR':

$CLR = W_{box} - w_1 - w_2 - w_3$

$\sigma_{CLR} = [(\partial CLR/\partial W_{box})^2 * \sigma_{Wbox}^2 + (\partial CLR/\partial w_1)^2 * \sigma_{w1}^2 + (\partial CLR/\partial w_2)^2 * \sigma_{w2}^2 + (\partial CLR/\partial w_3)^2 * \sigma_{w3}^2]^{1/2}$

$\partial CLR/\partial W_{box}$ = partial derivative of CLR_{NOM} with respect to overall box width = 1, σ_{Wbox} = standard deviation of W_{box}
$\partial CLR/\partial w_1$ = partial derivative of CLR_{NOM} with respect to cube #1 width = -1, σ_{w1} = standard deviation of w_1
$\partial CLR/\partial w_2$ = partial derivative of CLR_{NOM} with respect to cube #2 width = -1, σ_{w2} = standard deviation of w_2
$\partial CLR/\partial w_3$ = partial derivative of CLR_{NOM} with respect to cube #3 width = -1, σ_{w3} = standard deviation of w_3

My target box width is W_{box} = 10 inches. My target $cube_1$, $cube_2$ and $cube_3$ widths are w_1, w_2, w_3 = 3.25 inches. Now I can calculate the nominal clearance in my assembly: CLR_{NOM} = 10 – 3.25 – 3.25 – 3.25 = 0.25 inches.

Now, I need to get the variation in each cube width, to plug into the equation for the standard deviation of the assembly, σ_{CLR}. The question to answer: 'what **PRECISION** is required in all three cube widths for a *6-Sigma* capability in having greater than a zero value for clearance (i.e., three cubes always fit snugly in the box)?

What is '6-Sigma'? It's a term describing the application of Probability Science to reduce variation in a process, where only 3 defects are generated in 1,000,000 tries. That means I would make only 3 assemblies whose three cubes don't fit snugly in their boxes (1×10^6), or 999,997 asemblies that do, or 99.9997% goodness!

I start by assuming the average assembly clearance of 0.25 inches is evenly distributed across all three cubes, so each cube must be precisely made to a width of **3.25 ± .08"** in order to have a clearance greater than zero.

How likely is it that 1,000's of cubes can be randomly mass-produced with widths never varying beyond .08" from their target of 3.25", so that there are only 3 failed assemblies? That likelihood is 1×10^6 (1 chance in a million).

Anyone seeing this level of precision in the independent variables (the cubes) of the system (the assembly) would reasonably conclude this was designed by an INTELLIGENT MIND!

Fine-Tuned Precision in the Universe: 25 measureable Variables[18]

3.2

#	Item	Issue
1	Electro-magnetic Force	For life to exist, > 40 different elements must be able to bond to form molecules. But molecular bonding depends on 2 factors: 1) strength of electromagnetic force, and 2) ratio of electron mass to proton mass. If electromagnetic force was any larger: atoms would hold onto electrons so tightly that no sharing of electrons between other atoms would occur. If this force were any weaker: atoms wouldn't hang onto electrons at all, so again no sharing. In either case, molecules could never form, making life *impossible*.
2	Electrons	If the number of electrons doesn't equal the number of protons to a precision that is greater than **1 part in 10^{37}**, electromagnetic forces in the universe would overwhelm gravitational forces such that it would be *impossible* to form galaxies, stars and planets.
3	Electron-to-Proton Mass	The size and stability of electron orbits around the nuclei of atoms depends on the ratio of electron mass to the proton mass. If the ratio of electron-to-proton mass is not very delicately balanced, the chemical bonding required for life chemistry is *impossible*.
4	Neutron-to-Proton Mass	The neutron is 0.138% more massive than the proton. This extra mass relative to the proton determines the rate at which neutrons decay into protons, and protons into neutrons. If the neutron were **0.1%** less massive, protons would decay so readily into neutrons that all the stars in the universe would have rapidly collapsed into either neutron stars or black holes. So…the neutron's mass must be fine-tuned to < 0.1% or life in the universe is *impossible*.
5	Strong Nuclear Force	If too weak, protons and neutrons wouldn't stick together – only HYDROGEN would exist (it has just one proton and no neutrons in its nucleus). If too strong, protons and neutrons would be so attracted to each other that none would remain alone in the universe. In that case, there would be no hydrogen (only heavy elements). Life is impossible without hydrogen. How delicate is the balance for the strong nuclear force? If it was **2%** weaker, or **0.3%** stronger, than it actually is: life would be *impossible* at any time and any place within the universe.
6	Weak Nuclear Force	If stronger, the matter in the universe would quickly convert into heavy elements. If weaker, the matter in the universe would stay as only the lightest elements. Thus, those elements essential for life (C, O_2, N_2, Ph) would either not exist at all or in too small quantities for all life-essential chemicals to be built, making life *impossible*.
7	Force of Gravity	The strength of gravity determines how hot a star's nuclear furnace in its core burns. A planet that sustains life must be supported by a star that is stable and long-burning. If gravitational force was stronger: stars would be so hot they'd burn up too quickly for life. If gravitational force was any weaker: stars would never get hot enough to ignite nuclear fusion. In such a universe, no elements heavier than H and He would be produced, making life *impossible*
8	Nuclear Energies of He, Be, C, O_2	1970-1980: Fred Hoyle discovered that an incredible fine-tuning of the nuclear ground state energies for He, Be, C and O_2 was necessary for any kind of life to exist. These energies cannot be higher or lower with respect to each other by > 4% without creating a universe that has not enough oxygen or carbon, making life *impossible*. Hoyle (an atheist): *"a superintellect has monkeyed with the physics, as well as with chemistry and biology."*
9	Expansion of Universe	If the universe expanded too rapidly: matter would *disperse* so efficiently that none of it would clump enough to form galaxies. Without galaxy formation, no stars would form. Without star formation, no planets would form. Without planet formation, life is *impossible*. If the universe expanded too slowly: matter would *clump* so efficiently that the entire universe would collapse into a super-dense lump before any solar-type stars could form. How delicate is the universe expansion rate? It must be precise to within **1 part in 10^{55}** from its actual rate or life is *impossible*.
10	Electro-magnetic Force-to-Force of Gravity	If the electromagnetic force relative to the gravitational force increased by only **1 part in 10^{40}**, only small stars could form. If this ratio decreased by **1 part in 10^{40}**, only large stars could form. But life is *impossible* without small and large stars. We need large stars: only within their thermonuclear furnaces can most life-essential elements be made. We need small stars (such as our sun): only they burn long enough and stable enough to sustain planetary life.

#	Item	If…	Why no Life…	If…	Why no Life…
	Fine-Tuned Precision in the Universe: 25 measureable Variables[18]				
11	Mass Density of Universe	Larger	Too much deuterium (De) from the big bang – stars would burn too rapidly	Smaller	Insufficient helium (He) from the big bang – too few heavy elements would form
12	Velocity of Light	Faster	Stars would be too luminous	Slower	Stars not luminous enough
13	Age of Universe	Older	No solar-type stars in a stable burning phase in the right part of the galaxy	Younger	Solar-type stars in stable burning phase wouldn't form
14	Initial Uniformity of Radiation	Smoother	Stars and galaxies would not have formed	Coarser	Universe would be mostly black holes and empty space
15	Fine Structure Constant (a number used to describe the fine structure splitting of spectral lines)	Larger	No stars > 0.7 solar masses could exist	Smaller	No stars < 0.7 solar masses could exist
16	Avg. distance between stars	Larger	Heavy element density too thin for rocky planets to form	Smaller	Planetary orbits would become destabilized
17	Decay rate of a Proton (avg decay rate > 4×10^{32} years)	Greater	Life would be exterminated by the release of radiation	Smaller	There wouldn't be enough matter in the universe for life
18	Carbon-to-Oxygen Energy Level	Larger	Insufficient oxygen in the universe to support life	Smaller	Insufficient carbon in the universe to support life
19	Ground State Energy for Helium (He)	Larger	Insufficient carbon and oxygen in the universe to support life	Smaller	Insufficient carbon and oxygen in the universe to support life
20	Decay Rate of Beryllium (Be)	Slower	Heavy element fusion would generate catastrophic star explosions	Faster	No elements produced beyond berillium (no life chemistry possible)
21	Initial excess of nucleons over anti-nucleons	Greater	There would be too much radiation for planets to form	Smaller	Not be enough matter for galaxies or stars to form
22	Polarity of the Water Molecule	Greater	Heat of fusion and vaporization would be too great for life to exist	Smaller	Heat of fusion and vaporization would be too small for life's existence (liquid water would become too inferior a solvent for life chemistry to proceed – ice would not float, leading to a runaway freeze-up)
23	Supernovae Eruptions	Too Close, Frequent or Late	Radiation would exterminate life on earth	Too Far, Infrequent or Soon	Not enough heavy element ashes for formation of rocky planets
24	White Dwarf Binaries	Too Many or Late	Disruption of planetary orbits from stellar density (life on earth would be exterminated)	Too Few or Soon	Insufficient Flourine (Fl) produced for life chemistry
25	Ratio: exotic-to-ordinary matter	Smaller	Galaxies would not form	Larger	Universe would collapse before solar type stars form

Why the Anthropic Principle points to a *Personal* Creator:
Life requires the *PRECISE CONTROLS* of multiple, independent variables

Dr. Hugh Ross (1945 -) – PhD Astronomy from Univ. of Toronto, BS Physics from Univ. of British Columbia; former Research Fellow at CalTech (studying quasars and galaxies);..youngest person ever to serve as Director of observations for Vancouver's branch of the Royal Astronomical Society of Canada; Founder of 'Reasons to Believe' Apologetics ministry, author of "**The Creator & the Cosmos**"[18] ➔ The following are excerpts quoted from his article "Anthropic Principle: A Precise Plan for Humanity" (January 1, 2002):

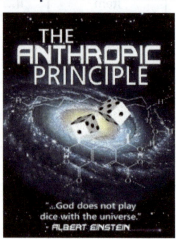

"The Anthropic Principle says that the universe appears 'designed' for the sake of human life. More than a century of astronomy and physics research yields this unexpected observation: the emergence of humans and human civilization requires physical constants, laws, and properties that fall within certain narrow ranges—and this truth applies not only to the cosmos as a whole but also to the galaxy, planetary system, and planet humans occupy. To state the principle more dramatically, a preponderance of *physical evidence* points to humanity as the central theme of the cosmos.

Support for the anthropic principle comes from an unmistakable trend line within the data: the more astronomers learn about the universe and the requirements of human existence, the more severe the limitations they find governing the structure and development of the universe to accommodate those requirements. In other words, additional discoveries are leading to more indicators of large-scale and small-scale fine-tuning.

In 1961, astronomers acknowledged just two characteristics of the universe as "fine-tuned" to make physical life possible. The more obvious one was the ratio of the gravitational force constant to the electromagnetic force constant. It cannot differ from its value by any more than **one part in 10^{40}** (one part in ten thousand trillion trillion trillion) without eliminating the possibility for life. Today, the number of known cosmic characteristics recognized as fine-tuned for life—any conceivable kind of physical life—stands at **thirty-eight**. Of these, the most sensitive is the space energy density (the self-stretching property of the universe). Its value cannot vary by more than **one part in 10^{120}** and still allow for the kinds of stars and planets physical life requires.

Evidence of specific preparation for human existence shows up in the characteristics of the solar system, as well. In the early 1960s astronomers could identify just a few solar system characteristics that required fine-tuning for human life to be possible. By the end of 2001, astronomers had identified more than 150 finely-tuned characteristics. In the 1960s the odds that any given planet in the universe would possess the necessary conditions to support intelligent physical life were shown to be less than one in ten thousand. In 2001 those odds shrank to less than one in a number so large it might as well be infinity (10^{173}).

An amount of *scientific evidence* in support of the anthropic principle fills several books. The authors' religious beliefs run the gamut from agnosticism to deism to theism, but virtually every research astronomer alive today agrees that the universe manifests exquisite fine-tuning for life.

The Revolt Against a Revolution This view of humanity as the focal point of the cosmos represents the historic overthrow of an idea rooted in an ancient revolution, the Copernican revolution. For the first fifteen centuries of the Christian era, Western science assumed that Earth's inhabitants, humans in particular, occupied the central position in the universe. When Nicolaus Copernicus revived the ancient Greek proof that the Sun, rather than Earth, holds the central position in Earth's system of planets, a new scientific perspective took root.

From this perspective, the Copernican principle, emerged the philosophical notion that humans occupy no privileged or exceptional position in the universe. For the past four hundred years, this principle has been the reigning paradigm of science and society. And, during the past forty years, an extension of it, the Mediocrity principle, has grown increasingly prevalent. The Mediocrity principle asserts that humanity is not special in any way and that human origin and development have likely been duplicated on billions of other sites throughout the cosmos.

The Anthropic principle, emerging almost simultaneously with the Mediocrity principle, emphatically contradicts it, exposing a distortion of Copernican thinking. The Anthropic principle makes this obvious and crucial distinction: while humanity's place in the universe is not *spatially* central, it does not necessarily follow that humanity's place is not central, or special, in *any* way.

Few people yet realize that current cosmological research demonstrates a physical universe with no spatial center. All the matter and energy of the universe reside on the three-dimensional surface of the expanding four-dimensional universe. Just as all Earth's cities reside on the planet's two-dimensional surface and none can be identified as geographically central to all others, likewise none of the galaxies, stars, and planets hold the center position on the cosmic 3-D surface.

In one sense, the Anthropic principle is possible because Copernicus was right. What makes humanity's location in the cosmos unique, or special, is that Earth resides away from the center of any astronomical system, such as Earth's galaxy. Humanity lives in a unique location—and moment—in cosmic space-time that allows not only for the possibility of human existence but also for the opportunity to discover that <u>human existence represents a miracle, a special case</u>.

Earth's particular location gives humans a special window to the solar system, the Milky Way galaxy, and the universe itself. In virtually any other galaxy or at any other location in Earth's galaxy and at every other time in cosmic history, the view to the surrounding area would be so unstable and/or so occluded that the form, structure, size, and other characteristics of the galaxy and universe would remain obscure to any sentient observers.

Earth's creatures enjoy a special view to the splendors of the cosmos. Nowhere else and at no other time in the universe would such glory be visible. <u>The importance of the Anthropic principle can hardly be overstated. It returns legitimacy and respectability to the human species as a worthy, even *primary*, subject of scientific research</u>. Further, the Anthropic principle has the potential to bring about a paradigm shift arguably as profound as any shift in human remembrance.

Cosmic Anticipation As early as the 1980s, physicist Paul Davies concluded that the *physical evidence* for design of the universe and of Earth for human life could rightly be described as overwhelming. Today, no physicist or astronomer who has researched the question denies that the universe, the Milky Way galaxy, and the solar system possess compelling hallmarks of <u>intentional design for human life</u>. Many researchers have commented over the past twenty years that it seems the universe 'knew' humans were coming.

The Christ Connection Those people who need hard *data* to affirm their sense of destiny can find it. The space-time theorems of general relativity prove that an *Entity* transcending matter, energy, space, and time is the *cause* of the universe in which humanity lives. Of all the gods, forces, or principles that people have proposed throughout human history to explain the existence and operation of the universe, only <u>the God of the Bible</u> is consistent with the characteristics of the *cause* established in these space-time theorems. Only the Bible predicts and explains the anthropic principle.

Some skeptics have attempted to trivialize the anthropic principle with the assertion that humans simply would not be here to observe the universe unless the extremely unlikely did somehow happen to take place. British philosopher Richard Swinburne responded to this notion with a simple illustration. He points out that the survivor of a firing squad execution would not attribute their survival to a lucky accident. Rather, they would conclude that either the rifles were loaded with blanks or that each of the executioners missed on purpose. The measured fine-tuning of the universe tells us that <u>Someone purposed for humans to exist for a certain period of time</u>.

Another argument claims that there is nothing remarkable about the fine-tuning of the universe *if* an infinitude of universes exist, each with a different set of characteristics. In this case, chance could dictate that at least one would manifest the characteristics necessary for human life. The fallacy in this appeal represents a form of the gambler's fallacy. A gambler might conclude that an ordinary coin could land on heads a hundred thousand consecutive times if he rationalizes that $2^{100,000}$ coins exist (though he cannot see them), each being flipped 100,000 times by $2^{100,000}$ coin flippers. Statistically, one of these coins could come up heads 100,000 times. Such thinking is considered fallacious, however, because the gambler has no evidence for the existence of the other coins, coin flippers, or distinct results. With a sample size of one, the only rational conclusion to draw is that someone "fixed" the coin to land on heads. In the case of the universe, no *evidence* can be found for the existence of other universes. In fact, the principles of relativity dictate that the space-time envelope of a universe that contains observers can never overlap that of any other universe(s). Thus, the sample size for human observers is one and always will be one, and the conclusion that <u>Someone purposed, or fixed, the universe for human existence</u> remains compelling.

Testing the Conclusion The anthropic principle invites testing. A skeptic not yet persuaded that the fine-tuning of the universe reflects more than a lucky coin toss can choose to examine the universe, the "coin," more closely. If the anthropic principle and its implications for transcendent design are false, research will discover declining *evidence* for fine-tuning and existing *evidence* will be erased by new data. If, on the other hand, the anthropic principle and its implications are true, research will yield an increase in both the number of fine-tuned characteristics and the degree of fine-tuning. Based on the accumulating *evidence*, to bet on the anthropic principle seems safer than taking another breath. The anthropic principle energizes humanity's climb on the pinnacles of Truth."

Hebrews 11:1,3

*"Faith is the substance of things hoped for, the EVIDENCE of things not seen.
By faith we UNDERSTAND that the worlds were framed by the word of God,
So that the things which are seen were not made of things which are visible."*

PSALM 8:3-4 God *PERSONALLY CARES* for me: Earth's precise *LOCATION*   3.3

"When I consider Your ①HEAVENS, the ②WORK of Your fingers, the moon and the stars which You have ③ORDAINED. What is man, that You are ④MINDFUL of him, and the son of man that You ⑤VISIT him? For You have made him a little lower than the angels, and You have crowned him with ⑥GLORY and ⑦HONOR."

① HEAVENS = *"shamayim"* = plural (like *"Elohim"*) = "space-time-mass universe" (same as Gen. 1:1, Ps 19:1)
② WORK = *"ma'āśeh"* = activity, actions ('work of Your fingers' = the 'handiwork of God')
③ ORDAINED = *"kûn"* = fixed in place; established or set to stand; erected
④ MINDFUL = *"zâkar"* = to remember or think about; to mark or record in memory
⑤ VISIT = *"pâqad"* = to oversee something with care and attentiveness
⑥ GLORY = *"kâbôd kâbôd"* = splendor, weight, significance (see Exo. 40:35, Ps19:1, Isaiah 43:7)
⑦ HONOR = *"hâdâr"* = excellency as in prizing or attaching great value to (see 1Chron. 16:27, Prov. 31:25)

Item	Fact	Significance
Earth's Protection against Impact Threats from Asteroids	Planets, comets and asteroids closest to the Sun orbit it at greater speeds than the outer planets. So any asteroid impacting the closest planets (Mercury, Venus, Earth, Mars) would do devastating damage. Highest density of asteroids in our Solar System is at 2 AU's (astronomical units) from the Sun. Planets closer to the main asteroid belt suffer frequent asteroid collisions.	**Mars**, being the closest planet to this main asteroid belt, takes most of asteroid impacts. Without Mars, Earth would be the closest planet. Mercury and Venus are farther from the main asteroid belt, but asteroids that do occur in their region are moving extremely fast, so when they do get hit it's a real mess. For Earth: we are in the optimal range for our asteroid belt, and optimally protected by Mars.
Earth's Location in the *Spiral* "Milky Way" Galaxy	There are 3 types of galaxies: *Spiral* galaxies are ≤ 5% of the 3 types, with conditions allowing generation of metal-rich stars and orderly star orbits (essential for life). *Elliptical* galaxies don't allow heavy metals to form (in order to have life, star systems must form late enough so they can incorporate this heavy element-enriched material). *Irregular* galaxies have a very active nuclei, which spew out life-destroying radiation and material, besides also lacking sufficient quantities of heavy elements essential for life.	Earth is located within the **spiral Milky Way galaxy**, which is the optimal galaxy for life: a late-type, metal-rich, spiral galaxy with orderly orbits and comparatively little danger to planets between spiral arms. In 1966: astronomers Carl Sagan and Iosef Shlovskii calculated that using only two of the many critical parameters needed for a planet to support life (1 = host star's chemical properties, 2 = planet's location relative to its host star in its galaxy), only **.001%** of all stars could have a planet that could support life.
Earth's Position away from the nucleus of Milky Way Galaxy	Earth's magnetic field and atmosphere shield surface life from most radiation, but there are very dangerous radiation bursts in our galaxy: AGN's (active galactic nucleus) outbursts, supernovae and gamma ray bursts. These radiation sources are much more threatening in the inner regions of the Milky Way because more stars are concentrated there.	The only form of protection from massive radiation sources is LOCATION. The worst location is in the Milky Way's bulge, with scorching radiation and stars with elliptical orbits. The safest place to be during an AGN outburst is in the **Milky Way's outer disk**, far from its nucleus. This is exactly where the Earth just happens to be located.
Earth's Position in the Milky Way Galaxy	Earth is located closest to the Perseus spiral arms of the Milky Way galaxy. This is one of the best places to learn about stars, galactic structures and cosmology. The Milky Way galaxy, based on its composition, is the **best type of galaxy (spiral) for scientific discovery and safety** (giant black holes lurk in massive elliptical galaxies).	M. Denton[26]: *"Our relatively peripheral position on the spiral arm of a rather ordinary galaxy is indeed rather fortunate. If we had been stationed in a more central position – say, near the galactic hub – it is likely our knowledge of the universe and other galaxies might not have been as extensive. Perhaps astronomy and cosmology as we know these subjects would never have developed."*
Earth's Distance from the Sun	Our distance from the Sun is **most optimal** not only for life but for *studying* life (in creating models of stars, scientists *begin* with the Sun and extrapolate lower/ higher temperatures and luminosities to describe stars).	If Earth closer: we'd be a hothouse with a thick atmosphere like Venus. If Earth farther: we'd have a thicker and obstructive atmosphere (greater amt. of CO_2 to keep H_2O on its surface), which is hostile to animal life.

Earth is optimally located with in SOLAR SYSTEM:

Protected from asteroids by Mars, Mercury and Venus.

Earth's Solar System is optimally located within the MILKY WAY GALAXY:

1) Protected from radiation bursts in the AGN (Active Galactic Nucleus) by being located in the outer disk.

2) Located in Perseus Arm, we are in an optimal place for scientific observation and discovery.

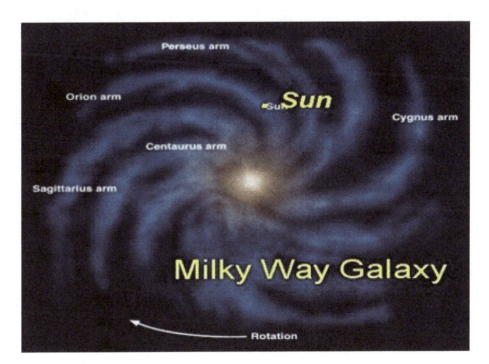

Psalm 115: 14-16
*"May the Lord give you increase more and more, and you and your children.
May you be blessed by the Lord, who made heaven and earth.
The heaven, even the heavens, are the Lord's,
but the EARTH He has given to the CHILDREN OF MEN."*

JOB & ISAIAH — God *PERSONALLY CARES* for me: Earth's precise *DESIGN* — 3.4

JOB 12: 8-9 *"...SPEAK TO THE EARTH, AND IT WILL TEACH YOU.... Who among all these does not know that the hand of the Lord has done this, in whose hand is the life of every living thing, and the breath of all mankind?"*

ISAIAH 45:18 *"...thus says the Lord, who created the heavens, who is God, who formed the earth and made it, who has established it, who did not create it in vain, who formed it to be INHABITED: 'I am the Lord, and there is no other.'"*

Item	Fact	Significance
Earth's Water	Its denser as a liquid than a solid, so it *floats* when it freezes. So… ice on the surface insulates the water underneath from losing more heat. It has very high *latent heats* when changing from a solid to a liquid to a gas (more heat is needed to vaporize 1g of water than the same amount of any other substance). So… it takes an unusually large amount of heat to convert liquid water to vapor.	**Life couldn't exist**: Water's *density* prevents lakes and oceans from freezing from the bottom up! Water's *latent heat* allows small bodies of water (ponds, lakes) to exist – otherwise, they would evaporate. Water's *latent heat* allows larger animals to regulate their body temperatures (otherwise, they couldn't dissipate heat and would die).
Earth's Carbon	The only element that, when combined with other key atoms of H, N, O and Ph, gives these molecules information-storage capacity by forming DNA and RNA (carriers of information) and amino acids and protein (life's building blocks)	Without it, **complex life couldn't exist** (no other element comes close). But CO_2 levels must be delicately balanced for life: the farther a planet is from its host star, the more CO_2 it needs to keep warm, but too much CO_2 prevents survival of large mobile creatures, who need O-rich air and low CO_2 levels.
Earth's Water (Hydrologic) Cycle and Carbon Cycle	Energy from the Sun evaporates H_2O into clouds, bringing rain, returning H_2O and CO_2 to plants, the soil and oceans. Heat from Earth's interior comes to the surface, sets the mantle in motion (plate tectonics, earthquakes, etc), building mountains and releasing CO_2 into the atmosphere by volcanoes. Carbon in the atmosphere makes its way to sea floor, going back into earth's mantle, gets reheated and returns to the surface as CO_2	1) cycling carbon and oxygen (in the forms of water and CO_2) keeps nutrients, water and land available for life to exist. 2) without recycling, earth would be lifeless: you couldn't mix the life-essential nutrients in earth's sunlight-drenched surface waters. 3) without recycling, global temperatures couldn't be regulated within the narrow ranges required – so **complex life couldn't exist**.
Earth's Precise Orbit and Axial Tilt = 23.5°±1.2°	Earth's orbit is nearly a perfect circle, and the Earth's axis of rotation tilts 23.5° from a line perpendicular to the plane formed by the Earth's orbit around the Sun. This rotational angle varies by only ±1.2° over 1,000's of years! The direction of the rotational axis stays nearly fixed in space, even as the Earth revolves around the Sun once each year. As a result, when the Earth is at a certain place in its orbit, the northern hemisphere is tilted toward the Sun and experiences summer. Six months later, when the Earth is on the opposite side of the Sun, the northern hemisphere is tilted away from the Sun and experiences winter. The seasons reverse in the southern hemisphere.	1) If the tilt angle was very small: it would prevent rain distribution across the earth (an **absolute requirement for life**). 2) 23.5° is just the right amount to allow wind patterns across the Earth to change throughout the year, which allows for seasonal rain showers to regions that otherwise would never see rain. 3) If the tilt angle were very large: when the North Pole leans sunward ½ of year, most of the northern hemisphere would have months of scorching daylight (many times hotter than Death Valley), but then freezingly cold months and perpetual nights during the 2nd ½ of year. What causes a large tilt angle? If our **Moon** was as small as Mars' 2 moons, we'd tilt 60°!
Earth's Moon and Ocean Tides	Our perfectly-tuned Moon: its just the right size to produce Earth's "just-right" 23.5° tilt angle as it "pulls" on the Earth by gravity. Tides are caused by gravity interacting between Earth and Moon. The Moon's pull makes oceans bulge out toward it. Another bulge occurs on the opposite side, since the Earth is also being pulled toward Moon (and away from the water on the far side). Since Earth is rotating while this happens, two tides ("low" and "high") occur each day.	Tides mix nutrients from the land with the oceans. 1/3 of tidal energy occurs on ocean floor, which drives the ocean's currents. These strong currents regulate Earth's climate by circulating heat (like a big regulator). If the Earth and Moon did not interact so perfectly to produce Earth's tides, nutrients would not get mixed and circulated but would be stagnated (**life couldn't exist** – we'd have a stagnated pool of slime).

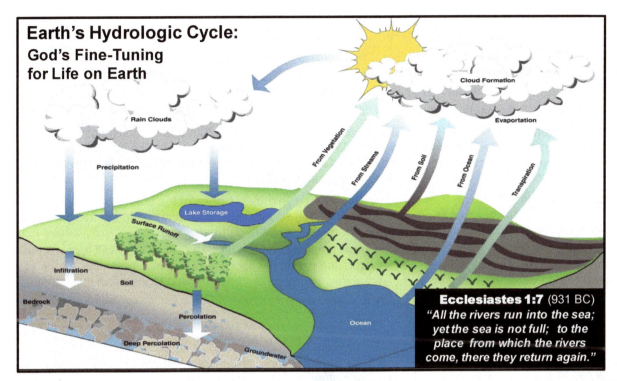

The hydrologic cycle is the continuous circulation of water among the oceans, continents, and atmosphere. It is a machine endlessly in motion, powered by the sun's energy and assisted by gravity. It has been circulating nearly the same water since the first clouds formed and the first rains fell on our earth (very little is ever lost or gained).

The continents contain about 2.5% of our planet's water, mainly in the polar ice caps and ground water. The atmosphere accounts for only about 0.0001%. The oceans hold the remaining 97.5% of our planet's water. About 90% of the water entering oceans is in the form of precipitation - rain and snow falling directly on the oceans. Runoff from the land accounts for the remaining 10%. The only significant outlet for ocean water is evaporation by the sun's energy (heat). On average, a molecule of water will remain in the oceans about 3,000 years before being transferred back to the atmosphere by evaporation.

Water evaporated into the atmosphere stays there about ten days before being dropped as condensation (rain, snow, etc.) back into the oceans or onto the land. Water precipitated onto land can (1) infiltrate the ground, becoming ground water that slowly flows to the sea, (2) flow across the surface, entering a system of streams and lakes which eventually flows to the sea, or (3) become glacial ice, eventually flowing to the sea.

This is a simple description of a complex machine: not all water travels completely through the cycle every time. Some evaporates from streams, lakes and glacial ice before reaching the sea, and plants use alot of water and transfer it back to the atmosphere by a process called transpiration. The system does not lose or gain water, but the way water is distributed over different areas of the globe does change, causing floods and droughts.

The Earth: A Circle Floating in Space

Isaiah 40:22 (750 BC) *"It is He who sits above the ①CIRCLE OF THE EARTH, and its inhabitants are like grasshoppers, who stretches out the heavens like a curtain, and spreads them out like a tent to dwell in."*

Job 26:7 (1200 BC) *"He stretches out the north over empty space; He ②HANGS THE EARTH ON NOTHING."*

① "circle" = Hebrew "chug" = circle (the Bible teaches that the earth is a sphere)

② "hangs" (*"tâlâh"* = suspends) the Earth on "nothing" (*"blyîimâh"* = nothing whatsoever)

The Bible states that God "suspends the Earth, which is in the shape of a circle or sphere, on absolutely nothing, in empty space." These verses clearly state what is now a scientific fact: the circular Earth is unsupported by any other object – it literally is floating in space. Photos taken from space show Earth as a sphere floating in the cosmic void. The Earth literally hangs on nothing, just as the Bible teaches.

Edgar Mitchell (Apollo 14 Astronaut): *"When I went to the moon I was a pragmatic test pilot. But when I saw the planet Earth floating in the vastness of space the presence of divinity became almost palpable and I knew that life in the universe was not just an accident."*

PSALM 19: 4b-6   The "Sun of Righteousness"   3.5

"In them (the heavens) He has placed a tabernacle for the sun, which is like a bridegroom coming out of his chamber, and rejoices like a strong man to run its race. Its rising is from one end of heaven, and its circuit to the other end; and there is nothing hidden from its heat."

Psalm 19:4,6 = "Tabernacle for the sun" = "abode of the Son"; "rises from 1 end, circuit to other end"

- Jonathan Edwards (1703-1758)[25]: "The Dispensation of the Rising of the Sun of Righteousness"
"*The Psalmist says that 'God has placed a tabernacle for the sun in the heavens': so God the Father had prepared an abode in heaven for Jesus Christ; He had set a throne for Him there, to which He ascended after He rose. But at the end of the gospel day He will descend again to the earth.*"

- God as Creator placed the sun in its heavenly position to give a *daily picture* of the true "Sun of Righteousness".
- Each new day, the sun appears to rise out of the earth; after it has risen, it ascends up to the midst of heaven, and then at that end of each day it appears to us to descend again to earth.
- Jesus Christ, the transcendent God of the universe, descended from heaven (where He dwelt with His Father), to earth in order to redeem man. When He rose from the grave, He ascended up to heaven on His throne at the right hand of the Father. He has promised that one day, He will return and descend to the earth in judgment.

John 3:13 *"No one has ascended to heaven but He who came down from heaven, that is, the Son of Man who is in heaven."*

Hebrews 1:8,13 "Christ on His throne"	Revelation 19:11-14 "Christ descending to earth in judgment"
"But to the Son He says, 'Your throne, O God, is forever and ever; a scepter of righteousness is the scepter of Your kingdom.' But to which of the angels has He ever said, 'Sit at My right hand, till I make Your enemies Your footstool'?"	*"Then I saw heaven opened, and behold, a white horse. And He who sat on him was called Faithful and True, and in righteousness He judges and makes war. His eyes were like a flame of fire, and on His head were many crowns. He had a name written that no one knows except Himself. He was clothed with a robe dipped in blood, and His name is called The Word of God. And the armies of heaven, clothed in fine linen, white and clean, followed Him on white horses."*

Psalm 19:5 = "like a bridegroom coming out of his chamber"

- The Sun of Righteousness rises from the grave, just as the sun appears to rise from the earth in the morning, coming forth as a bridegroom. The gospel dispensation begins with the resurrection of Jesus Christ as the King of heaven and earth and the bridegroom of His church, purchasing His spouse whom He loved with His own blood.

Romans 7:4 *"Therefore, my brethren, you also have become dead to the law through the body of Christ, that you may be married to another, even to Him who was raised from the dead, that we should bear fruit to God."*

Malachi 4:2 *"But to you who fear My name, the Sun of Righteousness shall arise with healing in His wings."*

Psalm 61:3-4 *"For You have been a shelter for me, and a strong tower from the enemy. I will abide in Your tabernacle forever. I will trust in the shelter of Your wings."*

Psalm 91:4 *"He shall cover you with His feathers, and under His wings you shall take refuge..."*

- Jesus = bridegroom, mankind = bride: uniting man's nature with the Holy Spirit into 1 person is His marriage.
- C.H. Spurgeon[25]: *"...the Word became flesh and dwelt among us in the world that He might thereby make our peace, reconciling God to man and man to God. By this happy match the Son of God is become the Son of Man, even flesh of our flesh and bone of our bones; and the sons of men are made the sons of God. My sin is His sin, and His righteousness is my righteousness. He who knew no sin, for my sake was made sin, and I having no good thing, am made the righteousness of God in Him (2Corin. 5:21)".*

2Corinthians 11:2 *"...I am jealous for you with godly jealousy. For I have betrothed you to one husband, that I may present you as a chaste virgin to Christ."*

Psalm 19:5 = "rejoicing like a strong man to run its race"

- Christ, when He rose, rose as a man of war, as the Lord strong and mighty, the Lord mighty in battle. He rose to conquer His enemies and to show forth His glorious power in subduing all things to Himself, especially death.

1Cor. 15:25-26 *"...He must reign till He has put all enemies under His feet. The last enemy that will be destroyed is death."*

Hebrews 12:1-2   "Look to Jesus as our example as we "run our race"
ITS NOT THE JOURNEY - IT'S THE PRIZE AT THE JOURNEY'S END

"... let us lay aside every weight, and the sin which so easily ensnares us, and let us run with endurance the race that is set before us, looking unto Jesus, the author and finisher of our faith, who for THE JOY THAT WAS SET BEFORE HIM ENDURED THE CROSS, despising the shame, and has sat down at the right hand of the throne of God."

Psalm 19:6 = "nothing Is hidden from its heat"

- <u>Jesus Christ exposes every person's true need</u>: The saving knowledge of Jesus Christ is the light penetrating the darkness of man. Nothing can hide from His light: He convicts everyone of their need to repent from their sin.

John 1:5 *"...the light SHINES IN THE DARKNESS, and the darkness did not comprehend it."*

John 3:19-21 *"...this is the condemnation, that the light has come into the world, and men loved darkness rather than light, because their deeds were evil. Everyone practicing evil HATES THE LIGHT and does not come to the light, lest his deeds be exposed. But he who does the truth comes to the light, that his deeds may be clearly seen, that they have been done in God."*

- <u>Jesus Christ gives the warmth of salvation to the dead and lost</u>: The saving knowledge of the light of Jesus Christ delivers a person out of the darkness of death into the light of eternal life:

Psalm 36:9 *"...with You is the fountain of life: in Your light we see light."*

John 9:5 *"As long as I am in the world, I am the Light of the world.."*

Thomas Playfree[25]: *"As the physical sun goes from the uttermost parts of the heavens and runs to the end of it again, the spiritual Sun of Righteousness is borne around the world, that He might be not only the 'glory of His people Israel' but also 'a light to the Gentiles', and 'all the ends of the earth might see the salvation of our God.'"*

C.H. Spurgeon[25]: *"Just as nothing on earth or in the air is hidden from the sun's heat, nothing is hidden from His light or His heat. He not only enlightens the understanding, so that it shall see and know the truth, but He softens the heart, so that it shall love the truth, and calls forth fruit from it, and ripens the fruit He has called forth."*

- <u>Psalm 1:1-12   Jesus Christ's Omniscience (vs. 1-6) and Omnipresence (vs. 7-12)</u>
    - verses 1-6 = nothing *inside* of me is hidden from the Lord
    - verses 7-12 = Christ always watches *over* me – I can't do anything outside His loving watchcare (Job 34:21)

- <u>Jesus Christ will require me to give an account of how I lived (Romans 14:12, Proverbs 15:3)</u>:

Hebrews 4:13 *"...there is no creature hidden from His sight, but all things are naked and open to the eyes of Him to whom we must give an account."*

The Sun: My Daily Reminder of Jesus Christ

God designed the Sun on Day 4 of creation week, as the "great light" at the center of our Solar System which is the "light-giver" (the source of earth's light is the Sun - Genesis 1:16).	Jesus Christ is the only source of eternal life: John 1:4-5 *"In Him was life, and the life was the light of men."*. John 8:12 *"I am the Light of the world. He who follows Me shall not walk in darkness, but have the light of life."*	 Earth shown for size comparison
The Sun's energy output is constant (within a few tenths of 1%). Most stars are very unstable: their energy output varies drastically, making life around them **impossible**.	Malachi 3:6 *"...I am the Lord. I do not change."* Hebrews 13:8 *"Jesus Christ is the same yesterday, today and forever."* Hebrews 1:12 *"... You are the same, and Your years will not fail."*	
The Sun dwarfs the earth. We must be protected from its rays and must never approach too close or be burned up - it is 1,000,000 miles wide and 300,000X heavier than earth (one million earths can fit inside the sun) - it is an extremely hot ball of gas: average surface temperature is 10,000°F	Isaiah 40:22 *"It is He who sits above the circle of the earth, and its inhabitants are like grasshoppers....."* Exodus 33:18,20 *"Then he said, 'Please, show me Your glory.' But He said, 'You cannot see My face; no man shall see Me, and live.'"* Hebrews 12:28-29 *"...let us have grace, by which we may serve God acceptably with reverence and godly fear....our God is a consuming fire."*	
The Sun is the *only star* in our Solar System (very rare since stars exist in groups). If this wasn't true, life is **impossible** (nearby stars would pull the earth so close to the sun at one point to boil everything, and so far away at another time to freeze all life).	John 14:6 *"No one comes to the Father except through Me."* Matt. 17:2,3,6,8 *"...Jesus...was transfigured before them. His face shone like the sun, and His clothes became as white as the light... Moses and Elijah appeared to them, talking with Him.....when the disciples heard it, they fell on their faces and were greatly afraid... when they had lifted up their eyes, they saw no one but Jesus only."*	

Ps 113:3   *"From the rising of the sun to its going down, the Lord's name is to be praised."*

Dr. Jay Richards, "Privileged Planet"[26]: Fine-Tuning & Anthropic Principle — 3.6

'The Privileged Planet'   (How Our Place in the Cosmos is Designed for Discovery)

"Our planet is exquisitely fit not only to support life, but also to give us he best view of the universe, as if Earth were designed both for life and for scientific discovery."

Dr. Jay W. Richards – PhD Philosophy and Theology from Princeton Theological Seminary; Senior Fellow at the Discovery Institute's Center for Science and Culture ➔ The following is quoted from "**The Privileged Planet**"[26], co-authored with astronomer Guillermo Gonzalez, on the delicate precision in the universe as seen in the Anthropic Principle, Corotation Circle and CHZ:

1) Anthropic Principle = "If Earth's local environment were simply a random slice in space, the probability of life would be infinitesimally small. The seemingly arbitrary and unrelated constants in physics have one strange thing in common: these are precisely the values needed to have a universe capable of supporting life."

Francis Crick (co-founder, DNA molecule): *"An honest man, armed with all the KNOWLEDGE available to us now, could only state that in some sense, the origin of the universe appears at the moment to be almost a miracle, so many are the conditions which would have to be satisfied to get it going."*

Paul Davies ("The Mind of God")[8]: *"Through my scientific work I have come to believe more and more strongly that the physical universe is put together with an ingenuity so astonishing that I can't accept it merely as a brute fact. I can't believe our existence in this universe is a quirk of fate, an accident of history, an incidental blip in the great cosmic drama. The present structure of the universe, so sensitive to minor alterations in numbers, has been rather carefully thought out. The seemingly miraculous concurrence of these numerical values must remain the most compelling evidence for COSMIC DESIGN."*

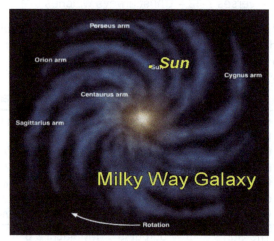

2) Corotation Circle = Solar System's *position* in the spiral Milky Way Galaxy: The orbital period of the stars equals the orbital period of the spiral arm pattern. Stars outside and inside the corotation circle cross the spiral arms more often. This is a very bad thing because giant molecular clouds lurking within the spiral arms pose many threats to life (radiation, black holes, impacts, bursts, etc.): life could not exist on a planet if spiral arm crossing occurred too often. Our Sun (and the Solar System in which Earth resides) just happens to reside in the Corotation Circle of the Milky Way Galaxy. So, not only are we in a stable position to avoid crossing the spiral arms, we are in a clear position to OBSERVE our universe around us.

3) Circumstellar Habitable Zone (CHZ) = Earth's *position* to the *SUN* in the Solar System: That region around a host star where liquid water can exist on a planet's surface in the host star's vicinity for extended periods. This definition is based on the assumption that life will flourish if this minimum Zone requirement is met. The main factor influencing this zone is <u>the relationship of the planet in question to its host star</u> (for us, the Sun). The most important factors (*all of which are met by the Sun and the Earth*) are as follows:
  a) location of a planet to any existing asteroid belt (asteroids are detrimental to a planet),
  b) planet's atmosphere (ex: the farther a planet is from its host star, the more CO_2 its atmosphere needs to keep it warm; if too thin, it will freeze on its dark side and bake on its lighted side; if too thick, complex life could not exist since it requires a balanced amount of carbon vs. oxygen),
  c) planet's location in the CHZ (inner edge vs. outer edge, as a planet's capacity to support complex life is much more likely when it is closer to the inner edge, as is Earth to the Sun),
  d) host star's constancy of its energy output (strong flares from a host star such as an M dwarf increase the relative X-ray radiation 1,000X compared to that from the Sun, resulting in UV radiation reaching a planet's surface of much greater intensity than could support life; on the other hand, the Sun's constancy of its levels of UV radiation maintains the ozone shield in the Earth's atmosphere),
  e) UV radiation's consistent oxidizing presence in the planet's atmosphere (the Sun's UV radiation provides a steady dissociation of H-rich light molecules, such as methane and water, in Earth's atmosphere – this loss of the H allows oxygen to become so abundant in Earth's atmosphere),
  f) host star's mass (massive stars have more rapid luminosity changes, which lead to drastic climate changes and greater populations of asteroids),
  g) planet's orbit (highly elliptical orbits lead to large temperature swings; Earth's orbit almost perfect circle),
  h) planet's chemical ingredients in its core (only certain kinds of cores can generate a life-protecting magnetic field, as is the case with Earth).

Dr. Guillermo Gonzales, Astrophysicist, PhD Astronomy, senior fellow of Discovery Institute Center for Science & Culture. The following are excerpts from his April 1, 2002 article "**Our Rare Sun**": "As astronomers are learning more about the solar system's surroundings and are able to better place the Sun in its proper context, they are showing the Sun to be rare indeed. They are also discovering that the conditions required for life are far more numerous and narrow than commonly believed. These findings, along with the many examples of fine-tuning in chemistry, biochemistry, physics, and cosmology, argue against *chance* explanations. A nonchance explanation called intentional design implies both mind and will. And I call that intentionality a *God* thing.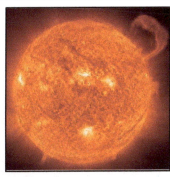

To assert that some of the Sun's parameters must be fine-tuned to within a narrow range to permit life on Earth is reasonable. This assertion is called the Weak Anthropic Principle. Earth's Sun is unlike other stars in these characteristics. Because these parameters must fall within a certain narrow range for Earth life to be possible, their convergence within that range argues for fine-tuning. And fine-tuning argues for a Fine-Tuner, more frequently referred to as God, the Creator.

Uncommon Parameter #1 = MASS The Sun is among the 4 to 8% most massive stars in the galaxy. While the Sun's mass is below midrange, it is far above the average value. The Sun's mass affects the fine-tuning necessary for the existence of life on Earth in a couple of ways. First, the lifetime of a star on the main sequence (its stable burning period) strongly depends on its mass. While on the main sequence, a star fuses its abundant hydrogen fuel relatively slowly, leading to a gradual increase of luminosity. The most massive stars last only a few million years on the main sequence. Stars twice the Sun's mass last just under two billion years, while stars half the Sun's mass last nearly 60 billion years! Thus, the more massive stars don't last long enough for Earth-like complex life to come on the scene. This makes the fact that the Sun is not among the roughly 3% most massive stars understandable. If it were, we wouldn't be here. But what about lower mass stars? Because low mass stars are less luminous than the Sun, a planet must orbit it closely to maintain liquid water on its surface. But, low mass stars tend to have flares similar in strength to those on the Sun. This means that the relative effects of flares will be more severe for life on a planet orbiting a low mass star. What's more, low mass stars are cooler and emit less ultraviolet radiation. This feature might seem like an advantage, but it's not. Ultraviolet radiation hitting a planet's atmosphere regenerates its ozone layer. The stronger its ozone shield, the better a planet protects itself from sudden increases in the ultraviolet radiation either from strong flares or nearby supernovae. Thus, the Sun offers better protection to strong transient radiation events than do lower mass stars.

Uncommon Parameter #2 = COMPOSITION Using high-resolution spectroscopy, astronomers can determine the relative abundances of over thirty chemical elements in the atmosphere of a solar-type star. They've known since the middle of the twentieth century that the compositions of stars are not all the same. As detector technology and stellar atmosphere modeling software have improved, astronomers have been able to study more subtle stellar composition variations. Beginning about ten years ago such data have shown the Sun's metallicity to be moderately above average when compared to nearby stars. Restricting the comparison to stars similar in age to the Sun (4 to 5 billion years) makes the Sun appear even more rare in metal richness. Only now are nearby stars forming with the metallicity as high as the Sun's.

Uncommon Parameter #3 = STABILITY A highly stable star, the Sun's light output varies by only 0.1% over a full sunspot cycle (approximately 11 years), though it may vary a bit more on longer timescales. The low amplitude of variations in the Sun's energy output keeps Earth's climate from experiencing excessively wild climate swings.

Uncommon Parameter #4 = LOCATION The Sun is located very close to the Corotation Circle - that place in the disk where the orbital period of the stars equals the orbital period of the spiral arm pattern. Stars both outside and inside the corotation circle cross spiral arms more often. Earth's proximity to the corotation circle may be of considerable importance, given that this configuration maximizes time intervals between spiral arm crossings.

Uncommon Parameter #5 = ORBIT Compared to nearby stars of similar age, the Sun's orbit in the plane of the disk is more nearly circular, and its vertical motion is smaller....having a nearly circular orbit also helps Earth avoid spiral arm crossings. We certainly don't want those arms crossing too often, given the high frequency of supernovae that occur there."

Guillermo Gonzalez, Ph.D., is an assistant professor of astronomy at Iowa State University. His specialties are high-resolution quantitative stellar spectroscopy and astrobiology. He has published his research in many astronomical journals, including the *Astrophysical Journal*, *Astronomical Journal*, *Astronomy & Astrophysics*, *Solar Physics*, and *Monthly Notices of the Royal Astronomical Society*.

Let's Review Some of What We've Learned about Design & Fine Tuning

Without the **precise four forces** to govern the behavior of matter, life in the Universe is impossible.

Physical laws of the Universe can be written in **math equations** on one side of one sheet of paper!

Without the **finely tuned values of > 50 variables** (accurate and precise), life in the Universe is impossible.

Accuracy with Precision around a standard

Without it's many **precise physical properties**, life in the Milky Way Galaxy is impossible.

Without it's many **precise physical properties**, life in the Solar System is impossible.

Material objects are made of minute particles with **precise chemical properties** or life in the Universe is impossible.

Here are 8 Facts about the Universe to which all scientists agree...

Together these 8 Facts make a strong case for a Universe that is *DESIGNED, CREATED* (Psalm 19:1-3)

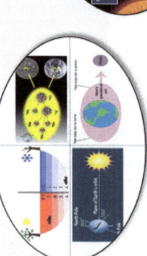

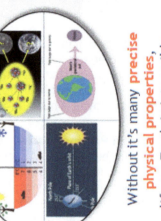

Without it's many **precise physical properties**, life on Earth is impossible.

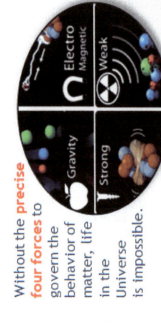

Without it's **precise, continuous water circulation**, life on Earth is impossible.

PSALM 19:7-11 God's Word, not His creation, points me to Him — 3.7

After David contemplates the majesty of God's creation, he jumps to the majesty of God's Bible. He mixes praise and prayer together as he comes to a full understanding of God's message: His creation shows His glory (vs. 1-6), His word shows His grace (vs. 7-11), and David sees his own need for God's grace in his life (vs. 12-14).

God gives six different names and adjectives to describe His Bible, then six different results I get by following it:

Psalm 19:7a *"The LAW of the Lord is perfect, converting the soul"*
- "law" = the Torah ("the law for life"); the standard by which every action is measured
- "of the Lord" = not mans' laws – the Bible is God's laws
- "perfect" = complete (thorough in every respect, totally comprehensive)
- "converting the soul" = God's law is so comprehensive that it changes me to the core of who I am as a person.

Psalm 19:7b *"The TESTIMONY of the Lord is sure, making wise the simple"*
- "testimony" = "to bear witness"; used only in this verse in all the Psalms
- "of the Lord" = God is bearing witness to *Himself*...as if raising His hand and solemnly taking an oath.
- "sure" = reliable or durable; similar to verb for "amen" ("the testimony of the Lord is amen")
- "simple" = literal meaning is "openness", or a *"simpleton"* = a person whose mind is like a house with front and back doors always open ("stuff comes in, then goes out") – can't discern right from wrong.
- God is saying that His testimony is so reliable that it can take a simpleton, who has no clue where they're going and why, and turn them into a person of wisdom (make him or her skilled at daily living).

Psalm 19:8a *"The STATUTES of the Lord are right, rejoicing the heart"*
- "statutes of the Lord" = God's rulings, pronouncements, principles
- "right" = life is a maze of choices; God's principles set the right path so we don't get lost (Psalm 119:).
- Jeremiah 15:   God says there is JOY that comes to the human heart when it rightly understands His Bible!

Psalm 19:8b *"The COMMANDMENT of the Lord is pure, enlightening the eyes"*
- "commandment of the Lord" = God's orders or divine decrees; things that God insists we do or keep doing.
- "pure" = radiant, unclean – an absence of anything impure – like our phrase "CRYSTAL CLEAR"
- "enlightening the eyes" = any person who picks it up can understand it

Psalm 19:9a *"The FEAR of the Lord is clean, enduring forever"*
- "fear of the Lord" = an attitude of the heart that seeks a right relationship with the Source of that fear.
- "clean" = without blemish (uncompromised, undefiled) – its FULL-STRENGTH from cover to cover
- "enduring forever" = the Bible's 2 enduring things: 1) the God who made us; 2) the deepest needs of the heart.

Psalm 19:9b *"The JUDGMENTS of the Lord are true and righteous altogether"*
- "judgments of the Lord" = God's verdicts, pronouncements of consequence, and / or punishments for sin.
- "true and righteous" = God doesn't operate according to His mood: He is consistent, fair and precise.

**Psalm 19's message: The Bible is God's specific revelation of Himself; Creation is not
While Creation puts God's existence on display, the Bible is God's clear, complete authority**

PSALM 19:11 What *REWARD* is there for "keeping" God's Word?   **3.8**

"by them Your servant is ①WARNED. And in ②KEEPING them there is great ③REWARD."

① WARNED = Hebrew "*zâhar*" = enlightened, taught to beware, admonished

2Tim. 3:16-17 *"All Scripture is given by inspiration of God, and is profitable for doctrine, for reproof, for correction, for instruction in righteousness, that the man of God may be complete, thoroughly equipped for every good work."*

Ps 119:9,11 *"How can a young man cleanse his way? By taking heed according to Your word. Your word I have hidden in my heart, that I might not sin against You."*

C. Spurgeon[25]: *"We are warned by the Word of our duty, our danger, and our remedy... So few men take the warning so graciously given. None but servants of God will do so, for they alone regard their Master's will."*

② KEEP = Hebrew "*shâmar*" = to watch over; to hedge (as in protecting); to guard by diligently observing

- God = our "Keeper"

Genesis 28:15 *"Behold, I who am with you will KEEP you wherever you go..."*

John 17:12 *"While I was with them in the world, "I KEPT them in Your name. Those whom You gave Me I have KEPT..."*

- God has commanded me to "keep" some important things

Genesis 2:15 *"Then the Lord God took the man and put him in the garden of Eden to tend and KEEP it."*

Proverbs 4:23 *"KEEP your heart with all diligence, for out of it spring the issues of life."*

Deuteronomy 7:12 *"...because you listen to these judgments and KEEP and do them, the Lord your God will KEEP with you the covenant and the mercy which He swore to your fathers."*

John 14:15 (Luke 6:46) *"If you love Me, you will KEEP My commandments."*

1Timothy 5:22 *"Do not...share in other people's sins; KEEP yourself pure."*

③ REWARD = Hebrew "*êqeb*" = wages or compensation given to His children at the end of their lives

- we don't *earn* wages of debt...we *win* great wages of grace (same as Hebrew "*śâkâr*" in Genesis 15:1)

Genesis 15:1 *"After these things the word of the Lord came to Abraham in a vision, saying, 'Do not be afraid, Abram. I am your shield, your exceedingly great REWARD.'"*

- **Psalm 19:11's rewards are earned at the "end" of one's labor.**

C. Spurgeon[25]: *"The main reward is yet to come. The word here signifies the HEEL, as if the reward would come to us at the end of life when the work is done and not while the labor was in the hand. Our light affliction, which is but for a moment, is not worthy to be compared with the glory which shall be revealed in us. Then we shall know the value of the Scriptures if we commit ourselves to them today."*

Hebrews 6:10 *"...God is not unjust to forget your work and labor of love which you have shown toward His name..."*

Galatians 6:9 *"...let us not grow weary while doing good, for in due season we shall reap if we do not lose heart."*

- **But God also rewards me as I live out my life daily....as I SEEK Him and His will for me.**

Hebr. 11:6 *"he who comes to God must believe that He is, and that He is a REWARDER of those who diligently seek Him."*

> **Treasury of David[25], Psalm 19:   God's promise of inward confidence and peace when He trains me**
> *"God didn't say 'by keeping them', but 'in keeping them': Righteousness has its own reward...and a quiet conscience is in itself no slender reward for obedience, though few men think so and act accordingly."*
>   Hebrews 12:11 *"...no discipline seems to be joyful for the present, but grievous; nevertheless, afterward it yields the peaceable fruit of righteousness to those who have been trained by it."*

Psalm 9:10 *"...those who know Your name will put their trust in You; You, Lord, have not forsaken those who SEEK You."*

Psalm 27:1,8 *"The Lord is my light and my salvation; whom shall I fear? The Lord is the strength of my life; of whom shall I be afraid? When You said, 'Seek My face,' my heart said to You, 'Your face, Lord, I will seek.'"*

Jeremiah 29:11-13 (Proverbs 3:5-6) *"...I know the thoughts that I think toward you," says the Lord, "thoughts of peace and not of evil, to give you a future and a hope. Then you will call upon Me and go and pray to Me, and I will listen to you. And you will SEEK Me and find Me, when you search for Me with ALL YOUR HEART."*

Isaiah 30:15 *"...thus says the Lord God, the Holy One of Israel: 'In returning and rest you shall be saved; in quietness and confidence shall be your strength.'"*

Romans 8:28 *"...we KNOW that all things work together for good to those who love God, to those who are the called according to His purpose..."*

> Adrien Rogers: *"People who spend their lives seeking happiness never find it. God says to find joy and success in life, seek His righteousness (Joshua 1:7-8, Matt. 5:6, 6:33)."*

Ps 119:10 *"With my whole heart I have SOUGHT You; Oh, let me not wander from Your commandments!"*

PSALM 19:12-14   Christian "WISDOM" = walking daily in *His Light*   3.9

"Who can understand his errors? Cleanse me from ①SECRET FAULTS. Keep back Your servant also from ②PRESUMPTUOUS SINS; let them not have dominion over me. Then I shall be blameless, and I shall be innocent of much transgression. Let the ③WORDS OF MY MOUTH and the ③MEDITATION OF MY HEART be acceptable in Your sight, O Lord my strength and my Redeemer."

- After David surveys God's work (creation) and word (Scripture), he goes to Ps 19's 3rd book: his conscience.
- As in the 1st 2 books, God is the author. I don't even know myself, but He does (1Corin. 13:12, Jerem. 17:9-10).
- <u>concession</u>: my life is full of errors - many I don't even know I'm doing (Isaiah 53:6, Ps 119:176, Rom. 7:18)
- <u>confession</u>: I can't cleanse myself from the sin that seeks to dominate me – I am dependent on God, who knows the true intentions of my heart behind my words and actions, to forgive me as I come to Him in repentance.
- C.H. Spurgeon[25]: *"Who can tell how often he offends God? No man. The hairs of a man's head may be told, the stars appear in multitude, but no arithmetic can number our sins. Before we can recount 1,000 we shall commit 10,000 more….like Hydra's head, while we are cutting off 20 by repentance, we find 100 more grown up."*

- <u>The desire of a person seeking God's standard of holiness</u> =
- Romans 7:14-15 = to be cleansed and delivered from the private (secret) sins, that continually work within me.
- Acts 24:16 = to have a conscience (inward man) that doesn't offend God nor sin against fellow man.
- Jerem. 17:5, Prov. 3:5-6 = to put no confidence in my own ability; to completely surrender to God's will for me.

- <u>Sin's desire</u>: dominate me (Gen. 4:7), ensnare and destroy me in its cycle (Heb.12:1, 1Peter 5:8).

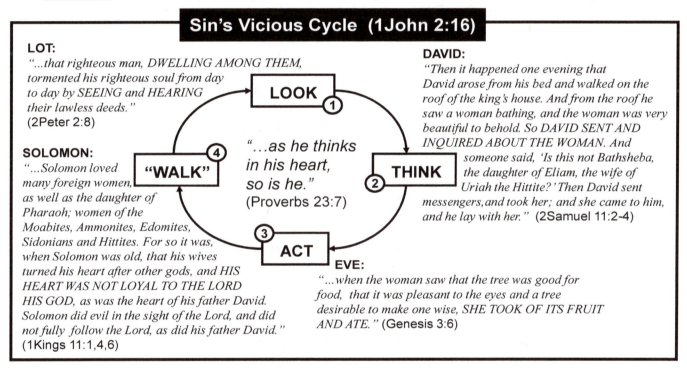

① **Psalm 19:12 = "Secret Faults"** (Numbers 15:22-26 = unintentional) → Paul's sin of *ignorance*
1Timothy 1:12-15   why Paul is "chief among sinners" *"…I obtained mercy because I did it IGNORANTLY in unbelief."*
Acts 8:1,3 (Acts 9:1-2)   Paul ruthlessly murdered innocent Christians *"As for Saul, he made havoc of the church, entering every house, and dragging off men and women, committing them to prison."*

- J. MacArthur[27]: Paul's former life before Christ
- "Paul was a Pharisee ("separated ones"): a small (≈ 6,000), legalistic sect of the Jews known for rigidly adhering to the law. Their goal: apply OT directly to life through a complex system of tradition and works righteousness.
- Paul considered himself blameless and completely righteous in the eyes of God and man by his keeping of the Law (Phil. 3:6). He outwardly kept the Law, but he was sinful and self-righteous. He was a proud and lost legalist.
- Paul's zeal for his religious beliefs led him to full-scale attack of the early church (Phil. 3:6): to the Jew, "zeal" was the highest single virtue of religion. It combines love and hate. Because Paul loved Judaism, he hated whatever might threaten it. So the elimination of the early Christians became his passion.
- Jesus and John the Baptist called Pharisees "snakes", "hypocrites", "fools", "blind guides" (Matt. 3:7, 23:13-33).

Paul's humiliation and exaltation:	
Acts 9:2-9	Christ brings this arrogant Pharisee "Saul" to his knees.
Galatians 2:20	Saul's former ignorance is replaced with the "light" of the knowledge of Christ's love for Him.
Phil. 3:7-14	"Paul", a new man, has a new "zeal": he forgets his past, pressing on to know Jesus.

② **Psalm 19:13 = "Presumptuous Sins"** (Numbers 15:30-31 = "deliberate") ➔ David's *premeditated* sins

2Sam. 11:3-5,14-15,26-27 adultery and murder *"the thing that David had done was evil in the eyes of the Lord."*
2Samuel 12:1,9-10,12,14 David's sin finds him out *"...you did it secretly, but I will do this thing before all Israel..."*

- J. MacArthur[27]: David's self-centered actions before God's conviction
- "To intensify the sin of adultery, both OT and NT state Bathsheba was Uriah's wife (2Sam. 12:10, Matt.1:6).
- Eliam (father of Bathsheba) and Uriah (husband of Bathsheba) were "mighty men of David" (2Sam. 23:34,39), making David's sins even more detestable since he planned them against some of his most trusted men.
- David failed twice to cover up his adultery, when Uriah refused to go home to Bathsheba and lay with her (2Sam. 11:6-13). In frustration and panic he plots Uriah's murder, having Uriah deliver his own death warrant.
- Graphic Proof = the extremes people go to pursue sin and in the absence of restraining grace (David knew the Law: Exodus 20:13-14, Levit. 24:17; he understood he was directly breaking God's word to get what he wanted)."

David's humiliation and exaltation:	
2Sam. 12:1-14	God exposes his premeditated murder and adultery, pronouncing judgment on his household.
Psalm 51	David worships the Lord in a prayer of *Repentance* for what he did to Uriah and Bathsheba.
Psalm 32	David worships the Lord in a prayer of *Joy for Forgiveness* for what he did.

③ **Psalm 19:14 = "Mouth & Heart"** (Jeremiah 17:9 = "out of a wicked heart") ➔ Peter's *denial* of Christ

Matthew 26:33-35 Peter boasts he will never betray Jesus *"...Even if I have to die with You, I will not deny You!"*
Matthew 26:40-41,55-56 Peter (and all the disciples) forsake Jesus *"...then all the disciples forsook Him and fled."*
Matthew 26:69-75 Peter "calls down curses" in an effort to convince the crowd that he doesn't even know Him.

- J. MacArthur[27]: Peter's self-centered life before Christ's crucifixion
  - "As long as Jesus was nearby, Peter was full of courage, doing and saying the miraculous
  - Matthew 14:22-23 Peter walks on water.
  - Matthew 16:13-20 Peter proclaims Jesus is the Christ.
  - Matthew 26:47-54 Peter takes on the Roman legions when they try to take Jesus."

Peter's humiliation and exaltation:	
Matthew 26:69-75	When Peter gets separated from Jesus, he is a failure (apart from Jesus, he's a coward).
John 21:15-19	Jesus confronts Peter directly with the question of the depth of his love for Him.
Acts 4:1-13	Peter, a new man in Christ, has a new "zeal": he is filled with the power of the Holy Spirit.

If these great saints made such terrible mistakes: what chance do I have?

The goal of the Christian life = live my life according to God's wisdom – but how?

1. I must **surrender** myself: trust the control of my life to the Lord Jesus Christ, who is the wisdom of God incarnate (1Corinthians 1:24 and Colossians 2:2-3).
2. I must **apply** myself: Proverbs 2:1-4 tells me the steps to acquiring God's wisdom
   a) focus your attention ("incline your ear")
   b) apply yourself fully ("apply your heart to understanding")
   c) hunger to understand ("cry out for discernment, lift up your voice for understanding")
   d) diligently seek out the meaning ("seek her as silver, and search for her as for hidden treasure")
3. I must **examine** myself: Galatians 6:1-8 warns me not to deceive myself – I will reap whatever I sow.
4. I must **discipline** myself: Ps 119:9-11 calls me to hide His sword (Eph. 6:17) in my heart : this is a *lifestyle*.

> **We often forget that there is a difference between worldly wisdom and God's wisdom**
> Proverbs 21:30 *"There is no wisdom or understanding or counsel against THE LORD."*
> Psalm 90:12   *"...TEACH us to NUMBER OUR DAYS, that we may gain a heart of wisdom."*

Chapter 4   Argument #5 for God = *DESIGN* in Animal Kingdom

4.1

Order, Complexity and Precision in Living Organisms infer an Intelligent Designer

> "Premise #1 =   Order, Complexity and Precision in living systems infer an intelligent design.
> Premise #2 =   There is order, complexity and precision in living organisms.
> Conclusion =   Therefore, there must be a Intelligent Designer of Life."

JOB 12:7,9 *"...ask the BEASTS, and THEY WILL TEACH YOU; and the BIRDS OF THE AIR, and THEY WILL TELL YOU... Who among all these does not know that the HAND OF THE LORD HAS DONE THIS, in whose hand is the life of every living thing, and the breath of all mankind?"*

#1) BAT ECHOLOCATION

Close to 1,000 species of bats exist worldwide, with amazing features that man has studied and learned from, to create technologies we use everyday. Job 12 tells man to study His animals, and their unique designs will TEACH us how to create new technologies that we as His special creations can use.

The largest bat colony on earth, with a population reaching 50 million, lives in America. Freetails fly at 60 mph, and as high as 10,000 feet. It is so large that it can be easily observed by airport radar

1) <u>Bats are the only mammals that fly</u>: Bats' wings are highly articulated, with more than two dozen independent joints and a thin flexible membrane covering them. The theory that the bats' unique wing structure evolved from some type of gliding squirrel-like animal has no scientific basis at all. Their wings are specially designed for flight.

2) <u>Bats hang upside down</u>: You won't find any "early ancestor" that did this (it's a totally unique trait of bats). Hanging upside down allows them to do 2 things easily:

(a) they can takeoff - bats' wings can't lift them into flight from a dead stop, and their hind legs are so small and underdeveloped that they can't run to build up takeoff speed. By hanging upside down, they fall into flight).

(b) they conserve energy - a bat's talons are connected to their upper body by tendons, not muscle, so they hang upside down without exerting any energy (unlike other animals, who have muscles that contract when grasping things... and this takes energy and tires the muscles over time). A bat finds something to grip, relaxes its body. Its own weight pulls down on the tendons connected to the talons, locking the talon joints, and the bat's weight keeps them closed. The bat only has to exert energy to release its grip, flexing muscles that pull its talons open.

3) <u>Bats have **ECHOLOCATION**</u>: Bats send out high-pitched sound waves (undetectable by the human ear) using their mouth or nose. When the sound hits an object an echo comes back to the bat for analysis. The bats know the *direction* and *angle* of the echo as it comes back from the object, as well as the *time* it takes for the echo to return. So, now the bat knows where the echoes are coming from AND how far away things are. The echolocation system in bats is so precise that it can identify a tiny insect's size, shape, texture and exact location from the sound of its echo. In fact, it's so precise that the bat can avoid obstacles no wider than a piece of thread. Sound travels very fast, so this happens almost instantly. Since the bats also are very fast they know exactly where they are while they are flying blind.

RADAR = Bats taught us echolocation – It stands for **RA**dio **D**etecting **A**nd **R**anging. Radar uses radio waves to bounce off of objects, just like bats use sound waves. Radar is used today in many areas of our lives (airports track airplanes by radar, weathermen use a form of radar known as Doppler radar to track rain, snow, storms, tornadoes and hurricanes). By the way.... dolphins and whales taught man echolocation underwater – it's called **SONAR** (**SO**und **NA**vigation **R**anging). Have you ever seen the movie "U571", about a German submarine captured by American seamen and their race to escape their German pursuers? The Germans use depth charges to try and destroy the captured sub. How do they know where to drop the charges? Or the movie "The Hunt for Red October", where a Russian submarine captain defects and the American submarine pursuing it locates it underwater in a vast ocean. How did the Americans find it? Sonar... which man learned from animals. If you've ever used a fish-finder, its sonar technology used to find fish and to know how deep the water is.

How RADAR Works = Radar copies bats' echolocation – it's made up of two parts. A <u>transmitter</u> sends out very powerful sound waves, and a super-sensitive <u>receiver</u> decodes the size, shape, and location of the object from the returning sound wave after it bounces off it.

But at first we couldn't get radar to work because the receiver couldn't withstand the powerful signal from the transmitter (receivers are ultra-sensitive to sound, and the transmitter's outgoing signal simply overwhelmed it). What scientists figured out: they had to design in a *fast switch* that turns the sensitive receiver off every time a radar pulse is sent out. Where did scientists learn this technology?

<u>**We have to give God the glory for the bat**</u> = Bats have the "fast switch" built in to the design, that ensures their radar system works. Muscles in their ears are the receivers for the echoes, and these muscles close the ears for split seconds when the bats are sending out their high pitched signals! Without this feature, the bat's navigational system would be useless. Below is information illustrating not only how amazing the bats' echolocation system is, but also how much more precise it is compared to anything man has attempted to make as we imitate the bat.

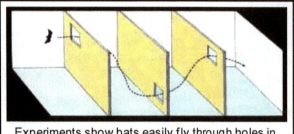

Experiments show bats easily fly through holes in walls to locate their prey... in complete darkness.

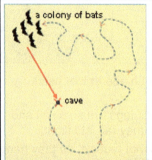

Bats wander around once they leave their cave, but they always fly back to their cave in a straight route from wherever they are. It is incredible how they are able to navigate so precisely back to the cave from no matter where they are.

	BAT (eptesicus)	RADAR (SCR-268)	RADAR (AN/APS-10)	SONAR QCS - T
Weight of system (kg)	0,012	12,000	90	450
Peak Power Output (W)	0.00001	75,000	10,000	600
Dimetre of Target (m)	0.01	5	3	5
Echolocation Efficiency Index	2×10^9	6×10^{-5}	3×10^{-2}	2×10^{-3}
Relative Figure of Merit	1	3×10^{-14}	$1,5 \times 10^{-11}$	10^{-12}

The bats' echolocation is millions of times more efficient and accurate than manmade radar and sonar. The table above clearly illustrates these properties. "Echolocation efficiency index" is range divided by the product weight times power times target diameter. "Relative figure of merit" compares the echolocation efficiency indexes with the bat as 1.

According to Darwin, the bat "figured out" through natural selection, over millions of years, that it needed this ability... and through selective adaptation this favorable trait of echolocation gradually developed as the bat grew the muscles and related tissue to do the job as it struggled to survive.   *REALLY???*

So these brilliant scientists copy God's technology for use in their man-made radar, but they can't get God's design to work repeatedly with precision without *engineering it in*. So the evidence is right in front of them: It takes *EXTERNAL INFORMATION* to be added to a system to create precision in functionality, or you won't get the desired output.

The bats' radar system wasn't made over time by the bat. **Job 12** tells us to look to the Lord for the Source of the external information, and **Romans 1:20** says we can *CLEARLY SEE* the invisible qualities of His character, by simply studying the things He has made (like the bat).

<u>Here's the problem with man</u>: when we refuse to give Him the glory, **Romans 1:21-22** says we may profess to those around us that we're really brilliant, but we end up looking really foolish in the theories we make up (i.e., evolution is the source for the bats' echolocation). Our "science" is foolishness even to children (they can tell that our theories don't make any common sense).

#2) GODWIT MIGRATION[33] (Jeremiah 8:7, Job 39:26)

"During the 2012 Olympics, Usain Bolt set Olympic and World records in the 100 and 200 meters, and the 4x100 relay. A human running at a speed of close to thirty miles per hour is quite impressive, but neither Usain Bolt nor any other human can maintain such a speed for more than a few seconds. Marathon runners may be able to run 26.2 miles without stopping, but no one averages more than 13 miles per hour while running great distances. Although the human body is a meticulously designed 'machine', which functions perfectly for its intended purpose on Earth, there are limits to what a person can do.

When these limits are compared to the speed and distance a particular bird flew some time ago, one gains a greater appreciation for God's wondrous creation.

In February 2007, scientists from the U.S. Geological Survey fitted 16 shorebirds, known as bar-tailed godwits, with satellite transmitters. One of the godwits, dubbed E7, made its way from New Zealand to Alaska over the next three months, flying 9,340 miles with one five-week-long layover near the North Korea-China border. After nearly four months, the godwit began its uninterrupted flight back to New Zealand. Amazingly, this little bird, which normally weighs less than one pound, flew **7,145 miles in nine days without stopping, averaging 34.8 mph**.

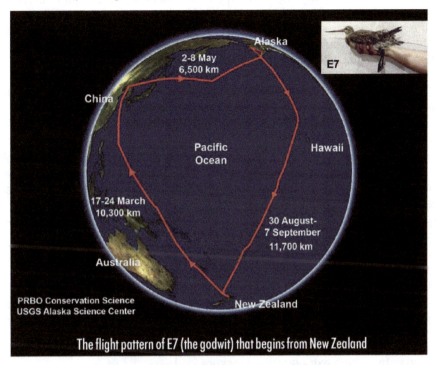

The flight pattern of E7 (the godwit) that begins from New Zealand

Without taking a break to eat, drink, or rest, the godwit flew 'the equivalent of making a roundtrip flight between New York and San Francisco, and then flying back again to San Francisco without ever touching down'. Equally impressive, the godwit's approximately 16,500-mile, roundtrip journey ended where it began. Without a map, a compass, or even a parent, godwits can fly tens of thousands of miles without getting lost.

Scientists have studied the migration of birds for decades and still cannot adequately explain this 'age-old riddle'. Their stamina and sense of direction is mind-boggling. We know more about how birds might achieve their epic flights around the world, but there are still far more mysteries than there are explanations. The tiny songbird that reappeared to build its nest in the apple tree outside your window—and we know from banding that it can indeed be exactly the same bird—has been to South America and back since you saw it last. How can that be?

Try as they might, evolutionists attempting to explain the complexities of bird migration can only offer woeful (and often contradictory) theories. How can a person reasonably conclude that non-intelligence, plus time, plus chance, results in a one-pound, bar-tailed godwit repeatedly, year after year, flying the exact same route of 7,145 miles in nine days without stopping for food, water, or rest?

The awe and wonder should be directed toward neither mindless evolution nor the birds themselves, but to the 'great and awesome God' (Daniel 9:4) who has done 'wondrous works' and 'awesome things' (Psalm 106:22), including endowing birds with the amazing trait we call "instinct." Truly, it is not by evolution or man's wisdom that a bird 'soars, stretching his wings toward the south' (Job 39:26). Rather, 'the stork in the sky knows her seasons; and the turtledove and the swift and the thrush observe the time of their migration' (Jeremiah 8:7, NASB), because all-knowing, all-powerful Jehovah is the Creator of them all."

#3) GIRAFFE BLOOD CIRCULATION[34]

"The height of an 18-foot giraffe, the tallest of all land animals, is quite daunting. The clumsy-looking giraffe's ability to run 34 miles per hour is very impressive. Its minimal sleep requirements—only about 30 minutes a day, often broken up into several short naps—and its ability to go weeks without drinking is remarkable. Its 18-inch, prehensile tongue, eight-foot-long tail, and six-foot-tall newborns are all very striking. Most remarkable, however, is the design of the giraffe's **circulatory system**.

A giraffe's brain is about eight feet higher than its heart. In order to get blood from its heart up to its brain, a giraffe must have an enormous heart that can pump blood extremely hard against gravity. What's more, it must maintain such blood pressure as long as the giraffe's neck is vertically in the air.

This long-necked mammal is equipped with a two-foot-long, twenty-plus-pound, thick-walled heart that is large enough and strong enough to pump blood eight feet high—creating blood pressure that is about twice that of any other large mammal, and as much as three times that of the average person.

But what about when a giraffe suddenly lowers its head several feet *below* its heart to get a drink of water? What happens to all of the blood that the heart normally pumps so powerfully against gravity to the brain? If the design of the giraffe were merely left up to time and chance, the first time a giraffe tried to lower its neck to get a drink of water, the heart would pump so much blood to the brain that blood vessels in the brain would explode, or the brain would fill up with blood so quickly that the giraffe would pass out. How does the giraffe keep from having brain bleeds, or from feeling woozy and passing out every time it bends down and raises back up? A *National Geographic* article on giraffes explains: 'To withstand the surge of blood to and from the brain as its neck sweeps up and down, the giraffe has developed control valves in the jugular veins and a special network of blood vessels in its head. Known as the **rete mirabile caroticum**—wonder net of the carotids—this circulatory buffer keeps blood pressure constant in the brain'.

A giraffe has intricate valves in its jugular veins that help control how much blood gets to the brain during those times when a giraffe has its head lowered. Working together with these valves is a network of blood vessels that controls the flow of blood into the head. Then, when the head is raised, the same net counters the danger of blackouts from reduced blood pressure.

One might wonder how giraffes, which stand on their feet most of the day and have such high blood pressure, keep their lower extremities from pooling with blood. The fact is, even though the blood vessels in the lower legs are under great pressure (because of the weight of fluid pressing down on them), giraffes have a very tight sheath of thick skin over their lower limbs that maintains high extravascular pressure. Similar to a fighter pilot's G-suit that exerts pressure on the body and legs of the wearer under high acceleration and prevents blackout…. leakage from the capillaries in the giraffe's legs, due to high blood pressure, is also probably prevented by a similar pressure of the tissue fluid outside the cells. In addition, the walls of the giraffe's arteries are thicker than those in any other mammal.

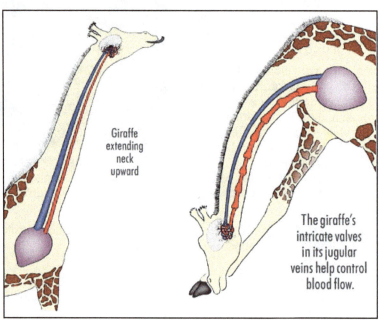

Giraffe extending neck upward

The giraffe's intricate valves in its jugular veins help control blood flow.

So, the giraffe has:
1) a complex pressure-regulation system,
2) unique "valves" that prevent overpressure when it lowers its head,
3) a network of blood vessels that helps stabilize blood pressure as the giraffe moves its neck up and down,
4) a heart powerful enough to send an adequate amount of blood eight feet upwards against gravity,
5) arteries in the lower part of its body thick enough to withstand the high blood pressure,
6) skin tight enough to force blood back upward and keep capillaries in its lower extremities from bursting, and
7) oversized lungs to hold 12 gallons of air, that compensate for the volume of dead air in its 10-foot long trachea (without this extra air-pumping capacity a giraffe would breathe the same used air over and over).

National Geographic would have us believe 'nature' provided giraffes with this 'special equipment'. Supposedly, giraffes' specialized, necessary, 'unique' control valves are 'remarkable adaptations' that 'developed'. In other words, multiplied millions of years of evolution have modified the giraffe's anatomy to allow this stretched-version mammal to function. How do the mindless, purposeless, random processes of time and chance adequately explain unique valves, a complex pressure-regulation system, a wonder net that keeps blood pressure constant in the brain (whether the giraffe's neck is raised or lowered), a heart, lungs, and arteries all just the right size, etc.? And how did all of these sophisticated body parts came about simultaneously?

The amazingly intricate design of the giraffe's circulatory system, as well as the rest of its anatomy and physiology, demand a better explanation than the random, chance processes of evolution. The fact is, the giraffe is brilliantly designed—a wonder of God's creation."

#4) CAMEL BLOOD CELLS[34]

"Camels belong to the family Camelidae, along with their new-world relatives llamas and alpacas, and they are divided into two species: *Camelus bactrianus*, or Bactrian camel, and *Camelus dromedarius*, or Dromedary camel. The Dromedary, also called the Arabian camel, has long been referred to by Bedouins as 'God's gift'.

A camel's thick eyebrows and double row of eyelashes keep sand out of its eyes. These are just two amazing features God designed for the camel to survive in its post-Fall habitat. From their nose to their feet, camels are perfectly suited to their desert environments: the harsh, hot winds and sand of the deserts of Africa, the Middle East, and Asia.

To protect them from sandstorms, camels were given nostrils that they can open and close; they also have bushy eyebrows, fur-lined ears, and double rows of curly eyelashes for the same protective purpose. The tough, leathery skin on their knees pads the joints as they kneel, and their special foot pads spread as they walk, to keep them from sinking into the sand. Even more remarkable is the camels' ability to withstand the intense, arid heat of the desert. Unlike any other mammal, camels can raise and lower their own body temperature, thereby conserving precious water.

Camels also have a unique metabolism that allows them to store enormous amounts of water in their bloodstream, while **oval-shaped red blood cells**, exclusive to the camel, tolerate both dehydration (lack of water) and osmosis (storing water). Camels can drink more than twenty gallons of water in a ten-minute period—a feat that would kill almost any other mammal—then store the water in their blood for up to two weeks.

The Dromedary camel is designed for the arid deserts of Africa and the Middle East. You can tell a Dromedary from a Bactrian by the number of humps the camel has and the length of the camel's hair. The long, shaggy hair of this Bactrian camel makes it suited for its life in the deserts of northern India.

Two obvious differences between the Dromedary and the Bactrian camels are the number of humps and the length of their hair. A one-hump camel is a Dromedary, and a two-hump camel is a Bactrian. The Dromedary has relatively short hair, enabling it to live in the extreme heat of the Arabian Desert. The Bactrian camel has long, shaggy hair, better suited for the cooler temperatures of Asia.

The Dromedary camel is designed for the arid deserts of Africa and the Middle East. You can tell a Dromedary from a Bactrian by the number of humps the camel has and the length of the camel's hair

The long, shaggy hair of this Bactrian camel makes it suited for its life in the deserts of northern India

A camel's **hump**, or humps, once popularly thought to contain water, in fact contain fat, which is used as fuel when food is scarce. Metabolizing this stored fat is also how camels utilize the water stored in their bloodstream. So, the misconception that the hump contains water is not so far from the truth after all! Camels can live without food for up to a month, by which time their hump, or humps, have become floppy and fallen to one side. However, the hump is restored when camels feed and build up their fat storage.

But how did the camel come to be suited for such a harsh, hot, sandy environment? A common misconception among evolutionists is that creationists believe God created each animal exactly as we see it today. But if this were true, many of the camel's design features would have been at best superfluous in the "very good" world of the Garden of Eden.

In Genesis 1:24, God said, *'Let the land produce living creatures according to their kinds'* (NIV). The original camel 'kind' would have contained in its genetic code the information to produce 'modern' camels, as well as their relatives, such as the llama. God, in His omniscience, may have placed in His original perfect creation everything it would need to survive in a world cursed by sin.

The camel's extraordinary tale of survival in one of the harshest climates is a beautiful testimony to the foreknowledge and amazing creativity of an infinite God who cares deeply about His creation."

Melinda Christian, a staff member of Answers in Genesis for the past six years, graduated from Calvary Bible College in Kansas City, Missouri. Melinda is an avid writer and has also edited a number of recent AiG publications.

#5) BOMBARDIER BEETLE DEFENSE SYSTEM

Genesis 1:24-25 *"God said, 'Let the earth bring forth the living creature according to its kind; cattle and CREEPING THING and beast of the earth, each according to its kind', and it was so. And God made the beast of the earth according to its kind, cattle according to its kind, and everything that CREEPS ON THE EARTH according to its kind. And God saw that it was good."*

John MacArthur ('The Battle for the Beginning')[7]: *"The Bombardier beetle is found mainly in the deserts of New Mexico. It was created with a unique defense mechanism that is impossible to explain by evolutionary theory.*

The beetle produces two chemicals in separate reservoirs in its abdomen. The two chemicals, hydroquinone and hydrogen peroxide, are harmless by themselves but potentially explosive when combined. When attacked, the beetle releases the chemicals through a movable jet at the rear of its abdomen. Catalytic **enzymes** *in a tiny reaction chamber just inside the expulsion valve set the chemical reaction in motion, and at precisely the right moment, the beetle aims his abdomen turret and releases the explosive mixture in the face of its predator.*

The combined chemicals instantly reach the temperature of boiling water, creating a surprise and a deterrent that is powerful enough to discourage most predators.

The beetle can fire up to five shots in rapid succession, and he instinctively knows how to time the explosion so that it occurs a moment after the chemicals are expelled, never in the reaction chamber where it would destroy the beetle.

How does the beetle know how to do this? Could such a complex system possibly have developed through some natural evolutionary process?

Consider what all the bombardier beetle's defense system entails: The beetle must be able to produce just the right chemicals, keep them in **separate reservoirs**, *and bring them together at the right time with the necessary catalytic enzymes. He must also possess all the equipment and ability necessary to combine the explosives, aim the mixture accurately, and fire precisely before the moment of explosion.*

Is it reasonable to think an evolving creature could develop such a system, with so many interdependent parts, through a process of individual, random genetic changes? The answer is clear: the bombardier beetle is the product of intelligent design."

Creation Magazine, "The Amazing Bombardier Beetle", Dec. 1, 1989

"The tiny bombardier beetle could not possibly have evolved. His defense mechanism is amazingly complicated, and could only have been created with all the parts working together perfectly. From twin 'exhaust tubes' at his tail, this beetle fires into the face of his enemies boiling-hot noxious gases with a loud pop. How can this be?

German chemist Dr Schildknecht discovered that the beetle mixes two chemicals (hydrogen peroxide and hydroquinone) which would usually form a dirty ugly mixture. The well-designed beetle uses a special **'inhibitor'** chemical to keep the mixture from reacting. How then can the explosion instantaneously occur when needed?

Dr Schildknecht discovered that in the beetle's specially designed combustion tubes are two **enzymes** called catalase and peroxidase which make chemical reactions go millions of times faster. These chemicals catalyze the extremely rapid decomposition of hydrogen peroxide into water and oxygen and the oxidation of hydroquinone into quinone, causing them to violently react and explode.

Common sense tells us that this amazing little insect cannon which can fire four or five 'bombs' in succession could not have evolved piece by piece. Explosive chemicals, inhibitor, enzymes, glands, combustion tubes, sensory communication, muscles to direct the combustion tubes and reflex nervous systems—all had to work perfectly the **very first time ('irreducible complexity')**."

Chapter 5   Argument #6 for God = *IRREDUCIBLE COMPLEXITY*   5.1
Precise Biochemical Processes in Living Organisms infer an Intelligent Designer

> *"Premise #1 = Irreducibly Complex systems or processes infer an intelligent design.*
> *Premise #2 = There is irreducible complexity in the biochemical makeup of living organisms.*
> *Conclusion = Therefore, there must be a Intelligent Designer of Life."*

PSALM 139:1-4   God's OMNISCIENCE = He knows me perfectly

vs. 1 *"Lord, You have ①SEARCHED me and ②KNOWN me."*

① SEARCHED = *"châqar"* = to examine intimately; to mine, as in searching for precious metals

God doesn't just review what's going on within me – He *mines* me like precious gold every moment of everyday (He scrutinizes my every thought and action in the same way He regulates the details of the universe)

② KNOWN = *"yâda"* = to have intimate knowledge through a relationship (kinsman)

David doesn't say "Lord, You know all things"….but, "You know *me*" (God knows and understands me); David uses the past tense: God's infallible knowledge of me has always existed, and continues to this day.

Isaiah 49:14-16   Another aspect of God's Character = DEVOTION

"But Zion said, 'The Lord has forsaken me, and my Lord has forgotten me.' Can a woman forget her nursing child, and not have compassion on the son of her womb? Surely they may forget, yet I will not forget you. See, I have inscribed you on the palms of My hands; your walls are continually before Me."

God explains His *DEVOTION* to Israel by using their Jewish custom of puncturing their hands with a symbol of their city and temple (Exodus 13:9); and the seal of devotion between two lovers (Song of Solomon 8:6).

---

vs. 2-4 *"You ①KNOW my sitting down and my rising up; You ③UNDERSTAND my thought afar off. You ④COMPREHEND my path and my lying down, and are acquainted with all my ways. For there is not a word on my tongue, but behold, O Lord, You ②KNOW it altogether."*

③ UNDERSTAND = *"bîyn"* = discern, fully grasp intellectually

④ COMPREHEND = *"zârâh"* = winnow or sift (similar to verse 1, for "search" or "mine"); *"all my ways"* extends to:

<u>my every movement</u> (*"sitting down and rising up"*) = any action is seen, known, and read by Jehovah my Lord.
<u>my thoughts</u> (*"…afar off"*) = He knows what I am thinking and what I will think 15 seconds or 15 years later.
<u>my actions</u> (*"my path and my lying down, all my ways"*) = whether it's in public, private, social…
<u>my words</u> (*"You know each word on my tongue altogether"*) = before I speak them, He knows them in my heart.

YAHWEH ROI   "The God who SEES and KNOWS me"

Genesis 16:13   *"Then she called the name of the Lord who spoke to her, YAHWEH ROI, for she said 'Have I also here seen Him who sees me?'"*

Prov. 15:3   *"The eyes of the Lord are in every place, keeping watch on the evil and the good."*

2Chron. 16:9   *"For the eyes of the Lord run to and fro throughout the whole earth, to show Himself strong on behalf of those whose heart is loyal to Him."*

Psalm 139:16   *"Your eyes saw my substance, being yet unformed."*

C.H. Spurgeon[25]: God's perfection knowledge of me   *"God can do nothing imperfectly; He knows everything perfectly, and He knows everything perfectly at once. All the powers of the Godhead are solely employed in the observation and examination of the conduct of one individual. Thus God, without confusion, beholds as distinctly the actions of every man, as if that man were the only created being, and the Godhead were solely employed in observing him. Let this thought fill your mind with awe and with remorse."*

John 2:23-25 → Jesus = only He sees and knows the real me

"Now when He was in Jerusalem at the Passover, during the feast, many believed in His name when they saw signs which He did. But Jesus did not commit Himself to them, because He knew all men, and had no need that anyone would testify of man, for HE KNEW WHAT WAS IN MAN."

Irreducible Complexity (IC): Reveals *Design*, Falsifies "*Natural Selection*"

Charles Darwin[1]: *"If it could be demonstrated that any complex organ existed which could not possibly have been formed by numerous, successive, slight modifications, my theory would absolutely break down."*

The argument that certain biological systems are too complex to have evolved from simpler, or "less complete" predecessors, and are also too complex to have arisen naturally through chance mutations. It supports the idea that an intelligent designer was involved in the creation of life (the theory of evolution requires no designer).

The founder of IC as it applies to **Intelligent Design**, biochemistry professor Michael Behe, defines an irreducibly complex system as one "composed of several well-matched, interacting parts that contribute to the basic function, wherein the removal of any one of the parts causes the system to effectively cease functioning". Examples are the complexity of the eye, the blood clotting cascade, or the motor in a cell's flagellum.

Michael Behe[16]: *"Irreducibly complex systems are very difficult to form by successive modifications. "*

"Some systems seem very difficult to form by such successive modifications -- I call them irreducibly complex. An everyday example of an irreducibly complex system is the humble mousetrap. It consists of (1) a flat wooden platform or base; (2) a metal hammer, which crushes the mouse; (3) a spring with extended ends to power the hammer; (4) a catch that releases the spring; and (5) a metal bar that connects to the catch and holds the hammer back. You can't catch a mouse with just a platform, then add a spring and catch a few more mice, then add a holding bar and catch a few more. All the pieces have to be in place before you catch *any* mice. "

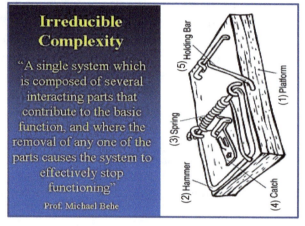

Irreducible Complexity
"A single system which is composed of several interacting parts that contribute to the basic function, and where the removal of any one of the parts causes the system to effectively stop functioning"
Prof. Michael Behe

Michael Behe[16]: *"Natural selection can only choose among systems that are already working, so irreducibly complex biological systems pose a powerful challenge to Darwinian theory."*

"Irreducibly complex systems appear very unlikely to be produced by numerous, successive, slight modifications of prior systems, because any precursor that was missing a crucial part could not function. Natural selection can only choose among systems that are already working, so the existence in nature of irreducibly complex biological systems poses a powerful challenge to Darwinian theory."

N. Pearcey[28]: Molecular Biology and IC: A powerful combination that breaks down Evolution

"...his (Darwin) theory utterly fails to account for it (IC). Why? Because a system of coordinated, interlocking parts like this can only operate after all the pieces are in place – which means they must appear simultaneously, not by any gradual, piece-by-piece process. Behe coined the term 'irreducible complexity' to refer to the minimum level of complexity that must be present before such a tightly integrated system can function at all.

Natural selection is said to work on tiny, random improvements in function – so it does not kick in until there is at least *some* function to select from. But irreducibly complex systems don't have *any* function until a minimum number of parts are in place – so those parts themselves cannot be products of natural selection. A minimum number of interacting pieces must be present before natural selection even begins to operate.

In Darwin's day, scientists knew next to nothing about biochemistry. Living things were **'black boxes'**, their inside workings a mystery. It was easy to speculate about large-scale scenarios where fins gradually turned into legs, or legs into wings, since no one had a clue as to have limbs and organs actually worked from the inside. It's as though we were to ask how a stereo system is made and the answer was: by plugging a set of speakers into an amplifier and adding a CD player, radio receiver, and tape deck. What we really want to know is how things like speakers and CD players themselves were assembled. What is *inside* those plastic boxes?

Today, through the use of the **electron microscope**, the 'black box' of the cell has been opened, and biologists are intimately familiar with its inside workings. The older broad-stroke speculations about fins becoming legs won't cut it anymore. Today any theory of life's origin must explain **molecular systems**.

Critics charge that IC is an argument from 'personal incredulity'. But they are missing the point. IC is a *logical* argument about how wholes are constructed from parts. An **aggregate** structure, like a sand pile, can be built up gradually by adding a piece at a time – one grain of sand after another. But an **organized** structure, like a computer, is built according to a pre-existing blueprint or design. Each interlocking piece is structured to contribute to the functioning of the whole – which is possible only after a minimal number of pieces are in place.

The logical question: are living structures aggregates or organized wholes? The answer is clear: not only on the level of body systems, but also within each tiny cell, living structures are incredibly complex organized wholes. The most plausible theory, then, is that the pieces were put together according to a preexisting blueprint."

"Darwin's Black Box" by Dr. Michael Behe[16]

Dr. Michael J. Behe is an American biochemist currently serving as Professor of Biochemistry at Lehigh University. He is best known for his argument of Irreducible Complexity (IC) as evidence for intelligent design in the complexity we now find in biochemical systems. Dr. Behe also serves as Senior Fellow on the Discovery Institute's Center for Science and Culture, and is one of the strongest proponents of Intelligent Design Theory.

Darwin's Black Box –
The Biochemical Challenge to Evolution

"There is an elephant in the roomful of scientists who are trying to explain the development of life. The elephant is labeled 'intelligent design.'

Life on earth at its most fundamental level, in its most critical components, is the product of intelligent activity." Michael Behe, Page 193

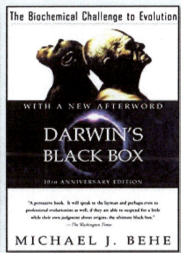

"For the Darwinian theory of evolution to be true, it has to account for the molecular structure of life. It is the purpose of this book to show that it does not." (page 25)

"Life is lived in the details, and it is molecules that handle life's details. The cumulative results show with piercing clarity that life is based on machines – machines made of molecules!" (page 4)

The main thesis behind Irreducible Complexity is that biochemical systems are now being discovered which are too complex to be explained by Darwinian evolution, with the alternative, and superior, explanation being intelligent design. In the book's introduction, Dr. Behe explains his why his work in Intelligent Design demands a hearing: *"Understanding how something works is not the same as understanding how it came to be. Understanding the origin of something is different from understanding its day-to-day workings. As a writer who wants people to read my work, I have a dilemma: people hate to read details, yet the story of the impact of biochemistry on evolutionary theory rests solely in the details!"*

He challenges the scientific community to explain biochemical complexity's origins: *"Science has made enormous progress in understanding how the chemistry of life works, but the elegance and complexity of biological systems at the molecular level have paralyzed science's attempt to explain their origins. There has been virtually no attempt to account for the origin of specific, complex biomolecular systems, much less any progress."*

Dr. Behe titles his book "Darwin's Black Box" because he takes us on a journey through the major discoveries in biology and biochemistry that reveal a miniature world of complex, purposefully designed "machines" that scream for an intelligent cause. These discoveries were beyond Darwin's reach when he wrote 'The Origin of Species'. The world of the cell and the workings of life processes were a 'black box'. Behe takes us inside the box.

On page 193, Dr. Behe explains how design's overwhelming detection in biochemistry leads to the conclusion of intelligent activity: *"There is an elephant in the roomful of scientists who are trying to explain the development of life. The elephant is labeled 'Intelligent Design.' To a person who does not feel obliged to restrict his search to unintelligent causes, the straightforward conclusion is that many biochemical systems were designed. They were designed not by the laws of nature, not by chance and necessity; rather, they were PLANNED. The designer knew what the systems would look like when they were completed, then took steps to bring the systems about. Life on earth at its most fundamental level, in its most critical components, is the product of intelligent activity."*

Throughout the 11 chapters of his book, Dr. Behe asks us 113 questions to make it easy for anyone with a desire to do what Dr. Behe had hoped when he wrote this book: to "dig into the details".

PSALM 94:9 *"He who planted the ear, shall He not hear? HE WHO FORMED* (Hebr. *"yâtsar"*) *THE EYE, shall He not see?"*

Charles Darwin[1]: "The eye to this day gives me a cold shudder. To suppose that the eye, with all its inimitable contrivances for adjusting the focus to different distances, for admitting different amounts of light, and for the correction of spherical and chromatic aberration, could have been formed by natural selection, seems, I freely confess, absurd in the highest possible degree."

The Biochemical "7 Steps" of "Sight"[16]

1. A photon of light striking the retina changes the shape of the molecule **11-cts-retinal**. This changes the shape of the much larger protein **rhodopsin** (to which its attached), creating new molecule **metarhodopsin II**.

2. Metarhodopsin II now sticks to another protein **transducin** (before bumping into metarhodopsin II, transducin had been tightly bound to a small molecule called **GDP**. GDP now falls off transducin).

3. Once GDP detaches from transducin, the molecule **GTP** binds to it. This multi-molecule GTP-transducin-metarhodopsin II now binds to a protein **phosphodiesterase** (found in the cell's inner membrane).

4. This triggers phosphodiesterase to lower the concentration of **cGMP** molecules in the cell (much like pulling the plug in a bathtub lowers the water level).

5. When the cGMP concentration drops, the **ion channel** closes, causing the positively-charged **sodium ion** level to reduce (since they are still being pumped out).

6. The reduction in sodium ion levels within the cell causes an imbalance of charge across the cell membrane, causing an electric current to be transmitted down the **optic nerve** to the brain.

7. VISION = The brain's interpretation of this electrical signal coming from the optic nerve

ion channel = Another cell membrane protein that binds cGMP. It is a gateway that regulates the number of sodium ions in the cell. Normally, the ion channel lets sodium ions flow into the cell while another protein pumps them out, thus keeping the sodium ion level at a tight range.

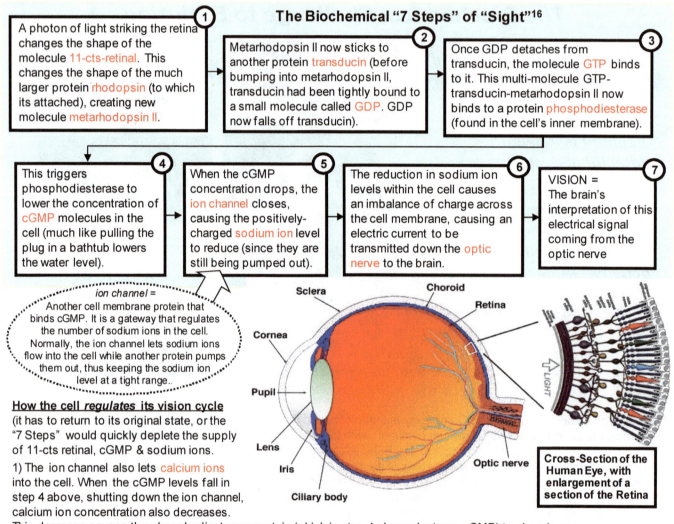

Cross-Section of the Human Eye, with enlargement of a section of the Retina

How the cell *regulates* its vision cycle (it has to return to its original state, or the "7 Steps" would quickly deplete the supply of 11-cts retinal, cGMP & sodium ions.

1) The ion channel also lets **calcium ions** into the cell. When the cGMP levels fall in step 4 above, shutting down the ion channel, calcium ion concentration also decreases. This decrease causes the phosphodiesterase protein (which in step 4 above destroys cGMP) to slow down.

2) As the calcium ion levels start falling, another protein called **guanylate cyclase** starts *resynthesizing* cGMP.

3) While all this is going on: the metarhodopsin II (of step 1 above) is being chemically modified by a protein called **rhodopsin kinase**, producing a modified rhodopsin which then binds to another protein known as **arrestin**. This arrestin prevents the rhodopsin from activating more of the transducin (from step 2 above).

4) But the **trans-retinal** that originally was formed by attaching 11-cts-retinal to rhodopsin must be reconverted back to 11-cts-retinal, then redo step 1 above (be bound again to rhodopsin) in order to start the visual cycle over again. To accomplished this, trans-retinal is chemically modified by a protein into **trans-retinol** (a form that contains 2 more hydrogen atoms). A 2nd protein then converts the trans-retinol molecule to 11-cts-retinol.

5) A 3rd protein removes the previously added H atoms to form the original **11-cts-retinal** - THE CYCLE IS COMPLETE.

R. Swenson[15]: *"While today's digital hardware is extremely impressive, it is clear that the human retina's real-time performance goes unchallenged. To simulate 10 milliseconds of the complete processing of even a single nerve cell from the retina would require the solution of about 500 simultaneous nonlinear differential equations 100X and would take at least several minutes of processing time on a Cray supercomputer. Keeping in mind that there are 10,000,000 or more such cells interacting with each other in complex ways, it would take a minimum of 100 YEARS of Cray time to simulate what takes place in your eye many times every second."*

PSALM 94:9 *"HE WHO PLANTED* (Hebr. *"nátá"*) *THE EAR, shall He not hear? He who formed the eye, shall He not see?"*

The Ear = The Microprecision of God's Design[15]
- Just as the eye converts photons into electrical signals to the optic nerve, that can be "seen" by the brain, the ear converts sound waves into electrical signals that can be "heard" by the brain via the auditory nerve.
- The reason "sound" happens at all is because of the design of the ear, not the energy in sound waves
  - a noise loud enough to pain the ear measures only 0.01 watt of energy
  - faintest sound audible by the ear has a pressure of 0.0002 dyne/ cm^2 (1 dyne = push of a healthy mosquito)
- "Binaural Summation" = the organ of Corti makes lightning-fast calculations to tell the brain where sound data came from. It can tell sound's origin based on a 0.00003-second difference in the arrival from one ear to the other.

Design of my Ear:
The **auricle** is designed to collect and focus sounds into the auditory canal. The inside surface of the auditory canal is covered with cells and hairs that secrete a thick, waxy product to protect the ear against external dirt. The **eustachian tube** functions to balance air pressure in the middle ear. At the end of the middle ear is the **cochlea** that has an extremely sensitive hearing mechanism. At the end of the ear canal towards the start of the middle ear is the **eardrum**.

How I hear sounds[15]
My eardrum is as thick as a piece of paper and exquisitely sensitive to any vibration. Even sound waves that move my eardrum by less than the diameter of a hydrogen molecule are perceived by my brain as a sound. My ear can hear a cricket chirping 1/2 mile away on a still night. My ear has 1 million moving parts. On the inner surface of my eardrum are the smallest bones in the body: the hammer, anvil and stirrup. As my eardrum vibrates, the motion is transmitted by the 3 bones to the cochlea and the organ of Corti, where there are 1,000's of exquisitely sensitive hair cells. The vibration transferred to the hair cells is converted into an electrical impulse for transmission to the brain by the auditory nerve.

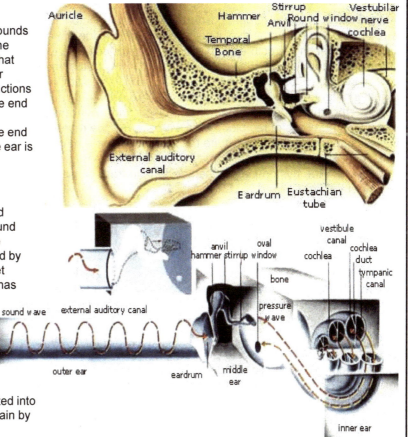

The "6-Step" hearing process ➔ Another Irreducibly Complex system
The system enabling me to hear is unimaginably complex, made of different structures that have been carefully designed in the minutest detail. This system could not have come into existence by random chance, "step by step", because the lack of the smallest detail would render the entire system useless.

Step 1 = sound waves are collected by the auricle and then hit the eardrum, which sets the bones in the middle ear vibrating (so sound waves are translated into mechanical vibrations).

Step 2 = these inner ear bones (hammer, anvil, stirrup) vibrate the so-called "oval window".

Step 3 = the "oval window" sets the fluid inside the cochlea in motion (here, the mechanical vibrations are transformed into nerve impulses which will travel to the brain through the vestibular nerves).

Step 4 = inside the cochlea, there are canals filled with fluid. The cochlear canal contains the "organ of corti" which is the sense organ of hearing. This organ is composed of hair cells. The vibrations in the fluid of the cochlea are transmitted to these hair cells through the basilar membrane, on which the organ of corti is situated.

Step 5 = the inner and outer hair cells vibrate according to the incoming sound frequency, so I can hear different sounds. Outer hair cells convert sound vibrations into electrical impulses and send them to the vestibular nerve.

Step 6 = the information from both ears meet in the superior olivary complex of the brain. The auditory pathway organs are the inferior colliculus, medial geniculate body and the auditory cortex. Both cochleas in our ears send signals to both hemispheres of the brain.

"An Eye for Creation"
9/1/1996: Creation Magazine interviews eye-disease researcher Dr George Marshall

Dr George Marshall, an eye-disease researcher from the University of Glasgow, Scotland, obtained his Bachelors of Science degree in Biology at the University of Strathclyde in 1984. He conducted research into bone marrow cancer at the University of Sheffield for 3 years until he was diagnosed with a serious, normally incurable illness.

He was dramatically healed of this in November 1987 and soon obtained a Masters degree in Medical Science from Sheffield. He then worked at the University of Manchester before taking up a post at the University of Glasgow in 1988. He obtained his Ph.D. in Ophthalmic Science at Glasgow in 1991 and was elected to Chartered Biologist status and to membership of the Institute of Biology in 1993. He is now Sir Jules Thorn Lecturer in Ophthalmic Science.

➢ Dr George Marshall [GM]: I pointed out that the principal reason why the eye cannot be regarded as being wired backward (as some evolutionists claim) was hidden in a footnote in your Creation Magazine (CM) article. The light-detecting structures within photoreceptor cells are located in the stack of discs. These discs are being continually replaced by the formation of new ones at the cell body end of the stack, thereby pushing older discs down the stack. Those discs at the other end of the stack are 'swallowed' by a single layer of retinal pigment epithelial (RPE) cells. RPE cells are highly active, and for this they need a very large blood supply—the choroid. Unlike the retina, which is virtually transparent, the choroid is virtually opaque, because of the vast numbers of red blood cells within it. For the retina to be wired the way that Professor Richard Dawkins suggested, would require the choroid to come between the photoreceptor cells and the light, for RPE cells must be kept in intimate contact with both the choroid and photoreceptor to perform their job. Anybody who has had the misfortune of a hemorrhage in front of the retina will testify as to how well red blood cells block out the light.

- CM: Then what do you think of the idea that the eye is wired backward?

➢ GM: The notion the eye was wired backward occurred to me as a 13-year-old when studying eye anatomy in science class. It took me 2 years of lecturing on human eye anatomy to realize why the eye is wired the way it is. The idea that the eye is wired backward comes from a lack of knowledge of eye function and anatomy.

- CM: How do you react to the notion that the human eye is the product of evolution?

➢ GM: The more I study the human eye, the harder it is to believe that it evolved. Most people see the miracle of sight. I see a miracle of complexity on viewing things at 100,000 times magnification. It is the perfection of this complexity that causes me to balk at evolutionary theory.

- CM: Can you give our readers some idea of just how complex the eye is?

➢ GM: The *RETINA* is probably the most complicated tissue in the whole body. Millions of nerve cells interconnect in a fantastic number of ways to form a miniature 'brain'. Much of what the photoreceptors 'see' is interpreted and processed by the retina long before it enters the brain.

- CM: A computer program has allegedly 'imitated' the evolution of an eye. Do you accept this?

➢ GM: Those who produced this model would acknowledge that the model is such a gross oversimplification that cannot be cited as a proof. May I quote a colleague's reaction [Dr John Hay, B.Sc., Ph.D., M.Sc., C.Biol., F.I.Biol.]: 'Computer simulation of evolutionary processes such as that described have three important flaws.

Flaw #1 = the findings imply that the development which is being measured over so many generations is independent of development of other structures which are necessary for function.

Flaw #2 = the changes observed from the simulation are dependent on the original data input which clearly is consequent to human design of the sequences/regions to be worked on and also the program(s) which are used for the simulation. These are not, therefore, random.

Flaw #3 = there is translation error in such simulations involving computer hardware/software. This can take the form of electronic error in single bits which are coding for a particular digit. Over many loops in this performance, intrinsic error can be magnified considerably. Was the simulation repeated using different PCs etc.? One feels that these three arguments are essential to any computer simulation package of evolutionary processes."

➢ GM: 'My first point indicated that even if there is an eye, it will be useless unless the organism has the neural and/or the mental processes to utilize information perceived by the eye. How can a chance mutation provide this complexity in several different structures? The argument has usually been that there is a plausible intermediate series of eye-designs in living animals, e.g. *Euglena* has an eyespot; other organisms have a "cup" which acts as a direction finder. 'However, the organism which defies this evolution is *Nautilus*. It has a primitive eye with no lens, which is somewhat surprising considering that its close relative, the squid, has one. This organism has (apparently!) been around for millions of years but has never "evolved" a lens despite the fact that it has a retina which would benefit from this simple change.'

"An Eye for Creation" (continued)

9/1/1996: Creation Magazine interviews eye-disease researcher Dr George Marshall, Univ. of Glasgow, Scotland

- **CM:** Do you believe that accepting creation as portrayed in Genesis is essential to your Christian faith?
- **GM:** Yes! On not literally accepting the Genesis account of creation one is left with a major problem—what Scriptures do you accept as true and what Scriptures do you reject as false? Only by accepting the whole of Scripture as the inspired Word of God does one avoid this dilemma. There are Scriptures that are a source of stumbling to the intellect. My practice is to 'pigeon-hole' them temporarily and never allow them to be a stumbling block to my faith. It's amazing how many of these knotty problems have subsequently resolved themselves. Thus Genesis creation may initially appear to be hard to accept, but it strikes me that evolution is equally if not more problematic to believe.
- **CM:** What advice would you have for Christian students, or for Christians in a science course?
- **GM:** Three things I would say:

First: recognize that science can become a 'religion' in its own right. Watch any TV program involving nature and you would think that evolution is an established fact. People get bombarded with this so often that they accept it without thinking. Scientists say something, so the general public (the 'worshippers') accept it without question. Scientists are much more cautious about one another's findings.

Second: science is not static. The science of today is quite different in many ways from the science of yesterday, and will probably bear little resemblance to the science of tomorrow. People once believed in 'spontaneous generation' which could be 'proved' by putting an old sack and a few bits of cheese in a dark corner. Mice spontaneously generated out of the sack. We laugh at such notions, but I suspect that in a hundred years' time people will laugh at some of our scientific notions.

Third: one can still become an eminent scientist without accepting evolutionary dogma; the ability to produce sound science in the laboratory is not diminished by one's stance on creation.

The Eye as a Machine: Designed so I can see

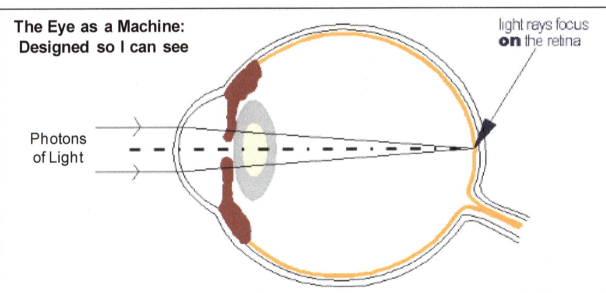

A good way to think of a machine is as "thought expressed in matter for an intended purpose". We just studied the biochemical details of how, once photons of light reach the retina, they are translated from light to electrical impulses that travel on my optic nerve to my brain, so I can "see".

The mechanical assembly of the eye is an engineering marvel. As a machine, it focuses random photons of light at the eyeball such that these now non-random light rays target the retina to initiate the biochemical process.

Here's a basic explanation: When light contacts my eye, it is bent as it passes through the cornea, aqueous humor, lens, and vitreous humor. It is then directed onto the retina, which is made up of rods (which adjust for brightness) and cones (which adjust for hue). Light changes the shape of 11-cts-retinal, which then causes a change in shape of rhodopsin in the rods... and the process of sight follows the biochemical steps outlined on previous pages, culminating with electrical impulses transmitted to the brain via the optic nerve.

Psalm 119:73 *"Your hands have made me and fashioned me; give me understanding, that I may learn Your commandments."*

M. Behe[16]: "Microbiology kills Darwin's theory that the Human Eye evolved"

"In the 19th century, the *anatomy* of the eye was known in detail. The **pupil** acts as a shutter to let in enough light to see in sunlight or nighttime darkness. The **lens** gathers light and focuses it on the **retina** to form a sharp image. The **muscles** allow it to move quickly. Different colors of light, with different wavelengths, would cause a blurred image, but the eye's **lens** changes density over its surface to correct for chromatic aberration.

> THE EYE: IRREDUCIBLY COMPLEX
> These sophisticated methods astounded everyone who was familiar with them. Scientists of the 19th century knew that if a person lacked any of the eye's many integrated features, the result would be a severe loss of vision or outright blindness. They concluded that the eye could function only if it were nearly intact.

Charles Darwin knew about the eye, too. The Origin of Species dealt with many objections to his theory of evolution by natural selection. He discussed the problem of the eye in a section of the book appropriately entitled 'Origin of Extreme Perfection and Complication. In Darwin's thinking, evolution could not build a complex organ in one or a few steps; radical innovations such as the eye require generations of organisms to slowly accumulate beneficial changes in a gradual process. He realized that if in one generation an organ as complex as the eye suddenly appeared, it would be tantamount to a miracle. Unfortunately, gradual development of the human eye appeared to be impossible, since its many sophisticated features seemed interdependent. For evolution to be believable, Darwin had to convince the public that complex organs could form in a step-by-step process.

He succeeded brilliantly. Darwin didn't try to discover a pathway that evolution might have used to make the eye. Rather, he pointed to modern animals with different kinds of eyes (ranging from the simple to the complex) and suggested that the evolution of the human eye might have involved similar organs as intermediates. Here's Darwin's argument paraphrased: *'Although humans have complex camera-type eyes, many animals get by with less. Some tiny creatures have just a simple group of pigmented cells – not much more than a light-sensitive spot. That simple arrangement can hardly be said to confer vision, but it can sense light and dark, and so it meets the creature's needs. The light-sensing organ of some starfishes is somewhat more sophisticated. Their eye is located in a depressed region. Since the curvature of the depression blocks off light from some directions, the animal can sense which direction the light is coming from. The directional sense of the eye improves if the curvature becomes more pronounced, but more curvature also lessens the amount of light that enters the eye, decreasing its sensitivity. The sensitivity can be increased by placement of material in the cavity to act as a lens; some modern animals have eyes with such crude lenses. Gradual improvements in the lens could then provide increasingly sharp images to meet the requirements of the animal's environment.'*

Darwin convinced much of the world that an evolutionary pathway leads from the simplest light-sensitive spot to man's sophisticated camera-eye. **But the question of how vision began remained unanswered**. Darwin did not even try to explain where his starting point – the relatively simple light-sensitive spot – came from. He dismissed the question of the eye's ultimate origin: *'How a nerve comes to be sensitive to light hardly concerns us more than how life itself originated.'* He had an excellent reason for declining the question: **it was completely beyond 19th century science.** How the eye works – that is, what happens when a photon of light 1st hits the retina – simply could not be answered at that time. As a matter of fact, no question about the underlying mechanisms of life could be answered (how did animal muscles cause movement? How did photosynthesis work? How was energy extracted from food? How did the body fight infection?). No one knew. **To Darwin, vision was a black box.** Now that the black box of vision has been opened, it is no longer enough for an evolutionary explanation of that power to consider only the anatomical structures of whole eyes. **Each of the anatomical steps and structures that Darwin thought were so simple actually involves staggeringly complicated biochemical processes** that cannot be papered over with rhetoric.

> Biochemistry offers a Lilliputian challenge to Darwin. Anatomy is, quite simply, irrelevant to the question of whether evolution could take place on the molecular level. Until recently, evolutionary biologists could be unconcerned with the molecular details of life because so little was known about them. Now the black box of the cell has been opened, and the infinitesimal world that stands revealed must be explained.

Evolution ▶ some people would rather be blind than ask for God's free gift of sight

John 9:39-41 *"'For judgment I have come into this world, that those who do not see may see, and that those who see may be made blind.' Then some of the Pharisees who were with Him heard these words, and said to Him, 'Are we blind also?' Jesus said to them, 'If you were blind, you would have no sin, but now you say "We see". Therefore your sin remains.'"*

R. Swenson ("More than Meets the Eye")[15]: *"We are all born with the same optics but that doesn't mean that we all can 'see'. Spiritual eyes are an entirely different piece of equipment. When Jesus walked among us, some saw Him and some didn't. They all had the same eyes, yet some were spiritually blind, 'ever seeing but never perceiving.' There is coming a day when all shall be made clear, for at that time 'every eye will see Him.' From my own personal experience, let me assure you that if we have eyes willing to see, God won't hide His glory from us."*

GENESIS 9:3-4 "BLOOD = God's Irreducibly Complex Design for Life"   5.3

"Every moving thing that lives shall be food for you. I have given you all things, even as the green herbs. But you shall not eat flesh with its LIFE, that is, its BLOOD."

Deuteronomy 12:15-16,23-25 *"...you may slaughter and eat meat within all your gates, whatever your heart desires, according to the blessing of the Lord your God which He has given you; the unclean and the clean may eat of it, of the gazelle and the deer alike. Only YOU SHALL NOT EAT THE BLOOD; you shall pour it on the earth like water.... Be sure that you do not eat the blood, for THE BLOOD IS THE LIFE; you may not eat the life with the meat. You shall not eat it; you shall pour it on the earth like water. You shall not eat it, that it may go well with you and your children after you, when you do what is right in the sight of the Lord."*

Blood = "God's Design for *Physical* Life"[20]

"As important as it is, the heart would be useless without blood to pump. Blood is the fluid that carries the precious oxygen and nutrients to each of our cells. The average-sized human body contains about 6 quarts of blood, which is circulated completely every 1-3 minutes. About 55% of blood is an amber-colored liquid called plasma, which is more than 90% water. Blood also contains fibrinogen, a protein that helps blood clot, as well as nutrients, hormones, enzymes, antibodies, and the body's waste products.

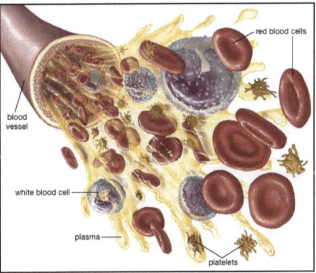

3 main components of blood:

1) Red blood cells = There are trillions of these oxygen-carrying cells in the entire body, and each one contains hundreds of millions of molecules of hemoglobin, which enables the cell to collect oxygen in the lungs and release it in the tissues. Red blood cells have a life span of only 4 months and must be replaced constantly. Your bone marrow produces replacement red blood cells at a rate of 1.5 million every second.

2) White blood cells = Outnumbered by red blood cells 750 to 1, they defend against foreign intruders (bacteria, viruses) by actively consuming them - a process called phagocytosis - or by producing antibodies, which are proteins that kill or otherwise interfere with the intruder's normal functions. White blood cells are different from most cells in the human body in their ability to move throughout the body. They can travel against the flow of blood and can pass through the walls of capillaries and into damaged and diseased tissue in search of infection.

3) Platelets = tiny disks are not actually cells but fragments of very large cells found in bone marrow. When blood vessels are damaged, the platelets release a substance that initiates blood clotting to inhibit the loss of blood."

Blood Clotting = "Autopilot Protection System"[16]

"Blood behaves in a certain way… and blood clotting is a very complex, intricately woven system consisting of a score of interdependent protein parts…all of which must work within very tight restrictions to avoid disaster. The absence of, or defects in, any one of a number of the components causes the entire system to fail (blood won't clot at right time or in the right place).

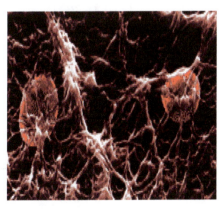

When a container of liquid (a carton of milk, or a tank of gas) springs a leak, the fluid drains out. The rate of flow depends on the thickness of the liquid (maple syrup leaks out more slowly than milk), but it all leaks out. There is no active process that resists the leaking fluid from draining out.

But when I get a cut, it bleeds until a CLOT stops the flow. When the pressurized blood circulation system is punctured, a clot must form quickly or the animal bleeds to death. But if the clot forms at the wrong time or place, it may block circulation as it does in heart attacks and strokes. So blood clotting must be tightly controlled so the clot forms only when and where it is supposed to. Yet blood clotting is on *AUTOPILOT* – our bodies are not only self-diagnosing, but self-repairing (more on Von Neumann machines later)!

<u>Blood Clotting is an Irreducibly Complex system</u>: Biochemical research shows there are many factors involved in blood clotting, and none of them can be missing for the process to occur. The formation, limitation, strengthening and removal of a blood clot form an integrated biological system. If one factor fails, the whole system of clot-formation fails."

Blood Clotting: Auto-Catalytic Cascade

Blood clotting is an *auto-catalytic cascade* (one protein activates a second protein, which activates a third protein, etc.), accelerating the production of more of the same proteins. This process of Blood Clotting involves multiple, different proteins. Some of these proteins are involved in *forming* the clot. Others are responsible for *regulating* clot-formation. Regulating proteins are needed because there should only be clots forming at the site of a wound, not in the middle of flowing arteries. Other proteins take care of *removing* the clot once it is no longer needed.

The diagram below provides a visual representation of Michael Behe's explanation for how the cascading effect of one protein activates the successive protein in the chain reaction leading to a blood clot.

The Clotting cascade: Depends critically on *TIMING and SPEED* at which the reactions occur[16]

- An animal would solidify if thrombin activated proconvertin at the wrong time
- An animal would bleed to death if proaccelerin or antihemophelic factor were activated too slowly
- An animal would die if thrombin activated protein C much faster than it activated proaccelerin
- An animal would die if anithrombin inactivated Stuart factor as fast as it was formed
- An animal would die if plasminogen was activated immediately when clot forms (it would dissolve the clot)

The Clotting Cascade: This complex biochemical system can't arise through natural selection[16]

"M. Behe's detailed discussion illustrates the impossibility of a problem that has resisted the determined efforts of top-notch scientists for four decades. Blood coagulation is a paradigm of staggering complexity that underlies even apparently simple bodily processes.

Faced with such complexity beneath even simple phenomena, Darwinian theory falls silent. The clotting cascade is a breathtaking balancing act in which a menagerie of biochemicals – sporting various decorations and rearrangements conferred by modifying enzymes – bounce off one another at precise angles in a meticulously ordered sequence. The audience rises to its feet in sustained applause."

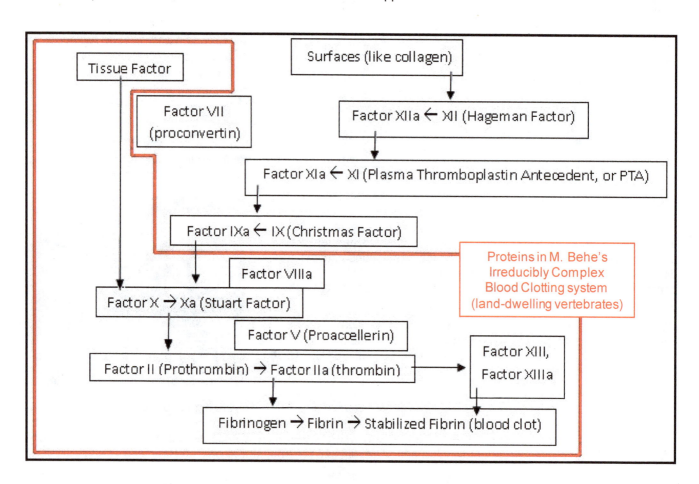

"Blood Clotting 101": What happens when I cut myself? Now I'm way smarter than a 5th grader

1. When a cut occurs, Hageman Factor[1] sticks to the surface of cells near the wound. Bound Hageman Factor reacts with another enzyme called HMK[2] to produce Activated Hageman[3].

2. Pre Kallikrein[4] reacts with Activated Hageman to produce Kallikrein[5].

3. PTA[6] reacts with Activated Hageman and HMK to produce Activated PTA[7].

4. Proconvertin[8] is activated by Activated Hageman Factor to produce Convertin[9].

5. Christmas Factor[10] reacts with Activated PTA and Convertin to produce Activated Christmas Factor[11].

6. Antihemophilic Factor[12] is activated by Thrombin[13] to produce Activated Antihemophilic Factor[14].

7. Stuart Factor[15] reacts with Activated Christmas Factor and Activated Antihemophilic Factor to produce Activated Stuart Factor[16].

8. When a cut occurs, Tissue Factor[17] (its only found outside of cells) is brought in near the wound where it reacts with Convertin and Stuart Factor to also produce Activated Stuart Factor.

9. Proaccelerin[18] is activated by Thrombin to produce Accelerin[19].

10. GLU-Prothrombin[20] reacts with Prothrombin[21] and Vitamin K[22] to produce GLA-Prothrombin[23] (Prothrombin cannot be activated in the GLU form - it must be formed into the GLA form. In this process ten amino acids must be changed from glutamate to gama carboxy glutamate.)

If bleeding takes place anywhere in the body, all the proteins responsible for halting that bleeding immediately travel to the injured tissue. Clotting, which takes place with the cooperation of a great many proteins, is an irreducibly complex process that evolution can't explain.

11. GLS-Prothrombin[24] is then able to bind to Calcium[25]. This allows GLA-Prothrombin to stick to surfaces of cells. Only intact modified Calcium-Prothrombin Complex can bind to the cell membrane and be cleaved by Activated Stuart and Accerlerin to produce Thrombin.

12. Prothrombin-Ca[26] (bound to cell surface) is activated by Activated Stuart to produce Thrombin.

13. Prothrombin also reacts with Activated Stuart and Accelerin to produce Thrombin.

14. Fibrinogin[27] is activated by Thrombin to produce Fibrin[28]. Threads of Fibrin are the final clot. However, it would be more effective if the Fibrin threads could form more cross links with each other.

15. FSF[29] (Fibrin Stabilizing Factor) is activated by Thrombin to form Activated FSF[30].

16. As Fibrin reacts with Activated FSF, multiple cross ties are made with Fibrin filaments to form an effective clot.

What exactly happens to remove the clot after the blood flow is stopped?

17. The blood protein Plasminogin[31] is activated by + - Pa[32] to produce Plasmin[33]. This acts like tiny chemical scissors which cuts up the Fibrin filaments of the clot.

18. The rate at which the clot is broken up is controlled by yet another blood protein named Alpha 2 Antiplasm[34], which in turn inactivates Plasmin. One of the most important parts of this blood clotting machine is the ability it has to keep the clotting localized to the area of the wound and to stop the clotting cascade. Most heart attacks and strokes are caused by blood clots lodging. You could say the blood-clot is the biggest killer of human beings.

19. Antithrombin[35] inactivates Activated Christmas Factor, Activated Stuart Factor and Thrombin.

20. Protein C[36] is activated by Thrombin to produce Activated Protein C[37].

21. Activated Protein C inactivates Accelerin and Activated Antihemophilic Factor.

22. Finally, Thrombomodulin[38] (lines inside of your blood vessels) prevents Thrombin from activating Fibrinogin.

Blood Clotting ≈ 38 Proteins, each with a specified function, linked in an Irreducibly Complex process (failure of any of these proteins to do its job means failure for the entire process and death to the animal)

How do evolutionists explain the process of Blood Clotting?
(the following is based on excerpts from M. Behe's book "Darwin's Black Box"[16], pages 90-96)

Dr. Russell Doolittle (professor of biochemistry at the Center for Molecular Genetics at the University of California at San Diego) wrote an article in *Thrombosis and Homeostasis* in which he attempted to answer the question, "How in the world did this complex and delicately balanced process evolve?"

In his article, meant for other professionals, Dr. Doolittle used the following phrases in his explanation: *"Tissue Factor appeared...", "Prothrombin appears...", "Fibrinogin is born...", "Antithrombin appears...", "Plasminogin is generated...", Antiplasmin arises...", "TPA springs forth...". "Proconvertin is duplicated from Stuart Factor."*

Michael Behe has the following observations about Dr. Doolittle's explanation of clotting evolution:

"At no step--not even one--does Dr. Doolittle give a model that includes numbers or quantities; without numbers there is no science. When a merely verbal picture is painted of the development of such a complex system there is absolutely no way to know if it would actually work. When such crucial questions are ignored we leave science and enter the world of Calvin and Hobbes".

Behe's major objection to the "state of the art" evolutionary models is his concern for irreducible complexity. Darwinian evolution is theorized to be directed by "natural selection." Natural selection only selects from the structures and biochemistry that are present and cannot work on some kind of future structure.

The engine of Darwinian evolution only works if there is something to select--something that is useful right now, not in the future. Even if we accept his scenario for purposes of discussion, however, by Doolittle's own account no blood clotting appears until at least the third step.

"The formation of tissue factor at the first step is unexplained, since it would then be sitting with nothing to do. In the next step (prothrombin popping up already endowed with the ability to bind tissue factor, which somehow activates it) the poor proto-prothrombin would also be twiddling its thumbs with nothing to do until, at last, a hypothetical thrombin receptor appears at the third step and fibrinogin falls from heaven at step four. Plasminogin appears in one step, but its activator (TPA) does not appear until two steps later. Stuart factor is introduced in one step and somehow tissue factor decided that this is the complex it wants to bind. Virtually every step of the suggested pathway faces similar problems". In order to have a controlled clotting mechanism you have to have 2 proteins for each step. Both the pro enzyme (non-activated) and its activator are required.

Behe calculated the odds of getting just the factor TPA and its activator at 1×10^{31} (1 time in 10^{31} opportunities). To compound the problem, if *"...a protein appeared in one step with nothing to do, then mutation and natural selection would tend to eliminate it."* To prevent this from happening, evolutionists are forced to imagine large clusters of proteins evolving all at once. Is it not more sensible to believe God created the whole mechanism fully functional and ready to go? It does not go against reason to believe that intricate design, especially when irreducible complexity is involved, demands an intelligent Designer.

On the other hand, it does go against reason to "believe" that natural, pure chance changes in DNA (mutations) are capable of producing a process that is so irreducibly complex such as "simple" blood clotting.

The irreducible complexity inherent in many biochemical systems not only precludes the possibility that they evolved by Darwinian natural selection, but concludes that intelligent design is necessary. Yet the complexity of these systems has gone largely unnoticed and greatly unreported to the general public.

M. Behe: *"Why does the scientific community not greedily embrace its startling discovery? Why is the observation of design handled with intellectual gloves? The dilemma is that while one side of the elephant is labeled intelligent design, the other side might be labeled God."*

Behe's sophisticated argument has garnered the attention of many within the scientific community. His book has been reviewed in the pages of Nature, Boston Review, Wall Street Journal, and on many Internet sites. While some have genuinely engaged the ideas and offered serious rebuttal, most have sat back on Darwinian authority and claimed that Behe is just lazy or hasn't given the evolutionary establishment enough time.

Jerry Coine (Nature (9/19/1996, p.227-228): *"There is no doubt that the pathways described by Behe are dauntingly complex, and their evolution will be hard to unravel. Unlike anatomical structures, the evolution of which can be traced by fossils, biochemical evolution must be reconstructed from highly evolved living organisms, and we may forever be unable to envisage the first proto-pathways. It is not valid, however, to assume that, because one man cannot imagine such pathways, they could not have existed."* That raises the question if it is valid to assume there is no Designer, because certain scientists cannot 'imagine such pathways'. Irreducible complexity stands out as a large obstacle for evolution. Many pro-design scientists are studying the same thing as their pro-evolution colleagues. While the one group attributes this to a Designer, the other group attributes it to a process called 'natural selection'. Let the facts prove which explanation is most justifiable."

The question for Evolutionists: *How does Natural Selection explain Blood Clotting, from a 'simple' to a 'complex' form, if it only functions as a whole, with all systems included?*

Blood = "God's Design for *Eternal* Life: the *Forgiveness* of my *sin*"

<u>Leviticus 17:11</u> "only blood can atone for my soul" ➔ *"...the life of the flesh is in the blood, and I have given it to you upon the altar to make atonement for your souls; for IT IS THE BLOOD THAT MAKES ATONEMENT for the soul."*

<u>Leviticus 16:30,34</u> "only blood makes me clean before God" ➔ *"...on that day* (Day of Atonement) *the priest shall make atonement for you, to cleanse you, that you may be clean from all your sins BEFORE THE LORD."*

<u>Hebrews 9:7,11-12</u> "God can only be approached through blood" ➔ *"...into the second part the high priest went alone once a year, NOT WITHOUT BLOOD, which he offered for himself and for the peoples' sins... but Christ came as High Priest of the good things to come... not with the blood of goats and calves, but WITH HIS OWN BLOOD HE ENTERED THE MOST HOLY PLACE once for all, having obtained eternal redemption."*

---

by Jesus' blood, the Father:
justifies me, forgives me, brings me near to Him, reconciles me to Him, makes peace with me

Rom. 3:23-26 *"All have sinned and fall short of the glory of God, being justified freely by His grace through redemption that is in Christ Jesus, whom God set forth to be a propitiation by HIS BLOOD, through faith, to demonstrate His righteousness, because in His forbearance God had passed over the sins that were previously committed, to demonstrate at the present time His righteousness, that He might be just and* THE JUSTIFIER *of the one who has faith in Jesus."*

Eph. 1:7 *"In Him we have redemption through HIS BLOOD, the* FORGIVENESS *of sin, by the riches of His grace."*

Eph. 2:13 *"...in Christ Jesus you who once were far off have been* MADE NEAR *by the BLOOD OF CHRIST."*

Col. 1:19-22 *"...it pleased the Father that in Him all the fullness should dwell, and by Him to reconcile all things to Himself, by Him, whether things on earth or in heaven, having* MADE PEACE *through THE BLOOD of His cross. And you, who were once alienated and enemies in your mind by wicked works, yet now* HE HAS RECONCILED *in the body of His flesh through death..."*

➔ **FORGIVE = *"aphesis" and "paresis"*** Blood allows Him to dismiss my sin by "passing over" it (remission)
Exodus 12:21-23 *"Moses called for all the elders of Israel and said to them, 'Pick out and take lambs for yourselves according to your families, and kill the Passover lamb. And you shall take a bunch of hyssop, dip it in the BLOOD that is in the basin. And none of you shall go out of the door of his house until morning. For the Lord will pass through to strike the Egyptians, and when He sees the BLOOD on the cross piece at the top of your door, and on the two doorposts, the Lord will PASS OVER the door and not allow the destroyer to come into your houses to strike you.'"*

1Corinthians 5:7 (Rom. 3:25-26) *"For indeed Christ, our PASSOVER, was sacrificed for us."*

Matt. 26:27-28 *"Then He took the cup, and gave thanks, and gave it to them, saying, 'Drink from it, all of you. For this is the BLOOD of the new covenant, which is shed for many for the REMISSION of sins."*

➔ **FORGIVE = *"aphiēmi"*** Blood cancels the punishment my sin requires (my offense is never brought up)
1John 1:7-9 *"...if we walk in the light as He is in the light, we have fellowship with one another, and the BLOOD OF JESUS CHRIST His Son cleanses us from all sin. If we say we have no sin, we deceive ourselves, and the truth is not in us. If we confess our sins, He is faithful and just to FORGIVE us our sins and to cleanse us from all unrighteousness."*

➔ **FORGIVE = *"charizomai"*** Blood bestows His unconditional favor (I am under no obligation for my offense)
Colossians 2:13-14 *"And you, being dead in your trespasses and the uncircumcision of your flesh, He has made alive together with Him, having FORGIVEN you all trespasses, having wiped out the certificate of debt with its requirements that was against us, which was contrary to us. And He has taken it out of the way, having NAILED IT TO THE CROSS."*

➔ **ATONE = *"hilastērion" and "hilasmos"*** Blood covers my sin
- Leviticus 17:11   only by shedding blood can my sins be forgiven
- Leviticus 22:24-25   only a perfect sacrifice for my sin is acceptable to God
- Hebrews 10:1-4,11 atonement just covers my sin – it can't permanently cancel it

The Blood of Jesus Christ = the only acceptable Solution for my sin's terminal disease

Solution #1	"my Lamb without blemish" (perfect and sinless)	1Peter 1:19, 1John 3:5
Solution #2	"my Willing Substitute" (offered Himself 1X as payment on my behalf)	Hebrews 9:14
Solution #3	"my Reconciliation with the Father" (peace)	Col. 1:20-22, Rom. 5:1
Solution #4	"my Confident Access to the Father" (God's throne = Holy of Holies)	Heb. 10:19-20

God's *Holiness* demands blood be shed …. God's *Love* makes that blood His own

I apply His blood ONCE for *Justification* ← Hebrews 10:14 ➔ I apply His cross DAILY for *Sanctification*

PSALM 139:5-12   God's *OMNIPRESENCE* = He surrounds me completely   **5.4**

vs. 5 *"You have ①HEDGED me ②BEHIND and ③BEFORE, and ④LAID Your hand upon me."*
① HEDGED = *"tsûr"* = confined, surrounded (as if besieged by an army on all sides of the city walls)
② BEHIND = *"âchôr âchôr"* = He either records my sins or, by His grace, chooses to not remember them
    Job 10:14 *"If I sin, then You mark me (charge my account – Ps 32:2), and will not acquit me of my iniquity."*
    Psalm 103:12 *"As far as the east is from the west, so far has He removed our iniquities from us."*

③ BEFORE = *"qedem qêdmâh"* = He foreknows my actions and thoughts, and provides for all my needs
    Psalm 103:14 *"...He knows our frame ("understands our constitution"); He remembers that we are dust."*
    Matthew 6:31 *"...do not worry, saying 'What shall we eat?' or "What shall we drink?" or 'What shall we wear?'. For after all these things the Gentiles seek. For your heavenly Father knows that you need all these things."*

④ LAID (Your hand) = *"shîyth"* = gripped by the Lord (God is very near – there is no escaping from Him)
   □ good illustration: a prisoner marching alongside a guard, gripped by the officer in charge.
   □ past tense: it doesn't say he 'will' lay His hand on me – He already has (it's a done deal).
    John 17:11 *"Holy Father, KEEP (Greek "tēreō" = continue to preserve by tightly guarding) through Your name those whom You have given Me, that they may be one as We are one."*

vs. 6 *"Such ⑤KNOWLEDGE is too ⑥WONDERFUL for me; it is high, I cannot attain it."*
⑤ KNOWLEDGE = *"da'ath"* = awareness; to know in the sense of have understanding of the subject
    Hosea 6:6 *"...I desire mercy and not sacrifice, and the KNOWLEDGE of God more than burnt offerings."*
    Hosea 4:6 *"My people are destroyed for their lack of KNOWLEDGE. Because you have rejected KNOWLEDGE, I will reject you from being priest for Me; because you have FORGOTTEN the law of your God, I will FORGET your children."*

- <u>Deuteronomy 8:11-20</u> ➔ God warns me - "Don't FORGET (Hebrew *"shâkach"* = to be oblivious due to lack of attention) ➔ sound like America today? God commands me to *commit* what I've been taught to *memory*, then *live out* my understanding via *obedience*

⑥ WONDERFUL = *"pâlîy"* = awesome; same as Hebr. *"yârê"* = fearful; extreme to an awesome degree
    Psalm 130:4   *"...there is forgiveness with You, that You may be FEARED (revered, held in awe and wonder)"*
    Psalm 66:3   *"How AWESOME (fearful, wonderful to the extreme) are Your works..."*
    Psalm 139:14 *"I will praise You, for I am FEARFULLY WONDERFULLY (awesome to the extreme) made."*

God's gift of my BRAIN – how I receive and understand information

Isaac Asimov[15]: "In a man is a 3-pound brain, which, as far as we know, is the most complex and orderly arrangement of matter in the universe."

I can't fully understand God's omnipresence, but He designed me with an incredibly complex BRAIN to know and reason things out.

My Brain = my "Control Center":
- it holds and sorts out 1×10^{14} bits of information (has a storage capacity 1,000X that of a Cray-2 supercomputer. Forty-five miles of nerves run through my body, picking up electrical impulses that move at almost 250 mph.
- Cerebrum: controls my voluntary actions (running, walking, etc.) and my body's sensations (pain, learning, emotions),
- Cerebellum: controls my *involuntary* actions (balance, posture, breathing, blood pressure).

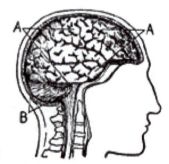

Human brain:
A, cerebrum;
B, cerebellum.

M. Denton[20]: "The Incredibly Complex Human Brain" "The human brain consists of about 10,000,000,000 nerve cells. Each nerve cell puts out between 10,000 – 100,000 connecting fibers by which it makes contact with other nerve cells in the brain. Altogether, the total number of connections in the brain approaches 1×10^{15}, or a thousand million million. Despite the enormity of the number of connections, the forest of fibers is not a chaotic random tangle but a highly organized network. The fibers are unique communications channels following their own specially ordained pathway through the brain. Because of the vast number of unique connections, our most sophisticated engineering techniques would take an eternity to assemble an object even remotely resembling the brain. This raises the obvious question:

Could any purely random process ever have assembled the human brain in the time available?

Psalm 139:7 *"Where can I go FROM Your Spirit? Or where can I flee FROM Your presence?"*

• David doesn't say "where can I go TO Your Spirit?" He makes it *personal* to himself, and says it's impossible to escape FROM the *omnipresence* of God – He is everywhere.

• Not only can't I hide from His sight (Omniscience) – I can't get away from God's immediate, constant PRESENCE. Whether I like it or not, I'm as near to God 24/7 as my soul is to my own body.

Romans 2:15, 1:19-20 God *reveals* Himself internally and externally	Acts 17:26-28 God *surrounds* me: I should desire (seek) *Him*
- My Conscience: *"...(Gentiles) show the work of the law written in their hearts, their conscience also bearing witness, and between themselves their thoughts accusing or else excusing them."* **- Created World:** *"...what may be known of God is manifest in them, for He has shown it to them. For since the creation of the world His invisible attributes are clearly seen, being understood by the things that are made, even His eternal power and Godhead, so that they are without excuse."*	*"...He has made from 1 blood every nation of men to dwell on all the face of the earth, and has determined their preappointed times and the boundaries of their habitations, so that they should SEEK the Lord, in the hope that they might grope for Him and find Him, though HE IS NOT FAR FROM EACH ONE OF US, for in Him we live and move and have our being, as also some of your own poets have said, 'For we are also His offspring* (kin).*'"*

vs. 8 *"If I ascend into heaven, You are there; If I make my bed in hell, ①BEHOLD, You are there."*
 - ascending to heaven to avoid God: flying into the fire to avoid its heat ("out of the frying pan into the fire")
 - descending to the lowest imaginable depths of the dead to avoid God: I'd find His justice there.
① BEHOLD = Hebr. *"hinnêh"* = lo, see = it may seem amazing to meet with God in hell compared to heaven. The presence of God produces very different effects between these 2 places:
 - in heaven = the bliss of seeing Him face-to-face forever (1John 3:2)
 - in hell = the terror of experiencing God's just punishment for sin forever (Luke 16:19-31)

vs. 9-10 *"If I take the wings of the morning, and dwell in the ③UTTERMOST PARTS of the sea, even there Your hand shall ②LEAD me, and Your right hand shall ②HOLD me."*

• If I flew faster than light, and found a place in the deepest oceans unknown to anyone, God is already there.
② LEADS (Hebr. *"nâchâh"* = governs) and ② HOLDS (Hebr. *"âchaz"* = seizes) me, even as a fugitive from Him.
③ UTTERMOST PARTS = Hebr. *"achărîyth"* = in its entirety → same as used in **Hebrews 7:25** for how He saves me (He who saves to the uttermost is with me, or HOLDS and LEADS me, to the uttermost parts of the sea)

vs. 11-12 *"If I say, 'Surely the darkness shall cover me,' even the night shall be light about me; Yea, the darkness shall not hide from You, but the night shines as the day; darkness and light are alike to You."*

• Evil people hate light because their evil deeds are exposed in the light, They think darkness hides them. They don't understand God sees just as well in darkness as in light. He doesn't need light to see (He made them both).
C. Spurgeon[25]: *"Men are so foolish to prefer darkness for their evil deeds; but so impossible is it for anything to be hidden from the Lord that they might as well transgress in broad daylight... the ungodly are duped by their notions of God (Ps 73:11), yet if they would consider for a moment they would conclude that he who could not see in the dark could not be God, and he who is not present everywhere could not be the Almighty Creator."*

YAHWEH SHAMMAH	"The God who is always PRESENT with me"
Ezek. 48:35 *"The way around shall be 18,000 cubits, the name of the city from that day shall be YAHWEH SHAMMAH."*	
Revelation 21:3 *"I heard a loud voice from heaven saying, 'Behold, the tabernacle of God is with men, and He will dwell with them, and they shall be His people, and God Himself WILL BE WITH THEM and be their God.'"*	
Where would I be without His presence in my life?	
God's glory = present in heaven God's power = present on earth God's justice = present in hell God's grace = present in His people	If He denied us His *powerful* presence = we'd fall into nothing If He denied us His *gracious* presence = we'd fall into sin If He denied us His *merciful* presence = we'd fall into hell

JEREMIAH 23:24 *"'Can anyone hide himself in secret places, so I shall not see Him?' says the Lord. 'Do I not fill heaven and earth?'"*

Chapter 6 Argument #7 for God = The *LANGUAGE* of Life
The Biochemical information in the Cell and it's DNA infers an Intelligent Designer

> "Premise #1 = Intelligent information infers an intelligent design.
> Premise #2 = There is specific information in the cellular DNA of living organisms.
> Conclusion = Therefore, there must be an Intelligent Designer of Life."

Psalm 139: 13-18   God's *OMNIPOTENCE* = He designed me fearfully

vs 13 *"You have ①FORMED my inward parts; You have ②COVERED me in my mother's womb."*

① FORMED = "qânâh" = fashioned; possessed; owned: God owns my innermost parts; He doesn't just search and observe (omniscient) and indwell (omnipresent) my mind and heart – He owns my innermost, secret soul.

Ezekiel 18:4 *"... ALL SOULS ARE MINE; the soul of the father as well as the soul of the son is Mine..."*

Daniel 5:23 *"...the God who holds your breath in His hand and OWNS ALL YOUR WAYS, you have not glorified."*

② COVERED = "sâkak" = interweaved; knitted together: in David's most secret place (not yet born), God not only personally guards but intimately puts David's parts together as one intricately weaving a cloth or basket.

vs 14 *"I will praise You, for I am fearfully wonderfully made; marvelous are Your works, and that my soul ③KNOWS very well."*

③ KNOWS = "yâdà" = intimately understands (same as Psalm 139:1, Jeremiah 1:5); David has complete confidence in God as his Designer (before he was born) and his Lord (directing his pathway through life).

vs 15-16 *"My frame was not hidden from You, when I was made in secret, skillfully ④WROUGHT in the lowest parts of the earth. Your eyes saw my substance, being yet ⑤UNFORMED. And in Your book they all were written, the days ⑥FASHIONED for me, when as yet there were none of them."*

④ WROUGHT = "râqam" = embroidered, as in needlework (God weaved my veins, sinews, bones together)

⑤ UNFORMED = "gôlem" = imperfect; He sees and knows me before I appear in a physical body
  Jeremiah 1:5 *"Before I formed you in the womb I KNEW YOU..."*

⑥ FASHIONED = "yâtsar" = formed or molded into shape, as in potter purposefully working with clay to shape it

CH Spurgeon[25]: *"My form, my shape, and everything about me were appointed by God before they had existence. God saw me when I could not be seen. He wrote about me when there was nothing of me to write about."*

Every day:	My Body:
- I exercise 7 million brain cells.	1) has 45 miles of nerves, with electric impulses traveling at 250 mph
- my heart beats 103,689 times.	2) by age 70, my heart has beat 2.5 billion times and pumped 48,000,000 gallons of blood
- my blood travels 168,000,000 mi.	
- I move 750 major muscles.	3) one drop of my body's water: 5 million red blood cells, 10,000 white cells and 300,000 platelets.
- I inhale 438 cubic feet of air.	
- I speak 48,000 words.	4) the microorganisms that live in and on my body make up 10% of my body weight (dried, without water).
- I give off 85.6°F of heat.	
- I lose 7.8 pounds of waste.	5) a in^2 of human skin contains 20 ft of blood vessels, 1,300 nerve cells, 100 sweat glands and 3 million cells.
- I sweat 1.43 pints of water.	
	6) a in^2 of human skin has 32 million bacteria on it.
	7) I lose 600,000 skin particles/ hour, or 40 lbs in my lifetime
	8) of the100,000 hairs on my head, I lose 50-100 hairs everyday, but they are replaced that same day.
	9) each second 10,000,000 cells die and are replaced in my body.
	10) my ears and nose don't stop growing during my entire lifetime.
	11) bone = living tissue with blood and nerves; only 2% of bone are cells, but these cells destroy old bone and replace it with new bone
	12) my skeleton replaces itself every 7 yrs
	13) bone marrow = blood cell factory (red blood cells, platelets, white blood cells) producing 1 trillion cells daily
	14) bone: strong as granite when compressed, 25X stronger when pulled
	15) femur = stronger than reinforced concrete (bears 1,200 psi with each step; can withstand a force of 6 tons before fracturing

Jeremiah 1:5   *"Before I FORMED (Hebr. "yâtsar" = molded into shape, as a potter with clay) you in the womb, I KNEW (Hebr. "yâda" = intimately understood) you..."*

"DNA: Put in Perspective when compared to LEGOS", by John Leonard (May 27, 2013)

"Behold, a life-size replica of a Star Wars X-Wing fighter, made out of LEGOs. According to this article in New York magazine, the full scale model required 5,335,200 LEGOs and took 32 master builders working more than 17,000 hours to complete. The LEGO X-Wing has a wing span of 44 feet, weighing 44,000 pounds. Any parent whose kids enjoyed LEGOs has a memory of stepping barefoot on one of the ubiquitous plastic blocks. But don't worry about the LEGO X-Wing; it's all glued together as one piece. Now whether or not you are a fan of the toy building blocks, you'll have to admit the LEGO X-Wing fighter is one impressive creation.

Star Wars X-Wing Fighter
5,335,200 LEGOs

Compared to the DNA molecule, however, the LEGO X-Wing is actually quite simple. Over five million building blocks were used? That's nothing compared to the **6 billion** bits of information called nucleotides that comprise a DNA molecule, the "LEGO" of life. The complex instructions coded into DNA provide the blueprint for an organism that is produced through an ordered and specific process of development into a body plan. For abiogenesis to have occurred, either the enormously improbable event occurred in which DNA self-organized just in time for some fortuitous catalyst caused inanimate matter to come to life…or, some sort of help was involved.

In fact, two-time Nobel Prize-winning scientist Ilya Prigogine said 'The statistical probability that organic structures and the most precisely harmonized reactions that typify living organisms would be generated by accident, is zero' (N. Gregair, A. Babbyabtz, Physics Today 25, pp. 23-28).

While I have tremendous respect for the work of scientists such as Dr. Prigogine, I must reject his suggestion that the probability of abiogenesis without divine intervention is literally zero, because that implies we have absolute certainty about the origin of life. I'm perfectly satisfied with the probability of abiogenesis without the assistance of supernatural intelligence as very near zero, because the simple acknowledgement that God is infinitely more probable because the only alternative to accidental is intentional. The powerful entity that has both the means and ability to execute on that intent could only be God.

My atheist friends can protest as much as they would like, but I'm not concerned with winning friends or influencing people. I'm only interested in the truth. According to the Big Picture, as described in my book 'Counterargument for God', you can't answer an existential question by only looking at a small fraction of the evidence. If you fairly look at the evidence, it becomes readily obvious that "accidental" speciation cannot simply explain our existence through purely natural events, not if an accidental Big Bang and abiogenesis by blind luck are virtually impossible. As we learn from our observations of the Big Picture, the only alternative to God is extraordinary good luck. Luck too good to be true."

DNA: The "Book of Life" The following are excerpts Dr. Ravi Zacharias's book, 'The Grand Weaver': "Some time ago I had the privilege to speak at a conference at Johns Hopkins University on the theme "What Does It Mean to Be Human?" Before my address, Francis Collins, the director of the Human Genome Project and the co-mapper of human DNA, presented his talk. He spoke of the intelligibility and marvel of the book of life, filled with more than 3 billion bits of information.

In his last slide, he showed two pictures side by side. On the left appeared a magnificent photo of the stained-glass rose window from Yorkminster Cathedral in Yorkshire, England, its symmetry radiating from the center, its colors and geometric patterns spectacular—clearly a work of art purposefully designed by a gifted artist. Its sheer beauty stirred the mind. On the right side of the screen appeared a slide showing a cross section of a strand of human DNA. The picture did more than take away one's breath; it was awesome in the profoundest sense of the term —

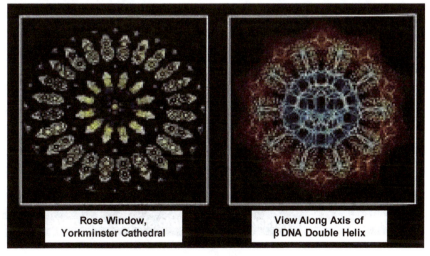

Rose Window, Yorkminster Cathedral

View Along Axis of β DNA Double Helix

not just beautiful, but overwhelming. And it almost mirrored the pattern of the rose window in Yorkminster…

The audience gasped at the sight, for it saw itself… Because of this design we can think in profound ways… we can map out the human genome and in it see the evidence of a great Cartographer. We can plan and now see a great Planner. We can sing and now see poetry in matter. We speculate and see the intricacies of purpose… At Johns Hopkins that day we saw the handiwork of the One who made us for himself."

The Double Helix DNA: God's detailed *LANGUAGE* that "fashions" me[15]

6.2

• Within each of the 100,000,000,000,000 cells in my body are twenty-three pairs of chromosomes made of tightly coiled DNA; the DNA carries 100,000 genes, each of which makes one specific protein.

• genes = my hereditary units carrying the instructions on how to recreate my entire body (they dictate everything from my hair and eye color to how my body processes sugar and how tall I am).

• proteins = the building blocks of life (the 100,000-plus proteins in my body do everything needed for me to live).

• DNA = long strand, consisting of two thin pieces of filament, wound tightly together in a twisted double helix (discovered by Francis Crick and James Watson in 1953, and won them the Nobel Prize).

"DNA 101": I am smarter than a 5th Grader

• The single-cell DNA molecule determines everything from whether I am left- or right-handed to my eye color to my foot size to whether I am at risk of heart disease.

• It is constructed of 3 repeating ingredients: 1) a sugar, 2) a phosphate (they combine to form DNA's "ladder", and they're always the same), and 3) a base (forms the DNA molecule's side chains, or the ladder's horizontal "rungs")
  - there are 4 different bases used in the "rungs": A = Adenine   C = Cytosine   G = Guanine   T = Thymine
  - Adenine only combines with Thymine; Guanine only combines with Cytosine

• 3,000,000 pairings of the 4 bases of the rungs (a staggering level of mathematical and biochemical complexity).

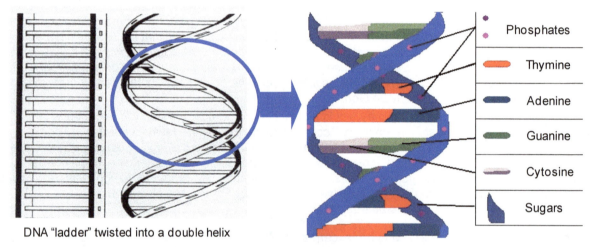

DNA "ladder" twisted into a double helix

• **DNA is complex**[15]
  - the DNA in 1 cell is > 5 feet long and so thin its only 50 *trillionths* of an inch wide, weighing only 1/50th of an ounce
  - if I could take this single-cell DNA and compress it down, it would be tinier than a speck of invisible dust
  - if I took all the DNA from my body's 100,000,000,000,000 cells and squeezed it together, it fits inside an ice cube
  - if I took the DNA from my 100,000,000,000,000 cells and stretched it end-to-end, it reaches over 10 billion miles
  - if my body's minimum 10-billion mile length of DNA was read out loud, at 3 bases every second (A, T, C, G, etc.), with a 40-hour reading week, it would take 132 years to complete.
  - because my body's cells are continually replaced with new ones, the cell's DNA is also "replicated" with incredible accuracy (DNA's "spellchecker" is an enzyme that examines newly-copied DNA; when an error is found, that piece is replaced; DNA's replication process makes only 1 error in a billion copy steps).

• **DNA has a specialized message**[15]
  - "genetic alphabet" = the 4 bases of the "rungs" in the "ladder" of DNA's double helix communicate a message
  - just as the specific order of letters in words communicate a unique message in a sentence, the specific *ORDER* of A, T, C and G in DNA's double helix in each cell determines the unique genetic makeup (what kind of life it is).

Isaiah 43:7 *"Everyone who is called by My name, whom I have created for My glory; I have FORMED (Hebr. "yâtsar" = molded into shape, as a potter with clay) him, yes, I have made him."*

Stephen Meyer, PhD: DNA = "God's Library of Life"[8]

• One of the most extraordinary discoveries of the 20th century was that DNA actually *STORES INFORMATION* (the detailed instructions for assembling **proteins**) in the 4-character chemical code (A, C, G, T). But here's the question: "What is the *SOURCE* of DNA's assembly instructions responsible for creating the proteins?"

- This foundational question has caused all naturalistic accounts of the origin of life to break down. If you can't explain where the information comes from, you haven't explained life, because it's the information that makes the molecules function as a living being.
- DNA is like a library. Each organism assesses the information it needs from DNA so it can build its critical components. In DNA, the long lines of A, C, G and T's are precisely arranged to create protein (to build just 1 protein, you need 1,200 – 2,000 letters or bases).

F. Turek: "The Key Question for Evolutionists"[9]

- All living thing's DNA doesn't consist of random letters but letters in a very specific order (just like real books).
- Staunch Darwinist Richard Dawkins admits that the message found in just the tiny 1-celled amoeba is has as much information in its DNA as 1,000 complete sets of the Encyclopedia Britannica (in other words, if you were to spell out all of the A, T, C and G in the "primitive" amoeba, the letters would fill 1,000 complete sets of encyclopedias!
- If simple messages like 'Take out the garbage – Mom', 'Mary loves Scott', and 'Drink Coke' require an intelligent being, then why doesn't a message 1,000 encyclopedias long require one?"

Using Probability Science (again): Could DNA's messaging have formed by Chance?

Statistics has proven that coincidence does not play a role in the formation of the coded information within DNA. The probability of the coincidental formation of even a single gene out of the 200,000 genes making up DNA is so low that even the notion of impossible remains weak. Frank Salisbury, an evolutionist and biologist, makes the following statement about this 'impossibility':

"A medium protein might include about 300 amino acids. The DNA gene controlling this would have about 1,000 nucleotides in its chain. Since there are four kinds of nucleotides in a DNA chain, one consisting of 1,000 links could exist in 4^{1000} forms. Using a little algebra we can see that $4^{1000} = 10^{600}$. Ten multiplied by itself 600 times gives the figure 1 followed by 600 zeros! This number is completely beyond our comprehension."

Even if we assume that all the necessary nucleotides are present in a medium, and that all the complex molecules and enzymes to combine them were available, the possibility of these nucleotides being arranged in the desired sequence is 1 in 4^{1000}, in other words, 1 in 10^{600}. Briefly, the probability of the coincidental formation of the code of an average protein in the human body in DNA by itself is 1 in 1 followed by 600 zeros.

This number, which is beyond even being astronomical, means in practice 'zero' probability. This means that such a sequence has to be effected under the control and knowledge of a wise and conscious power. There is zero probability of it happening by 'accident', 'chance', or 'coincidence'.

The probability of the coincidental formation of the code of an average protein in the human body in the DNA by itself is 1 in 10^{600}. We can write this number out as follows: 10^{600} = 1, 000,000,000,000,000,000,000,000,000, 000,000,000,000,000,000,000,000,000,000,000,000,000,000,000,000,000,000,000,000,000,000,000,000,000,000, 000,000,000,000,000,000,000,000,000,000,000,000,000,000,000,000,000,000,000,000,000,000,000,000,000,000, 000,000,000,000,000,000,000,000,000,000,000,000,000,000,000,000,000,000,000,000,000,000,000,000,000,000, 000,000,000,000,000,000,000,000,000,000,000,000,000,000,000,000,000,000,000,000,000,000,000,000,000,000, 000,000,000,000,000,000,000,000,000,000,000,000,000,000,000,000,000,000,000,000,000,000,000,000,000,000, 000,000,000,000,000,000,000,000,000,000,000,000,000,000,000,000,000,000,000,000,000,000,000,000,000,000, 000,000,000,000,000,000,000,000,000,000,000,000,000,000,000,000,000,000,000,000,000,000,000,000,000,000, 000,000,000,000,000,000,000,000,000,000,000,000,000,000,000,000,000,000,000.

Francis Crick, the biochemist who discovered the structure of DNA and an ardent evolutionist, won a Nobel prize with respect to the research he had made on the subject. In his book entitled "Life Itself: It's Origin and Nature", Crick testifies to the miraculous structure of DNA and states that the origin of life appears at the moment to be "almost a miracle." Even in Crick's view, life could never originate on earth spontaneously.

References: 1) F. Salisbury, "Doubts about Modern Synthetic Theory of Evolution",1, p. 6.
2) Francis Crick, "Life Itself: It's Origin and Nature", New York, Simon and Schuster, 11, p. .

Psalm 119:73 *"Your hands have made and FASHIONED (Hebr. "kûn" = directed, set in order as in framing) me; give me understanding, that I may learn Your commandments."*

THE CELL: God's micro-machinery that designs and sustains me — 6.3

Michael Denton[20]: *"It is astonishing to think that this remarkable piece of machinery, which possesses the ultimate capacity to construct every living thing that has ever existed on Earth, from a giant redwood to the human brain, can construct all its own components in a matter of minutes and… is of the order of several thousand million million times smaller than the smallest piece of functional machinery ever constructed by man."*

What is a Cell?

1) The smallest living units of all living things; discovered in 1665 by British scientist Robert Hooke who observed them in his optical microscope (he called them "cells" because their structure was like a tiny room or monk's cell).

2) Some organisms are made up of just one cell (e.g. bacteria and protozoans), but animals are multicellular (an adult human body has ≈ 100,000,000,000,000 cells, with each containing ≈ a trillion atoms).

3) Each cell has basic requirements to sustain it. The body's organs are built around providing the trillions of cells with those basic needs (such as oxygen, food, and waste removal). If people's cells are healthy, then they are healthy. All physiological processes, growth, development and disease can be described at the cellular level.

4) My body's most important communications are not my thoughts, but the messages between and within my cells (like hundreds of different circuits all wired to receive specific messages and generate specific responses).

M. Behe[8] and R. Swenson[15]: Cell = A Self-Contained Metropolis of Specialized, Complex Communication

1) Each cell in my body contains an all-powerful city hall (nucleus) surrounded by factories, archives, communications centers and power plants. Each cell nucleus contains the complete DNA for me.

- Nucleus = the information processing and administration center ("city hall")
- Mitochondria = the "power plant" for energy production via **ATP** (see description of irreducibly complex ATP)
- Ribosome = the "factory" where new cell components are manufactured
- Endoplasmic Reticulum = the "factory" for protein processing
- Golgi Apparatus = the distribution and shipping department
- Lysosome = the garbage disposal center
- Peroxisome = the detox center

2) Each cell lives in the community with its neighbors, doing its own specialized part.

3) Each cell generates its own electric field, which at times is larger than the electric field near a high-voltage power plant.

4) Each cell has an internal clock, switching on and off every 2-26 hours, never varying.

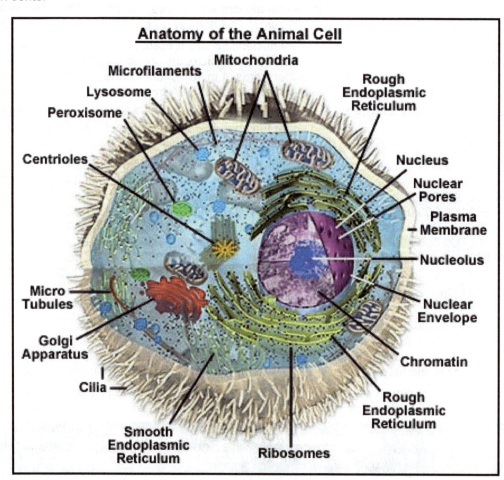

Anatomy of the Animal Cell

M. Behe[16]: The Cell's Microscopic Transportation System
"Not only is the ribosome amazing in that it manufactures new components, but now you're faced with the challenge of getting these new components into the right rooms where they can operate. To do that, you need another complicated system (just like you need a lot of things in place for a Greyhound bus to take someone from Philadelphia to Pittsburgh).

Each cell has a number of compartments, like rooms in a house. Each of these compartments is sealed off by a membrane (like the walls and door of a room) that is thinner than a spider's web and must function precisely or the cell will die. These components are designed to work in 1 room but not in another.

Here's an extremely simplified description the cell's "transportation system":

1) molecular trucks: they are enclosed and have motors attached to them.

2) highways: for these trucks to travel along

3) "ticket" attached to each protein: to make sure you let the protein onto the right molecular truck; you've got to be able to identify which components are supposed to go into which truck (it doesn't do any good if you just grab any protein that comes along because each one needs to go to a specific room)

4) truck route: the truck has to know where it's going (there must be signal on the truck itself and a complimentary signal on the compartment where the truck is supposed to unload its cargo)

5) cargo unloading mechanism: when the truck arrives where it's supposed to go, it pulls up to the dock and the cargo its carrying has to get out of the truck and into the compartment. It turns out that this is an active process that involves other components reorganizing each other, physically opening things up, and allowing the material to go inside.

"So you've got numerous components, all of which have to be in place or nothing works. If you don't have a signal, if you don't have the truck, you're pretty much out of luck. Now, does this microscopic transportation system sound like something that self-assembled by gradual modifications over the years? I don't see how it could have been. To me, it has all the earmarks of being designed."

R. Swenson[15]: The Cell's Never-ending Renewing of Me
"My cells are continually being torn down, remodeled and replaced. Think of it like this: if my body was a house, and my house was the size of Texas, imagine knocking down the walls in a million rooms every second and hastily rebuilding them again with new materials.

Every couple of days I replace all the cells lining the intestine. Every couple of weeks I replace all the cells of the skin. Every seven years I replace my entire skeleton.

It's almost as if God, working at the speed of light, is continuously tinkering with His invention. When Paul wrote 'Thought outwardly we are wasting away, yet inwardly we are being renewed day by day,' apparently he was correct on both the spiritual and physical levels."

Vs 17-18 *"How precious also are Your THOUGHTS to me, O God! How great is the sum of them! If I should count them, they would be more in number than the sand; when I awake, I am still with You."*

- David doesn't say *"When I awake, I return to You"*... David says "I am still with You". My communion with God is continuous and unbroken – He never leaves me

  Luke 15:31 *"He said to him, 'Son, you are always with Me, and all that I have is yours.'"*

  Matthew 28:20 *"...I am with you always, even to the end of the age."*

- <u>Who is the God of the Bible</u>? A Personal Creator who first carefully "fashioned me", then who *THINKS UPON ME CONTINUALLY* (at first, from eternity before I existed, then moment by moment while I live, then when time is no more) and thinks upon me endlessly (more than the innumerable grains of sand)!

Dr. Richard Swenson ('More than meets the Eye')[15]: "Put Your Faith in the Lord"

"If God put this all together, He must be very clever. And powerful. And precise. Does He know the position of all of these subatomic particles, all the time – even when they come in and out of existence in less than a trillionth of a second? Yes. He does.

The point is: such a God can be trusted with the details of my life. After rearranging subatomic particles all morning, the specifics of my life probably seem a bit unchallenging to Him."

Jeremiah 29:11 *"'For I know the THOUGHTS I have towards you', says the Lord; 'THOUGHTS of peace and not of evil, to give you a future and a hope.'"*

A.E. Wilder-Smith[11]: The Cell, DNA & ATP: *INFORMATION THEORY*   6.4

- **"Machine"** = thought expressed in matter with purpose (I am the highest-order "Von Neumann Machine")
- **"Von Neumann Machine"** = the more complex machines require more components and information

"The overwhelming evidence against Darwinian theory today lies in the discipline of which Darwin and his contemporaries knew just nothing, namely in the discipline of INFORMATION THEORY.

It is this new dimension opened up by information theory which has overwhelmed Darwin's type of thought. For it alone explains the sudden arisal of new species in the fossil record. It is information theory alone which is able to present reasonable ideas on its own subject as seen in the DNA molecule. Only information theory can explain the genesis of self replicating information storage and retrieval systems in biology.

In the present volume we have, therefore, endeavored to present and to develop a *scientifically sound theory* based on the INFORMATION FACTOR as a scientific alternative to Darwinian hypotheses.

Darwin thought that natural random phenomena, sifted and filtered by natural selection, could turn up biology. We know today what Darwin did not and indeed could not know, namely that biology's very heart depends upon an information storage and retrieval system which cannot conceivably arise in the random forces of natural law, but must arise in SURPRISE EFFECTS or INFORMATION which cannot be derived from natural laws

Darwin, had he lived in our era, would have put biology and its genesis down to the following formula:
'Matter + Time + Energy = Primeval Life', followed by 'Primeval Life + Time + Natural Selection = Evolution'.

It is a fact of science that in order to generate any machine the factor information "I" must be hybridized with matter. In the box below, we suggest that in order to arrive at the mechanisms (i. e . machine phenomena) of biology, the same factor "I" is just as necessary as factor t (= time) and factor energy.

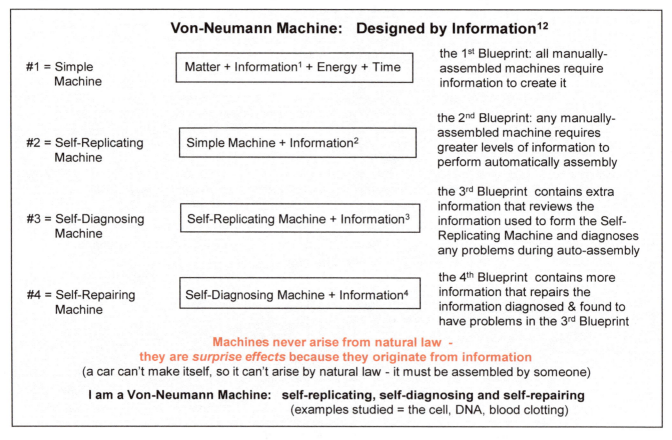

The alternative we here offer to Darwinian theory remains strictly scientific in that it recognizes one vital fact: - the necessity of factor "I" before any machine can be generated from raw matter, This generalization comprises and includes biological mechanisms.

We offer no explanation as to the source of factor "I". That is a matter, according to Noam Chomsky, beyond the capacity of the human mind, because it is and remains a true surprise effect (i. e. not derived from natural law in its generation). It would need therefore genuine revelation to solve the problem of the origin of factor "I".

The alternative we offer concerns the common sense necessity today in the age of computers of such a factor "I" in the synthesis of all machines including the mechanical and biological ones. The above facts have nothing to do with religious convictions. The facts are simply a scientific matter and as such we present them here as leading to a scientific alternative to evolutionary theory. "

ATP → The Cell's Energy Information Source to accomplish Life's work[22]

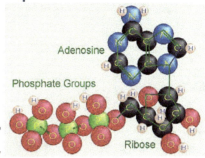

Arguably the second most important molecule behind DNA, ATP is the currency of the cell. When the cell needs to use energy such as when it needs to move substances across the cell membrane via the active transport system, it "pays" with molecules of ATP.

R. Swenson[15]: "Every cell contains 100's of these miniature ATP motors embedded in the surfaces of the mitochondria. Each motor is 200,000X smaller than a pinhead. At the center of the ATP molecule is a tiny wheel that turns at ≈ **6,000 rpm** and produces 3 new ATP molecules per rotation."

How fast does ATP's motor spin? The fastest production car made today Is the CCR supercar made by Swedish manufacturer Koenigsegg, reaches a top speed of 241 mph with a torque of 5,700 rpm. *So how is it possible that a microscopic motor, which is vastly more complicated to design, could have arisen by chance (given enough time) and outperform the highest performing man-made motor today?* It's reasonable to believe the ATP's performance is by DESIGN, not chance.

A single cell uses about 10 million ATP molecules per second to meet its metabolic needs, and recycles all of its ATP molecules about every 20-30 seconds. The enormous amount of activity that occurs inside each of the approximately one hundred trillion human cells is shown by the fact that at any instant each cell contains about *one billion* ATP molecules. This amount is sufficient for that cell's needs for only a few minutes and must be rapidly recycled. Given a hundred trillion cells in the average male, about 10^{23} or one sextillion ATP molecules normally exist in the body. For each ATP "the terminal phosphate is added and removed 3 times each minute".

The total human body content of ATP is only about 50 grams, which must be constantly recycled every day. The source of energy for constructing ATP is food; ATP is simply the carrier and regulation-storage unit of energy. A daily intake of 2,500 food calories translates into a turnover of a whopping 180 kg (400 lbs) of ATP.

ATP is an energy-coupling agent and not a fuel. It is not a storehouse of energy set aside for some future need. Rather it is produced by one set of reactions and is almost immediately consumed by another. ATP is formed as it is needed, primarily by oxidative processes in the mitochondria.

The ATP is used for many cell functions including *transport work* moving substances across cell membranes. It is also used for *mechanical work*, supplying the energy for muscle contraction. It supplies energy not only to the heart muscle (for blood circulation) and skeletal muscle (such as for gross body movement), but also to the chromosomes and flagella so they can carry out their many functions. A major role of ATP is in *chemical work*, supplying energy to synthesize the thousands of types of macromolecules that the cell needs to exist.

Without ATP, life is impossible. It is a perfectly designed molecule that provides the proper size energy packet for thousands of classes of reactions that occur in all forms of life. Even viruses rely on an ATP molecule identical to that used in humans. The ATP energy system is quick, highly efficient, produces a rapid turnover of ATP, and can rapidly respond to energy demand changes (Goodsell, 1996, page 79).

We are just beginning to understand how the ATP molecule works. Each ATP molecule is over 500 atomic mass units (500 AMUs). In manufacturing terms, the ATP molecule is a machine with a level of organization on the order of a research microscope or a standard television (Darnell, Lodish and Baltimore, 1996).

Among the questions evolutionists must answer include the following, *"How did life exist before ATP?" "How could life survive without ATP since no form of life we know of today can do that?"* and *"How could ATP evolve and where are the many transitional forms required to evolve the complex ATP molecule?"* No answers exist because only a perfect ATP molecule can properly carry out its role in the cell.

ATP = An Irreducibly Complex Machine. A potential ATP candidate molecule would not be selected by evolution until it was functional. Life could not exist without ATP or a molecule with the same function. ATP could have been created only as a unit to function immediately in life. The same is true of the other energy molecules used in life such as GTP.

Although other energy molecules can be used for certain cell functions, none comes close to satisfactorily replacing ATP's many functions. Over 100,000 other molecules like ATP have been designed to enable humans to live, and all the same problems related to their origin exist for them all. Many macromolecules that have greater detail than ATP exist, and **in order for life to exist all of them must work together as a unit**.

No transitional forms exist to bridge these 4 methods by evolution. According to the concept of irreducible complexity, these ATP producing machines must have been manufactured as functioning units and they could not have evolved by Darwinism mechanisms. Anything less than an entire ATP molecule will not function and a manufacturing plant which is less then complete cannot produce a functioning ATP (Behe, 1996).

Let's Review Some of What We've Learned About Design in Animals and People

Brain's highly organized network of 10,000,000,000 nerve cells processes billions of signals in billionths of seconds.

Eye's irreducible complexity transforms light photons to electricity so I can see.

Ear's irreducible complexity transforms sound waves to mechanical vibrations to electricity so I can hear.

Blood's irreducibly complex clotting system runs on autopilot so I don't bleed to Death.

There are 9 selected Facts about Animals and Humans...

Together these 9 Facts make a strong case for Living Things being *DESIGNED* (Job 12:7,9... Psalm 139)

Bombadier beetles' irreducibly complex defense system allows them to fire explosive chemicals without blowing themselves up.

Giraffes' irreducibly complex pressure-regulating valve system prevents their 25-pound heart from blowing their brains out when they take a drink..

The 1-pound godwit flies the exact same 7,145-mile migratory route year after year in 9 days without stopping for food, water or rest.

Bat echolocation is millions of times more efficient than any man-made radar or sonar.

DNA in my cells has all the detailed info. to create me!

Chapter 7   Argument #8 for God = The Human *SOUL*   7.1
Mankind's free will and moral consciousness infer an Intelligent Creator

> "Premise #1 =   Freedom to make moral choices cannot be explained by natural laws.
> Premise #2 =   Each person has the capacity to make conscious moral choices.
> Conclusion =   Therefore, moral consciousness was caused by something else, and this cause was God."

Psalm 139: 23-24   My Heart = where my God becomes my Lord

*"①SEARCH me, O God, and ②KNOW my ⑤HEART; ③TRY me, and know my anxieties;
and see if there is any wicked way in me, and lead me in the ④WAY everlasting."*

In Ps 139:1, David said God *had* mined him. Now, he *asks* God to exercise His Lordship over him: because my nature is to deceive myself, God must reveal the hidden sinful areas within me if I am to "crucify the outer man".

① SEARCH = *"châqar"* = penetrate, mine, examine intimately, dig, as in searching for precious metals
② KNOW = *"yâda"* = understand by careful observation
③ TRY = *"bâchan"* = to examine and prove through testing (as when going through a trial)
④ WAY = *"derek"* = extended journey as along a pathway or road
⑤ HEART = *"lêb", lêbâb"* = my SOUL = interior-most organ; center of my will, feelings and intellect; the *invisible, immaterial* center of who I am (used over 190 times throughout the Old Testament)

David, like Paul (Romans 7) and Jeremiah (Jerem. 17), knows that God must *SEARCH* the hidden, dark corners of his heart and *EXPOSE* David's wicked ways to him, or David will be *DECEIVED* by his own sinful nature.

My PHYSICAL Heart – God's amazing Design

- Scientists still don't know what causes the human heart to automatically begin the "auto-rhythmic" beating function that permits us to have physical existence.
- <u>my heart</u>: weighs < 1lb, body's hardest working muscle, incredibly reliable mechanical pump
  1) my heart beats ≈ 100,000 times in one day (million times in a year) without me ever having to think about it (during my lifetime, my heart will beat more than 2.5 billion times)
  2) my body has ≈ 6 quarts of blood; my heart pumps 9 pints per minute, or 1,500 gallons of blood every day, or 1 million barrels during my lifetime (enough to fill 3 super tankers).
  3) my heart can create enough pressure that it could squirt blood at a distance of 30 feet.
- <u>my heart's only job</u> = circulate blood throughout the body
  1) my body's blood circulates through my body 3X every minute (in 1 day, my blood travels 12,000 miles – that's 4 times the distance across the US from coast to coast).
     it pumps my body's O_2-poor blood to the lungs, where CO_2 is released and more oxygen absorbed.
  3) it then collects the oxygenated blood as it comes from the lungs and pumps it to every part of the body, delivering O_2 to the body's cells, which need it to survive.
  4) along the way, blood also passes through the abdomen, past cells that line the intestines and stomach, where it picks up nutrients that it will distribute to other parts of the body.

My SPIRITUAL Heart: how does God show me who I really am on the *inside*? ➔ **The BIBLE**

The Bible: FIRE
Jerem. 5:14, 23:29

Jeremiah 5:14, 23:29 *"Thus says the Lord God of hosts: 'Because you speak this word, behold, I will make My words in your mouth ①FIRE, and this people wood, and it shall devour them. Is not My word like a ①FIRE?' says the Lord."*

① FIRE = Hebr. *"êsh"* = raging fire; flaming hot
 a) general application: God's word is like fire because it *consumes peoples' hearts.*
 b) When I read the Bible, it is God's power to *BURN* the useless things out of my life.

The Bible: a SWORD   Eph. 6:17   Hebr. 4:12

Ephesians 6:17 *"...the ②SWORD of the Spirit, which is the word of God.*
Hebrews 4:12 *"...the word of God is living and powerful, and sharper than any 2-edged sword, piercing even to the division of soul and spirit, and of joints and marrow, and is a discerner of the thoughts and intents of the HEART."*

② SWORD = Gr. *"machaira"* = a small knife, 6-18" long, used for hand-to-hand combat.
If the fire of God's word doesn't get my attention, the SWORD will. It quickly CUTS to the heart of the matter.

Jeremiah 23:29 *"Is not My word like... a ③HAMMER that breaks the rock in pieces?"*
③ HAMMER = Hebr. "patûysh" = pounding hammer for smashing things into pieces
If you are thinking "The Bible has never been a fire or a sword to me", it's because your heart is so hard that God's words bounce right off it (Proverbs 28:14)!

What is a "Hard Heart"? I may not be in conscious rebellion against God...but my heart no longer feels God's conviction (my heart has grown insensitive to His voice). How can I tell if it's happened to me? When I am repeatedly exposed to a truth and refuse to apply it (I hear the truth over and over again – and I just keep ignoring it). My degree of hard-heartedness = the difference between what grieves me vs. what grieves God (when what grieves God no longer grieves me, my heart is hard).

James 1:23-25 *"...if anyone is a hearer of the word and not a doer, he is like a man observing his natural face in a mirror; for he ④OBSERVES HIMSELF, goes away, and immediately forgets what kind of man he was. But he who looks into the perfect law of liberty and continues in it, and is not a forgetful hearer but a doer of the word, this one will be blessed in what he does."*

④ OBSERVES = Gr. *"katanoeō"* = carefully studies himself (I look in the Bible and God shows me something about myself that I can grasp fully)

The Bible is like a mirror: it shows me what I need to fix (how stupid is it to see in a mirror that I have ketchup on my face, and then I just leave it there?)

Psalm 139:24	God's Power: He *LEADS* me in "the way everlasting"
He wants me to be "still"	Because He is "still"
• I must "cease raging" to know His presence Ps 46:10 *"BE STILL, and KNOW that I am God."* "still" = Heb. *"râphâh"* = "be feeble"; "don't panic"; "cease raging" (only time used in O.T.) "know" = Heb. *"yâda"* = "understand by observing"; discern, comprehend Prov. 14:16 *"..a fool RAGES and is self-confident."* "rages" = Heb. *"âbar"* = overruns, provokes • Trusting God = "rest quietly" in His presence Ps 4:4-5 *"Be angry, and do not sin. Meditate within your heart on your bed, and BE STILL.* (Heb. *"dâmam"* = "rest"; "wait")*... Offer the sacrifices of righteousness, and put your trust in the Lord."*	• God's character = gentleness and quietness 1Ki 19:11-12 *"'Go out, and stand on the mountain before the Lord,'... the Lord passed by, and a great and strong wind tore into the mountains and broke the rocks in pieces before the Lord, but the Lord was not in the wind; and after the wind an earthquake, but the Lord was not in the earthquake; and after the earthquake a fire, but the Lord was not in the fire; and after the fire a STILL, small voice."* (Heb. *"d'mâmâh"* = "quiet"; "delicate whisper") Ps 23:2 *"...He LEADS me beside the STILL waters."* (Heb. *"m'nûchâh"* = "peaceful", "restful", "calm") • God's salvation = His work that makes peace between us Isaiah 32:17 *"The work of righteousness shall be PEACE, and the effect of righteousness, QUIETNESS and assurance forever."*

"The Way Everlasting"= Peace with God through Christ my Lord
Mark 4:39 (Ps 107:29) *"Jesus arose and rebuked the wind, and said to the sea, 'Peace, BE STILL!', and the wind ceased and there was a great calm."* ("phimóo" = "cease raging")

R. Swenson[15]: "Trusting in His Sovereignty and Power = Why I'm at peace"
"God's power and precision is undeniable. His sovereignty is on display. So why do we live in such a stupor? How can such power fail to dominate our every thought and action? It's not that God failed to clearly demonstrate His nature or that He has been lax in instructing us. We are SLOW TO UNDERSTAND. Our eyesight is dim. This world is too much for us. But when we do understand the sovereignty, power, design, majesty, precision, genius, intimacy and caring of an Almighty God, It takes away our fear. It allows us to sleep at night and trust Him with the running of His own universe. It allows us to seek His will rather than follow our own mind. The more we trust in God's power, the less we worry about our weakness. The more we trust in God's sovereignty, the less we fret about our future."

Romans 5:1 *"Having been justified by FAITH, we have PEACE with God*
(Eph. 2:14, Phil. 4:7) *through our Lord Jesus Christ"*

Matthew 22:37 "My Conscience and Intelligence (heart, soul and spirit)" 7.2

"You shall love the Lord your God with all your HEART, with all your SOUL and all your MIND."
"heart" (*"kardia"*) = feelings, thoughts   "soul" (*"psuchē"*) = immaterial part   "mind" (*"dianoia"*) = intelligence

➔ **Who I am: just a complex, evolved machine?**
Marvin Minsky (MIT Prof., evolutionist)[8]: *"The human brain is a computer made of meat."*
Francis Crick (geneticist)[8]: *"Humans are the behavior of a vast assembly of nerve cells and their molecules."*

➔ **If I am a machine: where did my intelligence come from?**   René Descarte: *"I think, therefore I am"*
Acts 17:11 *"These were more fair-minded than those in Thessalonica, in that they received the word with all readiness of ①MIND, and ②SEARCHED the Scriptures daily to find out whether these things were so."*
① READINESS OF MIND = Greek *"prothumia"* = intellectually willing; predisposed
② SEARCHED = Greek *"anakrinō"* = scrutinize, investigate, examine

Phil. 2:2-5   *"...let this ③MIND be in you which was also in Christ Jesus..."*
③ MIND = Greek *"phroneô"* = disposition, inward interest or reflection
Ezra 7:10 *"Ezra ④PREPARED his ⑤HEART to seek the Law of the Lord, to do it, and to teach statutes and ordinances in Israel."*
④ PREPARED = Hebrew *"kûn"* = erected or fixed; applied or established in a firm way
⑤ HEART = Hebrew *"lâbâb"* = the innermost organ; refers to my mind or understanding

---

Michael Ruse (Darwinist)[8]: "Science can't explain man's intelligence and his capacity to self-examine"
"Why should a bunch of atoms have thinking ability? Why should I, even as I write now, be able to reflect on what I am doing and why should you, even as you read now, be able to ponder my points, agreeing or disagreeing, deciding to refute me or deciding that I am just not worth the effort? No one, certainly not the Darwinian as such, seems to have an answer for this... the point is that there is no scientific answer."

J.P. Moreland[8]: "The Human Soul = More Evidence for Divine Creation and against Evolution"
- *"How do you get something totally different – conscious, living, thinking, feeling, believing creatures – from matter that doesn't have that? That's the point – you can't get something from nothing!*
- *You either have 'In the beginning were particles,' or 'In the beginning was the Logos'. If you start with particles, and the history of the universe is about particles rearranging, you may end up with a more complicated arrangement of particles, but you still end up with particles. You're not going to have minds or consciousness.*
- *However, it makes sense that if you begin with an infinite mind, then you can explain how finite minds could come into existence. What doesn't make sense - and which many evolutionists are conceding – is the idea of getting a mind to squirt into existence by starting with brute, dead, mindless matter. That's why some of them are trying to get rid of consciousness by saying it's not real and that we're just computers.*
- *The Christian worldview begins with thought and feeling and belief and desire and choice. That is, God is conscious. God has thoughts. He has beliefs, desire and awareness, He's alive, He acts with purpose. We start there. And because we start with the mind of God, we don't have a problem explaining the origin of our mind."*

➔ **What is my "consciousness"?**   ⑥ CONSCIENCE = Gr. *"suneidēsis"* = moral awareness; self-perception
Acts 24:16 *"...I myself always strive to have a ⑥CONSCIENCE without offense toward God and man."*
- it's what I am aware of when I self-reflect or introspect (when I pay attention to what's going on inside of me).
- It's not the same as behavior – it's what *causes* behavior. It's my thoughts, emotions, desires, beliefs that make me alive and aware. If consciousness didn't exist: I wouldn't be *aware* of things around me (a state trooper pulling behind me with lights flashing causes a "panic attack" before I even know why I'm being pulled over).
- God gave me *pain* to warn my body, and a *conscience* to alert me to right vs. wrong (Rom. 2:14-15).
John 8:7-9 *"'He who is without sin among you, let him throw a stone at her first'. Again He stooped down and wrote on the ground. Those who heard it, being convicted by their ⑥CONSCIENCE, went out one by one, beginning with the oldest even to the last. And Jesus was left alone, and the woman standing in the midst."*

➔ **What is my "soul"?**   ⑦ SOUL = Hebr. *"nephesh"*, Gr. *"psuchē"* = breath; immaterial, invisible "vitality"
Ps 139:14 *"... I am fearfully and wonderfully made; marvelous are Your works, and that my ⑦SOUL knows very well."*
- the "I", or ego, or self, that contains our consciousness and animates our body.
- it is immaterial and distinct from the body (that's why the body becomes a corpse when the soul leaves it).
1Ki 17:21-22 *"...he ... cried out to the Lord and said, 'O Lord my God, I pray, let the child's ⑦SOUL come back to him.' Then the Lord heard the voice of Elijah; and the ⑦SOUL of the child came back to him and he revived."*
- Matthew 10:28 "Jesus describes the body and soul as separate entities": *"Don't fear those who kill the body but cannot kill the ⑥SOUL. But fear Him who is able to destroy both ⑦SOUL and body in hell."*

J.P. Moreland[8]: "Who I really am is invisible" *"A person is really invisible. My soul and conscience are invisible (which makes it hard to conceptualize them), while my body is visible. If I were just my conscience, when my conscience was different, I'd be a different person. But I can be the same person even though my conscience changes, so I can't be the same as my conscience.*

I've got to be the 'self', or soul, that contains my conscience. The same holds for my body. I can't be divided into pieces. I'm either a person or I'm not. But my brain and body can be divided. So I can't be the same as my body.

We don't learn about people by studying their bodies. We learn about people by finding out how they feel, what they think, what they're passionate about, what their worldview is... we get 'inside' people to learn about them.

There's more to me than my conscious life and body. I am a 'self', or an 'I', that cannot be seen or touched unless I reveal myself by my behavior or my talk. I have free will because I am a 'self', or a soul, not just a brain."

➔ **What are 3 evidences that validate I possess an immaterial "soul" with a "conscience"?**

Barry Beyerstein (brain scientist)[8]: *"Just as the kidneys produce urine, the brain produces consciousness."*

Many people don't believe people have an immaterial soul. They believe conscience is purely material, resulting from biological development. But there are 3 evidences that contradict "physicalism" and validate my spirituality:

#1) I reflect on things from a first-person (subjective or personal) point of view.
Each person has their own, unique point of view on any subject. If everything was just physical, it would be described in the third-person (objective, impersonal).

Luke 2:19 *"...Mary kept all these things and pondered them in her heart."*

J.P. Moreland[8]: "My soul: the inner and private 'me'"
"By simply introspecting, I have a way of knowing about what's happening in my mind that is not available to anyone else (my spouse, my best friend, my neurosurgeon). A scientist could know more about what's happening in my brain than I do, but he or she can't know more about what's happening in my mind than I do. He has to ask me. The human soul is vastly complicated because it's made in the image of God. We self-reflect and think."

#2) I have a free will: I can make choices (I'm more than just a physical brain).
Physical matter is governed by the laws of nature. If I'm just a material object, everything I do is fixed (I'm a computer that acts according to the programming I've received). So whatever is going to happen is already rigged by my makeup and environment, so I can't be held responsible for my behavior since I wasn't free to choose it.

1Kings 18:21 *"...Elijah came to all the people and said, "How long will you falter between two opinions? If the Lord is God, follow Him; but if Baal, then follow him."*

#3) I have a "disembodied" state (I don't "cease to exist" when I die; my soul lives on for eternity).
The Bible teaches that when I die, my soul leaves my body and awaits the resurrection of my body from the dead. But if I'm just a brain, it's impossible for me to exist outside my body.

Luke 23:42-43 *"...he said to Jesus, 'Lord, remember me when You come into Your kingdom.' And Jesus said to him, 'Assuredly, I say to you, today you will be with Me in Paradise.'"*

➔ **What is my "spirit"?**   "spirit" = Gr. *"pneuma"* = breath; immaterial, invisible part of me

Romans 8:16 *"The Spirit Himself bears witness with our SPIRIT that we are children of God."*

1Thes. 5:23 *"...may the God of peace Himself sanctify you completely; and may your whole SPIRIT* (pneuma), *SOUL* (psuchē) *and BODY* (soma) *be preserved blameless at the coming of our Lord Jesus Christ."*

Heb. 4:12 *"...the word of God is ... sharper than any 2-edged sword, piercing even to the division of SOUL* (psuchē) *and SPIRIT* (pneuma), *and of joints and marrow, and is a discerner of the thoughts and intents of the HEART* (kardia)".

Vine's Expository Dictionary: "The language of Hebrews 4:12 suggests the difficulty in distinguishing between the soul and the spirit, alike in their nature and in their activities. For example, in **Matthew 26:38** Jesus says His soul feels the emotions of extreme sorrow, while in **John 13:21** Jesus says His spirit feels the emotions of distress.

Putting this all together = JOHN 3:3   What it means to be "BORN AGAIN"

"Born twice, die once; born once, die twice"

My spirit must be born a second time to escape the second death (Revelation 21:8).

The spirit = the "inner man" designed by God to be His dwelling place
The soul = the invisible, "outer man" containing the mind, will, emotions
The body = the "flesh" (material organism animated by the soul and spirit)

JOHN 14:23 = I am indwelt by the Holy Spirit in UNION with my human spirit: I turn control of "me" over to Him; He indwells my spirit and governs my soul. My body is now useable to visibly express my *new life* (born again) in Christ (Matt. 5:16 - I glorify God through my outward expression of my new "crucified life")

Men and Women are 3-part beings: Spirit, Soul, Body

1 Thes. 5:23 *"Now may the God of peace Himself sanctify you completely; and may your whole SPIRIT, SOUL and BODY be preserved blameless at the coming of our Lord Jesus Christ."*

Genesis 2:7 *"And the Lord God formed man out of the dust of the ground (BODY), and breathed into his nostrils the breath of life (SPIRIT); and man became a living being (SOUL)."*

Hebrews 4:12 *"For the word of God is powerful, and sharper than any 2-edged sword, piercing even to the division of SOUL and SPIRIT, and of joints and marrow, and is a discerner of the thoughts and intents of the HEART."*

- **Man's SPIRIT = "pneuma"** – the *inner man* (invisible, immaterial, eternal) designed by God to be His dwelling place (because of the curse, man is dead in his spirit, without God - only through the new birth does He indwell man).

Ezekiel 36:27 *"I will put My Spirit within you and cause you to walk in My statutes, and you will keep My judgments and do them."*

Galatians 2:6 *"And because you are sons, God has sent forth the Spirit of His Son into your hearts, crying out, 'Abba, Father!'"*

1 John 3:24 *"And by this we know that He abides in us, by the Spirit whom He has given us."*

1 Corinthians 2:14 *"But the natural man does not receive the things of God, for they are foolishness to him; nor can he know them, because they are spiritually discerned."*

- **Man's SOUL = "psuche"** – the body's *outer man* which, like the spirit, is invisible and immaterial; it encompasses both your MIND (reasoning/ the will) and HEART (morals/ emotions/ feelings); your true, secret character (only God sees).

1 Samuel 16:7 *"...the Lord said to Samuel, 'Do not look at his appearance or at the height of his stature, because I have rejected him. For the Lord does not see as man sees; man looks at the outward appearance, but the Lord looks at the heart."*

Psalm 44:21 *"Would not God search this out? For He knows the secrets of the heart."*

Jeremiah 17:9 *"The heart is deceitful above all things, and incurably sick - who can know it? I, the Lord, search the heart, I test the mind, to give to everyone according to his ways, and according to the fruit of his doings."*

- **Man's BODY = "soma"** – the physical nature of man (distinct from the spirit "pneuma" and the soul "psuche"); the visible part of man that is the container of the soul and spirit, and expresses on the outside the decisions made by the soul on the inside.

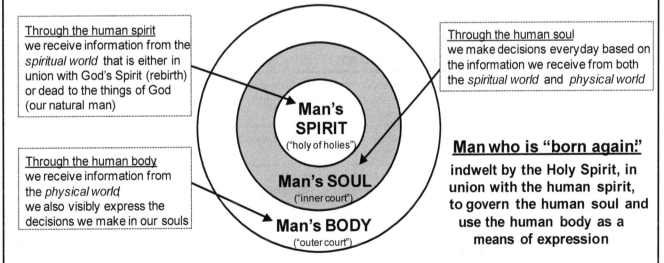

Through the human spirit we receive information from the *spiritual world* that is either in union with God's Spirit (rebirth) or dead to the things of God (our natural man)

Through the human soul we make decisions everyday based on the information we receive from both the *spiritual world* and *physical world*

Through the human body we receive information from the *physical world*; we also visibly express the decisions we make in our souls

Man's **SPIRIT** ("holy of holies")
Man's **SOUL** ("inner court")
Man's **BODY** ("outer court")

Man who is "born again:" indwelt by the Holy Spirit, in union with the human spirit, to govern the human soul and use the human body as a means of expression

Chapter 8 — How Darwinian Evolution is taught in Schools

From Dr. Jonathan Wells's Book "Icons of Evolution": 10 Questions to ask your biology teacher about Darwinian Evolution[17]

1. **ORIGIN OF LIFE.** Why do textbooks claim that the MILLER-UREY EXPERIMENT shows how life's building blocks may have formed on the early Earth -- when conditions on the early Earth were probably nothing like those used in the experiment, and the origin of life remains a mystery?

2. **DARWIN'S TREE OF LIFE.** Why don't textbooks discuss the "Cambrian explosion," in which all major animal groups appear together in the fossil record fully formed instead of branching from a common ancestor -- thus contradicting the evolutionary tree of life?

3. **HOMOLOGY.** Why do textbooks define homology as similarity due to common ancestry, then claim that it is evidence for common ancestry -- a circular argument masquerading as scientific evidence?

4. **VERTEBRATE EMBRYOS.** Why do textbooks use drawings of similarities in vertebrate embryos as evidence for their common ancestry -- even though biologists have known for over a century that vertebrate embryos are not most similar in their early stages, and the drawings are faked?

5. **PEPPERED MOTHS.** Why do textbooks use pictures of peppered moths camouflaged on tree trunks as evidence for natural selection -- when biologists have known since the 1970's that the moths don't normally rest on tree trunks, and all the pictures have been staged?

6. **DARWIN'S FINCHES.** Why do textbooks claim that beak changes in Galapagos finches during a severe drought can explain the origin of species by natural selection -- even though the changes were reversed after the drought ended, and no net evolution occurred?

7. **ARCHAEOPTERYX.** Why do textbooks portray this fossil as the missing link between dinosaurs and modern birds -- even though modern birds are probably not descended from it, and it's supposed ancestors do not appear until millions of years after it?

8. **MUTANT FRUIT FLIES.** Why do textbooks use fruit flies with an extra pair of wings as evidence that DNA mutations can supply raw materials for evolution -- even though the extra wings have no muscles and these disabled mutants cannot survive outside the laboratory?

9. **HUMAN ORIGINS.** Why are artists' drawings of ape-like humans used to justify materialistic claims that we are just animals and our existence is a mere accident -- when fossil experts cannot even agree on who our supposed ancestors were or what they looked like?

10. **EVOLUTION A FACT?** Why are we told that Darwin's theory of evolution is a scientific fact -- even though many of its claims are based on misrepresentations of the facts?

Answers from EVOLUTION: Who am I? Why am I here? Where did I come from?	
I'm the winning result of millions of totally random mutations between organisms over millions of years, as my species fought for survival in a harsh world… - Scientific evidence: Peppered Moths, Darwin Finches	Natural selection
Originating by a luck-of-the-draw event when living matter suddenly came from nonliving… - Scientific evidence: Miller-Urey Experiment	Abiogenesis
And I kept evolving from an original, common ancestral organism…. - Scientific evidence: Darwin's Tree of Life, Embryology, Homologous Structures	Common Ancestor
With many transitional steps as I developed from that original ancestor to a human being… - Scientific evidence: Fossil Record	Transitional Forms
So I'm here on earth for no specific purpose…..William Provine (Cornell Univ. Biologist)[14] "If Darwinism is true, then there are five inescapable conclusions: 1) there's no evidence for God, there's no life after death, 3) there's no absolute foundation for right and wrong, 4) there's no ultimate meaning for life, 5) people don't really have free will."	Secular Humanism

What our kids learn in High School: 11 Evidences for Darwinian Evolution   8.1
Biology II, Lees Summit HS, Lees Summit, MO
"Biology – Concepts and Connections, 5th Edition" (Neil A. Campbell, Jane B. Reece, Martha R. Taylor, Eric J. Simon)

① **Miller-Urey Experiment – "Life from Non-Life" (module 16.3)** = "Miller was the first to show that amino acids and other organic molecules *could have been* generated on a lifeless Earth. Miller's experiments were a test of a hypothesis about the origin of life developed in the 1920's by Russian biochemist A.I. Oparin and British geneticist J.B.S. Haldane. Oparin and Haldane independently proposed that the conditions on early Earth *could have* generated a collection of organic molecules that in turn *could have* given rise to the first living organisms. They reasoned that present-day conditions on Earth do not allow the spontaneous synthesis of organic compounds simply because the atmosphere is rich in O_2. Oxygen is corrosive: as a strong oxidizing agent, it tends to disrupt chemical bonds by extracting electrons from them. However, before the early prokaryotes added O_2 to the air, Earth *probably* had a reducing (electron-adding) atmosphere instead of an oxidizing one. An early reducing atmosphere *could have caused* simple molecules to combine, forming more complex ones.

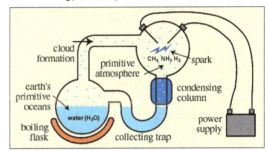

Miller and Urey predicted that organic molecules would form from inorganic ones under conditions like those on early Earth. A flask of warmed water represented the primeval sea. The 'atmosphere' consisted of a mixture of water vapor, H_2, CH_4, and NH_3 – the gases that scientists in the 1950's thought prevailed in the ancient world. Electrodes discharged sparks into the gas mixture to mimic lightning. Below the spark chamber, a glass jacket called a condenser surrounded the apparatus. Filled with cold water, the condenser cooled and condensed the water vapor in the gas mixture, causing 'rain', along with any dissolved compounds, to fall back into the miniature sea... After the experiment proceeded for a week, Miller found a variety of organic compounds in the solution, including some of the amino acids that make up the proteins of organisms.

Since the 1950's, Miller and other researchers have made most of the 20 amino acids commonly found in organisms, as well as sugars, lipids, the nitrogen bases present in the nucleotides of DNA and RNA, and even ATP. These laboratory studies support the idea that many of the organic molecules that make up living organisms *could have* formed before life itself arose on Earth.

Scientists now think that the composition of the atmosphere of early Earth was somewhat different from what Miller *assumed* in his historic first experiment. Some scientists doubt that the early earth atmosphere played a direct role in early chemical reactions. Controversy exists over whether the atmosphere contained enough H_4 and NH_3 to be reducing. Growing evidence indicates that the early atmosphere as a whole was chemically neutral, made up primarily of N_2 and CO_2. Still, it is possible that small 'pockets' of the early atmosphere – perhaps near volcanic openings – were reducing." ← **Refuting Evidence = Miller-Urey Experiment Lesson 8.2**

② **Fossil Record (module 13.3)** = "The fossil record testifies that organisms have evolved in a historical sequence. The oldest known fossils, dating from about 3.5 billion years ago, are prokaryotes. Molecular and cellular evidence also *indicates* that prokaryotes were the ancestors of all life. Fossils in younger layers of rock reveal the evolution of various groups of eukaryotic organisms. One example is the successive appearance of the different classes of vertebrates (animals with backbones). Fishlike fossils are the oldest vertebrates in the fossil record. Amphibians are next, followed by reptiles, then mammals and birds.

The evolutionary view of life predicts that we would find signs in the fossil record of linkages between ancient extinct organisms and species living today. Indeed, paleontologists have discovered many fossils that link past and present. For example, a series of fossils documents the changes in skull shape and size that occurred as mammals evolved from reptiles. And another series of fossils indicates that whales evolved from four-legged land mammals that lived some 55 million years ago." ← **Refuting Evidence = Cambrian Explosion Lesson 8.11**

③ **Punctuated Equilibrium (module 14.10)** = Many evolutionary biologists since Darwin's time, and even Darwin himself, have been struck by how few sequences of fossils have ever been found that clearly show a gradual, steady accumulation of small changes in evolutionary lineages. Instead, most fossil species appear suddenly in a layer of rock and persist essentially unchanged through several layers (strata) until disappearing from the record of the rocks as suddenly as they appeared. Paleontologists Niles Eldredge and Stephen Jay Gould coined the term PUNCTUATED EQUILIBRIUM to describe these abrupt episodes of speciation punctuating long periods of little change, or equilibrium... The model *suggests* that the evolution of our *hypothetical* butterflies actually occurs in spurts... Even though the emergence of this species actually took thousands of years, the overall history of the lineage as depicted in the fossil record *may seem* to fit the punctuated equilibrium model."
← **Refuting Evidence = Transitional Forms - The Fossil Record Lesson 8.11**

④ **Comparative Embryology (module 13.4)** = "The comparison of early stages of development is another major source of evidence for the common descent of organisms. One sign that vertebrates evolved from a common ancestor is that all of them have an embryonic stage in which they have structures on the sides of the throat called PHARYNGEAL POUCHES. At this stage, the embryos of fishes, frogs, snakes, birds and mammals look relatively alike. They take on more and more distinctive features as development progresses. For example, pharyngeal pouches develop into gills in fishes, but into parts of the ears and throat in humans." ← Refuting Evidence = Embryology Lesson 8.4

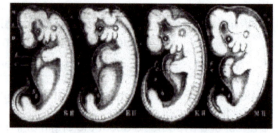

⑤ **Comparative Anatomy & Homologous Structures (module 13.4)** = "The comparison of body structures in different species. Anatomical similarities between many species give signs of common descent. Similarity in characteristics that results from common ancestry is known as **homology**. As Figure 13.4A shows, the same skeletal elements make up the forelimbs of humans, cats, whales, and bats, all of which are mammals. The functions of these forelimbs differ. A whale's flipper does not do the same job as a bat's wing, so *if these structures had been uniquely engineered, we would expect that their basic designs would be very different*. However, their structural similarity would not be surprising if all mammals descended from a common ancestor with the same basic limb elements. The *logical explanation* is, in fact, that the arms, forelegs, flippers, and wings of different mammals are variations on a common anatomical plan that has become adapted to different functions. Biologists call such similarities in different organism's **homologous structures** – features that often have different functions but are structurally similar because of common ancestry.

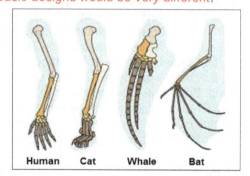

Comparative anatomy testifies that evolution is a remodeling process in which ancestral structures that originally functioned in one capacity become modified as they take on new functions – the kind of process that Darwin called 'descent with modification.' We see many signs that evolution remodels structures rather than creating them anew. For example, the human spine and knee joint were derived from ancestral structures that supported four-legged mammals. Almost none of us will reach old age without experiencing knee or back problems. *If these structures had been designed specifically to support our bipedal posture, we would expect them to be less subject to painful ailments*." ← Refuting Evidence = Homologous Structures Lesson 8.5

⑥ **Vestigial Organs (module 13.4)** = "These are structures of marginal, if any, importance to the organism, and are remnants of structures that served important functions in the organism's ancestors. The small hind-leg and foot bones of modern whales are examples of vestigial organs. The skeletons of some snakes retain vestiges of the pelvis and leg bones of walking ancestors. Because limbs are a hindrance to a snake's way of life, natural selection favored snake ancestors with successively smaller limbs."
← Refuting Evidence = Vestigial Organs Lesson 8.6

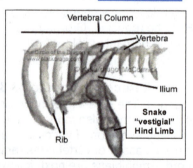

⑦ **Refinement, Expatiation & the Vertebrate Eye (module 14.11)** =
"The Darwinian theory of gradual change can account for the evolution of intricate structures such as the eyes or of new body structures such as wings. In most cases, complex structures have evolved in increments from simpler versions having the same basic function – a process of REFINEMENT. In others, we can trace the origin of evolutionary novelties to the gradual adaptation of existing structures to new functions.

As an example of the process of gradual refinement, consider the amazing camera-like eyes of vertebrates and squids. *Evidence* today supports the *hypothesis* that all complex eyes evolved from a simple ancestral patch of photoreceptor cells through a series of incremental modifications that benefited the owners at each stage. Figure 14.11 illustrates the range of complexity in the structure of eyes among mollusks living today. Some mollusks have very simple eyes. Others have eye cups that have no lenses or other means of focusing images. In those mollusks that do have complex eyes, the organs *probably* evolved in small stages of adaptation.

Throughout their evolutionary history, eyes retained their basic function of vision. But evolutionary novelty can also arise through the gradual acquisition of new functions. The term EXPATIATION refers to a structure that evolved in one context and later was adapted for another function. This term *suggests* that a structure can become adapted to alternative functions... natural selection can only result in the improvement of a structure in the context of its current utility." ← Refuting Evidence = The Eye Chapter 5, Lessons 5.1, 5.2

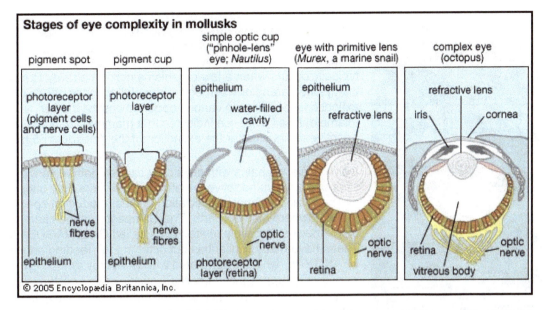

⑧ **Bird Evolution & Flight (module 14.11)** = Feathers could not have evolved as an adaptation for flights. Their first utility *may have been* for insulation… The ancestors of birds were *probably* relatively small, agile, bipedal dinosaurs that also would have benefited from a light frame. It is *possible* that longer, winglike forelimbs and feathers, which increased the surface area of these forelimbs, were co-opted for flight after functioning in some other capacity, such as mating displays, thermoregulation, and camouflage (functions that feathers still serve today). The first flights *may have been* only extended hops to pursue prey or escape from a predator. Once flight itself became an advantage, NATURAL SELECTION would have remodeled feathers and wings to fit their additional functions. ← Refuting Evidence = Transitional Forms - The Fossil Record **Lesson 8.11**

⑨ **Archaeopteryx & Transitional Forms of Dinosaurs-to-Birds (module 15.1)** = "Did birds evolve from dinosaurs? Evolutionary biologists have been pondering this question for decades. If birds evolved from dinosaurs, then, in a sense, dinosaurs are not really extinct, but rather are flying around today. Some biologists find this idea absurd and accept the older view that birds evolved from an earlier group of reptiles, the pseudosuchians, which are more closely related to today's crocodiles and alligators than dinosaurs. How can biologists investigate a question like this?

A fossil of the earliest known bird, called Archaeopteryx, was discovered in 1861, just two years after Darwin's publication of The Origin of Species. As you can see, it is a partial skeleton with impressions of feathers. Although some early scientists speculated on the kinship between dinosaurs and birds, it wasn't until the 1970's that John Ostrom, of Yale University, published a series of papers that ignited the controversy over the connection between birds and dinosaurs. Using *evidence* from the five Archaeopteryx fossils available, he systematically analyzed the parts of the skeleton, arguing that many of the features of this primitive bird were dinosaur-like. He went so far as to contend that if it weren't for the feather imprints, an Archaeopteryx specimen could easily have been classified as a theropod dinosaur.

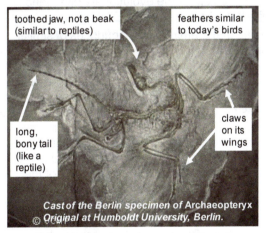

Few experts agreed with Ostrom at first because they were convinced that birds evolved from a reptile group very different from the theropods. But his arguments were interesting and sufficiently well developed to provoke a reaction. Others began to present opposing *evidence*… Meanwhile, Ostrom and others sought more support for their bird-dinosaur *hypothesis*. A new method for evaluating evolutionary relationships, called CLADISTICS, was emerging about the time that Ostrom was gathering his evidence… cladistics analysis strongly supported Ostrom's conclusions.

Today, the *hypothesis* that birds originated from dinosaurs is widely accepted. But debate continues about how the ancestor of birds first learned to fly. Scientists have investigated two possibilities. In one scenario, small, ground-running dinosaurs chasing prey or escaping predators used feathers to gain extra lift as they jumped into the air. In another scenario, dinosaurs climbed trees and then glided back down to the ground…. The evolution of birds and their ability to fly continues to be an intriguing and challenging scientific inquiry." ← Refuting Evidence = Transitional Forms - Archaeopteryx **Lesson 8.11**

⑩ **Natural Selection: Adaptive Radiation & Galapagos Finches (modules 14.8, 14.9)** =

"The evolution of many new species from a common ancestor introduced to a new and diverse environment. Adaptive radiation typically occurs when a few organisms make their way to new, unexploited areas or when environmental changes cause numerous extinctions, opening up various opportunities for the survivors. For example, fossil evidence indicates that mammals underwent a dramatic adaptive radiation after the extinction of the dinosaurs 65 million years ago.

Isolated island chains with physically diverse habitats are often the sites of explosive adaptive radiations. Colonizers may undergo multiple allopathic and sympatric speciation events, producing species that are found nowhere else on Earth. The Galapagos island chain has a total of 14 species of closely related birds called GALAPAGOS FINCHES. These have many similarities but differ in their feeding habits and their BEAK TYPE, which is correlated with what they eat.

Evidence accumulated since Darwin's time indicates that all 14 finch species evolved from a single small population of ancestral birds that colonized on the islands… The effects of the adaptive radiation of Darwin's finches are evident in the many types of beaks, specialized for different foods.

Some theories wait a long time to be tested. Such was the case with Darwin's 150-year-old *hypothesis* that the beaks of the diverse Galapagos finch species had adapted to different food sources through natural selection. Then came the classic research of PETER and ROSEMARY GRANT." ← **Refuting Evidence = Natural Selection & Darwin Finches Lesson 8.9**

⑪ **Molecular Biology & DNA (module 13.4)** = "In recent decades, advances in molecular biology have enabled biologists to read a molecular history of evolution in the DNA sequences of organisms. Siblings have greater similarity in their DNA and proteins than do unrelated individuals of the same species. And if two species have genes with sequences that match closely, biologists conclude that these sequences *must have been* inherited from a relatively recent common ancestor. In contrast, the greater the number of sequence differences between species, the *less likely* they share a close common ancestor. Molecular comparisons between diverse organisms have allowed biologists to develop *hypotheses* about the evolutionary divergence of major branches on the TREE OF LIFE.

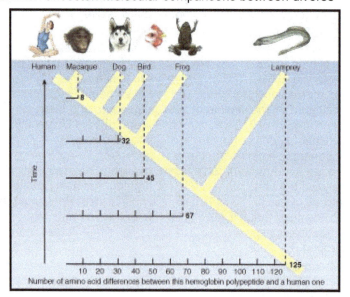

Studies of the amino acid sequences of similar (homologous) proteins in different species have been a rich source of *data* about evolutionary relationships. When comparing the amino acid sequence of human hemoglobin, the protein that carries oxygen in the blood, with the sequences of the hemoglobin of five other vertebrate animals, you can see that 95% of the amino acids of the rhesus monkey polypeptide are identical to the human polypeptide, whereas only 14% of the lamprey amino acids are the same as those in human hemoglobin. These amino acid comparisons lead to a *hypothesis* about evolutionary relationships: Rhesus monkeys are much more closely related to humans than are lampreys; mice, chickens, and frogs fall in between. It turns out this hypothesis agrees with earlier conclusions from comparative anatomy and embryology.

Darwin's boldest hypothesis is that all life-forms are related. About 100 years after Darwin made this claim, molecular biology has provided strong *evidence* for it: all forms of life use DNA and RNA, and the genetic code are essentially universal. This genetic language has been passed along through all the branches of evolution ever since it's beginning in an early form of life." ← **Refuting Evidence = DNA, ATP Chapter 6, Lesson 6.2**

Is the *circumstantial evidence* strong enough to convince us that what our teenagers are taught in high school about Origins can be presented to them as factual?

Scrutinizing Darwinian Evolution → Life from Non-Life: Miller-Urey Experiment 8.2

Genesis 1:20-23 *"...God said, 'Let the waters abound with an abundance of living creatures, and let birds fly above the earth across the face of the firmament of the heavens.' So God created every great sea creature and every living thing that moves, with which the waters abounded, according to their kind, and every winged bird according to its kind. And God saw that it was good. And God said, 'Be fruitful and multiply, and fill the waters in the seas, and let birds multiply on the earth.' So the evening and the morning were the fifth day."*

> Spontaneous Generation (a.k.a. "abiogenesis"): living organisms originate directly from lifeless matter

Dr. Henry Morris (*Scientific Creationism*[4]): "The Origin of Life"

"No doubt one of the most difficult stages in the evolutionary process would be the transition from non-life to life, from non-replicating chemicals to self-replicating systems. Nevertheless, if the evolution model is valid, this transition must have occurred, and it must have occurred by natural processes which can be explained in terms of the same laws of nature which operate today.

That being true, it should be expected as a basic prediction from the evolution model that the processes themselves still operate today and therefore that the evolution of life from non-life also is taking place today.

When empirical observations show that such evolution is not occurring today, then the evolution must be modified with another secondary assumption, namely, that there were different conditions in the earth's primeval atmosphere and hydrosphere than those which exist at present.

Again, the simplicity and potency of the creation model is apparent. It does not have to explain why life is not evolving from non-life today: it predicts this situation. Life, according to creationism, was a unique work of the creation period and is therefore not being created today."

How the Miller-Urey Experiment became so famous[17]:

- 1950's: scientists were in hot pursuit of the origin of life. Around the world, scientists were examining what kind of environment would be needed to allow life to begin.
- 1953: Stanley L. Miller and Harold C. Urey (Univ. of Chicago) = conducted an experiment which would change the approach of scientific investigation into the origin of life.

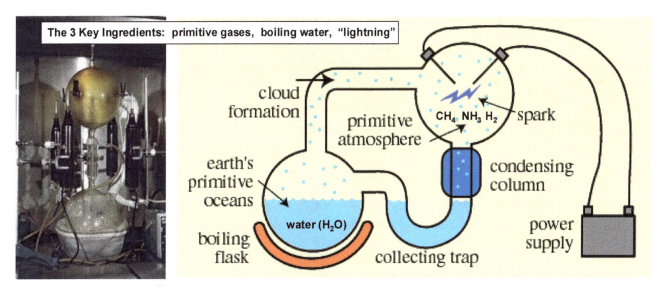

- Miller took methane (CH_4), ammonia (NH_3), hydrogen (H_2) and water (H_2O), believed to be the major components of the early Earth's atmosphere, and put them into a **closed system** (hydrogen is the main element in the universe; when it reacts with carbon, nitrogen and oxygen – common elements on the earth – you form CH_4, NH_3 and H_2O).
- He needed to pump energy into the system to get the gases to form chemicals. So he ran an **electric current**, to simulate **lightning storms** believed to be a common energy source on the early earth.
- Week 1: Miller observed that as much as 10-15% of the carbon was now in the form of organic compounds. 2% of the carbon had formed some of the **amino acids** which are used to make proteins.
- Experiment's "claim to fame": showed that organic compounds such as amino acids, which are essential to cellular life, could be made easily under the conditions that scientists believed were present on early earth.

Why Miller-Urey Experiment is so important to understand:
Lee Strobel ("The Case for a Creator"[8]): *"The moment I first learned of Miller's success, my mind flashed to the logical implication: if the origin of life can be explained solely through natural processes, then God was out of a job! After all, there was no need for a deity if living organisms could emerge by themselves out of the primordial soup and then develop naturally over the eons into more and more complex creatures (a scenario that was illustrated by Darwin's 'Tree of Life')".*

How the Miller-Urey Experiment became so infamous[17]:
It failed to simulate conditions of the early Earth, so it has little or nothing to do with the origin of life

1) **Earth's atmosphere today is 21% O_2** (PROBLEM: life's building blocks can't form in an oxygen atmosphere)
   - "oxidizing": cells need O_2 to produce energy through aerobic respiration by *breaking down* organic molecules
   - "reducing": our cells synthesize (*build up*) organic molecules in order for us to grow, heal or reproduce
   - compartments in our living cells *exclude oxygen* from the process of reducing since it is fatal (free oxygen, while beneficial to oxidation, actually destroys organic molecules)
   - Laboratory Step 1: scientists must REMOVE OXYGEN in the experiment to form any organic compound, so they guess that Earth's primitive atmosphere was not strongly oxidizing (as it is today) but was reducing.
   - Laboratory Step 2: once they remove oxygen, they then hypothesized that LIGHTNING in a reducing atmosphere (no oxygen) can spontaneously produce organic molecules needed for life.

   > Scientific evidence #1:   the early earth atmosphere contained OXYGEN (since there was water vapor)
   > Paleobiologist Kenneth Towe, 1996: *'The early earth very likely had an atmosphere that contained free oxygen."*

2) **Earth's early atmosphere had little ammonia and methane** (PROBLEM: Miller-Urey must have both present)
   - The case against AMMONIA: it absorbs UV radiation from sunlight, and is rapidly destroyed by it
   - The case against METHANE: if large amounts had been present in the primitive atmosphere, the earliest rocks would contain a high proportion of organic molecules – they don't.
   - Because hydrogen is so light, it can't be held by earth's gravity and it escapes into outer space. Without hydrogen, there's nothing to reduce CO_2 and nitrogen, which means METHANE and AMMONIA get oxidized (broken down) and thus cannot have been major parts of the early atmosphere.

   > Scientific evidence #2:   the early earth atmosphere did not contain HYDROGEN
   > Origin-of-Life Scientists Sidney Foxe and Klaus Dose, 1977: *"Not only did the Miller-Urey experiment start with the wrong gas mixture, but it also did not satisfactorily represent early geological reality because no provisions were made to remove HYDROGEN from the system (during a Miller-Urey experiment hydrogen gas accumulates, becoming up to 76% of the mixture, but on the early Earth it would have escaped into space)."*

3) **No experiment has ever produced organic material without starting with ammonia and methane**
   - Heinrich Holland (Princeton Univ. geochemist): *"Mixtures of carbon dioxide, nitrogen and water yielded NO amino acids at all. Yields and variety of organic compounds produced in these experiments decrease considerably as methane and ammonia are removed from the starting mixtures."*

   > Scientific Conclusion: Miller-Urey Experiment fails when more realistic ingredients are used
   > Origin-of-Life Scientists Sidney Foxe and Klaus Dose, 1977: *"No amino acids are produced by sparking a mixture of water vapor, carbon dioxide and nitrogen, even when we exclude oxygen."*

Disgraceful: The National Academy of Sciences[17]
- Remember Bruce Alberts (president, US National Academy of Sciences)? *"Science and lies cannot coexist."*
- Look at what Bruce Alberts says about the Miller-Urey experiment::
   - "Molecular Biology and the Cell" (graduate-level textbook used in universities): *"...organic molecules are likely to have been produced under such conditions. The best evidence for this comes from laboratory experiments."*
   - "1999 NAS Booklet": *"Experiments conducted under conditions intended to resemble those present on primitive Earth have resulted in the production of some of the chemical components of proteins."*
- Jonathan Wells ("Icons of Evolution"[17]): *"The National Academy of Sciences is the nation's premier science organization, commissioned by Congress in 1863 to advise government on scientific matters. Its members include many of the best scientists in America. Do they really approve of misleading the public about the evidence for evolution? Or is it being done without the members' knowledge? What are the American people supposed to think?"*

Scrutinizing Darwinian Evolution → Common Ancestor: Darwin's Tree of Life   8.3

Charles Darwin[1] (defining COMMON ANCESTRY): *"I view all beings not as special creations, but as the lineal descendants of some few beings which lived long before the first bed of the Cambrian system was deposited."*

Darwin believed any organic being descended from one primordial form. He pictured the history of life as a TREE, with the universal common ancestor as its root and modern species as its "green and budding twigs".

Genesis 1:11-12, 21-22, 24-25 "Special Creations, in Adult Form, made by God Himself"

- *"...God said, 'Let the earth bring forth grass, and the herb that yields seed, and the fruit tree that yields fruit ACCORDING TO ITS KIND, whose seed is in itself, on the earth'; and it was so. And the earth brought forth grass, the herb that yields seed according to its kind, and the tree that yields fruit, whose seed is in itself according to its kind. And God saw that it was good."*.

- *"...God created great sea creatures and every living thing that moves, with which the waters abounded, ACCORDING TO THEIR KIND, and every winged bird ACCORDING TO ITS KIND. And God saw that it was good."*

- *"...God said, 'Let the earth bring forth the living creature ACCORDING TO ITS KIND: cattle and creeping thing and beast of the earth, each ACCORDING TO ITS KIND; and it was so. And God made the beast of the earth ACCORDING TO ITS KIND, and everything that creeps on the earth ACCORDING TO ITS KIND. And God saw that it was good."*

Henry Morris, "The Genesis Record"[3]: *"There was no evolutionary struggle for existence among the animals, for 'God saw that it was good'. Neither could one kind evolve into a different kind, because God made each category 'after its kind.' This phrase **'after its kind' (Hebrew word for kind = min)** occurs 10X in Genesis 1. God designed each organism to reproduce after its own kind, not after some other kind. Thus, the evolutionary theory that all living things are interrelated by common ancestry and descent is directly refuted here in Genesis 1."*

Darwin's "Tree of Life"

Johnathan Wells, "Icons of Evolution"[17]: *"Of all the icons of evolution, the tree of life is most pervasive, because descent from a common ancestor is the foundation of Darwin's theory."*

Ernst Mayr (noted evolutionist): *"There is probably no biologist left today who would question that all organisms now found on the earth have descended from a single origin of life."*

QUESTION: If all living things descended from a common ancestor, why are they so different?

Darwin's answer: *"Branching-Tree"* he believed that minor variations within the original ancestral species were gradually amplified over many generations into larger differences that separated species from one another.

As he put it, 'the small differences distinguishing varieties of the same species, steadily tend to increase, till they equal the greater differences between species.'

So the large differences that separate, for example, the class of mammals from the class of insects, emerged only after a very long history of small differences accumulated over time, with the end result being the emergence of a human being & a fruit fly from the original common ancestor.

"Natural Selection": the agent acting within the Tree of Life – it accumulates slight, successive, favorable variations in short & slow steps (it can't produce any great or sudden modifications).

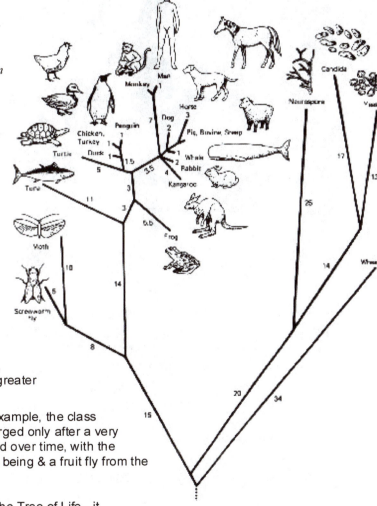

Scrutinizing Darwinian Evolution → Common Ancestor: Embryology   8.4

Charles Darwin[1] (defining EMBRYOLOGY): *"The leading facts in EMBRYOLOGY, which are second to none in importance, are explained on the principle of variations in the many descendants from some one ancient progenitor. These leading facts are that the embryos of the most distinct species belonging to the same class are closely similar, but become, when fully developed, widely dissimilar."*

Ernst Haeckel (1834 – 1919): German biologist who drew up the picture shown below, of embryos from various classes of vertebrates, showing them as virtually identical in earliest stages but totally different as they develop.

Jonathan Wells (Icons of Evolution)[17]: *"Haeckel's embryos seem to provide such powerful evidence for Darwin's theory that some version of them can be found in almost every modern textbook that deals with evolution. Yet biologists have known for over 100 years that Haeckel faked his drawings – vertebrate embryos never look as similar as he made them out to be."*

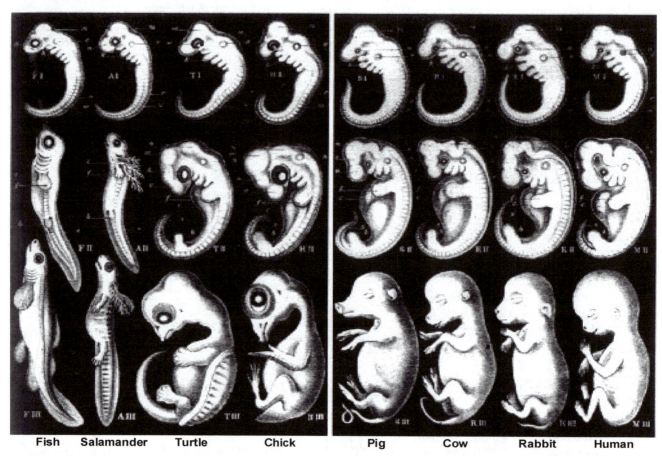

Fish   Salamander   Turtle   Chick   Pig   Cow   Rabbit   Human

- **Haeckel's Infamous Embryo Pictures:** six ways he biased the sample and deliberately distorted the truth

    1) he chose only those embryos that came closest to fitting his theory (there are seven vertebrate classes: he chose only the five that looked the most similar, and left out jawless and cartilaginous fishes entirely).
    2) for amphibians, he chose the salamander embryo instead of the frog, which looks very different.
    3) ½ his embryos are mammals, all of which are from one order (placentals); he omitted the other mammals (egg layers, pouch-brooding marsupials).
    4) vertebrate embryos in reality vary tremendously in size (from <1 mm up to 10 mm), but Haeckel portrayed them as being the same size.
    5) embryonic somites (blocks of cells on either side of backbone) vary a lot in real life – from 11 to > 60. Haeckel drew them as being all about the same number.
    6) he portrayed embryos at midway development because they do appear more similar. The earliest stages, which are the basis for Darwin's evolutionary claim of descent from a common ancestor, are very different (it is a known observation that early embryos are very different, then converge in appearance midway through development, only then becoming increasingly more different as they continue toward adulthood).

- **Comparing Embryos: Early, Intermediate, Late Stages of Development**

Jonathan Wells (Icons of Evolution)[17]: *"The earliest stages, which are the basis for Darwin's evolutionary claim of descent from a common ancestor, are very different…"*

Steve Jay Gould (May 2000 edition of "Natural History"): *"Haeckel exaggerated the similarities by idealizations and omissions….his drawings are characterized by inaccuracies and outright falsification."*

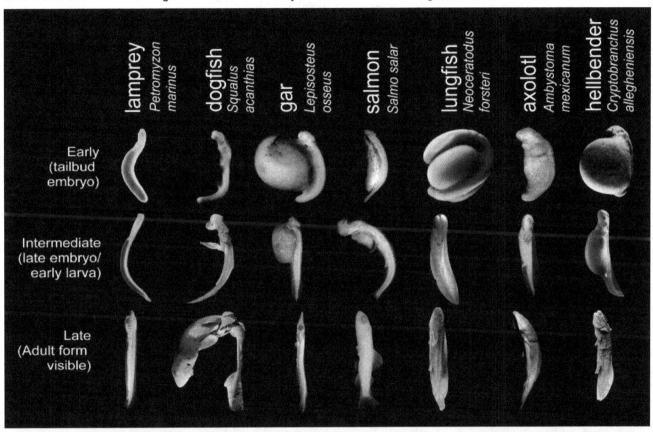

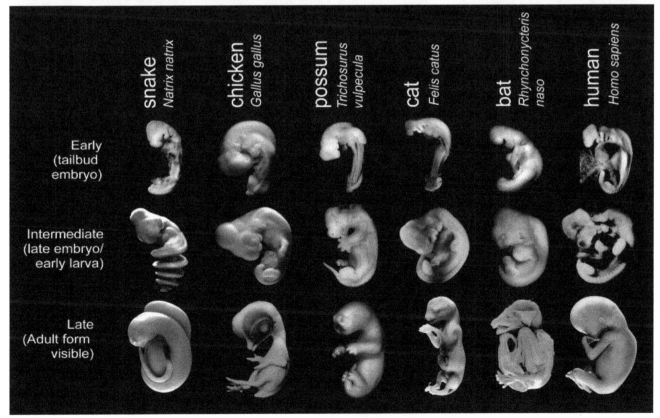

- **Karl Ernst von Baer (1792 - 1876):** Opponent of Darwinian Evolution via Embryonic Evidence[17]
    a) Before the publication of Origin of Species, he was Europe's most famous embryologist (not Haeckel). He knew that embryos never look like the adult of another species, and he saw no embryonic evidence for Darwin's theory that the various classes of vertebrates shared a common ancestor. Yet Darwin quoted him as his source for embryonic evidence for evolution!
    b) Von Baer lived long enough to object to Darwin's misuse of his observations, and he was a strong critic of Darwinian evolution until his death in 1876, but Darwin persisted in citing him anyway, making him look like a supporter of the very doctrine of evolutionary parallelism in embryos that he explicitly rejected.
- Haeckel's "Recapitulation Theory" = "Ontogeny recapitulates Phylogeny"
  ("Development is a Replay of Ancestry")
    a) "ontogeny" = embryonic development of an individual
       "phylogeny" = evolutionary history of the species
    b) Haeckel maintained that embryos "recapitulate" their evolutionary history by "passing through" the adult forms of their ancestors as they develop. Whenever a new feature develops in an organism, it is "tacked on" to the END of development, so ancestral forms always appear earlier in development than more recently evolved features.
    c) "tacking on" new evolutionary features makes no sense: "A house is not a cottage with an extra story on tacked on. A house is the alteration of the whole building (foundation, timbers, roof) even if the bricks are the same."

> **The Important difference between Von Baer's Research and Haeckel's: The Scientific Method**
> Von Baer based his laws on empirical observations made from laboratory experiments, where he intended to refute any theories that did not fit the evidence.
> Haeckel made deductions from evolutionary theory instead of performing experiments to test the things he observed in nature (Haeckel made a theoretical deduction, NOT an empirical inference).

- Adam Sedgwick (embryologist, 1894): *"there is no stage of development in which the unaided eye would fail to distinguish between them with ease...every embryologist knows that embryonic differences exist and could bring forward numerous instances of them. I need only say with regard to them that a species is distinct and distinguishable from its allies from the very earliest stages all through the development."*

> **Von Baer rejected Darwinism because it accepts evolutionary theory before looking at the embryonic evidence.**
>
> **Modern Darwinists haven't changed: despite repeated evidence, Haeckel's embryos stay in textbooks and Darwinian theory must not be challenged.**

Scrutinizing Darwinian Evolution → Common Ancestor: Homology 8.5

Charles Darwin[1] (defining *HOMOLOGY*) = *"that relationship between parts which results from their development from corresponding embryonic parts."*

If widely separated groups of organisms originated from a common ancestor, they should have basic features in common. The degree of resemblance between organisms indicates how closely related they are in evolution:

• in deciding how closely related two animals are, a comparative anatomist looks for structures which, though they may serve quite different functions in the adult, are fundamentally similar, suggesting a common origin. Such structures are described as homologous.

• groups with little in common are assumed to have diverged from a common ancestor much earlier in geological history than groups which have a lot in common;

• in cases where similar structures serve different functions in adults, it may be necessary to trace their origin and embryonic development, to look for more similarities derived from a common ancestor.

Adaptive Radiation = when a group of organisms share a homologous structure which is specialized to perform a variety of functions in order to adapt different environmental conditions and modes of life.

Mammal Forelimbs: In all tetrapods (i.e. from amphibians to mammals), forelimbs and hindlimbs conform to the pentadactyl pattern - limbs have a single proximal bone (humerus), two distal bones (radius and ulna), a series of carpals (wrist bones), followed by a series of five metacarpals (palm bones) and phalanges (digits).

Principle of Homology: Evolutionists claim that since the forelimb structure of tetrapods is the same, they originated at their embryonic development from a common ancestor. Through evolution, their forelimbs have been modified, to serve different functions in adaptation to different environments and modes of life.

Monkey: forelimbs are much elongated to form a grasping hand for climbing and swinging among trees.
Pig: 1st digit is lost, the 2nd and 5th digits reduced. Last 2 digits are stouter, with a hoof to support the body.
Horse: forelimbs are adapted for support and running by great elongation of the 3rd digit bearing a hoof.
Mole: has a pair of short, spade-like forelimbs for burrowing.
Anteater: uses its enlarged third digit for tearing down ant hills and termite nests.
Whale: forelimbs become flippers for steering and maintaining equilibrium during swimming.
Bat: forelimbs turned into wings by elongation of 4 digits; hook-like 1st digit is free for hanging from trees.

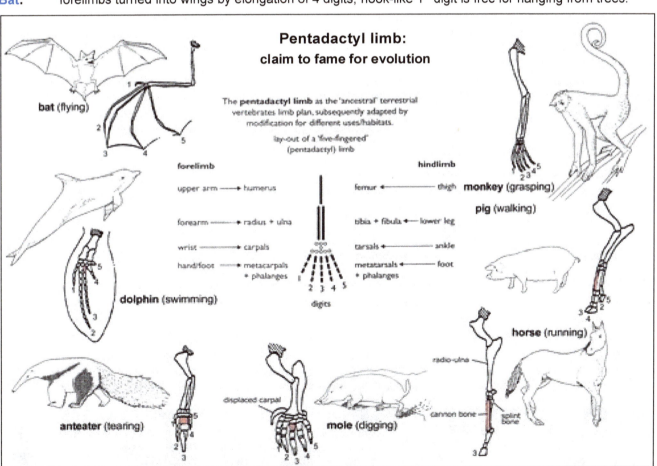

Pentadactyl limb: claim to fame for evolution

The pentadactyl limb as the 'ancestral' terrestrial vertebrates limb plan, subsequently adapted by modification for different uses/habitats.

lay-out of a 'five-fingered' (pentadactyl) limb

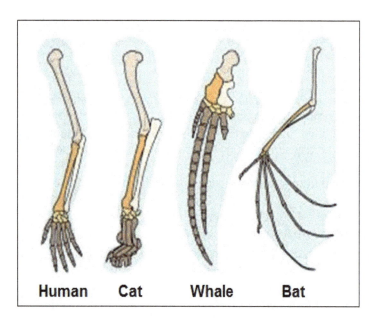

Encyclopedia Britannica:

"The indirect evidence for evolution is based primarily on the significance of similarities found in different organisms. Similarity of plan can easily be explained if all descended with modification from a common ancestor, by evolution, and the term HOMOLOGOUS is used to denote corresponding structures formed in this way.

In vertebrate animals, the skeleton of the forelimb is a splendid example of homology, in the bones of the upper arm, forearm, wrist, hand and fingers, all of which can be matched, bone for bone, in a rat, cat, dog, horse, bat, mole, porpoise, whale, or man.

The example is all the more telling because the bones have become modified in adaptation to different modes of life but have retained the same fundamental plan of structure, inherited from a COMMON ANCESTOR."

→ **Homologous Structures: Why they actually point to a *Creator*[20]**

- Darwin often mocked his creationist opponents for arguing that God simply chose to restrict Himself to the same pentadactyl design when He designed the flipper of a whale or the wing of a bird or the hand of a man: *"Nothing can be more hopeless than to attempt to explain this similarity of pattern in members of the same class by the doctrine of final causes… can we only say that it pleased the Creator to construct all the animals and plants in each great class on a uniform plan? This is not a scientific explanation."*[1]

- <u>What Darwin didn't know</u>: Molecular Biology (Electron Microscope) opened up a whole new world of scientific discovery at the CELL level – here's 3 powerful reasons for special creation and not evolution through homology:

#1. At EMBRYONIC development, structures are UNIQUE CREATIONS (not homologous)

a) "The validity of the inheritance from a common ancestor would be greatly strengthened if embryological and genetic research showed that homologous structures were specified by *homologous genes*, and followed homologous patterns of embryological development. But homologous structures are often specified by non-homologous genetic systems. This is exactly OPPOSITE to Darwin's definition of homology."

b) In early stages of egg cell division in amphibians, reptiles and mammals, it is obvious even to an untrained zoologist the early developmental stages are completely different for these three vertebrate classes.

c) Because of the great dissimilarity of early stages of embryonic development in the vertebrate classes, organs and structures considered homologous in adult vertebrates can't be traced back to homologous cells or early embryo stages. Homologous structures are UNIQUELY CREATED, arrived at by different routes!

#2. Homologous structures in different adult species: the SAME GENE is species-specific!

a) "genes" = units of heredity in the chromosomes (threadlike bodies found in cell nucleus that carries the genes) which control the development of the hereditary character of that organism.

b) Michael Denton (Molecular Biologist): *"The effects of the same gene in development of different vertebrates are surprisingly diverse. For example, one gene in birds that controls the formation of air sacs and downy feathers is the same gene in vertebrates that controls the development of lungs and kidneys."*[19]

#3. Many cases exist of homologous structures which can't be explained by common ancestry

a) the forelimbs and hindlimbs of all terrestrial vertebrates conform to the pentadactyl pattern explained above and are amazingly similar in bone structure and embryonic development – but no evolutionist would ever claim that the hindlimb evolved from the forelimb, or that forelimbs and hindlimbs evolved from a common source.

- **Two Questions to challenge any evolutionary biologists' position on homologous structures:**
  1. How do you explain the independent origin of very complex structures which are incredibly similar?
  2. How can you claim random accumulation of tiny advantageous mutations over time?

Michael Denton ("Evolution: A Theory in Crisis" [20]**)** → *"Without HOMOLOGY, there would be little need for a theory of common descent with modification. The facts of comparative embryology and anatomy provide NO EVIDENCE for evolution in the way conceived by Darwin."*

Vestigial Organs infer Common Ancestry? Imperfections infer anti-Design?[16] 8.6

➜**VESTIGIAL ORGANS** Instead of saying that a useful structure contains flaws that should not have been allowed, the writer points to some feature that has no apparent use at all. Often the feature resembles something that is actually used in other species, and so appears to be something that was in fact used at one time but then lost its function. For example, biologist Douglas Futuyma cites the 'rudimentary eyes of cave animals; the tiny, useless legs of many snakelike lizards; and the vestiges of the pelvis in pythons' as *evidence that evolution has occurred*... but he never explains how a real pelvis or eye developed in the first place, so as to be able to give rise to a vestigial organ later on, yet both the functioning organ and the vestigial organ require explanation. I do not purport to understand everything about design or evolution – far from it; *I just cannot ignore the evidence for design*... it is scientifically unsound to make any assumptions of the way things ought to be.

"useless" legs: vestigial organs?

Ken Miller talks about several genes that produce different forms of hemoglobin in humans: The (sixth ß–globin) gene is... nearly identical to that of the other five genes. Oddly, however, this gene... plays no role in producing hemoglobin. Biologists call such regions 'pseudogenes', reflecting the fact that however much they may resemble working genes, in fact they are not. The theory of intelligent design cannot explain the presence of nonfunctional pseudogenes unless it is willing to allow that the designer made serious errors, wasting millions of bases of DNA on a blueprint full of junk and scribbles. Evolution, in contrast, can easily explain them as nothing more than failed experiments in a random process of gene duplication that persist in the genome as evolutionary remnants.'

Problem 1 = Because we have not yet discovered a use for a structure does not mean that no use exists. The tonsils were once considered to be useless organs, but an important function in immunity has been discovered for them... hemoglobin pseudogenes, although they are not used to make proteins, may be used for other things that we don't know about... The point here is that Miller's assertion rests on assumptions only.

Problem 2 = Even if pseudogenes have no function, evolution has "explained" nothing about how pseudogenes arose. In order to make even a pseudocopy of a gene, a dozen sophisticated proteins are required: to pry apart the two DNA strands, to align the copying machinery at the right place, to stitch the nucleotides together in a string, to insert the pseudocopy back into the DNA, and much more. In his article Miller has not told us how any of these functions might have arisen in a Darwinian step-by-step process, nor has he pointed to articles in the scientific literature where we can find the information. He can't do that, because the information is nowhere to be found.

➜ **IMPERFECTIONS** "In the discussions about intelligent design, no objection is more frequently repeated. It can be briefly summarized: 'If there exists an intelligent agent who designed life on earth, then it would have been capable of making life that contained no apparent flaws; furthermore, it would have done so.... But just because something does not fit our idea of the way things ought to be, doesn't make it an argument against design.

Problem 1 = The argument demands perfection. Clearly, designers who have the ability to make better designs do not necessarily do so. The argument from imperfection overlooks the possibility that the designer might have multiple motives, with engineering excellence oftentimes relegated to a secondary role.... The key to intelligent-design theory is not whether a 'basic structural plan is the obvious product of design.' The conclusion of intelligent design for physically interacting systems rests on the observation of separate, well-fitted components to achieve a function that is beyond any of the components themselves.

Problem 2 = The argument depends on a psychoanalysis of the unidentified designer...the reasons that a designer would or would not do anything are virtually impossible to know unless the designer tells you specifically what those reasons are. One only has to go into a modern art gallery to come across designed objects for which the purposes are completely obscure (to me at least). The point of scientific interest is not the internal state of the designer but *whether one can detect design*.

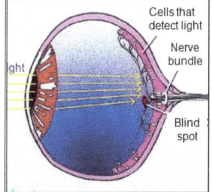

Problem 3 = The argument (from imperfection) frequently use their psychological evaluation of the designer as positive evidence for undirected evolution. The reasoning can be written as a syllogism:
1) A designer would have made the vertebrate eye without a blind spot.
2) The vertebrate eye has a blind spot.
3) Therefore Darwinian evolution produced the eye.

The scientific literature contains no evidence that natural selection working on mutation can produce either an eye with a blind spot, an eye without a blind spot, an eyelid, a lens, a retina, rhodopsin, or retinal. The debater has reached his conclusion in favor of Darwinism based solely on emotional feeling of the way things ought to be.

Scrutinizing Darwinian Evolution → Natural Selection via DNA Mutations **8.7**

> Charles Darwin[1] (defining NATURAL SELECTION): *"...it may be asked, how is it that varieties, which I have called incipient species, become ultimately converted into good and distinct species, which in most cases obviously differ from each other far more than do the varieties of the same species? How do these groups of species, which constitute what are called distinct genera, and which differ from each other more than do species of the same genus, arise? All these results... follow inevitably from the struggle for life. Owing to this struggle for life, any variation, however slight and from whatever cause proceeding, if it be in any degree profitable to an individual of any species, in its infinitely complex relations to other organic beings and to external nature, will tend to the preservation of that individual, and will generally be inherited by its offspring. The offspring, also, will thus have a better chance of surviving, for, of the many individuals of any species which are periodically born, but a small number can survive. I have called this principle, by which each slight variation, if useful, is preserved, by the term Natural Selection..."*

Darwin's theory of evolution has 4 main parts:

1) The original organism, and all subsequent life, changes over time. The ones living today differ from those in the past. The fossil record should provide ample evidence for this view.

2) All organisms are related. They are descended from a common ancestor. Similarities of organisms are classified together – they shared traits inherited from their common ancestor.

I have called this principle, by which each slight variation, if useful, is preserved, by the term of Natural Selection.
- Charles Darwin (1809 - 1882)

3) Change is gradual and slow, taking place over a long time. This should be supported by the fossil record, and is consistent with the fact that no naturalist had observed the sudden appearance of a new species.

4) The mechanism of evolutionary change is **natural selection**. This was the essential part of Darwin's theory.

What is Darwinian "Natural Selection"? "Survival of the fittest": the continual small variations between individuals of a species, as observed in nature, confers differing degrees of advantage or disadvantage in the struggle for existence. Individual organisms with favorable traits are more likely to survive and reproduce than those with unfavorable traits. Those with significant advantages would thus survive longer to transmit these characteristics by inheritance to their descendants (favorable, heritable traits become more common in the next generation). Given enough time, this passive process results in completely new and higher types of organisms.

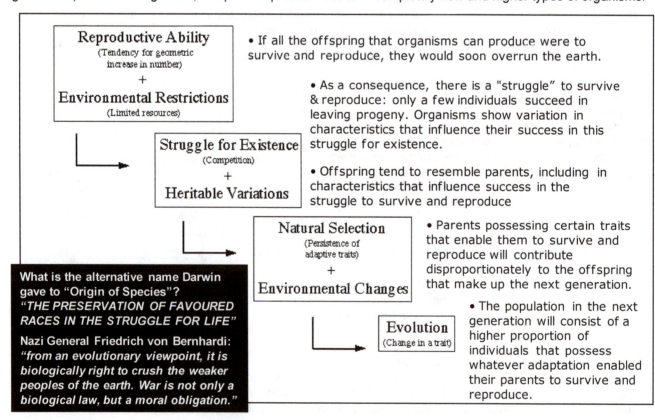

What is the alternative name Darwin gave to "Origin of Species"?
"THE PRESERVATION OF FAVOURED RACES IN THE STRUGGLE FOR LIFE"

Nazi General Friedrich von Bernhardi: *"from an evolutionary viewpoint, it is biologically right to crush the weaker peoples of the earth. War is not only a biological law, but a moral obligation."*

The *Scientific Definition* of Natural Selection (Henry Morris, PhD, "Scientific Creationism"[4])

"Modern molecular biology, with its penetrating insight into the remarkable genetic code implanted in the DNA system, has confirmed that normal variations operate only within the range specified by the DNA for that particular type of organism. Thus, variation within a species is <u>HORIZONTAL</u> (enabling it to adapt to its environment and thus survive), not <u>VERTICAL</u> (leading to the development of higher, more complex kinds of organisms). No truly novel characteristics, which could produce higher degrees of order or complexity, can ever appear.

In fact, natural selection acts to prevent vertical variation since these novelties are useless and harmful for survival until at least fully developed. It is significant that evolutionists have never yet been able to document, either in the living world or the fossil world, an incipient organ or structure leading to a future useful feature!

Natural selection can only act on variants which come to it via the genetic potentialities implicit in the DNA structure for its particular kind – IT CANNOT GENERATE ANYTHING NEW ITSELF."

DNA MUTATIONS: Agents of Natural Selection that drive Evolution?

Dr. A.E. Wilder Smith[11]: "Chance Mutations and Natural Selection eliminate the need for God"

"The theory of evolution seeks not only to explain... the mechanism by which the changes have occurred under natural and known laws or conditions. The mechanism postulated is one involving modifications arising by CHANCE. These changes may be known as MUTATIONS; they occur in genetic material by chance. The chance mutations, which give the possessor an advantage over organisms not possessing the same, help it to survive in the struggle for existence. As a result, the possessors will become more numerous and leave more offspring than the unsuccessful organisms not possessing the chance mutation in the genetic material.

Darwinism seeks to establish that a single primitive living cell could work itself up 'automatically' to a complex higher organism. No God or higher Being would be necessary to direct this process. Mutation by chance and struggle for existence (natural selection) would automatically produce this upward trend in complexity of life. It is on just this basis that evolutionists deny the necessity of the God postulate – the whole postulate of design is rendered unnecessary by the automaticity postulated for the evolutionary process."

Definition of "Mutation", taken from MedicineNet.com: "A permanent change, a structural alteration, in the DNA or RNA. In humans and many other organisms, mutations occur in DNA. However, in retroviruses like HIV, mutations occur in RNA which is the genetic material of retroviruses. In most cases, such changes are neutral and have no effect or they are deleterious and cause harm, but occasionally a mutation can improve an organism's chance of surviving and of passing the beneficial change on to its descendants. *Mutations are the necessary raw material of evolution.* Mutations can be caused by many factors including environmental insults such as radiation and mutagenic chemicals. Mutations are sometimes attributed to random chance events."

Charles Colson[35]: "What exactly is a Mutation?"
"Since a gene is like a coded set of instructions, a mutation is akin to a typing error – a changed letter here, and altered punctuation mark there, a phrase dropped, or a word misspelled. These typing errors are the only source of novelty in the genetic code. But already there is an obvious problem. If you introduce a typing error into a report you are writing, it is not likely to improve the report. An error is more likely to make nonsense than to make better sense. And the same is true of errors in the genetic code. Most mutations are harmful, often lethal, to the organism, so that if mutations were to accumulate, the result would likely be DEVOLUTION than evolution."

<u>What is a "Harmful mutation"?</u>: A mutation that creates non-functional proteins in the DNA of cells by causing errors in protein sequencing. Each cell depends on thousands of proteins to function in the right places at the right times. When a mutation alters a protein that plays a critical role in the body, a medical condition known as a "genetic disorder" can result. Once DNA damage results in a mutation, the mutation cannot be repaired by the cell's built-in DNA repair mechanism because the cell's enzymes only recognizes abnormal structures for repair, but the mutation's protein sequence is recognized as normal DNA structure so it cannot be repaired.

<u>What is a "Beneficial mutation"?</u>: An example where a mutation that changes the DNA's protein sequences actually enables the mutant organism to withstand particular environmental stresses better than normal organisms would be Sickle-cell disease (a blood disorder in which the body produces an abnormal type of hemoglobin in the red blood cells). One-third of all native inhabitants of Sub-Saharan Africa carry the Sickle-cell gene, because in areas where malaria is common, there is a survival value in carrying only a single sickle-cell gene (sickle cell trait). Those with only one of the two alleles of the sickle-cell disease are more resistant to malaria, since the infestation of the malaria plasmodium is halted by the sickling of the cells which it infests.

Jonathan Wells[17]: "DNA Mutations + Natural Selection ≠ the Raw Materials for Evolution"

"In Darwin's theory, evolution is a product of two factors: natural selection and heritable variations. Natural selection molds populations by preserving favorable variations that are passed on to succeeding generations. Small-scale evolution within a species (such as we see in domestic breeding) makes use of variations already present in a population, but large-scale evolution (such as Darwin envisioned) is impossible unless new variations arise from time to time. According to modern neo-Darwinism, genes consisting of DNA are the carriers of hereditary information; information encoded in DNA sequences directs the development of the organism; and new variations originate as MUTATIONS, or ACCIDENTAL CHANGES IN THE DNA.

According to new-Darwinism, beneficial DNA mutations provide the raw materials necessary for large-scale evolution. Beneficial mutations are rare, but they do occur. For example, mutations can have biochemical effects that render bacteria resistant to antibiotics or insects resistant to insecticides. But biochemical mutations cannot explain the large-scale changes in organisms that we see in the history of life. Unless a mutation affects MORPHOLOGY – the shape of the organism – it cannot provide the raw materials for morphological evolution.

Since mutations leading to antibiotic and insecticide resistance are clearly beneficial in certain environments, biology textbooks invariably list them as evidence that mutations provide the raw materials for evolution. Many textbooks also list sickle-cell anemia, because the same mutation that causes the crippling genetic disease can also, in a milder form, benefit infants growing up in malaria-ridden areas.

In all of these cases, however, the evolution that occurs is trivial. The raw materials for large-scale evolution must be able to contribute to fundamental changes in an organism's SHAPE AND STRUCTURE… MORPHOLOGICAL MUTATIONS can provide raw materials for morphological evolution, and evidence for such mutations is surprisingly thin. Since direct evidence has been so hard to come by, neo-Darwinists can only assume that genetic differences are the cause of morphological differences."

Charles Colson[35]: "Darwin's Theory of Morphological Evolution fails as Real Science"

"How did Darwin devise a theory of unlimited change from such examples of limited change (such as breeding Sugar Beets, Dogs, Race Horses, and Darwin's own breeding of rock pigeons)? He took the changes he had OBSERVED and extrapolated them back into the distant past – which he had NOT OBSERVED… Neither Darwin nor anyone else has ever actually witnessed evolution occurring. It is a conjecture going far beyond any observed facts... And therein lies the FATAL FLAW in Darwin's theory. Centuries of experiments show that change produced by breeding does not continue at a steady rate from generation to generation. Instead, change is rapid at first, then levels off, and eventually reaches a limit that breeders cannot cross.

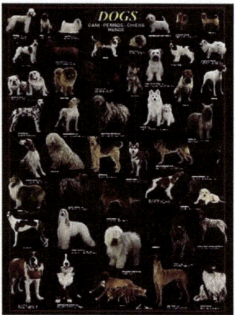

Since breeding does nothing more than shuffle existing genes, the only way to drive evolution to new levels of complexity is to introduce new genetic material. And the only source of new genetic material in nature is MUTATIONS. In today's neo-Darwinism, the central mechanism for evolution is RANDOM MUTATION and NATURAL SELECTION.

Mutations alter the details in EXISTING STRUCTURES – like eye color or wing size – but they do not lead to the creation of NEW STRUCTURES. The fruit flies have remained fruit flies. Like breeding, genetic mutations produce only minor, limited change. Furthermore, the minor changes observed do not accumulate to create major changes – the principle at the heart of Darwinism. Hence, mutations are not the source of the endless, limitless change required by evolutionary theory. Whether we look at breeding experiments or laboratory experiments, the outcome is the same – change in living things remains strictly limited to variations on the theme. We do not see the emergence of new and more complex structures.

The same pattern holds throughout the past, as we see in the FOSSIL RECORD. The overwhelming pattern is that organisms appear fully formed, with variations clustered around a mean, and without transitional stages leading up to them. The fossil record as a whole gives persuasive evidence against Darwinism.

Despite what the textbooks say, Darwin did not prove that nature is capable of crossing those 'fixed limitations'. He suggested only that it was theoretically possible – that minor changes might have accumulated over thousands of years until a fish became an amphibian, an amphibian became a reptile, and a reptile became a mammal. But after more than 150 years, it has become clear that Darwin's speculation flies in the face of all the results of breeding and laboratory experimentation, as well as the pattern in the fossil record.

The simple words from the first chapter of Genesis will stand firm: 'And God created every living thing to reproduce AFTER THEIR KIND (Genesis 1:11-12, 21, 24-25)".

The Peppered Moth & Industrial Melanism: Creation's Natural Selection[4]

"A classic example of normal variation within a species that is offered as evidence of present-day evolution is the PEPPERED MOTH of England, which "evolves" from a dominant light coloration to a dominant dark coloration as the tree trunks grew darker with pollutants during the advancing industrial revolution. This was not evolution in the true sense at all but only variation. Natural selection is a conservative force, operating to keep kinds from becoming extinct when the environment changes.

'The peppered moth experiments beautifully demonstrate natural selection – or survival of the fittest – in action, but they do not show evolution in progress, for however the populations may alter in their content of light, intermediate, or dark forms, all the moths remain from beginning to end Biston betularia.'

The phenomenon of variation and natural selection, rather than explaining evolution in the way Darwin thought, is a marvelous example of the creationist's principle of conservation in operation. The creation model predicts that since the Creator had a purpose for each kind of organism created, He would institute a system which would not only assure its genetic integrity but would be such as to maintain its identity as a SPECIFIC KIND while, at the same time, allowing it to ADJUST ITS CHARACTERISTICS (within limits) to changes in the environment. Otherwise, even very slight changes in its habitat, food supply, etc., might cause its extinction."

2 moths resting on the dark bark of an oak tree near the industrial city of Liverpool, U.K

The same 2 moths on a nearby beech tree covered by green algae & lichen.

Typica & melanic moths resting on light-colored lichen on an oak tree in rural Wales.

Peppered moths resting on 3 different tree trunks. Note the differences in camouflage efficiency

How Peppered Moths became so famous[17]:

- "Melanism": During Britain's industrial revolution, moths near heavily polluted cities became "melanic" colored.
- **Bernard Kettlewell (1950's):** Famous experiments that suggested natural selection in action. Predatory birds ate light-colored moths ("typica") that rested on pollution-darkened tree trunks, while the melanic form was hidden better on these darker tree trunks. So the melanic form survived and reproduced at greater numbers.
- P.M. Sheppard (geneticist, 1975): "This phenomenon with peppered moths is the most spectacular evolutionary change ever witnessed and recorded by man".

After anti-pollution legislation was passed in the 1950's, industrial melanism declined. As pollution decreased, the percentage of melanics west of Liverpool dropped, while the percentage of typicals rose. This seemed to match the theory of natural selection (industrial melanism in moths was due to camouflage and predatory birds).

How Peppered Moths became infamous[17]:

1) Kettlewell *staged* his photos of moths on tree trunks (it was later found they do not rest on tree trunks). He also released the moths in daylight, when birds preyed on his moths, and they weren't in their natural hiding places.

2) Extensive field studies in England and the US (1970's – 1980's) revealed no conclusive evidence for advantages to either "typica" or "melanic" moths in either type of environments (see data on next page).

Jerry Coyne, Univ. of Chicago, evolutionary biologist (1998): *"From time to time, evolutionists re-examine a classic experimental study and find, to their horror, that it is flawed or downright wrong. The 'prize horse in our stable of examples' is in bad shape, and, while not yet ready for the glue factory, needs serious attention."*

Problems with Peppered Moth Theories: The U.K. and The Netherlands

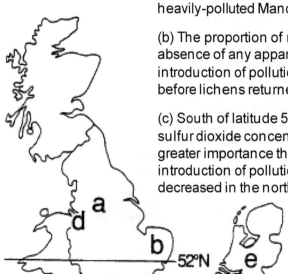

(a) Despite theoretical predictions, the proportion of melanics around heavily-polluted Manchester never reached 100%.

(b) The proportion of melanics in East Anglia reached 80% despite the absence of any apparent pollution (Lees and Creed 1975); after the introduction of pollution control legislation, typicas became predominant before lichens returned to the trees.

(c) South of latitude 52*N, the relatively poor correlation of melanism with sulfur dioxide concentration suggested that non-industrial factors were of greater importance than selective predation (Steward 1977a,b); after the introduction of pollution control legislation, the proportion of melanics decreased in the north, as expected, but increased in the south.

(d) The frequency of typicas on Wirral Peninsula increased dramatically before the return of lichens to tree trunks.

(e) The decline of melanism in The Netherlands has been accompanied by an increase not only in typicas, but also in an intermediate form almost as dark as melanics.

Problems with Peppered Moth Theories: The United States

(a) 1970's: the frequency of melanics in an unspoiled forest in southwestern Virginia was about double the frequency in polluted Blacksburg 18 km away; neither lichen cover nor gene flow could explain the difference.

(b) 1971-1978: melanics remained at 52% in a low-pollution area in central eastern Pennsylvania.

(c) Melanics occurred at low frequencies in western and central Massachusetts even though trees were neither devoid of lichens nor blackened by soot.

(d) Between the 1960's and 1990's, melanics in southeastern Michigan increased and decreased in parallel with those in England, but without any perceptible changes in lichen cover.

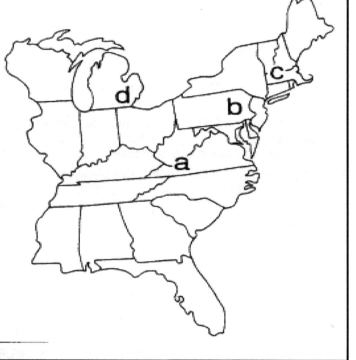

Galapagos Finches & Adaptive Radiation: Creation's Natural Selection[4]   8.9

- While Darwin was in the Galapagos Islands in 1835, he collected specimens of 13 different finches scattered among the 2 dozen volcanic islands. These finches differ mainly in the size and shape of their **beaks**.
- Darwin's Theory: a single species diverges into several varieties, then into several different species, through the action of natural selection (since the beaks of these finches are adapted to the different foods they eat, it seems reasonable to theorize that the various species evolved from a common ancestor via natural selection).
- **College Textbook "A": Darwin's Finches = Living Example of Evolution in Action**

"The Galapagos have been called a living laboratory where speciation can be seen at work. A few million years ago, one species of finch migrated to the rocky Galapagos from the mainland of Central or South America. From this one migrant species would come many -- at least thirteen species of finch evolving from the **single ancestor**.

On various islands, finch species have become adapted for different diets: seeds, insects, flowers, leaves, etc. This process in which one species gives rise to multiple species that exploit different niches is called **ADAPTIVE RADIATION**. The ecological niches exert the selection pressures that push the populations in various directions.

The ancestral finch was a ground-dwelling, seed-eating finch. After the burst of speciation in the Galapagos, a total of 14 species would exist: three species of ground-dwelling seed-eaters; three others living on cactuses and eating seeds; one living in trees and eating seeds; and seven species of tree-dwelling insect-eaters.

Scientists long after Darwin spent years trying to understand the process that had created so many types of finches that differed mainly in the size and shape of their beaks.

Most recently, Peter and Rosemary Grant have spent many years in the Galapagos, seeing changing climatic conditions from year to year dramatically altering the food supply. As a result, certain of the finches have lived or died depending on which species' beak structure was best adapted for the most abundant food -- just as Darwin would have predicted."

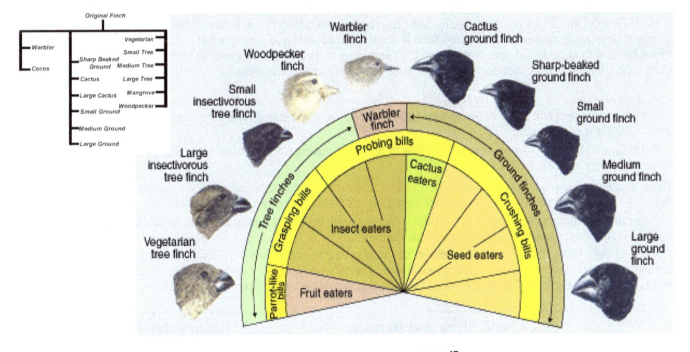

Examining the Evidence: "The Legend of Darwin's Finches"[17]

- **Darwin was (and still is) given credit for something he never studied nor said**

While Darwin was in the Galapagos Islands in 1835, he collected nine of the thirteen species that now bear his name, but he identified only six of them as finches.

Except in two cases, Darwin failed to observe any differences in their diets, and even in those cases he failed to correlate diet with beak shape.

Darwin was so unimpressed by the finches that he made no effort while in the Galapagos to separate them by island. Only after returning to England did ornithologist John Gould sort them out by geography, but much of the data Darwin provided was wrong.

Frank Sulloway (Science Historian, "Darwin and His Finches: The Evolution of a Legend", 1982): *"Darwin possessed only a limited and largely erroneous conception of both the feeding habits and the geographical distribution of these birds. Darwin was increasingly given credit after 19 for finches he never saw and for observations and insights about them he never made. As for the claim that the Galapagos finches impressed Darwin as evidence of evolution, nothing could be further from the truth."*

The Legend lives - High School and College textbooks claim the finches gave Darwin the idea of evolution!
1. *"Biological Science"* (Gould and Keeton, 1996): *"The finches played a major role in leading Darwin to formulate his theory of evolution by natural selection".*
2. *"Biology"* (Raven and Johnson, 1999): *"The correspondence between the beaks of the thirteen finch species and their food source immediately suggested to Darwin that evolution had shaped them."*
3. *"Biology: Visualizing Life"* (George Johnson, 1998): *"Darwin attributed the differences in bill size and feeding habits among these finches to evolution that occurred after their ancestor migrated to the Galapagos Islands. Imagine yourself in Darwin's place....writing journal pages that Darwin could have written."*

- **There is no evidence for the theory of natural selection driving evolution from a common ancestor**

Peter and Rosemary Grant (1973 – 1983): "OSCILLATING SELECTION" - pioneering research on the medium ground finch (one of the thirteen species) on the island Daphne Major (extensive measurements on beak size): based on weather conditions (changing beak size between dry and wet seasons)

1977: Drought Season
- A severe drought reduced medium ground finch population to only 15% because of the lack of small, soft seeds, which they depended on for survival (only tougher, larger seeds remained during the drought).
- The 15% that survived all had larger bodies and their beaks were 5% larger than normal (≈ ½ millimeter, or the thickness of a thumbnail). This slight change was allowed these birds to live off the tough, large seeds.
- Conclusion: natural selection favored birds with larger beaks, capable of cracking tough, large seeds.

1982-1983: El Niňo
- Heavy rains (> 10X normal rainfall, 50X more than fell during the drought). Plant life exploded, and medium ground finch population exploded as well.
- Peter Grant, Lisa Gibbs (*Nature*, 1987): "we observed a reversal in the direction of selection due to climate change: large adult size is favored when food is scarce because the supply of small, soft seeds is depleted. Only those birds with large beaks can crack open the remaining large and hard seeds. In contrast, small adult size is favored in years following wet conditions, because the food supply is dominated by small soft seeds."

Oscillating Selection: direct evidence of natural selection, but this will never produce a new species
- Jonathan Weiner (*The Beak of the Finch*, 1994): "Selection had flipped. The birds took a giant step backward, after their giant step forward."
- Peter Grant (*Scientific American*, 1991): "The population, subjected to natural selection, is oscillating back and forth with every shift in climate."

Peter and Rosemary Grant (1982 – 1983): "HYBRID FINCHES" - the thirteen species, as they breed, are actually MERGING into one population (not diverging, as Darwin required for a new species).
- Peter and Rosemary Grant (*Science*, 1992): "The superior fitness of *hybrids* among populations of Darwin's finches calls into question their designation as species."
- Peter Grant, 1993: "If species were defined by inability to interbreed, we would recognize only two species of Darwin's finch on Daphne Major, not the usual four. The three populations of ground finches on Genovesa would similarly be reduced to one. At the extreme, six species would be recognized in place of the current fourteen."

Finch Beak Sizes and Merging: The Truth isn't being published[17]

- Remember what the National Academy of Sciences said? *"Science and lies cannot coexist".*
- That's not what they publish...1994 booklet on evolution for teachers leaves out that beak sizes oscillate based on weather conditions, actually returning to normal. Instead, here's what it says: *"Darwin's finches are a compelling example of origin of species: a single year of drought on the islands can drive evolutionary changes in finches. If droughts occur about once every 10 years, a new species of finch might arise in only about 200 years."*

Let's not confuse the reader with the fact that selection was reversed after the drought, thereby producing no long-term evolutionary change!

Philip Johnson (Wall Street Journal, 1999): Direct Response to the NAS 1999 Booklet
"When our leading scientists have to resort to the sort of distortion that would land a stock promoter in jail, you know that they are in trouble."

Can we reconcile the Bible with Natural Selection?

8.10

Evolution teaches that nature "selects" the most fit individuals in a population as they struggle for survival in their environment. As the most fit survive and produce offspring, the weakest die off and the strongest prosper. PROBLEM: The Bible directly opposes "survival of the fittest"

"God's power works through my *weakness*"

2Corin. 12:9-10 *"'...My grace is sufficient for you, for MY STRENGTH IS MADE PERFECT IN WEAKNESS.' Therefore most gladly I will rather boast in my infirmities, that the power of Christ may rest upon me. Therefore I take pleasure in infirmities, in reproaches, in needs, in persecutions, in distresses, for Christ's sake. For when I am weak, then I am strong."*

Isaiah 40:28-29 *"Have you not known? Have you not heard? The everlasting God, the Lord, the Creator of the ends of the earth, neither faints nor is weary. There is no searching of His understanding. HE GIVES POWER TO THE WEAK, and to those who have no might He increases strength."*

"Jesus called people to put their trust in *Him*"

Matthew 11:28-29 *"Come to Me, all you who labor and are heavy laden, and I will give you rest. Take My yoke upon you and learn from Me, for I AM GENTLE and lowly in heart, and you will find rest for your souls."*

Matthew 9:36 *"...when He saw the multitudes, HE WAS MOVED WITH COMPASSION FOR THEM, because they were weary and scattered, like sheep having no shepherd."*

"Jesus calls people to be like *Him*"

Philippians 2:3-5 *"Let nothing be done through selfish ambition or conceit, but in lowliness of mind let each esteem others better than himself. Let each look out not only for his own interests, but also the interests of others. Let THIS MIND be in you which was also in Christ Jesus..."*

Acts 20:35 *"I have shown you in every way, by laboring like this, that YOU MUST SUPPORT THE WEAK. And remember the words of the Lord Jesus, that He said, 'It is more blessed to give than to receive.'"*

"*Mercy* is a virtue"

Matthew 5:7 *"Blessed are the MERCIFUL, for they shall obtain mercy."*

Proverbs 19:22 *"What is desired in a man is LOVINGKINDNESS (mercy)"*.

Christianity ➔ Its about Denying "Me" and *GIVING* to Others, not Struggling to Survive

① *"CHARIZOMAI"*: to bestow or grant freely upon another; used almost exclusively in reference to God, who gives without expecting anything in return

Romans 8:32 *"He who did not spare His own Son, but delivered Him up for us all, how shall He not with Him also freely ①GIVE us all things?"*

Luke 7:21 *"He cured many people of their illnesses, afflictions, and evil spirits; to many blind He ①GAVE sight."*

② *"PARADIDŌMI"*: to hand over or deliver up; referring to Christ, always connected with His LOVE

John 3:16 *"...God so LOVED the world that He ②GAVE His only begotten Son, that whoever believes in Him should not perish but have everlasting life."*

Galatians 2:20 *"I have been crucified with Christ; it is no longer I who live, but Christ lives in me; and the life which I now live in the flesh I live by faith in the Son of God who LOVED me and ②GAVE Himself for me."*

③ *"METADIDŌMI"*: to share (to "spend out") my own life and the things I have generously with another

1) <u>my spiritual gifts</u> (exhortation, teaching, prayer, etc.) - God commands us to SHARE or GIVE out of the abundance of the gifts He has blessed us with (exercise your gifts....don't waste them)

2) <u>my material blessings</u> (financial, possessions) – God says when I share with those in need, out of my own grateful heart, it is fruit credited to my account.

Romans 12:8 *"He who exhorts, in exhortation; he who ③GIVES, with liberality; he who leads, with diligence; he who shows mercy, with cheerfulness."*

Ephesians 4:28 *"Let him who stole steal no longer, but rather let him labor, working with his hands what is good, that he may have something to ③GIVE him who has need."*

Mark 8:34-35 *"Whoever desires to come after Me, let him deny himself, take up his cross, and **FOLLOW ME**. Whoever desires to save his life will lose it, and whoever loses his life for My sake and the gospel's will save it."*

Scrutinizing Darwinian Evolution → Transitional Forms: Fossil Record 8.11

Charles Darwin[1] (defining TRANSITIONAL FORMS): *"By the theory of natural selection, all living species have been connected with the parent-species of each genus, by differences not greater than we see between the natural and domestic varieties of the same species at the present day. As a result, the number of intermediate and transitional links, between all living and extinct species, must have been inconceivably great. The absence of these intermediate forms can only be attributed to the imperfection in the geological record."*

The Bible: "God created once, then things decay", not "new species by transitional forms"

• God created everything there is and ever will be one time at the beginning

John 1:1-3 *"In the beginning was the Word, and the Word was with God, and the Word was God. He was in the beginning with God. ALL THINGS WERE MADE THROUGH HIM, and without Him nothing was made that was made."*

Colossians 1:16-17 *"...by Him all things were created that are in heaven and that are on the earth, visible and invisible, whether thrones or dominions or principalities or powers. ALL THINGS WERE CREATED THROUGH HIM and FOR HIM. And He is before all things, and in Him all things consist."*

• After God created everything, nothing has ever evolved into something new (things decay and break down)

Ecclesiastes 1:9-10 *"...there is nothing new under the sun. Is there anything of which it may be said, 'See, this is new'? It has already been in ancient times before us."*

Romans 8:20-21 *"...the whole creation was subject to futility, not willingly, but because of Him who subjected it in hope; because the creation itself also will be delivered from the bondage of CORRUPTION (decay)..."*

Archaeopteryx ("ancient wing"): The Transitional Form that confirms Darwin's theory?

Discovered in 1861, Hermann von Meyer (limestone quarry in Solnhofen, Germany): this limestone is very fine-grained and used in lithography (printing process), so this fossil is preserved in exquisite detail.

Harvard Univ. Darwinist Ernst Mayr: *"Archaeopteryx is the almost perfect link between reptiles & birds."*

• **The "Dethroning" of Archaeopteryx: it's just another "Feathered Dinosaur"**

1) There are too many structural differences between it and modern birds for modern birds descend from it.
   (a) Larry Martin (Univ. Kansas paleontologist): *Archaeopteryx is not ancestral of any group of modern birds. Instead, it is the earliest known member of a totally extinct group of birds."*

2) Archaeopteryx fails Evolutionary Test #1: the origin of flight
   (a) "trees down theory" = ancestors of birds were 4-legged reptiles that climbed trees; they evolved into flying by leaping from trees (first gliding, then flight). *REJECTED AS HIGHLY IMPROBABLE.*
   (b) "ground up theory" = ancestors of birds were 2-legged reptiles that ran on the ground; they evolved into flying by developing long forelimbs while reaching for prey in combination with jumping as they chased it.
   (c) "ground up" is wrong = 2-legged reptiles that ran on ground appear in fossil record AFTER Archaeopteryx.

3) Archaeopteryx fails Evolutionary Test #2: **CLADISTICS** (method of analyzing fossils using Darwin's theory)
   (a) "living things are classified into groups based on their anatomical similarities, so all groupings become ancestor-descendant sets (organisms can only be grouped together if they share a common ancestor)."

(b) THE PROBLEM = cladistics concludes that the right candidates for Archaeopteryx's ancestor were 2-legged dinosaurs, which came AFTER Archaeopteryx! So no fossil record exists to show Archaeopteryx is a transition from a reptile to a bird: it's a feathered dinosaur.

- Henry Gee (Chief Science writer for *Nature*, 1999): *"Once upon a Archaeopteryx stood alone as the earliest fossil bird. Its uniqueness made it an icon, conferring on it the status of an ancestor. But the existence of other bird ancestors shows that Archaeopteryx is just another dinosaur with feathers."*

The Fossil Record: *ZERO* transitional forms destroys Darwin's "Tree of Life"

- Pierre-P. Grasse (evolutionary biologist): "Paleontology (study of fossil record) is the foundation of Evolution"
"Zoologists and botanists are nearly unanimous in considering evolution as a fact and not a hypothesis. I agree with the position and base it primarily on documents provided by paleontology (the fossil history of the world). Naturalists must remember that the process of evolution is revealed only through FOSSIL FORMS. A knowledge of paleontology is therefore a prerequisite; only paleontology can provide them with the evidence of evolution and reveal its course or mechanisms."[14]

- National Academy of Sciences: "Transitional Forms have been discovered many times"
"Hundreds of thousands of fossil organisms found in well-dated sequences represent a SUCCESSION OF FORMS THROUGH TIME and manifest many EVOLUTIONARY TRANSITIONS. There have been so many discoveries of intermediate forms between fish and amphibians, between amphibians and reptiles, between reptiles and mammals, and even along the primate line of descent that it is often difficult to identify categorically the line to which a particular genus or species belong"[14]

- Darwin ("Origin of Species"): "Where are the Transitional Forms?"
"Since innumerable transitional forms must have existed, why do we not find them embedded in countless numbers in the crust of the earth? Why is not every geological formation and every stratum full of such intermediate links? Geology does not reveal any such finely graduated organic chain; and this perhaps is the most obvious and GRAVEST OBJECTION against my theory."[1]

- Steven J. Gould (Harvard Univ. paleontologist): "Fossils show no evidence of Transitional Forms"
"The fossil record with its abrupt transitions offers NO SUPPORT for gradual change...all paleontologists know that the fossil record contains precious little in the way of intermediate forms; transitions between major groups are abrupt."

The Cambrian Explosion: The Discovery that reinforces a *DESIGNER*

- 1980's: fossil excavations revealed an incredible variety of fully-formed organisms abruptly appearing at the same time (NOT organisms following evolutionary theory of gradual development over long time periods):
  Burgess Shale in Canada   Sirius Passet in northern Greenland   Chengjiang in southern China

- The Cambrian Explosion's challenge to Evolution:
  1) it's not so much the abrupt appearance of highly-developed animals, or in the extent of the diversity of them, but in the fact that higher orders of animals (phylum and classes) appear abruptly, right from the start.
  2) Darwin's theory claims that higher-order animals (phyla, classes) emerge only AFTER a long history of divergence from lower categories (species, genera, families, orders). But in the Cambrian explosion, we see just the OPPOSITE happening: higher-order animals suddenly appear.
  3) There has never been a single fossil discovered that shows animal development from a common ancestor (no "ancestors", "intermediates", or "transitional forms" from lower-to-higher order).

- Lee Strobel ("The Case for a Creator"[8]): The Cambrian Explosion destroys the Tree of Life
"The Cambrian explosion has been called the 'Biological Big Bang' because it gave rise to the sudden appearance of most of the major animal divisions that are still alive today, as well as some that are extinct. Here's what the record shows: there were some jellyfish, sponges and worms prior to the Cambrian period. Then at the beginning of the Cambrian – boom! – all of a sudden we see arthropods (insects, crabs), echinoderms (starfish, sea urchins), chordates (vertebrates), and more. This is absolutely contrary to Darwin's Tree of Life. These animals, so different in their body plans, appear fully developed, all of a sudden, in what paleontologists have called the single most spectacular phenomenon in the fossil record."

- Henry Morris ("Scientific Creationism"[4]): The Cambrian Explosion points to God
"There is obviously a tremendous gap between 1-celled microorganisms and the high complexity and variety of the many invertebrate phyla of the Cambrian. If the former evolved into the latter, it seems impossible that no transitional forms between any of them would ever be preserved or found. A much more likely explanation for these gaps is that they represent permanent gaps between CREATED KINDS. Each organism has its own structure, specifically DESIGNED for its own purpose, not accidentally evolved by random processes."

"Darwin's Doubt" by Dr. Stephen Meyer[39]

Dr. Stephen C. Meyer is an American PhD Professor in the Philosophy of Science (obtained at the University of Cambridge). He is best known for Intelligent Design argument as seen in the complexity in biochemical systems.

Dr. Meyer directs the Seattle-based Discovery Institute's Center for Science and Culture, and is the leading proponent of Intelligent Design Theory. He has authored two best-selling books on Intelligent Design: 'Darwin's Doubt: The Explosive Origin of Animal Life and the Case for Intelligent Design', and 'Signature in the Cell: DNA and the Evidence for Intelligent Design', which was named a Book of the Year by the Times of London.

His work in Intelligent Design is introduced in this quote from his website 'stephencmeyer.org': *"The Origins of Information: Exploring and Explaining Biological Information the 21st century, the information age has finally come to biology. We now know that biology at its root is comprised of information rich systems, such as the complex digital code encoded in DNA. Groundbreaking discoveries of the past decade are revealing the information bearing properties of biological systems.*

Philosopher of science Dr. Stephen C. Meyer is examining and explaining the amazing depth of digital technology found in each and every living cell, such as nested coding, digital processing, distributive retrieval and storage systems, and genomic operating systems. Meyer is developing a more fundamental argument for intelligent design that is based not on a single feature like the bacterial flagellum, but rather on a pervasive feature of all living systems. Alongside matter and energy, Dr. Meyer shows that there is a third fundamental entity in the universe needed for life: information."

Darwin's Doubt –
The Explosive Origin of Animal Life and the Case for Intelligent Design

"Each of the features of the Cambrian animals and the Cambrian fossil record that render neo-Darwinism and other materialistic theories inadequate as causal explanations also happen to be features of systems known from experience to have arisen as the result of intelligent activity."

Stephen Meyer, Page 358

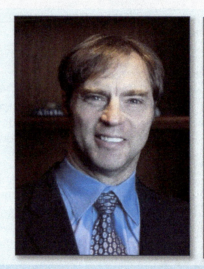
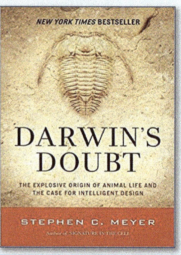

"No undirected physical or chemical process has demonstrated the capacity to produce specified information starting from 'purely physical or chemical precursors.'" (page vi)

"The fundamental problem confronting neo-Darwinism, as with chemical evolutionary theory, is the problem of the origin of new biological information." (page ix)

In the prologue, Dr. Meyer explains why his work on the Cambrian Fossil Explosion as evidence for Intelligent Design demands a hearing: *"Scientists now know that building a living organism requires information, and building a fundamentally new form of life from a simpler form of life requires an immense amount of new information. Thus, wherever the fossil record testifies to the origin of a completely new form of animal life – a pulse of biological innovation – it also testifies to a significant increase in the information content of the biosphere."*

He then challenges the scientific community with the need to explain how information could possibly originate from an evolutionary process: *"Whenever we find functional information – whether embedded in a radio signal, carved in a stone monument, etched on a magnetic disc, or produced by an origin-of-life scientist attempting to engineer a self-replicating – and we trace that information back to its ultimate source, invariably we come to a mind, not merely material process. For this reason, the discovery of digital information in even the simplest living cells indicates the prior activity of a designing intelligence at work in the origin of the first life."*

The Cambrian Explosion = Evidence for Genesis ch. 1

Below is a simplified explanation of the way animal life is thought to have evolved. Beginning with raw chemicals, simple life-forms such as algae supposedly formed several billion years ago. By some evolutionary process, creatures gradually got more and more complex. Eventually, you get the complex life we have today.

But there is the reality of what is called the "Cambrian Explosion.", given a time period of around 600 million years ago by secular science. There are two major findings within the Cambrian Explosion fossil record that completely discredit Evolutionary Theory but completely credit Creation Theory:

1) Before the Cambrian Explosion, the only fossil life is simple single-celled algae and bacteria. Then we suddenly find over 5,000 species of complex invertebrate fossils, such as sponges, jellyfish, worms and mollusks. There is no explanation for this. If evolution is true, we should find transitional fossils. There are none.

2) Within the strata of the Cambrian Explosion, we also do not find any transitional forms between invertebrates and fish, which are considered by Evolutionary Theory to be the earliest vertebrates. If evolution is true, fish evolved from invertebrates, but there are no transitional forms found in the Cambrian rocks. It's as if fish were just suddenly there, having no ancestors.

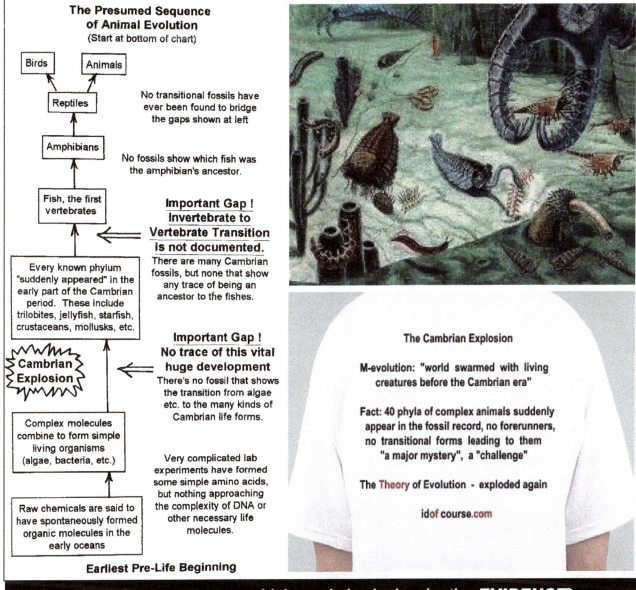

What the experts say – which one is backed up by the EVIDENCE?

| Richard Dawkins, Evolutionist ("The Blind Watchmaker", p. 229): *"It's as though they (Cambrian fossils) were just planted there, without any evolutionary history."* | God (Genesis 1:20-21): *"Let the waters abound with an abundance of living creatures... so God created great sea creatures and every living thing with which the waters abounded, according to their kind..."* |

Scrutinizing Darwinian Evolution → The HUMAN Fossil Record   8.12

Charles Darwin[1] (defining *HUMAN ORIGINS*) =
"Man bears in his bodily structure clear traces of his descent from some lower form."

What Darwin's Theory *says*:
People are modified descendants of an ancestor we shared with other animals

What Darwin's Theory *means*:
People are nothing but animals

What Darwin's Theory *says*:
Peoples' distinctive features are due to natural selection acting randomly on small variations over a long time

What Darwin's Theory *means*:
People are not the preordained goal of any directed purpose

**What our teenagers are being taught: "Modern Biology" (Holt, Rinehart, Winston)
Advanced Biology class, Lees Summit High School, Lees Summit, MO:**

- "To understand the story of human evolution, we must understand both our ancestry and our relationship to our closest living kin. Humans are members of the ancient mammalian order **Primates**. Many of our behaviors and characteristics are similar to other primates, and some are uniquely human."

- Anthropoid Primates = marmosets, monkeys, apes, **humans**.
  Prosimian Primates = lemurs, lorises, tarsiers

- "Compared with other primates, anthropoids have a large brain relative to their body size. The fossil record shows that as primates evolved, brain size increased."

- "Of the anthropoid species, the chimpanzees may be the most closely related to humans. Comparisons of chimpanzee and human DNA have shown a high degree of similarity. This similarity suggests that humans and chimpanzees may have shared an ancestor less than 6 million years ago. It is important to understand, however, that humans are not descended from chimpanzees or from any other modern ape. Rather, modern apes and humans are probably descended from a more primitive apelike ancestor."

- "Scientists who study the fossil remains of early hominids have inferred the evolutionary trends toward a larger brain and bipedalism. The fossils of hominids, unlike those of apes and their ancestors, show a whole spectrum of unique adaptations for upright walking."

- "Starting in early part of the 20th century, scientists have worked continuously to establish a robust fossil record of human evolution. This work has been rewarded by the discovery of many hominid life-forms, some of which are clearly identifiable as a known type, while others appear to be transitions between known types. As scientists fill in the puzzle of human evolution, they have been surprised by some of their discoveries: dead-end branches of the family tree, as well as evidence that 2 or more quite different hominid forms may have coexisted."

- "An early, now-extinct form of our species, Homo sapiens, probably arose from Homo erectus about 800,000 years ago. Over the years, evidence of hominid forms that were transitional between H. erectus and H. sapiens have been found. Thus, H. sapiens and H. erectus may have coexisted for more than 700,000 years."

**If our High School Textbooks are telling the truth….
Why have no Missing Links ever been found?**

Duane A. Schmidt[30]: *"…as the fossil evidence mounted, hopes for the missing link, which it was supposed to contain, shrank. Darwin said that given enough fossils we would find proof…*

Marvin L. Lubenow, in his brilliant book Bones of Contention, reported, 'the total number of hominid (man) fossil individuals discovered to date exceeds 6,000.' This is hardly a limited number of fossils to work with."

Why haven't human fossils solved the issue of mans' origins?
1) A few scattered bones doesn't make a full skeleton: random fossil bones can be reconstructed in a variety of different ways (it's all speculation how the few bones found at a site actually fit together).
   Constance Holden ("Science")[17]: *"The primary scientific evidence is a pitifully small array of bones from which to construct man's evolutionary history."*
2) A few scattered bones make it impossible to determine ancestor-descendant relationships: it's hard enough with written records to trace someone's lineage back a few hundred years. When you're dealing with a fragments of fossil records over 1,000's of years, it's effectively impossible.
   Henry Gee (*Nature*)[17]: *"No fossil is buried with its birth certificate…the time that separate fossils is so huge that we can't say anything definite about their connection through ancestry and descent. To take a line of fossils and claim that they represent a lineage is not a scientific hypothesis that can be tested, but an assertion that carries the same validity as a bedtime story – amusing, perhaps even instructive, but not scientific."*

If the fossils can't explain human origins, where do human evolution stories come from?
1) Paleoanthropology = The study of human origins
2) Ian Tattersall (American Museum of Natural History)[17]: *"Paleoanthropologists are STORYTELLERS: the patterns we perceive are as likely to result from our unconscious mindsets as from the evidence itself."*
3) Misia Landau (*Narratives of Human Evolution*)[17]: when paleoanthropologists want to explain what really happened in human evolution they use four main events, none of which can be tied to scientific evidence:
   (a) moving from trees to the ground   (b) developing an upright posture
   (c) acquiring intelligence and language (d) developing technology and society

What has science taught us about human origins?
1) Where paleoanthropologists agree: The human species does have a history…many fossils have been found that appear genuine, with both ape-like and human-like features (see pages of fossils).
2) Where paleoanthropologists disagree: can't decide which fossils represent ancestors of modern humans or extinct side branches of Darwin's infamous "tree".
   (a) "out of Africa" camp = modern humans first evolved in Africa and then spread throughout the world.
   (b) "multiregional camp" = humans evolved in many places simultaneously.
   (c) Neanderthals and Cro-Magnums = humans or our ape-like ancestors (we have extensive fossil evidence of these early peoples as humans, not ape-like ancestors! But paleoanthropologists can't agree).
3) There is no agreed-upon theory of human evolution: there are so many gaps in information to reach any sound conclusions, so the public is told theories based on 'biases, preconceptions and assumptions'
   (a) F. Clark Howell (Berkeley evolutionary biologist, 1996)[17]: *"explanatory models of human evolution are a house of cards – remove one card, and the whole structure of inference is threatened with collapse."*
   (b) Jonathan Wells[17]: *"The general public is rarely informed of the deep-seated uncertainty about human origins that is reflected in statements by scientists. Woven into the mythical accounts of human evolution is usually the message that we are nothing more than animals, and our existence is a mere accident."*

The "Science" of Paleontology and The History of Fossil Discoveries…
Still No Missing Link!

The following pages contain a fairly comprehensive list of what has been claimed as significant "human fossil" finds. There is little consensus among paleoanthropologists as to whether or not any of these fossils can be claimed to be human, nevermind reaching a consensus on what the human "family tree" is. The diagram to the right illustrates today's more popular view held by Evolutionists on the Human "Family Tree".

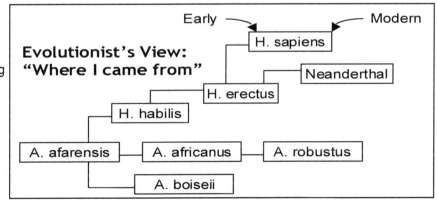

The History of the *Evidence* for "Missing Links"

➢ **Going from Bad Science…..**

LUCY
Nearly all experts agree Lucy was just a 3 foot tall chimpanzee.

HEIDELBERG MAN
Built from a jawbone that was conceded by many to be quite human.

NEBRASKA MAN
Scientifically built up from one tooth, later found to be the tooth of an extinct pig.

PILTDOWN MAN
The jawbone turned out to belong to a modern ape.

PEKING MAN
Supposedly 500,000 years old, but all evidence has disappeared.

NEANDERTHAL MAN
At the Int'l Congress of Zoology (1958) Dr. A.J.E. Cave said his examination showed that this famous skeleton found in France over 50 years ago is that of an old man who suffered from arthritis.

NEWGUINEA MAN
Dates way back to 1970. This species has been found in the region just north of Australia.

CROMAGNON MAN
One of the earliest and best established fossils is at least equal in physique and brain capacity to modern man… so what's the difference?

MODERN MAN
This genius thinks we came from a monkey.

"Professing themselves to be wise they became fools." (Romans 1:22)

➢ **To Outright False Facts…..**

The following quote is taken from the textbook "Modern Biology" (Holt, Rinehart, Winston), used in the Advanced Biology class at Lees Summit High School in Lees Summit, MO:

"An early, now-extinct form of our species, Homo sapiens, **probably** arose from Homo erectus about 800,000 years ago. Over the years, **evidence** of hominid forms that were transitional between H. erectus and H. sapiens **have been found**. Thus, H. sapiens and H. erectus **may have** coexisted for more than 700,000 years."

Charles Darwin[2] *"False facts are highly injurious to the progress of science, for they often endure long…"*

"Bones of Contention" by Professor Marvin Lubenow[41]

Marvin Lubenow is professor of Bible, theology and apologetics at Southern California Seminary in El Cajun, California. He spent more than 35 years researching the human fossil issue and frequently speaks and writes to defend the creationist position. He holds a Master of Science in Anthropology from Eastern Michigan University, and Master of Theology from Dallas Theological Seminary.

Bones of Contention –
A Creationist Assessment of Human Fossils

"We are unique and alone now in the world. There is no other animal species that truly resembles our own.

A physical and mental chasm separates us from all other living creatures.

There is no other bipedal mammal. No other mammal controls and uses fire, writes books, travels in space, paints portraits, or prays. This is not a question of degree. It is all or nothing.

There is no semi-bipedal animal, none that makes only small fires, writes only short sentences, builds only rudimentary spaceships, draws just a little bit, or prays just occasionally."

Martin Lubenow, Page 306

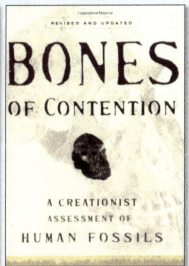

"The certainty with which evolutionists state that human evolution is a fact is a reflection of their philosophical belief, not of the objective evidence. The evidence for human evolution is not solid enough to convict a known thief of petty larceny." (page 327)

His first edition of "Bones of Contention", published in 1992, was a critique of the human fossil record as evidence for evolution. This updated edition, published in 2004, contains updated developments in the field of human evolution and the latest fossil discoveries. In this latest edition, Lubenow argues "the whole of evolution is dead."

He also expounds on the use of Darwinian evolution in its earliest days of publication, when "scientific racism", which claimed white Europeans were superior to other races, was heralded as scientific truth.

He elaborates on how the racism inherent in evolution is being camouflaged today, claiming the current model of choice, the "Out of Africa" or "African Eve" model for human evolution, although it lacks solid fossil evidence, is preferred by evolutionary scientists because it better hides the racism present in all evolutionary models.

Here are a few of Lubenow's statements that make his book a worthwhile read for those wanting a deeper understanding of the human fossil record:

1) Creationism itself is not what causes emotions to flare. The term "creationism" screams "God"! That's why it is so emotional. And that's why many people who do not personally know God embrace evolution (p. 16).

2) Darwin never saw any human fossils, although he published a book on human evolution in 1871 (p. 22).

3) The problem is not with the fossils. It is with the interpretation of the fossils (p. 25).

4) Most people today believe that Darwin disproved biblical creationism and proved evolution. The Darwinian Revolution, one of the most significant revolutions of all time, is generally thought to be the establishment of the concept of evolution on a solid, empirical basis. Not so. In the words of Harvard biologist Ernst Mayr, the Darwinian Revolution was actually a philosophical revolution from a theistic worldview to a worldview in which God was not involved in any way (p. 93).

5) The sin of evolution, and I use that term literally, is that evolution gives humans an allegedly scientific justification for racism (p. 139).

The Scientific Evidence: I am not descended from animals   8.13

Duane A. Schmidt (And God Created Darwin)[30]: *"Darwin admitted difficulty in coming to grips with the idea that man came from an ape. As a former divinity student he knew the consequences of what he proposed…"*

> Darwin[2]: *"My objective is to show there is no fundamental difference between man and the higher animals in their mental faculties. The difference in mind between man and higher animals, great as it is, certainly is one of degree and not of kind."*

- **Example 1: Language** *"…if what he meant by 'DEGREE' is that a human being can learn 20,000 words and the most intelligent ape seems at best to grasp minimal values from a few words… but Darwin balks at calling the differing abilities to use those words as the difference in 'KIND' which it is. Using words intelligently is a chasm away from pointing to a piece of candy when the keeper says 'candy' to his trained ape."*

- **Example 2: Favorable Mutations** *"Natural selection is supposed to be an engine that causes population shift to improve, ever on the lookout for small favorable mutations to capture in a descendant population. If this is true, what happened to the DE-EVOLUTION of man's ability to smell, run, see, and fly? What happened to man's instincts that his ape ancestors had? Surely those instincts would serve him better that the slow rearing and the lengthy puberty process man now endures?"*

- **Example 3: Body Fur** *"Man is not densely covered with fur (or even hair, scales, or feathers). Evolutionists say we lost our heavy, hairy covering but are unsure just why. Perhaps we could not lose a covering we never had? Desmond Morris claimed we lost our fur covering to become a 'naked ape' because we overheated as we chased down game. I wonder what game man has ever chased down? Or any hominid for that matter?"*

- **Example 4: The Foramen Magnum** *"Anatomically the head of man joins his backbone at more of a right angle than an ape's, which allows him to stand erect. This is because the foramen magnum, the hole beneath the vertebrae, is beneath the cranium and the ape's foramen magnum is more behind his skull. Major difference there and easy to spot on fossil skulls… this gradual 'shift' of the foramen magnum, from the rear of the skull to beneath it, is depicted ever so convincingly in drawings. Funny thing: none of these depicted changes, in all those museum displays and textbook drawings, can be backed up by even one example in the fossil world."*

- **Example 5: Self-Awareness** *"Man's behavior is learned, plus we know all this about ourselves. An animal knows, but he doesn't know that he knows. Even Dobzhansky admitted that the human animal is the only animal that 'distinguishes what is from what ought to be.' But without self-awareness man's ethics are empty calisthenics."*

- **Example 6: Lack of Instincts** *"As opposed to animals who live by instinct rather than wits, man has few instincts. Our progeny must be taught, schooled, and led into maturity, whereas animals need not be… animal instincts for fishing, flying and killing are so well-infused into those species' young that they perform those functions even if they have never seen a parent…they were born knowing how, as if a human child could be born knowing how to read. The animal world has tricks we human beings have not mastered. How could it advantage the child to lose the instincts that rule the animal world?"*

- **Example 7: Handling and Controlling Fire** *"Michael Denton, in 'Nature's Destiny', lays the uniqueness of human life at man's ability to handle and control fire. This talent led him to develop metallurgy, then technology and, ultimately, to probe the universe. Since no subhuman species is known to possess the talent of the fireplace, the argument has validity."*

> **"Man is complex…awareness of himself and his destiny did not develop by chance.**
> **The single question remains: where is the Watchmaker?"**

The Biblical Evidence: I am uniquely created by God

The Bible details three wonderful descriptions of how mankind was first created by God. Each of them reflect His preordained purpose for a special, intimate relationship with every single person He creates.

① God created me *PERSONALLY*

- **The Lord merely spoke his created animals into existence….**

Genesis 1:20-21, 24-25 *"…God SAID, 'Let the waters abound with an abundance of living creatures, and let birds fly above the earth across the face of the firmament of the heavens. So God created great sea creatures and every living thing that moves, with which the waters abounded, according to its kind, and every winged bird according to its kind. And God saw that it was good … God SAID, 'Let the earth bring forth the living creature according to its kind: cattle and creeping thing and beast of the earth, each according to its kind; and it was so. And God made the beast of the earth ACCORDING TO ITS KIND, and everything that creeps on the earth according to its kind. And God saw that it was good."*

Genesis 2:9 *"Out of the ground the Lord formed every beast of the field and every bird of the air, and brought them to Adam to see what he would call them."*

- **But He personally created me to be *LIKE HIM*….**

Genesis 1:26-27 *"… 'Let Us make man in OUR IMAGE, according to OUR LIKENESS; let them have dominion over the fish of the sea, over the birds of the air, and over the cattle, over all the earth and over every creeping thing that creeps on the earth.' So God created man in His image; in the image of God He created them; male and female He created them."*

Henry Morris (Biblical Creationism[5]): "Adam's body was carefully formed by GOD'S OWN HANDS (not, like the animals, merely by the divine spoken Word) out of the 'dust of the ground,' the basic elements of earth matter from which all physical systems had been made. Then Eve's body was formed by God out of the materials in Adam's side, probably both flesh and blood, as well as bone. They were not formed by any evolutionary process from a population of hominids, as modern pseudo-intellectuals have deceived themselves into believing."

② God created me *PURPOSEFULLY*

- **God's will = Gr. "THELEMA"** (His purpose for every single person)

Colossians 1:9-10 *"For this reason we also, since the day we heard it, do not cease to pray for you, and to ask that you be filled with the KNOWLEDGE OF HIS WILL in all wisdom and spiritual understanding; that you may have a walk worthy of the Lord, fully pleasing Him, being fruitful in every good work and increasing in the knowledge of God…."*

③ God created me *PROVISIONALLY*

Before He created me, God planned He would PROVIDE for my rebellion against His will. He created me knowing I would one day reject Him, but with His plan to bring me back to Him (He went from creating me to restoring me).

Genesis 2:16-17   God warns man of the consequences of not obeying Him
"…the Lord God commanded the man, saying, 'Of every tree of the garden you may freely eat; but of the tree of the knowledge of good and evil you shall not eat, for in the day that you eat of it you shall surely die."

Genesis 3:21   God's 1st sacrifice of an animal to cover their nakedness – He points to the future "Lamb of God"
"…for Adam and his wife the Lord God made tunics of skin, and clothed them."

Romans 3:23-26   Jesus = God's only acceptable sacrifice for our removal of sin
"…for all have sinned and fallen short of the glory of God, being justified freely by His grace through the redemption that is in Christ Jesus, whom God set forth to be a PROPITIATION by His blood through faith, to demonstrate His righteousness, because in His forbearance God has PASSED OVER the sins that were previously committed, to demonstrate at the present time His righteousness, that He might be just and the justifier of the one who has faith in Jesus."

> **Jeremiah 29:11**   *"For I know the thoughts that I think toward you, says the Lord, thoughts of peace and not of evil, to give you a future and a hope."*

Let's Review Some of What We've Learned about why Evolution is False

Homology: Similar structures have independent origins at genetic level (evidence for creation, not evolution).

Natural Selection: Galapagos finch beak sizes oscillate, but they have always stayed finches.

Fossil Record: "It offers no support for gradual change; there is precious little in the way of intermediate forms." Stephen J. Gould

Embryology: Haeckel's embryos were a deliberate distortion to promote evolution.

There are 9 Facts about Evolution to which all scientists agree...

Cambrian Explosion: 40 phyla of complex animals suddenly appear without transitions; fish suddenly appear without transitions.

Common Ancestry: Darwin's Tree of Life a man-made invention (no evidence).

Together these 9 Facts make a strong case *against Darwinian Evolution*

Transitional Forms: Archaeopteryx is not a dinosaur-to-bird; it's a feathered dinosaur.

Miller-Urey Experiment: Proving life can arise from non-life (abiogenesis) failed.

Human Evolution: The Missing Link (ape-to-man) doesn't exist - it's a fairy tale.

GLOSSARY OF TERMS → Creation vs. Evolution

Paleoanthropology = The study of human origins.

Anthropology = The science that deals with the origins, customs, etc. of life.

Paleontology = The study of the forms of life which existed in former geologic periods.

Creation = God, in His Bible, provides the accurate and reliable account of origins and the history of the earth. The statements made in God's Word should be able to be backed up and supported by physical evidence from the world that God has created. The Scriptures are used as a key for understanding the principle of origins and the history of the earth.

Creation Science = Creation Science is usually defined by the media as the Genesis account of creation - what is normally taught in the Sunday School classroom. The charge is continually repeated but it is not true. Creation science is scientific evidence, not religious dogma. Both creation and evolution have profound religious, philosophical implications, yet, both may be investigated scientifically. Chief Justice Rienquist and Justice Scallia pointed out that creation science involved the study of biology, paleontology, genetics, astronomy, astrophysics, probability analysis and biochemistry. They concluded that this discipline was the study "of scientific data supporting the theory that the physical universe and life within it appeared suddenly and have not changed substantially since appearing...Creation Science is a strictly scientific concept that...does not require the presentation of religious doctrine."

What is meant by "Intelligent Design?" (William Dembski)

"Intelligent Design begins with the observation that intelligent causes can do things which undirected natural causes cannot. Undirected natural causes can place scrabble pieces on a board, but cannot arrange the pieces as meaningful words or sentences. To obtain a meaningful arrangement requires an intelligent cause. This intuition, that there is a fundamental distinction between undirected natural causes on the one hand and intelligent causes on the other, has underlain the design arguments of past centuries. Intelligent Design presupposes neither a creator nor miracles. Intelligent Design detects intelligence without speculating about the nature of the intelligence."

"Intelligent Design entails that naturalism in all forms be rejected. Metaphysical naturalism, the view that undirected natural causes wholly govern the world, is to be rejected because it is false. Methodological naturalism, the view that for the sake of science, scientific explanation ought never exceed undirected natural causes, is to be rejected because it stifles inquiry. Nothing is gained by pretending science can get along without intelligent causes. Rather, because intelligent causes are empirically detectable, science must ever remain open to evidence of their activity."

"For Intelligent Design the first question is not how organisms came to be (though this question needs to be addressed), but whether they demonstrate clear, empirically detectable marks of being intelligently caused."

Irreducible Complexity = When a single system, composed of several well-matched, interacting parts that contribute to its basic function, has any 1 of these parts removed such that it causes the system to cease functioning. An Irreducibly complex system cannot be produced directly (that is, by continuously improving the initial function, which continues to work by the same mechanism) by slight, successive modifications of a precursor system, because any precursor to an irreducibly complex system that is missing a part is by definition nonfunctional.

Evolution = The belief that inorganic material evolves into simple cells and later into advanced life without any input from a divine being.

Theistic Evolution[14] = The belief in a God who acts in space and time, but scientific naturalism does not allow the consideration of positive evidence for a creator. Physical objects, including organisms, are explained only by physical causes. All organisms share a common ancestor, and the 1st organisms arose via physical causes from nonliving things. In essence, the activity of God is invisible to human science.

Spontaneous Generation = The supposed spontaneous origination of living organisms directly from lifeless matter (also known as "abiogenesis"); most common hypothesis: chemicals produced in the primitive Earth's atmosphere dissolved in the primordial seas to form a "hot dilute soup", from which the 1st living cells emerged.

Descent with Modification = Because evolutionary biologists acknowledge that the "event" which led to the origin of the first living cells was so improbable that it happened only once, they then assume that these few original cells gave rise to the millions of different species we have today.

Natural = Selection	"Survival of the fittest" (Charles Darwin's "Origin of Species"): small variations between individuals of a species, as observed in nature. Selection confers differing degrees of advantage or disadvantage in the struggle for existence. Individual organisms with favorable traits are more likely to survive and reproduce than those with unfavorable traits. Those with significant advantages survive longer to transmit these characteristics by inheritance to their descendants (favorable, heritable traits become more common in the next generation). Given enough time, this process results in new and higher types of organisms.
Adaptive = Radiation	The process in which one species gives rise to multiple species that exploit different niches. The ecological niches exert the selection pressures that push the populations in various directions.
Mutation[4] =	A real structural change in a gene, of such character that something novel is produced, and not merely a reworking of something already there. In some way, the linkages in a segment of the DNA molecules are changed, so that different "information" is conveyed via the genetic code in the formation of the structure of the descendant. This phenomenon of mutation is thus a most important component of the evolution model. The evolution model postulates this mechanism of "mutation" to produce the required upward progress in complexity which characterizes the model in its broadest dimension.
Genes =	Units of heredity in the chromosomes (threadlike bodies found in cell nucleus that carries the genes) which control the development of the hereditary character of that organism.
Cambrian = Explosion	A geological period thought to have begun $\approx$ 540 million years. The Cambrian explosion has been called the 'Biological Big Bang' because it caused the sudden appearance of most of the major animal divisions that are still alive today. The record shows there were some jellyfish, sponges and worms before the Cambrian period. Then – boom! – all of a sudden we see arthropods (insects, crabs), echinoderms (starfish, sea urchins), chordates (vertebrates), etc. This is absolutely contrary to Darwin's Tree of Life.
Punctuated = Equilibrium	Invented in the 1's by Stephen J. Gould and paleontologist Niles Eldredge, it states that evolution occurred only in selected sites and rapidly, instead of the gradual idea which Darwin believed (as well as many of today's scientists). This theory maintains that evolution happened so fast that no fossils were left behind (as Marvin Lubenow states: *"Punctuated Equilibrium must be the only theory in the history of science which claims to be scientific and then explains why evidence for it cannot be found."*)

➔ Physics

Molecule =	The smallest physical unit of an element or compound that can exist separately and still keep the properties of the original substance.
Atom =	The basic structure from which all matter is composed, in the same manner as a brick is the basic structure from which a wall is built. Although atoms are too small to be seen with our eyes, scientists have long had indirect evidence for the existence of atoms. We can now use the world's most powerful scanning tunneling microscopes to "see" the magnified images of atoms and to study surface reaction sites on an atom-by-atom basis. To get an idea of how small an atom is, consider that a small gold coin may contain over 20,000,000,000,000,000,000,000 atoms. In one breath of air, we breathe 6×10^{23} oxygen atoms. Atoms are made of small particles called protons, neutrons, and electrons. Each of these particles is described in terms of measurable properties, including mass and charge. Mass is the amount of matter that an object contains. The proton and neutron have roughly the same mass and have approximately one thousand times the mass of the electron. The proton and electron have equal, but opposite, electrical charges. A neutron does not have an electrical charge. The attractive electric force between the positively-charged protons in the nucleus and the negatively-charged electrons around the nucleus holds the atom together.
Element =	A substance made up of a single type of atom. It can't be broken into simpler components by chemical processes. There are naturally occurring elements. They may be solids, liquids, or gases. The elements are distributed unevenly, with some much more common than others. The ten most abundant elements on earth (oxygen, silicon, aluminum, iron, calcium, magnesium, nickel, sulfur, titanium, hydrogen) make up more than 99% of our planet.
Atomic = Nucleus	In an atom, the protons and neutrons clump together in the center and are called the nucleus. Because the protons are positively charged, the nucleus has a positive electric charge. The electrons of the atom move rapidly around the nucleus. If we attempt to detect an electron in an atom, we might find evidence of it located almost anywhere around the nucleus.

However, if we repeat this experiment many times, the electron is likely to be located in certain regions of space surrounding the nucleus. We might think that the electron is rapidly moving around the nucleus and our experiment "catches" the electron as an instantaneous "snapshot" of it in motion.

The probability of finding the electron in any region of space can then be described by a cloud that rapidly thins out as one goes farther from the nucleus. The density of the cloud at any point is the probability of finding the electron at that point. Most of an atom is empty space. The nucleus of the atom contains almost all of the mass of the atom. A greatly enlarged atom might look like a marble (the nucleus) inside an empty football stadium (the electron probability cloud).

Strong = Nuclear Force : The force governing the degree to which protons and neutrons stick together in atomic nuclei. It is as short-range as it is strong, extending only to the atomic nucleus. Its value is so delicately set that any change in it, whether stronger or weaker, would make life impossible on earth.

Weak = Nuclear Force : The force governing the conversion of protons to neutrons and vice-versa, and the interaction of neutrinos with other particles. Without this force, there would not be enough essential elements available for life.

Light[24] = Something that makes things visible or illuminates (electromagnetic radiation to which the organs of sight react). It has both *particle-like* properties and *wave* properties (light sometimes behaves like invisible particles called *photons*, while it can also display *wavelengths* that act like water waves or sound waves). Scientists accept this unusual dual nature of light without completely understanding it. Light is pure, beautiful, and beyond human understanding. No wonder God Himself is called "light" (1John 1:5) and Jesus calls Himself the "Light of the world" (John 8:12).

We are familiar with *visible* light from the Sun (rainbows, blue skies, red sunspots come from the separation of sunlight into its spectral colors). But the Sun and other stars also emit kinds of *invisible* light that our eyes cannot see (radio waves, microwaves, UV and infrared, x-rays and gamma rays). If we could see them, the heavens would be brilliantly illuminated with energy.

1st Law of Thermo-Dynamics[7] = "The Law of Conservation of Energy". Energy cannot be destroyed; neither is it being created. Systems that use energy do not use it up; they merely convert it to different forms of energy – heat, motion, sound, light, or chemical or electromagnetic energy (remember that Einstein's famous theorem, $E = MC^2$ – energy equals mass times the speed of light squared – teaches that matter is simply another form of energy. That means matter, like energy, cannot be destroyed, it can only be converted to another form. The amount of energy within any system remains constant unless outside forces interact with the system.

The only way to *increase* the energy in an energy-using system is for an external force to do work on that system – adding heat, fuel, or kinetic energy to it. Likewise, energy will *decrease* in a system only if it is transformed out of the system as heat, light, or some other form of energy.

2nd Law of Thermo-Dynamics = "The Law of Increasing Disintegration". There exists a universal principle of change in nature which is downhill, not uphill (as evolution requires). "In any physical change that takes place by itself the entropy always increases. All changes are in the direction that the entropy increases.

This proven Law is exactly opposite to the evolution model, which is based on the never-observed theory that systems move toward higher and higher levels of complexity and increased organization (rather than disintegration).

Entropy = A measure of the quantity of energy *not* capable of conversion into work. The entropy measures the degree of disorder associated with the energy. Energy must always flow in the direction that the entropy increases.

➜ Earth, Space and the Universe

Astronomy = The science that deals with the material universe beyond the earth's atmosphere.

Cosmology = The study of the origin and general structure of the universe. "To study the origin and development of the universe is to investigate the basis for any meaning and purpose to life. Cosmology has deep theological and philosophical ramifications. If the universe is not created or is in some manner accidental, then it has no objective meaning, and consequently, life, including human life, has no meaning. A mechanical chain of events determines everything. Morality and religion may be temporarily useful but are ultimately irrelevant. The universe becomes ultimate reality. On the other hand, if the universe is created, then there must be reality beyond the confines of the universe. The Creator is that ultimate reality and wields authority over all else. The Creator is the source of life and establishes its meaning and purpose. The Creator's personality defines personality. The Creator's character defines morality."[18]

Fine-Tuned Universe = The idea that conditions that allow life in the universe can only occur with the tightly restricted values of the universal physical constants, and that small changes in these constants would correspond to a very different universe, not likely conducive to the establishment and development of matter, astronomical structures, or life as it is presently known.

Circumstellar Continuously Habitable Zone (CCHZ)[26] = That region over which all the instantaneous CHZ's overlap for some extended period of time. It is much narrower that the CHZ, and the position of this zone varies from star to star. Low-mass host stars, being less luminous than the Sun, have small, close-in CCHZ's (the opposite is true for more massive stars).

Big Bang[24] = A popular, secular explanation for the origin of the universe. It states that the entire physical universe (all the matter and energy, and even the 4 dimensions of space and time) burst forth from a state of infinite (or near infinite) density, temperature and pressure. The universe expanded from a volume much smaller than the period at the end of this sentence….and it continues to expand.

The process began supposedly with the explosion of a "kernel" of mass energy, about 15 billion years ago. As the energetic radiation spread outward, temperatures slowly cooled enough for hydrogen and helium atoms to form. About 10 billion years ago, the 1st stars began to form from the cooling gas in the young universe. This star-forming process eventually gave rise to the Milky Way and other galaxies.

Steady-State Theory = In 1948, three British astrophysicists (Herman Bondi, Thomas Gold, Fred Hoyle), proposed the Steady-State theory that creation of matter is a law of nature (nothing can transcend the realm of nature), not a one-time miracle from outside nature. Skipping past any attempt to explain the expansion of the universe, they proposed that the voids resulting from expansion are filled by the continual, spontaneous self-creation of new matter.

This theory would imply that a universe with no beginning and no end should manifest a "steady population of stars and galaxies, at various stages of development, that is proportional to the time required to pass through these stages (there would be, upon examination, a balanced number of newly-formed, young, middle-aged, elderly, and extinct stars and galaxies). This theory has been discredited due to astronomical evidence (General Theory of Relativity, Hubble Law, Cosmic Background Radiation, Universal Expansion) that suggests the universe is in fact changing over time..

Galaxy = A large system of stars (an "island universe") held together by mutual gravitation; Earth is part of the Milky Way Galaxy (the faintly luminous band stretching across the heavens, composed of innumerable stars too distant to be seen clearly with the naked eye.

Galileo first identified a galaxy in when, through a telescope, he recorded viewing "a congeries of innumerable stars". Galaxies come in 3 basic types:
a) spiral galaxy = comprise only 5% of the 3 types: they appear as flattened disks (where most of their stars reside), which are only about 1% as thick as their diameter (Earth is in a spiral galaxy); they get their name from the beautiful spiral pattern formed by their young stars and bright nebulae;
b) elliptical galaxy = star formation ceases before the interstellar medium becomes enriched enough with heavy metals (in order to have life, stars systems must form late enough so they can incorporate this heavy element-enriched material).
c) irregular galaxy = "catchall for what's left; they have a very active nucleus, which spew out life-destroying radiation and material, besides also having insufficient quantities of heavy elements essential for life.

Star = A heavenly body that appears as a luminous point in the sky at night. It is a hot, opaque ball of gas that continuously broadcasts light in all directions, conveying information about itself and its local environment over vast distances. Stars play 2 essential life-support roles: as sources of most chemical elements and as steady suppliers of energy. The 2 measurable properties of a star are its luminosity (absolute brightness) and surface temperature.

Solar System = The Sun with all the celestial bodies that revolve around it. The Solar System is unique in the universe. There is almost an innumerable quantity of stars, but that doesn't mean any of them have planets. The only Solar System about which we have any information is our own. No astronomer has ever viewed any other planet outside the Solar System in his telescope and has no real evidence that any exists.

White Dwarf = An earth-sized, highly-dense dying star, which pulsate and rotate with periods measured in minutes. Some display a rich pattern of pulsating periods, allowing astronomers to derive all their important properties.

Red Giants[24] = The largest stars known to exist in the universe. Their diameters reach > 500X that of our Sun (the Sun's diameter is 8,000 miles, which is about 4X the distance between Earth and the Moon).

Meteoroid = Any of the small bodies, often remnants of comets, traveling through space.

Meteor = A fiery streak in the sky produced by a meteoroid passing through the earth's atmosphere.

Asteroid = Any of the 1,000's of small bodies that revolve about the Sun in orbits mostly between Mars and Jupiter. They pose a very real threat of collision, creating devastating damage depending on their speed and size.

Comet = A celestial body moving about the sun, consisting of a central mass surrounded by a misty envelope, that may form a tail that streams away from the sun. It is transient, dropping in the inner Solar System unannounced from who-knows-where.

Quasar[26] = The name stands for "quasi-stellar" objects. They are mysterious celestial bodies, from 4 to 10 billion light-years distant, that are the most luminous and distant objects in the visible universe. They are believed to be galaxies in their early stages, when their central black holes are growing rapidly by accreting gases (before disappearing into the black hole, the gas forms a very hot, bright accretion disk around it. It's this accretion disk that makes quasars so bright).

Pulsar[26] = An exotic type of massive star that results from that star's explosion, which blows its outer layers apart, leaving behind a very dense, furiously spinning neutron core. They emit highly directional radiation, and this strong beaming allows us to measure a pulsar's rotation period precisely (using radio telescopes). Because of this ease in measuring, we can precisely determine orbital characteristics of bodies orbiting about a pulsar, test various aspects of Einstein's Theory of General Relativity in weak and strong gravity limits, and learn about properties of matter at varying nuclear densities.

Black Hole[24] = A fearsome object, distorting space, time and common sense: so densely packed that not even light can escape their horizons. They are invisible, weigh billions of tons, and are smaller than a kernel of corn. Since stars must collapse when they run short of fuel, if it is heavy enough there will be no limit to its contracting. It will 1st shrink to the size of the moon, then a basketball. Finally it will have no size at all, as gravity crushes the entire star into a mathematical point.

The only meaningful size reference is a "twilight zone" region around the collapsed star, possibly extending outward for millions of miles. Anything entering this region can't withstand the inward gravity pull of the collapsed star. Even light cannot escape, hence the name "black hole".

Although black holes can't be seen directly, there are ways to detect them in space since they affect nearby stars, tearing them apart and producing x-rays in the process.

Redshift = The redshift of a galaxy is a measure of its radial velocity, and it can be measured using a spectrograph to determine the Doppler shift

Quark = An elementary particle and a fundamental constituent of matter. Quarks combine to form composite particles called hadrons, the most stable of which are protons and neutrons. Quarks are never directly observed or found in isolation; they can be found only within baryons or mesons. For this reason, much of what is known about quarks has been drawn from observations of the hadrons themselves.

There are six types of quarks, known as *flavors*: up, down, strange, charm, bottom, and top. Up and down quarks have the lowest masses of all quarks. The heavier quarks rapidly change into up and down quarks through the process of particle decay. Because of this, up and down quarks are generally stable and the most common in the universe, whereas strange, charm, top, and bottom quarks can only be produced in high energy collisions (such as those involving cosmic rays and in particle accelerators).

Quarks have various intrinsic properties, including electric charge, color charge, mass, and spin. Quarks are the only elementary particles in the Standard Model of particle physics to experience all four fundamental interactions, also known as *fundamental forces* (electromagnetism, gravitation, strong interaction, and weak interaction). For every quark flavor there is a corresponding type of antiparticle, known as an *antiquark*, that differs from the quark only in that some of its properties have equal magnitude but opposite sign.

The quark model was independently proposed by physicists Murray Gell-Mann and George Zweig in 1964. Quarks were introduced as parts of an ordering scheme for hadrons, and there was little evidence for their physical existence until deep inelastic scattering experiments at the Stanford Linear Accelerator Center in 1968. All six flavors of quark have since been observed in accelerator experiments.

➔ Microbiology

Cell = The basic unit of all living things, discovered in 1665 by British scientist Robert Hooke who first observed them in his crude (by today's standards) 17th century optical microscope. Hooke coined the term "cell" when he described the microscopic structure of cork like a tiny, bare room or monk's cell. Every living thing has cells. Some organisms are made up of just 1 cell (e.g. bacteria and protozoans), but animals, including human beings, are multicellular. An adult human body is composed of ≈ 100,000,000,000,000 cells! Each cell has basic requirements to sustain it, and the body's organ systems are largely built around providing the many trillions of cells with those basic needs (such as oxygen, food, and waste removal).

There are about 200 different kinds of specialized cells in the human body. Ideas about cell structure have changed considerably over the years. Early biologists saw cells as simple membranous sacs containing fluid and a few floating particles. Today's biologists know that cells are infinitely more complex than this. Therefore, a strong knowledge of the various cellular organelles and their functions is important to any physiologist. If a person's cells are healthy, then that person is healthy. All physiological processes, growth and development, and disease can be described at the cellular level.

Tissue = When many identical cells are organized together (such as muscle tissue, nervous tissue, etc).

Organ = Various tissues organize for a common purpose (the stomach is an organ, the skin, the brain).

Nerve Cells = They are in the nervous system and function to process and transmit information. They are the core (neurons) components of the brain, spinal cord and peripheral nerves. They use chemical and electrical synapses to relay signals throughout the body.

Epithelial Cells = Among other things, they secrete, absorb, protect, transport between cells, detect sensations. They line both the outside (skin) and the inside cavities of bodies.

Exocrine Cells = They secrete products through ducts, such as mucus, sweat, or digestive enzymes. The products of these cells go directly to the target organ through the ducts (example: bile from the gall bladder is carried directly into the duodenum via the bile duct).

Endocrine Cells = They are like exocrine cells, but they secrete their products into the bloodstream instead of through a duct. The products of the endocrine cells go throughout the body in the blood stream but act on specific organs (example: the hormone estrogen acts specifically on the uterus and breasts of females).

Red Blood Cells = They collect oxygen in the lungs and deliver it through the blood to the body tissues.

White Blood Cells = They are produced in the bone marrow and fight infectious disease and foreign objects in the immune system. They are found in the circulatory system, lymphatic system, spleen, and other body tissues.

Cell Nucleus = Largest of the organelles, it serves as the information processing and administrative center of the cell. It has 2 major functions: it stores the cell's hereditary material, or DNA, and it coordinates the cell's activities, which include growth, intermediary metabolism, protein synthesis, and reproduction (cell division)..

Cell Membrane = The boundary of the cell that separates internal metabolic events from the external environment and controls the movement of materials into and out of the cell. This membrane is very selective about what it allows to pass through; this characteristic is referred to as "selective permeability" (it allows oxygen and nutrients to enter the cell while keeping toxins and waste products out).

Golgi Apparatus = The distribution and shipping department for the cell, they modify and package cellular products in sacs called vesicles (small spherically shaped sacs that bud from the ends of a Golgi apparatus) so that the products can cross the cell membrane and exit the cell. Vesicles often migrate to and merge with the plasma membrane, releasing their contents outside the cell.

Mitochondria = Tiny saclike structures found near the nucleus that serve as the cell's main power generators, converting oxygen and nutrients into energy by generating ATP, the universal form of energy used by all cells. They convert food nutrients such as glucose, to a fuel (ATP) that the cells of the body can use.

Centrioles = Rod-like structures composed of 9 bundles which contain 3 microtubules each. They are very important in cellular division, where they arrange the mitotic spindles that pull the chromosome apart.

Ribosomes = Tiny organelles composed of ≈ 60% RNA and 40% protein, they play an active role in the complex process of making protein, where they serve as the structures that facilitate the joining of amino acids. Each ribosome is made of a large and small subunit which are made up of ribosomal proteins and RNAs.

Lysosomes = Sac-like compartments in the Golgi apparatus whose main function is digestion: they contain powerful enzymes that break down harmful cell products and waste materials, cellular debris and foreign invaders such as bacteria, and then force them out of the cell.

Peroxisomes = Common in liver and kidney cells, they break down lipids and detoxify harmful chemicals. Peroxisomes self-replicate by enlarging and dividing. They can convert hydrogen peroxide, a toxin made of O_2 to O.

Endoplasmic Reticulum = "Endoplasmic" means "within the plasma", and "reticulum" means "network". A complex, 3D internal membrane system that plays an important role in making proteins and shuttling cellular products, metabolizing fats, and producing various materials. *Rough endoplasmic reticulum* is the site where proteins not destined for the cytoplasm are synthesized, while *smooth endoplasmic reticulum* synthesizes and degrades lipids and stores calcium ions. In liver cells, the smooth ER is involved in the breakdown of toxins, drugs, and toxic byproducts from cellular reactions.

Chromosomes = Tiny strings of DNA that populate the nuclei of cells. They are 23 pairs of chromosomes (each pair has contributions from mother and father). They hold thousands of genes.

What is DNA?[15]

People—like mollusks, ibex, mosquitoes or petunias for that matter—aren't magic. They don't just appear. They're made and remade according to regimented recipes stored in the deoxyribonucleic acid (DNA) contained in their cells. The celebrated double helix not only houses key information about you but also has the power to replicate and translate itself into action. As one expert advises, think of DNA as a blueprint that builds itself into a house and then maintains itself.

Each rung of DNA's twisted ladder is made up of a pair of chemical bases—adenine, cytosine, thymine and guanine (known by their letters, A, C, T and G). The bases are a choosy bunch: A pairs only with T, and C pairs only with G. The ladder's vertical struts are long strands of phosphate and sugar molecules. A base and its attached strut comprise a nucleotide.

Genes = Long lines of chemical bases on the DNA molecule that code for particular proteins. They are the basic hereditary units that dictate everything from your hair and eye color to how your body processes sugar and how tall you are. Genes are homebodies. They stay in the nucleus. When one is "expressed," it is transcribed into a molecule called messenger RNA, which hustles out of the nucleus to ribosomes—protein-manufacturing plants in the cell's cytoplasm. The messenger RNA runs through the ribosomes, and the protein molecule is created. Genes also have a great influence on our susceptibility to disease. But keep things in perspective: Genes exist primarily to create you and maintain your health. As science writer Matt Ridley emphasizes in his book Genome, "Genes are not there to cause diseases."

Genome = The sum total of a living thing's DNA is called its genome. Humans are now believed to have about 25,000 to 30,000 genes. Just don't get cocky about being an oh-so-complex organism. Chimps, mice and even zebrafish have roughly the same number of genes. Even Arabidopsis thaliana, commonly known as mustard grass, has 25,000 genes. The number of genes does not determine your place on evolution's pecking order; it's what's done with them that really matters.

Proteins = Biochemical compounds that are the cells' building blocks and carry out most of their processes. The 100,000-plus kinds of proteins in humans make virtually everything happen in the body. They comprise muscles and tendons, transport nutrients to cells, carry oxygen molecules throughout the body, shuttle messages between cells and are catalysts for the body's chemical reactions (enzymes). If the cell is the factory, the proteins are the machines on the factory floor which carry out individually or in groups all the essential activities on which the life of the cell depends.

Amino Acids = Small organic compounds, consisting of about 20 atoms, which make up a protein. Of the hundreds of amino acids known to science, only 20 are utilized by living systems in the construction of proteins.

Enzymes = Biological molecules that accelerate chemical reactions. Almost all chemical reactions in a cell need enzymes in order for life to happen. Enzymes are proteins made from amino acids. An enzyme is formed by stringing together a unique chain of 100-1,000 amino acids in a very specific order and shape. That shape allows the enzyme to carry out specific chemical reactions.

This page intentionally left blank

FSE University

Book 3 of 4

Reliability of the Bible, Person of Jesus Christ

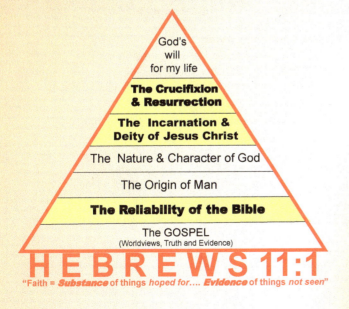

Who am I?

HEBREWS 11:1
"Faith = *Substance* of things *hoped for*.... *Evidence* of things *not seen*"

THE BIBLE: Are my Questions being answered? Who's telling the Truth?

Randall Baer, New Age Leader: "Inside the New Age Nightmare"[14]

- *"Like many new-agers, I was brought up in a middle-to-upper middle class home. Both parents were trained professionals: my father was a medical doctor and my mother a nurse. Family life was based on Christian morals, the Protestant work ethic, and an emphasis on education.*
- *In my early teens I started to become interested in religion. At home, we rarely discussed religious issues, leaving such topics to be covered in Sunday School and church. However, I never really felt any powerful experiences with Jesus, and my **questions** only multiplied as more and more doubts arose.*
- *I was friends with a navy chaplain, and I thought he could guide me toward the **truth**. One day I asked him, 'Can you tell me why some people are agnostics and atheists? I'd really like to know God, but I have so many doubts.' He told me, 'Perhaps some other time, but not now, Randall. You are too young.' My frustration began to increase – I had to find the truth.*
- *During the same time, I attended an adult Bible Study where I was the only teenager there – I was 14. One day I asked everyone, '**Why** should I believe in God? **Why** should I read the Bible? **Why** should I attend church?' The group sat in silence – I felt I had asked forbidden questions – my questions went completely unanswered.*
- *I no longer wanted to attend what I perceived as sterile, lifeless church services and study groups. I knew what I was searching for wasn't there. In the years ahead, I heard many New Agers tell a similar story."*

Jehovah's Witnesses: "New World Translation of the Holy Scriptures"
"But honesty compels us to remark that, while each (of the Evangelical Bible translators, such as Wycliffe, Tyndale) has its points of merit, they have fallen victim to the power of human traditionalism in varying degrees. Consequently, religious traditions have gone unchallenged and uninvestigated. These have been interwoven into the translations to color the thought. The Son of God taught that the traditions of creed-bound men made the commandments and teachings of God of no power and effect. *The endeavor of the New World Translation Committee has been to avoid this snare of religious traditionalism.*"

Mormons: "Book of Mormon"
"The stated purpose of the Book of Mormon is universal: to witness to the world the truth and divinity of Jesus Christ, and his mission of salvation through the gospel He taught. The sealed book, 'The Book of Mormon', *is predicted by Biblical prophecy and by its own declaration to be a confirming, additional revelation from God...*"

Unity Church: "What Unity Teaches"
"Christians hold to the Bible as the supreme exponent of spiritual principle. They believe that the Bible is the greatest and most deeply spiritual of all the Scriptures, though they realize that other Scriptures, such as Zend-Avesta, the Teachings of Buddha, the Koran, the Writings of Confucius, *contain expressions of eminent spiritual truth. The Unity religion is a religion which took the best from all religions.*"

Roman Catholicism: "Traditions added through History"

The Council of Ephesus, 431:	Mary is to be worshipped as the 'Mother of God'
Dowager Empress Irene of Constantinople, 788:	Worship of the cross and images, relics (ex: rosary)
Pope John XV, 995:	Canonize dead saints
Pope Innocent III, 1215:	Transubstantiation (wafer becomes actual body of Christ)
Pope Innocent III, 1215:	Confess sins to priests
The Council of Valencia, 1229:	Bible was forbidden to laymen
The Council of Florence, 1438:	Doctrine of Purgatory added as a dogma of faith
The Council of Trent, 1545:	Tradition is of equal authority with the Bible
Pope Pius IX, 1854:	Immaculate Conception of Mary, Infallibility of the Pope

Proverbs 30:5-6 *"Every word of God is PURE; He is a shield to those who put their trust in Him. Do not add to His words, lest He reprove You, and you be found a liar."*

Revelation 22:18-19 *"I testify to everyone who hears the words of the prophecy of this book: 'If anyone adds to these things, God will add to him the plagues that are written in this book; and if anyone takes away from the words of the book of the prophecy, God shall take away his part from the Book of Life, from the holy city, and from the things which are written in this book."*

Isaiah 8:20 *"To the law and to the testimony! If they do not speak according to this word, it is because there is no light in them."*

Galatians 1:9 *"... if anyone preaches any other gospel to you than what you have received, let him be accursed."*

Answering 24 of the Most Common Skeptic's Questions about the Bible

#	Skeptic's Charge	Lesson	Page
1	What's so unique about the Bible? It's no different than any other book	1.1	256
2	Can the Bible make a practical difference in my life?	1.4	264
3	Since the original writings don't exist (we only have copies of copies), how can you *know* if the contents of an ancient piece of literature are reliable and accurate?	2.1	268
4	How accurate and error-free is the New Testament? It has changed so much through time, is there really any way to trust what it says? Wasn't it just written by men?	2.1	269
5	But what about the time gap of 50-100 years between the actual events and the copies of the original manuscripts which we have? Even though we have thousands of copies, could errors have crept in that make the existing copies unreliable?	2.1	270
6	Aren't there about 400,000 textual errors in the early copies of the gospels? Since we only have copies of copies of the original documents over time, it's become so full of errors that we can't know what the original records actually said.	2.1	270
7	How accurate and error-free is the Old Testament? It has changed so much through time, is there really any way to trust what it says? Wasn't it just written by men?	2.4	278
8	How accurate are the Old Testament copies we have compared to the text of the 1st century? Since the oldest copies of Hebrew MSS we have are 895 AD, how do we know they were accurately transmitted?	2.5	281
9	Has archaeology confirmed or refuted the accuracy and historicity of the Bible?	3.1	286
10	Only the Bible records the Hittites as a significant kingdom. Most experts either regarded their mention as historically worthless, people invented as a fictional story or given status as a great nation when in fact they were non-existent or quite insignificant.	3.2	289
11	Only the Bible (mainly Jonah, Nahum and Isaiah) records the Assyrians, with their capital of Nineveh, as a significant, powerful kingdom. Most experts regarded the biblical accounts of Nineveh as historically worthless, invented as a fictional story.	3.3	294
12	Why would God need to give fulfilled prophecies in the Bible? Is He so hard for people to understand that He needs to 'prove' Himself?	4.1	305
13	Is there historical evidence, outside the Bible, that prophecies in the Bible are true?	4.1	305
14	What sources are there apart from the Bible that confirm its accuracy and reliability? Do other historical sources confirm or deny the Bible's internal testimony?	5.1	332
15	Did Jesus Christ really exist?	5.2	334
16	What about the testimonies of the people who were alive during that time? Do they stand behind what Jesus said, or is there anyone contradicting Him?	6.1	336
17	Christ's Resurrection is a story with no facts to back it up. You have to believe it by faith.	6.2	339
18	There are 6 popular theories set forth by those who do not believe in a physical, bodily resurrection of Jesus Christ. Can you show all of them are false?	6.3	341
19	Jesus didn't die on the Cross. He survived the crucifixion, so therefore His supposed resurrection never happened.	6.4	344
20	What is so unique about Jesus Christ? He may have been a good moral teacher, and He may even have said things that give me motivation to try to be a better person. But what's so great about Him that a world religion would claim Him as their leader?	7.1	354
21	Jesus never directly claimed to be God.	7.3	357
22	History is full of people who've claimed to be the Messiah. Why should I believe Jesus Christ is and all the others are fakes?	7.4	360
23	Didn't Jesus' followers add Isaiah 53 to the Old Testament after He died?	7.10	368
24	Isaiah 53 is about the nation of Israel as God's Suffering Servant. How can you use Isaiah 53 as proof of Jesus Christ as the Messiah fulfilling Old Testament Scripture?	7.10	368

CHAPTER 1   The Uniqueness and Reliability of the Bible

<u>Skeptic's Charge #1</u>:   What's so unique about the Bible? It's no different than any other book.

How Webster's Dictionary defines "unique" as "one and only; different from all others; having no like or equal". We'll demonstrate the uniqueness of the Bible from all other literature by investigating five areas:
1) The Bible's Continuity
2) The Bible's Circulation
3) The Bible's Translation
4) The Bible's Influence
5) The Bible's Survival

To demonstrate how reliable the Bible is in giving us the Word from God, we turn to Josh McDowell's work in his book 'The New Evidence that Demands a Verdict'[1]. He uses the three-part testing methodology of secular military historian Dr. Chauncey Sanders, as outlined in Dr. Saunder's book "Introduction to Research in English Literary History". The Chapters of this book (see below) are arranged based on applying Dr. Saunder's three tests to the Bible, and the box below explains the substance of his three tests.

Chapter 2	New & Old Testament	Test #1 = Bibliographic Test	p. 268
Chapter 3	Archaeology	Test #2 = External Evidence Test	p. 286
Chapter 4	Fulfilled Prophecy	Test #3 = Internal Evidence Test	p. 305
Chapter 5	Non-Biblical Sources	Test #2 = External Evidence Test	p. 332
Chapter 6	Eyewitness Accounts	Test #3 = Internal Evidence Test	p. 336

---

3 Tests to validate the Historicity and Reliability of any piece of Ancient Literature

TEST #1: Bibliographic Test
This test examines the textual transmission of the manuscripts through time. Since we don't have the original hand-written documents, how reliable are the copies we do have in terms of the *number* of manuscripts and the *time interval* between the original writing and the earliest existing copy?

- New Testament ⇒ Manuscript Evidence
- Old Testament ⇒ Dead Sea Scrolls

TEST #2: External Evidence Test
This test evaluates sources outside the document: "do *other* historical documents confirm or deny the internal testimony provided by the documents themselves? What sources exist apart from the literature under examination that confirm its accuracy, reliability and authenticity?"

- Archaeology
- Non-Biblical Sources

TEST #3: Internal Evidence Test
This test asks the question "Does the internal evidence of the document itself contain any inaccuracies or contradictions that would bring to question its reliability and trustworthiness? It is based on *Aristotle's dictum*: "The benefit of the doubt is given to the document itself, and we won't assume fraud or error unless we can prove contradictions by the author within the text or known factual inaccuracies."

- Fulfilled Prophecy
- Eyewitness Accounts

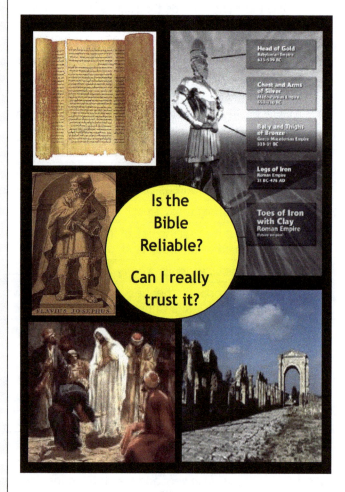

Is the Bible Reliable? Can I really trust it?

Top 5 Reasons Skeptics give for rejecting the Authority of the Bible[6]

Reason #1: "The Bible is just a bunch of stories. Noah's Ark? Adam and Eve? Yeah, right! And Superman and Cinderella too, I suppose?"

Reason #2: "The Bible is filled with contradictions. How can I take a book seriously that doesn't even agree with itself? One guy says this; another guy says that!"

Reason #3: "The Bible is outdated. I don't respect people from 200 years ago; so what could I possibly learn from a book that was written more than 2,000 years ago?"

Reason #4: "I believe that an individual's faith is a very personal matter; its different for each person. You don't get that from a book. It comes from deep within."

Reason #5: "The Bible is not scientific. It's filled with all kinds of inaccuracies that are offensive to the modern intellectual. Only the most naïve and simplistic could ever take seriously a book written by a bunch of fishermen or whatever."

If someone asks you "Why do you believe what the Bible says?".... how would you answer?
There is much *evidence* that proves we can *trust* the Bible as truth. As Christians, we don't check our brains at the door. OUR FAITH IS HISTORICAL, FACTUAL and DEFENSEABLE: our goal is to equip people, to say with confidence that *"I believe the Bible because it is true"*, not *"the Bible is true because I believe it"*.

Dan Brown, 'The Da Vinci Code'[13] - "The Bible can't be trusted since it came from man" (p. 250)

• "From Da Vinci's notebook on polemics and speculation," Teabing said, indicating 1 quote in particular. "I think you'll find this relevant to our discussion." Sophie read the words. *"Many have made a trade of delusions and false miracles, deceiving the stupid multitude"* – Leonardo Da Vinci. "Here's another," Teabing said, pointing to a different quote. *"Blinding ignorance does mislead us. O! Wretched mortals, open your eyes!"* - Leonardo Da Vinci.

• Sophie felt a chill. "Da Vinci is talking about the Bible?"…Teabing smiled. "And everything you need to know about the Bible can be summed up by the great canon doctor Martyn Percy." Teabing cleared his throat and declared, "The Bible did not arrive by fax from heaven." "I beg your pardon?"

• "The Bible is a product of man, my dear. Not of God. The Bible did not fall magically from the clouds. Man created it as a historical record of tumultuous times, and it has evolved through countless translations, additions and revisions. Historically there has never been a definitive version of the book."

John 17:17 *"Sanctify them by Your truth. Your word is TRUTH."*
Psalm 138:2 *"…You have magnified Your WORD above all Your name."*

Dan Brown, 'The Da Vinci Code'[13] - "What you end up believing can't be confirmed" (p. 276-277, 288)

• "But what good is a documented genealogy of Christ's bloodline?" Sophie asked. "It's not proof. Historians could not possibly confirm its authenticity." Teabing chuckled. "No more so than they can confirm the authenticity of the Bible." Sophie had never thought of it that way.

• "The Sangreal documents simply tell the other side of the Christ story. In the end, which side of the story you believe becomes a matter of faith and personal exploration…"

• "Those who look at Church scandals and ask, who are these men who claim to speak the truth about Christ and yet lie to cover up the sexual abuse of children by their own priests?" Teabing paused. "What happens to those people, Robert, if persuasive scientific evidence comes out that the Church's version of the Christ story is inaccurate, and that the greatest story ever told is, in fact, the greatest story ever sold?"

Acts 1:3 *"The former account I made, O Theophilus, of all that Jesus began both to do and teach, until the day in which He was taken up, after He through the Holy Spirit had given commandments to the apostles whom He had chosen, to whom He also presented Himself alive after His suffering by MANY INFALLIBLE PROOFS, being seen by them during 40 days and speaking of the things pertaining to the kingdom of God."*

Dr. Henry Morris[5]: "It comes down to TRUTH"

"The effective use of Christian evidences requires diligent study and preparation. It is most likely a Christian's unwillingness to study and learn the evidential facts that is the reason many argue for not using them but rather quote Scripture and give one's testimony. But don't forget that Buddhists, Jehovah's Witnesses, Christian Scientists, and even Communists can also quote their scriptures and give happy testimonies of how much their religion has done for them. The question is: 'IS IT TRUE?'".

THE BIBLE: Reasonable, Intellectual, True

---

① The Bible is: REASONABLE   "REASON" = the verb DIALEGOMAI
- to discuss openly, rationalize with others and raise objections as in open debate
- to compute as during examination; to bring together different viewpoints and reckon them up

---

Isaiah 1:18   *"Come, let us REASON together", says the Lord. "Though your sins are like scarlet, they shall be as white as snow; though they are red as crimson, they shall be as wool."*

Acts 17:2-3   *"Paul, as his custom was, went in to them, and for 3 Sabbaths he REASONED with them FROM THE SCRIPTURES, explaining and demonstrating that Christ had to suffer and rise again from the dead, and saying, "This Jesus whom I preach to you is the Christ."*

Acts 17:17,19:8 *"Therefore he REASONED in the synagogue with the Jews and with the Gentile worshipers, and in the marketplace daily with those who happened to be there. And he went into the synagogue and spoke boldly for three months, REASONING and PERSUADING concerning the things of the kingdom of God."*

Acts 18:4,19   *"And he REASONED in the synagogue every Sabbath, and persuaded both Jews and Greeks. And he came*
Acts 18:27-28   *to Ephesus, and left them there; but he himself entered the synagogue and REASONED with the Jews. And when he arrived, he greatly helped those who believed through grace; for he vigorously refuted the Jews publicly, SHOWING FROM THE SCRIPTURES that Jesus is the Christ."*

---

② The Bible is: INTELLECTUAL   "DEFENSE" = the noun APOLOGIA
- a verbal defense of what one has done or of truth which one believes
- I should know what I believe and why I am a Christian

1Peter 3:15   *"But sanctify the Lord God in your hearts, and always be ready to GIVE A DEFENSE to everyone who asks you a REASON for the hope that is in you, with meekness and fear."*

Proverbs 15:28 *"The heart of the righteous STUDIES how to answer…."*

Matthew 22:37   *"You shall love the Lord your God with all your heart, with all your soul, with all your MIND."*

Romans 12:2   *"And do not be conformed to this world, but be transformed by the renewing of your MIND…"*

Ephesians 4:23 *"…and be renewed in the spirit of your MIND, and that you may put on the new man which was created according to God, in righteousness and true holiness."*

---

③ The Bible is: TRUE, FOREVER, FROM GOD   "TRUTH" = the noun ALETHEIA
- actual, factual, conforms to reality

John 17:17   *"Sanctify them by Your truth. Your word is TRUTH."*

Revelation 21:5 *Then He who sat on the throne said, "Behold, I make all things new." And He said to me, "Write, for these words are TRUE and faithful."*

Psalm 119:89   *"FOREVER, O Lord, Your word is settled in heaven."*

Psalm 119:151   *"You are near, O Lord, and all Your commandments are TRUTH."*

Psalm 119:160   *"The entirety of Your word is TRUTH, and every one of Your righteous judgments endures FOREVER."*

Matthew 24:35   *"Heaven and earth will pass away, but My words will by no means pass away."*

2Tim. 3:16-17   *"All Scripture is given by inspiration OF GOD, and it is profitable for doctrine, for reproof, for correction, for instruction in righteousness…"*

1Thes. 2:13   *"…when you received the word of God which you heard from us, you welcomed it not as the word of men, but as it is in TRUTH, the WORD OF GOD, which also effectively works in you who believe."*

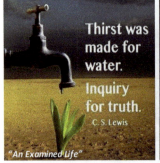
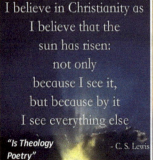
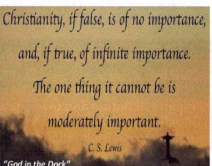

THE BIBLE: Unique in Continuity, Circulation, Translation, Influence 1.2

① **The Bible is unique in its CONTINUITY**

It was written over a period of 1,600 years (16 centuries!)	It was written over 40 generations of people	It was written in times of: war (David) peace (Solomon)
It was written on 3 continents: Asia Africa Europe	It was written in 3 languages: Hebrew (Old Testament) Aramaic ("language" of Near East) Greek (New Testament)	It was written in differing moods: great joy (Acts) great despair (Jeremiah)
It was written by > 40 authors from every walk of life: Moses = political leader Peter = fisherman Amos = herdsman Joshua = military general Nehemiah = cupbearer Daniel = prime minister Luke = doctor Solomon = king Matthew = tax collector Paul = rabbi	It was written in many different places: Moses - wrote in the wilderness Jeremiah - wrote in a dungeon Daniel - wrote on a hillside and in a palace Paul - wrote inside prison walls Luke - wrote while traveling John - wrote on the island of Patmos Joshua - wrote during battles David wrote - while being pursued	Its subject matter contains hundreds of *controversial topics* (i.e., topics that, when discussed, create debate and differing opinions (such as sin, homosexuality, eternal life) – yet throughout the entire Bible, each writer is in *perfect harmony and agreement* with all the others, despite the above-mentioned facts about how it was written

F.F. Bruce (Rylands Prof. of Bible Criticism and Exegesis, Univ. of Manchester)[1]

• "The Bible appears to be a collection of literature – mainly Jewish. If we inquire into the circumstances under which the various biblical documents were written, we find that they were written at intervals over a space of nearly 1600 years. The writers wrote in various lands, from Italy in the west to Mesopotamia and possibly Persia in the east.

• The *writers* themselves were a heterogeneous group of people, not only separated from each other by hundreds of years and hundreds of miles, but belonging to the most diverse walks of life.

• The *writings* themselves belong to a great variety of literary types: history, law (civil, criminal, ethical), religious poetry, lyric poetry, parable and allegory, biography, personal memoirs, prophetic and apocalyptic.

• For all that, the Bible possesses a UNITY which binds the whole together. Any part of the human body can only be properly explained in reference to the whole body. And from Genesis to Revelation, any part of the Bible can only be properly explained in reference to the whole Bible."

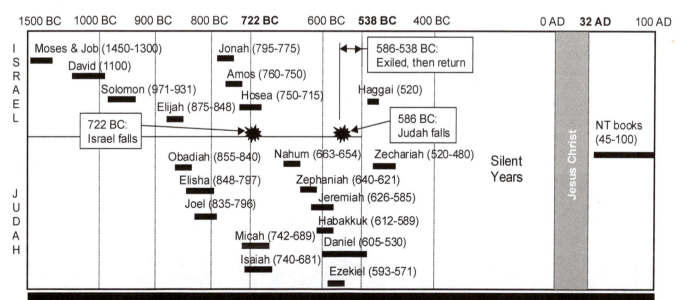

The Bible: written over 1600 years, 40 different authors, separated from each other by 1,500 miles and everyone writes in complete harmony (no one disagrees on even 1 controversial topic)!

Josh McDowell ("Evidence that Demands a Verdict")[1]
- "A representative of the *Great Books of the Western World* came to my house recruiting salesmen for their series. He spread out the chart of the *Great Books of the Western World* series. After spending some time going over these books, we spent an hour and a half going over the Bible.
- I challenged him to take just 10 authors in his *Great Books* series, all from one walk of life, one generation, one place, one time, one mood, one continent, one language and just one controversial subject. Then I asked him, 'Would these authors agree?' He said, 'No'. Two days later he committed his life to Jesus Christ."

② The Bible is unique in its CIRCULATION and TRANSLATION

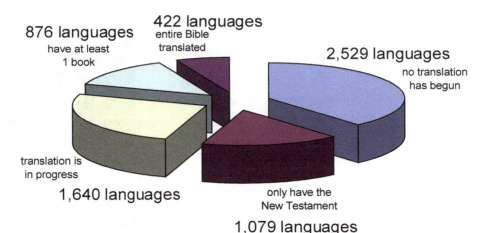

- 876 languages have at least 1 book
- 422 languages entire Bible translated
- 2,529 languages no translation has begun
- translation is in progress 1,640 languages
- only have the New Testament 1,079 languages

1) The Bible has been read by more people, and published in more languages, than any other book.
2) There have been more copies produced of its entirety and more sections than any other book in history.
3) Latin Vulgate (NT): first major book printed (on Gutenberg's printing press).
4) British and Foreign Bible Society: "to meet the demands for Bibles, they have to publish…
   - 1 copy every 3 seconds day and night
   - 22 copies every minute day and night
   - 1,369 copies every hour day and night
   - 32,876 copies every day in the year

   all these Bibles are then shipped to various parts of the world in 4,583 cases weighing 490 TONS.
5) There are BILLIONS of Bibles in circulation worldwide (by far, it is unique among literature for its circulation).
6) Wycliff Translators, 2006: there are 6,912 different languages in the world (world's population at 6.5 billion people). The above chart shows how these languages stack up in having Bible translations available to them.

③ The Bible is unique in its INFLUENCE on other Literature

1) Cleland B. McAfee ("The Greatest English Classic")[1]:
   "If every Bible in any considerable city were destroyed, the Bible could be restored in all its essential parts from the quotations on the shelves of the city's Public Library. There are works, covering almost all the great literary writers, devoted essentially to showing how much the Bible has influenced them."

2) Kenneth Scott Latourette (Yale University historian)[1]:
   "It is evidence of his importance, of the effect that he has had upon history and presumably, of the baffling mystery of his being that no other life on this planet has evoked so huge a volume of literature among so many peoples and languages, and that, far from ebbing, the flood continues to mount."

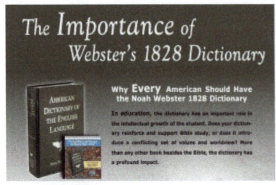
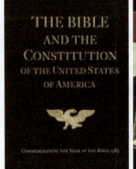
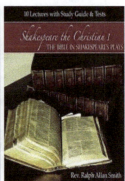

④ The Bible is unique in its **SURVIVAL**

1) SURVIVAL THROUGH TIME:
- Because it was written on papyrus (material that perishes), it had to be copied and recopied for 100's of years before the printing press was invented.
- The Bible has more manuscript evidence than any 10 pieces of classical literature combined!
- Bernard Ramm[1]: *"Jews preserved their Bible as no other manuscript has ever been preserved. They kept tabs on every letter, syllable, word and paragraph. They had special classes of men (scribes, lawyers, massoretes) within their culture whose sole duty was to preserve and transmit these documents with nearly perfect fidelity. Whoever counted the letters and syllables of Plato? Aristotle? Heroditus? Eurypides?"*

2) SURVIVAL THROUGH CRITICISM:
- H.L. Hastings[1]: *"If this book was not the book of God, men would have destroyed it long ago. Emperors and poets, kings and priests, princes and rulers have all tried their hand at it – they die, and the Bible still lives."*
- Bernard Ramm[1]: *"No other book has been so chopped, knived, sifted, scrutinized and vilified. What book on philosophy or religion or psychology has been subject to such a mass attack as the Bible?"*

Voltaire (François-Marie Arouet),1694-1778: French Enlightenment writer, historian, philosopher and skeptic who was famous for his attacks on the Catholic Church, and his advocacy of freedom of religion, freedom of expression, and separation of church and state. He recognized the benefits that Christianity brought to mankind, as seen in this quote from his 'Philosophical Dictionary' in 1764: *"Christianity: A religious system attributed to Jesus Christ, but really invented by Plato, improved by St. Paul, and finally revised and corrected by the Fathers, the councils, and other interpreters of the Church. Since the foundation of this sublime creed, mankind has become better, wiser, and happier than before. From that blessed epoch the world was forever freed from all strife, dissensions, troubles, vices, and evils of every kind; an invincible proof that Christianity is divine, and that it is to be possessed of the very devil himself to dare to commit such a creed or doubt its origin."* But his constant criticism against the church stemmed from his conviction that Christianity was more of a judgmental belief system than a belief system founded on the grace of God, as seen in this quote: *"Christians have been the most intolerant of all men."*

One of his most recognized quotes was his assertion that within 100 years of his death, the Bible would become extinct, disappearing from the face of the earth: *"One hundred years from my day there will not be a Bible in the earth except one that is looked upon by an antiquarian curiosity seeker."* But at age 83, it's Voltaire who has become extinct. The Bible continues to outsell all books.

3) SURVIVAL THROUGH PERSECUTION:
- **Diocletian** (303 AD): issues official edict to stop Christian worship, and destroy their Scriptures.
- **Constantine** (328 AD): Eusebius records that the Christian emperor Constantine gave the edict to have 50 perfect copies of the Bible prepared at the government's expense.

The "Martyrs of Abitene", 303AD

They were Christians who lived in Abitene, a city of the Roman province called "Africa Proconsularis," today's Tunis. They were victims of the persecutions under **Emperor Diocletian**, who ordered that *"the sacred texts and holy testaments of the Lord and the divine Scriptures be found, so that they could be burnt; the Lord's basilicas were to be pulled down; and the celebration of sacred rites and holy reunions of the Lord were to be prohibited"* (Acts of the Martyrs, I).

Disobeying the emperor's orders, a group of 49 Christians of Abitene gathered weekly in one of their homes to celebrate Sunday Mass. Taken by surprise during one of their meetings, they were arrested and taken to Carthage to Proconsul Anulinus to be interrogated.

When the Proconsul asked them if they kept the Scriptures in their homes, the martyrs answered courageously that "they kept them in their hearts," revealing that they did not wish to separate faith from life.

During their torture and torment, the martyrs uttered exclamations such as: "I implore you, Christ, hear me," "I thank you, O God," "I implore you, Christ, have mercy." Along with their prayers they offered their lives and asked that their executioners be forgiven.

Among the testimonies is that of **Emeritus**, who affirmed fearlessly that he received Christians for the celebration. The Proconsul asked him: "Why have you received Christians in your home, transgressing the imperial dispositions?" Emeritus answered: "Sine dominico non possumus" ("We cannot live without Sunday").

The Diocletian Persecution
taken from Eusebius of Caesarea, *Ecclesiastical History*, book VIII. (A.D. 324)

Eusebius (263-340) was an eyewitness to many martyrdoms in Caesarea during the persecution commenced by Diocletian in 303. This persecution lasted 10 years and was ended by Constantine's Edict of Milan (313).

- "...This persecution began with the brethren in the army. But as if without sensibility, we were not eager to make the Deity favorable and propitious; and some, like atheists, thought that our affairs were unheeded and ungoverned; and thus we added one wickedness to another. And those esteemed our shepherds, casting aside the bond of piety, were excited to conflicts with one another, and did nothing else than heap up strifes and threats and jealousy and enmity and hatred toward each other, like tyrants eagerly endeavoring to assert their power.

- Then, truly, according to the word of Jeremiah, 'The Lord in his wrath darkened the daughter of Zion, and cast down the glory of Israel from heaven to earth, and remembered not his foot-stool in the day of his anger. The Lord also overwhelmed all the beautiful things of Israel, and threw down all his strongholds.' And according to what was foretold in the Psalms: 'He has made void the covenant of his servant, and profaned his sanctuary to the earth, - in the destruction of the churches, - and has thrown down all his strongholds, and has made his fortresses cowardice. All that pass by have plundered the multitude of the people; and he has become besides a reproach to his neighbors. For he has exalted the right hand of his enemies, and has turned back the help of his sword, and has not taken his part in the war. But he has deprived him of purification, and has cast his throne to the ground. He has shortened the days of his time, and besides all, has poured out shame upon him.'

- All these things were fulfilled in us, when we saw with our own eyes the houses of prayer thrown down to the very foundations, and the Divine and Sacred Scriptures committed to the flames in the midst of the market-places, and the shepherds of the churches basely hidden here and there, and some of them captured ignominiously, and mocked by their enemies. When also, according to another prophetic word, 'Contempt was poured out upon rulers, and he caused them to wander in an untrodden and pathless way.'

- But it is not our place to describe the sad misfortunes which finally came upon them, as we do not think it proper, moreover, to record their divisions and unnatural conduct to each other before the persecution. Wherefore we have decided to relate nothing concerning them except the things in which we can vindicate the Divine judgment. Hence we shall not mention those who were shaken by the persecution, nor those who in everything pertaining to salvation were shipwrecked, and by their own will were sunk in the depths of the flood. But we shall introduce into this history in general only those events which may be useful first to ourselves and afterwards to posterity. Let us therefore proceed to describe briefly the sacred conflicts of the witnesses of the Divine Word.

- It was in the nineteenth year of the reign of Diocletian, [A.D. 303] in the month Dystrus, called March by the Romans, when the feast of the Saviour's passion was near at hand, that royal edicts were published everywhere, commanding that the churches be leveled to the ground and the Scriptures be destroyed by fire, and ordering that those who held places of honor be degraded, and that the household servants, if they persisted in the profession of Christianity, be deprived of freedom."

March 5.--ST. ADRIAN and March 7.-- ST. EUBULUS, Martyrs. (from the book 'The Lives of the Fathers, Martyrs and Other Principal Saints', by Reverend Alban Butler, 1887) In the seventh year of Diocletian's persecution, continued by Galerius Maximianus, when Firmilian, the most bloody governor of Palestine, had stained Caesarea with the blood of many illustrious martyrs, Adrian and Eubulus came out of the country called Magantia to Caesarea, in order to visit the holy confessors there. At the gates of the city they were asked, as others were, whither they were going, and upon what errand. They ingeniously confessed the truth, and were brought before the president, who ordered them to be tortured and their sides to be torn with iron hooks, and then condemned them to be exposed to wild beasts. Two days after, when the pagans at Caesarea celebrated the festival of the public Genius, Adrian was exposed to a lion, and not being dispatched by that beast, but only mangled, was at length killed by the sword. Eubulus was treated in the same manner two days later. The judge offered him his liberty if he would sacrifice to idols; but the Saint preferred a glorious death, and was the last that suffered in this persecution at Caesarea, which had now continued twelve years, under three successive governors, Flavian, Urban, and Firmilian, Divine vengeance pursuing the cruel Firmilian, he was that same year beheaded for his crimes, by the emperor's order, as his Predecessor Urban had been two years before.
Reflection.--It is in vain that we take the name of *Christians*, or pretend to follow Christ, unless we carry our crosses after Him. It is in vain that we hope to share in His glory, and in His kingdom, if we accept not the condition. We cannot arrive at heaven by any other road but that which Christ held, who bequeathed His cross to all His elect as their portion and inheritance in this world."

William Tyndale: Translating the Bible for the "Common Man"[8]

- Most of the reformers, Luther, Zuingle, Calvin, Knox, and others have acquired that name by their preaching, their writings, their struggles, and their actions. It is not so with WILLIAM TYNDALE, the principal reformer of England.

- All his activity was centered in preparing a translation of the Holy Scriptures for the peasants in the surrounding counties; an edition of the Bible in which he would use the language of the common people. Tyndale's famous quote as he worked was: *'If God preserves my life, I will cause a boy that driveth a plow to know more of the Scriptures than the pope.'*

- His fellow-countrymen profited by the work of his life. As early as 1526 more than twenty editions of Tyndale's New Testament had been circulated over the kingdom.

- Tyndale said: *"The Word of God never was without persecution — no more than the sun can be without his light. By what right doth the pope forbid God to speak in the English tongue? Why should not the Sermons of the Apostles, preached no doubt in the mother-tongue of those who heard them, be now written in the mother-tongue of those who read them?"*

- As he said below, Tyndale did not think of proving the divinity of the Bible by learned dissertations: *"Scripture derives its authority from Him who sent it. Would you know the reason why men believe in Scripture? It is Scripture. It is itself the instrument which outwardly leads men to believe, whilst inwardly, the spirit of God Himself, speaking through Scripture, gives faith to His children."*

- In August 1536, Tyndale appeared before the court. 'You are charged,' said his judges, 'with having infringed the imperial decree which forbids any one to teach that faith alone justifies.' It was not his own cause that he undertook to defend, but the cause of the Bible.

- Tyndale said: *"While all human religions make salvation proceed from the works of man, the divine religion makes it proceed from a work of God. He must believe in the perfect work of Christ which reconciles him completely with God; then he has peace, and Christ imparts to him, by his Spirit, a holy regeneration. Yes, we believe and are at peace in our consciences, because that God who cannot lie, hath promised to forgive us for Christ's sake."*

- The imperial government prepared at last to complete the wishes of the priests – his execution was scheduled for **Friday, the 6th of October, 1536**.

- But while the government had wished to show the people the punishment of a heretic, they only witnessed the triumph of a martyr. Tyndale was calm as he exclaimed: *"I call God to record that I have never altered, against the voice of my conscience, one syllable of his Word. Nor would do this day, if all the pleasures, honors, and riches of the earth might be given me."*

- While the executioner was fastening him to the post, the reformer exclaimed in a loud and suppliant voice: *"Lord, open the king of England's eyes!"* They were his last words. Instantly afterwards he was strangled, and flames consumed the martyr's body.

- 'Such,' says John Foxe, 'is the story of that true servant and martyr of God, William Tyndale, who, for his notable pains and travail, may well be called the Apostle of England in this our later age. '

Psalm 116:15 *"Precious in the sight of the Lord is the death of His saints."*

2 Timothy 3:16 "God has deeply invested in His Bible" — 1.4

"All Scripture is given by INSPIRATION of God, and is profitable for doctrine, for reproof, for correction, for instruction in righteousness…"

Charles Ryrie, "A Survey of Bible Doctrine": *"Not many years ago, all you had to say to affirm your belief in the inspiration of the Bible was that you believed the Bible was the Word of God. That was it. But as people have sliced and criticized and hacked the Bible to bits, it became necessary to add that you believed the Bible was the **inspired** Word of God. Later you had to include the **verbally inspired** Word of God. Then to mean the same thing, you had to say the **plenary, verbally inspired** Word of God. Today one has to say the **plenary, verbally inspired, infallible** Word of God. So many people have tried to undermine God's Word that you have to be really clear about what you mean."*

- **inspired** = "theopneustos": 2-part word meaning "God-breathed" (God literally "breathed the words" into the hearts and minds of human authors, who wrote them down according to their own styles and personalities). What we have recorded in the Bible are God's very words, inspired by the Holy Spirit.

2 Peter 1:20-21 *"…knowing this first, that no prophecy of Scripture is of any private interpretation, for prophecy never came by the will of man, but holy men of God spoke as they were MOVED BY THE HOLY SPIRIT."*

While man's will didn't create the Scriptures, God worked through the author's individual personalities. He supernaturally flowed His word-for-word truth through the personality and mind of each author:
PETER = excitable, enthusiastic, very verbal, very strong and forward in his expression.
PAUL = logical, analytical, methodical, point-by-point – lawyer-like in his flawless defense.
JOHN = tenderhearted, loving, comforting in the way he talks to his audience ("my children"…)

John 14:26 *"But the Helper, the Holy Spirit, whom the Father will send in my name, He will teach you all things, and bring to your remembrance all things that I said to you."* (translation: "when it's time to write down the record of My life, I will have sent the Holy Spirit to indwell you, and He will bring to your mind all the words that I am speaking now.")

- **plenary** = God wrote the ENTIRE BIBLE, not just parts, from Genesis 1:1 through Revelation 22:21.

- **verbal** = God didn't just choose the concepts – He chose the very words. The Holy Spirit communicated the specific words – not just the paragraph headings.

Revel. 22:19 *"…if anyone takes away from the WORDS of the book of this prophecy, God shall take away his part from the Book of Life, from the holy city, and from the things which are written in this book."*

Notice: it says that if anyone takes away from the *words* of this book – not the concepts, not the thoughts… the *words*. God does not want anyone messing with His Book.

- **infallible** = the Bible is 100% accurate in all it asserts and constitutes ALL TRUTH.

Psalm 119:160 *"The entirety of Your word is truth, and every one of Your righteous judgments endures forever."*

Psalm 19:7-11 God tells me what the Bible is good for…

Skeptic's Charge #2: Can the Bible make a practical difference in my life? God answers this question for us! He uses five different names for Scripture, six different adjectives to describe it, and then gives six different results I can get by just following the Bible:

1) *"The LAW of the Lord is perfect, converting the soul;*
2) *the TESTIMONY of the Lord is sure, making wise the simple;*
3) *the STATUTES of the Lord are right, rejoicing the heart;*
4) *the COMMANDMENT of the Lord is pure, enlightening the eyes;*
5) *the FEAR of the Lord is clean, enduring forever;*
6) *the JUDGMENTS of the Lord are true and righteous altogether. More to be desired are they than gold. Yea, than much fine gold. Sweeter also than honey and the honey in the combs. Moreover by them Your servant is warned, and in keeping them there is great reward."*

Names	Adjectives	Results
Law	→ perfect	→ converting the soul
Testimony	→ sure	→ making wise the simple
Statutes	→ right	→ rejoicing the heart
Commandment	→ pure	→ enlightening the eyes
Fear	→ clean	→ enduring forever
Judgments	→ true & righteous altogether	→ warning & rewarding God's servant

Psalm 19:7a *"The law of the Lord is perfect, converting the soul"*
- "law" = the Torah ("the law for life, rule for living"); the norm or standard by which every action is measured
- "of the Lord" = not mans' laws – the Bible is God's laws
- "perfect" = complete (all-sided, all encompassing, thorough in every respect, totally comprehensive)
- "converting the soul" = transform
  1) God's word can convert our sin-filled soul (the part of us that lives forever and relates to God).
  2) God promises His law is so totally comprehensive that whatever the condition of the individual soul, His Word can transform it from top to bottom, from inside to outside, from past to future.
  3) Scripture changes me to the very core of who I am as a person.

Psalm 19:7b *"The testimony of the Lord is sure, making wise the simple"*
- "testimony" = "to bear witness"; used only in this verse in all the Psalms
- "of the Lord" = God is bearing witness to *Himself*...as if raising His hand and solemnly taking an oath.
- "sure" = reliable or durable; similar to verb for "amen" ("the testimony of the Lord is amen") everything God says is right on – God, in His word, tells it like it is.
- "simple" = literal meaning is "openness", or a *"simpleton"*
  1) a person whose mind is like a house with front and back doors open ("stuff comes in, then goes out")
  2) this person has no capacity to discern right from wrong, valuable from useless.
  3) the world is full of simpletons: people who value what is worthless and disdain what is priceless.
- God is saying that His testimony is so reliable that it can:
  1) take a simpleton, with no clue where they're heading and why, and turn them into a person of wisdom.
  2) take a vacillating simpleton, who cannot discern right from wrong, and make him or her skilled at daily living.
- Wisdom to the Greek: it was to know   (Acts 17:16-21)
  Wisdom to the OT Hebrew: it was to do   (Proverbs)

Psalm 19:8a *"The statutes of the Lord are right, rejoicing the heart"*
- "statutes of the Lord" = God's rulings, pronouncements, principles
- the world has its "principles" too: "you only go around once, so go for the gusto"
                                        "God helps those who help themselves"
- "right" = God's principles are 100% RIGHT in everything they assert –life is a maze of choices everyday, and God's principles set the right path to navigate so we don't get lost (Psalm 119:105).
- Jeremiah 15:16   there is JOY that comes to the human heart when it rightly understands His Bible!

Psalm 19:8b *"The commandment of the Lord is pure, enlightening the eyes"*
- "commandment of the Lord" = God's orders or divine decrees; things that God insists we do or keep doing.
- "pure" = radiant, clean – an absence of impurity or visual impediment – like our phrase "CRYSTAL CLEAR"
- "enlighten the eyes" = any person who picks it up can understand it (remember what William Tyndale said, as he prepared to create the English translation of the Bible? *"If God preserves my life, I will cause a boy that driveth a plow to know more of the Scriptures than the pope."*)

Psalm 19:9a *"The fear of the Lord is clean, enduring forever"*
- "fear of the Lord" = an attitude of the heart that seeks a right relationship with the Source of that fear.
- "clean" = without blemish (undiminished, uncompromised, undefiled) – its FULL-STRENGTH from cover to cover (there isn't a single piece of the Bible that is of any inferior quality that it could lead you astray).
- The point: if you fear the Lord in this life, you will not have to fear Him in the life to come, because the fear of the Lord is clean (contrast Hebrews 10:31 and Matthew 10:28 with Luke 12:31-32).
- "enduring forever" = the Bible is never out of date nor needing revision – circumstances change, cultures and world leaders come and go...but God's word is always current and stable in our toughest times (Isaiah 33:6) because it deals with two things that never change: 1) the God who made us; 2) the needs of our heart.

Psalm 19:9b *"The judgments of the Lord are true and righteous altogether"*
- "judgments of the Lord" = God's verdicts, pronouncements of consequence, and/ or punishments for sin.
- "true and righteous" = when He announces or executes a judgment, it is absolutely truthful and righteous. God doesn't operate according to His mood or personal circumstance: He is consistent, fair and precise.

Psalm 19:11 *"...by them Your servant is warned, and in keeping them there is great reward."*

What the Bible can do in My Life: 8 Pictures of God's Word   1.5

Jeremiah 15:16 "*Your words were found, and I ate them, and Your word was to me the joy and rejoicing of my heart*"

Jeremiah 20:8-9 "*…the word of the Lord was made to me a reproach and a derision daily. Then I said, 'I will not make mention of Him, nor speak anymore in His name.' But His word was in my heart like a burning fire shut up in my bones; I was weary of holding it back, and I could not.*"

Ezra 7:10 "*Ezra prepared his heart to study the Law of the Lord, and to do it, and to teach statutes and ordinances in Israel.*"

#1. The Bible is FIRE

The Bible: FIRE
Jerem. 5:14, 23:29

"*Thus says the Lord God of hosts: 'Because you speak this word, behold, I will make My words in your mouth FIRE, and this people wood, and it shall devour them. Is not My word like a FIRE?' says the Lord.*"

c) The context of this verse is God's judgment on Judah for their idolatry and rebellion.
d) This also has a general context: the Bible is like fire because it *consumes peoples' hearts*.
e) When I read the Bible, it has the power of God to *burn the useless things out of my life*.

#2. The Bible is a SWORD

"*…and the SWORD of the Spirit, which is the word of God. For the word of God is living and powerful, and sharper than any 2-edged sword, piercing even to the division of soul and spirit, and of joints and marrow, and is a discerner of the thoughts and intents of the heart.*"

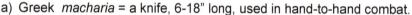
The Bible: a SWORD   Eph. 6:17   Hebr. 4:12

a) Greek *macharia* = a knife, 6-18" long, used in hand-to-hand combat.
b) Sometimes, the fire of God's word doesn't get our attention. But the SWORD will, because God says it quickly CUTS to the heart of the matter. That's because God KNOWS my very thoughts and intentions. His word exposes them to me if I'm too blind or in denial.
c) As the sword was the soldier's only weapon, so God's Word is the only needed weapon, infinitely more powerful than any of Satan's because it is ultimate truth.
d) While God's word can comfort and strengthen believers in Christ, it is a tool of judgment and execution for those who trust in themselves. For those who appear to be Christians on the outside but never committed themselves to Christ on the inside, God's word *exposes* their shallow beliefs and fake intentions.

#3. The Bible is a HAMMER

The Bible: a HAMMER
Jerem. 23:29

"*Is not My word like a fire?' says the Lord. And like a HAMMER that breaks the rock in pieces?*"

If you are thinking "The Bible has never been a fire or a sword to me", it's because your heart is so hard that God's words bounce right off it! Proverbs 28:14   "*Happy is the man who is always reverent, but he who HARDENS HIS HEART will fall into calamity.*"

What is a "Hard Heart"?   my heart may not be in conscious rebellion against God…but my heart no longer feels God's conviction (my heart has grown insensitive to His voice)

How can I tell if it's happened to me? When I am repeatedly exposed to a particular truth and refuse to embrace and apply it (I hear the truth over and over again – and I just keep ignoring it)

#4. The Bible is SEED

The Bible: SEED
1Peter 1:23

"*…having been born again, not of corruptible SEED but incorruptible, through the word of God which lives and abides forever. Now the parable is this: the SEED is the word of God.*"

a) a seed starts very small and takes time to grow, needing continual attention. God's Word starts to work in my heart, but it takes time (sometimes, I have to hear the same thing many times before it takes hold and I get it).

   Isaiah 28:9-10 "*Whom will He teach knowledge? And whom will he make to understand the message? Those just weaned from milk? Those just drawn from the breasts? For precept must be upon precept, precept upon precept, line upon line, line upon line, here a little, there a little.*"

b) planted in my heart (memorize, meditate), the Bible will bear fruit and transform my life, but I must have a willingness to plant the seed within me by my faith that He, in time, will keep His promise to work in my life.

   Luke 8:15 "*…the ones that fell on the good ground are those who, having heard the word with a noble and good heart, KEEP IT and bear fruit with PATIENCE.*"

   Philippians 1:6 "*…He who has begun a good work in you will complete it until the day of Jesus Christ.*"

#5. The Bible is MILK

"...as newborn babes, desire the pure MILK of the word, that you may grow thereby..."

a) newborn babies don't need to be taught the fact that they need milk – they're born with their mouths open.
b) what mom's milk is to a newborn, the Bible is to a sincere person of faith.
c) Milk = the elementary or basic things of the Bible (doctrinal truths) – my foundation I must learn in order to grow:
   Hebrews 5:12 *"...though by this time you ought to be teachers, you need someone to teach you again the first principles of the oracles of God; and you have come to need MILK and not solid food."*
d) just as people will cry and despair when they are starving and cannot get physical food, people are anxious, fearful and discouraged when they neglect God's only provision for their spiritual nourishment.

#6. The Bible is MEAT

"...everyone who partakes only of milk is unskilled in the word of righteousness, for he is a babe. But SOLID FOOD belongs to those who are of full age; that is, those who by reason of use have their senses exercised to DISCERN both good and evil."

a) after I've known Jesus for a period of time, I start asking myself, "Isn't there more?"
b) as I grow, I can't live only on milk – I need meat. It's the same with being a Christian.
c) Once I have that sure foundation of MILK (Jesus is my Savior and Lord, the Bible is God's word, my sins are forgiven through His death and resurrection), the MEAT is where I grow in my WALK (I practice discernment and holiness in my daily living – the "meat" sanctifies me from the inside-out).
   Romans 6:4 *"...we were buried with Him through baptism into death, that just as Christ was raised from the dead by the glory of the Father, even so we also should WALK in newness of life."*
   Galatians 5:16 *"...walk in the Spirit, and you shall not fulfill the lust of the flesh."*

#7. The Bible is LIGHT

"Your word is a lamp unto my feet and a LIGHT to my path."

a) the Bible works in my life so that I don't walk around dead or blind to life's dangers, making dumb mistakes that could have been avoided if I simply had known the WAY I should go
   Isaiah 59:10 *"We grope for the wall like the blind, and we grope as if we had no eyes; we stumble at noonday as at twilight; we are as dead men in desolate places."*
   Isaiah 30:21 *"Your ears shall hear a word behind you, saying, 'This is the way, walk in it', whenever you turn to the right hand or whenever you turn to the left."*
b) Anyone who has been unsure about an important decision knows the value of God's Word to light their path.

#8. The Bible is a MIRROR

"...if anyone is a hearer of the word and not a doer, he is like a man observing his natural face in a mirror; for he observes himself, goes away, and immediately forgets what kind of man he was. But he who looks into the PERFECT LAW OF LIBERTY and continues in it, and is not a forgetful hearer but a doer of the work, this one will be blessed in what he does."

a) "observes himself" = "carefully studies himself" (I look in the Bible and God shows me something about myself that I can grasp fully)
b) the Bible shows me myself! It confronts me with truth and convicts me about my true and deepest need. But the true value of a mirror isn't just in showing us an imperfection – it reveals the thing needing to be fixed, so that I can now ACT on what I've been shown (how stupid is it to see in a mirror that I have ketchup on my face, and then I just leave it there?)

"I have kept Your Word hidden in my heart, that I might not sin against You."
Psalm 119:11

CHAPTER 2 — Bibliographic Test: NEW TESTAMENT

Skeptic's Charge #3: Since the original writings don't exist (we only have copies of copies), how can you *know* if the contents of an ancient piece of literature are reliable and accurate (can you *test* its trustworthiness)?

How did they record and preserve writings back in Bible times? The Bible was written on papyrus: a reed growing in waters of Egypt and Syria. The English word "paper" is from the Greek word for papyrus.

The oldest papyrus writings date to 2400 BC. Papyrus was the preferred writing material up to the 3rd century AD (then animal skins).

TEST #1: Bibliographic Test

This test exams the textual transmission of the manuscripts through time. Since we don't have the original hand-written documents, how reliable are the copies we do have in terms of the *number* of manuscripts and the *time interval* between the original writing and the earliest existing copy?

- New Testament ⇒ Manuscript Evidence
- Old Testament ⇒ Dead Sea Scrolls

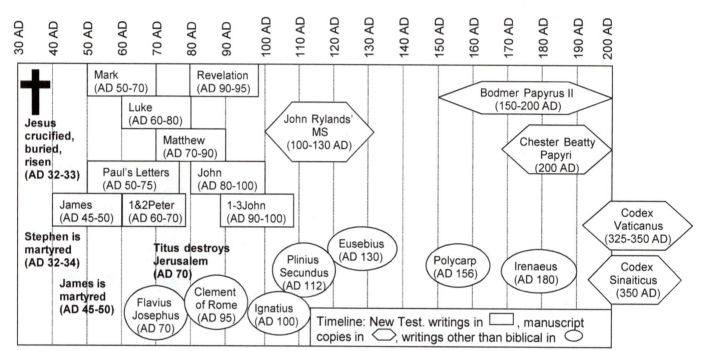

William F. Albright, PhD John Hopkins Univ., Pres. of International Org. of OT Scholars, Archaeologist: "We can say emphatically that there is no longer any solid basis for dating any book of the New Testament after about AD 80, two full generations before the date between 130 and 150 given by the more radical NT critics."

Geisler and Nix (Professors of Theology and Biblical Studies): "Only 1/8 of all the variants in the NT have any weight, as most of them are merely mechanical matters such as spelling or style. Of the whole, only 1/60 rise above trivialities, or can assumed to be called "substantial variations'. Mathematically this computes to a text that is **98.33% PURE**."

Sir Frederick George Kenyon (1863-1952): Director of British Museum, President of the British Academy from 1917 to 1921. Kenyon was a noted scholar of ancient languages, and made a lifelong study of the Bible, especially the New Testament as an historical text. His book 'Our Bible and the Ancient Manuscripts (1895)' shows how Egyptian papyri and other archaeological evidence corroborates historical events in the Gospels. He wrote on the historicity of the New Testament: *"The last foundation for any doubt that the Scriptures have come down to us substantially as they were written has now been removed."* He also was very outspoken on the reliability of the New Testament as evidenced by the incredible number of manuscripts available to test its transmission through time: *"No fundamental doctrine of the Christian faith rests on a disputed reading. The number of NT manuscripts, of early translations from it, and of quotes from it in the oldest Church writers, is so large that it is practically certain that the true reading of every doubtful passage is preserved in some one or other of these ancient authorities. THIS CAN BE SAID OF NO OTHER ANCIENT BOOK IN THE WORLD."* ('The Bible & Archaeology'. New York: Harper & Row, 1940).

- <u>Skeptic's Charge #4</u>:   How accurate and error-free is the <u>New Testament</u>? How do we know? It has changed so much through time, is there really any way to trust what it says? Wasn't it just written by men?
- <u>The Answer</u>: The NT is over *98.33% PURE* in its translation through history – it is by far the most accurate and reliable book ever written (there is no close second). In the table below we apply one of the several tests used to authenticate a book's historicity and accuracy – the manuscript evidence :

How many years have passed from when the book was written to the earliest hand-written copy we have? The more years between our earliest copy and the author's initial writing, the greater the chance it was inaccurately translated (it has changed through time).

How many hand-written copies do we have, to compare against each other? The more hand-written copies we have, the more evidence to see if the book was changed through time as it was recopied.

Remember what Dan Brown wrote, in "The Da Vinci Code"?: *"The Bible is a product of man, my dear. Not of God. The Bible did not fall magically from the clouds. Man created it as a historical record of tumultuous times, and it has evolved through countless translations, additions and revisions."* Is he right?

BIBLIOGRAPHIC TEST: MANUSCRIPT EVIDENCE

Author (Name and Book)	When Written	Date of Earliest Manuscript we have	Years from 1st written to earliest manuscript	# Copies we have
SOPHOCLES	496-406 BC	1000 AD	1,400 years	193
HERODOTUS *(History)*	480-425 BC	900 AD	1,300 years	8
THUCYDIDES *(History)*	460-400 BC	900 AD	1,300 years	8
EURIPIDES *(History)*	480-406 BC	1100 AD	1,500 years	9
PLATO *(Tetralogies)*	427-347 BC	900 AD	1,200 years	7
ARISTOPHANES	450-385 BC	900 AD	1,200 years	10
ARISTOTLE	384-322 BC	1100 AD	1,400 years	49
DEMOSTHENES	383-322 BC	1100 AD	1,300 years	200
CAESAR *(Gallic Wars)*	100-44 BC	900 AD	1,000 years	10
LUCRETIUS	died 53 BC	?	1,100 years	2
PLINY SECUNDUS *(History)*	61-113 AD	850 AD	750 years	7
SUETONIUS *(De Vita Caesarum)*	75-160 AD	950 AD	800 years	8
TACITUS *(Annals)*	100 AD	1100 AD	1,000 years	20
HOMER *(Iliad)*	900 BC	400 BC	500 years	1,757
NEW TESTAMENT	**40-100 AD**	**125 AD**	**25 YEARS**	**> 24,000**

THE NEW TESTAMENT CAN BE TRUSTED

- The Manuscript evidence: the New Testament is by far the most reliably translated book ever written.
- Its historicity and accuracy through time has no close second.
- Only 25 years exist from when the authors wrote it down and the earliest hand-written copy we have (John Ryland manuscript), and over 24,000 hand-written copies exist that match to 98% accuracy!

Examining the Evidence: The Time Gap from the Original Manuscripts

- <u>Skeptic's Charge #5</u>: But what about the time gap of 50-100 years between the actual events and the copies of the original manuscripts which we have? Even though we have thousands of copies, could errors have crept in that make the existing copies unreliable? Bart Ehrmann (Prof. New Testament, Univ. North Carolina, and world-renowned textual critic) makes the point that the earliest copies we do have contain the greatest number of transmission errors, while the later copies were then transmitted with much fewer errors. Wouldn't this suggest the earliest copies are not reliable, and we simply continued transmitting unreliable copies over time?

- <u>The Answer</u>: We have a huge treasure of manuscripts and fragments of manuscripts (over 24,000), with the earliest being Prof. Dan Wallace's recent fragment from the Gospel of Mark that dates to the first century A.D., placing within 50 years of the originals. From these, we can categorize the transmission errors by each type and location, and get a good impression as to what the original documents said (we cannot be 100% certain, but from the evidence we can be more than reasonably certain).

<u>There are 18 2nd Century manuscripts</u>: The **Gospels were completed between 50-100 A.D.**, which means the early copies are within 100 years. When these early manuscripts are put together, more than 43% of the NT is accounted for from copies no later than the 2nd Century.

<u>There are 99 manuscripts dating before 400 AD</u>: One of these, the Codex Sinaiticus, is the complete New Testament. So the gap between the original autographs and the earliest manuscripts is very small when we apply the same standard to all other classical ancient literature taught today in our universities as reliable (see previous page).

If we are going to be skeptical about the Bible, then we need to be much more skeptical about the works of any other ancient history. Or, we can say the opposite: we can be many times more confident in the reliability of the Bible. It is far and away the most reliable ancient document.

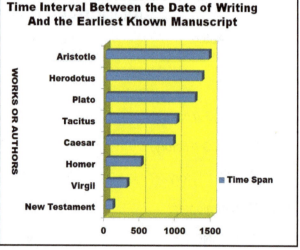

Examining the Evidence: The Transmission Errors in the Biblical Manuscripts

- <u>Skeptic's Charge #6</u>: Aren't there about 400,000 textual errors in the early copies of the gospels? Since we only have copies of copies of the original documents over time, it's become so full of errors that we can't know what the original records actually said. I've heard that scribes would fall asleep, misspell, take their eyes off the manuscript, or other mistakes anyone would make.

 Dr. Daniel B. Wallace (1952 -): PhD Dallas Theological Seminary; Prof. New Testament Studies; senior New Testament editor of the NET Bible and coeditor of the NET-Nestle Greek-English diglot. His expertise is textual criticism; founder of The Center for the Study of New Testament Manuscripts (csntm.org); His postdoctoral work includes work on Greek grammar at Tyndale House in Cambridge, textual criticism studies at the Institut für neutestamentliche Textforschung in Münster, and the Universität Tübingen, Germany. He is in demand as a speaker at churches, colleges, and conferences.

Appearing recently on the John Ankerburg Show, Dr. Wallace explained these 400,000 errors in the gospels, explaining how textual critics have categorized these errors into four types:

1) <u>Spelling & Nonsense Errors</u>: These errors occur when a scribe wrote a word that makes no sense in its context, usually because they were tired or took their eyes off the page. Some of these errors are quite comical, such as "we were horses among you" (Gk. hippoi, "horses," instead of ēpioi, "gentle," or nēpioi, "little children") in 1 Thessalonians 2:7 in one late manuscript. These errors are easily corrected.

2) <u>Minor Changes</u>: These minor changes are as small as the presence or absence of an article "the" or changed word order, which can vary considerably in Greek.

3) <u>Meaningful but not Plausible</u>: These errors have meaning but aren't a plausible reflection of the original text. For example, 1 Thessalonians 2:9, instead of "the gospel of God" (the reading of almost all the manuscripts), a late medieval copy has "the gospel of Christ." There is a meaning difference between God and Christ, but the overall manuscript evidence points in one direction, making the error plain and not plausibly part of the original.

4) <u>Meaningful and Plausible</u>: These are errors that have meaning and that the alternate reading is plausible as a reflection of the original wording. *These types of errors account for **less than 1%** of all textual variants and typically involve a single word or phrase.*

Not a single transmission error affects any Christian doctrine

Copyist Errors, Estimations, and the Biblical Text
(quoted in full from website 'TEKTON, Education & Apologetics Ministry')

"Many critics of Christianity express indifference to the principles of textual criticism when it comes to explaining claims of error in the Biblical text. They reject all explanations involving copyist error, even though they are of the same type used by textual critics in secular studies to resolve difficulties. And this being the case, we may refute their arguments by seeing what they would result in if carried to their logical conclusion.

The works of Tacitus contain a known numerical error which has been faulted to a copyist mistake. Two geographic locations are described as being 25 miles apart. But we know that the locations are actually *125 miles apart*. Hence Tacitean and classical scholars deduce that a copyist error changed the original CXXV to XXV. Now using this example, consider what one skeptic's objections do to the science of textual criticism:

'The common apologetic defense that somebody copied something incorrectly, is wholly unsupportable in light of the fact that the originals no longer exist. How do they know it was copied wrong?' Likewise, the originals of Tacitus no longer exist. How do we know it was copied wrong? 'If the conflict exists in the copies, then it is logical to assume it is present in the originals as well, absent evidence to the contrary.' So then: It is logical to assume that the error in Tacitus was in the original? We have no evidence to the contrary --- not even a variant or other document with another number, as we have in the Bible in most cases.

'...the apologists can hardly argue copyist errors to explain contradictions, then assert inerrancy in all other parts of the Bible.' So we can't use a copyist error to explain Tacitus, then assert his reliability elsewhere? Our writer says more on this subject, calling copyist-error explanations a "gimmick" or an "excuse" – but the bottom line is that there are certified TEXTUAL-CRITICAL METHODS for resolving such problems in any ancient text, and a bare dismissal of these is not a sufficient argument against them.

'...since the alleged originals no longer exist and with so much disagreement among the allegedly accurate copies, there is no way scholars can ever know for sure what the originals actually said. Any version on the market must be a product of educated guesses, consensus, and weighing the validity of manuscripts.' Secular textual critics, who operate under the same basic rules as biblical ones, would be very surprised to hear that there is "no way" to know "for sure" what original said. Of course, one might speculate that a given work by Tacitus on history was once a guide for dental hygiene practices, but the level of certainty for recovery is far, far higher than the implication above insists.

And so, how do we discover a copyist error? An overriding supposition in textual criticism assumes error in copying *before* assuming error in the original --- this is simply good manners. It is presumptuous to assume error upon the creator of a work, as it is far more likely, given the time and the number of hands an ancient document has usually passed through, that a copyist erred. This is so whether we have corroborating evidence or not.

The second factor is, indeed if there is corroborating evidence supporting what appears to be a more correct reading. For Tacitus, all we have is the mere fact that the 2 locations referenced are known to be about 125 miles apart. But we have better evidence for most Biblical problems of this sort. Take these verses from the KJV, where they have not been corrected with text-critical principles:

- *1 Kings 4:26 And Solomon had 40,000 stalls of horses for his chariots, and 12,000 horsemen.*
- *2 Chron. 9:25 And Solomon had 4,000 stalls for horses and chariots, and 12,000 horsemen; whom he bestowed in the chariot cities, and with the king at Jerusalem.*

Which is correct? Textual critics have determined that the second is correct, and 1 Kings has been hit by a copyist error, citing as support the reading found in 2 Chronicles. Archaeological data indicating that 4,000 would be an appropriate number of stalls for a nation the size of ancient Israel, whereas 40,000 would be very excessive. 4,000 comports better with the number of horsemen. There is sufficient explanation for a change. Tekton associate Eric Vestrup notes that *there is a reasonable probability that a scribe copied incorrectly, for "40" is spelled* **aleph-resh-bet-ayin-yodh-mem** *with "4" being spelled* **aleph-resh-bet-ayin-heh**, *the only difference being the plural "-im" ending in "40" while "4" has the singular feminine ending*. Compare this now with a skeptic's commentary when a fellow skeptic pointed out the high probability of a copyist error in this instance:

'First, although the alleged originals no longer exist, there are thousands of manuscripts claiming to be accurate copies of the alleged originals. When scholars decided to write the following versions--KJ, RS, ML, AS, NASB, MT, LV, JB, NIV, TEV, NWT, and etc.--they went through either some, many, most, or all of the manuscripts, compared what was said in each, reached a common consensus, and chose to use 40,000 in 1 Kings 4:26 and 4,000 in 2 Chron. 9:25. In order for there to have been a copyist error, the same incorrect figure had to have been copied in scores if not hundreds and thousands of manuscripts, certainly not one or two. Are you saying hundreds, if not thousands, of copyists made precisely the same error when they copied 1 Kings 4:26 and 2 Chron. 9:25 from the autographs? They not only copied incorrectly but made the same erroneous change?...What do you think are the odds of that happening?...The attempt by biblicists to pawn this problem off on one lone copyist or scribe in some monastery somewhere who happened to make one simple mistake is rather amusing, in light of the fact that thousands of manuscripts are involved with the same verse.'

Our skeptic here is indifferent to the actual process of textual composition in ancient times and the matter of textual "families". He has envisioned a single original which was the source of *all* copies, when in fact the lack of materials and skilled scribes in ancient times dictates that there were very few copies made to begin with, so that there is no instance of a single scribe transcribing the same error into hundreds, thousands, etc. manuscripts. What there would be is a single scribe making the error once, an error which is then preserved as successive single manuscripts are transcribed, until such time as mass copying procedures and schools existed -- and then, the error is preserved in thousands of manuscripts. It happened with Tacitus, and it happened with the Bible.

'Second, even if there were a copyist mistake, you could never be sure which figure was copied incorrectly. Was it the 40,000 figure that should have been 4,000 or the 4,000 figure that should have been 40,000? Because you could never know for sure, you might just as well expunge these two parts of the Bible. One is definitely incorrect, and you'll never know which.'

This is of course false, as we have seen above. Beyond that, should we expunge that part of Tacitus that contains the numerical error?

'Third, and very important, is the fact that the manuscripts contradict one another, and until the original is produced, the contradiction stands. Biblicists are asking us to ignore a contradiction staring us in the face, in favor of a theory that can in no way be substantiated. The fact is that the contradiction stands, and will continue standing until evidence is produced to the contrary. The burden of proof lies on he who alleges. Because the contradiction is clear and obvious, I am under no obligation to prove a contradiction exists in manuscripts which biblicists can't even prove existed. Biblicists, on the other hand, are obligated to prove there was no contradiction in the original writings, which they are wholly incapable of doing.'

So, likewise, the error "stands" in Tacitus -- and I could say: "Greco-Roman historians are asking us to ignore an error staring us in the face, in favor of a theory that can in no way be substantiated. The fact is that the error stands, and will continue standing until evidence is produced to the contrary. The burden of proof lies on he who alleges. Because the error is clear and obvious, I am under no obligation to prove an error exists in manuscripts which Greco-Roman historians and textual critics can't even prove existed. Greco-Roman historians and textual critics, on the other hand, are obligated to prove there was no error in the original writings, which they are wholly incapable of doing." It would be interesting to see our skeptic deliver this message before an audience of professional historians and textual critics. "

Dr. B.B. Warfield: Historical and Exegetical *EVIDENCE* for Biblical Inerrancy

Benjamin Warfield, (1851-1921): Prof. Systematic Theology, Princeton Theological Seminary; four PhD's in Biblical Theology: *"If we compare the present state of the New Testament text with that of any other ancient writing, we must ... declare it to be marvelously correct. Such has been the case with which the New Testament has been copied-a care which has doubtless grown out of true reverence for its holy words....* The New Testament [is] unrivaled among ancient writings in the purity of its text as actually transmitted and kept in use."[5].

Quoting from his book 'Inspiration and Authority of the Bible', Dr. Warfield uses *inductive reasoning* to argue for biblical inerrancy (versus today's typical deductive presupposition that the Bible is inspired by God).. *"Now if this doctrine is to be assailed on critical grounds, it is very clear that, first of all, criticism must be required to proceed against the evidence on which it is based. This evidence… is twofold. First, there is the ① exegetical evidence that the doctrine held and taught by the Church is the doctrine held and taught by the Biblical writers themselves. And secondly, there is the whole ② mass of evidence—internal and external, objective and subjective, historical and philosophical, human and divine—which goes to show that the Biblical writers are trustworthy as doctrinal guides. If they are trustworthy teachers of doctrine and if they held and taught this doctrine, then this doctrine is true, and is to be accepted and acted upon as true by us all. In that case, any objections brought against the doctrine from other spheres of inquiry are inoperative; it being a settled logical principle that so long as the proper evidence by which a proposition is established remains unrefuted, all so-called objections brought against it pass out of the category of objections to its truth into the category of difficulties to be adjusted to it. If criticism is to assail this doctrine, therefore, it must proceed against and fairly overcome one or the other element of its proper proof. It must either show that this doctrine is not the doctrine of the Biblical writers, or else it must show that the Biblical writers are not trustworthy as doctrinal guides."*

Argument ① = Exegetical: if the those who wrote the Bible actually held to the doctrine of biblical inerrancy, and were trusted to teach that doctrine to others, then this doctrine is true."

Argument ② = Historical: "If criticism is to assail this doctrine… It must show that this doctrine is not the *historical* doctrine of the Biblical writers." In this book, we apply Dr. Chauncey Saunder's three tests (bibliographic, internal evidence and external evidence) to determine the historical trustworthiness of the authors in their documentation of the Bible. To Dr. Warfield's challenge, his inductive arguments have been proven true. For more details on this topic, see also Dr. Daniel Wallace's internet article 'My Take on Inerrancy', dated August 10, 2006.

Expert Testimony on the Historicity of Luke

2.2

Sir William Mitchell Ramsay (1851-1939): Scottish archaeologist and New Testament scholar; leading authority on the history of Asia Minor; first Professor of Classical Archaeology at Oxford University and pioneered the study of antiquity in what is today western Turkey; nine honorary doctorates from British, Continental and North American universities. He was one of the original members of the British Academy, was awarded the Gold Medal of Pope Leo XIII in 1893 and the Victorian Medal of the Royal Geographical Society in 1906. The following excerpts are taken from W. Ward Gasque's '*Sir William M. Ramsay: Archaeologist and New Testament Scholar. A Survey of His Contribution to the Study of the New Testament*' (Grand Rapids: Baker Book House, 1966:

"During Ramsay's days as a university student, the study of apostolic history was dominated by Ferdinand Christian Baur (1792-1860) and his so-called Tübingen School. Reading Acts and the letters of Paul in the light of the Hegelian dialectic interpretation of history and the assumption that only four Pauline epistles were undoubtedly genuine (Galatians, Romans, 1and 2 Corinthians), they radically altered the traditional understanding of New Testament history… Their conclusions demanded a very late date for most of the New Testament writings, especially Acts. When he first began his work in Asia Minor, Ramsay's views concerning the Book of Acts were under the influence of this school of thought. 'I had read a good deal of modern criticism about the book,' he wrote, and dutifully accepted the current opinion that it was written during the second half of the second century by an author who wished to influence the minds of people in his own time by a highly wrought and imaginative description of the early Church.'

In his search for information bearing on the geography and history of Asia Minor he at first paid slight attention to the early Christian authorities. He had gained the impression in his studies that these were quite unworthy of consideration for a historian; anything having to do with religion belonged to the realm of the theologians, not that of the historians. When he spent time copying Christian inscriptions in his earliest years of travel, he felt the time to be wasted... Finally, in a desperate search for any information of a geographical and antiquarian nature, he began to study the journeys of Paul in this region of the world as described in the Book of Acts. He hardly expected to find any information of value regarding the condition of Asia Minor in the time of Paul; rather, he thought he would find material bearing upon the second half of the second century of the Christian era, i.e. the age (he thought) in which the author of Acts lived.

In his book '*The Bearing of Recent Discoveries on the Trustworthiness of the New Testament*'[18], Ramsay tells how he came to change his mind on the subject… Instead of assuming the book to be untrustworthy in regard to its avowed historical situation, he now began to approach Acts with an open mind that it might after all prove to be accurate in any given detail: 'Luke's narrative was trustworthy, it was for me exceptionally valuable, as giving evidence on a larger scale. There was nothing else like it. No other ancient traveler has left an account of the journeys which he made across Asia Minor [Xenophon gives little more than names and distances]; and if the narrative of Paul's travels rests on first-class authority, it placed in my hands a document of unique and exceptional value to guide my investigations. To determine the value of this narrative was a fundamental condition for my future work.'

Over the years the opinion gradually forced itself upon him that Luke's history of early Christian origins was unsurpassed for its accuracy. Further study of Acts XIII.-XXI. showed that the book could bear the most minute scrutiny of an authority for the facts of the Aegean world, and that it was written with such judgment, skill, art, and perception of the truth as to be a model of historical statement.

When he was invited to visit the United States two years later for lectures at Auburn Seminary (and incidentally at Harvard, Johns Hopkins, and Union Seminary, New York), he had thoroughly worked through the whole of Acts and had come to a definite conclusion. He stated the view at which he had arrived in St. Paul the Traveler (the publication of his American lectures): 'Our hypothesis is that Acts was written by a great historian, a writer who set himself to record the facts as they occurred, a strong partisan indeed, but raised above partiality by his perfect confidence that he had only to describe the facts as they occurred, in order to make the truth of Christianity and the honor of Paul apparent.... I shall argue that the book was composed by a personal friend and disciple of Paul, and if this be once established there will be no hesitation in accepting the primitive tradition that Luke was the author. The author of Acts is not to be regarded as the author of historical romance, legend, or third or second-rate history. Rather he is the writer of an historical work of the highest order, a work to be compared with that of Thucydides, the greatest of the Greek historians.'

Dr. Norman Geisler, '*In all, Luke names 32 countries, 54 cities and 9 islands without an error.*"
(Baker Encyclopedia of Christian Apologetics', 1998)

Collection of just some of the Scholarship for Historicity of Luke

New Testament Claim	Higher Criticism	Archaeology corroborates Luke
Luke 2:1-3 Luke mentions Quirinius as governor of Syria.	Scholars discarded Luke's claim since there was no records of Quirinius as governor at that time.	An inscription was found in Antioch ascribing Quirinius as governor in Syria around 7BC. Then, Josephus documents Quirinius as governor in Syria in 6AD. Now, scholars believe he was governor twice.
Luke 2:1-3 Luke mentions the census, and that everyone had to return to his ancestral home.	Scholars discarded Luke's claim since there was no records of any census being taken.	Archaeology confirmed the Romans held censuses every 14 years, begun under Augustus and beginning in neither 23-22BC or a little later, in 9-8BC. Lastly, a papyrus was discovered in Egypt giving instructions for conducting a census, and we know that regular censuses were taken in Egypt, Gaul and Cyrene. So it makes sense that Luke is documenting the fact that taking censuses was a repeated event.
Luke 3:1 Luke mentions "Lysanius tetrarch of Abilene" in announcing Jesus' public ministry.	Scholars discarded Luke's claim since the Lysanius of record was a ruler of Chalcis, from 40-36 B.C.	An inscription dating during the time of Tiberius, who ruled from 14-37 A.D., was found recording a temple dedication which names Lysanius as the "tetrarch of Abila" near Damascus, validating Luke's claim.
Acts 14:6 Luke records 'Paul and Barnabas, on account of an angry mob, fled from Iconium to Lystra and Derbe, cities of Lycaonia, and the surrounding region'.	Scholars discarded Luke's claim since ancient geographical knowledge at the time set Iconium as a city of Lycaonia. Scholars viewed this as an obvious error.	Iconium was not a part of Lycaonia during this time, but was made part of Phrygia from 37AD – 72AD, an entirely different district of Asia Minor. The people were of a different stock, and they spoke a different language from that of the Lycaonians. Also, the connection between Zeus and Hermes as associated gods in this region is further demonstration of the authenticity of Luke's narrative.
Acts 17:6 Luke calls the civil authorities in Thessalonica by the word *'politarchs'*.	No classical ancient literature existed which uses the word *'politarchs'* for civil rulers.	Archaeology has discovered 19 inscriptions that use the title of *'politarchs'* for civil authorities of a region, and 5 of these are in Thessalonica.
Acts 18:12-17 Paul was brought before Gallio, the proconsul of Achaea.	No records existed to substantiate the existence of Gallio when Paul was traveling on his missionary journeys (50AD).	At Delphi an inscription of a letter from Emperor Claudius was discovered, which includes the words "Lucius Junios Gallio, my friend, and the proconsul of Achaia . . ." Historians date the inscription to 52 A.D., corresponding to the apostle's stay in 51AD.
Acts 16:12 Luke refers to Philippi as a 'part' or 'district' of Macedonia, using Gr. word *'meris'*.	The Greek word *'meris'* is never used to describe a district from any other literature.	Archaeological excavations show this very word, *'meris'*, was used to describe the divisions of the district of Macedonia.
Acts 19:22, Romans 16:23 Erastus, a coworker of Paul, is named the Corinthian city treasurer.	No records up that time existed to substantiate the existence of Erastus as treasurer of Corinth (50AD)..	Archaeologists, excavating a Corinthian theatre in 1928, discovered this inscription: "Erastus in return for his aedilship laid the pavement at his own expense." The pavement was laid in 50 A.D. The designation of treasurer describes the work of a Corinthian aedile.
Acts 19:23-29 Luke writes of the riot of Ephesus, with a civic assembly (Ecclesia) occurring in the theater.	No records exist outside of Luke that documents this.	An inscription describes silver statues of Artemis ('Diana' in KJV) being placed in the 'theater during a full session of the Ecclesia'.
Acts 28:7 Luke calls Plubius, the chief man on the island of Malta, "first man of the island."	Scholars questioned this strange title and deemed it unhistorical.	Inscriptions have recently been discovered on the island that indeed gives Plubius the title of "first man."

Expert Testimony on the Text of the New Testament

Bruce Manning Metzger (1914 – 2007); widely considered one of the most influential New Testament (NT) scholars of the 20th century (Greek, NT and NT Textual Criticism); PhD NT Studies, Prof. NT, Princeton Theological Seminary; editor of the United Bible Society's standard Greek NT (starting point for most NT translations). His most noteworthy scholarly contribution to NT studies include: 1) *The Text of the NT: Its Transmission, Corruption, and Restoration* (1964), 2) *The Early Versions of the NT: Their Origin, Transmission, and Limitations* (1977), 3) *The Canon of the: Its Origin, Development, and Significance* (1987).

The following excerpts are quoted from Lee Strobel's interview with Dr. Metzger in "The Case for Christ"[4]:

➔ How can we be sure the biographies of Jesus were handed down to us in a reliable way?

"I'll be honest with you," I said to Metzger. "When I first found out that there are no surviving originals of the New Testament, I was really skeptical. I thought, If all we have are copies of copies of copies, how can I have any confidence that the New Testament we have today bears any resemblance whatsoever to what was originally written? How do you respond to that? This isn't an issue that's unique to the Bible; it's a question we can ask of other documents that have come down to us from antiquity," he replied. "But what the New Testament has in its favor, especially when compared with other ancient writings, is the unprecedented multiplicity of copies that have survived."

"Why is that important?" I asked.

"Well, the more often you have copies that agree with each other, especially if they emerge from different geographical areas, the more you can cross-check them to figure out what the original document was like. The only way they'd agree would be where they went back genealogically in a family tree that represents the descent of the manuscripts."

"OK," I said, "I can see that having a lot of copies from various places can help. But what about the age of the documents? Certainly that's important as well, isn't it?"

"Quite so," he replied. "And this is something else that favors the New Testament. We have copies commencing within a couple of generations from the writing of the originals, whereas in the case of other ancient texts, maybe five, eight, or ten centuries elapsed between the original and the earliest surviving copy. In addition to Greek manuscripts, we also have translations of the gospels into other languages at a relatively early time - into Latin, Syriac, and Coptic. And beyond that, we have what may be called secondary translations made a little later, like Armenian and Gothic. And a lot of others-Georgian, Ethiopic, a great variety."

"How does that help?"

"Because even if we had no Greek manuscripts today, by piecing together the information from these translations from a relatively early date, we could actually reproduce the contents of the New Testament. In addition to that, even if we lost all the Greek manuscripts and the early translations, we could still reproduce the contents of the New Testament from the quotations in commentaries, sermons, letters, and so forth of the early church fathers."

➔ Of the entire New Testament, what is the earliest portion that we possess today?

Metzger didn't have to ponder the answer. "That would be a fragment of the gospel of John, containing material from chapter eighteen. It has five verses-three on one side, two on the other - and it measures about two and a half by three and a half inches," he said.

"How was it discovered?"

"It was purchased in Egypt as early as 1920, but it sat unnoticed for years among similar fragments of papyri. Then in 1934 C. H. Roberts of Saint John's College, Oxford, was sorting through the papyri at the John Rylands Library in Manchester, England. He immediately recognized this as preserving a portion of John's gospel. He was able to date it from the style of the script."

"And what was his conclusion?" I asked. "How far back does it go?"

"He concluded it originated between A.D.100 to 150. Lots of other prominent paleographers, like Sir Frederic Kenyon, Sir Harold Bell, Adolf Deissmann, W, H. P. Hatch, Ulrich Wilcken, and others, have agreed with his assessment. Deissmann was convinced that it goes back at least to the reign of Emperor Hadrian, which was A.D. 117-138, or even Emperor Trajan, which was A.D. 98-117."

That was a stunning discovery. The reason: skeptical German theologians in the last century argued strenuously that the fourth gospel was not even composed until at least the year 160 - too distant from the events of Jesus' life to be of much historical use. They were able to influence generations of scholars, who scoffed at this gospel's reliability. "This certainly blows that opinion out of the water," I commented.

"Yes, it does," he said. "Here we have, at a very early date, a fragment of a copy of John in a community along the Nile River in Egypt, far from Ephesus in Asia Minor, where the gospel was probably originally composed."

This finding has literally rewritten popular views of history, pushing the composition of John's gospel much closer to the days when Jesus walked the earth. While papyrus manuscripts represent the earliest copies of the New Testament, there are also ancient copies written on parchment, which was made from the skins of cattle, sheep, goats, and antelope.

"We have what are called uncial manuscripts, which are written in all-capital Greek letters," Metzger explained. "Today we have 306 of these, several dating back as early as the third century. The most important are Codex Sinaiticus, which is the only complete New Testament in uncial letters, and Codex Vaticanus, which is not quite complete. Both date to about A.D. 350.

"A new style of writing, more cursive in nature, emerged in roughly A.D. 800. It's called minuscule, and we have 2,856 of these manuscripts. Then there are also lectionaries, which contain New Testament Scripture in the sequence it was to be read in the early churches at appropriate times during the year. A total of 2,403 of these have been cataloged. That puts the grand total of Greek manuscripts at 5,664."

In addition to the Greek documents, he said, there are thousands of other ancient New Testament manuscripts in other languages. There are 8,000 to 10,000 Latin Vulgate manuscripts, plus a total of 8,000 in Ethiopic, Slavic, and Armenian. In all, there are about 24,000 manuscripts in existence.

→ **What about discrepancies among the various manuscripts?**

"With the similarities in the way Greek letters are written and with the primitive conditions under which the scribes worked, it would seem inevitable that copying errors would creep into the text," I said. "And in fact, aren't there literally tens of thousands of variations among the ancient manuscripts that we have?"

"Quite so", Metzger conceded

"Doesn't that therefore mean we can't trust them?" I asked, sounding more accusatory than inquisitive.

"No sir, it does not," Metzger replied firmly. "First let me say this: Eyeglasses weren't invented until 1373 in Venice, and I'm sure that astigmatism existed among the ancient scribes. That was compounded by the fact that it was difficult under any circumstances to read faded manuscripts on which some of the ink had flaked away. And there were other hazards-inattentiveness on the part of scribes, for example. So yes, although for the most part scribes were scrupulously careful, errors did creep in. But there are factors counteracting that. For example, sometimes the scribe's memory would play tricks on him. Between the time it took for him to look at the text and then to write down the words, the order of words might get shifted. He may write down the right words but in the wrong sequence. This is nothing to be alarmed at, because Greek, unlike English, is an inflected language."

"Meaning . . . " I prompted him.

"Meaning it makes a whale of a difference in English if you say, 'Dog bites man' or 'Man bites dog'-sequence matters in English. But in Greek it doesn't. One word functions as the subject of the sentence regardless of where it stands in the sequence; consequently, the meaning of the sentence isn't distorted if the words are out of what we consider to be the right order. So yes, some variations among manuscripts exist, but generally they're inconsequential variations like that. Differences in spelling would be another example."

Still, the high number of "variants," or differences among manuscripts, was troubling. I had seen estimates as high as two hundred thousand of them.' However, Metzger downplayed the significance of that figure. "The number sounds big, but it's a bit misleading because of the way variants are counted," he said. He explained that if a single word is misspelled in two thousand manuscripts, that's counted as two thousand variants.

I keyed in on the most important issue. "How many doctrines of the church are in jeopardy because of variants?"

"I don't know of any doctrine that is in jeopardy," he responded confidently.

"So the variations, when they occur, tend to be minor rather than substantive?"

"Yes, yes, that's correct, and scholars work very carefully to try to resolve them by getting back to the original meaning. The more significant variations do not overthrow any doctrine of the church. Any good Bible will have notes that will alert the reader to variant readings of any consequence. But again, these are rare."

So rare that scholars Norman Geisler and William Nix conclude, "The New Testament, then, has not only survived in more manuscripts than any other book from antiquity, but it has survived in a purer form than any other great book – a form that is 99.5 percent pure." However, even if it's true that the transmission of the New Testament through history has been unprecedented in its reliability, how do we know that we have the whole picture?

→ **How do we know that the twenty-seven books of the New Testament represent the best and most reliable information?** It was time to turn to the question of the "CANON", a term that comes from a Greek word meaning "rule," "norm," or "standard" and that describes the books that are accepted as official in the church and included in the New Testament.' Metzger is considered a leading authority in that field.

"How did the early church leaders determine which books would be considered authoritative and which would be discarded?" I asked. "What criteria did they use in determining what would be included in the New Testament?"

"Basically, the early church had three criteria," he said. "First, the books must have apostolic authority-that is, they must have been written either by apostles themselves, who were eyewitnesses to what they wrote about, or by followers of apostles. So in the case of Mark and Luke, while they weren't among the twelve disciples, early tradition has it that Mark was a helper of Peter, and Luke was an associate of Paul."

"Second, there was the criterion of conformity to what was called the rule of faith. That is, was the document congruent with the basic Christian tradition that the church recognized as normative? And third, there was the criterion of whether a document had had continuous acceptance and usage by the church at large."

"They merely applied those criteria and let the chips fall where they may?" I asked.

"Well, it wouldn't be accurate to say that these criteria were simply applied in a mechanical fashion," he replied. "There were certainly different opinions about which criterion should be given the most weight. But what's remarkable is that even though the fringes of the canon remained unsettled for a while, there was actually a high degree of unanimity concerning the greater part of the New Testament within the first two centuries. And this was true among very diverse congregations scattered over a wide area."

"So," I said, "the four gospels we have in the New Testament today met those criteria, while others didn't?"

"Yes," he said. "It was, if I may put it this way, an example of survival of the fittest! In talking about the canon, Arthur Darby Nock used to tell his students at Harvard, 'The most traveled roads in Europe are the best roads; that's why they're so heavily traveled.' That's a good analogy. British commentator William Barclay said it this way: 'It is the simple truth to say that the New Testament books became canonical because no one could stop them doing so.' We can be confident that no other ancient books can compare with the New Testament in terms of importance for Christian history or doctrine. When one studies the early history of the canon, one walks away convinced that the New Testament contains the best sources for the history of Jesus. Those who discerned the limits of the canon had a clear and balanced perspective of the gospel of Christ. Just read these other documents for yourself. They're written later than the four gospels, in the second, third, fourth, fifth, even sixth century, long after Jesus, and they're generally quite banal. They carry names - like the Gospel of Peter and the Gospel of Mary - that are unrelated to their real authorship. On the other hand, the four gospels in the New Testament were readily accepted with remarkable unanimity as being authentic in the story they told."

"You have to understand that the canon was not the result of a series of contests involving church politics. The canon is rather the separation that came about because of the intuitive insight of Christian believers. They could hear the voice of the Good Shepherd in the gospel of John; they could hear it only in a muffled and distorted way in the Gospel of Thomas, mixed in with a lot of other things. "When the pronouncement was made about the canon, it merely ratified what the general sensitivity of the church had already determined. You see, the canon is a list of authoritative books more than it is an authoritative list of books. These documents didn't derive their authority from being selected; each one was authoritative before anyone gathered them together. The early church merely listened and sensed that these were authoritative accounts.

"For somebody now to say that the canon emerged only after councils and synods made these pronouncements would be like saying, 'Let's get several academies of musicians to make a pronouncement that the music of Bach and Beethoven is wonderful.' I would say, 'Thank you for nothing! We knew that before the pronouncement was made.' We know it because of sensitivity to what is good music and what is not. The same with the canon."

In terms of which documents were accepted into the New Testament, generally there has never been any serious dispute about the authoritative nature of twenty of the New Testament's twenty seven books - from Matthew through Philemon, plus 1Peter and 1John. This includes the four gospels that represent Jesus' biographies.

The remaining seven books, though questioned for a time by some early church leaders, "were finally and fully recognized by the church generally," according to Geisler and Nix.

As for the "pseudepigraphia," the proliferation of gospels, epistles, and apocalypses in the first few centuries after Jesus-including the Gospels of Nicodemus, Barnabas, Bartholomew, Andrew, the Epistle of Paul to the Laodiceans, the Apocalypse of Stephen, and others-they are "fanciful and heretical ... neither genuine nor valuable as a whole," and "virtually no orthodox Father, canon or council" considered them to be authoritative or deserving of inclusion in the New Testament."

In fact, I accepted Metzger's challenge by reading many of them myself. Compared with the careful, sober, precise, eyewitness quality of Matthew, Mark, Luke, and John, these works truly deserve the description they received from Eusebius, the early church historian: "Totally absurd and impious." They were too far removed from Jesus' ministry to contribute anything meaningful to my investigation, having been written as late as the fifth and sixth centuries, and their often mythical qualities disqualify them from being historically credible.

Q9: "All these decades of scholarship, of study, of writing textbooks, of delving into the minutiae of the New Testament text-what has all this done to your personal faith?" I asked.

"Oh," he said, sounding happy to discuss the topic, "it has increased the basis of my personal faith to see the firmness with which these materials have come down to us, with a multiplicity of copies, some of which are very, very ancient. On the contrary," he stressed, "it has built it. I've asked questions all my life, I've dug into the text, I've studied this thoroughly, and today I know with confidence that my trust in Jesus has been well placed." He paused while his eyes surveyed my face. Then he added, for emphasis, "Very well placed."

Bibliographic Test: OLD TESTAMENT

Skeptic's Charge #7: How accurate and error-free is the Old Testament? It has changed so much through time, is there really any way to trust what it says? Wasn't it just written by men?

We do not have the abundance of copies, nor the close time gap between copies and original writings, as with the New Testament, but we do have over 14,000 manuscripts and fragments of the Old Testament of three main types:

1) About 10,000 from the Cairo Geniza (storeroom) find of 1897, dating back as far as about AD. 800;
2) About 190 from the Dead Sea Scrolls find of 1947-1955, the oldest dating back to 250-200 B.C.; and
3) At least 4,300 assorted other copies.

The short time (150 years) between the original Old Testament manuscripts (completed around 400 B.C.) and the first extensive copies (about 250 B.C.), coupled with over 14,000 copies that have been discovered, ensures the trustworthiness of the Old Testament text. The earliest quoted verses (Numbers 6:24-26) date from 800-700 B.C.

Earliest Hebrew (Talmud) Copies	Date of Copy	Time Gap from OT	Contents
Dead Sea Scrolls (by Essenes)	250 BC – 50AD	150 years	entire OT except Esther
Cairo Codex	895 AD	1,295 years	all major and minor prophets
Aleppo Codex	900 AD	1,300 years	majority of OT
Codex of the Prophets of Leningrad	916 AD	1,316 years	Isaiah, Jeremiah, Ezekiel, 12 minor prophets
British Museum Codex	950 AD	1,350 years	Genesis - Deuteronomy
Reuchlin Codex of the Prophets	950 AD	1,350 years	most major & minor prophets
Babylonicus Petroalitanus	1,008 AD	1,408 years	entire OT

Why don't earlier copies of the Old Testament exist?: The Jews regarded the NEWEST copies of their manuscripts as the most valuable because the new copies were the most perfect and free from any physical damage. The older copies were systematically sent to the '*gheniza*' (a small building attached to the side of the synagogue) to be either stored away, with no intention to be used again, or deliberately destroyed.

How were the earliest copies of the Old Testament made?: The Talmudists were Old Testament scribes from 100AD – 500AD. They followed precise regulations every time they transcribed the OT Scriptures. Any roll where any of the regulations (see below) were not followed were held in a 'gheniza' until buried or burned.

Talmudist Regulations for Transcribing the Old Testament

1. A synagogue roll must be written on clean skins of animals; the skins used for a finished roll must contain a certain number of columns, equal throughout the copy of the entire codex (the codex is made of many individual rolls).
2. The length of each column must be 48-60 lines, and the column's width must be exactly 30 letters.
3. Between each consonant there must be only the space of a hair or thread.
4. Between every new section there must be only the length of 9 consonants.
5. Between every book there must be only the length of 3 lines.
6. An authentic copy must be used in transcribing the new copy, and the scribe must not deviate at all from it.
7. Nothing can be written by memory. The scribe looks at each letter on the authentic copy before him.
8. The ink used to copy the Scripture must be black and made according to a certain recipe.
9. The copyist must wash his whole body and then sit in full Jewish dress.
10. The copyist must not begin to write the name of God with a pen newly dipped in ink.

Following the Talmudists were the Masoretes, who were the Jewish scholars from 500AD – 950AD and gave the final form, in use today, of the Hebrew text of the Old Testament. They accepted the tedious task of editing and standardizing the text, which is known today as the 'Masoretic Text.' They, like the Talmudists, were extremely meticulous in their transmissions, with no erasures allowed but starting over again if any errors were made during transcription.

Expert Testimony on the Reliability of the Old Testament

Dr. Robert R. Wilson (1856-1930): William Henry Green Professor of Semitic Languages and Old Testament Criticism at Pronceton Theological Semoinary, PhD Princeton Univ.; fluent in 45 languages, including Hebrew, Aramaic and Greek, as well as all the languages into which the Scriptures had been translated up to 600 AD; In the late 1920s, he left Princeton to teach at the new, conservative Westminster Theological Seminary. Among his other works, Wilson contributed articles to the International Standard Bible Encyclopedia, a noted Bible reference of the early 20th century.

Skeptic's Question: The discovery of the Dead Sea Scrolls provides incontrovertible evidence of the accurate transmission of the Old Testament from its original autographs down to the time of Jesus Christ. But we have a 1,000-year time gap between the earliest entire copy we have (Cairo Codex, 895 AD) and the Dead Sea Scrolls. How can we be confident that the Old Testament we have today in our bibles contains the original writings of the authors, and has been faithfully preserved today?

At the age of 25, Dr. Wilson dedicated his life (into his seventy's) to verifying the reliability and historicity of the Old Testament. He opposed the school of higher criticism, which held that the Bible was inaccurate on many points and not historically reliable.

In his famous treatise he entitled 'What is an Expert?' Dr. Wilson challenged these so-called higher criticism "experts" at their own game: *"I defy any man to make an attack upon the Old Testament on the ground of evidence that I cannot investigate. I can get at the facts if they are linguistic. If you know any language that I do not know, I will learn it."* He spent over fifteen years focused on learning the major languages of the Old Testament era, to ensure he pursued a scholarly approach to the historical Old Testament narrative.

Professor Wilson wrote, *"I have come to the conviction that no man knows enough to attack the veracity of the Old Testament. Every time when anyone has been able to get together enough documentary 'proofs' to undertake an investigation, the biblical facts in the original text have victoriously met the test"* (quoted in R. Pache, 'The Inspiration and Authority of Scripture').

In his life-long study of the accuracy of the original manuscripts, he concluded, *"No man knows enough to assail the truthfulness of the Old Testament. . . . I try to give my students such an intelligent faith in the Old Testament Scriptures that they will never doubt them as long as they live."* (Robert Dick Wilson, 'Is the Higher Criticism Scholarly?' 1922).

In his book 'The Scientific Investigation of the Old Testament'[19], Dr. Wilson documents the major findings of fifty years of scholarly research. Here we'll highlight two of his points:

1) since the Hebrew Old Testament has no vowels, his textual criticism focused on researching the approximately 1,250,000 consonants in the Old Testament text, comparing their form and usage to other ancient writings.

2) In studying the pagan kings in the Old Testament, he discovered that he could tie their names in the Old Testament back to their own native writings. He documented that, for these pagan kings, there are 195 consonants in their names. In the Old Testament manuscripts, only three of the 195 consonants are in question as to spelling. This level of accuracy is absolutely incredible in ancient literature! For example, when he investigated the same use of these names in other literature outside the kings' own writings for the same time period, the names were so poorly spelled that without the Old Testament as the standard scholars had no confidence who exactly these kings were (for example, in the history documented by Ptolemy, an ancient writer, his list of the Babylonian kings has all eighteen misspelled). But again, the Old Testament nails it – we can trust it to be an extremely accurate historical document of the names, lineage and reigns of these pagan kings.

Josh McDowell, in his book 'Evidence that Demands a Verdict'[1], quotes Dr. Wilson on his statement that the Old Testament has proven its incredible trustworthiness as a history book of the ancient world:

"There are about 40 kings living from 2,000BC – 400BC. Each appears in the Old Testament in chronological order, with references to the kings of the same country and those of other countries. Mathematically, this equals 1 chance in 75,000,000,000,000,000,000,000,000 that this level of accuracy is mere chance circumstance.

My 45 years of study has led me to a firmer faith that the Old Testament gives a true historical account of the history of the Israelite people. In 144 cases of transliteration from Egyptian, Assyrian, Babylonian and Moabite into Hebrew, and in 40 more cases of the opposite, the evidence shows that for 2,300 - 3,900 years the text of the proper names in the Hebrew Bible has been transmitted with utmost minute accuracy.

That the original scribes should have written them with such close conformity to correct philological principles is a wonderful proof of their thorough care and scholarship. That the Hebrew text should have been transmitted by copyists through so many centuries is a phenomenon unequaled in the history of literature."

Expert Testimony on Archaeology & the Biblical Record

William Foxwell Albright (1891-1971) was an evangelical American Methodist archaeologist, biblical scholar, linguist, and expert on ceramics. He was born in Coquimbo, Chile to Protestant missionaries Wilbur Finley and Zephine Viola Foxwell Albright. He married Dr. Ruth Norton in 1921, and they had four sons.

Albright pursued his undergraduate studies at Upper Iowa University and received his Ph.D. in 1913 from the Oriental Seminary at Johns Hopkins University, where he later taught from 1929 to 1959. He was also the director of the American School of Oriental Research at Johns Hopkins. He published over 800 books and articles, including 'Yahweh and the Gods of Canaan', 'The Archaeology of Palestine', 'From the Stone Age to Christianity', and 'The Biblical Period from Abraham to Ezra'. He is world-famous for confirming the authenticity of the Dead Sea Scrolls. He edited the Anchor Bible for Jeremiah, Matthew and Revelation.

Using Scientific Archaeology to demonstrate Biblical Reliability: *"To the Christian, Palestine has a personal attraction as the cradle of his faith and the enduring witness to the genuineness of the documents upon which that faith is primarily based. Only by seeking to understand the Bible with all available information (new archaeological discoveries) would one be able to see revelation as a logical, consistent whole, and to combine his data into a solid foundation for confidence in the purposes of God and the destiny of man."*

He used his combination of Christian interpretation and historical analysis of the Bible to demonstrate the historical reliability of the Old Testament. *"We see scientific methods and discoveries judged by Marxist and racist gauges instead of by independent scientific standards."* In such a world, Albright pleaded, we need a return to Biblical (Christian) faith.

Albright demonstrated how scientific archaeology served to construct knowledge about the Bible and its historical context. He identified himself as a Christian humanist deeply committed, as he privately wrote in 1918, to creating a "common ground where scientific rationalism and evangelical faith can meet."

His writings were addressed to evangelical Christian readers. Archaeology, he said, was an ally of Christian conviction, not its enemy. Archaeology laid bare the birthplace of the Bible. No one could detect divine providence in history so clearly as "the reverent archaeologist, whose one great aim is to know the past as it really was, and to deduce the laws which govern the development of man toward that ultimate goal which the Creator has set for him."

Albright continued the pioneering efforts to defend the accuracy and trustworthiness of the Bible by subjecting centuries of pious guesses as to locations of biblical places and events to precise topographical and linguistic scrutiny. Insofar as they offered evidence of historical continuities between ancient biblical and modern locations, such modern names served the cause of scientific exploration.

At the Forefront of Biblical Archaeology: From 1920-1930, editors and feature writers for the New York Times treated the discovery of biblically related places as highly newsworthy. Reports from the field were often taken to suggest that the Bible after all could be trusted. "Bible Sites Found by Archaeologists," announced one news report, "Prof. Albright Identifies Ruins of Jonah's Home Town and Place Where Joshua Routed Foes; Finds Support Genesis; Topography of Fourteenth Chapter Upheld by Discovery of Town of Ham and Other Landmarks".

Reporting on a visit to the ruins of a synagogue at Tel Hum, Albright once wrote that *"we can only hope that it will soon be possible for the German fathers, who own the site of Capernaum [Tel Hum], to continue their digging, and to reveal to our eyes the Capernaum where Jesus walked and talked."* A year later, he would report that while standing among the excavations in Samaria, *"one may well feel the nearness of the great prophet [Elijah] as one stands in the ruins of Ahab's palace!"*

Writing in the Bulletin of the American school, Albright told his readers that: *"These unassuming mounds among the hills of Ephraim and Benjamin are of the greatest interest to us, since they represent authentic monuments of the Israelite past. Every stone and potsherd they conceal is hallowed to us by association with the great names of the Bible. Who can think of the tells which mark ancient Mizpah and Gibeah without a thrill, as memory calls up the shade of Samuel, and the heroic figure of Saul?"*

Defender of Biblically-Based Faith: In his 1922 essay, Albright wrote: *"When European dictators are trying to eradicate Judaism and Christianity, it is incredible folly to attack the Bible because it was written in a day when the sun was still believed to revolve around the earth. The religious and empirical insights of the Bible remain unsurpassed and have sustained our western civilization for nearly 2,000 years since the collapse of pagan culture."*

As Albright developed an increasingly large body of technical writings, his studies reaffirmed the trustworthiness of the Bible, the providential triumph of Christianity, and the superiority of Christian Bible-based "holy land" cultural values.

The Dead Sea Scrolls: Why they are so valuable 2.5

- <u>Skeptics' Charge #8</u>: How accurate are the OT copies we have compared to the text of the 1st century? Since the oldest copies of Hebrew MSS we have are 895 AD, how do we know they were accurately transmitted? Besides that, isn't it possible the disciples just added prophecies of Jesus into the Old Testament after His death, so there would be irrefutable evidence that He was the Old Testament Messiah?

- <u>How they were found</u>: In 1947, Bedouin shepherds, searching for a stray goat in the Judean Desert, entered a vacant cave and found sealed jars filled with ancient scrolls. That initial discovery by the Bedouins yielded 7 scrolls and began a search that lasted nearly 10 years, eventually producing 1,000's of scroll fragments from 11 caves. These scrolls are fragments from which 500 books of the Old Testament have been constructed.

- <u>How old they are</u>: Archaeologists also located and excavated the Qumran ruins (located on a barren terrace between the cliffs where the caves were found and the Dead Sea). Using paleography (handwriting), Accelerated Mass Spectrometry (AMS) testing, numismatics (coins) and pottery, experts established the date of the majority of the scrolls to **125-50 BC**. They are older than any other surviving manuscripts of the Hebrew Old Testament by over **1,000 years** (previously, the oldest complete Hebrew MSS possessed was from 895 AD).

- <u>Who the Essenes were</u>: The scrolls were kept and preserved by the Essenes, a Jewish sect who inhabited Qumran (among other locations) from ≈ 125BC to 68AD, when the Romans destroyed the settlement. They were ardent students of Scripture and separated themselves from the world, regarding themselves as "God's elect", the true "sons of light" who would only fight in the final battle with the "sons of darkness" at the end of the world.

- <u>THE INCREDIBLE EXACTNESS OF THE 2 ISAIAH SCROLLS (IQIsaiah^a and IQIsaiah^b)</u>:

a) IQIsaiah^a is the oldest manuscript of a complete Old Testament book (IQIsaiah^b is 75% complete), dating before Christ (125 BC). They are made of 17 pieces of leather, sewn together into a roll over 24 feet long.

b) The Isaiah Scrolls match word-for-word with our standard Hebrew Bible in over 95% of the text (with the 5% being minor variations that are variations in spelling over time). This demonstrates the incredible accuracy of the copyists of the Scriptures over this 1,000 year period (since the previous earliest copy "Cairo Codex").

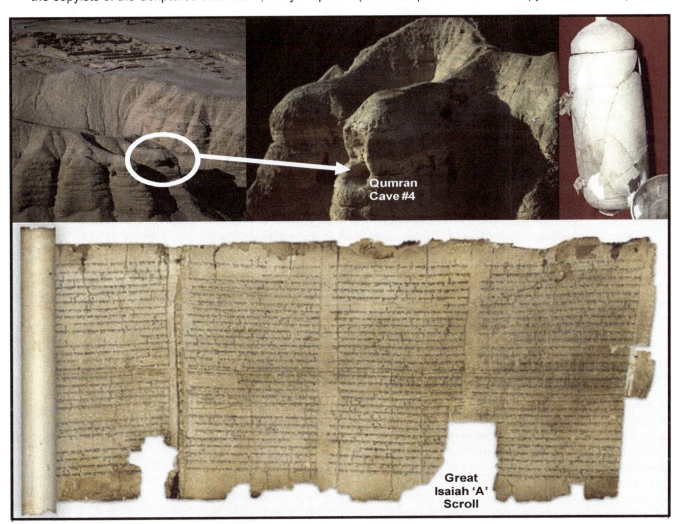

Qumran Cave #4

Great Isaiah 'A' Scroll

The 1QIsaiah^a Scroll (125 BC): 19 Proofs of Isaiah's Prophecies of Jesus Christ in 730 BC

John 5:39 *"You search the Scriptures, for in them you think you have eternal life; these are they which testify of Me."*

Isaiah 7:14 → Messiah's Virgin Birth *"...the Lord Himself will give you a sign. 'Behold, the virgin shall conceive and bear a Son, and shall call His name Immanuel.'"*	**Matt. 1:21-23** *"'...she will bring forth a Son, and you shall call His name Jesus, for He will save His people from their sins.' Now all this was done that it might be fulfilled which was spoken by the Lord through the prophet, saying: 'Behold, a virgin shall be with child, and bear a Son, and they shall call His name Immanuel', which is translated, 'God with us'."*
Isaiah 9:1-2 → The Light out of Galilee *"...By the way of the sea, beyond the Jordan, in Galilee of the Gentiles. The people who walked in darkness have seen a great light; those who dwell in the land of the shadow of death, upon them a light has shined."* **Isaiah 42:6-7 → The Light to the Gentiles** *"I, the Lord, have called You in righteousness, and will hold Your hand; I will keep You and give You as a covenant to the People, as a light to the Gentiles, to open blind eyes, to bring out prisoners from the prison, those who sit in darkness from the prison house."*	**Matt. 4:12-16** *"Now when Jesus heard that John had been put in prison, He departed to Galilee. And leaving Nazareth, He came and dwelt in Capernaum, which is by the sea, in the regions of Zebulun and Naphtali, that it might be fulfilled which was spoken by Isaiah the prophet, saying: 'The land of Zebulun and the land of Naphtali, the way of the sea, beyond the Jordan, Galilee of the Gentiles: the people who sat in darkness saw a great light, and upon those who sat in the region and shadow of death Light has dawned.'"* **Luke 2:30-32** *"...my eyes have seen Your salvation, which You have prepared before the face of all peoples. A light to bring revelation to the Gentiles, and the glory of Your people Israel."*
Isaiah 9:6 → The Authority of Lord Messiah *"For unto us a Child is born, unto us a Son is given, and the government will be upon His shoulder. And His name will be called Wonderful, Counselor, Mighty God, Everlasting Father, Prince of Peace."*	**Luke 2:10-11** *"... the angel said to them, 'Do not be afraid, for behold, I bring you good tidings of great joy which will be to all people. For there is born to you this day in the city of David a Savior, who is Christ the Lord."* **John 3:16** *"... God so loved the world that He gave His only begotten Son, that whoever believes in Him should not perish but have everlasting life."* **Matt. 28:18** *"... Jesus came and spoke to them, saying, 'All authority has been given to Me in heaven and on earth.'"*
Isaiah 9:7 → Messiah's Eternal Kingdom *"Of the increase of His government and peace there will be no end, upon the throne of David and over His kingdom, to order it and establish it with judgment and justice from that time forward, even forever."*	**Luke 1:31-33** *"... behold, you will conceive in your womb and bring forth a Son, and shall call His name Jesus. He will be great, and will be called the Son of the Highest; and the Lord God will give Him the throne of His father David. And He will reign over the house of Jacob forever, and of His kingdom there will be no end."*
Isaiah 11:1-2 → The Holy Spirit is with Him *"There shall come forth a Rod from the stem of Jesse, and a Branch shall grow out of his roots. The Spirit of the Lord shall rest upon Him, the Spirit of wisdom and understanding, the Spirit of counsel and might, the Spirit of knowledge and of the fear of the Lord."*	**Mark 1:10-11** *"...immediately, coming up from the water, He saw the heavens parting and the Spirit descending upon Him like a dove. Then a voice came from heaven, 'You are My beloved Son, in whom I am well pleased.'"*
Isaiah 28:16 → The Messiah is our Foundation *"...Thus says the Lord God: 'Behold, I lay in Zion a stone for a foundation, a tried stone, a precious stone, a sure foundation; whoever believes will not act hastily.'"*	**Matt. 21:42** *"Jesus said to them, 'Did you never read in the Scriptures: 'The stone which the builders rejected has become the chief cornerstone. This was the Lord's doing, and it is marvelous in our eyes'?"*
Isaiah 29:13 → The Messiah is to be worshipped *"...the Lord said: 'Inasmuch as these people draw near to Me with their mouths and honor Me with their lips, but have removed their hearts far from Me, and their fear toward Me is taught by the commandment of men."*	**Matthew 15:7-9** *"Hypocrites! Well did Isaiah prophesy about you, saying: 'These people draw near to Me with their mouth, and honor Me with their lips, but their heart is far from Me. And in vain they worship Me, teaching as doctrines the commandments of men.'"*

The 1QIsaiaha Scroll (125 BC): 19 Proofs of Isaiah's Prophecies of Jesus Christ in 730 BC

John 5:39 *"You search the Scriptures, for in them you think you have eternal life; these are they which testify of Me."*

Isaiah 35:4-6 → Messiah's Healing Ministry "Say to those who are fearful-hearted, 'Be strong, do not fear! Behold, your God will come with vengeance, with the recompense of God; He will come and save you.' Then the eyes of the blind shall be opened, and the ears of the deaf shall be unstopped. Then the lame shall leap like a deer, and the tongue of the dumb sing. For the waters shall burst forth in the wilderness, and streams in the desert."	**Luke 7:20-23** *"When the men had come to Him, they said, 'John the Baptist has sent us to You, saying, 'Are You the coming One, or do we look for another?' And that very hour He cured many people of their infirmities, afflictions, and evil spirits, and to many who were blind He gave sight. Then Jesus answered and said to them, 'Go and tell John the things you have seen and heard: that the blind see, the lame walk, the lepers are cleansed, the deaf hear, the dead are raised, the poor have the gospel preached to them. And blessed is he who is not offended because of Me."*
Isaiah 40:3-5 → Messiah's forerunner "The voice of one crying in the wilderness: 'Prepare the way of the Lord; make straight in the desert a highway for our God. Every valley shall be exalted, and every mountain and hill shall be made low; the crooked places shall be made straight, and the rough places smooth; the glory of the Lord shall be revealed, and all flesh shall see it together; for the mouth of the Lord has spoken.'"	**Matthew 3:1-3** *"In those days John the Baptist came preaching in the wilderness of Judea, and saying, 'Repent, for the kingdom of heaven is at hand!' For this is he who was spoken of by the prophet Isaiah, saying: 'The voice of one crying in the wilderness: Prepare the way of the Lord, make His paths straight.'"* **John 1:14** *"And the Word became flesh and dwelt among us, and we beheld His glory, the glory as of the only begotten of the Father, full of grace and truth."*
Isaiah 40:10-11 → The Great Shepherd "...the Lord God shall come with a strong hand, and His arm shall rule for Him, and His work before Him. He will feed His flock like a shepherd; He will gather the lambs with His arm, and carry them in His bosom, and gently lead those who are with young."	**John 10:11-14** *"I am the good shepherd. The good shepherd gives His life for the sheep. But he who is a hireling and not the shepherd, ... sees the wolf coming and leaves the sheep and flees; and the wolf catches the sheep and scatters them. The hireling flees because he is a hireling and does not care about the sheep. I am the good shepherd; and I know My sheep, and am known by My own."*
Isaiah 42:1-4 → Messiah's Meekness "Behold! My Servant whom I uphold. My Elect One in whom My soul delights! I have put My Spirit upon Him; He will bring forth justice to the Gentiles. He will not cry out, nor raise His voice, nor cause His voice to be heard in the street. A bruised reed He will not break, and smoking flax He will not quench; He will bring forth justice for truth. He will not fail nor be discouraged, till He has established justice in the earth.."	**Matthew 12:15-21** *"...when Jesus knew it, He withdrew from there; and great multitudes followed Him, and He healed them all. And He warned them not to make Him known, that it might be fulfilled which was spoken by Isaiah the prophet, saying: 'Behold! My Servant whom I have chosen, My Beloved in whom My soul is well pleased; I will put My Spirit upon Him, and He will declare justice to the Gentiles. He will not quarrel nor cry out, nor will anyone hear His voice in the streets. A bruised reed He will not break, and smoking flax He will not quench, till He sends forth justice to victory. And in His name Gentiles will trust.'"*
Isaiah 49:5-6 → God's Salvation for mankind "...now the Lord says, who formed Me from the womb to be His Servant, to bring Jacob back to Him, so that Israel is gathered to Him (for I shall be glorious in the eyes of the Lord, and My God shall be My strength), indeed He says, 'It is too small a thing that You should be My Servant, to raise up the tribes of Jacob, and to restore the preserved ones of Israel; I will also give You as a light to the Gentiles, that You should be My salvation to the ends of the earth.'"	**Matthew 23:37** *"O Jerusalem, Jerusalem, the one who kills the prophets and stones those who are sent to her! How often I wanted to gather your children together, as a hen gathers her chicks under her wings, but you were not willing!"* **Luke 2:30-32** *"...my eyes have seen Your salvation, which You have prepared before the face of all peoples. A light to bring revelation to the Gentiles, and the glory of Your people Israel."* **John 14:6** *"I am the way, the truth, and the life. No one comes to the Father except through Me."*

The IQIsaiahᵃ Scroll (125 BC): 19 Proofs of Isaiah's Prophecies of Jesus Christ in 730 BC

John 5:39 *"You search the Scriptures, for in them you think you have eternal life; these are they which testify of Me."*

Isaiah 50:5-7 ➔ Messiah's Obedience *"The Lord God has opened My ear; and I was not rebellious, nor did I turn away. I gave My back to those who struck Me, and My cheeks to those who plucked out the beard. I did not hide My face from shame and spitting. For the Lord God will help Me; therefore I will not be disgraced; therefore I will set My face like a flint, and I know that I will not be ashamed."*	▶ **Matthew 26:39** *"He went a little farther and fell on His face, and prayed, saying, 'O My Father, if it is possible, let this cup pass from Me; nevertheless, not as I will, but as You will.'"* **Matthew 26:67** *"Then they spat in His face and beat Him, and others struck Him with rods, saying, 'Prophesy to us, Christ! Who is the one who struck You?'"* **John 8:29** *"He who sent Me is with Me. The Father has not left Me alone, for I always do those things that please Him."*
Isaiah 52:13-15 ➔ Messiah: 1ˢᵗ humiliated, then one day exalted *"Behold, My Servant shall deal prudently; He shall be exalted and extolled and be very high. Just as many were astonished at You, so His visage was marred more than any man, and His form more than the sons of men; so shall He sprinkle many nations. Kings shall shut their mouths at Him; for what had not been told them they shall see, and what they had not heard they shall consider."*	▶ **Matthew 27:27-31** *"....the soldiers of the governor took Jesus ..... and gathered the whole garrison around Him. And they stripped Him and put a scarlet robe on Him. When they had woven a crown of thorns, they put it on His head, and a reed in His right hand. And they bowed the knee before Him and mocked Him, saying, 'Hail, King of the Jews!' Then they spat on Him, and took the reed and struck Him on the head. Then when they had mocked Him, they took the robe off Him, put His own clothes on Him, and led Him away to be crucified."* **Phil. 2:9** *"...God also has highly exalted Him and given Him a name which is above every name..."*
Isaiah 55:1-3 ➔ Messiah's plea to mankind *"Ho! Everyone who thirsts, come to the waters; and you who have no money, come, buy and eat. Yes, come, buy wine and milk without price. Why do you spend money for what is not bread, and your wages for what does not satisfy? Listen diligently to Me, and eat what is good, and let your soul delight itself in abundance. Incline your ear, and come to Me. Hear, and your soul shall live; and I will make an everlasting covenant with you – the sure mercies of David."*	▶ **John 7:37-38** *"On the last day, that great day of the feast, Jesus stood and cried out, saying, 'If anyone thirsts, let him come to Me and drink. He who believes in Me, as the Scripture has said, out of his heart will flow rivers of living water.'"* **Matthew 13:44** *"...the kingdom of heaven is like treasure hidden in a field, which a man found and hid; and for joy over it he goes and sells all that he has and buys that field."* **Matthew 11:28-29** *"Come to Me, all who labor and are heavy laden, and I will give you rest. Take My yoke upon you and learn from Me, for I am gentle and lowly in heart, and you will find rest for your souls."* **Acts 13:33-34** *"God has fulfilled this day for us their children, in that He has raised up Jesus...He raised Him from the dead, no more to return to corruption, He has spoken thus: 'I will give you the sure mercies of David.'"*
Isaiah 59:16-17 ➔ Messiah's Salvation *"He saw that there was no man, and wondered that there was no intercessor; therefore His own arm brought salvation for Him; and His own righteousness, it sustained Him. For He put on righteousness as a breastplate, and a helmet of salvation on His head; He put on the garments of vengeance for clothing, and was clad with zeal as a cloak."*	▶ **Mark 6:5-6** *"Now He could do no mighty work there, except that He laid His hands on a few sick people and healed them. And He marveled because of their unbelief."* **Ephesians 6:13-17** *"...take up the whole armor of God, that you may be able to withstand in the evil day, and having done all, to stand. Stand therefore, having girded your waist with truth, having put on the breastplate of righteousness, and having shod your feet with the preparation of the gospel of peace; above all, taking the shield of faith with which you will be able to quench all the fiery darts of the wicked one. And take the helmet of salvation, and the sword of the Spirit, which is the word of God."*

The 1QIsaiah^a Scroll (125 BC): 19 Proofs of Isaiah's Prophecies of Jesus Christ in 730 BC
John 5:39 *"You search the Scriptures, for in them you think you have eternal life; these are they which testify of Me."*

Isaiah 61:1-2 ➔ Messiah's Mission *"The Spirit of The Lord God is upon Me, because the Lord has anointed Me to preach good tidings to the poor; He has sent Me to heal the brokenhearted, to proclaim liberty to the captives, and the opening of the prisons to those who are bound; to proclaim the acceptable year of the Lord, and the day of vengeance of our God...."*	▶ **Luke 4:18-21** *"...He came to Nazareth, where He had been brought up. And as His custom was, He went into the synagogue on the Sabbath day, and stood up to read. And He was handed the book of the prophet Isaiah. And when He had opened the book, He found the place where it was written: 'The Spirit of the Lord is upon Me, because He has anointed Me to preach the gospel to the poor. He has sent Me to heal the brokenhearted, to preach deliverance to the captives, and recovery of sight to the blind, to set at liberty those who are oppressed, to preach the acceptable year of the Lord.' Then He closed the book, and gave it back to the attendant and sat down. And the eyes of all who were in the synagogue were fixed on Him. And He begun to say to them, 'Today this Scripture is fulfilled in your hearing.'"* **Luke 21:20,22,24** *"...when you see Jerusalem surrounded by armies, then know that its desolation is near. For these are the days of vengeance, that all things which are written may be fulfilled...and Jerusalem will be trampled by Gentiles until the times of the Gentiles are fulfilled."*
Isaiah 61:2-3 ➔ Messiah brings Comfort and Joy *"...to comfort those who mourn. To console those who mourn in Zion, to give them beauty for ashes, and the oil of joy for mourning. The garment of praise for the spirit of heaviness, that they may be called trees of righteousness, the planting of the Lord, that He may be glorified."*	▶ **Matthew 5:4** *"Blessed are those who mourn, for they shall be comforted."* **John 15:11** *"These things I have spoken to you, that My joy may remain in you, and that your joy may be full."* **2Corinthians 5:21** *"...He made Him who knew no sin to be sin for us, that we might become the righteousness of God in Him."* **Matthew 5:16** *"Let your light so shine before men, that they may see your good works and glorify your Father in heaven."* **1Peter 2:12** *"...having your conduct honorable among the Gentiles, that when they speak against you as evildoers, they may, by your good works which they observe, glorify God in the day of visitation."*

Here's three easy to read but detailed sources of information on the Dead Sea scrolls if you want to dig deeper on your own, from people who have not only spent extensive time studying the scrolls but are recognized experts in their field on them.

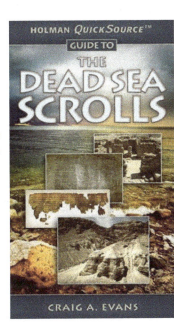
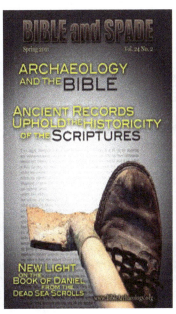

CHAPTER 3   External Evidence Test = ARCHAEOLOGY   3.1

Skeptic's Charge #9: Has archaeology confirmed or refuted the accuracy and historicity of the Bible?

Nelson Glueck (Jewish Archaeologist)[1]: *"No archaeological discovery has ever controverted a biblical reference. We can attest to the incredibly accurate historical memory of the Bible, and particularly so when it is fortified by archaeological fact."*

William F. Albright (PhD John Hopkins Univ., Pres. of International Org. of OT Scholars, Archaeologist)[1]: *"There can be no doubt that archaeology has confirmed the substantial historicity of the OT tradition. The excessive skepticism shown toward the Bible by important 18th and 19th century schools of the past has been progressively discredited. Discovery after discovery has established the accuracy of innumerable details, bringing increased recognition to the Bible as a valuable source of history."*

Millar Burrows (Yale University, Archaeologist)[1]: *"The excessive skepticism of many liberal theologians stems not from a careful examination of the available data, but from an erroneous predisposition against the supernatural. On the whole, archaeological work has unquestionably strengthened confidence in the reliability of the Scriptural record."*

THE WALLS OF JERICHO   Joshua 6:2-5,20 (Hebr. 11:30)

<u>Excavation of Jericho, 1930-1936</u>: A signed statement by members of the expedition was made to document the incredible finding, as quoted by the expedition leader, John Garstang: *"As to the main fact, then, there remains no doubt: the walls fell outwards so completely that attackers would be able to clamber up and over the ruins into the city. Why is this so unusual? Because walls of cities that are attacked from the outside do not fall outwards, they fall inwards."*

Jericho excavations of John Garstang showing remains after Israelite destruction in 1400 BC.

THE KINGS OF MESOPOTAMIA   Genesis 14:8-12

Higher critical scholarship used this account in Genesis 14 to discredit the Bible because no mention of these kings had ever been found in any source except the Bible ("they never existed – the Bible adds their names as part of a fable").

The Ebla Tablets: discovered in 1968 at Tell Mardikh excavation (Northern Syria). Ebla was a city of 260,000 people in 2300 BC. It was destroyed by Naram-Sim in 2250 BC. These tablets refer to all 5 cities (Sodom, Gomorrah, Admah, Zebolim and Zoar) and on one tablet the Cities are listed in the exact same sequence as Genesis 14.

Ebla Tablet

THE ROMAN CENSUS   Luke 2:1-3

Higher scholarship used Luke 2:1-3 to discredit Luke because no mention of a census, of people returning to their ancestral home, or of Quinirius as governor of Syria had ever been found in any source other than the Bible.

<u>Archaeological Findings:</u>
1. Censuses were 1st instituted under Augustus in 9-8 BC (matches with Luke) and held every 14 years.
2. Manuscript discovery in Egypt: *"Because of the approaching census it is necessary that all those residing for any cause away from their homes should at once prepare to return to their own governments in order that they may complete the family registration of the enrollment and that tilled lands may retain those belonging to them."*
3. An inscription discovered in Antioch names Quinirius as governor of Syria twice – once in 7 BC, again in 6 AD.

THE PAVEMENT   John 19:13

Higher critical scholarship used this account in John 19 to discredit the Bible because no mention of a "Pavement" had ever been found in any source but the Bible (therefore it never existed – it was added to "dress up the account.").

W. Albright, 'The Archaeology of Palestine': *"The Pavement was the court of the Tower of Antonia, the Roman military headquarters in Jerusalem. It was buried after the fall of Jerusalem, when the city was rebuilt in the time of Hadrian."*

Archaeology & the Bible: Ba'al Worship
(excerpts from Dennis Bratcher article, CRI/ Voice Institute)

By the 7th king of Edom, the most prevalent religious system of the Edomites, and in general the Canaanites, was the worship of **Ba'al**. What we know of the basic elements of the Ba'al myth actually comes from two groups of texts. The Babylonian creation hymn Enuma Elish describes a great battle among the gods, primarily between **Marduk**, Babylon's champion of the gods, and **Tiamat**, the primeval ocean or the "deep." Sometimes Tiamat is portrayed as a great serpentine beast, the dragon of chaos or the dragon of the sea. Marduk overcame Tiamat and her forces and after splitting her body into two parts, made the sky, stars, sun, and moon from one half, and the earth from the other. From the blood of Tiamat's defeated husband Kingu, one of the lesser gods, Ea (Enki) then created humanity to be servants of the gods so they would never have to work again. Marduk continued to bring order into the chaos caused by Tiamat, establishing the cycles of nature.

This theme of a cosmic battle among the gods personifies the struggle for life. This cosmic battle occurred anew each year and was reenacted in cultic ritual. Marduk represents the forces of order, the coming of spring with its renewal of life and the end of the reign of the chaos and death of winter. Marduk is the spring sun that gives life and renewed energy to the earth. Tiamat represents those forces that threaten human existence, the threat of a disordered world in which springtime never comes. Creation, in Babylonian thinking, was an ongoing struggle between order and chaos, a way of thinking related to the uncertainties of life in the ancient world.

The second group of texts come from **Ugarit**, in northern Syria. They are chiefly concerned with the emergence of **Ba'al** as the leader of the gods. Ba'al was the "Storm God", the bringer of rain, and thus fertility, to the land. Ba'al gave assurance of some stability in the physical world that would allow continued human existence.

There was rivalry among the gods and a struggle erupted between **Yamm**, the sea, and Ba'al, the rain. With the help of his sister **Anat**, the goddess of war, and **Astarte**, the goddess of earth and fertility,

Various carvings of Ba'al, the "Storm God"

Ba'al defeated Yamm, and his cohorts, **Tannin**, the dragon of the sea, and **Loran** (or Lothan, Isaiah 27:1), the serpent with seven heads. The gods built a magnificent house for Ba'al so that he could be at rest and provide abundant rain for the earth. But Ba'al was challenged by **Mot** (or Mut), the god of death and the underworld. Mot temporarily triumphed and Ba'al disappeared into the underworld. Anat and **Shapash**, the sun god, found Ba'al, brought him back to life, and restored him to his house.

Worship of Ba'al involved magic and rituals (including prostitution), which were to bring vitality to Ba'al in his struggle with Mot. Sexual acts by both male and female temple prostitutes were performed to arouse Ba'al who then brought rain to make Mother Earth fertile. The emphasis is on **rain**. The needed water cannot be the a flood or the salt water of Yamm (the Sea). It is life-giving rain, falling at the proper time.

While there are no surviving Canaanite religious texts, the Old Testament accounts of Ba'al worship correspond closely to the existing versions of the Ba'al myth and what is known of religious practices in surrounding areas. Israel's problem was not that they totally abandoned Yahweh for the worship of Ba'al, but that they added the worship of Ba'al to their worship of Yahweh (called **syncretism**). They had one God (Yahweh) for crises and another god (Ba'al) for everyday life. When crops were abundant, Ba'al was praised for his abundant rain. But during times of drought, not only was lack of rain a threat to survival, it was also a sign that Ba'al was unhappy. It is this context that the "contest" between **Elijah** and the prophets of Ba'al carries such significance. The issue is really who controls the rain, Ba'al or Yahweh.

Hosea and **Jeremiah** use of the metaphor of adultery or prostitution to describe the problem of Israel's Ba'al worship. The prophets condemn Ba'al worship as a sign of being unfaithful to their covenant relationship with Yahweh. This is also in the context for Yahweh being a **"jealous" God**. The idea here is that if God alone is God, as Deuteronomy 6:4 asserts, Israel cannot worship both Yahweh and Ba'al.

The Israelites struggled with Ba'al worship until the Exile. During the reign of **Ahab** and **Jezebel** (850BC), it was the state religion in the Northern Kingdom. Largely due to Jeremiah's insistence that the nation would fall because of Ba'al worship, the problem faded after the return from exile in 538BC. The **Judaism** that emerged after the exile in the reforms of **Ezra** and **Nehemiah** was passionately monotheistic, and has remained so ever since. It was partly that passion for monotheism that arose from purging Ba'al worship that led Judaism to reject **Jesus** as the Son of God. For many faithful Jews, that sounded too much like a return to a polytheistic syncretism.

Archaeology & the Bible: The Philistines

The Philistines were a people who occupied the southern coast off Canaan, their territory being named Philistia. They occupied the five cities of Gaza, Ashkelon, Ashdod, Ekron and Gath, along the coastal strip of southwestern Canaan, that belonged to Egypt up to the closing days of the Nineteenth Dynasty (ended 1185 BC). Genesis 10:13 lists them as descendants of **Ham**. The Philistines held a monolpoly on iron smithing, a skill they possibly acquired during conquests in Anatolia. These carvings of ancient Philistine warriors were found among ruins at Thebes, Egypt. They are dated to around 1200 BC (the time of Joshua).

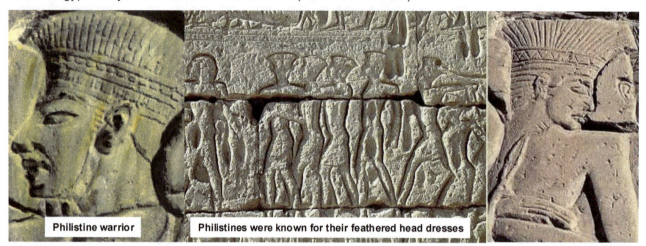

Philistine warrior

Philistines were known for their feathered head dresses

The Bible contains roughly 250 references to the Philistines or Philistia, referring to them as "uncircumcised", just like the Hamitic peoples, such as Canaanites, which the Bible relates encountered the Israelites following the Exodus (1Samuel 17:26-36, 2Samuel 1:20, Judges 14:3). The Bible records several battles between Israel and the Philistines, such as David defeating Goliath in single combat (1 Samuel 17).

The Philistines were culturally related to the Mycenean world and came from a point of origin in the Aegean thought by most scholars to have been Crete. Deuteronomy 2:23 records that the Caphtorites came from Crete, destroyed the Avvites and took their land. They conquered the coastal Caananite population, and together the conquered people and the invaders created a blended, west-Semitic speaking culture that we call Philistine.

The Philistines formed part of the "Sea Peoples" who attacked Egypt during the 19th Dynasty. Though they were eventually repulsed by **Ramses III**, he resettled them to rebuild the coastal towns in Canaan. Papyrus Harris I details the achievements of the reign of Ramses III. In the brief description of the outcome of the battles in Year 8 is the description of the fate of the Sea Peoples. Ramses tells us that, having brought the imprisoned Sea Peoples to Egypt, he *"settled them in strongholds, bound in my name. Numerous were their classes like hundred-thousands. I taxed them all, in clothing and grain from the storehouses and granaries each year."*

The Philistines lost their independence to **Tiglath-Pileser III** of Assyria by 732 BC, and revolts in following years were all crushed. **Nebuchadnezzar II** of Babylon eventually conquered all of Syria and the kingdom of Judah, and the former Philistine cities became part of the Neo-Babylonian Empire. There are few references to the Philistines after this time. However, Ezekiel 25:16 and Zechariah 9:6 mention the Philistines, so that they still existed as a people after the Babylonian invasion. The Philistines disappear as a distinct group by the late 5th century BC, the mixed people of the former Philstine cities having been converted to Judaism by the Hasmoneans.

Dagon

Philistine sanctuary of Tell Qasileh, consecrated to Dagon

Philistine culture was almost fully integrated with that of the Canaanites. The deities they worshiped were the Canaanite gods Ba'al, Astarte and Dagon (the fish god - see Judges 16:23; 1 Sam 5:2-5).

Archaeology & the Bible: The Hittite Empire 3.2

Canaanite tribe descended from Heth (Gen.10:1,9,15), driven out of Canaan by Israel under Joshua.

Skeptic's Charge #10: "Only the Bible records the Hittites as a significant, powerful kingdom. Most experts either regarded their mention as historically worthless, people invented as a fictional story or given status as a great nation when in fact they were (depending on the "expert") non-existent or quite insignificant."

Gen. 23:10	Abraham bought a burial place for Sarah from Ephron the Hittite.
Gen. 25:8-9	Abraham is buried in the cave bought from Ephron the Hittite.
Gen. 26:34-35	At age 40, Esau takes Hittite women for wives.
Exo. 23:20-23	God lists the Hittites as people to be conquered and destroyed.
Deuter. 7:1-2	God lists the Hittites as people to not form a covenant with.
Joshua 3:9-10	Joshua lists the Hittites as people to drive out of Canaan.
Joshua 11:1-9	The Hittites join the nations that resist Joshua's advance, only to be defeated at the waters of Merom.
Judges 3:4-6	Intermarriage occurs between the Hebrews and the Hittites.
1Samuel 26:6	Hittites are enrolled in David's army.
2Samuel 11:3	David inquires after Bathsheba, the wife of Uriah the Hittite (Uriah mentioned in 2Samuel 23:39).
1Kings 9:20-21	Hittites are listed as some of the people Solomon enslaves for use as forced labor.
1Kings 11:1-6	Hittite women are listed as some of the wives Solomon takes, in direct disobedience to the Lord.

Historical Liberal Criticism: If the Hittites even existed, they were very insignificant
Excerpts from "The Empire of the Hittites" by William Wright (1884)

" The Rev. T. K. Cheyne, Fellow of the same College, writing on the Hittites in the new edition of 'Encyclopedia Britannica', treats the Bible statements regarding the Hittites as unhistorical and unworthy of credence. Referring to the mention of the Hittites in the Book of Genesis, he says: 'The lists of these pre-Israelitish populations cannot be taken as strictly historical documents', 'they cannot be taken as of equal authority with Egyptian and Assyrian inscriptions'; and, carrying out his comparison, he adds: 'Not less unfavorable to the accuracy of the Old Testament references to the Hittites is the evidence deducible from proper names'.

Professor W. F. Newman, in speaking of the Hittites, says, 'The unhistorical tone is too manifest to allow of our easy belief in it'. He thinks 'there was a real event at bottom', for Xenophon in his Anabasis speaks of dangerous night panics in the Greek and Persian hosts, and therefore the Syrian army may have fled in a sudden panic. 'But', he adds of the Bible account, 'the particular ground of alarm attributed to them does not exhibit the writer's acquaintance with the times in very favorable light'. 'No Hittite kings can have compared in power with the king of Judah, the real and near ally, who is not named at all'. 'Nor is there a single mark of acquaintance with the contemporaneous history'.

Professor W. F. Newman discredits the incident because he thinks the Hittites were too insignificant to have caused alarm to the Syrian hosts."

The findings of Archaeology:

The Clay Tablets of Assyria and Egypt (dating 1287 BC) = 10,000 clay tablets discovered in 1906-1907 at Boghazkoi in Central Turkey which record, among other things, a fierce battle between Ramses II and the Hittites at Kadesh on the Orotes River and a military treaty between the Hittites and the Egyptians. Also, Egyptian artists depicted the Hittites as having features that identify them today as ancestors of the Armenian race.

The Hittite palace near Antioch in Syria (dating 1600 BC) = Sir Leonard Woolley (famous for his discoveries at Abraham's city of Ur): "The frequent references in the Old Testament to Hittites living in Syria and Palestine in the Patriarchal age, which have often been rejected as anachronisms, have proven sound history."

William F. Albright ("Recent Discoveries in Bible Lands")[1]: "In 1871 some inscriptions in a previously unknown type of hieroglyphic script were discovered at Hamath in Syria, and 8 years later A.H. Salce identified the script with that of inscriptions known from Asia Minor. The biblical term 'Hittite' was doubted by many, but it has proved to be correct."

John Elder ("Prophets, Idols and Diggers")[1]: "One of the striking confirmations of Bible history to come from the science of archaeology is the recovery of the Hittite people and their empires. Here is a people whose name appears again and again in the Old Testament, but who in secular history had been completely forgotten and whose very existence was considered to be extremely doubtful."

The Hittite Civilization: its legacy found only within the Bible and archaeology
- 2 periods of great Hittite power: the 1st in 1800 BC and the 2nd around 1400 – 1200 BC.
- 1400-1200 BC: the Hittites are powerful during **Suppiluliuma's** reign. Contact was very strong with Egypt.
- 1200 BC: Boghazkoi fell, but Hittite influence remained strong in Carchemish, Hamath and North Syria.
- The Assyrians start to dominate, and finally absorb the Hittites into their culture:
  - Assyrian emperor Tiglathphileser I (1100 BC) fought with the Hittites and other peoples of Western Asia.
  - Assyrian emperor Ashurnaisirpal (885-860 BC) put Sangara, king of Carchemish, under tribute.
  - Assyrian emperor Sargon II (717 BC) captures Carchemish.

> **Fred Wright** (*"Highlights of Archaeology in Bible Lands"*)[1]:
> *"The Bible picture of the Hittites fits in perfectly with what we know of the Hittite nation from the monuments. As an empire they never conquered the land of Canaan itself, although Hittite local tribes did settle there at an early date. Nothing discovered by the excavators has in any way discredited the Biblical account. Scripture accuracy has once more been proven by the archaeologists."*

Who were the Hittites (1600BC – 717 BC)?

The Hittites were a people who once lived in what is modern Turkey and northern Syria. Most of what we know about them today comes from ancient texts that have been recovered. The first indication of their existence occurred in about 1900 BC, in the region that was to become Hatti. There, they established the town of Nesa. Over the next 300 years, their influence grew until in about 1680 BC, a true empire was born.

This original kingdom was founded by a leader known as **Labarna**, and the kingdom was expanded by later rulers all across Anatolia and down to the Mediterranean Sea. So strong was this kingdom that in 1595 BC, they were able to raid Babylon. However, the kingdom was only as strong as the current ruler, and within about 120 years, it began to crumble.

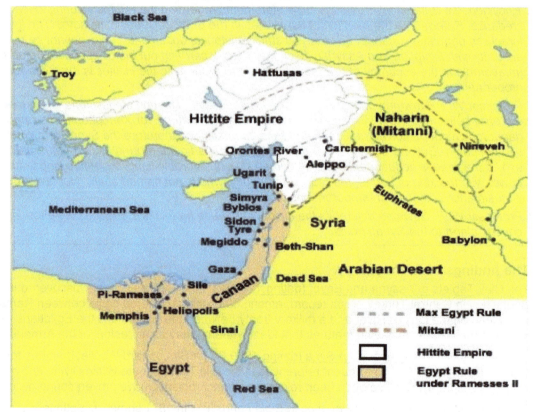

In Egypt, when their empire became weak as it did during three intermediate periods, usually due to a decentralization of government, the Nubians to the south (Egypt's only true neighbors) most often prospered.

They frequently took back land gained by the Egyptians when Egypt was strong, only to lose it once more when Egypt recovered.

So it apparently was with the Hittites. As their empire weakened around 1500 BC, the Mitanni empire to the south seems to have gained in strength. The control over the Hittite kingdom soon passed to the rulers of the Hangilbat region, who apparently forged alliances with the Egyptian kings. Within what was left of the old Hittite kingdom, a new ruling class of aristocracy took over. This weak Middle Kingdom lasted for about 100 years.

While the old Hittite kingdom was indeed strong, the new Hittite kingdom, lasting from about 1400-1193BC was even more powerful. In fact, at the time, it was one of the most powerful kingdoms in the known world, rivaling Egypt, Babylonia and Assyria. During this period, the Hittites were almost constantly at war, either in order to claim territory from their neighbors, or to protect their territory from other neighbors.

The Hittites and Egypt

It was at this time (1400-1193BC) we see the greatest contact, or at least the most extensively documented contact, between the Hittites and the Egyptians.

At its greatest level of power this Hittite empire, along with the other great powers of the Ancient Near East, all wished to dominate and exploit the economic resources and trade of the Syria region. At this time, Syria was the crossroads of world commerce. Products from the Aegean entered the Near East by ports such as Ugarit, whose ships dominated maritime trade in the eastern Mediterranean.

Hittite soldier   Hittites battling Egyptians

The merchandise from these ships was then distributed over an extensive network of trade routes, which were also used by merchants who brought raw materials such as precious metals, tin, copper and other merchandise from as far away as Iran and Afghanistan to trade in the emporia of Syria. Hence, Syria offered a considerable motive for the predatory powers of the region. Therefore, it is perhaps understandable that the great powers of Egypt, Mitanni and Hatti expended much effort, along with blood to control this vitally strategic region.

The maximum extent of the Hittite Empire ca. 1300 BC is shown in red, the Egyptian sphere of influence in green. The approximate extent of the Hittite Old Kingdom under Hantili I (ca. 1590 BC) is shown in darker red.

Relief of Suppiluliuma II, last known king of the Hittite Empire.

In the first half of the 14th century BC, the Hittite kingdom was ruled by **Suppiluliuma**, who began a successful campaign against the Kingdom of Mitanni in northern Syria. In his earliest campaigns in Syria, Suppiluliuma conquered the Mitanni states of Aleppo, Alalakh, Nuhashshe and Tunip in northern Syria. In the second Syrian war, he crossed the River Euphrates into Ishuwa and marched south. He surprised Mitanni, attacking the empire directly and sacking the capital Washukkanni. The small kingdoms in Syria then fell to him one after the other.

This resulted in the destruction of a status quo in the region, which was the culmination of the peace treaty between Egypt and the Kingdom of Mitanni arranged during the reign of Tuthmosis IV. In fact, it was the early efforts of the Hittite kingdom to whittle away at the Mitanni Empire that had caused the truce between Egypt and Mitanni in the first place, so that they might avoid a two-front war with the Hittites on one side and the Egyptians on the other. However, these efforts did not stop the Hittites from the destruction of the Mitanni empire, and in the end, the Egyptians had to contend with the Hittites over the Syrian region as the Mitanni empire fell apart.

Suppiluliuma sought initially to avoid conflict with Egypt. Egypt held central and southern Syrian territories for some 200 years, reaping considerable wealth from them. The perception that these borders marked the true boundaries of the Egyptian empire of this period had become impressed on the Egyptian mind as fixed. In all likelihood, Egypt would take strong measures against any power that encroached upon that region.

These territories included the city state of Kadesh, and the Hittite king had actually sought to avoid any occupation of that city. However, the king of Kadesh, operating as he believed was in the interests of his Egyptian overlord, attempted to block the Hittite advance southwards. He was defeated and the leading men of the city, including both the king and his son, Aitakama, were carried off to Hattusa, the Hittite capital of this period.

Yet the Hittites returned Aitakama, who took back control of Kadesh, seemingly renewing the status of the city as a vassal of Egypt, so the Egyptians were placated. However, within a short time of his return, Aitakama began to act in a manner that suggested he may well have become a stooge for the Hittite ruler, as rulers of other Egyptian vassal cities reported attempts by him to subvert them to the Hittite cause.

Egypt was finally forced to act in order to protect its territories. Though sparsely documented, an Egyptian assault on Kadesh in the reign of Akhenaten is now assumed to have occurred, and failed. Afterwards, the city formally passed into the hands of the Hittites, and its recovery became the focus of Egyptian military efforts down until the 19th Dynasty reign of Ramses II, though the first substantial efforts were made by Ramesses II's father, Seti I.

With a strong Hittite military presence in Syria that was not offset by any similar Egyptian equivalent, the balance of power shifted in the region and soon other vassal states of Egypt fell to the Hittites without bloodshed.

The Hittite Military

The Hittite military was built around the **chariot** and infantry, but they also employed considerable mercenary troops during their campaigns. Just as in Egypt, the chariotry attracted men from nobility, while the infantry was of lesser status. However, unlike the Egyptians, the chariot was the Hittite principal offensive weapon. This difference also extended to the very design and implementation of their chariotry. They viewed the chariot as essentially an assault weapon designed to crash into and break up groups of enemy infantry. It was a much heavier vehicle then that of the Egyptians, with a central axle strong enough to carry a 3-man crew. It was also less maneuverable and slower than its Egyptian counterpart.

When used under ideal conditions, the Hittite chariotry was very effective. It would open the way for their infantry to follow through and finish off the enemy. The infantry were armed with long thrusting spears and short stabbing daggers similar to those employed by their chariotry.

As an enemy of Egypt, **Ramesses II** condescendingly spoke of them as "effeminate ones" because the Hittites wore their hair long. But he would learn quickly that the Hittite warriors were every bit as brave and formidable as the Egyptian army, for the stage was set for the first battle in history that was well documented at Kadesh. He would eventually meet, fight, made peace with, and even marry into the Hittite empire, all within his long reign.

The Lion Gate at Hattusa, Turkey. This was 1 of the 2 city gates. The arc is typical for Hittite architecure. Hattusa was the capital of the Hittite empire. It was located near the modern-day village formerly known as Boğazköy (now named Boğazkale in Corum Province, Turkey), & was set in a loop of the Kizil Irmak river in central Anatolia.

The Line of Hittite Kings

KING	ROYAL RELATIONSHIP	CHRONOLOGY
Pithana		early 18th c.
Anitta	son of Pithana	mid 18th c.
Labarna	first known Hittite king	1680-1650
Hattusili I	nephew/adopted son of Labarna	1650-1620
Mursili I	grandson/adopted son of Hattusili I	1620-1590
Hantili	assassin and brother-in-law of Mursili I	1590-1560
Zidanta I	son-in-law of Hantili	1560-1550
Ammuna	son of Hantili	1550-1530
Huzziya I	son of Ammuna?	1530-1525
Telipinu	son of Zidanta I?/brother-in-law of Ammuna	1525-1500
Tahurwaili	?	
Alluwamna	son-in-law of Huzziya I	
Hantili II	son of Alluwamna	1500-1450
Zidanta II	?	
Huzziya II	?	
Muwatalli I	?	
Tudhaliya II	son of Huzziya II?	1450-1420
Arnuwanda I	son-in-law of Tudhaliya II	1420-1400
Tudhaliya III	son of Arnuwanda I	1400-1380
Tudhaliya	son of Tudhaliya III	1380?
Hattusili II	?	
Suppiluliuma I	son of Tudhaliya III or Hattusili II	1380-1340
Arnuwanda II	son of Suppiluliuma I	1340-1339
Mursili II	son of Suppiluliuma I	1339-1306
Muwatalli II	son of Mursili II	1306-1282
Mursili III	son of Muwatalli II	1282-1275
Hattusili III	son of Mursili II	1275-1250
Tudhaliya IV	son of Hattusili III	1250-1220
Karunta	son of Muwatalli/cousin of Tudhaliya IV	?
Arnuwanda III	son of Tudhaliya IV	1220-1215
Suppiluliuma II	son of Tudhaliya IV	1215-1200

Archaeology & the Bible: The Assyrian Empire   3.3

The Assyrians were a northern Semitic people that gained ascendancy in the regions of Mesopotamia, Syria, Palestine, Armenia, and even Egypt, in a period ranging from 1200-612BC.

Skeptic's Charge #11: "Only the Bible (mainly Jonah, Nahum and Isaiah) records the Assyrians, with their capital of Nineveh, as a significant, powerful kingdom. Most experts regarded the biblical accounts of Nineveh as historically worthless, invented as a fictional story."

What is the prophetic significance of "Nahum"?

- *Nahum* (663-654 BC) means "consolation" and is a short form of *Nehemiah* ("consolation of Yahweh").
- The book of *Nahum* is a specific declaration by God against Nineveh, prior to her destruction in 612 BC. About 150 years before *Nahum*, *Jonah* declared Nineveh's destruction, and they repented (795-775 BC).
- But soon afterwards the city returned to the violence and idolatry of earlier king Assurnasirpal (he believed in extreme cruelty towards captives of war, to terrorize surrounding nations).

Nineveh - biblical accounts:

- First mentioned in Genesis 10:11 ($\approx$ 1600 BC), with no mention for another 820 years until *Jonah* ($\approx$ 780 BC), where Nineveh is the flourishing capital of the Assyrian empire (2Kings 19:36, Isaiah 37:37).
- Besides Nahum, Zephaniah 2:13-15 ($\approx$ 630 BC) predicts Nineveh's destruction along with the fall of the Assyrian empire, which historically occurred in 612 BC.
- Jesus mentions Nineveh 800 years after *Zephaniah*, in Matthew 12:41 and Luke 11:32 ($\approx$ 70 AD).

Nineveh – ARCHAEOLOGY confirms PROPHECY:

- Up until the 1840's, knowledge of the great Assyrian empire and its magnificent capital was nearly zero. Other cities that perished had left ruins to mark their sites and tell of their former greatness; but of Nineveh, not a single vestige seemed to remain (even its location was a matter of guessing). In fulfillment of prophecy, Nineveh was buried out of sight, and no one knew its grave.
- After being lost for more than 2,000 years, Nineveh with all its palaces was discovered by archeologist Austen Henry Layard in 1847, revealing the life and manners of this ancient people, their arts of war and peace, their religious practices, their architecture, and the magnificence of their monarchs.
- The streets of Nineveh have been explored, the inscriptions on the bricks and tablets and sculptured figures have been read, and now the secrets of Assyrian history have been brought to light.

Nineveh - the library of King Assurbanipal (grandson of Sennacherib):

- Incredible find: $\approx$10,000 tablets, all written with Assyrian characters. They contain a record of the history, laws, and religion of Assyria. The library contains also old Accadian documents, which are the oldest extant documents in the world, dating as far back as the time of Abraham (the alphabet existed back when Moses wrote Genesis!).

Nineveh - the greatest of all ancient cities:

- Nineveh stretched 30 miles along the river Tigris and 10 miles from the river back toward the hills. Its position on the great highway between the Mediterranean and Indian Ocean brought in incredible wealth.
- Josh McDowell ("Evidence that Demands a Verdict")[1]: *"The specifications for the size and might of Nineveh made it one of the greatest cities in the ancient world:*
  - *The inner wall of Nineveh was 100 feet tall (10-story bldg.) and 50 feet thick (6-7 cars abreast)*
  - *The top of the wall had room for 3 chariots side-by-side, with towers 200 feet tall (20-story building)*
  - *The city was surrounded by a 150-foot wide moat, and a total circumference of the city of 7 miles*
  - *The distance from the inside of the inner wall to the inside of the outer wall was almost 1/2 mile".*

Assyrian soldiers at Nineveh

the magnificent walls of Nineveh

Cuneiform tablet: the fall of Nineveh

Bible & Assyrian Library: Assyria, Israel & Judah

Shalmaneser III (858-824 BC)	Adad-nirari III (810-783 BC)	Tiglath-pileser III (744-727 BC)	Shalmaneser V (726-722 BC)	Sargon II (722-705 BC)	Sennacherib (704-687 BC)	Esarhaddon (680-669 BC)	Assurbanipal (669-627 BC)
Ahab king in Israel (874-858 BC)	**Jehoahaz** king in Israel (814-798 BC)	**Menahem** king in Israel (752-742 BC)	**Hoshea** king in Israel (732-722 BC)	2Kings 17:24-41 Sargon II resettles Samaria with foreigners, because Israel refuses to follow the Lord.	**Hezekiah** king in Judah (716-687 BC)	**Manasseh** king in Judah (697-643 BC)	 Egypt breaks free in 652 BC...
Jehu king in Israel (841-814 BC)	2Kings 13:1-5 Jehoahaz calls on God for deliverance from Syria	2Kings 15:17-20 Tiglath-pileser (Pul) enters Israel; Menahem pays him tribute, and Tiglath withdraws	2Kings 17:1-23; 2Kings 18:10-12 Hoshea paid tribute to Tiglath-pileser, but he revolted twice against Assyria after Tiglath-pileser.		2Kings 18:13-16 while Sennacherib attacked Lachish, Hezekiah at first paid him tribute.	2Kings 21:1-18, 2Chronicles 33:1-20	Scythians attack Assyria in 626 BC: empire begins to crumble....
			After 2nd revolt (722 BC), Sargon II attacked Israel, taking her away captive. All this was because Israel refused to follow the Lord.	Isaiah 20:1 Sargon II attacks Judah (712 BC) and surrounding nations	2Kings 18:17-37, 2Kings 19:1-37; Isaiah 36:1-22, Isaiah 37:1-38 Sennacherib mocks Hezekiah & blasphemes God, demanding Judah surrender. Isaiah prophesies Sennacherib's destruction.	Manasseh's evil reign leads to Judah being taken by Esarhaddon.	Chaldean king Nabopolassar (626-605 BC) conquers Babylon, moves against Assyria...
		Pekah king in Israel (752-732 BC)					Chaldeans & Medes form alliance, attack Nineveh in 612 BC - collapses in 3 months. Medes & Babylonians divide up its spoils.
		Ahaz king in Judah (735-716 BC) 2Kings 15:29, 16:1-9; Isaiah 7:1-17, 8:1-8 Ahaz rushes to Tiglath-pileser & pays him tribute, Tiglath-pileser defeats Syria & kills king Rezin, takes control of northern Israel & deports its people to Assyria.					

Jonah (795-775 BC)
Jonah 3:4-10 Adad-nirari III repents, God doesn't destroy Nineveh

Isaiah (740-680BC)

Nahum (663-654BC)

"Black Obelisk of Shalmaneser III"(6.5' tall): it depicts Jehu kneeling as he pays tribute, giving gifts to Shalmaneser III (only existing representation found of a king of Israel).

Adad-nirari III Annals found at Nimrud, 803BC: he attacks Syria, who then stops it's attack on Israel to defend itself against him

Sargon II Inscription (720 BC): capture & deportation of Israel

"Taylor Prism" Sennacherib invades Judah (701 BC)

Esarhaddon "Prism B" capture of Manasseh (Judah)

Nabonidus Stele: Sennacherib's sons murder him (681 BC) (2Kings 19:35-37)

Nineveh's Library: Archaeology confirms Biblical History!

Archaeology and the Kings of Assyria

3.4

Assyrian Kings Who Had Contact With Israel & Judah

- Shalmaneser III (858-824 B.C.)
- Shamshi-Adad V (823-811 B.C.)
- Adad-Nirari III (810-783 B.C.)
- Shalmaneser IV (782-773 B.C.)
- Ashur-dan III (772-755 B.C.)
- Ashur-Nirari V (754-745 B.C.)
- Tiglath-pileser III (744-727 B.C.)
- Shalmaneser V (726-722 B.C.)
- Sargon III (721-705 B.C.)
- Sennacherib (704-681 B.C.)
- Esarhaddon (680-669 B.C.)
- Ashurbanipal (668-633 B.C.)
- Ashur-eti-ilani (632-629 B.C.)
- Sin-shum-lishir (628-624 B.C.)
- Sin-shar-ishkum (623-612 B.C.)
- Ashur-uballit (611-608 B.C.)

Sennacherib

Assurbanipal

Shalmaneser III (858-824)

Shalmaneser III, the son and successor of Ashurnasirpal, was his father's equal in both brutality and energy. His inscriptions record his considerable achievements but do not conceal his failures. His campaigns were directed mostly against Syria. While he was able to conquer northern Syria and make it a province, in the south he could only weaken the strong state of Damascus and was unable, even after several wars, to eliminate it. In 841 he laid unsuccessful siege to Damascus.

In 841, King Jehu of Israel was forced to pay tribute (see **"Black Obelisk of Shalmaneser III"** below). In his invasion of Cilicia, Shalmaneser had only partial success. The same was true of the kingdom of Urartu in Armenia, but he did capture immense quantities of lumber and building stone. The king and the general Dayyan-Ashur went several times to western Iran, where they found such states as Mannai in northwestern Iran and, farther away in the southeast, the Persians. They also encountered the Medes during these wars.

Black Obelisk of Shalmaneser III:

- language = Akkadian (neo-Assyrian)
- black limestone, 2.0 meters tall
- picture of Israel king Jehu bowing, paying tribute
- discovered 1846, site = present-day Nimrud (Iraq)
- archaeologist = Austen Henry Layard
- location = British Museum (inventory #BM WAA 118885

In Babylonia, Marduk-zakir-shumi I ascended the throne about the year 855. His brother Marduk-bel-usati rebelled against him, and in 851 the king was forced to ask Shalmaneser for help. Shalmaneser was only too happy to oblige. When the usurper had been finally eliminated (850), Shalmaneser went to southern Babylonia, which at that time was almost completely dominated by Aramaeans. There he encountered the Chaldeans, mentioned for the first time in 878 BC, and whom Shalmaneser made tributaries.

During his long reign he built temples, palaces, and fortifications in Assyria as well as in the other capitals of his provinces. His artists created many statues and stelae. The bronze doors from the town of Imgur-Enlil (Balawat) in Assyria portray the course of his campaigns and other undertakings in rows of pictures, often very lifelike. Hundreds of delicately carved ivories were carried away from Phoenicia, and many of the artists along with them; these later made Kalakh a centre for the art of ivory sculpture.

Shalmaneser III & Assyrian cruelty

Shalmaneser III attacking Hamath (Isaiah 37:11-13)

In the last four years of Shalmaneser's reign, he appointed his younger son Shamshi-Adad as the new crown prince. Forced to flee to Babylonia, **Shamshi-Adad V** (823-811BC) managed to regain the kingship with the help of Marduk-zakir-shumi I. As king he campaigned with varying success in southern Armenia and Azerbaijan, later turning against Babylonia. He won several battles against the Babylonian kings Marduk-balassu-iqbi and Baba-aha-iddina (818-812BC) and pushed through to Chaldea. Babylonia remained independent, however.

Adad-nirari III (810-783)

Shamshi-Adad V died while Adad-nirari III was still a minor. His Babylonian mother, Sammu-ramat, took over the regency, governing until 806. The Greeks, who called her Semiramis, credited her with legendary accomplishments, but historically little is known about her. Adad-nirari later led several campaigns against the Medes and also against Syria and Palestine. In 804BC he reached Gaza, but Damascus proved invincible. He also fought in Babylonia, helping to restore order in the north.

Shalmaneser IV (783-773 BC) fought against Urartu, then at the height of its power under King Argishti (780-755 BC). He successfully defended eastern Mesopotamia against attacks from Armenia. On the other hand, he lost most of Syria after a campaign against Damascus in 773 BC. The reign of **Ashur-dan III** (772-755 BC) was shadowed by rebellions and by epidemics of plague. Of **Ashur-nirari V** (754-746 BC) little is known.

In Assyria, many of the conquered lands were combined to form large provinces. The governors of these provinces sometimes acquired considerable independence, particularly under the weaker monarchs after Adad-nirari III. The influx of displaced peoples into the cities of Assyria created large metropolitan centers. The spoils of war, together with an expanding trade, created a well-to-do commercial class. There was much new building. A standing occupational force was needed in the provinces, and these troops grew steadily in proportion to the total military forces. There are no records on the training of officers or on military logistics. The civil service also expanded, the largest administrative body being the royal court, with thousands of functionaries and craftsmen in the several residential cities. In religion, the official cults of Ashur and Ninurta continued, while the religion of the common people went its separate way.

In Babylonia not much was left of the feudal structure; the large landed estates fell prey to the inroads of the Aramaeans, who were at first half nomadic. The leaders of their tribes and clans replaced the former landlords. Agriculture on a large scale was no longer possible except on the outskirts of metropolitan areas. The many Babylonian schools for scribes may have prevented the emergence of an Aramaean literature. In any case, the Aramaeans seem to have been absorbed into the Babylonian culture. The religious cults in the cities remained essentially the same. The Babylonian empire was slowly reduced to poverty, except in some of the cities.

> **The Neo-Assyrian Empire (746 – 610BC)** No other period of Assyrian history has an abundance of sources as those for the interval from 745-640BC. About 2,400 letters have been published. Usually the senders and recipients of these letters are the king and high government officials. Among them are reports from royal agents about foreign affairs and letters about cultic matters. Treaties, oracles, queries to the sun god about political matters, and prayers of or for kings contain a great deal of additional information. There are paintings and wall reliefs, which are often very informative.

Tiglath-pileser III (745-727), Shalmaneser V (726-722)

The decline of Assyrian power after 780BC was notable. Syria and considerable lands in the north were lost. A military coup deposed King Ashur-nirari V and raised a general named Tiglath-pileser III to the throne, who brought the empire to its greatest expanse. He reduced the size of the provinces in order to break the partial independence of the governors. He also invalidated the tax privileges of cities such as Ashur and Harran in order to distribute the tax load more evenly over the entire realm. Military equipment was improved substantially.

Tiglath-pileser III (Pul)
(2Kings 15:19-20)

Tiglath-pileser III's warriors conquering a city

Prisoners of Tiglath-pileser III led into captivity

In 746BC he went to Babylonia to aid Nabu-nasir (747-734BC) in his fight against Aramaean tribes. Tiglath-pileser defeated the Aramaeans and then made visits to the large cities of Babylonia. There he tried to secure the support of the priesthood by patronizing their building projects. Babylonia retained its independence. In 743BC he went to Syria, defeating there an army of Urartu. The Syrian city of Arpad, which had formed an alliance with Urartu, did not surrender so easily. It took Tiglath-pileser three years to conquer Arpad. He massacred the inhabitants and destroyed the city.

In 734BC Tiglath-pileser invaded southern Syria and the Philistine territories in Palestine, going as far as the Egyptian border. **Damascus** and **Israel** tried to resist him, seeking to ally with **Judah**. But **Ahaz of Judah** asked Tiglath-pileser for help. In 733BC Tiglath-pileser devastated **Israel** and forced it to surrender large territories. In 732BC he advanced upon Damascus, first devastating the gardens outside the city and then conquering the capital and killing the king, whom he replaced with a governor. The queen of southern Arabia, Samsil, was now obliged to pay tribute, being permitted in return to use the harbor of **Gaza**, which was in Assyrian hands.

When King Nabonassar of Babylonia died, the Aramaean Ukin-zer crowned himself king. In 731BC Tiglath-pileser fought and beat him and his allies, but he did not capture Ukin-zer until 729BC. This time he did not appoint a new king for Babylonia but assumed the crown himself under the name Pulu (**Pul** in the Old Testament).

In his old age he focused on improving his capital, **Kalakh**. He rebuilt the palace of Shalmaneser III, filled it with treasures from his wars, and decorated the walls with bas-reliefs of warlike character, as if designed to intimidate the onlooker with their presentation of gruesome executions. These pictorial narratives on slabs, sometimes painted, have also been found in Syria, at the sites of several provincial capitals of ancient Assyria.

Tiglath-pileser was succeeded by his son **Shalmaneser V** (726-722), who continued the policy of his father. As king of Babylonia, he called himself Ululai. Almost nothing is known about his enterprises, since his successor destroyed all his inscriptions. The Old Testament relates that he marched against **Hoshea** of **Israel** in 724BC after Hoshea had rebelled. He was probably assassinated during the long siege of Samaria. His successor maintained that the god Ashur had withdrawn his support of Shalmaneser V for acts of disrespect.

Sargon II (721-705)

Assuming the old name of **Sharru-kin** (Sargon in the Bible), meaning "Legitimate King," he assured himself of the support of the priesthood and the merchant class by restoring privileges they had lost, particularly the tax exemptions of the great temples. The change of sovereign in Assyria triggered another crisis in Babylonia. An Aramaean prince from the south, Marduk-apal-iddina II (the biblical Merodach-Baladan), seized power in Babylon in 721BC and was able to retain it until 710BC with the help of Humbanigash I of Elam.

A first attempt by Sargon to recover Babylonia miscarried when Elam defeated him in 721BC. During the same year the Samaria was captured. The Samarian upper class was deported, and **Israel** became an Assyrian province. **Samaria** was repopulated with Syrians and Babylonians. **Judah** remained independent by paying tribute. In 720BC Sargon squelched a rebellion in Syria that had been supported by Egypt. Then he defeated both Hanunu of Gaza and an Egyptian army near the Egyptian border.

From 717-716BC he campaigned in northern Syria, making **Carchemish** (Hittite stronghold) one of his provinces. He went to Cilicia to prevent further encroachments of the Phrygians under King Midas (Assyrian: Mita). In order to protect his ally, the state of Mannai, in Azerbaijan, Sargon embarked on a campaign in Iran in 719BC and incorporated parts of Media as provinces of his empire. In 714BC, under the leadership of the crown prince Sennacherib, the Assyrian army infiltrated Urartu, which was also threatened from the north by the Cimmerians. Many of their messages and reports have been preserved. The longest inscription ever composed by the Assyrians about a year's enterprise (430 very long lines) is dedicated to this Urartu campaign of 714BC.

The strong points of Urartu must have been well fortified. Sargon tried to avoid them by going through the province of Mannai and attacking the Median principalities on the eastern side of Lake Urmia. In the meantime, hoping to surprise the Assyrian troops, Rusa of Urartu had closed the narrow pass lying between Lake Urmia and Sahand Mount. Sargon, anticipating this, led a small band of cavalry in a surprise charge that developed into a great victory for the Assyrians. Rusa fled and died. The Assyrians destroyed all the cities, fortifications, and even irrigation works of Urartu. They did not conquer Tushpa (the capital) but took possession of the mountain city of Musasir. The spoils were immense.

Sargon was now free to settle accounts with Marduk-apal-iddina of Babylonia. Abandoned by his ally Shutruk-Nahhunte II of Elam, Marduk-apal-iddina found it best to flee, first to his native land on the Persian Gulf and later to Elam. Because the Aramaean prince had made himself very unpopular with his subjects, Sargon was hailed as the liberator of Babylonia. He complied with the wishes of the priesthood and at the same time put down the Aramaean nobility. He was satisfied with the modest title of governor of Babylonia.

Sargon resided in Kalakh, but he then found a new capital north of Nineveh. He called the city Dur-Sharrukin--"Sargonsburg" (modern **Khorsabad**). He erected his palace on a high terrace in the northeastern part of the city.

The temples of the main gods, smaller in size, were built within the palatial rectangle, which was surrounded by a special wall. This arrangement enabled Sargon to supervise the priests better than had been possible in the old, large temple complexes. Desiring that his palace match the vastness of his empire, Sargon planned it in monumental dimensions. Stone reliefs of two **winged bulls** with human heads flanked the entrance ; they were much larger than anything comparable built before. The walls were decorated with long rows of bas-reliefs showing scenes of war and festive processions. A comparison with a well-executed stela of the Babylonian king Marduk-apal-iddina shows that the fine arts of Assyria had far surpassed those of Babylonia.

Sargon II
(Isaiah 20:1)

Sargon II Winged Bull

Sargon II inscription (720 BC): capture & deportation of northern kingdom of Israel

Sargon never completed his capital, though from 713-705BC tens of thousands of laborers and hundreds of artisans worked on the great city. Yet, with the exception of some magnificent buildings for public officials, only a few durable edifices were completed in the residential section. In 705BC, in a campaign in northwestern Iran, Sargon was ambushed and killed. His corpse remained unburied, to be devoured by birds of prey. Sargon's son Sennacherib, who quarreled with his father, believed with the priests that his death was a punishment from the neglected gods of the ancient capitals.

Sennacherib (704-681)

With Sennacherib (Assyrian: Sin-ahhe-eriba), Assyria acquired an exceptionally clever and gifted, though often extravagant, ruler. His father is not mentioned in any of his many inscriptions. He left the new city of Dur-Sharrukin at once and resided in Ashur for a few years, until in 701BC he made **Nineveh** his capital, where he built a huge palace adorned with reliefs, some of them depicting the transport of colossal bull statues by water and by land. Many of the rooms were decorated with pictorial narratives in bas-relief telling of war, building activities, battles in the lagoons, the life in the military camps and the deportations.

Sennacherib's building projects were impressive. For example, when Nineveh needed water for irrigation, his engineers diverted the waters of a tributary of the Great Zab River. The canal had to cross a valley at Jerwan. An aqueduct was constructed of about 2 million limestone blocks with 5 huge archways over the brook in the valley. The bed of the canal on the aqueduct was sealed with cement containing magnesium. Parts of this aqueduct still stand today. Sennacherib wrote of these and other technological accomplishments in detail, with illustrations.

Sennacherib had considerable difficulties with Babylonia. In 703BC Marduk-apal-iddina again crowned himself king with the aid of Elam, proceeding at once to ally himself with other enemies of Assyria. After nine months he was forced to withdraw when Sennacherib defeated a coalition army consisting of Babylonians, Aramaeans, and Elamites. The new puppet king of Babylonia was Bel-ibni (702-700BC), who had been raised in Assyria.

In 702BC Sennacherib raided western Iran. In 701BC was his most famous campaign, against Syria and **Palestine**, to gain control over the main road from Syria to Egypt in preparation for campaigns against Egypt. When Sennacherib's army approached, Sidon immediately expelled its ruler, Luli, who was hostile to Assyria. The other allies either surrendered or were defeated. An Egyptian army was defeated at Eltekeh in Judah.

Sennacherib laid siege to Jerusalem, and King **Hezekiah** was called upon to surrender, but he refused (Hezekiah is reported to have paid tribute to Sennacherib on at least one occasion). An Assyrian officer tried to incite the people of Jerusalem against Hezekiah, but failed. In view of the difficulty of surrounding a mountain stronghold such as **Jerusalem**, and of the minor importance of this town for the main purpose of the campaign, Sennacherib cut short the attack and left Palestine with his army, which according to the Old Testament (2 Kings 19:35) was decimated by an epidemic. The number of Assyrian dead is reported to have risen to 185,000.

Sennacherib exiles Lachish of Judah (Isaiah 36:1-2)

Taylor Prism: Sennacherib Records his conflict with Hezekiah (2Kings 18:13-19:34)

Siloam inscription: Hezekiah bores a tunnel that brings in an underground water supply during attack of Jerusalem by Sennachrib (2Kings 20:20-21)

Nabonidus Stele: murder of Sennacheib by his sons (681 BC) (2Kings 19:35-37)

In 700BC, Bel-ibni of Babylonia broke union with Assyria. Sennacherib defeated Bel-ibni and replaced him with Sennacherib's oldest son, Ashur-nadin-shumi. Sennacherib then prepared to attack Elam, which had supported Babylonian rebellions. The overland route to Elam had been cut off and fortified by the Elamites. Sennacherib had ships built in Syria and at Nineveh. The ships from Syria were moved on rollers from the Euphrates to the Tigris. The fleet sailed downstream to the southern coastline of Elam. The Elamites launched a counteroffensive by land, occupying Babylonia. Not until 693BC were the Assyrians again able to fight their way through to the north.

In 689BC, Sennacherib conquered and destroyed Babylon's temples. The waters of the Arakhtu Canal were diverted over the ruins, and the inner city remained uninhabited for eight years. Many Assyrians were indignant at this, believing that the Babylonian god Marduk must be offended by destroying his temple carrying off his image. Marduk was also an Assyrian deity, to whom many Assyrians turned in time of need. A political-theological propaganda campaign was launched to explain to the people that what had taken place was in accord with the wish of most of the gods. A story was written in which Marduk, because of a transgression, was captured and brought before a tribunal. Only a part of this literature is extant. Even the great poem of the creation of the world, the Enuma elish, was altered: the god Marduk was replaced by the god Ashur.

In 681BC there was a rebellion. Sennacherib was assassinated by one or two of his sons in the temple of the god Ninurta at Kalakh. This god, along with the god Marduk, had been badly treated by Sennacherib, and the event was widely regarded as punishment of divine origin.

Esarhaddon (680-669)

Ignoring the claims of his older brothers, an imperial council appointed Esarhaddon (Ashur-aha-iddina) as Sennacherib's successor. The choice is all the more difficult to explain in that Esarhaddon, unlike his father, was friendly toward the Babylonians. It can be assumed that his mother, Zakutu (Naqia), who came from Syria or Judah, used all her influence on his behalf to override the national party of Assyria. The theory that he was a partner in plotting the murder of his father is improbable. He was able to procure the loyalty of his father's army. His brothers fled to Urartu. In his inscriptions, Esarhaddon always mentions both his father and grandfather.

Defining the destruction of Babylon explicitly as punishment by the god Marduk, the new king soon ordered the reconstruction of the city. He referred to himself only as governor of Babylonia and through his policies obtained the support of the cities of Babylonia. At the beginning of his reign the Aramaean tribes were still allied with Elam against him, but Urtaku of Elam (675-664BC) signed a peace treaty and freed him for campaigning elsewhere.

In 679BC he stationed a garrison at the Egyptian border, because Egypt, under the Ethiopian king Taharqa, was planning to intervene in Syria. He put down with great severity a rebellion of the combined forces of Sidon, Tyre, and other Syrian cities. The time was ripe to attack Egypt, which was suffering under the rule of the Ethiopians and was by no means a united country. Esarhaddon's first attempt in 674-673BC miscarried. In 671BC, however, his forces took Memphis, the Egyptian capital.

Esarhaddon inscription: restoration of Babylon (670 BC)

Occasional threats came from the mountainous border regions of eastern Anatolia and Iran. Pushed forward by the Scythians, the Cimmerians in northern Iran and Transcaucasia tried to gain a foothold in Syria and western Iran. Esarhaddon allied himself with the Scythian king Partatua by giving him one of his daughters in marriage. In so doing he checked the movement of the Cimmerians. Nevertheless, the apprehensions of Esarhaddon can be seen in his many offerings, supplications, and requests to the sun god. These were concerned less with his own enterprises than with the plans of enemies and vassals and the reliability of civil servants.

The priestesses of Ishtar had to reassure Esarhaddon constantly by calling out to him, "Do not be afraid." Previous kings, as far as is known, had never needed this kind of encouragement.

At home Esarhaddon faced serious difficulties from the court. His oldest son had died early. The national party suspected his second son, Shamash-shum-ukin, of being too friendly with the Babylonians. His third son, **Ashurbanipal**, was given the succession in 672BC, Shamash-shum-ukin remaining crown prince of Babylonia.

Another matter was Esarhaddon's failing health. He regarded eclipses of the moon as particularly alarming omens, and, in order to prevent a fatal illness from striking him at these times, he had substitute kings chosen who ruled during the three eclipses that occurred during his 12-year reign. The replacement kings died or were put to death after their brief term of office. During his off-terms Esarhaddon called himself "Mister Peasant." This practice implied that the gods could not distinguish between the real king and a false one.

Esarhaddon enlarged and improved the temples in both Assyria and Babylonia. He also constructed a palace in Kalakh, using many of the picture slabs of Tiglath-pileser III. The works that remain are not on the level of those of either his predecessors or of Ashurbanipal. He died while on an expedition to put down a revolt in Egypt.

Ashurbanipal (668-627)

After the death of his father, Ashurbanipal assumed the kingship as planned. He may have owed his fortunes to the intercession of his grandmother Zakutu, who had recognized his superior capacities. He tells of his diversified education by the priests and his training in armor-making as well as in other military arts.

He may have been the only king in Assyria with a scholarly background. As crown prince he also had studied the administration of the vast empire. The record notes that the gods granted him a record harvest during the first year of his reign. There were also good crops in subsequent years. During these first years he also was successful in foreign policy, and his relationship with his brother in Babylonia was good.

In 668BC he put down a rebellion in Egypt and drove out King Taharqa, but in 664BC the nephew of Taharqa, Tanutamon, gathered forces for a new rebellion. Ashurbanipal went to Egypt, pursuing the Ethiopian prince far into the south. His decisive victory moved Tyre and other parts of the empire to resume regular payments of tribute. Ashurbanipal installed Psamtik (Greek: Psammeticbos) as prince over the Egyptian region of Sais.

In 656BC Psamtik dislodged the Assyrian garrisons with the aid of Carian and Ionian mercenaries, making Egypt again independent. Ashurbanipal did not attempt to reconquer it. A former ally of Assyria, Gyges of Lydia, had aided Psamtik in his rebellion. In return, Assyria did not help Gyges when he was attacked by the Cimmerians. Gyges was killed. His son Ardys paid tribute to Assyria, as a lesser evil than being conquered by the Cimmerians.

When Elam attacked Babylon in 653BC, Ashurbanipal sent a large army and defeated them, killing the king. Elam was no longer strong enough to assume an active part on the international scene.

Ashurbanipal's royal bodyguards warring in Babylon (640 BC)

Ashurbanipal on chariot

Ashurbanipal conquering city of Hamanu in Elam

This victory had serious consequences for Babylonia. Shamash-shum-ukin formed a secret alliance in 656BC with the Iranians, Elamites, Aramaeans, Arabs, and Egyptians which was directed against Ashurbanipal, attacking Assyria in 652BC. Ashurbanipal, taken by surprise, soon pulled his troops together. The Babylonian army was defeated, and Shamash-shum-ukin was surrounded in his fortified city of Babylon. His allies were not able to hold their own against the Assyrians. The city of Babylon was under siege for three years. It fell in 648BC amid scenes of horrible carnage, Shamash-shum-ukin dying in his burning palace.

Elam's refusal in 647BC to extradite an Aramaean prince was used as pretext for a new attack that drove deep into its territory. The assault on the capital of Susa followed in 646BC, destroying the city and taking vast spoils. The upper classes were exiled to Assyria and other parts of the empire, and Elam became an Assyrian province. Assyria extended its domain to southwestern Iran. Cyrus I of Persia sent tribute to Nineveh, hoping perhaps to secure protection for his borders with Media. Little is known about the last years of Ashurbanipal's reign.

Ashurbanipal left more inscriptions than any of his predecessors. He founded the great **palace library** in **Nineveh** (modern Kuyunjik), which is today one of the most important sources for the study of ancient Mesopotamia. Important works were kept in more than one copy, some intended for the king's personal use. In his inscriptions Ashurbanipal tells of becoming an enthusiastic hunter of big game, acquiring a taste for it during a fight with marauding lions. In his palace at Nineveh the long rows of hunting scenes show what a masterful artist can accomplish in bas-relief; with these reliefs Assyrian art reached its peak. In the series depicting his wars, particularly the wars fought in Elam, the scenes are overloaded with human figures.

Rebuilt Library of Ashurbanipal on the Campus of the University Mosul, Iraq

	The Assyrian Empire & Kingdom of Judah		3.5
722 B.C.	Sargon II reigns in Assyria.		
717 B.C.	the fall of Carchemish sends Assyria into turmoil.		
717-715 B.C.	prophetic ministries of Isaiah and Micah	Isa 13:1-19:25; 28:1-35:10; Mic 3:1-12; Psa 82	
715-686 B.C.	Hezekiah succeeds Ahaz in Judah.	2 Kgs 16:19-20; 18:2-7; 2 Chr 28:26-29:2	
715 B.C.	Hezekiah enacts reforms and drives back the Philistines.	2 Kgs 18:8; 2 Chr 29:3-31:21; Psa 50, 81	
712 B.C.	Assyria conquers weakened Philistia		
712-710 B.C.	Isaiah goes stripped and barefoot to prophesy Assyria's humiliation of Egypt and Cush.	Isa 20:1-6	
710 B.C.	Isaiah prophesies against the nations.	Isa 21:1-27:13	
709 B.C.	the birth of Hezekiah's son Manasseh.	2 Kgs 21:1	
705-681 B.C.	Sennacherib reigns in Assyria.		
c. 705 B.C.	Simeon's conquest of Gedor.	1 Chr 4:34-43	
702 B.C.	Hezekiah's illness and miraculous recovery.	2 Kgs 20:1-11; 2 Chr 32:24-26; Psa 69; Isa 38:1-22	
702 B.C.	Hezekiah meets with Babylon concerning the Assyrian threat.	2 Kgs 20:12-19; Isa 39:1-8	
701 B.C.	Assyria conquers Ammon and besieges Judah; an angel slaughters the enemy forces.	2 Kgs 18:13-19:36; 2 Chr 32:1-23; Psa 46, 48, 75, 76, 84; Isa 36:1-37:37	
701-686 B.C.	Hezekiah prospers and forgets God in his last years	2 Chr 32:27-32	
c. 700 B.C.	Isaiah's prophecies for future generations.	Isa 40:1-66:24	
697 B.C.	12-year-old Manasseh begins reign with Hezekiah.	2 Kgs 21:1	
c. 690 B.C.	Micah's later prophecies	Mic. 4:1-7:20	
686-642 B.C.	Hezekiah's evil son Manasseh reigns in Judah.	2 Kgs 20:20-21:9; 2 Chr 32:32-33:9	
681-669 B.C.	Esarhaddon reigns in Assyria	2 Kgs 19:37; Isa 37:38	
c. 680 B.C.	Isaiah is martyred by Manasseh.	2 Chr 32:32; Heb 11:37	
668-627 B.C.	Ashurbanipal reigns in Assyria.		
664 B.C.	the birth of Manasseh's son Amon.	2 Kgs 21:19	
663 B.C.	the fall of Egypt's supposedly invincible city Thebes	Nah. 3:8	
660 B.C.	the founding of Byzantium		
c. 650 B.C.	the birth of Jeremiah.		
648 B.C.	the birth of Amon's son Josiah; Assyria carries Manasseh into captivity.	2 Kgs 21:10-16; 22:1; 2 Chr 33:10-11	
646 B.C.	Manasseh's repentance and return from captivity.	2 Chr 33:12-13, 18-19	
645 B.C.	Nahum prophesies on Assyria, Manasseh rebels.	2 Chr 33:14-17; Nah 1:1-3:19	
642-640 B.C.	Manasseh's evil son Amon reigns in Judah.	2 Kgs 21:17-22; 2 Chr 33:20-23	
640 B.C.	Amon is assassinated, his son Josiah becomes king.	2 Kgs 21:23-26	
640-609 B.C.	Josiah reigns as Judah's best king.	2 Kgs 22:1-2; 2 Chr 34:1-2	
634 B.C.	the birth of Josiah's son Eliakim (Jehoiakim)	2 Chr. 36:5	
633 B.C.	Josiah begins seeking God	2 Chr 34:3	
633-621 B.C.	Ahur-etil-ilani reigns in Assyria.		
632 B.C.	the birth of Josiah's son Jehoahaz.	2 Chr 23:31	
c. 630 B.C.	Zephaniah urges reform.	Zeph. 1:1-3:20	
629 B.C.	Josiah's early reforms.	2 Chr 34:4-7	

	The Assyrian Empire & Kingdom of Judah	
623 B.C.	the birth of Ezekiel; Josiah rediscovers the Torah and begins major reforms	2 Kgs 22:3-23:21; 2 Chr 33:29-33; 34:8-28; Psa 119; Ezek 1:1
622 B.C.	Judah celebrates the Passover.	2 Kgs 23:22-27; 2 Chr 35:1-19
621-612 B.C.	Sin-shur-ishkun reigns in Assyria.	
618 B.C.	Nebuchadnezzar's uncle Mattaniah (Zedekiah) born.	2 Chr 36:11
615 B.C.	the birth of Jehoiakim's son Jehoiachin (Jeconiah).	2 Chr 36:9
614 B.C.	Asshur falls to Cyaxares the Mede and is taken by Nabopalassar.	
612 B.C.	Nineveh is destroyed.	
612-609 B.C.	Ashur-ubalit reigns as the last king of Assyria.	
609-594 B.C.	Pharaoh Neco II reigns in Egypt.	
609 B.C.	Josiah and Necho fight Assyria; Josiah is killed in battle. His son Jehoahaz succeeds him.	2 Kgs 23:28-33; 2 Chr 35:20-36:3
609 B.C.	Necho imprisons Jehoahaz; he makes Eliakim king and renames him Jehoiakim.	2 Kgs 23:34; 2 Chr 36:4
609-539 B.C.	Judah's seventy years of service to Babylon.	Jer 25:11-12
609-598 B.C.	the evil reign of Jehoiakim in Judah.	2 Kgs 23:35-37; 2 Chr 36:5
608-605 B.C.	Jeremiah's prophecies	Jer 7:16-20:18; 25:1-26:24
605 B.C.	the deportation of Daniel and others to Babylon	Dan 1:1-2
605-560 B.C.	Nebuchadnezzar reigns in Babylon; he expels the Egyptians from Palestine and destroys Assyria.	Hab 1:1-3:19
605-602 B.C.	Nebuchadnezzar controls Judah.	2 Kgs 24:1
605-604 B.C.	Jeremiah's ministry continues.	Jer 36:1-32; 45:1-51:64
604 B.C.	Babylon destroys Philistia; Daniel and friends tested.	Dan 1:3-2:49
604 B.C.	the birth of Lao-tze in China.	
602 B.C.	the birth of Darius the Mede.	Dan 5:31
602 B.C.	God sends hordes of Arameans, Moabites, and Ammonites against Judah.	2 Kgs 24:2-4
600 B.C.	Rechabites' obedience vs. Judah's disobedience.	Jer 35:1-19
598 B.C.	Jehoiachin succeeds Jehoiakim, reigns 3 months.	2 Kgs 24:5-9; 2 Chr 36:6-9
597 B.C.	Nebuchadnezzar deports Jehoiachin; he makes Mattaniah king, changes his name to Zedekiah.	2 Kgs 24:10-17; 2 Chr 36:10-11; Psa 88, 89, 102; Jer 52:28
597-586 B.C.	the reign of Zedekiah.	2 Kgs 24:18-20; 2 Chr 36:12; Jer 52:1-2
597 B.C.	Jeremiah prophesies captivity.	Jer 21:1-24:10; 27:1-31:40
593 B.C.	the early prophecies of Ezekiel in Babylon.	Ezek 1:1-4:17
592 B.C.	Ezekiel prophesies desolation for Judah.	Ezek 5:1-19:14
591 B.C.	Ezekiel's continued prophecies.	Ezek 20:1-23:49; 25:1-17
589-587 B.C.	Zedekiah rebels against Babylon.	2 Kgs 24:20; 2 Chr 36:13-16; Jer 52:3
589 B.C.	Jerusalem's fall is imminent.	Jer 34:1-7
588 B.C.	as the siege of Jerusalem begins and more Jews are deported, Ezekiel tells the parable of the boiling pot.	2 Kgs 25:1; Jer 52:29; Ezek 24:1-27.
588-586 B.C.	Jeremiah's and Ezekiel's final warnings.	Jer 32:1-33:26; 34:8-22; 37:1-39:18; Ezek 26:1-31:18
586 B.C.	the fall of Jerusalem; Jeremiah remains behind.	2 Kgs 25:2-21; 1 Chr 9:1; 2 Chr 36:17-21; Jer 39:1-14; 52:4-27; Lam 1:1-5:22

CHAPTER 4   Internal Evidence Test = FULFILLED PROPHECY   4.1

Skeptic's Charge #12:   Why would God need to give fulfilled prophecies in the Bible? Is He so hard for people to understand that He needs to 'prove' Himself?

#1. Isaiah → To Reveal Himself as Sovereign (He alone is God)

Isaiah 44:6-8 *"Thus says the Lord, the King of Israel, and His Redeemer, the Lord of hosts: "I am the First and the Last; besides Me there is no other God. AND WHO CAN PROCLAIM AS I DO? Then let him declare it and set it in order for Me, since I appointed the ancient people. And the things that are coming and shall come, let them show these to them. Do not fear, nor be afraid; HAVE I NOT TOLD YOU FROM THAT TIME, AND DECLARED IT? You are My witnesses. Is there a God besides Me? Indeed THERE IS NO OTHER ROCK; I KNOW NOT ONE."*

Isaiah 42:9, 46:9-10 *"The former things have come to pass, and new things I declare; BEFORE THEY SPRING FORTH I tell you of them.... REMEMBER THE FORMER THINGS OF OLD, for I am God, and there is no other; I am God, and there is none like Me, declaring the end from the beginning, and FROM ANCIENT TIMES THINGS THAT ARE NOT YET DONE."*

Isaiah 48:3-5 *"I have declared the former things from the beginning; they went forth from My mouth, and I caused them to hear it. SUDDENLY I DID THEM, AND THEY CAME TO PASS. Because I knew that you were obstinate, and your neck was an iron sinew, and your brow bronze, Even from the beginning I have declared it to you; before it came to pass I proclaimed it to you, lest you should say, 'My idol has done them, and my carved image and my molded image have commanded them.'"*

#2. 1Peter 1:19-21 → To Strengthen the faith of believers

"We have the prophetic word MADE MORE SURE, which YOU DO WELL TO HEED as a light that shines in a dark place, until the day dawns and the morning star rises in your hearts; knowing this first, that no prophecy of Scripture is of any private interpretation, for prophecy never came by the will of man, but holy men of God spoke as they were moved by the Holy Spirit."

#3. New Testament → To Point us to Jesus Christ

Revelation 19:10 *"... Worship God! For THE TESTIMONY OF JESUS IS THE SPIRIT OF PROPHECY."*

John 5:39 *"You search the Scriptures, for in them you think you have eternal life; and these are they which testify of Me."*

Acts 10:43 *"To Him all the prophets witness that, through His name, whoever believes in Him receive remission of sins."*

Skeptic's Charge #13:   Is there historical evidence, outside the Bible, that prophecies in the Bible are true?

What's the chance the 12 prophecies below all happened by chance?

Peter Stoner[15]: "The probability of just these prophecies coming true (of the 100's in the Bible) is **5.76×10^{59} to 1**.

#	Prophecy	Odds
#1.	Tyre	75,000,000:1
#2.	Nineveh	> 100,000,000:1
#3.	Thebes & Memphis	1,000:1
#4.	Babylon	5,000,000,000:1
#5.	Moab and Ammon	1,000:1
#6.	Petra and Edom	10,000:1
#7.	Samaria	40,000:1
#8.	Gaza and Ashkelon	12,000:1
#9.	Jericho	200,000:1
#10.	Palestine	200,000:1
#11.	Zion Plowed	100:1
#12.	Jerusalem	80,000,000,000:1

How do we visualize a number like 5.76×10^{59}? If this was the number of silver dollars we had, they could fill 1×10^{28} solid silver balls the size of the sun (the sun is 1,000,000 times the volume of the earth). We then *mark 1 of these silver dollars*, and then stir the whole bunch of them up before putting them into these balls the size of the sun. If we then *blindfold* someone, take him over to all these 1×10^{28} great balls of silver dollars, and ask him to *pick out the 1 silver dollar that we marked*, his chances of choosing the right one would be **5.76×10^{59} to 1**. It is absurd that he would have any chance of finding the right silver dollar. The chance of these 12 prophecies all coming true equals the blindfolded person finding the right silver dollar. But these prophecies, and many more not examined here, all came true to the smallest detail.

NUMBERS 23:19   *"God is not a man, that He should lie, nor a son of man, that He should repent. Has He said, and WILL HE NOT DO IT? Or has He spoken, and WILL HE NOT MAKE IT GOOD?"*

Prophecy #1: The Destruction of TYRE 3,000BC-1,600AD 4.2

EZEKIEL 26:1-3	"Many nations will be against Tyre"
EZEKIEL 26:7-11	"Nebuchadnezzar will destroy Tyre's mainland city"
EZEKIEL 26:4	"Tyre will be a bare rock; flat like the top of a rock"
EZEKIEL 26:12	"Its debris will be thrown into the water"
EZEKIEL 26:5	"Fishermen will spread nets over the site"
EZEKIEL 26:14	"It will never be rebuilt again"
EZEKIEL 26:21	"It will never be found again"

* Probability of all these prophecies being fulfilled = 1:75,000,000

What is Tyre?

<u>3,000 BC</u>: Tyre was founded originally as a mainland settlement with an island city just off shore.

<u>1,000-815 BC</u>: Hiram, King of Tyre, joined 2 islets by landfill. Expansion began when traders from Tyre founded Carthage in North Africa. Eventually its colonies spread around the Mediterranean and Atlantic, bringing to the city a flourishing maritime trade.

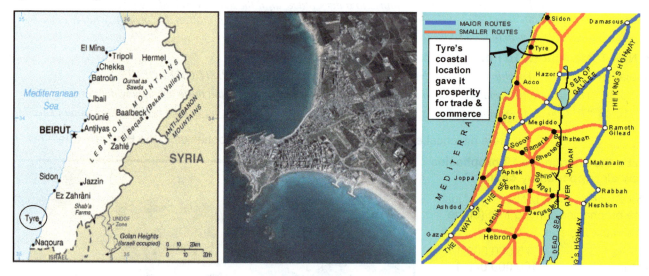

<u>600 BC</u>: Nebuchadnezzar, King of Babylon, laid siege to the walled city for 13 years. Tyre stood firm, but it was probable that at this time the residents of the mainland city abandoned it for the safety of the island.

<u>332 BC</u>: Alexander the Great set out to conquer Tyre in the war between the Greeks and the Persians. Unable to storm the city, he blockaded Tyre for 7 months. He used the debris of the abandoned mainland city to build a dam and then used his siege engines to breach the city walls. He was so enraged at the Tyrians' defense and the loss of his men that he destroyed half the city. The town's 30,000 residents were massacred or sold into slavery.

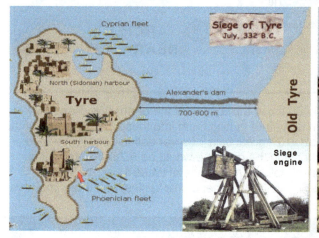

<u>64 BC</u>: Tyre and the whole of ancient Syria fell under Roman rule. The Romans built great important monuments in the city, including an aqueduct, a triumphal arch and the largest hippodrome in antiquity.

<u>634 AD</u>: Tyre was taken by the Islamic armies. The city offered no resistance and continued to prosper under its new rulers, exporting sugar as well as objects made of pearl and glass. This was a time when Tyre was adorned with fountains and its bazaars were full of all kinds of merchandise, including carpets and jewelry of gold and silver. Thanks to Tyre's strong fortifications it was able to resist to onslaught of the Crusaders until 1124 AD.

<u>1291 AD</u>: Tyre was conquered by the Mamlukes (after about 180 years of Crusader rule).

<u>1600AD</u>: Tyre fell to the Ottomans. At the end of World War I Tyre was integrated into the new nation of Lebanon.

EZEKIEL 26:1-3 "MANY NATIONS WILL BE AGAINST TYRE" *"And it came to pass in the 11th year, on the first day of the month, that the word of the Lord came to me, saying, "Son of man, because Tyre has said against Jerusalem, 'Aha! She is broken who was the gateway of the peoples; now she is turned over to me; I shall be filled. She is laid waste.' "Therefore thus says the Lord God: 'Behold, I am against you, O Tyre, and will cause many nations to come up against you, as the sea causes its waves to come up."*

- 1st Siege (585 BC) = <u>NEBUCHADNEZZAR</u>[1]: ENCYCLOPEDIA BRITANNICA: "After a 13-year siege (585-573 BC) by Nebuchadnezzar II, Tyre made terms and acknowledged Babylonian rule. In 583 BC Tyre, with the rest of Phoenicia, fell under the rule of Persia".

- 2nd Siege (333 BC) = <u>ALEXANDER THE GREAT</u>[1]: ENCYCLOPEDIA BRITANNICA: "In his war on the Persians, Alexander III, after defeating Darius III at the battle of Issus (333BC), marched southward toward Egypt, calling on the Phoenician cities to open their gates, as it was part of his plan to deny their use to the Persian fleet. The citizens of Tyre refused to do so, and he took them".

- 3rd Siege (314 BC) = <u>ANTIGONUS</u>[1]: NINA JIDEJIAN ("TYRE THROUGH THE AGES",1969): "Returning from successful wars in Babylonia, Antigonus easily reduced the cities of Phoenicia but met with firm resistance from Tyre. 18 years had passed since Alexander had seized Tyre and the city had recovered rapidly...after a siege of 15 months Tyre was reduced by Antigonus."

- 4th Siege (690 AD) = <u>THE MUSLIMS</u>[1]: JOSEPH MICHAUD ("HISTORY OF THE CRUSADES", 2 volumes): "After the taking and destruction of Ptolemais, the Sultan sent one of his emirs with a body of troops to take possession of the city of Tyre. This city, seized with terror, opened its gates without resistance. This city, which had not afforded the least succor to Ptolemais in the last great struggle, believed themselves protected by a truce. They were massacred, dispersed, and lead into slavery."

EZEKIEL 26:7-8 "NEBUCHADNEZZAR WILL DESTROY THE MAINLAND CITY"

"For thus says the Lord God: 'Behold, I will bring against Tyre from the north Nebuchadnezzar king of Babylon, king of kings, with horses, with chariots, and with horsemen, and an army with many people. He will slay with the sword your daughter villages in the fields; he will heap up a siege mound against you, build a wall against you, and raise a defense against you. He will direct his battering rams against your walls, and with his axes he will break down your towers. Because of the abundance of his horses, their dust will cover you; your walls will shake at the noise of the horsemen, the wagons, and the chariots, when he enters your gates, as men enter a city that has been breached. With the hooves of his horses he will trample all your streets; he will slay your people by the sword, and your strong pillars will fall to the ground."

- 3 years after this prophecy, Nebuchadnezzar laid siege to mainland Tyre. When he broke the gates down, he found the city almost empty. Most of the people moved by ship to an island 1/2-mile off the coast. The mainland city was destroyed in 573 BC, but the city on the island remained powerful for several hundred years afterward.

EZEKIEL 26:4 "TYRE WILL BE SCRAPED FLAT LIKE THE TOP OF A ROCK" *"They shall destroy the walls of Tyre and break down her towers; I will also scrape her dust from her, and make her like the top of a rock."*

- PHILIP MYERS ("GENERAL HISTORY FOR COLLEGES and HIGH SCHOOLS"[1]): "In 332 BC Alexander the Great reduced it to ruins. She recovered in a measure from this, but never regained the place she had previously held in the world. The larger part of the site of the once great city is now bare as the top of a rock - a place where fishermen that still frequent the spot spread their nets to dry."

mainland Tyre "scraped flat" like the top of a rock

EZEKIEL 26:12 "DEBRIS THROWN IN THE WATER"

"They will plunder your riches and pillage your merchandise; they will break down your walls and destroy your pleasant houses; they will lay your stones, your timber, and your soil in the midst of the water."

mainland Tyre's debris thrown into the water

- ENCYCLOPEDIA BRITANNICA[1]: "In his war on Persia, Alexander, after defeating Darius III at the battle of Issus in 333 BC, marched southward toward Egypt, calling on the Phoenician cities to open their gates, as it was part of his plan to deny their use to the Persian fleet. The citizens of Tyre refused to do so, and Alexander laid siege to the city. Possessing no fleet, he demolished old Tyre on the mainland, and with the debris built a mole 200 ft. wide across the straits separating the old and new towns, erecting towers and war engines at the farther end."

- JOSEPH FREE ("ARCHAEOLOGY and BIBLE HISTORY"[1]): "Ezekiel's prophecy concerning the laying of the stones, the timber, and the dust in 'the midst of the water' was specifically fulfilled when Alexander's engineers built the mole, and used remains of the city of Tyre, laying them in the water."

- CURTIUS (Loeb Classical Library: "Quintius Curtius IV", 2. 18-19[1]) on Alexander's construction of the causeway: "Much material was available from Mount Libanus (trees for beams) and the old city of Tyre supplied stones and dirt".

EZEKIEL 26:5 "FISHERMEN SPREAD NETS OVER IT"

"It shall be a place for spreading nets in the midst of the sea, for I have spoken,' says the Lord God; 'it shall become plunder for the nations."

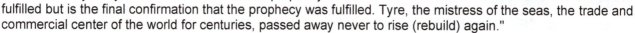

- NINA JIDEJIAN ("TYRE THROUGH THE AGES"[1]): "The 'Sidonian' port of Tyre is still in use today. Small fishing vessels lay at anchor there. The port has become a haven today for fishing boats and a place for spreading nets. The destiny of Tyre according to the prophet is a place where fishermen would spread their nets. The existence of a small fishing village upon the site of the ancient city of Tyre does not mean that the prophecy is not fulfilled but is the final confirmation that the prophecy was fulfilled. Tyre, the mistress of the seas, the trade and commercial center of the world for centuries, passed away never to rise (rebuild) again."

- HANS-WOLF RACKL ("ARCHEOLOGY UNDERWATER"[1]): "Today hardly a single stone of the old Tyre remains intact. Tyre has become a 'place to dry the fish nets', as the prophet predicted."

- PHILIP MYERS ("GENERAL HISTORY FOR COLLEGES and HIGH SCHOOLS"[1]): "In 332 BC Alexander the Great reduced it to ruins. She recovered in a measure from this, but never regained the place she had previously held in the world. The larger part of the site of the once great city is now bare as the top of a rock - a place where fishermen that still frequent the spot spread their nets to dry."

EZEKIEL 26:14 "IT WILL NEVER BE REBUILT AGAIN"
"I will make you like the top of a rock; you shall be a place for spreading nets, and you shall never be rebuilt, for I the Lord have spoken," says the Lord.

- FLOYD HAMILTON ("THE BASIS FOR THE CHRISTIAN FAITH"[1]): "Other cities destroyed by enemies had been rebuilt; Jerusalem was destroyed many times, but always has risen again from the ruins... But 25 centuries ago a Jew in exile over in Babylonia looked into the future at the command of God and wrote the words, 'Thou shalt be built no more!' The voice of God has spoken and old Tyre today stands as it was for 25 centuries, a bare rock, uninhabited by man! Today anyone who wants to see the site of the old city can have it pointed out to him along the shore, but there is not a ruin to mark the spot. It has been scraped clean and has never been rebuilt."

EZEKIEL 26:21 "IT WILL NEVER BE FOUND AGAIN"
"I will make you a terror, and you shall be no more; though you are sought for, you will never be found again," says the Lord God.

- NINA NELSON ("YOUR GUIDE TO LEBANON"[1]): "I went to visit Tyre on a summer's day. The town was sleepy, the harbor still. Fishing boats were putting out to sea. Pale turquoise fishing nets were drying in the sun."

**Tyre was destroyed in 1291 and was never rebuilt.
Today it is just a small fishing village, where fishermen spread their nets to dry.**

> **Prophecy #2: The Destruction of NINEVEH** 2,000 - 612BC **4.3**
>
> NAHUM 1:10 "Would be destroyed in a state of drunkenness"
> NAHUM 1:8, 2:6 "Would be destroyed in an 'overflowing flood'"
> NAHUM 3:13 "Would be burned"
> NAHUM 3:19 "Would be totally destroyed ('Your wound is incurable') and become desolate"
>
> * Probability of all these Prophecies being fulfilled = >1:100,000,000

- **What is the prophetic significance of "Nahum"?**

John MacArthur: "The book of Nahum (663-654) is a straightforward prophetic announcement of judgment against Assyria and her capital Nineveh for their cruel atrocities and idolatrous practices."

God distinguishes between His enemies and His children	
His enemies	**His children**
Nahum 1:2-3 *"God is jealous and the Lord avenges; the Lord avenges and is furious, the Lord will take vengeance on His adversaries, and He reserves WRATH for His ENEMIES; the Lord is slow to anger and great in power, and will not at all acquit the wicked."* **Rom. 8:7** *"...the carnal mind is ENMITY against God; for it is not subject to the law of God, nor indeed can it be."* **James 4:4** *"Do you not know that friendship with the world is enmity toward God? Whoever therefore wants to be a friend of the world makes himself an ENEMY of God."* **Eph. 2:1-3** *"...you He made alive, who were dead in trespasses and sins, in which you once walked according to the course of the world, according to the prince of the power of this air, the spirit who works in the sons of disobedience, among whom also we all once conducted ourselves in the lusts of the flesh, fulfilling the desires of the flesh and of the mind, and were by nature children of WRATH..."*	**Nahum 1:7** *"The Lord is good, a stronghold in the day of trouble; and He knows those who TRUST in Him."* **Heb. 11:6** *"...without FAITH it is impossible to please Him, for he who comes to God must believe that He is, and that He is a rewarder of those who diligently seek Him."* **Rom. 5:1** *"...having been justified by FAITH, we have peace with God through our Lord Jesus Christ..."* **Eph. 2:11-13** *"...remember that you, once Gentiles in the flesh – who are called Uncircumcision by what is called the Circumcision made in the flesh by hands – that at that time you were without Christ, being ALIENS from the commonwealth of Israel and STRANGERS from the covenants of promise, having no hope and WITHOUT GOD in the world. But now in Christ Jesus you who once were FAR OFF have been made NEAR by the blood of Christ."*

NAHUM 1:10 "DESTROYED IN A STATE OF DRUNKENNESS" *"For while tangled like thorns, and while drunken like drunkards, they shall be devoured like stubble fully dried."*

- BERNARD RAMM ("Protestant Christian Evidences"[1]): "Part of the success of the Medes was due to the optimism of the Ninevites who assumed the enemy was permanently repulsed and gave themselves to drinking and feasting."

- DIODORUS OF SICILY, 26 and 27.50[1]: "Camped outside the city walls, the king of Assyria, who had been unaware of his deteriorating position militarily and over-aware of his victories against the enemies, became lax in his vigilance and began to indulge his soldiers in a feast of animals and much wine and drinking. This fact of decline in the Assyrian's defenses reached the enemy general, Arbaces, through deserters, and a night attack was pursued. With great success, Arbaces's organized troops routed the disorganized camp of the Assyrians and sent them back in flight to their city with great losses. This battle, decided apparently entirely by the Assyrian drunkenness and disorganization, was the final scene before the actual battle for the city itself - the siege."

NAHUM 1:8, 2:6 "DESTROYED IN A FLOOD" *"But with an overflowing flood He will make an utter end of its place, and darkness will pursue His enemies. The gates of the rivers are opened, and the palace is dissolved."*

- GLEASON ARCHER ("A Survey of OT Introduction"[1]): "NAHUM 2:6 contains a remarkably exact prediction, for subsequent history records that a vital part of the city walls of Nineveh was carried away by a great flood, and its ruin of the defensive system permitted the besieging Medes and Chaldeans to storm the city without difficulty."

- GEORGE BADGER ("The Nestorians and Their Rituals"[1]): "The fact of the flood here recorded (NAHUM 1:8, 2:6) literally fulfills the prophecy of Nahum and accounts for a stratum of pebble and sand which has been found a few feet below the surface of the river in the mounds of Koyoonjuk and Nimrud."

- DIODORUS OF SICILY, 26 and 27.50[1]: "Realizing the precarious situation he was in, the Assyrian leader, Sardanapallus, made preparations for the defense of his city as well as his kingdom. A prophecy was in the land which stated, 'No enemy will ever take Nimus by storm unless the ruler shall first become the city's enemy.' Sardanapallus decided this would never be and therefore felt secure. The enemy of the Assyrians was very happy with its success to this point, but could not break down the mighty city walls. The inhabitants had great amounts of food stored away, and as a result, the city remained a resistance to the attackers for 3 years. But after 3 years and heavy rains, the river, swelling wide, broke down a distance of the city walls and flooded a portion of the city. The king panicked, believing the aforementioned prophecy had been completed. He gave up hope and ordered his kingly possessions as well as his concubines, etc., into a portion of his palace, burned the whole thing down. The siegers, learning of the break in the wall, attacked this point, forcing entry into the city, and took over as victors of the whole city. Arbaces was crowned its king and given supreme authority."

NAHUM 3:13 "WOULD BE BURNED" *"Surely, your people in your midst are woman! The gates of your land are wide open for your enemies; fire shall devour the bars of your gates."*

- M. E. L. MALLAWAN ("Numrud and Its Remains"[1]): "The condition in which we found it (throne room at Shalmanessar) was a dramatic illustration of the final sack: the wall plaster had been packed hard and burnt yellow by the flames and then blackened with soot which had penetrated into the brickwork itself. The intense heat had caused the south wall to bend inwards at a dangerous angle and the floor of the chamber itself was buried under a great pile of burnt debris over a metro and a half in depth, filled with ash, charcoal, small antiquities...there were also many hundreds of mutilated fragments of ivory carvings burnt black and gray, sometimes to a high polish from the heat. I have in my day witnessed the debris of many an ancient fire - at Ur of the Chaldees, at Nineveh, at Arpachiyah, on sites in the Habur and Balih valleys - but never have I seen so perfect an example of a vengeful bonfire, loose-packed as bonfires are, the soot still permeating the air as we approached. After this great holocaust parts of the walls toppled over into the chamber, which was filled to a total height of 3 meters with mud brick. The hard upper packing, amounting to another metro and a half of debris over that of the bonfire, thus finally sealed the contents which were left undisturbed until we reached them in 1958."
- DIODORUS OF SICILY, 26 and 27.50[1]: "Extensive traces of ash which represent the sack of the city by the Babylonians, Scythians, and Medes in 612 BC have been observed in many parts of the Acropolis. Thereafter the city ceased to be important."

NAHUM 3:19 "TOTALLY DESTROYED ('YOUR WOUND IS INCURABLE') and BE DESOLATE"
"Your injury has no healing, your wound is severe. All who hear news of you will clap their hands over you, for upon whom has not your wickedness passed continually?"

- JOSEPH P. FREE ("ARCHAEOLOGY AND BIBLE HISTORY"[1]): "A century ago such familiar biblical cities as Nineveh were shapeless mounds, the very identity of which, in some cases, had been forgotten."
- EDWARD CHIERA ("THEY WROTE ON CLAY: THE BABYLONIAN TABLETS SPEAK TODAY"[1]): "If the tourist of today, after all that has been written about the ancient civilizations of Babylon and Assyria, fails to get an accurate conception of what the past was, one can easily imagine that the first travelers crossed and recrossed the land without suspecting that they were close to the historical sites of Babylon and Nineveh. Even scientifically-minded travelers who knew from the Bible of the existence of these two cities, and attempted to find them, several times passed over their very ruins without knowing it."
- MERRILL UNGER ("UNGER'S BIBLE DICTIONARY"[1]): "In 612 BC the ancient splendid city and capital of the Assyrian empire was so completely obliterated, according to its prophesied decimation by Hebrew prophets, that it became like a myth until its discovery by Sir Austen Layard and others in the 19th century. The site has now been extensively excavated."
- GEORGE MEISINGER ("THE FALL OF NINEVEH"[1]) speaks to the critics who jeered at even the prior existence of Nineveh: "The priceless records of this once dauntless empire had been withheld from the annals of world history until the 19th century. Sir Henry Layard, the English pioneer archaeologist, was the first to unlock the mysteries of this nation - a nation which had refused to yield her secrets to mankind for so long. Yet, almost from the turn of Layard's spade, the city of Nineveh began to surrender hundreds and then thousands of informative clues to the past. For centuries the only knowledge that such an empire existed was to be found in the direct and indirect statements of Scripture. As the centuries rolled by, and as no archaeological evidence turned up to "substantiate" the biblical record, doubt began to grow as to whether such a people ever existed. The historian puzzled; the skeptic jeered the Scriptural accounts. So complete was Assyrian's extinction!"

**Nineveh was destroyed in 612BC and was never rebuilt.
Today it is a preserved archaeological dig, discovered by Austen Layard in 1847.**

Prophecy #3: THEBES & MEMPHIS 3,100BC - 641AD 4.4

EZEKIEL 30:13	"Destroy the idols of Memphis"
EZEKIEL 30:14	"Thebes will be destroyed ('broken up') and fired"
EZEKIEL 30:15	"Thebes: I will cut off the multitude of..."
EZEKIEL 30:13	"There will no longer be a native prince from Egypt"

* Probability of all these Prophecies being fulfilled = 1:1,000

What is Memphis?

Memphis, founded around 3100BC, is the legendary city of **Menes**, the King who united Upper and Lower Egypt. This name dates from 2055–1640BC, and is frequently found in ancient Egyptian texts.

Early on, Memphis was a fortress from which Menes controlled the land and water routes between Upper Egypt and the Delta. He founded the city by creating dikes to protect the area from Nile floods. Later, Memphis became the administrative and religious center of Egypt. So dominating is the city during this era that we refer to it as the Memphite period.

It was one of the largest and most important cities in the ancient world, demonstrated by its persistent tendency over 8 dynasties to be the Capital of Egypt. The city reached a peak of prestige as a center for the worship of **Ptah**, the god of creation and artworks. The **alabaster sphinx** guarding the Temple of Ptah serves as a memorial of the city's former power and prestige.

Alabaster Sphinx

In 671BC the **Assyrians**, led by king **Esarhaddon** captured Memphis. His forces sacked and raided the city, slaughtered villagers and erected piles of their heads. Esarhaddon returned to his capital Nineveh and erected a victory stele showing the son of Taharqa in chains. After he left, Egypt rebelled against Assyrian rule.

Ashurbanipal, succeeding his father, led a massive invasion in 664BC. Memphis was again sacked and looted, and the king **Tantarmani** was defeated, putting a definitive end to the Kushite reign over Egypt. Power then returned to the Saite pharaohs, who reconstructed and even fortified structures in the city.

Under the **Persians**, Memphis was made their administrative headquarters. A Persian garrison was permanently installed within the city, probably in the great north wall, near the domineering palace of **Apries**. The nationalist awakening came with the rise to power of **Amyrtaeus**, in 404BC, who ended the Persian occupation. He was defeated and executed at Memphis in 399BC by pharaoh **Nepherites I**. In 343BC, Egypt (under **Nectanebo II**) was again defeated by the Persian emperor **Artaxerxes III** at **Pelusium**. He retreated to Memphis and was then forced to flee to Nubia.

In 332BC **Alexander the Great** was crowned pharaoh in the Temple of Ptah and took control of Egypt from the Persians. When he died in Babylon (323BC), **Ptolemy** brought his body to Memphis. Claiming that he had officially expressed a desire to be buried in Egypt, he then carried the body of Alexander to the heart of the temple of Ptah, and had him embalmed by the priests.

With the arrival of the **Romans**, Memphis lost its place permanently in favor of **Alexandria**. The rise of the cultic religion of Serapis, and **Christianity** taking root deep into the country, spelled the complete ruin of the ancient cults of Memphis.

In 641AD the **Muslims** conquered Memphis and established their new capital a short distance north at **Fustat**. Memphis was abandoned and became a source of stone for the surrounding settlements. Today, other than the scattered ruins, most of the city is gone, or lies beneath cultivated fields, Nile silt and local villages.

Ezekiel (592-570BC) predicted the following future events on Thebes and Memphis:

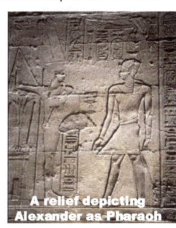
A relief depicting Alexander as Pharaoh

EZEKIEL 30:13 "DESTROY THE IDOLS OF MEMPHIS" *'Thus says the Lord God: "I will also destroy the idols, and cause the images to cease from Noph; there shall no longer be princes from the land of Egypt; I will put fear in the land of Egypt."'*

- ROBERT JAMESON ("A COMMENTARY: CRITICAL, EXPERIENTIAL & PRACTICAL ON THE OLD & NEW TESTAMENT"[1]): "Memphis, the capital of Middle Egypt, and the stronghold of 'idols': though no record exists of Nebuchadnezzar's destroying these, we know from Herodotus that Cambyses took Pelusium, the key to Egypt, by placing before his army dogs, cats, etc., all held sacred in Egypt, so that no Egyptian would use any weapon against them. He slew Apis, the sacred ox, and burned other idols of Egypt. To contrast the two cities of Memphis and Thebes, we must remember: Thebes would be broken up and the people cut off; Memphis would have its idols destroyed, which meant virtually the entire city.

- FLOYD HAMILTON ("THE BASIS OF THE CHRISTIAN FAITH"[1]) comments on this important difference: "Now if we compare Memphis with Thebes, where idols are still standing in great numbers, and where the images are still seen on the temple walls, the wonder of the fulfilled prophecy grows even more amazing. How did it happen that the prophecies about the two cities were not interchanged? How did it happen that it was not Thebes where the idols were destroyed, and Memphis which was to exist and yet be broken up? How did it happen that among all the ruined cities of Egypt, Memphis was selected for the peculiar fate of having its idols destroyed?"

EZEKIEL 30:14 "THEBES WILL BE DESTROYED ('BROKEN UP') AND FIRED" *"I will make Pathros desolate, set fire to Zoan, and execute judgments in No."*

- JOHN URQUHART ("THE WONDERS OF PROPHECY"[1]): "The judgments against Thebes ("No" in the above Scripture) were so strong, historians have unrealizingly presented the fulfillment's. Ezekiel lived during Nebuchadnezzar's reign, and 13 years after this king was gone and the Persians were the dominant empire, Cambyses (525 BC) invaded Egypt and hammered at the defenseless brow of Thebes as much destruction as anyone so crazy could deliver. He burned the temples and tried to destroy the colossal statues. Thebes rose quickly from this but carried a limp she would never shake off. Strabo is recorded to have observed Thebes in 25 BC and claimed that the city was broken up into multiple villages, in which form it has remained even in modern times - broken up and disunited. It seems phenomenal to note that the prophecy stipulated even the condition in which it would forever remain."

- AMELIA EDWARDS ("A THOUSAND MILES UP THE NILE"[1]) is recorded to have observed the scattered and sparse relics of ancient grandeur: "Much of what remains is hardly worth the effort of observing; and the leftovers are so few, they can be listed with ease. One can hardly believe that a great city ever flourished on this spot."

EZEKIEL 30:15 "THEBES: I WILL CUT OFF THE MULTITUDE OF..." *"I will pour My fury on Sin, the strength of Egypt; I will cut off the multitude of No."*

- JOHN URQUHART ("THE WONDERS OF PROPHECY") says: "Even then, Thebes remained among the top cities financially in the area. Yet about 89 BC, a siege was laid to the city which lasted three years. When Thebes finally did fall, it fell into eternal oblivion. It was virtually leveled, thus fulfilling Ezekiel 30:14-15. Its multitude was cut off and never returned."

EZEKIEL 30:13 "THERE WILL NO LONGER BE A NATIVE PRINCE FROM EGYPT" *'Thus says the Lord God: "I will also destroy the idols, and cause the images to cease from Noph; there shall no longer be princes from the land of Egypt; I will put fear in the land of Egypt."'*

- This final prediction has been neglected, but applies even today. This prophecy concerning the absence of a native prince from Egypt has been completely fulfilled. The prediction did not claim eternal anarchy, but that her government would be headed by foreigners.

| Prophecy #4: The Destruction of BABYLON | 2,112 - 536BC | 4.5 |

ISAIAH 13:19	"Babylon to be like Sodom and Gomorrah"
ISAIAH 13:20, JEREM. 51:24-26	"Never inhabited again"
ISAIAH 13:20	"Tents will not be placed there by Arabs"
ISAIAH 13:20	"Sheepfolds will not be there"
ISAIAH 13:21-22	"Desert creatures will infest the ruins"
JEREMIAH 51:26	"Stones will not be removed for other construction projects"
JEREMIAH 51:43	"The ancient city will not be frequently visited"
ISAIAH 14:23	"Covered with swamps of water"

* Probability of all these Prophecies being fulfilled = 1:5,000,000,000

What is Babylon?

Babylon means "babilu" (gate of god). It is an ancient city in the plain of shinar on the Euphrates River, about 50 miles south of Modern Baghdad. Babylon was founded by **Nimrod** of Genesis 10, who developed the world's first system of idolatry, which God condemned (Genesis 11). It later became the capital of the Babylonian Empire.

Babylon was overwhelming in size and appearance. The International Standard Bible Encyclopedia[1], and the historical records of Herodotus[1], give these details on the size and might of Babylon (even greater than Nineveh):

- 196 square miles: 14-mile sides, 56-mile circumference
- The city was surrounded by a 30-foot moat, with double walls
- The outer wall was 311 feet high (30-story building), 87 feet wide (8 chariots abreast, or 11 cars across)
- The city had 100 gates of solid brass
- The city had 250 watchtowers, 100 feet higher than the outer walls

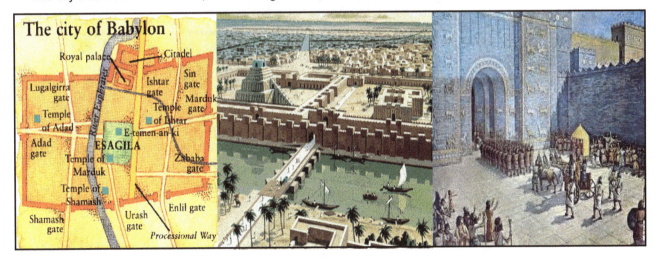

Who were the Babylonians?

The Babylonian Empire was the most powerful state in the ancient world after the fall of **Assyria** in 612BC. Its capital **Babylon** was beautifully adorned by king **Nebuchadnezzar**. Even after the Babylonian Empire was overthrown in 539BC by the Persian king **Cyrus the Great**, Babylon remained an important cultural center.

The city of **Babylon** first appears around 2112BC after the fall of the Empire of the Third Dynasty of Ur, which had ruled the city states of the alluvial plain between the rivers **Euphrates** and **Tigris**. The kings of the nation of the Amorites are known as the First Dynasty of Babylon (1894-1595BC). The area was reunited by **Hammurabi**, a king of Babylon of Amorite descent (1792-1750BC). From his reign on, the alluvial plain of southern Iraq was called **Babylonia**. It is one of the most fertile and rich parts of the ancient world.

There was no stopping the increasing power of the **Hittite** Empire (in Anatolia) and the **Kassite** tribes in the Zagros. It was impossible for the Babylonians to fight against all these enemies at the same time, and they started to lose grip. In 1595BC the Hittite king Mursilis I advanced along the Euphrates, sacked Babylon, and took away the statue of the supreme god of Babylonia, **Marduk**. After this raid, the Kassite tribes took over the city.

In the 13th century, the Babylonian rulers had to respect Assyrian kings like **Shalmaneser** and Tikulti-Ninurta, who captured Babylon and took away the image of Marduk. Another local power was **Elam**. In the 12th century, its armies looted Babylon. Now it was their turn to capture the statue of **Marduk** as well as the famous stele with the laws of king Hammurabi, which was discovered during an excavation in the Elamite capital **Susa**.

god Marduk (798BC)   Sacred Dragon of Marduk

Under king **Aššurnasirpal II** (883-859BC), the Assyrian empire started to grow again. One of the great challenges was the integration of Babylonia, which was Assyria's twin-culture and too highly esteemed to be reduced to the status of province. **Tiglath-pileser III** (744-727BC) united the two countries in a personal union. But the Babylonians twice claimed their independence under king Marduk-apla-iddin (710BC and 703BC; the biblical **Merodach Baladan**). The second revolt was punished harshly by the Assyrian leader **Sennacherib**, who sacked the city and deported its inhabitants to Nineveh. Sennacherib's successor **Esarhaddon** allowed the people to return, but the relation between Assyria and the Babylonians remained tense. **Aššurbanipal** (668-631BC) made his brother Šamaš-šuma-ukin viceroy of the southern part of Mesopotamia, but while he was involved in other wars, the Babylonian king revolted, and it took Aššurbanipal several years before he had restored order. In 627BC, after the death of Aššurbanipal, the Assyrian king Sin-šar-iškun sent two of his relatives to be governors of Babylon. They were expelled by a Babylonian soldier named **Nabopolassar**, who had once fought in the Assyrian army but now started a kingdom for himself. According to the Babylonian chronicle known as **ABC2**, he was recognized as king on 23 November 626BC. Nabopolassar continued the struggle against Assyria, which he wanted to overthrow.

In 617BC, Nabopolassar laid siege to Aššur, the religious capital of Assyria. The Assyrians repelled him, but in 615BC the **Medes**, a tribal federation living in modern Iran, intervened. Nabopolassar signed a treaty with their king **Cyaxares**, cemented by a royal wedding of his son, the Babylonian crown prince **Nebuchadnezzar**, to the Mede princess Amytis. The united Medes and Babylonians laid siege to the Assyrian capital **Nineveh** in May 612BC. The siege lasted for three months. In July, the city fell. King Sin-šar-iškun, who had once been in charge of Babylon, committed suicide.

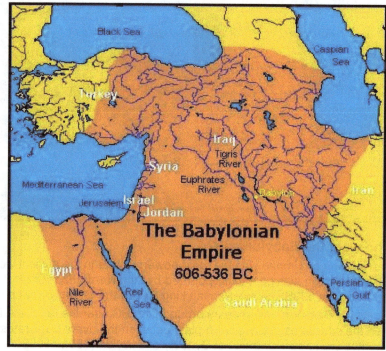

When Nabopolassar died in 606BC, Nebuchadnezzar began Babylonian expansion to the west, capturing **Jerusalem** in 597BC. When Jerusalem's king Jehoiakim revolted, the city was captured again in 586BC, and its people deported to Babylonia, as described in 2Kings 24:1 and the book of **Daniel**. This was the beginning of the Babylonian Captivity of the Jews. To the west, only **Tyre** resisted, and it fell in 575BC. The great monarchy of the ancient Near East had received a new elite: the Assyrians had been replaced by the Babylonians.

Nebuchadnezzar died in 562BC, succeeded by his son Amel-Marduk, who was immediately murdered and replaced by his brother-in-law Neriglissar (559-556BC), who was replaced by a new king, **Nabonidus**, who obtained power by a coup d'état. The reason may have been that Neriglissar was a commoner - rich, but without royal blood. The man most likely behind the coup was the king's son **Belshazzar** (Daniel chapter 5).

In 539BC, the Persian king **Cyrus** attacked and captured Babylon. His son **Cambyses** was made viceroy. This spelled the eventual end of the Babylonian empire by 536BC. Cyrus now became ruler of Syria and Palestine as well. The book of **Ezra** describes how Cyrus allowed the Jews, who were exiled to Babylon, to return home.

Isaiah (783-704 BC) and **Jeremiah** (626-586 BC) predicted these future events on Babylon:

ISAIAH 13:19 "BABYLON TO BE LIKE SODOM and GOMORRAH" *"And Babylon, the glory of the kingdoms, the beauty of the Chaldeans' pride, will be as when God overthrew Sodom and Gomorrah."*

- AUSTEN LAYARD ("DISCOVERIES AMONG THE RUINS OF NINEVEH AND BABYLON"[1]): "...the site of Babylonia naked and hideous waste. Owls start from the scanty thickets and the foul jackal skulks through the furrows. Truly, 'the glory of the kingdoms and the beauty of the Chaldees' excellency is as when God overthrew Sodom and Gomorrah."

- ENCYCLOPEDIA BRITANNICA[1]: "Until the 19th century the knowledge of Babylonia and Assyria was based on the Old Testament and a few Greek writers. Not until after the discovery of ancient monuments and written documents in the two countries, and especially after the decipherment of the cuneiform script and the languages written in this script, did the history and civilization of Babylonia and Assyria become known."

- GERALD A. LARUE ("BABYLON AND THE BIBLE"[1]): "Immediately the struggle for portions of the empire began among Alexander's generals after his death. Babylon was wracked by political struggles and battles for control and by the plundering activities of the troops of the contending parties. Possession of the city was shuttled back and forth until finally it became the property of the Seleucids. So badly shattered was the once beautiful city that it was apparent that reconstruction would be as costly as building a new city and the Seleucids decided on the latter course. The city of Seleucid was constructed on a site 40 miles north of Babylon on the Tygris river and one by one business establishments and commercial interests moved out of Babylon to Seleucia."

- ROBERT KOLDEWEY ("THE EXCAVATION OF BABYLON"[1]): "The city walls, for instance, which in other ancient towns measure 3 meters, or at most 6-7 meters, in Babylon are fully 17-22 meters thick. On many ancient sites the mounds piled above the remains are not more than 2 or 3 to 6 meters high, while here we have to deal with 12-24 meters, and the vast extent of the area that was once inhabited is reflected in the grand scale of the ruins."

JEREMIAH 51:24-26, ISAIAH 13:20 "NEVER INHABITED AGAIN" *"And I will repay Babylon and all the inhabitants of Chaldea for all the evil they have done in Zion and in your sight," says the Lord. "Behold, I am against you, O destroying mountain who destroys all the earth," says the Lord. "And I will stretch out My hand against you, roll you down from the rocks, and make you a burnt mountain. They shall not take from you a stone for a corner nor a stone for a foundation, but you shall be desolate forever," says the Lord.*

"It will never be inhabited, nor will it be settled from generation to generation; nor will the Arabian pitch tents there, nor will the shepherds make their sheepfolds there."

- GERALD A. LARUE ("BABYLON AND THE BIBLE"[1]): "During the reign of Augustus (27BC-14AD) Strabo visited the site and commented 'The great city has become a desert.' And Trajan visited Babylon in 116AD during his campaign against the Parthians and found, according to Cassius, 'mounds and legends of mounds.' 54 miles south of modern Baghdad lie the desolate, sand-swept ruins of once the proud city of Babylon."

- EDWARD CHIERA ("THEY WROTE ON CLAY: THE BABYLONIAN TABLETS SPEAK TODAY"[1]): "The sun has just now disappeared, and a purple sky smiles, unmindful of the scene of desolation...a dead city! I have visited Pompeii and Ostra, but those cities are not dead: they are only temporarily abandoned. The hum of life is still heard and life blooms all around...here only is real death... I should like to find a reason for all this desolation. Why should a flourishing city, seat of an empire, have completely disappeared? Is it the fulfillment of a prophetic curse that changed a superb temple into a den of jackals?"

- MERRILL UNGER ("UNGER'S BIBLE DICTIONARY"[1]) says: "On October 13, 539BC, Babylon fell to Cyrus of Persia and from that time on the decay of the city began. Xerxes plundered it. Alexander the Great thought to restore its great temple, in ruins in his day, but was deferred by the prohibitive cost. During the period of Alexander's successors the area decayed rapidly and soon became a desert."

ISAIAH 13:20 "TENTS WILL NOT BE PLACED THERE BY ARABS" *"It will never be inhabited, nor will it be settled from generation to generation; nor will the Arabian pitch tents there, nor will the shepherds make their sheepfolds there."*

- FLOYD HAMILTON ("THE BASIS OF CHRISTIAN FAITH"[1]): "Travelers report that the city is absolutely uninhabited, even by Bedouins. There are various superstitions current among the Arabs that prevent them from pitching their tents there, while the character of the soil prevents the growth of vegetation suitable for the pasturage of flocks."

- NORA B. KUBIE ("ROAD TO NINEVEH"[1]): "The workmen for Austen Layard refused to set up near the abandoned ruins of Babylon. A sense of mystery and dread hung over the crumbling heaps of brick and sand."

ISAIAH 13:20 "SHEEPFOLDS WILL NOT BE THERE" *"It will never be inhabited, nor will it be settled from generation to generation; nor will the Arabian pitch tents there, nor will the shepherds make their sheepfolds there."*

• PETER STONER ("SCIENCE SPEAKS: AN EVALUATION OF CERTAIN CHRISTIAN EVIDENCES"[1]): "There are no sheepfolds about Babylon."

ISAIAH 13:21-22 "DESERT CREATURES WILL INFEST THE RUINS" *"But wild beasts of the desert will lie there, and their houses will be full of owls; ostriches will dwell there, and wild goats will caper there. The hyenas will howl in their citadels, and jackals in their pleasant palaces. Her time has come, and her days will not be prolonged."*

• AUSTEN LAYARD ("DISCOVERIES AMONG THE RUINS OF NINEVEH AND BABYLON"[1]): "Wild beasts of the desert lie there; and their houses are full of doleful creatures; and owls dwell there, and satyrs dance there. And the wild beasts of the island cry in the desolate houses, and dragons in their pleasant places, for her day has come. A large gray owl is found in great numbers, frequently in flocks of nearly 100, in the low shrubs among the ruins of Babylon."

• GEORGE DAVIS ("BIBLE PROPHECIES FULFILLED TODAY"[1]): "Professor Kerman Kilprect, the well-known archaeologist, in his book 'EXPLORATIONS IN BIBLE LANDS IN THE 19TH CENTURY', says:'...what a contrast between the ancient civilization and the modern degradation. Wild animals, boars, and hyenas, jackals, and wolves, and an occasional lion infest the jungle.'"

• EDWARD CHIERA ("THEY WROTE ON CLAY: THE BABYLONIAN TABLETS SPEAK TODAY"[1]) says: "Under my feet are some holes which have been burrowed by foxes and jackals. At night they descend stealthily from their haunts in their difficult search for food, and appear silhouetted against the sky. This evening they appear to sense my presence and stay in hiding, perhaps wondering at this stranger who has disturbed their peace. The mound is covered with white bones which represent the accumulated evidence of their hunts."

JEREMIAH 51:26 "STONES WILL NOT BE REMOVED FOR CONSTRUCTION PROJECTS" *"They shall not take from you a stone for a corner nor a stone for a foundation, but you shall be desolate forever," says the Lord.*

Today: Ruins of the ancient city of Babylon with one of Saddam Hussain's palaces in the background.

• PETER STONER ("SCIENCE SPEAKS: AN EVALUATION OF CERTAIN CHRISTIAN EVIDENCES"[15]): "Bricks and building materials of many kinds have been salvaged from the ruins for cities round about, but the rocks, which were imported to Babylon at such great cost, have never been moved."

JEREMIAH 51:43 "THE ANCIENT CITY WILL NOT BE FREQUENTLY VISITED" *"Her cities are a desolation, a dry land and a wilderness, a land where no one dwells, through which no son of man passes."*

• PETER STONER ("SCIENCE SPEAKS: AN EVALUATION OF CERTAIN CHRISTIAN EVIDENCES"[15]): "Though nearly all ancient cities are on prominent tourist routes, Babylon is not, and has very few visitors."

ISAIAH 14:23 "COVERED WITH SWAMPS OF WATER" *"I will also make it a possession for the porcupine, and marshes of muddy water; I will sweep it with the broom of destruction," says the Lord of hosts.*

• NORA B. KUBIE ("ROAD TO NINEVEH"[1]) says: "Not a blade of grass would grow in the peculiar soil, blanched as if with a deadly poison, and the reedy swamps round about breathed a miasma of fever. Layard looked out over the malarial swamp called by the Arabs 'The Desert of Waters'...after the city's fall, the great engineering works of Babylonia were neglected, the irrigation canals became choked up, and the rivers overflowed."

• ENCYCLOPAEDIA BRITANNICA[1]: "A large part of the old city buried under a deep bed of silt remains to be found, and the Babylon of Hammurabi, of which only the slenderest traces have been detected, now lies beneath the water table."

• AUSTEN LAYARD ("DISCOVERIES AMONG THE RUINS OF NINEVEH AND BABYLON"[1]) says: "The great part of the country below ancient Babylon has now been for centuries one great swamp...the embankments of the rivers, utterly neglected, have broken away, and the waters have spread over the face of the land."

> **CONCLUSION #1: "Compare BABYLON (Prophecy #4) to EGYPT (Prophecy #3)"** FLOYD HAMILTON ("THE BASIS OF CHRISTIAN FAITH"[1]) challenges us to "notice the difference between the prophecies concerning BABYLON and EGYPT: the Babylonian nation was to disappear, Egypt to continue as a base nation and has continued as a base nation. How did it happen that both of these unlikely events came to pass exactly according to the way in which prophecy was worded, and the names were not exchanged?"
>
> **CONCLUSION #2: "Look at which God of History Remains Today"** There were many centers of religious worship in the ancient world: Memphis-Thebes, Babylon, Nineveh, and Jerusalem among them. The pagan deities which men said claimed an equal footing with the one God, Yahweh, never did last, especially after Jesus Christ. Yet Yahweh refuses to even consider Himself on equal terms with these pagan gods, and even went further by condemning the cities in which these gods flourished. It is one thing to issue threats, but the point here is to look at history. Which city out of the above listed has remained?

Babylon: Ancient History Brought to Life (from "ARMY LIVE", Official Blog of the US Army, July 22, 2009)

AL HILLAH, Iraq – High-reaching walls, ancient statues and a past filled with wonders and fame are an intrinsic part of Babylon. Maj. Gen. Rick Nash, Multi-National Division – South commanding general, Brig. Gen. Gerald Lang, MND-S deputy commanding general for support, Command Sgt. Maj. Doug Julin, MND-S senior enlisted leader and other Soldiers and civilians visited the site July 18 to see what this ancient city has to offer for Iraq.

"The mission (to Babylon) was to educate those on the command staff and some of the primary staff members on the importance of the religious aspects of this country and what there is to offer," said Julin. "Even though we are at war there are some very important things we have to preserve here and help them preserve as well."

Babylon's story is not only one of great length, but also one of much fame and historical significance. To archaeologists, the historic significance comes from the age of Nebuchadnezzar II in approximately 600 BC. This was called the Golden Period. Most of the great parts were built during this age, the Hanging Gardens

Maj. Gen. Rick Nash, Multi-National Division – South commanding general, looks over what is left of the foundation of Ishtar's Gate. (U.S. Army photo by Sgt. Debralee P. Crankshaw)

which were one of the Seven Wonders of the World and, in addition to that, the construction of Babylon tower and other (structures) here, like the walls, temples and palaces.

The tour of the site begins by passing through a re-creation of the **Ishtar Gate**. This gate was originally built by Nebuchadnezzar II in 575 BC. It was dedicated to Ishtar, the goddess of love and war. It was built with glazed blue tiles with alternating rows of dragons and bulls. The dragons were a tribute to Marduk, the god of water, vegetation, judgment and magic. The bulls were dedicated to the rain god, Adad. The re-creation was built in the 1930's with site tiles. The foundation of the original gate remains at the site.

There is also significance in the city for those interested in war and military commanders. Alexander the Great conquered the city in 331 BC. Babylon became the center of his empire for his 12-year campaign against the Persians and India. He died in Babylon in 323 BC. His generals fought for control of his empire, causing the citizens of Babylon to disperse. Babylon never regained its position as a great world power.

To religious people, Babylon also has a strong significance. "Babylon is a very important empire and city in the Old Testament. It figures prominently in the development of the Jewish faith as well as the Christian faith," said Chap. (Lt. Col.) John Morris, MND-S command chaplain. "Muslims revere

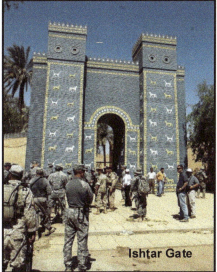
Ishtar Gate

many of the prophets who were in Babylon who were mentioned in the Old Testament," said Morris. "Christians understand Babylon from the New Testament. It's mentioned prominently in the Book of Revelation as a city and as a metaphor for a gigantic civilization in opposition to God. So, that empire and that city are important for people of monotheist faiths to understand the development of their faith."

Today, surveys are being conducted to determine the possibility of making Babylon a historic and tourism site. For people like Morris, this is an exciting prospect as he saw the visit as a unique opportunity. "To be there today for me personally as a person of faith and a Christian is a sacred privilege," he said.

Prophecy #5: MOAB & AMMON 1,200 - 580BC   4.6

EZEKIEL 25:1-4	"Will be taken by Easterners who will live off the fruits of the land"
EZEKIEL 25:1-4	"Men of the east" will make Ammon a site for their palaces"
JEREMIAH 48:47, 49:5-6	"People of old Moab and Ammon will reinhabit their land"

* Probability of all these Prophecies being fulfilled = 1:1,000

Who were the Moabites & Ammonites?

Moab is the historical name for a mountainous strip of land in modern-day Jordan running along the eastern shore of the Dead Sea. It was home to the kingdom of the Moabites, a people often in conflict with their Israelite neighbors to the west. Their capital was **Dibon**, located next to the modern Jordanian town of **Dhiban**.

In Genesis, the Moabites are described as relatives of the Israelites, both peoples tracing their descent back to a common ancestor, **Terah**. Terah's son **Haran** fathered **Lot**, whose son **Moab** was born after an incestuous relationship between Lot and his eldest daughter (Genesis 19:30-38). Moab was the son of **Abraham's** nephew Lot by his elder daughter, while **Ammon** was Moab's half-brother by a similar union of Lot with his younger daughter after the destruction of **Sodom**. The close ethnicity of Moab and Ammon is confirmed by history, while their kinship with the **Israelites** is proven by the linguistic evidence of the **Moabite Stone** (aka **Mesha Stele**).

The Moabites were friendly with the **Egyptians**, having kinship ties with them through **Joseph**. The Moabites welcomed Egyptian protection provided by border fortresses that enabled Egypt to control the Sinai. One of these forts was at Ir-Moab, on the Arnon River. During Joseph's era Egypt traded with **Damascus**, moving goods through Moab.

Mesha Stele

The Moabites' existence is proven by archeological findings, especially the **Mesha Stele**, with this inscription from Mesha, King of Moab: *"I am Mesha, son of Chemosh, king of Moab. My father was king of Moab for thirty years and I became king after my father: and I built this sanctuary to Chemosh (one of the many Canaanite gods) in Qerihoh, a sanctuary of refuge: for he saved me from all my oppressors and gave me dominion over all my enemies. Omri was king of Israel and oppressed Moab many days, for Chemosh was angry with his land. And his son succeeded him and he also said I will oppress Moab. In my days he said this, but I got the upper hand of him and his house: and Israel perished for ever... I have had the ditches of Qerihoh dug by Israelite prisoners.."*

TIME Magazine (December 18, 1995 Vol. 146, No. 25): *"The skeptics' claim that King David never existed is now hard to defend. Last year the French scholar Andre Lemaire reported a related "House of David" discovery in Biblical Archaeology Review. His subject was the Mesha Stele (also known as the **Moabite Stone**), the most extensive inscription ever recovered from ancient Palestine. Found in 1868 at the ruins of biblical Dibon and later fractured, the basalt stone wound up in the Louvre, where Lemaire spent seven years studying it. His conclusion: the phrase "House of David" appears there as well. As with the Tel Dan fragment, this inscription comes from an enemy of Israel boasting of a victory--King Mesha of Moab, who figured in the Bible. Lemaire had to reconstruct a missing letter to decode the wording, but if he's right, there are now two 9th century references to David's dynasty ".*

When Israel came out of the desert wilderness on their way to Canaan, Moses asked the king of Moab to allow Israel to pass through his country, promising to stay on the highway and offering to pay for any water which the people or animals would drink. But the king refused to grant Moses permission (Judges 11:17).

Deuteronomy 23:3-6 states that because neither the Moabites nor Ammonites provided any assistance to the Israelites, they were to be excluded from the assembly of worshipers (*"They did not come to meet you with food and drink when you were on your way out of Egypt, and even hired **Balaam**, son of Beor, to oppose you by cursing you."*) In these verses, God forbade Israel to do anything beneficial for the nations of Moab and Ammon.

The Israelites were allowed to harass Moab, but were forbidden to wage war on them, so they defeated **Midian** as a result of the advice that Balaam gave that led to a plague in punishment for the worship of idols at Baal Peor. This applied only to the men, but the women were permitted to convert. That is why **King David**, who descended from **Ruth**, (a Moabite) could be king and his grandson **Rehoboam** son of **Solomon** had a mother from Ammon.

<u>The Religion of the Moabites & Ammonites</u>: They were polytheists, and induced the Israelites to join in their sacrifices (Numbers 25:1-3). The chief god of the Moabites was **Chemosh** (Jeremiah 48:7,13). The Israelites sometimes referred to them the "people of Chemosh" (Numbers 21:29). The chief god of the Ammonites was **Molech**, or Baal Moloch.

Molech was represented as a huge bronze statue, depicted as a man with the head of a bull. The statue was hollow, and inside a fire burned which colored the Molech a glowing red. **Human sacrifices** were offered to him, as by Mesha, who gave up his son and heir (2Kings 3:26-27). Children were placed on the hands of the statue, which were raised to the mouth (as if Molech were eating) and the children fell into the fire and were consumed. The people gathered before Molech and danced, the sounds of flutes and tambourines drowning out the children's' screams.

Nevertheless, King Solomon built, for this "abomination of Moab," a "high place" (1Kings 11:7) that was not destroyed until the reign of Josiah (2Kings 23:12-13). The Moabite Stone also mentions a female counterpart of Chemosh, **Ashtar-Chemosh**, and a god **Nebo** probably the well-known Babylonian divinity **Nabu**.

<u>Pride was the trademark of the Moabites and Ammonites</u>: Moab was financially secure (Isaiah 15:7; Jeremiah 48:7,36) and had never suffered adversity as other nations (Jeremiah 48:11). They were used to plentiful harvests of "summer fruits" and wine (Isaiah 16:9-10; Jeremiah 48:32-33). As a result of their prosperity, Moab's pride, where they even "magnified himself against the Lord" (Jeremiah 48:26), was held in contempt by God (Jeremiah 48:29-30 and Isaiah 16:6). Jeremiah also mentioned Ammon's confidence in earthly riches and their foolish, boastful pride (Jeremiah 49:4).

The Ammonites brought God's wrath upon themselves by rejoicing at Judah's fall and the destruction of God's temple (Ezekiel 25:1-3; 21:28-32). Jeremiah said Moab literally "skipped for joy" to see Judah's anguish (Jeremiah 48:27), and Ammon had pleasure in Judah's suffering, **Ezekiel** lamented, "Thou hast clapped thine hands, and stamped with the feet, and rejoiced in heart with all thy despite against the land of Israel" (Ezekiel 25:4-7). The same bitter destruction by **King Nebuchadnezzar** awaited them (Jeremiah 25:21; 27:1-6; 48:38-39).

Although he was in captivity, hundreds of miles away, God told Ezekiel to choose the spot of ground where Nebuchadnezzar would divide his Babylonian army, sending one arm against Judah and the other to Rabbath, the capitol of Ammon (Ezekiel 21:18-22). Nebuchadnezzar overran Judah, and the Ammonites brutally seized the unprotected territory of Gilead, accomplishing their long-held desire to take from Israel the land which Moses took from the Amorites (Judges 11:12-13; Jeremiah 49:1). God then promised to play the part of Israel's near-kinsman and give Israel what the Ammonites possessed (Jeremiah 49:2). **Amos** and **Jeremiah** both prophesied that Rabbath, the capitol, and the cities of Ammon would be burned with fire (Amos 1:14; Jeremiah 49:2).

Over half a century later, when Judah returned from Babylonian captivity, **Tobiah the Ammonite** was one of the chief antagonists to Nehemiah, trying to stop the Jews' rebuild of Jerusalem's walls (Nehemiah 2:10; 4:7-8).

<u>Although Moab and Ammon were almost always antagonistic toward Israel, the exceptions are remarkable</u>:

1) When David was being sought by King Saul, he was granted refuge in Moab, and even was allowed to bring his parents to Moab for safety (1Samuel 22:3-4). During this time, **Nahash**, king of Ammon, showed kindness to David as well, for which David was very grateful (2Samuel 10:1-2). This friendship with David continued through one of Nahash's sons, Shobi (2Samuel 17:27), even though Nahash's other son, Hanun, who reigned in the place of his father, started a war with David by abusing David's ambassadors (2Samuel 10).

2) Among those warriors in David's army who had proved themselves to be most trustworthy and valiant was a man from Moab and one from Ammon (1Chronicles 11:39,46). Much later, when Judah's King **Joash** turned from righteousness and murdered the prophet Zechariah, he was assassinated by two of his own servants, one an Ammonite and the other a Moabite (2Chronicles 24:25-26).

3) The story of **Ruth** shows friendly relations between **Moab** and **Bethelehem**, one of the towns of the tribe of Judah. By his descent from Ruth, David had Moabite blood in his veins. He committed his parents to the king of Moab's protection (who may have been his kinsman), when hard pressed by **King Saul** (1 Samuel 22:3,4).

But here all friendly relations stop forever. The next time the name is mentioned is in the account of David's war, where he made the Moabites pay tribute.

Jeremiah (626-586BC) and **Ezekiel** (592-570BC) predicted the following future events on Moab and Ammon:

EZEKIEL 25:1-4 "WILL BE TAKEN BY EASTERNERS WHO WILL LIVE OFF FRUITS OF THE LAND"; "MEN OF EAST WILL MAKE AMMON A SITE FOR PALACES" *The word of the Lord came to me, saying, "Son of man, set your face against the Ammonites, and prophesy against them. Say to the Ammonites, 'Hear the word of the Lord God! Thus says the Lord God: "Because you said, 'Aha!' against My sanctuary when it was profaned, and against the land of Israel when it was desolate, and against the house of Judah when they went into captivity, indeed, therefore, I will deliver you as a possession to the men of the East, and they shall set their encampments among you and make their dwellings among you; they shall eat your fruit, and they shall drink your milk."*

• HOWARD VOS ("FULFILLED PROPHECY IN ISAIAH, JEREMIAH & EZEKIEL"[1]):"So rich and powerful was the nation of the Ammonites when Jeremiah wrote 'Ammon shall be a desolate heap' that it seemed very unlikely that such a catastrophe would ever occur. The emir Abdullah of the East, ruler of Transjordania, built his palace there, fulfilling another prophecy that the men of the East shall possess Ammon and set dwellings and palaces in her. In recent days the emir has distinguished himself as director of the Arab legion, which has taken such an active part in the fighting with the Jews in Palestine. Today the city of Ammon has a population of over 20,000, is a stopping place of the Damascus-Hejaz railway, and has officials of other nations numbered among its population. The men of the East do inherit her at the present."

JEREMIAH 48:47, 49:5-6 "PEOPLE OF MOAB & AMMON WILL REINHABIT THEIR LAND" *"Yet I will bring back the captives of Moab in the latter days," says the Lord. "Thus far is the judgment of Moab. Behold, I will bring fear upon you," says the Lord God of hosts, "From all those who are around you; you shall be driven out, everyone headlong, and no one will gather those who wander off. But afterward I will bring back the captives of the people of Ammon," says the Lord.*

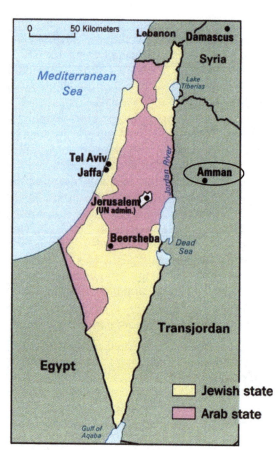

• GEORGE DAVIS ("BIBLE PROPHECIES FULFILLED TODAY", 1931[1]): "Both lands are making rapid strides forward after their long sleep of centuries. **Ammon**, the capital of Transjordan, is the old Rabbath of the Ammonites, that was captured by Joab and the Israelites acting under the direction of King David. Only a dozen years ago Ammon was a mere village of 200-300 people. Today it is a flourishing city with of 20,000 people and is the residence of the ruler of Transjordan, the emir Abdellah."

• JOSH MCDOWELL ("EVIDENCE THAT DEMANDS A VERDICT"[1]): "Possibly the people inhabiting Moab and Ammon are not the ancient Moabites and Ammonites, but even if this possibility were to be entertained, is it too much of a stretch of the imagination to see it happening in the future?"

• HOWARD VOS ("FULFILLED PROPHECY IN ISAIAH, JEREMIAH & EZEKIEL"[1]) says: "The impact of this material has been so great that a writer in a purely secular encyclopedia with a tremendous circulation has said: 'But Israel remained a great power while Moab disappeared. It is true that Moab was continuously hard pressed by desert hordes; the exposed condition of the land is emphasized by the chains of ruined forts and castles which even the Romans were compelled to construct. But the explanation is to be found within Israel itself, and especially in the work of the prophets.'"

Prophecy #6: The Destruction of SAMARIA 880BC - 66AD 4.7

HOSEA 13:16	"The city will fall violently"
MICAH 1:6	"Become 'as a heap in the field'"
MICAH 1:6	"Vineyards will be planted there"
MICAH 1:6	"It's stones will be poured down into the valley"
MICAH 1:6	"It's foundations shall be discovered"

* Probability of these Prophecies being fulfilled = 1:40,000

What is Samaria?

Originally the name "**Samaria**" denoted the territory of the tribes of Ephraim and half of Manasseh. It was bounded by **Galilee** to the north, Judea to the south, the Mediterranean Sea to the west, and the Jordan River to the east. It corresponds roughly to the northern portion of the modern West Bank territory.

Samaria was built by King **Omri** in 880BC. IKings 16:24 says the hill was purchased by King Omri from a man named Shemer for 2 talents of silver. Omri made it his capital.

Omri's son **Ahab**, the next king, put up "an altar for Baal in the temple of Baal" in Samaria (IKings 16:32) under the influence of his Phoenician wife **Jezebel**. Omri's dynasty ended with the revolution of **Jehu**, the founder of the new dynasty, who destroyed Ahab's shrine (2Kings 10:18-28).

About 721BC, Assyrian king **Sargon II** captured it, and its inhabitants were transported into captivity (2Kings 17:6). It was in this area that the Assyrians settled deportees from other countries alongside the remnants of the Israelite population, who in time became known as the **Samaritans**. The new inhabitants worshiped their own gods, and appealed to Sargon II for Israelite priests to instruct them on how to worship the "God of that country." The resulting religion mixed worship of the Hebrew god with other gods of the nations from which they had been brought.

Samaritanism is a religion closely related to Judaism but not considered part of it, and its adherents are not considered to be Jews. Samaritanism uses the **Torah** as its holy book. Their temple was at Mount Gerizim, not Jerusalem, and was destroyed by the Maccabees in the second century BC. The antagonism between Samaritans and Jews is important in understanding the New Testament stories of the "Good Samaritan" and the **Samaritan Woman**. After the Jews' return from the Babylonian Exile, they began to rebuild the Temple in Jerusalem. The Samaritans, with their center at Shechem, offered to help but were rejected. This began the antagonism between Jews and Samaritans (Ezra 4; Nehemiah 2:10).

During the 4th century BC, the Samaritans built their center at Samaria. In 332BC the city was captured by **Alexander the Great**, who settled Macedonian veterans there. Then in 108BC it was conquered and utterly destroyed by John Hyrcanus, and the Hasmoneans imposed Judaism on its Samaritan inhabitants. In 63BC Pompey annexed Samaria to the Roman province of Syria. Augustus gave the capital of Samaria to **Herod**, who rebuilt it into one of the most magnificent cities in Palestine and renamed it Sebaste in honor of the Roman emperor **Augustus** (Greek, Sebastos). In 6 AD it became part of the Roman province of **Judea**. During the First Jewish Revolt in 66 AD it was destroyed then rebuilt. In the late Roman period the city declined and became an unimportant village in the Byzantine period.

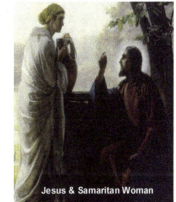
Jesus & Samaritan Woman

Samaria's wealth stemmed from agriculture (wheat and barley in the valleys, grapes and olives in the hill country), and the fact that one of the main branches of the Via Maris (the coastal highway) ran through it.

Christian tradition places the tomb of **John the Baptist** at Samaria (several churches were constructed there for this reason, the latest by the Crusaders in the 12th Century).

Hosea (748-690 BC) and **Micah** (738-690 BC) predicted the devastation of this city, with specific prophecies.

HOSEA 13:16 "THE CITY WILL FALL VIOLENTLY" *"Samaria is held guilty, for she has rebelled against her God. They shall fall by the sword, their infants shall be dashed in pieces, and their woman with child ripped open."*

- INTERNATIONAL STANDARD BIBLE ENCYCLOPEDIA[1]: "Sargon took Samaria in 722 BC. Not only did Samaria fall by the sword in 722 BC, but also in 331 BC by Alexander the Great and a third time in 120 BC by John Hyracanus, all conquerors causing great damage and death to the citizens of Samaria. Even the skeptic who would contend that the destruction of Samaria came after the event will not be able to disagree about the rest of the ramifications."

MICAH 1:6 "BECOME AS A HEAP IN THE FIELD" *"Therefore I will make Samaria a heap of ruins in the field, places for planting a vineyard; I will pour down her stones into the valley. And I will uncover her foundations."*

- JOHN URQUHART ("THE WONDERS OF PROPHECY"[1]): Henry Maundrell's reaction in 1697 to what he witnessed: "Sabaste is the ancient Samaria, the imperial city of the ten tribes after their revolt from the house of David...this great city is now wholly converted to gardens, and all tokens that remain to testify that there has ever been such a place, are only on the north side, a large square piazza encompassed with pillars, and on the east some poor remains of a great church."

- "ISRAEL: AN UNCOMMON GUIDE", by JOAN COMAY[1]: "The remains of magnificent buildings of that period, as well as great circular towers...can easily be identified today."

MICAH 1:6 "VINEYARDS WILL BE PLANTED THERE, IT'S STONES WILL BE POURED DOWN THE VALLEY, IT'S FOUNDATIONS SHALL BE DISCOVERED" *"Therefore I will make Samaria a heap of ruins in the field, places for planting a vineyard; I will pour down her stones into the valley. And I will uncover her foundations."*

Ruins of Samaria

- JOHN URQUHART ("THE WONDERS OF PROPHECY"[1]): "As it was then found, it has since remained, 'The whole hill of Sebastieh,' says Robinson, 'consists of fertile soil; It is now cultivated to the top, and has upon it many olive and fig trees. The ground has been ploughed for centuries; and hence it is now in vain to look for the foundations and stones of the ancient city.' The stones of the great city have been taken up by the cultivators and piled together or thrown down the hillsides, that its site might be turned into fields and vineyards."

- VAN DE VELDE (from Uruqhart's "THE WONDERS OF PROPHECY"[1]): calls Samaria "a pitiable hamlet, consisting of a few squalid houses, inhabited by a band of plunderers...the shafts of a few pillars only remain standing to indicate the sites of the colonnades...Samaria, a huge heap of stones! Her foundations discovered, her streets ploughed up, and covered with corn fields and olive gardens...Samaria has been destroyed, but her rubbish has been thrown down into the valley; her foundation stones, those grayish ancient quadrangular stones of the time of Omri and Ahab, are discovered, and lie scattered about on the slope of the hill."

- FLOYD HAMILTON ("THE BASIS OF THE CHRISTIAN FAITH"[1]): "Today the top of the hill where Samaria stood is a cultivated field with the foundations of the columns marking the place where the palaces and mansions stood. At the foot of the hill, in the valley, lie the foundations of the stones of the city..."

- JOAN COMAY ("ISRAEL: AN UNCOMMON GUIDE"[1]): "The remains of magnificent buildings of that period, as well as great circular towers...can easily be identified today."

Prophecy #7: GAZA-ASHKELON   2,000BC - 1,250AD   4.8

AMOS 1:8	"Philistines will not continue"
JEREMIAH 47:5-7	"Baldness shall come upon Gaza"
ZEPHANIAH 2:4-5	"Desolation shall come on Ashkelon"
ZEPHANIAH 2:6	"Shepherds and sheep will dwell around Ashkelon"
ZEPHANIAH 2:7	"Remnant of House of Judah will reinhabit Ashkelon"

* Probability of all these Prophecies being fulfilled = 1:12,000

What is Gaza-Ashkelon?

Ashkelon is mentioned 13 times in the Old Testament. It was the oldest (2000-1550BC) and largest seaport in **Canaan**, a large city of the **Philistines**, north of **Gaza**, with 15,000 people living inside walls 1.5 miles long, 50 feet high and 150 feet thick. On the sea it was defended by a high natural bluff.

The Philistines primarily worshipped **Ba'al** and **Dagon** (see Lesson 3.1). One of Ashkelon's most striking archaeological findings was a bronze and silver calf dating to over 3,500 years ago, about that time of Exodus 32:19: *"When Moses approached the camp and saw the calf and the dancing, his anger burned and he threw the tablets out of his hands, breaking them to pieces at the foot of the mountain"*

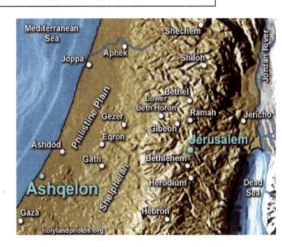

Amarna Letters

Another incredible find of archaeology was the **Amarna Letters** (382 clay tablets written over 30 years in Akkadian cuneiform), discovered around 1887, which include letters from King **Yidya** of Ashkelon (1350BC) to Egyptian pharaoh **Akhenaten**. They are an historical record of Egyptian relations with **Babylon**, **Assyria**, the **Mitanni**, the **Hittites**, **Syria** and **Canaan**.

The **Philistines**, who conquered Ashkelon about 1150BC, fought constantly with the **Israelites** and the kingdom of Judah. This seaport was the last of the Philistine cities to hold out against **Nebuchadnezzar**, who destroyed it in 604BC, taking the people into exile and completely ending the Philistine era. With the annihilation of the Philistine occupation, Ashkelon was rebuilt and became an important Hellenistic seaport. Queen **Cleopatra VII** used Ashkelon as her place of refuge when her brother and sister exiled her in 49BC.

Ashkelon was the birthplace of **Herod the Great**. **Josephus** records that Herod built several monuments there: bath houses, elaborate fountains and large colonnades. The city remained loyal to Rome during the First Revolt, 66–70AD, and in the following centuries it grew to be an important center.

The Crusades: Ashkelon was an important city due to its location near the coast and between the Crusader States and Egypt. In 1099AD, shortly after the siege of Jerusalem, an Egyptian Fatimid army was defeated by a Crusader force at the Battle of Ascalon. This battle is widely considered to have signified the end of the **First Crusade**. In 1153, during the **Second Crusade**, the city was captured by a Crusader army led by King Baldwin III of Jerusalem. In 1187 Saladin took Ashkelon as part of his conquest of the Crusader States following the Battle of Hattin. In 1191, during the **Third Crusade**, Saladin demolished the city because of its potential strategic importance to the Christians, but the leader of the Crusade, King Richard I of England, constructed a citadel upon the ruins. The Egyptians regained Ashkelon in 1247 during As-Salih Ayyub's conflict with the Crusader States. In 1250AD the Egyptian Mamluk dynasty came into power, and the Sultan ordered Ashkelon to be destroyed. As a result of this destruction, the site was abandoned by its inhabitants and fell into disuse.

Ashkelon Today: After the Israel War of Independence (1948) its regrowth began. Today Ashkelon is a bustling resort, home of one of the most popular marinas in the eastern Mediterranean.

Amos (775-750BC), **Jeremiah** (626-586BC) and **Zephaniah** (640-621BC) predicted future events on Gaza-Ashkelon:

AMOS 1:8 "PHILISTINES WILL NOT CONTINUE" *"I will cut off the inhabitant from Ashdod, and the one who holds the scepter from Ashkelon; I will turn My hand against Ekron, and the remnant of the Philistines shall perish," says the Lord God.*

- GEORGE DAVIS ("BIBLE PROPHECIES FULFILLED TODAY"[1]): "Not only was Ashkelon destroyed but the entire nation of the Philistines was 'cut off' precisely as predicted by the prophet Ezekiel 2500 years ago. The Philistines have been destroyed so completely that there is not a single Philistine living anywhere in the world today."

JEREMIAH 47:5-7 "BALDNESS SHALL COME UPON GAZA" *"Baldness has come upon Gaza, Ashkelon is cut off with the remnant of their valley. How long will you cut yourself? O you sword of the Lord, how long until you are quiet? Put yourself up into your scabbard, rest and be still! How can it be quiet, seeing the Lord has given it a charge against Ashkelon and against the seashore? There He has appointed it."*

- PETER STONER ("SCIENCE SPEAKS: AN EVALUATION OF CERTAIN CHRISTIAN EVIDENCES"[15]): "A city of Gaza still exists", writes "so for a long time the prophecy with respect to Gaza was thought to be in error. Finally a careful study was made of the location of Gaza, as described in the Bible, and it was found that the new city of Gaza was in the wrong location. A search was made for the old city and it was found buried under the sand dunes. It had indeed become bald. What better description could you give a city buried under sand dunes than to say that it had become bald?"

- JOHN URQUHART ("THE WONDERS OF PROPHECY"[1]): "...but meanwhile the prophecies had been so fully accomplished that the ancient city of Gaza could lift no protest against the mistake that was being made. The modern town is not built, as Dr. Keith afterwards discovered, on the site of the old, and is not therefore the subject of the prophecies. The great Gaza of the Philistines lay two miles nearer the shore and is now a series of sandhills, covered with minute but manifold remains. It is so forsaken that there is not a single hut resting on its site. It is so bald that neither pillar nor standing stone marks the place where the city stood, nor is there a single blade of grass on which the weary eye can rest."

ZEPHANIAH 2:4-5 "DESOLATION SHALL COME ON ASHKELON" *"For Gaza shall be forsaken, and Ashkelon desolate; they shall drive out Ashdod at noonday, and Ekron shall be uprooted. Woe to the inhabitants of the seacoast, the nation of the Cherethites! The word of the Lord is against you, O Canaan, land of the Philistines: 'I will destroy you; so there shall be no inhabitant."*

- GEORGE DAVIS ("BIBLE PROPHECIES FULFILLED TODAY"[1]): "Judgment fell upon the Philistines precisely as predicted. Sultan Bibars destroyed Ashkelon in 1270 AD and filled up its harbor with stones. Since that time, for nearly 700 years, the once mighty city of Ashkelon has lain waste and desolate."

- FLOYD HAMILTON ("THE BASIS OF THE CHRISTIAN FAITH"[1]): "There was a Turkish garrison in Ashkelon as late as the 17th century, but since that time it has been deserted. Portions of the wall with its ruined towers and battlements still remain, although Ashkelon alone of all the cities of the plain has walls still standing."

ZEPHANIAH 2:6 "SHEPHERDS AND SHEEP WILL DWELL AROUND ASHKELON" *"The seacoast shall be pastures, with shelters for shepherds and folds for flocks."*

- PETER STONER ("SCIENCE SPEAKS: AN EVALUATION OF CERTAIN CHRISTIAN EVIDENCES"[15]): "But in 270 AD Sultan Bibars destroyed it, and it has become the grazing place for many flocks of sheep. It is dotted with shepherds' huts and sheepfolds."

ZEPHANIAH 2:7 "REMNANT OF HOUSE OF JUDAH WILL REINHABIT ASHKELON" *"The coast shall be for the remnant of the house of Judah; they shall feed their flocks there; in the houses of Ashkelon they shall lie down at evening. For the Lord their God will intervene for them, and return their captives."*

- GEORGE DAVIS ("BIBLE PROPHECIES FULFILLED TODAY"[1]): "Following the establishment of the state of Israel the Jews recognized the splendid location of the old city of Ashkelon on the seacoast of their country. They decided to make it a beautiful city of Israel's new state. The Jerusalem Post says the new city of Ashkelon has been 'designed on the lines of a garden city. After long centuries of mighty Ashkelon lying waste and desolate, it is now being transformed into a garden city. The coast of the Mediterranean is indeed for 'the house of Judah', and 'in the house of Ashkelon shall they lie down in the evening. Long desolate Ashkelon has been revived from its ruins of centuries, and is becoming a garden city. And God has visited His people Israel and turned away their captivity and caused them to inhabit once desolate and now restored Ashkelon!"

Prophecy #8: The Destruction of PETRA & EDOM 1,010 - 312BC   4.9

ISAIAH 34:13	"Become a desolation"
JEREMIAH 49:18	"Never populated again"
EZEKIEL 25:14	"Conquered by heathen, Conquered by Israel"
EZEKIEL 35:5, ISAIAH 34:6-7	"Shall have a bloody history"
EZEKIEL 25:12-13	"Make Edom desolate as far as the city of Teman"
ISAIAH 34:13-15	"Wild animals will inhabit the area"
ISAIAH 34:10, EZEKIEL 35:7	"Cessation of trade"
JEREMIAH 49:17	"Spectators will be astonished"

* Probability of all these Prophecies being fulfilled = 1:10,000

What is Petra?

In the movie 'Indiana Jones and the Last Crusade', Sean Connery plays Indie's father whose obsession is to find the Holy Grail. Their quest to find the sacred relic leads them to the ruins of a lost city which was conquered by the crusaders back during medieval times. To find the city, the two travel by horseback through a winding narrow canyon, with towering granite walls on both sides. The canyon opens up onto a spectacular view of a city with its walls and pillars literally carved into the face of the massive rock cliffs that surround the area.

This city, which most moviegoers are probably unaware of, is the rock fortress of **Petra**, a major city of the Biblical **Edomites**. The city of Petra is one of the greatest discoveries of biblical archaeology. Petra, from the Greek word for "rock", was a crossroad for civilizations. By 700 BC some of the earliest known farmers lived north of Petra, making it contemporary with Jericho. The Petra Basin is watered by the Spring of Moses, from which the nearby modern town of Wadi Mousa gets its name. It is here that **Moses** struck a rock with his staff to extract water (Numbers 20:10-13). Aaron, brother of Moses, died nearby and is buried atop Mount Hora (aka Mount Aaron).

Who were the Edomites?

The Edomites were the descendants of Jacob's brother **Esau** (Genesis 36:43). They lived in the mountainous regions south of the Dead Sea. Edom is the Aramaic word for "red". They controlled the trade routes between the Arabian Peninsula and Damascus in what is today **Syria**.

Esau was always against his brother **Jacob**. He plotted once to kill Jacob because he had deceived his father Isaac into giving him the blessing of the first-born. Later, when Israel needed passage on their way to the promised land, Esau's descendants denied Israel permission to travel through their territory. Because of their constant hostility against Israel, God declared their fate in Malachi 1:2-4 (..."Yet Jacob I have loved; But Esau I have hated, and laid waste his mountains and his heritage for the jackals of the wilderness.").

From 550BC to 400BC the Edomites were overrun by Nabatean Arabs who ransacked their territory. Although Petra was inhabited by others up until the Crusaders conquered it, the city was completely deserted until being rediscovered by archaeologists in the late 1800's. Once a mighty fortress on a major trade route between North Africa and Europe, now it is a wasteland of stones, thorns and thistles, crawling with snakes, lizards, and owls by night, while birds of prey can be seen circling the sky's overhead by day.

ISAIAH 34:13 "BECOME A DESOLATION" *"And thorns shall come up in its palaces, nettles and brambles in its fortresses; it shall be a habitation of jackals, a courtyard for ostriches."*

JEREMIAH 49:18 "NEVER POPULATED AGAIN" *"As in the overthrow of Sodom and Gomorrah and their neighboring cities," says the Lord, "No one shall abide there. Nor shall a son of man dwell in it."*

- DAVID HIGGINS ("THE EDOMITES CONSIDERED HISTORICALLY & PROPHETICALLY"[1]): "The awful fate of Edom and its causes are clear. Edom would become a desolate wilderness because she had mistreated Israel (in contrast, Joel 3:20 predicts the perpetuity of Judah and Jerusalem. All the other prophetic utterances against Edom which followed were but a development of these two verses of Joel (Joel 3:19-20): 'Egypt shall be a desolation, and Edom a desolate wilderness, because of the violence against the people of Judah, for they have shed innocent blood in their land. But Judah shall abide forever, and Jerusalem from generation to generation.' Isaiah 34 predicts that, where once men and their palaces and fortresses were prominent, wild animals and weeds would become conspicuous. Travelers in Edom have marveled at the fulfillment of this prophecy down to the very details. Again and again the desolation of Edom is foretold. In the time of the prophets such a prediction seemed most unlikely of fulfillment. Even after the Edomites had been pushed out, the Nabateans developed a flourishing civilization that lasted for centuries. But God had said, 'I will lay the cities waste.' Today the land stands deserted, a mute testimony to the sure word of the Lord. Petra is a remarkable example of the literal fulfillment of this prophecy. This great ancient capital with its theater seating 4,000, its temples, its altars and its monuments, is now silent and alone, decaying with the passage of time."

EZEKIEL 25:14 "CONQUERED BY HEATHEN & CONQUERED BY ISRAEL" *"I will lay My vengeance on Edom by the hand of My people Israel, that they may do in Edom according to My anger and according to My fury; and they shall know My vengeance," says the Lord God.*

- GEORGE L. ROBINSON ("SARCOPHAGUS OF AN ANCIENT CIVILIZATION; PETRA, EDOM & THE EDOMITES"[1]): "After Saul's death, the Edomites took the first opportunity afforded them of showing their hatred of Israel. While David was occupied in North Syria smiting Hadadezer, king of Zobah, Edom seems to have invaded the southern part of Judah, even threatening Jerusalem. But upon David's return the much older kingdom of Edom was terribly reduced by the younger kingdom of Israel; 18000 of the Edomites being smitten in the valley of salt at the south end of the Dead Sea. David conquered Edom, which remained subservient to Judah even during the time of the divided monarchy, until the rule of Jehoram."

- HOWARD VOS ("FULFILLED PROPHECY IN ISAIAH, JEREMIAH & EZEKIEL"[1]): "The freedom which Edom gained from Judah proved to be only the preparation for more bondage - this time to Assyria. With the passing of Assyrian virility, Chaldean hordes swept down from Transjordan, gobbling up Edom with the rest of the nations."

- BERNARD RAMM ("PROTESTANT CHRISTIAN EVIDENCES"[1]): "That the Jews conquered them (Edomites) is proved by reference to 1Maccabees 5:3 and to Josephus' Antiquities. They were attacked successively by John Hyrcanus and Simon of Gerasa. Therefore, the prediction that the Jews too would conquer them has been fulfilled."

- DAVID HIGGINS ("THE EDOMITES CONSIDERED HISTORICALLY & PROPHETICALLY"[1]) says: "It was predicted in Ezekiel 25:14 that Israel would be used by God to take vengeance on Edom. Considering the fact that Israel was then in the Babylonian captivity, such a prophecy probably seemed ludicrous. Yet, some four centuries later the prediction finds its fulfillment in Judas Maccabeus and John Hyrcanus. Thousands of Edomites were slain and the nation was forced to submit to Jewish circumcision, and for all practical purposes they became Jews."

EZEKIEL 35:5-6, ISAIAH 34:6-7 "SHALL HAVE A BLOODY HISTORY" *"Because you have had an ancient hatred, and have shed the blood of the children of Israel by the power of the sword at the time of their calamity, when their iniquity came to an end, therefore as I live," says the Lord God, "I will prepare you for blood, and blood shall pursue you; since you have not hated blood, therefore blood shall pursue you."*

"The sword of the Lord is filled with blood, it is made overflowing with fatness, and with the blood of lambs and goats, with the fat of the kidneys of rams. For the Lord has a sacrifice in Bozrah, and a great slaughter in the land of Edom. The wild oxen shall come down with them, and the young bulls with the mighty bulls; their land shall be soaked with blood, and their dust saturated with fatness."

- DAVID HIGGINS ("THE EDOMITES CONSIDERED HISTORICALLY AND PROPHETICALLY"[1]): "A study of Edom's history has already borne this out. Assyria invaded the land and reduced Edom to servitude. The coming of Nebuchadnezzar took its toll. The migration of the Nabateans reduced their numbers - 40,000 Edomites died at the hands of Judas Maccabeus."

EZEKIEL 25:12-13 "MAKE EDOM DESOLATE AS FAR AS THE CITY OF TEMAN" *Thus says the Lord God: "Because of what Edom did against the house of Judah by taking vengeance, and has greatly offended by avenging itself on them, Therefore thus says the Lord God: "I will also stretch out My hand against Edom, cut off man and beast from it, and make it desolate from Teman; Dedan shall fall by the sword."*

- FLOYD HAMILTON ("THE BASIS OF THE CHRISTIAN FAITH"[1]): "And strange as it may seem, Teman, or Maan as it is called today, is still a prosperous town, on the eastern border of the land of Edom, and the only city in all that land that is not deserted! Could any more marvelous fulfillment of prophecy be found than this? Think what small chance there would be of a mere man picking out only one city in the whole land as the one city that should live down the centuries, while all the other cities shared in the general fate of destruction and desolation! God alone could foretell such a result, and the book which contains such prophecies must be His book!"

ISAIAH 34:13-15 "WILD ANIMALS WILL INHABIT THE AREA" *"And thorns shall come up in its palaces, nettles and brambles in its fortresses; it shall be a habitation of jackals, a courtyard for ostriches. The wild beasts of the desert shall also meet with the jackals, and the wild goat shall bleat to its companion; also the night creature shall rest there, and find for herself a place of rest. There the arrow snake shall make her nest and lay eggs and hatch, and gather them under her shadow; there also shall the hawks be gathered, everyone with her mate."*

- GEORGE SMITH ("THE BOOK OF PROPHECY"[1]): "Captain Mangles, who visited these ruins, says that when surveying the scenery of Petra, 'The screaming of eagles, hawks and owls, who were soaring over our heads in considerable numbers, seemingly annoyed at anyone approaching their lonely habitation, added much to the singularity of the scene.' It was also declared, 'It shall be a habitation for dragons (or serpents). I laid his heritage waste for the dragons of the wilderness.' Dr. Shaw represented the land of Edom, and the desert of which it now forms a part, 'as abounding with a variety of lizards and vipers, which are very numerous and troublesome.' And Volney relates that 'The Arabs, in general, avoid the ruins of the city of Idumea, on account of the enormous scorpions with which they swarm.' 'So plentiful', as observed by Mr. Cory, 'are the scorpions in Petra, that, though it was cold and snowy, we found them under the stones, sometimes two under one stone!'"

ISAIAH 34:10, EZEKIEL 35:7 "CESSATION OF TRADE" *"It shall not be quenched night or day; its smoke shall ascend forever. From generation to generation it shall lie waste; no one shall pass through it forever and ever."*
"Thus I will make Mount Seir most desolate, and cut off from it the one who leaves and the one who returns."

- ENCYCLOPEDIA BRITANNICA[1]: "Petra was already in decline at the time of the Islamic invasion in the 7th century. In the 12th century the Crusaders built a castle there called Sel. Otherwise, the site was occupied only by wandering tribesmen, and it was in this condition when rediscovered by the Swiss traveler J.L. Burckhardt in 1812."

- GEORGE L. ROBINSON ("THE SARCOPHAGUS OF AN ANCIENT CIVILIZATION"[1]): "Since Burckhardt's discovery of this wild desert metropolis in 1812, only occasional explorers and a comparatively small number of tourists have ventured to run the risk of visiting its ruins."

JEREMIAH 49:17 "SPECTATORS WILL BE ASTONISHED" *"Edom also shall be an astonishment; everyone who goes by it will be astonished and will hiss at all its plagues."*

- ALEXANDER KEITH ("EVIDENCE OF THE TRUTH OF THE CHRISTIAN RELIGION"[1]): "I would that the skeptic could stand as I did, among the ruins of this city among the rocks, and there open the sacred Book and read the words of the inspired penman, written when this desolate place was one of the greatest cities in the world. I see the scoffer arrested, his cheek pale, his lip quivering, and his heart quaking with fear, as the ruined city cries out to him in a voice loud and powerful as that of one risen from the dead, - though he would not believe Moses and prophets, he believes the handwriting of God Himself in the desolation and eternal ruin around him."

- GEORGE L. ROBINSON ("THE SARCOPHAGUS OF AN ANCIENT CIVILIZATION"[1]): "Petra is a place which astonishes and baffles, but above all fascinates. Your first visit is an event in your life. Elemental feelings stir; again you know what awe is and humility. You have a sense of God's work through man and without man. If you have never experienced the sensation before, here at last you come under the spell of mystery. The place seems so remote, so unrelated to its surroundings...so undiscoverable. What other city has been lost for thousands of years and at last, when stumbled upon by accident, has had still so much of its glory left with which to astonish the amazed traveler?"

- HENRY MORRIS ("THE BIBLE AND MODERN SCIENCE"[1]): "Edom and the Edomites are mentioned time and time again in the Bible, but were completely forgotten in secular history until the 19th century, when references to them were found in Egyptian and Assyrian monuments. Finally the preserved remains of their capital city, Petra, 'the Rock City', were discovered. Thus the critics, who had maintained the Edomites to be legendary, were again routed."

| Prophecy #9: | PALESTINE | 1,200BC - Today | 4.10 |

LEVITICUS 26:31,33	"Palestine cities will resemble waste"
LEVITICUS 26:31	"Desolation will come over the sanctuaries"
LEVITICUS 26:32,33	"Desolation will come over the land"
LEVITICUS 26:32	"Palestine will be inhabited by enemies"
LEVITICUS 26:33	"Jews will be persecuted"
EZEKIEL 36:33-35	"Palestine will be reinhabited by Jews, cities will revive and the land farmed"

* Probability of all these Prophecies being fulfilled = 1:20,000

What is Palestine?

Palestine is a name used to describe a geographic region between the Mediterranean Sea and the Jordan River, and various adjoining lands. As a geographic term, Palestine is the area that today includes **Israel** and the Israeli-occupied Palestinian territories, as well as part of **Jordan**, and some of both **Lebanon** and **Syria**. The Arabic word for Palestine is **Philistine**. The Bible calls the region **Canaan** (Numbers 34:1-12), while the part of it occupied by Israelites is designated Israel. The events of the four Gospels take place almost entirely in this country, which in Christian tradition thereafter became known as the **Holy Land**.

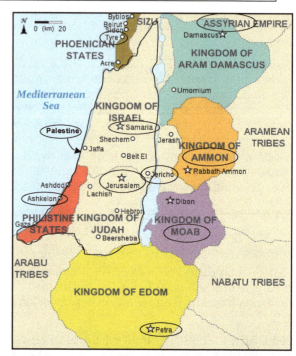

- 1200-1020 BC = The Kingdom of Israel was centered in Jerusalem over an area approximating modern-day Israel and the Palestinian territories (see map). An archaeological textual reference to the territory of Palestine is found in the **Merneptah Stele**, containing a recount of Egyptian king Merneptah's victories in the land of Canaan, mentioning Gezer, Ashkelon and Yanoam, along with Israel.

- 1020 BC = the Kingdom of Israel was established, with Saul as its first king.

- 1000 BC = **Jerusalem** became the capital of King David's kingdom, and shortly afterwards the First Temple was constructed by King **Solomon**.

- 930 BC = Israel split into the northern kingdom of Israel and the southern kingdom of Judah. These kingdoms co-existed in the greater Palestine area with **Edom** to the South of **Judah** and **Moab** and **Ammon** to the East of the River Jordan. One of the most important archaeological findings from this era is the **Mesha Stele** (850BC), bearing an inscription by the Moabite King Mesha, discovered in 1868 at **Dhiban** (biblical "Dibon," capital of Moab) now in **Jordan**. The Stele is the earliest known reference to the sacred Hebrew name of God – YHWH. It also is the most extensive inscription that refers to ancient Israel.

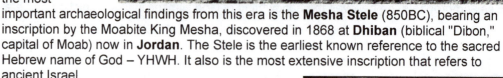
From the Merneptah Stele "Israel is wasted, its seed is no longer"

Mesha Stele

- 722-720 BC = the northern Kingdom of Israel was destroyed by the Assyrians and the Israelite tribes were exiled. An important finding from the southern Kingdom of Judah is the Siloam Insxcription (700 BC), which celebrates the successful digging from both sides of the Jerusalem wall to create the water tunnel and pool of **King Hezekiah** (see 2Kings 20:20).

- 586 BC = the **Babylonians** conquered the southern kingdom of Judah and Jerusalem. The **First Temple** was destroyed. Most of the surviving Jews were deported to **Babylonia**.

- 538 BC = the Babylonian Empire fell to the **Persian Empire**, and the Jews were allowed to return to the Land of Israel, and it was during this period that the Second Temple in Jerusalem was built.
- 333 BC = The Persian Empire fell to Greek general **Alexander the Great**. After his death, his conquests were divided among his generals, while the region of the Jews ("Judah" or **Judea** as it became known) was first part of the **Ptolemaic Dynasty** and then part of the **Seleucid Empire**.
- 140-37 BC = An independent Jewish kingdom existed under th **Hasmonean Dynasty**. The fascination in Jerusalem for Greek culture resulted in a movement to break down the separation of Jew and Gentile. Disputes between the leaders of the reform movement, Jason and Menelaus, eventually led to civil war and the intervention of **Antiochus IV Epiphanes**. Subsequent persecution of the Jews led to the **Maccabean Revolt** under the leadership of the Hasmoneans. After a century of independence disputes, the Roman army of **Pompey** controlled the kingdom.
- 37 BC-3 AD = Roman rule was solidified when **Herod** was made king. Around the time of the birth of **Jesus Christ**, Roman Palestine was in a state of disarray and direct Roman rule was re-established. While most inhabitants became Romanized, the Jews found Roman rule to be unbearable. The early **Christians** were terrorized and oppressed.
- 66-73 AD = As a result of the First Jewish-Roman War, **Titus** sacked Jerusalem and destroyed the Second Temple, leaving only supporting walls, including the Western Wall.
- 132-211 AD = Roman emperor **Hadrian** unsuccessfully tried to expel the Jews from Judea. Large Jewish populations remained in Samaria and Galilee. Hadrian renamed Jerusalem "Aelia Capitolina" and built temples to honor Jupiter.
- 330-536 AD = Emperor **Constantine I** converted to Christianity, making it the official religion of Palestine. In 536AD **Justinian I** promoted the governor at Caesarea to proconsul, expanding Palestine prosperity under the Christian Empire. The cities of Palestine, such as Caesarea Maritima, Jerusalem, Scythopolis, Neapolis, and Gaza reached their peak population in the late Roman period.
- 630-1914 AD = The **Muslims** defeated the empire's forces decisively at the Battle of Yarmouk in 636AD. Jerusalem fell in 638AD and Caesarea around 642AD. The Islamic prophet **Muhammad** established a new unified political polity in the Arabian peninsula at the beginning of the seventh century, seeing a rapid expansion of a vast Muslim Arab Empire. This empire conquered Palestine and it remained under the control of Islamic Empires for most of the next 1300 years. In 691AD, the **Dome of the Rock** was built on the site where the Islamic prophet Muhammad is believed by Muslims to have begun his nocturnal journey to heaven, on the Temple Mount.

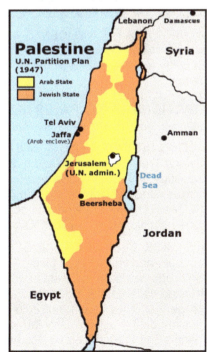

- 1882-1914 AD = The beginning of **Zionist immigration**. The "First Aliyah" was the first widespread wave of Jewish migration to Palestine, coming mostly from Eastern Europe and Yemen. An estimated 25,000–35,000 Jews immigrated during the First Aliyah. This first wave created several settlements in Israel such as Rishon LeZion, Rosh Pina, Zikhron Ya'aqov and Gedera. **Tel Aviv** was founded on land purchased from Bedouins north of Jaffa. In the "Second Aliyah" (1904-1914), 40,000 Jews immigrated, mostly from Russia and Poland. This second wave is credited with reviving the **Hebrew** language, establishing it as the standard language for Jews in Israel. Ottoman rule over the eastern Mediterranean lasted until World War I when the Ottomans sided with **Germany**. During World War I, the Ottomans were driven from much of the region by the **British Empire** during the dissolution of the Ottoman Empire.
- 1917-1948 AD = British foreign minister Arthur Balfour issued the **Balfour Declaration**, which promised a Jewish national home in Palestine. The **British Mandate for Palestine** was issued by the League of Nations to Great Britain on Sept. 29, 1923. Great Britain oversaw Palestine between 1920 and 1948, a period known as the "British Mandate." Two states were established within the Mandate territory, Palestine and Transjordan. The preamble of the mandate declared: *"Whereas the Principal Allied Powers have also agreed that the Mandatory should be responsible for putting into effect the declaration originally made on November 2nd, 1917, by the Government of His Britannic Majesty, and adopted by the said Powers, in favor of the establishment in Palestine of a national home for the Jewish people, it being clearly understood that nothing should be done which might prejudice the civil and religious rights of existing non-Jewish communities in Palestine, or the rights and political status enjoyed by Jews in any other country."*

Moses (1520-1400 BC) and **Ezekiel** (592-570BC) predict the future of this city. While Moses, in *Leviticus*, centers on the destruction of Palestine, Ezekiel predicts its future Jewish reinhabitation and revitalization. The specific prophecies are:

LEVITICUS 26:31,33 "PALESTINE CITIES WILL RESEMBLE WASTE" *"I will lay your cities waste and bring your sanctuaries to desolation, and I will not smell the fragrance of your sweet aromas. I will scatter you among the nations and draw out a sword after you; your land shall be desolate and your cities waste."*

- JOHN URQUHART ("THE WONDERS OF PROPHECY"[1]): "The warning has been with the Jews ever since they first entered the Promised Land. Moses in Leviticus warned that if they completed the sin against the divine plan of Yahweh, the horrible fate would fall upon them as listed in Leviticus 26:31-33. The fulfillment of the Jewish scattering seemed to impair fulfillment concerning the cities' desolation. The new landowners rebuilt the cities and the land was far from desolate. With Constantine on the throne, new churches grew on famous spots of Bible history. The land became so strong that the Persian invasion (7th century) under Chosroes was delayed when going through this. Later, Jerusalem held out 4 months against Arab attackers. The Crusaders (11th century) still saw the strength of the cities in Palestine, yet the prophecy concerning the cities was no empty threat, and long since recognized as fulfilled."

- WERNER KELLER ("THE BIBLE AS HISTORY"[22]): "Archaeologists have found no material evidence of Israel's existence in Palestine after the year 70AD, not even a tombstone with a Jewish inscription. The synagogues were destroyed, even the house of God in quiet Capernaum was reduced to ruins. The inexorable hand of destiny had drawn a line through Israel's part in the concert of nations."

- FLOYD HAMILTON ("THE BASIS OF CHRISTIAN FAITH"[1]): "According to this prophecy, the cities of the land should be a waste and the land a desolation. Palestine today is a land of ruins. In almost no other land are the ruins of cities and villages so numerous as they are in Palestine today. The land that formerly supported such a large population, is now barren and capable of supporting only a mere fraction of its former population."

LEVITICUS 26:31 "DESOLATION WILL COME OVER THE SANCTUARIES" *"I will lay your cities waste and bring your sanctuaries to desolation, and I will not smell the fragrance of your sweet aromas."*

- JOHN URQUHART ("THE WONDERS OF PROPHECY"[1]): "In 70AD the Roman legions smashed, tore and ripped at the marrow of the land, and the inhabitants frantically resisted the invaders. Consequently, the Romans showed even less mercy, and everything that stood for Judaism was destroyed. The temple was smashed and burned. The abominable figure of a pig rested over the gate of Bethlehem. Since that time, the Jew has never sacrificed and the old practice was brought to an abrupt halt."

LEVITICUS 26:32,33 "DESOLATION WILL COME OVER THE LAND" *"I will bring the land to desolation, and your enemies who dwell in it shall be astonished at it. I will scatter you among the nations and draw out a sword after you; your land shall be desolate and your cities waste."*

- MARK TWAIN ("INNOCENTS ABROAD"[1]) wrote about the way he saw Palestine in 1869: "There is not a solitary village throughout its whole extent - not for 30 miles in either direction. There are 2 or 3 small clusters of Bedouin tents, but not a single permanent habitation. One may ride 10 miles hereabouts and not see 10 human beings."

LEVITICUS 26:32 "PALESTINE WILL BE INHABITED BY ENEMIES" *"I will bring the land to desolation, and your enemies who dwell in it shall be astonished at it."*

- JOHN URQUHART ("THE WONDERS OF PROPHECY"[1]): "The Jewish dispersion is a well-known fact of history. They were dug up and gutted out, but this did not happen completely with the first Roman destruction of Palestine. In this, the Jews were crushed and trounced, but not really dispersed. This prediction was totally fulfilled in 135AD, when all of the land was confiscated and sold to Gentiles by Hadrian. From then on, Gentiles, the Jews' enemy, have been in control of Palestine and though the land has changed hands often, the owners have held two characteristics, Gentile background and hostility to Jews."

- SAMUEL CLEMENS ("INNOCENTS ABROAD"[1]) gives a great description of a vicious enemy: "We rested and lunched, and came to this place, Ain Mellahah (the boys call it 'Baldwinsville'). It was a very short day's run, but the dragoman does not want to go further, and has invented a plausible lie about the country beyond this being infested by ferocious Arabs, who would make sleeping in their midst a dangerous pastime. Well, they ought to be dangerous. They carry a rusty old weather-beaten flintlock gun, with a barrel that is longer than themselves; it has no sight on it; it will not carry farther than a brickbat, and is not half so certain. And the great sash they wear in many a fold around their wastes has 2 or 3 absurd old horse-pistols in it that are rusty from eternal disuse - weapons that would hang fire just about long enough for you to walk out of range, and then burst and blow the Arab's head off. Exceedingly dangerous these sons of the desert are."

LEVITICUS 26:33 "PEOPLE OF ISRAEL WILL DISPERSE" *"I will scatter you among the nations and draw out a sword after you; your land shall be desolate and your cities waste."*

- JOHN URQUHART ("THE WONDERS OF PROPHECY"[1]) quotes Rabbi-Nowitz who investigated the area for possible Jewish repopulating: "But meanwhile the doom remains. Rabbi-Nowitz, who went in 1882 to Palestine with the view of determining whether the 'tribes of the wandering foot and weary beast' might not find a refuge in their ancient home, had to abandon the idea. He was compelled to admit that the poverty of the soil and the oppression of the Turkish government make return an impossibility."

LEVITICUS 26:33 "JEWS WILL BE PERSECUTED" *"I will scatter you among the nations and draw out a sword after you; your land shall be desolate and your cities waste."*

- JOHN URQUHART ("THE WONDERS OF PROPHECY"[1]) says: "The history of the Jews is persecution. But the fire poured on their heads was also, in some measure, caused by their own brutality. They helped the Persians capture Jerusalem (7th century) and massacred their Christian prisoners, as well as the Persian Christian captives. The move backfired. It was not so much later that Peter the Hermit began the first Crusade - not in the Holy Land but in Germany where, to protect their 'Christian' homeland, Gentiles furiously slaughtered all Jews in sight all along the route. Fifty years later the same craze swept the Rhineland. Jews suffered in every popular uprising of that land."

- JOHN URQUHART ("THE WONDERS OF PROPHECY"[1]) again says: "England was little better; robbed and hazed by commoner and noble, 500-1500 Jews died in one incident in York. All their property was taken at the end of the 1200's, and they were brutally expelled from the kingdom and not readmitted until Charles II. Mobs in Paris rose against them in 1239 and acted very similarly to Germans. Between about 1400 and 1794, the Jews were outlawed from all of France. The story in Spain is even worse, and well known is the hatred in many other unmentioned countries. The contempt and hatred with which the Jews are still regarded there and elsewhere on the continent are well known, and the trembling of heart of which the prophet spoke has not ceased even now."

- MILMAN ("HISTORY OF THE JEWS"[1]) points out "These periods of insanity seem not to be sparked by any special incident, but appear to seep up to the surface from some deep, hidden hate which knows no bounds. The Jews were blamed for the Black Plague. Also, the Flagellants, a crazed movement of enthusiasts, marched behind a crucifix and tortured themselves for their sins and, as blind fanatics will, mis-reasoned that, to the glory of God and atonement for sin, they plundered and massacred Jews of Frankfurt and elsewhere. The Jews could find no fair protection under the law. They spread around and wandered from place to place: Germany, Brunswick, Austria, Franconia, Rhineland, Silesia, Brandenburg-Prussia, Bohemia, Lithuania, and Poland."

EZEKIEL 36:33-35 "PALESTINE WILL BE REINHABITED BY JEWS, CITIES WILL REVIVE & THE LAND WILL BE FARMED" *'Thus says the Lord God: "On the day that I cleanse you from all your iniquities, I will also enable you to dwell in the cities, and the ruins shall be rebuilt. The desolate land shall be tilled instead of lying desolate in the sight of all who pass by. So they will say, 'This land that was desolate has become like the garden of Eden; and the wasted, desolate, and ruined cities are now fortified and inhabited.'"*

- GEORGE DAVIS ("BIBLE PROPHECIES FULFILLED TODAY"[1]) says: "The return of more than a million Jews to the land of Israel, after being away from their ancient homeland for nearly 2000 years, is one of the most amazing and remarkable miracles of all time. And the astonishing thing about this modern return of the Jews to their homeland is this - it was foretold in detail by the prophet Jeremiah 2500 years ago."

- And as far as "THE LAND BEING TILLED", GEORGE DAVIS ("BIBLE PROPHECIES FULFILLED TODAY"[1]): "For many generations the Negev, in the southern part of Israel, has been largely a dry and isolated wilderness. There were some towns and villages in the Negev, but a large proportion of the inhabitants were roving bands of Bedouin. Today, portions of this long-barren land of the Negev are being cultivated, and are gradually being transformed from desert to fruitfulness and fertility."

- As far as "THE CITIES BEING REBUILT", GEORGE DAVIS ("BIBLE PROPHECIES FULFILLED TODAY"[1]): "For years, Beersheba was a sleepy Arab town with crude buildings and homes. But not long after the winning of the Nageb by the Jews in the Arab-Jewish war, there began to be a change in Beersheba. It came slowly at first. When I visited Beersheba in 1950, 2 years after the war, there were few visible signs of progress. 3 years later when I was again in Beersheba, the transformation of the city was in full swing. Modern houses were replacing old tumbled-down dwellings, as large numbers of Jews began to make their homes in Beersheba. They showed me an area outside the old city which was to be set apart for building factories. The population of the city was now increased to more than 20,000, and it is still growing and flourishing."

- JOSH MCDOWELL ("EVIDENCE THAT DEMANDS A VERDICT"[1]): "Palestine is a bustling place, and it is growing. After 1900 years of oppression, it is remarkable how suddenly, just since 1948, the Jews have built the nation which they have. Before that, they roamed from place to place; yet give them a place to stand and they move the world."

CHAPTER 5   External Evidence Test = NON-BIBLICAL SOURCES   5.1

Skeptic's Charge #14: What sources are there apart from the Bible that confirm its accuracy and reliability? Do other historical sources confirm or deny the Bible's internal testimony?

ANSWER: There are two major sources of external writings that support the Bible's internal testimony:
#1. The New Testament can be reconstructed in its entirety by using only the writings of the early church.
#2. Secular historians recorded significant events that supported the New Testament biblical accounts.

#1. Early Church Writings

Irenaeus (Bishop of Lyons in 180 AD), "Against Heresies III" *"Matthew published his gospel among the Hebrews in their own tongue, when Peter and Paul were preaching the gospel in Rome and founding the church there. After their departure (i.e. death, which strong tradition places at the time of the Neronian persecution in 64AD), Mark, the disciple and interpreter of Peter, himself handed down to us in writing the substance of Peter's preaching. Luke, the follower of Paul, set down in a book the gospel preached by his teacher. Then John, the disciple of the Lord, who also leaned on His breast, himself produced his Gospel, while living at Ephesus in Asia."*

Bruce Metzger (Prof. of NT Language and Literature, Princeton Univ.)[1]: "So extensive are the citations of the early Christian writers that if all other sources for our knowledge of the text of the New Testament were destroyed, they would be sufficient alone for the reconstruction of practically the entire New Testament."

#2. Secular Historians

Eusebius (Greek historian, 100AD), "Ecclesiastical History III" *"The elder (the apostle John) used to say this also: 'Mark, having been the interpreter of Peter, wrote down accurately all that he (Peter) mentioned, whether sayings or doings of Christ, not, however, in order. For he was neither a hearer nor a companion of the Lord; but afterwards, as I said, he accompanied Peter, who adapted his teachings as necessity required, not as though he were making a compilation of the sayings of the Lord. So then Mark made no mistake, writing down in this way some things as he (Peter) mentioned them; for he paid attention to this one thing, not to omit anything that he heard, not to include any false statement among them.'"*

Plinius Secundus (Governor of Bithynia, 112 AD), "Letter to Emperor Trajan" *"Having never been present at any trials of the Christians, I am unacquainted with the methods and limits to be observed either in examining or punishing them, whether any difference is to be made on account of age, or no distinction allowed between the youngest and the adult. Whether repentance admits to a pardon, or if a man has been once a Christian it avails him nothing to recant; whether the mere profession of Christianity, albeit without the commission of crimes, or only the charges associated therewith, are punishable. In the meantime, the method I have observed towards those who have been denounced to me as Christians is this: I interrogated them whether they were in fact Christians; if they confessed it, I repeated the question twice, adding the threat of capital punishment; if they still persevered, I ordered them to be executed. A placard was put up, without any signature, accusing a large number of persons by name. Those who denied they were, or had ever been, Christians, and who repeated after me an invocation to the gods, and who offered formal worship with libation and frankincense, before your statue, which I had ordered to be brought into court for that purpose, together with those of other gods, and who finally cursed Christ – none of which, it is said, those who are really Christians can be forced into performing – these I thought it proper to discharge. Others who were named by the anonymous informer at first confessed themselves Christians, and then denied it; true, they said, they had been of that persuasion but they had quitted it, some 3 years, others many years, and a few as much as 25 years previously. They all worshipped your statue and the images of the gods, and they cursed Christ."*

Cornelius Tacitus (Roman Historian, 115 AD), "Christus, the founder of the Christians"
"But not all the relief that could come from man, not all the bounties that the prince could bestow, nor all the atonements which could be presented to the gods, availed to relieve Nero from the infamy of being believed to have ordered the conflagration, the fire of Rome. Hence to suppress the rumor, he falsely charged with the guilt, and punished Christians, who were hated for their enormities. Christus, the founder of the name, was put to death by Pontius Pilate, procurator of Judea in the reign of Tiberius: but the pernicious superstition, repressed for a time broke out again, not only through Judea, where the mischief originated, but through the city of Rome also. Accordingly, an arrest was first made of all who pleaded guilty; then, upon their information, an immense multitude was convicted, not so much of the crime of firing the city, as of hatred against mankind."

Who was Flavius Josephus?   Paul Maier: *"Josephus: The Essential Writings"* [20]

The Importance of Josephus' writings "Apart from the Bible itself, Flavius Josephus is by far the most important historical source illuminating the entire biblical era. In terms of sheer quantity of data, Josephus provides probably 300 times as much information about Herod the Great as does the Gospel of Matthew, for example, or 10 times as much about Pontius Pilate. He also furnishes fascinating perspectives on Archelaus, Herod Antipas, the two Agrippas, Felix and Festus, as well as intriguing sidelights on John the Baptist, Jesus' half-brother James, and Jesus Himself. The fact that Josephus was born in Jerusalem only four years after the crucifixion of Jesus and wrote about the time the Gospels were composed adds to his value as a virtual eyewitness of events in later New Testament era. He also excels in his geographical and architectural descriptions of the land and its structures, and his accuracy is being progressively affirmed today by archaeological excavations. If Josephus had not existed, all our Bible dictionaries and commentaries would be substantially smaller."

The Life of Josephus (37AD – 100AD) "Born in 37 AD, he was the son of a priest named Matthias and a mother who descended from the royal Jewish family of the Hasmoneans. At age 16, he began studying the principal Jewish sects – Pharisees, Saducees, and Essenes – favoring the Essenes and living for 3 years in the wilderness as a disciple of a hermit named Bannus. But at age 19, he returned to Jerusalem and joined the Pharisees.

In 64 AD he traveled to Rome to intercede in behalf of some Jewish priests whom Felix, the Roman procurator, had sent to Nero for trial. It was during this visit that he was profoundly impressed with the power of Rome...it was the beginning of his 'Romanophile' tendencies. When he returned to Judea, the Jews were on the verge of rebellion against Rome. Josephus, unable to restrain his countrymen, joined the rebellion reluctantly and was appointed commander in Galilee, using Jotapata as his stronghold. But after a siege of 47 days by Vespasian, Jotapata fell. Josephus hid in a cave with some of the townspeople, where they all killed themselves rather than surrender except himself and one other. They emerged from the cave and surrendered. He was brought before Vespasian to be punished, but because of his previous reputation while in Rome he was freed. He added Vespasian's family name "Flavius" to his own. For the rest of the war he served the Romans as mediator and interpreter, appealing to the Jews to surrender. But the Jews vilified him as a coward and traitor.

After the war, he returned to Rome with the Flavians, where he spent the rest of his life. He settled in Vespasian's former mansion with full Roman citizen's rights as well as an imperial pension, from which he devoted himself to a literary career. When he died (around 100 AD), he was honored with a statue at Rome.".

Flavius Josephus, "Antiquities XVIII, 63" ➔ **Jesus the Christ** *"At this time there was a wise man called Jesus, and his conduct was good, and he was known to be virtuous. Many people among the Jews and the other nations became his disciples. Pilate condemned him to be crucified and to die. But those who had become his disciples did not abandon his discipleship. They reported that he had appeared to them three days after his crucifixion and that he was alive. Accordingly, he was perhaps the Messiah, concerning whom the prophets have reported wonders. And the tribe of Christians, so named after him, has not disappeared to this day."*

<u>Commentary</u>: "The above wording is more widely accepted by scholarship of the most famous, and most controversial, passage in "Antiquities". The initial wording in Josephus is suspected of being tampered with, since it so explicitly defends Jesus as the Messiah. Although Eusebius, in 324AD, also records the original Josephus writing, the above rendering matches the Arabic manuscript by 10th century Melkite historian Agapius, and is more widely accepted as accurate since Josephus would not have believed Jesus to be the Messiah nor in His resurrection (he remained a non-Christian Jew)."

Flavius Josephus, "Antiquities XX, 197" ➔ **James the brother of Jesus** *"Upon Festus' death, Caesar sent Albinus to Judea as procurator. But before he arrived, King Agrippa had appointed Ananus to the priesthood, who was the son of the elder Ananus. This elder Ananus, after he himself had been high priest, had 5 sons, all of whom achieved that office, which was unparalleled. The younger Ananus, however, was rash and followed the Saducees, who are heartless when they sit in judgment. Ananus thought that with Festus dead and Albinus still on the way, he would have his opportunity. Convening the judges of the Sanhedrin, he brought before them a man named James, the brother of Jesus who was called the Christ, and certain others. He accused them of having transgressed the law, and condemned to be stoned to death."*

Flavius Josephus, "Antiquities XVIII, 106" ➔ **John the Baptist** *"To some of the Jews, Herod's disaster seemed to be divine vengeance for his treatment of John, surnamed the Baptist. Although John was a good man and exhorted the Jews to lead righteous lives and practice justice toward their colleagues and piety towards God, Herod had put him to death. John taught that baptism must not be employed to obtain pardon for sins committed, but as a consecration of the body, implying that the soul was already purified by proper behavior. When others also joined the crowds around John and were greatly aroused by his preaching, Herod grew alarmed that such eloquence could lead to rebellion. Therefore, he decided that it would be better to strike first and get rid of him, rather than wait for an uprising. Although John was brought in chains to Machaerus and put to death in that stronghold, the Jews decided that the destruction of Herod's army was God's vindication of John."*

Lucian of Samosata (Greek Historian, 170 AD), "The Crucified Sage of the Christians"
"The Christians, you know, worship a man to this day – the distinguished personage who introduced their novel rites, and was crucified on that account… You see, these misguided creatures start with the general conviction that they are immortal for all time, which explains the contempt of death and voluntary self-devotion which are so common among them; and then it was impressed on them by their original lawgiver that they are all brothers, from the moment that they are converted, and deny the gods of Greece, and worship the crucified sage, and live after his laws. All this they take quite on faith, with the result that they despise all worldly goods alike, regarding them merely as common property."

What can we learn about Jesus from Lucian?
1) Jesus is called the 'crucified sage', the one who 'introduced their (Christians') novel rites' – so Lucian confirms Jesus as the founder of Christianity.
2) Lucian confirms the crucifixion of Jesus Christ.
3) Lucian helps us understand not only the behavior and practices of Christians in Lucian's time, but also the attitude of non-believers like Lucian towards Jesus and Christians (Jesus is recognized as a 'sage', but His teachings, and the tenets of Christian belief is generally regarded as nonsense. As Dr. Norman Geisler says, in the book 'Baker Encyclopedia of Christian Apologetics', *"Despite being one of the church's most vocal critics, Lucian gives one of the most informative accounts of Jesus and early Christianity outside the New Testament."*

Babylonian Talmud (70 AD – 200 AD), "Yeshu was hanged on the eve of the Passover"
Gary Habermas, in his book 'The Historical Jesus', quotes the following from the BabylonianTalmud: *"On the eve of the Passover Yeshu was hanged. For forty days before the execution took place, a herald went forth and cried, 'He is going forth to be stoned because he has practiced sorcery and enticed Israel to apostasy. Any one who can say anything in his favor, let him come forward and plead on his behalf.' But since nothing was brought forward in his favor he was hanged on the eve of the Passover."* (Babylonian Talmud, v. III, Sanhedrin 43a).

What can we learn about Jesus from this passage in the Talmud?
1) 'Yeshu' is the name 'Jesus', and is the one who 'practiced sorcery', which matches the New Testament (see Mark 3:22, Matt. 9:12,24,34, where Jewish authorities tried to attribute sorcery to Jesus' miracles)
2) The fact and timing of the crucifixion matches the New Testament (see John 19:14, Galatians).
3) The attitude of the religious leaders matches the New Testament (they tried to stone Him at first, but then they, not the Romans, insisted on crucifixion).

Answering the Skeptics' Charge #15:   Did Jesus Christ really exist?   **5.2**

William Lane Craig (1949 -): PhD Philosophy, Univ. of Birmingham ; Prof. of Philosophy, Talbot School of Theology, Biola Univ.; Authored or edited over 30 books, with Craig's primary contribution to philosophy of religion is his defense of two major positions that are used in his defense of the Christian faith: 1) Resurrection of Jesus Christ, and 2) The Kalam Cosmological Argument (based on the following three premises: a) everything that begins to exist has a cause of its existence). b) the universe began to exist, c) therefore, the universe has a cause for its existence. He is a very popular public debater, being very much in demand at universities to take the Christian position against the New Atheists.

The information below is taken from Dr. Craig's website, "Reasonable Faith", in the 'Q&A' section, and is his response to the topic "Stephen Law on the Non-existence of Jesus of Nazareth".

"When I first encountered this article (by Philosophy Professor Stephen Law, entitled 'Evidence, Miracles, and the Existence of Jesus,' Faith and Philosophy, 2011) in my debate preparation, my first thought was that only a philosophy journal would publish such a piece! This article would never have made it past the peer-review process for a journal of New Testament or historical studies.

Even a radical skeptic like Bart Ehrmann savages the so-called "mythicists" who claim that we have no good evidence that Jesus of Nazareth was a real person: 'Few of these mythicists are actually scholars trained in ancient history, religion, biblical studies or any cognate field, let alone in the ancient languages generally thought to matter for those who want to say something with any degree of authority about a Jewish teacher who (allegedly) lived in first-century Palestine. . . . But even taking these into account, there is not a single mythicist who teaches New Testament or Early Christianity or even Classics at any accredited institution of higher learning in the Western world. And it is no wonder why. These views are so extreme and so unconvincing to 99.99 percent of the real experts that anyone holding them is as likely to get a teaching job in an established department of religion as a six-day creationist is likely to land in a bona fide department of biology' (quoted from Ehrmann's article "Did Jesus Exist?" Huff Post (March 29, 2012). Law's argument for skepticism about Jesus would not be taken seriously by bona fide historical scholars. No wonder! Almost every premise in this argument is unjustified or false.

Law's Premise #1. Extraordinary claims require extraordinary evidence. This sounds so commonsensical, doesn't it? But in fact it is demonstrably false. Probability theorists studying what sort of evidence it would take to establish a highly improbable event came to realize that if you just weigh the improbability of the event against the reliability of the testimony, we'd have to be skeptical of many commonly accepted claims. Rather what's crucial is the probability that we should have the evidence we do if the extraordinary event had not occurred (see S. L. Zabell, "The Probabilistic Analysis of Testimony," Journal of Statistical Planning and Inference, 1988). This can easily offset any improbability of the event itself. In the case of the resurrection of Jesus, for example, this means that we must also ask, "What is the probability of the facts of the empty tomb, the post-mortem appearances, and the origin of the disciples' belief in Jesus' resurrection, if the resurrection had not occurred?" It is highly, highly, highly, improbable that we should have that evidence if the resurrection had not occurred.

Law's Premise #2. There is not extraordinary evidence for any of the divine/miraculous stuff in the NT documents. I suppose it depends on what you mean by "extraordinary," but the evidence for the facts of the empty tomb, Jesus' post-mortem appearances, and origin of the disciples' belief is such that the majority of scholars, even radical critics like Ehrmann, are convinced of their historicity. Moreover, there is no naturalistic theory proposed as an explanation of these three facts which has garnered the allegiance of a significant number of scholars. So the evidence for the central miracle of the New Testament is pretty extraordinary—even though, as mentioned above, that is not a pre-requisite of the verdict of historicity.

Law's Premise #4. Where testimony/documents combine both mundane and extraordinary claims, and there's excellent reason to be skeptical about the extraordinary claims, then there's pretty good reason to be skeptical even about the mundane claims, at least until we possess some pretty good independent evidence of their truth. Premise #4 has little to commend it, I suspect. We may be cautious in such cases—but skeptical? Legends blend historical claims with non-historical marvels, and the presence of the marvels doesn't imply that we should reject the historicity of the mundane claims.

Law's Premise #6. There's no good independent evidence for even the mundane claims about Jesus (such as that he existed). But premise #6 is the most obviously false premise in the argument. With respect to extra-biblical evidence Law is just misinformed. Jesus is mentioned in such ancient sources as Tacitus, Josephus, Mara bar Serapion, and Jewish rabbinic sources. If you're interested in reading these, Robert Van Voorst has collected these sources in his book 'Jesus outside the New Testament.' There is no reason to think that all of these sources are dependent exclusively on Christian tradition. For example, according to Van Voorst "the wording of almost every element" of Josephus' original text "indicates that Josephus did not draw it, directly or indirectly, from first-century Christian writings. 'Worse, what Law doesn't appreciate is that the sources in the NT itself are often independent of one another, so that we have independent evidence for many of the mundane, not to speak of the miraculous, events of Jesus' life. It is precisely that multiple, early, independent attestation to many of the events of Jesus' life that has persuaded historical scholars of the historicity of many of the events in the Gospel narratives. We have references to Jesus' burial in five independent sources and indications of the discovery of his empty tomb in no less than six independent sources, which is really quite extraordinary.

<u>But there are more reasons for denying Premise #6</u>:

1) Principle of Sufficient Cause: Law says that Alexander the Great must have existed because of the military dynasties left in his wake. But in the same way, Jesus must have existed because of the first-century Christian movement left in his wake. Attempts to explain this movement away as mythological have failed.

2) Embarrassment: Jewish Messianic expectations included no idea of a Davidic Messiah who, instead of throwing off Israel's enemies and establishing David's throne in Jerusalem, would be shamefully executed by them as a criminal. Jesus' crucifixion was something the early church struggled to overcome, not something it invented. Jesus' crucifixion is one datum upon which all historical scholars, even the most radical, agree.

3) Archaeology: Law accepts the historicity of Alexander the Great partly because of the archaeological evidence for the dynasties he founded. But how about Jesus? The Church of the Holy Sepulchre in Jerusalem has a very strong historical claim to be built over the actual tomb of Jesus of Nazareth. In 326-28 the mother of the Emperor Constantine, Helena, undertook a trip to Palestine and enquired where the tomb of Jesus was located. The locals pointed to a spot where a Temple to Aphrodite had stood for over a century. We have here a very old tradition as to the location of Jesus' tomb which is rendered probable by the facts that (i) the location identified was inside the extant walls of the city, even though the NT says it was outside the city walls. People didn't realize that the spot was, in fact, outside the original walls because they did not know the original walls' location. (ii) When Constantine ordered the temple to be razed and the site excavated, they dug down and found a tomb! But if this is the very tomb of Jesus, then we have archaeological evidence for his existence.

In sum, Law's argument is not a good one. Skepticism or even agnosticism about the historicity of Jesus of Nazareth is groundless. As Ehrmann concludes, 'Whether we like it or not, Jesus certainly existed.' (Bart Ehrmann, "Did Jesus Exist?" Huff Post, March 29, 2012)."

CHAPTER 6   Internal Evidence Test = Eyewitnesses   6.1

Skeptic's Charge #16: What about the testimonies of the people who were alive during that time? Do they stand behind what Jesus said, or is there anyone contradicting Him?

Answer: The New Testament writers wrote as *EYEWITNESSES*, from first-hand information.

What's the difference between a "defense attorney" and a "witness"?

Jesus never calls us to be attorneys (i.e., defend Him). He simply calls us to be His **witnesses**.
- Attorney = gather the facts of the case to be presented...
- Witness = truthfully testify to facts they have personally seen and heard that pertain to the case...

Acts 22:15 *"For you will be His WITNESSES to all men of what you have SEEN and HEARD."*

Luke 1:1-2 *"Inasmuch as many have taken in hand to set in order a narrative of those things which are most surely believed among us, just as those who from the beginning were EYEWITNESSES..."*

2Peter 1:16 *"For we do not follow cunningly devised fables when we made known to you the power of our Lord Jesus Christ, but we were EYEWITNESSES of His majesty."*

1John 1:1-2 *"That which was from the beginning, which we have heard, which WE HAVE SEEN WITH OUR EYES, which we have looked upon, and our hands have handled, concerning the word of life – the life was manifested, and WE HAVE SEEN, and BEAR WITNESS, and declare to you that eternal life which was with the Father and was manifested to us -..."*

Acts 2:32 *"This Jesus God has raised up, of which WE ARE ALL WITNESSES."*

Acts 3:14-15 *"But you denied the Holy One and the Just, and asked for a murderer to be granted to you, and killed the Prince of life, whom God raised from the dead, of which WE ARE WITNESSES."*

Acts 4:19-20 *But Peter and John answered and said to them, "Whether it is right in the sight of God to listen to you more than to God, you judge. For we cannot but speak the things which WE HAVE SEEN AND HEARD."*

Acts 26:26 *"For the king, before whom I also speak freely, knows these things; for I am convinced that none of these things escapes his attention, since THIS THING WAS NOT DONE IN A CORNER."*

F.F. Bruce (Rylands Professor of Bible Criticism and Exegesis, University of Manchester)[1]:
- "The earliest gospel preachers knew the value of **first-hand** testimony, and appealed to it time and time again. 'We are witnesses of these things', was their constant and confident assertion. And it can have been by no means so easy as some writers seem to think to invent words and deeds of Jesus in those early years, when so many of His disciples were about, who could remember what had and had not happened.
- And it wasn't only friendly eyewitnesses that the early preachers had to reckon with; there were others less well disposed who were also conversant with the main facts of the ministry and death of Jesus. The disciples could not afford to risk inaccuracies which would at once be exposed by those who would be only too glad to do so. On the contrary, one of the strong points in the original apostolic preaching is the confident appeal to the **knowledge** of the hearers; they not only said, 'We are witnesses of these things', but also, 'As you yourselves also know' (Acts 2:22). Had there been any tendency to depart from the facts in any material respect, the possible presence of hostile witnesses in the audience would have served as a further corrective."

Simon Greenleaf (Royall Professor of Law, Harvard University): *"An Examination of the Testimony of the Four Evangelists by the Rules of Evidence Administered in the Courts of Justice" (1846)[1]:*
- "The great truths which the apostles declared, were that Christ had risen from the dead, and that only through repentance from sin and faith in Him could men hope for salvation. This doctrine they asserted with **one voice, everywhere.** Their master had recently perished as a malefactor, by the sentence of a public tribunal. His religion sought to overthrow the religions of the whole world. The laws of every country were against the teachings of His disciples. The interests of all the rulers and great men in the world were **against** them. Propagating this new faith, they could expect nothing but contempt, opposition, persecutions, imprisonments, torments and cruel deaths.
- Yet this faith they zealously did propagate; and all these miseries they endured **rejoicing**. As one after another was put to a miserable death, the survivors only carried on their work with increased vigor and resolution. They had every possible motive to review carefully the grounds of their faith, and the evidences of the great facts and truths which they asserted; and these motives were pressed upon their attention with the utmost frequency.
- It was therefore impossible that they could have persisted in affirming the truths they narrated, had not Jesus actually **risen** from the dead, and had they not known this fact as certainly as any other fact. If it were possible for them to have been deceived, every human motive operated to lead them to discover and avow their error."

Think about it ➔ People don't WILLINGLY *die horrible deaths for what they* KNOW *is a lie*

PETER: Eyewitness to the Resurrection   (from coward to courage)

Matthew 14: 22-32 ➔ Peter does the miraculous with Jesus

• The disciples are on the Sea of Galilee, while Jesus is on the mountain praying. The boat is in a storm and they can't get to Capernaum. Suddenly, the disciples saw Jesus coming toward them, walking on the water, and they were scared (they thought it was a ghost) – but not Peter.

• Peter cries, "Is that You, Lord?" Jesus answers, "It is I". Peter asks, "Can I come?" Jesus said, "Come." Why didn't Peter just wait until Jesus reached the boat? That's not Peter. He probably said to himself, "Jesus is over there, I am over here – not good. I must go over there."

• It never entered Peter's mind that he normally can't walk on water. That wasn't even the problem. When he saw Jesus, his desire was to BE WITH HIM. But once he got on the waves, he looked down and thought, "What am I doing here?" He started sinking, but the Lord lifted him up.

The Point: When *near Jesus*, Peter did the miraculous. He and Jesus walked back together on the water.

Matthew 16: 13-20 ➔ Peter says the miraculous with Jesus

• Jesus asks His disciples, "Who do men say that I am?" They say, "Some people think You are Jeremiah, some say You are Elijah, some say You are a prophet." Jesus then asks, "But who do you say that I am?"

• Peter said, "You are the Christ, the Son of the living God." Jesus says, "Flesh and blood did not reveal this to you, Peter, but My Father in heaven did."

The Point: When *near Jesus*, Peter said the miraculous.

Matthew 26: 47-54 ➔ Peter has miraculous courage with Jesus

• The disciples are with Jesus in the garden of Gethsemane. Judas enters with ≈ 500 Roman soldiers. In front of these soldiers came the chief priests, and before the chief priests the servants of the priests.

• Peter is standing with Jesus when they laid hands on Him. That's all Peter needed. Since he didn't ever want to leave Jesus' side, he took the sword and started with the first guy in line, who was Malchus, the high priest's servant. Peter cuts off his ear (he probably was going for his head). Peter was ready to take on the Roman army.

The Point: When *near Jesus*, Peter had miraculous courage.

Matthew 26: 57-58, 69-75 ➔ Peter is a coward without Jesus

• As they led Jesus into the courtyard to be tried, Peter doesn't go with Jesus but followed behind "at a distance", staying outside near a campfire with the locals. He is now separated from Jesus.

• Two servants identify him in public as a follower of Jesus. Both times he denies knowing Jesus, each time his voice rising in defiance to the accusation. On the 3rd time, everyone around the fire accuses him as being a follower of the Lord. Now, he starts swearing oaths that he doesn't know Jesus.

The Point: When Peter was *separated from Jesus*, he is a failure. Apart from Christ, he is nothing.

Mark 16:1-13 ➔ Peter is in hiding: he fears for his life and no longer believes

• Only the women are brave enough to go to Jesus' tomb (the men stay in hiding in a closed room). In verse 7, the angel specifically tells Mary Magdalene to tell PETER that He is risen. But when she tells them, they all (including Peter) refuse to believe her.

The Point: When Peter believes *Jesus is dead*, he is afraid and faithless.

John 20:19-29 ➔ Peter stops hiding when Jesus appears

• The disciples are all hiding from the Jews because now that they believe Jesus is dead, they fear what the Jewish leaders will do to them. Then, Jesus appears to them, with the door never being opened to let Him in! He shows them His physical body, as proof He has risen from the dead. Thomas exclaims He is his "Lord and God".

Acts chapters 1- 4 ➔ Jesus has ascended to heaven (He physically left Peter)

ch. 2:14-41   Peter again says the miraculous: Peter preaches Christ to the multitudes - 3,000 people saved.

ch. 3:1-26, 4:1-4 Peter again does the miraculous: Peter heals a lame man, preaches - 5,000 more saved.

ch. 4:5-22   Peter again has miraculous courage: Peter boldly witnesses to the Sanhedrin while under arrest

---

How does Peter regain that boldness he had before Jesus was crucified?

2Peter 1:16 – Peter's *EYEWITNESS* to the *RESURRECTION* transformed him.

The Death, Burial and Resurrection of Jesus Christ (1Corinthians 15:1-19)

Excerpts from John Piper (February 28, 2007): "8 Reasons Why I Believe That Jesus Rose from the Dead"

1. Jesus Himself testified to His coming resurrection from the dead (Mark 8:31, Matt. 17:22, Luke 9:22). Even His accusers said that this was part of Jesus' claim (Matt. 27:63). The character of Jesus, revealed in the witnesses, has not been judged by most people to be a lunatic or a deceiver.

2. The tomb was empty on Easter (Luke 24:3, Matt. 28:11-15). The dead body of Jesus could not be found. There are four possible ways to account for this:

2.1 *His foes stole the body.* If they did (and they never claimed they did), they would have produced the body to stop the spread of the Christian faith in the very city where the crucifixion occurred. But they could not produce it.

2.2 *His friends stole the body.* Is it probable? Could they have overcome the guards at the tomb? More important, would they have begun to preach with such authority that Jesus was raised, knowing that he was not? Would they have risked their lives and accepted beatings for something they knew was a fraud?

2.3 *Jesus was not dead, but only unconscious when they laid him in the tomb.* He awoke, removed the stone, overcame the soldiers, and vanished from history after meeting with His disciples where He convinced them He was risen from the dead. He was obviously dead. The Romans saw to that. The stone could not be moved by one man from within who had just been stabbed in the side by a spear and spent six hours nailed to a cross.

2.4 *God raised Jesus from the dead.* This is what He said would happen. It is what the disciples said did happen. But as long as there is a remote possibility of explaining the resurrection naturalistically, people say we should not jump to a supernatural explanation. Is this reasonable? I don't think so. Why reject truth just because it's strange?

3. The disciples were transformed from men who were hopeless and fearful after the crucifixion (Luke 24:21, John 20:19) into men who were confident and bold witnesses of the resurrection (Acts 2:24, 3:15, 4:2). They explained their change was because they saw the risen Christ and were authorized as His witnesses (Acts 2:32). The most popular competing explanation is that their confidence was owing to hallucinations. There are numerous problems with such a notion. The disciples were not gullible, but level-headed skeptics both before and after the resurrection (Mark 9:32, Luke 24:11, John 20:8-9,25). Is the deep and noble teaching of those who witnessed the risen Christ the stuff of which hallucinations are made? What about Paul's great letter to the Romans? I find it hard to think of this giant intellect and deeply transparent soul as deluded or deceptive, and he claimed to have seen the risen Christ.

4. Paul claimed 500 others had also seen Him - many of them were still alive when he said this (1Corin. 15:6). What makes this so relevant is that this was written to Greeks who were skeptical of such claims when many of these witnesses were still alive. It was a risky claim if it could be disproved by a little firsthand research.

5. The existence of a thriving, empire-conquering early Christian church supports the truth of the resurrection. The church spread on the power of the testimony that Jesus was raised from the dead and that God had thus made Him both Lord and Christ (Acts 2:36). This is the message that spread all over the world. Its power to cross cultures and create one new people of God was a strong testimony of its truth.

6. The Apostle Paul's conversion supports the truth of the resurrection. He argues in Galatians 1:11-17 that his gospel comes from the risen Jesus Christ, not from men. Before his Damascus Road experience when he saw the risen Jesus, he was violently opposed to the Christian faith (Acts 9:1). But now he is risking his life for the gospel (Acts 9:24-25). His explanation: The risen Jesus appeared to him and authorized him to spearhead the Gentile mission (Acts 26:15-18). Can we credit such a testimony? This leads to the next argument.

7. The New Testament witnesses do not bear the stamp of dupes or deceivers. How do you decide whether to believe a person's testimony? When a witness is dead, we can base our judgment of him only on his writings and the testimonies of others about him. How do Peter, John, Matthew, Paul stack up? These men's writings do not read like works of gullible, easily deceived or deceiving men. Their personal commitment is sober and carefully stated. Their teachings are coherent and do not look like the invention of unstable men. Their moral and spiritual standard is high. And the lives of these men are totally devoted to the truth and to the honor of God.

8. There is glory in the gospel of Christ's death and resurrection as narrated by the biblical witnesses. John 16:13 teaches that God sent the Holy Spirit to glorify Jesus as His Son. The Holy Spirit does not do this by telling us that Jesus rose from the dead. He does it by opening our eyes to see the self-authenticating glory of Christ in the narrative of His life, death and resurrection. He enables us to see Jesus as He really was. He is irresistibly true and beautiful. 2 Corinthians 4:4,6 states that a saving knowledge of Christ crucified and risen is not the mere result of right reasoning about historical facts. It is the result of spiritual illumination to see those facts for what they really are: a revelation of the truth and glory of God in the face of Jesus Christ..."

Expert Testimony on the Historical Resurrection of Jesus Christ

6.2

Skeptic's Charge #17: Christ's Resurrection is a story with no facts to back it up. You have to believe it by faith.

Below are excerpts from Dr. William Lane Craig's opening statement in his March 28, 2006 debate with Dr. Bart Ehrmann on the Resurrection (College of Holy Cross, Worchester, MA) – full debate is on YouTube

"...as a result of my studies, I came to see that a remarkably good case can be made for Jesus' resurrection historically as well, and I hope to show tonight that the resurrection of Jesus is the best explanation of certain well-established facts about Jesus.

I want to sketch briefly how a historical case for Jesus' resurrection might look. In constructing a case for Jesus' resurrection, it's important to distinguish between the evidence and the best explanation of that evidence. This distinction is important because in this case the evidence is relatively uncontroversial. As we'll see, it's agreed to by most scholars. On the other hand, the explanation of that evidence is controversial. That the resurrection is the best explanation is a matter of controversy. Although Dr. Ehrmann says there cannot be any historical evidence for the resurrection, we'll see that what he really means is that the resurrection cannot be the best explanation of that evidence, not that there is no evidence. That leads me, then, to my first major contention, namely:

> **There are four historical facts which must be explained by any adequate historical hypothesis:**
> 1) Jesus' burial 2) The discovery of his empty tomb
> 3) His post-mortem appearances 4) The origin of the disciples' belief in his resurrection.

Let's look at that first contention more closely. I want to share four facts widely accepted by historians today.

Fact #1: After his crucifixion Jesus was buried by Joseph of Arimathea in a tomb. Historians have established this fact on the basis of evidence such as the following:

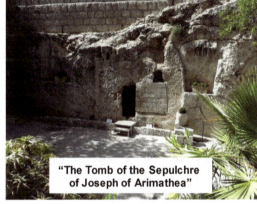

"The Tomb of the Sepulchre of Joseph of Arimathea"

1. Jesus' burial is multiply attested in early, independent sources. We have four biographies of Jesus, by Matthew, Mark, Luke, and John, which have been collected into the New Testament, along with various letters of the apostle Paul. Now the burial account is part of Mark's source material for the story of Jesus' suffering and death. This is a very early source which is probably based on eyewitness testimony and which the commentator Rudolf Pesch dates to within seven years of the crucifixion. Moreover, Paul also cites an extremely early source for Jesus' burial which most scholars date to within five years of Jesus' crucifixion. Independent testimony to Jesus' burial by Joseph is also found in the sources behind Matthew and Luke and the Gospel of John, not to mention the extra-biblical Gospel of Peter. Thus, we have the remarkable number of at least five independent sources for Jesus' burial, some of which are extraordinarily early.

2. As a member of the Jewish Sanhedrin that condemned Jesus, Joseph of Arimathea is unlikely to be a Christian invention. There was understandable hostility in the early church toward the Jewish leaders. In Christian eyes, they had engineered a judicial murder of Jesus. Thus, according to the late New Testament scholar Raymond Brown, Jesus' burial by Joseph is "very probable," since it is "almost inexplicable" why Christians would make up a story about a Jewish Sanhedrist who does what is right by Jesus (Raymond E. Brown, The Death of the Messiah, 2 vols., Garden City, N.Y.: Doubleday, 1994, 2: 1240-1). For these and other reasons, most New Testament critics concur that Jesus was buried by Joseph of Arimathea in a tomb. According to the late John A. T. Robinson of Cambridge University, the burial of Jesus in the tomb is 'one of the earliest and best-attested facts about Jesus' (John A. T. Robinson, 'The Human Face of God', Philadelphia: Westminster, 1973, p. 131).

Fact #2: On the Sunday after the crucifixion, Jesus' tomb was found empty by a group of his women followers. Among the reasons which have led most scholars to this conclusion are the following:

1. The empty tomb is also multiply attested by independent, early sources. Mark's source didn't end with the burial, but with the story of the empty tomb, which is tied to the burial story verbally and grammatically. Moreover, Matthew and John have independent sources about the empty tomb; it's also mentioned in the sermons in the Acts of the Apostles (2.29; 13.36); and it's implied by Paul in his first letter to the Corinthian church (I Cor. 15.4). Thus, we have again multiple, early, independent attestation of the fact of the empty tomb.

2. The tomb was discovered empty by women. In patriarchal Jewish society the testimony of women was not highly regarded. In fact, the Jewish historian Josephus says that women weren't even permitted to serve as witnesses in a Jewish court of law. Now in light of this fact, how remarkable it is that it is women who are the discoverers of Jesus' empty tomb.

Any later legendary account would certainly have made male disciples like Peter and John discover the empty tomb. The fact that it is women, rather than men, who are the discoverers of the empty tomb is best explained by the fact that they were the chief witnesses to the fact of the empty tomb, and the Gospel writers faithfully record what, for them, was an awkward and embarrassing fact. I could go on, but I think enough has been said to indicate why, in the words of Jacob Kremer, an Austrian specialist on the resurrection, 'By far most exegetes hold firmly to the reliability of the biblical statements concerning the empty tomb' (Jacob Kremer, Die Osterevangelien–Geschichten um Geschichte, Stuttgart: Katholisches Bibelwerk, 1977, pp. 49-50).

Fact #3: On different occasions and under various circumstances different individuals and groups of people experienced appearances of Jesus alive from the dead. This is a fact which is virtually universally acknowledged by scholars, for the following reasons:

1. Paul's list of eyewitnesses to Jesus' resurrection appearances guarantees that such appearances occurred. Paul tells us that Jesus appeared to his chief disciple Peter, then to the inner circle of disciples known as the Twelve; then he appeared to a group of 500 disciples at once, then to his younger brother James, who up to that time was apparently not a believer, then to all the apostles. Finally, Paul adds, "he appeared also to me," at the time when Paul was still a persecutor of the early Jesus movement (I Cor. 15.5-8). Given the early date of Paul's information as well as his personal acquaintance with the people involved, these appearances cannot be dismissed as mere legends.

2. The appearance narratives in the Gospels provide multiple, independent attestation of the appearances. For example, the appearance to Peter is attested by Luke and Paul; the appearance to the Twelve is attested by Luke, John, and Paul; and the appearance to the women is attested by Matthew and John. The appearance narratives span such a breadth of independent sources that it cannot be reasonably denied that the earliest disciples did have such experiences. Thus, even the skeptical German New Testament critic Gerd Lüdemann concludes, 'It may be taken as historically certain that Peter and the disciples had experiences after Jesus' death in which Jesus appeared to them as the risen Christ' (Gerd Lüdemann, 'What Really Happened to Jesus?', trans. John Bowden, Louisville, Kent.: Westminster John Knox Press, 1995, p. 8).

Fact #4: The original disciples suddenly and sincerely came to believe that Jesus was risen from the dead despite their having every predisposition to the contrary. Think of the situation the disciples faced following Jesus' crucifixion:

1. Their leader was dead. And Jewish Messianic expectations had no idea of a Messiah who, instead of triumphing over Israel's enemies, would be shamefully executed by them as a criminal.

2. Jewish beliefs about the afterlife precluded anyone's rising from the dead to glory and immortality before the general resurrection of the dead at the end of the world. Nevertheless, the original disciples suddenly came to believe so strongly that God had raised Jesus from the dead that they were willing to die for the truth of that belief.

But then the obvious question arises: What in the world caused them to believe such an un-Jewish and outlandish thing? Luke Johnson, a New Testament scholar at Emory University, muses, 'Some sort of powerful, transformative experience is required to generate the sort of movement earliest Christianity was' (Luke Timothy Johnson, 'The Real Jesus', San Francisco: Harper San Francisco, 1996, p. 136).

And N. T. Wright, an eminent British scholar, concludes, 'That is why, as an historian, I cannot explain the rise of early Christianity unless Jesus rose again, leaving an empty tomb behind him' N. T. Wright, 'The New Unimproved Jesus', Christianity Today, September 13, 1993, p. 26).

In summary, there are four facts agreed upon by the majority of scholars: Jesus' burial, the discovery of his empty tomb, his post-mortem appearances, and the origin of the disciples' belief in his resurrection.

Theories to Explain Away the Resurrection of Jesus Christ[2]

6.3

Skeptic's Charge #18: There are 6 popular theories set forth by those who do not believe in a physical, bodily resurrection of Jesus Christ. Can you show all of them are false?

➔ **The Swoon Theory (or Resuscitation Theory)** = *Jesus did not die, He only swooned*, therefore the disciples saw only a revived or resuscitated Christ. Christ was nailed to a cross and suffered from shock, pain and loss of blood. But instead of actually dying, He only fainted (swooned) from exhaustion. When He was placed in the tomb, He was still alive and the disciples, mistaking Him for dead, buried Him alive. After several hours, He revived in the coolness of the tomb, arose, and departed. Islam teaches the Swoon Theory (esp. Muslim scholar Ahmed Deedaf), as highlighted in the Qur'an, verse 4:155: *"and for their unbelief, and their uttering against Mary a mighty calumny, and for their saying, 'We slew the Messiah, Jesus son of Mary, the Messenger of God' -- yet they did not slay him, neither crucified him, only a likeness of that was shown to them".*

The Refutation = This theory completely ignores the evidences of His death and would require a greater miracle than the resurrection. For details on the physical evidence of His death on the Cross, see **Lesson 6.4** ("On the Physical Death of Jesus Christ - A Medical Examination of the Evidence"). According to this theory, the cool damp air of the tomb, instead of killing Him, healed Him. He split out of His garments, pushed the stone away, fought off the guards and shortly thereafter appeared to His disciples as the Lord of life.

The Linen Wrappings: The swoon theory cannot answer the problem of the linen wrappings lying undisturbed, exactly as they had been when around the body of Christ. Christ would have had to perform a miracle of wiggling out of the wrappings which were wound tightly about the body with over a hundred pounds of spices in the wrappings without someone to help unwrap Him, as in the case of Lazarus in John 11.

Matthew 28:6 *"He is not here, for He has risen, just as He said. Come, see the place where He was lying."*

Mark 16:6 *"He said to them, 'Do not be amazed; you are looking for Jesus the Nazarene, who has been crucified. He has risen; He is not here; behold, here is the place where they laid Him.'"*

Luke 24:12 *"But Peter arose and ran to the tomb; stooping and looking in, he saw the linen wrappings only; and he went away to his home, marveling at that which had happened."*

John 20:5-8 *"...and stooping and looking in, he saw the linen wrappings lying there; but he did not go in. Simon Peter therefore also came, following him, and entered the tomb; and he beheld the linen wrappings lying there, and the face-cloth, which had been on His head, not lying with the linen wrappings, but rolled up in a place by itself. So the other disciple who had first come to the tomb entered then also, and he saw and believed."*

The Circumstances of the Cross: These circumstances proved Christ died. He was dead in the judgment of the soldiers, in the judgment of Pilate, in the judgment of the Jews who requested the guard for the tomb, and in the judgment of the women who went to the tomb to further prepare the body by heaping spices over the body.

John 19:31-35 *"The Jews therefore, because it was the day of preparation, so that the bodies should not remain on the cross on the Sabbath for that Sabbath was a high day, asked Pilate that their legs might be broken, and that they might be taken away. The soldiers therefore came, and broke the legs of the first man, and of the other man who was crucified with Him; but coming to Jesus, when they saw that He was already dead, they did not break His legs; but one of the soldiers pierced His side with a spear, and immediately there came out blood and water. And he who has seen has borne witness, and his witness is true; and he knows that he is telling the truth, so that you also may believe."*

Mark 15:43-4 *"Joseph of Arimathea came, a prominent member of the Council, who himself was waiting for the kingdom of God; and he gathered up courage and went in before Pilate, and asked for the body of Jesus. And Pilate wondered if He was dead by this time, and summoning the centurion, he questioned him as to whether He was already dead. And ascertaining this from the centurion, he granted the body to Joseph."*

The Physical Condition of Christ after Crucifixion: If Christ had only swooned, He still would have been half dead. In His weakened condition He could not have walked the seven miles on the Emmaus road. It would have been impossible for someone to so quickly give the impression that He was the Conqueror of death and the grave, the Prince of Life. It was this belief which turned the disciples around and became the foundation of their ministries. In addition to the three things mentioned above, there are other circumstances that need to be explained like the removal of the stone and the guard over the tomb.

➔ **The Hallucination Theory** = Christ's post-resurrection appearances were really only supposed appearances because the people only had hallucinations. In this way, all the post-resurrection appearances can be dismissed.

The Refutation = How could 500 people have hallucinations at one time? Also, the appearances happened under different conditions and were spread out over different times. And, don't forget, the disciples were reluctant to believe in the resurrection in the first place! This involves a miracle of blindness to reason away the resurrection. The hallucination theory is simply not plausible because it contradicts laws and principles which psychiatrists say are essential to hallucinations. Psychiatrists claim: Only certain kinds of people have hallucinations.

These are usually high-strung, highly imaginative, and very nervous people. In fact, usually only paranoid or schizophrenic individuals have hallucinations. But Christ appeared to many different types of people. His appearances were not restricted to people of any particular psychological makeup.

Hallucinations are linked in an individual's subconscious--to his particular past experiences and this was certainly not a part of any past experience.

Hallucinations are usually restricted to when and where they occur. They usually occur in a nostalgic atmosphere or in a place of familiar surroundings which places the person to a reminiscing mood. They occur in people when there is a spirit of anticipation or hopeful expectation. The historical record shows no such anticipation existed. They were prone to disbelieve even after they were told of the resurrection.

Mark 16:11-16 *"And when they heard that He was alive, and had been seen by her, they refused to believe it. And after that, He appeared in a different form to two of them, while they were walking along on their way to the country. And they went away and reported it to the others, but they did not believe them either. And afterward He appeared to the eleven themselves as they were reclining at the table; and He reproached them for their unbelief and hardness of heart, because they had not believed those who had seen Him after He had risen. And He said to them, "Go into all the world and preach the gospel to all creation. He who has believed and has been baptized shall be saved; but he who has disbelieved shall be condemned."*

Luke 24:11-12 *"And these words appeared to them as nonsense, and they would not believe them. But Peter arose and ran to the tomb; stooping and looking in, he saw the linen wrappings only; and he went away to his home, marveling at that which had happened."*

John 20:24-30 *"But Thomas, one of the twelve, called Didymus, was not with them when Jesus came. The other disciples therefore were saying to him, "We have seen the Lord!" But he said to them, "Unless I shall see in His hands the imprint of the nails, and put my finger into the place of the nails, and put my hand into His side, I will not believe." And after eight days again His disciples were inside, and Thomas with them. Jesus came, the doors having been shut, and stood in their midst, and said, "Peace be with you." Then He said to Thomas, "Reach here your finger, and see My hands; and reach here your hand, and put it into My side; and be not unbelieving, but believing." Thomas answered and said to Him, "My Lord and my God!" Jesus said to him, "Because you have seen Me, have you believed? Blessed are they who did not see, and yet believed."*

➔ **The Impersonation Theory** = The appearances were not really Christ at all, but someone impersonating Him. This, the opponents say, is evident because in some cases they did not recognize Him at first (or at all).

The Refutation =

1. The disciples were reluctant to believe in the resurrection, were doubtful and would have been hard to convince unless it was really Him, as was the case with Thomas.

2. It would have been impossible to impersonate Christ's wounds. This was Christ's proof to Thomas that it was really Him (John 20:24).

3. At times their inability to recognize Him was a phenomenon of His glorified body brought about by His own purposes as in Luke 24:16, *"But their eyes were restricted that they should not recognize Him."*

4. These men had traveled with the Lord for three years and it is incredible that anyone could have gotten away with an impersonation particularly due to their reluctance to believe.

5. They were meeting in locked chambers in some instances, and He suddenly appeared in His glorified body. No one could impersonate such a miraculous act other than the resurrected Christ.

➔ **The Spiritual Resurrection Theory** = This states that Christ's resurrection was not a real physical resurrection. Proponents of this theory assert that Christ's body remained in the grave and His real resurrection was spiritual in nature. It was only told this way to illustrate the truth of spiritual resurrection.

The Refutation = Note what William Craig says in his book entitled, *Knowing the Truth About the Resurrection, Our Response to the Empty Tomb:* *"We need to see clearly that there can be positive theological implications of the resurrection only insofar as its historical reality is affirmed. While many theologians may find such a conviction hopelessly antiquated, the man in the street knows better. His common sense tells him that there is no reason why a dead man should be decisive for his existence today, and I agree with him. Once doctrinal teachings are detached from their historical realities, we have entered the arena of myth. And there is simply no good reason to prefer Christian myths over other myths or, for that matter, secular philosophies. The resurrection is only real for our lives today if it is a real event of history."* (Introduction, p. xiii).

A physical body did disappear from the tomb. If it was only a spiritual resurrection, then what happened to the body? History shows there was a body there and it disappeared. The enemies of Christ were never able to produce the body nor disprove the resurrection.

The resurrection accounts are not presented in symbolic language but as hard fact. John 20 is full of what Greek grammarians call vivid historical present tenses to stress the historical reality of the Gospel message. The record states He was touched and handled, that He had a body, and that He even ate with the disciple (Luke 24:30,41, John 21:12).

1Corinthians 15 teaches us that Christ not only arose, but that He arose bodily. He possessed a glorified body which had unique capacities. 1Corinthians 15:44 calls it a spiritual body, but it was nevertheless a physical body as well. Note the following facts about the body of Christ:
- He could appear in different forms (Mark16:12).
- He could eat though it was not needed for sustenance (Luke 24:30).
- He could appear and disappear and could pass through solid objects (John 20:19,26).
- He could pass in a moment from one place to another (Luke 24:31).

Philippians 3:21 shows that His body was glorious and unique, but nevertheless, still a body according to which our bodies will one day be fashioned. So, it was spiritual, glorified, and yet a physical body of flesh and bone.

→ **The Theft Theory** = The disciples stole the body and claimed that He rose from the dead.

The Refutation = Again, such a theory ignores the evidence of the linen wrappings and the empty tomb. If someone had stolen the body, they would have either taken the body and left the wrappings scattered or piled in a heap, but only resurrection could account for the position of the linen wrappings with the body absent.

Further, there is the question of the probability of who **could** and **would** steal the body under the circumstances.

1. The Romans would not; they were guarding it with their lives by Roman law. They had sealed the tomb and were protecting it against theft. The religious leaders had provided their own refutation against such a theory.

2. The women could not for they could not have removed the stone and were wondering who would remove it for them when they went early Sunday morning to finish burial preparations (Mark16:3-4).

3. The Jewish crowd would not - they actually requested a Roman guard protect the tomb against theft (Matthew 27:63-66). This last point is very significant because the presence of the Roman soldiers and the Roman seal over the door made the possibility of the religious leaders claims of theft nearly impossible.

4. The disciples would not because they were perplexed and scattered, huddled together in hidden rooms. Two had even left town and were on their way to Emmaus. The likelihood of these timid, scared Galilean disciples stealing the body of Jesus out from under the noses of a guard of highly disciplined and skilled Roman soldiers while they all slept (an offense punishable by death) is ridiculous.

Matthew 28:11-15 *"Now while they were on their way, behold, some of the guard came into the city and reported to the chief priests all that had happened. And when they had assembled with the elders and counseled together, they gave a large sum of money to the soldiers, and said, "You are to say, 'His disciples came by night and stole Him away while we were asleep.' "And if this should come to the governor's ears, we will win him over and keep you out of trouble." And they took the money and did as they had been instructed; and this story was widely spread among the Jews, and is to this day."*

→ **The Unknown Tomb Theory** = The disciples did not know where the tomb was located and could not have found the empty grave. This theory depends on the belief that those who were crucified were tossed into a common pit and were not allowed to be buried.

The Refutation = This theory also disregards totally the straightforward historical narrative about the events surrounding Christ's burial and the post-resurrection scene. The Gospel record indicates that Joseph of Arimathea took the body to his own private tomb--not a public mass burial ground. According to Scripture, the body of Christ was prepared for burial according to the burial customs of the Jews; the women sat opposite the tomb and watched. Not only did Joseph of Arimathea and the women know where the tomb was, so did the Romans--they placed a guard there.

Conclusion = None of these natural theories adequately deals with the evidence of the known facts that surrounded the resurrection of our Lord. The evidence says He arose and this resurrection marks Him as the Son of God (Romans 1:4), as the Savior of the world and the means of justification and peace with God through personal faith in Christ (Romans 4:25 through 5:1), or if one rejects the Risen Savior, as their judge at the day of judgment (Acts 17:30-31).

> **John 1:12** *"..as many as received Him, to them He gave the right to become children of God, even to those who believe in His name."*

Forensic Science: Expert Testimony on the Crucifixion of Jesus Christ

Skeptic's Charge #19: Jesus didn't die on the Cross. He survived the crucifixion, so therefore His supposed resurrection never happened.

The following Article, "On the Physical Death of Jesus Christ"[23], written in March 1986 by William D. Edwards, MD; Wesley J. Gabel, MDiv; Floyd E Hosmer, MS, AMI, is reproduced below in its entirety.

INTRODUCTION

The life and teachings of Jesus of Nazareth have formed the basis for a major world religion (Christianity), have appreciably influenced the course of human history, and, by virtue of a compassionate attitude towards the sick, also have contributed to the development of modern medicine. The eminence of Jesus as a historical figure and the suffering and controversy associated with his death have stimulated us to investigate, in an interdisciplinary manner, the circumstances surrounding his crucifixion. Accordingly, it is our intent to present not a theological treatise but rather a medically and historically accurate account of the physical death of Jesus Christ.

SOURCES

The source material concerning Christ's death comprises a body of literature and not a physical body or its skeletal remains. Accordingly, the credibility of any discussion of Jesus' death will be determined primarily by the credibility of one's sources. For this review, the source material includes the writings of ancient Christian and non-Christian authors, the writings of modern authors, and the Shroud of Turin. (1-40) Using the legal-historical method of scientific investigation, (27) scholars have established the reliability and accuracy of the ancient manuscripts. (26,27,29,31)

The most extensive and detailed descriptions of the life and death of Jesus are to be found in the New Testament gospels of Matthew, Mark, Luke, and John. (1) The other 23 books of the New Testament support but do not expand on the details recorded in the gospels. Contemporary Christian, Jewish, and Roman authors provide additional insight concerning the first-century Jewish and Roman legal systems and the details of scourging and crucifixion. (5) Seneca, Livy, Plutarch, and others refer to crucifixion practices in their works. (8,28)

Specifically, Jesus (or his crucifixion) is mentioned by the Roman historians Cornelius Tacitus, Pliny the Younger, and Suetonius, by non-Roman historians Thallus and Phlegon, by the satirist Lucian of Samosata, by the Jewish Talmud, and by the Jewish historian Flavius Josephus, although the authenticity of portions of the latter is problematic. (26) The Shroud of Turin is considered by many to represent the actual burial cloth of Jesus, (22) and several publications concerning the medical aspects of his death draw conclusions from this assumption. (5,11) The Shroud of Turin and recent archaeological findings provide valuable information concerning Roman crucifixion practices. (22-24) The interpretations of modern writers, based on a knowledge of science and medicine not available in the first century, offer additional insight concerning the possible mechanisms of Jesus' death. (2,17)

When taken in concert, certain facts -- the extensive and early testimony of both Christian proponents and opponents, and their universal acceptance of Jesus as a true historical figure; the ethic of the gospel writers, and the shortness of the time interval between the events and the extant manuscripts; and the confirmation of the gospel accounts by historians and archaeological findings (26,27) -- ensure a reliable testimony from which a modern medical interpretation of Jesus' death may be made.

GETHSEMANE

After Jesus and his disciples had observed the Passover meal in an upper room in a home in southwest Jerusalem, they traveled to the Mount of Olives, northeast of the city. Owing to various adjustments in the calendar, the years of Jesus' birth and death remain controversial. (29) However, it is likely that Jesus was born in either 4 or 6 BC and died in 30 AD. (11,29)

During the Passover observance in 30 AD, the last Supper would have been observed on Thursday, April 6 [Nisan 13], and Jesus would have been crucified on Friday, April 7 [Nisan 14]. (29)) At nearby Gethsemane, Jesus, apparently knowing that the time of his death was near, suffered great mental anguish, and, as described by the physician Luke, his sweat became like blood. (1)

Although this is a very rare phenomenon, **bloody sweat** (hematidrosis or hemohidrosis) may occur in highly emotional states or in persons with bleeding disorders. (18,20) As a result of hemorrhage into the sweat glands, the skin becomes fragile and tender. (2,11) Luke's descriptions supports the diagnosis of hematidrosis rather than eccrine chromidrosis (brown or yellow-green sweat) or stigmatization (blood oozing from the palms or elsewhere). (18,21) Although some authors have suggested that hematidrosis produced hypovolemia, we agree with Bucklin (5) that Jesus' blood loss probably was minimal. However, in the cold night air, (1) it may have produced chills.

TRIALS

Jewish Trials: Soon after midnight, Jesus was arrested at Gethsemane by the temple officials and was taken first to Annas and then to Caiaphas, the Jewish high priest for that year. (1) Between 1 AM and daybreak, Jesus was tried before Caiaphas and the political Sanhedrin and was found guilty of blasphemy. (1)

The guards then blindfolded Jesus, spat on him, and struck him in the face with their fists. (1) Soon after daybreak, presumably at the temple, Jesus was tried before the religious Sanhedrin (with the Pharisees and the Sadducees) and again was found guilty of blasphemy, a crime punishable by death. (1,5)

Map of Jerusalem at the time of Christ:
① Jesus left the Upper Room and walked with disciples to Mount of Olives and Garden of Gethsemane; ② where He was arrested and taken first by Caiaphas. After the first trial before political Sanhedrin at Caiaphas' residence, ③ Jesus was tried again before religious Sanhedrin, probably at the Temple; ④ Next, He was taken to Pilate, who sent Him to ⑤ Herod Antipas. ⑥ Herod returned Jesus to Pilate, and ⑦ Pilate finally handed Him over for scourging at Fortress of Antonia and crucifixion at Golgotha.

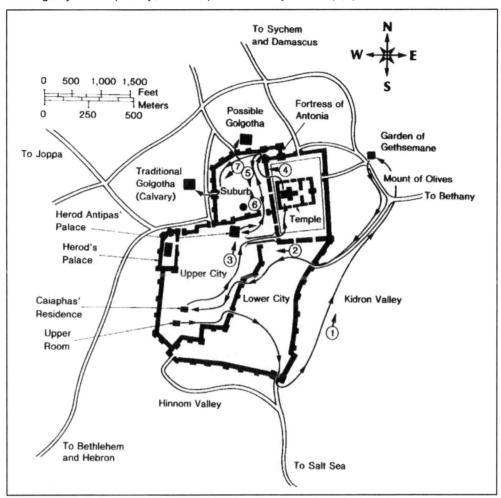

Roman Trials: Since permission for an execution had to come from the governing Romans, (1) Jesus was taken early in the morning by the temple officials to the Praetorium of the Fortress of Antonia, the residence and governmental seat of Pontius Pilate, the procurator of Judea. However, Jesus was presented to Pilate not as a blasphemer but rather as a self-appointed king who would undermine the Roman authority. (1)

Pilate made no charges against Jesus and sent him to Herod Antipas, the tetrarch of Judea. (1) Herod likewise made no official charges and then returned Jesus to Pilate. (1) Again, Pilate could find no basis for a legal charge against Jesus, but the people persistently demanded crucifixion. Pilate finally granted their demand and handed over Jesus to be flogged (scourged) and crucified. (McDowell (25) has reviewed the prevailing political, religious, and economic climates in Jerusalem at the time of Jesus' death, and Bucklin (5) has described the various illegalities of the Jewish and Roman trials.)

Health of Jesus: The rigors of Jesus' ministry (that is, traveling by foot throughout Palestine) would have precluded any major physical illness or a weak general constitution. Accordingly, it is reasonable to assume that Jesus was in good physical condition before his walk to Gethsemane.

However, during the 12 hours between 9 PM Thursday and 9 AM Friday, he had suffered great **emotional stress** (as evidenced by hematidrosis), abandonment by his closest friends (the disciples), and a **physical beating** (after the first Jewish trial). Also, in the setting of a traumatic and sleepless night, had been forced to walk more than 2.5 miles to and from the sites of the various trials. These physical and emotional factors may have rendered Jesus particularly vulnerable to the adverse hemodynamic effects of the scourging.

SCOURGING

Scourging Practices: Flogging was a legal preliminary to every Roman execution, (28) and only women and Roman senators or soldiers (except in cases of desertion) were exempt. (11) The usual instrument was a short whip (flagrum or flagellum) with several single or braided leather thongs of variable lengths, in which small iron balls or sharp pieces of sheep bones were tied at intervals. Occasionally, staves also were used. (8,12)

For scourging, the man was stripped of his clothing, and his hands were tied to an upright post. (11) The back, buttocks, and legs were flogged either by two soldiers (lictors) or by one who alternated positions. (5,7,11,28) The severity of the scourging depended on the disposition of the lictors and was intended to weaken the victim to a state just short of **collapse or death**. (8) After the scourging, the soldiers often taunted their victim. (11)

Medical Aspects of Scourging: As the Roman soldiers repeatedly struck the victim's back with full force, the iron balls would cause **deep contusions**, and the leather thongs and sheep bones would cut into the skin and subcutaneous tissues. (7) Then, as the flogging continued, the lacerations would tear into the underlying skeletal muscles and produce quivering ribbons of bleeding flesh. (27,25) Pain and blood loss generally set the stage for **circulatory shock**. (12) The extent of **blood loss** may well have determined how long the victim would survive on the cross. (3)

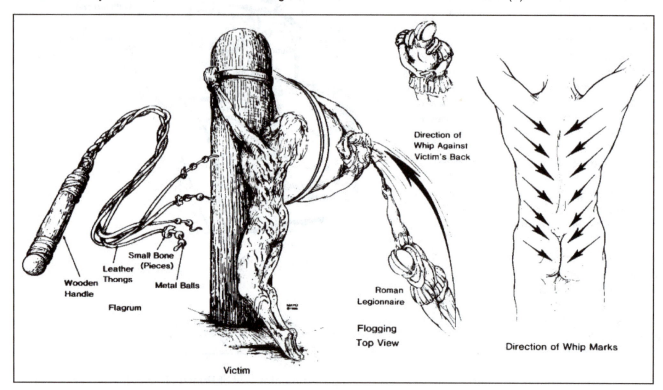

Scourging of Jesus: At the Praetorium, Jesus was severely whipped. (Although the severity of the scourging is not discussed in the four gospel accounts, it is implied in one of the epistles (1 Peter 2:24). A detailed word study of the ancient Greek text for this verse indicates that the scourging of Jesus was particularly harsh. (33) It is not known whether the number of lashes was limited to 39, in accordance with Jewish law. (5)

The Roman soldiers, amused that this weakened man had claimed to be a king, began to mock him by placing a robe on his shoulders, a crown of thorns on his head, and a wooden staff as a scepter in his right hand. (1) Next, they spat on Jesus and struck him on the head with the wooden staff. (1) Moreover, when the soldiers tore the robe from Jesus' back, they probably reopened the scourging wounds. (7)

The severe scourging, with its intense pain and appreciable blood loss, most probably left Jesus in a **preshock state**. Moreover, hematidrosis had rendered his skin particularly tender. The physical and mental abuse meted out by the Jews and the Romans, as well as the lack of food, water, and sleep, also contributed to his generally weakened state. Therefore, even before the actual crucifixion, Jesus' physical condition was at least serious and possibly critical.

CRUCIFIXION

Crucifixion Practices: Crucifixion probably first began among the Persians. (34) Alexander the Great introduced the practice to Egypt and Carthage, and the Romans appear to have learned of it from the Carthaginans. (11) Although the Romans did not invent crucifixion, they perfected it as a form of **torture** and **capital punishment** that was designed to produce a **slow death with maximum pain and suffering**. (10,17)

It was one of the most disgraceful and cruel methods of execution and usually was reserved only for slaves, foreigners, revolutionaries, and the vilest of criminals. (3,25,28) Roman law usually protected Roman citizens from crucifixion, (5) except perhaps in the case of desertion by soldiers.

In its earliest form in Persia, the victim was either tied to a tree or was tied to or impaled on an upright post, usually to keep the guilty victim's feet from touching holy ground. (3,11,30,34,38). Only later was a true cross used; it was characterized by an upright post (stipes) and a horizontal crossbar (patibulum), and it had several variations (11).

Although archaeological and historical evidence indicates that the low Tau cross was preferred by the Romans in Palestine at the time of Christ, (2,7,11) crucifixion practices varied in a given geographic region and in accordance with the imagination of the executioners, and the Latin cross and other forms also may have been used. (26)

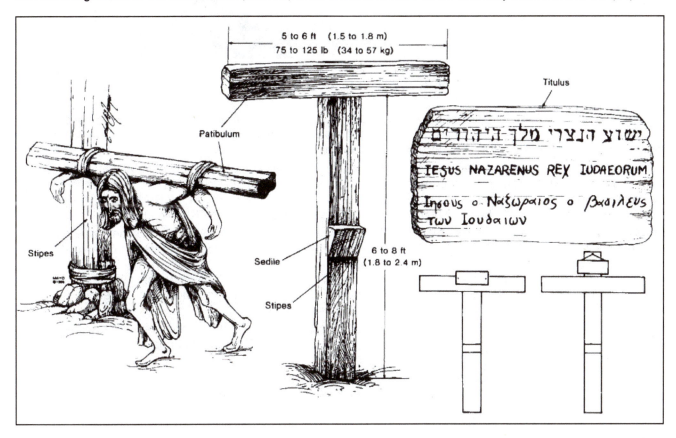

It was customary for the condemned man to **carry his own cross** from the flogging post to the site of crucifixion outside the city walls. (8,11,30) He was usually naked, unless this was prohibited by local customs. (11) Since the weight of the entire cross was probably well over 300 lb. (136 kg), only the crossbar was carried. (11) The patibulum, weighing 75 to 125 lb. (34 to 57 kg), (11,30) was placed across the nape of the victim's neck and balanced along both shoulders.

Usually, the outstretched arms then were tied to the crossbar. (7,11) The processional to the site of crucifixion was led by a complete Roman military guard, headed by a centurion. (3,11) One of the soldiers carried a sign (titulus) on which the condemned man's name and crime were displayed. (3,11) Later, the titulus would be attached to the top of the cross. (11) The Roman guard would not leave the victim until they were sure of his death. (9,11)

Outside the city walls was permanently located the heavy upright wooden stipes, on which the patibulum would be secured. In the case of the Tau cross, this was accomplished by means of a mortise and tenon joint, with or without reinforcement by ropes. (10,11,30) To prolong the crucifixion process, a horizontal wooden block or plank, serving as a crude seat (sedile or sedulum), often was attached midway down the stipes. (3,11,16) Only very rarely, and probably later than the time of Christ, was an additional block (suppedaneum) employed for transfixion of the feet. (9,11)

At the site of execution, by law, the victim was given a bitter drink of wine mixed with myrrh (gall) as a mild **analgesic**. (7,17) The criminal was then thrown to the ground on his back, with his arms outstretched along the patibulum. (11) the **hands could be nailed** or tied to the crossbar, but nailing apparently was preferred by the Romans. (8,11) The archaeological remains of a crucified body, found in an ossuary near Jerusalem and dating from the time of Christ, indicate that the nails were tapered iron spikes approximately 5 to 7 in (13 to 18 cm) long with a square shaft 3/8 in (1 cm) across. (23,24,30) Furthermore, ossuary findings and the Shroud of Turin have documented that the nails commonly were driven through the wrists rather than the palms. (22-24,30)

After both arms were fixed to the crossbar, the patibulum and the victim, together, were lifted onto the stipes. (11) On the low cross, four soldiers could accomplish this relatively easily. However, on the tall cross, the soldiers used either wooden forks or ladders. (11)

Next, the **feet were fixed to the cross**, either by nails or ropes. Ossuary findings and the Shroud of Turin suggest that nailing was the preferred Roman practice. (23,24,30) Although the feet could be fixed to the sides of the stipes or to a wooden footrest (suppedaneum), they usually were nailed directly to the front of the stipes. (11) To accomplish this, flexion of the knees may have been quite prominent, and the bent legs may have been rotated laterally (23-25,30)

When the nailing was completed, the titulus was attached to the cross, by nails or cords, just above the victim's head. (11) The **soldiers and the civilian crowd often taunted and jeered** the condemned man, and the soldiers customarily divided up his clothes among themselves. (11,25)

The length of survival generally ranged from three or four hours to three or four days and appears to have been inversely related to the severity of the scourging. (3,11) However, even if the scourging had been relatively mild, the soldiers could hasten death by **breaking the legs below the knees** (crurifragium or skelokopia). (3,11)

Not uncommonly, insects would light upon or burrow into the open wounds or the eyes, ears, and nose of the dying and helpless victim, and birds of prey would tear at these sites. (16) Moreover, it was customary to leave the corpse on the cross to be devoured by predatory animals. (3,11,12,28) However, by Roman law, the family of the condemned could take the body for burial, after obtaining permission from the Roman judge. (11)

Since no one was intended to survive crucifixion, the body was not released to the family until the soldiers were sure that the victim was dead. By custom, one of the Roman guards would **pierce the body with a sword** or lance. (3,11) Traditionally, this had been considered a spear wound to the heart through the right side of the chest -- a fatal wound probably taught to most Roman soldiers. (11) The Shroud of Turin documents this form of injury. (5,11,22) Moreover, the standard infantry spear, which was 5 to 6 ft (1.5 to 1.8 m) long (30) could easily have reached the chest of a man crucified on the customary low cross. (11)

Medical Aspects of Crucifixion: With a knowledge of both anatomy and ancient crucifixion practices, one may reconstruct the probably medical aspects of this form of slow execution. Each wound apparently was intended to produce intense agony, and the contributing causes of death were numerous.

The scourging prior to crucifixion served to weaken the condemned man and, if blood loss was considerable, to produce orthostatic hypotension and even hypovolemic shock. (8, 12) When the victim was thrown to the ground on his back, in preparation for transfixion of his hands, his scourging wounds would become torn open again and contaminated with dirt. (2,14) Furthermore, with each respiration, the painful scourging wounds would be scraped against the rough wood of the stipes. (7) As a result, blood loss from the back probably would continue throughout the crucifixion ordeal.

With arms outstretched but not taut, the wrists were nailed to the patibulum. (7,11) It has been shown that the ligaments and bones of the wrist can support the weight of a body hanging from them, but the palms cannot. (11)

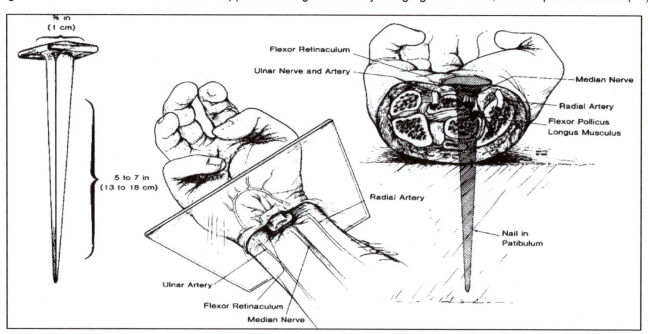

Accordingly, the iron spikes probably were driven between the radius and the carpals or between the two rows of carpal bones, (2,10,11,30) either proximal to or through the strong bandlike flexor retinaculum and the various intercarpal ligaments.

Although a nail in either location in the wrist might pass between the bony elements and thereby produce no fractures, the likelihood of painful periosteal injury seems great. Also, the driven nail would crush or sever the rather large sensorimotor median nerve. (2,7,11) The stimulated nerve would produce excruciating bolts of fiery pain in both arms. (7,9) Although the severed median nerve would result in paralysis of a portion of the hand, ischemic contractures and impalement of various ligaments by the iron spike might produce a clawlike grasp.

Most commonly, the feet were fixed to the front of the stipes by an iron spike driven through the first or second intermetatarsal space, just distal to the tarsometatarssal joint. (2,5,8,11,30) It is likely that the peroneal nerve and branches of the medial and lateral plantar nerves were injured by the nails.

Although scourging may have resulted in considerable blood loss, crucifixion per se was a relatively bloodless procedure, since no major arteries, other than perhaps the deep plantar arch, pass through the favored anatomic sites of transfixion. (2,10,11)

The major pathophysiologic effect of crucifixion, beyond the excruciating pain, was a marked interference with normal respiration, particularly exhalation. The weight of the body, pulling down on the outstretched arms and shoulders, would tend to fix the intercostal muscles in an inhalation state and thereby hinder passive exhalation. (2,10,11) Accordingly,

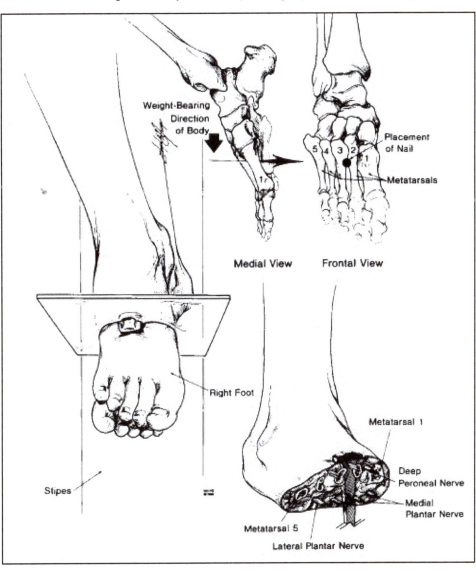

exhalation was primarily diaphragmatic, and breathing was shallow. It is likely that this form of respiration would not suffice and that hypercarbia would soon result. The onset of muscle cramps or tetanic contractions, due to fatigue and hypercarbia, would hinder respiration even further. (11)

Adequate exhalation required lifting the body by pushing up on the feet and by flexing the elbows and adducting the shoulders. (2) However, this maneuver would place the entire weight of the body on the tarsals and would produce searing pain. (7) Furthermore, flexion of the elbows would cause rotation of the wrists about the iron nails and cause fiery pain along the damaged median nerves. (7) Lifting of the body would also painfully scrape the scourged back against the rough wooden stipes. (2,7) Muscle cramps and paresthesias of the outstretched and uplifted arms would add to the discomfort. (7) As a result, each respiratory effort would become agonizing and tiring and lead eventually to asphyxia. (2,3,7,10)

The actual cause of death by crucifixion was multifactorial and varied somewhat with each case, but the two most prominent causes probably were hypovolemic shock and exhaustion asphyxia. (2,3,7,10) Other possible contributing factors included dehydration, (7,16) stress-induced arrhythmias, (3) and congestive heart failure with the rapid accumulation of pericardial and perhaps pleural effusions. (2,7,11) Crucifracture (breaking the legs below the knees), if performed, led to an asphyxic death within minutes. (11)

Death by crucifixion was *excruciating* (Latin, excruciatus, or "*OUT OF THE CROSS*").

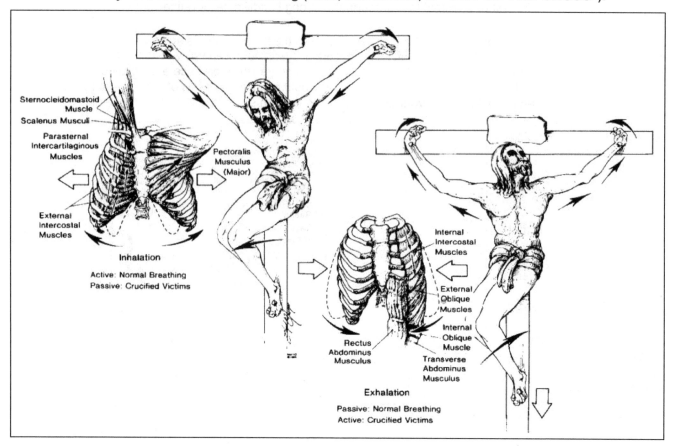

Crucifixion of Jesus

After the scourging and the mocking, at about 9 AM, the Roman soldiers put Jesus' clothes back on him and then led him and two thieves to be crucified. (1) Jesus apparently was so weakened by the severe flogging that he could not carry the patibulum from the Praetorium to the site of the crucifixion one third of a mile (600 to 650 m) away (1,3,5,7) Simon of Cyrene was summoned to carry Christ's cross, and the processional then made its way to Golgotha (or Calvary), an established crucifixion site.

Here, Jesus' clothes, except for a linen loincloth, again were removed, thereby probably reopening the scourging wounds. He then was offered a drink of wine mixed with myrrh (gall) but, after tasting it, refused the drink. (1) Finally, Jesus and the two thieves were crucified. Although scriptural references are made to nails in the hands (1), these are not at odds with the archaeological evidence of wrist wounds, since the ancients customarily considered the wrist to be a part of the hand. (7,11) The titulus was attached above Jesus' head. It is unclear whether Jesus was crucified on the Tau cross or the Latin cross; archaeological findings favor the former (11) and early tradition the latter. (38) The fact that Jesus later was offered a drink of wine vinegar from a sponge placed on the stalk of the hyssop plant (1) (approximately 20 in, or 50 cm long) strongly supports the belief that Jesus was crucified on the short cross.

The soldiers and the civilian crowd taunted Jesus throughout the crucifixion ordeal, and the soldiers cast lots for his clothing. (1) Christ spoke seven times from the cross. (1) Since speech occurs during exhalation, these short, terse utterances must have been particularly difficult and painful. At about 3 PM that Friday, Jesus cried out in a loud voice, bowed his head, and died. (1) The Roman soldiers and onlookers recognized his moment of death. (1)

Since the Jews did not want the bodies to remain on the crosses after sunset, the beginning of the Sabbath, they asked Pontius Pilate to order crucifracture to hasten the deaths of the three crucified men. (1) The soldiers broke the legs of the two thieves, but when they came to Jesus and saw that he was already dead, they did not break his legs. (1) Rather, one of the soldiers pierced his side, probably with an infantry spear, and produced a sudden flow of blood and water. (1) Later that day, Jesus' body was taken down from the cross and placed in a tomb. (1)

Death of Jesus

Two aspects of Jesus' death have been the source of great controversy, namely, the nature of the wound in his side (4,6) and the cause of his death after only several hours on the cross. (13-17). The gospel of John describes the piercing of Jesus' side and emphasizes the sudden flow of blood and water. (1) Some authors have interpreted the flow of water to be ascites (12) or urine, from an abdominal midline perforation of the bladder. (15)

However, the Greek word (pleura (32,35,36)) used by John clearly denoted laterality and often implied the ribs. (6,32,36) Therefore, it seems probable that the wound was in the thorax and away from the abdominal midline.

Although the side of the wound was not designated by John, it traditionally has been depicted on the right side. (4) Supporting this traditions is the fact that a large flow of blood would be more likely with a perforation of the distended and thin-walled right atrium or ventricle than the thick-walled and contracted left ventricle. Although the side of the wound may never be established with certainty, the right seems more probable than the left.

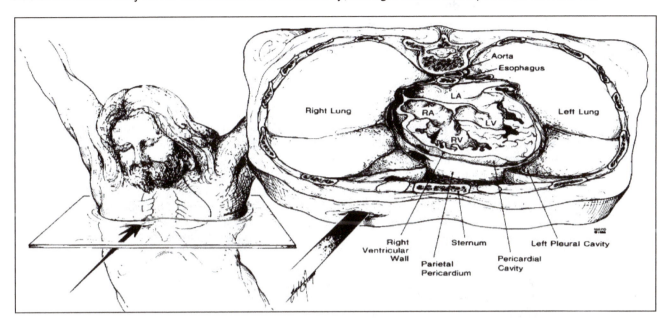

Some of the skepticism in accepting John's description has arisen from the difficulty in explaining, with medical accuracy, the **flow of both blood and water**. Part of this difficulty has been based on the assumption that the blood appeared first, then the water. However, in the ancient Greek, the order of words generally denoted prominence and not necessarily a time sequence. (37) Therefore, it seems likely that John was emphasizing the prominence of blood rather than its appearance preceding the water.

Therefore, the water probably represented serous pleural and pericardial fluid, (5-7,11) and would have preceded the flow of blood and been smaller in volume than the blood. Perhaps in the setting of hypovolemia and impending acute heart failure, pleural and pericardial effusions may have developed and would have added to the volume of apparent water. (5,11) The blood, in contrast, may have originated from the right atrium or the right ventricle or perhaps from a hemopericardium. (5,7,11)

Jesus' death after only three to six hours on the cross surprised even Pontius Pilate. (1) The fact that Jesus cried out in a loud voice and then bowed his head and died suggests the possibility of a catastrophic terminal event. One popular explanation has been that Jesus died of cardiac rupture. In the setting of the scourging and crucifixion, with associated hypovolemia, hypoxemia, and perhaps and altered coagulable state, friable non-infective thrombotic vegetations could have formed on the aortic or mitral valve. These then could have dislodged and embolized into the coronary circulation and thereby produced an acute transmural myocardial infarction. Thrombotic valvular vegetations have been reported to develop under analogous acute traumatic conditions. (39) Rupture of the left ventricular free wall may occur, though uncommonly, in the first hours following infarction. (40)

However, another explanation may be more likely. Jesus' death may have been hastened simply by his state of exhaustion and by the severity of the scourging, with its resultant blood loss and preshock state. (7) The fact that he could not carry his patibulum supports this interpretation. The actual cause of Jesus' death, like that of other crucified victims, may have been multifactorial and related primarily to hypovolemic shock, exhaustion asphyxia, and acute heart failure. (2,3,5-7,10,11) A fatal cardiac arrhythmia may have accounted for the apparent catastrophic terminal event.

Thus, it remains unsettled whether Jesus died of cardiac rupture or of cardiorespiratory failure. However, the important feature may be not how he died but rather whether he died. Clearly, the weight of historical and medical evidence indicates that Jesus was dead before the wound to his side was inflicted and supports the traditional view that the spear, thrust between his right ribs, probably perforated not only the right lung but also the pericardium and heart and thereby ensured his death. Accordingly....

> **"Interpretations based on the assumption that Jesus did not die on the cross appear to be at odds with modern medical knowledge."**

ARTICLE REFERENCES

1. Matthew 26:17-27:61, Mark 14:12-15:47, Luke 22:7-23:56, John 13:1-19:42, the "The Holy Bible" (New International Version). Grand Rapids, Mich. Zondervan Bible Publishers, 1978.
2. Lumpkin R: The physical suffering of Christ. "J Med Assoc Ala" 1978;47:8-10,47.
3. Johnson CD: Medical and cardiological aspects of the passion and crucifixion of Jesus, the Christ. "Bol Assoc Med PR" 1978;70:97-102.
4. Barb AA: The wound in Christ's side. "J Warbury Courtauld Inst" 1971;34:320-321.
5. Bucklin R: The legal and medical aspects of the trial and death of Christ. "Sci Law" 1970; 10:14-26.
6. Mikulicz-Radecki FV: The chest wound in the crucified Christ. "Med News" 1966;14:30-40.
7. Davis CT: The crucifixion of Jesus: The passion of Christ from a medical point of view. "Ariz Med" 1965;22:183-187.
8. Tenney SM: On death by crucifixion. "Am Heart J" 1964;68:286-287.
9. Bloomquist ER: A doctor looks at crucifixion. "Christian Herald", March 1964, pp 35 46-48.
10. DePasquale NP, Burch GE: Death by crucifixion. "Am Heart J" 1963;6:434-435.
11. Barbet P: "A Doctor at Calvary: The Passion of Our Lord Jesus Christ as Described by a Surgeon", Earl of Wicklow (trans). Garden City, NY, Doubleday Image Books, 1953, pp 12-18, 37-147, 159-175, 187-208.
12. Primrose WB: A surgeon looks at the crucifixion. "Hibbert J" 1949, pp 382-388.
13. Bergsma S: did Jesus die of a broken heart? "Calvin Forum" 1948;14:163-167.
14. Whitaker JR: The physical cause of the death of our Lord. "Cath Manchester Guard" 1937;15:83-91.
15. Clark CCP: What was the physical cause of the death of Jesus Christ? "Med Rec" 1890; 38:543.
16. Cooper HC: The agony of death by crucifixion. "NY Med J" 1883:38:150-153.
17. Shroud W: "Treatise on the Physical Cause of the Death of Christ and Its Relation to the Principles and Practice of Christianity" ed 2. London, Hamilton & Adams, 1871, pp 28-156, 489-494.
18. Allen AC: "The Skin: A Clinicopathological Treatise", ed 2. New York, Grune & Stratton Inc, 1967, pp 745-747.
19. Sutton RL Jr: "Diseases of the Skin", ed 11. St Louis, CV Mosby Co, 1956, pp 1393-1394.
20. Scott CT: A case of haematidrosis. "Br Med J" 1918;1:532-533.
21. Klauder JV: Stigmatization. "Arch Dermatol Syphilol" 1938;37:650-659.
22. Weaver KF: The mystery of the shroud. "Natl Geogr" 1980;157:730-753.
23. Tzaferis V: Jewish tombs at and near Giv'at ha-Mivtar, Jerusalem. "Israel Explor J" 1970;20:38-59.
24. Haas N: Anthropological observations on the skeletal remains from Giv'at ha-Mivtar. "Israel Explor J" 1970;20:38-59.
25. McDowell J: "The Resurrection Factor" San Bernardino, Calif, Here's Life Publishers, 1981, pp 20-53, 75-103.
26. McDowell J: "Evidence That Demands a Verdict: Historical Evidence for the Christian Faith." San Bernardino, Calif, Here's Life Publishers, 1979, pp 39-87, 141-263.
27. McDowell J: "More Than a Carpenter" Wheaton, Ill, Tyndale House Publishers, 1977, pp 36-71, 89-100.
28. Hengel M: "Crucifixion in the Ancient World and the folly of the Message of the Cross" Bowden J (trans) Philadelphia, Fortress Press, 1977, pp 22-45, 86-90.
29. Ricciotti G: "The Life of Christ" Zizzamia AI (trans). Milwaukee, Bruce Publishing Co, 1947, pp 29-57, 78-153, 161-167, 586-647.
30. Pfeiffer CF, Vos HF, Rea J (eda): "Wycliffe Bible Encyclopedia." Chicago Moody Press, 1975, pp 149-152, 404-405, 713-723, 1173,1174, 150-1523.
31. Greenleaf S: "An Examination of the Testimony of the four Evangelists by the Rules of Evidence Administered in the Courts of Justice." Grand Rapids, Mich, Baker Book House, 1965, p. 29.
32. Hatch E, Redpath HA: "A Concordance to the Septuagint and the Other Greek Versions of the Old Testament (Including the Apocryphal Books) Graz, Austria, Akademische Druce U Verlagsanstalt, 1975, p 1142.
33. Wuest KS: "Wuest Word Studies From the Greek New Testament for the English Reader." Grand Rapids, Mich. WB Eerdmans Publisher, 1973, vol 1, p 280.
34. Friedrich G: "Theological Dictionary of the New Testament", Bremiley G (ed-trans). Grand Rapids, Mich. WB Eerdmans Publisher, 1971, vol 7, pp 572,573,632.
35. Aradt WF, Gingrich FW: "A Greek-English Lexicon of the New Testament and Other Early Christian Literature." University of Chicago Press, 1057, p 673.
36. Brown F, Driver SR, Briggs CA: "A Hebrew and English Lexicon of the Old Testament With an Appendix Containing the Biblical Aramaic." Oxford, England, Clarendon Press, 1953, pp 841, 854.
37. Robertson AT: "A Grammar of the Greek New Testament in Light of Historical Research." Nashville, Tenn, Broadman Press, 1931, pp 417-427.
38. Jackson SM (ed): "The New Schaff-Herzog Encyclopedia of Religious Knowledge." New York, Funk & Wagnalls, 1909, pp 312-314.
39. Kim H-S, Suzuki M, Lie JT, et al: Nonbacterial thrombotic endocarditis (NBTE) and disseminated intravascular coagulation (DIC): Autopsy study of 36 patients. "Arch Pathol Lab Med" 1977;101:65-68.
40. Becker AE, van Mantgem J-P: Cardiac tamponade: A study of 50 hearts. "Eur J Cardiol" 1975;3:349-358.

Let's Review Some of What We've Learned about why the Bible is True

History – Assyrian Empire: Discovery of city of Nineveh and King Ashurbanipal's 10,000-tablets validate biblical records.

Archaeology: "Archaeological work has unquestionably strengthened confidence in the reliability of the Scriptural record." Millar Burrows (Yale Univ.)

Dead Sea Scrolls: Old Testament books, with prophecies pointing to Jesus Christ, date to 125BC.

Prophecy: Foretold events in the Bible have been verified historically.

There are 9 Facts about the Bible to which majority of scholars agree...

Manuscripts & Text Criticism: > 24,000 New Testament copies: no Christian doctrine rests on a disputed reading.

Nonbiblical Authors: 14 writers outside the Bible verify the contents of the Bible.

Together these 9 Facts make a strong case *for the truth of the Bible*

Uniqueness: Written by 40 authors on 3 continents over 1,500 years, with complete harmony.

Eyewitnesses: People don't willingly die horrible deaths for what they know is a lie.

Life-changing Impact: The Bible teaches, convicts, inspires.

CHAPTER 7 Argument #9 for God = The Person of *JESUS CHRIST* 7.1

Skeptic's Charge #20: What is so unique about Jesus Christ? He may have been a good moral teacher, and He may even have said things that give me motivation to try to be a better person. But what's so great about Him that a world religion would claim Him as their leader?

Answer: The New Testament records claim He was more than a man. He is the God-man.

Lesson		11 - Lesson Plan
7.2	John 8:56-59	⇨ The Deity of Jesus Christ
7.3	Dr. John H. Gerstner:	"A Primer on the Deity of Christ"
7.4	Genesis	⇨ The Lineage of Messiah
7.9	Daniel 9:24-26	⇨ The 1st Coming of Messiah
7.5	Isaiah 7:14	⇨ The Incarnation of Messiah
7.6	Joshua 1:9	⇨ Immanuel
7.7	Isaiah 9:6	⇨ God in the Flesh
7.8	Daniel 7:13	⇨ The Son of Man
7.12	John 1:3-5	⇨ The Creator, Life & Light
7.10	Isaiah 53:1-12	⇨ The Suffering Messiah
7.11	Psalm 22:1-31	⇨ The Crucifixion of Messiah

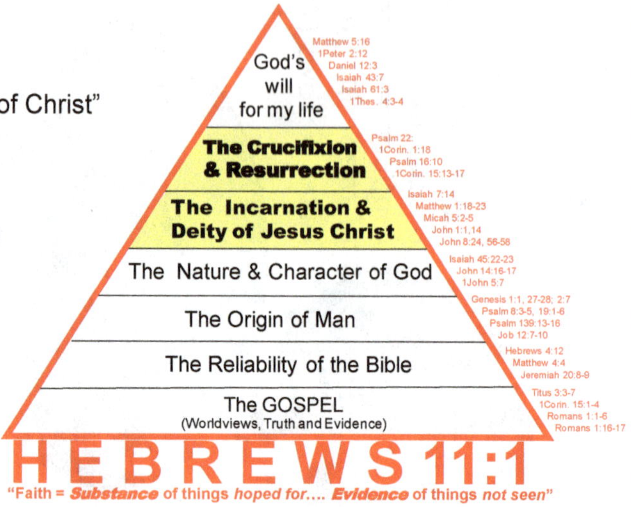
God's will for my life
Matthew 5:16
1Peter 2:12
Daniel 12:3
Isaiah 43:7
Isaiah 61:3
1Thes. 4:3-4
The Crucifixion & Resurrection
Psalm 22:
1Corin. 1:18
Psalm 16:10
1Corin. 15:13-17
The Incarnation & Deity of Jesus Christ
Isaiah 7:14
Matthew 1:18-23
Micah 5:2-5
John 1:1,14
John 8:24, 56-58
The Nature & Character of God
Isaiah 45:22-23
John 14:16-17
1John 5:7
The Origin of Man
Genesis 1:1, 27-28; 2:7
Psalm 8:3-5, 19:1-6
Psalm 139:13-16
Job 12:7-10
The Reliability of the Bible
Hebrews 4:12
Matthew 4:4
Jeremiah 20:8-9
The GOSPEL
(Worldviews, Truth and Evidence)
Titus 3:3-7
1Corin. 15:1-4
Romans 1:1-6
Romans 1:16-17
HEBREWS 11:1
"Faith = Substance of things hoped for.... Evidence of things not seen"

Back to Book 1, 'Worldviews, Truth and Evidence' ⇨ Scientific Examination of the Evidence

We list out 87 unique pieces of circumstantial evidence from the Old Testament that, when assembled together, form a mosaic of unique prophetic descriptions or events that any person in history must fulfill in order to be a candidate for the Messiah (God's 'Anointed King' who comes to earth as a man to deliver all of mankind from bondage to their sin and the penalty their sin enacts upon them).

Jesus is documented in the New Testament as fulfilling every one of these 87 prophecies. To demonstrate how reasonable it is to claim that Jesus Christ is the Messiah sent from God, we turn to the work of Dr. Peter Stoner and his application of PROBABILITY SCIENCE to just 8 of these 87 Old Testament prophecies.

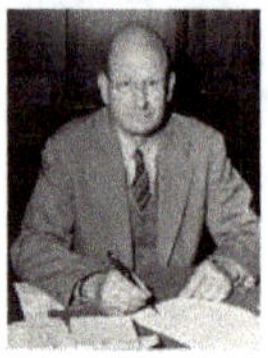

Peter Stoner (1888 – 1980): Chairman of the Mathematics and Astronomy Departments at Pasadena City College until 1953; Chairman of the science division, Westmont College, 1953–57; best known for his book '*Science Speaks*' that calculates probabilities for specific Bible prophecies. He was a co-founder of the American Scientific Affiliation, a Christian organization described as "a fellowship of men and women in science and disciplines that relate to science who share a common fidelity to the Word of God and a commitment to integrity in the practice of science."

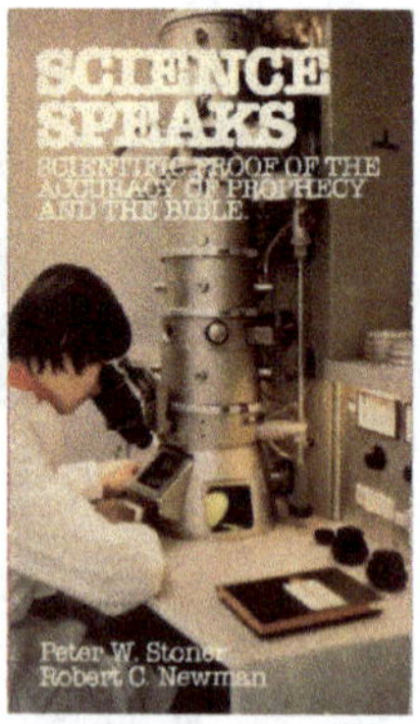
SCIENCE SPEAKS
SCIENTIFIC PROOF OF THE ACCURACY OF PROPHECY AND THE BIBLE
Peter W. Stoner
Robert C. Newman

In his book **"Science Speaks"**[15], Professor Stoner explains how he calculated the mathematical probabilities for biblical prophecies:

In order to ensure no bias goes into the calculations, he spread the work across nearly 600 university students, in twelve different classes, with each class working independently from the others in analyzing the detailed circumstances surrounding each prophecy.

Each of the twelve groups worked through each prophecy until they came to a consensus on their calculations. He then brought the twelve independent analyses together and compared their results, documenting the similarities and differences.

Then, he submitted his students' work to an independent committee of the American Scientific Affiliation, for peer review by a team of experts in probability science, who verified that his application of the science of probability to these prophecies was done correctly.

Quick Reminder from Book 1, Lesson 4.5: How we calculate probability of historical events

We can use statistics to calculate the odds that any historical event happened by chance by first capturing all the variables that influence that event. For example, the historical prophecy of the Messiah born in Bethlehem requires one of the variables to be "city". If there were 200 cities existing at the time, that one variable has a 1:200 chance for any person to be born in Bethlehem. Keep in mind this is just one variable (other variables could be number of births each month, gender, ethnic group, etc.). The job of the statistician is to define all variables, calculate each variable's odds of occurrence, then solve for the overall probability in question.

8 Old Testament Prophecies tested by Dr. Stoner (The Numbers refer to Book 1 Evidences)		
Old Testament Prophecy	**New Testament Fulfillment**	**Probability**
52 Messiah's forerunner (prepares arrival) (Isaiah 40:3, 730BC *"The voice of one crying in the wilderness: 'Prepare the way of the Lord; make straight in the desert a highway for our God.'"*)	John 1:22-23 *"...they said to him, 'Who are you, that we may give an answer to those who sent us? What do you say about yourself?' He said, 'I am the voice crying in the wilderness: "Make straight the way of the Lord," as the prophet Isaiah said.'"*	1 chance in 100 (1×10^2)
54 Messiah born in Bethlehem Ephrathah (Micah 5:2, 700 BC *"But you, Bethlehem Ephrathah, though you are little among the thousands in Judah, yet out of you shall come forth to Me the One to be ruler in Israel, whose goings forth are from of old, from the days of eternity."*)	Luke 2:4-7 *"Joseph went up from Galilee, out of the city of Nazareth, into Judea, to the city of David, called Bethlehem, because he was of the house and lineage of David, to be registered with Mary, his betrothed wife, who was with child... while they were there... she brought forth her firstborn Son..."*	1 chance in 280,000 (1×10^5)
64 Messiah enters Jerusalem on a donkey (Zechariah 9:9, 500BC *"Rejoice greatly, O daughter of Zion! Shout, O daughter of Jerusalem! Behold, your King is coming to you; He is just and having salvation, lowly and riding on a donkey, a colt, the foal of a donkey."*)	Matthew 21:2-3 *"...He said to them, 'Go into the village opposite you; and immediately you will find a donkey tied, and a colt with her. Loose them and bring them to Me. And if anyone says anything to you, you shall say, 'The Lord has need of them', and immediately he will send them."*	1 chance in 1,000 (1×10^3)
67 Messiah betrayed by a close friend (Psalm 41:9, 1,000BC *"Even my old familiar friend whom I trusted, who ate my bread, has lifted up his heel against me."*)	Luke 22:47-48 *"...Judas, one of the twelve, went before them and drew near to Jesus to kiss Him. But Jesus said to him, 'Judas, are you betraying the Son of Man with a kiss?'"*	1 chance in 1,000 (1×10^3)
71 Messiah is silent during accusations (Isaiah 53:7, 730BC *"He was oppressed and afflicted, yet He opened not His mouth. And as a sheep before its shearers is silent, so He opened not His mouth."*)	Matthew 27:12-14 *"...while He was being accused by the chief priests and elders, He answered nothing. Then Pilate said to Him, 'Do You not hear how many things they testify against You?' And He answered them not one word, so that the governor marveled greatly."*	1 chance in 1,000 (1×10^3)
73 Messiah betrayed for 30 pcs. of silver (Zechariah 11:12, 500BC *"Then I said to them, 'If it is agreeable to you, give me my wages; and if not, refrain.' So they weighed out for my wages 30 pieces of silver."*)	Matthew 26:14-15 *"Then one of the twelve, Judas Iscariot, went to the chief priests and said, 'What are you willing to give me if I deliver Him to you?' And they counted out to him 30 pieces of silver."*	1 chance in 1,000 (1×10^3)
74 30 pcs. of silver buys a potter's field (Zechariah 11:13, 500BC *"The Lord said to me, 'Throw it to the potter' – that princely price they set on me. So I took the 30 pieces of silver and threw them into the house of the Lord for the potter."*)	Matthew 27:5,7 *"...he threw down the pieces of silver in the temple and departed, and went and hanged himself. And they took counsel and bought with them the potter's field, to bury strangers in."*	1 chance in 100,000 (1×10^5)
79 Messiah is crucified (Psalm 22:16, 1,000BC *"...dogs have surrounded Me; the assembly of the wicked has enclosed Me. They pierced My hands and My feet."*)	John 19:17-18 *"He, bearing His cross, went out to a place called the Place of the Skull, which is called in Hebrew, Golgotha, where they crucified Him, and two others with Him..."*	1 chance in 10,000 (1×10^4)

QUESTION: What is the probability that one man fulfilled all eight of the above prophecies?

<u>Back to Book 1, Lesson 4.5</u> ⇨ Method 1: multiply each of the individual prophecy's probabilities of occurrence together to get the overall probability of one man meeting all eight prophecies.

$$P_{success} = (1 \times 10^2) \times (1 \times 10^5) \times (1 \times 10^3) \times (1 \times 10^3) \times (1 \times 10^3) \times (1 \times 10^3) \times (1 \times 10^5) \times (1 \times 10^4) = \mathbf{1 \times 10^{28}}.$$

That's saying for every 10,000,000,000,000,000,000,000,000,000 people, the odds are that about 1 of them would meet all eight prophecies. There are only 6,000,000,000 people on the earth. With Christ the only person in history fulfilling just eight prophecies (and remember, Book 1 lists 87), **what are the odds it's just coincidence?**

John 8:56-59   The Deity of Jesus Christ   7.2

"'Your father Abraham ①REJOICED to ②SEE My ③DAY, and he saw it and was glad.' Then the Jews said to Him, 'You are not yet 50 years old, and have You seen Abraham?' Jesus said to them, 'Most assuredly, I say to you, before Abraham was, ④I AM.' Then they took up stones to throw at Him, but Jesus hid Himself and went out of the temple, going through the midst of them, and so passed by."

① REJOICED = Gr. "*agalliaō*" = jumped for joy, overwhelmingly excited
② SEE = Gr. "*eidō*" = to see literally, to behold and fully comprehend
③ DAY = Gr. "*hemera*" = literal appearance in time; the time space between dawn and dark

What does Jesus mean in John 8:56? The use of past tenses (rejoiced, saw) seems to refer to something that occurred during Abraham's lifetime. Two strong possibilities:
• Genesis 15:1 = The Lord appears to him in a vision, declaring Himself to him for the first time as the great "I AM", in this context as Abram's "exceedingly great reward".
• Genesis 22:13-15 = This passage, known to rabbis as the *Akedah* ("Binding"), tells of Abraham finding the ram which will replace his son Isaac on the altar of sacrifice — an occasion of certain rejoicing.

④ I AM = Gr. "*ejgwV eijmiv*" The meaning of Jesus' statement in John 8:58 is:
"Before Abraham came into existence I, the "I AM," eternally was, am now, and shall be." Here is an *explicit claim to deity*, consistent with John's usage of *"ejgwV eijmiv"*.

• Although each time John uses "I AM" must be examined in context to see if it is referring to Exodus 3:13-15, it is clear it is the case here (especially in light of the response of the Jewish authorities in the following verse).

Exodus 3:13-15 *"Moses said to God, 'Indeed, when I come to the children of Israel and say to them, "The God of your fathers has sent me to you", and they say to me, "What is His name?", what shall I say to them?' And God said to Moses, "I AM WHO I AM". And He said, "Thus you shall say to the children of Israel, "I AM has sent me to you." Moreover God said to Moses, "Thus you shall say to the children of Israel, 'The Lord God of your fathers, the God of Abraham, the God of Isaac, and the God of Jacob, has sent me to you. This is My name forever, and this is My memorial to all generations.'"*

• John 8:59 = The significance of Jesus' claim to deity in verse 58 is fully understood by the Jewish authorities. They want to stone him. Leviticus 24:16 says anyone who blasphemes the name of God shall be stoned to death. John 10:33 says this is how the Jews answered Jesus when He asked them why they wanted to stone Him.

Leviticus 24:16 *"Whosoever BLASPHEMES the name of the Lord shall surely be put to death, and all the congregation shall certainly STONE him, the stranger as well as him who is born in the land. When he blasphemes the name of the Lord, he shall be put to death."*

John 10:33 *"The Jews answered Him, saying, 'For a good work we do not stone You, but for BLASPHEMY, and because You, being a Man, make Yourself God.'"*

C.S. Lewis ("Mere Christianity")[7]: You can't ignore Jesus' claim to Deity

"I am trying here to prevent anyone saying the really foolish thing that people often say about Him: "I'm ready to accept Jesus as a great moral teacher, but I don't accept His claim to be God." That is the one thing we must not say.

A man who said the sort of things Jesus said would not be a great moral teacher. He would either be a lunatic – on a level with the man who says he is a poached egg – or else he would be the Devil of Hell. You must make your choice. Either this man was, and is, the Son of God: or else a madman or something worse.

You can shut Him up for a fool, you can spit at Him and kill Him as a demon; or you can fall at His feet and call Him Lord and God. But let us not come with any patronizing nonsense about His being a great human teacher. He has not left that open to us. He did not intend to."

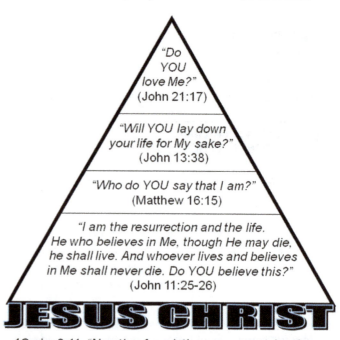

"Do YOU love Me?" (John 21:17)

"Will YOU lay down your life for My sake?" (John 13:38)

"Who do YOU say that I am?" (Matthew 16:15)

"I am the resurrection and the life. He who believes in Me, though He may die, he shall live. And whoever lives and believes in Me shall never die. Do YOU believe this?" (John 11:25-26)

JESUS CHRIST

1Corin. 3:11 *"No other foundation can anyone lay than that which is laid, which is Jesus Christ"*

Dr. John H. Gerstner: "A Primer on the Deity of Christ"[9]

Skeptic's Charge #21: Jesus never directly claimed to be God.

ANSWER: Below are nine proofs presented by Dr. Gerstner on the Deity of Jesus Christ. These proofs are excerpts taken from Dr. Gerstner's essay on the subject.

PROOF #1 = *"He who has seen Me has seen the Father."* **(John 14:9)**

There's no question in anybody's mind that the word "Father" here refers to the Deity. So when He says those words to Philip, His obvious meaning is, "He who has seen Me has seen God." Jesus is seriously and unmistakably saying that to see Him is to see God.

Jesus claims a one-to-one identy between Himself and the Father. Jesus didn't identify deity with His human nature or any other human being. In uttering those words, Jesus is in union with God. We have here Christ's own reference to the Christian doctrine of the INCARNATION, meaning "in the flesh." God in the flesh, Immanuel.

A normal person would feel blasphemous in saying. "He who has seen Me has seen the Father". That's because every person knows they are not God. The only way to make sense of that claim coming from the lips of a visible human being is that He, Jesus of Nazareth, is actually in a unique unity with God. It is so different from the way any other human being is related to God that He alone can say that to see Him is to see the Father. Jesus' statement is a clear claim of deity and simultaneously of incarnation.

PROOF #2 = *"I and the Father are one."* **(John 10:30)**

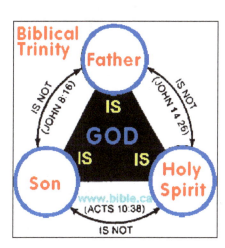

This sounds like, "He who has seen Me has seen the Father." But there is this difference: In saying, "I and the Father are one," He indicates not a one-to-one identity, but a "two-in-one" identity. He has in mind two persons when He says, "I and the Father are one." He is saying He is DISTINCT from the Father, at the same time that He is one with the Father. The statement, "He who has seen Me has seen the Father," stresses His identity with God. But, "I and the Father are one" speaks of both identity and diversity. It is a reference to two persons in one Godhead. Jesus is pointing to the Christian doctrine of the TRINITY. We have here the oneness of God or "monotheism," the unity of the divine essence or being. At the same time, we see that Christ is distinct from the Father. The Son and the Father are one in the same divine essence. Jesus as a member of the Trinity underlines His full deity.

PROOF #3 = *"You being a man make yourself to be God."* **(John 10:33)**

Jesus carries on a dialogue with certain "Jews who believed on Him." But before the chapter is over, those Jews who believed in Him were seen not to believe in Him. When Christ claimed to be deity, these professed believers realized they did not in fact believe in Him. They believed in the person they thought Jesus was. When they learned who Jesus claimed to be, they were outraged at Him.

It was in the course of the dialogue with these "believing" Jews that Jesus indicated that He came from the Father and indeed was one with the Father. These "disciples" were getting the message and not liking it. The more these "believers" learn about His claims to deity, the more they become hostile and outraged. Finally, they recognize that Christ unmistakably claims to be God.

In their book, that is blasphemy, because Jesus was a human being, and it is blasphemy for a human being to claim to be God. They picked up stones to kill Him because, as they said, *"You being a man make yourself to be God."* Here are different reactions to the same proposition of Jesus that He was indeed God incarnate. When Jesus said, *"He who has seen Me has seen the Father,"* He was speaking to His believing disciples. They accepted it. But this statement about Christ's deity was made to professed believers who really did not believe. Here we have the testimony of unbelievers to Christ's self-opinion as we have in the other chapter the testimony of believers to His belief about Himself. Both groups are confronted with the same Christ. One group accepts Him as divine and worships. The other group rejects Him as a blasphemer and endeavors to execute Him.

PROOF #4 = *"I am the vine, and you are the branches. He who abides in Me, and I in him, bears much fruit; for without Me you can do nothing."* **(John 15:5)**

Christ taught that He is the SOURCE of their life and their fruit-bearing, that is, their morality. He teaches the way of morality and that He is the way. Jesus often sets forth teachings and describes maxims, but He also talks about the source of power for fulfilling the moral law, as in the vine and branches. The morality He commands is fulfilled in those who don't simply hear what He says and obey it, but look to Him for the necessary strength to fulfill it.

In Matthew 5:16, He says, *"Let your light so shine before men that they may behold your good works and glorify your Father who is in Heaven."* In John 15, He explains where their good works actually come from: He, as the vine, is the source of life, which somehow fills His followers, producing in them a moral life.

Christ not only teaches morality but also claims that He Himself fulfills that morality in His followers. He revealed Himself as the source for fulfilling His own commandments. If most superficial "Christians" really understood this, they may then stop following His teaching. These people are real moralists. They try to be humble, but they really are proud of their character. They feel it's their character, and they don't need outside help to obey these commandments. If you told them that they could not carry out what Jesus taught without His power, they would not buy that.

They think Christ is admirable as a moral teacher addressing Himself to moral persons such as themselves. They agree with His ideas. They join with Him in following them. But depend upon Him for the power to do good? They would not accept that. They would want nothing more to do with Him. He would be insulting them.

Most people think this way at first. It's only when they realize how deep their depravity is and how little inclined they are to general morality that they begin to look around for help. Its once they do realize they are sinners, then they know that they need forgiveness.

If, as sinners, they sense that they cannot become new people unless they have a new principle of life within them, they may not realize at first that it's nothing less than Jesus Christ Himself dwelling in them and moving them to morality. But they learn quickly enough once He teaches them that.

Once you realize that you're a sinner, you know that you do not have the internal power to make your ethics rise up and walk. That's because you've become acquainted with your own heart and with the Christian doctrine. Christ, even in His moral teaching, implies His very deity. He Himself empowers us to fulfill His own laws by indwelling us as the vine indwells and energizes the branch to bear fruit. For Christ to indwell every Christian who bears moral fruit, He would have to be spiritual and not material, and He would have to be infinite. What else would that be except deity itself?

We must conclude from the teaching of Jesus Christ about morals that He Himself is the fulfiller of them, and that, therefore, He Himself must be the infinite divine Spirit.

PROOF #5 = **"The Sermon on the Mount" (Matthew 5-7)**

The Sermon on the Mount in Matthew is found in chapters 5 through 7. Here Christ says the type of thing that leaves no doubt. He assumes His own deity. For example, consider the Beatitudes in general. We're all familiar with these. Many of us have memorized them: "*Blessed are the poor in spirit, for theirs is the kingdom of heaven.*" "*Blessed are the peacemakers, for they shall be called the children of God.*" And so on. I'll not cite them all, but just note that Jesus speaks them with absolute finality and on His own authority alone.

The prophets would constantly say, *"Thus saith the Lord."* They would always ground the authority of their message not on themselves but on God, who had revealed His message to them. They make it clear they are the servants and He is the Lord. But with Jesus, the authority of His message does not depend upon a source outside Himself.

In the Beatitudes, on His own authority, He tells us who will inherit the kingdom of God, who will be the children of God, who will inherit the earth, and so on. No mere human being can say that on His own authority. He can give educated guesses. Or, if he is commissioned by God, he can say it in God's name, but not of himself. Yet this man Jesus spoke these things very calmly with a supreme and serene authority appropriate only to deity itself.

These things sound so natural coming from His lips that we don't notice extraordinary implications. He talks as if He is God, even when He doesn't say so directly. It doesn't seem strange to hear Jesus speak that way. It wouldn't be appropriate for anyone to speak that way unless He were divine. The reason people reading the Beatitudes miss their implicit argument for Jesus' deity is that it seems so natural coming from His lips.

PROOF #6 = *"Blessed are you when men shall revile you and say all manner of evil against you falsely for My sake. Rejoice and be exceedingly glad for so they persecuted the prophets that were before you."* **(Matthew 5:11-12)**

Jesus is saying that the prophets suffered for Him. And the prophets lived hundreds of years before Jesus. That implies that He was preexistent, a supernatural being. If He lived hundreds of years before that sermon, and people suffered for Him before He was born, then He existed in another form before taking human form.

The point is even more plain if you imagine an ordinary person making the kind of statement He does. Suppose, for example, someone stood behind a pulpit and said, "Blessed are John Calvin and Martin Luther and John Wesley and Jonathan Edwards because they suffered for my sake." It would not only be false, because, of course, they never knew me, or suffered for me, or would even think of suffering for me had they known me; it would also be absolutely absurd. I would have to be out of my mind to say a thing like that.

But Christ says it as a simple matter of fact. In perfect calmness and secure rationality He casually remarks that men hundreds and thousands of years before suffered for His sake. When you think of it, you realize what an overwhelming assertion of His deity that is.

PROOF #7 = *"It is said by them of old time, `Thou shalt not kill,' but I say unto you..."* or *"It is said by them of old time, `Thou shalt not commit adultery,' but I say unto you..."* **(Matthew 5:27-28)**

When Christ comments directly on the Bible, He's putting Himself on a level with Old Testament Scripture. For Him and His audience the Old Testament was the Word of God. In the same breath that He cites what His audience regarded as the inspired Word of God, He calmly says, "But I say to you." By putting His word on a level with what was revered as the Word of God, Christ puts Himself on a divine level.

Suppose someone from the pulpit said to a worshipping congregation, "Now, the Word of God says so and so. But I say unto you." You know what that congregation would say to me. "Who do you think you are?" Only one person may properly do such a thing: God Himself. The only one equal to God is God.

Jesus Christ certainly sounds as if He is making God His equal. If He were not God then, of course, He would be just as impertinent and blasphemous as anyone to say such a thing. His being a perfect man doesn't change the fact that He'd be infinitely beneath the infinite God. Moreover, a perfect man would never utter such blasphemy. Therefore, Jesus Christ is claiming to be God.

PROOF #8 = *"…whoever hears these sayings of Mine, and does them… now everyone who hears these sayings of Mine, and does not do them…"* **(Matthew 7:24-27)**

Jesus tells the well-known parable of the two men who built their houses on differing foundations. One man built on a rock; the other on sand. One of the houses, you remember, collapsed during a storm; the other stood. The point of it is that the man who built his house on a rock really was building on Christ. And the man who built on sand did not build on Christ or His teaching. Jesus is saying that if an individual believes in Him and His teaching and obeys Him, he will be able to go through the storms of life, and no doubt the storms of final judgment. If a person does not believe, he will be ruined in this world and the world to come.

For anyone else to say that would be consummate arrogance and, again, blasphemy. And yet, what is more natural than for a divine person to say such a thing. If Christ is divine, you could never understand His not saying it; and if He were not divine, you could never understand His saying it. It's that simple.

PROOF #9 = *"I never knew you."* **(Matthew 7:23)**

Jesus ends the Sermon on the Mount by describing the final judgment: *"In that day, men shall come before Me and say, `Lord, Lord. Have we not prophesied in Thy name? Have we not cast out devils in Thy name? Have we not done mighty works in Thy name?' And I shall say unto them, `Depart from Me ye workers of iniquity. I never knew you."*

Jesus is saying He's going to be the judge of the last day. He is going to reject some people at His judgment seat. There's only one judge of the last day: God Himself. Christ says He's the judge of the last day. Therefore, He is saying unmistakably that He is God.

These people before the judgment seat of Christ are saying that they prophesied in His name and did many great things. Can we be sure they're telling the truth? They wouldn't try to deceive that Judge. So, let's assume they really were prophets of Christ or preachers of the Word of God. They were even successful at casting out devils. We are assuming they did many mighty works, because they wouldn't dare lie about a matter like that before the judgment seat. They may have been liars in this world, but not before the all-wise God in the next world.

Why would Christ reject such persons? But that's the very point. They did these things in the name of Christ, no doubt. But they didn't do them in the SPIRIT OF CHRIST. They could be preachers of the Word. They could declare the true gospel. They could even deliver people out of darkness and into light, doing many other mighty works. But according to Jesus Himself, the Spirit of Christ isn't what motivates them when they do these things.

Evidence #1 for the Deity of Jesus Christ: MESSIAH'S LINEAGE

Skeptic's Charge #22: "History is full of people who've claimed to be the Messiah. Why should I believe Jesus Christ is and all the others are fakes?"

ANSWER: Look at the evidence: here's the details of MESSIAH's LINEAGE that anyone claiming to be Messiah must meet. No one in history ever has, except Jesus Christ.

1) Messiah must be a Hebrew In Genesis 22:18, God eliminates all other nations ("*In your seed all the nations of the earth shall be blessed...*").

✓ fulfilled in Jesus = Matthew 1:1 ("*... the genealogy of Jesus Christ, the Son of David, the Son of Abraham*").

2) Messiah must descend from Isaac Abraham had two sons, Isaac and Ishmael. God eliminates 1/2 of Abraham's lineage by stating Messiah will be a descendant of Isaac, not Ishmael. Genesis 21:12 ("*...in Isaac your seed shall be called*").

✓ fulfilled in Jesus = Matthew 1:2 ("*Abraham begot Isaac*").

3) Messiah must descend from Jacob Isaac had two sons, Jacob and Esau. God eliminates 1/2 of Isaac's lineage by stating Messiah will descend by Jacob, not Esau. Genesis 35:10 ("*Your name shall not be called Jacob anymore, but Israel shall be your name*") and Numbers 24:17 ("*A Star shall come out of Jacob; a Scepter shall rise out of Israel*").

✓ fulfilled in Jesus = Matthew 1:2 ("*Isaac begot Jacob*").

4) Messiah must descend from Judah Jacob had 12 sons. God eliminates 11/12 of Jacob's lineage by stating Messiah will descend by Judah. Genesis 49:10 ("*The scepter shall not depart from Judah, nor a lawgiver from between his feet, until Shiloh comes, and to Him shall be the obedience of the people*").

✓ fulfilled in Jesus = Matthew 1:2 ("*Jacob begot Judah*") and Hebrews 7:14 ("*...our Lord arose from Judah...*").

5) Messiah must descend from Jesse God eliminates all other households of Judah's tribe, narrowing it to one family, by stating Messiah will come from Jesse's family. Isaiah 11:1,10 ("*There shall come forth a Rod from the stock of Jesse, and a Branch shall grow out of his roots... in that day there shall be a Root of Jesse, who shall stand as a banner to the people; for the Gentiles shall seek Him, and His resting place shall be glorious.*")

✓ fulfilled in Jesus = Matthew 1:5 and Luke 3:32 ("*...Obed begot Jesse... Jesus, the son of Jesse*").

6) Messiah must descend from David Jesse had 7 sons. God eliminates 6/7 of Jesse's lineage by stating Messiah will be a descendant of David. Jeremiah 23:5 ("*...I will raise to David a Branch of righteousness; a King shall reign and prosper, and execute judgment and righteousness in the earth. In His days Judah will be saved, and Israel will dwell safely; now this is the name by which He will be called: THE LORD OUR RIGHTEOUSNESS*").

✓ fulfilled in Jesus = Matthew 1:6 and Luke 3:31 ("*...Jesse begot David the king... Jesus, the son of David*").

7) Messiah must be born in Bethlehem God eliminates all other cities in the world. Micah 5:2 ("*But you, Bethlehem Ephrathah, though you are little among the thousands of Judah, yet out of you shall come forth to Me the One who is to be ruler in Israel, whose goings forth have been of old, from everlasting*").

✓ fulfilled in Jesus = John 7:42 ("*Has not the Scripture said that the Christ comes from the seed of David and from the town of Bethlehem, where David was?*").

8) Messiah must arrive before the Temple is destroyed God narrows Messiah's arrival before 70AD, when Titus destroys the temple. Daniel 9:26 ("*..the people of the prince who is to come shall destroy the city and the sanctuary...*") and Malachi 3:1 ("*...the Lord, whom you seek, will suddenly come to His temple...*").

✓ fulfilled in Jesus = Mark 11:11 ("*... Jesus went into Jerusalem and into the temple. So when He had looked around at all things...*") and Mark 13:2 ("*Jesus said... 'Do you see these great buildings? Not one stone shall be left upon another that shall not be thrown down'*").

Evidence #2 for the Deity of Jesus Christ: THE INCARNATION 7.5
Isaiah 7:14 ➔ John 1:1-2,14

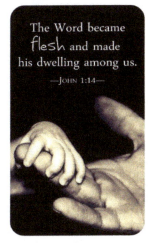

Isaiah 7:14 *"The Lord Himself will give you a sign. Behold, the ①VIRGIN shall conceive and bear a Son, and shall call His name ②IMMANUEL."*

John 1:1-2,14 *"③IN THE BEGINNING was the ④WORD, and the Word was with God, and the Word was God. He was in the beginning with God. And the Word became ⑤FLESH and ⑥DWELT among us..."*

① VIRGIN = Hebrew "*almah*" = virgin (one never having had sexual relations) – etymogically, '*almah*' is derived from the verb '*alam*', meaning 'to hide or conceal'.

Dr. Victor Buksbazen, 'Commentary on the Prophet Isaiah'[16]:

• *"The Hebrew word used here in Isaiah 7:14 is 'almah', and it is first used in the Old Testament in connection with Rebekah, the future bride of Isaac, in Genesis 24:43. But in Genesis 24:16, she is also called a 'virgin', and this time the Hebrew word is 'bethulah'. Both 'almah' and 'bethulah' can be used in the Old Testament for a virgin, but 'almah' is never applied to a married woman, while 'bethulah' is sometimes, which means it can also mean a married woman who is no longer a virgin (see Joel 1:8 and Deuteronomy 22:19)."*

• *"There are only 7 uses for 'almah' in the Old Testament - each time it's a virgin:*
Genesis 24:43 = applied to Rebekah, the future bride of Isaac
Exodus 2:8 = applied to Miriam, the sister of Moses
Psalm 68:25 = 'damsels' playing with timbrels (plural of 'almah', or 'alamoth')
Song of Solomon 1:3 and 6:8 = virgins of the royal court
Proverbs 30:19 = "the way of a man with a virgin"
Isaiah 7:14 = "Behold the virgin" = 'ha-almah'"

② IMMANUEL = Hebrew "*immânû'êl*" = 'with us is God'

③ IN THE BEGINNING = Gr. "*en archē*" ➪ John's appeal to the Jews: "in eternity past" = Greek equivalent of Genesis 1:1 ("in the beginning"); John is restating what the Jews know from their Torah, the pre-existence of God, except now he illuminates the Trinity in the first chapter of John: the Father = SOURCE of all things (Genesis 1:1), the Son = CREATOR of all things (Genesis 1:1), the Holy Spirit = ENERGIZER of all things (Genesis 1:2).

④ WORD = Gr. "*logos*" ➪ John's appeal to the Jews and Greeks: eternal mind, creative energy, eternal Cause; John used "Logos" because it was in common use everywhere. The Jew understands it as the wisdom of God; the Greek thinks of the rational principle of which all natural laws are expressed. But for John, the Word was not a principle, but a living Person who is divine and the source of life for all people.

⑤ FLESH = Gr. "*sarx*" = the human body that is visible (as opposed to the soul and spirit, which is invisible).

⑥ DWELT = Gr. "*skēnoō*" = "pitched his tent", "tabernacled". God fulfilled His promise in Isaiah 7:14 of Immanuel (Hebrew "*Immânû'êl*" = "God with us").

God's precision ➔ The Virgin Birth

Matthew ch 1: Jesus' **Deity** ("Son of God") by fulfilling OT requirement of descending from the house of David, since JOSEPH is in David's line. God made a covenant with David that His house would bring Messiah:

Matthew 1:1 *"The book of the genealogy of Jesus Christ, the Son of David, the Son of Abraham."*

2Samuel 7:16 *"...your house and your kingdom shall be established forever before Me...."*

Luke ch 3: Jesus' **humanity** ("Son of Man"), thus belonging not only to Israel but to the world, by tracing Jesus through MARY ➔ see Luke 2:1-5: she returned to Bethlehem because she descended from David).

5) Matt. 1:16 = Gr. relative pronoun "of whom" is *feminine singular*; Matthew shows the **virgin birth** thru Mary.

6) Luke 3:23 = only Joseph's name has no definite article ("as was supposed"); Luke shows the **virgin birth**.

7) Jeremiah 22:30 = King Jeconiah, an ancestor of Joseph (Matt. 1:11-12), was DISQUALIFIED from the Throne: *"Thus says the Lord: 'Write this man down as childless, a man who shall not prosper in his days; for none of descendants shall prosper, sitting on the throne of David, and ruling anymore in Judah.'"*
If Jesus was the physical son of Joseph, He would have inherited Jeconiah's curse.

8) But He was the physical son of David through MARY, not Joseph's seed – He inherited the throne of David without coming under the curse of Joseph's bloodline!

ROMANS 11:33 *"Oh, the depth of the riches both of the wisdom and knowledge of God!"*

Evidence #3 for the Deity of Jesus Christ: IMMANUEL

Joshua 1:9 ➔ Matthew 1:23

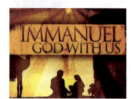

Joshua 1:9 *"Be strong, and of good courage; do not be afraid, nor be dismayed, for the Lord your God IS WITH YOU wherever you go."*

Matthew 1:23 *"Behold, a virgin shall be with child, and bear a Son, and they shall call His name 'IMMANUEL', which is translated, 'GOD WITH US.'"*

Albert Einstein (1879-1955) is one of the most recognized names in the world, and is probably the most famous scientist who ever lived. Time Magazine highlighted him as the "Person of the Century" in 1999. What many people may not know about him was his pronouncement to the scientific community, after reviewing the scientific evidence from Hubble's Telescope, that the universe was not static (which was the prevailing scientific theory at the time) but had a beginning, and therefore a Beginner, a "First Cause".

So who did Einstein identify as this "First Cause" who created everything in the beginning from nothing? In 1942, he met with three theologians at his home to discuss his views of who God is (Dov Hertzen, an orthodox rabbi, Brian McNaughton, a Catholic priest, and Mark Hartman, a liberal Protestant theologian). Though he confessed to the rabbis and priests who came to congratulate him on his discovery of God that he was convinced God brought the universe into existence and was intelligent and creative, he denied that God was personal. The clergy had a valid challenge to Einstein's denial: How can a Being who is intelligent and creative not also be personal?

But Einstein struggled with what he saw as an inconsistency in a Christian God who was all-powerful and all-good, but held people responsible for their choices: *'If this being is omnipotent, then every occurrence, including every human action, every human thought, and every human feeling and aspiration is also His work; how is it possible to think of holding men responsible for their deeds and thoughts before such an almighty Being? In giving out punishments and rewards He would to a certain extent be PASSING JUDGMENT ON HIMSELF. How can this be combined with the goodness and righteousness ascribed to Him?'* The clergy didn't have an answer that satisfied him, and he didn't look for the answer himself.

Einstein believed in a God who fit the description in Psalm 19, whose glory is revealed in a GENERAL sense, in the scientific evidence in the universe ("The heavens declare the glory of God..."). But Einstein did not believe this same God of creation could personally care for Him, and the clergy never pointed him to that same God who, in Joshua 1:9, promised to be personally with Him. God fulfilled that promise by revealing His glory in a SPECIFIC way, as John 1:14 says, by the Incarnation (the God of Joshua 1:9 comes to us and lives personally among us as IMMANUEL): *"The Word became flesh and dwelt among us, and we beheld His glory, the glory of the only begotten of the Father, full of grace and truth"*.

Why does this Creator God make Himself known to us personally?

At the Incarnation ➔   God comes to dwell with man as the God-man Jesus Christ.

But at the Cross ➔   God *PASSED JUDGMENT ON HIMSELF* when Jesus willingly took upon Himself the sins we all commit, offering His perfect life as the sacrifice to pay for our immorality, a punishment we deserved.

Through this sacrifice God reveals both His justice (crimes deserve punishment) and His deep love for us (Christ takes your punishment for you), offering each of us His free gift of reconciliation back to Him. He promises not only to forgive us through Christ but also to NEVER LEAVE US. In John 14:23, Jesus Himself promises He will dwell within anyone who sincerely asks Him to be their Lord and Savior for their sins: *"If anyone loves Me, he will keep My word; and My Father will love him, and We will come and MAKE OUR HOME WITH HIM."*

Adam Brown, the Navy Seal honored in the book 'Fearless'[12], believed in what Einstein never understood. 'Fearless' is a book written to celebrate the life of Adam Brown, who died in 2011 while on a mission in Afghanistan. What stood out to those who knew him was his devotion to Jesus Christ as his God and Savior, his source for his unbelievable courage (his favorite Bible verse was Philippians 4:13 – *"I can do all things through Christ who strengthens me."*). After his death, his father spoke to over two dozen of his Navy Seal buddies to make sure they understood that the key to eternal life is in Jesus Christ: *"Adam would have wanted me to tell y'all that there is hope, and if you'd like to see him again someday, you just need to invite Jesus into your heart."* This is the glory of God that we celebrate every Christmas season, that God has come to us – as Immanuel, Jesus Christ.

PSALM 116:15   *"Precious in the sight of the Lord is the death of His saints."*

IMMANUEL = God becomes a man and dwells with us

Matthew 1:23 *"'Behold, a virgin shall be with child, and bear a Son, and they shall call His name IMMANUEL, which translated 'God with us.'"*.

John 1:14 *"And the Word (Greek 'Logos') became FLESH and DWELT AMONG US."*

Joshua 1:5 *"No man shall be able to stand before you all the days of your life; as I was with Moses, so I will be with you. I WILL NOT LEAVE YOU NOR FORSAKE YOU."*

Isaiah 41:10 *"Fear not, for I AM WITH YOU."*

IN......	JESUS IS...	VERSE....
GENESIS	the ram at Abraham's altar	Genesis 22:7-14
EXODUS	the Passover Lamb	Exodus 12:21-27
LEVITICUS	the High Priest	Leviticus 9:15-18
NUMBERS	the Cloud by Day, and Pillar of Fire by Night	Numbers 9:15-16
DEUTERONOMY	the City of our refuge	Deuteronomy 19:1-13
JOSHUA	the scarlet thread out Rahab's window	Joshua 2:8-19
JUDGES	our Judge	Judges 2:16-18
RUTH	our kinsman Redeemer	Ruth 3:8-12
1st and 2nd SAMUEL	our trusted Prophet	1Samuel 3:19-20
KINGS and CHRONICLES	our reigning King	1Kings 2:1-4, 6:11-13
EZRA	our faithful Scribe	Ezra 7:1-16
NEHEMIAH	the Rebuilder of everything that is broken	Neh. 2:1-5, 10, 19-20
ESTHER	the Mordecai sitting faithful at the gate	Esther 2:19-23
JOB	our Redeemer who ever lives	Job 19:25-27
PSALMS	my Shepherd, and I shall not want	Psalm 23:1
PROVERBS and ECCLESIATES	our wisdom	Prov. 8:14, Eccle. 2:26
SONG OF SOLOMAN	the beautiful Bridegroom	Song of Sol. 2:4-10
ISAIAH	the Suffering Servant	Isaiah 53:1-12
JEREMIAH and LAMENTATIONS	the Weeping Prophet	Jer. 13:17, Lam. 1:16
EZEKIEL	the Wonderful 4-faced Man	Ezekiel 1:10
DANIEL	the 4th Man, in the midst of a fiery furnace	Daniel 3:24-25
HOSEA	my Love, who is forever faithful	Hosea 2:14-20
JOEL	baptizes us with the Holy Spirit	Joel 2:29-32
AMOS	our burden-bearer	Amos 2:13
OBADIAH	our Savior	Obadiah 1:17
JONAH	the foreign Missionary who takes the word of God to the world	Jonah 1:1-2
MICAH	the Messenger with beautiful feet	Micah 4:1-5, 5:1-5
NAHUM	the Avenger	Nahum 1:2
HABAKKUK	the Watchman who is ever praying for revival	Habakkuk 1:5, 2:1
ZEPHANIAH	the Lord, mighty to save	Zephaniah 3:17
HAGGAI	the Restorer of our lost heritage	Haggai 2:9
ZECHARIAH	our Fountain	Zechariah 13:1
MALACHI	the Sun of Righteousness with healing in His wings	Malachi 4:2
MATTHEW	the Christ, the Son of the living God	Matthew 16:16
MARK	the Miracle-worker	Mark 2:8-12
LUKE	the Son of Man	Luke 5:24
JOHN	the Door by which everyone of us must enter	John 10:9
ACTS	the Shining Light who appears to Saul on the road to Damascus	Acts 9:3-6
ROMANS	our Justifier	Romans 5:1
1CORINTHIANS	our Resurrection	1Corin. 15:12-20
2CORINTHIANS	our Sin-Bearer	2Corin. 5:21
GALATIANS	He redeems us from the law	Galatians 4:4-5
EPHESIANS	our unsearchable riches	Ephesians 3:8
PHILLIPPIANS	He supplies our every need	Philippians 4:19
COLOSSIANS	the fullness of the Godhead bodily	Colossians 2:9
1st and 2nd THESSALONIANS	our soon-coming King	1Th. 2:19, 2Th. 1:7-8
1st and 2nd TIMOTHY	the Mediator between God and man	1Timothy 2:5
TITUS	our Blessed Hope	Titus 2:13
PHILEMON	the friend who sticks closer than a brother	Philemon 1:16
HEBREWS	the blood of the everlasting covenant	Hebrews 13:20
JAMES	it is the Lord who heals the sick	James 5:14-15
1st and 2nd PETER	the Chief Shepherd	1Peter 5:4
1st, 2nd and 3rd JOHN	it is Jesus who has the tenderness of love	1John 4:7-10, 18-19
JUDE	the Lord coming with 10,000 saints	Jude 1:14
REVELATION	King of Kings and Lord of Lords	Revelation 19:11-16

Evidence #4 for the Deity of Jesus Christ: GOD IN THE FLESH
Isaiah 9:6

"Unto us a Child is born, unto us a Son is given, and the government will be upon His shoulder, and His name will be called ① Wonderful Counselor, ② Mighty God, ③ Everlasting Father, ④ Prince of Peace."

Isaiah 9:6 explains Christmas as a 12-day celebration. It officially begins on December 25th, with the celebration of Isaiah 9:6a (the birth of the Christ Child) and ends on January 6th, with the celebration of Isaiah 9:6b (the Day of Epiphany, or the Incarnation, when the Son is given). Isaiah the prophet, in 730BC (over 2,700 years ago) expected a God-given, supernatural Redeemer on the strength of God's promises in Isaiah 7:14 (predicts His birth) and Isaiah 9:6 (describes His Divine character). Let's examine His character as defined in the four names of Isaiah 9:6.

① **"Wonderful Counselor"** (*"Pele Yoetz"*) ⇨ In our bibles, "wonderful" is an adjective. But in the original Hebrew 'pele' is a noun, so Isaiah's first name for Jesus Christ is "Wonder Counselor". The bible first uses the word 'pele' in Judges 13:17-18, where Manoah asks the Angel of the Lord to tell him His name, so they may honor Him. He replies, *"Why do you ask My name, seeing it is 'pele' (a wonder/ a mystery)?"* In verse 22, Manoah proclaims this Angel to be God Himself. The point being made is that God ascribes to Himself the name of mystery and wonder, in the same way He ascribes holiness as one of His essential names. So this miraculous virgin-born Child, with the name '*Pele Yoetz*', is God Himself.

② **"Mighty God"** (*"El Gibbor"*) ⇨ Christ's name is "mighty God". But then, over 100 years later in Jeremiah 32:17-18, Christ is described as both '*El Gibbor*' and the ARM (Hebrew word '*zorah*') of the Lord: *"Ah, Lord God! Behold, You have made the heavens and the earth by Your great power and outstretched ARM. There is nothing too hard for You. You show lovingkindness to thousands, and repay the iniquity of the fathers into the bosom of their children after them – the great, the MIGHTY GOD ('El Gibbor'), whose name is the Lord of hosts."*

Why is this such a big deal? Jeremiah is crediting Jesus Christ as Mighty God in two direct ways: 1) the ARM of the Lord comes from Isaiah chapter 53 (the Suffering Servant who will die for our sins – see Lesson 7.10), and 2) the ARM who is the Creator of the universe (see John 1:3, Hebrews 1:1-2). Once again, this second name of 'El Gibbor' for the virgin-born Child points to His Deity.

③ **"Everlasting Father"** (*"Abhi ad"*) ⇨ Christ is called the "paternal Father of eternity". Our 'Mighty God' acts with paternal compassion towards His children. Matthew 9:36 describes Jesus the same way, as He was "*moved with compassion*" over the multitudes who were "*weary and scattered, like sheep, having no shepherd*". This same Jesus is described as "Everlasting" in Micah 5:2 (Micah wrote at the same time as Isaiah) *"But you, Bethlehem Ephrathah, though you are little among the thousands of Judah, yet out of you shall come forth to Me the One to be ruler in Israel, whose goings forth have been from old, from EVERLASTING."*

And remember in John 14:8-9, when Philip asks Jesus to show him the Father? What does Jesus tell Him? *"Philip said to Him, 'Lord, show us the Father, and it is sufficient for us.' Jesus said to him, 'Have I been with you so long, and yet you have not known Me, Philip? He who has seen Me HAS SEEN THE FATHER...'"*. Jesus is plainly telling us that everything you want to know about God the Father you can discover by looking to Me, the Child born to a virgin in Bethlehem.

④ **"Prince of Peace"** (*"Sar Shalom"*) ⇨ this means the "General over Prosperity, Safety and Peace". "Shalom" means much more than just the absence of war and strife. Isaiah is telling us the virgin-born Child is our General who oversees the quiet confidence in our hearts, by the historical evidence of the Cross, where Christ accomplished everything required to restore peace between us and our holy God.

Let's make this connection by tying together Old and New Testament verses: Isaiah 53:5 says *"He was wounded for our transgressions, He was bruised for our iniquities; the chastisement for OUR PEACE ('shalom') was upon Him, and by His stripes we are healed."* In Colossians 1:19-20, it's Jesus given the credit for bringing the 'shalom' between God and man by the Cross: *"It pleased the Father that in Him all the fullness should dwell, and by Him to reconcile all things to Himself, by Him, whether things on earth or things in heaven, having made PEACE through the BLOOD OF HIS CROSS.."*

So how does a person get this 'shalom', this quiet confidence in their hearts of an everlasting relationship with the Wonder Counselor, Mighty God, Everlasting Father? Romans 5:1 says it best - trust Jesus with your life:

"Having been justified by FAITH, we have PEACE with God through our Lord Jesus Christ."

Evidence #5 for the Deity of Jesus Christ: SON OF MAN

Daniel 7:13

"I was watching in the night visions, and behold, one like the SON OF MAN, coming with the clouds of heaven! He came to the Ancient of Days, and they brought Him near before Him. Then to Him was given dominion and glory and a kingdom, that all peoples, nations and languages should serve Him. His dominion is an everlasting dominion, which shall not pass away, and His kingdom the one which shall not be destroyed."

Jesus' favorite name for Himself was "Son of Man", occurring over 84 times in the Gospels. Josh McDowell, in his book 'He walked among Us'[3], says that only once in the New Testament is the title "son of man" used for someone other than Jesus, and that's in Hebrews 2:6, where quotes Psalm 8:4 and refers to a human being.

But the name "Son of Man" seems rather odd, maybe even a little unassuming. He would only rarely call Himself "Son of God", which sounds much more impressive, don't you think? And people kept trying to get Him to say He was the Christ, meaning "Anointed One", which would have made Him an instant celebrity. After all, we've demonstrated in several previous lessons that Jesus Christ is God in the flesh, so He certainly had every right to declare Himself as God. Maybe He could have used a PR firm to help Him with His image. Maybe if He had been a little more flamboyant back then, we Americans today would be more attracted to Him. After all, He'd fit right in with our celebrity culture, where we like to give people names that make them larger than life, especially in sports (like 'King James', or 'Neon Deon'). But Jesus felt the name "Son of Man" highlighted to His audience something critical about Himself that people needed to know.

We find our answer in the Old Testament. Only one time (of the 106 times it is used) does this name refer to God's Messiah. The other 105 times, it refers to a specific human being (Josh McDowell again explains that in these other 105 times, 91 times it's for Ezekiel and once for Daniel). That one Old Testament verse where the "Son of Man" points to God's Messiah, the Christ, is Daniel 7:13.

Guess which Old Testament verse for the "Son of Man" Jesus specifically applies to Himself at His trial, when He answers the Sanhedrin's question if He is God's promised Messiah? Mark 14:61-64 *"...the high priest asked Him, saying to Him, 'Are You the Christ, the Son of the Most High?' And Jesus said, 'I am. And you will see the SON OF MAN sitting at the right hand of the Power, and coming with the clouds of heaven.' Then the high priest tore his clothes and said, 'What further need do we have of witnesses? You have heard the blasphemy! What do you think?' And they all condemned Him to be deserving of death."*

Why did they condemn Jesus to be executed? They understood that Daniel 7:13 spoke of the Messiah, and they understood Jesus was claiming to be that Messiah (God in the flesh, the promised Savior of Daniel 7:13).

In their book 'More than a Prophet'[10], Emir and Ergun Caner (former followers of Islam who are now followers of Christ and PhD University Professors of Theology) do an excellent job of explaining Jesus' claim to Deity in Mark 14:62: *"We have heard uninformed Christians say that Jesus referred to His deity in references to the 'Son of God' and to His humanity in references to 'Son of Man.' That seems reasonable, but it just isn't so. The term 'Son of Man' carries with it both the presence of the Jewish Messiah and divine authority. The 'Son of Man' here (in Mark 14:62 – to – Daniel 7:13) has explicit authority:*
1) He approached the Ancient of Days and is led into His presence. Islam rejects any proximity with Allah;
2) He is given the authority of God;
3) He is given glory. Islam glorifies no one but Allah. If Christ is the 'Son of Man', He is worthy of worship;
4) He is given sovereign power. Islam believes only Allah is sovereign. If Christ is given sovereign power, He is again worthy of worship;
5) The 'Son of Man' is worshipped. Jesus called on others to worship Him as the 'Son of Man'."

Now we can go back and answer our earlier question: "Why did Jesus choose to call Himself by what appeared to us as such an unassuming name?" As usual, He expects us to use our brains. He is again, as in the previous Old Testament prophecies we've examined, pointing to the biblical evidence for our Christian faith, with its substance centered on Himself.

But there's a second, and equally important reason, and it's why we chose Daniel 7:13 as Evidence #5 for the Deity of Jesus Christ. It points to our God who, in complete humility, with no fanfare or PR firm, lowered Himself to become part of humanity, so He could fulfill His promise to us, to not only make Himself known to us, but make Himself totally accessible to us.

In describing the lowly nature of Jesus, C.S. Lewis said it best, *"If you want to get the hang of it (the Incarnation), think how you would like to become a slug or a crab."* I don't know about you, but it's just another example of His constant urging to reignite my passionate love for Him.

Evidence #6 for the Deity of Jesus Christ: MESSIAH's 1st COMING

Daniel 9:24-26

Verse 24: *"70 WEEKS are determined for your people and for your holy city, to finish the transgression, to make an end of sins, to make reconciliation for iniquity, to bring everlasting righteousness, to seal up vision and prophecy, and to anoint the most holy."*

Verse 25: *"Know therefore and understand, that from the going forth of the command to restore and build Jerusalem until Messiah the Prince, there shall be 7 WEEKS AND 62 WEEKS; the street shall be built again, and the wall, even in troublesome times."*

Verse 26: *And after the 62 weeks Messiah shall be cut off, but not for himself; and the people of the prince who is to come shall destroy the city and the sanctuary. The end of it shall be with a flood, and till the end of the war desolations are determined."*

> QUESTION: If Jesus is the Messiah sent by God, shouldn't the known historical date when He rode into Jerusalem on a donkey, and then was crucified, match the date we calculate from this prophecy in Daniel 9?

What is the prophetic significance of "Daniel"? Daniel's name means "God is my Judge". His writings bridge the entire Babylonian captivity (605 – 536BC). Daniel was kidnapped at about 15 years old (in 605 BC) and deported to Babylon to be brainwashed into Babylonian culture for the task of helping the Babylonians integrate the defeated Jews into their culture. "Daniel" was written to encourage the exiled Jews by revealing God's program for them, both during and after the time of Gentile power in the world.

What "Revelation" is to the New Testament, "Daniel" is to the Old Testament: 1) nine of the twelve chapters relate revelation through dreams and visions, and 2) the prominent theme of the 2 books is similar: God's sovereign control over the affairs of all rulers and nations, and their final replacement with the True King, Messiah.

In Babylon, Daniel received God's word concerning successive stages of Gentile world domination through the centuries until the greatest Conqueror, Messiah, would put down all Gentile lordship, after which He would usher in His glorious millennial kingdom.

The following breakdown of Daniel 9:24-26 is taken from Sir Robert Anderson's book *"The Coming Prince."*[11]

DANIEL 9:24   What are these "70 Weeks"?

The Hebrew word for *week* is *SHABUA*, which means "a period of seven." It can mean 7 days, weeks or years, but Daniel talks in years throughout his book, so it refers to YEARS. This prophecy deals with 70x7 = **490 Years**.

DANIEL 9:24   What is going to happen after these "70 Weeks"?

Daniel speaks of future events of the 1st and 2nd coming of Messiah, when all things in the Bible will be fulfilled:

- 1st COMING: finish the transgression   - Israel's apostasy will end   (Zech. 12:10, Rom. 11:25-26)

  make an end to sins   - judge sin with finality   (Hebrews 9:26)

  make reconciliation for iniquity   - Messiah's death   (Zech. 13:1, Rom. 3:23-26)

- 2nd COMING: bring everlasting righteousness - the millennial kingdom   (Rev. 21:22-27)

  seal up vision and prophecy   - no more revelation is needed

                                     - God completes things at 2nd coming (Isaiah 61:2, Luke 21:22)

  anoint the Most Holy   - the Holy Place in the millennial kingdom   (Ezekiel 40-48)

DANIEL 9:25   What command to rebuild Jerusalem is Daniel talking about?

Nehemiah 2:1-6 details the command by Artaxerxes, king of Persia, to rebuild Jerusalem on **March 14, 445 BC**:

- It happened in the 20th year of King Artaxerxes' reign, and he took the throne in Persia in 465 BC, so 20 years makes it 445 BC.

- It happened in the month of Nisan. Jewish custom says whenever the exact day isn't given, always use the 1st day of the month. But the 1st day of Nisan is always the 1st day after the new moon of the Passover- in 445 BC, this new moon was on March 13, 445 BC. So, the 1st day of Nisan was March 14, 445 BC.

- Daniel 9:25 says it was "during troublesome times". Nehemiah 4:17-18 says everyone had weapons while building the wall.

DANIEL 9:26   Does Jesus enter Jerusalem, then die, 483 years from March 14, 445BC?

- Daniel says "7 weeks and 62 weeks" after Artaxerxes' command marks the appearance and death of the Messiah. A year in Jewish calculations at Daniel's time was 360 days, so we can translate "69 weeks" into days:

   (69 weeks) * (7 years in 1 week) = 483 years   (483 years) * (360 days in 1 year) = **173,880 days**

- We know that Jesus entered Jerusalem on **April 6, 32AD** because:

  a) Luke 3:1 says Jesus began His ministry in the 15th year of Tiberius Caesar, or 29 AD (Caesar's reign began in 14 AD), and His ministry lasted 3 years to 32 AD. So the year He died was 32 AD.

  b) John 12:1 says Jesus went to Bethany 6 days before the Passover. Passover is always on 14 Nisan, which in 32 AD was April 10, 32 AD (Thursday). So 6 days earlier puts us at Friday, April 4, 32 AD.

  c) Jesus spent Saturday, April 5 (the Sabbath) with Lazarus at Bethany. John 12:12 says Jesus entered Jerusalem the next day.

Was Sunday, April 6, 32 AD....
173,880 DAYS from Artaxerxes' command on March 14, 445 BC to rebuild Jerusalem?

---

1) Artaxerxes's command =   March 14, 445 BC

2) Jesus enters Jerusalem =   April 6, 32 AD

3) Exact # days by current calendar (365 days/ year) =   477 years, 24 days =   174,129 days

4) Deduct 1 year, or 365 days (no "0" between 1 BC and 1 AD) = 174,129 days – 365 days =   173,764 days

5) Add 119 days for leap years =   173,764 days + 119 days =   173,883 days

6. Subtract 3 days for inaccuracy of 365-day calendar =   173,883 days – 3 days =   **173,880 days**
(its 1/128th of a day longer than the true solar year,
so every 128 years of Daniel's 483 years subtract 1 day – that's 3 days)

DANIEL 9:26   Is Jesus killed?

The Messiah will be *cut off, but not for himself*...the Hebrew word for "cut off" is YIKARET, which means a sudden, violent end. "Not for himself" means the Messiah is cut off by others. This is Jesus' **crucifixion**.

Now Jesus could arrange to ride into Jerusalem on a donkey on the exact day and fulfill **Zechariah 9:9**, but it would be impossible for Him to arrange His own execution as well.

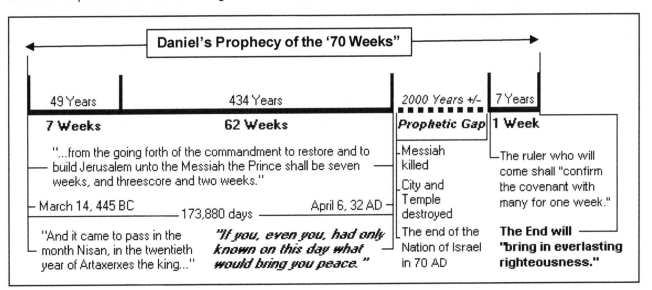

LUKE 19:41-44

Jesus Christ came to earth as a man, on the exact day He promised in the Old Testament, and fulfilled His promise to us of providing the way to eternal life by dying for our sins

"Now as He drew near, He saw the city and wept over it, saying, 'If you had known, even you, especially in this your day, the things that make for your peace! But now they are hidden from your eyes. For the days will come upon you when your enemies will build an embankment around you, surround you and close you in on every side, and level you, and your children within you, to the ground; and they will not leave in you one stone upon another, because YOU DID NOT KNOW THE TIME OF YOUR VISITATION."

Evidence #7 for the Deity of Jesus Christ: *The* SUFFERING MESSIAH
Isaiah 53:1-12

Skeptic's Charge #23: "How do you know Jesus' followers didn't add Isaiah 53 to the Old Testament after He died?"

Answer: The IQIsaiah[a] Scroll dates at least 125 years *BEFORE* Jesus Christ was born! Chapter 53 matches almost perfectly with our current Old Testament:

Josh McDowell ('Evidence that demands a Verdict')[1]: *"Of the 166 words in Isaiah 53, only 17 letters are in question. 10 of these letters are simply spelling changes (no impact on the meaning), 4 are stylistic differences (conjunctions), and the remaining 3 letters are in the word "light". In Isaiah 53, for the 166 words, there is only one word (3 letters) in question after 1,000 years of transmission, and this one word does not change the meaning of the passage."*

Skeptic's Charge #24: "Isaiah 53 is about the nation of Israel as God's Suffering Servant. How can you use Isaiah 53 as proof of Jesus Christ as the Messiah fulfilling Old Testament Scripture?"

Answer: Isaiah 53 can be shown to point to a person, not the nation of Israel. Then, with the discovery of the Dead Sea Scrolls to eliminate skeptics' charge #1, we can confidently trust the New Testament authors' (which included Jesus Himself) assertion that Isaiah 53 pointed to Jesus as its Messianic.

Dr. Victor Buksbazin[17]: in Acts 8:26-35, as the Ethiopian eunuch read Isaiah 53, he asked Philip *"of whom does the prophet say this, of himself or of some other man?"*

The Crusades

a) before the 11th century AD: Jewish tradition viewed Isaiah 53 as a portrait of God's Suffering Servant, the Messiah (this view is still held today by most Orthodox Jews). Examples: Targum of Johnathan ben Uziel (2nd century AD); Babylonian Targum (6th century AD); Midrash Rabbah and Yalkut Shimoni (rabbinical commentaries)

b) after 11th century AD: during the first CRUSADES in 1096 AD, the Crusaders identified the "infidels" as including the "Christ-killing Jews" who lived among them in Europe, and began a massacre of Jewish people. Most Jews were disgusted by anything Christianity believed or represented. Since Christians used Isaiah 53 as one of their main arguments for the messiahship of Jesus, the majority of Jewish scholars (but not all) reinterpreted this prophecy to refer to the nation of Israel, to blunt the Christian position."

c) While several modern, prominent Jewish scholars and liberal Christians interpret Isaiah 53 to be Israel as God's "Suffering Servant", Isaiah clearly reveals God's disgust towards Israel as a blind, disobedient servant:

Isaiah 1:2-6 "The Wickedness of the nation of Israel" *"I have nourished and brought up children, and they have rebelled against Me; the ox knows its owner and the donkey its master's crib; but Israel does not know, My people do not consider.' Alas, sinful nation, a people laden with iniquity, a brood of evildoers, children who are corrupters! They have forsaken the Lord, they have provoked to anger the Holy One of Israel, they have turned away backward. Why should you be stricken again? You will revolt more and more. The whole head is sick, and the whole heart faints. From the sole of the foot even to the head. There is no soundness in it."*

Isaiah 42:18-25 "The Deafness, Blindness and Disobedience of the nation of Israel" *"Who is blind but My servant, or deaf as My servant whom I send? Who is blind as he who is perfect, and blind as the Lord's servant? Seeing many things, but you do not observe; opening the ears, but he does not hear. The Lord is well pleased for His righteousness' sake; He will magnify the law and make it honorable. But this is a people robbed and plundered; all of them are snared in holes, and they are hidden in prison houses; they are prey, and no one delivers; for plunder, and no one says, 'Restore!' Who among you will give ear to this? Who will listen and hear for the time to come? Who gave Jacob for plunder, and Israel to the robbers? Was it not the Lord, He against whom we have sinned? For they would not walk in His ways, nor were they obedient to His law. Therefore He has poured on him the fury of His anger and the strength of battle; it has set him on fire all around, yet he did not know; and it burned him, yet he did not take it to heart."*

Isaiah 53	New Testament Fulfillment in Jesus Christ
Isaiah 53:1-2 ➔ *Messiah's Obscure Lineage* *"Who has believed our report? And to whom has the arm of the Lord been revealed? For He shall grow up before Him as a tender plant, and as a root out of dry ground. He has no form or comeliness; and when we see Him, there is no beauty that we should desire Him."*	**John 12:37-38** *"But although He had done so many signs before them, they did not believe in Him, that the word of Isaiah the prophet might be fulfilled, which he spoke: 'Lord, who has believed our report? And to whom has the arm of the Lord been revealed?'"* **Luke 2:7** *"...she brought forth her firstborn Son, and wrapped Him in swaddling clothes, and laid Him in a feed trough, because there was no room for them in the inn."* **Luke 2:22-24 (Levit. 12:8)** *"...they brought Him to Jerusalem to present Him to the Lord....and to offer a sacrifice according to what is said in the law of the Lord, 'A pair of turtledoves or 2 young pigeons.'"*

Isaiah 53	New Testament Fulfillment in Jesus Christ
Isaiah 53:3-4 ➔ ***Messiah's Rejection*** "He is despised and rejected by men, a Man of sorrows and acquainted with grief. And we hid, as it were, our faces from Him; He was despised, and we did not esteem Him. Surely He has borne our griefs and carried our sorrows; yet we esteemed Him stricken, smitten of God, and afflicted."	▶ **Matthew 13:54-57** *"...when He had come to His own country, He taught them in their synagogue, so that they were astonished and said, 'Where did this Man get this wisdom and these mighty works? Is this not the carpenter's son? Is not His mother called Mary? And His brothers James, Joses, Simon, and Judas? And His sisters, are they not all with us? Where then did this Man get all these things?' So they were offended at Him."* **John 1:10-11** *"He was in the world, and all things in the world were made through Him, and the world did not know Him. He came to His own, and His own did not receive Him."* **John 9:39-41** *"They answered and said to Him, 'Abraham is our father.' Jesus said to them, 'If you were Abraham's children, you would do the works of Abraham. But now you seek to kill Me, a Man who has told you the truth which I heard from God. Abraham would not do this. You do the deeds of your father.' They said to Him, 'We were not born of fornication; we have one Father – God.'"*
Isaiah 53:5-6,8 ➔ ***Messiah's Punishment for us*** "But He was wounded for our transgressions. He was crushed for our iniquities; the chastisement for our peace was upon Him, and by His stripes we are healed. All we like sheep have gone astray; we have turned, every one, each to His own way; and the Lord has laid on Him the iniquity of us all. He was taken from prison and from judgment; who will declare His generation? For He was cut off from the land of the living; for the transgressions of my people He was afflicted."	▶ **Romans 4:24-25** *"...it shall be imputed to us who believe in Him who raised up Jesus our Lord from the dead, who was delivered up because of our offenses..."* **1Peter 2:24-25** *"...who Himself bore our sins in His own body on the tree, that we, having died to sins, might live for righteousness – by whose stripes you were healed. For you were like sheep going astray, but have now returned to the Shepherd and Overseer of your souls."*
Isaiah 53:7 ➔ ***Messiah's Silence*** "He was oppressed and He was afflicted, yet He opened not His mouth; He was led as a lamb to the slaughter, and as a sheep before its shearers is silent, so He opened not His mouth."	▶ **Matthew 26:62-63** *"...the high priests arose and said to Him, 'Do You answer nothing? What is it that these men testify against You?' But Jesus kept silent."*
Isaiah 53:9 ➔ ***Messiah's Sinlessness*** "...they made His grave with the wicked – but with the rich at His death, because He had done no violence, nor was any deceit found in His mouth."	▶ **Matthew 27:38** *"Then two robbers were crucified with Him, one on the right and another on the left."* **Matthew 27:57-60** *"...there came a rich man from Arimathea, named Joseph, who himself had also become a disciple of Jesus. This man went to Pilate and asked for the body of Jesus. Then Pilate commanded the body to be given to him. And when Joseph had taken the body, he wrapped it in a clean linen cloth, and laid it in his new tomb which he had hewn out of the rock."* **1Peter 2:21-22** *"...to this you were called, because Christ also suffered for us, leaving us an example, that you should follow His steps: 'Who committed no sin, nor was deceit found in His mouth.'"*
Isaiah 53:10-11 ➔ ***Messiah's Sacrifice for us*** *"It pleased the Lord to crush Him; He has put Him to grief. When you make His soul an offering for sin, He shall see His seed, He shall prolong His days, and the pleasure of the Lord shall prosper in His hand. He shall see the travail of His soul and be satisfied. By His knowledge My righteous Servant shall justify many, for He shall bear their iniquities."*	▶ **Romans 8:32** *"He who did not spare His own Son, but delivered Him up for us all, how shall He not with Him freely give us all things?"* **2Corin. 5:21** *"...He made Him who knew no sin to be sin for us, that we might become the righteousness of God in Him."*
Isaiah 53:12 ➔ ***Messiah's Triumph*** *"...I will divide Him a portion with the great, and He shall divide the spoil with the strong, because He poured out His soul unto death, and He was numbered with the transgressors, and He bore the sin of many, and made intercession for the transgressors."*	**Colossians 2:15** *"Having disarmed principalities and powers, He made a public spectacle of them, triumphing over them in it."* **Mark 15:27-28** *"With Him they also crucified two robbers, one on His right and the other on His left, so the Scripture was fulfilled which says, 'And He was numbered with the transgressors.'"* **Luke 23:34** *"Then Jesus said, 'Father, forgive them, for they do not know what they do.'"*

JOHN 5:39 *"You search the Scriptures, because in them you think you have eternal life. But these are they that testify of Me."*

Evidence #8 for the Deity of Jesus Christ: The CRUCIFIXION

Psalm 22

vs 1 *"My God, My God, why have You forsaken Me? Why are You so far from helping Me, and from the words of My groanings?"*

vs 7-8 *"All those who see Me laugh Me to scorn; they shoot out the lip, and shake the head, saying 'He trusted in the Lord, let Him rescue Him; let Him deliver Him, since He delights in Him!'"*

vs 14-15 *"I am poured out like water, and ALL MY BONES ARE OUT OF JOINT; my heart is like wax; it has melted within Me. My strength is dried up like a potsherd, and MY TONGUE CLINGS TO MY JAWS; You have brought Me to the point of death."*

vs 16-18 *"Dogs have surrounded Me; the assembly of the wicked has enclosed Me; THEY PIERCED MY HANDS AND MY FEET; I can count all My bones. They look and stare at Me. They divide My garments among them, and for My clothing they cast lots."*

vs 24 *"...nor has He hidden His face from Him; but when He cried to Him, He heard."*

vs 30-31 *"A posterity shall serve Him. It will be recounted of the Lord in the NEXT GENERATION. They will come and declare His righteousness to A PEOPLE WHO WILL BE BORN, that HE HAS DONE THIS."*

Crucifixion was a cruel form of execution for slaves and rebels. The condemned man was nailed or tied to a wooden frame, then left to die. Originally the 'cross' was simply a stake that impaled the head of someone already dead, where the heads of executed men and women were placed on spikes at city gates or on battlement walls.

The **Assyrians**, who were masters of psychological warfare, probably invented a form of crucifixion around 800BC (or possibly the Persians later around 500BC). They impaled captives to mock and terrify their enemies. The heads or bodies held aloft on spikes were intended as a public display, a humiliation of the enemy.

One of the discoveries from the Assyrian library was this inscription from Assyrian King Assurnasirpal II (883-859BC): *"I built a pillar against his city gate, and I flayed all the chief men, and I covered the pillar with their skins. Some I walled up within the pillar; some I impaled upon the pillar on stakes, and others I bound to stakes round about the pillar. And I cut off the limbs of the officers. Many captives from among them I burned with fire, and many I took as living captives. From some I cut off their noses, their ears, and their fingers, of many I put out their eyes. I made one pillar of the living, and another of heads, and I bound their heads to posts round about the city."*

Crucifixion as understood today (nailed to a cross) was used by Alexander the Great (300BC), then by the Romans (100BC), who perfected this horrifying way of killing a criminal. It was finally abolished by the Emperor Constantine in 337AD. In the Roman Empire, crucifixion was not normally used for citizens or free men, but reserved for people lower down the social ladder. It was known as the 'slave's punishment'. Those higher up the social ladder, like Paul, could demand a quick death by decapitation, which was considered more humane. Herod Antipas had John the Baptist beheaded, possibly because he admired or feared him.

How do we know about crucifixion?

Mostly from written sources like the gospels (Matthew 27, Mark 15, Luke 23, and John 19). But there is evidence from archaeology. Bodies of executed criminals were usually dumped as rubbish, to be eaten by scavenging dogs. But in some cases, as with the death of Jesus, the body was retrieved by loved ones and given a decent burial.

In 1968, the remains of a crucified man were discovered in a burial cave at Giv'at ha-Mivtar, northeast of Jerusalem. This cave contained five ossuaries or bone boxes. In one of the ossuaries were the bones of a young man who had died in his mid-twenties, crucified at about the same time as Jesus. A 4.5" nail was still lodged in his heel bone. There was even a small wedge of wood remaining between the heel bone and the head of the nail, put there by some Roman soldier to hold the nail and his foot firmly in place. According to the ossuary box inscription, his name was 'Yehochanan', which in English is 'John'. Both his leg bones had been smashed, something done to hasten the death of the crucified man. The gospels describing Jesus' death emphasize that His leg bones were not smashed, since he died quickly.

Psalm 22 was written ~1000BC... at least 200 years BEFORE Crucifixion was even invented!

Evidence #9 for the Deity of Jesus Christ: CREATOR, LIFE, LIGHT
John 1:3-5

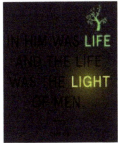

"All things were ①MADE ②THROUGH Him, and without Him nothing was made that was made. In Him was ③LIFE, and the life was the ④LIGHT of men. And the light shines in the ⑤DARKNESS, and the darkness did not comprehend it."

① MADE = Gr. *"ginomai"* = caused to be; came into being or existence

② THROUGH = Gr. *"dia"* = a primary preposition denoting the *CHANNEL* by which an action takes place; God the Father created the world ("all things") *through* God the Son, so Jesus, the Word, is the Creator God.

③ LIFE = Gr. *"zóē"* = physical and spiritual existence; John uses the word "life" 36X, far more than the synoptics.
  a) John doesn't say life had been created – he says throughout his gospel that life has always existed in Christ (we are dependent on His SUSTAINING POWER for our temporary, physical lives).
  b) More than physical life, John emphasizes that Jesus' gift of eternal life is to those who BELIEVE in Him:
  John 10:10 *"...I have come that they may have life, and that they may have it more abundantly."*
  John 11:25 *"...I am the resurrection and the life. He who believes in Me, though he may die, he shall live."*
  John 14:6   *"...I am the way, the truth, and the life."*
  John 17:3   *"...this is eternal life, that they may know You, the only true God, and Jesus Christ whom You have sent."*

④ LIGHT = Gr. *"phos"* = revealed radiance; luminescence, as in the Sun that shines

⑤ DARKNESS = Gr. *"skotia"* = dimness; obscurity; blindness; error/ falsehood; evil/ wrongdoing
  a) <u>Intellectually</u>: "light" refers to biblical TRUTH while "darkness" refers to ERROR or falsehood
  Psalm 119:105 *"Your word is a lamp unto my feet and a light unto my path."*
  Proverbs 6:23 *"...the commandment is a lamp, and the law is light; reproofs of instruction are the way of life."*
  b) <u>Morally</u>: "light" refers to HOLINESS or purity while "darkness" refers to SIN or wrongdoing
  John 3:19 *"...this is the condemnation, that the light has come into the world, and men loved darkness rather than light, because their deeds were evil. For everyone practicing evil hates the light and does not come to the light, lest his deeds should be exposed."*
  Romans 13:12 *"...let us cast off the works of darkness, and let us put on the armor of light."*
  1Thessalonians 5:4-5 *"...you, brethren, are not in darkness, so that this Day should overtake you as a thief. You are all sons of light and sons of the day. We are not of the night nor of darkness."*

In John 12:35-36: Jesus says He entered our *physical* world to make *spiritual* sons of light through *faith*: *"A little while longer the light is with you. Walk while you have the light, lest darkness overtake you; he who walks in darkness does not know where he is going. While you have the light, BELIEVE in the light, that you may become SONS OF LIGHT."*

- Jesus as the Light of mankind not only reveals who God is through His INCARNATION (see Isaiah 9:1-2), but He also reveals our darkness in sin by exposing it to the purity and holiness ("light") of His word:
  Psalm 36:9 *"...with You is the fountain of life; in YOUR LIGHT we see light."*
- Death and Darkness flee when the Life and the Light enter into the darkness:
  □ the blind receive their sight, both physically and spiritually (John 9)
  □ the dead are raised to new life, both physically and spiritually (John 11)

John 1:6-9   God's calling in my life = Be a *WITNESS* to the Light

"There was a man sent from God whose name was John. This man came for a ①WITNESS, to bear witness of the Light, that all through Him might believe. He was not that Light, but was sent to bear witness of that Light. That was the true Light, which gives light to every man who comes into the world."

① WITNESS = Gr. *"marturia"* = our English word MARTYR = to testify or declare in the open

- John uses "witness" 33x as a verb and 14x as a noun (his evangelistic and apologetic focus = Jesus is God)
- <u>What's a "martyr"?</u> Webster's Dictionary = "a person who chooses to suffer death rather than renounce their religion; a person who endures great suffering for a principle or cause"
- <u>The Application</u>: like John the Baptist, Jesus calls me to be a martyr - Acts 1:8 *"...you shall receive power when the Holy Spirit has come upon you; and you shall be My WITNESSES in Jerusalem, and in Judea and Samaria, and to the end of the earth."*

Let's Review Some of What We've Learned about why Jesus Christ is God

God in Flesh: Dead Sea Scroll of Isaiah dates to 125BC and records birth of a child who is Mighty God (Isaiah 9:6).

Immanuel: Jesus claimed to fulfill Old Testament promise that God would personally be with us (Isaiah 41:10).

Incarnation: Dead Sea Scroll of Isaiah dates to 125BC and records virgin birth (Isaiah 7:14) - which only Jesus fulfilled.

Lineage: 8 requirements for anyone claims to be Messiah only fulfilled in history by Jesus Christ.

Son of Man: Jesus's favorite name for Himself points to Daniel 7:13.

"And then they will see 'the Son of Man coming in the clouds' with great power and glory."

There are 10 Claims about Jesus Christ to which majority of scholars agree...

Together these 10 Claims make a strong case for *the Deity of Jesus Christ* (John 8:58)

Creator, Life, Light: Jesus constantly refers to Himself as the Creator, Light and the Source of Life in Old Testament.

Messiah's First Coming: Jesus fulfills Daniel 9:24-26 (and He says so in Luke 19:41-44).

Suffering Servant: Dead Sea Scroll of Isaiah dates to 125BC and records the suffering of a Person for our sins (Isaiah 53).

Crucifixion: Scholars agree Jesus was tried, scourged and crucified as foretold about Messiah in Old Testament (Isaiah 50, Psalm 22).

Resurrections: 4 historical facts that are best explained by Jesus's resurrection.

FSE University

Book 4 of 4

God's Will for My Life

Why am I here?

Chapter 1   GOD'S WILL = "Thelema"
His design (purpose) for each person

1.1

Colossians 1:9-10 *"For this reason we also, since the day we heard it, do not cease to pray for you, and to ask that you be filled with the KNOWLEDGE OF HIS WILL in all wisdom and spiritual understanding; that you may have a walk worthy of the Lord, fully pleasing Him, being fruitful in every good work and increasing in the knowledge of God...."*

Four RULES for knowing God's Will for my life[1]

- RULE #1:   Its not about me

    a) Since I didn't create myself, I can't know for what purpose I was created.

    Romans 9:21 *"But now, O Lord, You are our Father; we are the clay, and You our potter; and we all are the work of Your hand."*

    b) I only exist because God wills that I exist.

    Psalm 100:3 *"Know that the Lord, He is God; it is He who made us, and not we ourselves; we are His people, and the sheep of His pasture."*

    c) My purpose on earth is far greater than my personal ambitions, peace of mind, or happiness.

    Esther 4:14 *"For if you remain completely silent at this time, relief and deliverance will arise for the Jews from another place, but you and your father's house will perish. Yet who knows whether you have come to the kingdom for such a time as this?"*

- RULE #2:   Its all about Him

    a) I exist for His benefit, His glory, His purpose, His delight.

    Isaiah 43:7 *"Everyone who is called by My name, whom I have created for My glory; I have formed him, yes, I have made him."*

    Psalm 149:4 *"The Lord takes pleasure in His people..."*

    b) He wants to be first in my life.

    Exodus 34:14 *"...you shall worship no other god, for the Lord, whose name is Jealous, is a jealous God."*

- RULE #3:   Since God says He has a purpose for me, He must want me to know it

    a) My life only makes sense if I let God use me for His purpose (not try to use Him to achieve my plans).

    Genesis 50:20 *"But as for you, you meant evil against me; but God meant it for good, in order to bring it about as it is this day, to save many people alive."*

    b) I can choose my career, my spouse, my hobbies – but I don't get to choose my PURPOSE.

    Proverbs 19:21 *"There are many plans in a man's heart. Nevertheless the Lord's counsel – that will stand."*

- RULE #4:   God's purpose for me is in His Word

    a) The Bible = the Owner's Manual. It tells me why I'm here, how life works, what to avoid, how to please Him.

    Matthew 4:4 *"...Man shall not live by bread alone, but by every word that proceeds from the mouth of God."*

    b) My life is no accident – I was planned by God. Every detail (my gender, ethnicity, etc.) is His doing.

    Acts 17:26 *"He has made from one blood every nation of men to dwell on all the face of the earth, and has determined their preappointed times and the boundaries of their habitation."*

What is a person's "WILL"?

"That faculty of the mind which is exercised by deciding, among 2 or more objects, which one shall be embraced or pursued." The "Will" can be summed up in 3 steps:

DECIDING
Between different directions

DEDICATING
To my decision

DEMONSTRATING
My decision with action

➤ **Only SAVED people can know His will**

Ephesians 1:9 *"Having made known to us the mystery of HIS WILL, by HIS GOOD PLEASURE which He purposed in Himself."*

Colossians 1:9 *"For this reason we also, since the day we heard it, do not cease to pray for you, and to ask that you may be filled with THE KNOWLEDGE OF HIS WILL in all wisdom and spiritual understanding..."*

➤ **Only people who do God's will are SAVED**

Matthew 7:21 *"Not everyone who says 'Lord, Lord', shall enter the kingdom of heaven, but he who does the WILL OF MY FATHER in heaven."*

Matthew 12:50 *"For whoever does the WILL OF MY FATHER in heaven is My brother and sister and mother."*

1John 2:17 *"And the world is passing away, and the lust of it; but he who does the WILL OF GOD abides forever."*

John 9:31 *"We know that God does not hear sinners; but if anyone is a worshipper of God and does HIS WILL, He hears him."*

➤ **God works in SAVED people to do His will**

Philippians 2:13 *"...for it is God who works in you both to will and to do for HIS GOOD PLEASURE."*

Hebrews 13:20-21 *"Now may the God of peace who brought up our Lord Jesus from the dead, that great Shepherd of the sheep, through the blood of the everlasting covenant, make you complete in every good work TO DO HIS WILL, working in you what is WELL PLEASING IN HIS SIGHT, through Jesus Christ, to whom be the glory forever and ever."*

Jesus: Making God's Will His Daily PRIORITY

Matt. 6:10 *"Your kingdom come, YOUR WILL BE DONE, on earth as it is in heaven."*

Luke 22:42 *"Father, if it is Your will, remove this cup from Me; nevertheless NOT MY WILL BUT YOURS BE DONE."*

John 4:34 *"My food is to do THE WILL OF HIM who sent Me, and to finish His work."*

John 5:30 *"I can of Myself do nothing. As I hear, I judge; and My judgment is righteous, because I DO NOT SEEK MY OWN WILL BUT THE WILL OF THE FATHER who sent Me."*

John 6:38 *"For I have come down from heaven, not to do My own will, but the WILL OF HIM who sent Me."*

John 7:16-17 *"My doctrine is not Mine, but His who sent Me. If anyone wants to do HIS WILL, he shall know concerning the doctrine, whether it is from God or whether I speak on My own authority."*

Psalm 8:3-9   The Dignity God bestows on Man: FREE WILL

"When I ①CONSIDER Your heavens, the work of Your fingers, the moon and the stars, which You have ordained, what is man, that You are ②MINDFUL of him, and the son of man, that You ③VISIT him? For You have made him a little lower than the angels, and You have ④CROWNED him with ⑤GLORY and ⑥HONOR.
You have made him to have ⑦DOMINION over the works of Your hands; You have put ALL THINGS under his feet, all sheep and oxen – even the beasts of the field, the birds of the air, and the fish that pass through the paths of the seas. O Lord, our Lord, how excellent is Your ⑧NAME in all the earth."

① CONSIDER = Hebr. "râ'âh" = to discern or perceive by observation; to think something through
② MINDFUL = Hebr. "zâkar" = keeping in remembrance; thinking upon; giving attention to
③ VISIT = Hebr. "pâqad" = care for; oversee (as in guidance, holding accountable to a standard)
④ CROWNED = Hebr. "âtar" = encircled for protection
⑤ GLORY = Hebr. "kâbôd kâbôd" = splendor; significance or weight in terms of moral goodness
⑥ HONOR = Hebr "hâdar" = dignity; magnificence; excellency
⑦ DOMINION = Hebr. "mâshal" = rule; governance; power
⑧ NAME = Hebr. "shêm" = **CHARACTER**, as in expressing someone's honor or fame based on their attributes or qualities; inward **MORAL** quality or integrity that manifests itself in behavior

Verses 3-4: The same question here from David is an argument skeptics make today: the universe is so vast, how could anyone think humans have any significance at all? In Carl Sagan's 1994 book '*Pale Blue Dot: A Vision of the Human Future in Space*', Sagan uses the 1990 photograph of Earth taken by Voyager I to emphasize how insignificant Earth, and the human population, really is when compared to the enormity of space:

"The Earth is a very small stage in a vast cosmic arena. Think of the rivers of blood spilled by all those generals and emperors so that in glory and triumph they could become the momentary masters of a fraction of a dot. Think of the endless cruelties visited by the inhabitants of one corner of this pixel on the scarcely distinguishable inhabitants of some other corner. How frequent their misunderstandings, how eager they are to kill one another, how fervent their hatreds. Our posturings, our imagined self-importance, the delusion that we have some privileged position in the universe, are challenged by this point of pale light. Our planet is a lonely speck in the great enveloping cosmic dark. In our obscurity – in all this vastness – there is no hint that help will come from elsewhere to save us from ourselves."

Verse 5: But here is where David and Sagan diverge in their view of the significance of mankind. God has given something very special to people: **DIGNITY**. God has crowned people with the unique honor, as His children, to live our lives freely and make our own choices. We are not, as the Darwinian evolutionists would have us believe, robots programmed to behave in a certain way. We can decide to do what is right, or what is wrong, on our own.
• It's the same way we, as parents, raise our children: we give them the dignity as people to understand the conditions for living in our home, and the rules that mom and dad set for being part of their family, but we as parents allow our children to choose their own path.
• What about in your work? What if your boss never allowed you to advance in your career, but instead he or she treated you like a robot who only did what you were told, nothing more (anyone who has seen the movie '*The Devil wears Prada*' knows what I mean).
• Would you like to live in a communist country, where your future is decided for you? What about India, where your lot in life is set at birth by the rules of the Caste System, with no choice whatsoever.

Verses 6-8: Not only are we created by God with the dignity of free will, He has given mankind **DOMINION** over all of creation. With the authority given to man comes the RESPONSIBILITY to manage His creation for Him, according to the conditions He has given us in His law, while allowing us to choose whether or not we are willing to follow His conditions – just like good parents train their children.

Why are we, as humans, given such privilege by God? The answer is in **GENESIS 1:26-28, 2:7**. God has made people in HIS IMAGE. One of the noblest features of the divine likeness in man is our capacity to think. He expects us to cooperate with Him both consciously and intelligently, and to discriminate – rationally as well as morally – between what we are permitted to do and what we are prohibited from doing. While animals were created to behave by instinct, we were created to behave by **INTELLIGENT CHOICE** – free will.

The Caste System
- GODS
- BHRAMIN — Priests, Academics
- KSHATRYIA — Warriors, Kings
- VAISHYA — Merchants, Landowners
- SUDRA — Commoners, Peasants, Servants
- UNTOUCHABLES — Outcast-Out of Caste. Street sweepers, latrine cleaners

---

JOHN 7:17   "If anyone WANTS to do His will..."

PSALM 37:3-6 Finding God's *hidden will* for my life — 1.2

"①*TRUST in the Lord, and do good.;* ②*DWELL in the land, and* ③*FEED on His righteousness.* ④*DELIGHT yourself also in the Lord, and* **He shall give you the desires of your heart**. ⑤*COMMIT your way to the Lord, trust also in Him, and He shall bring it to pass. He shall bring forth your righteousness as the light, and your justice as the noonday.* ⑥*REST in the Lord, and* ⑦*WAIT patiently for Him;* ⑧*DO NOT FRET because of him who prospers in his way, because of the man who brings wicked schemes to pass.* ⑨*CEASE from anger, and* ⑩*FORSAKE wrath; do not fret – it only causes harm."*

God's Conditional Promise in Psalm 37:3-6 →	10 Responses He wants from me:	
① TRUST (in the Lord)	"bâtach" = bold confidence, as a refuge	Prov. 3:5; Isa. 26:4
② DWELL (in the land)	"shâkan" = permanently reside, inhabit, abide	Ps 37:29; Ps 68:6
③ FEED (on His righteousness)	"râ âh" = graze (as sheep with their shepherd)	Ps 23:1; Isa. 40:11
④ DELIGHT YOURSELF.(in the Lord)	"ânag" = to be in love with; sweetly affectionate	Ps 1:2; Deut. 10:15
⑤ COMMIT (to the Lord)	"gâlal" = wallow in; roll with; trust	Prov. 16:3
⑥ REST (in the Lord)	"dâmam" = to stop; to be still; to quiet myself	Ps 62:5; Lam. 3:26
⑦ WAIT PATIENTLY (for Him)	"chûl chîyl" = to bear, as in sorrow or distress	only O.T. use
⑧ DO NOT FRET (because of him…)	"râ'am" = tumble inward; crash; violently agitated	1Sam. 1:6
⑨ CEASE (from anger)	"râphâh" = let it alone; cut it off	no other O.T. use
⑩ FORSAKE (wrath)	"âzab" = relinquish; abandon; leave it behind	Ps 9:10

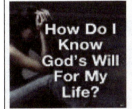

The Key to knowing God's Hidden Will = Doing His Revealed Will

When people think about God's will for their life, its usually about things that we can't see in our future: "How do I really know I'm following God's plan for my life… Should I take that job? Should I move to that city? Should I marry that person?

To "Delight myself in the Lord" =
To live according to His revealed will for me

"If you focus on living according to My will <u>as I revealed it to you in My Bible</u>, you can do anything you desire – I will give you the desires of your heart because your desires will be MY DESIRES for you."

10 Ways God has **REVEALED** His will to mankind

1. God the Son - is to suffer and die for our sins

Galatians 1:4 *"…who gave Himself for our sins, that He might deliver us from this present evil age, according to the WILL OF OUR GOD AND FATHER,…"*

Isaiah 53:10-11 *"Yet IT PLEASED THE LORD to bruise Him; He has put Him to grief. When you make His soul an offering for sin, He shall see His seed, He shall prolong His days, and the PLEASURE OF THE LORD shall prosper in His hand. He shall see the travail of His soul and BE SATISFIED."*

2. God the Father - wants to save people

John 6:40 *"…this is the WILL OF HIM who sent Me, that everyone who sees the Son and believes in Him may have everlasting life; and I will raise him up at the last day."*

John 5:21 *"For as the Father raises the dead and gives life to them, even so the Son gives life to WHOM HE WILL."*

James 1:18 *"Of HIS OWN WILL He brought us forth by the word of truth, that we might be a kind of firstfruits of His creatures."*

3. God the Father - ADOPTS saved people into His family

Ephesians 1:5 *"..having predestined us to adoption as sons by Jesus Christ to Himself, by the GOOD PLEASURE OF HIS WILL."*

Ephesians 1:11 *"in whom also we have obtained an inheritance, being predestined according to the purpose of Him who works all things according to the counsel of HIS WILL"*

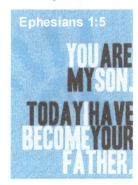

4. Saved people - are to be SANCTIFIED (set apart)

1Thessalonians 4:3,7 *"For this is the WILL OF GOD, your sanctification...for God did not call us to uncleanness, but in HOLINESS."*

Romans 12:2 *"And do not be conformed to this world, but be transformed by the renewing of your mind, that you may prove what is that good and acceptable and perfect WILL OF GOD."*

Hebrews 10:8-10 *"'Sacrifice and offering, burnt offerings, and offerings for sin You did not desire, nor had pleasure in them (which are offered according to the law)', then He said, 'Behold, I have come to do YOUR WILL, O GOD.' He takes away the first that He may establish the second. BY THAT WILL we have been sanctified through the offering of the body of Jesus Christ once for all."*

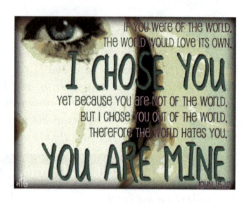

5. Saved people - are to be FILLED with the Holy Spirit

Ephesians 5:17 *"... do not be unwise, but understand what the WILL OF THE LORD is. And do not be drunk with wine, which is dissipation, but be filled with the Spirit..."*

6. Saved people - are to rejoice, pray and be THANKFUL

1Thessalonians 5:16-18 *"Rejoice always, pray without ceasing, in everything give thanks; for this is the WILL OF GOD in Christ for you."*

1John 5:14 *"...this is the confidence that we have in Him, that if we ask anything according to HIS WILL, He hears us."*

Romans 8:27 *"Now He who searches the hearts knows what the mind of the Spirit is, because He makes intercession for the saints according to THE WILL OF GOD."*

2Chronicles 7:14 *"If My people who are called by My name, will humble themselves, and PRAY, and seek My face, and turn from their evil ways, then I will hear from heaven, and will forgive their sin and heal their land."*

7. Saved people - are to OBEY Him

Ephesians 6:6 *"...not with eyeservice, as men-pleasers, but as servants of Christ, doing the WILL OF GOD from the heart..."*

Matthew 21:31 *"A man had two sons, and he came to the first and said, 'Son, go and work today in my vineyard.' He answered and said, 'I will not,' but afterward he regretted it and went. Then he came to the second and said likewise. And he answered and said, 'I go, sir,' but he did not. Which of the two did the WILL OF HIS FATHER?"*

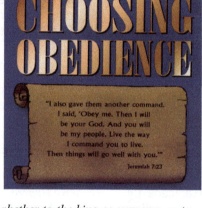

8. Saved people - are to SUBMIT

Ephesians 5:21 *"...submitting to one another in the fear of God."*

2Corin. 8:5 *"...this they did, not as we had hoped, but first gave themselves to the Lord, and then to us by THE WILL OF GOD."*

1Peter 2:13-15 *"... submit yourselves to every ordinance of man for the Lord's sake, whether to the king as supreme, or to governors, as to those who are sent by him for the punishment of evildoers and for the praise of those who do good. For this is the WILL OF GOD, that by doing good you may put to silence the ignorance of foolish men..."*

9. Saved people - are to do GOOD

Matt. 5:16 *"Let your light so shine before men, that they may see your GOOD WORKS and glorify your Father in heaven."*

John 15:8 *"By this My Father is glorified, that you BEAR MUCH FRUIT."*

John 3:21 *"...he who does the truth comes to the light, that his deeds may be clearly seen, that they have been done in God."*

10. Saved people - are to SUFFER for His sake

1Peter 3:17 *"It is better, if it is the WILL OF GOD, to suffer for doing good than for doing evil."*

1Peter 4:1-2 *"Since Christ suffered for us in the flesh, arm yourselves also with the same mind, for he who has suffered in the flesh has ceased from sin, that he no longer should live the rest of his time in the flesh for the lusts of men, but for the WILL OF GOD."*

1Peter 4:19 *"Therefore let those who suffer according to the WILL OF GOD commit their souls to Him in doing good, as to a faithful Creator."*

ISAIAH 61:1-3   God's Will is fully revealed in JESUS CHRIST   1.3

"The Spirit of the Lord God is upon Me, because the Lord has anointed Me to preach good tidings to the poor; HE HAS SENT ME to heal the brokenhearted, to proclaim liberty to the captives, and the opening of the prisons to those who are bound; to proclaim the acceptable year of the Lord, and the day of vengeance of our God; to comfort all who mourn, to console those who mourn in Zion, to give them beauty for ashes, the oil of joy for mourning, the garments of praise for the spirit of heaviness; that they may be called trees of righteousness, the planting of the Lord, that He may be glorified."

God's Will #1 = to JUSTIFY me	God's Will #2 = to SANCTIFY me	God's Will #3 = to be GLORIFIED thru me
• Preach good tidings to the poor • Heal the broken-hearted • Liberate the captives, open the prisons • Begin the acceptable year of the Lord • Comfort and console those who mourn • Give them beauty for ashes • Give them the oil of joy for mourning • Give them garments of praise for heavy spirits	• "Trees of Righteousness" • "Plantings of the Lord"	• "He may be glorified"

God's will: He is a SAVIOR

Luke 2:11 *"For there is born TO YOU this day in the city of David a SAVIOR, who is Christ the Lord."*

1Timothy 1:15, 2:3-4 *"This is a faithful saying and worthy of all acceptance, that Christ Jesus came into the world to SAVE SINNERS, of whom I am chief." "This is good and acceptable in the sight of God our SAVIOR, who desires all men be SAVED and to come to the knowledge of the truth."*

John 3:16-17 *"For God so loved the WORLD, that He gave His only begotten Son, that whoever believes in Him should not perish but have everlasting life. God did not send His Son into the world to condemn the world, but that the world through Him might be SAVED."*

Isaiah 45:22 *"Look to Me and be SAVED, ALL you ends of the earth! For I am God, and there is no other."*

Zephaniah 3:17 *"The Lord your God in your midst, the Mighty One, will SAVE; He will rejoice over you with gladness, He will quiet you in His love, He will rejoice over you with singing."*

God's Character: He FORGIVES before He judges

Psalm 86:5,15; 145:8-9 *"For You, Lord, are good, and ready to forgive, and abundant in mercy to all who call upon You. But You, O Lord, are a God full of compassion, and gracious, longsuffering and abundant in mercy and truth. The Lord is gracious and full of compassion, slow to anger and great in mercy. The Lord is good to all, and His tender mercies are over all His works."*

Numbers 14:18 *"The Lord is longsuffering and abundant in mercy, forgiving iniquity and transgressions, but He by no means clears the guilty, visiting the iniquity of the fathers on the children to the 3rd and 4th generation."*

Ezekiel 18:23, 33:11 *"Do I have any pleasure at all that the wicked should die?" says the Lord God, "and not that he should turn from his ways and live? "Say to them: 'As I live, says the Lord, 'I have no pleasure in the death of the wicked, but that the wicked turn from his way and live."*

God's Character: He is patient and merciful – He gives us time to REPENT

2Peter 3:9 *"The Lord is not slack concerning His promise, as some count slackness; but is LONGSUFFERING toward us, not willing that any should perish but all come to repentance."*

Ecclesiastes 8:11 *"Because the sentence against an evil work is NOT EXECUTED SPEEDILY, the heart of the sons of men is fully set in them to do evil."*

Isaiah 57:11 *"And of whom have you been afraid, or feared, that you have lied and not remembered Me, nor taken it to heart? Is it not because I HAVE HELD MY PEACE from of old, that you do not fear Me?"*

Psalm 50:21 *"These things you have done, and I KEPT SILENT; you thought that I was altogether like you; but I will reprove you, and set them in order before your eyes."*

Jesus Christ = God's WORK in Salvation

John 4:34 *"Jesus said to them, 'My food is to do the will of Him who sent Me, and to finish His WORK.'"*
John 5:17 *"Jesus answered them, 'My Father has been WORKING until now, and I have been working.'"*

Isaiah 59:9-17
The ARM of the Lord = Hebr "zeróah" = power, shoulder, strength, might

- *" Justice is far from us, nor does righteousness overtake us; we look for light, but there is darkness! For brightness, but we walk in blackness! We grope for the wall like the blind, and we grope as if we had no eyes; we stumble at noonday as at twilight; we are as dead men in desolate places. We all growl like bears, and moan sadly like doves; we look for justice, but there is none; <u>for salvation, but it is far from us</u>.*
- *For our transgressions are multiplied before You, and our sins testify against us; for our transgressions are with us, and as for our iniquities, we know them; in transgressing and lying against the Lord, and departing from our God, speaking oppression and revolt, conceiving and uttering from the heart words of falsehood. Justice is turned back, and righteousness stands afar off; for truth has fallen in the street, and equity cannot enter. So truth fails, and he who departs from evil makes himself a prey.*
- *Then the Lord saw it, and it displeased Him that there was no justice. He saw that there was no man, and wondered that there was no intercessor; therefore* **His own ARM brought salvation for Him***; and His own righteousness, it sustained Him. For HE put on righteousness as a breastplate, and a helmet of salvation on HIS head; HE put on the garments of vengeance for clothing, and was clad with zeal as a cloak."*

Isaiah 53:1,5-6
Jesus = The "ARM" ("zeróah") of the Lord

"Who has believed our report? And to whom has **the ARM of the Lord** *been revealed? But He was wounded for our transgressions, He was bruised for our iniquities; the chastisement for our peace was upon Him, and by His stripes we are healed. All we like sheep have gone astray; we have turned everyone each to his own way; and the Lord has laid on Him the sin of us all."*

2Corinthians 5:21 *"...He made Him who knew no sin to be sin for us, that we might become the righteousness of God IN HIM."*

Ephesians 6:13-17
I put on Jesus's ARMOR when He lives in me

"Therefore take up the whole armor of God, that you may be able to withstand in the evil day, and having done all, to stand. Stand therefore, having girded your waist with truth, having put on **the breastplate of righteousness***, and having shod your feet with the gospel of peace; and above all, taking the shield of faith with which you will be able to quench all the fiery darts of the wicked one. And take* **the helmet of salvation***, and the sword of the Spirit, which is the word of God."*

Romans 13:14 *"But* **put on the Lord Jesus Christ***, and make no provision for the flesh, to fulfill its lusts."*

God's Strong ARM is always at Work:

Jesus <u>FINISHED</u> His work to justify me (John 19:30), then <u>BEGAN</u> His work to sanctify me (Phil. 1:6)

John 19:30 *"...He said, "It is finished!" And bowing His head, He gave up His spirit".*

Philippians 1:6 *"...He who has begun a GOOD WORK IN YOU will complete it until the day of Jesus Christ..."*

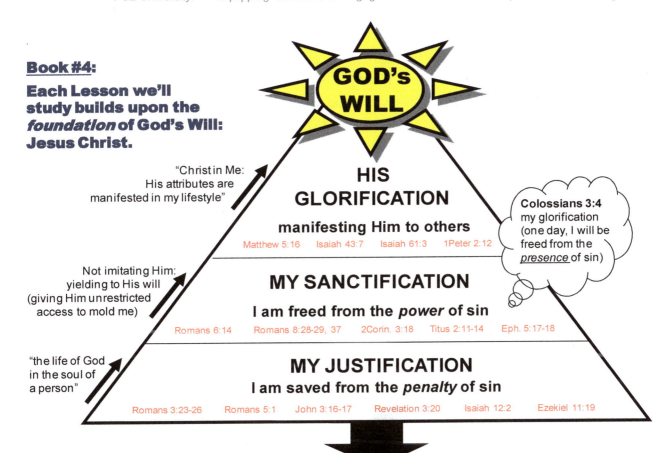

Chapter 2   God's Will: my JUSTIFICATION

Lesson		9 - Lesson Plan
2.1	Justification	"God's character = Just & Righteous"
2.2	Luke 18:9-14	"Jesus explains Justification"
2.3	Ephesians 2:4-9	"What is Saving Faith?"
2.4	Matthew 7:13-14	"God's Way of Salvation"
2.5	Matthew 16:24-25	"The Gospel According to Jesus"
2.6	Matthew 4:17	"What is Repentance?"
2.7	Genesis 15:5-12,17	"God's Gift of Salvation = Covenant"
2.8	Hebrews 9:16-18	"God's Gift of Salvation = Consecration"
2.9	Eternal Security: can it make a difference in how I live my life?	

Pyramid diagram – God's will for my life:
- The Crucifixion & Resurrection (Matthew 5:16, 1Peter 2:12, Daniel 12:3, Isaiah 43:7, Isaiah 61:3, 1Thes. 4:3-4, Psalm 22, 1Corin. 1:18, Psalm 16:10, 1Corin. 15:13-17)
- The Incarnation & Deity of Jesus Christ (Isaiah 7:14, Matthew 1:18-23, Micah 5:2-5, John 1:1,14, John 8:24, 56-58)
- The Nature & Character of God (Isaiah 45:22-23, John 14:16-17, 1John 5:7)
- The Origin of Man (Genesis 1:1, 27-28; 2:7, Psalm 8:3-5, 19:1-6, Psalm 139:13-16, Job 12:7-10)
- The Reliability of the Bible (Hebrews 4:12, Jeremiah 20:8-9, Titus 3:3-7)
- The GOSPEL (1Corin. 15:1-4, Romans 1:1-6, Romans 1:16-17)

HEBREWS 11:1   "Faith = *Substance* of things hoped for.... *Evidence* of things *not seen*"

JUSTIFICATION   2.1   *Greek "dikaioma"*

1) legal term in a court of law: a Judge's decision leading to a just sentence
2) to charge/ impute/ credit a person's account as just by declaring them Not Guilty for their crime (sin)

Courtroom — JUSTIFIED! Not Guilty!

➢ **GOD'S CHARACTER:** JUST (Heb. *"tsedaskaw"*) and RIGHTEOUS (Heb. *"yashar"*)
- "to be level or upright"; rightness, moral virtue based on a standard
- main focus = the quality and integrity of one's character (one's heart, as manifested in their lifestyle)
- God's holiness = He defines what is right vs. wrong living as extensions of who He is (His own character)

Isaiah 61:8 *"For I, the Lord, love justice...."*
Psalm 89:14 *"Righteousness and justice are the foundation of Your throne; mercy and truth go before Your face."*

➢ **GOD'S LAW:** He as JUDGE sets the right and just standard for judging sin

Romans 3:20 *"By the deeds of the law no flesh will be justified in His sight, for by the law is the knowledge of sin.."*
Romans 1:32 *"...knowing the righteous judgment of God, that those who practice such things are deserving of death."*
Psalm 7:11 *"God is a JUST JUDGE, and He is angry with the wicked everyday."*

➢ **GOD'S LAW:** He declares me Guilty for my sin when I trust in my WORKS

Gal. 5:4 *"You have become estranged from Christ, you who attempt to be justified by law; you have fallen from grace."*
Galatians 2:16 *"...knowing that a man is not justified by the works of the law but by faith in Jesus Christ, even we have believed in Christ Jesus that we might be justified by faith in Christ and not by the works of the law; for by the works of the law no flesh shall be justified."*

➢ **GOD'S GRACE:** He declares me Not Guilty ("righteous") for my sin when I trust CHRIST'S work

John 1:17 *"For the law was given through Moses, but GRACE and truth came through Jesus Christ."*
Acts 13:39 *"...and by Him everyone who believes is JUSTIFIED from ALL THINGS from which you could not be justified by the law of Moses."*
Romans 5:16 *"And the gift is not like that which came through the one who sinned. For the judgment which came from one offense resulted in condemnation, but the free gift which came from many offenses resulted in JUSTIFICATION."*
Romans 5:1 *"...having been JUSTIFIED by faith, we have peace with God through our Lord Jesus Christ..."*

- **GOD'S GRACE:** He IMPUTES ("credits") Christ's righteousness to me when I trust Christ's work

    John 5:24 *"Most assuredly, I say to you, he who hears My words and believes in Him who sent Me has everlasting life, and SHALL NOT COME INTO JUDGMENT, but has passed from death into life."*

    2Corin. 5:21 *"He made Him who knew no sin to be sin for us, that we might become the righteousness of God IN HIM."*

    Romans 3:24-26 *"...being justified freely by His grace THROUGH THE REDEMPTION THAT IS IN CHRIST JESUS, whom God set forth to be a propitiation by His blood, through faith, to demonstrate His righteousness, because in His forbearance God had passed over the sins that were previously committed, to demonstrate at the present time HIS RIGHTEOUSNESS, that He might be JUST and the justifier of the one who has faith in Jesus."*

    Gen. 15: 6 (Rom. 4:1-5) *"...he (Abraham) believed in the Lord, and HE ACCOUNTED IT TO HIM for righteousness."*

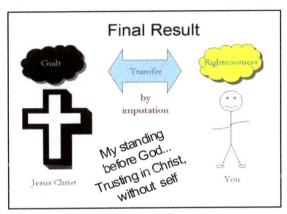

- **John MacArthur, "The Gospel According to Jesus"[2]**   an **INSTANTANEOUS** change

    "Justification may be defined as an act of God whereby He imputes to a believing sinner the full and perfect righteousness of Christ, forgiving the sinner of all unrighteousness, declaring him or her perfectly righteous in His sight, thus delivering the believer from all condemnation. This definition contains several elements:

    1.) imputed righteousness,
    2.) forgiveness of sins,
    3.) new standing before God, and
    4.) a reversal of God's wrath.

    It is a legal verdict that takes place in the court of God, not in the heart of the sinner. It is an instantaneous change of one's standing before God, not a gradual transformation that takes place within the one justified."

- **Charles C. Ryrie, "So Great Salvation"[10]**   Christ's righteousness **IMPUTED** to sinful man

    "How can a just God make a guilty person not guilty? Salvation is God making a swap: God IMPUTES our sin (He charges our sin account) to Christ and imputes Christ's righteousness to us! Jesus credited me with HIS righteousness, with all its rights and privileges, when I asked Him to save me.

    God only has 3 options as sinners stand in His courtroom:
    1). condemn them,
    2). compromise His righteousness and receive them the way they are, or
    3). change them into righteous people.

    If He can exercise the third option, then He can announce them righteous – this is to announce them 'Not Guilty', which is Justification."

- **Charles Stanley, "Eternal Security"[9]**   man's **SINFULNESS** imputed to Christ

    "As Jesus hung on the cross, His Father abandoned Him. This separation was so real that Jesus calls God differently: in John, He calls God 'My Father' 109X. But on the cross, Mark 15:34 says He calls Him 'My God' (*"Jesus cried out with a loud voice, 'Eloi, Eloi, lama sabachthani?' which translates, 'My God, My God, why have You abandoned Me?'"*). The intimacy was gone. Jesus was alone.

    Sin's penalty is death – it demands separation from God. Jesus willingly paid that penalty in my place.

    After paying sin's penalty, He went back into God's presence. How could He restore His relationship with God? His righteousness. Sin separates man from God, but Jesus had no sin. Nothing kept Him from reuniting with God.

    Read Hebrews 9:17, 10:14. Jesus' sinlessness makes Him the only acceptable sacrifice for ALL SIN for ALL TIME. There is no difference between sins you committed in the past and sins you'll commit in the future."

SIN: It's Definition / It's Operation

Sin's 7 Definitions in the Bible

1) Transgression = an overstepping of the law; the Divine boundary between good and evil
Psalm 51:1 *"... According to the multitude of Your tender mercies, blot out my TRANSGRESSIONS."*
Romans 2:23 *"You who make your boast in the law, do you dishonor God through BREAKING THE LAW?"*

2) Iniquity = an act inherently wrong, whether expressly forbidden or not
Romans 1:21 *"Although they knew God, they DID NOT GLORIFY HIM AS GOD, nor were they thankful, but became futile in their thoughts, and their foolish hearts were darkened."*

3) Error = a departure from what is right
Romans 1:18 *"The wrath of God is revealed from heaven against all ungodliness and UNRIGHTEOUSNESS of men, who suppress the truth in unrighteousness."*
1John 3:4 *"Whoever commits sin also commits lawlessness, and sin is LAWLESSNESS."*

4) Missing the Mark = a failure to meet the Divine standard
Romans 3:23 *"All have sinned and FALLEN SHORT of the glory of God."*

5) Trespass = the intrusion of self-will into the sphere of divine authority
Ephesians 2:1 *"You He made alive, who were dead in TRESPASSES and sins..."*

6) Lawlessness = spiritual anarchy
1Timothy 1:9-10 *"... the law was not made for a righteous person, but for the lawless and insubordinate, for the ungodly and for sinners, for the unholy and profane, for murderers of mothers, for manslayers, for fornicators, for sodomites, for kidnappers, for liars, for perjurers, and any other thing that OPPOSES SOUND DOCTRINE."*

7) Unbelief = an insult to Divine veracity
John 16:8-9 *"When He has come, He will convict the world of SIN, and of righteousness, and of judgment. Of SIN, because they DO NOT BELIEVE IN ME..."*

Sin's 5 Operations as explained in the Bible

1) Sin originated with Satan
Isaiah 14:12-14 *"How have you fallen from heaven, O Lucifer son of the morning! How you are cut down to the ground, you who weakened the nations! For you have said in your heart: 'I will ascend into heaven, I will exalt my throne above the stars of God, I will also sit on the mount of the congregation, on the farthest sides of the north. I will ascend above the heights of the clouds. I will be like the Most High.'"*

2) Sin entered the world through Adam
Romans 5:12 *"Just as through one man sin entered the world, and death through sin, and thus death spread to all men, because all sinned."*

3) Sin was, and is, universal (Christ alone the exception)
Romans 3:23 *"All have sinned and fallen short of the glory of God."*
1Peter 2:21-22 *"...Christ also suffered for us, leaving us an example that you should follow His steps: 'Who committed no sin, nor was guile found in His mouth.'"*

4) Sin incurs the penalties of spiritual and physical death
Genesis 2:17 *"Of the tree of the knowledge of good and evil you shall not eat, for in the day that you eat of it you shall surely die."*
Ezekiel 18:4 *"All souls are Mine; the soul of the father as well as the soul of the son is Mine; the soul who sins shall die."*
Romans 6:23 *"The wages of sin is death..."*

5) Sin has no remedy but in the sacrificial death of Jesus Christ made available by the gift of faith
Acts 4:12 *"... there is no other name under heaven given among men by which we must be saved."*
Hebrews 9:26 *"... now, once at the end of the ages, He has appeared to put away sin by the sacrifice of Himself."*
Acts 13:38-39 *"Let it be known to you, brethren, that through this Man is preached to you the forgiveness of sins, and by Him everyone who believes is justified from all things from which you could not be justified by the law of Moses."*

Summarizing What "Sin" Is:
1) an ACT = the violation of, or lack of obedience to, the revealed will of God
2) a STATE = the absence of righteousness
3) a NATURE = enmity towards God

LUKE 18:9-14   Jesus explains JUSTIFICATION

"Also He spoke this parable to some WHO TRUSTED IN THEMSELVES THAT THEY WERE RIGHTEOUS, and despised others: 'Two men went up to the temple to pray, one a Pharisee and the other a tax collector. The Pharisee stood and prayed thus within himself, 'God, thank You that I am not like other men – extortioners, unjust, adulterers, or even as this tax collector. I fast twice a week; I give tithes of all that I possess.'

And the tax collector, standing afar off, would not so much as raise his eyes to heaven, but beat his breast, saying, 'God, be merciful to me, a sinner!'

I tell you, this man went down to his house JUSTIFIED rather than the other; for everyone who exalts himself will be abased, and he who humbles himself will be exalted.'"

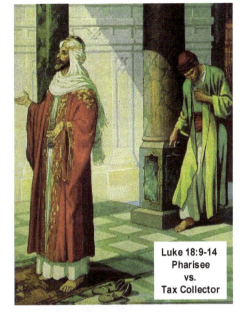

Luke 18:9-14
Pharisee vs. Tax Collector

"What is the most-quoted verse in the Bible?"

Habakkuk 2:4 *"Behold the proud, his soul is not upright in him; but THE JUST SHALL LIVE BY HIS FAITH."*

Galatians 3:11 *"But that no one is justified by the law in the sight of God is evident, for 'THE JUST SHALL LIVE BY FAITH.'"*

Hebrews 10:38 *"Now THE JUST SHALL LIVE BY FAITH; but if anyone draws back, My soul has no pleasure in him."*

Romans 1:17 *"...the righteousness of God is revealed from faith to faith; as it is written, 'THE JUST SHALL LIVE BY FAITH.'"*

The **REFORMATION**: Justification is by God's Grace alone through Faith in Christ alone

➔ **The Protestant Position**: Reformation began with Martin Luther, when he discovered through hours of studying Scripture (which the State Church prohibited people from reading on their own) the doctrine of justification by God's grace alone through faith alone, apart from works. His confrontation with the State Church climaxed when he posted his 95 Theses at the Castle Church in Wittenberg, Germany on October 31, 1517.

What are Luther's "95 Theses"?

- As part of a fund-raising campaign by Pope Leo X to finance the renovation of St. Peter's Basilica in Rome, Johann Tetzel, a Dominican priest, began selling INDULGENCES throughout Germany. Albert of Mainz (the Archbishop of Mainz in Germany) had borrowed heavily to pay for his high church rank and was deeply in debt. He agreed to allow the sale of the indulgences in his territory in exchange for a cut of the proceeds.

- Luther was not aware of this. Even though Luther's prince, Frederick III, and Prince George, Duke of Saxony, forbade the sale in their lands, Luther's parishioners traveled to purchase them.

- When people came to confession, they presented their indulgences (which they had paid for with silver money), claiming they no longer had to repent of their sins, since the document promised to forgive all their sins.

- Luther was outraged that they had paid money for what was theirs by right as a free gift from God. He felt compelled to expose the fraud that was being sold to the people. This exposure was to take place in the form of a public scholarly debate at the University of Wittenberg. The 95 Theses outlined the items to be discussed and issued the challenge to any and all comers. He nailed these 95 theses to the front door of the church at Wittenberg.

Martin Luther, "A Treatise on Christian Liberty" (Nov. 1520) *"That expression 'righteousness of God' was like a thunderbolt in my heart. I hated Paul with all my heart when I read that the righteousness of God is revealed in the gospel (**Romans 1:16-17**). Only afterward, when I saw the words that followed - namely, that it's written that the just shall live through faith (1:17) – and I consulted Augustine, I was cheered. When I learned that THE RIGHTEOUSNESS OF GOD IS HIS MERCY, and that HE MAKES US RIGHTEOUS THROUGH IT, a remedy was offered to me in my affliction. For it is faith alone, not good works, that makes the true Christian and saves him from hell. For it is faith in Christ that makes a man good; his good works follow from that faith. 'The tree bears fruit, the fruit does not bear the tree.'"*

➔ **Roman Catholic Theology:** The entire emphasis is on "holy living": you must *work* to achieve a new standing before God. It is not an instant verdict by God. Being instantly justified by faith in Christ is "legal fiction" to the Roman Catholic. The Protestant's doctrine was heretical because it makes their position of "holy living" useless.

The State Church (The Diet of Worms, April 17, 1521) *"Martin, your plea to be heard from Scripture is the one always made by heretics. You do nothing but renew the errors of Wyclif and Huss. How can you assume that you are the only one to understand the sense of Scripture? Would you put your judgment above that of so many famous men and claim that you know more than all of them? You have no right to call into question the most holy orthodox faith, instituted by Christ the perfect Lawgiver, proclaimed throughout the world by the Apostles, sealed by the red blood of martyrs, confirmed by the sacred councils, and defined by the Church…and which we are forbidden by the Pope and the Emperor to discuss, lest there be no end to debate. I ask you, Martin to answer candidly and without distinction: do you or do you not repudiate your books and the errors which they contain?"*

Martin Luther, "Response to the Church" (The Diet of Worms, April 17, 1521)
"Your Imperial Majesty and Your Lordships demand a simple answer. Here it is, plain and unvarnished. Unless I am convinced of error by the testimony of Scripture, since I put no trust in the unsupported authority of Pope or councils, since it is plain that they have often erred and often contradicted themselves, or by manifest reasoning, I stand convinced by the Scriptures to which I have appealed, and MY CONSCIENCE IS TAKEN CAPTIVE BY GOD'S WORD. I cannot and will not recant anything, for to act against our conscience is neither safe for us, nor open to us. **ON THIS I TAKE MY STAND**. *I can do no other. God help me. Amen."*

What is "SAVING" FAITH? 2.3 Greek "*pistis*" or "*pisteuo*"

- a firm conviction based upon hearing
- to "cling" to: a pledge of fidelity (commitment to promise), as in marriage vows
- a personal surrender to the invisible God, and the conduct inspired by that surrender (2Corinthians 5:7)
- its object is a Person: its not in God's promises (the occasion to exercise faith), but in God Himself

1) It comes from God: (note: see Truth #2 of the 8 Trurths for Eternal Security)

- The capacity of the human heart to understand who God is, His gift of eternal life, and His purpose for me.
- Faith and grace are **SUPERNATURAL GIFTS** (not man's response to God), placed in my heart by God.

Romans 5:15 *"...the gift of grace which is by Jesus Christ has abounded to many."*
Ephesians 2:8-9 *"..by grace are you saved through faith, and that not of yourselves; it is the gift of God, not of works, lest any man should boast."*

- Salvation is because of God's **LOVE**, not because of my faith (He saves me because he LOVES me)

Ephesians 2:4-5 *"...God who is rich in mercy because of His GREAT LOVE WITH WHICH HE SAVED US, even when we were dead in trespasses, made us alive together with Christ (by grace you have been saved through faith)..."*

2) It precedes **SIGHT** (I see after I trust):

- Faith accepts the evidence God gives me for Himself and gives the controls of my life to Him.
- Faith rests in His promise to save me from my sin. Then He gives me spiritual eyes to know Him as He leads me through life.

John 11:40 *"Jesus said 'Did I not say to you that if you would believe you would see the glory of God?'"*
2Corinthians 5:7 *"...we walk by faith, not by sight."*
Colossians 3:2 *"Set your mind on things above, not on things on the earth."*
Hebrews 11:1,3 *"Faith is the substance of things hoped for, the evidence of things not seen. By faith we understand that the worlds were framed by the word of God, so that the things which are seen were not made of things which are visible."*
2Corinthians 4:18 *"...while we do not look at the things which are seen, but at the things which are not seen. For the things which are seen are temporary, but the things which are not seen are eternal."*
John 20:29 *"...because you have seen Me, you have believed. Blessed are those who have not seen and yet have believed."*
Hebr. 11:27 *"By faith he forsook Egypt, not fearing the wrath of the king; for he endured as seeing Him who is invisible."*
Romans 8:24-25 *"For we were saved in this hope, but hope that is seen is not hope; for why does one still hope for what one sees? But if we hope for what we do not see, then we eagerly wait for it with perseverance."*
Romans 1:20 *"For since the creation of the world His invisible attributes are clearly seen, being understood by the things which are made, even His eternal power and Godhead, so that they are without excuse."*

3) It has its **SOURCE** in the Bible:

- Faith is born by hearing and reading the Bible (it activates faith within me).
- Faith grows by studying and meditating on the Bible (God blesses me when I make His word is a priority).

1Peter 1:23 *"...having been born again, not of corruptible seed but incorruptible, through the WORD OF GOD which lives and abides forever."*
Romans 10:17 *"So then faith comes by hearing, and hearing by the WORD OF GOD."*
1Peter 2:2 *"...as newborn babes, desire the pure milk of the Word, that you may grow thereby."*
Psalm 1:1-2 *"Blessed is the man who walks not in the counsel of the ungodly, nor stands in the path of sinners, nor sits in the seat of the scornful, but his delight is in the law of the Lord, and in His law he meditates day and night."*
Joshua 1:8 *"This Book of the law shall not depart from your mouth, but you shall meditate in it day and night, that you may observe to do according to all that is written in it. For then you will make your way prosperous... and have good success."*

Why do I *NEED* faith?

1) The only way a **HOLY** God will **FORGIVE** me
- Faith= God's channel to appropriate His grace to me
- Faith= God's only way to free me from condemnation of my sin. Only by faith can my sins be forgiven and I experience God's presence in my life.

Hebrews 11:6 *"But without faith it is impossible to please Him, for he who comes to God must believe that He is, and that He is a rewarder of those who diligently seek Him."*

Romans 5:1 *"Therefore, having been justified by faith, we have peace with God through our Lord Jesus Christ."*

2) Without faith, I cannot **OBEY** God:
- It enables me to live for Christ and obey His word.

Hebrews 11:8-9 *"BY FAITH Abraham OBEYED when he was called to go out to the place which he would afterward receive as an inheritance. And he went out, not knowing where he was going."*

How can I *RECEIVE* faith?

- The source of faith is the Bible, but the substance of faith is **ACTION** (my response to the Bible).
- Faith is the hand that reaches out to take God's free gift of eternal life (I must act on His offer).
- I first response to God's offer (acknowledge); the second response is from Him (appropriate):

God's Character = HOLY & PURE

- HOLY = "*hagios*" = separated from sin; set apart; moral perfection in personal character & conduct

Exodus 15:11 *"Who is like You, O Lord, among the gods? Who is like You, glorious in HOLINESS..."*

Leviticus 19:2 *"...you shall be holy; for I, the Lord your God, am HOLY."*

Matthew 5:48 *"You shall be PERFECT, just as your Father in heaven is perfect."*

- PURE = "*hagnos*" = undefiled, not contaminated (same root as "*hagios*")

Habakkuk 1:17 *"You are of PURER eyes than to behold evil, and cannot look on wickedness."*

James 3:17 *"...the wisdom that is from above is first PURE..."*

ACKNOWLEDGE (to admit or agree with God; to surrender to the authority of Jesus Christ as Savior and Lord)
- Trusting God for salvation means distrusting my ability to save myself.
- My relationship with God begins when I recognize and admit I have offended Him. I realize that only by turning to God through faith in Jesus can I be saved.
- In repentance I willingly turn away from my lifestyle and in faith I turn to Jesus, asking Him to take my sins upon Himself as my personal Savior, giving Him my life.

APPROPRIATE (to set apart or assign for a specific purpose; to take possession of)
- God gave His love to me while I was still a sinner because Jesus died for me while I was living my way, in disobedience to Him (John 3:16, Romans 5:8).
- My faith receives God's free gift of eternal life, which He appropriates to those who believe what He says and surrender to Him as their Savior and Lord (John 1:12).
- His promises to me and His principles for living my life go into action by His grace through my faith (Eph. 2:4).

- When people openly say they believe in Christ, does that mean they are saved?

John 2:23-25 *"Now when He was in Jerusalem at the Passover, during the feast, MANY BELIEVED IN HIS NAME when they saw the signs which He did. But JESUS DID NOT COMMIT HIMSELF TO THEM, because He knew all men, and had no need that anyone should testify of man, for HE KNEW WHAT WAS IN MAN."*

- People are saved when they surrender with their **HEART**, not their lips:

Romans 10:9 *"If you confess with your mouth the Lord Jesus Christ, and believe IN YOUR HEART that God raised Him from the dead, you will be saved. For with the HEART one believes unto righteousness..."*

Ezekiel 33:31 *"So they come to you as people do, they sit before you as My people, and they hear your words, BUT THEY DO NOT DO THEM; for with their mouth they show much love, but THEIR HEARTS PURSUE THEIR OWN GAIN."*

Matt. 15:8 *"They draw near to Me with their mouth, and honor Me with their lips, but THEIR HEART IS FAR FROM ME."*

Hebrews 3:12 *"Beware, brethren, lest there be in any of you an EVIL HEART OF UNBELIEF in departing from... God."*

> Psalm 130:3-4 *"If You, Lord, should mark iniquities, who could stand? But there is forgiveness with You, that You may be feared."*

FACTUAL FAITH → the kind that cannot save you

This type of faith depends on historic or scientific data. It trusts only in what is seen or evident. Every person has this faith – it's what we mean when we say "seeing is believing".

Factual Faith in the Old Testament – the book of EXODUS: God performed many miracles in front of people so they could see and know without any question that He was the true God and they should worship only Him.

- God parts the Red Sea (Exodus 14:13,31): *"Moses said to the people, 'Do not be afraid. Stand still, and SEE the salvation of the Lord, which He will accomplish for you today. For the Egyptians whom you see today, you shall see again no more forever.' Thus Israel SAW the great work which the Lord had done in Egypt; so the people feared the Lord, and believed the Lord and His servant Moses."*

- God says the physical signs He reveals prove He is God (Exodus 10:1-2): *"Now the Lord said to Moses, 'Go in to Pharaoh; for I have hardened his heart and the hearts of His servants, that I may SHOW THESE SIGNS of Mine before him, and that you may tell in the hearing of your son and your son's son the mighty things I have done in Egypt, and My signs which I have done among them, that they may KNOW that I am the Lord.'"*

- God uses nonbelievers to work signs (Exodus 11:9): *"The Lord said to Moses, 'Pharaoh will not heed you, so that My wonders may be MULTIPLIED in the land of Egypt."* (Romans 9:22-23 – *"What if God, wanting to SHOW His wrath and to make His power KNOWN, endured with much longsuffering the vessels of wrath prepared for destruction...").*

- God miraculously feeds the Israelites (Exodus 16:7-8,11-12): *"'In the morning you shall SEE the glory of the Lord; for He hears your murmurings against the Lord. But what are we, that you murmur against us?' And Moses said, 'This shall be SEEN when the Lord gives you meat to eat in the evening, and in the morning bread to the full; for the Lord hears your murmurings which you make against Him. And what are we? Your murmurings are not against us but against the Lord.' And the Lord spoke to Moses, saying, 'I have heard the murmurings of the children of Israel. Speak to them, saying, 'At twilight you shall eat meat, and in the morning you shall be filled with bread. And you shall KNOW that I am the Lord your God.'"*

Factual Faith in the New Testament – 'Doubting Thomas'

John 20:25,29 *"The other disciples therefore said to him, 'We have SEEN the Lord.' But he said to them, 'Unless I SEE in His hands the print of the nails, and put my finger into the print of the nails, and put my hand into His side, I WILL NOT BELIEVE.' Jesus said to him, 'Thomas, because you have SEEN Me, you have believed.'"*

Even though Thomas was with Jesus when He performed miracles, he refused to believe Jesus rose from the dead without physical evidence.

Factual Faith in the New Testament – Pharisees, Priests and Scribes

Matthew 27:41-42 *"Likewise the chief priests, also mocking with the scribes and elders, said, 'He saved others; Himself He cannot save. If He is the king of Israel, let Him now come down from the cross, and we will BELIEVE Him.'"*

Psalm 22:7-8 (1000 BC): *"All those who SEE Me laugh Me to scorn; they shoot out the lip, they shake the head, saying, 'He trusted in the Lord, let Him rescue Him, since He delights in Him!'"*

In Mark 8:11-12, Jesus would not give them the physical signs they wanted (i.e., factual faith) because they totally refused to believe Him unless He submitted to their tests: *"And the Pharisees came out and began to dispute with Him, seeking from Him a SIGN from heaven, testing Him. But He sighed deeply in His spirit, and said, 'Why does this generation seek a sign? Assuredly, I say to you, no sign will be given to this generation.'"*

In John 10:24-26, Jesus told the hostile crowds that the miracles they saw Him perform (His works) were all the proof they needed that He was their promised Messiah, so by refusing to believe in Him with all the factual evidence He gave them, they proved they didn't know Him: *"Then the Jews surrounded Him and said, 'How long do you keep us in doubt? If you are the Christ, tell us plainly.' Jesus answered them, 'I told you, and you do not believe. The works that I do in My Father's name, they bear witness of Me. But you do not believe, because you are not of My sheep.'"*

And also in Matthew 13:58 and Mark 6:5-6, Jesus would not perform miracles because He knew ahead of time they would not believe in Him no matter what He showed them: *"He did not do many mighty works there because of their unbelief.... Now He could do no mighty work there, except that He laid His hands on a few sick people and healed them. And He marveled because of their unbelief."*

TEMPORARY FAITH ➔ the kind that cannot save you

This type of faith is useless because it doesn't last. It flares up quickly and people get excited, but because of people's cares and the difficulties they face in the world it does not endure.

Temporary Faith in the Old Testament – Deuteronomy 32:20: After God leads them out of Egypt, they start sacrificing to the pagan gods around them, and had forgotten who their God was. God tells them point-blank that they are sinful because they have no faith: *"I will hide My face from them, I will see what their end will be, for they are a perverse generation, children in whom there is NO FAITH."*

Temporary Faith in the Old Testament – the book of EXODUS: The 3 examples below show that even though the Jews saw God do great miracles to deliver them, they blamed Him when things got hard.

- <u>Making bricks without straw</u>: When Moses and Aaron first tell the Jews that God will deliver them from the Egyptians, and they perform God's miracles before them to prove He is real, they say they believe: *"Moses and Aaron went and gathered together all the elders of the children of Israel. And Aaron spoke all the words which the Lord had spoken to Moses. Then HE DID THE SIGNS IN THE SIGHT OF THE PEOPLE. So the people BELIEVED; and when they heard that the Lord had visited the children of Israel and that He had looked on their affliction, then they bowed their heads and worshipped."* (Exodus 4:29-31)

But then Moses demands the Egyptians set the Jews free, and in anger they force the Jews to make bricks without straw. The Jews now reject Moses and show their lack of faith in God because of this hardship that the Egyptians put on them: *"So Moses spoke thus to the children of Israel; but THEY WOULD NOT HEED MOSES, because of anguish of spirit and cruel bondage."* (Exodus 6:9)

- <u>Manna and Quail from heaven</u>: The Israelites worship God after they just watched Him part the Red Sea and the Egyptian army be destroyed: *"Sing to the Lord, for HE HAS TRIUMPHED GLORIOUSLY! The horse and its rider He has thrown to the sea."* (Exodus 15:21)

But as they start their journey in the desert, they get hungry and can't find any food. So the first thing they do is complain that they should have ignored God and stayed in Egypt because He can't feed them, even though they just saw Him part an ocean: *"Then the whole congregation of the children of Israel MURMURED AGAINST MOSES AND AARON in the wilderness. And the children of Israel said to them, 'Oh, that we had died by the hand of the Lord in the land of Egypt, when we sat by the pots of meat and when we ate bread to the full! For you have brought us out into the wilderness to kill this whole assembly with hunger."* (Exodus 16:2-3)

- <u>Water from the Rock</u>: God gives the Israelites food all the forty years they were in the wilderness because He loves them: *"And the children of Israel ate manna forty years, until they came to an inhabited land; they ate manna until they came to the border of the land of Canaan."* (Exodus 16:35)

But now as they start their journey from the wilderness of Zin, they get thirsty. The first thing they do is complain again that they should have ignored God and stayed in Egypt because He can't take care of them. They actually doubt that God is with them, even though He is giving them food miraculously every day and He just parted the Red Sea: *"Therefore the people CONTENDED WITH MOSES, and said, 'give us water, that we may drink.' And Moses said to them, 'Why do you contend with Me? Why do you TEMPT THE LORD?' And the people thirsted there for water, and the people MURMURED AGAINST MOSES, and said, 'Why is it you have brought us up out of Egypt, to kill us and our children and our livestock with thirst?' So he called the name of the place Massah and Meribah, because of the contention of the children of Israel, and because they tempted the Lord, saying, 'IS GOD AMONG US OR NOT?'"* (Exodus 17:2-3,7)

Temporary Faith in the New Testament – afraid to side with Christ: There were leaders in Jerusalem who initially trusted in Jesus, but their actions show their faith was temporary because they wouldn't confess Christ for fear of what their peers would think: *"Nevertheless even among the rulers many believed in Him, but because of the Pharisees THEY DID NOT CONFESS HIM, lest they should be put out of the synagogue; for THEY LOVED THE PRAISE OF MEN MORE THAN THE PRAISE OF GOD."* (John 12:42-43)

Temporary Faith in the New Testament – the Stony Soil:
Jesus explains temporary faith by comparing the heart with stony soil: *"But he who received the seed on stony places, this is he who hears the word and immediately receives it with joy; yet HE HAS NO ROOT IN HIMSELF, but ENDURES ONLY FOR A WHILE. For when tribulation or persecution arises because of the word, immediately he stumbles."* (Matthew 13:20-21). *"But the ones on the rock are those who, when they hear, receive the word with joy; and THESE HAVE NO ROOT, who BELIEVE FOR A WHILE and in times of temptation fall away."* (Luke 8:13).

MATTHEW 7:13-14   God's Way of Salvation   2.4

"Enter by the narrow gate; for wide is the gate and broad is the way that leads to destruction, and there are many who go in by it. Narrow is the gate and difficult is the way which leads to life, and there are few who find it."

➔ **Each person must CHOOSE (free will)**

Deuteronomy 30:19 *"I call heaven and earth as witnesses today against you, that I have set before you life and death, blessing and cursing; therefore choose life, that both you and your descendants may live…"*

1Kings 18:21 *"Elijah came to all the people and said, 'How long will you falter between two opinions? If the Lord is God, follow Him; but if Baal, then follow him.'"*

Jeremiah 21:8 *"Now you shall say to this people, 'Thus says the Lord, "Behold, I set before you the way of life and the way of death."'"*

➔ **Each person must choose the RIGHT GATE**

John 10:9 *"I am the door. If anyone enters by Me, he will be saved, and will go in and out and find pasture."*
John 14:6 *"I am the way, the truth, and the life. No one comes to the Father except by Me."*
Acts 4:12 *"… there is no other name under heaven given among men by which we must be saved."*

"There is a way that seems right to a man, but its end is the way of death."
Proverbs 14:12

Broad Road   **turnstile**

"I am the way, the truth, and the life. No one comes to the Father except through Me."
John 14:6

Salvation is intensely personal: one-at-a-time, squeezing through, bringing nothing with you; believing is an individual act

"Your ears shall hear a word behind you, saying, 'This is the way, walk in it,' whenever you turn to the right hand or whenever you turn to the left."
Isaiah 30:21

John MacArthur[3]: "All the world's religions are based on human achievement. Biblical Christianity alone recognizes divine accomplishment - the work of Christ on humankind's behalf - as the sole basis for salvation. The narrow way and broad way do not contrast religion with paganism. Jesus is not setting the higher religions against the lower ones, or even Christianity against open immorality. The choice is between divine accomplishment and human achievement. Both systems claim to be the way to God. The wide gate is not marked 'This Way to Hell'; it is labeled 'Heaven', the same as the narrow. It just doesn't go there."

➔ **The right gate isn't "easy believism" – it will COST you something**

Luke 23:23-24 *"Then one said to Him, 'Lord, are there few who are saved?' And He said to them, 'STRIVE to enter through the narrow gate, for many, I say to you, will seek to enter and will not be able.'"*

- "STRIVE" = Gr. "*agonizomai*": an agonizing struggle, requiring extreme effort (1Corin. 9:25 = an athlete battling to win).

Matthew 11:12 *"… from the days of John the Baptist until now the kingdom of heaven suffers violence, and violent men take it by force."*

Luke 16:16 *"The law and the prophets were until John. Since then the kingdom of God has been preached and everyone is forcing his way into it."*

Acts 14:22 *"…strengthening the souls of the disciples, exhorting them to continue in the faith, and saying, 'We must through many tribulations enter the kingdom of God.'"*

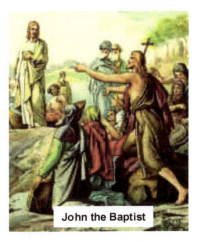

John the Baptist

➜ **"Counting the Cost":** The right gate is for those who **ADMIT** they have no hope without Christ

John 6:64-68 *"But there are some of you who do not believe." For Jesus knew from the beginning who they were who did not believe, and who would betray Him. And He said, "Therefore I have said to you that no one can come to Me unless it has been granted to him by My Father." From that time many of His disciples went back and walked with Him no more." The Jesus said to the twelve, "Do you also want to go away?" Then Simon Peter answered Him, "Lord, to whom shall we go? YOU HAVE THE WORDS OF ETERNAL LIFE."*

Matthew 9:13, 18:11 *"But go and learn what this means: 'I desire mercy and not sacrifice.' For I did not come to call the righteous, but SINNERS, to repentance. For the Son of Man has come to save that which was lost."*

John MacArthur[2]: "I am convinced the popular evangelistic message today actually lures people into a deception. Though it presents Christ as the Way, the Truth, and the Life, it omits the offense of the cross (the narrow way). Its focus is the love of God, but doesn't include God's wrath. It tells people they are deprived, not depraved. It is full of love and understanding, without mentioning the holy God who hates sin. There is no call to repent, no warning of judgment, no call for brokenness, no reason for deep sorrow over sin. It is a message of easy salvation, hasty decisions, false promises of health and happiness and material blessings. This is not God's way of salvation."

Jesus: He separates people into 2 Groups

- **2 Kinds of TREES:** Fruitful (good works) vs. Fruitless (evil works)

Matthew 7:17-20 *"..every good tree bears good fruit, but a bad tree bears bad fruit. A good tree cannot bear bad fruit, nor can a bad tree bear good fruit. Every tree that does not bear good fruit is cut down and thrown into the fire. Therefore by their fruits you will know them"*

- **2 Kinds of FOUNDATIONS:** Rock vs. on Sand

Matthew 7:24-27 *"Therefore whoever hears these sayings of Mine and does them, I will liken him to a wise man who built his house on the rock; and the rain descended, the floods came, and the winds blew and beat on that house; and it did not fall, for it was founded on the rock. Now everyone who hears these sayings of Mine and does not do them, will be like a foolish man who built his house on the sand: and the rain descended, the floods came, and the winds blew and beat on that house; and it fell. And great was its fall."*

- **2 Kinds of HEARTS:** Proud vs. Humbled

Luke 18:9-14 *"Also He spoke this parable to some who trusted in themselves that they were righteous, and despised others: 'Two men went up to the temple to pray, one a Pharisee and the other a tax collector. The Pharisee stood and prayed thus with himself, 'God, thank You that I am not like other men – extortioners, unjust, adulterers, or even this tax collector. I fast twice a week; I give tithes of all that I possess.' And the tax collector, standing afar off, would not so much as raise his eyes to heaven, but beat his breast, saying, 'God, be merciful to me, a sinner!' I tell you, this man went down to his house justified rather than the other; for everyone who exalts himself will be based, and he who humbles himself will be exalted."*

- **2 Kinds of SONS:** Obedient vs. Disobedient

Matthew 21:28-32 *"But what do you think? A man had 2 sons, and he came to the first and said, 'Son, go, work today in my vineyard.' He answered, 'I will not,' but afterward he regretted it and went. Then he came to the second and said likewise. And he answered and said, 'I go, sir,' but he did not go. Which of the two did the will of his father?" They said to Him, "The first". Jesus said to them, "Assuredly, I say to you that tax collectors and harlots enter the kingdom of God before you. For John came to you in righteousness, and you did not believe him, but tax collectors and harlots believed him; and when you saw it, you did not afterward regret it and believe him."*

- **2 Kinds of CRIMINALS**: Acceptance vs. Rejecting

Luke 23:39-43 *"Then 1 of the criminals who were hanged blasphemed Him, saying, 'If You are the Christ, save Yourself and us.' But the other, answering, rebuked him, saying, 'Do you not even fear God, seeing you are under the same condemnation? And we indeed justly, for we receive the due reward of our deeds; but this Man has done nothing wrong.' The he said to Jesus, 'Lord, remember me when You come into Your kingdom.' And Jesus said to him, 'Assuredly, I say to you, today you will be with Me in Paradise.'"*

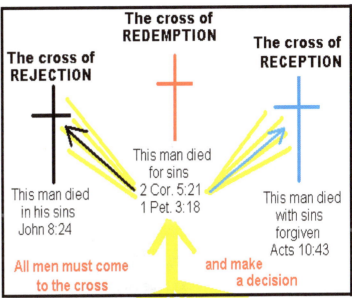

- **2 Kinds of NATIONS**:
  Sheep (know Him) vs. Goats (never knew Him)

Matthew 25:32-34, 41, 46 *"All the nations will be gathered before Him, and He will separate them one from another, as a shepherd divides his sheep from the goats. And He will set the sheep on His right hand, but the goats on the left. Then the King will say to those on His right hand, 'Come, you blessed of My Father, inherit the kingdom prepared for you from the foundation of the world.' Then He will also say to those on the left hand, 'Depart from Me, you cursed, into everlasting fire prepared for the devil and his angels. And these will go away into everlasting punishment."*

- **2 Kinds of SERVANTS**:
  Faithful vs. Faithless

Matthew 25:45-51 *"Who then is a faithful and wise servant, whom his master made ruler over his household, to give them food in due season? Blessed is that servant whom his master, when he comes, will find so doing. Assuredly, I say to you that he will make him ruler over all his goods.*

But if that evil servant says in his heart, 'My master is delaying his coming', and begins to beat his fellow servants, and to eat and drink with the drunkards, the master of that servant will come on a day when he is not looking for him and at an hour that he is not aware of, and will cut him in two and appoint his portion with the hypocrites. There shall be weeping and gnashing of teeth."

MARK 10:17-27 "The Rich Young Ruler: The <u>COST</u> of Eternal Life"

"Now as He was going out on the road, one came running, knelt before Him, and asked Him, "Good Teacher, what shall I do that I may inherit eternal life?" So Jesus said to him, "Why do you call Me good? No one is good but One, that is, God. You know the commandments: 'Do not commit adultery', 'Do not murder', 'Do not steal', 'Do not bear false witness', 'Do not defraud', Honor your father and your mother'." And he answered and said to Him,

"Teacher, all these things I have observed from my youth." Then Jesus, looking at him, LOVED HIM, and said to him, "One thing you still lack: Go your way, sell whatever you have and give to the poor, and you will have treasure in heaven; and come, TAKE UP THE CROSS, AND FOLLOW ME." But he was sad at this word, and went away grieved, for he had great possessions."

Then Jesus looked around and said to His disciples, "How HARD it is for those who have riches to enter the kingdom of God!" And the disciples were astonished at His words. But Jesus answered again and said to them, "Children, how HARD it is for those who TRUST IN RICHES to enter the kingdom of God!

It is easier for a camel to go through the eye of a needle than for a rich man to enter the kingdom of God." And they were ASTONISHED BEYOND MEASURE, saying among themselves, "Who then can be saved?" But looking at them, Jesus said, "With men it is impossible, but with God all things are possible."

JESUS'S STYLE OF EVANGELISM: "<u>COUNT</u> the Cost"

1. <u>Jesus didn't go after a "decision"</u>: Jesus started by preaching the law, not even mentioning faith. He didn't tell him to invite Him into his heart or accept Him as personal Savior. He certainly failed to get "closure".

2. <u>Jesus drove him away</u>: instead of getting him to make a "decision", Jesus laid out terms that were unacceptable to him. The young man left not because he heard the wrong message, and not even because he didn't believe, but because he refused to forsake his true love in order to follow Jesus as his true Lord.

WHAT THE RICH YOUNG RULER DID <u>RIGHT</u>

1. <u>He had the right motive</u> – he sought Jesus out and admitted he wasn't saved. He was empty – he had no joy. He didn't have the abundant life that only Jesus gives. He had everything else: youth, wealth and prominence (a religious leader in the synagogue). The disciples were "astonished beyond measure": in Jewish culture, if a religious leader with his credentials wasn't saved, who was?

2. <u>He had the right attitude</u> – he came in broad daylight, in public (unlike Nicodemus, who came at night in private), running to Jesus. He knelt before Jesus – a position of humility, in front of the crowd. His desperation was transparent to everyone there. Not only did he know he wasn't saved, he knew he NEEDED to be saved. He wanted eternal life so badly that he risked losing face with everyone who already thought he was a spiritual giant.

3. <u>He came to the right Source</u> – he knew of Jesus's power. He addressed Him as "*didaskalos*", or "teacher", and "*agathos*", meaning "good in internal essence". He wasn't just saying Jesus was a "good teacher". He believed Jesus was good in nature. He didn't understand Jesus was God, but he wanted His guidance on eternal life because he believed Jesus had it.

4. <u>He asked the right question</u> – he had a works-based religion, but he was asking a simple, honest question. He was seeking the truth.

WHAT THE RICH YOUNG RULER DID <u>WRONG</u>

1. <u>He was filled with pride</u> – Jesus knew he wanted salvation because he felt empty, not because he knew he was a sinner. Jesus didn't offer him relief for his restlessness. He confronted him with his sin. Real evangelism balances peoples' needs with the reality of the perfect law of God, so people can see their deficiency.

2. <u>He did not confess his guilt</u> – as a Pharisee, he kept the law's rituals, but he wasn't REPENTANT. Before the crowd, he claimed he kept the entire law. He believed he was righteous – he had no sense he was a sinner who offended God. Anyone not willing to confess their sin cannot receive forgiveness from God.

3. <u>He would not submit to Christ</u> – Jesus took him to what he held most dearly – his possessions. Jesus was saying, "I must be first place in your life." Jesus TESTED the rich young ruler, that he CHOOSE between Him and his possessions. He failed the test, and left as empty as he came. No matter what commandments he kept, he was UNWILLING to TURN from what he loved most. He wanted eternal life on his terms, not Jesus's.

> **Proverbs 13:7** *"There is one who pretends to be rich, but has nothing; another pretends to be poor, but has great wealth".*

The Gospel according to Jesus: saving faith is SURRENDER 2.5

Luke 2:11 *"...there is born to you this day on the city of David a SAVIOR, who is Christ THE LORD."*

Question: Luke 2:11 says Jesus is Savior and Lord. Can you accept Him as Savior but reject Him as Lord?
Answer: Jesus says no one coming to Him for salvation will reject His authority over their life. Missionary Jim Elliot said it best: *"A man is no fool who gives up what he cannot keep, to gain what he cannot lose."*

Matthew 16:24-25 Jesus said <u>to His disciples (the 12)</u>, *"If anyone desires to come after Me, let him ①DENY HIMSELF, ②TAKE UP HIS CROSS, and ③FOLLOW ME. For whoever desires to save his life will lose it, and whoever ①LOSES HIS LIFE for MY SAKE will find it. For what is a man profited if he gains the whole world, and loses his own soul?"*

Luke 14:25-30,33; 17:32-33 <u>"Great multitudes</u> went with Him. He turned and said to them: *"If anyone comes to Me and does not hate his father and mother, wife and children, brothers and sisters, yes, and ①HIS OWN LIFE also, he cannot be My disciple. And whoever does not ②BEAR HIS CROSS and ③COME AFTER ME cannot be My disciple. Which of you, intending to build a tower, does not sit down first and COUNT THE COST, whether he has enough to finish it – lest, after he has laid the foundation, and is not able to finish it, all who see it begin to mock him, saying, 'This man began to build and was not able to finish.' Likewise, whoever of you does not ①FORSAKE ALL THAT HE HAS cannot be My disciple. Remember Lot's wife. Whoever seeks to save his life will lose it, and whoever ①LOSES HIS LIFE will preserve it."*

Matthew 10:32-33; 37-39 (<u>to His 12 apostles</u>) *"Therefore whoever ③CONFESSES ME BEFORE MEN, him I will confess before My Father who is in heaven. But whoever denies Me before men, him I will also deny before My Father who is in heaven. He who loves father or mother more than Me is not worthy of Me. And he who loves son or daughter more than Me is not worthy of Me. And he who does not ②TAKE HIS CROSS and ③FOLLOW ME is not worthy of Me. He who finds his life will lose it, and he who ①LOSES HIS LIFE for MY SAKE will find it."*

John 12:25-26 (<u>to His 12 disciples</u>) *"He who loves his life will lose it, and he who ①HATES HIS LIFE in this world will keep it for eternal life. If anyone serves Me, let him ③FOLLOW ME; and where I am there My servant will be also. If anyone serves Me, him My Father will honor."*

John MacArthur[2]: "I do not like the term 'Lordship salvation'. It was coined by those who want to eliminate submission to Christ from the call of saving faith, and it implies that Jesus' lordship is a false addition to the gospel. As we see from Jesus' own words, 'lordship salvation' is biblical and historical evangelism."

① DENY MYSELF → Gr. "aparneomai" = disown; surrender control of my life to Jesus Christ

- See yourself as God sees you – a sinner who is in need of healing.
  Job 42:5-6 = despising my sinfulness when I compare myself to God's holiness ⇨ *"I've heard of You by the hearing of the ear, but now my eye sees You. Therefore I ABHOR myself and repent in dust and ashes."*

  Luke 5:31-32 = Understand that Jesus came to save only those who see themselves as sinful ⇨ *"Those who are well do not need a physician, but those who are sick. I have not come to call the righteous, but SINNERS, to repentance."*

- Surrender: a decisive saying of NO to yourself and YES to Him; putting Him on the **THRONE** of your life
  Phillippians 3:7-8 = my former achievements are counted as excrement ⇨ *"..what things were gain to me, these I have counted loss for Christ. But indeed I also count all things loss for the excellence of the knowledge of Christ Jesus my Lord, for whom I have suffered the loss of all things and count them as RUBBISH that I may gain Christ."*

② DIE TO MYSELF → "TAKE UP MY CROSS" = I crucify *me* so I gain *Him*

Roman crucifixion

- Choosing a life-or-death devotion (people knew what He meant; over 30,000 crucifixions had occurred during the time He said this to them)
- Daily choice of self-martyrdom (die to self) in order to live for Him as Lord over my life
  1Corinthians 15:31 *"I affirm, by the boasting in you which I have in Christ Jesus our Lord, I DIE DAILY."*
  Galatians 2:20 *"I have been CRUCIFIED with Christ; it is no longer I who live, but Christ lives in me..."*

- Jesus called me to be a **MARTYR**
  Acts 1:8 *"...you shall receive power when the Holy Spirit has come upon you; and you shall be My WITNESSES in Jerusalem, and in Judea and Samaria, and to the end of the earth."*

- "witnesses" = Greek *"martus"* = martyr ; a record or witness of Him
  what's a "martyr"? Webster's Dictionary = "a person who chooses to suffer death rather than renounce their religion; a person who endures great suffering for a principle or cause"

- Paraphrasing "Take up his cross": *"If anyone wishes to follow Me, be prepared to be led out to public execution, following My example"*.
Capital punishment was a <u>public event</u>. The condemned criminal was paraded through the streets to the place of execution, the crowd watching the entire event. On the way to execution, he obviously abandoned all earthly hopes and dreams he had for his life.

Crucifixions: Public Events

❸ **FOLLOW JESUS** ➔ Gr. "*akoloutheō*" = walk the same road; accompany; identify with

- To follow Jesus means surrendering to Him as my LORD (He saves me just as I am, if I am **WILLING** to OBEY).

Following Jesus = crucify self

Luke 6:46, Matthew 7:21 = If He is Lord, you will want to obey Him ➔ *"...why do you call Me 'Lord, Lord', and do not do the things which I say? Not everyone who says to Me, 'Lord, Lord,' shall enter the kingdom of heaven, but he who does the will of My Father in heaven."*

John 14:23-24 = Jesus tells me how I can show Him that I truly love Him ➔ *"If anyone loves Me, he will keep My word... He who does not love Me does not keep My words."*

John 13:17 = How to follow Jesus Christ ➔ *"If you know these things, happy are you if you DO them."*

MATTHEW: "Follow Me"

Matthew 9:9-13, Luke 5:27-32 *"...He went out and saw a tax collector named Levi, sitting at the tax office. And He said to him, 'Follow Me.' And he LEFT ALL, rose up, and followed Him. Then Levi gave Him a great feast in his own house. And there were a great number of tax collectors and others who sat down with them. But the scribes and the Pharisees murmured against His disciples, saying, 'Why do You eat and drink with tax collectors and sinners?' And Jesus answered and said to them, 'Those who are well do not need a physician, but THOSE WHO ARE SICK. But go and learn what this means: 'I desire mercy and not sacrifice.' For I have not come to call the righteous, but SINNERS, to repentance.'"*

Matthew: a "publican", or tax collector.

- <u>Cruel, arrogant, evil</u>: they bought tax franchises from the Roman Emperor, collecting taxes from their own people. Rome allowed them to cheat and steal from the people as long as Rome got their tax. They preyed especially on the poor, stopping them at any time and demanding whatever taxes they wanted, with the real threat of throwing them in prison if they didn't pay their demands.
- Tax collecting and prostitution were the most despised professions in Israel.
- Tax collectors were considered loyalists to Rome, so they were excommunicated from society.

Matthew: leaving it all behind to follow Jesus

- <u>There was no turning back</u>: Matthew not only gave up a very lucrative job, but he knew the minute he walked away, the Romans would replace him (there was no shortage of money-grubbing riffraff who would gladly take his job) and he would be an outcast.
- <u>Why did Matthew only invite society's lowlifes to the feast</u>? These were the only kinds of people he knew (no one else would associate with him). He didn't know the "elite" of Jewish society. His first impulse after deciding to follow Jesus was to bring his closest friends to meet Him.
- All 3 Gospel accounts of Tax Collectors are **favorable**. God saves sinners who repent: Luke 19:2-10 (Zaccheus), Luke 18:10-14 (parable of the publican and Pharisee), Luke 5:27-32 (call of Matthew)

Luke 15:1 *"Then all the TAX COLLECTORS and SINNERS drew near to Him to hear Him."*

Matthew 21:32 *"For John came to you in the way of righteousness, and you did not believe him, but TAX COLLECTORS and HARLOTS believed him; and when you saw it, you did not afterward relent and believe him."*

Luke 7:29-30 *"And when all the people heard Him, EVEN THE TAX COLLECTORS declared the righteousness of God, having been baptized with the baptism of John. But the Pharisees and experts in the law rejected the counsel of God for themselves, not having been baptized by him."*

What is REPENTANCE? 2.6

- **THE HEART OF N.T. PREACHING =**
REPENT and BELIEVE (Jesus, John the Baptist, the Apostles)

Matthew 4:17 *From that time Jesus began to preach and to say, "REPENT, for the kingdom of heaven is at hand."*

Matthew 3:1-2 *In those days John the Baptist came preaching...saying, "REPENT, for the kingdom of heaven is at hand!"*

Acts 20:21 *"Testifying to Jews, and to Greeks, REPENTANCE toward God and FAITH toward our Lord Jesus Christ."*

Luke 5:32 *"I have not come to call the righteous, but sinners to REPENTANCE."*

Luke 13:3,5 *"I tell you, but unless you REPENT you will all likewise perish."*

Acts 26:20 *"...declared first to those in Damascus and in Jerusalem, and throughout all the region of Judea, and then to the Gentiles, that they should REPENT, TURN TO GOD, and do works befitting repentance."*

- **AN ACT OF GOD** (not a human work)

Acts 11:18 *When they heard these things they became silent; and they glorified God, saying, "Then God has also granted to the Gentiles REPENTANCE TO LIFE."*

Acts 5:31 *"Him God has exalted to the right hand to be Prince and Savior, to give REPENTANCE to Israel and forgiveness of sins."*

2Timothy 2:25 *"...God perhaps will grant them REPENTANCE, so that they may know the truth."*

- **THE LIFESTYLE OF A BELIEVER** (not a 1-time act)

1John 1:8-10 (Psalm 32:5) *"If we say that we have no sin, we deceive ourselves, and the truth is not in us. If we CONFESS our sins, He is faithful and just to forgive us our sins and to cleanse us from all unrighteousness. If we say that we have not sinned, we make Him a liar, and His word is not in us."*

Luke 17:3-4 *"If your brother sins against you, rebuke him; and if he REPENTS, forgive him. And if he sins against you 7 times in a day, and 7 times in a day returns to you, saying 'I REPENT', you shall forgive him."*

REPENTANCE = engages the mind, emotions and will (3 different N.T. words)

Thayer's Greek Lexicon: "The change of mind ("metanoeo") where I hate my sins ("metamelomai"), and determine to change ("epistrephomai"); I recognize, am sorry for my sins, and make amends, which leads to good deeds."

1Thessalonians 1:9 *"...how you (1) TURNED TO GOD (2) FROM IDOLS to (3) SERVE the living and true God."*

- Repentance is not: a presalvation attempt to set my life in order, or fix my sin before turning to Christ in faith.
- Repentance is: God's command to recognize my sin and hate it, to turn my back on it and flee to Jesus.

- **"METANOEO" = INTELLECTUAL**
- recognizing my sin: I am personally responsible for my sin - it offends a holy God
- recognizing who God is: He can forgive my sin, if I turn to Him and away from it

Luke 11:32 *"The men of Nineveh will rise up in judgment with this generation and condemn it, for they repented at the preaching of Jonah, and indeed a greater than Jonah is here."*

Luke 15:7 *"... there will be more joy in heaven over one sinner who repents than over 99 just persons who need no repentance."*

- **"METAMELOMAI" = EMOTIONAL**
- not worldly sorrow: regret I got caught and have to pay the consequences
- true godly sorrow: deep sense of remorse that I have offended God

2Corinthians 10 *"... godly sorrow produces REPENTANCE TO SALVATION..."*

Luke 18:13-14 *"...the tax collector, standing afar off, would not so much as raise his eyes to heaven, but beat his breast, saying, 'God, be merciful to me a sinner!'"*

- **"EPISTREPHOMAI" = A WILLING CHANGE in direction**
- not outward behavior: God hates outward expression with no inward change
- true inward change: determined to leave "me" for "Him", it shows in my behavior

Matthew 3:8 *"Therefore bear fruits worthy of REPENTANCE."*

Matthew 23:25-26 *"... you cleanse the outside of the cup and dish, but inside they are full of extortion and self-indulgence. Blind Pharisee, first cleanse the INSIDE of the cup and dish, that the outside of them may be clean also."*

LUKE 15:11-32 The Prodigal Son: "Repentance to Salvation"

➔ **THE PRODIGAL vs. 11-16** "his contemptible behavior"

• in Jewish culture, for a son to demand his inheritance was equivalent to saying he wished his father was dead.

• he wasted no time leaving his father, who had raised and cared for him, to go live his way, on his terms.

• he quickly wasted the inheritance (fully knowing his lifestyle opposed everything his father had taught him).

• in his desperation, he joined another's household rather than return to his father (they only gave him pig food).

• "no one gave him anything": he soon learned people are glad to share in his wealth, but not in his poverty.

➔ **THE PRODIGAL vs. 17-21** "his repentance"

• his sorrow over his predicament is not repentance, but is the first step towards it (see 2Corinthians 7:9-10).

• "sinned against heaven and before you" = he now acknowledges his sin.

• he rehearses what he'll say to his father (he is determined to ask forgiveness and accept the consequences).

• repentant faith = total turnaround: unconditional surrender, humility (self-denial), willing to do what the father asks (submission to his father's will).

• vs. 20 shows he ACTED on his plan (see Matthew 21:28-32 – many say they will do something, but never do).

• his arrogance turned to meekness and humility. He was a different man from when he first left home.

➔ **THE FATHER vs. 12,20-24** "His love for the Prodigal"

• He didn't refuse his request for the inheritance, or punish him for his insolence – He graciously gives BOTH sons their share of the family wealth.

• He is the picture of the seeking heavenly Father – He was always watching for him, and RUNS to meet him.

• When repentant sinners turn to God, they see He's been looking for their return, and waiting to embrace them.

• He isn't interested in his son's confession – He orders a feast to celebrate his son's homecoming.

• He already FORGOT His son's sin – there is no punishment – only rejoicing that he has returned to Him.

• Romans 2:4 *"...the goodness of God leads you to repentance"*

• Luke 15:7 *"...there will be more joy in heaven over 1 sinner who repents than 99 just persons who need no repentance."*

➔ **THE FATHER vs. 12, 28** "His love for the older son"

• vs. 12: he also, with his younger brother, received his inheritance (but he stayed at home and worked).

• like the Prodigal, the older son is LOST – when he refuses to come in, the father goes and SEEKS him out.

➔ **THE OLDER SON vs. 25-30** "self-righteous, no love for His Father (serves out of duty)"

• vs. 28: he is angry over his father's compassion – he DISHONORS his father by refusing to join the celebration.

• the picture of the Pharisees: he refuses to eat with a sinner, even one who repents and returns.

• refuses to share in his father's joy (draws near the celebration, but won't come in the house).

• vs. 29: he doesn't see himself as sinful: he is as lost as his brother, but too PROUD to admit it.

• Doesn't understand his Father's heart: he can't tolerate sinners, especially flagrant ones (read Hosea 6:6).

• he takes great pride in his own righteousness, but refuses to submit to his father's will.

• vs. 30: calls the Prodigal "this son of yours", not "this brother of mine" – he won't relate to sinners.

The Gospel: "God graciously saves *repentant sinners* who **SURRENDER** to Him in *FAITH*."

PRODIGAL: 1.) sees his sin   2.) repents   3.) receives forgiveness   4.) enters his Father's joy

OLDER SON: 1.) sees only his righteousness   2.) unrepentant   3.) serves his father out of duty, not love

Those who acknowledge and turn from their sin = God the Father runs to them with open arms.

Those who think they deserve God's favor = excluded from the celebrated joy of a loving Father.

Genesis 15:5-12,17 God's Gift of Salvation = a COVENANT VOW 2.7

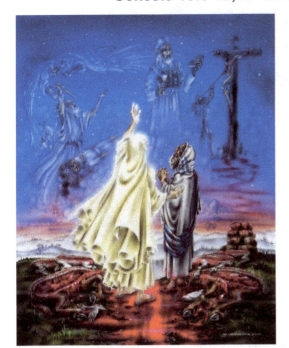

Covenant = Hebrew *"diatheke"*

1) to cut or divide by a sacrifice, thereby securing the obligation of each individual involved to fulfill his/ her vow
2) not a *contract*, which is a joint obligation → in a covenant, each individual is bound to their vow
3) not a *commitment*, where there is limited consequence if broken → in a covenant, there is a strict penalty to anyone making the covenant if that person fails to keep their vow(s)

vs. 5-7 God makes an **UNCONDITIONAL** promise to Abraham

vs. 8-10 God's 1st covenant (salvation by faith, through shed blood) requires a sacrifice – God has Abraham kill 1 each of the 5 acceptable animal sacrifices (cow, sheep, goat, pigeon, dove), cut them in half, then place the halves on opposite rows, in preparation for the covenant ceremony (Jeremiah 34:18-19).

vs. 11. The vultures symbolize Satan, as he tries to thwart God's plans. Abram's alertness to drive them away symbolizes the need for alertness in the believer so the enemy won't succeed.

vs. 12. God puts Abraham to sleep because the covenant doesn't involve any promise from him (in vs. 17, only God walks through the pieces as a promise)

vs. 17. Only God passes between the dead animals - the covenant places NO CONDITIONS on Abram - this is God's solemn vow to fulfill His promise to Abram for **JUSTIFICATION** by **GRACE** through **FAITH**.

The "smoking oven" and flaming torch" symbolize the presence of God (Exodus 19:18) and the cross of Christ

• The "smoking oven" symbolizes the SUFFERING that must first come, as God's wrath towards sin is satisfied through the sacrificial offering of a sinless, perfect Savior (Hebr. "smoke" = "àshan" = "burn with anger", as in Deuteronomy 29:20). This is a picture of the future cross where Jesus Christ will suffer for the sins of mankind (Isaiah 53; 2Corin. 5:21; Galatians 3:13-14)

• The "flaming torch" symbolizes the GLORY afterwards, as the Lord, who is the True Light of mankind, leads His people out of the bondage of sin into the freedom of God's forgiveness through His offering of Himself (Exodus 13:21-22; John 1:4-5, 9; John 8:12).

When two people performed this ceremony: they were literally saying to each party in the covenant *"may what happened to these animals also happen to me, if I break my covenant with you"*

God's Character = RELIABLE

2Chronicles 16:8-9 *"Were the Ethiopians and the Lubim not a huge army with very many chariots and horsemen? Yet, because you RELIED on the Lord, He delivered them into your hand. For the eyes of the Lord run to and fro throughout the whole earth, to SHOW HIMSELF STRONG on behalf of those whose heart is LOYAL to Him."*
RELY = Hebr. *"shaw-an"* = "to rest in; to depend on with full confidence"

Numbers 23:19 *"God is not a man, that He should lie. Nor a son of man, that He should repent. Has He not said, and will He not do it? Or has He spoken, and will He not make it good?"*

God's physical illustration of this spiritual truth of a covenant: MARRIAGE VOWS

"Do you, (GROOM or BRIDE's name), take (name) to be your wedded wife, to live together in marriage. Do you promise to love her, comfort her, honor and keep her for better or worse, for richer or poorer, in sickness and health, forsaking all others, being faithful to her so long as you both shall live?" (name): *"I do."*

1) Marriage isn't begun in vagueness and uncertainty (both people are fully aware, awake and conscious).
2) A vow before God = a promise where one person binds himself/ herself to an act of service to the other.
3) Making the marriage vow before God is serious business: He holds you accountable to **PAY** it:

Proverbs 20:25 *"It is a snare for a man to devote something rashly as holy, and afterward to reconsider his vows."*
Eccle. 5:4 *"When you make a vow to God, do not delay to pay it; for He has no pleasure in fools. Pay what you vowed."*

4) Keeping your marriage vows is WORK – but the vow you made was *"for better or for worse"*...

Isaiah 62:5 God's Character = **FAITHFUL**

"... as the bridegroom rejoices over the bride, so shall your God rejoice over you."

Jesus = the Bridegroom who keeps His vows

➔ "TO LIVE TOGETHER IN MARRIAGE"

John 14:23 *"If anyone loves Me, he will keep My word; and My Father will love Him, and WE WILL COME TO HIM AND MAKE OUR HOME WITH HIM."*

Revelation 21:3 *And I heard a loud voice from heaven saying, "Behold, the tabernacle of God is with men, and He will dwell with them, and they shall be His people, and God Himself will be with them and be their God."*

➔ "TO LOVE HER"

Ephesians 5:25 *"Husbands, love your wives just as CHRIST LOVED THE CHURCH and GAVE HIMSELF FOR IT."*

Galatians 2:20 *"I have been crucified with Christ; it is no longer I who live, but Christ lives in me; and the life which I now live in the flesh I live by faith in the Son of God, WHO LOVED ME and GAVE HIMSELF FOR ME."*

Jeremiah 31:3 *"The Lord has appeared from afar to me, saying, 'Yes, I have LOVED YOU with an EVERLASTING LOVE; therefore with lovingkindness I have drawn you."*

➔ "TO COMFORT HER"

2Corinthians 1:3-4 *"Blessed be the God and Father of our Lord Jesus Christ, the Father of mercies and God of all COMFORT, who comforts us in all our tribulation..."*

Isaiah 49:13 *"Sing, O heavens! Be joyful, O earth! And break out in singing, O mountains! For the Lord has COMFORTED HIS PEOPLE, and will have mercy on His afflicted."*

Isaiah 61:1-2 *"The Spirit of the Lord God is upon Me, because the Lord has anointed Me to preach good tidings to the poor; He has sent Me....to COMFORT THOSE WHO MOURN..."*

➔ "TO HONOR HER"

Philippians 2:3-5 *"Let nothing be done through selfish ambition or conceit, but in lowliness of mind let each ESTEEM OTHERS BETTER THAN HIMSELF. Let each look out not only for his own interests, but also the interests of others. Let this mind be in you which was ALSO IN CHRIST JESUS..."*

John 12:26 *"If anyone serves Me, him MY FATHER WILL HONOR."*

➔ "TO KEEP HER"

Genesis 28:15 *"Behold, I am with you and will KEEP YOU wherever you go..."*

John 17:12 *"While I was with them in the world, I KEPT THEM in Your name. Those whom You gave Me I HAVE KEPT..."*

John 10:27-28 *"My sheep hear My voice, and I know them, and they follow Me. And I give them eternal life, and they shall NEVER PERISH; neither shall anyone SNATCH THEM OUT OF MY HAND."*

➔ "FOR BETTER OR WORSE, FOR RICHER OR POORER, IN SICKNESS OR HEALTH"

Romans 8:35,37-39 *"Who shall separate us from the love of Christ? Shall tribulation, or distress, or persecution, or famine, or nakedness, or peril, or sword? Yet in all these things we are more then conquerors through Him who loved us. For I am persuaded that neither death nor life, nor angels nor principalities nor powers, nor things present nor things to come, nor height nor depth, nor any other created thing, shall be able to separate us from the love of God which is in Christ Jesus our Lord."*

➔ "FORSAKING ALL OTHERS"

Philippians 2:6-8 *"Who, being in the form of God, did not consider equality with God something to be held onto, but MADE HIMSELF OF NO REPUTATION, taking the form of a servant and coming in the likeness of men. And being found in appearance as a man, HE HUMBLED HIMSELF and became obedient TO THE POINT OF DEATH, even the death of the cross."*

Hebrews 12:2 *"...looking unto Jesus, the author and finisher of our faith, who for the joy that was set before Him ENDURED THE CROSS, DESPISING THE SHAME, and has sat down at the right hand of the throne of God."*

➔ "BEING FAITHFUL ONLY TO HER"

2Timothy 2:13 *"If we are faithless, He REMAINS FAITHFUL; He cannot deny Himself."*

Hebrews 13:5 *"... He Himself has said, 'I WILL NEVER LEAVE YOU NOR FORSAKE YOU.'"*

Salvation = a COVENANT MARRIAGE relationship with Jesus Christ

Hebrews 9:16-18   God's Gift of Salvation = a CONSECRATION

"...where there is a testament, there must also be the necessity of THE DEATH OF THE TESTATOR. For a testament is in full force after men are dead, since it has no power at all while the testator lives. Therefore not even the first covenant was CONSECRATED without blood."

Consecrate = "*enkainizo*" = separate unto, or dedicate, through *DEATH* (in Scripture, covenant promises are only activated by shedding blood; death of the sacrifice activates the promises into realities)

2Chronicles 7:5   *"King Solomon offered a sacrifice of 22,000 bulls and 120,000 sheep. So the king and all the people CONSECRATED the temple of God."*

- **Christ (the bridegroom) had to DIE to give LIFE to the church (His bride)**

2Corinthians 11:2 *"For I have betrothed you to ONE HUSBAND, that I may present you as a pure virgin to CHRIST."*
Acts 20:28 *"...take heed to yourselves and to all the flock, among which the Holy Spirit has made you overseers to shepherd the church of God which He PURCHASED WITH HIS OWN BLOOD."*
Hebrews 10:19-20 *"Therefore brethren, having boldness to enter the Holiest by the blood of Jesus, by a new and living way which He CONSECRATED for us through the veil, that is, His flesh..."*
Mark 14:24 *"He said to them, 'This is My blood of the NEW COVENANT (testament), which is shed for many."*
John 10:10-11 *"I have come that they may have LIFE, and that they may have it more abundantly. I am the good shepherd. The good shepherd gives HIS LIFE for the sheep."*
Mark 10:45 *"For even the Son of Man did not come to be served, but to serve, and to GIVE HIS LIFE a ransom for many."*

- **The husband's highest calling = consecration to his wife by DYING**

Ephesians 5:25 *"Husbands, LOVE YOUR WIVES, just as Christ loved the church and GAVE HIMSELF FOR IT."*
Romans 12:1 *"...present your bodies a LIVING SACRIFICE, holy, acceptable to God, which is your reasonable service."*
Matt. 16:24 *"If anyone desires to come after Me, let Him DENY HIMSELF, and TAKE UP HIS CROSS, and follow Me."*

Being Married to Jesus Christ is a consecration - it will cost me my LIFE

1. People don't have good marriages because they're not willing to consecrate themselves to each other.
2. A bad marriage: one or both are consecrated to something other than each other.

- **A life consecrated to the Jesus Christ = "No Matter What"**

Job 13:15-16 *"Though He slay me, YET I WILL TRUST HIM. Even so, I will defend my own ways before Him. He also shall be my salvation. For a hypocrite could not come before Him."*
Daniel 3:17-18 *"...our God whom we serve is able to deliver us from the burning fiery furnace, and He will deliver us from your hand, O king. BUT IF NOT, let it be known to you, O king, that we do not serve your gods, nor will we worship the gold image which you have set up."*
John 8:29 *"He who sent Me is WITH ME. The Father has not left Me alone, for I always do those things that PLEASE HIM."*
Psalm 27:1 *"The Lord is my light and my salvation: WHOM SHALL I FEAR? The Lord is the strength of my life; of whom shall I be afraid?"*
Isaiah 50:5-7: *"The Lord has opened My ear, and I was not rebellious, nor did I turn away. I gave My back to those who struck Me, and My cheeks to those who plucked out the beard. I did not hide My face from shame and spitting. For THE LORD GOD WILL HELP ME, therefore I will not be disgraced; ...I have SET MY FACE LIKE A FLINT, and I know that I will not be ashamed."*
Jeremiah 1:18-19 *"For behold, I have made you this day A FORTIFIED CITY and an IRON PILLAR, and bronze walls against the whole land; against the kings of Judah, against its princes, against its priests, and against the people of the land. They will fight against you, but they will not prevail against you. For I AM WITH YOU," says the LORD, "to deliver you."*
Ephesians 6:10 *"...be strong IN THE LORD, and in the power of HIS MIGHT."*

2CHRONICLES 16:9 → Isaiah 40:10 → Prov. 8:14 → 1Corin. 1:24 → Col. 1:27 → Phil. 4:13 → John 15:5
"The eyes of the Lord run to and fro throughout the whole earth, to SHOW HIMSELF STRONG on behalf of those whose heart is loyal to Him."

THE CROSS: Consecration's Power is in <u>BROKENNESS</u>

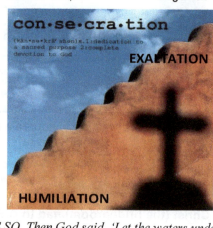

"Consecrated" is the Greek word *"enkainizo"*, meaning "dedicated to". And that requires *DEATH* to self to give *LIFE* to one another. And death to self can only be realized in one way – *BROKENNESS*. This isn't a new concept – this is God's design.

- **God's Act of <u>CREATION</u>** (Genesis 1:3,6-7,9,14,24)**...** was NOT His greatest revelation of His power

"God said, 'Let there be light'; and THERE WAS LIGHT. Then God said, 'Let there be a firmament in the midst of the waters, and let it divide the waters from the waters. Thus God made the firmament, and divided the waters which were under the firmament from the waters which were above the firmament; and IT WAS SO. Then God said, 'Let the waters under the heavens be gathered together into one place, and let the dry land appear'; and IT WAS SO."

- **God's Act of <u>REDEMPTION</u>...** The Creator's power is in His *breaking of Himself* for His creation

Matthew 26:38-39 *"Then He said to them, 'My soul is exceedingly sorrowful, even to death. Stay here and watch with Me.' He went a little further and fell on His face, and prayed, saying, 'O My Father, if it is possible, LET THIS CUP PASS FROM ME; nevertheless, not as I will, but as You will.'"*

Luke 22:44 *"Being in AGONY, He prayed more earnestly. And His sweat became like great drops of blood falling down to the ground."*

Hebrews 5:7 *"...who, in the days of His flesh, when He had offered up prayers and supplications, with VEHEMENT CRIES and TEARS to Him who was able to save Him from death, and was heard because of His GODLY FEAR..."*

Matthew 27:46 *"About the 9th hour Jesus cried out with a loud voice, saying, 'Eli, Eli, lama sabachthani?' that is, 'My God, My God, WHY HAVE YOU FORSAKEN ME?'"*

Isaiah 53:5,10 *"...He was wounded for our transgressions, He was bruised for our iniquities; the chastisement for our peace was upon Him, and by His stripes we are healed... It pleased the Lord to crush Him; He has put Him to grief."*

- **God's Power is <u>REVEALED</u> at the <u>CROSS</u>** - it is in *His brokenness* that God's power is revealed

1Corinthians 1:18,27 *"The message of the cross is foolishness to those who are perishing, but to us who are being saved it is the POWER OF GOD. And God has chosen the foolish things of the world to put to shame the wise, and God has chosen the WEAK THINGS of the world to put to shame the things which are mighty."*

Romans 1:16 *"I am not ashamed of the gospel, for it is the POWER OF GOD to salvation for everyone who believes..."*

Philippians 2:8 *"And being found in appearance as a man, He HUMBLED HIMSELF and became obedient to the point of DEATH, even the death of the CROSS."*

- **God's Power is <u>RELEASED</u> through the CROSS** - it is in *our brokenness* that God's power is released

Psalm 147:3 *"He heals the BROKENHEARTED and binds up their sorrows."*

Matthew 5:3 *"Blessed are the POOR IN SPIRIT, for theirs is the kingdom of heaven."*

Luke 4:18 *"The Spirit of the Lord is upon Me, because He has anointed Me to preach the gospel to the POOR. He has sent Me to heal the BROKENHEARTED..."*

Psalm 51:16-17 *"For You do not desire sacrifice, or else I would give it; You do not delight in burnt offering. The sacrifices of God are a BROKEN SPIRIT, a BROKEN and CONTRITE HEART – these, O God, You will not despise."*

Psalm 34:18 *"The Lord is near to those who have a BROKEN HEART, and saves such as have a contrite spirit."*

2Corin. 4:7 *"...we have this treasure in earthen vessels, that the excellency of the POWER may be of God and not of us."*

God's Design = <u>BROKENNESS</u>

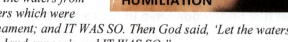

You must break the ...	To free the...	
Clouds	Rain	Genesis 7:11-12
Ground	Crop	Hosea 10:12; Jeremiah 4:3
Grain	Fruit	John 12:24; 1Corinthians 15:36
Bread	Nutrients	Acts 20:11
Body	Blood	Leviticus 17:11; Luke 22:20; 1Corinthians 11:24
Heart	Spirit	Matthew 5:3-4; Luke 4:18
1st man	1st woman	Genesis 2:7, 21-22
Creator	Creation	Matthew 26:26, 20:28; John 6:35; Ephesians 1:7, 2:13

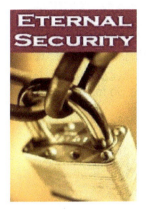

ETERNAL SECURITY: can it impact how I live? 2.9

#1: I can rejoice because God's will is to restore once and for all His broken relationship with His prize creation - me.

#2: Everything is at stake – if my salvation hinges on anything but Christ's finished work on the cross, I am in trouble.

#3: Where there is no assurance of God's acceptance, there is no peace. Where there is no peace, there is no joy. Where there is no joy, I can't love other people.

Charles Stanley, "Eternal Security: Can You be Sure?"[9]

➔ "I was raised in a Pentecostal Holiness Church, where you are taught to believe that salvation is by faith alone, but they do not believe in eternal security and frequently preached against it. At age 12, I made a public confession of faith and received Christ as my Savior. I'll never forget that June morning in 1944, because the overwhelming peace I felt has never left me to this day. But an internal battle raged in me - the problem was I was continually confessing my sins, begging for forgiveness, and hoping I wouldn't die before I had time to repent!

➔ At age 14 I joined the Baptist Church, where I first heard the phrase 'eternal security'. That's when I discovered not everyone believed as I did. But even at 14 I was a diligent student of the Bible, and I was eager to debate with anyone on eternal security. Armed with my Bible verses, no one could make a dent in my theology that you are saved by faith but you can lose your salvation.

➔ When I left for college, I was a staunch believer that a Christian can lose their salvation. Intellectually, I became more persuaded than ever as I saw many peoples' carnal lifestyles – people who claimed to be saved but showed no evidence they knew Jesus Christ.

➔ When I entered Southwestern Theological Seminary, I again hotly debated that you can lose your salvation. But it was here during my intense study of Scripture that my position began to change. I discovered that my salvation through faith alone cannot be reconciled with my belief that I can forfeit my salvation. If I must do something to keep from losing my salvation, salvation would be by faith and works.

➔ It was as if a light came on: I suddenly saw it in Scripture. I wanted to start shouting – I felt like a man freed from prison. I couldn't stop thanking God, especially since I had been wrong all these years. Then it struck me – I had been eternally secure since that day as a 12-year old when I went forward and asked Christ to save me. I realized how little I had really trusted God. **John 8:32** sums it up: *'You shall know the truth, and the truth shall make you free.'* Freedom comes from knowing the truth, bondage comes from missing it."

JOHN: Jesus PROMISES I can't lose my salvation

John 3:16 *"God so loved the world that He gave His only begotten Son, that whosoever believes in Him should not perish but HAVE EVERLASTING LIFE."*

John 3:36 *"He who believes in the Son HAS EVERLASTING LIFE; and he who does not believe in the Son shall not see life, but the wrath of God abides in Him."*

John 5:24 *"Most assuredly, I say to you, he who hears My word and believes in Him who sent Me HAS EVERLASTING LIFE, and shall not come into judgment, but has passed from death into life."*

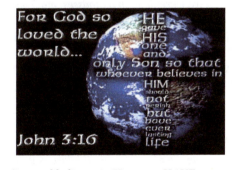

John 6:40 *"And this is the will of Him who sent Me, that everyone who sees the Son and believes in Him may HAVE EVERLASTING LIFE; and I will raise Him up at the last day."*

John 6:47 *"Most assuredly, I say to you, he who believes in Me HAS EVERLASTING LIFE."*

John 8:24 *"I say to you that you will die in your sins; for if you do not believe that I am He, you will die in your sins."*

John 8:51 *"Most assuredly, I say to you, if anyone keeps My word He shall NEVER SEE DEATH."*

John 10:9 *"I am the door. If anyone enters by Me, He WILL BE SAVED, and will go in and out and find pasture."*

John 10:27-30 *"My sheep hear My voice, and I know them, and they follow Me. And I give them eternal life, and THEY SHALL NEVER PERISH; neither shall anyone snatch them out of My hand. My Father, who has given them to Me, is greater then all; no one is able to snatch them out of My Father's hand. I and the Father are one."*

John 11:25-26 *Jesus said to her, "I am the resurrection and the life. He who believes in Me, though he may die, HE SHALL LIVE. And whoever lives and believes in Me SHALL NEVER DIE. Do you believe this?"*

John 17:3 *"And this is eternal life, that they may know You, the only true God, and Jesus Christ whom You have sent."*

8 PROOFS for Eternal Security

#1. Luke 19:10 *"…the Son of Man has come to seek and to save that which was lost."*
If Christ came to seek and to save that which was lost, and yet we can somehow become unsaved – and undo what Christ came to do – shouldn't God take us to heaven the moment we're saved, to insure we make it?

#2. Philippians 4:6 *"Be anxious for nothing, but in everything by prayer and supplication, with thanksgiving, let your requests be made known to God."*
If my salvation is not a settled issue, how can I be anxious for nothing?

#3. John 10:28 *"I give them eternal life, and they shall never perish; neither shall anyone snatch them out of My hand."*
If our salvation is not secure, how can Jesus say about those whom He gives eternal life, "and they shall never perish"? If even one man or woman receives eternal life and then loses it through some sin they commit, won't they perish? And by doing so, wouldn't that make Jesus a liar?

#4. Ephesians 1:13-14 *"In Him you also, after listening to the message of truth, the gospel of your salvation –having also believed, you were SEALED in Him with the Holy Spirit of promise, who is given as a pledge of our inheritance, with a view to the redemption of God's own possession, to the praise of His glory."*
2Corinthians 1:21-22 *"Now He who establishes us with you in Christ and anointed us is God, who also SEALED us and gave us the Spirit in our hearts as a pledge."*
What is the significance of God's seal if it can be continually removed and reapplied? What does it really seal? What is God really promising (pledging) if the promise can be removed?

#5. Revel. 3:5 *"He who overcomes shall be clothed in white garments; I will not erase his name from the book of life."*
Does it make any sense to say that salvation is offered as a solution for our sin, and then turn around and teach that salvation can be taken away because of our sin as well?

> **TRUTH #1:** The "Book of Life" was complete since the foundation of the world (Revel. 13:8, 17:8). God wrote everything before I did anything. I don't get my name added when I trust Him – I was in the Book all along.

#6. Ephesians 2:4-5,8-9 *"But God, who is rich in mercy, because of His GREAT LOVE with which He loved us, even when we were dead in trespasses, made us alive together with Christ (by grace you have been saved)…For by grace you have been saved through faith, and that not of yourselves; it is a gift of God, not of works, lest anyone should boast."*
If my faith maintains my salvation, what must I do to maintain my faith? Not maintaining my faith means I can lose it and thus my salvation. My faith is strengthened by prayer, Bible study, fellowship, evangelism. But if these works maintain my faith, and maintaining my faith is needed for salvation – then wouldn't I conclude that I'm saved by my good works?

> **TRUTH #2:** Faith is not the reason God saves me – Love is (salvation is through faith, not because of it).

#7. Luke 10:19-20 *"Behold, I have given you authority to tread upon serpents and scorpions, and over all the power of the enemy, and nothing shall injure you. Nevertheless do not rejoice in this, that serpents are subject to you, but REJOICE that your names are recorded in heaven."*
Can joy and insecurity coexist? Can I rejoice in a relationship that is only as secure as our behavior is consistent?

#8. Romans 4:5, 5:1 *"But to the one who does not work, but believes in Him who justifies the ungodly, his faith is accounted for righteousness. Having been justified by faith, we have peace with God through our Lord Jesus Christ."*
If my salvation hinges on my consistency of my faith, by what standard do I judge my consistency? Can I have any doubts at all? How long can I doubt? To what degree do I doubt? Is there a divine quota I better not exceed?

> **TRUTH #3:** My act of faith ("believe"), not my maintenance of faith, saves me (faith is the only way the saving work of Christ is applied to the individual. Salvation comes to a person at that moment in time when he or she places their trust in Christ and His death on the cross as the complete payment for their sin).
>
> **TRUTH #4:** Maintaining my faith ("assurance") is a struggle, but JESUS is my security (Christ's faithfulness to Christians is not contingent on their faithfulness to Him).

Chapter 3 God's Will: my Sanctification

15 - Lesson Plan

Lesson		
3.1	Sanctification	
3.2	Proverbs 18:10	"God's Wisdom: seen in His Character"
3.3	Proverbs 22:1	"God's Character: God's Concern"
3.4	Proverbs 21:3	"My Character: God's Definition"
3.5	Proverbs 4:23	"My Character: a heart issue"
3.6	Proverbs 23:26	"My Character: is relational"
3.7	Proverbs 16:3	"My Character: requires renewal"
3.8	Proverbs 20:9	"My Character: fights my nature"
3.9	Romans 6	"My Character: defeats my nature"
3.10	Proverbs 16:3	"My Reverence: my beginning"
3.11	Proverbs 3:34	"My Humility: draws God"
3.12	Proverbs 16:3	"My Submission: reveals my servanthood"
3.13	Proverbs 17:27	"My Meekness: reveals my understanding"
3.14	Proverbs 3:5-6	"My Faithfulness: requires risk"
3.15	Proverbs 3:34	"My Truthfulness: delights God"

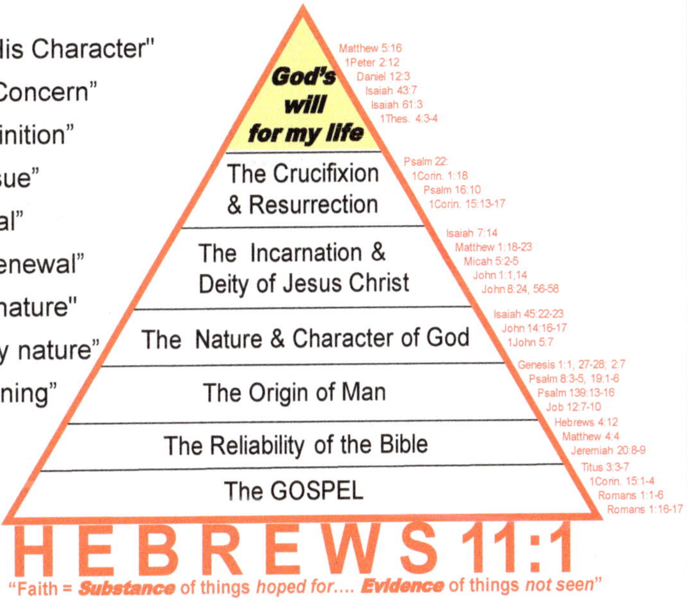
God's will for my life
Matthew 5:16
1Peter 2:12
Daniel 12:3
Isaiah 43:7
Isaiah 61:3
1Thes. 4:3-4
The Crucifixion & Resurrection
Psalm 22:
1Corin. 1:18
Psalm 16:10
1Corin. 15:13-17
The Incarnation & Deity of Jesus Christ
Isaiah 7:14
Matthew 1:18-23
Micah 5:2-5
John 1:1,14
John 8:24, 56-58
The Nature & Character of God
Isaiah 45:22-23
John 14:16-17
1John 5:7
The Origin of Man
Genesis 1:1, 27-28; 2:7
Psalm 8:3-5, 19:1-6
Psalm 139:13-16
Job 12:7-10
The Reliability of the Bible
Hebrews 4:12
Matthew 4:4
Jeremiah 20:8-9
The GOSPEL
Titus 3:3-7
1Corin. 15:1-4
Romans 1:1-6
Romans 1:16-17
HEBREWS 11:1
"Faith = Substance of things hoped for.... Evidence of things not seen"

SANCTIFICATION 3.1 *Greek "hagiasmos"*

For this is the will of God,
Your sanctification.
1 Th. 4:3

1) Separating believers to God, by God (HOLINESS)
   1Thess. 4:3,7 *"For this is the will of God, your sanctification.... for God did not call us to uncleanness, but in HOLINESS."*

2) The relationship with God entered by FAITH in Christ
   Acts 26:18 *"...to open their eyes and to turn them from darkness to light, and from the power of Satan to God, that they may receive forgiveness of sins and an inheritance among those who are sanctified by FAITH in Me."*

3) The SEPARATION of the believer from an evil lifestyle
   Romans 6:19 *"I speak in human terms because of the weakness of your flesh. For just as you presented your members as slaves of uncleanness, and of lawlessness leading to more lawlessness, so now present your members as slaves of righteousness unto SANCTIFICATION."*

4) Must be LEARNED from God, through the teaching of His word
   John 17:17 *"Sanctify them by Your truth. Your word is truth."*

5) Must be earnestly PURSUED by the believer
   Hebrews 12:14 *"PURSUE peace with all men, and holiness, without which no one will see the Lord."*

6) Can't be imputed – it is built upon by FOLLOWING Jesus Christ in obedience to the Word
   Matt 11:29 *"Take My yoke and learn from Me, for I am gentle and lowly in heart, and you will find rest for your souls."*
   John 13:15 *"For I have given you an EXAMPLE, that you should do as I have done to you."*

7) The HOLY SPIRIT = the Agent in sanctification
   2Thes. 2:13 *"But we are bound to give thanks to God always for you, brethren beloved by the Lord, because God from the beginning chose you for salvation through sanctification by the SPIRIT and belief in the truth..."*

> **5 Truths we'll study on Sanctification:**
> #1. Sanctification = Christ *FREED* me from the power of sin
> #2. Sanctification = God *CONFORMS* me into Christ-likeness
> #3. Sanctification = God wants to *FILL* me with the Holy Spirit ("walking dynamite")
> #4. Sanctification = God *GROWS* our relationship by renewing my *CHARACTER*
> #5. Sanctification = God *RENEWS* my character as I yield to His Lordship

#1. Sanctification = Christ freed me from the <u>POWER</u> of sin

Romans 6:6-7, 6:14 *"Knowing this, that our old man was crucified with Him, that the body of sin might be done away with, that we should no longer be slaves of sin. For he who has died has been freed from sin. For SIN SHALL NO LONGER HAVE DOMINION OVER YOU, for you are not under law but under grace."*

Galatians 5:16-18 *"I say then, 'Walk in the Spirit, and you shall not fulfill the lusts of the flesh. For the flesh lusts against the Spirit, and the Spirit against the flesh, and these are contrary to one another, so that you do not do the things that you wish. But if you are led by the Spirit, YOU ARE NOT UNDER THE LAW."*

John 8:34-36 *Jesus answered them, "Most assuredly, I say to you, whoever commits sin is a SLAVE OF SIN.. and a slave does not abide in the house forever, but a son abides forever. Therefore if the SON MAKES YOU FREE, you shall be free indeed."*

Isaiah 61:1 *"He has sent Me (Jesus Christ) to heal the brokenhearted, to proclaim LIBERTY TO THE CAPTIVES, and the OPENING OF THE PRISON TO THOSE WHO ARE BOUND..."*

Hebrews 2:14-15 *"Inasmuch then as the children have partaken of flesh and blood, He likewise shared in the same, that through death HE (JESUS) MIGHT DESTROY HIM WHO HAD THE POWER OF DEATH, that is, the devil, and RELEASE THOSE who through fear of death were all their lifetime subject to bondage."*

#2. Sanctification = God <u>CONFORMS</u> me into "Christ-likeness"

Romans 8:29-30,12:2 *"And we know that all things work together for good to those who love God, to those who are the called according to His purpose. For whom He foreknew He also predestined to be CONFORMED TO THE IMAGE OF HIS SON, the He might be the firstborn among many brethren." "And do not be conformed to this world, but BE TRANSFORMED BY THE RENEWING OF YOUR MIND, that you may prove what is that good and acceptable and perfect WILL OF GOD."*

2Corinthians 3:18 *"But we all, with unveiled face, beholding as in a mirror the glory of the Lord, are being TRANSFORMED INTO THE SAME IMAGE from glory to glory, just as by the Spirit of the Lord."*

Ephesians 4:22-24 *"...that you put off, concerning your former conduct, the old man which grows corrupt according to the deceitful lusts, and BE RENEWED IN THE SPIRIT OF YOUR MIND, and that you put on the new man which was created according to God, in righteousness and holiness."*

> **JESUS: Sanctified (set apart) by the Father to do His will**
>
> • <u>Psalm 40:6-8, John 4:34, John 12:49-50</u> = Jesus knew His Father's will because He listened and obeyed: *"Sacrifice and offering You did not desire; My ears You have opened; burnt offering and sin offering You did not require. Then I said, 'Behold, I come; in the scroll of the Book it is written of Me. I delight to do Your will, O My God, and Your law is within My heart."*
> Jesus said to them, *"My food is to do the will of Him who sent Me, and to finish His work." "For I have not spoken on My own authority; but the Father who sent Me gave Me a command, what I should say and what I should speak. And I know that His command is everlasting life. Therefore, whatever I speak, just as the Father told Me, so I speak."*
>
>
>
> • <u>John 5:30, 15:5, Romans 12:1</u> = willing to make myself nothing so He becomes everything: *"I CAN OF MYSELF DO NOTHING. As I hear, I judge; and My judgment is righteous, because I do not seek My own will but the will of the Father who sent Me." "I am the Vine, you are the branches. He who abides in Me, and I in him, bears much fruit; for WITHOUT ME YOU CAN DO NOTHING."*
> *"I beseech you therefore, brethren, by the mercies of God, that you present your bodies a LIVING SACRIFICE, holy, acceptable to God, which is your reasonable service."*

#3. Sanctification = God wants to <u>FILL</u> me with the Holy Spirit

Ephesians 5:15-18 *"See then that you walk carefully, not as fools but as wise, redeeming the time, because the days are evil. Therefore do not be unwise, but understand what THE WILL OF THE LORD is. And do not be drunk with wine, in which is dissipation, but be FILLED WITH THE SPIRIT."*

2Corinthians 3:17 *"Now THE LORD IS THE SPIRIT, and where the Spirit of the Lord is, there is liberty."*

1Corinthians 2:12-13 *"Now WE HAVE RECEIVED, not the spirit of the world but the Spirit who is from God, that we might know the things which have been freely given to us by God."*

➔ Christians are <u>COMPLETE</u> in Jesus Christ

Colossians. 2:3,9-10 *"...in whom are hidden all the treasures of wisdom and knowledge. For in Him dwells the fullness of the Godhead in bodily form, and YOU ARE COMPLETE IN HIM, who is the head of all rule and authority."*

2Peter 1:3 *".His divine power has given us ALL THINGS that pertain to life and godliness, through the knowledge of Him"*

John MacArthur *(Found: God's Will[4])* "All the richness of truth necessary for salvation, sanctification and glorification is found in Jesus Christ, who Himself is God revealed. Paul is stressing that believers are complete in Jesus in two ways: 1. Positionally = believers have received the imputed perfect righteousness of Christ. 2. His complete sufficiency = believers are eternally secure in their salvation and will persevere and grow because they have all heavenly resources necessary for spiritual maturity."

I must stop praying for what I already have	
"Lord, give me more of your **Spirit**."	1Corinthians 6:19 *"Or do you not know that your body is the temple of the Holy Spirit, who is in you, whom you have from God..."* Romans 8:9 *"You are not in the flesh but in the Spirit, if indeed the Spirit dwells in you... if anyone does not have the Spirit of Christ, he is not His."*
"Lord, give me more **love** for my neighbor."	Romans 5:5 *"...the love of God has been poured out in our hearts by the Holy Spirit who was given to us."*
"Lord, give me more of Your **grace**."	2Corinthians 12:9 *"My grace is sufficient for you, for My strength is made perfect in weakness."*
"Lord, give me **strength** for today."	Philippians 4:13 *"I can do all things through Christ who strengthens me."*
"Lord, **guide** me to do the right thing."	John 16:13 *"...when He, the Spirit of truth, has come, He will guide you into all truth..."*
"Lord, give me **peace** of mind."	Romans 5:1 *"...having been justified by faith, we have peace with God through our Lord Jesus Christ."*
"Lord, give me more **power**."	Acts 1:8 *"...you shall receive power when the Holy Spirit has come upon you"*
James 1:5-6	I must start praying for what He promises to give me
"If any of you lacks WISDOM, let him ASK OF GOD, who gives to all liberally and without reproach, and it will be given to him. But let him ask in FAITH, with no doubting, for he who doubts is like a wave of the sea driven and tossed by the wind. For let not that man suppose that he will receive anything from the Lord; he is a double-minded man, unstable in all his ways."	

➔ ACTS 1:8 Christians have access to the "<u>POWER</u>" of God   Greek word = "*dunamis*" = DYNAMITE

The attitude of many Christians: "I don't have the power to do it (witness, be patient, help someone I dislike)."

The reality of the Gospel: I received the Holy Spirit when He saved me. I am **WALKING DYNAMITE**

The reality of your problem: God promises that the power is there – it's the release of that power that is missing. There is a difference between POSSESSING the Holy Spirit and being **FILLED** with Him.

How He operates in your life: He lives within me, but do I allow Him to release His power, to fill my life, so that I can become what He wills for me? If I am not yielded to the Spirit I do not manifest Christ in my life. The Holy Spirit must permeate my life if I am to **RADIATE** (glorify) Him to others around me.

> **Spirit-filled Christians don't stumble around trying to find out what God wants –**
> **THEY JUST GO: yielding every decision (no matter how trivial) everyday to HIS control**

#4 & #5. Sanctification = Through my character, God <u>GROWS</u> our relationship and <u>RENEWS</u> me

GOD'S <u>CHARACTER</u> = His Will for My Life

This part of the "Faith: Substance & Evidence" series focuses on the SUBSTANCE behind my faith – the Character of God and His will for my life. This entire series is designed to strengthen me with the confidence to "know what I believe", living my beliefs with <u>CONVICTION</u> in an unsaved world that I live in.

How do I really know I'm following God's plan for my life? God says that one day I will stand before Him, and I'm supposed to be ready to give Him an account for how I lived? I want to be ready – HOW?

God's Answer: "I am working *IN YOU* (Philippians 1:6) to mold *YOUR CHARACTER* to that of *MY SON*, so *HIS CHARACTER* is radiated *THROUGH YOU* to those *AROUND YOU*."

When I allow God to work in me, I become a *LIVING WITNESS* to who He is (Matthew 5:16), fulfilling His great commission for me (Mark 16:15) and bringing GLORY to His name.

The Process: **"Climbing the Proverbs Ladder of CHARACTER"**: As the Lord imparts His wisdom in my heart.... my relationship with Him grows.... as He starts molding my character..... to bring Him glory.

CLIMBING THE "PROVERBS LADDER" John 1:51, Gen. 28:12
Living the Life that pleases God

Step	Description	Reference	#
	My Evangelism = fulfills Jesus's vision	Matt. 5:16	4.12
	My Suffering = grows my character	Rom. 5:3-4	4.11
for His glory	God's Suffering = fulfills righteousness	Hebr. 5:8	4.10
	My Diligence = prompts God's promises	Prov. 8:17	4.9
	My Giving = promises God's blessing	Prov. 21:26	4.8
	My Forgiveness = answer to bitterness	Prov. 14:10	4.7
	God's Forgiveness = His gift of love	Prov. 17:9	4.6
	God's Kindness/ Mercy = love in action	Prov. 19:22	4.5
	My Love for God = why I obey	Prov. 3:12	4.4
	God's Love for me = "agape"	Prov. 10:12	4.3
	My Truthfulness = delights Him	Prov. 12:22	3.15
	My Faithfulness = requires risk	Prov. 3:5-6	3.14
by molding my character	My Meekness = my understanding	Prov. 17:27	3.13
	My Submission = my servanthood	Prov. 16:3	3.12
	My Humility = attracts God to me	Prov. 3:34	3.11
	My Reverence = where I begin	Prov. 1:7	3.10
	My Character: can defeat my nature	Romans 6	3.9
	My Character: fights against my nature	Prov. 20:9	3.8
to grow our relationship	My Character: requires renewal	Prov. 28:13	3.7
	My Character: is relational	Prov. 23:26	3.6
	My Character: a heart issue	Prov. 4:23	3.5
	My Character: God's definition	Prov. 21:3	3.4
God puts His wisdom into my heart	God's Character: His concern	Prov. 22:1	3.3
	God's Wisdom: seen in His Character	Prov. 18:10	3.2

GOD'S WISDOM
seen in His MORAL CHARACTER

Proverbs 18:10 *"The NAME of the Lord is a strong tower; the righteous run to it and are safe."*

3.2

NAME = "shêm" = **CHARACTER**, as in expressing someone's honor or fame based on their attributes or qualities; inward **MORAL** quality or integrity that manifests itself in behavior.

- **Is there a difference between someone's nature and their character? How about GOD?**
  "nature" = the inherent, physiological characteristics of people or animals that direct their function and behavior. (example: the nature of fish is to swim and breath underwater, the nature of man is to walk and breath air).

- **How do we define what is MOROAL?**
  Webster's 1990 Dictionary = "living in accordance with an established set of principles of right or wrong conduct; capable of recognizing and then conforming to such principles."

  Webster's 1828 Dictionary = "Relating to the practice, manners or conduct of men as social beings in relation to each other, with reference to right and wrong. The word moral applies to actions that are good or evil, virtuous or vicious, and has reference to the law of God as the standard by which their character is to be determined."

- **What's the difference between morals and ETHICS?**

  - Del Tackett (Truth Project): *"Noah Webster's 1828 dictionary is based on a **biblical** worldview (the definitions are very different than today's Webster dictionary definitions). Morals have to do with an individual's conduct as related to good and evil. Ethics have to do with one's SYSTEM OF APPLICATION of the morals. One would be considered ethical if they live by good moral principles.*

  - R.C. Sproul (Truth Project): *"Morality looks at the verb 'IS'. Ethics looks at the word 'OUGHT'. The distinction has been obscured in our day. People use the term 'morality' and ethics as synonyms. That leads to **statistical** morality. We go around the nation seeing what people are DOING ('is'), rather than seeing if what they are doing conforms to what they OUGHT to be doing (example: if statistics show that cheating on your spouse has become a common practice, then the ethics of fidelity to your spouse is replaced by an acceptable moral practice of adultery). So 'good' ends up being determined by what IS instead of what OUGHT to be."*

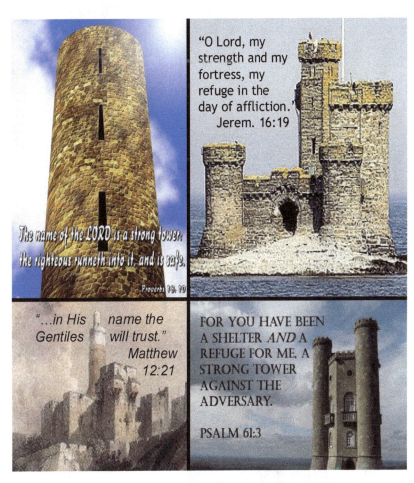

- **What's important = the SOURCE of my ethics (i.e., "system of application of my morals")**

  - Proverbs 23:27 (*"..as a man thinks in his heart, so is he."*)… My own personal morality is comprised of the set of my personal truth claims that I embrace so deeply that I believe they reflect what is really real, and therefore, they drive what I think, how I act and what I feel.

  - My inward (heart) ethical system that I make my own boils down to a **CHOICE** between God's system (as He reveals His ethics in His word, by His very character) and the world's system.

What is God's character like?
Proverbs 30:4 "What is His **NAME**, and what is His **SON'S** name, if you know?

Throughout Book 4, we'll examine...
GOD'S CHARACTER

1) He is just & righteous
(Lesson 2.1)

2) He is holy & pure
(Lesson 2.3)

3) He is reliable
(Lesson 2.7)

4) He is faithful
(Lesson 2.7)

5) He is moral
(Lesson 3.2)

6) He watches over me –
YHWH Roi
(Lesson 3.2)

7) He heals me –
YHWH Rapha
(Lesson 3.2)

8) He shepherds me –
YHWH Raah
(Lesson 3.2)

9) He becomes my
salvation –
YHWH Shua
(Lesson 3.2)

10) He is always there
for me –
YHWH Shammah
(Lesson 3.2)

11) He provides for me –
YHWH Yireh
(Lesson 3.2)

12) He protects me –
YHWH Nissi
(Lesson 3.2)

13) He sanctifies me –
YHWH M'Kaddesh
(Lesson 3.2)

14) He becomes my
righteousness –
YHWH Tsidkenu
(Lesson 3.2)

15) He guards my heart
(Lesson 3.5)

16) He became a
humble servant
(Lesson 3.11)

17) He is meek
(Lesson 3.12)

18) He is truthful -
He hates lying
(Lesson 3.14)

19) He is love
(Lesson 4.3)

20) He is kind & merciful
(Lesson 4.5)

21) He is forgiving
(Lesson 4.6)

22) He is giving
(Lesson 4.8)

23) He is diligent
in pursuing me
(Lesson 4.9)

24) He suffers for
my sake
(Lesson 4.10)

25) He is a rewarder
(Lesson 4.13)

Proverbs 18:10
*"The name of the Lord is a strong tower.
The righteous run to it and are safe."*

11 Names of our God that reveal His <u>MORAL CHARACTER</u>   (who He is)

He *SEES* me	He *HEALS* me	He *SHEPHERDS* me	He *SAVES* me
He is *THERE* for me	He gives me *PEACE*	He *PROVIDES* for me	He *PROTECTS* me
He *SANCTIFIES* me	He is my *RIGHTEOUSNESS*	He is always *WITH* me	

- **YAHWEH ROI**   "The God who sees me"

Genesis 16:13 *"Then she called the name of the Lord who spoke to her, YAHWEH ROI, for she said 'Have I also here seen Him who sees me?"*

Prov. 15:3 *"The eyes of the Lord are in every place, keeping watch on the evil and the good."*

2Chron. 16:9 *"For the eyes of the Lord run to and fro throughout the whole earth, to show Himself strong on behalf of those whose heart is loyal to Him."*

Psalm 139:16 *"Your eyes saw my substance, being yet unformed."*

- **YAHWEH RAPHA**   "The God who heals me"

Exodus 15:26 *"If you diligently heed the voice of the Lord your God and do what is right in His sight, give ear to His commandments and keep all of His statutes, I will put none of the diseases on you which I have brought on the Egyptians. For I am YAHWEH RAPHA."*

Exodus 23:25 *"So you shall serve the Lord your God, and He will bless your bread and your water. And I will take sickness away from the midst of you."*

Isaiah 53:4 *"Surely He has borne our illnesses."*

Matthew 9:35 *"Jesus went about all the cities and villages, teaching in their synagogues, preaching the gospel of the kingdom, and healing every sickness and every disease among the people."*

- **YAHWEH RAAH**   "The God who shepherds (feeds and watches over) me"

Genesis 48:15 *"God, before whom my fathers Abraham and Isaac walked, the God who has fed me all my life long to this day."*

Isaiah 40:10-11 *"The Lord shall come with a strong hand, and His arm shall rule for Him; His reward is with Him, and His work before Him. He will feed His flock like a Shepherd; He will gather the lambs with His arm, and carry them in His bosom, and gently lead those who are with young."*

John 10:11-14 *"I am the good Shepherd. The good shepherd gives His life for the sheep. But he who is a hired man and not the shepherd, one who does not own the sheep, sees the wolf coming and leaves the sheep and flees; and the wolf catches the sheep and scatters them. The hired man flees because he does not care about the sheep. I am the Good Shepherd; and I know My sheep, and am known by My own."*

- **YAHWEH SHUA**   "The God who saves me"

Isaiah 12:2 *"Behold, God is my salvation; I will trust and not be afraid. For YAH, the Lord, is my strength and my song; He also has BECOME MY SALVATION."*

Ps. 118:14,21 *"The Lord is my strength and my song, and He has become my salvation. I will praise You, for You have answered me, and have BECOME MY SALVATION."*

Exodus 15:2 *"The Lord is my strength and my song, and He has BECOME MY SALVATION."*

Matthew 1:21 *"..she will bring forth a Son, and you shall call His name JESUS, for He will save His people from their sins."*

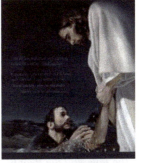

- **YAHWEH SHAMMAH**   "The God who is always there for me"

Ezek. 48:35 *"All the way around shall be 18,000 cubits, and the name of the city from that day shall be YAHWEH SHAMMAH."*

Revel. 21:3 *"I heard a loud voice from heaven saying, 'Behold, the tabernacle of God is with men, and He will dwell with them, and they shall be His people, and God Himself WILL BE WITH THEM and be their God.'"*

Psalm 27:10 *"When my father and my mother forsake me, then the Lord will take care of me."*

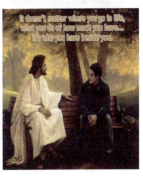

- **YAHWEH SHALOM** "The God who gives me peace"

Judges 6:24 *"So Gideon built an altar to the Lord, and called it YAHWEH SHALOM."*

Isaiah 54:10 *"For the mountains shall depart and the hills be removed, but My kindness shall not depart from you, nor shall My covenant of PEACE be removed", says the Lord, who has mercy on you."*

Colossians 1:19-20 *"It pleased the Father that in Him all the fullness should dwell, and by Him to reconcile all things to Himself, by Him, whether things on earth or things in heaven, having made PEACE through the BLOOD OF HIS CROSS.."*

Isaiah 53:5 *"...the chastisement for OUR PEACE was upon Him..."*

Romans 5:1 *"...we have PEACE with God through our Lord Jesus Christ."*

- **YAHWEH YIREH** "The God who provides for me"

Genesis 22:14 *"And Abraham called the name of the place, "YAHWEH YIREH", as it is said to this day, "in the mount of the Lord it shall be provided."*

Psalm 23:1 *"The Lord is my shepherd, I shall not LACK..."*

Eph. 3:20 *"Now to Him who is able to do exceedingly abundantly above all that we ask or think..."*

Phil. 4:19 *"And my God shall supply all your need according to His riches in glory by Christ Jesus."*

- **YAHWEH NISSI** "The God who protects me"

Exodus:17:15 *"And Moses built an altar and called its name YAHWEH NISSI."*

Exodus:14:13-14 *Moses said to the people, "Do not be afraid. Stand still, and see the salvation of the Lord, which He will accomplish for you today. For the Egyptians whom you see today, you shall see again no more forever. The Lord shall FIGHT FOR YOU, and you shall hold your peace."*

Psalm 27:1 *"The Lord is my light and my salvation – whom shall I fear? The Lord is the strength of my life – of whom shall I be afraid?"*

Isaiah 41:10 *"Fear not, for I am with you. Be not dismayed, for I am your God. I will strengthen you, yes, I will uphold you with My righteous right hand."*

Romans 8:37 *".. in all these things we are MORE THAN CONQUERORS through Him who loved us."*

- **YAHWEH M'KADDESH** "The God who sanctifies me"

Lev. 20:7 *"Sanctify yourselves therefore, and BE HOLY, for I am the Lord your God."*

Ezek. 37:28 *"The nations shall know that I, the Lord, sanctify Israel, when My sanctuary is in their midst forevermore."*

John 17:17 *"Sanctify them by Your truth. Your word is truth."*

1Thes. 5:23 *"Now may the God of peace Himself SANCTIFY YOU completely; and may your whole spirit, soul and body be preserved blameless at the coming of our Lord Jesus Christ."*

- **YAHWEH TSIDKENU** "The God who is my righteousness"

Jerem. 23:5-6 *"Behold, the days are coming, says the Lord, that I will raise to David a Branch of righteousness; a King shall reign and prosper, and execute judgment and righteousness in the earth. In His days Judah will be saved, and Israel will dwell safely. Now this is His name by which He will be called: YAHWEH TSIDKENU."*

2Corin. 5:21 *"He made Him who knew no sin to be sin for us, that we might become the RIGHTEOUSNESS OF GOD in Him."*

Rom. 3:21-26 *"The righteousness of God apart from the law is revealed, being witnessed by the Law and the Prophets, even the righteousness of God which is through faith in Jesus Christ to all and on all who believe. For there is no difference; for all have sinned and fallen short of the glory of God, being justified freely by His grace through the redemption that is in Christ Jesus, whom God set forth to be a propitiation by His blood, through faith, to DEMONSTRATE HIS RIGHTEOUSNESS, because in His forbearance God has passed over the sins that were previously committed, to demonstrate at the present time HIS RIGHTEOUSNESS, that He might be JUST and the justifier of the one who has faith in Jesus."*

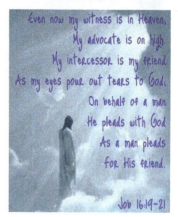

PSALM 20:7 "Some men trust in chariots, and some in horses; but we will remember the NAME of the Lord our God."

The Euthyphro Dilemna: How could God be the Source of "Good"?

William Lane Craig (1949 -   ): PhD Philosophy, Univ. of Birmingham ; Prof. of Philosophy, Talbot School of Theology, Biola Univ.; Authored or edited over 30 books, with Craig's primary contribution to philosophy of religion is his defense of two major positions that are used in his defense of the Christian faith: 1) Resurrection of Jesus Christ, and 2) The Kalam Cosmological Argument. He is a very popular public debater, being very much in demand at universities to take the Christian position against the New Atheists.

The information below is from Dr.Craig's website, "Reasonable Faith", in the 'Q&A' section, and is his response to Question #44 on the "Euthyphro Dilemna".

Question: "I wondered if you could help me out with some problems I'm having in dealing with the Euthyphro dilemma. As you know, the Euthyphro dilemma asks something along the lines of: 'Is the good good because God approves it, or does God approve it because it's good?'

EUTHYPHRO DILEMMA

Plato's dialouge Euthyphro is centered around two men, Euthyphro and Socrates, who discuss the Divine Command Theory. "Divine Command Theory is the view that morality is somehow dependent upon God, and that moral obligation consists in obedience to God's commands."¹

Socrates' (modified) question to Euthyphro:

IS SOMETHING MORALLY RIGHT BECAUSE GOD COMMANDS IT, OR DOES GOD COMMAND IT BECAUSE IT IS MORALLY RIGHT?

Right because God commands it
This conclusion would indicate that God has determined what is right or wrong arbitrarily and no moral principle is self-evident.

God commands it because it is right
This conclusion would indicate that what is morally right is independent of God's commands. Moral standards are sovereign from God and there is morality without God.

Valid moral philosophy cannot be contingent on arbitrary standards. The alternative conclusion means God is neither necessary nor sufficient for morality. This Socratic argument invalidates the Divine Command Theory as an effective moral philosophy.

The theist doesn't want to say that the Good is good simply because God happens to approve of it, since this makes morality arbitrary (call this Horn A). Nor does he want to say that God approves the Good because it is, in fact, good, since this seems to entail the existence of standards of goodness outside of God (call this Horn B).

The theist splits the horns of the dilemma by saying God is necessarily good, and **the source and standard of the Good is God's very nature**. On one hand, this avoids Horn B, since goodness, rather than existing outside of God, is part of God's very nature (and in fact depends upon Him for its existence). And it avoids Horn A, since God's will isn't arbitrary, but operates according to a definite moral standard (i.e. God's necessarily good nature).

But it seems that the atheist can now reformulate the dilemma to ask: 'Is God's nature good because of the way God happens to be, or is it good because it matches up to some external standard of goodness?'

It seems to me that the answer to the reformulated dilemma has to involve something like the claim that God's nature couldn't be anything but good - i.e. that God's nature doesn't just 'happen' to be a certain way. But I'm not sure what it means to say this, since unless we have a concept of the Good outside of God, this doesn't seem to amount to much, in the sense that it doesn't seem to place any restrictions on God's nature. I suspect the concept of possible worlds might be helpful here. But I'm not sure how or why.

<u>My suggestion for an argument would go something like this</u>:
(1) God is, by definition, a maximally great being.
(2) This entails His being metaphysically necessary and morally perfect.
(3) Therefore, by (2), God exists in all possible worlds.
(4) But, if moral values are objective, moral perfection tends towards a unique, maximal set of moral values.
(5) So, by (1), (3) & (4), it follows that God has the same moral character in every possible world.
(6) Therefore God's nature is good neither because of the way He happens to be nor because of His fitness with reference to an external standard of goodness.
—which answers the reformulated dilemma.

This sounds sort of OK to me. But I'm not convinced about (4). I'm also concerned that I've thought too hard about this and am starting to talk rubbish at this point. I seem to be going round in circles in my head. If you could spell things out very clearly and simply for me, I'd be extremely grateful.... Thx again! James

Dr. WL Craig Answer:

I think your intuitions are right on target, James! The argument you give just needs some adjustment. When the atheist says, "Is God's nature good because of the way God happens to be, or is it good because it matches up to some external standard of goodness?"...

The second horn of the dilemma represents nothing new - it's the same as the second horn in the original dilemma, namely, that God approves something because it's good, and we've already rejected that.

So the question is whether we're stuck on the first horn of the dilemma.

Well, if by "happens to be" the atheist means that God's moral character is a contingent property of God, that is to say, a property God could have lacked, then the obvious answer is, "No."

God's moral character is essential to Him; that's why we said it was part of His nature. To say that some property is essential to God is to say that there is no possible world in which God could have existed and lacked that property. God didn't just happen by accident to be loving, kind, just, and so forth. He is that way essentially.

You needn't worry about "what it means to say this, since unless we have a concept of the Good outside of God, this doesn't seem to amount to much." For this is to confuse moral ontology with moral semantics.

Our concern is with moral ontology, that is to say, the foundation in reality of moral values. Our concern is not with moral semantics, that is to say, the meaning of moral terms.

The theist is quite ready to say that we have a clear understanding of moral vocabulary like "good," "evil," "right," and so on, without reference to God. Thus, it is informative to learn that "God is essentially good."

Too often opponents of the moral argument launch misguided attacks upon it by confusing moral ontology with either moral semantics or, even more often, moral epistemology (how we come to know the Good).

If it be asked why God is the paradigm and standard of moral goodness, then I think premise (1) of your argument gives the answer: God is the greatest conceivable being, and it is greater to be the paradigm of goodness than to conform to it.

Your premise (2) is also true, which is why God can serve as the foundation of necessary moral truths, *i.e.*, moral truths which hold in every possible world.

I'm not sure what you mean by premise (4); but I think it's dispensable. All you need to say is that moral values (or at least many of them) are not contingent, but hold in every possible world.

Then God will ground these values in every possible world. That seems to me to settle the issue. So far from talking rubbish, it seems to me that you have directed us toward the correct answer!

**Quoting Dr. Craig once again from his "Reasonable Faith" website
(Question #261 Keeping Moral Epistemology and Moral Ontology Distinct, April 15, 2012)**

"The claim that moral values and duties are rooted in God is a Meta-Ethical claim about Moral Ontology, not about Moral Linguistics or Epistemology. It is fundamentally a claim about the objective status of moral properties, not a claim about the meaning of moral sentences or about the justification or knowledge of moral principles.

I'm convinced that keeping the distinction between moral epistemology and moral ontology clear is the most important task in formulating and defending a moral argument for God's existence of the type I defend.

A proponent of that argument will agree quite readily (and even insist) that we do not need to know or even believe that God exists in order to discern objective moral values or to recognize our moral duties.

Affirming the ontological foundations of objective moral values and duties in God similarly says nothing about how we come to know those values and duties. The theist can be genuinely open to whatever epistemological theories his secular counterpart proposes for how we come to know objective values and duties.

"Moral Ontology" = The foundation in reality of moral values. To say that God's commands constitute our moral duties is a claim of moral ontology.

"Moral Semantics" = The actual meaning of moral terms. It is always the right thing, in any discussion or debate over good versus evil, to make sure we understand what each of us, means by our terms.

"Moral Epistemology" = How people come to know what is objectively good. How we come to know our moral duties, the matter of moral epistemology, is irrelevant to any argument about God's existence."

Argument #10 for God = *The OBJECTIVE MORAL LAW*
The Existence of Objective Moral Law points to an intrinsically worthy Moral Law Giver

> "Premise #1 = If God does not exist, objective Moral Values and Duties do not exist.
> Premise #2 = Objective Moral Values and Duties exist.
> Conclusion = Therefore, God exists."

This argument is explained by Ravi Zacharias in his article 'Nonsense or New Life? Is the Christian faith intellectual nonsense? Does God really transform us?', written on May 9, 2012 which I quote in full below:

"'If God exists and takes an interest in the affairs of human beings, his will is not inscrutable,' writes Sam Harris about the 2004 tsunami in Letter to a Christian Nation. *The only thing inscrutable here is that so many otherwise rational men and women can deny the unmitigated horror of these events and think this is the height of moral wisdom. In his article "God's Dupes," Harris argues, 'Everything of value that people get from religion can be had more honestly, without presuming anything on insufficient evidence. The rest is self-deception, set to music.' Oxford zoologist Richard Dawkins similarly suggests that the idea of God is a virus, and we need to find software to eradicate it. Somehow if we can expunge the virus that led us to think this way, we will be purified and rid of this bedeviling notion of God, good, and evil. Along with a few others, these atheists call for the banishment of all religious belief. 'Away with this nonsense' is their battle cry. In return, they promise a world of new hope and unlimited horizons once we have shed this delusion of God.*

I have news for them, however—news to the contrary. The reality is that the emptiness that results from the loss of the transcendent is stark and devastating, philosophically and existentially. Indeed, the denial of an objective moral law, based on the compulsion to deny the existence of God, results ultimately in the denial of evil itself. Furthermore, one would like to ask Dawkins: Are we morally bound to remove that virus? Somehow he himself is, of course, free from the virus and can therefore input our moral data. In an attempt to escape what they call the contradiction between a good God and a world of evil, atheists try to dance around the reality of a moral law (and hence, a moral law giver) by introducing terms like "evolutionary ethics." The one who raises the question against God in effect plays God while denying God exists.

Now one may wonder: Why do you actually need a moral law giver if you have a moral law? The answer is because the questioner and the issue he questions always involves the **essential value of a person**. *You can never talk of morality in abstraction. Persons are implicit to the question and the object of the question. In a nutshell, positing a moral law without a moral law giver would be equivalent to raising the question of evil without a questioner. So you cannot have a moral law unless the moral law itself is intrinsically woven into personhood, which means it demands an intrinsically worthy person if the moral law itself is valued. And that person can only be God.*

In reality, our inability to alter what is actual frustrates our grandiose delusions of being sovereign over everything. Yet the truth is we cannot escape the existential rub by running from a moral law. Objective moral values exist only if God exists. Is it all right, for example, to mutilate babies for entertainment? Every reasonable person will say "no." **We know that objective moral values do exist. Therefore, God must exist.** *Examining those premises and their validity presents a very strong argument.*

Of course, the world does not understand what the absoluteness of the moral law is all about. Some get caught, some don't get caught. Yet who of us would like our hearts exposed on the front page of the newspaper today? Have there not been days and hours when like the apostle Paul, you've struggled within yourself, and said, "I do not understand what I do. For what I want to do I do not do, but what I hate I do…. What a wretched man I am! Who will rescue me from this body of death?" (Romans 7:15, 24). **Each of us knows this tension and conflict within if we are honest with ourselves.**

In that spirit, we ought to take time to reflect seriously upon the question, "Has God truly wrought a miracle in my life? Is my own heart proof of the supernatural intervention of God?" In the West where we go through seasons of new-fangled theologies, the whole question of "lordship" plagued our debates for some time as we asked, is there such a thing as a minimalist view of conversion? "We said the prayer and that's it." Yet how can there be a minimalist view of conversion when conversion itself is a maximal work of God's grace? "Old things are passed away; behold, all things are become new" (2 Corinthians 5:17). In a strange way we have minimized every sacred commitment and made it the lowest common denominator. What might my new birth mean to me?

That is a question we seldom ask. **Who was I before God's work in me, and who am I now?** *The first entailment of coming to know the God of transformation is the new hungers and new pursuits that are planted within the human will. I well recall that dramatic change in my own way of thinking. There were new longings, new hopes, new dreams, new fulfillments, but most noticeably a new will to do what was God's will. This new affection of heart—the love of God wrought in us through the Holy Spirit—expels all other old seductions and attractions.*

The one who knows Jesus Christ begins to see that her own misguided heart is impoverished and in need of constant submission to the will of the Lord—spiritual surrender. **The hallmark of conversion is to see one's own spiritual poverty.** *Arrogance and conceit ought to be inimical to the life of the believer. A deep awareness of one's own new hungers and longings is a convincing witness both to God and God's grace within."*

Examining Dr. Zacharias's Logic that the existence of Evil demonstrates that God exists

In many of his Q&A sessions at universities around the country, Ravi Zacharias is often asked "If God is good, why does evil exist?", or "How can an omnipotent, loving God allow so much evil and suffering in the world?" This age-old question was asked by the philosopher Epicurus, and is still asked today. The real question we need to first ask is "*Does the reality of evil in our world serve as evidence that God does not exist?*"

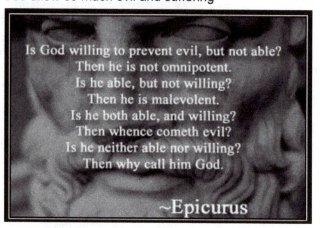

Once we've examined that question, we can ask the second question: "Why does God allow evil and suffering?" Let's break down Dr. Zacharias's answer that you cannot have a moral law without a moral law-giver.

Dr Zacharias point #1 = *"If you believe there is such a thing as good and evil, you must then posit a moral law on the basis of which to distinguish such."*

Dr Zacharias point #2 = *"If there is a moral law, then there must be a moral law-giver."*

Dr Zacharias point #3 = *"Now one may wonder: why do you actually need a moral law giver if you have a moral law? The answer is because the questioner and the issue he or she questions always involve the essential value of a person. You can never talk of morality in abstraction. Persons are implicit to the question and the object of the question. In a nutshell, positing a moral law without a moral law giver would be equivalent to raising the question of evil without a questioner. So you cannot have a moral law unless the moral law itself is intrinsically woven into personhood, which means it demands an intrinsically worthy person if the moral law itself is valued. And that person can only be God."*

1) Issues of morality are uniquely human – they are centered around the intrinsic VALUE of a person.
Ravi says above in point #3 that "*the questioner and the issue he or she questions always involve the essential value of a person.*" We only say it is evil for God to allow "bad" things to happen to people because ① we consider people intrinsically valuable. For example, children are not like our pets, that are our property. They are not as valuable as human beings, whether or not they are part of our immediate family. To illustrate further, if someone's dog were to savagely bite a 2-year old in the face, most of us would think it right that we put down the dog, regardless of how well behaved it is. But if a 2-year old savagely bites a dog in the face, no one would suggest we should put down the 2-year old. What's the difference? We all know our pets are property, but children have intrinsic value, whether they are part of our family or not. They are persons, not property.

2) The intrinsic VALUE of a person is the Foundation of Moral Laws.
Ravi again says in point #3 that "*you cannot have a moral law unless the moral law itself is intrinsically woven into personhood*". But the concept of "value" is relative, based on the one who decides to call something or someone valuable. Webster's Dictionary defines it as "attributing relative worth or merit to something." So the question becomes: is the value of each person absolutely recognized as binding on all people everywhere, regardless of time, culture or situation? It's back to the definition of "ethics ("ought")", the "application of a moral system". ② We hopefully all recognize that all people *ought* to be intrinsically valuable. So where does this sense of the "oughtness" of value of a person come from?

3) The intrinsic VALUE of a person demands the existence of God.
Ravi concludes in point #3 that "*it (moral law) demands an intrinsically worthy person if the moral law itself is valued. And that person can only be God.*" ③ So if the moral law must be based on the intrinsic value of all persons everywhere and at all times and in every situation, how could we possibly arrive at it subjectively? Could each of our relative ideas on morality all sinc up, or would we end up with multiple ideas of how to apply the moral law based on the situation or the people involved? An absolute standard for the worthiness of all persons, as Ravi explains, demands "an intrinsically worthy person." This "person" must be in themselves, by their very essence of who they are, worthy of high value." And Ravi claims there is only one real candidate for such a person – the personal God of the Bible.

HABAKKUK 2:13 *"You are of purer eyes than to behold evil, and cannot look on wickedness"*

C. S. Lewis ('Mere Christianity')[6]: 3 Arguments for the Objective Moral Law

> **Argument #1: Implied Practice** (people are inconsistent moral subjectivists)
> 1) If *ethics* ('the system of application of morals') is subjective, people view actions they consider "wrong" to only be wrong from their point of view.
> 2) But without exception, people view wrongs against themselves as actions that are really wrong.
> 3) Therefore moral values are objective and not subjective.
>
> "Whenever you find a man who says he does not believe in a real Right and Wrong, you will find the same man going back on this a moment later. He may break his promise to you, but if you try breaking it to him he will be complaining 'It's not fair' before you can say Jack Robinson. A nation may say treaties do not matter, but then, next minute, they spoil their case by saying that the particular treaty they want to break was an unfair one. But if treaties do not matter, and if there is no such thing as Right and Wrong--in other words, if there is no Law of Nature--what is the difference between a fair treaty and an unfair one? *Have they not let the cat out of the bag and shown that, whatever they say, they really know the Law of Nature just like anyone else?*"

Norman Geisler[18]: *"If you want to get to the heart of the matter and find out what someone really believes about values, find out what his expectations are. A person can easily say that people are of no greater value than things, but he will balk if you treat him like a cigarette butt and step on him. He still expects to be treated like a person with VALUE, even if he denies that worth with his words. Even someone who claims there are no values still values the right to his opinion and expects you to do the same. This fact helps us greatly in affirming ABSOLUTE VALUES because it makes values actually undeniable. Whenever someone denies absolute values, they expect to be treated as a person of absolute value."*

The obviousness of objective moral values = peoples' claim to have rights

If I have rights, then there is an objectively binding MORAL obligation on others to allow me to exercise those rights. Otherwise, the idea of rights makes no sense. If I have a right to life, that only makes sense if you have a moral obligation not to kill me.

> **Argument #2 = Underlying Moral Consensus** (people have consistent moral principles)
> 1) If morality were subjective, we'd find major differences of fundamental principles between moral codes.
> 2) But, although there are differences in moral codes between different times or countries, the differences are not very great - you can recognize the same law running through them all. The differences are around beliefs about fact rather than what constitutes right moral behavior.
> 3) Therefore, morality is objective rather than subjective.
>
> *"I only ask the reader to think what a totally different morality would mean. Think of a country where people were admired for running away in battle, or where a man felt proud of doublecrossing all the people who had been kindest to him. You might as well imagine a country in where two and two made five. Men have differed as regards what people you ought to be unselfish to—whether it was only your own family, or your fellow countrymen, or everyone. But they have always agreed that you ought not to put yourself first. Selfishness has never been admired. Men have differed as to whether you should have one wife or four. But they have always agreed that you must not simply have any woman you like."*

C.S. Lewis uses the example of putting witches to death to illustrate his point #2 above: *"...though the differences between people's ideas of Decent Behavior often make you suspect that there is no real natural Law of Behavior at all, yet the things we are bound to think about these differences really prove just the opposite... I have met people who exaggerate the differences, because they have not distinguished between differences of morality and differences of behavior about FACTS. For example, one man said to me, '300 years ago people in England were putting witches to death. Was that what you call the Rule of Human Nature or Right Conduct?' But surely the reason we do not execute witches is that we do not believe there are such things. If we did – if we really thought that there were people going about who sold themselves to the devil and received supernatural powers from him in return and were using these powers to kill their neighbors or drive them mad or bring bad weather, surely we would all agree that if anyone deserved the death penalty, then these filthy quislings did. There is no difference in moral principle here: the difference is simply about MATTER OF FACT. It might be a great advance in knowledge not to believe in witches: there is no moral advance in not executing them when you do not think they are there. You would not call a man humane for ceasing to set mousetraps if he did so because he believed there were no mice in the house."*

> **Argument #3 = Morality is Measurable** (people know when moral behavior improves or degrades)
> 1) If moral values are subjective, then moral codes cannot improve or degrade, since there is no objective standard by which to judge one code better than another.
> 2) But the work of people like Pol Pot, Adolf Hitler, or Osama Bin Laden versus Martin Luther King, William Wilberforce or Mother Teresa shows that moral codes can be made either more evil or more good.
> 3) Therefore, moral values are objective rather than subjective.

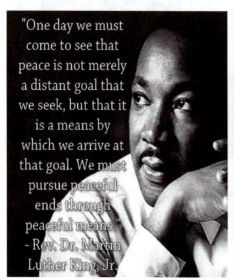

Morally Good: Risking your life to save another

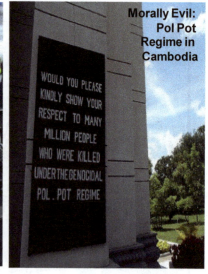

Morally Evil: Pol Pot Regime in Cambodia

GOD'S CHARACTER
is His Concern

Proverbs 22:1 *"A GOOD NAME is to be chosen rather than great riches."*

3.3

- **Character = *"shĕm"* = NAME, as in expressing someone's attributes or qualities.**

Proverbs 18:10 *"The NAME of the Lord is a strong tower; the righteous run to it and are safe."*

Isaiah 26:8 *"O Lord, we have waited for You; the desire of our soul is for YOUR NAME."*

Leviticus 19:12 *"...you shall not swear by MY NAME falsely, nor shall you profane the NAME of God: I am the Lord."*

Exodus 20:7 *"You shall not take the NAME of the Lord your God in vain, for the Lord will not hold him guiltless who takes His name in vain."*

- **"vain" = hollow or empty, without meaning or significance**
- **God's character is HOLINESS – it is so important to Him, that He made it 1 of the 10 commandments!**

Leviticus 10:1-3 *"Then Nadab and Abihu, the sons of Aaron, each took his censer and put fire in it, put incense on it, and offered profane fire before the Lord, which He had not commanded them. So fire went out from the Lord and devoured them, and they died before the Lord. Then Moses said to Aaron, 'This is what the Lord spoke, saying, "By those who come near Me, I MUST BE REGARDED AS HOLY; and before all the people I must be glorified."' So Aaron held his peace."*

Proverbs 27:21   *"A man is valued by what others say about him."*

EZEKIEL 36:20-28   God GUARDS how we show His character to others

"When they came to the nations, wherever they went, they profaned MY HOLY NAME – when they said of them, 'These are the people of the Lord, and yet they have gone out of His land.' But I had concern for MY HOLY NAME, which the house of Israel had profaned among the nations wherever they went.

Therefore say to the house of Israel, 'Thus says the Lord God: "I do not do this for your sake, O house of Israel, but for MY HOLY NAME'S sake, which you have profaned among the nations wherever you went. And I will sanctify MY GREAT NAME, which has been profaned among the nations, which you have profaned in their midst; and the nations shall know that I am the Lord", says the Lord God, "when I am hallowed in you before their eyes.

For I will take you from among the nations, gather you out of all countries, and bring you into your own land. Then I will sprinkle clean water on you, and you shall be clean; I will cleanse you from all your filthiness and from all your idols. I will give you a NEW HEART and put a NEW SPIRIT within you, I will take the heart of stone out of your flesh and give you a heart of flesh. I will put MY SPIRIT within you and cause you to walk in My statutes, and you will keep My judgments and do them.

Then you shall dwell in the land that I gave to your fathers; you shall be MY PEOPLE, and I WILL BE YOUR GOD."

EXODUS 9:13-16, 29:45-46   God puts His character on DISPLAY - He is a Personal Savior

"Then the Lord said to Moses, 'Rise early in the morning and stand before Pharaoh, and say to Him, "Thus says the Lord God of the Hebrews: 'Let My people go, that they may serve Me, for at this time I will send all My plagues to your very heart, and on your servants and on your people, THAT THEY MAY KNOW THAT THERE IS NONE LIKE ME IN ALL THE EARTH. Now if I had stretched out My hand and struck you and your people with pestilence, then you would have been cut off from the earth. But indeed for this purpose I have raised you up, that I may show My power in you, and that MY NAME MAY BE DECLARED IN ALL THE EARTH."

"I will dwell among the children of Israel and will be their God. And they shall know that I am the Lord their God, who brought them out of the land of Egypt, that I MAY DWELL AMONG THEM. I am the Lord their God."

The Father's character: revealed in His **ACTIONS**

Psalm 23:3 *"He leads me in the paths of righteousness for HIS NAME'S SAKE."*

Isaiah 43:25 *"I, even I, am He who blots out your transgressions for MY OWN SAKE; I will not remember your sins."*

Jeremiah 14:7,21 *"O Lord, though our iniquities testify against us, do it for YOUR NAME'S SAKE; Do not abhor us, for YOUR NAME'S SAKE; do not disgrace the throne of Your glory."*

The Father's character: revealed in the character of His **SON**

Matthew 6:9 *"Our Father, who art in heaven, hallowed be THY NAME."*

John 12:27-28 *"Now My soul is troubled, and what shall I say? 'Father, save Me from this hour?' But for this purpose I came to this hour. Father, glorify YOUR NAME."*

Philippians 2:9-11 *"God has highly exalted Him and given Him the name which is above every name, that at the NAME OF JESUS every knee should bow, of those that are in heaven, and of those on the earth, and of those under the earth, and that every tongue should confess that Jesus Christ is Lord, to the GLORY OF GOD THE FATHER."*

1Peter 2:23 *"...who, when He was reviled, did not revile in return; when He suffered, He did not threaten, but committed Himself to Him who judges righteously."*

The Father's character: revealed in the character of His **CHILDREN**

Isaiah 61:1-3 *"The Lord has sent Me to heal the brokenhearted, to proclaim liberty to the captives, and the opening of the prisons to those who are bound.....that they may be called trees of righteousness, the PLANTINGS OF THE LORD, that HE MAY BE GLORIFIED."*

Matthew 5:16 *"Let YOUR LIGHT so shine before men, that they may see your good works and GLORIFY YOUR FATHER in heaven."*

My character: revealed by my **ACTIONS**

Proverbs 21:3 *"To DO RIGHTEOUSNESS and JUSTICE is more acceptable to the Lord than sacrifice."*

Proverbs 20:11 *"Even a child is KNOWN BY HIS DEEDS, by whether what he does is pure and right."*

Proverbs 10:9 *"He who WALKS WITH INTEGRITY walks securely, but he who perverts his ways will become known."*

My character: defined by what's on the **INSIDE**

Proverbs 23:7 *"For AS A MAN THINKS IN HIS HEART, so is he."*

Proverbs 27:19 *"As in water face reveals face, so A MAN'S HEART REVEALS THE MAN."*

Proverbs 4:23 *"Keep your HEART with all diligence, for OUT OF IT spring the issues of life."*

PSALM 15: "Character is the key to **RELATIONSHIP**"

<u>TRUTH #1</u>: God's character, living within us in the Person of Jesus, sustains and nurtures us (John 14:23, Col. 1:27). But that doesn't mean everyone has the same intimacy with the Father – why not?

<u>TRUTH #2</u>: Psalm 15: "A person of character knows God intimately"

- There is a correlation between our character and our ability to know God intimately.
- The person who pursues character gains the privilege of experiencing a special relationship with the Father.
- Psalm 15 describes the difference between knowing God from a distance and knowing Him intimately.
- vs. 1: the Psalm begins by asking who is closest to the Father (who has an "inside track" to God Himself)?
- vs. 2-5: the answer to vs. 1 is "those with the character traits that God desires":
  - Their walk is blameless, they do what is right, and they tell the truth (verse 2)
  - They don't gossip nor slander others, they don't mistreat people (verse 3)
  - They side with those who are right, they keep their word (verse 4)
  - They lend money to the needy without interest, they don't take advantage for personal gain (verse 5)

Andy Stanley[11], "The REAL YOU"

- *"Your character is who you really are. It will impact how much you accomplish in this life. It will determine whether or not you are worth knowing. It will make or break every one of your relationships.*
- *Your character is instrumental in establishing how long you will be able to hold on to the fortune afforded you by hard work. Your character is the internal script that will determine your response to failure, success, mistreatment, and pain. It reaches into every single facet of your life. It is more far-reaching than your talent, your education, your background, or your network of friends. Those things can open doors for you, but your character will determine what happens once you pass through those doors.*
- *Your good looks and net worth may get you married; your character will keep you married. Your God-given reproductive system may enable you to produce children; your character will determine your ability to relate to and communicate with those children.*
- *Who will you be in 5 years? 10 years? I'm not referring to your role or job title. For just a moment, lay aside the dreams that involve your career or net worth. I'm talking about what you hope to find on the inside. What kind of person do you hope to become? Today, you took a step. You either moved closer to or further away from what you hope to be. Most people moved further away. A handful overcame the negative inertia of this fallen world and moved forward. But nobody – nobody – stood still.*
- *There are things that can put you at a disadvantage in the starting blocks of life. You don't choose your starting point. But you do have the opportunity and responsibility to choose where you end up. Character is not as much about what you are as it is what you are becoming. It is not an issue of where you are as it is where you're headed.*
- *And the development of your character is not a solo flight. It is not a 'be all you can be' kind of thing. The truth is, most of us are being all we can be. And that's the problem. Being all we can be isn't enough. We need to be what we aren't, and, left to our own devices, we can't become anything other than what we are.*
- *And so our merciful heavenly Father smiles and offers a very large hand...Romans 8:29,31 "For those He foreknew He also predestined to be conformed to the likeness of His Son...If God is for us, who can be against us?"*

My CHARACTER
God's definition

Proverbs 21:3 *"To DO righteousness and justice is more acceptable to the Lord than sacrifice."*

3.4

The Problem: Our cultural definition of Character is <u>SUBJECTIVE</u> (a "moving target")

- Everyone agrees that character is crucial – its something everyone expects from others. Without a clear definition, a "target to shoot for", we get easily deceived into thinking we are men and women of character, and that its everyone else who has a problem.
- My definition of character is whatever comes naturally to me, and character is what I wish I saw more of in you!
  - people with "character" behave friendly or nicely to others
  - people with "character" take a stand for their beliefs (nevermind the rightness or wrongness of those beliefs)
- C.S. Lewis[6]: *"Human beings all over the earth have this curious idea that they ought to behave in a certain way, and they can't really get rid of it. But whenever you find a man who says he doesn't believe in right or wrong, you will find the same man going back on this a moment later. He may break his promise to you, but if you try breaking one to him he'll be complaining, 'Its not fair'..."*

The Solution: the Biblical definition of Character is <u>OBJECTIVE</u> (a "set standard")

- Biblical character = has its source in the nature of the CREATOR, NOT the behavior patterns of mankind.
- Good Character = simply a reflection of God's character (the Father, Son and Holy Spirit)
  - God's character isn't meant to be a picture of the real thing – it is the real thing.
  - Because God's character is the real thing: we find ourselves ACCOUNTABLE to it.

  Isaiah 40:25 *"To whom then will you liken Me, or to whom shall I be equal?" says the Holy One.*
  John 14:9 *"Jesus said to him, 'Have I been with you so long, and yet you have not known Me, Philip? He who has seen Me has seen the Father; so how can you say, "Show us the Father"?'"*
  Colossians 1:15 *"He is the exact image of the invisible God, the firstborn over all creation."*

God's Definition of Character: "to do what is right regardless of <u>PERSONAL</u> <u>COST</u>"

Character Ingredient #1: I must ACKNOWLEDGE there is an OBJECTIVE STANDARD of right and wrong:
- this standard exists independent of my own emotions, experiences or desires.
- this standard is a permanent, unwavering benchmark by which I can measure my choices.

Deuteronomy 6:18 *"And you shall do what is right and good IN THE SIGHT OF THE LORD, that it may be well with you, and that you may go in and possess the good land of which the Lord swore to your fathers."*
Exodus 15:26 *"If you diligently heed the voice of the Lord your God and do what is right IN HIS SIGHT, give ear to His commandments and keep all His statutes, I will put none of the diseases on you which I have brought on the Egyptians. For I am the Lord who heals you."*
Proverbs 21:3 *"To do righteousness and justice is more acceptable TO THE LORD than sacrifice."*
Malachi 1:6 *"A son honors his father, and a servant his master. If then I am the Father, where is My honor? And if I am the Master, where is My reverence?"*

Character Ingredient #2: I must COMMIT to do what is right, in spite of what it costs me personally:
- I can overcome temptation because I make decisions based on a predetermined set of objective principles
- do what's right because it's the right thing to do

Isaiah 50:5-7 *"The Lord has opened My ear; and I was not rebellious, nor did I turn away. I gave My back to those who struck Me, and My cheeks to those who plucked out the beard; I did not hide My face from shame and spitting. For the Lord God will help Me; therefore I will not be disgraced; therefore I HAVE SET MY FACE LIKE A FLINT, and I know that I will not be ashamed."*
Daniel 3:16-18 *"Shadrach, Meshach, and Abed-Nego answered and said to the king, '...we have no need to answer you in this matter. If that is the case, our God whom we serve is able to deliver us from the burning fiery furnace, and He will deliver us from your hand, O king. But if not, let it be known to you, O king, that WE DO NOT SERVE YOUR GODS, nor will we worship the gold image which you have set up."*
Acts 4:18-20 *"They called them and commanded them not to speak at all nor teach in the name of Jesus. But Peter and John answered and said to them, 'Whether it is right in the sight of God to listen to you more than God, you judge. For we cannot but speak the things which we have seen and heard."*
Luke 6:46 *"But why do you call Me 'Lord, Lord,' and do not do THE THINGS WHICH I SAY?"*
John 13:17 *"If you know these things, happy are you if you DO THEM."*

"Want to know what your character is really like?" Self-examination of 3 Relationships

➤ Relationship #1: with GOD

Proverbs 23:26 *"My son, give Me your heart, and let your eyes observe My ways."*

Proverbs 3:5-6 *"Trust in the Lord with all your heart, and lean not on your own understanding. In all your ways acknowledge Him, and He shall direct your paths."*

John 8:29 *"He who sent Me is with Me. The Father has not let Me alone, for I always do those things that please Him."*

What does God hate?	What does God love?
Prov. 6:16-19 *"These 6 things the Lord HATES, yes, 7 are an ABOMINATION to Him: a proud look, a lying tongue, hands that shed blood, a heart that devises wicked plans, feet that are swift in running to evil, a false witness who speaks lies, and one who sows discord among the brethren."*	Prov. 8:31-32 *"...MY DELIGHT was with the sons of men. Now therefore, listen to Me, My children, for blessed are those who keep My ways. For whoever finds Me finds life, and obtains FAVOR from the Lord..."*
Prov. 28:9 *"One who turns away from hearing the law, even his prayer shall be an ABOMINATION."*	Prov. 16:20 *"He who heeds the word wisely will FIND GOOD, and whoever trusts in the Lord, HAPPY is he."*
Prov. 15:9 *"The way of the wicked is an ABOMINATION to the Lord..."*	Prov. 15:9 *"...HE LOVES him who follows righteousness."*
Prov. 15:8 *"The sacrifice of the wicked is an ABOMINATION to the Lord..."*	Prov. 15:8 *"...the prayer of the upright is HIS DELIGHT."*
Prov. 8:13 *"The fear of the Lord is to hate evil; pride, arrogance and the evil way and the perverse mouth I HATE."*	Prov. 8:17 *"I LOVE those who love Me, and those who seek Me diligently will find Me."*
Prov. 17:15 *"He who justifies the wicked, and he who condemns the just, both of them alike are an ABOMINATION to the Lord."*	Prov. 19:17 *"He who has pity on the poor lends to the Lord, and He will pay back what he has given."*
Prov. 14:31 *"he who oppresses the poor reproaches his Maker."*	Prov. 14:31 *"he who honors Him has mercy on the needy."*
Prov. 3:34 *"Surely He SCORNS the scornful..."*	Prov. 3:34 *"He gives GRACE to the humble."*
Prov. 12:22 *"Lying lips are an ABOMINATION to the Lord"*	Prov. 12:22 *"those dealing truthfully are His delight."*
Prov. 16:5 *"Everyone who is proud in heart is an ABOMINATION to the Lord..."*	Prov. 18:12 *"...before HONOR is humility."*
Prov. 15:25 *"The Lord will DESTROY the house of the proud...."*	Prov. 15:25 *"...but He will ESTABLISH the boundary of the widow."*
Prov. 28:13 *"Whoever covers his sins will NOT PROSPER..."*	Prov. 28:13 *"...but whoever confesses and forsakes them will have MERCY."*

➤ Relationship #2: with MYSELF

<u>GUILT</u> = what happens to me in that moment when I knowingly COMPROMISE my character. I become aware of a disparity between God's objective standard and my subjective one I'm living out. I feel distanced from Him.

<u>How I deal with guilt</u> = I tend to AVOID Him (I do the same thing when I have conflict with people. Rather than face it, I hide from it). I try to justify my behavior, but my guilty feelings only get worse.

<u>God's will for my life</u> = bring my character into conformity with His Son's (what He's doing INSIDE of me). Avoiding the pursuit of character is to jeopardize my RELATIONSHIP with God.

➤ Relationship #3: with OTHERS

The greatest obstacle to building truly good relationships is justified self-centeredness, a selfishness that, deep in our souls, feels entirely reasonable and therefore acceptable in light of how I've been treated.

Godly Character = not only submitting to God's objective standard of right and wrong, but also SURRENDERING to God my expectations of others, and loving other people (my neighbors) – even when they don't reciprocate.

Character is the "Oil in an Engine"[11]

The <u>closer</u> people get to each other, the greater the chance for <u>conflict</u> between them. Things cool down when people <u>back away</u> from each other. But God created people with an inherent <u>need</u> for each other. People cannot thrive by <u>avoiding</u> issues between them. We must resolve our differences to <u>grow</u> relationships.

God's character is "<u>others-oriented</u>" (I am commanded to focus on others' needs before my own). Without character, people close to each other will soon destroy each other (eventually, the friction that builds up over our differences takes it toll, so that people who were destined to be together tear each other apart).

Healthy, long-term relationships are evidence of the presence of strong character.

My CHARACTER
is a heart issue

Proverbs 4:23 *"KEEP YOUR HEART with all diligence, for out of it flow the issues of life."*

3.5

➢ **TRUTH #1**: My character requires a sensitive **HEART**
The more I love someone, the less I am able to tolerate the things that hurt them (when I really love someone, I am very sensitive to, and intolerant of, anything that causes them harm).
Proverbs 31:27 *"She WATCHES OVER the ways of her household, and does not eat the bread of idleness."*
Proverbs 29:15,17 *"The rod and reproof give wisdom, but a child LEFT TO HIMSELF brings shame to his mother. Correct your son and he will give you rest. Yes, he will give delight to your soul."*

My love for Jesus shows in my lifestyle. Does my lifestyle please Him? It's a question of **LORDSHIP**
Proverbs 16:3 *"Submit your works to the Lord, and your thoughts will be established."*
John 14:15 *"If you love Me, keep My commandments."*

➢ **TRUTH #2**: My character requires the "**RENEWAL**" process
What Character is NOT: doing what's good for me, or what's easy for me, or what comes naturally to me...
What Character IS: conforming myself to Christ's image by allowing Him to transform (renew) me
If I don't renew my mind, I won't be transformed. Things stay the way they are. I won't know the abundant life.
Proverbs 3:1 *"My son, do not forget My law, but let your HEART keep My commandments..."*
Romans 12:2 *"...do not be conformed to this world, but be transformed, by the RENEWING of your mind...",*

➢ **TRUTH #3**: God doesn't ask for my commitment – He asks for my "renewal"
Making a commitment is nothing but a sincere, external gesture – it says nothing about what's **INSIDE** me. Most of my promises are beyond my ability to keep them.
My Christianity isn't an event – it's a *lifelong process* of sensitizing my heart to seek His standards.
Proverbs 3:5-6 *"Trust in the Lord with all your HEART, and lean not on your own understanding. In all your ways ACKNOWLEDGE HIM, and He will direct your paths."*

➢ **TRUTH #4**: Renewing my heart requires me to see things from **HIS PERSPECTIVE**
How I interpret reality around me serves as the foundation for all my choices and decisions.
My spiritual maturity involves *learning* to see things from God's perspective (when I view things through His word, His commandments start making sense to me, my motivation to obey skyrockets, I want to please him).
Proverbs 8:32-34 *"Now therefore, LISTEN TO ME, My children, for blessed are those who keep My ways. Hear instruction and be wise, and do not disdain it. Blessed is the man who LISTENS TO ME..."*

God's Agenda[11]: "Clothe me with His **CHARACTER**"

Remember trying to dress your child when they were *newborns*? They'd twist and squirm as you tried to get their arms and legs into the clothes. I was only successful when I focused on "1 hole at a time". It was never easy - I had to wrestle them into their clothes. That's because they didn't understand the process of getting dressed until they *matured*. Then, little by little, they started catching on and cooperating. They'd see the shirt coming and lean their head toward it. They'd start putting their arms through the sleeves by themselves. Soon, things go easier as they *knew* what to expect. They knew where the "getting dressed" process would end up.

Developing character depends on my willingness to cooperate. God wants to clothe me with His character. But if I don't understand what He's trying to accomplish, or why, I'll make the process more difficult and time-consuming. Just like little babies, I often squirm and wriggle and resist what God is trying to do in my life.

But like the good parent that He is, God is working to shape my character – and He is relentless. Since the day I was born, conforming me to Him has been His priority. But while He is faithfully working to produce character in me, much of my progress depends on my heart's willingness to cooperate.

What's my agenda for me? Is my priority for my life the same as His? Or do I give lip service to my relationship with Jesus, inviting Him into my decisions only when I desperately need help or it fits my lifestyle? Imagine my potential for an abundant life if I worked with Him instead of around or against Him! As I renew my heart and mind, I start to understand and cooperate with His purposes for me, instead of fighting them.

Proverbs 3:11-12 *"My son, do not despise the chastening of the Lord, nor detest His correction; for whom the Lord LOVES He corrects, just as a father the son in whom HE DELIGHTS."*

Watch out for a "HARD HEART"

Proverbs 21:29 *"A wicked man HARDENS his face, but as for the upright, he understands his way."*
Proverbs 28:14 *"Happy is the man who is always reverent, but he who HARDENS his heart will fall into calamity."*
Proverbs 29:1 *"He who is often reproved, and HARDENS his neck, will suddenly be destroyed, and without remedy."*

- **What is a "Hard Heart"?**
  1. "overexposure and under-response to truth"
  2. my heart is not necessarily in conscious rebellion against God…but my heart no longer feels God's conviction (my heart has grown insensitive to His voice)

Andy Stanley[11]: "the Callused Heart"

"A similar thing happens to your hands when you work in the yard or lift weights without gloves. At first the rake or barbell rubs against the skin, and it hurts. There is a SENSITIVITY to the consequences created by the FRICTION. But after a while, the skin begins to TOUGHEN UP. Gradually, you develop calluses. Eventually, you feel NOTHING at all. Your skin gets so thick that it insulates your nerve endings, and you can't feel it anymore. The sensitivity is gone.

That's what happens to our hearts. When we repeatedly say no to God, our hearts become so hard that we no longer even detect His voice. He's still speaking, but WE CAN'T HEAR. He's still at work, but we are in no position to respond. We've lost our spiritual sensitivity."

- **How can I tell if its happened to me?**
  1. When I am repeatedly exposed to a particular truth and refuse to embrace and apply it (I hear the truth over and over again – and I just keep IGNORING it)
  2. When I REPEATEDLY say "no" to God in a particular area of life

Prov. 1:7 *"The fear of the Lord is the beginning of knowledge, but fools DESPISE WISDOM and INSTRUCTION."*
Prov. 12:1 *"He who loves instruction loves knowledge, but he who HATES REPROOF is stupid."*
Prov. 13:1 *"A wise son heeds his father's instruction, but a scoffer DOES NOT LISTEN to rebuke."*
Prov. 15:5 *"A fool DESPISES his father's instruction, but he who receives reproof is prudent."*
Prov. 15:10 *"Harsh correction is for him who forsakes the way, and he who HATES REPROOF will die."*
Prov. 15:32 *"He who DISDAINS INSTRUCTION despises his own soul, but he who heeds reproof gets understanding."*
Prov. 17:16 *"Why is there in the hand of a fool the purchase price of wisdom, since HE HAS NO HEART FOR IT?"*
Prov. 19:27 *"CEASE LISTENING TO INSTRUCTION, My son, and you will stray from the words of knowledge."*
Prov. 28:9 *"One who TURNS AWAY HIS EAR from hearing the law, even his prayer shall be an abomination."*

- **What's the long-term consequences?**
  1. Once I can't DISCERN the prompting of the Holy Spirit, I'm open to just about anything….
  2. Whenever His word conflicts with my lifestyle, I REDEFINE His standard so it fits me….
  3. I focus on areas of Scripture that come naturally, but de-emphasize those areas that cause FRICTION.
  4. I do this without even knowing I'm doing it: I value things based on how they fit my life and goals.
  5. I commit idolatry: I worship what makes me feel good about MYSELF, but ignore God's whole counsel.

Prov. 14:12 *"There is a way that SEEMS RIGHT to a man, but its end is the way of death."*
Prov. 16:2 *"All the ways of man are pure IN HIS OWN EYES, but the Lord weighs the spirits."*
Prov. 18:2 *"A fool has no delight in understanding, but in expressing HIS OWN HEART."*
Prov. 26:12 *"Do you see a man wise IN HIS OWN EYES? There is more hope for a fool than for him."*
Prov. 28:26 *"He who TRUSTS IN HIS OWN HEART is a fool, but whoever walks wisely will be delivered."*
Prov. 30:12 *"There is a generation that is pure IN ITS OWN EYES, yet it is not washed from its filthiness."*

- **The TRUE TEST: a simple equation**
  1. My degree of hard-heartedness = the difference between what grieves me vs. what grieves God.
  2. "Am I bothered by the things that BOTHER Him?"……"Is my heart in sync with His?"
  3. When what grieves God no longer grieves me, my heart is HARD.
  4. Do you know what God says in the Bible He loves and what He hates? How do these same things strike me? Am I PASSIONATE about them?

**If I know something I do grieves God, but I wonder if maybe He's overreacting a bit…
I've got work to do.**

When I stand before God, for what will He hold me most ACCOUNTABLE?

Proverbs 4:23 *"KEEP YOUR HEART with all diligence, for out of it spring the issues of life".*
Ecclesiastes 11:9 *"Rejoice, O young man, in your youth, and let your HEART cheer you in the days of your youth; walk in the ways of your HEART, and in the sight of your eyes; but know that for all these God will bring you into judgment."*

> **"HEART"** = *KARDIA* (English word "cardiac") and *PSUCHE* (English word "psyche")
> - A person's mental and moral activity, both rational (the will, reasoning) and emotional. A person's soul, or life.
> - It contains the "inner, hidden man" that is your true character that only God can see.

➔ **Can God SEE what I am really like?**
Proverbs 27:19 *"As in water face reveals face, so a man's HEART reveals the man."*
Matthew 6:21 *"For where your treasure is, there your HEART will be also."*
Psalm 44:21 *"Would not God search this out? For He knows the secrets of the HEART."*
1Samuel 16:7 *"Do not look at his appearance, or at the height of his stature, because I have refused him. For the Lord does not see as man sees; man looks at the outward appearance, but the Lord looks at the HEART."*
Jeremiah 17:10 *"I, the Lord search the HEART..."*

➔ **Its unfair: How can God hold me accountable for a heart I can't FIX?**
Jeremiah 17:9 *"The HEART is deceitful above all things, and incurably sick - who can understand it?"*
Proverbs 20:9 *"Who can say, 'I have made my HEART clean, and I am pure from my sin'?"*
Mark 7:21 *"For from within, out of the HEART of men, proceed evil thoughts, adulteries, fornications, murders, thefts, covetousness, wickedness, deceit, licentiousness, an evil eye, blasphemy, pride, foolishness."*

➔ **Why is my heart so MESSED UP?**
Jeremiah 16:12 *"And you have done worse than your fathers, for behold, each one walks according to the imagination of his own evil HEART, so that NO ONE LISTENS TO ME."*
Psalm 81:13 *"Oh, that my people would LISTEN TO ME, that Israel would walk in My ways."*
Isaiah 53:6 *"All we like sheep have gone astray; we have turned everyone each TO HIS OWN WAY."*
Matthew 23:37 *"O Jerusalem, Jerusalem, the one who kills the prophets and stones those who are sent to her! How often I wanted to gather your children together, as a hen gathers her chicks under her wings, but YOU WERE NOT WILLING."*

➔ **How do I fix my CONDITION?**
Ezekiel 11:19 *"I will give them one heart, and will put a new spirit within them, and take away the STONY HEART out of their flesh, and give them a HEART OF FLESH, that they may walk in My statutes and keep My judgments and do them; and they shall be My people and I will be their God."*
Prov. 23:26 *"My son, GIVE ME YOUR HEART, and let your eyes observe My ways."*
Prov. 3:5 *"Trust in the Lord with ALL YOUR HEART; don't lean on your own understanding."*
Mark 12:30 *"You shall love the Lord with ALL YOUR HEART, with all your soul, with all your mind, and with all your strength."*
John 15:5 *"I am the vine, you are the branches. He who abides in Me, and I in him, bears much fruit; for WITHOUT ME YOU CAN DO NOTHING."*
Philippians 4:13 *"I can do all things THROUGH CHRIST who strengthens me."*

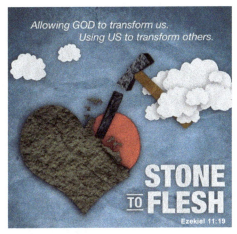

➔ ***Philippians 4:7*** *"...the peace of God, which passes all understanding, will GUARD your HEARTS and MINDS through Christ Jesus."*

Jesus' Character: He <u>GUARDS</u> my Heart

<u>MY PROBLEM</u>: I can't guard against sin on my own because my heart is infected with it! I have offended God by sinning against Him.

<u>HIS SOLUTION</u>: In **Isaiah 59:9-17** God Almighty takes the initiative. His ARM intercedes for me, to bring salvation to me, to live IN ME, to be my True Vine who guards my heart:

"Therefore justice is far from us, nor does righteousness overtake us; we look for light, but there is darkness! For brightness, but we walk in blackness! We grope for the wall like the blind, and we grope as if we had no eyes; we stumble at noonday as at twilight; we are as dead men in desolate places. We all growl like bears, and moan sadly like doves; we look for justice, but there is none; for salvation, but it is far from us.

For our transgressions are multiplied before You, and our sins testify against us; for our transgressions are with us, and as for our iniquities, we know them; in transgressing and lying against the Lord, and departing from our God, speaking oppression and revolt, conceiving and uttering FROM THE HEART words of falsehood. Justice is turned back, and righteousness stands afar off; for truth has fallen in the street, and equity cannot enter. So truth fails, and he who departs from evil makes himself a prey.

*Then the Lord saw it, and it displeased Him that there was no justice. He saw that there was no man, and wondered that there was no intercessor; therefore **His own ARM brought salvation for Him**; His own righteousness, it sustained Him. For HE put on righteousness as a breastplate, and a helmet of salvation on HIS head; HE put on the garments of vengeance for clothing, and was clad with zeal as a cloak."*

➔ JESUS = The "<u>ARM</u>" of the Lord   (Hebrew "zrô'âh" = power, strength, might)

In **Isaiah 53:1-6**, the mighty ARM of God is revealed in the person of Jesus our Savior, who came to fulfill God's promise made to man, to deliver us from our sin by paying the price (death) in our place (substitution):

*"Who has believed our report? And to whom has **the ARM of the Lord** been revealed? For He shall grow up before Him as a tender plant, and as a root out of dry ground. He has no form or comeliness, and when we see Him, there is no beauty that we should desire Him.*

He is despised and rejected of men. A man of sorrows and acquainted with grief. And we hid as it were our faces from Him. He was despised and we did not esteem Him. Surely He has borne our griefs and carried our sorrows. Yet we esteemed Him stricken, smitten by God, and afflicted.

But He was wounded for OUR TRANSGRESSIONS, He was bruised for OUR INIQUITIES, the chastisement for OUR PEACE was upon Him, and by His stripes WE ARE HEALED. All we like sheep have gone astray; we have turned everyone each to his own way; and the Lord has laid on HIM the sins of us all......"

➔ YHWH SHUA = JESUS: His <u>ARMOR</u> I wear when He lives IN me:

I can only be effective in guarding my heart if I surrender my soul (who I am; my very life) to Jesus, so He has complete access to my heart, to do with me whatever He wants. Then, He lives IN ME to be my Guardian.

Ephesians 6:13-17 *"Therefore take up the whole armor OF GOD, that you may be able to withstand in the evil day, and having done all, to stand. Stand therefore, having girded your waist with truth, having put on the breastplate of righteousness, and having shod your feet with the gospel of peace; and above all, taking the shield of faith with which you will be able to quench all the fiery darts of the wicked one. And take the helmet of salvation, and the sword of the Spirit, which is the word of God."*

Isaiah 12:2 *"Behold, God is my salvation, I will trust and not be afraid; for YAH, the Lord, is my strength and my song; He also has become my salvation."*

Colossians 1:27-28 *"To them God willed to make known what are the riches of the glory of the mystery among the Gentiles, which is CHRIST IN YOU, the hope of glory. Him we preach, warning every man and teaching every man in all wisdom, that we may present every man perfect IN CHRIST JESUS."*

John 14:17, 23 *"...even the Spirit of truth, whom the world cannot receive, because it neither sees Him nor knows Him; but you know Him, for HE DWELLS WITH YOU and WILL BE IN YOU."* Jesus ... said to him, *"If anyone loves Me, he will keep My word; My Father will love Him, and We will come to him and MAKE OUR HOME WITH HIM."*

My CHARACTER
is relational

Proverbs 23:26 *"My son, GIVE ME YOUR HEART, and let your eyes observe My ways."*

3.6

Question #1: It shouldn't be so hard to be a person of character, should it? Shouldn't I just naturally want to?
Answer #1: No. My natural bent is toward self-achievement (religious), not Christ-likeness (relational).

➢ The FLESH (the "Old Man") = The "Religious Approach" to life
My ability to do for God, and His corresponding obligation to do for me (my hard work is to be rewarded).
I measure my approval rating with God according to my deeds (good deeds = approval, bad deeds = rejection).
Why "religion" doesn't work: I have no power on my own to win God's approval; God's approval was settled at the Cross, won for me by Jesus; God's approval is a gift I accept, not a wage I must earn.

➢ The SPIRIT (the "New Man") = The "Relational Approach" to life
What God has done FOR me, and what He, who now INDWELLS me, is willing to do THROUGH me.
Trusting what Christ did on the cross, I received His life and began to personally relate with God (Jesus did for me what I could never do – He removed the barrier separating me from the Father by paying for my sins).
I couldn't save myself from sin's penalty, and I can't save myself from sin's power. It's a lifelong dependency.
Why "relationship" does work: I don't have to depend on me...I have a Father who loves me and does the work IN me. I must do my part: good intentions aren't enough – I must CHOOSE His ways over my own.

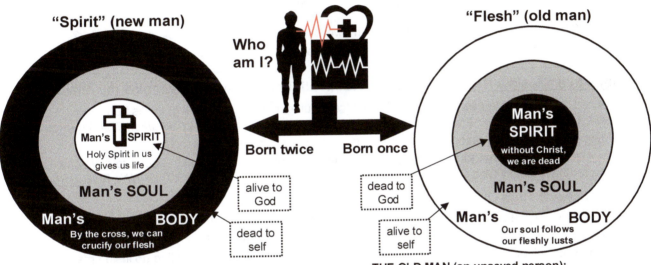

THE NEW MAN (a saved person):
• their spirit is *indwelt* by God's spirit (born again)
• their soul receives information from the *spiritual world* that is in union with God's Spirit
• can put their FLESH to DEATH daily (doesn't have to obey their flesh; there can be victory over habitual sin)

THE OLD MAN (an unsaved person):
• their spirit is DEAD to the things of God (natural man)
• their soul makes daily decisions based on information from their flesh (*physical senses*)
• they are SLAVES to their flesh - they can only resist their lusts in the power of their own will

➢ *God's desire for me = "WALK daily in His Spirit"*
Gal. 5:22-23 - These fruits are HIS character that He produces in and through me as I rely upon His strength.
1Corin. 15:31 - My pursuit of Christ's character hinges on my day-to-day dependency on the power of the Holy Spirit to mold me toward Christ-likeness. I must CRUCIFY the "old man" and "die with Christ" to my own desires.
Gal. 2:20 ⇨ Matthew 22:37 ⇨ John 3:16 - Through my LOVE RELATIONSHIP with God, I am finally capable of doing what I was incapable of doing on my own. That's what "walking in the Spirit" (Galatians 5:16) is all about.

Andy Stanley[11]: *"God does not command us to go out and attain on our own the virtues of Galatians 5:22-23. These are the fruits of the CHARACTER the Heavenly Father longs to produce through me as I learn to rely upon and draw upon His strength. Character is produced THROUGH me; it is not manufactured by me. My pursuit of Christ's character hinges on my day-to-day dependence on the power of the Holy Spirit to empower me toward Christ-likeness."* Through my RELATIONSHIP with God, I am finally capable of doing what I was incapable of doing on my own. And that's what "walking in the Spirit" (Galatians 5:16) is all about."

When Proverbs 23:26 says "give Me your heart", God wants to INDWELL me, to put on a "New Man". That's why Christians testify that their faith is intensely RELATIONAL.

The difference between the Christian and the unsaved is based on the RELATIONSHIP – who's in charge?

Christian: new man, alive to God, by His Spirit	**Unsaved: old man, dead to God, in the flesh**
Romans 8:1-2 *"There is therefore no condemnation to those who are in Christ Jesus, who do not walk according to the flesh, but according to the Spirit. For the law of the Spirit of life in Christ has made me free from the law of sin and death. But you are not in the flesh but IN THE SPIRIT, if indeed the Spirit of God dwells in you.."* **2Corinthians 5:17** *"...if anyone is in Christ, he is a NEW CREATION; old things have passed away; behold, all things have become new."*	**Ephesians 2:1-3** *"...you He made alive, who were DEAD in trespasses and sins, in which you once walked according to the course of this world, according to the prince of the air, the spirit who now works in the sons of disobedience, among whom also we all once conducted ourselves in the lusts of our flesh, fulfilling the DESIRES OF THE FLESH and of the mind, and were by nature children of wrath, just as the others."*

Christian: my flesh (old man) was put to death	**Unsaved: my flesh (old man) runs my life**
Galatians 2:20 *"I have been CRUCIFIED with Christ; it is no longer I who live, but Christ lives in me; and the life which I now live in the flesh I live by faith in the Son of God, who loved me and gave Himself for me."* **Coloss. 2:11** *"In Him you were also circumcised with the circumcision made without hands, by PUTTING OFF the body of sins of the flesh, by the circumcision of Christ."*	**1Peter 4:3-4** *"We have spent enough of our past lifetime in doing the will of the Gentiles – when we WALKED in filthiness, lusts, drunkenness, revelries, drinking parties, and abominable idolatries. In regard to these, they think it strange that you do not run with them in the same flood of dissipation, speaking evil of you."*

Question #2: So, as a "new man" in Christ, HOW can I work with the Holy Spirit to mold my character?
Answer #2: The 4 "Heart Habits" of the John 8:31 "Truth Process"

---

4 Steps to a "Healthy Heart": The John 8:31 Truth Process where He molds my character

Jesus defined "putting on the new man" as <u>ABIDING</u> (continuing, dwelling or staying) in His truth:
"If you abide in My word, you are My disciples indeed. And you shall know the truth, and the truth shall make you free."
This abiding process is an equation: Embrace His truth + Immerse myself in His teaching = Be Free
There are 4 "Heart Habits" that form this process of abiding and leading me to real freedom, to developing a holy character that pleases God (not freedom from circumstances). TRUTH PAVES THE WAY FOR <u>GROWTH</u>.

Step #1: Speak His truth <u>OUT</u> <u>LOUD</u>
- something powerful happens when I verbalize truth in the face of temptation, discouragement, or anxiety
- verbalizing truth moves me from assumption to reality – I am making a stand
- verbalizing truth will expose and squash any misdirected feelings that may be building up inside me:
  - if I feel afraid of how something may end up, I'll have a hard time being honest   (verbalize Prov. 12:22)
  - if I am worried someone may lose respect for me, I'll won't want to be accountable (verbalize Prov. 10:9)
  - if I stay angry over a past hurt, I won't forgive the next person who offends me   (verbalize Prov. 10:12)
  - if I feel offended by someone, I'll want to tell others, to help heal my wound   (verbalize Prov. 17:9)
  - if I stay bitter over how I was treated, I'll lash out at whoever upsets me next   (verbalize Prov. 16:32)

Step #2: <u>PERSONALIZE</u> His truth
- when I speak His truths, put them in the first person - see what these Proverbs sound like when personalized:
  Proverbs 16:3 *"If I commit my works to the Lord, then my thoughts will be established."*
  Proverbs 19:17 *"If I have pity on the poor I am lending to the Lord, and He will pay back to me what I have given."*
  Proverbs 28:13 *"If I cover my sins I will not prosper, but if I confess and forsake them I will have mercy."*

Step #3: <u>PRAY</u> His truth
- when I am praying, incorporate truths as a way of expressing back to Him my surrender to His word
- my prayers become an audible expression of my agreement with His plan for my character

Step #4: <u>MEDITATE</u> on His truth
- meditate = "to ponder by talking to myself"
- when I identify a character flaw I want to fix, meditating throughout the day on relevant verses draws Him close to me. His presence gives me the power to "stay the course" (it's a process, based on a relationship)
  Proverbs 4:5 *"He also taught me, and said to me, 'Let your heart RETAIN MY WORDS; keep My commands and live.'"*
  Psalm 1:2 *"His delight is in the law of the Lord, and in His law he MEDITATES day and night."*

My CHARACTER
requires renewal

Proverbs 28:13 *"He who covers his sins will not prosper, but whoever confesses and forsakes them will have mercy."*

3.7

➢ **TRUTH #1:** Renewing my mind has 2 parts: "put off the OLD man, "put on the NEW man"
Every facet of my behavior is tied back to something I believe (what I believe determines how I behave).
I must challenge the assumptions and beliefs that support my attitudes and worldview.
I must identify those things I have always believed that are not true, and STOP doing them ("put them off").
I must take deliberate action – create a PLAN for replacing the lies with truth ("put them on").
Colossians 3:9-10 *"Do not lie to one another, since you have PUT OFF the OLD MAN with his deeds, and have PUT ON the NEW MAN who is renewed in knowledge according to the image of Him who created him."*
Proverbs 4:24-27 *"PUT AWAY from you a deceitful mouth, and put perverse lips FAR from you. Let your eyes look straight ahead, and your eyelids look right before you. PONDER THE PATH of your feet, and let your ways be established. Do not turn to the right or to the left; remove your feet from evil."*

➢ **TRUTH #2:** "Putting off the old man" - God's renewal process begins with REPROVNG
Definition of REPROVE = "to bring conviction by exposing an area in someone's life that needs to change."
Synonyms = prove/ test, rebuke, convict, expose/ discover.
Ever have reproof come over you when:
 - you read Scripture (exposed an area of your life you were avoiding)?
 - you were seen doing something that dishonored the Lord?
 - a fellow Christian said or did something you knew was right, but you wouldn't also do it?

• PROVE or TEST

2Timothy 3:16 *"All Scripture is given by inspiration of God, and is profitable for doctrine, for REPROOF, for correction, for instruction in righteousness, that the man of God may be complete, thoroughly equipped for every good work."*

• EXPOSE or DISCOVER

John 3:20 *"For everyone practicing evil hates the light and does not come to the light, lest his deeds should be EXPOSED."*
Ephesians 5:11,13 *"...have no fellowship with the unfruitful works of darkness, but rather EXPOSE them. But all things that are EXPOSED are made manifest by the light, for whatever makes them manifest is light."*

• CONVICT or REBUKE

John 16:8 *"...when He has come, He will CONVICT the world of sin, and of righteousness, and of judgment."*
Hebrews 12:5-6 *"...you have forgotten the exhortation which speaks to you as to sons: 'My son, do not despise the discipline of the Lord, nor be discouraged when you are REBUKED by Him; for whom the Lord loves He chastens, and scourges every son whom He receives.'"*
Revelation 3:19 *"As many as I love I REBUKE and chasten. Therefore, be zealous and repent."*

PROVERBS: It's all about my willingness to receive God's reproofs

Prov. 1:23	*"Turn at My REPROOF; surely, I will pour out My Spirit on you; I will make My words known to you."*
Prov. 6:23	*"...the commandment is a lamp, and the law is light; REPROOFS of instruction are the way of life."*
Prov. 10:17	*"He who keeps instruction is in the way of life, but he who refuses REPROOF goes astray."*
Prov. 12:1	*"Whoever loves instruction loves knowledge, but he who hates REPROOF is stupid."*
Prov. 13:18	*"Poverty and shame comes to him who ignores correction, but he who regards REPROOF will be honored."*
Prov. 15:5	*"A fool despises his father's instruction, but he who receives REPROOF is prudent."*
Prov. 15:10	*"Harsh correction is for him who forsakes the way, and he who hates REPROOF will die."*
Prov. 15:31	*"The ear that hears the REPROOF of life will abide among the wise."*
Prov. 15:32	*"He who disdains instruction despises his own soul, but he who heeds REPROOF gets understanding."*
Prov. 17:10	*"REPROOF is more effective for a wise man than 100 blows on a fool."*
Prov. 19:25	*"...REPROVE one who has understanding, and he will discern knowledge."*
Prov. 29:1	*"He who is often REPROVED, and hardens his neck, will suddenly be destroyed, and that without remedy."*
Prov. 29:15	*"The rod and REPROOF give wisdom, but a child left to himself brings shame to his mother."*

QUESTION: why is Reproof so crucial to character?
ANSWERS: #1. renewal must take place in our <u>MINDS</u> (how we think), not our behavior (how we act).
#2. I must replace the world's lies with God's <u>TRUTH</u> (I am being lied to every single day).

The CONSEQUENCES: Believing the world's lies	
If I believe… I must be beautiful to be loved	I will focus on my physical appearance
If I believe… people can't be trusted	I won't have any close friends
If I believe… only strong people survive in this world	I won't be merciful
If I believe… happiness is based on accumulating things	I won't be generous
If I believe… I can't change	I won't
If I believe… people will laugh if they know I'm a Christian	I'll never share Jesus with anyone
If I believe… God accepts me based on my performance	I'll either work myself to death or give up altogether
The SOLUTION: I must <u>IDENTIFY</u> the "old man" beliefs that drive my behavior, or my behavior won't change. Proverbs 23:7 *"For AS A MAN THINKS IN HIS HEART, so is he."*	

<u>4 ways to identify false beliefs</u> – ask the Holy Spirit to reveal the lies holding me back from change

a) Evaluate the things you say or think (the excuses I make for sin)
   "I've always been this way"   "Everyone else is doing it"   "I can handle it – I'm different"
   "One time won't hurt"   "Nobody will know"   "But I'm in love"

b) Examine the areas in my life where I am overly sensitive
   If I overreact in situations where certain topics come up, I may have a false belief.
   Do people feel like they're walking on eggshells around me because I explode when they mention that topic?

c) Examine your strongest temptations
   What's the appeal?   What sort of conversations do I have with myself to justify it, if I know doing it is wrong?
   Until I expose and face the lies behind the temptation, I cannot apply the truth.

d) Examine areas where I have inordinate fears (fear is often a sign I'm believing a lie)
   Even though I know the facts, I'm afraid anyway.

> **TRUTH #3:** "Put on the new man" - God's renewal process ends with EMBRACING Truth

   Proverbs 23:23   *"Buy the TRUTH, and don't sell it…also wisdom and instruction and understanding."*
   John 8:32   *"…you shall know the TRUTH, and the truth shall make you free."*

Find the specific truths of God's word that counter the specific lies I've been told, and believed, all my life.
Gaining more knowledge isn't the answer to building character:
   - Knowledge doesn't necessarily result in a renewed mind (if it were the answer, we'd all be in seminary).
   - Satan has more knowledge of God than anyone – look at what good it did him….

God wants to renew my mind with truth, not just fill it with facts.

JESUS – He demonstrates the amazing power of TRUTH (Matthew 4:1-11)
After fasting forty days (over a month without food), Satan come to Him in His weakened state with three lies:
1) <u>Big Lie #1</u>: VERSE 3   Satisfying your hunger is more important than devotion to the Father
• The Father led Him into the wilderness – Jesus was following instructions, which included fasting.
• The temptation: my physical concerns outweigh my obedience (at the core of most temptations I face).
2) <u>Big Lie #2</u>: VERSE 6   Proving Himself by miracles is more important than devotion to the Father
• Jesus was a Man under the authority of His Father (John 5:19, John 12:49-50)
3) <u>Big Lie #3</u>: VERSE 9   Redeeming the world was more important than devotion to the Father
• Satan offered Jesus immediate control of all the world's kingdoms…if He'd just worship him for a moment.
• Satan offered a good thing – Jesus chose the best thing.
Have I filled my mind with enough "it is written" truths that, when I hear the lie, I respond with truth?

My Moral CHARACTER
fights against my immoral nature

Proverbs 20:9 *"Who can say, 'I have made my heart clean, and I am pure from my sin?'"*

3.8

WHY IS RENEWAL SO HARD TO DO?   the <u>FLESH</u> = Gr. "SARX"

- The outward body (also Gr. "soma") as opposed to the inward spirit or soul

John 1:14 *"And the Word became FLESH and dwelt among us, and we beheld His glory, the glory as of the only begotten of the Father, full of grace and truth."*

John 6:63 *"It is the Spirit who gives life; the FLESH profits nothing. The words I speak to you are spirit, and they are life."*

2Corinthians 10:3 *"For though we walk in the FLESH, we do not war according to the FLESH."*

- The weaker element in human nature

Matthew 26:41 *"Watch and pray, lest you fall into temptation. The spirit indeed is willing, but the FLESH is weak."*

Romans 6:19 *"I speak in human terms because of the weakness of your FLESH...."*

Romans 8:3 *"For what the law could not do in that it was weak through the FLESH, God did by sending His Son in the likeness of sinful FLESH, on account of sin: He condemned sin in the FLESH."*

- The unregenerate state of mankind

Romans 7:5 *"For when we were in the FLESH, the passions of sins which were aroused by the law were at work in our members to bear fruit to death."*

Romans 8:6-8 *"... to be FLESHLY MINDED is death, but to be spiritually minded is life and peace. Because the fleshly mind is enmity against God, for it is not subject to the law of God, nor indeed can be. So then those who are in the FLESH cannot please God."*

- The seat of sin in man (not the same thing as the physical body)

1John 2:16 *"For all that is in the world – the lust of the FLESH, the lust of the eyes, and the pride of life – is not of the Father but is of the world."*

"God is working to change me from the 'INSIDE-OUT'

Ezekiel 11:19-21 "Then I will give them one heart, and I will put a NEW SPIRIT within them, and take the stony heart out of their flesh, and give them a HEART OF FLESH, that they may walk in My statutes and keep My judgments and do them; and they shall be My people, and I will be their God. But as for those whose hearts walk after the heart of their detestable things and their abominations, I will recompense their deeds on their own heads", says the Lord God.

Ezekiel 36:26-27 "I will give you a NEW HEART and put a NEW SPIRIT within you; I will take the heart of stone out of your flesh and give you a heart of flesh. I will put MY SPIRIT WITHIN YOU and cause you to walk in My statutes, and you will keep My judgments and do them."

Jeremiah 31:33-34 "This is the covenant that I will make with the house of Israel after those days", says the Lord: "I will put My law in their MINDS, and write it on their HEARTS, and I will be their God, and they shall be My people."

Romans 7:14-23 explains the Problem: my flesh will never give up control without a FIGHT

Galatians 5:16-17 *"...walk in the Spirit, and you shall not fulfill the lusts of the FLESH. For the flesh lusts against the Spirit, and the Spirit against the flesh, and these are CONTRARY to one another; so that YOU DO NOT DO THE THINGS THAT YOU WISH."*

Ezekiel 18:29-32 *"Yet the house of Israel says, 'The way of the Lord is not fair.' O house of Israel, is it not My ways which are fair, and your ways which are not fair? Therefore I will judge you, O house of Israel, every one according to his ways," says the Lord God. "Repent and turn from all your transgressions, so that iniquity will not be your ruin. Cast away from you all the transgressions which you have committed, and get yourselves a NEW HEART and a NEW SPIRIT. For why should you die, O house of Israel? For I have no pleasure in the death of one who dies," says the Lord God. "Therefore turn and live!"*

- Paul's problem is the same as all people: once Jesus Christ comes into your heart as your Savior, your life does not become perfect because your sin nature (your flesh, also known as the OLD MAN) is not gone.

Charles Stanley: "We are sinful by our nature, not by our works"
"A hog has a hog's nature – no matter how much you clean him up, he will always go back to the slop. We have a sin nature. No matter how much good we do, we live for ourselves, in rebellion to God"

ROMANS 7:14-25 The Moral Law and the 'War Within'

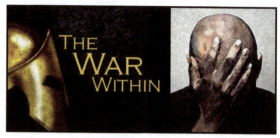

"For we know that the law is spiritual, but I am ①CARNAL, ②SOLD under ③SIN. For what I am doing, I do not understand. For what I will to do, that I do not practice; but what I hate, that I do. If then, I do what I will not to do, I agree with the law that it is good. But now, it is no longer I who do it, but SIN that dwells in me. For I know that in me (that is, in my ④FLESH) nothing good dwells; for to will is present with me, but how to perform what is ⑤GOOD, I do not find. For the good thing that I will to do, I do not do; but the ⑥EVIL I will not to do, that I practice. Now if I do what I will not to do, it is no longer I who do it, but SIN that dwells in me.

I find then a law, that EVIL is present with me, the one who wills to do GOOD. For I delight in the law of God according to the inward man. But I see another law in my members, ⑦WARRING AGAINST the law of my ⑧MIND, and bringing me into ⑨CAPTIVITY to the law of SIN which is in my members.

O wretched man that I am! Who will deliver me from this body of death? I thank God – through Jesus Christ our Lord! So then, with the MIND I myself serve the law of God, but with the FLESH the law of SIN."

① CARNAL = Gr. "*sarkikos*" = fleshly, temporal, unregenerate
② SOLD = Gr. "*piprasko*" = trafficked, as in slavery
③ SIN = Gr. "*harmaria*" = offense
④ FLESH = Gr. "*sarx*" = the weaker element in human nature, the unregenerate state of man
⑤ GOOD = Gr. "*kalos*" = intrinsically virtuous, valuable or worthy
⑥ EVIL = Gr. "*kakos*" = intrinsically worthless, depraved, wicked
⑦ WARRING AGAINST = Gr. "*antistrateuomai*" = attacking with intent to destroy
⑧ MIND = Gr. "*nous*" = intellect (encompasses my thoughts, feelings and my will)
⑨ CAPTIVITY = Gr. "*aichmalotizo*" = bondage, as a prisoner with no rights

What does this *'Moral War Within'* look like? In "The Reason for God"[14], Pastor Timothy Keller illustrates this as he retells Robert Louis Stevenson's classic 'The Strange Case of Dr. Jekyll and Mr. Hyde': "Dr. Jekyll comes to realize that he is 'an incongruous compound of good and evil.' His bad nature is holding his good nature back, he believes. He can aspire to do things, but he cannot follow through on them.

Therefore he comes up with a potion that can separate out his two natures. His hope is that his good self, which will come out during the day, will be free from the influence of evil and will be able to realize its goals. However, when he takes the potion at night and his bad side comes out, he is far more evil than he expected. He describes his evil self using classic Christian categories: 'I knew myself, at the first breath of new life, to be more wicked, tenfold more wicked, sold a slave to my original evil; and the thought in that moment, braced and delighted me like wine… every act and thought centered on self.'"

Keller explains how Dr. Jekyll's evil side, Mr. Hyde, got his name: "Edward Hyde is so named not because he is hideous but because he is hidden. He thinks solely of his own desires; he doesn't care in the slightest who he hurts in order to gratify himself. Stevenson is saying that even the best of people hide from themselves what is within – an enormous capacity for egotism, self-absorption, and regard for their own interests over those of others. We hide from ourselves our self-centered capacity for evil acts, but situations arise that act as a 'potion', and out they come.

Once Jekyll realizes he has the capacity for evil acts, he solemnly resolves not to take the potion anymore, and devotes himself to charity and good works, partially as atonement for what Edward Hyde has done, and partially as an effort to simply smother his selfish nature with acts of unselfishness. However, one day Dr. Jekyll is sitting on a bench in Regents Park, thinking about all the good he has been doing, and how much better a man he was, despite Edward Hyde, than the great majority of people: 'As I smiled… at the very moment of that vain-glorious thought, a qualm came over me, a horrid nausea and the most dreadful shuddering… I looked down… I was once more Edward Hyde.' For the first time Jekyll becomes Hyde involuntarily, without the potion, and this is the beginning of the end. Jekyll ends up killing himself.

Stevenson's insight here is, I think, profound. Why would Jekyll become Hyde without the potion? Like so many people, Jekyll knows he is a sinner, so he tries desperately to cover his sin with great piles of good works. Yet his efforts do not actually shrivel his pride and self-centeredness, they only aggravate it. Jekyll becomes Hyde, not in spite of his goodness, but because of his goodness." As with Paul in Romans 7:14-25, our problem is that even after Jesus Christ comes into your heart as your Savior, our sin nature (our flesh) is not gone. The battle within, over Lordship, begins: **WHO IS IN CHARGE?**

The Moral Law and the Battle within: Francis Collins

The following are excerpts from Chapter 1 ('From Atheism to Belief') of his book '**The Language of God**'[15]

American physicist-geneticist; PhD physical chemistry, Yale University; MD, Univ. NC, Chapel Hill; Director of the National Institutes of Health in Bethesda, Maryland; succeeded James Watson in 1993 as Director of National Human Genome Research Institute (NHGRI); noted for his discoveries of disease genes (cystic fibrosis, Huntington's disease, etc.); founder and president of the BioLogos Foundation.

"At first, I was confident that a full investigation of the rational basis for faith would deny the merits of belief, and reaffirm my atheism. But I determined to have a look at the facts, no matter what the outcome." Collins read, among many other books, 'Mere Christianity" by C.S. Lewis. Here is his conclusion: "…as I turned its pages… I realized that all of my own constructs against the plausibility of faith were those of a schoolboy. Lewis seemed to know all of my objections… he invariably addressed them within a page or two. When I learned subsequently that Lewis himself had been an atheist, who had set out to disprove faith on the basis of logical argument, I recognized how he could be so insightful about my path. It had been his path as well.

The argument that most caught my attention, and most rocked my ideas about science and spirit down to their foundation, was right there in the title of Book One: 'Right and Wrong as a Clue to the Meaning of the Universe.' While in many ways the 'Moral Law' that Lewis described was a universal feature of human existence, in other ways it was as if I was recognizing it for the first time. To understand the Moral Law, it is useful to consider, as Lewis did, how it is invoked in hundreds of ways each day without the invoker stopping to point out the foundation of his argument.

Disagreements are part of daily life. Some are mundane, as the wife criticizing her husband for not speaking more kindly to a friend, or a child complaining 'it's not fair', when different amounts of ice cream are doled out at a birthday party. Other arguments take on larger significance. In international affairs, some argue the United States has a moral obligation to spread democracy throughout the world, even if it requires military force, whereas some say that the aggressive, unilateral use of military and economic force threatens to squander moral authority. In the area of medicine, furious debates currently surround the question of whether or not it is acceptable to carry out research on human embryonic stem cells. Some argue that such research violates the sanctity of human life; others posit that the potential to alleviate human suffering constitutes an ethical mandate to proceed.

*Notice that in all these examples, each party attempts to appeal to an **unstated higher standard**. This standard is the MORAL LAW. It might be called the LAW OF RIGHT BEHAVIOR, and its existence in each of these situations seems unquestioned. What is being debated is whether one action or another is a closer approximation to the demands of that law. Those accused of having fallen short, such as the husband who is insufficiently cordial to his wife's friend, usually respond with a variety of excuses why they should be let off the hook. Virtually never does the respondent say, 'To hell with your concept of right behavior.'*

The Law of Human Nature can't be explained away as cultural artifact or evolutionary by-product, so how can we account for its presence? There is truly something unusual going on here. To quote C. S. Lewis, 'If there was a controlling power outside the universe, it could not show itself to us as one of the facts of the universe – no more than the architect of the house could actually be a wall or staircase or fireplace in that house. The only way in which we could expect it to show itself would be inside ourselves as an influence or a command trying to get us to behave in a certain way. And that is just what we do find inside ourselves. Surely this ought to arouse our suspicions?'

Encountering this argument at age 26, I was stunned by its logic. Here, hiding in my own heart as familiar as anything in daily experience, but now emerging for the first time as a clarifying principle, this Moral Law shone its bright white light into the recesses of my childish atheism, and demanded a serious consideration of its origin. Was this God looking back at me? And if it were so, what kind of God would this be? Would this be a deist God, who invented physics and mathematics and started the universe in motion about 14 billion years ago, then wandered off to deal with other, more important matters, as Einstein thought? No, this God, if I was perceiving Him at all, must be a THEIST God, who desires some kind of RELATIONSHIP with these special creatures called human beings, and has therefore instilled this special glimpse of Himself into each one of us. This might be the God of Abraham, but it was certainly not the God of Einstein.

There was another consequence to this growing sense of God's nature, if in fact He was real. Judging by the incredibly high standards of the Moral Law, one that I had to admit I was in the practice of regularly violating, this was a God who was HOLY and RIGHTEOUS. He would have to be the embodiment of GOODNESS. He would have to HATE EVIL, And there was no reason to suspect that this God would be kindly or indulgent."

PSALM 5:4 *"You are not a God who takes pleasure in wickedness, nor shall evil dwell with You."*

COLOSSIANS 3:3-10   Winning the Battle: "I must DIE to myself if I want to LIVE"

"For YOU DIED, and your life is hidden with Christ in God. When Christ WHO IS OUR LIFE appears, then you also will appear with Him in glory. Therefore PUT TO DEATH your members which are on the earth: fornication, uncleanness, passion, evil desire, and covetousness, which is idolatry. Because of these things the wrath of God is coming upon the sons of disobedience, in which you also once walked when you lived in them.

But now you must also PUT OFF all these: anger, wrath, malice, blasphemy, filthy language out of your mouth. Do not lie to one another, since you have PUT OFF THE OLD MAN with his deeds, and have PUT ON THE NEW MAN who is RENEWED IN KNOWLEDGE according to the image of Him who created him."

2Corinthians 5:14-17 *"For the love of Christ constrains us, because we judge thus: that if One died for all, then all died; and He died for all, that those who live should NO LONGER LIVE FOR THEMSELVES, but for Him who died for them and rose again. Therefore, from now on, we regard no one according to the flesh. Even though we have known Christ according to the flesh, yet now we know Him thus no longer… if anyone is in Christ, he is a NEW CREATION; old things have passed away; behold, ALL THINGS HAVE BECOME NEW."*

Ephesians 2:1-3 If you live for yourself: you are already DEAD *"And you He made alive, who were DEAD IN TRESPASSES AND SINS, in which you once walked according to the course of this world, according to the prince of the air, the spirit who now works in the sons of disobedience, among whom also we all once conducted ourselves in the lusts of our flesh, fulfilling the desires of the flesh and of the mind, and were by NATURE children of wrath, just as the others."*

Isaiah 59:10 *"We grope for the wall like the blind, and we grope as if we had no eyes; we stumble at noonday as at twilight, WE ARE AS DEAD MEN in desolate places."*

John 3:3-5

John 3:3-5 If you want to live: you must be CHANGED *"Jesus said to Him, 'Most assuredly, I say to you, unless one is BORN AGAIN, he cannot see the kingdom of God.' Nicodemus said to Him, 'How can a man be born when he is old? Can he enter a 2nd time into his mother's womb and be born?' Jesus answered, "Most assuredly, I say to you, unless one is born of water and the Spirit, he cannot enter the kingdom of God.'"*

Romans 13:14 *"But PUT ON the Lord Jesus Christ, and make no provision for the flesh, to fulfill its lusts."*

Romans 6:3-13 BAPTISM = burying the old man, raising the new man

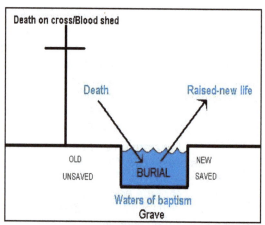

"…do you not know that as many of us as were baptized into Christ Jesus were baptized into his DEATH? Therefore we were BURIED WITH HIM through baptism into death, that just as Christ was raised from the dead by the glory of the Father, even so we also should walk in NEWNESS OF LIFE. For if we have been united together in the likeness of His death, certainly we also shall be in the likeness of His resurrection, knowing this, that OUR OLD MAN WAS CRUCIFIED with Him, that the body of sin might be DONE AWAY WITH, that we should no longer be slaves of sin. For he who has DIED has been freed from sin. Now if we died with Christ, we believe that we should also LIVE with Him, knowing that Christ, having been raised from the dead, dies no more. Death no longer has dominion over Him. For the death that He died, He died to sin once for all; but the life that He lives, He lives to God. Likewise you also, reckon yourselves to be DEAD INDEED TO SIN, but ALIVE TO GOD in Christ Jesus our Lord. Therefore do not let sin reign in your mortal body, that you should obey its lusts. And do not present your members as instruments of unrighteousness to sin, but present yourselves to God as being ALIVE FROM THE DEAD, and your members as instruments of righteousness to God."

Colossians 2:13-14 The Working of God: Change you by the CROSS
"… you, being dead in your trespasses and the uncircumcision of your flesh, He has made alive together with Him, having forgiven you all trespasses, having wiped out the certificate of debt with it's requirements that was against us, which was contrary to us. And He has taken it out of the way, having NAILED IT TO THE CROSS."

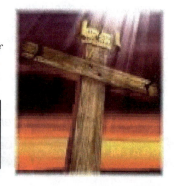

Phillippians 1:6
"…being confident of this very thing, that HE WHO HAS BEGUN A GOOD WORK IN YOU will complete it until the day of Jesus Christ."

"The Normal Christian Life" by Watchman Nee[22]

Watchman Nee (November 4, 1903 – May 30, 1972) was a leader of the original underground church in China, helping to establish local churches in China independent of foreign missionaries that has resulted in one of largest movements of Christianity the world has ever seen.

In 1922, he initiated church meetings in Fuzhou that sparked the beginning of local churches in China. During his 30 years in ministering the gospel of Jesus Christ, he published many books expounding on biblical truth, as well as establishing churches throughout China and leading many conferences to train Bible students and church workers.

Watchman Nee never attended theological schools or Bible institutes. His wealth of knowledge concerning God's purpose, Christ, the Spirit, and the church was acquired through studying the Bible. The Lord revealed many truths to him, which he taught to others, through his diligent study of the Word, which he explains in his book 'How to Study the Bible'.

The Normal Christian Life

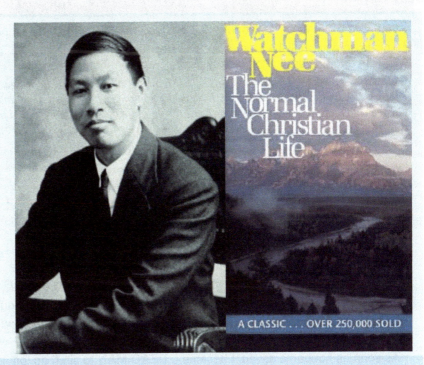

Watchman Nee on Romans 3:23 (man's thinking vs. God's thinking)

"Man's thought is always of the punishment that will come to him if he sins.

God's thought is always of the glory man will miss if he sins.

The result of sin is that we forfeit God's glory.

The result of redemption is that we are qualified again for glory.

God's purpose in redemption is glory, glory, glory." Page 109

"I must first have the sense of God's possession of me before I can have the sense of His presence with me. Once His ownership is established, then I dare do nothing in my own interests, for I am His exclusive property." (page 106)

He also built a collection of over 3,000 of the best Christian books throughout church history, including nearly all the classical Christian writings from the first century forward. His incredible ability to grasp and memorize important scriptural truths and spiritual principles from these books, combined with his deep understanding of God's Word, made him one of if not the most impactful church leader during China's Christian explosive growth.

As the Communist Revolution erupted in 1946 (led by the Communist Party of China and its leader, Chairman Mao Zedong), Nee was persecuted and imprisoned for his faith in 1952 at the age of 49, spending the 20 twenty years of his life in prison until his death in 1972.

Throughout the 14 chapters of his book, Watchman provides the following insights into what the "normal" Christian life looks like with their page references. His deep understanding of his own personal knowing and loving Jesus Christ can help all of us in our own personal journeys in our relationship with Jesus.

My Moral CHARACTER
can defeat my immoral nature

Romans 6:6-7,11,19 Precept 1 = "*Know*";
Precept 2 = "*Reckon*"; Precept 3 = "*Present*"

3.9

THREE KEYS TO VICTORY:		"The degree that I *DIE* will be the degree that I *LIVE* in God's grace" "I must lose to win; I must give in to Christ to go up"
"knowing"	An act of my spirit (Holy Spirit knowledge)	There are certain things I must know; if I am ignorant of God's Word, I cannot expect the power of God.
"reckoning"	An act of my will (head and heart acknowledge)	I must reckon on the facts I found in God's Word; there must be a decision I make to walk daily by faith.
"presenting"	An act of my body (by my reckoning)	I must present my body daily as a living sacrifice.

"KNOWING THIS"   Romans 6:6-7
"Knowing this, that our old man was crucified with Him, that the body of sin might be done away with, that we should no longer be slaves of sin. For he who has died has been freed from sin."

At the CROSS: I have positionally and personally **CRUCIFIED** my sin nature with Christ

▪ This is an accomplished fact by Jesus. Because of *His achievement* at the cross, I have been put to death with Him and declared righteous by God.

Galatians 2:20-21 *"I have been CRUCIFIED WITH CHRIST; it is no longer I who live, but Christ lives in me; and the life which I now live in the flesh I live by faith in the Son of God, who loved me and gave Himself for me. I do not set aside the GRACE of God; for if righteousness comes through the law, then Christ died for nothing."*

Galatians 5:24 *"...those who are Christ's have CRUCIFIED THE FLESH with its passions and desires."*

Galatians 6:14 *"...God forbid that I should glory except in the CROSS of our Lord Jesus Christ, by which the world has been CRUCIFIED to me and I to the world."*

Colossians 2:20-21 *"...if you DIED WITH CHRIST from the basic principles of the world, why, as though living in the world, do you subject yourselves to regulations – do not touch, do not taste, do not handle."*

2Corin. 5:21 *"He made Him who knew no sin to be sin for us, that we might become the RIGHTEOUSNESS OF GOD in Him."*

Colossians 2:13-14 *"And you, being dead in your trespasses and the uncircumcision of your flesh, He has made alive with Him, having forgiven you all trespasses, having wiped out the certificate of death with its requirements that was against us, which was contrary to us. And He has taken it out of the way, having NAILED IT TO THE CROSS."*

Because of the CROSS: I have *daily* access to God's **POWER** to conquer sin and crucify the sin nature in me.

▪ Because I am positionally IN CHRIST, I was also crucified, buried and rose again:
When Jesus died, I died   –   When Jesus was buried, I was buried   –   When Jesus rose, I rose to new life.

▪ As soon as I became saved, I became a **DEAD MAN** to sin (I no longer am a slave to my flesh – I don't have to respond to others' criticisms or offenses – because "*...the joy of the Lord is your strength.*" (Nehemiah 8:10).

▪ A corpse doesn't care about a lot of the things that we as humans get upset about.

1Corinthians 1:17-18 *"...Christ did not send me to baptize, but to preach the gospel, not with wisdom of words, lest the CROSS OF CHRIST should be made of no effect. For the message of the cross is foolishness to those who are perishing, but to us who are being saved it is the POWER OF GOD."*

Romans 1:16 *"...I am not ashamed of the gospel of Christ, for it is the POWER OF GOD to salvation for everyone who believes, for the Jew first and then the Greek."*

"RECKON"   Romans 6:11
"...you also reckon yourselves to be dead indeed to sin, but alive to God in Christ Jesus our Lord."

"reckon" = Gr "LOGIZOMAI" = accounting term for calculate or count on; to "take as fact what you believe is true"

▪ I operate each day by what I *know*, no matter what I *see* (knowing what God says vs. feelings or experience)
2Corinthians 5:7 *"For we walk by faith, not by sight."*
Colossians 3:2 *"Set your mind on the things above, not on things on the earth."*

▪ example: when I balance my checkbook, I record $ transactions, based on the facts of what I know. I "reckon" how I spend and save based on my accounting in my checkbook, even though I do not see the actual money.

- As a Christian: "reckoning" applies with the crucified life – I account according to the figures that God has presented to me in His statement.

Reckoning #1: Justification - Christ's death and resurrection are accomplished facts; I *believed* God's word on sin and salvation by grace through faith in Christ – Jesus' shed **BLOOD** was applied one time at my salvation.

Reckoning #2: Sanctification – now I must *walk by faith* everyday in God's grace and "reckon" my flesh to be dead – I must apply the **CROSS** daily in my life as I live the process of being set apart to God.

- God says my flesh has been crucified and is dead to sin. But if I do not *"reckon"* this to be so, I'll keep feeding my flesh instead of feeding my spirit. So I actually am allowing the "old man", my sin nature, to live and thrive.
- The Bible says I do not have to sin – which means I have **NO EXCUSE** when I do (it is my fault).

Romans 6:7 *"...he who has DIED has been FREED FROM SIN."*
Romans 6:14 *"...sin shall NOT HAVE DOMINION OVER YOU, for you are not under the law but under GRACE."*

- The power of sin is still living and very real, but I can access God's grace through the CROSS and "reckon" myself dead to sin's power (my history will always contain sin, but its no longer my desire to sin).
- I have a choice: I can believe God or believe my flesh
  - justification and sanctification both require walking in **FAITH**
  - God's grace, through His gift of faith, *saved* me; it takes God's grace, through His gift of faith, to *sanctify* me
- Living in victory over sin = living in grace through the power of His **RESURRECTION**

2Corin. 5:14-15 *"...the love of Christ MOTIVATES us, because we judge thus: that if One died for all, then ALL DIED; and He died for all, that those who live should live no longer for themselves, but for Him who died for them and rose again."*
Col. 3:3-5 *"For YOU DIED, and your life is HIDDEN WITH CHRIST in God. When Christ who is OUR LIFE appears, then you also will appear with Him in glory. Therefore PUT TO DEATH YOUR MEMBERS which are on the earth..."*

"PRESENT"   Romans 6:19
"...for just as you presented your members as slaves of uncleanness, and of lawlessness leading to more lawlessness, so now PRESENT your members as slaves of righteousness for holiness ."

"present" = Gr *"PARISTEMI"* = not passive surrender or "giving in"– its active **YIELDING**, as a PRISONER

- example: its not the criminal who stops "running from Him" and finally gives up; it's the criminal who turns himself in (he comes *to* Him and presents himself as His prisoner, extending his arms, saying "here I am, put on the cuffs, I'm your prisoner - do whatever You want with me).

Romans 12:1 *"I beseech you therefore brethren, by the mercies of God, that you PRESENT your BODIES a living sacrifice, holy, acceptable to God, which is your reasonable service."*
Colossians 1:21-22 *"...you, who once were alienated and enemies in your mind by wicked works, yet now He has reconciled in the body of His flesh through death, to PRESENT you holy, blameless, and irreproachable in His sight..."*
Colossians 1:28 *"Him we preach, warning every man and teaching every man in all wisdom, that we may PRESENT every man perfect in Christ Jesus."*

- Greek *"DULOS"* = bondservant; a "3rd level galley slave (the 3rd level was the ship's lowest level – these slaves' only job was to row; they knew there was no hope of escape - if the ship were rammed, or it sunk, they all died).

Romans 1:1 *"Paul, a BONDSERVANT of Jesus Christ, called to be an apostle, separated to the gospel of God..."*
Ephesians 3:1 *"For this reason I, Paul, the prisoner of Jesus Christ for the Gentiles..."*

- Sanctified ("holy") - not just separating myself FROM wrong things, but separating myself TO God, FOR God.

1Thessalonians 4:7 *"For God did not call us to uncleanness, but in HOLINESS..."*
Levit. 11:44 *"I am the Lord your God. You shall therefore SANCTIFY yourselves and you shall be HOLY; for I am holy."*
1Pet 1:15-16 *"as He who called you is holy, you also be holy in all your conduct, as it is written, 'be holy, for I am holy."*

- Biblical "death" never means ceasing to exist; its **SEPARATION** (God *separates* the old man from the new)

Ephesians 4:22-23 *"...put off, concerning your former conduct, the OLD MAN which grows corrupt according to the deceitful lusts, and be renewed in the spirit of your mind, and that you put on the NEW MAN which was created according to God, in righteousness and true holiness."*
2Corinthians 5:17 *"...if anyone is in Christ, he is a new creation; OLD THINGS HAVE PASSED AWAY... all things have become NEW."*

The "Journey of Spiritual Growth":
Applying the CRUCIFIED LIFE

Starting as a child (New Birth) ➔ Growing into the "New Man"

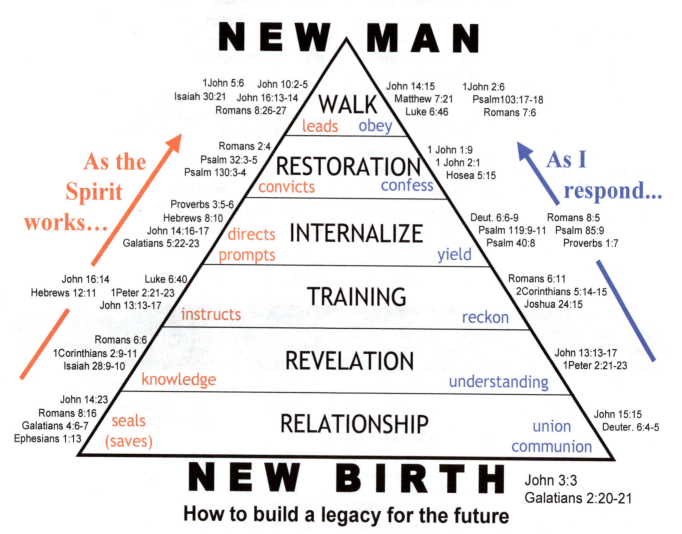

How to build a legacy for the future

As I study the Scriptures listed above for each "layer" in the pyramid:
- ➔ I'll see how the Holy Spirit works in my life to take me from a "new birth" (baby in Christ) and grow me into the "new man" (a mature Christian) who is "childlike" in my willingness to obey His commands.
- ➔ The key to growth in my Christian life (to progressively climb up the layers of the pyramid) is **RESPONDING** to the **LEAD** of the Holy Spirit, as He continually **WORKS** to mold me daily into the image of Jesus Christ.

John Stott[19]: "Who I am in Christ"

"We are to consider not only what we should be but what by God's grace we already are. We are constantly to recall what God has done for us and say to ourselves: God has...
1) united me with Christ in His death and resurrection.
2) obliterated my old life and given me an entirely new life in Christ.
3) adopted me into His family and made me His child.
4) put His Holy Spirit within me and so made my body His temple.
5) made me His heir.
7) promised me an eternal destiny in heaven.

This is what He has done for me and in me. This is who I am in Christ."

My **REVERENCE** is where I begin

Proverbs 1:7 *"The ①FEAR OF THE LORD is the beginning of knowledge, but fools despise wisdom and instruction."*

3.10

① FEAR = Hebr. *"yir'âh"* = morally reverent; afraid of His judgments

Prov. 28:14 *"Happy is the man who is always reverent, but he who hardens his heart will fall into calamity."*
Prov. 9:10 *"The fear of the Lord is the beginning of wisdom, and the knowledge of the Holy One is understanding."*
Prov. 8:13 *"The fear of the Lord is to hate evil; pride, arrogance and the evil way and the perverse mouth I hate."*
Prov. 10:27 *"The fear of the Lord prolongs days, but the years of the wicked will be shortened."*
Prov. 14:27 *"The fear of the Lord is a fountain of life, to avoid the snares of death."*
Prov. 15:33 *"The fear of the Lord is the instruction of wisdom, and before honor is humility."*
Prov. 22:4 *"By humility and fear of the Lord are riches and honor and life."*
Prov. 13:13 *"He who despises the word will be destroyed, but he who fears the commandment will be rewarded."*
Prov. 15:16 *"Better is a little with the fear of the Lord, than great treasure with trouble."*
Prov. 16:6 *"In mercy and truth atonement is provided for iniquity; and by the fear of the Lord one departs from evil."*
Prov. 19:23 *"The fear of the Lord leads to life, and he who has it will abide in satisfaction; he will not be visited with evil."*
Prov. 23:17-18 *"Do not let your heart envy sinners, but in the fear of the Lord continue all day long; for surely there is a hereafter, and your hope will not be cut off."*

> **What it means to "fear God"**

Meaning #1: not cowardice or timidity; being **FRIGHTENED** of His awesome power and righteous retribution:

Luke 12:5 *"But I will show you whom you should fear: Fear Him who, after He has killed, has power to cast into hell; yes, I say to you, fear Him!"*
Psalm 119:120 *"My flesh trembles for fear of You, and I am afraid of Your judgments."*
Isaiah 8:13 *"The Lord of hosts, Him you shall hallow; let Him be your fear, and let Him be your dread."*
Psalm 7:11 *"God is a just judge, and God is angry with the wicked every day."*
Ezekiel 22:13 *"Behold, therefore, I beat My fists at the dishonest profit which you have made, and at the bloodshed which has been in your midst."*

Isaiah 13:6-7,9,11,13 - we see a horrible picture of how awesome God is when He executes His Judgment against unbelievers, as He tells Babylon of the coming "day of the Lord" against them:
"Wail, for the day of the Lord is at hand! It will come as destruction from the Almighty. Therefore all hands will be limp, every man's heart will melt, and they will be afraid. Behold, the day of the Lord comes, cruel with both wrath and fierce anger, to lay the land desolate; and He will destroy its sinners from it. I will punish the world for its evil, and the wicked for their iniquity; I will halt the arrogance of the proud, and will lay low the haughtiness of the tyrants. Therefore I will shake the heavens, and the earth will move out of her place, in the wrath of the Lord of hosts and in the day of His fierce anger."

Meaning #2: a sincere dread of displeasing Him, such that it influences your **ATTITUDE** and inspires a constant carefulness in dealing with others. Jesus taught us this in **John 8:29**. While on earth He had complete confidence in everything He did because His motive was simple: to please His Father: *"And He who sent Me is with Me. The Father has not left Me alone, for I always do those things that please Him."*

Prov. 14:26 *"In the fear of the Lord there is strong confidence, and His children will have a place of refuge."*
Psalm 85:9 *"Surely His salvation is near to those who fear Him, that glory may dwell in our land."*
Psalm 89:7 *"God is greatly to be feared in the assembly of the saints, and to be held in reverence by those around Him."*
Psalm 112:1 *"Blessed is everyone who fears the Lord, who delights greatly in His commandments."*
Psalm 115:11,13 *"You who fear the Lord, trust in the Lord; He is their help and their shield, He will bless those who fear the Lord, both small and great."*
Psalm 118:4 *"Let those who fear the Lord now say, 'His mercy endures forever.'"*
Psalm 128:1 *"Blessed is everyone who fears the Lord, who walks in His ways."*
Psalm 130:4 *"But there is forgiveness with You, that You may be feared."*
Psalm 147:11 *"The Lord takes pleasure in those who fear Him, in those who hope in His mercy."*
Job 28:28 *"And to the man He said, 'Behold, the fear of the Lord, that is wisdom; to depart from evil is understanding.'"*
Isaiah 33:6 *"Wisdom and knowledge will be the stability of your times, and the strength of salvation; the fear of the Lord is His treasure."*
Isaiah 66:2 *"But on this one I will look: on him who is poor and of a contrite spirit, and who trembles at My word."*

Psalm 145:17-20   God's Love requires Him to judge Evil

"The Lord is ①RIGHTEOUS in all His ②WAYS, ③GRACIOUS in all His ④WORKS. The Lord is ⑤NEAR to all who call upon Him, to all who call upon Him in ⑥TRUTH. He will fulfill the desire of those who ⑦FEAR Him; He will also hear their cry and ⑧SAVE them. The Lord ⑨PRESERVES all who ⑩LOVE Him, but all the ⑩WICKED He will ⑩DESTROY."

① RIGHTEOUS = Hebr. *"tsaddiyq"* = lawful, just.
② WAYS = Hebr. *"derek"* = roads trodden upon; courses of life, modes of action chosen.
③ GRACIOUS = Hebr. *"châsyîd"* = kind, merciful
④ WORKS = Hebr. *"ma'áśeh"* = activity; transactions; labors
⑤ NEAR = Hebr. *"qârôb qârôb"* = allied with; kinsman to; the closest neighbor
⑥ TRUTH = Hebr. *"'emech"* = trustworthiness; faithfulness; certainty
⑦ FEAR = Hebr. *"yârê"* = morally reverent; afraid of His judgments
⑧ SAVE = Hebr. *"yâsha'"* = to free, deliver or rescue; to bring or delivery to safety
⑨ PRESERVES = Hebr. *"shâmar"* = puts a hedge around; guards; protects; diligently attends to
⑩ LOVE = Hebr. *"'ahâb 'ahêb"* = have affection for; care for in friendship
⑩ WICKED = Hebr. *"râshâ"* = morally wrong; ungodly
⑩ DESTROY = Hebr. *"shâmad"* = utterly desolate; pluck down; bring to nothing

---

Timothy Keller[14]: 'A God of Judgment can't be a God of Love?'

"In Christianity God is both a God of love and justice. Many people struggle with this. They believe that a loving God can't be a judging God... I have been asked literally thousands of times, 'How can a God of love be also a God filled with wrath and anger? If he is loving and perfect, he should forgive and accept everyone. He shouldn't get angry.'

I start my response by pointing out that all loving persons are sometimes filled with wrath, not just despite of but because of their love. If you love a person and you see someone ruining them – even they themselves – you get angry. As **Becky Pippert** puts in her book 'Hope Has Its Reasons': *Think how you feel when we see someone we love ravaged by unwise actions or relationships. Do you respond with benign tolerance as we might toward strangers? Far from it... Anger isn't the opposite of love. Hate is, and the final form of hate is indifference... God's wrath is not a cranky explosion, but a settled opposition to the cancer... which is eating out the insides of the human race He loves with His whole being.*'

Yale theologian **Miroslav Volf**, a Croatian who has seen the violence in the Balkans... writes below that it is the lack of belief in a God of vengeance that 'secretly nourishes violence': *'If God were not angry at injustice and deception and did not make a final end to violence – that God would not be worthy of worship... The only means of prohibiting all recourse to violence by ourselves is to insist that violence is legitimate only when it comes from God... My thesis that the practice of non-violence requires a belief in divine vengeance will be unpopular with many... in the West... (But) it takes the quiet of a suburban home for the birth of the thesis that human non-violence (results from the belief in) God's refusal to judge. In a sun-scorched land, soaked in the blood of the innocent, it will invariably die... (with) other pleasant captivities of the liberal mind.'*

Can our passion for justice be honored in a way that does not nurture our desire for blood vengeance? Volf says the best resource for this is belief in the concept of God's DIVINE JUSTICE. If I don't believe that there is a God who will eventually put all things right, I will take up the sword and will be sucked into the endless vortex of retaliation. Only if I am sure that there's a God who will right all wrongs and settle all accounts perfectly do I have the power to refrain.

Czeslaw Milosz, the Nobel Prize-winning Polish poet, wrote the remarkable essay 'The Discreet Charms of Nihilism'. In it he remembers how Marx had called religion 'the opiate of the people' because the promise of an afterlife (Marx said) led the poor and the working class to put up with unjust social conditions. But, Milosz continued: *'And now we are witnessing a transformation. A true opium of the people is a belief in nothingness after death – the huge solace of thinking that our betrayals, greed, cowardice, murders are not going to be judged... (but) all religions recognize that our deeds are imperishable.'*

Many complain that belief in a God of judgment will lead to a more brutal society. Milosz had personally seen, in both Nazism and Communism, that a loss of belief in a GOD OF JUDGMENT can lead to brutality. If we are free to shape life and morals any way we choose without ultimate accountability, it can lead to violence."

Volf and Milosz argument: "The doctrine of God's final judgment is a NECESSARY UNDERGIRDING for human practices of love and peacemaking."

Hell = The Greatest Monument to Human Free Will

Romans 1:24-25 *"God gave them up to uncleanness, in the lusts of their hearts, to dishonor their bodies among themselves who exchanged the truth of God for a lie, and worshipped and served the creature rather than the Creator…"*

Matthew 25:41 *"He will also say to those on the left hand, 'Depart from Me, you cursed, into the ⑤EVERLASTING ⑥FIRE ⑦PREPARED for the ⑧DEVIL and his angels…"*

Matthew 10:28 *"Do not ①FEAR those who kill the body but cannot kill the ②SOUL. But rather ①FEAR Him who is able to ③DESTROY both soul and body in ④HELL."*

① FEAR = Gr. *"phobeō"* = to be exceedingly frightened by or afraid of; to be in awe of; to reverence
② SOUL = Gr. *"psuchē"* = breath; spirit.
③ DESTROY = Gr. *"apollumi"* = cause to perish; it does not indicate annihilation, but ruination (see Matthew 9:17, where same verb is used when referring to wineskins being ruined).
④ HELL = Gr. *"geenna"* = valley of Hinnom (garbage dump outside the walls of Jerusalem), used as the name for the place, or state, of everlasting punishment. It was a smoldering fire where maggots fed off the garbage.
⑤ EVERLASTING = Gr. *"'aiōnios"* = perpetual; eternal (since the world began) – same word as in John 3:16
⑥ FIRE = Gr. *"pur"* = fire, as is in lightning
⑦ PREPARED = Gr. *"hetoimazô"* = to make ready
⑧ DEVIL = Gr. *"diabolos"* = Satan (specifically, false accuser, transducer, slanderer)

Timothy Keller (excerpts from 'The Reason for God', pages 78-82)[14]: "Modern people inevitably think that hell works like this: God gives us time, but if we haven't made the right choices by the end of our lives, he casts our souls into hell for all eternity. As the poor souls fall through space, they cry for mercy, but God says 'Too late! You had your chance! Now you will suffer!' This caricature misunderstands the very nature of evil.

The Biblical picture is that sin separates us from the presence of God, which is the source of all joy and indeed of all love, wisdom, or good things of any sort. Since we were originally created for God's immediate presence, only before His face will we thrive, flourish, and achieve our highest potential. If we were to lose His presence totally, that would be hell – the loss of our capability for giving and receiving love or joy.

A common image of hell in the Bible is that of **FIRE**. Fire disintegrates. Even in this life we can see the kind of soul disintegration that self-centeredness creates. We know how selfishness and self-absorption leads to piercing bitterness, nauseating envy, paralyzing anxiety, paranoid thoughts, and the mental denials and distortions that accompany them. Now ask the question, 'What if when we die we don't end, but spiritually our life extends on to eternity?' Hell, then, is the trajectory of the soul, living in a self-absorbed, self-centered life, going on forever.

In his fantasy 'The Great Divorce', C.S. Lewis describes a busload of people from hell who come to the outskirts of heaven. There they are urged to leave behind the sins that have trapped them in hell – but they refuse. Lewis's descriptions of these people are striking because we recognize in them the self-delusion and self-absorption that are 'writ small' in our own addictions: 'Hell begins with a grumbling mood, always complaining, always blaming others… but you are still distinct from it. You may even criticize it in yourself and wish you could stop it. But there may come a day when you can no longer. Then there will be no you left to criticize the mood or even to enjoy it, but just the grumble itself, going on forever like a machine. It is not a question of God 'sending us' to hell. In each of us there is something growing, which will BE HELL unless it is nipped in the bud.'

The people in hell are miserable, but Lewis shows us why. We see raging like unchecked flames their pride, their paranoia, their self-pity, their certainty that everyone else is wrong, that everyone else is an idiot! All humility is gone, and thus so is their sanity. They are utterly, finally locked in a prison of their own self-centeredness, and their pride progressively expands into a bigger and bigger mushroom cloud. They continue to go to pieces forever, blaming everyone but themselves. Hell is that, 'writ large'.

That is why it is a travesty to picture God casting people into a pit who are crying 'I'm sorry! Let me out!' The people on the bus from hell in Lewis's parable would rather have their 'freedom', as they define it, than salvation. Their delusion is that, if they glorified God, they would somehow lose power and freedom, but in a supreme and tragic irony, their choice has ruined their own potential for greatness. **Hell is, as Lewis says, 'the greatest monument to human freedom.'**

As Romans 1:24 says, 'God gave them up to… their desires.' All God does in the end with people is give them what they most want, including freedom from Himself. What could be more fair than that? Lewis writes:

'There are only two kinds of people – those who say "Thy will be done" to God or those to whom God in the end says, "Thy will be done." All that are in Hell choose it. Without that self-choice it wouldn't be Hell. No soul that seriously and constantly desires joy will ever miss it.'"

My HUMILITY
attracts God to me

Proverbs 3:34 *"God resists the PROUD, but gives grace to the HUMBLE."*

- Proud = *"HUPERĒPHANOS"* = "huper" = above, "phainomai" = to manifest → showing oneself above others
- Humble = *"TAPEINOS"* = low-lying, in the sense of my mind and position

> Rick Warren[1] : the best Definition of HUMILITY
>
> **"Humility is not thinking less of yourself; it is thinking of yourself LESS"**
> John 3:30 *"He must increase, but I MUST DECREASE."*
>
> - Humility is not putting yourself down or denying your strengths; rather, it is being honest about your weaknesses. The more honest you are, the more of God's grace you get. You will also receive grace from others. Vulnerability is an endearing quality; we are naturally drawn to humble people.
>
> - Pride blocks God's grace in our lives, which we must have in order to grow, change, heal and help others. We only receive God's grace by humbly admitting that we need it.
>
> - Humble people focused on serving others, not themselves. Self-important, stubborn pride destroys fellowship faster than anything else. Pride builds walls between people; humility builds bridges.

WHAT ARE THE 2 VIEWS ON "SELF" ?

The World	The Christian	
loves and worships	hates	Job 42:5-6
pleases and trusts	distrusts	Psalm 146:3-4, Jerem. 17:5
protects and guards	gives up, forsakes	Rom. 12:1, Luke 14:33
justifies, saves (the "victim")	condemns (the "guilty")	Ps 14:1-3, Ps 143:2, Rom. 3:10,19
develop, improve	abandon, empty	Matt. 18:3-4, 2Ki 5:8-17, Luke 4:27-28
important (self-respect)	nothing	Isa. 40:17, Isa. 2:22, Ps 39:5
focus	forget	Phil. 2:3
promote (lift up)	demote (lower)	Luke 14:7-11, Prov. 25:6-7
find	lose	Matt. 10:39

> **The Holy Spirit's main ministry = develop *CHRIST-LIKENESS* in me**
> (Galatians 5:22-23, Philippians 1:6)
>
> But He will either: resist me if I am proud (Proverbs 3:34, James 4:6,10)
>   break me, to bring me to that point of needing Him (2Kings 5:8-17)

C.S. Lewis[6]: "The Great Sin"

1) "There is one vice of which no man in the world is free; which everyone in the world loathes when he sees it in someone else; and of which hardly any people, except Christians, ever imagine that they are guilty themselves. I have heard people admit that they are bad-tempered, or that they cannot keep their heads about girls or drinking, or even that they are cowards. I do not think I have ever heard anyone who was not a Christian accuse himself of this vice. At the same time, I have seldom met anyone, who was not a Christian, who showed the slightest mercy to it in others. There is no fault which makes a man more unpopular, and no fault which we are more unconscious of in ourselves. And the more we have it ourselves, the more we dislike it in others.

2) The vice I am talking about is <u>PRIDE</u>; the virtue opposite to it, in Christian morals, is <u>HUMILITY</u>. You may remember, when I was talking about sexual immorality, I warned you that the center of Christian morals did not lie there. Well, now we have come to the center. The essential vice, the utmost evil, is pride. It was through pride that the devil became the devil. Pride leads to every other vice. It is the complete <u>ANTI-GOD</u> state of mind.

3) Pride is <u>COMPETITIVE</u> by its very nature. Pride gets no pleasure out of having something, only out of having more than the next man. We say that people are proud of being rich, or clever, or good-looking, but they are not. They are proud of being richer, or more clever, or better looking, than others. It is the comparison that makes you proud, the pleasure of being above the rest. Greed may drive men into competition if there is not enough to go around; but the proud man, even when he has gotten more than he wants, will try to get still more just to assert his power. Nearly all those evils in the world that people put down to greed or selfishness are really far more the result of pride.

4) It is pride which has been the chief cause of misery in every nation and every family since the world began. Other vices may sometimes bring people together: you may find good fellowship among drunken or unchaste people. But pride always means <u>ENMITY</u> - not only between man and man, but enmity to God. In God you come up against something which is in every respect immeasurably superior to yourself. Unless you know God as that- and, therefore, know yourself as nothing in comparison – you cannot <u>KNOW</u> God. A proud man is always looking down on things and people; and as long as you are looking down, you cannot see something that is above you.

5) That raises a terrible question: how is it that people who are eaten up with pride can say they believe in God and appear to themselves very religious? I am afraid it means they are worshipping an imaginary God. They tell themselves they are nothing in the presence of this phantom God, but are really imagining how He approves of them and thinks them far better than ordinary people. It was of those people Christ was thinking when He said some would preach about Him and cast out devils in His name, only to be told at the end of the world that He had never known them. Any of us may at any moment be in this death-trap.

6) Luckily, we have a test: whenever we find that our religious life is making us feel that we are good – above all, that we are better than someone else – we may be sure that we are being acted on, not by God, but by the devil. The real test of being in the God's presence is you either forget about yourself altogether or you see yourself as a small, dirty object. It is better to <u>FORGET</u> about yourself altogether.

7) Pride comes directly from <u>HELL</u>. It is purely spiritual, so it is far more subtle and deadly. Pride is often used to beat down the simpler vices. Teachers often appeal to a boy's pride, or self-respect, to make him behave decently. Many men have overcome cowardice, or lust, or ill-temper, by learning to think they are beneath his pride. The devil laughs. He is perfectly content to see you become chaste and brave and self-controlled provided he is setting up in you the dictatorship of pride – just as he would be quite content to see your ulcer cured if he was allowed to give you cancer. For pride is a spiritual <u>CANCER</u> – it eats up the very possibility of love, or contentment, or even common sense.

8) Pleasure in being praised is not pride. For here the pleasure lies not in what you are but in the fact that you have pleased someone you wanted to please. But the more you delight in yourself and the less you delight in praise, the worse you are becoming. When you delight wholly in yourself and do not care about praise at all, you have reached the bottom. The diabolical pride comes when you look down on others so much you do not care what they think of you.

9) We must not think pride is something God forbids because He is offended at it, or that humility is something He demands as due His own dignity – as if God was proud. He is not at all worried about His dignity. The point is, He wants you to <u>KNOW</u> Him; He wants to give Himself to you. If you really get into any kind of touch with Him you will, in fact, be humble – delightedly humble, feeling the infinite relief of having for once got rid of all the silly nonsense about your own dignity which has made you restless and unhappy all your life.

10) Do not imagine that if you meet a really humble man he will be what most people call 'humble' nowadays. He will not be a sort of greasy, apologetic person who is always telling you that, of course, he is nobody. Probably all you will think about him is that he seemed a cheerful, intelligent chap who took a real interest in what you said to him. He will not be thinking about being humble – he will not be thinking about <u>HIMSELF</u> at all.

11) If anyone would like to acquire humility, I can, I think, tell him the first step: it is to realize that one is proud. Nothing can be done before it. If you think you are not conceited, it means you are very conceited indeed."

My SUBMISSION
demonstrates my humility

Proverbs 16:3 *"COMMIT your works to the Lord, and your thoughts will be established"*

3.12

- "HUPEIKO" (to submit) and "HUPOTASSO" (to be placed under) = a military term meaning to be subject to

Why must I submit?

1. to silence the critics: The world is watching and looking for FAULTS in Christians. We have to eliminate the faults by living an exemplary life, that points to Jesus Christ.

1Peter 2:16 *"For this is the WILL OF GOD, that by doing good you may put to silence the ignorance of foolish men…"*

2Peter 3:15-16 *"…sanctify the Lord God in your hearts, and always BE READY to give a defense to everyone who asks you a REASON for the hope that is in you, with meekness and fear; having a good conscience, that when they DEFAME YOU AS EVILDOERS, those who revile your good conduct in Christ maybe ashamed."*

2. to glorify God to men: The world needs Christ. By submitting to the laws, and to each other within the bounds of Scripture, we will attract people to us, which is really an attraction to our Savior.

1Corin. 9:19,22-23 *"Though I am free from all men, I have made myself a SERVANT TO ALL, that I might win the more. I have become ALL THINGS to all men, that I might by all means save some. Now this I do for the GOSPEL'S SAKE…"*

Matt. 5:13-16 *"You are the SALT of the earth; but if the salt loses its flavor, how shall it be seasoned? It is then good for nothing but to be thrown out and trampled underfoot by men. You are the LIGHT of the world. A city set on a hill cannot be hidden. Nor do they light a lamp and put it under a basket, but on a lampstand, and it gives light to all in the house. Let your light SO SHINE BEFORE MEN, that they may see your good works and glorify your Father in heaven."*

John MacArthur ('Found: God's Will'[4]) "…if Christians learned to live the kind of life Peter described we would knock the world right off its pins. But sometimes the world can't distinguish us from itself. God wants us to be the kind of citizens in the world that will draw the attention of the world. We must be **DIFFERENT**. We need to have the qualities of salt and light. That involves submission, which is clearly commanded in Scripture."

I must submit to JESUS CHRIST as Sovereign Lord

James 4:7 *"Therefore SUBMIT to God."*

Romans 12:1 *"I beseech you therefore, brethren, by the mercies of God, that you present your bodies a LIVING SACRIFICE, holy, acceptable to God, which is your REASONABLE SERVICE."*

Hebrews 12:9 *"…we have had human fathers who corrected us, and we paid them respect. Shall we not much more readily be IN SUBJECTION to the Father of spirits and live?"*

Ephesians 1:22-23 *"And He put ALL THINGS UNDER HIS FEET, and gave Him to be head over all things to the church, which is His body, the fullness of Him who fills all in all."*

Philippians 3:20-21 *"For our citizenship is in heaven, from which we also eagerly wait for the Savior, the Lord Jesus Christ, who will transform our lowly body that it might be conformed to His glorious body, according to the working by which He is able even to SUBDUE ALL THINGS to Himself."*

1Peter 3:21-22 *"…Jesus Christ, who has gone into heaven and is at the right hand of God, angels and authorities and powers having been made SUBJECT to Him."*

Romans 10:2-4 *"For I bear them witness that they have a zeal for God, but not according to knowledge. For they being ignorant of God's righteousness, and seeking to establish their own righteousness, HAVE NOT SUBMITTED to the righteousness of God. For Christ is the end of the law for righteousness to everyone who believes."*

Romans 8:7 *"For the carnal mind is enmity against God; for it is NOT SUBJECT to the law of God, nor indeed can be."*

I must submit to OTHERS (my spouse, my parents, other believers)

1Peter 5:5-6 *"…you younger people, SUBMIT yourselves to your elders. Yes, all of you BE SUBMISSIVE TO ONE ANOTHER, and be clothed with humility, for 'God resists the proud, but gives grace to the humble.' Therefore HUMBLE yourselves under the mighty hand of God, that He may EXALT you in due time…"*

1Corin. 16:15-16 *"… you know the household of Stephanas, that it is the firstfruits of Achaia, and that they have devoted themselves to the ministry of the saints – that you also SUBMIT to such, and to everyone who works and labors with us."*

Ephesians 5:17,18,21 *"Therefore do not be unwise, but understand what the will of the Lord is. And do not be drunk with wine, in which is dissipation, but be filled with the Spirit, SUBMITTING TO ONE ANOTHER in the fear of the Lord."*

Ephesians 5:22-24 (Col. 3:18) *"Wives, SUBMIT to your own husbands, as to the Lord. For the husband is head of the wife, as also Christ is head of the church; and He is Savior of the body. Therefore, just as the church is SUBJECT to Christ, so let the wives be to their own husbands in everything. Wives, SUBMIT to your own husbands, as is fitting in the Lord."*

1Peter 3:1-2 *"…you wives, BE SUBMISSIVE to your own husbands, that even if some do not obey the word, they, without a word, may be won by the conduct of their wives, when they observe your chaste conduct accompanied by fear."*

I must submit to GOVERNMENT (ruling authorities)

1Peter 2:13-16 *"Therefore SUBMIT yourselves to every ordinance of man for the Lord's sake, whether to the king as supreme, or to governors, as to those who are sent by him for the punishment of evildoers and for the praise of those who do good. For this is the WILL OF GOD, that by doing good you may put to silence the ignorance of foolish men – as free, yet not using your liberty as a cloak for wickedness, but as servants of God."*

Rom. 13:1-7 *"Let every soul be SUBJECT to the governing authorities. For there is no authority except from God, and the authorities that exist are appointed by God. Therefore whoever resists the authority resists the ordinance of God, and those who resist will bring judgment on themselves. For rulers are not a terror to good works, but to evil. Do you want to be unafraid of the authority? Do what is good, and you will have praise from the same. For he is God's minister to you for good. But if you do evil, be afraid; for he does not bear the sword in vain; for he is God's minister, an avenger to execute wrath on him who practices evil. Therefore YOU MUST BE SUBJECT, not only because of wrath but also for conscience' sake. For because of this you also pay taxes, for they are God's ministers attending continually to this very thing. Render therefore to all their due: taxes to whom taxes are due, customs to whom customs, fear to whom fear, honor to whom honor."*

Titus 3:1 *"Remind them to be SUBJECT to rulers and authorities to obey, to be ready for every good work..."*

How do I know when I've submitted to God's will?
- I rely on Him to work things out, instead of trying to manipulate others, force my agenda, or control the situation.
- I stop worrying about being right – I'm more concerned with the other person than with defending myself.
- I see serving other people as an **OPPORTUNITY** instead of an OBLIGATION.

The Character of Jesus Christ: Submission = SERVING One Another in Love

Galatians 6:2 *"Bear one another's burdens, and so fulfill the LAW OF CHRIST."*

Matthew 22:36-40 *"Teacher, which is the greatest commandment in the law?" Jesus said to him, "You shall love the Lord your God with all your heart, with all your soul, and with all your mind. This is the first and greatest commandment. And the second is like it: you shall LOVE YOUR NEIGHBOR AS YOURSELF. On these 2 commandments hang all the Law and the Prophets."*

He showed us servanthood how by LIVING it:

Luke 2:51-52 *"Then He went down with them and came to Nazareth, and was SUBJECTED to them, but His mother kept all these things in her heart. And Jesus increased in wisdom and stature, and in favor with God and men."*

Matthew 20:26-28 *"...whoever desires to become great among you, let him be your SERVANT. And whoever desires to be first among you, let him be your SLAVE. Just as the Son of Man did not come to be served, BUT TO SERVE, and to give His life a ransom for many."*

Philippians 2:3-8 *"Let nothing be done through selfish ambition or conceit, but in LOWLINESS OF MIND let each esteem others BETTER THAN HIMSELF. Let each look out not only for his own interests, but also the interests of others. Let THIS MIND be in you WHICH WAS ALSO IN CHRIST JESUS, who, being in the form of God, did not consider it robbery to be equal with God, but MADE HIMSELF OF NO REPUTATION, taking the form of a SERVANT, and coming in the likeness of men. And being found in appearance as a man, HE HUMBLED HIMSELF, and became obedient to the point of death, even the death of the cross."*

John 13:12-17 *"So when He had washed their feet, taken His garments, and sat down again, He said to them, 'Do you know what I have done to you? You call Me Teacher and Lord, and you say well, for so I am. If I then, your Lord and Teacher, have washed your feet, you also ought to WASH ONE ANOTHER'S FEET. For I have given you an EXAMPLE, that you should do as I have done to you. Most assuredly, I say to you, a servant is not greater than his master, nor is he who is sent greater than he who sent him. If you know these things, happy are you if you DO them.'"*

What does John 13:17 mean?
God won't bless you ("happy") because you KNOW what He commands, but because you **do** what He commands.

His command to you is to **surrender** the controls of your life to Him, which is evidenced by your willingness to serve Him and others in His name.

Mark 9:33-35 *"... when He was in the house He asked them, 'What was it you disputed among yourselves on the road?' But they kept silent, for on the road they had disputed among themselves who would be the greatest. And He sat down, called the 12, and said to them, 'IF ANYONE DESIRES TO BE FIRST, HE SHALL BE LAST OF ALL AND SERVANT OF ALL.'"*

Romans 6:18 *"And having been set free from sin, you became SLAVES OF RIGHTEOUSNESS."*

Galatians 5:13 *"For you, brethren have been called to liberty; only do not use liberty as an opportunity for the flesh, but through love to SERVE ONE ANOTHER."*

My MEEKNESS
reveals my understanding

Proverbs 17:27 *"He who has knowledge spares his words, and a man of understanding is of a CALM SPIRIT."*

Slow to Anger = great UNDERSTANDING of God
Prov. 14:17 *"He who is QUICK-TEMPERED acts foolishly, and a man of wicked intentions is hated."*
Prov. 14:29 *"He who is SLOW TO WRATH has great understanding, but he who is impulsive exalts folly."*
Prov. 16:32 *"He who is SLOW TO ANGER is better than the mighty, and he who rules his spirit than he who takes a city."*
Prov. 19:11 *"The discretion of a man makes him SLOW TO ANGER, and it is to his glory to overlook a transgression."*
Prov. 20:3 *"It is honorable for a man to STOP STRIVING, since any fool can start a quarrel."*
Prov. 25:28 *"Whoever has NO RULE OVER HIS SPIRIT is like a city broken down, without walls."*

Under control = often means you THINK before speaking
Prov. 17:28 *"Even a fool is counted wise when he HOLDS HIS PEACE; when he shuts his lips, he is counted perceptive."*
Prov. 11:12 *"He who is devoid of wisdom despises his neighbor, but a man of understanding HOLDS HIS PEACE."*
Prov. 10:19 *"In the multitude of words sin is not lacking, but he who RESTRAINS HIS LIPS is wise."*
Prov. 13:3 *"He who GUARDS HIS MOUTH preserves life, but he who opens wide his lips shall have destruction."*
Prov. 21:23 *"Whoever GUARDS HIS MOUTH and tongue keeps his soul from trouble."*
Prov. 14:33 *"Wisdom rests quietly in the heart of him with understanding, but what is in the heart of fools is made known."*
Prov. 18:21 *"Death and life are in the power of the tongue, and those who love it will eat its fruit."*

Listening = understand the other person's VIEWPOINT before giving your opinion
Prov. 18:2 *"A fool has no delight in understanding, but in expressing his own heart."*
Prov. 18:13 *"He who answers a matter before he hears it, it is folly and shame to him."*
Prov. 29:20 *"Do you see a man hasty in his words? There is more hope for a fool than for him."*
Prov. 29:11 *"A fool vents all his feelings, but a wise man holds them back."*

God's Character = MEEK

Matthew 11:28-29 *"Come to Me, all you who labor and are heavy laden, and I will give you rest. Take My yoke upon you and learn from Me, for I am ①MEEK and lowly in heart, and you will find rest for your souls."*

Zechariah 9:9 (Matthew 21:5) *"Rejoice greatly, O daughter of Zion! Shout, O daughter of Jerusalem! Behold, your King is coming to you; He is just and having salvation, ①MEEK and riding on a donkey. A colt, the foal of a donkey."*

2Corinthians 10:1 *"Now I, Paul, myself am pleading with you by the ①MEEKNESS and gentleness of Christ..."*

Vincent's Word Studies in the New Testament, Vine's Expository Dictionary of Old and New Testament Words
① Meek = "*PRAÜS, PRAÜTÊS*" = mild, gentle in my spirit; an inward quality of *self-control* (Galatians 5:23).
<u>the Greeks</u>: "meek" was applied to people in terms of their *outward* conduct (suggests weak or effeminate).
<u>the Bible</u>: "meek" has a much higher meaning - it consists not only in a person's outward behavior, nor in his relations to his fellow men...it is an **INWARD** grace of the soul (a condition of mind and heart), and the exercises of meekness are first seen in submission to God's will (meekness is evidence of a spiritual relationship to God).

<u>Meekness toward God</u>: I accept God's dealings with me as good, and therefore without disputing or resisting (I see opposition, insult, persecution as God's permitted ministers of chastening, all the while bearing patiently "the contradiction of sinners against me" by forgiving and restoring the erring).

Meekness requires **HUMILITY**, which is not a natural quality but an outgrowth of a renewed nature (only the humble heart is meek, and as such, does not fight against God).

<u>Meekness toward others</u>: insults or injuries are permitted and used by God to chasten and purify His elect.

For a Christian, meekness is manifested by **SUBMISSION** (Galatians 6:1), where I am to forgive and restore lest I also be tempted (it springs from a sense of inferiority of the sinful creature to the holy Creator).

Matthew 5:5 *"Blessed are the MEEK, for they shall inherit the earth."*

Galatians 5:22-23 *"...the fruit of the Spirit is love, joy, peace, longsuffering, kindness, goodness, faithfulness, MEEKNESS, SELF-CONTROL. Against such there is no law."*

2Timothy 2:24-25 *"...a servant of the Lord must not quarrel but be MEEK to all, able to teach, patient, in humility correcting those who are in opposition, if God perhaps will grant them repentance, so that they may know the truth..."*

1Peter 3:15 *"...sanctify the Lord God in your hearts, and always be ready to give a defense to everyone who asks you a reason for the hope that is in you, with MEEKNESS and fear..."*

Why God didn't let Moses lead His people into the Promised Land

- In **Deuteronomy 32:51-52**, God tells Moses he will not lead the Israelites into the Promised Land, because his sin against Him resulted in God not being glorified in their eyes: *"...because YOU TRESPASSED AGAINST ME among the children of Israel at the waters of Meribah Kadesh, in the Wilderness of Zin, because you did not hallow Me in the midst of the children of Israel, yet you shall see the land before you, though you shall not go there, into the land which I am giving to the children of Israel."*

- God takes Himself very seriously: He told Moses in **Leviticus 10:3** that His character must be glorified as holy: *"By those who come near Me I must be regarded as holy; and before all the people I must be glorified."*

- What was Moses's sin against God? **Numbers 20:2-13** tells us what happened at Meribah Kadesh that caused Moses to lose his leadership role over the Israelites: *"Now there was no water for the congregation; so they gathered together against Moses and Aaron. And the people contended with Moses and spoke, saying: 'If only we had died when our brethren died before the Lord! Why have you brought up this congregation of the Lord into this wilderness, that we and our animals should die here? And why have you made us come out of Egypt, to bring us to this evil place? It is not a place of grain or figs or vines or pomegranates; nor is there any water to drink.' So Moses and Aaron went from the presence of the assembly to the door of the tabernacle of meeting, and they prostrated themselves on their faces. And the glory of the Lord appeared to them.*

Then the Lord spoke to Moses, saying, 'Take the rod; you and your brother Aaron gather the assembly together. SPEAK TO THE ROCK before their eyes, and it will yield its water; thus you shall bring water for them out of the rock and give drink to the congregation and their animals.' So Moses took the rod from before the Lord as He commanded him. And Moses and Aaron gathered the congregation together before the rock; and he said to them, 'Hear now, you rebels! Must WE bring water for you out of this rock?' Then Moses lifted his hand and STRUCK THE ROCK TWICE with his rod; and water came out abundantly, and the congregation and their animals drank. Then the Lord spoke to Moses and Aaron, 'Because YOU DID NOT BELIEVE ME, TO HALLOW ME in the eyes of the children of Israel, therefore you shall not bring this congregation into the land which I have given them.' This was the water of Meribah, because the children of Israel contended with the Lord, and He was hallowed among them."

- Was Moses faithless? Numbers 12:6-8 *"Then He said, 'Hear now My words: if there is a prophet among you, I, the Lord, make myself known to him in a vision, and I speak to him in a dream. Not so with My servant Moses; he is faithful in all My house. I speak to him face to face, even plainly, and not in dark sayings; and he sees the form of the Lord."*

Hebrews 11:24-27 *"By faith Moses, when he became of age, refused to be called the son of Pharaoh's daughter, choosing rather to suffer affliction with the people of God than to enjoy the passing pleasures of sin, esteeming the reproach of Christ greater riches than the treasures in Egypt; for he looked to the reward. By faith he forsook Egypt, not fearing the wrath of the king, for he endured as seeing Him who is invisible."*

- Was Moses proud? Numbers 12:3 *"Moses was very humble, more than all men who were on the face of the earth."*

- God actually says He had a special relationship with Moses unlike any other man alive - Exodus 33:9-11,14,17 *"...it came to pass, when Moses entered the tabernacle, that the pillar of cloud descended and stood at the door of the tabernacle, and the Lord talked with Moses. All the people saw the pillar of cloud standing at the tabernacle door, and all the people rose and worshipped, each man in his tent door. So the Lord spoke to Moses face to face, AS A MAN SPEAKS TO HIS FRIEND. And He said, 'My Presence will go with you, and I WILL GIVE YOU REST. Then the Lord said to Moses, 'I will also do this thing that you have spoken, for you have found grace in My sight, and I KNOW YOU BY NAME'"*

- Moses's sin: his lack of **MEEKNESS** was revealed in his outbursts of **ANGER**. In **Numbers 20:2-13**, as an *OLD MAN*, his uncontrolled anger over the peoples' complaints and rebellion against God cost him the leadership of Israel into Canaan. And In **Exodus 2:11-15**, as a *YOUNG MAN*, he was so incensed when he saw an Egyptian beating a Jew that he murdered the Egyptian, causing him to flee for his life into exile as a refugee: *"Now it came to pass in those days, when Moses was grown, that he went out to his brethren and looked at their burdens. And he saw an Egyptian beating a Hebrew, one of his brothers.*

So HE LOOKED THIS WAY AND THAT, and WHEN HE SAW NO ONE, he killed the Egyptian and hid him in the sand. And when he went out the 2nd day, behold, two Hebrew men were fighting, and he said to the one who did the wrong, 'Why are you striking your companion?' Then he said, 'Who made you a prince and a judge over us? Do you intend to kill me as you killed the Egyptian?' So Moses feared and said, 'Surely this thing is known!' When Pharaoh heard of this matter, he sought to kill Moses. But Moses fled from the presence of Pharaoh and dwelt in the land of Midian..."

My FAITHFULNESS
requires risk

Proverbs 3:5-6 *"Trust in the Lord with all your heart, and lean not on your own understanding. In all your ways acknowledge Him, and He will direct your paths."*

Proverbs: a book of FAITH
Proverbs 30:5 *"Every word of God is pure; He is a shield to those who put their TRUST in Him."*
Proverbs 3:26 *"For the Lord will be your CONFIDENCE, and will keep your foot from being caught."*
Proverbs 16:20 *"He who heeds the word wisely will find good, and whoever TRUSTS in the Lord, happy is he."*
Proverbs 20:6 *"Most men will proclaim their own goodness, but who can find a FAITHFUL man?"*
Proverbs 2:22 *"But the wicked will be cut off from the earth, and the UNFAITHFUL will be uprooted from it."*
Proverbs 28:26 *"He who TRUSTS in his own heart is a fool, but whoever walks wisely will be delivered."*

What is genuine faith?
1) A conviction, as opposed to simply a belief, that God can and will do what He promises.
2) Living life more on the edge –
   (a) God is in the *impossible*, not the **PREDICTABLE**   1Samuel 17: David vs. Goliath
      - if I can explain it myself, it probably wasn't the Lord   Judges 7: Gideon and 300 men
      - I won't *see* His power if I don't *need* it
   (b) God wants me to take a *risk*, not play it **SAFE**   Mark 2: men carry the paralytic
      - He wants me to exercise faith so He can show Himself to be faithful   Mark 5: woman with flow of blood
      - He wants me to stop being a *settler* and start being a *pioneer*
   (c) God wants me to have a *vision* before He gives the *provision*   Numbers 14: Caleb and Joshua
      - *method* will always precede the *means*
      - *faith* always comes before **SIGHT** (first I must trust, then I'll see)

John 11:40 *Jesus said to her, "Did I not say to you that if you would BELIEVE you would see the glory of God?"*
Hebrews 11:1,3 *"Faith is the substance of things hoped for, the evidence of things NOT SEEN. By faith we understand that the worlds were formed by the word of God, so the things which are seen were not made of things which are visible."*
2Corinthians 5:7 *"For we walk by faith, NOT BY SIGHT."*
2Corinthians 4:18 *"...while we do not look at the things which are seen, but at the things which are NOT SEEN. For the things which are seen are temporary, but the things which are not seen are eternal."*
John 20:29 *"...because you have seen Me, you have believed. Blessed are those who have NOT SEEN and yet have believed."*
Hebr. 11:27 *"By faith he forsook Egypt, not fearing the wrath of the king; he endured as seeing Him who is INVISIBLE."*
Colossians 3:2 *"Set your mind on things ABOVE, not on things on the earth."*
Romans 8:24-25 *"For we were saved in this hope, but hope that is seen is not hope; for why does one still hope for what one sees? But if we hope for what we DO NOT SEE, then we eagerly wait for it with perseverance."*

Dangerous Faith: Believing He really is WITH me

1Chronicles 28:20 *"...Be strong and of good courage, and do it; do not fear nor be dismayed, for the Lord God – my God – will be WITH YOU. He will not leave you nor forsake you, until you have finished all the work for the service of the house of the Lord."*

Isaiah 41:10 *"Fear not, for I am WITH YOU; be not dismayed, for I am your God. I will strengthen you. Yes, I will HELP YOU. I will UPHOLD YOU with My righteous right hand."*

Joshua 1:5,9 *"No man shall be able to stand before you all the days of your life; as I was with Moses, so I will be with you. I will not leave you nor forsake you. Have I not commanded you? Be strong and of good courage; do not be afraid, nor be dismayed, for the Lord your God is WITH YOU wherever you go."*

Deuteronomy 1:30-31 *"The Lord your God, who goes BEFORE YOU, He will fight FOR YOU, according to all He did for you in Egypt before your eyes, and in the wilderness where you saw how the Lord your God CARRIED YOU, as a man carries his son, in all the way that you went until you came to this place."*

Deuteronomy 3:22,7:21 *"You must not fear them, for the Lord Himself fights FOR YOU. You shall not be terrified of them; for the Lord your God, the great and awesome God, is AMONG YOU."*

Exodus 14:13-14 *"Do not be afraid. Stand still, and see the salvation of the Lord, which He will accomplish FOR YOU today. For the Egyptians whom you see today, you shall see again no more forever. The Lord will fight for you, and you shall hold your peace.'"*

Mark 5:22-34   "Dangerous Faith"   Max Lucado: "He Still Moves Stones"[12]

- "...one of the rulers of the synagogue came, Jairus by name. And when he saw Him, he fell at His feet and begged Him earnestly, saying, 'My little daughter lies at the point of death. Come and lay Your hands on her, that she may be healed, and she will live.' Jesus went with him, and a great multitude followed Him and thronged Him. Now a certain woman had a flow of blood for 12 years, and had suffered many things from many physicians. She had spent all that she had and was no better, but rather grew worse.
- When she heard about Jesus, she came behind Him in the crowd and touched His garment; for she said, 'If only I may touch His clothes, I shall be made well. IMMEDIATELY the fountain of her blood was dried up, and she felt in her body that she was healed of her suffering. And Jesus, immediately knowing in Himself that power had gone out of Him, turned around in the crowd and said, 'Who touched My clothes?' But His disciples said to Him, 'You see the multitude thronging You, and You say, 'Who touched Me?' And He looked around to see her who had done this thing. But the woman, fearing and trembling, knowing what had happened to her, came and fell down before Him and told Him the whole truth. And He said to her, 'DAUGHTER, your FAITH has made you well. Go in peace, and be healed of your affliction.'"

1) **Verses 25-26 She was physically and financially <u>EXHAUSTED</u> (a "bruised reed"):**
  (a) bleeding for 12 years (chronic menstrual disorder)
  (b) suffering many things (even from the doctors who were supposed to heal her)
  (c) spent all the money she had (financial strain for the cost of ongoing treatment)
  (d) her suffering kept increasing (she awoke everyday to suffering, with no cure)

2) **She was socially ostracized (unwanted in Jewish society):**
  (a) sexually (she could not touch her husband)
  (b) maternally (she could not bear children)
  (c) domestically (anything she touched was called unclean - no washing dishes, sweeping floors, etc.)
  (d) spiritually (she was not allowed in the temple)

3) **Verses 22-24, 27 She risks <u>EVERYTHING</u> to touch Him** →

  (a) He is surrounded by a huge crowd of people:
    - to touch Him, she must touch others around Him
    - if anyone recognizes her, she will be rebuked and thrown out
  (b) He is on the way to help Jairus's daughter:
    - he is a ruler in the synagogue (most important man in town)
    - she is a nobody (no money, no clout, no friends, no offering)
  (c) Her *faith* that He can help causes her to **DO** something
    - she can offer Him nothing, but is determined to reach Him
    - she is convicted that He will keep His promises (Matthew 5:6)
    - she DID something – she **SOUGHT** Him out

4) **Can I relate to her?**
  (a) She has nothing to offer Him, except her need. All she knew was He was there, and He was good. So she made the choice to seek Him out no matter what (she was convinced He would do what is right).
  (b) <u>Note Verse 34</u>: *only 1 person was commended that day for having faith*...and it wasn't a wealthy giver, a loyal follower, a renowned teacher. It was a shame-struck, penniless outcast who held on to her conviction that He would keep His promise to those who came to Him in their desperate need.
  Hebrews 11:6 *"But without faith it is impossible to please Him, for he who comes to God must believe that He is, and that He is a rewarder of those who diligently SEEK Him."*

5) **Verses 29-34 Jesus does 2 things that happen nowhere else in the Bible**
  (a) Jesus heals her before He even knows it (the power left Him instantaneously)
    - the deity of Christ was a step ahead of His humanity
    - her **NEED** summons His help (the Father knows her need and her heart, and sees her **ACTION**)
  (b) Jesus affectionately calls her **DAUGHTER** (it's the only time Jesus calls *any* woman *anywhere* daughter)
    - as soon as she *demonstrated* her faith, He immediately stopped and she received His full attention

---

2Corinthians 6:18   *"I will be a Father to you, and you shall be My sons and daughters", says the Lord Almighty.*

My TRUTHFULNESS delights Him

Proverbs 12:22 *"Lying lips are an abomination to the Lord, but those who deal truthfully are His delight."*

3.15

Truth and Truthful: adjective = *"ALĒTHĒS"* = sincere ("without wax") or genuine; accurate and honest
Lie or Liar: noun = *"PSUEDOS"* = false, deceit, unreal

> **Origin of the word sincere ("without wax"):** when a sculptor made a statue, he or she would fill in any imperfections (pits, holes, cracks) with wax, and then paint over the wax with a color that matched the natural plaster of the statue. Any imperfections would then be completely hidden. To judge the true value of the statue, a candle would be held up to the statue to heat its surface – any wax would melt away and expose the defects. The most valuable statues used no wax.

God hates lying (those who "USE WAX")

Proverbs 6:16-19 *"These 6 things the Lord hates, yes, 7 are an abomination to Him: a proud look, a LYING TONGUE, hands that shed innocent blood, a heart that devises wicked plans, feet that are swift in running to evil, a FALSE WITNESS who SPEAKS LIES, and one who sows discord among brethren."*

Proverbs 14:5 *"A faithful witness DOES NOT LIE, but a false witness will utter lies."*

Proverbs 13:5 *"A righteous man HATES LYING, but a wicked man is loathsome and comes to shame."*

Proverbs 19:9 *"A false witness will not go unpunished, and he who SPEAKS LIES shall perish."*

Proverbs 21:6 *"Getting treasures by a LYING TONGUE is the fleeting fantasy of those who seek death."*

Psalm 5:6 *"You shall destroy those who SPEAK FALSEHOOD; the Lord abhors the bloodthirsty and DECEITFUL man."*

Psalm 101:7 *"... He who TELLS LIES shall not continue in My presence."*

God looks for SINCERE people (those who tell the truth)

Prov. 3:3 *"Let not mercy and TRUTH forsake you; bind them around your neck, write them on the tablet of your heart."*

Joshua 24:14 *"Now therefore, fear the Lord, serve Him in SINCERITY and in TRUTH, and put away the gods which your fathers served on the other side of the River and in Egypt. Serve the Lord!"*

Exodus 18:21 *"...you shall select from all the people able men, such as fear God, men of TRUTH, hating covetousness; and place such over them to be rulers of thousands, rulers of hundreds, rulers of fifties, and rulers of tens."*

1Samuel 12:24 *"...fear the Lord, and serve Him in TRUTH with all your heart..."*

Ephesians 4:25 *"putting away lying, each one speak the TRUTH with his neighbor, for we are members of one another."*

QUESTION: Why does God take such a hard stance on truthfulness?
ANSWER: God's character is TRUTHFUL – God CANNOT LIE

Titus 1:2 *"...in hope of eternal life which God, who CANNOT LIE, promise before time began."*

Hebrews 6:18 *"...IT IS IMPOSSIBLE FOR GOD TO LIE..."*

Numbers 23:19 *"God is not a man, THAT HE SHOULD LIE, nor a son of man, that He should repent. Has He said, and will He not do it? Or has He spoken, and will He not make it good?"*

Isaiah 53:9 *"...they made His grave with the wicked, but with the rich at His death, because He had done no violence, NOR WAS ANY DECEIT FOUND in His mouth."*

Exodus 34:6 *"The Lord passed before him and proclaimed, 'The Lord, the Lord God, merciful and gracious, longsuffering, and abounding in goodness and TRUTH...'"*

Deuteronomy 32:4 *"He is the Rock, His work is perfect; for all His ways are justice, a God of TRUTH and without injustice; righteous and upright is He."*

SATAN: the Opposite of God – the "father of lies"

John 8:44 *"You are of your father the devil, and the desires of your father you want to do. He was a murderer from the beginning, and does not stand in the truth, because there is no truth in him. When he speaks a lie, he speaks from his own resources, for he is a LIAR and THE FATHER OF IT."*

> **Psychology Today Survey ("the devil is active in peoples' lives")**
> 1. More people say they cheat on their marriage partners than on their income taxes or expense accounts.
> 2. 50% people surveyed said if their tax return was audited, they'd get caught owing the government money.
> 3. 30% people admit to lying to a best friend this year, and 96% of these people feel guilty about it.
> 4. 50% people said that if they damaged another car in a parking lot, they'd drive away without leaving a note, even though 89% say this would be immoral.

WHY IS IT SO HARD SOMETIMES FOR ME TO TELL THE TRUTH?

Answer #1 = I don't LIKE the truth

Jeremiah 17:9 *"The heart is DECEITFUL above all things, and beyond cure; who can know it?"*

Ecclesiastes 9:3 *"...Truly the hearts of the sons of men are full of evil; madness is in their hearts while they live, and after that they go to the dead."*

- Jesus said knowing the *truth frees* me (John 8:32 - *"you shall know the truth, and the truth shall make you free."*)
- I learned at an early age the problem: "being honest has its unpleasant consequences" – better to tell "half-truths", or outright lies, and avoid all that unpleasantness.

Answer #2 = I don't TRUST the truth

Genesis 12:10-14   Abraham premeditates a lie because he doesn't trust God's promise to protect him
"Now there was a famine in the land, and Abram went down to Egypt to sojourn there, for the famine was severe in the land. And it came to pass, when he was close to entering Egypt, that he said to Sarah his wife, 'Indeed I know that you are a woman of beautiful countenance. Therefore it will happen, when the Egyptians see you, that they will say, 'This is his wife'; and they will kill me, but they will let you live. Please say you are my sister, that it may be well with me for your sake, and that I may live because of you."

1Samuel 27:1-12   David forms an alliance with the Philistines: he lies, steals, murders, for protection from Saul
"David said in his heart, 'Now I shall perish someday by the hand of Saul. There is nothing better for me than that I should speedily escape to the land of the Philistines; and Saul will despair of searching for me, to seek me anymore in any part of Israel. So I shall escape out of his hand. Then David arose and went over with the 600 men who were with him to Achish the son of Maoch, king of Gath.....now the time that David dwelt in the country of the Philistines was 1 full year and 4 months.
And David and his men went up and raided the Geshurites, the Girzites, and the Amalekites. For those nations were the inhabitants of the land from ancient times....whenever David attacked the land, he left neither man nor woman alive, but took away the sheep, the oxen, the donkeys, the camels, and the apparel, and returned to camp to Achish.
Then Achish would say, 'Where have you made a raid today?' And David would say, 'Against the southern area of Judah, or against the southern area of the Jerahmeelites, or against the southern area of the Kenites.' David would save neither man nor woman alive, to bring news to Gath, saying, 'Lest they should inform on us, saying, 'Thus David did.'' And so was his behavior all the time he dwelt in the country of the Philistines."

- God makes no distinction between a "white lie" and the above examples. He says any lie is sin – I am guilty whenever I lie (James 2:10 *"...whoever shall keep the whole law, and yet stumble in one point, he is guilty of all."*

What I do	Why I do it	What I call it	What God calls it
I flatter my boss	he will like me	"brown-nosing"	lying to my boss
I exaggerate things I say	people will admire me	"stretching the truth"	lying to others
I live beyond my means	people will respect me	"the American way""	living a lie

What is the most tragic "death" in my life due to my lies?   (Romans 6:23 *"...the wages of sin is death..."*)
1. My marriage?   My conscience?   My career?   My intimacy and peace?   My personal witness"?
2. The courtroom won't listen to the testimony of a perjured witness – neither will the world.
3. Why would the Lord use me as a witness if I won't tell the truth?
4. Can God trust me in the small things? If not, He will never give me greater things to do for Him because I have shown myself to be untrustworthy (Matthew 25:21).

Max Lucado, "A Heart Like Jesus"[13]   **'FACE THE MUSIC'**

"Many years ago a man conned his way into the orchestra of the emperor of China although he could not play a note. Whenever the group practiced or performed, he would hold his flute against his lips, pretending to play but not making a sound. He received a modest salary and enjoyed a comfortable living. Then one day the emperor requested a solo from each musician. The flutist got nervous. There wasn't enough time to learn the instrument. He pretended to be sick, but the royal physician wasn't fooled. On the day of his solo performance, the impostor took poison and killed himself. The explanation of his suicide led to a phrase that we now use often in our English language: "He refused to face the music.""

God's command: Ephesians 4:25 tells me to "face the music" by putting away lying

Chapter 4 — God's Will: His Glorification

Lesson	9 - Lesson Plan
4.1	Glorifying God
4.2	My Fruit
4.3	Glorifying God: Agape Love
4.4	Glorifying God: Kindness and Mercy
4.5	Glorifying God: Forgiving, Giving
4.6	Glorifying God: Diligence, Suffering
4.7	Glorifying God: Evangelism Fulfills the Vision of Jesus
4.8	The Reward System (Part 1)
4.9	The Reward System (Part 2)

God's will for my life
- The Crucifixion & Resurrection — Matthew 5:16, 1Peter 2:12, Daniel 12:3, Isaiah 43:7, Isaiah 61:3, 1Thes. 4:3-4
- The Incarnation & Deity of Jesus Christ — Psalm 22, 1Corin. 1:18, Psalm 16:10, 1Corin. 15:13-17
- The Nature & Character of God — Isaiah 7:14, Matthew 1:18-23, Micah 5:2-5, John 1:1,14, John 8:24, 56-58
- The Origin of Man — Isaiah 45:22-23, John 14:16-17, 1John 5:7
- The Reliability of the Bible — Genesis 1:1, 27-28; 2:7, Psalm 8:3-5, 19:1-6, Psalm 139:13-16, Job 12:7-10
- The GOSPEL — Hebrews 4:12, Matthew 4:4, Jeremiah 20:8-9, Titus 3:3-7, 1Corin. 15:1-4, Romans 1:1-6, Romans 1:16-17

HEBREWS 11:1
"Faith = *Substance* of things *hoped for*.... *Evidence* of things *not seen*"

GOD'S GLORY ◄ 4.1

Hebrew "*kâbôd kâbôḏ*"
Greek "*doxa*" or "*doxaro*"

- who God essentially is, as evidenced in how He reveals Himself
- to praise or honor God for His character, attributes and actions
- 3 ways God is glorified in this world: His creation, His Son, His children

God's will: its all about Him, not me

Isaiah 42:8 *"I am the Lord, that is My name; and MY GLORY I will not give to another."*

Revelation 15:4 *"Who shall not fear You, O Lord, and GLORIFY YOUR NAME? For You alone are holy. For all nations shall come and worship before You, for Your judgments have been manifested."*

Prov. 25:27 *"It is not good to eat much honey; so to seek one's own glory is not glory."*

God's will: create, save, forgive, sanctify for HIS SAKE

Isaiah 43:7 *"Everyone who is called by My name, whom I have **created** for My glory."*

Psalm 106:8 *"Nevertheless He **saved** them for His name's sake, that He might make His mighty power known."*

Isaiah 43:25 *"I, even I, am He who **blots out your transgressions** for My Own sake..."*

Psalm 23:3 *"...He leads me in the paths of **righteousness** for His name's sake."* →

Isaiah 61:3 *"...that they may be called trees of righteousness, the **plantings** of the Lord, that He may be glorified."*

1) God is glorified in: His CREATION

Psalm 19:1-3 *"The heavens declare the GLORY of God; and the expanse of heaven reveals the work of His hands."*

Psalm 8:1,3-4 *"O Lord, our Lord, how excellent is Your name in all the earth, You who SET YOUR GLORY above the heavens! When I CONSIDER Your heavens, the work of Your fingers, the moon and the stars, which You have ORDAINED. What is man, that You are mindful of him, and the son of man that you care for him?"*

Romans 1:19-20 *"...because what may be known of God is EVIDENT among them, for God has SHOWN IT TO THEM. For since the creation of the world HIS INVISIBLE ATTRIBUTES ARE CLEARLY SEEN, being understood by the things that are made, even HIS ETERNAL POWER AND DIVINE NATURE, so that they are without excuse."*

Isaiah 40:21,26 *"Have you not KNOWN? Have you not HEARD? Has it not been TOLD TO YOU from the beginning? Have you not UNDERSTOOD from the foundations of the earth? Lift up your eyes on high, and see WHO HAS CREATED THESE THINGS, who brings out their host by number; He calls them all by name by the greatness of His might and the strength of His power..."*

2) God is glorified in: His SON

John 1:14

John 1:14 *"The Word became flesh and dwelt among us, and we beheld HIS GLORY, the glory of the only begotten of the Father, full of grace and truth."*

John 14:13 *"...whatever you ask in My name, that I will do, that the Father may be GLORIFIED in the Son."*

John 12:27 *"Now My soul is troubled, and what should I say? 'Father, save Me from this hour?' But for this purpose I came to this hour. Father, GLORIFY Your name."*

John 11:39-40 *Jesus said, "Take away the stone". Martha, the sister of him who was dead, said to Him, "Lord, by this time there is a stench, for he has been dead 4 days." Jesus said to her, "Did I not say to you that if you would believe you would see the GLORY OF GOD?"*

Philippians 2:9-11 *"...God also has highly exalted Him and given Him a name which is above every name, that at the name of Jesus every knee should bow, of those that are in heaven, and of those on earth, and of those under the earth, and that every tongue should confess that Jesus Christ is Lord, to the GLORY of God the Father."*

Matthew 9:6-8 *"'But that you may know that the Son of Man has power on earth to forgive sins' – then He said to the paralytic, 'Arise, take up your bed, and go to your house.' And he arose and departed to his house. Now when the multitudes saw it, they were afraid and GLORIFIED God, who had given such power to men."*

Matthew 15:30-31 *"Then great multitudes came to Him, having with them those who were lame, blind, mute, crippled, and many others; and they laid them down at Jesus' feet, and He healed them. So the multitudes were afraid when they saw the mute speaking, the crippled made whole, the lame walking, and the blind seeing; and they GLORIFIED the God of Israel."*

3) God is glorified in: His CHILDREN (our transformed lives)

John 15:8

John 15:8 *"By this My Father is GLORIFIED, that you bear much FRUIT; so you will be My disciples."*

Matthew 5:16 *"Let your light so shine before men, that they may see your good works and GLORIFY YOUR FATHER in heaven."*

Galatians 1:23-24 *"...they were hearing only, 'He who formerly persecuted us now preaches the faith which he once tried to destroy.' And they GLORIFIED GOD in me."*

1Peter 2:12 *"...having your conduct honorable among the Gentiles, that when they speak against you as evildoers, they may, by your good works which they observe, GLORIFY GOD in the day of visitation."*

Psalm 126:1-2 *"When the Lord brought back the captivity of Zion, we were like those who dream. Then our mouth was filled with laughter and our tongue with singing. They said among the nations, 'The Lord has done great things for them.'"*

Proverbs 17:6 *"Children's' children are the crown of old men, and the glory of children is THEIR FATHER."*

My FRUIT  4.2 Greek "*karpos*"

works, deeds or character traits practiced; visible expression of the power that works inwardly and invisibly

The character of the fruit = the character of the POWER producing it

Matthew 7:16-20 *"You will know them by their FRUITS. Do men gather grapes from thornbushes or figs from thistles? Even so, every good tree bears good fruit, but a bad tree bears bad fruit. A good tree cannot bear bad fruit, nor can a bad tree bear good fruit. Every tree that does not bear good fruit is cut down and thrown into the fire. BY THEIR FRUITS YOU WILL KNOW THEM."*

The works of the flesh = the visible expression of HIDDEN SIN

Galatians 5:19-21 *"The works of the flesh are EVIDENT, which are: adultery, fornication, uncleanness, licentiousness, idolatry, sorcery, hatred, contentions, jealousies, outbursts or wrath, selfish ambitions, dissensions, heresies, envy, murders, drunkenness, revelries, and the like; of which I tell you beforehand, just as I also told you in time past, that those who PRACTICE such things will not inherit the kingdom of God."*

1Corinthians 6:9-10 *"Do you not know that the unrighteous will not inherit the kingdom of God? Do not be deceived. Neither fornicators, nor idolators, nor adulterers, nor homosexuals, nor sodomites, nor thieves, nor covetous, nor drunkards, nor revilers, nor extortioners will inherit the kingdom of God."*

James 3:14-15 *"If you have bitter envy and self-ambition in your hearts, do not boast and lie against the truth. This wisdom does not descend from above, but is earthly, sensual and demonic."*

The fruit of the Spirit = the visible expression of the INVISIBLE POWER of God

John 15:4-5,16 *"ABIDE IN ME, and I in you. As the branch cannot bear fruit of itself, unless it abides in the vine, neither can you, unless you abide in Me. I am the vine, you are the branches. He who abides in Me, and I in him, bears much fruit; for without Me you can do nothing. By this My Father is glorified, that YOU BEAR MUCH FRUIT; so you will be My disciples. You did not choose Me, but I chose you and appointed you that you should go and bear fruit, and that your fruit should remain, that whatever you ask the Father in My name He may give you."*

ABIDING In Christ = Greek "*MENO*" = to continue, remain or dwell in; to persistently devote as in cleaving
The fact that it means "remaining" is evidence that salvation has already taken place
The fruit of salvation = continuing service to Him

The fruit of the Spirit = brings PEACE

Hebrews 12:11 *"No chastening seems to be joyful for the present, but grievous; nevertheless, afterward it yields the PEACEABLE FRUIT OF RIGHTEOUSNESS to those who have been trained by it."*

James 3:17-18 *"The wisdom that is from above is first pure, then PEACEABLE, gentle, willing to yield, full of mercy and good fruits, without partiality and hypocrisy. Now the fruit of righteousness is sown in PEACE by those who make peace."*

> **Hebrews 3:6,12-14** Abiding and believing are the only genuine *EVIDENCES* of salvation

5 Biblical Fruits I can store for ETERNITY

#1. Developing Christ-like CHARACTER

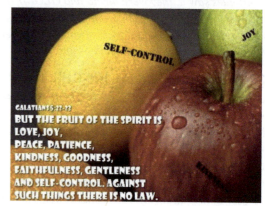

Every character trait developed in me that reflects His character is fruit that is very pleasing to Him.

Galatians 5:22-23 *"...the fruit of the Spirit is love, joy, peace, longsuffering, kindness, goodness, faithfulness, gentleness, self-control."*

Isaiah 57:15 *"I dwell in the high and holy place, with him who has a contrite and humble spirit, to revive the spirit of the humble, and to revive the heart of the contrite ones"*

Isaiah 66:2 *"But on this one will I look: on him who is poor and of a contrite spirit, and who trembles at My word."*

1Peter 3:3-4 *"Do not let your beauty be that outward adorning of arranging of hair, of wearing gold, or of putting on fine apparel; but let it be the hidden person of the heart, with the incorruptible ornament of a gentle and quiet spirit, which is very precious in the sight of God."*

2Peter 1:5-8 *"...giving all diligence, add to your faith virtue, to virtue knowledge, to knowledge self-control, to self-control patience, to patience godliness, to godliness brotherly kindness, and to brotherly kindness love. For if these things are yours and abound, you will be neither barren nor UNFRUITFUL in the knowledge of our Lord Jesus Christ."*

#2. Demonstrating Christ-like CONDUCT   Right character = Right Conduct

As I *learn* what pleases Him, my fruitful works conform to my increased knowledge of Him.

Colossians 1:10-11 *"...you may have a walk worthy of the Lord, fully pleasing Him, being FRUITFUL in every good work and increasing in the knowledge of God, strengthened with all might, according to His glorious power, for all patience and longsuffering with joy.."*

Hebrews 13:16, 20-21 *"...do not forget to do good and to share, for with such sacrifices God is well pleased. May the God of peace who brought up our Lord Jesus from the dead, that great Shepherd of the sheep, through the blood of the everlasting covenant, make you perfect in every good work to do His will, working in you what is WELL PLEASING IN HIS SIGHT, through Jesus Christ, to whom be the glory forever and ever."*

#3. Generous GIVING for the sake of others

I bear fruit when I cheerfully give to meet others' needs

Romans 15:26-28 *"It pleased those from Macedonia and Achaia to make a certain contribution for the poor among the saints who are in Jerusalem....if the Gentiles have been partakers of their spiritual things, their duty is also to minister to them in material things... when I have performed this and sealed to them this FRUIT, I shall go by way of you to Spain."*

Philippians 4:15-17 *"Now you Philippians know also that in the beginning of the gospel, when I departed from Macedonia, no church shared with me concerning giving and receiving but you only. For even in Thessalonica you sent aid once and again for my necessities. Not that I seek the gift, but I seek the FRUIT that abounds to your account."*

#4. LEADING others to Christ
my Christ-like character and conduct draws others who will want what I have

1Corinthians 16:15 *"...you know the household of Stephanas, that it is the FIRSTFRUITS of Achaia..."*

Psalm 89:1 *"...with my mouth will I MAKE KNOWN Your faithfulness to all generations."*

Psalm 107:2,22 *"Let the redeemed of the Lord SAY SO, whom He has redeemed from the hand of the enemy. Let them sacrifice the sacrifices of thanksgiving, and declare His works with rejoicing."*

#5. Praising and WORSHIPPING Him
I bear fruit with my lips by my offering of praise to Him

Hebrews 13:15 *"...by Him let us continually offer the sacrifice of praise to God, that is, the FRUIT OF OUR LIPS, giving thanks to His name."*

Isaiah 43:21 *"This people I have formed for Myself; they shall declare My praise."*

Psalm 27:6 *"...my head shall be lifted up above my enemies all around me; therefore I will offer sacrifices of joy in His tabernacle; I will sing, yes, I will sing praises to the Lord."*

Psalm 105:1-2 *"Oh, give thanks to the Lord! Call upon His name; make known His deeds among the peoples. Sing to Him, sing psalms to Him; talk of all His wondrous works."*

Jonah 2:9 *"I will sacrifice to You with a voice of thanksgiving; I will pay what I have vowed. Salvation is of the Lord."*

Why some people reject Christ: they watch CHRISTIANS!

1. Why does God save people? — To bring glory to Himself (His <u>nature</u> is to love and save us)
2. Why did Jesus come to earth? — To restore glory to the Father that He had, before we sinned (Rom. 3:23)
3. What is God's will for my life? — To restore His relationship with me, then use me to draw others to Him
4. Do people see Christ in my life? — God always puts my character before my performance

<u>2Corinthians 5:20</u> = THE WILL OF GOD: He wants me to be His ambassador, by living out His character to the unbelieving world around me. He knows those who, through my witness, will come to trust in Him.

<u>Ezekiel 36:21</u> = THE PROBLEM WITH ME: I want to glorify myself and live my way, instead of living His way. When people see it, they are turned off to God.

1. Bertrand Russell, Prof. of Philosophy, Nobel Prize Winner — **"Why I am not a Christian"**[21]

"I think that there are a good many points upon which I agree with Christ a great deal more than the professing Christians do. I do not know that I could go with Him all the way, but I could go with Him much further than most professing Christians can.

There is maxim of Christ which I think has a great deal in it, but I do not find it is very popular among some of our Christian friends. He says, 'If thou wilt be perfect, go and sell that which thou hast, and give to the poor.' That is a very excellent maxim, but, as I say, it is not much practiced.

All these, I think, are good maxims, although they are a little difficult to live up to. I do not profess to live up to them myself; but then, after all, it is not quite the same thing as for a Christian."

2. Anton Lavey, founder, First Church of Satan — **"Introduction to the Satanic Bible"**

"I would see men lusting after half-naked girls dancing at the carnival, and on Sunday morning and when I was playing the organ for tent-show evangelists at the other end of the carnival lot, I would see these same men sitting in the pews with their wives and children, asking God to forgive them and purge them of carnal desires. And the next Saturday night they'd be back at the carnival or some other place of indulgence. I knew then that the Christian church thrives on hypocrisy, and that man's carnal nature will win out no matter how much it is purged or scourged by any white-light religion."

3. John Stott, Pastor in England — **"Basic Christianity"**[20]

"The Christian landscape is strewn with the wreckage of derelict, half-built towers – the ruins of those who began to build and were unable to finish. For thousands of people still ignore Christ's warning and undertake to follow Him without first pausing to reflect on the cost of doing so. The result is the great scandal of Christendom today, so-called "nominal Christianity".

In countries to which Christian civilization has spread, large numbers of people have covered themselves with a decent, but thin, veneer of Christianity. They have allowed themselves to become somewhat involved; enough to be respectable but not enough to be uncomfortable. Their religion is a great, soft cushion. It protects them from the hard unpleasantness of life, while changing its place and shape to suit their convenience. No wonder the cynics speak of hypocrites in the church and dismiss religion as escapism."

GOD'S LOVE FOR ME
is called "Agape"

Proverbs 10:12 *"Hatred stirs up strife, but LOVE (ahavah) covers a multitude of sins."*

4.3

<u>Four Different words for LOVE in the language of Bible times</u>: from *emotional* to most *spiritual*

1) **EROS** = romantic, passionate, sentimental love
   - Greek word that isn't found in the NT, but its Hebrew equivalent is frequently used in the OT
   - often refers to the start of a marriage: the idea of yearning to unite with and possess the one loved
   - emotional: it can't sustain a relationship by itself, but its a response to a real, mature love relationship

2) **STORGE** = secure, safe, "old-shoe" love
   - natural affection and a sense of belonging to one another (part of a close-knit circle)
   - those in the relationship care for, and give the utmost loyalty, to one another
   - when the world shows itself as a cold, hard place, "storge" offers emotional refuge

3) **PHILEO** = companionship, "dear friend" love
   - while "eros" makes lovers, "phileo" makes dear, intimate friends
   - comradeship, sharing, communicating (the most intimate things aren't shared with anyone else)
   - only possible once a relationship exists (sharing both time and interests requires mutual vulnerability)

4) **AGAPE (NT), AHAVAH (OT)** = **selfless, sacrificial, serving, giving, unconditional love**
   - the only love that is totally unselfish – it gives and keeps on giving based on the needs of the one loved, without expecting anything in return or considering the cost involved
   - the only love NOT REQUIRING A RELATIONSHIP, that can be exercised immediately because…
     - it's a *choice of the will*, with no dependence on feelings (a mental attitude of conviction)
     - it's a love of action, not an emotion or a reaction or a response
     - it doesn't care if the person is indifferent or rejecting to the love
     - it doesn't consider how loveable the person is
   - unique to God (supernatural): He is the source…it is only accessible through Him
   - God loves all mankind with "apage" love, and He also has "phileo" love for those in a relationship with Him through Jesus Christ ("agape" values and serves, while "phileo" cherishes and enjoys)

1Corinthians 13:1-13 "The AGAPE Love of our God"

"Though I speak with the tongues of men and of angels, but have not LOVE, I have become as sounding brass and a clanging cymbal. And though I have the gift of prophecy, and understand all mysteries and all knowledge, and though I have all faith, so that I could remove mountains, but have not LOVE, I am nothing. And though I bestow all my goods to feed the poor, and though I give my body to be burned, but have not LOVE, it profits me nothing..

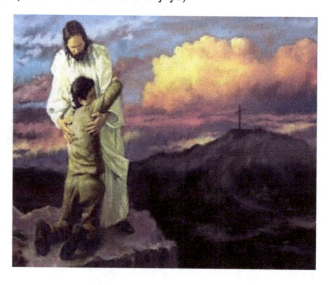

love suffers long and is kind
love does not parade itself
love does not behave rudely
love is not provoked
love rejoices in the truth
love believes all things
love endures all things

love does not envy
love is not puffed up
love does not seek its own
love thinks no evil
love bears all things
love hopes all things
love never fails.

But whether there are prophecies, they will fail; whether there are tongues, they will cease; whether there is knowledge, it will vanish away. For we know in part and we prophesy in part. But when that which is perfect has come, then that which is in part will be done away. When I was a child, I spoke as a child, I understood as a child, I thought as a child; but when I became a man, I put away childish things. . Now abide faith, hope and love, these three; but the greatest of these is (agape) LOVE."

4 Key Insights into God's Agape/ Ahavah Love

1) God's love first existed within the TRINITY

John 17:24-26 *"Father, I desire that they also whom You gave Me may be with Me where I am, that they may behold My glory which You have given Me; for YOU LOVED ME before the foundation of the world."*

John 14:31 *"...that the world may know that I LOVE THE FATHER, and as the Father gave Me commandment, so I do..."*

2) God expressed His love on the nation of ISRAEL

Deuteronomy 7:6-8 *"...the Lord your God has chosen you to be a people for Himself, a SPECIAL TREASURE above all the peoples on the face of the earth.. The Lord did not set His LOVE on you nor choose you because you were more in number than any other people, for you were the least of all peoples; but because the Lord LOVES YOU..."*

1Kings 10:9 *"Blessed be the Lord your God, who delighted in you, setting you on the throne of Israel! Because the Lord has LOVED ISRAEL FOREVER, therefore He made you king, to do justice and righteousness."*

Jeremiah 31:1-3 *"At the same time," says the Lord, "I will be the God of all the families of Israel, and they shall be My people." Thus says the Lord: "The people who survived the sword found grace in the wilderness – Israel, when I went to give him rest." The Lord has appeared of old to me, saying, "Yes, I have LOVED YOU with an everlasting love; therefore with lovingkindness I have drawn you."*

3) God showers His love on ALL MANKIND

John 3:16 *"For God so LOVED the world, that He gave His only begotten Son, that whoever believes in Him should not perish but have everlasting life."*

Romans 5:8 *"...God demonstrates His own LOVE toward us, in that while we were still sinners, Christ died for us."*

Ephesians 2:4-5 *"...God, who is rich in mercy, because of His great LOVE with which HE LOVED US, even when we were dead in trespasses, made us alive together with Christ (by grace you have been saved)..."*

Ephesians 5:2, 25 *"...walk in love, as Christ also has LOVED us and given Himself for us, an offering and a sacrifice to God for a sweet-smelling aroma. Husbands, love your wives, just as CHRIST ALSO LOVED THE CHURCH and gave Himself for it."*

1John 4:9-10,19 *"In this the love of God was manifested toward us, that God has sent His only begotten Son into the world, that we might live through Him. In this is love, not that we loved God, but that HE LOVED US and sent His Son to be the propitiation for our sins. We love Him because He first LOVED us."*

Titus 3:4-5 *"...when the kindness and the LOVE of God our Savior toward man appeared, not by works of righteousness which we have done but according to His mercy He saved us..."*

2Corinthians 5:14-15 *"The LOVE OF CHRIST constrains us, because we judge thus: that if One died for all, then all died; and He died for all, that those who live should live no longer for themselves, but for Him who died for them and rose again."*

4) God has a PERSONAL *"agape"* love for ME

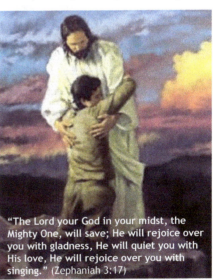

"The Lord your God in your midst, the Mighty One, will save; He will rejoice over you with gladness, He will quiet you with His love, He will rejoice over you with singing." (Zephaniah 3:17)

▸ God gets totally involved in my life because He desires a close relationship with me. His love is not for people as a group. God really loves *individual* people, like me.

▸ Jesus often focused on one person (Zaacheus, the woman at the well, the woman with the flow of blood, the cripple at the pool of Bethesda). He always took the time to respond to anyone around Him who reached out to Him in need. **Isaiah 53:2-3** says He understands my pain because He experienced it personally: *"He has no form or comeliness; and when we see Him, there is no beauty that we should desire Him. He is despised and rejected by men, a Man of sorrows and acquainted with grief. We hid, as it were, our faces from Him; He was despised, we did not esteem Him."* **Knowing He would be treated this way, He willingly subjected Himself to it.**

Galatians 2:20 = Paul's motivation to surrender his life to Christ's Lordship

"I have been crucified with Christ; it is no longer I who live, but Christ lives in me; and the life which I now live in the flesh I live by faith in the Son of God, who LOVED ME and gave Himself FOR ME."

What the World Believes:
Only the <u>BIBLE</u> reveals a God of Agape Love

ISLAM (Ergun and Emir Caner, "Unveiling Islam"[16]) – Middle East, Africa

<u>Allah: the "Distant One"</u>
The Allah we worshipped as Muslims was a remote judge.
When Christians speak of the intimacy and grace of God, it confuses a Muslim.
In all the terms and titles of Allah, one does not encounter terms of intimacy.
Even the most faithful and devout Muslim refers to Allah only as a servant to master; Allah is a distant sovereign.

<u>Allah: the "Cold Judge"</u>
Islam looks to a god of the scales, as opposed to the atoning Son of God.
Allah forgives only at the repentance of the Muslim, and all consequences for sin and the debt of guilt fall on the Muslim, who comes to Allah in terror, hoping for commutation of his sentence.
One sees a judge, as opposed to a God of Love.

<u>Allah: the "Hater"</u>
Allah's heart is set against the infidel.
He has no love for the unbeliever, nor is a Muslim to "evangelize" the unbelieving world.
Allah is to be worshipped, period.
The theme is conquest, not conversion, of the unbelieving world.

Middle East

Country	Population	Muslim		Christian	
Pakistan	156,483,155	150,349,015	96.1%	3,614,761	2.3%
Iran	67,702,199	67,038,717	99.0%	223,417	0.3%
Turkey	66,590,940	66,351,213	99.6%	213,091	0.3%
Uzbekistan	24,317,851	20,305,406	83.5%	316,132	1.3%
Iraq	23,114,884	22,386,765	96.9%	358,281	1.6%
Afghanistan	22,720,000	22,240,608	97.9%	4,544	0.0%
Saudi Arabia	21,606,691	20,057,491	92.8%	980,944	4.5%
Yemen	18,112,066	18,101,199	99.9%	9,056	0.1%
Syria	16,124,618	14,560,530	90.3%	822,356	5.1%
Turkmenistan	4,459,293	4,095,415	91.8%	120,401	2.7%
Oman	2,541,739	2,355,175	92.7%	64,560	2.5%
United Arab Emirates	2,441,436	1,623,555	66.5%	227,054	9.3%
Kuwait	1,971,634	1,723,800	87.4%	161,082	8.2%
	428,186,506	411,188,889	96.0%	7,115,678	1.7%

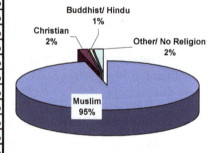

Africa

Country	Population	Muslim		Christian	
Nigeria	111,506,095	45,717,499	41.0%	58,652,206	52.6%
Egypt	68,469,695	59,239,980	86.5%	8,887,366	13.0%
Algeria	31,471,278	30,426,432	96.7%	91,267	0.3%
Sudan	29,489,719	19,168,317	65.0%	6,841,615	23.2%
Morocco	28,220,843	28,178,512	99.9%	14,110	0.1%
Somalia	10,097,177	10,092,128	100.0%	5,049	0.1%
Tunisia	9,585,611	9,553,020	99.7%	21,088	0.2%
Libya	5,604,722	5,408,557	96.5%	168,142	3.0%
Mauritania	2,669,547	2,665,276	99.8%	4,271	0.2%
	297,114,687	210,449,721	70.8%	74,685,114	25.1%

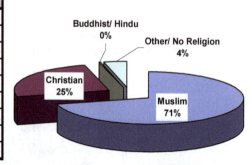

BUDDHISM (Lit-Sen-Chang, "Zen-Existentialism: The Spiritual Decline of the West") – Far East

Zen Buddhism is a subtle form of Atheism: it is the love of self first, last and always.

It denies the infinity and transcendence of a living, personal God.

It denies the need of a Savior, thus denying the true God and the gift of His grace, by exalting and deifying man.

Salvation can be secured by man's own power and wisdom.

In Zen Buddhism, there is no supernatural intervention. We bear the whole responsibility for our actions and no Sage whosoever he be has the right to encroach on our free will.

HINDUISM (Walter Martin, "The Kingdom of the Cults"[17]) – Far East

There is no single Hindu idea of God.

He can be pantheist (all existence), animist (all nonhuman objects such as rocks, trees, animals, etc.), polytheist (many gods to worship), henotheist (many gods, but only one worshipped), monotheist (only one god).

Hinduism believes that all souls are eternal and accountable for their actions throughout time.

There is no need for a personal relationship to a Savior, who by grace takes the punishment for their sins.

Rather, it is through "karma" (wheel of suffering) and "reincarnation" (soul inhabits successive human bodies) their bad actions are atoned for as they strive to achieve self-realization ("nirvana") through ritualistic sacrifice and discipline.

Far East

Country	Population	Other or No Religion		Buddhist/ Hindu		Muslim		Christian	
China	1,262,556,787	1039968025	82.4%	105,802,259	8.4%	25,251,136	2.0%	91,535,367	7.3%
India	1,013,661,777	45614780	4.5%	817,011,392	80.6%	126,707,722	12.5%	24,327,883	2.4%
Indonesia	212,991,926	3194879	1.5%	4,685,822	2.2%	171,032,517	80.3%	34,078,708	16.0%
Bangladesh	129,155,152	839508	0.7%	16,790,170	13.0%	110,595,557	85.6%	929,917	0.7%
Vietnam	79,831,650	29649475	37.1%	43,109,091	54.0%	558,822	0.7%	6,514,263	8.2%
Burma	45,611,177	1870058	4.1%	38,039,722	83.4%	1,733,225	3.8%	3,968,172	8.7%
North Korea	24,039,193	22551167	93.8%	1,081,764	4.5%	0	0.0%	406,262	1.7%
Nepal	23,930,490	552794	2.3%	21,728,885	90.8%	1,196,525	5.0%	452,286	1.9%
Malaysia	22,244,062	1379132	6.2%	5,916,920	26.6%	12,901,556	58.0%	2,046,454	9.2%
Sri Lanka	18,827,054	84722	0.4%	15,801,546	83.9%	1,506,164	8.0%	1,434,622	7.6%
Tajikistan	6,188,201	564364	9.1%	0	0.0%	5,538,440	89.5%	85,397	1.4%
Laos	5,433,036	1953176	36.0%	3,319,585	61.1%	59,763	1.1%	100,511	1.9%
Tibet	2,500,000	490000	19.6%	2,000,000	80.0%	5,000	0.2%	5,000	0.2%
	2,846,970,505	1,148,712,081	40.3%	1,075,287,156	37.8%	457,086,425	16.1%	165,884,842	5.8%

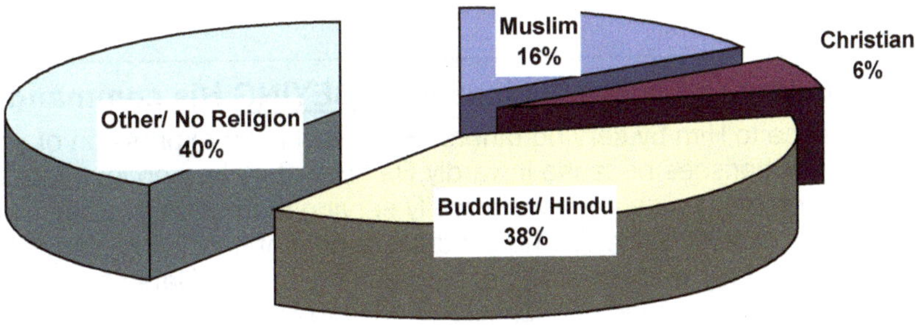

- Other/ No Religion 40%
- Buddhist/ Hindu 38%
- Muslim 16%
- Christian 6%

My LOVE FOR GOD
is why I obey

Proverbs 3:12 *"...whom the Lord LOVES He corrects, just as a father the son in whom he delights."*

4.4

What MOTIVATES me to want to do what God says? His wrath? His sovereignty? His love?
Hint: 2Corinthians 5:14-15

Old Testament: my love for God
- to cherish the object loved above all else; to connect my heart with the object loved; to fervently desire
- if I love God this way, I will show my love by my tenderness, mercy and patience towards others

Psalm 91:14-16 *"Because he has SET HIS LOVE UPON ME, therefore I will deliver him; I will exalt him on high, because he has known My name. He shall call upon Me, and I will answer him; I will be with him in trouble; I will deliver him and honor him. With long life I will satisfy him, and show him My salvation."*

Psalm 145:18-20 *"The Lord is near to all who call upon Him, to all who call upon Him in truth. He will fulfill the desire of those who fear Him; He also will hear their cry and save them. The Lord preserves all who LOVE HIM, but the wicked He will destroy."*

New Testament: my "agape" love for God
- I serve Him without expecting anything in return from Him or considering the cost involved
- I choose to love Him (I don't need Him to show His love for me before I love Him)
- John MacArthur ('The God Who Loves'[5]): *"The word AGAPE was not a common word in 1st-century culture until the New Testament made it so. When 1st-century Greeks thought of love, it was phileo or eros, never agape. This agape love became the **identifier** of a Christian, because Jesus and the early church fathers preached that the best evidence of a regenerate heart, and someone who truly knows God, is the demonstration of agape love."*

John 16:27 *"...the Father Himself loves you, because you have LOVED ME, and have believed that I came forth from God."*

Romans 8:28 *"...we know that all things work together for good to those who LOVE GOD, to those who are the called according to His purpose."*

1Corinthians 8:1-3 *"...if anyone thinks that he knows anything, he knows nothing yet as he ought to know. But if anyone LOVES GOD, this one is known by Him."*

New Testament: my "agape" love for God requires my "agape" love for OTHERS

John 13:34-35 *"A NEW commandment I give to you, that you LOVE ONE ANOTHER; as I have loved you, that you also love one another. By this all will know that you are My disciples, if you have love for one another."*

John 15:12-13, 17 *"This is My commandment, that you LOVE ONE ANOTHER as I have loved you. Greater love has no one than this, than to lay down one's life for his friends. These things I command you, that you LOVE ONE ANOTHER"*

Matt. 22:35-40 *"...one of them, a lawyer, asked Him a question, testing Him, and saying, 'Teacher, which is the great commandment in the law?' Jesus said to him, 'You shall love the Lord your God with all your heart, with all your soul, and with all your mind. This is the 1st and great commandment. And the 2nd is like it: "You shall LOVE YOUR NEIGHBOR as yourself." One these 2 commandments hang all the Law and the Prophets.'"*

1John 4:7-8 *"Beloved, let us LOVE ONE ANOTHER, for love is of God; and everyone who LOVES is born of God and knows God. He who does not love does not know God, for GOD IS LOVE."*

Jesus confronts the "Religious": Loving God means <u>OBEYING</u> His command to serve others

God wants you to show obedience to Him by serving others. He says it is an expression of your love for Him. Jesus chastised the scribes and Pharisees because inwardly He knew they had no love for God. They gave the outward appearance of serving others (inside, they were really serving themselves). They would tell the common people they were God's chosen leaders, who set the example of holy living. Jesus turned them upside-down by telling them NO.... they were enemies of God and children of Satan because they cared for themselves and served their own lusts, instead of sacrificial service to others.

Mark 12:28-34 Jesus reveals in public that true wisdom belongs to those who agape love God and others.

Luke 6:27-35 Jesus commands us to agape love those who hate us.

Luke 7:41-50 Jesus links God's forgiveness of my sins with my agape love for Him and others

Luke 10:25-37 Jesus counters the question of "who is my neighbor?" with "the Good Samaritan".

Genuine Love for God = OBEYING Him

God's message has never changed: true love for Him is always revealed through the ACTION of OBEDIENCE.

Beginning with Abraham, God showed the first step of obedience is trusting Him with my life, which brings a close love relationship between God and me.

Then, throughout history, God sent His prophets and ultimately His only Son to tell me that genuine love for Him is revealed through my KEEPING His commandments.

Matt. 21:23-32 Jesus uses this parable to expose the religious leaders' loveless, DISOBEDIENT hearts

John 8:39 *"They answered and said to Him, 'Abraham is our father.' Jesus said to them, 'If you were Abraham's children, you would DO the works of Abraham."*

John 6:40 *"And this is the WILL OF HIM who sent Me, that everyone who sees the Son and BELIEVES IN HIM may have everlasting life; and I will raise him up at the last day."*

John 6:28-29 *"Then they said to Him, 'What shall we DO, that we may work the works of God?' Jesus answered and said to them, 'This is the work of God, that you BELIEVE IN HIM whom He has sent.'*

Jesus makes it crystal clear: I don't love Him if I won't OBEY Him

John 14:15,21 *"If you love Me, KEEP MY COMMANDMENTS. He who has My commandments and keeps them, it is he who loves Me. And he who loves Me will be loved by My Father, and I will love him and manifest Myself to him."*

John 14:23-24 *"Jesus answered and said to him, 'If anyone loves Me, he will KEEP MY WORD; and My Father will love Him, and We will come to him and make our home with him. He who does not love Me does not keep My words; and the word which you hear is not Mine but the Father who sent Me.'"*

John 8:51 *"Most assuredly, I say to you, if anyone KEEPS MY WORD, he shall never see death."*

1 John 5:2-3 *"By this we know that we love the children of God, when we love God and KEEP HIS COMMANDMENTS. For this is the love of God, that we keep His commandments. And His commandments are not burdensome."*

1 John 2:3-5 *"...by this we know that we know Him, if we KEEP HIS COMMANDMENTS. He who says, 'I know Him,' and does not keep His commandments, is a liar, and the truth is not in him. But whoever keeps His word, truly the love of God is completed in him. By this we know that we are in Him."*

Matthew 7:21 *"Not everyone who says 'Lord, Lord,' shall enter the kingdom of heaven, but he who DOES THE WILL OF MY FATHER in heaven."*

Luke 6:46 *"But why do you call Me 'Lord, Lord,' and do not DO the things which I say?"*

God's Old Testament PROPHETS: Genuine love for God means obedience

Deuteronomy 6:4-5 *"Hear, O Israel: The Lord our God, the Lord is one! You shall LOVE THE LORD your God with all your heart, with all your soul, and with all your might."*

Deuteronomy 7:9-10 *"Know that the Lord your God, He is God, the faithful God who keeps covenant and mercy for a thousand generations with those who love Him and KEEP HIS COMMANDMENTS; and He repays those who hate Him to their face, to destroy them. He will not be slack with him who HATES HIM; He will repay Him to his face."*

Exodus 20:5-6 *"...I, the Lord your God, am a jealous God, visiting the iniquity of the fathers on the children to the 3rd and 4th generations of those who hate Me, but showing mercy to 1000's, to those who love Me and KEEP MY COMMANDMENTS."*

Deuteronomy 10:12-13 *"And now, Israel, what does the Lord your God require of you, but to fear the Lord your God, to walk in all His ways and to love Him, to serve the Lord your God with all your heart and with all your soul, and to KEEP THE COMMANDENTS of the Lord and His statutes which I command you today for your good?"*

Joshua 22:5 *"...take diligent heed to do the commandment and the law which Moses the servant of the Lord commanded you, to LOVE the Lord your God, to walk in all His ways, to KEEP HIS COMMANDMENTS, to hold fast to Him, and to serve Him with all your heart and with all your soul."*

Nehemiah 1:5 *"I pray, Lord God of heaven, O great and awesome God, who keep Your covenant and mercy with those who love You and OBSERVE YOUR COMMANDMENTS..."*

Ezekiel 33:30-32 *"...they speak to one another, everyone saying to his brother, 'Please come and hear what the word is that comes from the Lord.' So they come to you as people do, they sit before you as My people, and they hear your words, but THEY DO NOT DO THEM; for with their mouth they show much love, but with their hearts pursue their own gain.."*

Daniel 9:4 *"...I prayed to the Lord my God, and made confession, and said, 'O Lord, great and awesome God, who keeps His covenant and mercy with those who love Him, and with those who KEEP HIS COMMANDMENTS."*

GOD'S KINDNESS and MERCY
His Love in Action

Proverbs 19:22 *"What is desired in a man is KINDNESS."*

4.5

The Old Testament

- KINDNESS derives from the Arabic word that refers to a mother's built-in connection to her baby as seen when she breast-feeds: from where we get the phrase "full of the milk of human kindness".
- MERCY derives from the "mercy seat" of the ark of the covenant: refers to "covering, atoning or propitiating" – an extraordinary expression of the "heart-attitude" of tenderness and compassion.
- main context : God's abundant favor, tender affection and **LONGSUFFERING** toward His own people.

Proverbs 31:26 *"She opens her mouth with wisdom, and her tongue is the law of KINDNESS."*
Proverbs 21:21 *"He who follows righteousness and MERCY finds life, righteousness and honor."*
Proverbs 11:17 *"The MERCIFUL man does good for his own soul, but he who is cruel troubles his own flesh."*
Micah 6:8 *"He has shown you, O man, what is good; and what does the Lord require of you but to do justly, to love MERCY, and to walk humbly with your God?"*
Hosea 6:6 *"I desire MERCY and not sacrifice, and the knowledge of God more than burnt offerings."*

The New Testament

- KINDNESS (Greek *"chrēstos", "chrēsteuomai"*): graciousness and goodness of the heart - not merely as a quality, but as expressed in **ACTION** by mercy, tenderness and compassion towards others.
- MERCY (Greek *"eleos", "oiktirmos"*): outward expression of someone's pity and compassion towards another – it assumes the one giving mercy has resources adequate to meet the needs or ills of the one receiving it.
- Grace = God's attitude toward the law-breaker and rebel; Mercy = God's attitude toward those in distress.

Luke 6:35 *"...love your enemies, do good, and lend, hoping for nothing in return; and your reward will be great, and you will be sons of the Highest. For He is KIND to the unthankful and evil."*
1Corinthians 13:4 *"...love SUFFERS LONG and is KIND..."*
Romans 2:4 *"...do you despise the riches of His goodness (kindness), FORBEARANCE, and LONGSUFFERING, not knowing that the goodness (kindness) of God leads you to repentance?"*
Galatians 5:22-23 *"...the fruit of the Spirit is love, joy, peace, LONGSUFFERING, KINDNESS, goodness, faithfulness, gentleness, self-control."*
Ephes. 4:32 *"...be KIND to one another, tenderhearted, forgiving one another, just as God in Christ Jesus forgave you."*
Colossians 3:12 *"...put on tender MERCIES, KINDNESS, humbleness of mind, meekness, LONGSUFFERING,."*

The World's view of "Kindness" and "Mercy": A License to KILL

Margaret Sanger, founder of Planned Parenthood (quoted in "Women and the New Race", 1920):
"The most merciful thing a large family can do for one of its infant members is to kill it."

James Watson, Noble Prize winner and co-discoverer of DNA (Amer. Medical Assoc. *Prism* Magazine, 1993):
"Because of the limitations of present detection methods, most birth defects are not discovered until birth… however, if a child was not declared alive until 3 days after birth… the doctor could allow the child to die if the parents so choose and save a lot of misery and suffering."

Neal Boortz, "A Religious Case for Killing Terry Schiavo", 2005
"Do you believe in God's promise of everlasting life? Do you believe that the reward for a life well spent on this earth is a life with God in heaven after you die? … why do you so ardently desire that the soul of Terry Schiavo spend 5, 10, perhaps 30 years or more trapped in a useless and non-functioning body, unable to move on to whatever reward awaits her? Isn't 15 years enough?"

C.S. Lewis ('Virtue and Vice'[7]): *"There is kindness in love; but love and kindness are not bounded together, and when kindness is separated from the other elements of love, it involves a certain fundamental INDIFFERENCE to its object, even something like CONTEMPT of it.*

Kindness consents very readily to the removal of its object – we have all met people whose 'kindness' to animals is constantly leading them to kill animals 'lest they suffer. This kind of kindness cares not whether the object becomes good or bad, provided only that it escapes suffering. But if God is Love, He is, by definition, something more than mere kindness. And it appears, from all the records, that though He has often rebuked and condemned us, He has never regarded us with contempt."

PROPITIATION = God's "Mercy Seat"

- **New Testament** = *"hilaskomai"* = "to satisfy such that a kind, merciful and gracious attitude ensues"

The Greeks = "appease" or "propitiate" their gods by earning their favor through good works (in Greek literature, the natural attitude of their gods was not one of goodwill towards them).

The Bible = never used for any action by man to bring God into a favorable attitude of gracious disposition.

Romans 3:23-26 explains that it is God Himself who is *PROPITIATED* ("**GRACIOUSLY DISPOSED**") toward man, such that He can now meet with man, by providing for Himself the perfect sacrifice of Christ, who is the manifestation of the OT "mercy seat": *"...all have sinned and fallen short of the glory of God, being justified freely by His GRACE through the redemption that is in Christ Jesus, whom God set forth to be a PROPITIATION ("MERCY SEAT") by His BLOOD, through faith, to demonstrate His righteousness, because in His forbearance God has passed over the sins that were previously committed, to demonstrate at the present time His righteousness, that He might be just and the JUSTIFIER of the one who has faith in Jesus."*

God Himself has so dealt with sin that He can show **MERCY** to the believing sinner by removing their guilt and dismissing (passing over, or remission) their sins (the individual person is the **OBJECT** of His mercy).

Hebrews 2:17 (Hebrews 9:2-8, 11-12, 28) *"...in all things He had to be made like His brethren, that He might be a MERCIFUL and faithful High Priest in things pertaining to God, to make PROPITIATION for the sins of the people."*

- **Old Testament** = *"kapporeth"* = "mercy seat: cover of the ark of the Covenant" →

The cover of the ark of the covenant (New Testament "*HILASTERION*" = Propitiatory), described below in Exodus 25:17-22, is where the blood of an unblemished animal was poured out by the **HIGH PRIEST**, to atone for the sins of Israel: *"You shall make a MERCY SEAT of pure gold; 2-1/2 cubits shall be its length and 1-1/2 its width. And you shall make two cherubim of gold; of hammered work you shall make them at the 2 ends of the mercy seat. And the cherubim shall stretch out their wings above, covering the mercy seat with their wings, and they shall face one another; the faces of the cherubim shall be toward the mercy seat. You shall put the mercy seat on top of the ark, and in the ark you shall put the Testimony that I will give you. There I WILL MEET WITH YOU, and I will speak with you from above the mercy seat..."*

← Between the Shekinah glory cloud above the ark and the tablets of the law inside the ark was the blood-sprinkled cover; blood of the sacrifices was between God and His broken law! The cherubim guard God's holiness (Gen. 3:24). They are bent over the mercy seat, wings outstretched with their faces toward it, acknowledging that the blood satisfies God's holiness. Sinful man can approach and meet with God.

Ephesians 2:4-9 "God's mercy and kindness are revealed in Jesus Christ"

"...God, who is rich in MERCY, because of His great love with which He loved us, even when we were dead in trespasses, made us alive together with Christ (by grace you have been saved), and raised us up together, and made us sit together in the heavenly places in Christ Jesus, that in the ages to come He might show us the exceeding riches of His grace in His KINDNESS toward us in Christ Jesus. For by grace you have been saved through faith, and that not of yourselves; it is the gift of God..."

Luke 18:9-14: Pharisee vs. Tax Collector "Justification = Trusting in God's **MERCY**, not in myself"

Its blood upon God's mercy seat that makes propitiation for my soul (NOT my good works). God's Old Testament sacrifices pointed to His spotless Lamb, who gives me access behind the 2nd veil by His blood (Matthew 27:50-51).

Christ's work on the Cross = Christ annuls sin's power to separate me from a holy God. Because God is kind and merciful, He promised that IF I trust in Christ for my forgiveness, I WILL BE delivered from His justice.

PSALM 89:14 *"Righteousness and justice are the foundation of Your THRONE; mercy and truth go before Your FACE."*

GOD'S FORGIVENESS
His gift of Love

Proverbs 17:9 *"He who COVERS A TRANSGRESSION seeks love.."*

4.6

---

1) FORGIVE = *"aphiēmi"* = "to send away" (CANCEL or remove); main use is in forgiving debts and sins
   1st element in forgiveness = release from, and complete cancellation of, the *punishment* due the sin
   2nd element in forgiveness = removal of the *cause* of the offense (the sin itself is never again brought up)

2) FORGIVE = *"charizomai"* = "bestow unconditional FAVOR by forgiveness" (the offender has no obligation)

3) REMISSION = *"aphesis"*, *"paresis"* = a dismissal or release; a "passing by or over" of sin)

4) ATONEMENT = *"hilastērion"*, *"hilasmos"* = covering for sin; propitiation *(ark of the Covenant "mercy-seat")*

---

1) FORGIVE = CANCEL sin = *"aphiēmi"* (Matthew 9:2-8 "only God cancels the debt")

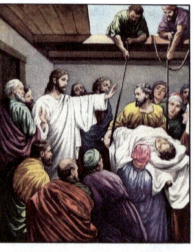

"And behold, they brought to Him a paralytic lying on a bed. And Jesus, seeing their faith, said to the paralytic, 'Son, be of good cheer; YOUR SINS ARE FORGIVEN ('aphiēmi') YOU.' And at once some of the scribes said within themselves, 'This Man blasphemes!'

But Jesus, knowing their thoughts, said, 'Why do you think evil in your hearts? For which is easier, to say, 'Your sins are forgiven you,' or to say 'Arise and walk'? But that you may know that the Son of Man has power on earth to forgive sins' – then He said to the paralytic, 'Arise, take up your bed and go to your house.' And he arose and departed to his house. Now when the multitudes saw it, they marveled and glorified God, who had given such power to men."

Acts 8:22 "Repent therefore of this your wickedness, and pray God if perhaps the thought of your heart may be FORGIVEN you."

Isaiah 1:18-19 "Come now, and let us reason together," says the Lord. "Though your sins are like scarlet, they shall be made white as snow; though they are red like crimson, they shall be as wool. If you are willing and obedient, you shall eat the good of the land, but if you refuse and rebel, you shall be devoured by the sword..."

Psalm 103:12 "As far as the east is from the west, so far has He REMOVED our transgressions from us."

Isaiah 43:25 "I, even I, am He who blots out your transgressions for My own sake; I WILL NOT REMEMBER YOUR SINS."

Isaiah 44:22 "I have BLOTTED OUT, like a thick cloud, your transgressions, and like a cloud, your sins. Return to Me, for I have redeemed you."

1John 1:7-9 "...if we walk in the light as He is in the light, we have fellowship with one another, and the blood of Jesus Christ His Son cleanses us from all sin. If we say we have no sin, we deceive ourselves, and the truth is not in us. If we confess our sins, He is faithful and just to FORGIVE us our sins and to cleanse us from all unrighteousness."

1John 2:12 "I write to you, little children, because your sins are FORGIVEN you for His name's sake."

2) FORGIVE = bestow UNCONDITIONAL favor = *"charizomai"* (Luke 7:39-47 "Mary Magdelene")

"Now when the Pharisees who had invited Him saw this, he spoke to himself, saying, 'This man, if He were a prophet, would know who and what manner of woman this is who is touching Him, for she is a sinner.' And Jesus answered and said to him, 'Simon, I have something to say to you.' And he said, 'Teacher, say it.'

'There was a certain creditor who had 2 debtors. One owed 500 denarii, and the other 50. And when they had nothing with which to repay, he FREELY FORGAVE them both. Tell Me therefore, which of them will love him more?' Simon answered, 'I suppose the one whom he FORGAVE more.' He said to him, 'You have rightly judged.'

Then He turned to the woman and said to Simon, 'Do you see this woman? I entered your house; you gave Me no water for My feet, but she has washed My feet with her tears and wiped them with the hair of her head. You gave Me no kiss, but this woman has not ceased to kiss my feet since the time I came in. You did not anoint My head with oil, but this woman has anointed My feet with fragrant oil. Therefore I say to you, her sins, which are many, are FORGIVEN, for she loved much. But to whom little is forgiven, the same loves little.' And He said to her, 'Your sins are FORGIVEN ('chaizomai').'"

2) FORGIVE = bestow UNCONDITIONAL favor = *"charizomai"* (John 8:3-11 "Adulterous Woman")

"Then the scribes and Pharisees brought to Him a woman caught in adultery. And when they had set her in the midst, they said to Him, 'Teacher, this woman was caught in adultery, in the very act. Now Moses, in the law, commanded us that such should be stoned. But what do you say?' This they said, testing Him, that they might have something of which to accuse Him.

But Jesus stooped down and wrote on the ground with His finger as if He did not hear. So when they continued asking Him, He raised Himself up and said to them, 'He who is without sin among you, let him throw a stone at her first.' And again He stooped down and wrote on the ground.

Then those who heard it, being convicted by their own conscience, went out one by one, beginning with the oldest even to the last. And Jesus was left alone, and the woman standing in the midst. When Jesus had raised Himself up and saw no one but the woman, He said to her, 'Woman, where are those accusers of yours? Has no one condemned you?' She said, 'No one, Lord'. And Jesus said to her, 'NEITHER DO I CONDEMN YOU. Go and sin no more.'"

Colossians 2:13-14 *"And you, being dead in your trespasses and the uncircumcision of your flesh, He has made alive together with Him, having FORGIVEN you all trespasses, having wiped out the certificate of debt with its requirements that was against us, which was contrary to us. And He has taken it out of the way, having nailed it to the cross."*

Ephesians 4:32 *"...be kind to one another, tenderhearted, forgiving one another, just as God in Christ FORGAVE you."*

Colossians 3:12-13 *"...as the elect of God, holy and beloved, put on tender mercies, kindness, humbleness of mind, meekness, longsuffering, bearing with one another, and forgiving one another, if anyone has a complaint against another, just as Christ FORGAVE you, so you also must do."*

3) REMISSION = PASS OVER sin = *"aphesis"* (Exodus 12:21-23 "The Passover in Egypt"))

"Moses called for all the elders of Israel and said to them, 'Pick out and take lambs for yourselves according to your families, and kill the PASSOVER LAMB. And you shall take a bunch of hyssop, dip it in the blood that is in the basin, and strike the lintel and the two doorposts with the blood that is in the basin. And none of you shall go out of the door of his house until morning. For the Lord will pass through to strike the Egyptians, and when He sees the blood on the cross piece at the top of your door, and on the two doorposts, the Lord will PASS OVER the door and not allow the destroyer to come into your houses to strike you.'"

1 Corinthians 5:7 *"For indeed Christ, our PASSOVER, was sacrificed for us."*

Matthew 26:27-28 *"Then He took the cup, and gave thanks, and gave it to them, saying, 'Drink from it, all of you. For this is the blood of the new covenant, which is shed for many for the REMISSION ('aphesis') of sins."*

Romans 3:25-26 *"...in His forbearance God has PASSED OVER the sins that were previously committed, to demonstrate at the present time His righteousness, that He might be just and the Justifier of the one who has faith in Jesus."*

Hebrews 9:22 *"...according to the law almost all things are cleansed with blood, and without shedding of blood there is no REMISSION."*

Hebrews 10:17-18 *"'Their sins and their lawless deeds I will remember no more.' Where there is REMISSION of these, there is no longer an offering for sin."*

Luke 24:45-47 *"And He opened their understanding, that they might comprehend the Scriptures. Then He said to them, 'Thus it is written, and thus it was necessary for the Christ to suffer and to rise from the dead the third day, and that repentance and REMISSION of sins should be preached in His name to all nations, beginning at Jerusalem.'"*

Mark 1:4 *"John came baptizing in the wilderness and preaching a baptism of repentance for the REMISSION of sins."*

Acts 2:38 *"... Repent, and let every one of you be baptized in the name of Jesus Christ for the REMISSION of sins."*

Acts 10:43 *"...all the prophets witness that, through His name, whoever believes in Him will receive REMISSION of sins."*

Acts 13:38-39 *"...let it be known to you, brethren, that through this Man is preached to you the REMISSION of sins; and by Him everyone who believes is justified from all things from which you could not be justified by the law of Moses."*

4) ATONEMENT = COVERING for sin = *"hilasmos"* (Romans 4:6-8 "God's forgiveness can't be earned)

"...David also describes the blessedness of the man to whom God imputes righteousness apart from works: 'Blessed are those whose lawless deeds are FORGIVEN ('hilasmos'), and whose sins are COVERED; blessed is the man to whom the Lord shall not impute sin..'"

➢ only by shedding BLOOD can my sins be forgiven

Leviticus 17:11 *"...the life of the flesh is in the blood, and I have given it to you upon the altar to make atonement for your souls; for it is the blood that makes ATONEMENT for the soul."*

➢ only a PERFECT SACRIFICE for my sin is acceptable to God

Ezekiel 46:13 *"You shall daily make a burnt offering to the Lord of a lamb of the 1st year without blemish; you shall prepare it every morning."*

Leviticus 22:24-25 *"You shall not offer to the Lord what is bruised or crushed, or torn or cut; nor shall you make any offering of them in your land. Nor from a foreigner's hand shall you offer any of these as the bread of your God, because their corruption is in them, and defects are in them. They shall not be accepted on your behalf."*

Ezekiel 46:13

➢ atonement just COVERS my sin – it can't permanently cancel it

Hebrews 10:4,11 *"It is not possible that the blood of bulls and goats could take away sin. And every priest stands ministering daily and offering repeatedly the same sacrifices, which can never take away sins."*

Hebrews 10:1-3 *"For the law, having a shadow of the good things to come, and not the very image of the things, can never with these same sacrifices, which they offer continually year by year, make those who approach perfect. For then would they not have ceased to be offered? For the worshippers, once purged, would have no more consciousness of sins. But in those sacrifices there is a REMINDER of sins every year."*

Hebrews 10:4,11

➢ Jesus Christ is the "Lamb without blemish" who PERMANENTLY CANCELS my sins

1John 3:5 *"...you know that He was manifested to TAKE AWAY our sins, and in Him THERE IS NO SIN.."*

Hebrews 9:14 *"...how much more shall the blood of Christ, who through the eternal Spirit offered Himself WITHOUT SPOT to God, purge your conscience from dead works to serve the living God?"*

Hebrews 10:12,14 *"But this Man, after He had offered one sacrifice for sins FOREVER, sat down at the right hand of God...for by one offering He has perfected forever those who are being sanctified."*

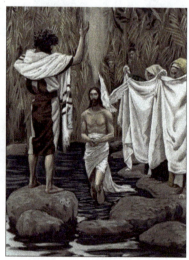

John 1:29 *"...John saw Jesus coming toward him and said, 'Behold, the Lamb of God who takes away the sins of the world.'"*

1Peter 1:19 *"...with the precious blood of Christ, as of a lamb without blemish and without spot."*

2Cor. 5:21 *"...He made Him who knew no sin to become sin for us, that we might become the righteousness of God in Him."*

Jesus = God's SCAPEGOAT for my sins

"Yom Kippur" = "The Day of Atonement" The most important day of the Jewish calendar, called "The Great Day", established by God as an everlasting statute (Leviticus 16:34). One day each year, God provided Israel with a COVERING for their sins, and each person stood clean before their holy God (Leviticus 16:30).

Ten days before, on "Rosh Hashanah" (Jewish "New Year"), the rabbis teach that God decides whether or not a person's name is written in the Book of Life (Exodus 32:32-33). Jews greet each other by saying "May you be INSCRIBED in the Book of Life".

"Day of Atonement" by Isidor Kaufmann, 1910

From "Rosh Hashanah" to "Yom Kippur", called the "10 Days of Penitence", each person is called to repentance. On "Yom Kippur", God's judgment on each person for the coming year is sealed. Jews greet each other on this day by saying "May you be SEALED in the Book of Life".

God's original intent for all Jews on "Yom Kippur" was to HUMBLE themselves (Levit. 16:29 = "inflict their souls"), recognizing their sinfulness and spiritual bankruptcy, acknowledging their total dependency on God and their need for a substitutionary sacrifice to ATONE for their sins.

"Yom Kippur" centered around the Temple and the High Priest, who offered animal sacrifices at the mercy seat of the ark of the Covenant in the "Holy of Holies", and the sacrifice of the "**Scapegoat**" (Leviticus 16).

What's the role of the "Scapegoat" in "Yom Kippur"?
1) Webster's Dictionary: Scapegoat = "a person made to bear the blame for others"
2) Vine's Expository Dictionary: Scapegoat = "the goat for Azazel (root word *āzal*), for *complete sending away*"

On "Yom Kippur", the high priest presents two goats before the Lord at the door of the Tabernacle, casting lots on them:
Goat #1 = was "for **JEHOVAH**". It is sacrificed as a sin offering (the shedding of blood for the remission of sin).
Goat #2 = was "for **AZAZEL**". The high priest lays his hands on this 2nd goat, confessing the sins of the people.

"Goat for Jehovah" "Goat for Azazel"

Leviticus 16:10, 21-22 says a man is chosen to lead the scapegoat into the wilderness and let it loose, to signify the one-time **REMOVAL** of sin from the nation of Israel, so that no people could rise in judgment against them:

"But the goat on which the lot fell to be the SCAPEGOAT shall be presented alive before the Lord, to make ATONEMENT UPON IT, and to let it go as the scapegoat into the wilderness.. Aaron shall lay both hands on the head of the live goat, confess over it all the iniquities of the children of Israel, and all their transgressions, concerning all their sins, putting them on the head of the goat, and shall send it away into the wilderness by the hand of a suitable man. The goat shall BEAR ON ITSELF ALL THEIR INIQUITIES to an uninhabited land; and he shall release the goat in the wilderness."

Jesus Christ = our final, 1-time atoning sacrifice for PERMANENT FORGIVENESS of sin

1) The "goat for Jehovah" = our *sin offering* (its innocent blood was sprinkled on the mercy seat behind the veil in the Holy of Holies – a picture of Christ's death as God's only acceptable sacrifice for forgiveness of our sins).

2) The "goat for Azazel" = our scapegoat, sent away into the wilderness as a picture of our justification before a holy God (our sins have been completely removed from us). He, as the "Scapegoat" for the world, is our PROPITIATION.

Isaiah 53:4-6 *"Surely He has borne our griefs & carried our sorrows; yet we esteemed Him stricken, smitten of God, and afflicted. But He was wounded for OUR TRANSGRESSIONS, He was bruised for OUR INIQUITIES; the chastisement for our peace was UPON HIM, and by His stripes we are healed. All we like sheep have gone astray; we have turned, every one to his own way; and THE LORD HAS LAID ON HIM the iniquity of us all."*

Hebrews 9:24-26   "Yom Kippur points to Christ's *SUFFICIENCY* on our behalf"

My FORGIVENESS
the answer to bitterness

Proverbs 14:10 *"The heart knows its own BITTERNESS and a stranger does not share its joy."*

4.7

What is bitterness?
1) a gift to me, left by the people who have wronged me, which I have received and guard tightly within my heart
2) the debt those who have wronged me owe to me until the day they are brought to justice
3) viewed by me as *rightfully mine* – once I allow **UNRESOLVED HURT** to become resentment and bitterness inside my heart, I feel more and more like the victim who is justified to demand payment for the debt owed to me

> Bitterness = *"PIKRIA"* = from the root word "pik" meaning "to cut"; pointed or sharp so as to stick or irritate the person a person's heart condition, not seen by men, but manifested in behavior or lifestyle self-centeredness that defiles and destroys from within: unforgiving, revengeful, evil speaking
>
> Hebrews 12:14-15 *"Pursue peace with all men, and holiness, without which no one will see the Lord; looking diligently lest anyone fall short of the grace of God; lest any ROOT OF BITTERNESS springing up cause trouble, and by this many become defiled."*
>
> Ephesians 4:30-31 *"...do not grieve the Holy Spirit of God, by whom you were sealed for the day of redemption. Let all BITTERNESS, wrath, anger, loud quarreling and evil speaking be put away from you, with all malice."*

How would you describe a "victim" of bitterness?
POWERLESS (no control over their lives, at the mercy of others); PRISONER (react to *circumstances*)

> ## Matthew 18:21-35 "Our Heavenly Father demands we FORGIVE"
>
> **vs. 21-22** *"Then Peter came to Him and said, 'Lord, how often shall my brother sin against me, and I FORGIVE him? Up to seven times?' Jesus said to him, 'I do not say to you, up to seven times, but up to seventy times seven.*
>
> <u>Amos 1:3,6,9,11,13</u> The rabbis taught forgiveness up to 3X since God forgave Israel's enemies up to 3X...so Peter felt he was really stretching at 7X. He assumed forgiveness was to benefit the offender...but after 7X, no more. Then, the offender "owes me", or its ok for me to "get even" for what has been taken from me.
>
> <u>Luke 17:3-4</u> Jesus taught that when a Christian asks to be forgiven, forgiveness was always to be granted.
>
> **vs. 23-25** *Therefore the kingdom of heaven is like a certain king who wanted to settle accounts with his servants. And when he had begun to settle accounts, one was brought to him who owed him 10,000 talents. But as he was not able to pay, his master commanded that he be sold, with his wife and children and all that he had, and that payment be made.*
> "talent" = largest denomination of currency...so 10,000 signified a huge amount of money owed. There was no way the debtor could repay the sum.
> <u>The analogy</u>: our debt to God for our sins cannot be paid – we deserve death (Romans 6:23).
>
> **vs. 26-27** *The servant therefore fell down before him, saying, 'Master, have patience with me, and I will pay you all.' Then the master of that servant was moved with compassion, released him, and forgave him the debt.*
> <u>Psalm 86:15</u> = Master's nature is **COMPASSION**. → Col. 2:13-14 = God wipes out the debt (total forgiveness).
>
> **vs. 28-30** *But that servant went out and found one of his fellow servants who owed him 100 denarii; and he laid hands on him and took him by the throat, saying, 'Pay me what you owe!' So his fellow servant fell down at his feet and begged him, saying, 'Have patience with me, and I will pay you all.' And he would not, but went and threw him into prison till he should pay the debt.*
> "100 denarii" = 3 month's wages...no comparison to 10,000 talents. But the man has no desire to show mercy.
> <u>The contrast</u>: while the servant was *brought* to his Master, he *sought out* a fellow servant who owed him.
>
> **vs. 31-35** *So when his fellow servants saw what had been done, they were very grieved, and came and told their master all that had been done. Then his master, after he had called him, said to him, 'You wicked servant! I forgave you all that debt because you begged me. Should you not also have had compassion on your fellow servant, just as I had pity on you?' And his master was angry, and delivered him to the torturers until he should pay all that was due to him. So My heavenly Father also will do to you if each of you, from his heart, does not FORGIVE his brother his trespasses."*
> **Hebrews 12:5** ("The Master is angry") = God delivers His children to be scourged if they refuse to forgive.

Eph. 4:32, Col. 3:12-13 → Christians forgive because Christ paid in full our UNPAYABLE DEBT

Proverbs 11:17 tells me why forgiving is so crucial to my **DEVELOPMENT** of Christ-like character:
"The merciful man does good for HIS OWN SOUL, but he who is cruel TROUBLES HIS OWN FLESH."

Unresolved hurt opens the gate of my heart. I actually **ALLOW** the destructive force of bitterness to come right in.

My mind doesn't have a delete button: memories of being hurt by someone don't just die. If I don't deal with the hurt through forgiveness, I will be consumed with wanting justice – I'll want the offender to pay the debt owed me.

My bitterness becomes an expression of my **SELF-CENTEREDNESS**: which is the anti-Christ type of character.

God's standard is **Philippians 2:3-4**. Men and women of character put others first, so holding on to the unresolved hurt sidelines me in my pursuit of Christ-like character.

Andy Stanley[11]: *"We have a tendency to view forgiveness as a gift to the one who offended us – as a benefit to that person. For this reason, we are hesitant to forgive. Why give something to someone who has already taken something from us? That doesn't make any sense. After all, we are the ones who are owed. But forgiveness is not a gift for someone else. Sure, it may involve granting a pardon for an offense. But that's just the beginning. The effects of forgiveness run much deeper. For the most part, it's a gift that was designed for us. Its something we give ourselves. Because when you consider everything that's at stake, the one who benefits the most from forgiveness is the one who grants it, not the one who receives it."*

The 3-Step Process of Forgiving Someone

Step #1: Charge the Defendant Identify what has been taken from me (I know what the person did, but I don't know exactly what the person took).

The problem: generalized forgiveness does not heal specific wounds. I may go through the motions of forgiving, but I won't experience the release from the hurt.

Forgiveness centers on canceling debts – so I must clearly identify the debt before I act to cancel it. Have I been blamed for something I didn't do? Have I been lied to? Has someone spread gossip about me that has stolen my reputation? Did my mother or father abandon me, or just never gave me the time I really wanted?

Step #2: Drop the Charges Instead of pressing charges.... I make the decision to drop the case. I must declare that the person who offended me doesn't owe me anything anymore.

My key: Forgiveness is not a feeling...it's a *DECISION*. I simply *CHOOSE* to cancel the debt.

My joy: its between my Father and I - He is pleased with me (I don't need to share it with the one who hurt me).

My temptation: to judge whether or not I have forgiven by how I *FEEL* toward the offender. But its not about me.

Step #3: Dismiss the Case I decide that I will not reopen the case.

My struggle: my feelings don't just automatically follow my decision to forgive, and my memory isn't erased (when those memories flood back in, my old feelings come back along with them).

I must **RENEW** my **MIND** all over again and face those memories when they come back (memories aren't my problem – its what I choose to do with them that determines their impact).

But I mustn't reopen the case – go back to Step #1 and pinpoint again that thing that was taken from me. Then, praise my Heavenly Father for giving me the grace and strength to "drop the charges" and forgive, reminding myself that what I have against the offender is NOTHING compared to what He forgave in me.

Don't accept the **lie** that I never really forgave – focus on the **TRUTH** that I made the decision to cancel the debt, so by God's promises the debt was cancelled.

What memories really are: opportunities to renew my mind with what I know is true and to rejoice in my own forgiveness. Truly forgiving someone doesn't always mean truly forgetting. But if I renew my mind, even painful memories become reminders of His goodness and grace and healing power in my life.

Ephesians 4:32 *"Be kind to one another, tenderhearted, FORGIVING one another, just as God in Christ also forgave you."*

Colossians 3:12-13 *"....as the elect of God, holy and beloved, put on tender mercies, kindness, humbleness of mind, meekness, longsuffering; bearing with one another, and FORGIVING one another, if anyone has a complaint against another; even as Christ forgave you, so you also must do."*

Forgiveness is non-negotiable if I truly want to pursue Christ-like character.

My GIVING
promises God's blessings

Proverbs 11:25 *"The GENEROUS soul shall be made rich, and he who waters will also be watered himself."*

4.8

Old Testament "GIVING" to supply that which is wanting; to generously meet the anxious **NEEDS** of another

Proverbs 22:9 *"He who has a bountiful eye will be blessed, for he GIVES of his bread to the poor."*
Proverbs 21:26 *"He covets greedily all day long, but the righteous GIVES and does not spare."*
Proverbs 21:13 *"Whoever shuts his ears to the cry of the poor will also cry himself and not be heard."*
Proverbs 3:9 *"Honor the Lord with your possessions, and the firstfruits of all your increase."*

Two Descriptions in the New Testament of God's Character of "Giving"

① *"CHARIZOMAI"*: to bestow or GRANT FREELY upon another; used almost exclusively in reference to God, who gives freely without expecting anything in return.

Romans 8:32 *"He who did not spare His own Son, but delivered Him up for us all, how shall He not with Him also freely GIVE us all things?"*
Luke 7:21 *"…He cured many people of their illnesses, afflictions, and evil spirits; and to many who were blind He GAVE sight."*
Galatians 3:18 *"…if the inheritance is of the law, it is no longer of promise; but God GAVE it to Abraham by promise."*
1Corin. 2:12 *"…Now we have received, not the spirit of the world, but the Spirit who is from God, that we might know the things which have been freely GIVEN to us by God."*

② *"PARADIDŌMI"*: to hand over or deliver up; in reference to Christ, this word is always connected with His **love**.

John 3:16 *"…God so LOVED the world that He GAVE His only begotten Son, that whoever believes in Him should not perish but have everlasting life."*
Galatians 2:20 *"I have been crucified with Christ; it is no longer I who live, but Christ lives in me; and the life which I now live in the flesh I live by faith in the Son of God who LOVED me and GAVE Himself for me."*
Ephesians 5:2, 25 *"…walk in love, as Christ also has LOVED us and GIVEN Himself for us, an offering and a sacrifice to God for a sweet aroma. Husbands, love your wives just as Christ also loved the church and GAVE Himself for it…"*

One Description in the New Testament of God's command that I exercise the character of "Giving"

③ *"METADIDŌMI"*: to impart or share (to "**SPEND OUT**") my life and the things I have generously with another.

<u>my spiritual gifts</u> (exhortation, teaching, prayer, etc.) - God commands us to SHARE or GIVE out of the abundance of the gifts He has blessed us with (exercise your gifts….don't waste them).

<u>my material blessings</u> (financial, possessions, etc.) – God says when I give to those in need, it is fruit credited to my account, revealing my repentant heart.

Romans 12:8 *"He who exhorts, in exhortation; he who GIVES, with liberality; he who leads, with diligence; he who shows mercy, with cheerfulness."*
Ephesians 4:28 *"Let him who stole steal no longer, but rather let him labor, working with his hands what is good, that he may have something to GIVE him who has need."*

The 4 Phases of Giving in my Life

Phase #1: *Understand:* 2Corinthians 9:7 says it's a <u>COMMANDMENT</u> from the Lord
"…let each one GIVE as he purposes in his heart, not grudgingly or of compulsion; for God loves a cheerful giver."

Phase #2: *Cultivate* a "Rom. 12:1, 2Corin. 8:1-5 Attitude" (He first gave to me, so I will give to Him and others)
"I urge you therefore, brethren, by the mercies of God, that you present your bodies a LIVING SACRIFICE, holy, acceptable to God, which is your reasonable service."
"…this they did, not as we had hoped, but first GAVE THEMSELVES to the Lord, and then to us by the will of God."

Phase #3: *Motivate* my giving out of <u>LOVE</u>… or 1Corinthians 13:3 warns that it's worthless
"…though I GIVE my body to be burned, but have not LOVE, it profits me nothing."

Phase #4: *Practice* Matthew 10:8 (grace living = grace giving….. so give according to the gifts given to me!)
"Freely you have received, FREELY GIVE."

What "Gifts" from God can I *give back* to Him?   How do I know if I have any?

GIFT #1: <u>PROPHECY</u> (the proclamation of God's divinely inspired word)
1Corinthians 14:3 *"He who prophesies speaks edification and exhortation and comfort to men."*
Acts 15:32 *"...Judas and Silas, themselves being prophets also, exhorted the brethren with many words and strengthened them."*
• Am I supernaturally endowed to apply God's Word to: 1) Edify (build up others in the faith; 2) Exhort (encourage others to do what is biblical); 3) Comfort (confirm the truth of God's word in situations requiring insight).
• The Positive: prophecy requires INSIGHT and DISCERNMENT – the ability to see things clearly in terms of the TRUTH of God's Word (right vs. wrong), having the courage to stand for that truth and bring conviction to others.
• The Negative: because I see truth so clearly, I must guard against being unforgiving (more judgmental than merciful), impulsive and hasty (don't think before speaking), and openly rebuking when disagreed with.

GIFT #2: <u>TEACHING</u> (the ability to present biblical truth in a way that establishes sound doctrine in those taught)
• Jesus = our model of a teacher (over 40X He is called "teacher" or "Master", but never "preacher").
Luke 24:25-27 *"...He said to them, 'O foolish ones and slow of heart to believe in all that the prophets have spoken! Ought not the Christ to have suffered these things and to enter into His glory?' And beginning at Moses and all the Prophets, He expounded to them in all the Scriptures the things concerning Himself."*

Luke 24:25-27

• Teachers: (1) combine the intellect, will and emotion; (2) avoid confusing people by presenting truth in a systematic, ordered manner.
• Every believer can and must teach others (<u>DISCIPLESHIP</u> is a good example), but some are supernaturally gifted to teach.

GIFT #3: <u>EXHORTATION</u> (the ability to comfort and encourage others toward righteousness and obedience)
• This gift is both firm and encouraging. It appeals to one's will and emotion, bringing both comfort and conviction.
• If you have this gift: you are approachable and naturally reach out to others (you are a "people person").
• It isn't bawling someone out – its coming alongside of, *encouraging* right decisions and bringing comfort.
1Timothy 2:1 *"I exhort first of all that supplications, prayers, intercessions, and giving of thanks be made for all men."*
Acts 14:21-22 *"...when they had preached the gospel to that city and made many disciples, they returned to Lystra, Iconium, and Antioch, strengthening the souls of the disciples, exhorting them to continue in the faith, and saying, 'We must through many tribulations enter the kingdom of God.'"*
• Barnabas: an excellent model (Acts 4:36 says he was nicknamed "son of encouragement").
Acts 9:26-27 *"when Saul had come to Jerusalem, he tried to join the disciples; but they were all afraid of him, and did not believe that he was a disciple. But Barnabas PULLED ALONGSIDE HIM and brought him to the apostles. And he declared to them how he had seen the Lord on the road, and that He had spoken to him, and how he had preached boldly at Damascus in the name of Jesus."*

GIFT #4: <u>GIVING</u> (the ability to invest resources in God's missions for maximum return on the investment)
• If you have this gift: you don't think of recognition or reward (you're motivated by love and loyalty to the Lord).
2Corinthians 8:8-9 *"I speak not by commandment, but I am testing the SINCERITY OF YOUR LOVE by the diligence of others. For you know the grace of our Lord Jesus Christ, that though He was rich, yet for your sakes He became poor, that you through His poverty might become rich."*

GIFT #5: RULING or <u>ADMINISTRATION</u> (the ability to organize, administrate, manage, lead)
1Corin. 12:28 *"...God has appointed these in the church: first apostles, second prophets, third teachers, after that miracles, then gifts of healings, helps, administrations, varieties of tongues."*
• Everyone is someone's leader in some way (Discipleship, Nursery, etc.).

GIFT #6: <u>MERCY</u> (the ability to show compassion and understanding to the needs and trials of others)
• If you have this gift: you know just the right thing to say or do in time of someone's crisis or need.
• Dorcas (Acts 9:36): a great example of someone known for her good works and almsdeeds ("deeds of mercy").

1 Corinthians 12:7   *Everyone* has at least 1 GIFT

My DILIGENCE
prompts a promise from God

Proverbs 8:17 *"I love those who love Me, and those who seek Me DILIGENTLY will find Me."*

4.9

> **What is "diligence"?** Hebrew *"SHÂCHAR, MISHMÂR, CHÂRÛTS CHÂRÛTS"* = "watchfulness; to seek after early, especially first thing in the morning; constant effort to exert oneself with persevering attention to the thing being done; to whole-heartedly attend to something (in contrast to what is merely superficial).
>
> Proverbs 4:23 *"Guard your heart with all DILIGENCE, for out of it spring the issues of life."*
> Proverbs. 11:27 *"He who DILIGENTLY seeks good finds favor, but trouble will come to him who seeks evil."*
> Proverbs 13:4 *"The soul of the sluggard desires but has nothing; but the soul of the DILIGENT shall be made rich."*

Our attention in "God's Will for my life" is on diligence as it relates to CHARACTER, to become the *person* that God wants me to be from the "INSIDE- OUT".

TRUTH #1: God is diligently seeking ME, to mold me as His own son or daughter

Luke 15:8 *"...what woman, having 10 silver coins, if she loses 1 coin, does not light a lamp, sweep the house, and SEEK DILIGENTLY until she finds it?"*

John 4:23 *"...the Father is SEEKING such to worship Him."*

Ever wonder why God's agenda seems to be at odds with mine? There are times in my life when God annoys me as I've tried to follow Him, just because of who He is - a perfect God who is diligent in molding me to be like Him! But when I try it my way, I quickly discover how incapable I am without Him...

God's Character = 40 Annoying Attributes of My Heavenly Father (or...why He's God and I'm not)	
He's invisible	Job 9:11 *"If He goes by me, I don't see Him..."*
He's a perfectionist	Matthew 5:48 *"...you shall be perfect, just as your Father in heaven is perfect."*
He's hard to please	Hebrews 11:6 *"Without faith its impossible to please Him, for he who comes to God must believe that He is, and He rewards those who diligently seek Him."*
He's way too generous with my possessions	Matthew 5:40 *"If anyone wants to sue you and take away your tunic, let him have your cloak also."*
He's OK with leaving things open-ended	Genesis 12:1 *"The Lord said to Abram, 'Get out of your country, from your kindred and from your father's house, to a land that I will show you.'"*
He's got all the time in the world	2Peter 3:8 *"...with the Lord 1 day is as 1,000 years, and 1,000 years as 1 day."*
He thinks my life is His	Ezekiel 18:4 *"Behold, all souls are mine."*
He thinks what He wrote 2,000 years ago still goes	Matthew 24:35 *"Heaven and earth will pass away, but My words will by no means pass away."*
He thinks I shouldn't worry	Matthew 6:27 *"Which of you by worrying can add 1 cubit to his stature?"*
He thinks I shouldn't get even	Prov. 20:22 *"Don't say, 'I will repay evil'; wait for the Lord; He will save you."*
He thinks I should be longsuffering	1Corinthians 13:4 *"Love suffers long and is kind."*
He thinks I should be forgiving	Ephesians 4:32 *"Be kind to one another, tenderhearted, forgiving one another, just as God in Christ also forgave you."*
He thinks I should pray for my enemies	Luke 6:27-28 *"Love your enemies; do good to those who hate you; bless those who curse you, and pray for those who spitefully use you."*
He thinks "No" is a sufficient answer	Deuteronomy 3:26 *"The Lord was angry with me on your account, and would not listen to me: 'Enough of that! Speak no more to Me of the matter!'"*
He thinks humility is a character quality I need	Luke 14:11 *"Whoever exalts himself will be humbled, and he who humbles himself will be exalted."*
He thinks delayed obedience is disobedience	Luke 9:62 *"'No one, having put his hand to the plow, and looking back, is fit for the kingdom of God.'"*
He thinks problems are a good way to make me stronger	James 1:2-3 *"My brethren, count it all joy when you fall into various trials, knowing that the testing of your faith produces perseverance."*

God's Character = 40 Annoying Attributes of My Heavenly Father (or...why He's God and I'm not)

He won't justify Himself to me	Job 38:4 *"Where were you when I laid the foundations of the earth? Tell me, if you know so much!"*
He won't let me take anything with me when I die	1Timothy 6:7 *"...we brought nothing into this world, and it is certain we can carry nothing out."*
He won't give up	Luke 15:4 *"What man of you, having 100 sheep, if he loses 1 of them, does not leave the 99 in the wilderness and go after the 1 which is lost until he finds it?"*
He doesn't make mistakes	Job 36:22-23 *"God is exalted by His power; who teaches like Him? Who has assigned Him His way, or who has said, 'You have done wrong'?"*
He doesn't fit His schedule to mine	John 11:21 *"Martha said to Jesus, 'Lord, if You had been here, my brother would not have died."*
He doesn't think my anger is justified nearly as often as I do	Jonah 4:9 *"God said to Jonah, 'Is it right for you to be angry about the plant?'"*
He isn't easy to follow	Mark 8:34 *"Whoever desires to come after Me, let him deny himself, take up his cross, and follow Me."*
He isn't politically correct	John 14:6 *"I am the way, the truth and the life. No one comes to the Father except through Me."*
He isn't interested in my excuses	Proverbs 24:12 *"If you say, 'Surely we did not know this,' does not He who weighs the hearts consider it?...will He not render to each man according to his deeds?"*
He isn't impressed by what I try to do for Him	Romans 4:2 *"If Abraham was justified by works, he has something of which to boast, but not before God."*
He isn't impressed by my appearance	1Samuel 16:7 *"The Lord does not see as man sees; for man looks at the outward appearance, but the Lord looks at the heart.'"*
He isn't impressed with how clever I am	1Corinthians 1:25 *"The foolishness of God is wiser than men, and the weakness of God is stronger than men."*
He isn't interested in making me look good	1Corinthians 4:9 *"I think that God has displayed us, the apostles, last, as men condemned to death: for we have been made a spectacle to the world..."*
He drags things out way too long	John 10:24 *"The Jews surrounded and said to Him, "How long do You keep us in suspense? If You are the Christ, tell us plainly."*
He takes everything personally	Matthew 25:40 *"The King will answer and say to them, 'Assuredly, I say to you, inasmuch as you did it to one of the least of these My brethren, you did it to Me.'"*
He wants me to trust Him just because of who He is	Isaiah 45:22 *"Look to Me, and be saved, all you ends of the earth! For I am God, and there is no other."*
He expects me to keep my word	Ecclesiastes 5:4 *"When you make a vow to God, do not delay to pay it; for He has no pleasure in fools."*
He keeps confusing my part-time resolve with some kind of full-time commitment	Deuteronomy 30:10 *"If you obey the voice of the Lord your God, to keep His commandments and His statutes which are written in this Book of the Law, and if you turn to the Lord your God with all your heart and with all your soul."*
He knows what I'm thinking	Genesis 18:12-13 *"Sarah laughed within herself, saying, 'After I have grown old, shall I have pleasure, my lord being old also?' The Lord said to Abraham, 'Why did Sarah laugh?"*
He sees right through me	Luke 6:46 *"Why do you call me 'Lord, Lord', and do not do the things that I say?"*
He makes it hard to be good	2Timothy 3:12 *"...all who live godly in Christ Jesus will suffer persecution."*
He decides when my time is up	Job 14:5 *"A man's days are determined, the number of his months is with You; You have appointed his limits, so that he cannot pass."*
He always wins	Acts 9:4-5 *"He fell to the ground, and heard a voice saying to him, 'Saul, Saul, why are you persecuting Me?' He said, 'Who are You, Lord?' And the Lord said, 'I am Jesus, whom you are persecuting. It is hard for you to kick against the goads.'"*

EZEKIEL 18:25 *"Yet you say, 'The way of the Lord is not fair'... is it not My way which is fair, and your ways which are not fair?"*

TRUTH #2: I must be diligent in <u>DESIRING</u> Jesus (He must be my #1 Priority)

Isaiah 55:1-2 *"Why do you spend money for what is not bread, and your wages for what does not satisfy? Listen DILIGENTLY to Me, and eat what is good; and let your soul delight itself in abundance. Incline your ear, and come to Me. Hear, and your soul shall live; and I will make an everlasting covenant with you – the sure mercies of David."*

Psalm 27:8 *"When You said, 'SEEK My face', my heart said, 'Your face, O God, I will SEEK.'"*

Psalm 77:1-2,6 *"I cried out to God with my voice – to God with my voice; and He gave ear to me. In the day of my trouble I SOUGHT the Lord; my hand was stretched out in the night without ceasing; my soul refused to be comforted. I call to remembrance my song in the night; I meditate within my heart, and my spirit makes DILIGENT search."*

Matthew 13:44-46 *"The kingdom of heaven is like treasure hidden in a field, which a man found and hid; and for joy over it he goes and SELLS ALL THAT HE HAS and buys that field. Again, the kingdom of heaven is like a merchant SEEKING beautiful pearls, who, when he had found 1 pearl of great price, went and SOLD ALL THAT HE HAD and bought it."*

TRUTH #3: Diligence in *obeying* Jesus because I've committed to His <u>LORDSHIP</u>

Psalm 119:4 *"You have commanded us to keep Your precepts DILIGENTLY."*

Deuteronomy 28:1-2 *"...it shall come to pass, if you DILIGENTLY obey the voice of the Lord your God, to observe CAREFULLY all His commandments which I command you today, that the Lord your God will set you high above all the nations of the earth. And all the blessings shall come upon you and overtake you, because you obey the voice of the Lord your God."*

2Peter 3:14 *"...beloved, looking forward to these things, be DILIGENT to be found by Him in peace, without spot and blameless."*

Hebrews 12:14-15 *"Pursue peace with all men, and holiness, without which no one will see the Lord: looking DILIGENTLY lest anyone fall short of the grace of God..."*

MAX LUCADO ('*A Heart Like Jesus*')[13]:   Hebrews 11:6

"...without faith it is impossible to please Him, for he who comes to God must believe that He is, and that He is a rewarder of those who DILIGENTLY seek Him."

Diligently: what a great word. Be diligent in your search. Be hungry in your quest. Step away from the puny pursuits of possessions and positions, and seek your king. The Bible tells of those weren't satisfied until they had *sought Him out*:

- the shepherds weren't satisfied to see *angels* – they had to see *Him* (Luke 2:8-17)
- the Magi didn't want to see the *light over Bethlehem* – they had to see the *Light of Bethlehem* (Matt. 2:1-2)
- Simeon didn't want to *see the world* before he died – he wanted to *see the world's Maker* (Luke 2:25-31)
- John and Andrew weren't satisfied to *hear John the Baptist* – they wanted to *live with Jesus* (John 1:35-39)
- Matthew wasn't satisfied with a *curbside talk* with Jesus – so he *took Jesus home* with him (Matt. 9:9-10)
- Zacchaeus wasn't satisfied to hear about Jesus – he went out on a limb to see Him (Luke 19:1-6)

God rewards those who truly **WANT** to find Him. Not those who seek doctrine or religion or systems or creeds. The reward goes to those who settle for nothing less than Jesus Himself. And what reward awaits those who seek Jesus? Nothing short of His **HEART**. Can you think of a greater gift than to be like Him?
2Corinthians 3:18 *"...as the Spirit of the Lord works within us, we become more and more like Him."*

Jesus felt no guilt -	He wants to remove mine
Jesus humbled Himself for His Father's work -	He wants my humble spirit so He can work in me
Jesus was always under control -	He wants me under His control
Jesus trusted completely in His Father -	He wants me to trust completely in Him
Jesus always told the truth -	He wants me to be a truthful person
Jesus showed love to the unlovable -	He wants His love to show through me
Jesus was kind and mercy to the undeserving -	He wants me to have the same
Jesus readily forgave anyone truly seeking it -	He wants me to be a forgiving person
Jesus gave everything for me -	He wants me to give everything for Him

Genesis 15:1 *"Do not be afraid, Abram. I am your shield, you exceedingly great reward."*
Colossians 1:27 *"the Lord sanctifies me through Jesus Christ in me"*

WHAT AREAS OF MY LIFE <u>REQUIRE</u> MY DILIGENCE?

Select the top 1 or 2 character qualities that you struggle with (all verses from Proverbs)

- ☐ Do I really FEAR the Lord (v.1:7)? — I won't grow at all if I don't submit to His will
- ☐ Am I on guard against PRIDE (v.3:34)? — God resists my prayers if I am self-seeking
- ☐ Am I in CONTROL of my temper (v.17:27)? — I don't understand God if I'm easily angered
- ☐ Do I really TRUST Him in all things (v.3:5-6)? — God wants me to take risks
- ☐ Do I tell the TRUTH (v. 23:23)? — God hates my lying
- ☐ Do I LOVE only when convenient (v.10:12)? — Loving others should cost me something
- ☐ Do I practice KINDNESS and MERCY (v.19:22)? — My good intentions won't make a difference
- ☐ Do I FORGIVE with "no strings attached" (v.17:9)? — Holding on to past hurts will destroy me
- ☐ Does my GIVING show my love (v.11:25)? — God wants to bless my heart
- ☐ Do I take my Christianity seriously (v. 8:17)? — God wants to be #1 in my life

---

5-Step Process to become more like Jesus

Philippians 2:12 *"...work out my own salvation, with fear and trembling, for it is God who works in me both to will and to do for His good pleasure."*

Step #1: HUNGER to grow in character (Proverbs 2:1-4)

"My son, if you receive My words, and treasure My commands within you, so that you INCLINE YOUR EAR to wisdom and APPLY YOUR HEART to understanding; yes, if you CRY OUT for discernment, and LIFT UP YOUR VOICE for understanding; if you SEEK HER AS SILVER, and search for her as for hidden treasure; then you will understand the fear of the Lord, and find knowledge of God."

Step #2: PRAY for God to give you the wisdom to apply that quality in your life (James 1:5-8)

"If any of you lacks wisdom, let him ASK OF GOD, who gives to all liberally and without reproach, and it will be given to him. But let him ask in faith, with no doubting, for he who doubts is like a wave of the sea driven and tossed by the wind. For let not that man suppose that he will receive anything from the Lord; he is a double-minded man, unstable in all his ways."

Step #3: FOLLOW Christians with the qualities you desire to cultivate in yourself (Philippians 3:17)

"Brethren, join in following my example, and NOTE THOSE who so walk, as you have us for an example."

Step #4: DEPEND on the Holy Spirit to lead you as you grow (John 16:7,13)

"...I tell you the truth. It is to your advantage that I go away; for if I do not go away, the Helper will not come to you; but if I depart, I will send Him to you... when He, the Spirit of truth, has come, HE WILL GUIDE YOU into all truth..."

Step #5: STUDY and MEMORIZE God's Word to grow (2Timothy 3:15, Ezra 7:10, Psalm 119:9,11)

"Be DILIGENT to present yourself approved of God, a worker who does not need to be ashamed, RIGHTLY DIVIDING THE WORD OF TRUTH."

"Ezra had prepared his heart to SEEK the Law of the Lord, and to do it, and to teach statutes and ordinances in Israel."

"How can a young man cleanse his way? By taking heed according to YOUR WORD. Your word I have HIDDEN IN MY HEART, that I might not sin against You."

GOD'S SUFFERING
fulfills His own righteousness

Hebrews 5:8 *"...though He was a Son, yet He learned obedience by the things which He SUFFERED."*

4.10

- *"PASCHO"* = refers to Christ's sufferings
- *"HUPOMENO"* = experience pain or distress inflicted by others
- <u>John MacArthur</u>: what it means for Jesus to "learn obedience through suffering"

"Christ did not need to suffer in order to conquer or correct any disobedience. In His deity (as the Son of God), He understood obedience completely. As the incarnate Lord, He humbled Himself to learn (Luke 2:51-52). He learned obedience for the same reason He bore temptation: to confirm His humanity and experience its sufferings to the fullest (Phil. 2:8). Christ's obedience was also necessary so that He could fulfill all righteousness (Matt. 5:17-18) and thus prove to be the perfect sacrifice to take the place of sinners (1Peter 3:18). He was the perfectly righteous One, whose righteousness would be imputed to sinners (Romans 3:24-26)."

God's will: JESUS would suffer for our sake

Acts 3:18 *"..those things which God foretold by the mouth of His prophets, that the Christ would SUFFER, He has fulfilled."*

Acts 26:22-23 *"...having obtained help from God, to this day I stand, witnessing both to small and great, saying no other things than those which the prophets and Moses said would come – that the CHRIST WOULD SUFFER, that He would be the first to rise from the dead, and would proclaim light to the Jewish people and to the Gentiles."*

Luke 24:46-47 *"... it was necessary for the Christ to SUFFER and to rise from the dead the 3rd day, and that repentance and remission of sins should be preached in His name to all nations, beginning at Jerusalem."*

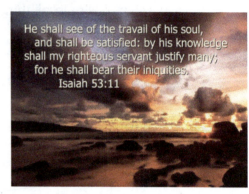

He shall see of the travail of his soul, and shall be satisfied: by his knowledge shall my righteous servant justify many; for he shall bear their iniquities.
Isaiah 53:11

Mark 8:31 *"He began to teach them that the Son of Man must SUFFER many things, and be rejected by the elders and chief priests and scribes, and be killed, and after 3 days rise again. Likewise the Son of Man is about to SUFFER at their hands."*

1Peter 3:18 *"Christ also SUFFERED ONCE FOR SINS, the just for the unjust, that He might bring us to God, being put to death in the flesh but made alive by the Spirit..."*

JEREMIAH: "Jesus in the O.T." – the WEEPING PROPHET

"Jeremiah" means "Jehovah throws", as in "laying down a foundation" ("Jehovah establishes, appoints, sends"). 627–586 BC (40 years): in a time of immorality, he preached repentance, then pending judgment (Babylon).

Jeremiah 1:4-8 = he was only 20-25 years old when he was called by God, but <u>God promised to be with Him</u>. He lived a solitary life of intense persecution = he was threatened often, tried for his life, put in stocks, publicly humiliated by a false prophet, thrown in a pit, and forced to flee from Jerusalem.

Jeremiah 20:8-11 = the prophet Jeremiah laments over how difficult it was, if he focused on his circumstances, to speak the truth and stand firm in his faith……but he remembered that <u>the Lord was always with him</u>:

"O Lord, You enticed me, and I was persuaded; You are stronger then I, and have prevailed. I AM A LAUGHING STOCK all the day; EVERYONE MOCKS ME. For when I spoke, I cried out; I shouted, 'Violence and plunder!' Because the Word of the Lord was made to me a reproach and a derision daily. Then I said, 'I will not make mention of Him, nor speak anymore in His name.' But His word was in my heart like a burning fire shut up in my bones; I was weary of holding it back, and I could not. All my acquaintances WATCHED FOR MY STUMBLING, saying, 'Perhaps he can be induced; then we will prevail against him, and we will take our revenge on him.'" But THE LORD IS WITH ME as a mighty, awesome one. Therefore my persecutors will stumble, and will not prevail. They will be greatly ashamed, for they will not prosper. Their everlasting confusion will never be forgotten."

JESUS = Our PERSECUTED Savior (just like Jeremiah)

Matthew 9:23-24 *"And when Jesus came into the ruler's house, and saw the flute players and the noisy crowd wailing, He said to them, 'Make room, for the girl is not dead, but sleeping." And they LAUGHED HIM TO SCORN."*

Luke 20:20 *"...THEY WATCHED HIM, and sent spies who pretended to be righteous, that they might seize on His words, in order to deliver Him to the power and the authority of the governor."*

Matthew 12:10-14 *"..there was a man who had a withered hand. And they asked Him, saying, 'Is it lawful to heal on the Sabbath?'– that they might BRING CHARGES AGAINST HIM. Then He said to them, 'What man is there among you who has 1 sheep, and if it falls into a pit on the Sabbath, will not lay hold of it and lift it out? Of how much more value then is a man than a sheep? Therefore it is lawful to do good on the Sabbath.' Then He said to the man, 'Stretch out your hand.' And he stretched it out, and it was restored as whole as the other. Then the Pharisees went out, and took counsel against Him, how they might DESTROY HIM."*

MARK 6:2-3 = the word "offended" used here is "SCANDALON", which means **STUMBLING STONE**
"And when the Sabbath had come, He began to teach in the synagogue. And many hearing Him were astonished, saying, 'Where did this Man get these things? And what wisdom is this which is given to Him, that such mighty works are performed by His hands! Is this not the carpenter, the son of Mary, and brother of James, Joses, Judas, and Simon? Are not His sisters here with us?' And THEY WERE OFFENDED AT HIM."

MATTHEW 27:28-31 = the soldiers mock, spit on Him, beat Him
"They stripped Him and put a scarlet robe on Him. When they had twisted a crown of thorns, they put it on His head, and a reed in His right hand. And they bowed the knee before Him and MOCKED HIM, saying, 'Hail, King of the Jews!' Then they spat on Him, and took the reed and struck Him on the head. Then when they had mocked Him, they took the robe off Him, put His own clothes on Him, and led Him away to be crucified."

MATTHEW 27:39-43 = everyone mocks Him as He is dying on the cross
"...those who passed by BLASPHEMED Him, wagging their heads and saying, 'You who destroy the temple and build it in 3 days, save Yourself! If You are the Son of God, come down from the cross.' Likewise the chief priests, also MOCKING with the scribes and elders, said, 'He saved others; Himself He cannot save. If He is the King of Israel, let Him now come down from the cross, and we will believe Him. He trusted in God; let Him deliver Him now if He will have Him; for He said, 'I am the Son of God.'"

JESUS = secure in His Father's promise to never LEAVE HIM (just like Jeremiah)

John 8:29 *"He who sent Me is WITH ME. The Father has not left Me alone, for I always do the things that please Him."*

John 16:32 *"The hour is coming yes, and now has come, that you will be scattered, each to his own, and will leave Me. And yet I am not alone, because THE FATHER IS WITH ME."*

John 10:17 *"My Father LOVES ME, because I lay down My life that I might take it again."*

Matthew 3:17 *"A voice came from heaven, saying, 'This is My beloved Son, in whom I AM WELL PLEASED.'"*

Isaiah 50:5-7 *"The Lord has opened My ear, and I was not rebellious; nor did I turn away. I gave My back to those who struck Me, and My cheeks to those who plucked out the beard. I did not hide my face from shame and spitting. For the Lord God will HELP ME; therefore I will not be disgraced; therefore I have set My face like a flint, and I KNOW that I will not be ashamed."*

God's will: I glorify Him as I suffer for HIS SAKE

2Timothy 2:12 *"...all who desire to live godly in Christ Jesus WILL SUFFER PERSECUTION."*

Phil. 1:29 *"For to you it has been granted on behalf of Christ, not only to believe in Him, but also to SUFFER for His sake."*

John 15:18-21 *"If the world hates you, you know that IT HATED ME before it hated you. If you were of this world, the world would love its own. Yet because you are not of this world, but I chose you out of the world, therefore THE WORLD HATES YOU. Remember the word that I said to you, 'A servant is not greater than his master.' If they persecuted Me, THEY WILL ALSO PERSECUTE YOU. If they kept My word, they will keep yours also. But all these things they will do to you FOR MY NAME'S SAKE, because they do not know Him who sent Me."*

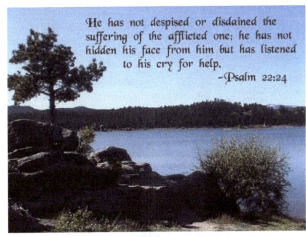

He has not despised or disdained the suffering of the afflicted one; he has not hidden his face from him but has listened to his cry for help.
-Psalm 22:24

1Peter 2:21-23 *"... to this YOU WERE CALLED, because Christ also suffered for us, LEAVING US AN EXAMPLE, that you should follow His steps: 'Who committed no sin, nor was deceit found in His mouth'; who, when He was reviled, did not revile in return; when He SUFFERED, He did not threaten, but committed Himself to Him who judges righteously..."*

God's plan: I suffer because the Gospel is OFFENSIVE

Galatians 5:11, 6:12 *"And I, brethren, if I still preach circumcision, why do I still suffer persecution? Then the OFFENSE OF THE CROSS has ceased. As many as desire to make a good showing in the flesh, these try to compel you to be circumcised, only that they may not suffer persecution for the CROSS OF CHRIST."*

1Timothy 4:10 *"For to this end we labor and SUFFER REPROACH, because we trust in the living God, who is the Savior of all men, especially of those who believe."*

2Timothy 1:12 *"For this reason I also suffer these things; nevertheless I am not ashamed, for I know whom I have believed and am persuaded that He is able to keep what I have committed to Him until that Day."*

2Corin. 5:9 - Pleasing God includes accepting the suffering that comes with taking His name
"Therefore we make it our aim, whether present or absent, to be well pleasing to Him."

Argument #11 for God = Evil & Suffering exist

1Peter 3:18 *"Christ ①SUFFERED once for our sins, the just for the unjust, that He might ②BRING us to God."*
① 'SUFFERED' = Gr. *'PASCHO'* = Christ personally experienced pain or distress inflicted upon Him by others
② 'BRING US' = Gr. *'PROSAGŌ'* = lead us (as a shepherd) towards, draw us near to

The following excerpts are taken from pages 25-31 of Timothy Keller's book 'The Reason for God'[14]

"Horrendous, inexplicable suffering, though it cannot disprove God, is nonetheless a problem for the believer in the Bible. However, it is perhaps an even greater problem for nonbelievers. **C.S. Lewis** described how he had originally rejected the idea of God because of the cruelty of life. Then he came to realize that evil was even more problematic for his new atheism. In the end, he realized that suffering provided a better argument for God's existence than one against it:

'My argument against God was that the universe seemed so cruel and unjust. But how had I got this idea of 'just' and 'unjust'… what was I comparing this universe with when I called it unjust? Of course I could have given up my idea of justice by saying it was nothing but a private idea of my own. But if I did that, then my argument against God collapsed too – for the argument depended on saying that the world was really unjust, not simply that it did not happen to please my private fancies… consequently atheism turns out to be too simple.' Lewis recognized that modern objections to God are based on a sense of fair play and justice. People, we believe, ought not to suffer, be excluded, die of hunger or oppression.

But the evolutionary mechanism of natural selection depends on death, destruction, and violence of the strong against the weak – these things are all perfectly natural. On what basis, then, does the atheist judge the natural world to be horribly wrong, unfair, and unjust? The nonbeliever in God doesn't have a good basis for being outraged at injustice, which, as Lewis points out, was the reason for objecting to God in the first place. If you are sure that this natural world is unjust and filled with evil, you are assuming the reality of some extra-natural (or supernatural) standard by which to make your judgment. The philosopher **Alvin Plantinga** said it like this:

'Could there really be such a thing as horrifying wickedness if there were no God and we just evolved? I don't see how. There can be such a thing only if there is a way that rational creatures are supposed to live… a secular way of looking at the world has no place for genuine moral obligation of any sort… and thus no way to say there is such a thing as genuine and appalling wickedness. Accordingly, if you think there really is such a thing as horrifying wickedness…, then you have a powerful… argument for the reality of God.'

> In short, the problem of tragedy, suffering and injustice is a problem for everyone. It is at least as big a problem for nonbelief in God as for belief. It is therefore a mistake, though an understandable one, to think that if you abandon belief in God it somehow makes the problem of evil easier to handle.

'So what if suffering and evil doesn't logically disprove God?', a person might say. 'I'm still angry. All this philosophizing does not get the Christian God 'off the hook' for the world's evil and suffering!' In response the philosopher **Peter Kreeft** points out that the Christian God came to earth to deliberately put Himself on the hook of human suffering. In Jesus Christ, God experienced the greatest depths of pain. Therefore, though Christianity does not provide the reason for each experience of pain, it provides deep resources for actually facing suffering with hope and courage rather than bitterness and despair.

To understand Jesus's suffering at the end of the gospels, we must remember how He is introduced at the beginning. The gospel writer John, in his first chapter, introduces us to the mysterious but crucial concept of God as tri-personal. The Son of God was not created but took part in creation and lived throughout all eternity 'in the bosom of the Father' (John 1:18) – that is, in a relationship of absolute intimacy and love. But at the end of His life He was cut off from the Father…

Christian theology has always recognized that Jesus bore, as the substitute in our place, the endless exclusion from God that the human race has merited. On the cross, Jesus's cry of dereliction – 'My God, My God, why have You forsaken Me?' – is a deeply relational statement. New Testament scholar **Bill Lane** writes: 'The cry has a ruthless authenticity… Jesus did not die renouncing God. Even in the inferno of abandonment He did not surrender His faith in God but expressed His anguished prayer in a cry of affirmation – 'My God, My God.' Jesus still uses the language of intimacy – 'My God' – even as He experiences infinite separation from the Father.'

If we again ask the question, 'Why does God allow evil and suffering to continue?' and we look at the Cross of Jesus, we still do not know what the answer is. However, we now know what the answer isn't. It can't be that He doesn't love us. It can't be that He is indifferent or detached from our condition. God takes our misery and suffering so seriously that He was willing to take it on Himself."

> If we embrace the Christian teaching that Jesus is God and that He went to the Cross, then we have deep consolation and strength to face the brutal realities of life on earth. We can know that God is truly IMMANUEL – God with us – even in our worst sufferings."

Naturalism: Is there any moral basis for Evil & Suffering?

Charles Darwin, *The Descent of Man* - our moral values are nothing but biological adaptations: *"If ... men were reared under precisely the same conditions as hive-bees, there can hardly be a doubt that our unmarried females would, like the worker-bees, think it a sacred duty to kill their brothers, and mothers would strive to kill their fertile daughters, and no one would think of interfering."*

Michael Ruse (PhD Philosophy of Biology, Florida State University): *"The position of the modern evolutionist ... is that humans have an awareness of morality ... because such an awareness is of biological worth. Morality is a biological adaptation no less than are hands and feet and teeth. ... Considered as a rationally justifiable set of claims about an objective something, ethics is illusory. I appreciate that when somebody says, 'Love thy neighbor as thyself,' they think they are referring above and beyond themselves. ... Nevertheless, ... such reference is truly without foundation. Morality is just an aid to survival and reproduction, ... and any deeper meaning is illusory."*

Richard Dawkins (PhD Evolutionary Biology) - atheism's depressing assessment of human worth: *"There is at bottom no design, no purpose, no evil, no good, nothing but pointless indifference. ... We are machines for propagating DNA. ... It is every living object's sole reason for being."*

> Objections to God often appeal to fair play and justice. But it is a mistake to think abandoning belief in God makes the problem of evil and suffering easier to handle.

Argument *against* Naturalism: Objective Moral Values

Dr. William Lane Craig: PhD Philosophy (Univ. of Birmingham), PhD Theology (Univ. Munich). Analytical philosopher, theologian and Christian apologist, focusing on philosophy of religion, metaphysics and philosophy of time. Founder of online ministry, *Reasonable Faith.Org*.

"**On a naturalistic view:** moral values are just the behavioral by-products of biological evolution and social conditioning.

Just as a troop of baboons exhibit co-operative and even self-sacrificial behavior because natural selection has determined it to be advantageous in the struggle for survival, so *homo sapiens* — their primate cousins — exhibit similar behavior for the same reason.

As a result of sociobiological pressures there has evolved among *homo sapiens* a sort of "herd morality" that functions well in the perpetuation of our species.

But **on the atheistic view:** there does not seem to be anything that makes this morality objectively true.

If there is no God, any basis for regarding that herd morality evolved by *homo sapiens* as objectively true seems to have been removed.

Take God out of the picture, and all you seem to be left with is an apelike creature on a tiny speck of dust beset with delusions of moral grandeur.

> **PSALM 14:1**   *"The fool has said in his heart, 'There is no God.'"*

What about *Natural* Evil and the Suffering it causes – why would God allow this?

Dr. Fazale Rana holds a PhD in chemistry with an emphasis in biochemistry from Ohio University, with Postdoctoral studies at the Universities of Virginia and Georgia. Before joining 'Reasons to Believe', he was a senior scientist in product development for Procter & Gamble. The following article, reprinted in its entirety, is entitled "Natural Evil or Moral Evil – Reasons to Believe", and was written by Dr. Rana on October 1, 2003.

"Why does God allow bad things to happen? How can He, if He is good and all-powerful? These questions identify the "problem of evil" that for many people represents a significant challenge to God's existence—and to personal faith.

Philosophers and theologians recognize two kinds of evil: moral and natural. Moral evil stems from human action (or inaction in some cases). Natural evil occurs as a consequence of nature—earthquakes, tornadoes, floods, diseases, and the like.

Natural evil seems to present a greater theological challenge than moral evil does. A skeptic might admit that God can be excused for the free-will actions of human beings who violate His standard of goodness. But natural disasters and disease don't result from human activity, they reason. Therefore, this type of "evil" must be attributed solely to God. Recent work, however, aimed at reducing cholera in rural Bangladeshi villages suggests how precarious this reasoning can be.

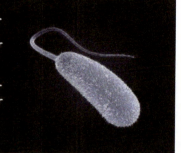

Imagine getting a horrible disease with terrible diarrhea, vomiting, and unbearable abdominal pain. Where you lose so much fluid and electrolytes in one day that it kills you. This is what is in store for you if you ingest parasitic *Vibrio cholerae*. *Vibrio cholerae* is a gram-negative, oxidase positive bacteria that is comma shaped. It has a single polar flagella and moves very rapidly. It lives in the water and also is a human parasite responsible for the horrible and historically consequential disease, Cholera.

Cholera, a disease characterized by diarrhea, extensive dehydration, and rapid death if not immediately treated, is caused by ingestion of the bacterium, Vibrio cholerae. This microbe naturally associates with a microscopic crustacean (copepod) that floats as part of the surface water zooplankton in Bangladesh. During the late spring and summer, phytoplankton blooms with rising water temperatures. This, in turn, leads to blooms of zooplankton and toxic levels of Vibro cholerae in rivers, lakes, and ponds.

Rural villages of Bangladesh rely heavily on surface water as a source of drinking water. As a (sometimes deadly) result, cholera outbreaks routinely occur in the fall after the zooplankton levels explode.[4] Bangladeshi villagers cannot turn to wells for drinking water since over half are contaminated with arsenic. Boiling surface water is rarely an option because wood fuel, used to sterilize the water, is scarce and expensive. In light of this seemingly hopeless situation, skeptics and Christians alike are justified to ask, "Why would an all-powerful and good God create a world in which Vibro cholerae is inevitably a part?"

In response to the cholera crisis, an international research team developed a simple filtration procedure to remove zooplankton (and accompanying Vibro cholerae) from surface water and deployed it in sixty-five rural Bangladeshi villages. The research team instructed the villagers to use an inexpensive cloth commonly found in households to filter drinking water. Laboratory studies demonstrated that the folded cloth retained zooplankton and removed about 99% of Vibro cholerae from the drinking water. In the field, the cases of cholera plummeted by 50% over a two year span. Moreover, the cholera cases reported were less severe, since the disease's impact depends on the amount of Vibro cholerae ingested.

The suffering caused by cholera—and other water-borne diseases—is rooted in man's failure to act, not in God's design. Vibro cholerae, a natural symbiont of zooplankton, comes into contact with human beings largely due to poverty and questionable resource and land management, not as an inevitable consequence of the natural order.

Even then, a simple filtration process offers protection from this microbe's devastating effects, allowing people to coexist with a natural realm that God pronounces good."

My SUFFERING
grows my character

Romans 5:3-4 *"...tribulation produces perseverance, and perseverance, character, and character, hope."*

4.11

• "SUMPASCHO" = refers to our sufferings with Christ   • "HUPOMENO" = endure pain or distress inflicted by others   • "SUNKAKOUCHEOMAI" = to suffer with, as comrades

God's desire: I REJOICE when I suffer for His sake

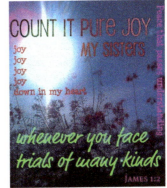

Acts 5:40-41 *"...when they had called for the apostles and beaten them, they commanded them that they should not speak in the name of Jesus, and let them go. So they departed from the presence of the council, REJOICING that they were counted worthy to SUFFER SHAME for the name of Jesus."*

1Peter 1:6-9 *"In this you GREATLY REJOICE, though now for a little while, if need be, you have been GRIEVED BY VARIOUS TRIALS, that the genuineness of your faith, being much more precious than gold that perishes, though it is TESTED BY FIRE, may be found to praise, honor, and glory at the revelation of Jesus Christ, whom you have not seen you love. Though now you do not see Him, yet believing, you rejoice with joy inexpressible and full of glory, receiving the end of your faith – THE SALVATION OF YOUR SOULS."*

1Peter 4:12-16 *"Beloved, do not think it strange concerning the FIERY TRIAL which is to try you, as though some strange thing happened to you, but REJOICE to the extent that YOU PARTAKE OF CHRIST'S SUFFERINGS, that when His glory is revealed, you may also be glad with exceeding joy. If you are INSULTED for the name of Christ, blessed are you, for the Spirit of glory and of God rests upon you. On their part He is blasphemed, but on your part He is glorified. But let none of you suffer as a murderer, a thief, an evildoer, or as a meddler in other peoples' matters. Yet if anyone SUFFERS AS A CHRISTIAN, let him not be ashamed, but let him glorify God in this matter."*

God's plan: I GROW through my suffering

1Peter 5:9-10 *"Resist him, steadfast in the faith, knowing that the same sufferings are experienced by your brotherhood in the world. But may the God of all grace, who called us to His eternal glory by Christ Jesus, AFTER YOU HAVE SUFFERED a while, perfect, establish, strengthen, and settle you."*

James 1:2-4 *"My brethren, count it all joy when you fall into various trials, knowing that the TESTING OF YOUR FAITH PRODUCES PERSEVERANCE. But let perseverance have its perfect work, that you may be mature and complete, lacking nothing."*

1Peter 4:1-2 *"...since Christ SUFFERED for us in the flesh, ARM YOURSELVES also with the same mind, for he who has suffered in the flesh has ceased from sin, that he no longer should live the rest of his time in the flesh for the lusts of men, but for the WILL OF GOD."*

God's promise: He will REWARD me at the end for my suffering for His sake

Matthew 5:10-12 *"Blessed are those who are PERSECUTED for righteousness' sake, for theirs is the kingdom of heaven. Blessed are you when they REVILE and PERSECUTE you, and say all kinds of evil against you falsely FOR MY SAKE. Rejoice and be exceedingly glad, for great is your REWARD in heaven, for so they persecuted the prophets before you."*

Hebrews 11:24-27 *"By faith Moses, when he became of age, refused to be called the son of Pharaoh's daughter, choosing rather to SUFFER AFFLICTION with the people of God than to enjoy the temporary pleasures of sin, esteeming the reproach of Christ greater riches than the treasures of Egypt, for he looked to the REWARD. By faith he forsook Egypt, not fearing the wrath of the king; for he endured as seeing Him who is invisible."*

Revelation 2:10 *"Do not fear any of those things which you are ABOUT TO SUFFER. Indeed, the devil is about to throw some of you into prison, that you may be tested, and you will have tribulation 10 days. Be faithful until death, and I will give you the CROWN OF LIFE."*

WHICH ONE AM I?

Deuteronomy 6:10-12 *"It shall be, when the Lord your God brings you into the land which He swore to your fathers, to give you large and beautiful cities which you did not build, houses full of all good things which you did not fill, hewn-out wells which you did not dig, vineyards and olive trees which you did not plant – when you have eaten and are full – then beware, lest you forget the Lord who brought you out of the land of Egypt, from the house of bondage."*	**Jeremiah 20: 8-9** *"Because the word of the Lord was made a reproach and a derision daily, then I said 'I will not make mention of Him, nor speak anymore in His name.' But His word was in my heart like a burning fire shut up in my bones. I was weary of holding it back, and I could not."*

The Persecuted Church (1Peter 5:9)   Areas dominated by Islam

The Voice of the Martyrs: Pakistan, 2004

"The morning of January 5, 2004, Pastor Mukhtar Barkat rose very early. His eldest daughter, Esther, was unable to visit for Christmas, and Mukhtar had arranged to catch the 4:00 AM train to Lahore, to see her and his grandchildren. That morning a thick fog had settled, making it very difficult to see. The pastor was only a few blocks from the train station when his attackers appeared. He probably never even saw them. He was discovered shortly after, bullets throughout his body. He left behind his wife and son.

He had started a small church of 50 members in the city of Khanewal 4 years earlier. He loved the Lord, and wanted to share the gospel with all who would listen. He led more than 200 Pakistanies to Christ during his 17 years in ministry. His services were broadcast throughout his neighborhood by several loudspeakers atop the church steeple. Mukhtar did this because the Muslims blasted their call to prayer 5X daily, so Christians should do the same. He studied the Koran, and often debated with Muslim scholars. His widow said "He was a convincing debator and a very effective speaker. The Muslim leaders became upset at his growing popularity among Christians and non-Christians alike.

About one year ago, he was summoned to the police station after Muslims formally complained against his church, saying the loudspeakers were too loud. He apologized, went back and lowered the volume but kept them going. Several days later some of the leading Muslim elders came and warned him that he would be killed if he continued the loudspeaker evangelism. He told them he did not fear death, and he would not stop."

→ About Pakistan: Pakistan gained independence from Britain in 1947, but has been very unstable ever since. Its people have suffered through three major wars, enduring military regimes and corrupted military dictatorships. Pakistan is an Islamic republic. Policy is increasingly dictated by an Islamic extremist minority sympathetic with Afghanistan's Taliban movement. Militant Islamic forces have initiated much violence against Pakistani Christians, many being falsely accused of breaking "Law 295c: blaspheming Mohammed", which is punishable by death, some even killed by mobs after being acquitted and released. The most menial tasks in society are reserved for the Christians. The Koran testifies that a follower of Allah is to hate Christians:

Surat 5:51 *"O true believers, take not the Jews and Christians for your friends. They cannot be trusted. They are defiled – filth."*

The Persecuted Church (1Peter 5:9)   Areas dominated by Buddhist, Hindu, No Belief

The Voice of the Martyrs: China, 2002

"Mr. Lau had been a very fervent Buddhist, highly regarded by the people of his village in Guangdong Province. But on a Friday night, he and his daughter had went with his sister to a Friday night meeting where the gospel had been preached, and they accepted Christ as their Savior and Lord and were baptized. Mr. Lau was so overflowing with excitement he removed all the idols from his home and began proclaiming the gospel to his fellow villagers. Several believed, and he began a prayer meeting at his home, and he even built a baptistry in front of his house. On July 21, 2002, 49 villagers boldly declared their faith in Christ by public baptism.

The next day Chinese police officers and officials of the state-controlled church (TSPM = Three-Self Patriotic Movement) interrogated Mr. Lau at his home and read the laws of state religion to him, telling him he had broken these laws. They warned him that if he preached about Jesus he would be arrested. They removed all Christian posters and hymn sheets from his home, and they told him that he must stop singing hymns in his 'unregistered house meetings.' They also warned that they could not protect him if he disobeyed – that 'anything could happen to the house church.'

On October 11, 2002, the police officers again went to Brother Lau's house and threatened him with arrest if he refused to close down his house meetings. At this time, they are watching him closely, and he is living under the threat of imprisonment and even death."

→ About China: China was declared the "People's Republic of China" in 1949 by Chairman Mao Zedong, who sought to purge society of anything that would point to religion, causing China's people to endure tremendous hardship ever since. China's human rights record is one of the worst in the world. Its system of "re-education through labor" holds hundreds of thousands each year in work camps, without even a court hearing.

In sheer numbers, China is the world's worst persecutor of Christians. More Christians are currently in Chinese prisons than all other prisons of the world combined. In one recent 18-month period, 500 top leaders of one group, the South China Church, were arrested and imprisoned. Five were sentenced to death, but their sentences were reduced as a result of international protests. In spite of government efforts, the Chinese Christian church is exploding: It is estimated that 1,200 CHINESE COME TO CHRIST EACH HOUR.

Prov. 28:1 *"The wicked flee when no one pursues, but the righteous are as bold as lions."*

My EVANGELISM
fulfills the Vision of Jesus

Matthew 5:16 *"Let your light so shine before men that they may see your good works and GLORIFY your Father in heaven"*

4.12

While on earth, Jesus was focused on His vision: building His church not only upon truth but one BUILT OUTWARD, like a **bridge** to the community (not inward, like an island). John 17:23 tells why this was so important to Him: *"...that the world may know that You have sent Me."*

A Christian at work

- **HIS VISION =** In the Sermon on the Mount, Jesus said Christians must **influence** the world by allowing HIM to shine through them.

- In **John 8:12**, Jesus said *He* is the Light. But in Matthew 5:16, He says *we* are the light. He is giving His vision: after His resurrection and ascension, we are the light because He lives in us (Col. 1:27)!

- **MY HOPE =** I can be **transformed** by Him, as He conforms me to be more and more **like** Him. That means I LIVE OUT what I believe. Then, He and His Father are glorified through me to an unbelieving world.

- I fulfill Acts 4:13, as I become **living proof** to an unsaved world that Jesus Christ in me is real: *"...when they saw the boldness of Peter and John, and perceived that they were uneducated and untrained men, they marveled and they realized that THEY HAD BEEN WITH JESUS."*

- I can bridge the void between the church and the world around me. 1Corinthians 1:26-29 says that only when I humble myself before Him can He **use me** to draw others to Him. This is God's will for my life.

The Vision of Jesus

His church would be built on 2 essential ingredients:
#1. the *TRUTH* of God's word
#2. the *BRIDGE* to reach the community

Matthew 5:16

	FROM...		TO...
serve	finding community within our church	→	impacting community as a church
	an island community	→	a bridge to the community
	stranger in the community	→	lighthouse in the community
	loving ourselves	→	loving the community
	turning our face inward	→	turning our face outward
	condemning the world's ills	→	conversing with the world's needs
	the church of my needs	→	the church of good deeds
sacrifice	receiving blessings	→	being a blessing
	self-focused	→	Christ-focused
	storing our resources	→	giving our resources away
send	church's seating capacity	→	church's sending capacity
	a holding tank	→	a launching pad
	being served	→	serving others
sanctified	lack of passion & direction	→	directing passion to meet needs
	comfortable & safe	→	risky, vulnerable, sacrificial
	status quo	→	change
	playing church	→	motivated as a church
	isolated	→	engaged
	what difference can I make?	→	what has God called me to do?

Is my *Church* a stranger to my community?
Am *I* personally influencing the community around me?

Mark 1:17 "Effective Evangelism = First '<u>COME</u> and See'... then '<u>GO</u> and Tell'"

"COME² after Me, and I will make you fishers of men."

The Bible teaches that before I can be effective in sharing with others the good news of what Jesus Christ has done in my life, I need to **KNOW** Him. I must have a relationship with Him in order to tell someone about Him.

Two New Testament words for "COME"	Two New Testament words for "GO"
Come¹ = *"erchomai"* = to accompany; to identify with Come² = *"deute"* = to follow after	Go³ = *"poreuomai"* = to take a journey; to travel Go⁴ = *"hupagō"* = to sink out of sight; to withdraw
John 1:37-39 Jesus invites the 1st disciples to come *"The 2 disciples heard him speak, and they followed Jesus. Then Jesus turned, and seeing them following, said to them, 'What do you seek?' They said to Him, 'Rabbi... where are You staying?' He said, 'COME¹ and SEE.'"*	**Matt. 28:19-20** Jesus says go and make disciples *"GO³ therefore and make disciples of all the nations, baptizing them in the name of the Father and of the Son and of the Holy Spirit, teaching them the things that I have commanded you..."*
John 7:37-38 Jesus says come and identify with Him *"...If anyone thirsts, let Him COME¹ to Me and drink. He who believes in Me, as the Scripture has said, 'out of his heart will flow rivers of living water.'"*	**Mark 16:15** Jesus says go and preach the gospel *"...GO³ into all the world and preach the gospel to every creature. He who believes and is baptized will be saved; but he who does not believe will be condemned."*
Matt. 19:14 Jesus says come to Him with childlike faith *"...Let the little children COME¹ to Me, and do not forbid them; for of such is the kingdom of heaven."*	**Matthew 22:9** Jesus says go into the world and invite everyone to come to the wedding *"...GO³ into the highways, and as many as you find, invite to the wedding."*
John 6:37 Jesus promises that anyone who comes and identifies with Him never loses their salvation *"...the one who COMES¹ to Me I will by no means cast out."*	**Mark 5:19-20** The N.T.'s 1st Missionary *"'...GO⁴ home to your friends, and tell them the great things the Lord has done for you, and how He has had compassion on you.' And he departed and began to proclaim in Decapolis all that Jesus had done for him...."*
Matt. 11:28 Jesus promises rest to all who come to Him *"COME² to Me, all you who labor and are heavy laden, and I will give you rest."*	**Mark 10:52-53** 1st faith, then sight – now I must go *"'...GO⁴ your way; your faith has made you well.' And immediately he received his sight and followed Jesus on the road."*
John 5:40 Jesus tells the crowd they aren't willing to come and identify with Him to be saved *"...you aren't willing to COME¹ to Me that you may have life."*	**John 15:16** Jesus says go and bear fruit in His name *"You did not choose Me, but I chose you and appointed you that you should GO⁴ and bear fruit..."*

What "God's Will for my life" is all about: growing in my relationship with Jesus Christ.

"The Starfish Thrower" (Loren Eiseley, Readers Digest, 1991)

Luke 15:4-7 "Heaven's applause is for **one** at a **time**"

"What man of you, having 100 sheep, if he loses 1 of them, does not leave the 99 in the wilderness and GO³ AFTER THE ONE which is lost until he finds it? And when he has found it, he lays it on his shoulders, rejoicing. And when he comes home, he calls together his friends and neighbors, saying to them, 'REJOICE WITH ME, for I have found my sheep which was lost! I say to you that likewise there will be more joy in heaven over ONE SINNER WHO REPENTS than over 99 upright persons who need no repentance."

"I awoke early, as I often did, just before sunrise to walk by the ocean's edge and greet the new day. As I moved through the misty dawn, I focused on a faint, faraway movement. I saw a boy, bending and reaching and waving his arms – dancing on the beach, no doubt in celebration of the perfect day soon to begin.

As I approached, I sadly realized that he was not dancing, but rather bending to sift through the debris left by the night's tide, stopping now and then to pick up a starfish and then standing, to heave it back into the sea. I asked the boy the purpose of the effort. 'The tide has washed the starfish onto the beach and they cannot return to the sea by themselves,' he replied. 'When the sun rises, they will die, unless I throw them back to the sea.'

I looked at the vast expanse of beach, stretching in both directions. Starfish littered the shore in numbers beyond calculation. The hopelessness of the boy's plan became clear to me and I pointed out, 'But there are more starfish on this beach than you can ever save before the sun is up. YOU CAN'T EXPECT TO MAKE A DIFFERENCE.'

He paused briefly to consider my words, bent to pick up a starfish and threw it as far as possible. Turning to me he simply said, 'I MADE A DIFFERENCE TO THAT ONE.'"

GOD'S REWARDS
4.13 Revelation 20:11-15
different for Christians vs. Non-Christians

"Then I saw a great white throne and Him who sat on it, whose face the earth and the heaven fled away. And there was found no place for them. And I saw the dead, small and great, standing before God, and THE BOOKS were opened. And another book was opened, which is the BOOK OF LIFE. And the dead were judged according to their works, by the things which were written in the books. The sea gave up the dead who were in it, and Death and Hades delivered up the dead who were in them. And they were judged, EACH ONE ACCORDING TO THEIR WORKS. Then Death and Hades were cast into the lake of fire. This is the 2nd death. And anyone not found written in the BOOK OF LIFE was cast into the lake of fire."

Revelation 20:11-15

The Books: 1) Contain all the deeds for those standing in line waiting to be judged. Each person in line will be judged according to what he or she had or had not done.
2) What is written doesn't decide where I spend eternity. My eternal destination depends on whether or not my name is written in the Lamb's Book of Life.

➢ The "BOOK OF LIFE"

Exodus 32:32-33 *"'Yet now, if You will forgive their sin – but if not, I pray, blot me out of YOUR BOOK which You have written.' And the Lord said to Moses, 'Whoever has sinned against Me, I will blot him out of My book.'"*

Psalm 69:27-28 *"Add iniquity to their iniquity, and let them not come into Your righteousness. Let them be blotted out of the BOOK OF THE LIVING, and not be written with the righteous."*

Daniel 12:1 *"At that time Michael shall stand up, the great prince who stands watch over the sons of your people; and there shall be a time of trouble, such as never was since there was a nation, even to that time. And at that time your people shall be delivered, everyone who is found WRITTEN IN THE BOOK."*

Malachi 3:16 *"Then those who feared the Lord spoke to one another, and the Lord listened and heard them; so a BOOK OF REMEMBRANCE was written before Him for those who feared the Lord and who meditate on His name."*

John MacArthur (*Exposition on Malachi*): "In the hearts of true worshippers who loved and served God, all the talk of judgment produced fear that they, too, might be swept away by God's wrath. To encourage the godly remnant, Malachi noted how the Lord hadn't forgotten those "who fear the Lord and meditate on His name." The Book of Remembrance may be a reference to the Book of Life where the names of God's children are recorded."

➢ God watches and TAKES NOTES

Proverbs 15:3, 5:21 *"The eyes of the Lord are in every place, KEEPING WATCH over the good and the evil. The ways of man are before the eyes of the Lord, and He weighs all his parts."*

Job 34:21 *"...His eyes are on the ways of man, and He sees all his steps."*

Psalm 33:15 *"He fashions their hearts individually; He CONSIDERS all their works."*

Nehemiah 13:14 *"Remember me, O my God, concerning this, and do not wipe out my good deeds that I have done for the house of God, and for its services!"*

Hebrews 4:13 *"...there is no creature hidden from His sight, but all things are naked and open to the eyes of Him to whom WE MUST GIVE AN ACCOUNT."*

➢ God requires EVERYONE to give an account of their life

Hebrews 9:27 *"...as it is appointed for men to die once, but after this the judgment."*

Romans 14:12 *"So then each of us shall give account of himself to God."*

1Peter 4:5 *"They will give an account to Him who will judge the living and the dead."*

Eccle. 11:9 *"Rejoice, O young man, in your youth. And let your heart cheer you in the days of your youth; walk in the ways of your heart, and in the sight of your eyes; but know that for all these GOD WILL BRING YOU INTO JUDGMENT."*

Psalm 10:13-14 *"Why do the wicked renounce God? He has said in his heart, 'You will not require an account.' But You have seen it, for You observe trouble and grief, to REPAY IT BY YOUR HAND."*

Charles Stanley[9]: "The Certainty of God rewarding you for your choices"

"Death is life's only certainty. Though we are not free to choose the moment of death, we have been given the opportunity to choose the destination.

The Bible presents only 2 options – HEAVEN or HELL. There is no third alternative."

Luke 16:24-31   The Rich Man and Lazarus – The Reality of Hell

The following is from Tim Keller's book 'The Reason for God'[14], pages 79-80

"Lazarus is a poor man who begs at the gate of a cruel rich man. They both die and Lazarus goes to heaven while the rich man goes to hell. There he looks up and sees Lazarus in heaven 'in Abraham's bosom': 'So he called to him, 'Father Abraham, have pity on me and send Lazarus to dip the tip of his finger in water and cool my tongue, because I am in agony in this fire.' But Abraham replied, 'Son, remember that in your lifetime you received your good things, while Lazarus received bad things, but now he is comforted here and you are in agony. And besides all this, between us and you a great chasm has been fixed, so that those who want to go from here to you cannot, nor can anyone cross over from there to us.' He answered, 'Then I beg you, father, send Lazarus to my father's house, for I have 5 brothers. Let him warn them, so that they will not also come to this place of torment.' Abraham replied, 'They have Moses and the Prophets; let them listen to them.' 'No, father Abraham,' he said, 'but if someone from the dead goes to them, they will REPENT.' He said to him, 'If they do not listen to Moses and the Prophets, they will not be convinced even if someone rises from the dead.'"

What is astonishing is that though their statuses have now been reversed, the rich man seems blind to what has happened. He still expects Lazarus to be his servant and treats him as his water boy. He doesn't ask to get out of hell, yet strongly implies that God never gave him and his family enough information about the afterlife.

Commentators have noted the astonishing amount of denial, blame-shifting, and spiritual blindness in this soul in hell. They have also noted that the rich man, unlike Lazarus, is never given a personal name. He is only called a 'Rich Man,' strongly hinting that since he built his identity on his wealth rather than on God, once he lost his wealth he lost any sense of self. In short, hell is simply one's freely chosen identity apart from God on a trajectory of infinity. We see this process 'writ small' in addictions to drugs, alcohol, gambling, and pornography.

When we build our lives on anything but God, that thing – though a good thing – becomes an enslaving addiction, something we have to have to be happy. Personal disintegration happens on a broader scale. In eternity, this disintegration goes on forever. There is increasing isolation, denial, delusion, and self-absorption. When you lose all humility you are out of touch with reality. No one ever asks to leave hell. The very idea of heaven seems to them a sham."

Chuck Swindoll (taken from 'Stress Fractures', 1990): *"It is the story of two men. While alive, their status could hardly have been more different. And when they died, again a contrast. One found himself in heaven; the other, in hell. Our attention falls upon the rich man who is pleading for relief and removal from his torturous surroundings. The scene is unpleasant to imagine, but it is nevertheless real. Neither here nor elsewhere does Jesus suggest this was merely a fantasy. The man in hell is in conscious torment. He is crying out for mercy. Being "far away" (v. 23) and permanently removed by "a great chasm" (v. 26), he is desperately alone, unable to escape from hell, as we read, "none may cross over" (v. 26). The horror is painfully literal, unlike the jokes often passed around regarding hell. Haunted with thoughts of other family members ultimately coming to the same place, the man begs for someone to go to his father's house and warn his brothers ". . . so that they will not also come to this place of torment" (v. 28).*

This is only one of many references to an eternal existence in hell. The New Testament, in fact, says more about hell than it does about heaven. Here are just a few characteristics of hell set forth in the New Testament:
1) It is a place of weeping and gnashing of teeth (Matthew 8:12).
2) It is a place where people scream for mercy, have memories, are tormented, feel alone, cannot escape (Luke 16:23-31).
3) It is a place of unquenchable fire (Mark 9:48) and 4) It is a place of darkness (Revelation 9:2).
5) It is a place of eternal damnation (Mark 3:29).
6) It is a place where God's wrath is poured out (Revelation 14:10).
7) It is a place of everlasting destruction (2Thessalonians 1:9).
The finality of all this is overwhelmingly depressing. We have little struggle believing that heaven will be forever, but for some reason we ignore that hell will be equally everlasting. To deny the permanence of hell is impossible without also removing the permanence of heaven. Each is a reality and each is ultimate finality."

EZEKIEL 18:30,32 *"Repent, and turn from all your transgressions, so that iniquity will not be your ruin. For I have no pleasure in the death of one who dies" says the Lord. "Therefore, TURN and LIVE!"*

Charles Stanley[9]: Answers to the Christian's questions on *"how now shall I live?"*

"Does my behavior matter once I am assured of my salvation? → You bet it does.
Are there any eternal consequences when I sin? → Absolutely.
Will eternity be the same for believers who lived for Christ vs. for themselves? → Not a chance.

God's Justice = moves Him to keep a careful record of those who remain faithful and those who do not.
God's Grace = moved Him to sacrifice His only Son to provide a way for our salvation.
God's Justice = causes Him to take special note of those believers willing to sacrifice for His Son."

<u>REMEMBER</u>: we are not talking about heaven and hell. A believer's works have nothing to do with *where* they spend eternity. But they have a lot to do with what a believer can expect once he or she gets there. Unknown to many Christians is that each of us has the opportunity to make another choice: besides choosing where we spend eternity, we can choose what it will be like once we get there. Eternity will not be the same for every believer."

PAUL: His life will COUNT for eternity

Paul paid close attention to his conduct

Acts 24:15-16 *"...there will be a resurrection of the dead, both of the just and the unjust. This being so, I myself always strive to have a conscience without offense toward God and men."*

Acts 23:1 *"Then Paul, looking earnestly at the council, said, 'Men and brethren, I have lived in all good conscience before God until this day.'"*

<u>Paul is a role model for me</u>: He always maintained his conduct, even during intense persecution and suffering at the hands of others, when he had every reason to take vengeance against them.

Acts 13:43-45 (Paul's conflict at Antioch) *"Now when the congregation had broken up, many of the Jews and devout proselytes followed Paul and Barnabas, who, speaking to them, persuaded them to continue in the grace of God. And the next Sabbath almost the whole city came together to hear the word of God. But when the Jews saw the multitudes, they were filled with envy, and contradicting and blaspheming, they opposed the things spoken by Paul."*

Acts 14:1-6 (Paul nearly killed at Iconium) *"Now it happened in Iconium that they went together to the synagogue of the Jews, and so spoke that a great multitude both of the Jews and of the Greeks believed. But the unbelieving Jews stirred up the Gentiles and poisoned their minds against the brethren. Therefore they stayed there a long time, speaking boldly in the Lord, who was bearing witness to the word of His grace, granting signs and wonders to be done by their hands. But the multitude of the city was divided: part sided with the Jews, and part with the apostles. And when a violent attempt was made by both the Gentiles and Jews, with their rulers, to abuse and stone them, they became aware of it and fled to Lystra and Derbe..."*

Acts 17:16-18 (Paul ridiculed in Athens) *"Now while Paul waited for them at Athens, his spirit was provoked within him when he saw that the city was full of idols. Therefore he reasoned in the synagogue with the Jews and with the Gentile worshippers, and in the marketplace daily with those who happened to be there. Then certain Epicurian and Stoic philosophers encountered him. And some said, 'What does this BABBLER want to say?' Others said, 'He seems to be a proclaimer of foreign gods,' because he preached to them Jesus and the resurrection."*

Paul's motivation for good conduct (what he did) – he will have his day in COURT

His gratitude for all Jesus did for him on the cross drove him to obedience. God's actions toward believers will depend on the believer's faithfulness to Him, as evidenced through obedience with a sincere heart attitude:

2Corinthians 5:9-10 *"...we make it our aim, whether present or absent, to be well pleasing to Him, for WE MUST ALL APPEAR BEFORE THE JUDGMENT SEAT OF CHRIST, that each one may receive the things done in the body, according to what he has done, whether good or bad."*

Ephesians 6:5-8 *"Servants, be obedient to those who are your masters according to the flesh, with fear and trembling, in SINCERITY OF HEART, AS TO CHRIST; not with eyeservice, as men-pleasers, but as servants of Christ, doing the will of God FROM THE HEART, with good will doing service, AS TO THE LORD, and not to men, knowing that whatever good anyone does, he will receive the same from the Lord, whether he is a slave or free."*

Colossians 3:22-25 *"Servants, obey in all things your masters according to the flesh, not with eyeservice, as men-pleasers, but in SINCERITY OF HEART, fearing God. And whatever you do, DO IT HEARTILY, AS TO THE LORD and not to men, knowing that from the Lord you will receive the reward of the inheritance; for you serve the Lord Christ. But he who does wrong will be repaid for the wrong which he has done, and there is no partiality."*

JESUS – the Rewarder of Christians for their WORK

Revel. 22:12 *"...I am coming quickly, and My reward is with Me, to give to everyone ACCORDING TO HIS WORK."*

Titus 2:13-14 *"...looking for the blessed hope and glorious appearing of our great God and Savior Jesus Christ, who gave Himself for us, that He might redeem us from every lawless deed and purify for Himself His own special people, ZEALOUS FOR GOOD WORKS."*

My REWARDS
4.14 1Corinthians 3:11-15
Based on my motives

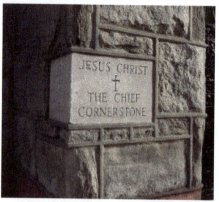

"No other foundation can anyone lay than that which is laid, which is Jesus Christ. Now if anyone builds on this foundation with gold, silver, precious stones, wood hay straw, each one's work will become EVIDENT; for the Day will declare it, because it will be revealed by fire; and the fire will TEST each one's work, of WHAT SORT IT IS. If anyone's work which he has built on it endures, he will receive a reward. If anyone's work is burned, he will suffer loss; but he himself will be saved, yet so as through fire."

<u>Charles Stanley[9]</u>: "Every believer's life will be evaluated on the basis of his or her contribution and commitment to the kingdom of God – of which Christ is pictured as the foundation."

Two kinds of CHRISTIANS

1) "<u>Gold, Silver, Precious Stones</u>" = quality materials representing dedicated, spiritual service to build the church
   - they are rewarded for their faithfulness because their heart attitude motivated them to serve out of love; their inner love shone through by their outer works.

   Hebrews 6:10 *"For God is not unjust to forget your work and labor of love which you have shown toward His name."*

2) "<u>Wood, Hay, Straw</u>" = inferior materials representing shallowness with no eternal value (not evil, but useless)
   - their works, one by one, burn up; in God's view, nothing they lived for has counted toward the kingdom.
   - their *heart attitude* is revealed to them - they spent their lives pursuing perishable, temporary things.

   Matthew 6:19-21 *"Do not lay up for yourselves treasures on earth, where moth and rust destroy and where thieves break in and steal; but lay up for yourselves treasures in heaven, where neither moth nor rust destroys and where thieves do not break in and steal. For where your treasure is, there your heart will be also."*

The JUDGMENT SEAT of Christ - 2Corinthians 5:9-10

"We make it our aim, whether present or absent, to be WELL PLEASING to Him. For we must all appear before the judgment seat of Christ, that each one may receive the things done in the body, according to what he has done, whether good or bad."

- <u>Two Major Issues for Believers</u> are settled at the Judgment Seat:

1) JUDGMENT ON WORKS: 1Corinthians 3:11-15
   - some rewarded for their faithfulness ("gold, silver, precious stones").
   - others ashamed for their earthly unfaithfulness ("wood, hay, stubble").

2) ETERNAL AUTHORITY (it won't be the same for all believers)
   - some believers will be entrusted with certain privileges, others will not.

   Matt. 25:21 *"Well done, good and faithful servant; you were faithful over a few things, I will make you ruler over many things. Enter into the joy of your Lord."*
   - some believers will be given more of the true riches, others less.

   Luke 16:10-11 *"He who is faithful over what is least is faithful also in much; and he who is unjust in what is least is unjust in much... if you have not been faithful in unrighteous mammon, who will commit to your trust the true riches?"*

- <u>Jesus's message to me</u>: He ties my faithful use of my earthly riches with my accumulation of treasure in heaven:

Luke 18:22 *So when Jesus heard these things, He said to him, "You still lack one thing. Sell all that you have and distribute to the poor, and you will have TREASURE IN HEAVEN; and come, follow Me."*

<u>Charles Stanley[9]</u>: "Privilege in the kingdom is determined by one's **FAITHFULNESS** in this life. This truth may come as a shock. Maybe you always thought that everyone would be equal in the kingdom of God. It is true that there will be equality in terms of our inclusion in the kingdom of God, but not in our rank and privileges. As He watches me live my life now, it is my willingness to use and invest what God has entrusted me with that determines how much He will entrust me with in His kingdom."

Galatians 6:7,9 *"Do not be deceived, God is not mocked; for whatever a man sows, that he will also reap. And let us not grow weary in doing good, for in due season we shall reap if we do not lose heart."*

The BEMA Seat of Christ: The 5 Crowns

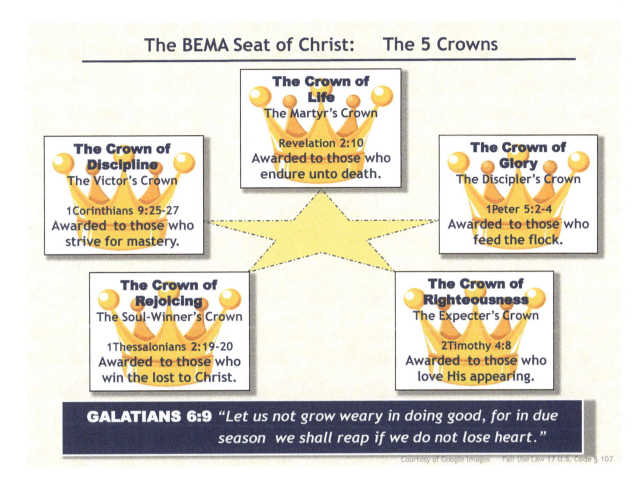

The Crown of Life
The Martyr's Crown
Revelation 2:10
Awarded to those who endure unto death.

The Crown of Discipline
The Victor's Crown
1 Corinthians 9:25-27
Awarded to those who strive for mastery.

The Crown of Glory
The Discipler's Crown
1 Peter 5:2-4
Awarded to those who feed the flock.

The Crown of Rejoicing
The Soul-Winner's Crown
1 Thessalonians 2:19-20
Awarded to those who win the lost to Christ.

The Crown of Righteousness
The Expecter's Crown
2 Timothy 4:8
Awarded to those who love His appearing.

GALATIANS 6:9 *"Let us not grow weary in doing good, for in due season we shall reap if we do not lose heart."*

The BEMA Seat of Christ: The 7 Revelation Privileges

1. Personal
To Eat of the Tree of Life
Revelation 2:7
Awarded to those who love Jesus Christ.

2. Persevere
Not hurt by the 2nd Death
Revelation 2:11
Awarded to those with a sound witness.

3. Persist
Stone with a New Name
Revelation 2:17
Awarded to those who overcome this world.

4. Protect
Morning Star & Authority
Revelation 2:26-29
Awarded to those who avoid this world's lies.

5. Pure
Divine Identification
Revelation 3:5
Awarded to those who have a pure walk.

6. Passion
A Throne Given
Revelation 3:21
Awarded to those with a fervent & pure heart.

7. Prove
A New Name Given
Revelation 3:12
Awarded to those who hold on to things of God.

MATTHEW 25:21
"Well done, good and faithful servant; you were faithful over a few things, I will make you ruler over many things. Enter into the joy of your Lord."